DICTIONARY OF FILMS

Dictionary of FILMS

Georges Sadoul

TRANSLATED, EDITED, AND UPDATED BY

Peter Morris

UNIVERSITY OF CALIFORNIA PRESS
BERKELEY AND LOS ANGELES

University of California Press
Berkeley and Los Angeles
Original edition © 1965 by Editions du Seuil,
Paris; translated by permission.
English translation © 1972 by The Regents
of the University of California
Library of Congress Catalogue Card No.: 74-136027
Designed by W. H. Snyder
ISBN: 0-520-01864-8 (cloth)
0-520-02152-5 (paper)

Preface

BY GEORGES SADOUL

At the present time, some 3,000 features are produced throughout the world in an average year. Perhaps 100,000 have been produced since 1930 and the beginning of sound.

In attempting to give a panorama of world cinema since its origins, I selected some 1200 films for this *Dictionary*. I set out to include films from lesser known countries and to give a place to major works from the "silent era."

I have seen at least 95% of the films I discuss. Those which, for various reasons, I have been unable to see, are described in the words of other authors. In addition, I have often had to refer to other critics for films which I have not been able to see again. An historian finds it difficult to re-see films after their initial releases and his memory is not always reliable. I can offer various examples of the fallibility of memory.

The film which made the strongest impression on me at the end of the "silent" period was Sternberg's *Underworld* (1927). I therefore felt it important to discuss it in detail with my students at the IDHEC (Institut des Hautes Études Cinématographiques, Paris) where I taught film history with Jean Mitry after 1944. I described to them in considerable detail an apartment, a stairway, stuffed birds — the lair occupied by the gangster (Bancroft). I described this repeatedly for five or six years until Henri Langlois discovered a print of *Underworld* for the Cinémathèque Française. As soon as possible I had it projected at IDHEC. But the apartment in the film bore no relation to that in my memory — which I had, I suppose, recalled from *The Drag Net,* an exactly contemporary film of Sternberg's in which Bancroft also appeared.

Even the film maker himself does not always have an exact recall of his own work. In 1941, the anti-fascist German writer, Friedrich Wolf, was a war correspondent for the Russians during the fighting near Moscow. He became separated from his unit during the terrible battle and ran into a Soviet patrol who took him for a Nazi parachutist spy because of his strong German accent. In order to identify himself he said he was the scriptwriter of *Professor Mamlock,* a 1938 Soviet film which had had considerable success in the USSR. He was asked to recount the story for the many soldiers who had seen it, but they judged his summary so inaccurate that he might have been shot if other military personnel had not arrived who identified him. Since I was unable to discuss this dramatic episode with Friedrich Wolf, I can't say whether his own memory was at fault or whether it was the soldiers who had remembered the film inaccurately.

In his book *The Art of Film,* Ernest Lindgren cites Pudovkin's 1928 analysis of a sequence from his own film *Mother* (1926) in which he described sequences which apparently didn't exist. Initially, I thought the British theoretician was right and agreed with him that the film maker, writing his text without re-seeing his film, had included scenes deleted at the editing stage or scenes in the shooting script which were never shot. Then, in Moscow, I saw the original Soviet version of *Mother* — very different from the English and French versions. I now think Lindgren was mistaken because he didn't know the original work but a distorted British adaptation in which sequences had been re-edited and several shots deleted.

Such practices were common in the "silent" period. They have not disappeared with sound. The French-dubbed version of Samuel Fuller's *Pick-Up on South Street* (1953) became *Le Port de la drogue* ("Drug Harbor") although the original plot dealt with spies, not drug traffickers.

Seeing a film once is not enough to know it well. I saw Feyder's *Thérèse Raquin* forty years ago at a time when I was not a film critic. I saw Lubitsch's *Oyster Princess* and Lupu Pick's *Shattered* even earlier while still a student. For these three films, difficult to re-see today and which I recall only in part, I have had recourse to the descriptions of Moussinac and Louis Delluc.

It is even possible to forget a film one has seen and about which one has written a review. For example, around 1950, I decided that I didn't know Ophüls' *La Tendre ennemie.* Later, I discovered an account of it written by me as a young critic and published in the weekly *Regards.* In the entry for this film I have included some phrases from this review which now seem so strange to me that they might have been written by another hand.

Therefore, if the brief résumés of some films seem inaccurate to readers this might be the fault either of the distortions of a foreign adaptation of the original version, or of the wording, or of my memory — or perhaps also of theirs.

For each film included in this *Dictionary* I have given a fairly complete list of credits, the running time (or length for silent films), a summary of the plot in two or three lines, and a critical appreciation. For documentation, I have drawn to a large extent from the *fiches filmographiques* published by the French Federation of Film Societies and from the *Index de la Cinématographie française* (now, alas, no longer published) whose 25 volumes contain the credits and synopses of 12,000 films released in France since 1946.

It is hoped that this modest *Dictionary of Films,* complementing my *Dictionary of Film Makers,* will be of some service to cinephiles, film society organizers and viewers of television (where "re-runs" are frequent). This volume will be undoubtedly the first of its kind published in the world since *Filmen* published in 1939–40 by the film historian, Ove Brusendorff, in Danish.The *Film Lexicon* announced in 1960 by Charles Reinert (in Germany) has never appeared. The *Filmlexicon delle Opere* (in Italian) which was to have followed the *Filmlexicon degli Autori* (in 7 volumes) is still unpublished.

This modest volume does not pretend to rival this latter long-awaited encylopedia, and has aimed above all at being easy to use, giving the credits of more than 1,000 important films produced in over 50 countries during 70 years, plus critical appraisals. Enthusiasts of certain important film genres such as the western, the musical, the horror film, the documentary, the cartoon, and the like, will undoubtedly feel these have been under-represented in this volume. The limitations of space have obliged me to neglect much and I hope that other specialized genre or national filmographies will be published one day.

For this *Dictionary of Films* we have restricted ourselves to providing the reader with such elements as will give him "a general idea" of the film referred to — without asking him in the least to share in the author's judgments or in his selection of films.

Introduction

TO THE ENGLISH EDITION
BY PETER MORRIS

In preparing the English edition of Georges Sadoul's *Dictionary of Films* I have been conscious of his own remarks regarding the fallibility of memory and have taken advantage of his invitation to amend the original wherever possible. The original edition testifies to his taste and critical perspective as a humanist film critic and it is my hope that I have retained the spirit of this in bringing it to English-speaking readers.

The technical data for each film have been checked against original sources, corrected where necessary and, in some cases, additional credits have been added. The somewhat brief plot summaries of the original have been expanded for most of the entries and certain additions or corrections of fact to the critical appraisals have been made. My translation has been a free one, seeking to capture the spirit of the original rather than always its literal meaning. For some entries I have felt it appropriate to include additional critical remarks, sometimes from a different viewpoint than Sadoul; these are indicated in the text by square brackets.

For some films, chiefly those which Sadoul indicated he had not seen (such as *Blackmail*) I have completely revised and re-written the entry. About a hundred new titles have been added, including not only those made in more recent years but also several earlier films I felt a work of this kind should cover (e.g., *Drifters, Frankenstein, The Merry Widow, On the Town*). I have also added to the original entry other remakes, additional versions of literary works, and films of the same title. In each case, entries written by me are indicated by an asterisk in front of the title. In all, the *Dictionary* has been expanded by some fifteen per cent.

Inevitably, errors creep into a volume of this scope. Corrections and additional information would be welcome for future editions.

The format has been revised so that each film is now entered under its original-language title (except for Chinese films which have proved elusive), with cross references from all known release titles. This approach will I hope not only provide film students with more accurate information but also avoid confusions about release and re-release titles — which often vary widely. Entries are arranged alphabetically by letter.

I have used the word "see" in cross references to distinguish between titles which are solely release titles of the original referred to (in which cases simple cross references are given) and those which are either (1) part of a trilogy and have been discussed in one entry (e.g., the *Pather Panchali* trilogy), or (2) the titles of remakes or other adaptations of literary works and hence discussed below the main entry (e.g. *The Long Night* which is the American remake of *Le Jour se lève*). In both these latter cases a "see" cross reference is given.

The year given for each film is the year production was completed. This is not always common practice but it seems more useful in discussing a film maker's work to know when he made it rather than when it was released. The practice of using release dates sometimes leads to absurdities, as with Renoir's *Une Partie de campagne* which was made in 1936 but not released until 1946. When the year of production is not the same as the year of release, I have given also this date (e.g., France 1936, released 1946); when production was spread over several years I have indicated this (e.g., Germany 1924, production began 1922).

I have followed French practice in entering French titles beginning with *Un* or *Une* under "U." However, such titles are always cross-referenced (e.g., *Chien Andalou (Un)* refers to *Un Chien Andalou*).

The running times of sound films are given in minutes; the length of silent films is given in feet — or in meters for European and Asian films, with an approximate footage equivalent for convenience. For certain early films, notably Japanese, it has proved impossible to identify original lengths accurately and, in such cases an approximate length has been given.

I am indebted to the Canadian Film Institute's Film Study Center and to the British Film Institute's Information Department, without access to which this volume could not have been prepared in its present form.

Abbreviations

Anim	Animation by/Animator
Art Dir	Art Director/Decor by/Designed by
Assist	Assistant
Assoc	Associate
Cast	Principal actors & actresses
Choreog	Choreography by/Dances directed by
Dir	Director/Directed by
Ed	Editor/Edited by
Mus	Music composed by/Composer
Photog	Photographer/Photographed by
Prod	Produced by (usually company)
q.v.	See
Scen	Scenarist/Script-writer/Written by

ADDED MATERIALS

Completely new entries added by the translator, or entries substantially revised, are indicated by asterisks next to the titles. Passages added to entries by the translator are enclosed in square brackets.

AAN SAVAGE PRINCESS India 1952. *Dir* Mehboob Khan *Scen* Chaudary, Ali Raza *Photog* Faredoon A. Irani *Art Dir* M. R. Acharekar *Mus* Naushad *Songs* Shakil Badayuni *Cast* Dilip Kumar, Nimmi, Nadira, Premnath, Mukri *Prod* Mehboob Productions, Bombay. 190 mins (130 mins foreign release). Technicolor (enlarged from 16mm Kodachrome).

A young, proud peasant (Kumar) defends the people's freedom against an arrogant prince (Premnath) who has usurped his father's throne and is attempting to seduce the hero's girl friend, Mangala (Nimmi). Mangala commits suicide to protect her virtue, the peasant kills the prince, marries his sister (Nadira), and reinstates the maharaja.

Aan was the first Indian film to reach a large international public. Notable for its seductive music, its beautifully photographed landscapes, its excellent décor, and its absorbing account of exotic adventures (the princess thrown to the lions, the camel stampede in the jungle, the cavalry battles, etc.). The construction is episodic, each scene being self-contained and separated from the next by a musical scene or a chorus. It had a successful release in London, but was most enthusiastically received in the Arab world and in Black Africa. Ten years later, its success was still evident and its songs were still heard on the radio and on records.

A BOUT DE SOUFFLE BREATHLESS France 1959. *Dir* Jean-Luc Godard *Scen* François Truffaut, Godard *Photog* Raoul Coutard *Ed* Cécile Decugis *Mus* Martial Solal *Cast* Jean-Paul Belmondo, Jean Seberg, Daniel Boulanger. *Prod* Imperia/SNC/ Les Films Georges de Beauregard. 89 mins.

A young gangster, Michel (Belmondo), after stealing a car, is returning to Paris when he casually kills a policeman on the highway. Penniless in Paris, he seeks out his American girl friend, Patricia (Seberg), and tries to persuade her to flee with him to Italy since Police Inspector Vital (Boulanger) is closing in. After helping Michel to hide, Patricia beytrays him to the police, who shoot him down in the street.

Godard's first feature is marked especially by its acerbic, derisive tone, its easy confidence, its personal, contemporary (if somewhat flowery) expression of story and language, its unconventional editing style, and its vision of Paris, where destiny overwhelms two lovers doomed to separation and death (as in *Quai des brumes*). This was Belmondo's first major role, and his interpretation of an anarchic criminal, confused, bitter, and cynical, made him famous. Jean Seberg, all feline ambiguity, has never been better directed.

[This is undoubtedly one of the seminal films of the Sixties. Its elliptical style, its reflection of the existentialist ethos, and its individualistic approach, affected many films that followed it. Godard's critical view of the cinema as a mixed form is reflected here in the use of a collage of film techniques in his mixing of the comic with the tragic and realism with melodrama, and in his "quotes" from other film makers and from gangster films.]

ACADEMICIAN IVAN PAVLOV AKADEMIK IVAN PAVLOV

*ACCATONE Italy 1961. *Dir* Pier Paolo Pasolini *Scen* Pier Paolo Pasolini based on his own novel *Una Vita Violenta* *Photog* Tonino delli Colli *Art Dir* Flavio Mogherini *Cast* Franco Citti, Franca Pasut, Roberto Scaringella, Adele Cambria,

1

Paolo Guidi *Prod* Cino del Duca/Arco. 120 mins.

In the slums of Rome, Accattone "The Sponger" (Citti) lives off the earnings of a prostitute. He falls in love with Stella (Pasut), tries to reform for her sake, but gives up. As he plans a theft with a friend, the police close in; Accattone escapes on a motorcycle but crashes and is killed.

Accattone is neorealism rejuvenated — with a vengeance. There is none of the sentimentalism that marks some of the postwar Italian films; for Pasolini, there is no solution to Accattone's problem, no escape possible from the vicious circle of despair, vice, and poverty.

This was Pasolini's first film, Its rough-edged style, its cool, unhysterical portrayal of corruption, cruelty, and violence, and its quiet lyricism marked one of the most significant directorial debuts of the Sixties.

ACE IN THE HOLE THE BIG CARNIVAL USA 1951. *Dir* Billy Wilder *Scen* L. Samuels, W. Newman, Billy Wilder *Photog* Charles B. Lang Jr. *Ed* Arthur Schmidt *Cast* Kirk Douglas, Jan Sterling, Richard Benedict, Bob Arthur, Porter Hall *Prod* Paramount. 111 mins.

A journalist (Douglas), trying to make a name for himself, organizes an enormous publicity stunt around a man who is trapped alive in a cave. He persuades the man's wife (Sterling) to join him in making money out of the resulting sensation. He has a change of heart when the man dies, but he is fatally stabbed by the wife.

[One of Wilder's most successful films: an acid, ruthless depiction of the journalist and the sensation-hungry crowds who flock to the caves.] Best sequence: the carnival organized around the cave where the man lies in agony.

ADIEU PHILIPPINE France/Italy 1962. *Dir* Jacques Rozier *Scen* Michèle O'Glor, Jacques Rozier *Photog* René Mathelin *Ed* Monique Bonnot *Cast* Jean-Claude Aimini, Yveline Céry, Stefania Sabatini, Vittorio Caprioli *Prod* Unitec-Alpha Productions-Euro International Films-Rome Paris Films. 106 mins.

Story of a television technician (Aimini) who, while waiting to be drafted, has a love affair with two inseparable girls. As much derived from *cinéma vérité* as from the *nouvelle vague,* this charming, fresh film is full of insight. The script was largely improvised.

ADVENTURE (THE) AVVENTURA (L')

ADVENTURER (THE) USA 1917. *Dir/Scen* Charles Chaplin *Cast* Chaplin, Edna Purviance, Eric Campbell, Albert Austin, Henry Bergman, Frank Coleman, Kono *Prod* Mutual. 1,845 ft.

The last and best of the Mutual series. Charlie, an escaped convict, rescues two wealthy women from drowning and is invited to their house, where he courts the daughter (Purviance). His rival suitor (Campbell) recognizes him, sends for the prison guards, and Charlie takes flight again. See *Dictionary of Film Makers* (Chaplin article) for Chaplin's analysis of the film's famous ice-cream gag.

ADVENTURES OF BARON MUNCHHAUSEN (THE) see BARON MÜNCHHAUSEN

ADVENTURES OF OKTYABRINI (THE) POKHOZDENIYA OKTYABRINI

AELITA USSR 1924. *Dir* Yakov Protazanov *Scen* Fyodor Otsep, Alexei Faiko, based on the novel by Alexei Tolstoy *Photog* Yuri Zhelyabuzhsky, E. Schöneman *Art Dir* Sergei Kozlovsky (sketches by Isaac Rabinovich, Victor Simov) *Cast* Yulia Solntseva, Nikolai Batalov, Igor Ilinsky, Konstantin Eggert, Nikolai Tseretelli, V. Orlova *Prod* Mezhrabpom–Russ. 1,841 meters. (approx. 6,000 ft.).

A young Russian soldier (Batalov) and an engineer who has invented a rocket (Tseretelli) land on Mars, where the soldier starts a revolution among the slaves of the planet's ruler, Queen Aelita (Solntseva).

Protazanov, who had been working in Berlin and Paris since 1917, had the best facilities placed at his disposal for this production. Though not an important example of his Russian work, it has merit because of its stylized, theatrical settings and costumes and its realistic depiction of Moscow during the era of the New Economic Policy (NEP). The dazzling beauty of Solntseva (who shortly after married Dovzhenko) made the film a great success, and many babies born that year were named Aelita. The film is especially notable for the superb performances of Ilinsky (as the detective) and Batalov.

AEROGRAD FRONTIER USSR 1935. *Dir/ Scen* Alexander Dovzhenko *Photog* Eduard Tisse, Mikhail Gindin *Mus* Dmitri Kabalevsky *Cast* Semyon Shagaida, Stepan Shkurat, Sergei Stolyarov, I. Melnikova *Prod* Mosfilm/Ukrainfilm. 81 mins.

In the Siberian taiga, the frontier guards prevent the infiltration of Japanese spies and prepare for the building of an airport.

Aerograd conveys marvelously the atmosphere of the wild and marshy forests, with a beautifully lyrical finale showing the flight of the airplanes. The most remarkable sequence is that in which the frontier guard learns that his best friend, an old hunter, is a spy and saboteur. *Aerograd* is a noble, complex, and very engaging work, though not one of Dovzhenko's great films.

AFFAIRE DREYFUS (L') France 1899. *Dir/ Prod* Georges Méliès. 618 ft.

The first "feature" of the great film maker was produced at a time when the Dreyfus case was at its height. It is a very engaging film, sympathetic to Dreyfus. Its ten realistic scenes were based on magazine prints and photographs and were made in a studio. The film was produced for foreign distribution; its screening in France would have provoked brawls in the audience.

OTHER FILMS on the Dreyfus case:
— *L'Affaire Dreyfus* France 1908. *Dir* Ferdinand Zecca.
— *Dreyfus* Germany 1930. *Dir* Richard Oswald.
— *Dreyfus* Britain 1931. *Dir* Milton Rosmer & F. W. Kraemer *Cast* Sir Cedric Hardwicke.
— *I Accuse* Britain 1957. *Dir* José Ferrer *Cast* José Ferrer.
See also *The Life of Emile Zola*

AFFAIRE EST DANS LE SAC (L') IT'S IN THE BAG France 1932. *Dir* Pierre Prévert *Scen* Jacques Prévert from an original script by A. Rathony *Photog* A. Gibory, Eli Lotar *Ed* Louis Chavance *Mus* Maurice Jaubert *Art Dir* Lou Bonin, Reichenko (based on sets by Lucien Aguettant & Jacques Colombier) *Cast* Jean-Paul Dreyfus, Etienne Decroux, Lucien Raimbourg, Marcel Duhamel, Jacques Brunius, Jacques Prévert, Guy Decomble, Julien Carette, Jean Deninx, Lou Bonin, Lora Hays, Gildès, Daniel Gilbert *Prod* Pathé-Nathan. 47 mins.

A hat maker (Decroux) and a young man (Dreyfus) plot to kidnap the daughter of a multimillionaire by putting her in a sack. In the end, the boy marries the heiress, and the multimillionaire takes the hatter for a jester. This nonsense comedy abounds in poetic gags. The retort: "I want a béret, a proper French béret" is an allusion to the headgear worn by French fascists in 1930. This political allusion is not surprising since the actors were from the "October Group," a company of the extreme left founded by J.-P. Dreyfus (Le Chanois). This important work by Prévert did not have a single commercial showing, yet has become a classic.

AFRICAN QUEEN (THE) Britain 1951. *Dir* John Huston *Scen* James Agee, John Huston based on novel by C. S. Forester *Art Dir* Wilfred Singleton *Photog* Jack Cardiff *Ed* Ralph Kemplen *Mus* Allan Gray *Cast* Humphrey Bogart, Katharine Hepburn, Robert Morley *Prod* Romulus-Horizon (Sam Spiegel). 103 mins. Technicolor.

A prim English spinster, Rose (Hepburn), and a slovenly Canadian riverboat captain, Charlie (Bogart), become enemy aliens in German East Africa when war breaks out in 1914. They attempt to escape in the riverboat and Rose persuades Charlie to attack a German gunboat with homemade missiles. After running the gauntlet of guns, jungle storms, and mosquitoes, they are captured by the Germans; but luck is with them and the gunboat is sunk. During the journey they fall in love.

Shot largely on location, but with the addition of studio scenes (the back projection is very apparent because of the color). The emphasis in the film is on the change in the characters of Rose and Charlie and on the stupidity of war. Bogart, in the role of the dissolute riverboat captain, gives a superb and many-layered performance (for which he won an Oscar), but he is more than matched by Hepburn's authoritative creation of the shy spinster; the scenes of their dawning love for each other are a delight. This is one of Huston's favorite films.

AFTER THE THIN MAN see THIN MAN (THE)

3

AGE D'OR (L') France 1930. *Dir* Luis Buñuel *Scen* Luis Buñuel, Salvador Dali *Assist Dir* Jacques Brunius *Photog* Albert Dubergen *Art Dir* Schilzneck *Ed* Luis Buñuel *Cast* Gaston Modot, Lya Lys, Max Ernst, Pierre Prévert, Caridad de Laberdesque, Lionel Salem, Liorens Artryas, Ibanez, Duchange, Madame Noizet, José Artigas, Jacques Brunius *Prod* Vicomte de Noailles. 63 mins.

Principal sequences: the quasi-scientific documentary about scorpions; the starved, wretched Majorcan bandits (Prévert, Ernst) who eventually collapse exhausted on the cliffs; the ceremony of the laying of the foundation stone for "Imperial Rome" disturbed by a man (Modot) lying on the ground lustfully making love to a woman; scenes of Rome; two policemen drag the man (Modot) down the street; his fantasy of his mistress (Lys) as he looks at a photograph; later, he frees himself from his captors by producing an official-looking document and before leaving in a taxi kicks a blind man; a large reception in the Marquis of X's magnificent villa near Rome, where the guests ignore various strange incidents (a farm cart led through the ballroom, a fire); the gamekeeper shoots his son; the man (Modot) arrives carrying a woman's dress, slaps the face of the Marquise, and then takes his mistress (Lys) into the garden where they embrace passionately; their love-making is frustrated and interrupted by a phone call from an angry Minister of the Interior who says (over newsreel shots of fire and crowds fleeing), "You are the only one to blame for what has happened, murderer," and then kills himself; the man returns to his lover but she leaves him to make love with an old conductor of an orchestra that is giving a concert in the garden; the despair of the man in his lover's bedroom as he throws various objects out of the window — a pine tree on fire, a live archbishop, a stuffed giraffe, feathers; in the finale, the four survivors of the "most brutal of orgies" leave the chateau led by the Duke of Blangis (criminal hero of de Sade) dressed as Jesus.

The production of *L'Age d'or* was financed by a patron of the arts, the Vicomte de Noailles, and Buñuel was given complete creative freedom. His contribution was fundamental: nearly all the main themes of his work are to be found in the film. It was originally to have been called "the frozen waters of egotistical calculation" (an expression of the Communist Manifesto).

In a manifesto included in the program of *L'Age d'or* written and illustrated by many surrealists, it was said: "The foundations are laid, conventions become dogma, policemen push people around just as they do in everyday life. And, just as in everyday life, accidents occur in bourgeois society while that society pays no attention whatsoever. But such accidents (and it must be noted that in Buñuel's film they remain uncorrupted by plausibility) further weaken an already rotting society that is trying to prolong its existence artificially through priests and policemen . . . But it is LOVE that brings about the transition from pessimism to action; Love, denounced in the bourgeois demonology as the root of all evil. For Love demands the sacrifice of every other value: status, family, and honor."

In addition to extolling *L'amour fou,* the film violently attacks religion and the social order — the Freudian symbolism of which is due mainly to Dali. Examples of this include the indifference of the Marquis (his face covered with flies) and his guests to two laborers crossing the room in a farm cart and to a maid overcome by a fire; the gamekeeper who shoots a child; the skeletons of the bishops on the rocks.

L'Age d'or was presented to the Board of Censors as the dream of a madman and obtained a screening permit. The first few weeks of screenings at Studio 28 were unmarked by incidents. On the evening of December 3, 1930, members of the fascist League of Patriots and of the Anti-Semitic League interrupted the screening, shouting "Down with the Jews," throwing stink bombs and purple ink at the screen; furnishings were destroyed and paintings (by Dali, Max Ernst, Man Ray) were slashed. As a result the film was banned by police commissioner Chiappe. *L'Age d'or* is very much a reflection of its own era and of the 1930 surrealist revolt.

AGE OF INFIDELITY MUERTE DE UN CICLISTA

AGUAS BAJAN TURBIAS (LAS) MUDDY WATERS RUN DOWN Argentina 1952. *Dir* Hugo del Carril *Scen* Eduardo Borras, Gori Muñoz based on the novel by

Varela *Photog* José-Maria Beltran *Mus* Riberro *Cast* Hugo del Carril, Adriana Benetti. 82 mins.

A group of maté gatherers are treated like slaves by a trader but revolt against his tyranny.

One of the few films of merit produced in Argentina during the Peron years. It is based on a novel by Varela, who was in prison when it was made and whose name is not included in the credits. Its theme is very similar to Mario Soffici's earlier *Prisoners of the Earth* (*q.v.*).

A.H.Q. Hong Kong 1957. *Dir* Yuen Yang-an *Scen* Yuen Yang-an based on the novel by Lu Hsun *Cast* Kuan Hsiang *Prod* Great Wall Studio, Hong Kong.

Based on the famous work by the Chinese writer, Lu Hsun, it tells of a peasant who befriends unfortunates. The perfect black humor and social polemic of the novel have been incorporated into this honestly produced and very well-acted film.

AIN EL GHEZAL THE GIRL FROM CARTHAGE Tunisia 1924 *Dir/Photog* Scemana Chikly *Scen* Haydé Chikly *Cast* Haydé Chikly, Ahmed Dziri, Abdelgassen Ben Taleb, Hadj Hadi Dehali.

The daughter of a caid (Dehali), in love with a poor man (Dziri), rejects a rich Tunisian (Taleb) and is killed by mercenaries.

Without doubt the first Arabian feature. It was made in North Africa by a cameraman who had been working since 1898 for newsreels and the Cinema Service of the Army. The production was assisted by the *bey,* who allowed the film to be made in his gardens and in a religious school. The film was shot entirely in natural sets and "shows a fantasia, a marriage, a local celebration, and the like" (*Mon Ciné* October 30, 1924).

AIR FORCE USA 1943. *Dir* Howard Hawks *Scen* Dudley Nichols *Photog* James Wong Howe *Cast* John Garfield, Harry Carey, Gig Young, Arthur Kennedy *Prod* Warner Brothers. 124 mins.

US air combat in the Pacific. Hawks, who was a pilot, shows the heroism and horrors of the air battles with a virile brutality.

AITANGA Norway 1942. *Dir* Helge Lunde *Scen* Helge Lunde based on the novel by F. W. Remmler *Photog* Per Johnson *Cast* Signe Hasso, Georg Lokkeberg, Alfred Maurstadt. 85 mins.

The son (Lokkeberg) of a hunter falls in love with a mountain girl (Hasso). He fights with her fiancé (Maurstadt) and kills him. But the murder doesn't separate the lovers.

Made in natural settings in the Great North, the film is notable for its picturesque portrayal of Lapp costumes and wild animals. The photography is somewhat overstylized.

AJAANTRIK THE PATHETIC FALLACY India 1958. *Dir* Ritwik Ghatak *Scen* Subodh Gosh.

An excellent picaresque comedy-fantasy about a taxi driver's love for his aging taxi; set in a variety of regions in Bengal.

AKADEMIK IVAN PAVLOV ACADEMICIAN IVAN PAVLOV USSR 1949. *Dir* Grigori Roshal *Photog* V. Gardanov, M. Magid *Art Dir* Y. Enei, A. Wechsler *Mus* Dmitri Kabalevsky *Cast* A. Borisov, Nina Alisova, V. Chestnokov, N. Plotnikov *Prod* Lenfilm. 110 mins.

The life and work of Pavlov (1846–1936), famous for his theory of conditioned reflexes. It was successful because of its many scientific sections, Borisov's powerful performance, and Papava's script, which depicted Pavlov not as a "yes-man" but as a passionate nonconformist.

AKAHIGE RED BEARD Japan 1965. *Dir.* Akira Kurosawa *Scen* Masato Ide, Hideo Iguni, R. Kikushima, A. Kurosawa based on a novel by Shugoro Yamamoto *Photog* A. Nakai, T. Saito *Mus* M. Sato *Art Dir* Y. Muraki *Cast* Toshiro Mifune, Yuzo Kayama, M. Kuwano, Terumi Niki *Prod* Toho-Kurosawa. 185 mins. Tohoscope.

In the early 19th century, a recently graduated doctor, Yasumoto (Kayama), is posted to an impoverished clinic run by Dr. Niide (Mifune), whose patients call him "Red Beard." Having hoped for a position as a society doctor, Yasumoto cannot accept Red Beard's contention that doctors fight poverty as well as illness. After assisting in various cases, he finally begins to conform to the clinic's rules and rescues a girl, Otoyo (Niki), who had been ill-treated in a brothel. When he himself falls ill, Otoyo nurses him. Finally, when he is offered a society position, he turns it down to stay at the clinic with Red Beard.

Kurosawa himself has called this a "monument to goodness in man." This remarkable "Education sentimentale," Dostoevskian in overtones, [has been much criticized for its "sentimentality," its proposition that good begets good. Kurosawa challenges the viewer to react cynically and then shows that the cynicism is meaningless. Kurosawa's style is simple, yet every scene is full of revealing details and images of extraordinary beauty. Mifune gives a superb performance in an extremely difficult role.]

A LA CONQUETE DU POLE THE CONQUEST OF THE POLE France 1912. *Dir* Georges Méliès. 1,350 ft.

A group of explorers and flyers arrive at the Pole and become involved with the Giant of the Snows.

This is perhaps the most perfect film in the Méliès series of "Voyages" and science fiction films, because of its elegance, the rhythm of its construction, the perfect harmony of the sets, and the grandiose machinery that operates the Giant. It was not very successful commercially, mainly because Zecca mutilated it and because Pathé sabotaged its release, but also because its style and esthetic belonged to 1900 and not to the period of Thomas Ince, Griffith, Feuillade, L. Perret, Mario Caserini, etc. For the public in 1912 the film was extremely outmoded. Nonetheless it is a masterpiece and has since become a classic.

ALAMO (THE) USA 1960. *Dir* John Wayne *Scen* James Edward Grant *Photog* William H. Clothier, Todd-AO *Ed* Stuart Gilmore *Mus* Dmitri Tiomkin *Cast* John Wayne, Richard Widmark, Laurence Harvey, Richard Boone, Frankie Avalon, Linda Cristal *Prod* Batjac/Alamo. 193 mins. Technicolor.

In 1836 in Texas (then Mexican), a group of North American mercenaries led by David Crockett (Wayne), James Bowie (Widmark), and General Sam Houston (Boone), are besieged in the monastery-fortress of Alamo and are massacred to the last man.

It was with the cry, "Remember the Alamo!" that the United States after 1845 conquered Texas, New Mexico, Arizona, and California. The story of the Alamo has inspired numerous American films (notably by Griffith and Ince). The sensational effects of this chauvinistic epic by actor-director John Wayne made it a great commercial success. Stuart Gilmore's sensitive and effective editing is the most notable aspect of the film.

ALEXANDER NEVSKY USSR 1938. *Dir* S. M. Eisenstein *Assist Dir* D. Vasiliev, V. Ivanov *Scen* Pyotr Pavlenko, S. M. Eisenstein *Photog* Eduard Tisse *Art Dir* I. Shpinel, N. Soloviov, K. Yeliseyev (based on designs by Eisenstein) *Mus* Prokofiev *Cast* Nikolai Cherkassov, Nikolai Okhlopkov, Andrei Abrikosov, Valentina Ivashova, Dmitri Orlov, Varvasa Massalitinova *Prod* Mosfilm. 112 mins.

In 1242, in the region of Russia menaced by Mongolian raids, Prince Alexander Nevsky (Cherkassov) learns in Novgorod that the Teutonic Knights are invading Russia. Some of the leaders wish to make peace with the invaders but the people mobilize and choose Nevsky as their commander. Although the Teutonic Knights win several victories and take Pskov, they are finally defeated in the great Battle on the Ice and the victorious people march into the liberated city of Pskov.

Eisenstein conceived the film as cinematic opera based on a bold, contrapuntal relationship between Prokofiev's score and the film's visual rhythm. It astonished those who saw it in 1939 and many foreign critics scorned its operatic approach, which they found difficult to accept. Had they read Eisenstein's theoretical writings they would not have been misled by his novel approach. "Curiously enough," wrote Eisenstein, "unlike my colleagues, *Alexander Nevsky* was my first sound film. I would have liked very much to experiment at leisure, to try some of the ideas that had haunted me during the years I watched sound films from a distance. But the guns booming at Lake Khasan shattered my intentions. There was no time for day-dreaming . . . it seemed impossible to ensure an organic unity of music and picture in the short time allotted to us. It seemed impossible to find and reproduce that wonderful inner synchronization of plastic and musical images, that is, to achieve that in which actually lies the secret of audio-visual impression. . . . This is where the magician Sergei Prokofiev came to my rescue." An intimate collaboration sprang up between the two great artists: "Both music and 'visual' music, that is, the representation, must be composed on the same principle. Here the experience of montage construction in the silent film comes in handy. The silent film demanded that the music develop in shot sequences along and in conformity with the narrative presentation of events. . . . The repetition of an expressive combination of sounds, which is indispensable in music, is present in the rhythmical and montage groups of representations too." Once the "symphonic" construction of the film and the new relationship created between filmmaker and musician is understood, this carefully designed film no longer seems to be "cold."

"Patriotism is my theme," wrote Eisenstein, as Russia was awaiting the attack of new Teutonic hordes. He was sure any such attack would be defeated: in 1938 he wrote "This is the fate in store for all who may dare attack our country." The patriotic feeling that pervades *Alexander Nevsky* gave considerable warm sentiment to several scenes, particularly those depicting the atrocities committed by the Teutons at Pskov. Eisenstein was struck by the contemporary relevance of *Alexander Nevsky:* "The striking thing was the similarity between the events described in the chronicles and epics and the events of our own days." And in 1938 he described the Teutonic Knights' "terrible, invincible wedge formation" in this way: "Imagine the prow of a battleship, or a powerful tank magnified to the size of one hundred iron-clad horsemen advancing in serried ranks. . . . Imagine finally the 'thin edge' of this giant iron wedge, cutting into the very midst of the enemy soldiers, stupefied by the terrible mass of steel bearing down on them: instead of the knights' faces they see steel visors with cross-shaped openings." He apparently also had other armored formations in mind and, in the first draft, swastikas were present on the Teutons' helmets.

The Battle on the Ice dominates the film but its visual and aural power should not allow one to forget the other superb sequences of cinematic opera that pass from pastoral to lamentation and end in a triumphal cantata. *Alexander Nevsky* marks a decisive turning point in Eisenstein's work, one in which he moved from the masses as hero to individual and tragic heroes, characterized and shaped by their historic missions.

ALIAS NICK BEAL see FAUST

ALL ABOUT EVE USA 1950. *Dir* Joseph L. Mankiewicz *Scen* Joseph L. Mankiewicz *Photog* Milton Krasner *Ed* Barbara McLean *Art Dir* Lyle Wheeler, George W. Davis *Mus* Alfred Newman *Cast* Bette Davis, Anne Baxter, George Sanders, Gary Merrill, Celeste Holm, Marilyn Monroe, Hugh Marlowe *Prod* 20th Century-Fox. 138 mins.

A young actress, Eve (Baxter), becomes famous and replaces her rival (Davis), after having been introduced to her by a friend (Holm), the wife of a successful author (Marlowe), and winning her confidence. This conventional but intelligent satire of the theatrical world is most notable for the acting. Although Bette Davis was hailed at Cannes for her performance, the film is dominated by Anne Baxter. Even she, however, yields for a moment to a petite newcomer, Marilyn Monroe, who appears in a short scene.

ALL QUIET ON THE WESTERN FRONT USA 1930. *Dir* Lewis Milestone *Scen* Del Andrews, Maxwell Anderson, George Abbott based on the novel by Erich Maria Remarque *Photog* Arthur Edeson *Ed* Edgar Adams, Milton Carruth *Art Dir* Charles D. Hall, W. R. Schmidt *Mus* David Broekman *Cast* Lew Ayres, Louis Wolheim, John Wray, Raymond Griffith, Slim Summerville *Prod* Universal. 140 mins. (current versions 104 mins.).

The brutality of warfare for the ordinary soldier on both sides of the line on the French front in 1916. Young recruits (Ayres, Summerville, and others) are initiated by a veteran (Wolheim) and brutalized by a noncommissioned officer (Wray). [Milestone, who originally began it as a silent film but completed it with sound, managed to retain many of the pictorial values and editing rhythms from silent films in a period when most sound films were static photographed plays.]

Its polemic against war and its horrors led to its being attacked by the Nazis, who were close to power in 1930. Their demonstrations against the film as injurious to German interests led to its being withdrawn from theaters. When the film was released again twenty years later, it still retained much of its original power.

ALL THAT MONEY CAN BUY see FAUST

ALONE ODNA

ALOUETTE ET LA MESANGE (L') France 1922. *Dir* André Antoine *Scen* André Antoine, Grillet *Cast* Henry Krauss, Pierre Alcover, and nonprofessional actors.
In 1924 Antoine said to André Lang about this still unreleased film: "I had had an idea for a film: the life of boatmen on the canals in Flanders. I send Grillet ahead to look for a location. I arrive with the artists. We leave Antwerp on one barge and we go up the Escaut. Since everything was shot on the voyage this enhanced the photography. Very striking! It ended with a man being sucked into the mud one night and the next day the barge floated anew tranquilly in the light and the silence."
According to this description it seems that Antoine used a neorealistic approach twenty years before the Italians.

*ALPHAVILLE, UNE ETRANGE AVENTURE DE LEMMY CAUTION ALPHAVILLE France/Italy 1965. *Dir/Scen* Jean-Luc Godard *Photog* Raoul Coutard *Mus* Paul Mizraki *Ed* Agnès Guillemot *Cast* Eddy Constantine, Anna Karina, Akim Tamiroff, Howard Vernon *Prod* Chaumiane/Filmstudio. 98 mins.
Special agent Lemmy Caution (Constantine) crosses intergalactic space to Alphaville to discover what happened to his predecessor, Henri Dickson, (Tamiroff) and to Professor von Braun (Vernon). He is assisted by von Braun's daughter (Karina). He discovers Alphaville is ruled by von Braun through his computer, Alpha 60, which eliminates everything that does not conform. He witnesses Dickson's death but eventually destroys von Braun and the computer. A film about alienation in a technological society. Richard Roud has written: "*Alphaville* has been described as 'Tarzan versus IBM' (and this in fact was the original title). Nominally a science fiction film, *Alphaville* is really about the horrors of today, not tomorrow. And Alpha 60, Capital of the electronic world, is the Paris of today, Capital of Pain. Visually, it was Godard's most striking film since *Vivre sa vie*, a kind of consolidation of all the earlier films, and a signpost of the more abstract approach of more recent films."

*AMANT DE CINQ JOURS (L') FIVE DAY LOVER/INFIDELITY France/Italy 1960. *Dir* Philippe de Broca *Scen* Daniel Boulanger, Philippe de Broca based on the novel by Françoise Parturier *Photog* Jean-Bernard Penzer *Art Dir* Bernard Evein *Mus* Georges Delerue *Cast* Jean Seberg, Jean-Pierre Cassel, Micheline Presle, François Périer *Prod* Ariane Filmsonor/Mondex/Cineriz. 86 mins.
A bored young housewife, Claire (Seberg), has a brief affair with Antoine (Cassel), ignorant of the fact that he is her best friend's (Presle) lover. At a party, the friend breaks the romantic illusion and Claire returns to her husband (Périer) and her habit of wandering the city in search of unexpected friends.
Philippe de Broca, who has inherited something of the mantle of Lubitsch, displays in this sophisticated comedy (de Broca's third) of sexual mores, wit, charm, and a deftness in depicting character. Jean-Pierre Cassel gives an excellent performance in a role similar to those he had in *The Love Game* and *The Joker:* a charming, brilliant dilettante at his best only in the company of women.

AMANTS (LES) THE LOVERS France 1958. *Dir* Louis Malle *Scen* Louis Malle based on *Point de Lendemain* by Dominique-Vivent, Baron Denon *Photog* Henri Decae *Art Dir* Bernard Evein, Jacques Saulnier *Ed* Léonide Aznar *Cast* Jeanne Moreau, Alain Cuny, Jean-Marc Bory, José-Louis de Villalonga, Gaston Modot *Prod* Nouvelles Editions de Films. 88 mins. Dyaliscope.
A rich, provincial woman (Moreau) married to a busy newspaper owner (Cuny) seeks excitement in Paris and takes a lover (de Villalonga). But her husband becomes suspicious. As she returns home, she meets a young man (Bory) and invites him to stay the evening. That night they realize their love cannot be denied and, after spending the night together, drive away.
This bold and poetic portrait of love was Louis Malle's first success. Its best sequence is satirical: the dinner at the chateau. The weakest sequence is per-

haps the lyrical love scene in the park. Its beautiful erotic scenes (which could have been scabrous but are always modest) contributed greatly to the film's international success.

AMERE VICTOIRE BITTER VICTORY France 1957. *Dir* Nicholas Ray *Scen* Gavin Lambert, Nicholas Ray, René Hardy based on *Bitter Victory* by René Hardy *Photog* Michel Kelber *Ed* Léonide Azar *Art Dir* Jean d'Eaubonne, Marc Frédéric, Petitot *Mus* Maurice le Roux *Cast* Curt Jurgens, Richard Burton, Ruth Roman, Raymond Pellegrin *Prod* Transcontinental Films/Robert Laffont Productions. 100 mins. (90 mins. Britain, 82 mins USA.) CinemaScope.

In 1942, the commander (Jurgens) of a desert patrol in Lybia allows a scorpion to mortally sting his wife's (Roman) lover (Burton) and then destroys the witness (Pellegrin) to his crime. His mission accomplished, he is welcomed as a hero.

Though the film contains certain weaknesses (particularly in the first part), the desert scenes, shot in Africa, are very striking. The most beautiful sequence, in which an officer under orders must put his wounded comrade out of pain, is extremely moving. Curt Jurgens gives a reasonable performance but is somewhat unconvincing as a British officer.

AMERICAN IN PARIS (AN) USA 1951. *Dir* Vincente Minnelli *Scen* Alan Jay Lerner *Photog* Alfred Gilks, John Alton *Art Dir* Cedric Gibbons, Preston Ames *Mus* George Gershwin *Ed* Adrienne Fazan *Choreog* Gene Kelly *Cast* Gene Kelly, Leslie Caron, Oscar Levant, Nina Foch, Georges Guetary *Prod* MGM. 116 mins. Technicolor.

An American painter (Kelly) living in Paris is desired by a millionairess (Foch) but prefers a pretty girl (Caron), who is, however, the fiancée of his French friend (Guetary).

This cinematic ballet is not a series of vaudeville acts but more like an opera in which the dances and the music are an integral part of the dramatic action (though the plot is quite conventional). The film's appeal relies mainly on the lavish dances, choreographed by Gene Kelly, and the settings, which are a succession of homages to the great French painters Toulouse-Lautrec, Raoul Dufy, Utrillo, Renoir, etc. Gene Kelly and Leslie Caron are magnificent. The final musical sequence is unparalleled as an example of film choreography. Winner of five Academy Awards.

AMERICAN TRAGEDY (AN) USA 1931. *Dir* Josef von Sternberg. *Scen* Josef von Sternberg, Samuel Hoffenstein based on the novel by Theodore Dreiser *Photog* Lee Garmes *Art Dir* Hans Dreier *Cast* Phillips Holmes, Sylvia Sidney, Frances Dee, Irving Pichel *Prod* Paramount. 90 mins.

"The script of *An American Tragedy* was first offered by Paramount to the famous Eisenstein. He prepared an outline that stressed the political aspects of the work, making of it an anticapitalist propaganda film that boosted his relationship with Moscow. Paramount therefore entrusted Sternberg with the task of making it into an unbiased dramatic film, a feat in which he was completely successful" (press release, 1931). ["I eliminated the sociological elements, which, in my opinion, were far from being responsible for the dramatic incident which Dreiser had concerned himself" (Joseph von Sternberg). An austere, detached version of the novel, in many ways more honest (and certainly more vigorous) in its dissection of a small-town tragedy than Stevens's later, more respectful, but pedestrian, version.]

See also PLACE IN THE SUN (A)

AMICHE (LE) THE GIRL FRIENDS Italy 1955. *Dir* Michelangelo Antonioni *Scen* Suso Cecchi d'Amico, Alba de Céspedes based on *Tra donne sole* by Cesare Pavese *Photog* Gianni di Venanzo *Art Dir* Gianni Polidori *Mus* Giovanni Fusco. *Cast* Eleanora Rossi Drago, Valentina Cortese, Gabriele Ferzetti, Franco Fabrizi, Madeleine Fischer, Yvonne Furneaux, Ettore Manni *Prod* Trionfalcine. 90 mins.

Clelia (Rossi Drago) sets up a fashion house in Turin and makes friends with a model (Fischer), a potter (Cortese), a rich idler (Furneaux), a painter (Ferzetto), a designer (Fabrizi). The model is driven to suicide by the rich woman and Clelia leaves the town.

The Pavese novel on which the film is based was freely adapted.

Antonioni says that he loved its account of "females and their interior lives — I have been told that Pavese and I are somewhat similar. His intellectual ex-

9

periences coincided tragically with his personal experiences (he committed suicide in 1955). Could the same be said of me? Doesn't the fact I'm here in the process of making films suggest optimism? For me, I want to have my characters part of their surroundings and not to separate them from their everyday environment. Also you won't find one single *champ-contre-champ* in *Le Amiche*. The technique is instinctive and derives from a desire to follow the characters in order to unveil their innermost hidden thoughts."

AMONG PEOPLE see DETSVO GORKOVO

AMORE IN CITTA LOVE IN THE CITY Italy 1953. *Dir* Michelangelo Antonioni, Federico Fellini, Cesare Zavattini, Alberto Lattuada, Carlo Lizzani, Francesco Muselli, Dino Risi *Scen* Zavattini, Aldo Buzzi, Luigi Chiarini, Luigi Malerba, Tullio Pinelli and others *Photog* Gianni di Venanzo *Art Dir* Gianni Polidori *Mus* Mario Nascimbene *Cast* nonprofessionals *Prod* FaroFilm. 110 mins. (Lizzani episode removed from foreign release versions at the instigation of the Italian Government.)

A six-part episode film, based on true situations. It was the first (and only) edition of a film journal to be called "The Spectator." 1. "Paradise for Three Hours" (Risi) — in the highly charged atmosphere of a cheap dance hall in Rome, where clerks, truck drivers, and servant girls meet and part again in a kind of formalized ritual involving an awkward, yet hectic, physical contact. 2. "When Love Fails" (Antonioni) — unsuccessful suicides recount their own stories of why they had wanted to commit suicide, blaming disappointment in love. 3. "Love Cheerfully Arranged" (Fellini) — a client (Fellini) of a matrimonial agency pretends he is looking for a wife for his friend who has delusions of being a werewolf. 4. "Paid Love" (Lizzani) — a survey of prostitution using girls "picked up" by the camera in streets, cafés, and rooms and interviewed by a reporter. 5. "The Love of a Mother" (Zavattini/Maselli) — based on a major Italian news story in which Catherina Rigoglioso, soon after she was released from prison, relives her story for the camera. As an unmarried mother she discovers that society will assume its responsibilities toward her child only

if she abandons it. 6. "Italy Turns Around" (Lattuada) — 20 sexy Italian beauties were let loose on the male population of Rome whose reactions were observed by hidden cameras.

Zavattini was the inspirational force behind this significant film, which marked an evolution of neorealism toward what later became known as *cinéma-vérité*. The style of films like *Bicycle Thieves* becomes in this film either a direct recording of actuality ("Paradise for Three Hours," "Italy Turns Around") or a reconstruction of real events with the protagonists acting out their own dramas ("The Love of a Mother," "When Love Fails"). These latter two episodes are the best, especially "The Love of a Mother" in which "realism surpasses all artistic prudence" (Bazin).

This film brought together the principal Italian film-making hopes of the Fifties. But the 1954–60 crisis and the producers' lack of understanding hindered the careers of Maselli, Lizzani, and Risi; even Fellini and Antonioni (then unknown) had difficulties.

AMOUR D'UNE FEMME (L') France/Italy 1953. *Dir* Jean Grémillon *Scen* René Wheeler, Jean Grémillon, René Fallet *Photog* Louis Page *Mus* Henri Duttileux *Ed* Louisette Hautecoeur *Cast* Micheline Presle, Massimo Girotti, Gaby Morlay, Marc Cassot *Prod* L.P.C. (Pierre Gerin)/Films Costellazione. 100 mins.

On an island, a young lady doctor (Presle), the friend of a teacher (Morlay), loves an engineer (Girotti), who leaves her because she is hindering his career.

An important and noble film on the female psyche and the relationship between men and women. It was a total commercial failure and was, unfortunately, the last feature of a great film maker.

AMOURS DE LA REINE ELISABETH (LES) QUEEN BESS, HER LOVE STORY/QUEEN ELIZABETH France 1912. *Dir* Louis Mercanton, Henri Desfontaines *Scen* Eugène Moreau *Art Dir* Théâtre Sarah Bernhardt, Paris *Cast* Sarah Bernhardt, Lou Tellegen, Romani, Maxudian, Chameroy, Decoeur *Prod* Histrionic Film. 3,093 ft. *Queen Elizabeth* is a photographed version of the play that Sarah Bernhardt wanted to adapt for the screen ("This is my one chance for immortality," she is reported to have said). However, as Delluc said, this is an attempt at romantic beauty but has nothing to do with the cinema.

The film played an important part in American film history. Acquired by Adolph Zukor for $28,000, it was released in the USA as the first of the "Famous Players in Famous Plays." It made its first appearance at the specially rented Lyceum Theater in New York on July 12, 1912 surrounded by publicity suggesting that one could see the divine Sarah "in the flesh." Sarah Bernhardt herself had said "It gives me great pleasure to know that my masterpiece will from now on be available to anyone who wants to see it." The film's subsequent career in the States, through Al Lichtman's efforts, was very successful and earned Zukor $80,000. Its success enabled him to become a producer under the name Famous Players (which later became Paramount).

[The acting is largely statuesque, sometimes even pantomimic; long explanatory titles are used throughout. However, the success of this film did much to reduce prejudice against the "movies" and establish a new role for longer films.]

AND GOD CREATED WOMAN ET DIEU CRÉA LA FEMME

AND WOMAN . . . WAS CREATED ET DIEU CRÉA LA FEMME

AND YET WE LIVE DOKKOI IKITEIRU

ANGEL AND SINNER see PYSHKA

ANGELE HEARTBEAT France 1934. *Dir* Marcel Pagnol *Scen* Marcel Pagnol based on *Un de Beaumugnes* by Jean Giono *Cast* Fernandel, Orane Demazis, Jean Gervais. 90 mins. approx.

The story of a young woman who returns to her native village with an illegitimate child. Without question this is Pagnol's greatest film and Fernandel's best role, an unforgettable tragic portrayal.

ANGEL EXTERMINADOR (EL) THE EXTERMINATING ANGEL Mexico 1962. *Dir* Luis Buñuel *Scen* Luis Buñuel from a story by Buñuel and Luis Alcoriza *Photog* Gabriel Figueroa *Ed* Carlos Savage *Art Dir* Jesus Bracho *Cast* Silvia Pinal, Enrique Rambal, Jacqueline Andere, José

Baviera, Augusto Benedico *Prod* Uninci and Films 59. 95 mins.

Nobile (Benedico) invites to his sumptuous house a number of guests, who, when they wish to go home, discover they are unable to leave the music room. They remain isolated there for days, their social façade collapses, and they are reduced to eating sheep that arrive unexpectedly. The "spell" is suddenly shattered and the survivors of the "Raft of Medusa" go to church to celebrate their deliverance with a "Te Deum." However, when the service is over, the congregation is unable to leave; sheep enter the cathedral.

The key to this film might be a Mexican proverb: "After 24 hours corpses and guests smell bad." As with *El*, this typical Buñuelian film seems like a new episode for *L'Age d'or*. It has been defined by Buñuel as "a metaphor, a deeply felt, disturbing reflection of the life of modern man, a witness to the fundamental preoccupations of our time. Its images, like the images in a dream, do not reflect reality, but themselves create it." This marvelous film is something of a summary of Buñuel's life and work.

ANGEL STREET GASLIGHT (Britain)

ANGELS WITH DIRTY FACES USA 1938. *Dir* Michael Curtiz *Scen* John Wexley, Warren Duff *Photog* Sol Polito *Cast* James Cagney, Pat O'Brien, Humphrey Bogart, Ann Sheridan, George Bancroft *Prod* Warner Brothers. 97 mins.

A gangster (Cagney) works with a pastor (O'Brien) to rehabilitate the street boys of his district. A typical example (with an excellent cast) of a series of social melodramas that featured the Dead End Kids and were made as follow-ups to *Dead End* (*q.v.*). A few more films of this type were made but eventually the Dead End Kids turned into comedians.

ANGES DU PECHE (LES) France 1943. *Dir* Robert Bresson *Scen* R. P. Bruckberger, Robert Bresson, Jean Giradoux *Photog* Philippe Agostini *Art Dir* René Renoux *Mus* Jean-Jacques Grunenwald *Ed* Yvonne Martin *Cast* Renée Faure, Jany Holt, Sylvie, Marie-Hélène Dasté, Mila Parély, Silvia Monfort *Prod* Synops-Robert Paul. 73 mins.

A proud, sophisticated girl (Faure) enters a convent at Béthanie devoted to the rehabilitation of young girls. She becomes attached to one of them (Holt), a rebellious delinquent, and has trouble with the mother superior (Sylvie). She refuses to accept a punishment and runs away. Later she returns secretly to the convent and dies of exhaustion while pronouncing her vows. The delinquent gives herself up to the police.

Robert Bresson's first feature is notable for the intelligent and down-to-earth manner with which he handled a difficult subject, though Jean Giradoux's laconic and penetrating dialogue plays an important role. The sets are mediocre but Bresson's creation of a closed world is a symphony in black and white. This and Agostini's camerawork more than make up for the defects.

ANIKI BOBO Portugal 1942. *Dir* Manuel de Oliveira *Scen* based on Rodrigues de Fuertas *Photog* Antonio Mendes *Mus* Jaime Silva Filho *Cast* Nascimento Fernandes, Vitaldos Santos, and various children. 90 mins. approx.

A semidocumentary of the everyday life of children in the streets of Porto, the rallying cry of the children being "Aniki Bobo." The style, the atmosphere, and the use of nonprofessional actors might suggest that *Aniki Bobo* was influenced by Italian neorealism, though it was in fact made five years before *Sciuscià*. This sensitive film, though sometimes a little sentimental, is an important work — and not only for Portugal, though it was the best film produced there for forty years (1920–60).

ANIMAL CRACKERS USA 1930. *Dir* Victor Heerman *Scen* Morrie Ryskind based on the musical play: book by George S. Kaufman and Morrie Ryskind, music and lyrics by Bert Kalmar and Harry Ruby. *Photog* George Folsey *Cast*, Groucho, Chico, Harpo, and Zeppo Marx, Lilian Roth, Margaret Dumont *Prod* Paramount. 98 mins.

The Marx Brothers attend a party given by Mrs. Rittenhouse (Dumont) at her large house on Long Island at which she hopes to reap the social honors of the season.

One of the great Marx Brothers films, full of extraordinary gags; yet it suffers somewhat by being adapted from a musical comedy in which staged musical sequences break up the pace of the action.

*ANIMAL FARM Britain 1954 (production began 1952). *Dir* John Halas, Joy Batchelor *Scen* Lothar Wolff, Borden Mace, Philip Stapp, John Halas, Joy Batchelor based on the novel by George Orwell *Anim Dir* John Reed *Mus* Matyas Seiber *Voices* (of all animals) Maurice Denham *Prod* Halas and Batchelor. 73 mins. Technicolor.

An animated version of the George Orwell political satire in which the animals of a poorly kept farm revolt against their despotic owner and establish a "socialist" regime. The most "intelligent" are the pigs, who betray the others and establish a dictatorship, which is finally overthrown by the other animals.

Produced at about the same time as *La Bergère et le Ramoneur* (*q.v.*) this animated political fable is not as imaginative in design or execution as its French parallel. Orwell's original narrative is faithfully followed, with the exception of the final episode in the film where the animals stage a counterrevolution.

Seventy artists, 750 scenes, and 300,000 drawings were involved in the production. Despite its generally unadventurous design, it was a notable experiment of British animation and had considerable influence on the development of the cartoon film in Britain.

ANNEE DERNIERE A MARIENBAD (L') LAST YEAR AT MARIENBAD France/Italy 1961. *Dir* Alain Resnais *Scen* Alain Robbe-Grillet *Photog* Sacha Vierny *Mus* Francis Seyrig *Art Dir* Jacques Saulnier *Éd* Henri Colpi, Jasmine Chasney *Cast* Delphine Seyrig, Giorgio Albertazzi, Sacha Pitoeff. 94 mins. Dyaliscope.

A film extremely difficult to summarize, since to describe it in terms of "plot" and "character" both limits and defines it. In a large baroque palace, a man (Albertazzi) says that the previous year he met a woman (Seyrig) with another man who is perhaps her husband (Pitoeff). Is he lying or is she? This does not matter in a film whose editing alternates past, present, and future, the real and the imaginary. In the closed milieu of the palace and the rigidly formal garden, a kind of (non-Euclidean) geometrical dance develops with high society people revolving like Van Gogh's prisoners, asking questions that are unanswered and leaving sentences unfinished. This is, without doubt, a stylistic exercise and there are suggestions of the *cinéma des vamps*. However, some people in France in the early Sixties felt the film depicted a particular ruling class. Though a difficult film, it has had considerable international success.

ANOTHER THIN MAN see THIN MAN (THE)

A NOUS LA LIBERTE France 1931. *Dir* René Clair *Assist Dir* Albert Valentin *Scen* René Clair *Photog* Georges Périnal *Art Dir* Lazare Meerson *Mus* Georges Auric *Cast* Raymond Cordy, Henri Marchand, Rolla France, Paul Oliver, Vincent Hyspa *Prod* Tobis. 95 mins.

Two friends escape from prison and the first (Marchand) sacrifices himself for the second (Cordy), who becomes a big manufacturer of records. After Marchand is freed, he becomes employed in his friend's factory and recognizes him. The factory owner takes away a large sum of money in order to escape blackmail but a storm blows the bank notes away to a crowd of officials who grab them. The factory owner then escapes the police with the help of his old friend and they become happy vagabonds, while the factory continues to function for the benefit of the workers. Clair said to Charensol about this film: "At the time I was closest to the extreme left. I wanted to attack the Machine, which led men into starvation instead of adding to their happiness. I was wrong to use the operetta formula but I thought it would enhance the satirical nature of the film more than would a realistic style."

Conceived when the economic crisis and unemployment in the Western world were being attributed to automation, this film contains excellent sequences that have become classics. Especially notable is the parallel of working on an assembly line in prison and in the factory; the regimentation of workers and prisoners in Meerson's futuristic and deliberately inhuman sets. Another justly famous sequence: the officials in top hats fighting for the bank notes in the storm. Excellent acting by Cordy and Marchand (an unknown actor who remained so). Very good music by Auric, especially the final chorus. "My old friend, life is beautiful (. . .) One can laugh and

sing all together. One can love and drink all together. For us, for us, is freedom."

The film's failings lie less in its Utopian, though ironic, theme than in a certain cold formality in its perfect images and editing, a coldness that counteracts the warmth of the two principals.

When *Modern Times* was finished in 1935, Tobis (which was controlled by Goebbels) sued for copyright infringement against Chaplin, who had clearly been influenced by the assembly line scenes. But René Clair, whose Henri Marchand character was derived from Chaplin, brought the suit to an end when he said: "All of us flow from a man whom I admire and I am honored if he was inspired by my film."

ANTOINE ET ANTOINETTE France 1947. *Dir* Jacques Becker *Scen* Françoise Giroud, Maurice Griffe, Jacques Becker *Photog* Pierre Montazel *Mus* Jean-Jacques Grunewald *Art Dir* Robert-Jules Garnier *Ed* Marguerite Renoir *Cast* Roger Pigaut, Claire Mafféi, Annette Poivre, Gaston Modot *Prod* Gaumont. 95 mins.

The life and loves of a salesgirl (Mafféi) in Uniprix and of a printing worker (Pigaut). They win the lottery, he loses the ticket, but they eventually find it.

One of the first French films that dealt naturally and warmly with the lives of Parisian workers, it depicts the happiness and difficulties of a young couple in love living in a little attic apartment in postwar Paris. This sensitive film was part of French "neorealism," a movement that never reached fruition.

APACHE USA 1954. *Dir* Robert Aldrich *Scen* James R. Webb based on the novel *Bronco Apache* by Paul I. Wellman *Photog* Ernest Laszlo *Ed* Alan Crosland *Cast* Burt Lancaster, Jean Peters, John McIntyre *Prod* Hecht-Lancaster. 87 mins. Technicolor.

After the surrender of Geronimo, a young Indian (Lancaster) refuses to yield to white domination, marries a white girl (Peters), and resists the American armies while his son is born.

One of the first antiracist westerns, directed effectively and warmly by a noteworthy director. Good performance by Lancaster as an Indian. Excellent use is made of the natural settings in which the film was largely shot.

APARAJITO see PATHER PANCHALI

APART FROM YOU see KIMI TO WAKARETE

A PROPOS DE NICE France 1929–30. *Dir/ Scen/Ed* Jean Vigo *Photog* Boris Kaufman. 2,450 ft.
While not a documentary (a word not then accepted) it is a "document," though one with a "point-of-view" in the style of Dziga Vertov. It was in fact photographed by Vertov's brother, Boris Kaufman.
Vigo outlined his theme in his first synopsis: "Nice is, above all, a town living a game: the great hotels, the tourists, the roulette, the paupers. Everything is doomed to die." Vigo found the "paupers more interesting than the tourists" and as a result his film rests mainly on the contrast between the idlers sprawled in the sun, the Promenade des Anglais, and the poor sections of the old town. In the end, Vigo's theme of the "game" was less important than his portrayal of the carnival, which he depicted as a kind of dance of death intercut with ridiculous funeral statues and *kino-eye* improvised shots of idlers. This lyrical, violent, and subversive social polemic is full of black humor and biting sarcasm. Into it are incorporated several visual metaphors: the waxed, naked feet; the woman who suddenly appears naked in a chair; the tourist suddenly "paralyzed." It is a short film but a great one: "An example of true cinema, but also an attack on a particular kind of world."

APUR SANSAR see PATHER PANCHALI

ARAYA Venezuela 1958. *Dir* Margot Benacerraf.
The best film ever produced in Venezuela, it depicts daily life in the feudal salt marshes with a style that is both poetic and realistic. It was acclaimed by FIPRESCI at Cannes.

ARE WE ALL MURDERERS? NOUS SOMMES TOUS DES ASSASSINS

ARGILA (literally CLAY) Brazil 1940. *Dir* Humberto Mauro *Scen* Humberto Mauro *Photog* Manuel Ribeiro *Ed* Waston Macedo *Mus* Villalobos *Cast* Carmen Santos, Celso Guimaraes, Bandeira Duarte. 90 mins. approximately.
A sophisticated woman (Santos) falls in love with a ceramics maker and "re-news" the art of Indian ceramics. A conventional story but one around which Humberto Mauro (the strongest personality of the Brazilian cinema from 1920–40) creates his own special style: a refined visual sense of atmosphere and the countryside.

ARMY GAME (THE) see TIRE AU FLANC

ARRIVEE D'UN TRAIN EN GARE DE LA CIOTAT see LUMIÈRE FILMS

ARROSEUR ARROSE (L') see LUMIÈRE FILMS

ARSENAL USSR 1929. *Dir/Scen/Ed* Alexander Dovzhenko *Photog* Danylo Demutsky *Art Dir* Isaac Shpinel, Vladimir Muller *Cast* S. Svashenko, A. Buchma, M. Nademsky *Prod* VUFKU. 1,820 meters (6,060 ft.).
The war of 1914: the misery in the countryside and the horrors at the front. Revolutionary fraternization; mutineers return home in a train that is derailed. In Kiev, the nationalists reveal themselves; the Bolshevik reaction; the arsenal goes on strike, the bourgeois are confused, and there is fighting in the streets. The strikes are finally defeated and the Whites shoot the hero (Svashenko).
One of Dovzhenko's best films, almost as brilliant as *Earth*. Outstanding sequences: the peasants' misery symbolized by a starving horse on arid ground; the hysteria of the nationalists parading the portrait of Shevtshenko and installing it like an icon in front of the saints' candles (which the portrait blows out when it flaps); the difficult meeting of soldiers and communist workers, the fat and bespectacled nationalists' spokesmen, and the glib Social Democrats; the strike that brings the machinery to a halt and the terrified bourgeois in their distant apartments listening to the silence; the derailed train, with the famous metaphor of a crushed accordion (which is repeated in *La Bataille du Rail*) and the hero who says when he is revived: "I will be a mechanic" (the titles are an essential element in the film); his "death" at the end, when he struggles forward, his shirt open at his naked breast, while the Whites riddle him with bullets.
The story (which was difficult to follow in some re-edited foreign versions) is coherent and moving in the original version, a romantic and lyrical masterpiece of the silent era.

ARYAN (THE) USA 1916. *Dir.* William S. Hart, Clifford Smith *Scen* C. Gardner Sullivan *Photog* Joseph August, Clyde de Vinna *Cast* William S. Hart, Bessie Love, Louise Glaum, Hershall Mayall, Gertrude Claire, S. C. Smith *Prod* Thomas Ince for Triangle. 4,600 ft. approx.

"The Story of a White Human Heart Turned Black" (Triangle publicity). A gold prospector (Hart) is cheated by a woman (Glaum) and robbed. Swearing vengeance on the whole white race and on women in particular, he becomes the leader of a band of outlaws. Later some emigrants cross his path and among them is a girl (Love). "The hard cruel face of a man who has learned to hate looks into the trusting countenance of a girl whose whole life has known nothing but love and trust" (Triangle publicity). At first her pleas for his help have no effect, but she trusts him: "He is a white man . . . although he lives among half-breeds and Indians, and she knows he will run true to the creed of his race — to protect its women" (Triangle publicity). In the end, he justifies the girl's faith in him.

In France, "during an especially poor period (1916), *The Aryan* made artists think" (Moussinac). Since Thomas Ince alone was given credit for the film, Delluc considered him "the first poet of the screen," because he brought to Paris the great epic sense of the western. So great was the adulation for Ince in Paris, that films were attributed to him that he hadn't even produced: *A Sister of Six* (directed by Sidney Franklin, produced by Griffith, 1916); *Her Fighting Chance* (directed by Edwin Carew, 1917). Saloons, gold prospectors, cowboys, all the glamour of the Far West and authentic American themes were connected to Ince's name — even though this had been introduced by astute distributors.

[As Sadoul notes, Ince did not direct this film and, in fact, did not direct any of Hart's films. Hart himself considered *The Aryan* one of his best. It is especially notable for a delicate and sensitive performance by Bessie Love in her first major role.]

ASHES AND DIAMONDS POPIOL I DIAMANT

ASPHALT Germany 1929. *Dir.* Joe May *Scen* Rolf Vanloo, Fred Majo, Hans Szekely *Photog* Günther Rittau *Cast* Gustav Fröhlich, Betty Amann, Else Heller, Albert Steinrück, Hans Adalbert Schlettow *Prod* UFA. 2,575 meters (9,200 ft. approx.).

A young policeman (Fröhlich) becomes involved with a flighty woman (Amann) and unintentionally kills his rival. He is arrested by his father, himself a policeman, but is exonerated by his mistress. Excellent sets and a seductive heroine *à la* Louise Brooks. However, it is a complete commercialization of the *Kammerspiel* style [into which Joe May poured everything: chiaroscuro, superimpositions, a murder seen through a mirror, suggestive shadows. The result is merely a skillful and pretentious imitation of the avant-garde.]

ASPHALT JUNGLE (THE) USA 1950. *Dir* John Huston *Scen* Ben Maddow, John Huston based on the novel by W. R. Burnett *Photog* Harold Rosson *Art Dir* Cedric Gibbons, Randall Duell *Mus* Miklos Rosza *Ed* George Boemler *Cast* Sam Jaffe, Sterling Hayden, Louis Calhern, Jean Hagen, James Whitmore, Marc Lawrence, Marilyn Monroe *Prod* MGM. 112 mins.

A brilliant criminal, Reimenschneider (Jaffe), is released from prison, where he had perfected a plan for a million dollar jewel robbery. Backing for the plot is provided by an apparently respectable lawyer (Calhern), and the gang members are collected, among whom are a killer, Dix Handley (Hayden), and a driver (Whitmore). The crime is successful. The lawyer plans a double cross but Dix shoots him and goes into hiding with Reimenschneider. Meanwhile, the police are on their trail and, after a betrayal, close in and either kill or arrest all the gang.

A tense, well-directed thriller, whose style is largely American "neorealism." The planning and execution of the robbery are described in a sort of light-hearted documentary manner. The characters of the master criminal and the lawyer have real psychological depth. Of marginal interest is the appearance of a newcomer to films called Marilyn Monroe.

REMAKES:

*Badlanders (The) USA 1958. *Dir* Delmer Daves *Scen* Richard Collins based on the novel by W. R. Burnett *Cast* Alan Ladd, Ernest Borgnine, Katy Jurado *Prod*

MGM. 87 mins. Metrocolor. Cinema-Scope. A western version of the novel about a robbery at a gold mine.

— *Cairo* USA 1963. *Dir* Wolf Rilla *Scen* Joanne Court based on *The Asphalt Jungle* by W. R. Burnett *Photog* Desmond Dickinson *Cast* George Sanders, Richard Johnson, Faten Hamama, Walter Rilla *Prod* MGM. 91 mins.

A conventional thriller involving a theft from the Cairo Museum.

ASSASSINAT DU DUC DE GUISE (L') ASSASSINATION OF THE DUC DE GUISE France 1908. *Dir* Charles le Bargy, André Calmettes *Scen* Henri Lavedan *Art Dir* Bertin *Mus* Saint-Saëns *Cast* Le Bargy, Albert Lambert, Gabrielle Robinne, Berthe Bovy, Dieubonné *Prod* Film d'Art. 921 ft.

Henri III (Le Bargy) summons the Duc de Guise (Lambert). Despite the uneasiness of his mistress (Robinne) he goes to the Château de Blois and is assassinated.

The scenario by Lavedan (of the Académie Française) was published in *L'Illustration* and is a skillful visual story. The performance by Le Bargy (of the Comédie Française) is a fine characterization, intelligent, though a bit hammy. Emile Bertin's sets reproduced the historic rooms of the Château de Blois. Saint-Saëns' score (the first written for a film) was hailed as a "masterpiece of symphonic music."

In 1932 the film was declared "a lasting monument to grandeur and folly," but in 1922, D. W. Griffith had said to Robert Florey: "My best memory of the cinema? The sensation given me twelve years ago by a marvelous film, *L'Assassinat du duc de Guise*. It was a complete revelation. If only your compatriots had been able to continue producing such films as that (taking new methods into account, of course), they would today be the first and foremost film makers in the world." One might perhaps consider this exaggerated if Carl Dreyer had not also expressed his complete admiration in 1927.

The cinematic revolution that this work created was analyzed with precision by Victorin Jasset in 1911: "All the previous rules were discarded. The artists didn't run about, they stayed immobile and obtained a growing intensity of effect . . . Le Bargy created his character with a revealing wealth of detail. A beginner used new methods and his were the better. Apart from a few technical rules, nothing remains of the old school; it was the downfall of the old principles. The film's influence has been enormous, though initially it was practically nonexistent. It opened the eyes of the Americans."

The success of *Duc de Guise* determined the development of the Film d'Art in the USA and in the whole of Europe, especially in Italy. This film, formerly unjustly discredited, is a key work.

OTHER VERSIONS:

— *Assassinat du duc de Guise* France 1897. *Dir* Georges Hatot *Prod* Société Lumière. 50 ft. approx.

ASSOMMOIR (L') GERVAISE

ATALANTE (L') LE CHALAND QUI PASSE France 1934. *Dir* Jean Vigo *Scen* Jean Guinée, Jean Vigo, Albert Rièra *Photog* Boris Kaufman, Louis Berger *Art Dir* Francis Jourdain *Mus* Maurice Jaubert *Ed* Louis Chavance *Cast* Jean Dasté, Dita Parlo, Michel Simon, Gilles Margaritis, Louis Lefèvre, Maurice Gilles, Raya Diligent, René Blech *Prod* J. L. Nounez-Gaumont. 89 mins. (original length).

A barge captain, Jean (Dasté), marries a peasant girl, Juliette (Parlo), who is in search of adventure, and takes her with him on the barge "L'Atalante." Also living on the barge are an elderly, grizzled, eccentric mate, Père Jules (Simon), who really runs the barge, and a moronic Boy (Lefèvre). The girl is frustrated by the lack of adventure and dreams of the excitement of Paris. When they go ashore, she quarrels with her husband, they separate, and the barge goes on without her. Both husband and wife despair, but are reunited through good luck and with the mate's help.

The original script (the work of an unknown writing under a pseudonym) was commissioned to Vigo. He adapted it freely and turned it into his masterpiece, in which realism is united with surrealistic poetry to create a violent and powerful lyricism. Michel Simon's Père Jules is certainly one of the great creations of the cinema. Principal sequences: the wedding in a Normandy village and the strange bridal procession from church to barge; the mate's cabin stuffed with bric-à-brac, an old phonograph, musical boxes, swordfish, pictures of prostitutes, innumerable cats, and the pickled hands of a dead friend;

the cheap dance hall where a peddler (Margaritis) — who is also cyclist, tumbler, one-man-band, and lady charmer — enchants the wife; the arrival in the suburbs with open areas dominated by electric pylons; the wife wandering lonely and lost in Paris, the theft of her purse, and the crowd's near-lynching of the alleged thief; the despair of the husband as he dives underwater to discover the face of his lost love; Jules's finding the wife and her wordless return to the barge.

"His overflowing imagination permitted him to improvise with astonishing facility. It wasn't the words that inspired him, but faces, objects, landscapes" (Albert Rièra). "He used everything around him: the sun, the moon, snow, night. Instead of fighting unfavorable conditions, he made them play a part" (Boris Kaufman).

L'Atalante was well received by the critics but not by professionals. The distributors (using Louis Chavance) altered Vigor's editing and deleted some sequences in order to make it what they thought would be more commercial. They added a theme song, a then popular sentimental melody, "Le Chaland qui passe," which became the title of the film. It opened in Paris the same day that Vigo was buried, having died of leukemia. It was a total commercial disaster and soon disappeared from the screens. Elie Faure (a friend of Vigo's father, the anarchist Almereyda) had earlier hailed the film in these terms: "L'Atalante. Humanity. The humanity of the poor. No sparkling crystal on tablecloths. Dish cloths hanging up. Casseroles. Buckets. Bread. A bottle of wine. Humble sparks in the half-light enhanced by the fog from the river. The elusive shadows of Rembrandt meeting Goya's sly shadows among the rough furnishings. . . The spirit of Jean Vigo's work is classical, almost violent and always tormented, fevered, overflowing with ideas and with fantasy; truculent; a virulent and even demoniacal romanticism that still remains humanistic."

AT GREAT COST DOROGOI TSENOI

*AT LAND USA 1944. *Dir/Photog/Ed* Maya Deren *Assist* Alexander Hammid (Hackenschmied), Hella Heyman *Cast* Maya Deren, Alexander Hammid. 16 mins. (silent).

Together with *Meshes of the Afternoon* (*q.v.*), this film marked the renaissance of the American experimental film. Maya Deren (like many later "underground" film makers) insisted that her films had no story, since dramatic narratives and plots belonged to literature. For her the cinema, as a peculiarly temporal and spatial art, should concern itself with dynamic relationship in a relativistic universe. Her own description of the film at its premiere (1946) stated that it was "a film in the nature of an inverted Odyssey, where the universe assumes the initiative, and confronts the individual with a continuous fluidity toward which, as a constant identity, he seeks to relate himself."

ATLANTIDE (L') France 1921. *Dir* Jacques Feyder *Scen* Jacques Feyder based on the novel by Pierre Benoit *Photog* Georges Specht, Victor Morin *Art Dir* Manuel Orazi *Mus* Jemain *Cast* Stacia Napierkowska, Jean Angelo, Georges Melchior, Marie-Louise Iribe *Prod* Thalman. 8,300 ft.

Two men, Saint-Avit (Melchior) and Morange (Angelo), discover part of the lost continent of Atlantis and fall under the spell of Queen Antinea (Napierkowska). One dies because he refuses her love, the other escapes but finds he cannot live without her.

The film cost two million francs and was at the time the most expensive film made in France. "The sand is the star of this film," said Delluc and indeed the most interesting aspect of this film is that the exteriors were shot in North Africa, in the Toggourt region of the Sahara. The desert scenes are far more memorable and meaningful than either the opulent *grande-dame* performance by Napierkowska or the interiors shot in an improvised studio in Algiers in the *Cabiria*-like sets of Orazi.

The film was financed by the Thalman Bank, then sold to Aubert, and was a tremendous commercial success in France (a reserved seat run for over a year) and abroad.

This was Feyder's first directorial effort and his later career showed him worthy of better than this. However, it is still stimulating and exciting in parts and both Melchior and Angelo were well directed by Feyder.

OTHER VERSIONS:
— *die Herrin von Atlantis* Germany 1932.

17

Dir. G. W. Pabst *Scen* Ladislau Vajda, Hermann Oberländer based on the novel by Pierre Benoit *Photog* Eugen Schüfftan, Ernst Koerner *Art Dir* Erno Metzner *Cast* Brigitte Helm, Gustav Diessl, Tela Tschaï, Heinz Klingenberg, V. Sokolov, Florelle *Prod* Nero-Film. 2,384 meters (7,900 ft. approx.). (Also produced in French and English versions.)

A cold and decorative film with mannered photography. Brigitte Helm resembles a wax model more than the seductive Queen Antinea.

— *The Siren of Atlantis* USA 1948. *Dir* Gregg G. Tallas. 74 mins.

— *Atlantis, the Lost Continent* USA 1961. *Dir* George Pal. 90 mins. Metrocolor.

— *Antinea, l'Amante della citta sepolta* (*The Lost Kingdom*/*L'Atlantide*) France /Italy 1961. *Dir* Edgar G. Ulmer. 100 mins. Technirama. Eastman Color.

AT 3:25 PARIS QUI DORT

ATOM-BOMBED CHILDREN (OF HIROSHIMA) GENBAKU NO KO

ATONEMENT OF GOSTA BERLING (THE) GÖSTA BERLINGS SAGA

ATTACK USA 1956. *Dir* Robert Aldrich *Scen* James Poe based on the play *The Fragile Fox* by Norman Brooks *Photog* Joseph Biroc *Art Dir* William Glasgow *Mus* Frank Devol *Ed* Michael Luciano *Cast* Jack Palance, Eddie Albert, Robert Strauss, Lee Marvin *Prod* The Associates and Aldrich Company. 104 mins.

Clashes between American soldiers during the fighting of 1944. A somewhat theatrical film but violent and convincing. Aldrich has said: "The film is, for me, a sincere plea for peace, a kind of document . . . My hero (Palance) shows this best when he is tempted to kill the cowardly captain (Albert) responsible for the death of his men. I wanted to show my contempt and hatred for this captain, in making him a sadist even at the risk of making him appear grotesque."

AUBERGE ROUGE (L') France 1923. *Dir* Jean Epstein *Scen* Jean Epstein based on *Une ténébreuse affaire* by Balzac *Photog* Raoul Abourdier, Roger Hubert, Robert Lefèbvre *Cast* Gina Manès, Léon Mathot, Jacques Christiany, Courtois *Prod* Pathé. 5,900 ft. approx.

A film told mainly through numerous flashbacks during the course of a banquet attended by people in very decorative costumes. It was, for its time, an attempt at psychological cinema and original editing in which "objects, playing cards, jewels, take over the screen and become characters" (H. Langlois).

AUBERGE ROUGE (L') THE RED INN France 1951. *Dir* Claude Autant-Lara *Scen* Jean Aurenche, Pierre Bost *Photog* André Bac *Art Dir* Max Douy *Mus* René Cloërec *Ed* Madeleine Gug *Cast* Fernandel, Françoise Rosay, Julien Carette, Gregoire Aslan, Didier d'Yd, Nane Germon, Marie-Claire Olivia *Prod* Memnon Films. 95 mins.

In 1833, in the Ardèche Mountains, travelers in a public carriage take refuge in an inn. The innkeepers (Rosay, Carette) plot to kill and rob them. A debauched and gluttonous monk (Fernandel) rescues them from this unhappy situation, but soon after leaving the inn, the carriage plunges over a precipice.

An excellent success by Autant-Lara and his team, stylistically polished, with a rough Voltairean satire that is lively but lacks bitterness. The theme was suggested to Aurenche by "the bloodstained inn of Peyrebelle." The characters of the travelers are only sketched, but the three principals are all excellent. One of Fernandel's best roles.

AU RAVISSEMENT DES DAMES Belgium 1913. *Dir* Alfred Machin *Photog* Jacques Bizeuil *Art Dir* R. Morand *Cast* Fernande Dépernay *Prod* Belge-Cinéma Film. 265 meters.

A large shop pays its salesgirls badly and starves them. They become tubercular and their dresses contaminate the rich clients. One of the rare "social" films of its time.

AUSTERNPRINZESSIN (DIE) THE OYSTER PRINCESS Germany 1919. *Dir* Ernst Lubitsch *Scen* Hans Kräly, Ernst Lubitsch *Photog* Theodor Sparkuhl *Art Dir* Kurt Richter *Cast* Ossi Oswalda, Harry Liedtke, Victor Janson, Julius Falkenstein, Kurt Bois *Prod* Union-Film. 4,200 ft.

An American millionaire, the "oyster king" (Janson), and his daughter (Oswalda) invade an old aristocratic Prussian family in order to buy a title for the daughter by marriage with a prince (Liedtke).

An elaborate, sophisticated satire, though

sometimes facile and vulgar, incorporating some of the boldness of Berlin cabarets. Delluc, though he referred to its "coarseness," added, "the most interesting examples of the decorative German style can be found in this film. It has a first class intellectual line and style. Audiences will love those scenes staged with a forceful rhythm, creating at the end an almost anguished atmosphere. Some scenes, such as that in the waiting room, are something of a masterpiece." In that corridor, with its black and white stones, the character, distressed and alone, carefully walks on but a single square, creating in this way a kind of dance.

AUTOMOVIL GRIS (EL) THE GREY MOTOR CAR Mexico 1919. *Dir/Photog* Enrique Rosas, Joaquin Coss *Scen* Miguel Necochea, Enrique Rosas *Cast* Dora Vila, Maria Teresa Montoya, Mercedes Ferriz, Juan Canals, Joaquin Coss.
This serial is one of the most beautiful silent films. It re-creates in the natural setting of Mexico a series of extortions and murders committed by bandits during the Revolution (then quite recent). The directors were undoubtedly much influenced by Feuillade, but, surprisingly, they knew how to portray the life of ordinary Mexicans at the turn of the century. A sound track was added later and the film is still being screened fifty years after its production.

AUTOUR D'UNE CABINE France 1894. *Dir* Emile Reynaud *Mus* Gaston Paulin 45 meters. 636 scenes.
The first masterpiece of the animated cartoon was laboriously painted by hand, frame by frame. It opened with beach scenes (gulls, beach huts, bathers) which led into a scuffle between a Parisian man and a "Copurchic," overly curious about the beauty of a Parisian girl in the beach hut. It lasted over ten minutes because Reynaud used a variety of tricks during projection. A section from the film was brought to life again in *Naissance du Cinéma*. It is an astonishing sequence, notable for the humor of the three characters, the gracefulness of their gestures, and the use of color and backgrounds (projected separately). It is to be hoped that *Autour d'une cabine* will one day be transferred entirely on to film, since the Cinémathèque Française is conserving the original materials.
See also *Pauvre Pierrot*

AUTUMN AFTERNOON (AN) SAMMA NO AJI

AVANT LE DELUGE France 1953. *Dir* André Cayatte *Scen* Charles Spaak, André Cayatte *Photog* Jean Bourgoin *Mus* J.-J. Grunenwald *Ed* Paul Cayatte *Art Dir* Jacques Colombier *Cast* Bernard Blier, Marina Vlady, Jacques Castelot, Isa Miranda, Line Noro, Balpêtré, Paul Frankeur *Prod* U.G.C.-Documento Films. 80 mins.
Some adolescents (Vlady, etc.) form a gang and, led on by a shady character (Castelot), become mixed up in a crime and are brought before the courts, to the despair of their rich parents (Blier, Frankeur, Balpêtré, Miranda, Noro).
This film is the best of the "Judicial series" that made Cayatte famous in a number of countries. Spaak's script is mainly of interest for its exact depiction of the panic that gripped some of the French bourgeois at the end of 1951 when the Korean War almost became a world war.

AVVENTURA (L') THE ADVENTURE Italy/France 1960. *Dir* Michelangelo Antonioni *Scen* Elio Bartolini, Tonino Guerra, Michelangelo Antonioni *Photog* Aldo Scavarda *Mus* Giovanni Fusco *Ed* Eraldo da Roma *Art Dir* Piero Poletto *Cast* Monica Vitti, Gabriele Ferzetti, Lea Massari, Dominique Blanchar, Renzo Ricci, James Adams *Prod* Cino Del Duca/Produzioni Cinematografiche Europee/Société Cinématographique Lyre. 145 mins.
A party of rich Italians land on an uninhabited island. A young woman (Massari) quarrels with her lover, an architect (Ferzetti), and disappears. No trace of her can be found, although one of her girl friends (Vitti) refuses to give up. With the architect, she searches for her all over Sicily, but in the end they forget her and become lovers.
Antonioni has characterized his film: "I have been struck by the fragility of human relationships, by the moral, political and even physical instability of the modern world in which the physical becomes metaphysical and in which the frontier between science and science fiction hardly exists. Every day we live an *adventure,* ideological or sentimental. Our drama is non-communication and it is this feeling that dominates the characters in my film, which I preferred to set in a rich environment because feelings

there are not dependent on material circumstances. These are men and women who try to lead normal lives but who encounter so many difficulties that they are unable to avoid the final catastrophe. The film is as much optimistic as it is pessimistic. In the final image, the man is facing the wall and the woman facing outwards into space. They remain bound by resignation, pity, tolerance, the remainder of their vital burden. I wanted to show Sicily without folkloric affectations, the country as it is, as naturally as possible, but in relation to the characters and their anguish."

Main sequences: the disappearance of the young woman during the cruise; the arrival in a new, but deserted, small town; the day spent in a rich villa; the party in a baroque palace (real, but suggestive of Marienbad); the final scene between the couple after she discovers him with another woman.

Antonioni was in difficult straits after completing this film. It was badly received in Italy and was jeered and whistled at during the Cannes Festival. However, it did obtain a Jury Award and later was a great success in Paris and elsewhere, a success that established Antonioni's international reputation.

AWARA THE VAGABOND India 1953. *Dir* Raj Kapoor *Scen* K. A. Abbas based on his own novel *Photog* R. Karmaker *Art Dir* M. R. Acharekar *Mus* Ravi Shankar, Jaikishan *Choreog* Mrs. Simke *Cast* Raj Kapoor, Prithviraj, Nargis, R. N. Singh *Prod* R.K. Films. 99 mins.

As in *Le Coupable* (by François Coppée), a magistrate tries to condemn an unjustly accused delinquent (Kapoor), and realizes that it is his own son. A sumptuous Bombay super production directed by the most famous Indian actor, it includes several dream and ballet sequences.

AZIMA (EL) THE WILL/DETERMINATION Egypt 1939. *Dir/Scen* Kamal Selim *Art Dir* Wali Eldin Samey *Cast* Hussein Sedky, Fatma Rouchdy, Anwar Wagdy, Abdel Aziz Khalil *Prod* MISR. 110 mins. approx.

The son of a poor barber graduates from school but has difficulty earning his living. He is unjustly fired but finally wins the girl he loves (Rouchdy) and defeats his rival, a rich butcher.

This artistic portrait of the working-class districts of Cairo is unquestionably the best pre-1945 Egyptian film. ["Selim's film had a really overwhelming success . . . There were several reasons for this: the author-director dealt with a social problem drawn from Egyptian life; for the first time the audience was offered a sound, suitable subject without any intrusion of songs and dances; the film involved a scrupulous study of everyday Egyptian types . . . Kamal Selim spent several months wandering through the working-class districts of Cairo, studying the types whose behavior he planned to copy" (Galal El Charkawi).]

El Azima may be justly compared with some of the great prewar French films. It was certainly influenced by "poetic realism," since Selim knew and admired the work of Renoir, Carné, Clair, and Duvivier.

AZ PRIJDE KOCOUR THAT CAT/CASSANDRA CAT/WHEN THE CAT COMES Czechoslovakia 1963. *Dir* Vojtech Jasny *Scen* Jiri Brdecka, Vojtech Jasny *Photog* Jaroslav Kucera *Mus* S. Havelka *Cast* Jan Werich, Emilie Vasaryova, Vladimir Brodsky, Jari Sovak *Prod* Statny Film. 108 mins. Color. CinemaScope.

An original and delightful fantasy-comedy in which a magic cat reveals the true nature of everyone he looks at. Excellent color and blending of everyday life and fantasy.

BAB EL HADID CAIRO STATION/IRON GATE
Egypt 1957. *Dir* Youssef Shahin *Scen*
Abdel Hay Adib, Mohammed Abou
Youssef *Cast* Fairid Charwki, Hend
Rostom, Youssef Shahin, Hassan Baraudy.
90 mins. approx.
Filmed in Cairo's railway station (known
as the "Iron Gate"), *Bab el Hadid* tells
the story of Kinawi (Shahin), a crippled
newspaper vendor who is in love with
Hannouma (Rostom), a lemonade seller
who in turn is planning to marry the
handsome porter, Abu Seri (Charwki),
who earns a great deal of money. Kinawi
plans murder in his tortured mind . . .
"The images are disturbing; Kinawi is
finally put into a straitjacket and taken
away as the crowds come and go each
day through the station. Shahin's shots
were long and at times deliberately uncomfortable; he held on a face long
enough for the audience to see through
it without a single word being uttered.
The station was society, the people in it
were its citizens, and Kinawi was its
victim." (Based on Galal El Charkawi's
*Essay on the History of the Cinema in
the UAR.*)
The film was well received at the 1958
Berlin Festival and just missed winning
the Grand Prix. It is the best film of
this young director, who also brilliantly
played the part of the crippled and demented Kinawi.

BABI RYAZANSKYE WOMEN OF RYAZAN
USSR 1927. *Dir* Olga Preobrazhenskaya
Co-Dir Ivan Pravov *Scen* Olga Vishnev-
skaya, Boris Altschuler *Photog* Konstan-
tin Kuznetsov *Art Dir* Dmitri Kolupayev
Cast Kuzma Yastrebetsky, G. Bobynin,
Yelena Maximova, Emma Tsessarskaya,
R. Puzhnaya *Prod* Sovkino. 1,845 meters.
Life in a small Russian village in the
Ryazan district at the time World War I

broke out, and the story of a father's
desire for his son's bride.
Olga Preobrazhenskaya had been a star
in prerevolutionary films. In this film
(the fourth she directed), she reveals
her belief in the strength of a simple
plot, and her penchant for portraying
folk traditions and for conveying a sense
of the beauty and freshness of her native countryside. An unforgettable shot
is that in which the wind and clouds
blow over the wheat fields, announcing
the declaration of war. *Women of
Ryazan* enjoyed a considerable success
both in the Soviet Union and abroad.

BABY DOLL USA 1956. *Dir* Elia Kazan
Scen Tennessee Williams *Photog* Boris
Kaufman *Ed* Gene Milford *Art Dir*
Richard Sylbert *Mus* Kenyon Hopkins
Cast Karl Malden, Carroll Baker, Eli
Wallach, Mildred Dunnock *Prod* New-
town (Elia Kazan). 114 mins.
A "poor white" southerner (Malden)
lives in a large broken-down home with
"Baby Doll," a nymphette (Baker) who,
despite his efforts, is still a virgin. He
has an argument with a Mexican
(Wallach) who seduces Baby Doll, and
as he is planning revenge is arrested by
the police.
Tennessee Williams is often handled
badly on the screen but this is one of
his, and one of Kazan's, best films. Although the drama centers around the
attractive nymphette, Baby Doll, it is
underneath a drama of ownership, close
to Balzac and Zola, and presents a
realistic portrait of the South. The natural sets, the décor, and the objects
surrounding the characters play a major
role. Exceptional performances by Carroll
Baker and stage actor Eli Wallach. After
this film, "Baby Doll" became a well-
known name for a certain style of
pajamas.

BACHELOR PARTY (THE) USA 1957. *Dir* Delbert Mann *Scen* Paddy Chayefsky *Photog* Joseph La Shelle *Ed* William B. Murphy *Mus* Paul Madeira *Cast* Don Murray, E. G. Marshall, Jack Warden, Patricia Smith, Carolyn Jones, Nancy Marchand, Karen Norris, Philip Abbott *Prod* Norma Productions for United Artists. 93 mins.

A young, ambitious husband (Murray), learning his wife is pregnant and alarmed at the prospect of fatherhood, spends an alcoholic and intensely stag night out with the boys (Marshall, Warden, etc.), who like him are all middle-class and bitter.

This story of somewhat pitiable men is told by Chayefsky with humor, understanding, sympathy, and a critical sense of American social realities and the ordinary man. Chayefsky, a graduate of television, is more truly responsible for this success than is the mediocre director, Delbert Mann.

BADLANDERS (THE) see ASPHALT JUNGLE

BAJAJA BAYAYA/PRINCE BAYAYA Czechoslovakia 1950. *Dir* Jiri Trnka *Scen* Trnka based on a fairy tale by Bozena Nemcova (with narration of poems by V. Nezval) *Photog* L. Hajek, E. Franek *Mus* Vaclav Trojan *Anim* B. Pojar, J. Karpas, B. Sramek, Z. Hrabe, S. Latal. 70 mins. Agfacolor.

A young peasant becomes a knight and fights monsters to win the king's daughter. The most architectural of Trnka's films, and the one in which he began to move closer to the style of "ciné-opera." Its medieval scenery and characters are based on little-known Czech Gothic tableaux that have their own peculiar style and modernisms.

BAKER'S WIFE (THE) FEMME DU BOULANGER (LA)

BALLADA O SOLDATE BALLAD OF A SOLDIER USSR 1959. *Dir* Grigori Chukrai *Scen* Valentin Yoshov, Grigori Chukrai *Photog* Vladimir Nikolayev, Era Saveleva *Ed* M. Timofeiva *Mus* Mikhail Ziv *Cast* Vladimir Ivashov, Shanna Prokhorenko, Antonina Maximova, Nikolai Kruchkov, Ievgeni Urbanski *Prod* Mosfilm. 89 mins. During World War II, a nineteen-year-old soldier (Ivashov) puts two Nazi tanks out of combat and receives six days' leave from his general (Kruchkov).

During a difficult journey home, he meets a very young girl (Prokhorenko), with whom, after various adventures, he falls deeply and chastely in love. He leaves her without knowing her address and finally arrives home, where he has scarcely time to embrace his mother, before having to return to the front.

This sensitive, romantic work (which received an award at Cannes in 1960) shows the heroics, horrors, and cowardices of war as they appear to an ordinary soldier. Best sequences: the panic of the hero faced with the tanks; the meeting with a woman deceiving her husband, who is away at war; the journey by truck along the shattered roads; the romance and the abrupt separation in the overloaded trains; the final meeting with the mother.

"In this film," Chukrai has said, "I wanted to speak to my comrades, men of my age who became soldiers as soon as they left school. I wanted to show what sort of man my hero was. Discarding battle scenes, I looked for a subject that would show war for what it is."

BALLADE VAN DE HOGE HOED (DE) BALLAD OF THE TOP HAT Netherlands 1936. *Dir/Scen/Prod* Max de Haas. 30 mins.

An earthy, humorous view of Amsterdam seen through the adventures of a battered top hat, which sails along the canals and is treated differently by various owners. A successful experimental film by a good Dutch director.

BALLAD OF A SOLDIER BALLADA O SOLDATE

BALLAD OF THE NARAYAMA NARAYAMA BUSHI-KO

BALLAD OF THE TOP HAT BALLADE VAN DE HOGE HOED (DE)

BALLET MECANIQUE (LE) France 1924. *Dir* Fernand Léger *Assist* Dudley Murphy *Photog* Man Ray, Dudley Murphy *Mus* George Antheil *Cast* Kiki. 1,260 ft.

Léger, influenced by Abel Gance's *La Roue*, almost abandoned his paint brush for the camera with this avant-garde film. He was interested at that time in pictures "of objects sometimes isolated, sometimes grouped in contrasts". He also wrote: "The idea for the film came to me in order to be certain of the plastic possibilities of these new elements expressed in movement. The repetitions of shapes, of slow or rapid rhythms, allowed extremely rich possibilities. An object could become, all on its own, a tragic, comic or spectacular sight. It was an adventure in the land of wonders. I would have liked to use fragments of objects. But it would have become too abstract an experience, inaccessible to an ordinary audience. For this reason the editing alternated fragments and ordinary reality. True cinema is the image of the object totally unknown to my eyes." The film corresponds to its title, being composed of mechanical objects, displays, and similar unrelated bits of reality. Two women are shown (one of whom is Kiki), also a newspaper headline ("On a volé un collier de 1,000,000"), and a section of *Charlot cubiste,* an uncompleted animated film undertaken by Léger in 1920. His American technical collaborator, Dudley Murphy, eventually continued his film-making career in the USA and Mexico.

BALLON ROUGE (LE) THE RED BALLOON France 1956. *Dir* Albert Lamorisse *Scen* Albert Lamorisse *Photog* Edmond Séchan *Mus* Maurice Le Roux *Ed* Pierre Gillette *Cast* Pascal Lamorisse. 34 mins. Technicolor
A small boy (Lamorisse) chases a flying red balloon through the Belleville section of Paris.
Not a documentary, but a large-budget short (25,000 balloons were used costing half a million francs). It was an enormous international success. Despite a Grand Prix at Cannes it was often attacked by French critics for its (inevitable) special effects and its (often real) affectations. Outside France, the film was acclaimed as an immortal masterpiece of lyrical poetry. Very good use of color, with the red balloon enhancing the greyness of Paris.

BALTIC DEPUTY (THE) DEPUTAT BALTIKI

BAMBI USA 1942. *Dir* Walt Disney *Anim* David Hand *Scen* Larry Morey based on a story by Felix Salten *Mus* Frank Churchill, Edward Plumb *Prod* Walt Disney Productions. 70 mins. Technicolor.
A pretty little fawn, Bambi, and his doe mother resist winter and fire. After having played with the other animals (among whom are a rabbit and an owl), Bambi

becomes a stag and "marries" the young doe, Féline.
With its animals with long eyelashes, and its delicacy and affected sentimentality, the film counted on moving young and old alike. It was presented with great success during the war in the USSR (where Disney was then almost unknown) and exerted considerable influence.

BANDE A PART BAND OF OUTSIDERS/OUTSIDERS France 1964. *Dir* Jean-Luc Godard *Scen* Jean-Luc Godard based on *Fool's Gold* by Dolores Hitchens *Photog* Raoul Coutard *Mus* Michel Legrand *Ed* Agnès Guillemot, Françoise Collin *Cast* Anna Karina, Claude Brasseur, Sami Frey *Prod* Anouchka Films/Orsay Films. 95 mins.
Franz (Frey) and Arthur (Brasseur) plan to burglarize the suburban villa where their girl friend Odile (Karina) is staying. They only find a small portion of the large sum of money they had hoped to find, and Arthur is killed. Franz and Odile leave Paris.
"These three characters are truly 'a band of outsiders.' They are more honest with themselves than with others. They are not among those who want to be cut off from the world, it is the world that is far from them" (Godard).
[Godard's first attempt since *Breathless* to make a gangster film intended, as he said, to "sell a lot of tickets," was as much of a commercial failure as his other films. Godard creates the closed-in, fairy-tale world of his three characters with penetrating insight. As Pauline Kael wrote: "The distancing of Godard's imagination induces feelings of tenderness and despair which brings us closer to the movie-inspired heroes and the wide-eyed ingénue than to the more naturalistic characters of ordinary movies . . . The world of *Band of Outsiders* is both 'real' — the protagonists feel, they may even die; and yet 'unreal' because they don't take their own feelings or even death very seriously, as if they weren't important to anybody, really. Their own identity is in their relationship with each other."]

BANDERA (LA) ESCAPE FROM YESTERDAY France 1935. *Dir* Julien Duvivier *Scen* Julien Duvivier, Charles Spaak based on the novel by Pierre Mac Orlan. *Photog* Jules Kruger, Marc Fossard *Mus* Jean

Wiener, Roland Manuel *Art Dir* Jacques Krauss *Ed* Marthe Poncin *Cast* Jean Gabin, Robert Le Vigan, Pierre Renoir, Gaston Modot, Annabella, Viviane Romance, Margo Lion, Noël Roquevert *Prod* Société Nouvelle de Production. 100 mins.

After murdering a man in Paris, Pierre Gilieth (Gabin) flees to Spain and joins the Foreign Legion. He courts and eventually marries Aicha (Annabella), a beautiful Arab dancing girl. He is tracked down by a police informer (Le Vigan), but after they both volunteer to defend a dangerous outpost, a reconciliation takes place. Gilieth shows great heroism but finally dies with his captain (Renoir), leaving only the informer to tell the tale to the reinforcements.

La Bandera was dedicated to General Franco, then unknown and commanding the Legion in Spanish Morocco. With its handsome legionnaires fighting against Arab bandits on location in Spanish Morocco, this is a well-made film in the "slice of life" style, although it made excessive use of oblique angle shots.

BANDIT (THE) CANGACEIRO (O)

BANDITI A ORGOSOLO BANDITS OF ORGOSOLO Italy 1961. *Dir* Vittorio De Seta, *Scen* Vittorio De Seta, Vera Gherarducci *Photog* Vittorio De Seta *Ed* Jolanda Benvenuti *Mus* Valentino Bucchi *Cast* Michele Cossu, Peppeddu Cuccu, and other Sardinian people *Prod* Titanus. 98 mins.

A shepherd shelters some bandits and is suspected of being an accomplice. He eventually becomes a bandit himself. Very good documentary-like direction, slowly paced and with very carefully composed photography.

BAND OF OUTSIDERS BANDE À PART

BANK (THE) CHARLIE AT THE BANK USA 1915. *Dir/Scen* Charles Chaplin *Photog* Rollie Totheroh *Cast* Chaplin, Edna Purviance, Billy Armstrong, Charles Insley Leo White, Fred Goodwins, Carl Stockdale *Prod* Essanay. 1,700 ft.

Charlie, working as a janitor in a bank, dreams he rescues the stenographer (Purviance) from bank robbers and thus wins her affection. He wakes to find she is still accepting the attentions of the cashier (Stockdale). One of the first comedies in which the gags are woven into a well-constructed story: Charlie entering a large vault, then bringing out a mop and pail; the letter torn in three in order to fit into the box; cleaning between the feet of clients who totally ignore him. Somewhat of a transition between the Keystone films and Chaplin's later social criticism.

BANYA THE BATH HOUSE USSR 1962. *Dir* Sergei Yutkevich *Co-Dir* Anatoli Karanovich *Scen* Yutkevich based on the play by Vladimir Mayakovsky *Art Dir* Felix Zbarsky *Mus* Rodion Shchedrin. 51 mins. (36 mins. in general release version). Color.

A free adaptation of a 1928 satirical play by Mayakovsky, brought up-to-date and directed against "the big machine," symbol of the personality cult. The authors use ingeniously all the techniques of animation (puppets, paper cut-outs, drawings, special effects) in retaining a Twenties-period style.

BAREFOOT CONTESSA (THE) USA/Italy 1954. *Dir* Joseph L. Mankiewicz *Scen* Joseph L. Mankiewicz *Photog* Jack Cardiff *Mus* Mario Nascimbene *Ed* William Hornbeck *Cast* Humphrey Bogart, Ava Gardner, Edmond O'Brien, Marius Goring, Valentina Cortesa, Rossano Brazzi *Prod* Figaro for United Artists. 128 mins. Technicolor.

A dancer in a cheap Madrid cabaret, Maria Vargas (Gardner), is discovered by American film director Harry Dawes (Bogart), who is accompanied by his playboy backer and Muldoon (O'Brien), a publicity agent. In Hollywood she quickly becomes a star and has several affairs. She finally falls in love with Count Vincenzo Torlato-Favrine (Brazzi), the last of his line. On their wedding night he tells her he is impotent and, desperate, Maria goes to the chauffeur and becomes pregnant. Vincenzo shoots her and the chauffeur. (The story is told in a series of four flashbacks at Maria's funeral.)

Claude Chabrol considers the script Stendhalian because its central figure is as unfairly treated as Armance. However, it is better compared to the *circa* 1914 Italian romantic, fashionable dramas. Beautiful photography, especially in the unifying sequence — Maria's burial in an Italian cemetery.

*BARIERA THE BARRIER Poland 1966. *Dir/Scen* Jerzy Skolimowski *Photog* Jan Laskowski *Art Dir* Roman Wolyniec, Z. Straszewski *Mus* Krzysztof Komeda *Ed* H. Prugar *Cast* Jan Nowicki, Joanna Szczerbic *Prod* Kamera Film Unit. 83 mins.

A medical student (Nowicki) abandons his studies in order to avoid the social assembly line and, setting out in search of the "good" things in life, meets a girl (Szczerbic) who drives a streetcar. After a tangle of situations and encounters, they are parted, but meet again at the end.

The Barrier confirmed Skolimowski's earlier promise as a director with extraordinary talent and certainly one of the most exciting Polish directors of the Sixties. In the film, Skolimowski is concerned with the contemporary Polish mentality and the restless, dissatisfied younger generation of "cop-outs." His narrative line is only an excuse for a series of visual reflections, metaphors, and symbolic events tied together by a basic idea of creating a confrontation of attitudes and feelings. He balances his style on the edge between reality and dreams and achieves a profound density in subject matter and an unusually subtle style. As Michael Kustow wrote: "It has a jester's freedom, the confidence of a man who knows his world deeply, who has measured the possibilities his history allows, and can rise to the surface holding scraps and fragments together in strange combinations which may seem mad, but make desperate sense."

BARON MUNCHHAUSEN Rudolf Raspe's stories of this popular braggart were first published in English in 1785. He is known as "Baron de Crac" in French, "Castana" in Spanish, "Prasil" in Czech, etc.

— France 1911. *Dir* Georges Méliès *Prod* Star Film/Pathé. 235 meters. A somewhat ponderous comedy.

— France 1913. *Dir* Emile Cohl. Paper cut-out silhouette film.

— *Germany 1920. *Dir* Richard Felgenauer. Animated film.

— *The Adventures of Baron Münchhausen* USA 1929. *Dir* Paul Peroff. Animated film.

— *Münchhausens Abenteuer* Germany 1943. *Dir* Josef von Baky *Scen* Berthold Bürger (Erich Kästner) *Photog* K. Irmenschet *Art Dir* Emil Hasler, Otto Gülstorff *Cast* Hans Albers, Ilse Werner, etc. *Prod* UFA. 134 mins. Agfacolor.

Large-budget film presented impressively for the 25th Anniversary of UFA and the 10th of Hitlerian cinema. Several successful tricks — the Baron riding a cannonball, the flowerwomen, etc.

— *Baron Prasil* Czechoslovakia 1962. *Dir/Scen/Art Dir* Karel Zeman *Photog* Jiri Tarantile *Mus* Z. Liska *Cast* Milos Kopecky, Jana Brejchova, Jan Werich. 81 mins. Agfacolor.

Following the development he began with *Invention of Destruction* (*q.v.*), the celebrated Czech animator became a brilliant artist with this charming film. He employed a number of special effects and made particular use of old engravings in the design. Its excellent and discreet color is one factor that allows one to compare it with the work of Georges Méliès.

[*Note:* Hans Richter made two attempts to produce a version of Baron Münchhausen. The first, in 1937 in Zürich, was to have had Georges Méliès design the sets. Méliès' death in 1938 put a stop to the production. Also in Zürich, in 1939, he tried again with financial backing from Jean Renoir's distributor and with Jacques Prévert, Jacques Brunius, and Maurice Henry as scenarists. Preparation of the sets was well under way when the war ended the project.]

*BARRAVENTO TEMPEST/THE TURNING WIND Brazil 1961. *Dir* Glauber Rocha *Scen* Luiz Paulino dos Santos, Glauber Rocha *Photog* Tony Rabatoni *Mus* Washington Bruno Da Silva based on Bahian folk music *Ed* Nelson Pereira dos Santos *Cast* Aldo Teixeira, Antonio Luiz Sampaio, Luiza Maranhao, Lucy Carvalho, Lidio dos Santos, *Prod* Iglu Films. 110 mins. (80 mins in some versions.)

One of the key films in the new Brazilian cinema, this elliptical film is at once a portrait of the folkloric and religious aspects of the fishing villages in Bahia and a denunciation of the exploitation of the fishermen and the role of "macumba" in keeping them subjugated. "Barravento" (the turning wind or tempest) is the name given by the fishermen to any violent change in nature, love, or social environment and, more particularly, to any change in the minds of men that destroys their old superstitions. As such, the title embodies Rocha's own response to the struggle between old and new forces in Brazil. The film is visually rich and expressive, with the violent passages counterpointed by scenes of intense lyrical beauty.

BARREN LIVES VIDAS SECAS

BARRIER (THE) BARIERA

BAS-FONDS (LES) THE LOWER DEPTHS/THE UNDERWORLD France 1936. *Dir* Jean Renoir *Scen* Jean Renoir, Charles Spaak, J. Companeez, E. Zamiatine based on the play by Maxim Gorky *Assist* Jacques Becker *Photog* Jean Bachelet *Art Dir* Eugène Lourié, Hugues Laurent *Ed* Marguerite Renoir *Cast* Jean Gabin, Louis Jouvet, Vladimir Sokolov, Robert Le Vigan, Gabrielle, René Génin, Sylvain, Suzy Prim, Junie Astor *Prod* Albatros. 92 mins.
Renoir did not try to create a Russian atmosphere, but set the action in an unidentified country. The film is mainly spoiled by mediocre (and too flashy) acting, although the Fête sequence is good. "The work is uneven, badly balanced, not homogeneous enough. The subject is badly suited to Renoir's naturalistic temperament" (Henri Langlois, 1937).
— *China 1948. Dir* Tso-Lin Wang. Good things have been said of this Gorky transposition, made with Chinese actors in Shanghai in a somewhat neorealistic style.
See also *Donzoko*

BATAILLE DU RAIL (LA) THE BATTLE OF THE RAILS France 1945. *Dir* René Clément *Scen* René Clément, Colette Audry *Photog* Henri Alekan *Mus* Yves Baudrier *Ed* J. Desagneaux *Cast* Tony Laurent, Leroy, Desagneaux, Clarieux, Daurand, Lozach, Pauléon, Rauzéna, Redon, Salina, Woll, and the French railwaymen. *Prod* Coopérative générale du Cinéma français. 80 mins.
A series of documentary reconstructions based on a script suggested to Colette Audry by the stories of members of the Resistance: 1941, the secret crossings of the demarcation line; 1942, sabotage and the execution of hostages; 1943, a train attack by partisans, who are defeated; 1944, at the moment of disembarkation, the troop train "Apfelkern" is diverted and finally derailed. Epilogue: the liberation.
René Clément's first feature is one which equaled *Rome, Open City,* though not *Paisa.* It should have received the international success of Rossellini's film but was badly distributed outside France. It was originally begun as a short with the support of the "Résistance Fer" and the F.F.I. Best sequences: the execution of the hostages; the crossing of the line; the odyssey of the convoy "Apfelkern" and its derailment (actuality footage). The finale and the battle with the partisans are weaker. Excellent portrayals by the actors, not all nonprofessionals, but all unknown or anonymous.

BATH HOUSE (THE) BANYA

BATTLE OF BRITAIN (THE) see WHY WE FIGHT (SERIES)

BATTLE OF CHINA (THE) see WHY WE FIGHT (SERIES)

BATTLE OF RUSSIA (THE) see WHY WE FIGHT (SERIES)

BATTLE OF THE RAILS (THE) BATAILLE DU RAIL (LA)

BATTLESHIP POTEMKIN BRONENOSETS 'POTYOMKIN'

BATTLE STRIPE MEN (THE)

BAYAYA BAJAJA

BEAU SERGE (LE) HANDSOME SERGE France 1958. *Dir/Scen* Claude Chabrol *Assist Dir* Philippe de Broca, Claude de Givray, Charles Bitsch *Photog* Henri Decae *Mus* Emile Delpierre *Ed* Jacques Gaillard *Cast* Gérard Blain, Jean-Claude Brialy, Michèle Meritz, Bernadette Lafont, Jeanne Perez, Edmond Beauchamp, Claude Cerval, André Dino *Prod* AJYM. 97 mins.
A young Parisian, François (Brialy), convalescing in his native village in Auvergne, finds his childhood friend, Serge (Blain) has become a drunkard and, it seems to him, entered a bad marriage with Yvonne (Meritz). After a love affair with Marie (Lafont), Yvonne's younger sister, François interferes naively in Serge's life but finally comes to understand and accept reality.
Produced on a low budget in natural settings in Sardent (Creuse), a village that Chabrol knew well, *Le Beau Serge* was his first and remains his best film. Major sequences: François' arrival in the village and his first sight of Serge;

the free-for-all at the dance; the discussion in the snow with Serge and Yvonne; the dramatic finale in the depth of a winter night when François goes through his personal Calvary.

[*Le Beau Serge* is often credited as the first of the *nouvelle vague* films, though Varda's *La Pointe Courte* preceded it by three years.]

BEAUTE DU DIABLE (LA) Italy/France 1949. *Dir* René Clair *Scen* René Clair, Armand Salacrou *Photog* Michel Kelber *Art Dir* Léon Barsacq *Mus* Roman Vlad *Ed* James Cuenet *Cast* Michel Simon, Gérard Philipe, Nicole Besnard, Carlo Ninchi, Raymond Cordy, Gaston Modot, Paolo Stoppa, Simone Valère *Prod* Universalia/Enie/Franco-London Film. 96 mins.
A "Mediterranean version" of the Faust legend. In Italy about 1830, Professor Faust (Simon) receives the gift of youth from Mephistopheles (Simon). He becomes the poor Knight Henri (Philipe), meets Marguerite (Besnard), and is accused of having killed the professor, who has disappeared. He agrees to sign a pact with Mephistopheles, who has given him the trust of the Prince (Ninchi) and the love of the Princess (Valère), and has promised him the all-powerful gift of atomic arms. In a mirror, Henri sees the future with horrific visions of the evils of science, breaks the pact, and puts the devil in flight with a popular revolt. Redeemed by Marguerite's love, he turns with her towards the dawning heavens . . .
René Clair has said of this ambitious film: "There are several themes of indestructible richness. These are those of which an author should be wary. But why a new *Faust*, one asks, and in a different period? The character becomes strangely clear . . . The great drive that pushed the alchemists has continued until the era of atomic discoveries. And my contemporaries have the privilege of taking part in the spectacle of a humanity which, having sold its soul to science, tries to forestall the damnation of the world towards which its own efforts are leading it."
The key scene is the best sequence: Mephistopheles shows Faust his future — dictatorship founded on ruins and murders — in a large baroque mirror. But the Knight, Henri, "refuses to accept the judgment of destiny." The performance by Michel Simon is equalled by Gérard Philipe, each in one of his best roles. The direction is elegant, but the décor is a little overblown, the producer having insisted on spending the (ephemeral) riches of Universalia.
In *Comédies et Commentaires* (1959) Clair wrote: "The scenes with Marguerite appear dragged out, because she is not indispensable. The theme is the conflict between Faust and Mephistopheles." He judges "objectively remarkable" the idea that Mephistopheles becomes Faust and vice versa. "Since it is Faust who invokes him, it is of Faust himself that he is the image." This metaphor was barely understandable to the public and was even less clear than the somewhat allusive atomic theme.
René Clair noted the reaction of certain English viewers: "But Faust did sign the pact. He should accept its clauses. What he did isn't right." For these islanders, divine grace itself could not oppose the rules of traditional British honesty.
See also *Faust*

BEAUTIES OF THE NIGHT BELLES DE NUIT (LES)

BEAUTY AND THE BEAST BELLE ET LA BÊTE (LA)

BEAUTY FROM NIVERNAISE (THE) BELLE NIVERNAISE (LA)

BEDAZZLED see FAUST

BEFORE DAWN REIMEI IZEN

*BELLE DE JOUR France/Italy 1967. *Dir* Luis Buñuel *Scen* Luis Buñuel, Jean-Claude Carrière based on the novel by Joseph Kessel *Photog* Sacha Vierny *Art Dir* Robert Clavel *Ed* Walter Spohr *Cast* Catherine Deneuve, Jean Sorel, Michel Piccoli, Geneviève Page, Pierre Clementi *Prod* Paris Film/Five Films. 100 mins. Eastman Color.
Séverine (Deneuve) is in love with her husband, Pierre (Sorel), but is left frigid by his love-making. Henri (Piccoli) tries to seduce her; she rejects him, but is fascinated to learn that a friend supplements her income by working in a brothel. She joins a house run by Madame Anaïs (Page) and the physical fulfillment she finds there increases her love for Pierre. A young gangster (Clementi) tries to persuade her to live with him but she refuses and leaves the brothel. The

gangster shoots Pierre out of jealousy; later Henri tells the paralyzed Pierre the truth about Séverine but the couple remain together.

Buñuel stated this would be his last film (though he has since made two more) and a greater testament to his cinematic genius could not be imagined. A hypnotic and exquisite film into which he poured the quintessence of all his beliefs on the nature of good and evil, of eroticism, love, and morality. Buñuel's refusal to judge his characters allows the viewer to go beyond moral distinctions and reach, with Séverine, a sense of liberation.

BELLE EQUIPE (LA) THEY WERE FIVE France 1936. *Dir* Julien Duvivier *Scen* Charles Spaak, Julien Duvivier *Photog* Jules Krüger, Marc Fessard *Art Dir* Jacques Krauss *Mus* Maurice Yvain *Ed* Marthe Poncin *Cast* Jean Gabin, Charles Vanel, Viviane Romance, Raymond Aimes, Robert Lynen, Raymond Cordy, Raphaël Medina *Prod* Ciné Arys. 94 mins. (78 mins U.S.).

Five unemployed Parisian workers win 100,000 francs in the Lottery and combine to open a pleasure garden and restaurant. Things do not go smoothly and their numbers are depleted until only two are left. One (Gabin) quarrels with the other (Vanel) over the love of the latter's beautiful, but unfaithful, wife (Romance). There are two versions of the ending. In the "tragic" version (for the upper-class theaters) one man kills the other and the workers' cooperative fails. In the happy version (for regular theaters, also used in the English release version) the two men send the wife away and the brave unemployed become carefree proprietors.

The first part of this film is excellent, showing the unemployed during the Thirties, their discovery of the banks of the Marne, their strong desire to become independent, their common fight against adversity and hardship. There is also a sense of the *Front Populaire* in this film that reflects the period in which it was made. Although Vanel, Gabin, and Viviane Romance (in her first major role) are perfect, as melodramatic intrigue piles on melodramatic intrigue the film becomes less interesting.

The film seems like a natural continuation of Renoir's *Crime de M. Lange* (*q.v.*). Renoir, when he heard Spaak's theme of the film, wanted very much to direct it, but Duvivier refused to give up his option.

BELLE ET LA BETE (LA) BEAUTY AND THE BEAST France 1946. *Dir* Jean Cocteau *Co-Dir/Technical Advisor* René Clément *Scen* Jean Cocteau based on the story by Mme. Leprince de Beaumont *Photog* Henri Alekan *Art Dir* René Moulaert. Carré *Costumes* Escoffier, Castillo *Artistic Dir* Christian Bérard *Mus* Georges Auric *Make Up* Arakélian *Cast* Jean Marais, Josette Day, Mila Parély, Marcel André, Michel Auclair, Nane Germon *Prod* André Paulvé. 95 mins.

Beauty (Day) saves her father (André) by giving herself to the Beast (Marais). Because she loves him, he is transformed into a handsome prince.

A sumptuous film fantasy, superbly photographed. The sets by Christian Bérard contribute to the visual enchantment and Arakélian's make-up creations are splendid. One of Cocteau's greatest successes as a film maker.

BELLE NIVERNAISE (LA) THE BEAUTY FROM NIVERNAISE France 1923. *Dir* Jean Epstein *Scen* Jean Epstein based on a novel by Alphonse Daudet *Photog* Paul Guichard, Léon Donnot *Ed* Jean Epstein *Cast* Blanche Montel, David Evremond, Maurice Touzé, Géo Charliot, Max Bonnet *Prod* Pathé. 5,900 ft. approx.

The life of bargemen traveling the rivers and canals. "One of the most perfect, classical, and exquisite works of French silent cinema. With its barely perceptible rhythm, and its perfect simplicity, it is the film that France can best offer to match the Swedish masterpieces" (Henri Langlois).

BELLES DE NUIT (LES) NIGHT BEAUTIES/ BEAUTIES OF THE NIGHT France/Italy 1952. *Dir/Scen* René Clair *Photog* Armand Thirard, Robert Juillard, Louis Née *Art Dir* Léon Barsacq *Mus* Georges van Parys *Cast* Gérard Philipe, Martine Carole, Gina Lollobrigida, Magali Vendeuil, Paolo Stoppa, Raymond Bussières, Bernard LaJarrige, Raymond Cordy, Jean Paradès *Prod* Franco-London-Film/ Rizzoli. 89 mins.

An obscure and discontented provincial music teacher (Philipe) escapes into his dreams, where he meets several versions of the ideal woman. First, he goes back to the turn of the century where, as a successful composer, he meets a lady (Carole); then as a romantic and handsome soldier during the conquest of Algeria (1830) he meets a voluptuous girl (Lollobrigida) in a harem; then during his French Revolution exploits, he meets another love (Vendeuil); then another with the Musketeers; finally he dreams of being among the cavemen in Gaul. In the end, he forces himself to stay awake and notices the garage proprietor's lovely daughter.

Clair's initial idea was to make "a comic *Intolerance*," but this film is not at all comparable to Griffith's. Even if it has "no other ambition than to entertain" it soon becomes boring. Songs are interspersed among the action, and the refrain: "How beautiful it was to be twenty years old when the children of *la Patrie,* clarions sounding, tambours beating, went to pacify Algeria," had a double-edged meaning in the late Fifties. However, it does have attractive sets, costumes, and colors and, not least of all, Gina Lollobrigida, glowing with youthful beauty.

BEN HUR The story of a Jew's captivity by the Romans, his release, and his final triumph, set in the time of Christ.
— USA 1907. *Dir* Sidney Olcott, Frank Oakes Rose *Scen* Gene Gauntier based on the novel by Lew Wallace *Prod* Kalem. 1 reel.

Produced without the authorization of the novelist or the copyright holders. The publishers of the book and the producers of the play sued Kalem for breach of copyright and Kalem settled for $25,000 in 1911. This was the first recognition of an author's rights in film versions of his work. [The director, Olcott, himself said: "I took a cameraman down to the track and shot the race (a chariot race publicity stunt). A couple of interiors added to this and presto, *Ben Hur* was screened."]
— USA 1925 (production began 1923). *Dir* Fred Niblo *Co-Dir* Christy Cabanne, Hal Roach *2nd Unit Dir* B. Reaves Eason *Scen* Bess Meredyth, Carey Wilson based on the novel by Lew Wallace *Photog* Karl Struss, René Guissart, Clyde de Vinna, Percy Hilburn, George Meehan and others *Art Dir* Horace Jackson, Ferdinand Pinney Earle *Ed* Lloyd Nosler *Cast* Ramon Novarro, Francis X. Bushman, Carmel Myers, May McAvoy, Betty Bronson, Leo White *Prod* M.G.M.

10,450 ft. Reissued with music and sound effects in 1931. (Charles Brabin was original director, George Walsh the original Ben Hur, and June Mathis the original scriptwriter.)

The film cost four million dollars, an enormous sum for the time, and MGM did not recover their investment despite the film's commercial success. The Goldwyn company began production in 1923 in Rome using thousands of extras. The merger that created MGM led to a reconsideration and, in 1924, production was begun anew in Hollywood with different director, scriptwriters, and cast. Of the original cast, only Bushman (as Messala) and Carmel Myers were retained. MGM's loss on the film led to the imposition of the block booking system for other MGM programs.

Moussinac judged the film in 1927: "Enormous material means and technical facilities have been used to produce an edifying, but stupid, story. Color sequences in the Saint-Sulpice "Road to the Cross" style. A film that recalls the earlier Italian cinema. There are two sensational and successful (which is better) attractions: a sea battle and a chariot race. The latter especially is remarkable. And two images that border on grandeur but lack radiance. *Ben Hur?* A lucky dip."
— USA 1959. *Dir* William Wyler *2nd Unit Dir* Andrew Marton, Yakima Canutt, Mario Soldati *Scen* Karl Tunberg based on the novel by Lew Wallace *Photog* Robert L. Surtees *2nd Unit Photog* Piero Portalupi *Art Dir* William A. Horning, Edward Carfagno *Sets* Hugh Hunt *Mus* Miklos Rozsa *Ed* Ralph E. Winters, John D. Dunning *Cast* Charlton Heston, Stephen Boyd, Haya Harareet, Jack Hawkins, Hugh Griffith *Prod* M.G.M. 217 mins. Technicolor. Camera 65 Panavision.

"Fifteen million dollars, ten years in preparation, a year in production, 496 speaking roles, 100,000 extras, 8 hectares of sets, enough negative used to stretch around the world" (publicity). Moussinac's critique of the second *Ben Hur* could equally well be applied to the third. The battle at sea is dull but the chariot race is excellent, especially in stereophonic sound. The race alone required four months of rehearsals and three months to produce. Wyler left the direction of it to his assistants, specialists in westerns. The commercial success of this version surpassed even that of the second and it has been reissued several times.

BERG-EJVIND OCH HANS HUSTRU THE OUT-LAW AND HIS WIFE Sweden 1917. *Dir* Victor Sjöström *Scen* Victor Sjöström, Sam Ask based on the play by Johan Sigurjönssen *Photog* J. Julius (Julius Jaenzon) *Art Dir* Axel Esbensen *Cast* Victor Sjöström, Edith Erastoff, John Ekman, Nils Aréhn, Jenny Tschernichin-Larsson *Prod* Svenska Biografteatern. 2,781 meters (9,200 ft. approx.).

In Iceland in the mid-19th century, Berg-Ejvind (Sjöström), outlawed for stealing sheep, is given work on a farm by a rich widow, Halla (Erastoff), who becomes his mistress. The local bailiff (Aréhn) grows jealous and tries to arrest Berg-Ejvind, but he flees to the mountains where he is joined by Halla. They have a child and five years of happiness before they are betrayed. Finally, alone in the snow, they commit suicide.

"The most beautiful film in the world" according to Louis Delluc, who added, "Sjöström has directed it with a stylistic breadth that needs no comment. He has shown himself to be a commanding and humane actor, just as his partner and a third actor: the countryside."

The mountains, a geyser, the mountain stream where the outlaws drown the child, the snow where they are driven to their death, are the real characters in this drama. Its story is as spare as the sets for the family farm, simply and effectively designed by Axel Esbensen. It was with this film in mind (Sjöström's best with *The Wind*) that Moussinac wrote in 1924: "The décor is used with singular power to accentuate the character of a scene, explain and complete a gesture or an expression, or reveal the dramatic psychology; choosing their "natural depths" with the greatest care, using the creative force of the light in the studios with a rare understanding, the Swedes leave nothing to chance. They consider carefully and if they let themselves be carried away, they know when to stop."

BERGERE ET LE RAMONEUR (LA) MR. WON-DERBIRD/THE SHEPHERDESS AND THE CHIMNEY SWEEP. France 1953. *Dir* Paul Grimault *Scen* Jacques Prévert, Paul Grimault *Mus* Joseph Kosma *Ed* Gilbert Natot *Voices* (*French version*) Pierre Brasseur, Serge Reggiani, Anouk Aimée (*English version*) Peter Ustinov, Claire Bloom, Max Adrian, Denholm Elliot, Alec Clunes *Prod* André Sarrut. 63 mins. Technicolor.

Animated film. A dictator (King Charles V and III make VIII, and VIII makes XVI) tyrannizes Tachycardie. He accuses a shepherdess and a chimney sweep of "young love" and throws his police and motorized forces against them. But a bird (Mr. Wonderbird) saves them, destroys the royal palace, and delivers the people of the lower town, who live in the shadows.

Prévert's scenario, echoing somewhat the theme of *Metropolis,* is a stirring fantasy, and Grimault's inventions work very well. Best sequences: the chase; the description of the extravagant royal palace; the appearance of the terrifying robot; the portraits of the dictator, printed and distributed by the thousands; the happy ending re-establishing the harmony of the countryside.

Grimault had worked six or seven years on this film (the first feature-length animated film produced in France) when a conflict with the producer forced its completion. Many of the scenes were colored or reworked contrary to his intentions, but he lost the court case, which he brought with Prévert, to regain possession of his film. Although mutilated and deformed, it marked, nonetheless, a major stage in the development of animation.

BERLIN U.S.S.R. 1945. *Dir* Yuli Raizman, *Assist* Nikolai Shpikovsky *Photog* Leon Saakov, Roman Karmen, E. Volk and forty others *Mus* A. Roitman *Prod* Central Newsreel Studios. 69 mins.

A remarkable documentary, produced during the battle for Berlin. Striking shots: the Red flag raised on the Reichstag; Goebbels and his family burnt after their suicide; the terrified civilians wandering among the ruins.

See also *Padeniye Berlina* (*The Fall of Berlin*)

BERLIN, DIE SINFONIE DER GROSSTADT BERLIN, THE SYMPHONY OF A GREAT CITY Germany 1927. *Dir* Walther Ruttman *Scen* Walther Ruttman, Karl Freund, based on an idea by Carl Mayer *Photog* Reimar Kuntze, Robert Baberske, Läszlo Schäffer *Mus* Edmund Meisel *Prod* Fox-Europa, supervised by Karl Freund. 7,020 ft. 78 mins.

A cross section of the life and rhythm of a late spring day in Berlin, from dawn to midnight. It is a symphony of visual impressions, admirably edited, and based on the ideas and methods of Dziga Vertov. Some of the sequences are metaphorical: the crowds and cattle; the legs of dancers, two pairs of legs going to a hotel, a montage of legs; a sleeping man compared to an elephant.

The director said in 1928: "Since I began in the cinema, I had the idea of making something out of life, of creating a symphonic film out of the millions of energies that comprise the life of a big city. The possibility of such a film arose the day I met Karl Freund, who had the same ideas. During several weeks, as early as 4 a.m., he and I had to photograph the dead city. It is strange that Berlin tried to escape my efforts to capture its life and rhythm with my lens. We were constantly tormented by the hunter's fever, but the most difficult parts were those of the sleeping city. It is easier to work with moving things than to give the impression of absolute repose and the calm of death. For the night scenes, the chief cameraman, Reimar Kuntze, developed a hypersensitive film stock so that we could avoid using artificial light." [Curiously enough, in an interview in 1929 Karl Freund said that *he* developed the special film in addition to inventing several contrivances to hide the camera during filming. Carl Mayer withdrew from the production in the early stages, disagreeing with Ruttman's superficial and formalized approach to the depiction of life in a city.]

At this time censorship prevented many from seeing Vertov's more militant films. Ruttman's very successful film spread Vertov's theories worldwide and exercised considerable influence everywhere, from Japan to Brazil.

BEST YEARS OF OUR LIVES (THE) USA 1946. *Dir* William Wyler *Scen* Robert E. Sherwood, based on *Glory for Me* by MacKinlay Kantor *Photog* Gregg Toland *Ed* Daniel Mandell *Mus* Hugo Friedhofer *Art Dir* George Jenkins, Perry Ferguson *Cast* Myrna Loy, Fredric March, Dana Andrews, Virginia Mayo, Teresa Wright, Harold Russell, Cathy O'Donnell *Prod* Sam Goldwyn Productions. 172 mins.

Three men return from the war: Fred, a young air force officer (Andrews); Al, a middle-aged soldier who was formerly a banker (March); and Homer, a sailor (Russell) who has lost both arms and had them replaced by artificial ones. Fred finds his hasty "war" marriage to Marie (Mayo) a mistake and cannot settle into his prewar job of serving in a drugstore. The banker, with occasional drinking excursions, settles down into getting to know his wife (Loy) and daughter (Wright) and making bank loans. The sailor has to overcome the pity he assumes is felt by his fiancée (O'Donnell), family, and friends. In the end, Fred marries the banker's daughter. Hailed in 1946 as a masterpiece, this film contributed to an overestimation of Wyler's talents. Marred by a conventional happy ending, it was nonetheless a sincere portrayal of the difficulties and problems of readjustment in postwar America. One remembers, especially, Dana Andrews's performance, visiting a pilot's cemetery or fighting a client in a bar who had told him he was wrong about war and that he should now be ready to fight the Reds.

BETE HUMAINE (LA) JUDAS WAS A WOMAN France 1938. *Dir* Jean Renoir *Scen* Jean Renoir based on the novel by Zola *Photog* Curt Courant *Art Dir* Eugène Lourié *Mus* Joseph Kosma *Ed* Marguerite Renoir *Cast* Jean Gabin, Julien Carette, Fernand Ledoux, Jean Renoir, Simone Simon, Jenny Hélia, Blanchette Brunoy *Prod* Paris Films. 99 mins.

Lantier (Gabin), a railway mechanic and hereditary alcoholic, is pushed into crime. He becomes the lover of Séverine (Simon), who wants him to kill her husband, Roubaud (Ledoux), himself a criminal, but he ends by strangling her.

Renoir, after the unmerited failure of *La Marseillaise* (*q.v.*), agreed to make this film because Gabin very much wanted to play a railway worker. He had less than vague memories of the novel, which is far from being one of Zola's best, and is one in which the three protagonists are modern Atridae, whose heredity condemned them to worse crimes. With some hesitation he rejected an adaptation by Roger Martin Du Gard that concluded with the declaration of war in August 1914, and finally himself wrote a scenario that mainly retained "a love story of the railroads" from the original novel.

The opening sequence showing, in a documentary style, the Paris-Le Havre run seen from a train, is a masterpiece of editing and perfect simplicity. It is comparable to another sequence, less impressionistic but still very beautiful, showing the life of the migrant railway workers. In this way, Renoir depicted Lantier's social milieu by showing him at work. His impulse to murder is powerfully but quietly expressed in the brief scene showing his desire to kill a woman (Brunoy) who had given herself to him while a train was passing. Later, the drama becomes more involved and three sequences are equally admirable: the killing committed by Roubaud in an express; the attempt to kill him in the nocturnal setting of the railway tracks; the final strangling of Séverine, intercut with a railway workers' fair, while a voice on the soundtrack sings a turn-of-the-century ballad.

"I try to discover the unity of action before considering the unity of place and time," wrote Renoir. *La Bête Humaine* is far superior to *La Grande Illusion* and was far from being a commercial failure. However, some critical attacks hampered its success. M. Vinel (Rebatet), though he did not deny the qualities of the film, set the pattern in *L'Action Française:* "In politics, Renoir is out of the same Jewish-Democratic lineage as Zola. We hope we will not see him again in the miry rut of the class cinema."

The acting is of exceptional quality. It is one of Gabin's great roles and Carette responds intelligently to his performance. Simone Simon is a Séverine of tragic proportions, while Ledoux, as the callous Roubaud, is remarkable.

See also HUMAN DESIRE

BETWEEN WORLDS MÜDE TOD (DER)

BICYCLE THIEVES LADRI DI BICICLETTE

BIDONE (IL) THE SWINDLERS Italy/France 1955. *Dir* Federico Fellini *Scen* Fellini, Ennio Flaiano, Tullio Pinelli *Photog* Otello Martelli *Art Dir* Dario Cecchi *Mus* Nino Rota *Ed* Mario Serandrei, Guiseppe Vari *Cast* Broderick Crawford, Richard Basehart, Franco Fabrizi, Giulietta Masina, Lorella De Luca *Prod* Titanus/S.G.C. 108 mins.

A trio of petty swindlers — Augusto (Crawford), Picasso (Basehart), and Roberto (Fabrizi) — trick two old peasant women with a story of buried treasure and later deceive a group of slum dwellers into making payments on nonexistent houses. They would like to break into higher criminal circles but Picasso is nagged by his wife Iris (Masina), who wants him to break with his cronies, while Augusto worries about his daughter Patrizia (De Luca), who wants to become a teacher. She discovers the truth about her father when he is arrested for an earlier crime. When he is released, he learns Roberto has left and Picasso has returned to his wife. He joins another group and, disguised as a priest, is forced to give comfort to the paralyzed daughter of a peasant he is cheating. Overcome by remorse, he tells the gang he has returned the money but they beat him up and take the money, which he was in fact saving for his daughter. He slowly dies of his wounds on a deserted mountain road.

Best sequences: the swindlers dressed as priests conning the peasant woman; the evening in a nightclub and the cabaret; a midnight party at the home of an old accomplice who became rich; Augusto's remorse over the paralytic girl; Augusto's death, like a solitary wolf, on the mountain road.

This tragic film was not successful, probably because the title suggests a comedy. Stylistically it is both gently nostalgic and harshly realistic. Its forceful dramatic theme is suggestive of Gogol's *Dead Souls*. Very beautiful photography, with occasionally somewhat surrealistic images, notably in the opening sequence that shows the swindlers in the country dressed in. cassocks.

BIENVENIDO, MR. MARSHALL WELCOME, MR. MARSHALL Spain 1952. *Dir* Luis G. Berlanga *Scen* Juan Bardem, Luis Berlanga, Miguel Mihura *Photog* Manuel Berenguer *Art Dir* Francisco Canet Cubel *Mus* Jesus G. Lopez *Ed* Pepita Orduna *Cast* Lolita Sevilla, José Isbert, Manolo Moran, Alberto Romea, Elvira Quintilla *Prod* UNINCI. 86 mins.

In a poor Castillian town, the mayor (Isbert) learns that the representatives of the Marshall Plan are visiting Spain and his village and imagines they will bring prosperity to the countryside. Together with an impresario (Moran) he organizes a special folkloric reception, but the procession of officials goes through the village without stopping.

Berlanga and Bardem were both starting their film-making careers when they made this satire. Its success revived the Spanish cinema after fifteen years' hibernation. Certainly part of its success must be credited to co-scenarist Bardem, but the picaresque tone of the film belongs properly to Berlanga. The poverty of Spain is described with simple effectiveness and contrasted with the grotesque "Spanish fiesta" with its shawls, mantillas, castanets, bull fighters, etc., organized to seduce "Mr. Marshall." Its accurate portrait of the social structure of the Spanish countryside, with its ruined Hidalgos, its priests, and its rich landowners, is excellent. The town remains a collective personality from which only the mayor, beautifully portrayed by the great actor, José Isbert, stands out.

BIG CARNIVAL (THE) ACE IN THE HOLE

BIG DAY (THE) JOUR DE FÊTE

BIG FAMILY (THE) BOLSHAYA SEMYA

BIG HOUSE USA 1930. *Dir* George Hill *Dir* (*French/German version*) Paul Fejos *Scen* Frances Marion, Joe Farnham, Martin Flavin *Photog* Harold Wenstrom *Art Dir* Cedric Gibbons *Ed* Blanche Sewell *Cast* Chester Morris, Wallace Beery, Lewis Stone, Robert Montgomery, Leila Hyams, Karl Dane *Cast* (*German version*) Heinrich George, Gustave Diesl, Egen von Jordan, von Twardowski *Dial* Hans Clever, Ernst Toller, E. W. Brandes *Cast* (*French version*) André Berry *Prod* Cosmopolitan for MGM. 88 mins. (Also made in Italian and Spanish versions).
A prison revolt directed against the Warden (Stone) is led by a murderer (Beery), and a thief (Morris) expecting his parole. A young prisoner (Montgomery) saves the hostages but the revolt itself is successful.
A powerful criticism of the penitentiary system, totally unromantic, and inspired by a spate of revolts in American prisons. The script and the superb soundtrack (both of which won an Oscar) are devoted to portraying the atmosphere of prison life as seen through the eyes of a young convict. "Montgomery cast against type, but turning in a convincing performance, dramatizes the process by which a selfish, tough kid is made into a criminal. The scenes of his admission to prison are clinically thorough" (John Baxter) Beery is excellent as the brutish convict whose growing sense of power culminates in the riot, — an outbreak that begins in the vast dining hall as mess tins are thrown in the air and continues through the exciting fighting sequences to the climax.
This is one of the first major successes of the American sound film and one that appears to have been of equal quality in all versions. George Hill killed himself in 1934, having made only a handful of films.

BIG KNIFE (THE) USA 1955. *Dir* Robert Aldrich *Scen* James Poe from the play by Clifford Odets *Photog* Ernest Laszlo *Art Dir* William Glasgow *Ed* Michael Luciano *Mus* Frank DeVol *Cast* Jack Palance, Ida Lupino, Wendell Corey, Shelley Winters, Rod Steiger, Everett Sloane *Prod* Associates and Aldrich. 111 mins.
A famous Hollywood star, Charlie Castle (Palance), feels he has compromised himself and wants to break away. His wife, Marion (Lupino), agrees with him but Charlie's producer, Hoff (Steiger), blackmails him into a new contract because Charlie had killed a pedestrian in a car accident and let his publicity agent (Sloane) take the rap. When Dixie (Winters), an extra who had been with Charlie in the car, threatens to talk, she is beaten up and then killed in an accident. Meanwhile, Marion has left Charlie for another man. Despairing, Charlie commits suicide.
"My producer is a combination of Louis B. Mayer, Jack Warner and Harry Cohn," Robert Aldrich has said. "Its theme is how, no matter what the environment, whether in arts or business, the natural freedom of man, his possibility for self-expression is being hampered by amoral, tyrannical bosses. At the same time, the film is directed against certain typical Hollywood characters."
The three-act play, which Aldrich adapted cinematically, is ultimately a polemic against Hollywood, its gossip columnists, press agents, unscrupulous producers, and stars — stars who are victims of their own fame, of the big knife, the system that killed Marilyn Monroe as it did Charlie. None of the Hollywood characters portrayed are reduced to a formula and Hoff, the producer, is a very complex personality, an all-too-human monster. Luxurious sets contribute to the oppressive atmosphere in which Jack Palance is a kind of Frankenstein's monster hunted down and destroyed by his creator.

BIG PARADE (THE) USA 1925. *Dir* King Vidor *Scen* Laurence Stallings, Harry Behn *Photog* John Arnold *Ed* Hugh Wynn *Mus* David Mendoza, William Axt *Titles* Joseph Farnham, *Cast* John Gilbert, Renée Adorée, Hobart Bosworth, Karl Dane, Claire McDowell, Tom O'Brien, George K. Arthur *Prod* MGM. 11,519 ft.

A young American (Gilbert), stirred into thinking of the heroics of war, enlists. He arrives in France, courts a beautiful peasant girl (Adorée), is wounded in the fighting, and finally marries the young girl.

After directing this film King Vidor said: "The war has now become a human thing, and after ten years the human values predominate, everything else becoming insignificant. We have searched for the individual side more than the mass. We have shown the heart struggles of the hero, his girl, his mother, and his comrades. We have not ignored the enormity of what was going on around them, but we have seen it through their eyes. The human comedy emerges from a terrifying tragedy. The poetry and the romance, the atmosphere, the rhythm and the tempo all find their proper place. Some units of the Second Division that fought in the Argonne have re-created the battles for us and a "Boche" (today a peaceful American citizen) told us the exact positioning of the German machine guns. When a nation declares war, the people fight it without asking why. But the last war posed a question for all time: Why are there wars? I am certainly not in favor of wars but I did not want to preach against them."

The Big Parade was, however, presented in France under the slogan "A film to make you hate war" with the praise of Marshall Joffre ("All my compliments for this beautiful spectacle") and of General Gouraud ("I must tell you what a splendid evening I had").

The much-mutilated French version provoked, as did the publicity, the indignation of the left. Moussinac judged the film "false, artificial, vulgar, no human accent, not a cry of truth." This is too strong: the scenes of military training, the endless lines of troops and trucks moving up to the front, the faces of the soldiers, are moving and true. But Vidor was wrong in thinking he had created "a surprising realism in the scenes of French village life." In these scenes, Renée Adorée "dressed like a burlesque miller's wife" (Moussinac) is as ridiculous as the papier-maché sets. The film had a worldwide success and made its director famous.

BIG SLEEP (THE) USA 1946. *Dir* Howard Hawks *Scen* William Faulkner, Leigh Brackett, Jules Furthman, based on the novel by Raymond Chandler *Photog* Sidney Hickox *Mus* Max Steiner *Art Dir* Carl Jules Weyl *Ed* Christian Nyby *Cast* Humphrey Bogart, Martha Vickers, Lauren Bacall, John Ridgely *Prod* Warner Brothers. 114 mins.

A private dectective, Marlowe (Bogart) is retained to deal with a case of blackmail. Carmen (Vickers), the youngest daughter, is a drug addict and Vivian (Bacall), her sister, is involved with bad company. Dealing with gangsters and disposing of various corpses, Marlowe solves the problem, sends Carmen for psychiatric treatment, and falls in love with Vivian.

The director has said that he didn't really understand Chandler's novel, but its typically Chandler atmosphere and plot are beautifully caught by Hawks in this *film noir*. It has also been defined by Nino Frank as a new kind of detective story: "The essential question is less who committed the crime than to see how the protagonist behaves. The only thing that is important is the enigmatic psychology of one or the other, enemies and friends at the same time." Humphrey Bogart's presence is an essential asset to the film, as is that of his wife, Lauren Bacall. A dark, sensual film, full of oppressive atmosphere.

*BIRDS (THE) USA 1963. *Dir* Alfred Hitchcock *Scen* Evan Hunter based on the story by Daphne Du Maurier *Photog* Robert Bucks, with Ub Iwerks as special effects adviser *Art Dir* Robert Boyle *Ed* George Tomasini *Cast* Tippi Hedren, Rod Taylor, Suzanne Pleshette, Jessica Tandy *Prod* Alfred Hitchcock for Universal-International. 119 mins. Technicolor.

A chance meeting in a pet shop impels Melanie (Hedren) to follow Mitch (Taylor) to Bodega Bay on the California coast. There she meets his mother (Tandy) and a schoolteacher who is in love with him (Pleshette). Inexplicably all the birds in the area begin to attack the inhabitants.

As commercially successful as his other films, *The Birds* perhaps aroused more critical controversy than any other Hitchcock film. For non-*aficionados,* this was as involving and enjoyable as his others, but weighed down by symbolic pretentiousness, by Hitchcock trying to live up to his reputation as a "serious" director. For others, such as Robin Wood: "The birds are a concrete embodiment of the arbitrary and unpredictable, of whatever makes human life and human relationships precarious, a reminder of the fragility and instability that cannot be ignored or evaded, and beyond that, of the possibility that life is meaningless and absurd.

"The opening shots of the film, as so often in Hitchcock, state the theme with almost diagrammatic simplicity. Melanie Daniels crosses a street in San Francisco; overhead, birds mass in ominous dark clouds. She enters an expensive pet shop; she is surrounded by birds in ornamental cages. Outside, reality, with its constant menace of instability; inside, the 'safe' artificial world that sophisticated human beings fabricate and call reality. The light comedy of the opening sequence is not merely there to lull the spectator into a state of unpreparedness for the coming horrors. The triviality is the point: the triviality of constant, even habitual playacting.

"In these opening scenes, Melanie's behaviour and attitude, even her stance, are unnatural and dehumanizing — life rendered insignificant in the gilded cage of artificiality."

BIRTH OF A NATION (THE) USA 1915. *Dir* D. W. Griffith *Scen* D. W. Griffith, Frank E. Woods, Thomas Dixon, Jr. based on *The Clansman* and partly *The Leopard's Spots* by Thomas Dixon, Jr. *Assist Dir* Raoul Walsh, W. S. Van Dyke, Jack Conway, George Siegman *Ed* D. W. Griffith *Photog* G. W. Bitzer *Mus Arranged* Joseph Carl Breil, D. W. Griffith *Cast* Henry B. Walthall, Mae Marsh, Miriam Cooper, Josephine Crowell, Spottiswoode Aitken, Lillian Gish, Ralph Lewis, Elmer Clifton, Robert Harron, Wallace Reid, Joseph Henaberry, Donald Crisp, Elmo Lincoln, Raoul Walsh, Eugene Pallette, Sam de Grasse, George Siegman, Walter Long *Prod* Epoch (D. W. Griffith, Harry E. Aitken). Original release length 13,058 ft.; later cut to 12,500 ft.; existing versions about 11,700 ft. (195 mins.). Also reissued in a sound version.

In the mid-19th century, the rich Dr. Cameron, his wife (Crowell), their son Ben (Walthall), daughter Margaret (Marsh), and their other children live happily in the South and are visited by their friends from Pennsylvania, Phil (Lewis) and Elsie (Gish) Stoneman. The Civil War breaks out and the families are caught up on opposite sides of the fight. Ben Cameron, "the little Colonel," is wounded but nursed back to health by Elsie Stoneman, whom he loves, as Phil does Margaret. After the North's victory, Congressman Stoneman demands the punishment of the South, Lincoln refuses, but Stoneman sends a mulatto, Silas Lynch (Siegman), to organize an "army of the people" and later moves South with Elsie and Phil to carry out his equality program. The Reconstruction Period and the reign of the carpet-baggers: Ben becomes leader of the Ku Klux Klan to avenge the death of his younger sister at the hands of a Negro militiaman (Long). Lynch demands that Elsie marry him while the Negro militia lay siege to the Camerons. Ben and the clansmen rescue them and the two couples are married.

"The Ku Klux Klan saved the life of a people and revived the young South, writing one of the most dramatic chapters in Aryan history." This is the way the Reverend Thomas Dixon defined the main thesis of *The Clansman,* a very mediocre, ultraracist, propaganda novel, dedicated to his Uncle "Colonel Leroy McAfee, Grand Titan of the Ku Klux Klan." Griffith, the son of a southern Colonel ruined by the war, preserved the spirit of the novel and its bloodthirsty "Negroes" (played by black-face white actors). The film was first presented in Los Angeles (February 8, 1915) as *The Clansman.* The title was later changed because, according to Griffith, "the reestablishment of the South with its rights was the Birth of a New Nation." The extreme bias of a number of sequences provoked violent protests from liberal Americans, the National Association for the Advancement of Colored People, the President of Harvard University, and periodicals like *The Nation* and *The New Statesman.*

In New York, Chicago, Boston, etc., race riots broke out and there were many injuries. *The Birth of a Nation* was banned for its racism in Europe, where some "colored" troops had fought with the Allied armies. When in 1921 the film was finally given a permit for showing in France, it was only with numerous deletions. It remained banned in French occupation zones in Germany, where nationalists had been accusing Senegalese troops of rape and murder. The film was never shown in Tsarist Russia, nor, of course, in the USSR.

Its influence on the development of film art in Europe could only have occurred much later than 1915. It was not influential in the USSR, despite claims to the contrary. But it was very significant in the USA, as much on the industry itself as on the art of film. Its production cost $100,000 while its receipts reached 15 million dollars. Its $2.00 reserved-seat engagement in theaters created a new viability for exhibitors and allowed the production of longer, major feature films. It gave birth to "Hollywood" and its domination, first of the American cinema, then of world cinema.

The film contains sequences of great beauty. If one ignores the racist propaganda, the scene in which the young Flora Cameron is driven to her death by a Negro trying to rape her is admirable for the perfection of its editing and the dramatic use of natural settings. It also ends with a magnificent climactic scene, whose crosscutting has become classic. Griffith cuts from scenes of the Camerons trying to fight off the Negro militia to the clansmen galloping across streams to save them.

The high point of the film is the Battle of Petersburg. The burning of Atlanta with lines of refugees on the roads intercut with scenes of violent fighting is superbly handled and concludes with a "field covered with dead on which night falls." With this, one can unreservedly accept Griffith as the sympathetic, humane and tolerant man he showed himself to be elsewhere, if one ignores the racial question. He was much affected by the demonstrations against his film and showed, in *Hearts of the World,* a white soldier kissing his wounded black comrade. Griffith, as he proved in *Intolerance,* was sincerely liberal and progressive when he avoided depicting the Negro with the blind prejudice of a southerner.

BIRUMA NO TATEGOTO THE HARP OF BURMA/THE BURMESE HARP Japan 1956.

Dir Kon Ichikawa *Scen* Natto Wada based on the novel by Michio Takeyama *Photog* Minoru Yokoyama *Mus* Akira Ifukube *Ed* Masanori Tsujii *Cast* Shoji Yasui, Rentaro Mikuni, Tatsuya Mihashi, Taniye Kitabayashi *Prod* Nikkatsu. 116 mins.

In Burma during the Japanese collapse, Private Mizushima, (Yasui), who plays a Burmese harp, becomes wounded and separated from his unit, which is taken prisoner. He is nursed back to health and, dressed as a Buddhist monk, begins the long trek to the camps. On the way he sees many corpses of his countrymen and finally realizes his task is to honor the unknown dead by burying them. One day he passes his old unit but makes them understand he wishes to remain in Burma.

A lyrical, epic film, in which the horrors of war are matched by the beauty of nature, the assertion of human dignity, and moving music.

BITTER RICE RISO AMARO

BITTER VICTORY AMÈRE VICTOIRE

BLACKBOARD JUNGLE USA 1955. *Dir* Richard Brooks *Scen* Richard Brooks based on the novel by Evan Hunter *Photog* Russell Harlan *Art Dir* Cedric Gibbons, Randall Duell *Mus* Charles Wolcott *Ed* Ferris Webster *Cast* Glenn Ford, Anne Francis, Louis Calhern, Vic Morrow, Sidney Poitier, John Hoyt, Margaret Hayes. *Prod* MGM. 101 mins.

In a poor section of New York, a new teacher (Ford) has difficulty educating his tough and rebellious class, dominated by Artie West (Morrow) and a Negro (Poitier). He rescues a colleague, Lois (Hayes), from an attack by one of the boys and is himself beaten up. His wife (Francis) is upset by rumors of an affair between him and Lois and their child is born prematurely. Eventually he arouses his pupil's interest and when West attacks him with a knife the other boys in the class disarm him. Though it would be an exaggeration to talk of "an American Vigo," Richard Brooks' film is a vigorously realistic study of juvenile delinquency, of the American social environment, and of the relationship between Blacks and Whites. The youth played by Sidney Poitier is the most dignified, courageous, and lucid character in the class. After winning a just cause, he affirms "We shall not go back," a phrase that alludes to the fight for racial equality (of which this film was one of the first Hollywood recognitions). When *Blackboard Jungle* was screened at the Venice Film Festival, it provoked a diplomatic protest from Mrs. Luce, then American Ambassador in Rome.

BLACK GOD AND THE WHITE DEVIL (THE)
DEUS E O DIABO NA TERRA DO SOL

*BLACKMAIL Britain 1929. *Dir* Alfred Hitchcock *Scen* Alfred Hitchcock, Charles Bennett, Benn W. Levy based on the play by Charles Bennett *Photog* Jack Cox *Ed* Emile de Ruelle *Art Dir* Wilfred C. and Norman Arnold *Mus* Hubert Bath, Henry Stafford *Cast* Anny Ondra, John Longden, Sara Allgood, Charles Paton, Donald Callthorp, Cyril Ritchard (Anny Ondra's voice dubbed by Joan Barry) *Prod* British International/Wardour. 7,398 ft. 81 mins.
Alice White (Ondra) kills in self-defense an artist (Ritchard) who tries to rape her. Her fiancé, Frank Webber, (Longden), a detective assigned to the case, realizes the girl's involvement and learns the truth when a blackmailer, Tracy (Callthorp), tries to blackmail him. However, Webber contrives to make the police suspect Tracy, who is killed in a spectacular chase on the roof of the British Museum.
Blackmail was made first as a silent film but was later released as Britain's first sound film, in part reshot and in part dubbed. Although largely unsuccessful commercially, *Blackmail* is one of the best of the early sound films, notable for its subjective, imaginative use of sound to emphasize the drama of the images (e.g. in the "knife" sequence). The freedom of using postsynchronized sound in a previously shot silent film allowed Hitchcock to experiment with the expressive use of sound in a way not possible for films shot as original sound films. *Blackmail* suggests already Hitchcock's penchant for setting his adventures of the extraordinary within a framework of actuality. The realistic feeling for London localities is excellent: the empty streets at dawn, the police station, the little shop with the living room at the back. Interesting also is that Hitchcock sets the scene for his story with an opening reel (as he did with *The Lodger*) that is almost documentary in character and has no narrative connection with the main plot. *Blackmail* has sometimes been described as quasi-expressionist, but it is more likely Hitchcock was influenced by the expressive, pictorial values of the German cinema and sought to incorporate these in a more conventional narrative.
FILMS WITH THE SAME TITLE:
— *USA 1920. *Dir* Dallas Fitzgerald *Cast* Viola Dane, Wyndham Standing *Prod* Metro.
— USA 1939. *Dir* H. C. Potter *Cast* E. G. Robinson, Gene Lockhart, Ruth Hussey *Prod* MGM. 81 mins.
An escaped convict, innocent of his crime, tries to build a new life but is betrayed by the real criminal.
— *USA 1947. *Dir* Lesley Selander *Cast* Ricardo Cortez, William Marshall, Adele Mara *Prod* Republic. 65 mins.
Blackmail plot against a millionaire leads to two murders.

BLACK ORPHEUS ORFEU NEGRO

BLACK PIRATE (THE) USA 1926. *Dir* Albert Parker *Scen* Douglas Fairbanks (under pseud. Elton Thomas), Jack Cunningham *Photog* Henry Sharp *Art Dir* Oscar Borg, Dwight Franklin *Cast* Douglas Fairbanks, Billie Dove, Donald Crisp, Sam de Grasse *Prod* Douglas Fairbanks for United Artists. 8,500 ft. approx. Technicolor.
An acrobatic fairy tale using a vaguely Robin Hood theme. It was Douglas Fairbanks' last successful spectacular film. It was also the first feature in two-color Technicolor, a process whose dominant greenish-blue fitted well into the sea and underwater scenes. The most famous sequence is that in which Fairbanks captures a galleon single-handed after slitting the sails in two by sliding down them with a sword.

BLACKSMITH (THE) USA 1922. *Dir/Scen* Buster Keaton, Mal St. Clair *Cast* Buster Keaton, Virginia Fox *Prod* Associated First National *Assoc Prod* Comique Films Corp. 2 reels.
Blacksmith makes marvelous use of objects for comic effect (the horseshoes arranged like shoes in their boxes), but it is above all a frenzy of destruction involving an amazon woman, a white horse, and a very luxurious car.

BLADE AF SATANS BOG LEAVES FROM SATAN'S BOOK Denmark 1919 (released 1921). *Dir* Carl Theodor Dreyer *Scen*

Edgar Høyer based on the novel *Satans Sorger* by Marie Corelli, script rewritten by Dreyer *Photog* George Schnéevoigt *Art Dir* Alex Bruun, Jens G. Lind, Carl Dreyer *Cast* Helge Nissen (Satan) 1. *In Palestine* — Halvart Hoff, Jacob Texiere, Erling Hausson 2. *The Inquisition* — Halander Helleman, Ebon Strandin, Johannes Meyer 3. *The French Revolution* — Tenna Kraft, Emma Wiehe, Edith Pio 4. *The Red Rose of Finland* — Carlo Wieth, Clara Pontoppidan, Carl Hillebrandt *Prod* Nordisk. 7,000 ft. approx.
Satan, through the ages, betraying Christ and Marie-Antoinette, becoming Grand Inquisitor, and Commissar of a group of Bolsheviks in Finland during the Civil War. This film, an attack on the French and Russian Revolutions, contains some beautiful moments, notably the traveling shot in an inn. The best episode is that of the Passion of Christ, produced in a natural and direct style in the open air.

BLAUE ENGEL (DER) THE BLUE ANGEL Germany 1930. *Dir* Josef von Sternberg *Scen* Josef von Sternberg based on the novel *Professor Unrat* by Heinrich Mann (Carl Zuckmayer, Karl Vollmoeller, Robert Liebman credited with script) *Photog* Günther Rittau, Hans Schneeberger *Art Dir* Otto Hunte, Emil Hasler *Lyrics and Songs* Friedrich Hollaender *Cast* Emil Jannings, Marlene Dietrich, Hans Albers, Kurt Gerron, Rosa Valetti, Eduard von Winterstein *Prod* UFA (in German and English Versions). 114 mins.
An authoritarian teacher (Jannings) meets Lola (Dietrich), a nightclub singer and falls in love with her. He marries Lola and travels with the troupe, managed by Mazeppa (Albers), selling sexy photos of his wife. He becomes a clown and on returning to his own town and old classroom becomes aware of his downfall and tries to strangle his faithless wife.
Erich Pommer, the producer, asked Sternberg to come to Berlin to direct a story that was felt to be particularly suited to UFA's great star, Jannings: the downfall of an honorable middle-aged man. Sternberg had to find a Lola and finally chose the then obscure Marlene Dietrich, who had appeared in four or five small parts in films in 1927–29. With a feather boa, top hat, and black stockings over beautiful naked legs, she was a sensual and fascinating character who was more the star of the film than

Jannings or Hans Albers. Her sexy voice, her song "Falling in Love Again," and her appealing freshness made Marlene Dietrich into a new kind of vamp, one which she embodied for thirty years. "It was Sternberg," she has said, "who discovered me; until then I was nothing. He believed in me, made me work, gave me all his knowledge, his experience, his energy, and this created my success." Jannings, as usual, is superb in his portrayal of the ruin of an honorable man.
Blue Angel owes much to the cameramen and designers, who created an impressively German atmosphere and a sense of cabaret life. Its designs are derived from *Kammerspiel,* a style that had already influenced Sternberg.
The film has little dialogue and the excellent songs integrate well with the action.
— *The Blue Angel* USA 1959. *Dir* Edward Dmytryk *Cast* Curt Jurgens, Mai Britt.
[It would be difficult to match the original, but this version hardly tried.]

BLAZING SUN (THE) SERAA FIL WADI

BLIND DATE CHANCE MEETING Britain 1959. *Dir* Joseph Losey *Scen* Ben Barzman, Millard Lampell based on the novel by Leigh Howard *Photog* Christopher Challis *Art Dir* Edward Carrick *Mus* Richard Bennett *Ed* Reginald Mills *Cast* Hardy Kruger, Stanley Baker, Micheline Presle *Prod* Independent Artists. 95 mins.
A young man (Kruger) is suspected of the murder of his mistress (Presle). He reconstructs their life together and is finally proved innocent by Inspector Morgan (Baker).
A superb study of behavior and character, using a police investigation as background and many flashbacks. Remarkable direction of the three main characters on largely studio sets. [Losey has said: "Because it was a very unrealistic story — a very trite story, and a rather incredible story in terms of contrivance — (I felt it essential) that we give it as much interest in terms of observation and reality as we could, and that the characters be very rich . . . It certainly is fantastic the degree to which the English class structure influences practically every Englishman's life, either in rebellion against it or acceptance of it, or simply through their being gotten at by it without realising it."]

*BLIND HUSBANDS USA 1918. *Dir/Art Dir* Erich von Stroheim *Scen* Stroheim from his story *The Pinnacle Photog* Ben Reynolds *Cast* Erich von Stroheim, Gibson Gowland, Francelia Billington, Sam De Grasse, Fay Holderness *Prod* Universal. 8 reels.

A callow, carnal Austrian officer (Stroheim) on holiday in the mountains seduces the wife (Billington) of a rich American (De Grasse).

Stroheim's first film is, like the later *The Devil's Passkey* and *Foolish Wives* (*q.v.*), concerned with the eternal triangle: a continental seducer, an idle, unsatisfied wife looking for romance, an obtuse American husband seemingly bent only on making money. An accumulation of circumstantial details, of character mannerisms, and of psychological understanding gives significance to the trite plot of this sexual comedy-drama.

BLONDE IN LOVE (A) LASKY JEDNE PLAVOV-LASKY

BLOOD FEAST FIN DE FIESTA

BLOOD OF A POET (THE) SANG D'UN POÈTE (LE)

BLOOD OF BEASTS (THE) SANG DES BÊTES (LE)

BLOWUP Britain 1966. *Dir* Michelangelo Antonioni *Scen* Michelangelo Antonioni, Tonino Guerra based on a short story by Julio Cortazar *Photog* Carlo di Palma *Ed* Frank Clarke *Art Dir* Assheton Gorton *Mus* Herbert Hancock *Cast* David Hemmings, Vanessa Redgrave, Sarah Miles, Peter Bowles *Prod* Bridge Films for MGM. 111 mins. Eastman Color (print by Metrocolor).

A fashion photographer (Hemmings) by chance takes shots of a woman (Redgrave) which appear on being enlarged, to perhaps show a murder; but perhaps the murder is in his imagination.

"It is a film that carries few autobiographical elements. I believe in this story, but from outside it" (Antonioni). In a superb depiction of "post-Victorian" London, Antonioni followed up the ideas of *L'Avventura* on the uncertainty of recalling the moment that has already passed.

["If not the greatest, *Blow Up* seems to me easily the most likeable of Antonioni's later films; and its freshness and vivac-

ity make one look forward to his future work with an eagerness one would scarely have anticipated in the days of *La Notte* and *L'Eclisse* . . . What one first notices about *Blow Up* is its tempo, its effect of spontaneity, its lack of mannerisms." (Robin Wood). *Blow Up* is the only one of Antonioni's films to reach a relatively wide commercial market. Its success was probably due equally to its sexual scenes and the audiences' delight in puzzling out the meaning. However, Antonioni's attempt to depict the difficulty of any individual grasping "objective" reality and his bold, stylistic use of color make this his most accomplished (if not best) film since *L'Avventura*.]

BLUE ANGEL (THE) BLAUE ENGEL (DER)

BLUE EXPRESS GOLUBOI EKSPRESS

BOLSHAYA SEMYA THE BIG FAMILY USSR 1954. *Dir* Josef Heifitz *Scen* V. Kochetov, S. Kara based on the novel *The Zhurbins* by V. Kochetov *Photog* S. Ivanov *Art Dir* V. Volin, V. Savostin *Mus* V. Pushkov *Cast* Sergei Lukyanov, Boris Andreyev, Alexei Batalov, V. Kouznietzova *Prod* Lenfilm. 108 mins. Agfacolor.

A family of shipbuilders in a port: the grandfather (Lukyanov), the father (Andreyev), the sons (Batalov, Kouznietzova), etc. An unpretentious, often lyrical portrait of the daily life of Soviet workers. It is faithful to the original novel but somewhat superior.

BONHEUR (LE) HAPPINESS France 1965. *Dir/Scen* Agnès Varda *Photog* Jean Rabier, Claude Beausoleil *Ed* Janine Verneau *Art Dir* Hubert Monloup *Cast* Jean-Claude Drouot, Claire Drouot, Sandrine Drouot, Olivier Drouot, Marie-France Boyer *Prod* Parc Film/Mag Bodard. 79 mins. Eastman Color.

A cabinet maker (Drouot) loves his wife (Claire Drouot) but also his mistress (Boyer). The wife is killed (suicide or accident) and he remakes his life with his mistress. This light, "happy story of a kind of artisan milieu in the Paris suburbs" (Agnès Varda) would have stirred up less argument or indignation if it had been titled "A Great Misfortune."

BONNES FEMMES (LES) France/Italy 1959. *Dir* Claude Chabrol *Scen* Paul Gégauff, Claude Chabrol *Photog* Henri Decaë *Ed*

Jacques Gaillard *Cast* Bernadette Lafont, Lucile Saint-Simon, Clothilde Joano, Stéphane Audran *Prod* Paris Film Productions/Panitalia. 104 mins.

The life and pleasures of four young Parisian salesgirls, showing them at work in the Bastille district of Paris, in the swimming pool, in the country, and at the Pacra Concert. One girl thinks she has found true love when she spends a day in the country with an enigmatic motorcyclist, but instead he murders her. "The cinema of contempt" is a phrase that has been used in referring to this satire, which could not overcome lamentable acting. Some consider it to be Chabrol's best film. It was a total commercial failure.

*BONNIE AND CLYDE USA 1967. *Dir* Arthur Penn *Scen* David Newman, Robert Benton *Photog* Burnett Guffey *Art Dir* Dean Tavoularis *Mus* Charles Strouse *Ed* Dede Allen *Cast* Warren Beatty, Faye Dunaway, Michael J. Pollard, Gene Hackman, Estelle Parsons, Denver Pyle *Prod* Tatira/Hiller for Warner Brothers/Seven Arts. 111 mins. Technicolor.

Loosely based on fact, this is the story of Clyde Barrow (Beatty), Bonnie Parker (Dunaway) and their cohorts (Pollard, Hackman, Parsons) who, after a wild life of crime, meet their eventual death at the hands of a sheriff (Pyle).

Undoubtedly Arthur Penn's best film, a perfectly judged blend of comedy, violence, and love. The almost childlike world of fantasy which Bonnie and Clyde create around themselves, their arrogant yet innocent belief in their own myth, is excellently depicted through Burnett Guffey's evocative photography and the superb performances of Warren Beatty and Faye Dunaway.

BOOMERANG USA 1946. *Dir* Elia Kazan *Scen* Richard Murphy based on an article by Anthony Abbott (*pseud* of Fulton Oursler) *Photog* Norbert Brodine *Art Dir* Richard Day, Chester Gore *Ed* Harmon Jones *Cast* Dana Andrews, Jane Wyatt, Lee J. Cobb, Sam Levene, Cara Williams, Arthur Kennedy *Prod* Louis de Rochemont for 20th Century-Fox. 88 mins.

Based on a true story: a district attorney (Andrews) proves that an accused man (Kennedy) is innocent of the murder of a minister and in doing so faces the hostility of a small town. Kazan's second feature, and his first success, is directed in a semidocumentary style, partly due to Louis de Rochemont, who had inaugurated the semirealist trend in the States with Hathaway's *The House on 92nd Street*. It has a liberal approach but ends up rather drab and colorless.

BORDER STREET ULICA GRANICZNA

BORINAGE Belgium 1933. *Dir/Scen/Photog/Ed* Joris Ivens/Henri Storck. (Sound version prepared in the USSR: *Ed* Helen van Dongen *Mus* Hans Hauska) *Prod* E.P.I. 36 mins.

An inquiry into conditions in the Borinage coal-mining district near Brussels. The Borinage was the scene of a strike of many months duration and the home of miners living in poverty and misery. The film was made illegally under difficult conditions and a very low budget, with the Belgian police often chasing the two film makers from the scene. Many scenes were photographed in direct, almost *cinéma vérité* style, though others were reconstructed. A "staged" workers' demonstration became, during the filming, an actual demonstration that the police tried to suppress. This militant documentary was the first (apart from the then unreleased *Land without Bread*) of its kind and importance produced in the Western world. It is quite rightly one of the works Ivens himself thinks highly of, since it has a power and an unforgettable feeling of authenticity. Originally made silent, a sound version was made in the USSR (using additional scenes photographed in Moscow).

BORN YESTERDAY USA 1950. *Dir* George Cukor *Scen* Albert Mannheimer based on the play by Garson Kanin *Photog* Joseph Walker *Ed* Charles Nelson *Art Dir* Harry Horner *Mus* Frederick Hollander *Cast* Judy Holliday, William Holden, Broderick Crawford *Prod* Columbia. 103 mins.

A tycoon, Harry Brock (Crawford), who has made his fortune by crooked dealings in scrap iron, arrives in Washington with his mistress, Billie Dawn (Holliday), a former chorus girl of astonishing ignorance. He hires a writer, Paul Verrall (Holden), to educate her, only to learn — when Billie calls him a Fascist and threatens to expose him —

that Paul has taught her not only manners but the principles of democracy. In the end she decides only to curb his activities and they leave together.

A typical sophisticated comedy, but also a satire about a woman rebelling against her "sugar daddy" and his crooked dealings. One of Cukor's best comedies, with a remarkable performance by Judy Holliday.

BOROM SARRET Sénégal 1963. *Dir/Scen* Ousmane Sembéne *Photog* Christian Lacoste *Cast* Ly Abdoulaye. 18 mins.

The story of a morning in the life of a poor taxi driver and his misadventures in the rich section of Dakar.

This penetrating short film was directed by a Senegalese novelist in two language versions: French and Oulov (a West African language). It is the first truly important film to be made by a black African (almost seventy years after the cinema was invented) and was awarded a prize at the 1963 Tours Festival.

BOUDU SAUVE DES EAUX BOUDU SAVED FROM DROWNING France 1932. *Dir* Jean Renoir *Scen* Jean Renoir based on the play by René Fauchois *Assist Dir* Jacques Becker *Photog* Marcel Lucien, Asselin *Art Dir* Hugues Laurent, Jacques Castanier *Ed* Suzanne de Troyes *Cast* Michel Simon, Charles Granval, Max Dalban, Jean Dasté, Séverine Lerczinska, Jean Gehret, Jacques Beckuer, Marcelle Hainia *Prod* Michel Simon/Jean Gehret. 88 mins.

A Parisian antiquarian bookseller (Granval) saves a magnificently scruffy tramp, Boudu (Simon), from suicide in the Seine. Boudu insists his rescuer is now responsible for him and goes to live in his house. Boudu totally disregards proprieties, seduces the wife (Hainia), and then the maid (Lerczinska). He marries the maid, but falls accidentally into the river after the ceremony, rediscovers his liberty, and returns to his wanderings.

Renoir staked much on this film, which was produced with complete freedom but was a complete commercial failure until the enthusiasm of film societies rescued it after 1945. It was based on a famous play that ended with Boudu accepting his responsibilities. Renoir changed the ending and made it a justification of joyful anarchy, contrasting this against the middle-class bookseller's plodding towards material comforts. Renoir gave Michel Simon as much freedom as he wanted in the interpretation of the role and he creates an enchanting character. The sets for the apartment are excellent; it is in this restricted world that most of the action is based, after an excellent description of Paris and its quays and until the final lyrical scene — the uninhibited freedom of the suburban countryside. Especially notable is the sound of a bugle while Boudu is seducing the wife, the image itself showing only a patriotic color print. *Boudu* is in some ways Renoir's *A nous la liberté* (*q.v.*), but it is very uneven in quality, with genius often giving way to disorder.

BOUE (LA) FIÈVRE

BOULE DE SUIF PYSHKA

BOYARS' PLOT (THE) IVAN GROZNY

BRASA DORMIDA Brazil 1927–28. *Dir/Scen* Humberto Mauro *Photog* Edgar Brasil *Cast* Nita Rey, Luiz Sorace, Maximo Serrano.

A poor young man, working in a sugar refinery, becomes engaged to the daughter of the proprietor after having uncovered a saboteur and his accomplices. This film was begun by the self-taught director, Mauro, in 1925 in Cataguez (a small town in the state of Minas Geraes) and was completed with the help of film enthusiasts in Rio and the producer, A. de Barros. The plot is ordinary and dull but the direction is often superb.

There is a good characterization of the half-caste villain (whose straightened hair becomes suddenly curly again) and a feeling for the use of simple details in characterization. Mauro (the best Brazilian director from 1920–1950) had a remarkable ability to use details in close-up and create a sense of "filmic space." There is also a lyrical use of the drama of natural sets, such as the love scene in a large tropical forest involving a snake.

BREATHLESS A BOUT DE SOUFFLE

BRIDE OF FRANKENSTEIN (THE) see FRANKENSTEIN

BRIDGE (THE) BRUG (DE)

BRIDGE ON THE RIVER KWAI (THE) Britain 1957. *Dir* David Lean *Scen* Michael Wilson (name removed from credits), Pierre Boulle from his own novel *Photog* Jack Hildyard *Ed* Peter Taylor *Art Dir* Donald M. Ashton *Mus* Malcolm Arnold *Cast* Alec Guinness, William Holden, Jack Hawkins, Sessue Hayakawa *Prod* Sam Spiegel, Horizon Productions. 161 mins. Technicolor. CinemaScope.

In Malaya during the Second World War, an English colonel, Nicholson (Guinness), is taken prisoner with his men. Under the orders of a Japanese colonel (Hayakawa), he is forced to have his men construct a bridge that an American commando (Holden) has been ordered to destroy.

In the original novel by Pierre Boulle, the bridge remained intact. The film becomes a satire on militarism because the colonel begins by helping the enemy in order to maintain the morale of his troops and ends by defending "his" bridge, trying to ignore the fact that he assisted a Japanese offensive.

This large-budget super production was a worldwide success, mainly because of its spectacular effects, Alec Guinness' performance, its careful style, and its somewhat folkloric atmosphere. However, it may also be because its moral was a general reflection of the years from 1955–1960. During this period an agonizing reappraisal took place, showing that many (not only those in the colonial armies), through narrow-mindedness, betrayed the cause they believed they served, even though they were as sincere as Colonel Nicholson.

BRIEF ENCOUNTER Britain 1945. *Dir* David Lean *Scen* Noel Coward based on "Still Life" from the *Tonight at 8:30* series *Photog* Robert Krasker *Art Dir* L. P. Williams *Ed* Jack Harris *Cast* Celia Johnson, Trevor Howard, Stanley Holloway, Cyril Raymond *Prod* Cineguild. 86 mins.

In a railway station, a suburban housewife and mother (Johnson) who is bored by her husband (Raymond) meets a doctor (Howard) who is himself married. They fall in love, but she is honest, and allows him to leave the country while she returns to her husband.

Incorrectly greeted as a masterpiece in 1946, this is nevertheless a very fine British film.

Though it established David Lean's rep-utation, it had little success in England, where it was attacked as "quasi-adulterous." Although Noel Coward is a man of the theater, his script is cinematic and revived the use of the flashback.

Brief Encounter's value lies above all in its documentary-like description of provincial, middle-class English life, using both sets and realistic details: the couple's home; the small town with its ridiculous statues; Saturday shopping; the tea room; a canal and the lockkeeper's home; and, above all, the railway buffet, the center of the action. There are also several comic bits: a gossiping woman, a waitress chattering with her customers and a parody of a fast-talking American trailer. Under her silly hat, Celia Johnson is moving, as is Trevor Howard.

*BRIGADOON USA 1954. *Dir* Vincente Minnelli *Scen* Alan Jay Lerner from his own musical play *Mus* Frederick Loewe *Choreog* Gene Kelly *Photog* Joseph Ruttenberg *Art Dir* Cedric Gibbons, Preston Ames *Ed* Albert Akst *Cast* Gene Kelly, Van Johnson, Cyd Charisse *Prod* MGM. 102 mins. Ansco Color. CinemaScope.

Two Americans (Kelly, Johnson) in Scotland wander into Brigadoon, a small village that only comes to life for one day every century, and meet an attractive young girl (Charisse).

In spite of its strong list of credits (including choreography by Gene Kelly), *Brigadoon* is one of Minelli's most disappointing films. His attempt to create a whimsical Scottish dream world fails badly, mainly because of the dull color photography, unimaginative use of CinemaScope, and poorly staged musical numbers.

BRINGING UP BABY USA 1938. *Dir* Howard Hawks *Scen* Dudley Nichols, Hager Wilde based on a story by Hager Wilde *Photog* Russell Metty *Mus* Roy Webb *Art Dir* Van Nest Polglase, Perry Ferguson *Ed* George Hively *Cast* Cary Grant, Katharine Hepburn, May Robson, Charlie Ruggles, Barry Fitzgerald *Prod* RKO. 102 mins.

An academic scientist (Grant) gets involved with a dizzy rich girl (Hepburn) and a domesticated leopard, Baby. It escapes and they capture instead a wild leopard escaped from a circus. But everything sorts itself out and they are married in the end.

One of the best American screwball comedies of the Thirties, in which Hawks used his typical comic theme of dignity destroyed: a scientist falls in the mud and down stairs, is garbed in a lady's dressing gown, blinded by feathers, and finally collapses on top of a dinosaur's skeleton.

BROKEN BLOSSOMS USA 1919. *Dir* D. W. Griffith *Scen* D. W. Griffith based on *The Chink and the Child* in Thomas Burke's *Limehouse Nights Photog* G. W. Bitzer *Special Effects* Hendrick Sartov *Mus Arrang* Louis F. Gottschalk, G. W. Griffith *Cast* Lillian Gish, Richard Barthelmess, Donald Crisp, Norman Selby *Prod* D. W. Griffith for United Artists. 6,013 ft.

Set in the Limehouse district of London, the story of a Chinaman's (Barthelmess) chaste love for a young girl (Gish), persecuted by her brutal father (Crisp). Her father is defeated in a boxing match and beats the child to death. The Chinaman kills the father then commits suicide.

"The Chink and the Child was completed in eighteen days and nights. In rehearsals we timed the film so perfectly that, when it was first cut and put together, there was only 200 ft. over. There were no retakes . . . The budget was $90,000 and the returns exceeded a million" (Lillian Gish autobiography).

"We find here the eternal and the basic antithesis involved in the fight between beauty and ugliness, good and evil. This contrast creates naturally the choice of similar rhythms for the film, a slow rhythm being set against a fast one. In this way, brutality and crime are made more meaningful when faced with the harmonious beauty of love and dreams. What I especially remember are the perfect boxing sequences and the mute admiration of the yellow man for the young girl he has helped and idolized. A small number of simple sets are sufficient, but they are used with great art and conscience. One hardly need say that the artist has transposed life" (Léon Moussinac).

This film was made before the style of *Kammerspiel* developed in Germany and perhaps influenced it. It is a tragedy with a dramatic structure based on a mainly instinctive use of the three unities rule and parallel editing (analyzed by Léon Moussinac). The film was made entirely in the studio but Griffith created a marvelous atmospheric sense of Limehouse: the foggy street and houses, the Chinaman's shop and miserable room.

The climax is masterful, with Lillian Gish cringing and spinning desperately in a closet as her father breaks the door down with an ax and then beats her to death with a whip handle. Lillian Gish is entirely believable as the young girl (though she was then 30) and her creation of the role is exceptional. One especially remembers the smile she made by pushing the corners of her mouth up with her fingers. Barthelmess succeeds in making the Chinaman touching and convincing, but Donald Crisp's Brute is too heavy-handed, "the boxer's gestures often become grimaces" (Moussinac). Apart from this small failing, *Broken Blossoms* is Griffith's most perfect, and perhaps his most engaging, film even though it was made quickly and cheaply.

REMAKE:

— *Broken Blossoms* Britain 1936. *Dir* John (Hans) Brahm, *Scen* Emlyn Williams based on the story by Thomas Burke *Cast* Emlyn Williams, Dolly Haas, Arthur Margetson. 84 mins.

Griffith had previously planned a remake in Britain and was originally assigned to this production, but resigned during the early stages. It was not a commercial success, despite Brahm's and Williams' attempt to introduce a harsh realism. The acting is good, especially Williams as the Chinaman and Margetson as the Brute.

PARODY:

— *Broken Bottles* Britain 1920. *Cast* Leslie Henson. 2 reels.

A burlesque version that parodies not only the story but also the acting and photography.

BRONENOSETS POTYOMKIN BATTLESHIP POTEMKIN USSR 1925. *Dir* Sergei M. Eisenstein *Assist* Grigori Alexandrov with Alexander Antonov, Mikhail Gomarov, A. Levshin, Maxim Strauch *Scen* S. M. Eisenstein, Nina Agadzhanova-Shutko *Photog* Eduard Tisse, V. Popov *Art Dir* Vasili Rakhals *Titles* Nikolai Aseyev *Mus* Edmund Meisel *Cast* Antonov, Alexandrov, Vladimir Barsky, Levshin, Gomarov, Strauch *Prod* Goskino. 4,589 ft. (Sound version issued in 1950 with music by E. Krioukov. 65 mins.).

In 1958, a jury of historians from 26 countries ranked *Potemkin* as the "best film in the world" by 100 votes out of 117 cast. In 1948, an international referendum had decided the same.

On 19 March, 1925, the commission responsible for the 20th Anniversary celebrations of the 1905 Revolution assigned most of the films to seven or eight directors. Among these was the 27-year-old S. M. Eisenstein. He soon prepared a script, *The Year of 1905,* in collaboration with Nina Agadzhanova-Shutko, a militant who had been involved in the revolutionary period. The manuscript was hundreds of pages long and would have recounted the complete history of that year from January to December, including the dozens of events that took place in 20 or 30 towns. The production began in Leningrad in July but was interrupted by bad weather. After filming several scenes in Baku, Eisenstein and his collaborators went to Odessa. There, he developed the idea of reducing *The Year of 1905* to a single one of its episodes: the "Potemkin" mutiny, an event which took up only one page in the original script. Using this simple outline, the film was made in six or seven weeks (end of September to the beginning of November 1925). Several sequences and details of the action were improvised during shooting. The film was barely finished by the morning of its official premiere, December 21, 1925, at the Bolshoi Theater in Moscow. It was enthusiastically received at the premiere, as it was in Berlin, London, Amsterdam, and New York.

It was given its premiere in Paris by the Ciné Club of France at l'Artistic, rue de Douai. It was acclaimed by many important directors and by the surrealists. But the film was banned (as it was in many countries) by the French censor until 1952.

Potemkin includes 1,300 shots. Main sequences:

1. *Men and Maggots* Sailors sleeping in their hammocks and arguing; the maggoty beef; the little bearded M. O. (a driver from Odessa) looks over his spectacles at the crawling meat: "These are not maggots"; the men gather together again, buy jam and refuse the soup.

2. *Drama on the Quarterdeck* The men are assembled on the quarterdeck; the captain arrives: "Those who think the soup is good take two steps forward"; the threat of hanging the "mutineers"; the rush towards the gun turret; the men remain behind and are covered with tarpaulins to be shot; the priest (an Odessa gardener) blesses the shooting party; the refusal to fire; the mutineers

seize arms; the officers and the priests thrown into the sea; the "ringleader" (Vakulinchuk) wounded and thrown into the sea.

3. *Appeal from the Dead* Odessa deserted; the ship's boat brings in the body of Vakulinchuk; its display on the quay; the crowd enlarges until the whole town is involved; story of a woman; a derider corrected; the call to insurrection; meeting on the battleship.

4. *The Odessa Steps* The crowd on the steps acclaiming the sailors, when suddenly the first shots are fired; the boots of the soldiers walk over the bodies; the child is killed; the mother who reclimbs the steps holding her dead son; a mother, high on the steps, is hit and her body pushes her child's pram down the steps; the descent of the pram; a woman with her eye slashed under her pince-nez; the guns of the "Potemkin" fire on the generals' headquarters; the stone lion appears to rear up.

5. *Meeting the Squadron* Meeting on the battleship; the boat gets under way; a night of suspense; the squadron appears on the horizon; the decks are cleared for action; the guns loaded; the signal "Join Us"; the ships of the squadron covered by men crying "Brothers, brothers, brothers" as the "Potemkin" passes victoriously through the squadron.

Eisenstein's refusal to use an individual hero was derived from theories of the Prolekult Theater. In the two revolutionary groups (the battleship and the town itself) individuals are reduced to recognizable types, each appearing only briefly. Eisenstein laid great stress on the meaning of small details and objects, such as the surgeon's pince-nez, which reflects his whole character: "the dangling eyeglasses were made to symbolize their owner helplessly struggling among the seaweed after the sailors had thrown him overboard" (Eisenstein). In one of his theoretical articles, Eisenstein compared the close-up with the figure of speech known as the synecdoche: "When can a particular episode take the place of the whole logically and completely? Only in cases where the detail, the part, the particular episode is typical. In other words, when it reflects the whole like a piece of broken mirror . . . Maggoty meat became a symbol of the inhuman conditions in which the whole mass of the exploited classes . . . lived. The quarterdeck scene is equally characteristic of the cruelty with which tsarism crushed every attempt at protest . . . The refusal to shoot at the crowd, the masses, the people, at their own brothers was extremely typical of the time . . . The mourning over the body of Vakulinchuk was one of the countless instances when the funerals of revolutionary heroes became impassioned demonstrations . . . The scene on the Odessa steps is a synthesis of the slaughter in Baku and the January 9 Massacre (and) the Black Hundred pogromists who set fire to a theater in Tomsk where a meeting was in progress. And the finale of the film with the battleship sailing majestically past the Admiral's squadron . . . is symbolic of the 1905 Revolution as a whole . . . The "Potemkin" was no more than an individual episode, but one reflecting the greatness of the whole" (Eisenstein, *Notes of a Film Director*).

Eisenstein invented at least two episodes that became "history" for many "historians"; the tarpaulin scene, and the events on the steps, which actually took place elsewhere in Odessa.

"The Odessa Steps" sequence is the high point of the film and is a sequence Eisenstein analyzed in detail in a 1939 article: "Organic Unity and Pathos in the Composition of Potemkin."

The international success of the film was doubtless due to the unrivaled perfection of its form, but it was also due to its humanitarianism and to the enthusiasm that impregnated its revolutionary subject. With *Potemkin* the Soviet Cinema burst on to the international film scene and the effects of its breakthrough have not yet disappeared.

BRUG (DE) THE BRIDGE Netherlands 1927/28. *Dir/Photog/Ed/Scen* Joris Ivens. 306 meters. (1,000 ft. approx.)

A kind of film symphony, influenced by Vertov and Ruttmann, on the functional movements of a large railway swing bridge in Rotterdam.

Man is absent, but not his life and work, in this, the first film Ivens made alone.

BRUTE FORCE USA 1947. *Dir* Jules Dassin *Scen* Richard Brooks based on the novel by Robert Patterson *Photog* William Daniels *Art Dir* Bernard Herzbrun, John F. DeCuir *Mus* Miklos Rozsa *Ed* Edward Curtiss *Cast* Burt Lancaster, Hume Cronyn, Charles Bickford, Yvonne de Carlo *Prod* Universal. 98 mins.

Prison melodrama about a sadistic prison officer, Captain Munsey (Cronyn), and six men in Cell R. 17 led by Joe Collins (Lancaster). The men plan to break out and revenge themselves on Munsey who, however, discovers the plot. The men are all killed but not before Joe throws Munsey to his death from a watchtower. This is Dassin's first success. Its style and chiaroscuro photography were much influenced by European films, especially those of Marcel Carné. There are metaphorical allusions to Nazism, and Munsey is portrayed as an American fascist, worthy of the S.S., who plays a record of *Tannhauser* while torturing his victims. Burt Lancaster gives a remarkable portrayal of a convict.

BUCHSE DER PANDORA (DIE) LULU/PANDORA'S BOX Germany 1928/29. *Dir* G. W. Pabst *Scen* G. W. Pabst, Ladislaus Vajda based on the plays *Erdgeist* and *Büchse der Pandora* by Frank Wedekind *Photog* Günther Krampf *Art Dir* Andrei Andreiev, Gottlieb Hesch *Cast* Louise Brooks, Fritz Kortner, Gustav Diessl, Franz Lederer, Daisy d'Ora, Carl Goetz, Alice Roberte *Prod* Nero-Film. 8,800 ft.

Lulu (Brooks), whose rich lover, Schön (Kortner), is engaged to the daughter of a Minister of the Interior, forces him to marry her. His son (Lederer) becomes infatuated with her and she kills Schön on their wedding night. She escapes during her trial and leaves with the son, but they are poverty-stricken. She becomes a prostitute in London where she is killed by Jack the Ripper (Diessl).

The French censors ripped into this film and turned it into a totally different film from the original: Schön's son becomes his secretary; Lulu is acquitted instead of being condemned to death; her Lesbian friend (Roberte) becomes a childhood friend, and Jack the Ripper disappears entirely. In order to "end the film on a ridiculously moral note" (Pabst), Lulu joins the Salvation Army.

Above everything else in this film, one remembers the exceptional personality of Louise Brooks, who had been asked to come to Europe after her appearance in Hawks's *A Girl in Every Port* (q.v.).

"In *Pandora's Box* and *Diary of a Lost Girl* we have the miracle of Louise Brooks. Her gifts of profound intuition may seem purely passive to an inexperienced audience, yet she succeeded in stimulating an otherwise unequal director's talent to the extreme. Pabst's remarkable evolution must thus be seen as an encounter with an actress who needed no directing, but could move across the screen causing the work of art to be born by her mere presence. Louise Brooks, always enigmatically impassive, overwhelmingly exists throughout these two films. We now know that Louise Brooks is a remarkable actress endowed with uncommon intelligence, and not merely a dazzlingly beautiful woman.

"Pandora's Box is a silent film. As such it does very well without the words which Wedekind — the author of the two plays *Erdgeist,* and *Die Büchse der Pandora,* which Pabst condensed into one film — deemed indispensable to bring out the erotic power of this singular 'earthly being,' endowed with animal beauty, but lacking all moral sense, and doing evil unconsciously" (Lotte Eisner).

Lulu is also a Pandora spilling her miseries around her. She is a German "femme fatale," not a Latin one, led towards her destiny through a variety of remarkably created atmospheres. Writes Lotte Eisner: "Nobody has ever equaled Pabst's portrayal of the backstage fever on the opening night of a big show, the hurrying and scurrying during the scene changes, the stage seen from the wings as the performers go on and off and bound forward to acknowledge their applause at the end of their act, the rivalry, complacency, and humor, the bewildering bustle of stagehands and electricians — a stupendous whirl of artistic aspirations, colorful detail, and a facile eroticism . . . She is the center of attraction, and Pabst succeeds in devising an infinite variety of seduction scenes to show her to advantage, as when Dr. Schön comes into the flat wondering how to tell his mistress that he is getting married. The camera catches his nervousness as he paces up and down the room; the ash from his cigarette burns a table runner, and he fiddles with a bibelot, as Jannings had fidgeted with a liqueur glass in *Variety.* Then a skillful shot-and-reverse-shot shows us Lulu observing him. She sinks back into the cushions, moves, lies on her front half-reared like a sphinx, while Schön goes up to her and sits down. The camera dives and scrutinizes Lulu's impassive features, lingering over the perfect sweep of her face, the pearl-like quality of her skin, the fringe of her lacquered hair, the sharp arch of her eyebrows, and the trembling shadow of her lashes.

"Another passage offers a subtle variant: in the prop-room Lulu throws herself on to the divan, and the camera moves up to the white nape of her neck, and slips along her legs as they kick with impatience. The two lovers wrestle and sink into a long embrace. These scenes are extremely erotic, but quite free from vulgarity."

Equally remarkable is the marriage ceremony that ends in murder; the trial with Lulu in her widow's weeds; a nocturnal orgy on the ship; London in the fog; Lulu's cheap room in London, where Jack the Ripper becomes fascinated by a knife in a loaf of bread.

OTHER VERSIONS:

— *Die Büchse der Pandora* Germany 1919. *Dir* Arzen Csérepy *Cast* Asta Nielsen.

— *Erdgeist* Germany 1923. *Dir* Leopold Jessner *Scen* Carl Mayer based on the play by Frank Wedekind *Cast* Asta Nielsen, Rudolf Forster Albert Bassermann, Alexander Granach *Prod* Richard Oswald Films. 7 reels.

— *Lulu/No Orchids for Lulu* Austria 1962. *Dir* Rolf Thiele *Scen* Herbert Reinecker based on the plays by Frank Wedekind *Photog* Michel Kelber *Cast* Nadja Tiller, O. E. Hasse, Hildegard Knef. 100 mins.

A heavy-handed, almost absurd version.

BURLESQUE ON CARMEN CARMEN

BURMESE HARP (THE) BIRUMA NO TATEGOTO

BUS STOP USA 1956. *Dir* Joshua Logan *Scen* George Axelrod based on the play by William Inge *Photog* Milton Krasner *Art Dir* Mark-Lee Kirk, Lyle R. Wheeler *Cast* Marilyn Monroe, Don Murray, Arthur O'Connell *Prod* 20th Century-Fox. 94 mins. Eastman Color. Cinema-Scope.

Bo Decker (Murray) and Virgil (O'Connell) meet Cherie (Monroe) at a rodeo and Bo tries to persuade her to marry him. She refuses, but he nevertheless takes her on the bus home with him. The bus is forced to stop at a roadside café and the bus driver puts an end to Bo's rudeness and abduction by fighting him, but Cherie leaves with him by choice in the end.

Though based on a play, the film is not too stagey and is an honest success for

Joshua Logan. Cherie is one of Monroe's best roles.

BUTCHER BOY (THE) USA 1917. *Dir* Roscoe (Fatty) Arbuckle *Cast* Buster Keaton, Fatty Arbuckle, Al St. John, Josephine Stevens, Arthur Earle, Agnes Neilson. 2 reels.

The first in a series produced by Fatty Arbuckle between 1917–19 for Paramount Famous Players. While there is the usual violence, sadism, and slapstick, there are some expressive gags. And, for the first time, he had as co-stars, Buster Keaton and Al St. John.

BUTTERFLY LOVERS LIANG SHAN-PO AND CHU YING-TAI

BWANA DEVIL USA 1952. *Dir/Scen* Arch Oboler *Photog* Joseph Biroc *Cast* Robert Stack, Barbara Britton, Nigel Bruce *Prod* Gula for United Artists. 79 mins. Ansco Color. Natural Vision (3D).

In British East Africa, American hunters fight a lion (Bwana Devil) that terrorizes the superstitious natives and halts the building of a railroad.

A low-budget film with a puerile script that would not have merited mention if it had not been the first made in 3-D: when viewed through polarized lenses it had a stereoscopic effect. Released with the slogan, "A lion in your lap," it was a great commercial success. For a while, it appeared that 3-D might have as good a future as CinemaScope and Cinerama (anounced also in 1951–52), but its appeal quickly passed.

BYELEYET PARUS ODINOKY LONE WHITE SAIL USSR 1937. *Dir* Vladimir Legoshin *Scen* Valentin Katayev based on his own novel *Photog* Bentision Monastirsky, G. Garibian *Mus* M. Rauchberger *Cast* Igor But, Boris Runge, A. Melnikov, A. Chekayevsky *Prod* Soyuzdetfilm. 82 mins.

The revolutionary events in Odessa during the 1905 "Potemkin" mutiny as seen by two young boys, one the son of a professor and the other of a fisherman.

A film full of poetry and charm, owing in part to Katayev's beautiful story but also to Legoshin's ability to handle child actors. Legoshin had been a collaborator of Donskoy (who had not yet begun the *Gorki* trilogy) and was temperamentally close to him. This, however, is his only successful film.

BY THE LAW PO ZAKONU

CABINET DES DR. CALIGARI (DAS) THE CAB-
INET OF DR. CALIGARI Germany 1919 (released 1920). *Dir* Robert Wiene *Scen*
Carl Mayer, Hans Janowitz *Photog* Willy
Hameister *Art Dir* Hermann Warm,
Walter Reiman, Walter Röhrig *Cast*
Werner Krauss, Conrad Veidt, Lil Dagover, Friedrich Feher, Hans Heinrich
von Twardowski *Prod* Decla-Bioscop.
1,703 meters. (5,600 ft. approx.)
About 1830, Dr. Caligari (Krauss) ex-
hibits a somnambulist, Cesare (Veidt), in
a fairground. Cesare tells a student that
he will die "before dawn." The student is
murdered and his friend (Feher) suspects Caligari. Caligari orders Cesare to
kill a young woman (Dagover) but he
attempts to kidnap her instead, is hunted,
and dies from exhaustion. Caligari escapes into a lunatic asylum, of which
it is learnt he is the director, but is finally
unmasked as insane. At the end the whole
fable is explained as the invention of an
inmate (Feher) of an asylum who imagines the director (Krauss) of the hospital is "Caligari."
Erich Pommer, the producer added this
ending to the script by the Austrian Carl
Mayer, based on an idea by the Prague
poet, Hans Janowitz. They included in
their original story various memories of
the War and had intended it as a satire
on Prussian authoritarianism, which
changed men into robots as Caligari did
with the somnambulist Cesare. Pommer's
new ending reversed the meaning.
Pommer inisisted that the sets and costumes should be in the style of the *Der
Sturm* expressionist group, which included the painters Röhrig and Reiman
and the designer Hermann Warm. This
group was saying at the time "Films
should be living drawings," and this idea
was fulfilled in their film. Fritz Lang was
originally chosen as director (he would
have used the painter Coubine) but

other commitments forced his replacement by a second-rate film maker, Robert
Wiene, whose job basically was to direct
the three excellent actors that Pommer
had hired: Werner Krauss, Conrad Veidt,
and Lil Dagover. The film was produced
in two or three weeks on a small budget.
Backgrounds were for the most part
painted canvas.
Caligari was captivating mainly because
of its visual experiments. Expressionism
was born in Munich around 1912 and
spread quickly in the defeated and chaotic Germany of 1919. It invaded the
theater, billboards, streets, and shop
fronts. *Caligari's* series of tableaux and
the colorful effect of its painted backdrops was almost a return to Méliès and
to filmed theater, but using entirely new
esthetics that were in harmony with the
postwar confusion. True film expressionism developed later in Germany; it was
based less on the theater and can be
clearly distinguished from its precursor,
"caligarism."
The scenario was based on the great
German tradition of fantasy, on the tradition of the romantics, Chamisso and
Hoffman, and on medieval stories. But
it also contained the philosophic fable
of a man fascinated by and made into a
criminal by an all-powerful authoritarian
master. It is in this sense that Siegfried
Kracauer saw in it a trend leading from
"Caligari to Hitler," a sort of "cortège
of monsters and tyrants." Although one
shouldn't over-stress Kracauer's thesis,
it must be admitted that as early as 1918,
the brilliant scenarist, Carl Mayer, meta-
phorically portrayed in *Caligari* the fate
of Germany from 1939 to 1949 (the first
Nazis appeared in 1919).
Some of the most famous scenes: the
doctor unveils Cesare standing in his coffin; the white bedroom where Cesare
kidnaps the young girl and the wall he

rests against; his flight across the roofs and his capture on a little bridge; Caligari in prison. But these superbly composed pictures are often more striking in stills than on the movie screen. They are striking because of their excesses: shots of Werner Krauss as Caligari in top hat and thick glasses, and especially of Conrad Veidt, looking like a skeleton in his black tights.

"Du Must Caligari Werden" ("You will become Caligari") was the catch phrase Pommer used to publicize the film. From its first showing (Marmorhaus, Berlin, Feb. 26, 1920) it was a great success. It swept America and France, where Delluc gave it its first showing, though at first people discussed it as "the work of the Boche" and pointed out its "dangerous" overtones.

Note: The original title of this film is sometimes incorrectly given as *Kabinett des Dr. Caligari*. The word *Cabinet* was used in the original to give it an "archaic" sense.

— *The Cabinet of Dr. Caligari* USA 1962. *Dir* Roger Kay *Scen* Robert Bloch *Cast* Glynis Johns, Dan O'Herlihy. 105 mins. CinemaScope.

An inept, psychological melodrama that is not a remake but simply uses the title.

CABINET OF DR. CALIGARI (THE) CABINET DES DR. CALIGARI (DAS)

CABIRIA Italy 1914 (production began 1912). *Dir* Giovanni Pastrone (Piero Fosco) *Scen* Gabriele D'Annunzio, Giovanni Pastrone *Photog* Segundo de Chomon, Giovanni Tomatis, Augusto Battagliotti, Natale Chiusano *Mus* Ildebrando Pizzeti *Cast* Lidia Quaranta, Umberto Mozzato, Bartolomeo Pagano, Italia Almirante (Manzini), Alex Bernard, V. de Stefano, Enrico Gemelli, Luigi Chellini, *Prod* Itala Film. 12 reels, about 10,000 ft. (Later released in 8-, 9-, and 10-reel versions, and in 1932 re-released in an abridged sound version.)

During the Second Punic War, a Roman Patrician, Fulvio (Mozzato), and his slave, Maciste (Pagano), save Queen Sophonisbe and a young Sicilian slavegirl, Cabiria (Quaranta) who was about to be sacrificed. After Archimedes (Gemelli) saves Syracuse, Cabiria, who has become the Queen's confidante, sees her kill herself after Scipio's (Chellini) victory. Once again she is almost sacrificed

to Baal, but Maciste saves her and she marries Fulvio.

Pastrone, an enterprising Italian producer, wrote the script. Before directing it (under the name Piero Fosco), he asked Gabriele D'Annunzio if he would put his name to it. He accepted without further ado after being paid 50,000 gold lire, but restricted himself to rewriting the pompous titles and to naming the heroes, then announced to all and sundry that he had composed a "Greco-Roman-Punic drama." It was the first production to cost over a million dollars. Enormous and sumptuous sets were built in Turin while exteriors were shot in Tunisia, Sicily, and the Alps.

Main sequences: the sacrifices to Baal, with the bronze statue swallowing up the children in the flames; the siege of Syracuse and Archimedes setting fire to the Roman fleet with burning mirrors; the shipwreck of the heroes; Hannibal's armies and elephants in the snows of the Alps; Maciste's exploits after the fall of Carthage.

Cabiria brought about many revolutionary innovations in film technique. This is especially true in its systematic use of the traveling shot, which sometimes allowed Pastrone to isolate his characters (who appeared in close-up as the camera tracked forward) and sometimes allowed him to emphasize the perspectives of the enormous sets (constructed of shining, false marble blocks).

The acting (more restrained than is often said) is dominated by the Herculean Pagano, a docker from Genoa who had been discovered and hired by Pastrone. *Cabiria* was a world-wide success (including Japan) and its technical innovations and spectacular sets revolutionized the cinema. The film had an especially strong impact in the USA, where it profoundly influenced Cecil B. DeMille and the producers of *Ben Hur,* among others. It also influenced Griffith, who studied *Cabiria* closely before making the Babylonian sequence of *Intolerance*. The character of Maciste became accepted as myth and has since been used in scores of Italian spectaculars.

CABIRIA (THE NIGHTS OF) NOTTI DI CABIRIA

CACCIA TRAGICA THE TRAGIC HUNT/THE TRAGIC PURSUIT Italy 1947. *Dir* Giuseppe De Santis *Scen* Giuseppe De Santis, Michelangelo Antonioni, Umberto Barbaro, Carlo Lizzani, Cesare Zavattini *Photog*

Otello Martelli *Ed* Mario Serandrei *Art Dir* Carlo Egidi *Mus* Giuseppe Rosati *Cast* Massimo Girotti, Andrea Checchi, Vivi Gioi *Prod* A.N.P.I. for Lux Film. 89 mins.

In the Po delta, peasants hunt a bandit (Checchi) and his mistress (Gioi) who have stolen money from the cooperative and kidnapped the wife of one of the peasants as a hostage. In the end, they pardon the bandit.

The first film of De Santis, notable for its conviction and its vigorous technique. In the opening sequence, a crane shot moves from a particular to a general view that shows the peasants in the misty fields still full of unexploded mines. At the end, the bandit leaves across the open fields as the peasants throw sods of earth at him. The plot is somewhat suggestive (intentionally so) of the peripatetic style of *The Exploits of Elaine*.

*CADUTA DEGLI DEI (LA) THE DAMNED/ GÖTTERDÄMMERUNG German Federal Republic/Italy 1969. *Dir* Luchino Visconti *Scen* Nicola Badalucco, Enrico Medioli, Luchino Visconti *Photog* Armando Nannuzzi, Pasquale De Santis *Art Dir* Enzo Del Prato, Pasquale Romano *Mus* Maurice Jarre *Ed* Ruggero Mastroianni *Cast* Dirk Bogarde, Ingrid Thulin, Helmut Berger, Renaud Verley, Albrecht Schönhals, Umberto Orsini, René Kolldehoff *Prod* Praesidens Film/Pegaso Film. 164 mins. Eastman Color.

Germany immediately following the burning of the Reichstag: the family of steel industrialist, Baron Joachim von Essenbeck (Schönhals), is divided politically in its support for the Nazis and in a power struggle for control of the firm. Essenbeck's daughter-in-law, Sophie (Thulin) persuades her lover and the firm's manager, Friedrich Bruckmann (Bogarde), to form an alliance with Aschenbach (Griem), a fanatical Nazi. They denounce Herbert (Orsini), vice-president and an anti-fascist, help him escape, then shoot the Baron. Friedrich is made heir. Konstantin (Kolldehoff), the new vice-president blackmails Sophie's son, Martin, to gain control for himself but being a member of the SA, is killed by Friedrich during the Night of the Long Knives. Friedrich and Sophie are now completely in the power of Aschenbach, who sets out to destroy them. Sophie goes mad after making love to her own son and, after a mock wedding, she and Friedrich commit suicide.

The Damned is dominated not so much by decadence (although Visconti's portrayal of this is powerful enough) but by the amoral manner in which all the characters use each other and in the end are destroyed by an evil stronger than their own. Visconti's view is fatalistic: once society begins to slide, nothing (not even the small "l" liberal, Herbert) can prevent its ultimate collapse.

Visconti uses a baroque, almost rococo, expressionist style. The strange, non-naturalistic, colors and make-up are perhaps the only ones appropriate to his Stygian theme.

CAESAR AND CLEOPATRA Britain 1945. *Dir* Gabriel Pascal *Scen* George Bernard Shaw assisted by Marjorie Deans based on the play by George Bernard Shaw *Photog* Robert Krasker, Jack Cardiff, F. A. Young, Jack Hildyard *Art Dir* John Bryan, Oliver Messel *Mus* Georges Auric *Cast* Claude Rains, Vivien Leigh, Stewart Granger, Flora Robson, Francis L. Sullivan, Cecil Parker *Prod* Gabriel Pascal Productions. 126 mins. Technicolor.

This film is reported to have cost a million pounds sterling, and was an almost total failure, despite G. B. Shaw, an intelligent performance by Claude Rains, and an appearance by the young male star, Stewart Granger.

See also *Cleopatra*

CAIRO see ASPHALT JUNGLE (THE)

CAIRO STATION BAB EL HADID

CALIGARI CABINET DES DR. CALIGARI (DAS)

CALLE MAYOR GRAND'RUE/ THE LOVE-MAKER Spain/France 1956. *Dir/Scen* Juan Antonio Bardem *Photog* Michel Kelber *Art Dir* Enrique Alarcon *Ed* Marguerite de Ochoa *Mus* Joseph Kosma *Cast* Betsy Blair, José Suarez, Yves Massard, Dora Doll, Lila Kedrova. 95 mins.

In a provincial town a group of dissatisfied young men decide one of them (Suarez) will court a 35-year-old spinster (Blair) for a joke. She falls desperately in love. He becomes conscience-stricken when he realizes the difficulty of the situation and ends by loving her. A friend (Massard) tells her the truth.

Using a very similar plot to *Les Grandes*

manoeuvres (*q.v.*), this is a perceptive portrait of small-town life in contemporary Spain — the religious processions, the rich young men with their dreary round of pleasures, and the women trapped by age-old customs.

CAMERAMAN (THE) USA 1928. *Dir* Edward Sedgwick *Scen* Clyde Bruckman, Lex Lipton, Richard Schayer *Photog* Elgin Lessley, Reggie Lanning *Ed* Hugh Wynn *Cast* Buster Keaton, Marceline Day, Harry Gribbon, Harold Goodwin, Sidney Bray *Prod* Joseph M. Schenck, MGM *Assoc Prod* Buster Keaton Productions. 6,995 ft.

Buster Keaton, a street photographer, falls in love with Sally (Day), a girl working for MGM and, to win her, becomes a newsreel cameraman. He begins dismally, failing with every reel he shoots, but eventually triumphs. In his first attempt to use the camera, Keaton is enamoured of trick shots and illusionary devices. His first newsreel could be described like this: "Some horses, tails in front of them, gallop backwards over hurdles that replace themselves afterwards; some beautiful water nymphs dive up from the water onto the diving board; then a battleship leaves the high seas and sails down the streets of New York, which might explain the panic of passers-by struggling to get on a bus."

Other famous gags: Keaton running around asking everyone if they know the beautiful girl he has photographed; playing a game of baseball alone in an empty stadium; the cannon on a battleship that goes off under his nose after he has ignored the warning "No entry"; the bus trip, seated on the mud guard; bathing in the sea with the fat man, who undresses in the same cabin, and his difficulty in leaving the water without his bathing trunks; the fight with the cop; the festival and fight in Chinatown, with Keaton encouraging the fighters; the monkey filming Keaton's rescue of the drowning girl; Buster Keaton phlegmatically accepting the typical New York welcome intended not for him but for Lindbergh. One of the best and most perfect of the Keatons. "*The Cameraman*, this Newsreel by Buster Keaton of a newsreel by Buster Keaton, is probably his masterpiece" (P. Demun).

CAMMINO DELLA SPERANZA (IL) THE PATH TO HOPE/THE ROAD TO HOPE. Italy 1950.

Dir Pietro Germi *Scen* Pietro Germi, Federico Fellini, Tullio Pinelli *Photog* Leonida Barboni *Ed* Rolando Benedetti *Mus* Carlo Rustichelli *Cast* Raf Vallone, Elena Varzi, Saro Urzi, Franco Navarra. *Prod* Lux Films. 105 mins.

When the sulphur mines close in Sicily, a confidence trickster, Ciccio (Urzi) tells the unemployed that he can find them work in France. Among those who leave on the voyage are a widower, Saro (Vallone), and a bandit, Vanni (Navarra). Ciccio tries to abandon them in Naples but is prevented; in Lombardy they try to help with the harvest but are declared "blacklegs" (strike breakers). Vanni is jealous of his girl friend's interest in Saro and at the French frontier they fight and Vanni is killed. The frontier guards take pity on the group and allow them to enter France.

This film was based on real incidents and could have been the *Paisa* of the Italian unemployed. It comes nowhere near achieving this — the ending is weak and melodramatic, even though two or three episodes are very convincing.

*CAMPANADAS A MEDIANOCHE CHIMES AT MIDNIGHT/FALSTAFF Spain/Switzerland 1965. *Dir* Orson Welles *Scen* Orson Welles based on Shakespeare's *Richard II, Henry IV, Parts I & II, Henry V, The Merry Wives of Windsor Photog* Edmond Richard *Art Dir* José Antonio de la Guerra, Mariano Erdorza *Mus* Angelo Francesco Lavagnino *Ed* Fritz Mueller *Cast* Orson Welles, Keith Baxter, John Gielgud, Margaret Rutherford, Jeanne Moreau, Marina Vlady *Prod* Internacional Films Espanola/Alpine. 119 mins.

Falstaff's (Welles) friendship with Prince Hal (Baxter), and his rejection when Henry IV (Gielgud) dies and Hal becomes King.

This "lament for Merrie England" (Welles) has some of the nostalgic feeling that pervades *The Magnificent Ambersons* (*q.v.*) and, by any measure of Welles's work, is at least its equal. The film moves inexorably from the jolly world of taverns and wenches toward a sense of dankness and decay where all around is talk of death, and probes the strange relationship of two men who liked, but totally misunderstood, each other. The acting of the three leads is matchless and Margaret Rutherford makes a marvelous Mistress Quickly.

CANGACEIRO (O) THE BANDIT Brazil 1953. *Dir/Scen* Lima Barreto *Photog* Chick Fowle *Ed* Oswald Hafenrichter *Mus* Gabriel Migliori *Cast* Alberto Ruschel, Marisa Prado, Milton Ribiero *Prod* Companhia Cinematografica-Vera Cruz. 105 mins.

Bandits (called "cangaceiros") commit many crimes in northeastern Brazil, the Sertan. Their chief (Ribiero) and his lieutenant (Ruschel) kidnap a teacher (Prado) and the lieutenant falls in love with her. After several fights, the two men are killed.

The cangaceiros were peasants ruined by feudalism who became honorable bandits (almost like Robin Hood in their characteristics). The film is based on actual accounts of their exploits in the early part of the 20th century. The reason for the cangaceiros' behavior is only hinted at in a script that tends to romanticize them and dresses them in a picturesque manner with plumed cocked hats. However, Lima Barreto well conveys a sense of the poetry of the open desert space of the Sertão and makes this adventure story lively and suspenseful. Very beautiful photography by the Englishman, Fowle, together with authentic Brazilian music. This film marked the high point of the Vera Cruz Studios (a São Paulo company that didn't last long) and directly stemmed from Cavalcanti's efforts, since he recruited those who made it even though by then he himself had already left the Studios.

CANTO DO MAR (O) SONG OF THE SEA Brazil 1954. *Dir/Ed* Alberto Cavalcanti *Scen* José Mauro de Vasconcelos, Alberto Cavalcanti *Photog* Cyril Arapoff *Art Dir* Ricardo Sievers *Mus* Guerra Peixe *Cast* nonprofessionals *Prod* Kino Films. About 80 mins.

Cavalcanti's masterpiece, during the sound period at least, in which he rediscovered his native country and the town of Recife where he had lived as a child. The film is mainly a portrait of the dramatic poverty of this tropical town; the continual influx of the hungry, driven from the Sertão by drought and destitution; the rites, more African than Christian, of the "Candombles"; the population living in straw huts; the vast beaches; and the daily difficulties of life. Unfortunately, it was never shown in Europe and had only a brief career in Brazil.

*CARABINIERS (LES) THE SOLDIERS/THE RIFLEMEN France/Italy 1963. *Dir* Jean-Luc Godard *Scen* Jean-Luc Godard, Roberto Rossellini, Jean Gruault based on the play *I Carabinieri* by Benjamino Joppolo *Photog* Raoul Coutard *Ed* Agnès Guillemot, Lila Lakshmanan *Art Dir* Jean-Jacques Fabre *Mus* Philippe Arthuys *Cast* Marino Mase, Albert Juross, Jean Brassat, Gérard Poirot, Geneviève Galéa, Catherine Ribeiro *Prod* Rome-Paris Films/Laetitia. 80 mins.

Two carabiniers (Poirot, Brassat) bring draft papers for Ulysse (Mase) and Michel-Ange (Juross), two peasants who must leave their wives (Ribeiro and Galéa) to fight for the king. Everywhere they go they send postcards of their conquests to the women. They return as victors but, when the time comes to collect their reward, they learn the king has signed a peace treaty and they are considered war criminals. They are shot.

"This film is a fable, a tale wherein realism serves only to preserve and reinforce the imaginary. And so it is that the actions and events described in this film could take place anywhere . . . the characters are placed neither psychologically, nor morally, nor even less sociologically. Everything happens on the animal level and even this is filmed from a vegetable, i.e. Brechtian point of view" (Godard, Introduction to the scenario of *Les Carabiniers*). "Everything will be very realistic, in a purely theatrical perspective — we will see war scenes, commando style, as in Fuller's films, with some newsreel footage" (Godard).

When *Les Carabiniers* opened in Paris in May 1963, critical and public reaction was so antagonistic ("consists of nothing but wretchedly filmed shots, piled up for better or worse, and tied together by faulty continuity") that the film was almost immediately withdrawn. Its commercial career elsewhere was equally disastrous, but it remains one of Godard's most important films. His ability to get under the surface of his theme (war as simply a quest for possessions) is seen best in this film. As Michel Cournot almost grudgingly remarked: "We are neither attracted nor moved by Godard's film: we are totally exasperated, nauseated, and impatient for it to end . . . (It) explodes the misunderstandings and ambiguities that make war films bearable. Stupid by virtue of intelligence, revolting by virtue of honesty, disjointed by a rigorous spirit, *Les Carabiniers* proves, in the end . . . that it is morally impossible to make a successful war film."

CARMEN GYPSY BLOOD Germany 1918. *Dir* Ernst Lubitsch *Scen* Hanns Kräly, Norbert Falk based on the opera by Bizet and the story by Prosper Merimée *Photog* Alfred Hansen *Art Dir* Karl Machus, Kurt Richter *Cast* Pola Negri, Harry Liedtke, Magnus Stifter *Prod* Union-UFA. 1,784 meters.

This was Lubitsch's first important film and the second time he had directed Pola Negri, who played a role that made her an international star. Very beautiful sets. Although the source was credited as the Bizet opera, the story is much closer to Merimée, including the use of the framing story of its being a tale told by a traveler over the campfire (in hand-tinted color in the original).

— France 1926. *Dir* Jacques Feyder *Scen* Jacques Feyder based on the story by Prosper Merimée *Assist* Charles Barrois, Maurice Silver, Charles Spaak *Photog* Maurice Desfassiaux, Paul Parguel *Art Dir* Lazare Meerson *Mus* Ernesto Halffter Esrich *Cast* Raquel Meller, Louis Lerch, Gaston Modot, Victor Vina *Prod* Albatros-Films. 8,750 ft.

A super-production designed as a vehicle for the singer Raquel Meller. It lacks rhythm and warmth and is of interest mainly for its beautiful scenes of the Spanish countryside.

OTHER VERSIONS:
— France 1909. *Dir* André Calmettes (?)
— Spain 1910 and 1914. *Dir* R. de Baños.
— USA 1913. *Cast* Marguerite Snow.
— USA 1913. *Cast* Marion Leonard. (From the Bizet opera.)
— USA 1915. *Dir* Raoul Walsh *Cast* Theda Bara *Prod* Fox.
— USA 1915. *Dir* Cecil B. De Mille *Cast* Geraldine Farrar, Wallace Reid *Prod* Lasky.
— *Loves of Carmen* USA 1927. *Dir* Raoul Walsh *Cast* Dolores del Rio, Victor McLaglen *Prod* Fox.
— *Britain 1932. *Dir* Cecil Lewis, Walter Mycroft *Cast* Marguerite Namara. (Based on the Bizet opera.)
— Germany 1933. *Dir* Lotte Reiniger. (Short, silhouette film based on the Bizet opera.)

— *Argentina 1939. *Dir* Florian Rey *Cast* Imperio Argentina.
— France/Italy 1942–44. *Dir* Christian-Jaque *Cast* Viviane Romance, Jean Marais.
— *The Loves of Carmen* USA 1948. *Dir* Charles Vidor *Cast* Rita Hayworth, Glenn Ford.
— *Carmen Proibita* Italy/Spain 1953. *Dir* M. G. Scotese *Cast* Anna Esmerelda, Fausto Tozzi. (Modern version.)
— *Carmen 63* Italy/France 1963. *Dir* Carmine Gallone *Cast* Giovanna Ralli, Jacques Charrier. (Modern version.)
— *Carmen Baby* USA/Germany/Yugoslavia 1967. *Dir* Radley Metzger *Cast* Uta Levka, Claude Ringer.
See also *Carmen Jones*

CARMEN CHARLIE CHAPLIN'S BURLESQUE ON CARMEN / BURLESQUE ON CARMEN USA 1916. *Dir/Scen* Charles Chaplin *Photog* Rollie Totheroh *Cast* Chaplin, Edna Purviance, Ben Turpin, Jack Henderson, Leo White, John Rand, May White, Wesley Ruggles *Prod* Essanay. 3,750 ft.
[Less of a burlesque of Merimée or Bizet than of the two American films of *Carmen* made in 1915. "He had intended it to be released in two reels December 18, 1915. But after he left Essanay, discarded material and new scenes were added, thus expanding the picture to a four-reeler. A subplot concerning Turpin and the gypsies is cross-cut with the action proper, Turpin and Chaplin never meeting" (Theodore Huff).]
This is not one of the best of the Essanay series but is the first in which Chaplin played a straight role (in the final tragic scene). Delluc wrote: "He died as part of the film. Two seconds, one charming, the other magnificent. I never want to see again a tenor in the last act of the opera."

CARMEN JONES USA 1954. *Dir* Otto Preminger *Scen* Harry Kleiner *Book and lyrics* Oscar Hammerstein II *Photog* Sam Leavitt *Art Dir* Edward L. Ilou *Ed* Louis R. Loeffler *Mus* Georges Bizet arranged by L. Birnbaum, George Brand and directed by Herschel Burke Gilbert *Cast* Harry Belafonte, Dorothy Dandridge, Joe Adams (with the dubbed voices for the songs of respectively Le Vern Hutcherson, Marilyn Horne, Marvin Hayes), Pearl Bailey, Olga James *Prod* 20th Century-Fox. 103 mins. De Luxe Color. CinemaScope.

Based on a moderized, all-Negro version of the opera (written for Broadway by Oscar Hammerstein II) in which Carmen (Dandridge) becomes a worker in a parachute factory, Don José (Belafonte) a GI Sergeant who deserts, and the bullfight a boxing match. The merits of this adaptation are debatable mainly because the dramatic progression is weaker. However, it had a first-rate cast, splendid black voices, excellent direction, and largely natural sets. This is one of Preminger's best films. It was shown only once in France in 1965, 10 years after its production, since the rights to the opera were not in the public domain.

CARNET DE BAL LIFE DANCES ON/ CHRISTINE France 1937. *Dir* Julien Duvivier *Scen* Jean Sarment, Pierre Wolff, Bernard Zimmer, Henri Jeanson, Julien Duvivier. *Photog* Michel Kelber, Philippe Agostini, P. Levent *Mus* Maurice Jaubert *Ed* A. Versein *Cast* Marie Bell, Harry Baur, Louis Jouvet, Françoise Rosay, Pierre Blanchar, Raimu, Fernandel, Pierre-Richard Willm *Prod* Lévy-Strauss Sigma. 109 mins.

A childless widow (Bell) remembers a ball 20 years earlier and, through an old dance program, seeks out those who were once her suitors. She finds almost all of them are failures, their once-great ambitions having dwindled. One has become an abortion doctor in Marseilles (Blanchar), one a shady lawyer (Jouvet), another religious (Baur), another a hairdresser (Fernandel). Even the old dance hall itself now seems small and unromantic. Her only real love has committed suicide, leaving a son and a half-mad mother (Rosay). Disillusioned, she returns home and adopts the son.

The best episodes are those with Jouvet and Blanchar. This is an uneven film, at times quite mediocre, with pretentious dialogue. However, it does offer a compact sample of prewar French stars.

CARNIVAL IN FLANDERS KERMESSE HÉROÏQUE (LA)

CARROSSE D'OR (LE) THE GOLDEN COACH France/Italy 1952. *Dir* Jean Renoir *Scen* Jean Renoir, Renzo Avanzo, Guilia Macchi, Jack Kirkland based on *Le Carosse de Saint-Sacrement* by Prosper Merimée *Photog* Claude Renoir *Art Dir* Mario Chiari *Mus* selections from Vivaldi *Cast* Anna Magnani, Duncan Lamont, Paul Campbell, Ricardo Rioli, Odoardo Spadaroz *Prod* Panaria Film/Hoche Productions. 100 mins. Technicolor.

Set in 18th-century Peru, this film is the story of three loves of a beautiful actress, Camilla (Magnani): Felipe, a soldier who finally goes to live among the Indians; Ramon, a vain bullfighter; and the Viceroy (Lamont). The Viceroy gives Camilla a golden coach he had ordered for himself but she gives it to the church to save him from humiliation.

The script was based very freely on the Merimée story and little of its original anticlerical attitude is evident. There are several allusions to the ever-present colonial war but Renoir takes as his theme the contrast between theater and life. This is summed up in the speech by the leader of Camilla's acting troupe, who wonders whether the characters on the stage are more real than those off it.

However, this is mainly a beautiful spectacle with superb color, costumes, and sets. Magnani gives a memorable performance as Camilla and, against hers, the other acting pales into insignificance. There doesn't seem to be much of a link between *La Règle du jeu* (*q.v.*) and this film, except that with it Renoir returned to the Europe he had abandoned after his masterpiece of poetry and social criticism in 1939.

*CASABLANCA USA 1942. *Dir* Michael Curtiz *Scen* Howard Koch, Julius J. Epstein, Philip G. Epstein based on an unproduced play *Everybody Comes to Rick's* by Murray Burnett, Joan Alison *Photog* Arthur Edeson *Art Dir* Carl Jules Weyl *Mus* Max Steiner with songs by M. K. Jerome, Jack Scholl, and Herman Hupfeld *Ed* Owen Marks *Cast* Humphrey Bogart, Ingrid Bergman, Paul Henreid, Claude Rains, Conrad Veidt, Sidney Greenstreet, Peter Lorre, Dooley Wilson *Prod* Warner Brothers. 102 mins.

Rick Blaine (Bogart) runs a nightclub in Casablanca, part of unoccupied French territory. Victor Laszlo (Henreid), a famous fighter against the Nazis, arrives with his wife, Ilsa (Bergman), with whom Rick had had an affair in Paris but who had left him suddenly without explanation. The French police prefect, Captain Renault (Rains), is under orders by the Gestapo Major Strasser (Veidt) to keep Laszlo from leaving Casablanca. Rick has a blank exit visa stolen by a crook (Lorre), later shot by the police, but he at first refuses to help Laszlo. Ilsa realizes she is still in love with Rick. Pretending to her that he is only helping her husband escape while she remains with him in Casablanca, Rick forces Captain Renault to ensure that both Victor and Ilsa leave while he remains behind.

An incisive, witty, and enchanting film that is certainly Curtiz' best. It represents the ultimate in the Bogart myth: his Rick Blaine is cynical and tough, hardened by life's misfortunes, yet still sentimental and idealistic. The dialogue is full of quotable Bogart lines ("What's your nationality?" "I'm a drunkard"; "You despise me, Rick, don't you?" "If I gave you any thought I probably would").

Ingrid Bergman has recalled that there was no finished shooting script for the film. That it continues to delight audiences is due not only to Bogart and the trenchant dialogue, but also to Arthur Edeson's evocative camerawork, the effectively integrated music, and the inspired casting in the character roles. Notable among these is Claude Rains's charming and amoral Captain Renault and Sidney Greenstreet's fezzed, amiably corrupt proprietor of the Blue Parrot. *Casablanca* won Academy Awards for Best Picture, Best Direction, and Best Screenplay.

CASA DEL ANGEL (LA) THE HOUSE OF THE ANGEL/END OF INNOCENCE Argentina 1957. *Dir* Leopoldo Torre Nilsson *Scen* Beatriz Guido, Leopoldo Torre Nilsson, Martin Mentasti based on the novel by Beatriz Guido *Photog* Anibal Gonzales Paz *Art Dir* Emilio Rodriguez *Mus* Juan Carlos Paz *Cast* Elsa Daniel, Lautaro Murua, Guillermo Battaglia *Prod* Argentina Sono Film. 75 mins.

Set in Argentina in the Twenties, the story of the sensual awakening of a rich young girl (Daniel). Her family is involved in a political intrigue whose victim is the man she loves (Murua). A poetic, yet realistic, portrait of the Argentinian ruling class.

CASINO ROYALE see *Goldfinger*

CASQUE D'OR GOLDEN MARIE/GOLDEN HELMET France 1952. *Dir* Jacques Becker *Scen* Jacques Becker, Jacques Companeez *Photog* Robert Le Febvre *Art Dir* Jean d'Eaubonne *Costumes* Georgette Fillon *Mus* Georges Van Parys *Ed* Marguerite Renoir *Cast* Simone Signoret, Serge Reg-

giani, Claude Dauphin, Raymond Bussières, William Sabatier *Prod* Speva Films/Paris Films. 96 mins.

In the Belleville district of Paris in the summer of 1898, Marie, (Signoret) known as "Casque d'or," bored with her lover, Roland (Sabatier), meets Manda (Reggiani) at a small riverside dance hall. They are immediately attracted to each other but Roland (a member of a gang of "apaches") challenges Manda and they fight. Later, Manda visits the Ange Gabriel; Leca (Dauphin), the gang's leader, who is himself infatuated with Marie, invites the two men to fight with knives and Manda kills Roland. Though the police are not looking for him, Manda and Marie leave for two days' joyful idyll in the country. Leca informs the police that Manda's friend Raymond (Bussières) is guilty, then tells Manda, who gives himself up to the police to clear his friend. Learning of Leca's treachery, he and Raymond escape with Marie's help. He kills Leca, again gives himself up to the police, and is guillotined.

Received badly by the French critics but enthusiastically by the English, this is now considered by many as Becker's masterpiece. The story was based on historical fact – the case of Manda and Leca gained widespread publicity at the time through the cutthroat rivalry of two newspapers and was responsible for the introduction of the word "apache" into the language. Becker has said of the film: "I don't like criminals. A 'perfect crime' thriller is dependent on psychiatry. I'm not interested in recounting clinical cases, but in human beings. I found the visuals during the writing of the script. As I wrote it, visualizing the scenes, I gave only the minimum essential dialogue to the characters . . . Companeez was only involved in the last fifth of the script." (Notably in suggesting the motivation for Manda's final surrender to justice.)

Notable sequences: the apaches at a riverside dance hall; the description of Belleville; the fight in the Ange Gabriel; the idyllic love scenes between Manda and Marie in the countryside; the sordid execution of Manda.

Becker made *Casque d'or* more than just a period gangster film. It is a film of great plastic beauty, a moving portrait of life in Belleville in a style that recalls old engravings and the films of Feuillade.

The costumes, the behavior of the characters, the sense of mood and background, all combine to make the film more than a mere historical reconstruction. Becker makes his characters truly come to life: Leca, a thoroughly antipathetic traitor, played by Claude Dauphin; Raymond, a sympathetic and loyal friend of Manda's who has taken to crime; the complex and sensuous Marie in which role Simone Signoret, in the full bloom of her beauty, gives the performance of her career. However, Serge Reggiani dominates the film as Manda, a craftsman driven to murder and the guillotine by his love for Casque d'or.

CASSANDRA CAT AZ PRIJDE KOCOUR

*CAT AND THE CANARY (THE) USA 1927. *Dir* Paul Leni *Scen* Alfred Cohn, Robert F. Hill based on the play by John Willard *Photog* Gilbert Warrenton *Art Dir* Charles D. Hall *Cast* Laura La Plante, Creighton Hale, Forrest Stanley, Tully Marshall, Flora Finch, Gertrude Astor, Arthur Carewe *Prod* Universal. 7,600 ft.
A comedy-horror film with a complex plot that has since become a standard theme. A group of relatives of a rich man assemble in his rotting mansion to hear his will. If the heir (La Plante) proves insane, a second heir will be named. One man dies and the night brings many terrors to the heir, only the hero (Hale) realizing it is a plot. In the morning the mystery is solved: the "Cat" is the second heir.
A great commercial success that had an enormous influence on American horror films in its use of expressionistic devices. Paul Leni (in his first American film) made superb use of sets, lighting, and a camera that seems to glide about the house to create a mood and a real sense of mystery. Only the comic scenes have not survived the passage of time.
OTHER VERSIONS:
— *The Cat Creeps* USA 1930. *Dir* Rupert Julian *Scen* Gladys Lehman based on the play by John Willard *Photog* Hal Mohr, Jerry Ash *Cast* Helen Twelvetrees, Raymond Hackett, Jean Hersholt, Lilyan Tashman *Prod* Universal. 71 mins.
— *The Cat and the Canary* USA 1939. *Dir* Elliot Nugent, *Scen* Walter De Leon, Lynn Starling based on the play by John Willard *Photog* Charles Lang *Cast* Bob Hope, Paulette Goddard, Gale Sonder-

gaard, John Beal *Prod* Paramount. 74 mins.
[A successful comedy vehicle for Bob Hope, with little else to recommend it except Gale Sondergaard's performance as the sinister housekeeper and some effective camerawork.]

*CAT PEOPLE USA 1942. *Dir* Jacques Tourneur *Scen* DeWitt Bodeen *Photog* Nicholas Musuraca *Art Dir* Albert d'Agostino, Walter E. Keller *Mus* Roy Webb *Ed* Mark Robson *Cast* Simone Simon, Kent Smith, Tom Conway, Jane Randolph *Prod* RKO. 73 mins.
A beautiful Balkan girl, Irena Dubrovna (Simon), who believes she is descended from people who can turn into cats under emotional stress, marries Oliver Reed (Smith) a naval architect. Irena visits a psychiatrist, Dr. Judd (Conway), but he scoffs at her fears. Irena's obsession destroys Oliver's love and he turns for consolation to Alice (Randolph) a co-worker in his office, who admits she loves him. One night in Central Park she hears and senses a great cat. Dr. Judd desires Irena and tries to kiss her; his claw-torn and bloody body is found in her apartment. Hunted and desperate, Irena releases a black panther from the zoo. Oliver and Alice find her body in front of the empty cage.
The first in the series of eleven low-budget horror films that Val Lewton produced at RKO during the early Forties whose approach depended on the power of suggestion, on hints at an unknown terror. It was an enormously successful formula and had great public appeal: *Cat People* was shot in 24 days, cost $134,000, and grossed over four million dollars.
Lewton and Tourneur show nothing directly (except for one shot of a black panther) but use shadows and sound, preying on audiences' fear of the dark and the unknown to create their mood. Carlos Clarens sees the film as "a variation on the werewolf theme, the case history of an obsession, a study in frigidity (or possibly repressed Lesbianism)." Some of the power of the shock sequences has disappeared with the years but its atmosphere and inexorably mounting suspense are as potent as ever.
— *The Curse of the Cat People* USA 1944. *Dir* Robert Wise, Gunther Fritsch *Photog* Nicholas Musuraca *Scen* DeWitt

Bodeen *Mus* Roy Webb *Cast* Simone Simon, Kent Smith, Jane Randolph, Ann Carter, Julia Dean *Prod* RKO. 70 mins.

Not a sequel to *Cat People*, the title having been imposed on Lewton by the studio. It has nothing to do with cats, being an obsessive study of a child's loneliness, similar to *The Turn of the Screw*, in which a seven-year-old girl (Carter), who is ignored by the adults around her, finds companionship with the ghost of her dead, insane mother. James Agee found it "full of the poetry and danger of childhood" and it is certainly more psychologically satisfying than *Cat People*. Robert Wise was given his first chance to direct when Gunther Fritsch was drafted into the army.

CAUGHT IN A CABARET THE WAITER/JAZZ WAITER/FAKING WITH SOCIETY USA 1914. *Dir/Scen* Charles Chaplin, Mabel Normand *Photog* Frank D. Williams *Cast* Chaplin, Mabel Normand, Harry McCoy, Alice Davenport, Chester Conklin, Minta Durfee, Mack Swain, Alice Howell *Prod* Keystone. 1,560 ft.

The first film directed and written by Chaplin. As a waiter in a tough cabaret, he saves Mabel from a robber. Posing as a duke, he is invited to her garden party. Later, the guests go slumming and discover Charlie is only a waiter; pandemonium follows. The sequences in the cabaret are excellent, somewhat suggestive of those in *A Dog's Life* (*q.v.*)

CAVALCADE USA 1933. *Dir* Frank Lloyd *Scen* Reginald Berkeley, Sonya Levien based on the play by Noel Coward *Photog* Ernest Palmer *Mus* Sammy Lee *Ed* Margaret Clancy *Art Dir* William Darling *Cast* Clive Brook, Diana Wynyard, Herbert Mundin, Ursula Jeans, Una O'Connor *Prod* Fox. 110 mins.

The glorious pages of British history from 1899 to 1918 as seen by Robert and Jane Marryot (Brook, Wynyard) and a middle-class family. This exultation of English nationalism, pompously directed, is of interest mainly for its ingenious script. It was a great success and led to other films that adopted the *Cavalcade* formula, showing historic events through the eyes of ordinary people. It won Academy Awards for Best Picture, Best Direction, and Best Art Direction.

OTHER VERSIONS:

— *USA 1955. *Dir* Lewis Allen *Cast* Michael Wilding, Merle Oberon *Prod* TCF Television. 44 mins.

CAVALIER OF THE GOLDEN STAR KAVALER ZOLOTI ZVEZDY

CELA S'APPELLE L'AURORE (literally, IT IS CALLED THE DAWN) France/Italy 1955. *Dir* Luis Buñuel *Scen* Luis Buñuel, Jean Ferry from the novel by Emmanuel Roblès *Photog* Robert Le Febvre *Art Dir* Max Douy *Mus* Joseph Kosma *Ed* Marguerite Renoir *Cast* Georges Marchal, Lucia Bose, Giani Esposito, Julien Bertheau, Nelly Borgeaud, Henri Nassiet, Gaston Modot *Prod* Films Marçeau/ Laetitia Film. 108 mins.

On Corsica, a young company doctor, Valerio (Marchal), feeling sympathetic to the workers under his care who are exploited by his own company, rejects the pleas of his wife, Angela (Borgeaud), to leave for Nice. When she leaves for a holiday, he meets and falls in love with Clara (Bose), a beautiful young widow. Sandro (Esposito) is fired by the company director and he and his tubercular wife are evicted from their home. His wife dies as a result of this and Sandro shoots the director. Valerio hides him, and, despite questioning by the police chief (Bertheau) and pressure from Angela and her father (Nassiet), he refuses to betray him or let Clara hide him. When discovery seems inevitable, Sandro escapes from Valerio's house and shoots himself.

Although badly received at the time of its release and still almost unknown, Buñuel himself places this among his three or four best. Certainly, it is among his most rigorous, "the humanist equivalent of a Calvinist proposition" (Raymond Durgnat).

He found some of his themes in the original novel by Roblès: "the love capable of reconciling man with the idea of life," the help which a truly noble man must give to another, even a criminal, hunted by the police (in the story, one driven to crime by social injustice) and the violent criticism of the establishment, especially the police.

The character who dominates the film is the police chief (penetratingly depicted by Henri Nassiet), who is not at all an illiterate brute but an admirer of Dali, whose "Crucifixion" decorates his office, and of the plays of Paul Claudel (a right-wing, Catholic poet). Intelligent, suspicious, yet polite, he is, for Buñuel, "the main character because of his attitudes to society, life, and love, and also because of certain typical details: the handcuffs sitting on the copy of Claudel's works. By chance, naturally. Also his reprimand of a policeman for hitting a prisoner. It seems this is unfashionable. So much the worse. It suits me." (Buñuel is here referring to a criticism that attacked this lack of "orthodoxy.")

CELUI QUI DOIT MOURIR HE WHO MUST DIE France/Italy 1957. *Dir* Jules Dassin *Scen* Ben Barzman, Jules Dassin from the novel by Nikos Kazantzaki *Christ Recrucified Photog* Jacques Natteau *Art Dir* Max Douy *Ed* Robert Dwyre, Pierre Gillette *Mus* Georges Auric *Cast* Jean Servais, Carl Möhner, Pierre Vaneck, Melina Mercouri, Fernand Ledoux, René Lefèvre, Maurice Ronet, Gregoire Aslan, Roger Hanin, Gert Froebe. 126 mins. CinemaScope.
In 1921, in a Greek village under Turkish domination headed by Agha (Aslan), Pope Grigoris names for the annual Passion Play, Manolios (Vaneck) for Christ, Katerina (Mercouri) for Mary Magdalene, Michaelis (Ronet) for John, and Panayotaros (Hanin) for Judas.
A group of starving refugees arrive led by Pope Fotis (Servais). Pope Grigoris thinks aiding them will disturb relations with the Turks and refuses help. However, Manolios, Katerina, and others give help, while Michaelis tries to give them his property when his father dies. Grigoris rouses the villagers to prevent this and Manolios leads the refugees into the village. Agha arrests him, hands him over to Grigoris, and he is stabbed by Panayotaros.
The novel was adapted by Barzman and Dassin in the style of a large social fresco, contrasting the "collaborators" in the village with the misery of the refugees hunted in the mountains. There are some good epic scenes but also weak ones. It is the most ambitious and the most sincere of Dassin's European films.

CELULOZA/POD GWIAZDA FRYGIJISKA A NIGHT OF REMEMBRANCE/UNDER THE PHRYGIAN STAR Poland 1954. (A two-part film.) *Dir* Jerzy Kawalerowicz *Scen* Igor Newerly, Jerzy Kawalerowicz from the novel by Igor Newerly *Photog* Seweryn Kruszynski *Cast* Josef Nowak, Lucyna Winnicka, T. Szmigielowna, Stanislaw Milski, Part I, 125 mins; Part II, 125 mins.
Depicts the fight of a militant and of the workers against the Pilsudski regime around 1930. Kawalerowicz' first successful film. It is too long and overblown but has some excellent episodes and is an entertaining reconstruction of the social relations that characterized Poland between the wars.

CESAR see MARIUS

CESTA DUGA GODINU DANA THE ROAD A YEAR LONG Yugoslavia 1958. *Dir* Giuseppe De Santis *Scen* De Santis, Maurizio Ferrara, and others *Photog* Pasquale de Santis *Cast* Silvano Pampanini, Elenora Rossi-Drago, Massimo Girotti. 159 mins. Ultrascope.
The construction of a road by peasants in an underdeveloped region of Italy despite the opposition of the authorities. A powerful and truthful film, unfortunately still unknown.

CHAIRY TALE (A) HISTOIRE D'UNE CHAISE Canada 1957. *Dir* Norman McLaren *Co-Dir/Cast* Claude Jutra *Mus* Ravi Shankar *Prod* National Film Board of Canada. 10 mins.
A man (Claude Jutra) in a fight with a chair that refuses to be cajoled into being sat upon. A trick film using several devices dear to the hearts of some early trick film makers (editing, reverse action, etc.) but also several new ones, notably "pixilation" (frame-by-frame photography of people or objects). This is an animated ciné-ballet, full of rhythm and irony.

CHALAND QUI PASSE (LE) ATALANTE (L')

CHANCE MEETING BLIND DATE

CHANG USA 1927. *Dir/Photog/Ed* Ernest B. Schoedsack, Merian C. Cooper *Prod* Paramount. 6,536 ft.
Dramatized documentary of the life of Kru and his family in the jungle of Thailand. His growing of rice and raising of animals is often thwarted by predatory animals. Kru leads an expedition against them which culminates in the killing of a giant tiger. Then a herd of elephants (the Chang) invade and destroy the village but, under Kru's leader-

ship, the villagers capture and domesticate the elephants and rebuild their homes.

Paul Morand, who had met the directors in the Far East, says of the film: "What *Nanook* was for the snow, *Chang* is for the Asiatic jungle. Man still plays there the same role that our ancestors played in the primeval forests. The effort of these two solitary turners of the crank gives sedentary Westerners their last glimpses of Earthly Paradise." If the comparison with Flaherty is exaggerated, *Chang* was nevertheless, at the end of the silent period, an interesting documentary construction in which the two film makers "directed" the natives and animals of the Siamese jungle in order to tell a story they knew would have public appeal.

CHAPAYEV USSR 1934. *Dir* Sergei and Georgy Vasiliev *Scen* Sergei and Georgy Vasiliev based on the account by Dmitri Furmanov *Photog* Alexander Sigayev, A. Xenofontov *Art Dir* I. Makhlis *Mus* Gavril Popov *Cast* Boris Babochkin, B. Blinov, Varvara Myasnikova, Leonid Kmit, I. Pevtsov *Prod* Lenfilm. 94 mins. Based on a biography by Dmitri Furmanov (Blinov), who had been Chapayev's (Babochkin) political commissar, it depicts the exploits and battles of the individualistic Red Army commander who fought against the Whites during the Civil War in 1919.

Famous sequences: the constant friction and arguments between the ebullient Chapayev and the reasonable Furmanov; the battle plan explained with potatoes set around the table; the love scene between a Red partisan (Kmit) and a partisan girl (Myasnikova) whom he taught how to handle a machine gun; Chapayev trapped in a house; his death as he tries to escape by swimming the river.

The high point of the film is undeniably the famous scene of "the psychological attack": the Whites mount an assault in a paradelike formation with the dead and wounded being immediately replaced by others, equally impeccably arrayed. The Reds are close to panic, but a machine gun finally forces the Whites to retreat. Based on an authentic episode of the Civil War, this evocation of the past was also somewhat of a prophecy of the future in which the mechanical inhumanity represented by the enormous parades at Nuremburg mounted an assault on Europe that was finally broken by partisans as unprepared but as committed as those in *Chapayev*. In the French underground and during the Spanish Civil War a number of freedom fighters became known by the name of this hero, popularized in a film that had a great success in the USSR and abroad, and which marked a decisive turning point in the Soviet cinema.

In planning the film, Sergei and Georgy Vasiliev (who had themselves taken part in the Civil War) and their actors lived in the country for many months with soldiers and officers, many of whom had fought with Chapayev. They observed their behavior, listened to their stories, noted their orders and their tone of voice, and synthesized their research in a detailed shooting script that incorporated most of their plans and ideas.

The directors and their actors created heroic but human types: Chapayev in his Cossack cloak with its large epaulettes, his fur hat, broad gestures, and petulance. Furmanov, strutting in his military tunic and his leather belt, phlegmatic, introspective, and persuasive. The White General Borozdin (Pevtsov), who loved good music and was not contemptuous of his opponents, is at the same time both humane and cruel.

The dialogue, with its typically Russian humor, is excellent. Their heroes are not monolithic, black-and-white characters. There is in them, and in their relationships, a human quality, and Chapayev is not shown as an infallible leader.

The direction is effective, handled without spectacular effects and, like the photography, is powerful and sometimes of epic proportions. And as Dovzenko said: "When Chapayev came from behind a hill, Eisenstein himself would have forgotten if he fought in long shot, medium shot, or close-up, if the noise of the boots had been synchronized with the gallop of the horses, if the damned shots disappeared in a dissolve or in the grave." Its success, its emotional power, its artistic and historic importance, put Chapayev among the ten masterpieces of the Soviet cinema.

[Sergei and Georgy Vasiliev were *not* brothers, but assumed the pseudonym of 'the Brothers Vasiliev' while they were both still editors.]

CHAPEAU DE PAILLE D'ITALIE (UN) UN CHAPEAU DE PAILLE D'ITALIE

CHAPLIN (series) USA 1914–1921

One can include in this series the approximately 60 shorts that carried in their title in France (but not in the USA) the name "Charlot", from *Making a Living* (1914) to *The Idle Class* (1921). Not all can be analyzed and only a dozen or so examples have been included in this dictionary. It should be noted that Chaplin directed, wrote and acted in all these films. "Charlie's" character evolved greatly between 1914 and 1921. In the Keystone series, Chaplin is wretched and rascally, but stronger and more wicked than the rest. Little by little, during 1914–15, he became the "little man" and after 1916, the "tramp." At this point, Charlie came to represent the immigrants of the 1910's, the unemployed who lived by chasing work and maintaining a precarious existence.

CHARETTE FANTOME (LA) see KÖRKARLEN

CHARLIE AT THE BANK BANK (THE)

CHARLIE CHAPLIN'S BURLESQUE ON CARMEN CARMEN

CHARLIE, THE PERFECT LADY WOMAN (A)

CHEAT (THE) USA 1915. *Dir* Cecil B. De Mille *Scen* Hector Turnbull *Art Dir* Wilfred Buckland *Photog* Alvin Wyckoff *Cast* Fanny Ward, Jack Dean, Sessue Hayakawa, James Neill *Prod* Famous Players/Lasky/Paramount. 42 mins.

A society lady (Ward) gambles with the funds of the Red Cross and is forced to borrow from a rich Japanese (Hayakawa). She then refuses to become his mistress. Furious, he brands her with a red-hot iron. Her husband (Dean) kills the Japanese but is acquitted when his wife reveals her brand in court.

This film was not very successful in the USA, where it was banned in a number of States, but it was a huge success in Paris because of its shocking and outspoken theme and was hailed by some as a masterpiece. Delluc reacted against this infatuation by describing it as a "cinematic Tosca" and wrote: "Lord, preserve us from masterpieces . . . which this isn't anyway."

The Cheat was powerfully directed by De Mille, a man trained in the theater who knew how to depict lurid and sensational scenes (such as that in which Hayakawa marks the naked shoulder of Fanny Ward with the red-hot brand from his collection) and great spectacle (the trial and acquittal, a large charity fête). On the other hand, De Mille owed much to his art director and to the cameraman Alvin Wyckoff, who created an expressive visual style known as "Lasky lighting" with chiaroscuro effects that were as famous then as were those of *Citizen Kane* 25 years later.

REMAKES:

— *The Cheat* USA 1923. *Dir* George Fitzmaurice.

— *The Cheat* USA 1931. *Dir* George Abbott.

— *Forfaiture* France 1937. *Dir* Marcel L'Herbier.

CHEAT (THE) ROMAN D'UN TRICHEUR (LE)

CHELOVEK NO. 217 GIRL NO. 217 USSR 1944. *Dir* Mikhail Romm *Scen* Yevgeni Gabrilovich, Mikhail Romm *Photog* Boris Volchok, E. Zavelova *Mus* Khachaturian *Art Dir* Yevgeni Enei *Cast* Yelena Kuzmina, Anna Lisyanskaya, Vasili Zaichikov *Prod* Mosfilm and Tashkent Studio. 101 mins.

A young Russian girl (Kuzmina) is deported to Nazi Germany and acquired by a German family as a slave. She kills a member of the SS and escapes during a bombing raid.

A powerful and dramatic portrayal of the slavery of deported Russian women. Good performance by Kuzmina and interesting sets by Enei.

CHELOVEK S KINOAPPAROTOM THE MAN WITH THE MOVIE CAMERA USSR 1928. *Dir/Scen/Ed* Dziga Vertov *Assist* Yelizaveta Svilova *Photog* Mikhail Kaufman *Prod* VUFKU. 1830 meters.

"In the prologue, a movie theater whose seats and screen prepare themselves for the screening. Then we are projected from the screen into life. A cameraman, always moving about perched on a car, records the motion of the town with all its activities, from every angle in the most varied arrangements. The man with the camera penetrates into houses, work places, ending on the beach which becomes populated in the evening. In between, we are shown the 'man of the screen,' the editor, playing and creating with these images. At the end, the camera escapes from the hands of its master and, in the movie house, does a little turn of its own" (Delmas).

"There are different 'movements,' a 'theme,' but also a 'melody' and an 'accompaniment': the personality behind the camera and the same personality in the camera, the eye in the camera, the camera in the eye, the spectator-actor and the actor-spectator, their film and our film. The attitude of a poet enamoured of the world, who strives to group multiple forms in a vision called, around 1920, 'simultaneous' and 'multiplanar.' *The Man with the Movie Camera* seems very close to "Documentaires" by Cendrars or even a poem by Apollinaire" (Decaudin).

This film is not a Soviet version of *Berlin, Symphony of a Great City* (inspired by Kaufman's earlier *Moscow*) but an application of the "life as it is lived" method and at the same time a portrait of a large collective city, since the scenes in Moscow mingle with those in Odessa.

Vertov selected his brother, the cameraman Mikhail Kaufman, as his hero, and shows him in the street and in the most extraordinary places. He uses all the resources of editing, but also uses trick photography, animation, slow motion, and speeded-up shots. In one sequence some women in a cab, realizing that the cameraman is following them, smirk and gesture at the camera; here the director makes the camera itself play a role in the drama. At the end, the camera takes a bow after a montage sequence that recapitulates the "themes and variations" of this film made manifest.

CHIEN ANDALOU UN CHIEN ANDALOU

CHIENNE (LA) ISN'T LIFE A BITCH? France 1931. *Dir* Jean Renoir *Scen* Jean Renoir from the novel by Georges de la Fouchardière *Photog* Theodore Sparkuhl, Roger Hubert *Art Dir* Gabriel Scognamillo *Ed* Marguerite Renoir *Cast* Michel Simon, Janie Marèze, Georges Flament, Jean Gehret, Alexandre Rignault, Madeleine Berubet *Prod* Braunberger/Richebé. 85 mins.

An unhappily married middle-aged bank clerk (Simon) falls for a prostitute (Marèze). She robs and deceives him and he eventually kills her. He is not suspected, however, and her pimp (Flament) is convicted in his place while he becomes a tramp.

The original novel was mediocre and could have only offered to Michel Simon

a role in the Jannings style. But out of the melodrama Renoir created a very realistic social portrait of certain aspects of Montmartre life. Even in this, his first sound feature, Renoir used depth of field and sound effects to characterize the personalities in their social milieu, such as the shabby lodgings of the bank clerk, with its courtyard window looking straight onto another window, and the leitmotiv of a clumsy piano exercise endlessly repeated.

The film was a commercial failure because a comedy was expected of Michel Simon and the humorist La Fouchardière, but it was well received by the French critics.

See also *Scarlet Street*

CHIKAMATSU MONOGATARI A STORY FROM CHIKAMATSU/THE CRUCIFIED LOVERS Japan 1954. *Dir* Kenji Mizoguchi *Scen* Yoshikata Yoda, Matsutaro Kawaguchi based on stories of Chikamatsu Monzaemon *Photog* Kazuo Miyagawa *Art Dir* Hiroshi Mizutani *Mus* Fumio Hayasaka *Cast* Kazuo Hasegawa, Kyoko Kagawa, Yoko Minamida, Eitaro Shindo *Prod* Daiei. 110 mins.

Set in the 17th century, the story of an illicit love between a merchant's wife (Kagawa) and her husband's servant. They flee together but are captured and crucified according to the ancient punishment for adultery.

One of the greatest films of Mizoguchi, who gained his reputation by making a group of films depicting the condition of women in various periods.

[The film was based on a story by Chikamatsu (a renowned 17th-century writer) and derived from a Bunraku play (traditional theater similar to Kabuki). The syle of the film bears no relation to the play and Mizoguchi did not call the film by its proper name. It is similar to calling "Hamlet," in a film version, "A Tale From Shakespeare."

It is perhaps Mizoguchi's most intense and concentrated study of social mores in feudal Japan and among his most visually sensuous films. His replacement of the original happy ending with a tragic one in which the lovers die, condemned by their inequality of caste, gives his version an additional poignancy.]

CHILDHOOD OF MAXIM GORKI (THE) DETSVO GORKOVO

CHILDREN OF HIROSHIMA GENBAKU NO KO

CHILDREN OF PARADISE (THE) ENFANTS DU PARADIS (LES)

CHILDREN OF THE ATOM BOMB GENBAKU NO KO

CHILDREN OF THE EARTH DHARTI KE LAL

CHIMES AT MIDNIGHT CAMPANADAS A MEDIANOCHE

CHINA EXPRESS GOLUBOI EKSPRESS

CHISTOIE NEBO CLEAR SKY/CLEAR SKIES USSR 1961. *Dir* Grigori Chukrai *Scen* Daniel Khrabrovitsky *Photog* Sergei Polvanov *Cast* Nina Drobysheva, Evgeny Urbansky *Prod* Mosfilm. 98 mins. Sovcolor.

Sasha, a young girl (Drobysheva), falls in love with a handsome pilot (Urbansky) on leave during World War II, becomes pregnant, then hears he has been shot down. She remains faithful to him and finally he returns, embittered but still in love with her. Because he allowed himself to be captured by the Germans, he is thrown out of the Party. Only after Stalin's death is the verdict against him reversed.

The first part of this film (a traditional, sentimental love story) doesn't jibe with the second (unjust persecution and the personality cult). Although there are touching lyrical sequences in the first part, it is the second — a true cry from the heart — that gives the film its depth. Remarkable sequence: after being condemned by a bureaucrat in an office furnished with a gigantic statue of Stalin, the hero wonders if it isn't right for him to be called a coward and a traitor even though everything suggests the opposite. The acting is uneven.

CHORUS OF TOKYO TOKYO NO GASSHO

CHRISTINE CARNET DE BAL

CHRISTMAS IN JULY USA 1940. *Dir/Scen* Preston Sturges *Photog* Victor Milner *Cast* Dick Powell, Ellen Drew, Raymond Walburn, Franklin Pangborn, *Prod* Paramount. 70 mins.

The story of a young couple (Powell, Drew) and a winning lottery ticket. This is a lively satire of the American "ordinary guy" with some excellent char-acter roles, notably Franklin Pangborn as a nervous radio announcer and Raymond Walburn as a coffee tycoon.

CHRONICLE OF A SUMMER CHRONIQUE D'UN ÉTÉ

CHRONIQUE D'UN ETE CHRONICLE OF A SUMMER France 1961. *Dir* Jean Rouch *Scen* Jean Rouch, Edgar Morin *Photog* Roger Morillère, Raoul Coutard, Jean-Jacques Tarbès, Michel Brault *Ed* Jean Ravel, Nina Baratier, Françoise Colin, *Cast* Jean Rouch, Edgar Morin, Marceline, Mary-Lou, Angelo, Jean-Pierre, Jacques, Jean (workers), Régis, Céline, Jean-Marc, Nadine, Landry, Raymond (students), etc. *Prod* Argos. 90 mins.

Cinéma-vérité was an expression Rouch used to describe the approach he used in this film; it was derived (inaccurately) from Dziga Vertov's "kino-pravda."

The cameraman used the "living" camera, a highly portable lightweight camera connected to a synchronized sound recorder. The film's theme is an inquiry among passers-by in Paris during the summer of 1960, beginning with the question "Are you happy?" The interviewer (the sociologist, Edgar Morin) then stepped in and, using psychodrama techniques, tried to reveal the true personality of the person being interviewed. Famous sequences: the statement by the ex-deportee, Marceline, in a deserted Paris on August 15th; Mary-Lou's confession; black students discovering the significance of a number tattooed on an arm by the Nazis in Auschwitz; a worker at the Renault factory returning to work. The film rarely uses totally improvised scenes and the directors never photographed people without their knowledge. The camera is not concealed and itself plays a very real role in the drama; its presence transforms some of the interviewees (Angelo, Mary-Lou, Marceline) into nonprofessional actors who end up by giving performances, consciously or not.

CHUTE DE LA MAISON USHER (LA) THE FALL OF THE HOUSE OF USHER France 1928. *Dir* Jean Epstein *Scen* Jean Epstein based on Edgar Allan Poe's *The Fall of the House of Usher* and *The Oval Portrait Assist* Luis Buñuel *Photog* Georges Lucas, Jean Lucas *Art Dir* Pierre Kefer *Cast* Marguerite Gance (Mme. Abel Gance), Jean Debucourt, Charles Lamy,

Pierre Hot *Prod* Jean Epstein. 4,923 ft. Epstein's film used another story by Poe, *The Oval Portrait,* in addition to the title story. "The cinematic equivalent of Debussy. An absolute mastery of editing and rhythm in which slow motion, super-impressions, moving camera shots, and the mobile camera combine to play a totally ungratuitous role. The lighting of the sets transforms them and imparts a sense of mystery. The actors were merely objects" (Henri Langlois).
See also *Fall of the House of Usher*

CIEL EST A VOUS (LE) France 1943. *Dir* Jean Grémillon *Scen* Albert Valentin, Charles Spaak *Photog* Louis Page *Art Dir* Max Douy *Mus* Roland Manuel *Cast* Madeleine Renaud, Charles Vanel, Jean Debucourt, Léonce Corne *Prod* Les Films Raoul Ploquin. 105 mins.
A female pilot (Renaud) wins the world's distance-flying record for women with the help of her husband (Vanel), the owner of a small provincial service station.
Based on an actual happening in 1935, this film is less about aviation than about average Frenchmen sacrificing everything for their ideals. This theme gave the film a special impact when it was first shown in February 1944, when the *maquis* were becoming seriously involved in the fighting. "The director has not hidden the pettiness of ordinary people, the silliness of a festival, a doctor's (Corne) manias, the morose discipline in orphanages, and the bitterness of some women attacking a spirit they don't understand. Yes, we live in a country that is rife with the deplorable taste of Henry II dressers, but also one in which the favorite myth of schoolchildren has been that of Bernard Palissy burning his Henry II dresser, his floors, and his house for an ideal. And we love also, in Zola's *La Débâcle,* the brave little bourgeois from Sedan who, taken into battle, fights calmly and, together with our soldiers, saves our honor. Grémillon's heroes are real; here is the image of French heroism, this child born with no other defense than a piece of leather and a pebble. Patriotism beats in these simple images" (*Confluences,* April 1944, Claude Jacquier (G.S.)) The fighting in the spring and summer of 1944 disorganized the French cinema and prevented this beautiful film from achieving the success it deserved. Its images have much of the feeling of neorealism but its lack of success prevented it from becoming the seminal film of a French neorealism movement.

CIRCLE OF LOVE RONDE (LA)

CIRCUS (THE) USA 1928. *Dir/Scen* Charles Chaplin *Photog* Rollie Totheroh, Jack Wilson, Mark Marlott *Art Dir* Charles D. Hall, William E. Hinckley, *Cast* Charles Chaplin, Allan Garcia, Merna Kennedy, Betty Morrissey, Harry Crocker, Henry Bergman, Stanley Sanford, John Rand, George Davis, Steve Murphy, Doc Stone *Prod* Chaplin for United Artists. 7 reels, about 6,500 ft.
A tramp (Chaplin) is mistaken for a pickpocket and takes refuge in a circus, where he gets a job as a handyman and studies to be a clown. In the ring, he is kicked by a donkey and his funny reactions raise him to be star clown. He falls in love with an equestrienne (Kennedy) until a handsome tightrope walker (Crocker) wins her. He is fired for protecting the girl and the girl runs away also, but he nobly returns for the tightrope walker. After they marry, he decides to stay behind.
This film has a perfect dramatic structure; there are some scenes full of pathos (the tramp being funny when he doesn't intend to be) and the ending is tragic. Famous sequences: Chaplin's tightrope act during which the safety device breaks and he is attacked by three escaped monkeys; the wild chase through a hall or mirrors; his imitation of traditional clown acts (suggestive of *Limelight*); his being locked in the lion's cage; the ending, with Chaplin sadly watching the wagons depart in the early morning in front of a circle of sawdust left by the circus.

CIRK THE CIRCUS USSR 1936. *Dir/Scen* Gregori Alexandrov *Photog* Vladimir Nilsen *Mus* Isaac Dunayevsky *Cast* Lyubov Orlova, Melkinova, Volodin, Stoliarov, etc. *Prod* Mosfilm. 89 mins.
The misadventures of an American singer (Orlova) who has had a black child. An entertaining musical comedy with good dance and vaudeville sequences, though not as successful as Alexandrov's earlier *Jazz Comedy* (*q.v.*)

CISARUV SLAVIK THE EMPEROR'S NIGHTINGALE Czechoslovakia 1948. *Dir/Art Dir*

Jiri Trnka *Scen* Jiri Brdecka, Jiri Trnka based on Hans Christian Andersen *Photog* E. Franek, F. Pecenka *Live Action Dir* M. Makovec *Mus* V. Trojan. 67 mins. Agfacolor.

Based on the fairy tale about a young emperor who drives a real nightingale away in favor of a mechanical toy nightingale, falls ill, and is saved by the return of the nightingale.

Trnka's first feature-length puppet film is a warmhearted yet serious work, notable for its set designs, puppetry, and color.

CITIZEN KANE USA 1941. *Dir* Orson Welles *Scen* Herman J. Mankiewicz, Orson Welles *Photog* Gregg Toland *Art Dir* Van Nest Polglase *Sets* Darrell Silvera *Mus* Bernard Herrmann *Ed* Robert Wise *Cast* Orson Welles, Joseph Cotten, Dorothy Comingore, Agnes Moorehead, Ruth Warrick, Everett Sloane, George Coulouris, Ray Collins, William Alland *Prod* Mercury for RKO. 119 mins.

An all-powerful press magnate, Kane (Welles), dies in his fabulous castle, Xanadu, his last word being "rosebud." A newsreel in the *March of Time* style leads a reporter (Alland) to seek the meaning behind the word and perhaps find the meaning of Kane. Thatcher's (Coulouris) memoirs about Kane evoke his youth and his mother (Moorehead). The journalist questions Bernstein (Sloane), now an old man, who tells how Kane ran his newspaper and fomented the war with Cuba (1897). Then Leland (Cotten), also old, recounts Kane's marriage to a president's niece (Warrick), his meeting with his mistress (Comingore), and his unfortunate foray into politics. The reporter questions the second wife in a nightclub; she tells of her useless attempts to become an opera singer and her retreat with Kane into the fabulous Xanadu. At the end, as some of Kane's belongings are being burned in a furnace, we see among them the sled "Rosebud," which he had loved as a child.

Orson Welles, who had become famous for his radio broadcast "The War of the Worlds," was given for this, his first film (at age 25), absolute authority over the script [largely the work of Herman J. Mankiewicz, who shared screen credit — and an Oscar — with Welles] and the choice of actors. He chose his actors

from the Mercury Theater, which he had founded and directed, and took the millionaire newspaper magnate William Randolph Hearst as his model for Kane. Hearst tried to prevent the film's release but succeeded only in increasing the publicity for it.

Before making his first film Welles had carefully studied films preserved at the Museum of Modern Art in New York. Although he took some of his techniques from these films, he refined them to a new and personal level: "depth of field" (superbly used by the photographer Gregg Toland), flashbacks showing the same man described differently by various witnesses who knew him, ceilings on the sets, low-angle shots and chiaroscuro photography.

The most striking sequences: the "actuality" montage in the style of a *March of Time* newsreel; Kane's childhood in a landscape of snow and a family boardinghouse run by his mother; the entrance of the turn-of-the-century chorus girls at the end of a banquet; Kane's election meetings held under his portrait, a hundred times life-size; his hard work on the newspaper; his married life falling into luxurious boredom; the voice lessons of his untalented mistress and her failure at the Opera (with a brilliant crane shot); the unreal, sonorous emptiness of Xanadu with its enormous monumental rooms where the second Mrs. Kane works incessantly on gigantic jigsaw puzzles; the final scene after his death, showing Kane's accumulated treasures and junk in an immense warehouse.

The essence of the film lies in its story, comparable to a great modern novel, and in its often expressionistic style. It studies Kane from every aspect, accentuating his egotism and his loneliness. Welles (who himself had some of Kane's characteristics incarnated Kane and, despite some misuse of make-up, is an imposing presence who pushes all the other actors (including Joseph Cotten, Agnes Moorehead, Everett Sloane) into the background.

Well received by the critics and audiences in New York, the film was not understood by the public at large. Its commercial failure allowed the new officials of RKO to get rid of Welles. However, the film has continued to exert an enormous international influence and was included among the 12 Best Films of All Time at Brussels in 1958.

CITY GIRL see OUR DAILY BREAD

CITY LIGHTS USA 1931. *Dir/Scen/Mus* Charles Chaplin *Assist Dir* Harry Crocker, Henry Bergman, Albert Austin *Photog* Rollie Totheroh, Gordon Pollock, Mark Marlott *Art Dir* Charles D. Hall *Cast* Charles Chaplin, Virginia Cherrill, Florence Lee, Harry Myers, Allan Garcia, Hank Mann, Henry Bergman *Prod* Chaplin for United Artists. 87 mins.

An unemployed man (Chaplin) falls in love with a blind flower girl (Cherrill) and becomes involved with an eccentric millionaire (Myers), who is generous when drunk but mean when sober. After trying to earn money as a street sweeper, then as a boxer, he takes a large sum to enable the blind girl to have an operation to regain her sight. He is arrested and on leaving prison finds the blind girl cured.

Apart from several slapstick sequences (an evening in a nightclub, a boxing match, etc.) the film is a "comedy romance in pantomime," a bittersweet tragedy. It was two years in production and although talkies had become established, Chaplin made it without dialogue, using only musical accompaniment and sound effects.

Famous sequences: the solemn unveiling of the Statue to Prosperity revealing the unemployed Chaplin asleep on the center figure; the meeting with the flower girl, who offers him a flower thinking he has just got out of a rich man's car, and his understanding her blindness only when she throws (unknowingly) a bucket of water at him; the drunken millionaire whom Chaplin meets by the river as he tries to drown himself by tying a heavy stone to himself; Chaplin swallowing a whistle, which causes a taxi to stop and several dogs to appear; the comic boxing sequences; the tragic closing scene in which the cured girl is running a flower shop. She offers the ragged tramp a coin, suddenly recognizes her benefactor, and says, with obvious bewilderment, "You?" Chaplin, holding a flower, merely smiles poignantly at her.

This simple story is told in the restrained and sparse style of the great classics, but each detail was the result of arduous and time-consuming work. In one of the opening scenes, Chaplin climbs through a luxurious car tied up in a traffic jam and finds himself facing the blind flower girl who, having heard the car door slamming, mistakes him for a millionaire. This brief scene, the basis of the film and essential to an understanding of the dramatic development, took many weeks of work with numerous rehearsals and corrections to make it entirely to the point.

Despite its simple style and story, social polemic is quietly and continuously present, in addition to such overt allusions as the Statue to Prosperity guarded by armed men symbolizing police and war.

The film cost Chaplin (his own producer and financially somewhat embarrassed after his divorce) a great deal of money. Its first screenings in the United States were disappointing. However, when he presented it in Europe it became an enormous and profitable international success.

CITY STREETS USA 1931. *Dir* Rouben Mamoulian *Scen* Oliver P. Garrett, Max Marcin based on a story by Dashiell Hammett *Photog* Lee Garmes *Cast* Gary Cooper, Sylvia Sidney, William Boyd, Paul Lukas *Prod* Paramount. 82 mins.

The Kid (Cooper), lieutenant in a gang of bootleggers, falls in love with Nan (Sidney). He is imprisoned for refusing to betray a murderer, his father. After various tragic adventures, the lovers escape the gang.

Mamoulian's second film was a conventional, but moving, gangster melodrama whose skillful location shooting creates a constant impression of the big city. This was Sylvia Sidney's second film (the part had been originally written for Clara Bow) and both she and the young Gary Cooper give marvelous performances.

Its visual style, somewhat impressionistic, was possibly influenced by *Underworld*, notably in its use of cut-in, symbolic objects — the dove outside the prison, the montage of porcelain cats in a jealousy scene, etc. Especially beautiful is the scene in the prison visiting room, with the bars and the shadows separating the two faces. *City Streets* is also notable for its sound track, including an early use of overlapping dialogue as Sylvia Sidney recalls her past.

CITY SYMPHONY TOKAI KOYOGAKU

CIULINII BARAGANULUI THE THISTLES OF

65

THE BARAGON Romania 1957. *Dir* Louis Daquin *Scen* Louis Daquin, Alexendru Struteanu, A. Tudal based on the novel by Panait Istrati *Photog* André Dumaître *Cast* Nuta Chirlea, Ana Vladescu, Ruxandra Ionesco, Clorin Piersic. 110 mins.
A child (Chirlea), who has seen her father starve to death on the road, joins a revolt of Romanian peasants about 1905. A beautiful and very moving film, notable for its landscapes, its collective heroes, and the presence of the child observing the events.

CIVILIZATION: OR HE WHO RETURNED USA
1916. *Dir* Thomas H. Ince (with Raymond B. West and Reginald Baker) *Scen* C. Gardner Sullivan *Photog* Irwin Willat *Mus* Victor Schertzinger *Cast* Enid Markey, Howard Hickman, J. Barney Sherry, Hershell Mayall, Charles French, Lola May, George Fisher, Frank Burke *Prod* Triangle. 12 reels. (Reissued in a sound version in 1931, 68 mins.).
Set in a mythical kingdom in the 20th century. The king (Mayall) declares war on his neighbors to satisfy a personal lust for power despite the efforts of a pacifist (Burke) and a secret army of women pledged to end the fighting. Count Ferdinand's (Hickman) fiancée (Markey) tries to persuade him not to join, but he refuses and is wounded on a submarine. During his illness he has visions of heaven and hell and sees Christ (Fisher). When he recovers he lives as a reincarnation of Christ and is sentenced to death. Later, the king also has a vision of Christ and signs a peace treaty.
[*Civilization* was one of the three pacifist films made in 1916. (*Intolerance* and Brenon's *War Brides* with Nazimova were the others) and its appeal to the market was nicely calculated. After "studying the pulse of the box office and the motion-picture public's reaction to the *Battle Cry of Peace* and war propaganda, Ince decided there was a market for the other side of the situation" (Terry Ramsaye).] The publicity claimed that it cost a million dollars but its budget ($100,000) did not match that of *Birth of a Nation*. It enjoyed a tremendous commercial success in the USA ($800,000 gross) and was said to have helped to re-elect President Wilson on his platform, "He kept us out of the war." However, the entry of the USA into the war in 1917 brought an end to its circulation. [Even though it was an antiwar film, it was the first of those "produced with the cooperation of the US Navy."] However, the versions of this antiwar film shown in France and Italy in 1917 became prowar. Colette wrote of it: "The delicate details are not missing since that is all there is and there is too much of it. A swarm of extras, of mediocre leading roles. The allegory (with all the risks and perils of its use) plays a large part. I regret the tangibility of a Christ who chats with a kaiser . . . There are hundreds of scenes about which I cannot complain: the warlike cavalcades, explosions of underwater mines, ambulances that blow up and the ever-present mud. Some frenetic cuts (60 pictures to the minute) give a tumultuous impression of the earth trembling everywhere. It is an artist who composed such scenes as that of the poor mother clutching her three little ones to her, while in front of her march the shadows of helmets and shouldered bayonets."

CLEAR SKY CHISTOIE NEBO

CLEO DE 5 A 7 CLEO FROM 5 TO 7 France/
Italy 1961. *Dir/Scen* Agnès Varda *Photog* Jean Rabier *Art Dir* Bernard Evein *Ed* Jeanne Verneau *Mus* Michel Legrand *Cast* Corinne Marchand, Antoine Bourseiller *Prod* Rome-Paris Films. 90 mins.
Ninety minutes exactly (the length of the film) in the life of a singer (Marchand) who learns that she has cancer and meets a young soldier (Bourseiller) about to leave for the Algerian War. Produced mainly in the streets of Paris, this is a moving poem of love and death.

CLEOPATRA
— USA 1934. *Dir* Cecil B. De Mille *Scen* Waldemar Young, Barlett Cormack, Vincent Lawrence *Photog* Victor Milner *Art Dir* Hans Dreier *Mus* Rudolph Kopp *Cast* Claudette Colbert, Warren William, Herbert Wilcoxon, Gertrude Michael, Joseph Schildkraut, Irving Pichel, C. Aubrey Smith, Charles Morris *Prod* Paramount. 101 mins.
A carnivalesque Paramount extravaganza, remembered mainly for the bath scene by Claudette Colbert (which was thrown in as a gimmick), the dozens of seminaked girls, and the scene in which Cleopatra seduces Mark Antony (Wilcoxon).

— USA 1963. *Dir* Joseph L. Mankiewicz *Scen* Joseph L. Mankiewicz, Ranald Mac-Dougall, Sidney Buchman based on various classical sources and on *The Life and Times of Cleopatra* by C. M. Franzero *Photog* Leon Shamroy *Art Dir* John De Cuir and others *Ed* Dorothy Spencer *Mus* Alex North *Cast* Elizabeth Taylor, Richard Burton, Rex Harrison, Roddy McDowall, George Cole, Pamela Brown, Gregoire Aslan, etc. *Prod* 20th Century-Fox/J.L.M./Walwa. 243 mins. DeLuxe Color. Todd-AO.

The incredible expenditures on this film, the most costly ever made (40 million dollars) led to the removal of Spyros Skouras as head of Fox. Despite its cost and its record length, it hardly surpassed the earlier *Cleopatra*'s. One might apply to it Delluc's comment about Italian films in 1920: "When you don't see three, you see a hundred thousand." The large number of extras was combined with the love affairs of somewhat senile actors. It seemed to last, this Cleo, from five to seven, instead of four hours.

OTHER VERSIONS:
— France 1899. *Dir* Georges Méliès.
— France 1909. *Prod* Film d'Art.
— USA 1912. *Dir* Charles Gaskill *Cast* Helen Gardner.
— *Cleopatra* USA 1917. *Dir* J. Gordon Edwards *Cast* Theda Bara *Prod* Fox. 11 reels.
See also: *Caesar and Cleopatra*

CLOAK (THE) SHINEL

CLOSELY OBSERVED TRAINS OSTRE SLEDO-VANE VLAKY.

CLOSELY WATCHED TRAINS OSTRE SLEDO-VANE VLAKY.

CLUB OF THE BIG DEED (THE) S.V. D.

CLUTCHING HAND (THE) EXPLOITS OF ELAINE (THE)

COCHECITO (EL) THE WHEELCHAIR Spain 1959. *Dir* Marco Ferreri *Scen* Marco Ferreri, Rafael Azcona based on a novel by Azcona *Photog* Juan Julio Baena *Art Dir* Enrique Alarcon *Ed* Pedro del Rey *Cast* José Isbert, Pedro Porcel, J. L. Lopez Vasquez *Prod* Films 59. 88 mins.

An old man (Isbert), whose rich family refuses to give him a motorized wheelchair, poisons them with rat poison and buys himself his "cochecito." A mordant satire of the Spanish bourgeois in which the Milanese, Ferreri, displays his black humor and his beloved "monsters."

COEUR FIDELE THE FAITHFUL HEART France 1923. *Dir/Scen* Jean Epstein *Photog* Paul Guichard assisted by Stuckert, Leon Donnot *Cast* Leon Mathot, Gina Manès, Edmond Van Daele, Benedict *Prod* Pathé. 6,500 ft. approx.

The rivalry between the villainous Petit-Paul (Van Daele) and the honest-working Jean (Mathot) for a woman, Marie (Manès). Set in Marseille and its suburbs.

Jean Epstein's masterpiece, famous especially for the rapid cutting in the fair sequence, where the swirl of a merry-go-round and the movement of its figures serve as counterpoint to a brawl between the two men. This is one of the films which, while made at the time of impressionism, is more suggestive of "poetic realism" because of its sense of landscape and its characters drawn from everyday life.

["There is in the dream of his characters at the seashore a so-perfect comprehension of what the cinema can and should be, that one has the impression of finding oneself abruptly facing truth" (René Jeanne, 1926). "It reveals a technical knowledge that is resolutely oriented towards stylization, not by *trompe l'oeil* but by giving new value to reality" (Georges Bourgeois, 1923).]

COME AND GET IT ROARING TIMBER USA 1936. *Dir* Howard Hawks, William Wyler *Scen* Jane Murfin, Jules Furthman based on the novel by Edna Ferber *Photog* Gregg Toland, Rudolph Maté *Ed* Edward Curtiss *Mus* Alfred Newman *Cast* Edward Arnold, Joel McCrea, Frances Farmer, Walter Brennan, Andrea Leeds *Prod* Goldwyn for United Artists. 105 mins.

An ambitious lumber-camp boss, Barney Glasgow (Arnold), is in love with Lotta Morgan (Farmer), but leaves her for a more profitable marriage with Evvie (Leeds). Twenty-five years later, he returns to visit his old friend Swan (Brennan), who married Lotta (now dead). Barney is attracted by Lotta's daughter (Farmer) and disaster and scandal threaten. When his son Richard (McCrea) falls for the daughter also, they have a violent quarrel and Barney returns to his senses and his wife.

It seemed to many French critics in 1936 that Hawks had directed the first part of the film and Wyler the second. However, Hawks was the principal director since only the last few minutes of the film were directed by Wyler after Hawks was taken off it by Goldwyn. It is a vigorous portrait of pioneer America with a powerful performance by Edward Arnold. Frances Farmer plays a dual role.

COME BACK AFRICA USA 1959. *Dir* Lionel Rogosin *Scen* Lionel Rogosin, Lewis N'Kosi, Bloke Modisane *Photog* Ernest Artaria, Emil Knebel *Cast* Zaccharia, Vinah, Miriam Makeba, and the people of Johannesburg. *Prod* Lionel Rogosin. 90 mins.

A semidocumentary story of Zaccharia, a Zulu peasant, whom the drought forces to work in the mines, then to establish himself in the shanty town of Johannesburg where he rejoins his wife, Vinah, who is killed by a bandit.

Rogosin, an American film maker, produced this film clandestinely in South Africa with the help of Black organizations, while the ultraracist government thought he was making a different film. It is a superb example of *cinéma vérité*, the script having been created by Rogosin following an investigation among blacks who had suffered through racism. Remarkable sequences: the work in the mines; the streets of Johannesburg; working for a white family, then in a garage; life in the shanty town; imprisonment by the police; a political discussion between Blacks; Zaccharia's final despair, crying and beating the table.

COMPADRE MENDOZA (EL) Mexico 1934. *Dir* Fernando de Fuentes *Scen* M. Magdaleno, J. Bustillo Oro, Fernando de Fuentes *Photog* Ross Fisher *Art Dir* Beleho *Cast* Carmen Guerrero, Alfredo del Diestro, Antonio R. Frautro. 90 mins. approx.

During the Revolution "Comrade" Mendoza, a rich landowner, changes according to the circumstances from a supporter of Zapata into a counterrevolutionary who executes his former "friends."

One of the best Mexican films during the years 1932 to 1942, a rich period in Mexican cinema. It is a brisk satire whose good humor, lively sense of observation, and memories of the Mexican Revolution (then still very recent) contribute to its portrayal of "Comrade" Mendoza as a true social type.

CONCRETE JUNGLE CRIMINAL (THE)

CONDAMNE A MORT S'EST ECHAPPE (UN) UN CONDAMNÉ À MORT S'EST ÉCHAPPÉ

CONFIDENTIAL REPORT MR. ARKADIN Spain 1955. *Dir/Scen/Art Dir* Orson Welles *Photog* Jean Bourgoin *Mus* Paul Misraki *Ed* Renzo Lucidi *Cast* Orson Welles, Patricia Medina, Robert Arden *Prod* Sevilla Studios/Mercury. 99 mins.

The wealthy Mr. Arkadin (Welles), threatened with blackmail by a young man (Arden) who is courting his daughter (Medina), searches out his own past. In Spain, Paris, Tangier, Amsterdam, and Munich, Arkadin finds his old accomplices and destroys them to preserve his own security, but ends by committing suicide.

Orson Welles has described his hero: "Arkadin is a self-made man in a corrupt world. He didn't try to make himself better than this world but, as a prisoner of it, is its best expression."

As with Kane, "It is concerned with an international tycoon who is surrounded by mystery. It required a true police investigation in order to lift the veil that cloaked the criminal origins of his immense fortune. His thirst for power shattered love, for Mr. Arkadin saw his daughter removed from him by the adventurer whom he had commissioned to remove the traces of his past. The artificial universe of the hero collapses and his suicide is this time the only decent conclusion" (Maurice Bessy). Not only did Welles embody Arkadin, but in the English version (it was made also in Spanish) he dubbed the voices of 18 actors.

Confidential Report is a return to the general theme of *Citizen Kane*, but in another period. It was not edited by Welles, who has consequently somewhat disowned it. But the script is very much his and carries the recognizable signature of his powerful spirit and the ideas that preoccupy him.

CONFLAGRATION ENJO

CONGRESS DANCES KONGRESS TANZT (DER)

*CONNECTION (THE) USA 1961. *Dir* Shirley Clarke *Scen* Jack Gelber *Photog* Arthur J. Ornitz *Art Dir* Richard Sylbert *Mus* Freddie Redd *Cast* Warren Finnerty, Jerome Raphel, Jim Anderson, Carl Lee, Barbara Winchester, Roscoe

Browne, William Redfield *Prod* Shirley Clarke/Lewis Allen. 110 mins.

Shirley Clarke's first feature is an adaptation of Jack Gelber's play about a group of heroin addicts waiting for their "connection" to bring them a fix. The original stage production used the device of a "play within a play"; in the film version a documentary director moves into the addicts' pad to make a realistic study of their lives. Little by little he becomes involved in their story until he is talked into trying a fix.

Shirley Clarke shot the film through the two cameras used by the director and the other cameraman, with the cameras and technicians occasionally getting in each other's sightlines. As the director becomes more involved, the other cameraman continues relentlessly recording what happens despite orders to cut.

For an equivalent of *The Connection*'s almost Pirandellian manipulations of reality one would have to return to Vertov's *Man With the Movie Camera* (*q.v.*). *The Connection* recognizes and uses the inevitable distortion that the film camera brings to recording even the appearance of reality. The technique may have only limited general application but it works brilliantly in this film. The acting (the cast is largely that of the stage production) is uniformly admirable.

The Connection set another precedent. It was one of the first films to enlist the support of private investors. Some 200 backers invested a total of $167,000, a procedure until then used only for financing stage productions. The film was shot in 19 days on a single set in New York. During its first commercial run, the film was seized by police on an obscenity charge but was later cleared in the courts.

CONQUEST OF THE POLE À LA CONQUÊTE DU PÔLE

CONTACT MAN (THE) see FAUST

CONTEMPT MÉPRIS (LE)

CONTINENTE PERDUTO THE LOST CONTINENT Italy 1954. *Dir* Mario Craveri *Co-Dir* Leonardo Bonzi, Enrico Gras, Francesco A. Lavagnino, Giorgio Moser *Photog* Mario Craveri, Gianni Raffaldi, Franco Barnett *Mus* Francesco A. Lavagnino *Ed* Mario Serandrei. 82 mins. CinemaScope. Ferraniacolor.

This pseudo documentary produced in the Far East is the height of trickery. Its bombastic images are underlined by grandiloquent music and a rapturous commentary. Its natural successors were *Mondo Cane* and that film's scores of imitations.

COPS USA 1922. *Dir/Scen* Buster Keaton, Eddie Cline *Cast* Buster Keaton, Virginia Fox *Prod* Associated First National *Assoc Prod* Comique Film Corp. 2 reels.

The same Keaton perfection in which the gags are impeccably timed and none are dragged on too long. Buster Keaton is first a clumsy driver, then is pursued by a horde of policemen. Even though it is derived from Mack Sennett, this faultless comedy has the special Keaton genius in every scene.

COQUILLE ET LE CLERGYMAN (LA) SEASHELL AND THE CLERGYMAN (THE) France 1928. *Dir* Germaine Dulac *Scen* Antonin Artaud *Photog* Paul Guichard *Cast* Alex Allin. 2,576 ft.

A clergyman (Allin), committed by his calling to celibacy but in love with a romantic beauty, is afflicted by sexual torments he is unable to resolve.

The film is composed of a series of episodes using Freudian imagery to express the clergyman's mental anguish. Antonin Artaud, dissatisfied with the way Germaine Dulac handled his script, incited a violent and memorable demonstration by the surrealists against Dulac at the Studio des Ursulines. Despite Artaud's dissatisfaction, Dulac's film is a sincere and honest experiment whose sequences in the streets of Paris are especially notable.

[The British Board of Film Censors rejected the film with the comment: "It is so cryptic as to have no apparent meaning. If there is a meaning, it is doubtless objectionable."]

CORBEAU (LE) THE RAVEN France 1943. *Dir* Henri-Georges Clouzot *Scen* Louis Chavance, Henri-Georges Clouzot *Photog* Nicholas Hayer *Art Dir* André Andreiev, Herman Warm *Mus* Tony Aubain *Cast* Pierre Fresnay, Pierre Larquey, Ginette Leclerc, Héléna Manson, Micheline Francey, Noël Roquevert, Bernard Lancret, Balpétré, Brochard *Prod* Continental. 92 mins.

In a small French town, poison-pen letters are sent to the inhabitants and provoke tensions and suicides. Suspected in turn are a doctor (Fresnay), a crippled girl with loose morals (Leclerc), and a sick woman (Manson). Finally, it is discovered that the guilty one is a well-liked old man (Larquey).

Based on a prewar true story (the poison-pen letters of Tulle), *Le Corbeau* is basically an ingeniously suspenseful thriller with the audience being led to believe that each character in turn is the guilty one on the basis of the psychological motivation.

The film was produced by the German company, Continental, which stressed the film's setting in their publicity: "A typical small French town." This provoked a violent denunciation of the film in the clandestine *Les Lettres Françaises* by George Adam and Pierre Blanchar. *Le Corbeau* was banned in France for two years after the Liberation and its director suspended for six months.

It is well directed and acted and contains Ginette Leclerc's best role. One of her scenes shows two faces under a swinging light alternating between shadow and light as she says "You think that goodness is light and darkness is evil. But where is the darkness? Where the light?"

REMAKE:
— *The 13th Letter* USA 1951. *Dir* Otto Preminger *Scen* Howard Koch based on the original screenplay *Photog* Joseph La Shelle *Art Dir* Lyle Wheeler, Maurice Ransford *Mus* Alex North *Cast* Charles Boyer, Linda Darnell, Michael Rennie, Constance Smith, Françoise Rosay *Prod* 20th Century-Fox. 84 mins.

[Set in a village in Quebec, Preminger's version is less vicious and more human than Clouzot's but also less engrossing. It is also almost an exact copy: there are no plot changes, the dialogue is almost identical, and there are many scenes that have been copied in detail, such as the lamp-swinging scene. Françoise Rosay as the suicide's mother is excellent.]

*CORNER IN WHEAT (A) USA 1909. *Dir* D. W. Griffith *Scen* D. W. Griffith based on the novel *The Pit* by Frank Norris *Photog* G. W. Bitzer *Cast* Frank Powell, W. Christie Miller, Kate Bruce, Jeanie Macpherson, Henry B. Walthall, James Kirkwood *Prod* Biograph. 990 ft.

Based on a novel by Frank Norris, this film contrasts the life of a poor farmer with the activities of a tycoon dealing in wheat. It was Griffith's first film of social

comment and was unusual at the time for its attempt to propound a "liberal" message. His use of parallel action to contrast the two situations anticipates his later use of the device. In the end, the tycoon is asphyxiated in a grain pit.

COSTER BILL OF PARIS see CRAINQUEBILLE

COUNTERPLAN VSTRECHNYI

COUPABLE (LE) France 1917. *Dir* André Antoine *Scen* André Antoine based on the play by François Coppée *Photog* Trimbach (?) *Cast* Romuald Joubé, Grétillat, René Rocher, Sylvie, Sephora Mossé, Léon Bernard, Mona Gondre (the young boy).

A procurer (Joubé), a witness against his illegitimate son, recognizes him and accuses himself of the crime.

Antoine turned François Coppée's melodramatic play into a film in which the studio-based trial scenes alternate with flashbacks set in natural backgrounds. Particularly pleasing is its portrait of Paris in 1916 (when it was shot) with its grey cobblestone streets. The actors are quietly directed.

COUSINS (LES) THE COUSINS France 1958. *Dir/Scen* Claude Chabrol, *Dialogue* Paul Gégauff *Photog* Henri Decaë *Art Dir* Jacques Saulnier, Bernard Evein *Mus* Paul Misraki *Ed* Jacques Gaillard *Cast* Gérard Blain, Jean-Claude Brialy, Juliette Mayniel, Claude Cerval, Geneviève Cluny *Prod* AJYM. 110 mins.

Charles (Blain), a young maladroit student from the provinces, comes to live in Paris with his sophisticated, bullying cousin, Paul (Brialy). Charles falls in love with Florence (Mayniel) but she becomes Paul's mistress. In their examinations, Paul passes effortlessly while Charles fails. Confused, Charles kills himself.

Les Cousins was a great commercial success mainly for its somewhat glamorized portrait of student life and especially for the sequence showing carefree young people enjoying a night "on the town." Best sequences: the arrival in Paris; the student scenes; the evocation of the SS. The suspense ending is contrived and overly ingenious.

[The acting is the film's principal merit with Brialy and Blain playing similar contrasting roles to those they played in *Le Beau Serge*.]

COVERED WAGON (THE) USA 1923. *Dir* James Cruze *Scen* Jack Cunningham based on a novel by Emerson Hough *Photog* Karl Brown *Ed* Dorothy Arzner *Cast* Ernest Torrence, Tully Marshall, J. Warren Kerrigan, Lois Wilson, Alan Hale *Prod* Famous Players–Lasky. 9,200 ft.

One of the great silent westerns because of its breadth and its authenticity. It tells of a party of pioneer settlers who journey to the West by wagon train. Made with exteriors in Nevada and Utah, this film was considered by Robert Sherwood as "the one great American epic the screen has produced." It has also been characterized by Lewis Jacobs as: "Forthright, impressive, and vigorous. It brought a breath of fresh air into the jazz-ridden film world. So authentic had Cruze tried to make the film that he declared: 'There wasn't a false whisker in the film. The dust raised by the wagons was real dust, the Indians were real Indians, the beards on the pioneers were real beards.' But opposed to such *plein-air* documentation was the weak and illogical story; the heroine who remains ridiculously clean despite desert winds, snow storms, and Indian attacks; the inconsequential and interminable romance; and the conventional Wild West Indian attacks . . . Such faults kept the film from really being what it might have become — an honest, profound, and moving social document on a heroic scale . . . It did have unusual qualities in its representation of the Old West — the broad countryside, the vast sky and earth, the abundance of space and air — which, together with its realistic execution, stamped the film as distinctive. But it was very far short of a masterpiece."

The Covered Wagon was a phenomenal box-office success for which the producer, Zukor, gave himself the credit.

CRAB-CANNING SHIP (THE) KANI-KOSEN

CRAINQUEBILLE France 1922. *Dir/Art Dir* Jacques Feyder, *Scen* Jacques Feyder based on the story by Anatole France *Photog* Léonce H. Burel, Forster *Cast* Maurice de Féraudy, Françoise Rosay, Félix Oudart, Numès, Jean Forest *Prod* Les Films Trarieux/A. Legrand. 1,800 meters (6,000 ft. approx.).

A street merchant (de Féraudy) is unjustly accused by Police Agent 64 (Oudart) of having cried "Death to the cows" and is sent to prison. When he is released, he becomes a tramp and befriends a small boy (Forest).

"I really don't remember that there were so many things in my novel," said Anatole France after having seen the film. Although *Crainquebille* is best known for its somewhat impressionistic effects (the trial scene with the enormous judge looming over the tiny Crainquebille), Feyder also brought to it a personal vision of Paris and of the working-class districts through which this film heralded the poetic realism of the Thirties. *Crainquebille* was deeply admired by Griffith and has become a classic. Striking performance by de Féraudy.

OTHER VERSIONS:

— **Crainquebille/Coster Bill of Paris* France 1933. *Dir* Jacques de Baroncelli *Cast* M. Tramel, Gaston Modot (used Starevich puppets in the dream sequence). 6 reels.

— *Crainquebille* France 1954. *Dir* Ralph Habib *Cast* Yves Deniaud. 87 mins.

CRANES ARE FLYING (THE) LETYAT ZHU-RAVLI

CRAZY PAGE (A) KURUTTA IPPEIJI

CRAZY RAY (THE) PARIS QUI DORT

CRIME DE MONSIEUR LANGE (LE) THE CRIME OF MONSIEUR LANGE France 1935. *Dir* Jean Renoir *Scen* Jacques Prévert based on an idea by Jean Renoir, Jean Castanier *Photog* Jean Bachelet *Assist Dir* Pierre Prévert *Art Dir* Jean Castanier, Robert Gys *Mus* Jean Wiener, song by Joseph Kosma *Ed* Marguerite Renoir *Cast* René Lefèvre, Jules Berry, Florelle, Nadia Sibirskaïa, Sylva Bataille, Marcel Levesque, Maurice Baquet, Henri Guisol, Marcel Duhamel, Jacques Brunius, Jean Dasté, Sylvain Itkine, Max Morise, René Génin *Prod* Oberon. 84 mins.

M. Lange (Lefèvre) works in a publishing house in Paris, where his boss, the lecherous Batala (Berry) exploits him and the other workers. In his spare time Lange writes stories about the West that Batala publishes. With his creditors on his heels, Batala absconds and is believed to have been killed in a train crash. Lange and the other employees form a cooperative and have great success with Lange's stories. Meanwhile Valentine (Florelle), a laundress, is in love with Lange, as is Estelle (Sibirskaïa), another laundress, with the concierge's son (Baquet). Batala suddenly reappears dressed as a priest and claims his business. Lange shoots Batala and flees with Valentine.

"A bizarre work that clearly bore the mark of the year in which it was made, with its exploiting capitalists, its workers' cooperative, its daughter of the people violated by an evil boss" (Bardèche and Brasillach, 1943). "Its interest is beyond technique and cinema as such, in the profound meaning of the film and the message of its *auteurs*. It is all the more remarkable that the work owes its spiritual style to the harmony of two unshakably original temperaments: Prévert brought his liveliness and mordancy, Renoir the sympathy of his true romanticism" (Roger Leenhardt, 1936).

It is quite true that this film bears the mark of the *Front Populaire* and in spirit is a kind of philosophical tale. At the end, Lange tells the police of his crime and finds himself absolved: it is acceptable to have removed an evil proprietor. The center of the action, and almost the only set, is the courtyard of a Parisian working-class apartment block with its concierge (Levesque), its washerwomen in the courtyard, the printing shop, and the office of the proprietor. It is here that the courageous workers organize a front against Batala to establish a prosperous cooperative.

During the production, Renoir and Prévert were often at odds and never worked together again. Prévert (and his friends from the "October Group") had much influence on the film's theme. It was produced on a very low budget with a poor sound process that makes the brilliant dialogue often incomprehensible. One of the most famous gags: Batala, disguised as a priest, crying "A priest!" as he is dying.

*CRIME WITHOUT PASSION USA 1934. *Dir/Scen* Ben Hecht, Charles MacArthur based on their own *Caballero of the Law Photog/Assoc Dir* Lee Garmes *Special effects* Slavko Vorkapich *Cast* Claude Rains, Margo, Whitney Bourne, Paula Trueman, Charles Kennedy, Esther Dale *Prod* Paramount. 80 mins.

A "perfect crime" thriller in which a lawyer, Lee Gentry (Rains), murders Carmen Brown (Margo) and suffers the consequences.

Made at the Astoria Studios in New York, where Hecht and MacArthur had hopes of founding a new school of filmmaking to rival Hollywood. Claude Rains (whose only previous film role had been an invisible one in *The Invisible Man*) made an impressive debut as the shyster lawyer who is a pawn of fate, and with the film's success became an established star. It was Margo's first film, though she has appeared in only a handful of films since. Helen Hayes appears as an extra in a hotel lobby.

Slavko Vorkapich devised two of his most famous "montages" for the film. "One of these, dealing with the symbolic unleashing of the Furies, might be cited as a sort of rapid-fire index to the grammar of the film, of what can be accomplished with visual screen technique" (Ezra Goodman).

*CRIMINAL (THE) CONCRETE JUNGLE Britain 1960. *Dir* Joseph Losey *Scen* Alun Owen, Jimmy Sangster, *Photog* Robert Krasker *Ed* Reginald Mills *Mus* Johnny Dankworth *Art Dir* Scott Macgregor *Cast* Stanley Baker, Sam Wanamaker, Margit Saad, Gregoire Aslan, Jill Bennett, Patrick Magee *Prod* Merton Park Studios. 97 mins.

Johnny Bannion (Baker) is released from prison where he has been in conflict with the Chief Warden (Magee). He is met by Mike Carter (Wanamaker), a liaison man with the gang, with whom he plans the robbery of a race track. He falls in love with Suzanne (Saad) and makes a former girl friend (Bennett) jealous. The robbery is successful, Bannion hides the money, but is betrayed and arrested again. Back in prison he learns Carter has Suzanne and bribes Frank Saffron (Aslan) to plan an escape. He tries to rescue Suzanne but Carter shoots him and he dies in the field where the money is hidden.

This is perhaps the quintessential Losey, "a comment on a society that has made money its god and hence imprisoned itself in a vicious circle" (Robin Wood). Losey has commented on his antihero: "Bannion was modeled after someone that I know who is very active in the so-called underworld. And a man who, if his life had taken another direction, could have been a great executive, could have done anything he wanted to, because he has brains, he has humour, he has power . . . And this is what I tried to present in Bannion, that this is waste, that the prison system hasn't changed, that it doesn't help, that it is a reflection of the society outside, that it has its own organisation, its own immediate parallels. It is at once more loyal, more sentimental, more violent, but it's the same thing and one creates the other."

The film is full of memorable sequences: the opening sequence in the prison as Kelly returns; Bannion's apartment and his first meeting with Suzanne; Bannion, dying from gunshot wounds, staggering desperately across the barren field where the money is hidden, and his dread of the afterlife as he dies; the final image of a group of prisoners shuffling around in a circle.

Bannion, a man of intense creative spirit destroyed by the corrupt, deadening forces of society, is brilliantly played by Stanley Baker in his best role.

CRIMINAL LIFE OF ARCHIBALDO DE LA CRUZ (THE) ENSAYO DE UN CRIMEN

CRIMSON CURTAIN (THE) RIDEAU CRAMOISI (LE)

CRIN BLANC, CHEVAL SAUVAGE WHITE MANE/WILD STALLION France 1953. *Dir* Albert Lamorisse *Photog* Edmond Séchan. 47 mins.

The adventures of a small boy and a white horse in the Camargue region of France. Very beautiful photography but rather affected. It was a great commercial success.

CROIX DE BOIS (LES) France 1932. *Dir* Raymond Bernard *Photog* Jules Kruger *Cast* Gabriel Gabrio, Pierre Blanchar, Charles Vanel.

This was entirely produced and acted by war veterans. It was so impressive that in November 1962, 30 years after its production, a veteran of World War I tried to kill himself after seeing it on television.

REMAKE:

— *The Road to Glory* USA 1936. *Dir* Howard Hawks *Scen* William Faulkner, Joel Sayre based on the film by Raymond Bernard *Photog* Gregg Toland *Art Dir* Hans Peters *Mus* Louis Silvers *Ed* Edward Curtis *Cast* Fredric March, Warner Baxter, Lionel Barrymore, Gregory Ratoff, June Lang. 100 mins.

Chauvinistic melodrama palliated by some pleasing performances. There is no relationship between this film and

Hawks's first feature of the same title (1926) which is a romance with May McAvoy, Leslie Fenton and Ford Sterling.

CRONACHE DI POVERI AMANTE Italy 1954. *Dir* Carlo Lizzani *Scen* Amidei, Dagnino, M. Mida, Carlo Lizzani based on the novel by Vasco Pratolini *Photog* Gianni di Venanzo *Mus* Mario Zafred *Cast* Anna-Maria Ferrero, Antonella Lualdi, Marcello Mastroianni, Gabriele Tinti, Cosetta Greco, Adolfo Consolini, 102 mins.

Set in Florence in 1925, the loves of a young man (Tinti), the Fascist raids, and the anti-Fascist fight.

An undeniable achievement that beautifully creates the atmosphere of the original novel. Most of the action centers around the Via del Corno (an old Florentine street) with its blacksmith, Maciste (Consolini), and his young daughters (Ferrero, Lualdi, Greco). The best sequence is "the night of the apocalypse" during which the Blackshirts hunt down and massacre the anti-Fascists, including Maciste.

The production used 1925 fashions intelligently. The film just missed the *Palme d'or* at Cannes but its release was held up by deliberate government interference.

CROSSFIRE USA 1947. *Dir* Edward Dmytryk *Scen* John Paxton based on *The Brick Foxhole* by Richard Brooks *Photog* Roy Hunt *Art Dir* Albert d'Agostino, Alfred Herman *Ed* Harry Gerstad *Cast* Robert Young, Robert Mitchum, Robert Ryan, Gloria Grahame. *Prod* RKO. 86 mins.

During the demobilization period, a group of GI's led by Montgomery (Ryan) murder a Jew but are caught by a patient policeman (Young). (In the original novel, it was a homosexual who was murdered.)

An antiracist polemic that uses the trappings of a thriller, with a typical script, photography, and violence. It is a striking portrait of disturbed demobilized soldiers awaiting an unsure tomorrow. Dmytryk's best film.

CROSSROADS JUJIRO

CROWD (THE) USA 1928. *Dir* King Vidor *Scen* King Vidor, John V. A. Weaver, Harry Behn *Photog* Henry Sharp *Art Dir* Cedric Gibbons, Arnold Gillespie

Ed Hugh Wynn *Cast* James Murray, Eleanor Boardman, Bert Roach, Estelle Clark *Prod* MGM. 98 mins.

The life of an ordinary American (Murray) and his wife (Boardman). King Vidor wrote of this film: "In the opening scenes of *The Crowd* we showed a group of people entering and leaving a large office building in downtown New York; then the camera tilted up framing a design of multitudinous windows and disclosing the great height of the structure. The camera traveled up the building, passing many floors and windows, until it stopped at one floor and moved into one window. Through the window one could discern hundreds of desks and clerks. The camera moved through the window and started an angled descent toward one desk and one clerk — our "hero" concentrating on his monotonous duties. This camera maneuvre was designed to illustrate our theme — one of the mob, one of the crowd . . . "

Under the influence of Murnau, Dupont, Lang, and Lubitsch, King Vidor made much use of the moving camera as an expressive device. Famous sequences: the shabby apartment of the man; his anxious wait for the birth of his son in a hospital with endless corridors; the crowds in the street indifferent to the death of his son; the final scene. But, according to Vidor: "Finally the picture was sent out with two endings, so that the exhibitor could take his choice. The realistic ending showed Murray with his wife in a variety theater, laughing at a clown. Since he managed to enjoy life and therefore conquer it, in this simple and inoffensive way, the camera moved back and up to lose him in the crowd as it had found him. In the course of the narrative he had not made a million dollars or committed a heinous crime, but he had managed to find joy in the face of adversity." The optimistic interpretation offered by the director of the "realistic" ending is not the only one possible. Because the "hero" laughs at a clown dressed up as the kind of out-of-work man he himself had been, he abdicates all human dignity. And, like him, the crowd mocks itself as it is shaken by idiotic laughter. This often bitter film, Vidor's masterpiece, was very courageous in attempting to depict the life of the "little man." It was not, as is often claimed, a commercial failure: it grossed a million dollars, twice its production costs.

CROWS AND SPARROWS China 1949. *Dir* Cheng Chun-li *Scen* Chen Bai-chen, Cheng Chun-li, Chao Tan, Shen Fu, Hsu Tao, Wang Ling-gun *Cast* Chao Tan, Wei Ho-ling, Sun Tao-lin *Prod* Kun Lun Studio, Shanghai. 100 mins., approx.

An excellent satiric portrayal, in an almost neorealistic style, of the last days of the Kuomintang. It shows a greedy landlord, the tenants of a small house, galloping inflation, speculation, and the chaos that preceded the defeat of the Kuomintang in 1949. The film was produced under that regime but was banned. It was finally completed after Mao Tse-tung's victory.

CRUCIFIED LOVERS (THE) CHIKAMATSU MONOGATARI

CRY (THE) GRIDO (IL)

CUBAN LOVE SONG (THE) USA 1931. *Dir* W. S. (Woody) Van Dyke *Scen* C. Gardiner Sullivan, Bess Meredyth, John Colton, Gilbert Emery, Robert E. Hopkins, Paul Hervey Fox *Photog* Harold Rosson *Mus* Herbert Stothart *Cast* Lawrence Tibbett, Lupe Velez, Jimmy Durante, Ernest Torrence, Louise Fazenda, Karen Morley *Prod* MGM. 90 mins.

Based on the then popular song, "Peanut Vendor," this is the story of a young Cuban girl (Velez) in love with a handsome sailor (Tibbett) who deserts her.

Bertolt Brecht, who liked this film, showed it in 1932 to Lily Brik, who recognized in it a story outline from the papers of Mayakovsky. However, according to a 1948 interview with Albert Lewin, the producer, neither he nor his colleagues had ever met Mayakovsky and the original script was written after the poet's death in 1930. The mystery of how Mayakovsky could have written an outline for a film produced many months after his death has never been solved.

*CUBA SI! France 1961. *Dir/Photog* Chris Marker *Mus* E. G. Mantici, J. Calzada *Ed* Eva Zora *Prod* Films de la Pléiade. 58 mins.

"And here is the film which is nearest to my heart, and not merely because it is the last. Shot rapidly in January, 1961, during the first alert period (you know — at the time when the majority of French papers were hooting over Fidel's paranoia in imagining himself threatened with invasion), it aims at communicating, if not the experience, at least the vibrations, the rhythm of a revolution that will one day perhaps be held to be the decisive moment of a whole era of contemporary history. It also aims at countering the monstrous wave of *misinformation* (one has to use the English word, but it will enter the French language, just as the thing itself has entered French life) in the major part of the press. It is interesting that it was the same Minister who tolerated in the press and sanctioned on the radio the most outrageous untruths at the moment of the invasion of April '61, who had the nerve to ban *Cuba Si!* in the name of historical truth, while at the same time casting against the honesty of the film and its author the most ungraceful insinuations. But since it takes two to engage in polemics, I shall not pursue the matter here . . . " (Chris Marker's preface to the script of *Cuba Si!*).

Undoubtedly the best film on the Cuban Revolution and its impact — an eloquent, personal record of history in the making. Perhaps its most typical sequence is that in which, during an interview with Castro, Marker inserts shots from an old Robin Hood film.

*CUL-DE-SAC Britain 1966. *Dir* Roman Polanski *Scen* Roman Polanski, Gerard Brach *Photog* Gilbert Taylor *Art Dir* Voytek *Mus* Komeda *Ed* Alastair McIntyre *Cast* Donald Pleasence, Françoise Dorléac, Lionel Stander, Jack MacGowran, William Franklyn *Prod* Compton/Tekli. 111 mins.

Albert (MacGowran) and Richard (Stander), two wounded gangsters, arrive on an isolated island where Richard forces the middle-aged effeminate owner, George (Pleasence), and his sluttish wife, Teresa (Dorléac), to bury Albert, who has died of his wounds. When some friends arrive, Richard is forced to act as George's manservant. Teresa flirts with Cecil (Franklyn), one of the visitors, and finally George orders all the visitors off the island. When Richard hears from his boss that he is to find his own solution to the predicament, he threatens the couple, but George seizes the gun and shoots him. Cecil reappears and Teresa leaves with him.

Polanski's second film in Britain is a somewhat Pinteresque study in sexual humiliation that at its worst is affected and contrived and at its best matches anything Polanski has done. The key scenes are: that in which Teresa forces George to act out her role in a nightie; the scene where George confesses his obsession with Teresa; and the scene where George discovers the sexual exhilaration of violence when he shoots Richard.

Donald Pleasence's performance as George is a brilliant tour-de-force and Jack MacGowran gives a delightful comic performance in his brief appearance as Albert in the opening scenes. This is a key film to an understanding of Polanski's development.

CUMBRES BORRASCOSAS ABISMOS DE PASIÓN Mexico 1952. *Dir* Luis Buñuel *Scen* Luis Buñuel, Arduino Maiuri, Julio Alejandro based on *Wuthering Heights* by Emily Brontë *Photog* Augustin Jimenez *Art Dir* Edward Fitzgerald *Ed* Carlos Savage *Cast* Irasema Dilian, Jorge Mistral, Lilia Prado *Prod* Tepeyac (Oscar Dancigers). 90 mins.

Buñuel had been anxious to film Brontë's *Wuthering Heights* in 1932. When he finally made it in Mexico 20 years later, it is clear that the action has been transposed to a Spanish-speaking country. Nonetheless, and especially in the last reel (where Heathcliff violates Catherine's tomb), the film conveys a sense of the "abyss of passion" worthy of Emily Brontë.

See also *Wuthering Heights*

CURSE OF THE CAT PEOPLE see CAT PEOPLE

CURSE OF THE DEMON NIGHT OF THE DEMON

CZECH YEAR (THE) SPALICEK

CZLOWIEK NA TORZE MAN ON THE TRACK Poland 1956. *Dir* Andrzej Munk *Scen* Jerzy Stefan Stawinski, Andrzej Munk based on a short story by Stawinski *Photog* Romuald Kropat *Art Dir* Roman Mann *Cast* Kasimierz Opalinski, Zygmunt Maciejewski, Zygmunt Zintel, Zygmunt Listkiewicz *Prod* Kadr. 89 mins.

An old engineer (Opalinski) is held responsible for an accident in which he died, but an investigation proves that in fact he behaved heroically.

"The audience is led to understand the tragedy of an old man in an atmosphere of suspicion that causes him to be considered politically unreliable. The film shows an attitude of the management, based more on presumptions than facts, that is unjust to people who have often suffered a moral and physical downfall" (Brochure for the film.)

This courageous and polemical film is the masterpiece of a young Polish director whose early death was a great loss to the cinema. The story is told in a series of flashbacks from the inquiry held in an atmosphere heavy with suspicion. At the end, when the truth is revealed, someone says: "Open the windows," a gesture that symbolized the end of an error-filled period. Kasimierz Opalinski gives a remarkable performance as the old railway worker.

DALEKA CESTA DISTANT JOURNEY Czechoslovakia 1949. *Dir* Alfred Radok *Scen*
Erik Kolar, Mojmir Drvota, Alfred Radok *Photog* Josef Strecha *Mus* Jiri Stern-
wald *Cast* Blanka Waleska, Otomar
Krejca, Victor Ocasek. 90 mins. approx.
One of the best postwar Czechoslovakian
films. As in the Polish film *Ostatni etap*
(*q.v.*), it describes the daily life in a
concentration camp, though its style is
quite different.
André Bazin said that it was notable for
its complete sparseness and that it was
"overloaded with esthetic references."
But, he added, "surprisingly the most
questionable characteristics of expressionism paradoxically justify themselves
with a new profundity, in a virginal
realism. The elaborate décor, the symbolic high-contrast lighting, the unusual
camera angles, the staginess of certain
scenes — all the devices that one believed
outdated are here used logically to convey the reality of a nightmare. The film
is a return to the world of Kafka, and,
more curiously, to that of de Sade."

DAMA S SOBATCHKOI THE LADY WITH THE
LITTLE DOG USSR 1959. *Dir* Josef Heifitz
Scen Josef Heifitz based on the story by
Chekhov *Photog* Andrei Moskvine, D.
Meschiev *Art Dir* B. Manevitch, I. Kap-
lan *Mus* N. Simonian *Cast* Alexei Batalov, Ya Savvina *Prod* Lenfilm. 90 mins.
In Yalta at the turn of the century, Anna
(Savvina), an unhappily married lady,
meets a married man (Batalov), and they
have an affair. However, after he returns
to Moscow he realizes he is truly in love.
He seeks out Anna and they continue to
meet furtively over the years, attempting
to discover a solution to their dilemma.
This is perhaps the best adaptation of a
Chekhov story. Heifitz beautifully conveys the warmth and understanding of
the original story of a love affair that
seems to hold hope of nothing in the future but unhappiness for both partners.

DAMES DU BOIS DE BOULOGNE (LES) THE
LADIES OF THE BOIS DE BOULOGNE France
1945. *Dir* Robert Bresson *Scen* Robert
Bresson based on a story from Diderot's
Jacques le fataliste Dialogue Jean Cocteau *Photog* Philippe Agostini *Art Dir*
Max Douy *Ed* Jean Feyte *Mus* Jean-
Jacques Grünenwald *Cast* Maria Casarès,
Paul Bernard, Elim Labourdette, Lu-
cienne Bogaert *Prod* Films Raoul Ploquin. 90 mins.
Based on a Diderot story about a jealous
woman (Casarès) who is abandoned by
her lover (Bernard) and who takes revenge on him, with the assistance of
his mother (Bogaert), by making him
marry a semiprostitute (Labourdette).
For his second feature, Bresson used a
Diderot story that he transposed into a
modern period, though he tried to abstract the action from any particular time
and place. Originally the story had been
"a terrible example of a woman's revenge" that forced an aristocrat to marry
a prostitute and who, consequently, could
no longer be received at court nor in
society. Bresson's transposition of the
story to modern times clearly had to lose
the strength of this dramatic device.
The film was produced during the last
months of the German occupation of
France and during the difficult winter
that followed the Liberation. Despite
Bresson's attempt to abstract the theme
of the film from its own time, it reflects
precisely the year it was produced — a
reflection that is not due simply to the
fashions, cars, or "the sound of a windshield wiper against a page of Diderot"
(André Bazin). It was originally to have
been titled "Les Dames du Port-Royal"
(Place Port-Royal, now Place Louvois,
in front of the Bibliothèque Nationale)

and this led to Bresson being accused of "Jansenism."

Two characters dominate the film: Maria Casarès (whose best screen performance this is), spinning her vengeful web in a white setting full of rare furnishings, and Elina Labourdette dancing in her apartment in black stockings and top hat. Alain Cuny had been originally selected to play the nobleman but the producers mistakenly insisted on Paul Bernard for the role. His background in cynical roué roles did not serve him well. Cocteau's dialogue, although it was based on Diderot, is a little too ornate.

André Bazin's criticism of this film is very much to the point: "Bresson has taken the risk of transferring one realistic story into another realistic context. The result is that these two examples of realism destroy each other, the passions displayed emerge out of the characters as if from a chrysalis . . . On the other hand, his stylized treatment of it does not have the pure abstract quality of a symbol. It is rather a dialectic presentation of the concrete and the abstract by a reciprocal interplay of seemingly incompatible elements" (1951).

Les Dames du Bois de Boulogne was a total commercial failure but its reputation has increased over the past twenty years.

DAMNED (THE) MAUDITS (LES) (Clément)

DAMNED (THE) CADUTA DEGLI DEI (LA) (Visconti)

*DAMNED (THE) THESE ARE THE DAMNED Britain 1961. *Dir* Joseph Losey *Scen* Evan Jones based on the novel *The Children of Light* by H. L. Lawrence *Photog* Arthur Grant *Art Dir* Don Mingaye *Design Consultant* Richard MacDonald *Mus* James Bernard *Ed* James Needs, Reginald Mills *Cast* Macdonald Carey, Shirley Ann Field, Viveca Lindfors, Alexander Knox, Oliver Reed *Prod* Hammer/Swallow. 87 mins. Hammerscope.

Somewhere near Weymouth, in a secret project, some children whose mothers have been contaminated by nuclear radiation during their pregnancies are being educated by Bernard (Knox) and the military authorities to take over the world after a nuclear war. An American, Simon (Carey), lands in Weymouth and becomes involved with Joan (Field) and a gang of "teddy boys" led by Joan's

brother, King (Reed). They also meet an artist, Freya (Lindfors), whose studio is on the cliffs near the secret project and who knows Bernard. They accidentally discover the project. The children rebel and Simon, Joan, and King try to rescue them but are fatally affected by the radiation. The children are recaptured by force and Bernard shoots Freya.

Although superficially a science fiction film, and one of Losey's best works, this is much more a moral fable of a world gone insane. Bernard's authoritarianism (though he is a reasonable and decent man) and King's vicious violence are symptoms of the same malaise, while Simon and Joan's abdication of responsibility (until it is too late) are indicative of the kind of society in which Bernard and King can flourish. Only Freya is completely free of viciousness or indifference and, while Simon, Joan, and King destroy themselves, she must be deliberately shot for the project to survive.

DAMSEL IN DISTRESS (A) USA 1937. *Dir* George Stevens *Scen* P. G. Wodehouse, Ernest Pagano, S. K. Lauren based on the novel by P. G. Wodehouse *Mus* George Gershwin *Choreog* Hermes Pan *Cast* Fred Astaire, George Burns, Gracie Allen, Joan Fontaine *Prod* RKO. 100 mins.

A musical comedy based on the novel by P. G. Wodehouse about a peer's daughter who is in love with an American but is dominated by his hostile aunt. One of Fred Astaire's best musicals. Academy Award for Dance Direction, 1937.

OTHER VERSION:
— *USA 1920. *Dir* Albert Capellani *Scen* based on the novel by P. G. Wodehouse *Cast* June Caprice, Creighton Hale, W. H. Thompson, Charlotte Granville *Prod* Pathé.

DANGEROUS MEETINGS (THE) LIAISONS DANGEREUSES 1960 (LES)

DANIEL AND THE DEVIL see FAUST

DARKNESS AT NOON MAHIRU NO ANKOKU

*DARLING . . . Britain 1965. *Dir* John Schlesinger *Scen* Frederic Raphael *Photog* Ken Higgins *Art Dir* Ray Simm *Mus* Johnny Dankworth *Ed* James Clark *Cast* Julie Christie, Dirk Bogarde, Laurence Harvey, Roland Curram *Prod* Vic/Appia. 127 mins.

A pretty, spoiled model, Diana Scott (Christie), recounts the story of her life: her foolish marriage, her love for journalist Robert Gold (Bogarde), with whom she lived, her affair with Miles Brand (Harvey) to further her career, her pregnancy and abortion, and her marriage to a wealthy Italian Prince after Robert rejects her.

Schlesinger's third feature, a slick attack on the affluent society, was a commercial success. Ultimately superficial and pointless, it is more memorable for Julie Christie's performance (which won an Academy Award and made her a star) than for Schlesinger's stylistically modish direction.

DAUGHTERS OF CHINA China 1949. *Dir* Ling Tsu-Feng, Ti-Chiang *Scen* Yen Yi-Yen *Photog* Chien Chiang *Ed* Ming Wei, Lin Yü-Ying *Prod* Northeastern Film Studios. 85 mins.

During the Sino-Japanese War, eight young girls join the partisans and die in battle. Similar to *Chapayev* (*q.v.*), this is a good example of the early postrevolutionary Chinese cinema. [Particularly memorable are scenes showing the life of the partisans, the long march, the two farmers bringing rice to the partisans, and the final scene by the river.]

DAVID AND LISA USA 1962. *Dir* Frank Perry *Scen* Eleanor Perry based on a book by Dr. Theodore Isaac Rubin *Photog* Leonard Hirschfield *Mus* Mark Lawrence *Art Dir* Paul M. Heller *Ed* Irving Oshman *Cast* Keir Dullea, Janet Margolin, Howard da Silva. 94 mins.

Two mental patients, a young man (Dullea) and a young woman (Margolin), fall in love in a psychiatric hospital.

This moving film was produced independently by Paul Heller and was a great success in art houses. It is one of the best films to come from the independent New York school.

DAWN PATROL (THE) THE FLIGHT COMMANDER USA 1930. *Dir* Howard Hawks *Scen* Howard Hawks, Don Totheroh, Seton I. Miller based on *The Flight Commander* by John Monk Saunders *Photog* Ernest Haller, Elmer Dyer (air scenes) *Ed* Ray Curtiss *Cast* Richard Barthelmess, Douglas Fairbanks Jr., Neil Hamilton, Frank McHugh, Clyde Cook *Prod* Howard Hughes for First National. 95 mins.

In 1915 on the French front, the squadron leader (Hamilton) of a group of American volunteer pilots is hated because of the squadron's high death rate. He is replaced by his loudest critic (Barthelmess), who soon discovers the inevitability of death, and then by another leader (Fairbanks).

Howard Hawks (who had been a pilot in the war) drew on his memories and experiences in making this virile and violent film.

REMAKE:

— *USA 1938. *Dir* Edmund Goulding *Scen* as original version *Cast* Errol Flynn, Basil Rathbone, David Niven, Donald Crisp. *Prod* Warners. 103 mins. A glamorized version using the original script and many of the original flying sequences from Hawk's film.

DAYBREAK JOUR SE LÈVE (LE)

DAY IN THE COUNTRY (A) UNE PARTIE DE CAMPAGNE

DAY OF WRATH VREDENS DAG

DAY SHALL DAWN JAGO HUA SAVERA

DAYS OF HOPE ESPOIR

DEAD END USA 1937. *Dir* William Wyler *Scen* Lillian Hellman based on the play by Sidney Kingsley *Photog* Gregg Toland *Art Dir* Richard Day *Mus* Alfred Newman *Ed* Daniel Mandell *Cast* Sylvia Sidney, Joel McCrea, Humphrey Bogart, Claire Trevor, Wendy Barrie and the Dead End Kids (Huntz Hall, Leo Gorcey, Bobby Jordan, Gabriel Dell, Bernard Punsley, Billy Halop) *Prod* Samuel Goldwyn for United Artists. 93 mins.

Crime takes two gangsters, Baby Face Martin (Bogart) and Dave (McCrea), back to the slum district where they were born. With a young girl (Sidney) they lead astray a gang of slum children (Hall, Gorcey, etc).

"(The story) takes place in East Side Manhattan, where the mansions of the big outside world rub shoulders with the slums. A lively script shows us how slum children are led into crime. Six youths (Leo Gorcey, Bobby Jordan, Huntz Hall, Gabriel Dell, Bernard Punsley, and Billy Halop) give an astonishingly natural performance. The publicity pretended that they were all found in the streets and that their appearance as the "Dead End Kids" led to their becoming Hollywood celebrities. One admires in them the 'reflection of a lost childhood' and the 'mark of the gutter' but, in fact, they were all professional actors" (Maurice Lapierre). *Dead End* also offered an affective Sylvia Sidney and Humphrey Bogart performing in the kind of role he was to make his own.

Wyler had intended to shoot the film on location in the New York slums but Goldwyn insisted on the use of studio sets. These were designed by Richard Day (who had worked with Stroheim) and are extremely effective. Gregg Toland's photographic genius was first evidenced in this film.

See also: *Angels With Dirty Faces*

DEAD OF NIGHT Britain 1945. *Dir* Alberto Cavalcanti, Robert Hamer, Charles Crichton, Basil Dearden *Scen* John Baines, Angus McPhail based on stories by H. G. Wells, E. F. Benson, John Baines, Angus McPhail *Photog* Jack Parker, H. Julius *Mus* Georges Auric *Cast* Mervyn Johns, Roland Culver, Anthony Berger, Googie Withers, Sally Ann Howes, Michael Redgrave, Basil Radford *Prod* Ealing Studios. 104 mins.

An omnibus of stories (five episodes plus a linking story) of the supernatural. The linking story (Basil Dearden) describes an architect's series of recurrent dreams. 1. "Hearse Driver" (Basil Dearden) — a driver dreams of an accident and avoids it. 2. "Christmas Party" (Alberto Cavalcanti) — some children meet a young ghost. 3. "Haunted Mirror" (Robert Hamer) — a mirror reveals a past crime to its purchaser. 4. "Golf" (Charles Crichton) — two golf players fight a phantom. 5. "Ventriloquist" — a deranged ventriloquist is at odds with his dummy.

This omnibus of ghost stories is still entertaining, though the best episode is undoubtedly Cavalcanti's "Ventriloquist." Cavalcanti was very much the driving force of this film, which gave Charles Crichton and Robert Hamer their first chance to direct.

DEATH OF A CYCLIST MUERTE DE UN CICLISTA

DEATH OF A SALESMAN USA 1951. *Dir* Laslo Benedek *Scen* Stanley Roberts based on the play by Arthur Miller *Photog* Frank F. Planer *Art Dir* Cary Odell *Mus* Alex North *Ed* William Lyon *Cast* Fredric March, Mildred Dunnock, Kevin McCarthy, Cameron Mitchell *Prod* Stanley Kramer/Columbia. 115 mins.

A traveling salesman (March) loses his job when he reaches sixty. He recalls his past and concludes that, despite his attempts to be a "good guy," life has gone sour for him, that he has not held faith with his wife (Dunnock), and that his two sons (McCarthy, Mitchell) have little regard for him. He commits suicide.

A successful adaptation of Arthur Miller's portrait of the American middle class, notable for its skillful use of flashbacks and Fredric March's faultless performance.

DECORATOR (THE) WORK

DEFIANT ONES (THE) USA 1958. *Dir* Stanley Kramer *Scen* Nathan E. Douglas, Harold Jacob Smith *Photog* Sam Leavitt *Mus* Ernest Gold *Cast* Tony Curtis, Sidney Poitier, Theodore Bikel, Charles McGraw, Lon Chaney, Jr. *Prod* Lomitas-Curtleigh for United Artists. 97 mins.

Two prisoners, one white, John Jackson (Curtis), the other black, Noah Cullen (Poitier), escape but cannot break the chains that bind them. Eventually, their hatred of each other gives way to understanding.

An antiracist polemic, sympathetic and warm, but somewhat too didactic.

DEJA S'ENVOLE LA FLEUR MAIGRE THE FRAIL FLOWERS ARE DISAPPEARING/THE LANK FLOWER HAS ALREADY FLOWN Belgium 1960. *Dir/Scen* Paul Meyer *Photog* Freddy Rents *Ed* Paul Meyer, Rose Tuytschaver *Mus* Arsène Souffriau *Cast* the inhabitants of Flénu. 83 mins.

The difficult life of miners, many of whom are unemployed, in the depression-ridden Borinage district. Its unusual poetry and harsh realism make this the best Belgian feature since 1940.

* DEMANTY NOCI *Diamonds of the Night* Czechoslovakia 1964. *Dir* Jan Nemec *Scen* A. Lustig, Jan Nemec based on a story by Arnost Lustig *Photog* Jaroslav Kucera *Cast* Antonin Kumbera, Ladislav Jansky. 68 mins.

The story of four days in the lives of two young Jewish prisoners (Kumbera, Jansky) who escape from a train during the war. The story is interspersed with visions and dreams evoked by the anguish, hunger, and fear they are living through. Nemec's experiments in intercutting raw, almost journalistic sequences of the hunt for the boys with Kafka-like visions works brilliantly in evoking a constant state of apprehension and an emotional feeling of war — even if the film is occasionally a little self-indulgent. There is virtually no dialogue.

Nemec was 27 when he made this film, having previously made only a short at the Prague Film School.

DEPUTAT BALTIKI THE BALTIC DEPUTY USSR 1937. *Dir* Alexander Zharki, Josef Heifitz *Scen* Zharki, Heifitz, D. Del, Leonid Rakhmanova *Photog* M. Kaplan *Mus* M. Timofeyev *Art Dir* Nikolai Suvorov, V. Kalyagin *Cast* Nikolai Cherkassov, M. Damasheva, A. Melnikov, Oleg Zhakov *Prod* Lenfilm. 100 mins.

In 1917, an old professor (Cherkassov) is rude to a group of starving people but eventually realizes his place is with them and the Revolution. He is elected to the Soviet by the sailors of the Baltic fleet.

Partly based on the biography of the Russian scientist K. A. Timiriazev, this is both an excellent psychological drama of one man and a careful historical reconstruction. This was Cherkassov's first major role and he gives a brilliant portrayal of the 75-year-old professor, though he himself was then only 32.

DERNIERES VACANCES (LES) France 1947. *Dir* Roger Leenhardt *Scen* R. Breuil, Roger Leenhardt *Photog* Philippe Agostini *Art Dir* Léon Barsacq *Mus* Guy Bernard *Ed* Myriam *Cast* Berthe Bovy, Renée Devillers, Pierre Dux, Jean d'Yd, Odile Versois, Michel François. 95 mins.

During a holiday in a country house in the south of France in the Twenties, a boy (François) and a young girl (Versois) who have grown up together discover the first awakenings of adult emotions, while the father (Dux) and the family debate the necessity of selling the family estate and go through their own amorous intrigues.

This was the first of Leenhardt's two features and its nostalgic account of the difficulties in the "verdant paradise of adolescent love" has much of the personal style and feeling of an autobiographical novel. Those attempting to make the *Grand Meaulnes* of the cinema most often fall into the trap of trying to create guileless "poetry" that ends up looking false and absurd. Leenhardt's film is one of the exceptions that proves the rule and has become a minor classic. Though the two young people are the main characters, Leenhardt also creates a striking social portrait of the adults, members of a declining middle class, focused against the background of the somewhat run-down family estate.

Leenhardt did not make his second feature (*Le Rendez-vous de minuit*) until 1961.

DERNIER MILLIARDAIRE (LE) France 1934. *Dir/Scen* René Clair *Photog* Rudolf Maté, Louis Née *Art Dir* Lucien Aguettand, Lucien Carré *Mus* Maurice Jaubert *Ed* Jean Pouzet *Cast* Max Dearly, Renée Saint-Cyr, Marthe Mellot, Raymond Cordy, José Noguero, Paul Olivier *Prod* Pathé-Natan. 90 mins.

With her small principality of Casinario near bankruptcy, the queen (Mellot) arranges a marriage between the princess (Saint-Cyr) and a financier, Banco (Dearly), whom she had made dictator. Banco contracts megalomania and creates havoc at court and with the financial system. The princess elopes with a romantic bandleader (Noguero). Banco is betrothed to the queen then reveals he is not a millionaire.

Because Clair's script was more of a satire on dictatorships than on high finance, the German, Tobis, to whom he was contracted, rejected it. When Clair finally filmed it for Pathé, an extreme right-wing government held power in France. At its premiere in September on the Champs-Elysées, audience reaction was as negative as it was for *La Règle du jeu* five years later. "The somewhat creaking humor of the first half passed in silence, but in the second some whistles could be heard," reported Georges Charensol.

The barter scenes during the economic crisis are the most famous: a customer pays the café with a hen and, receiving two chickens and an egg as change, leaves the egg as a tip. In another scene, a gambler stakes a gun and receives a heap of guns as his winnings.

This satire of dictatorships, financial speculators, and courtly etiquette, though lacking the rhythm and balance of Clair's best work, is still incisive. Max Dearly,

as the financial dictator, gives an excellent performance.
[It was a total failure in France, though it did well in some other countries, notably Japan and the Soviet Union. In Britain, it was re-released during the war as an anti-Fascist film.]

DERNIER TOURNANT (LE) see OSSESSIONE

DESCENDANT OF GHENGIS KHAN (THE) POTOMOK CHINGIS-KHAN

DESERTO ROSSO (IL) THE RED DESERT Italy/France 1964. *Dir* Michelangelo Antonioni *Scen* Michelangelo Antonioni, Tonino Guerra *Photog* Carlo Di Palma *Art Dir* Piero Poletto *Mus* Giovanni Fusco, and electronic music compositions by Vittorio Gelmetti *Ed* Eraldo Da Roma *Cast* Monica Vitti, Richard Harris, Carlo Chionetti *Prod* Film Duemila/Cinematografica Federiz/Francoriz. 116 mins. Eastman Color.
In Raverne, which has become an industrial wasteland, a neurotic young woman (Vitti) married to an engineer (Chionetti) searches in vain for a meaning in life and takes a lover (Harris).
Antonioni has said: "The milieu in which Giuliana lives accelerates the personality's breakdown . . . (but) it isn't the milieu that gives birth to the breakdown; it only makes it show. One may think that outside of this milieu, there is no breakdown. But that's not true. Our life . . . is dominated by 'industry.' And 'industry' shouldn't be understood to mean factories only, but also and above all, products. These products are everywhere, they enter our homes, made of plastics and other materials unknown barely a few years ago; they overtake us wherever we may be. With the help of publicity . . . they obsess us . . . I have gone back to the source of that sort of crisis which, like a torrential river, swelled a thousand tributaries, divides in a thousand arms in order, finally, to submerge everything and spread everywhere."
Antonioni's most accomplished film, if not his best. The personal drama of the heroine is integrated with the plasticity of the setting and with its social implications. The photography is very carefully composed, often reminiscent of abstract art and expressing with brilliant visual sense "the color of the emotions." For the auteur, *The Red Desert* could

be seen as a "bleeding desert, alive, full of the flesh of men".

DESERT WEDDING NOCES DE SABLE (LES)

DESTINY MÜDE TOD (DER)

DESTINY OF A MAN SUDBA CHELOVEKA

DETERMINATION AZIMA (EL)

DETSVO GORKOVO THE CHILDHOOD OF MAXIM GORKY; OUT IN THE WORLD/AMONG PEOPLE; MY UNIVERSITIES (trilogy). USSR 1938–40. *Dir* Mark Donskoy *Scen* Mark Donskoy, I. Gruzdev based on Gorky's memoirs. *Photog* Pyotr Yermolov *Art Dir* I. Stepanov. *Mus* Lev Schwartz *Prod* Soyuzdetfilm.
Part I: *Detsvo Gorkovo/The Childhood of Maxim Gorky* 1938. *Cast* Varvara Massalitinova, M. Troyanovski, Alexei Lyarsky. 101 mins.
Part II: *V lyudyakh/Out in the World/Among People/In the World* 1939. *Cast* Alexei Lyarsky, M. Troyanovski, Varvara Massalitinova. 98 mins.
Part III: *Moi universiteti/My Universities* 1940. *Cast* Y. Valbert, Stepan Kayukov, Nikolai Dorokhin, Lev Sverdlin. 104 mins.
Part I: Little Alexei Peshkov (Lyarsky) is raised by an authoritarian grandfather (Troyanovski), a courageous grandmother (Massalitinova), and two rival uncles. His home makes a strong impression on the young boy who, one day, leaves his grandparents to make his own way in the world.
Part II: Alexei (Lyarsky) works as a servant, then becomes an assistant cook on a transport ship, then an assistant to a painter of icons.
Part III: As a young man (Valbert) unable to study at Kazan, he meets the boatmen of the Volga, the dockers, the workers, the intellectuals, and the revolutionaries, and eventually becomes the writer, Maxim Gorky.
The expression "revolutionary romanticism" applies perfectly to these three very beautiful films whose value is increased by their fidelity to Gorky's original autobiographical works. Those who have visited Nijni-Novgorod (today called Gorky) and the house (now a museum) where the writer spent his childhood, have found the precise atmosphere re-created by Donskoy. His warm yet pitiless depiction of life in

Tsarist Russia is magnificent: the poorly lit, muddy little streets, the drunkards, the brutalities, and the tenderness of the ordinary people. One can almost sense the smell of squalor, rags, cabbage, gherkins, black bread, and vodka. Those who have visited Gorky country are also struck by the tremendous lyrical spirit of the Volga, between the heights to the west and the Tartar Steppes to the east. Donskoy also brings this lyricism to his trilogy, which is his most moving achievement and is, with the *Maxim* trilogy (*q.v.*), among the best Russian films of the Thirties. However, its style is a little jarring and some of the best sequences are separated by less successful episodes.

DEUS E O DIABO NA TERRA DO SOL THE BLACK GOD AND THE WHITE DEVIL Brazil 1964. *Dir/Scen* Glauber Rocha *Photog* Valdemar Lima *Mus* Heitor Villalobos with songs composed and performed by Sergio Ricardo *Ed* Glauber Rocha, Rafael Justo, Valverde *Cast* Iona Magalhães, Geraldo del Rey, Othon Bastos. 102 mins.
In impoverished Northeastern Brazil, a poor peasant changes from a fanatic preacher into a "cangaceiro," a bandit of honor. Everybody is massacred by the big landowners.
Rocha's fourth feature (made when he was 26) introduced *cinema novo* to the outside world and characterized the film makers' concern with the agrarian situation and the "cangaceiro" peasant of barren Northeastern Brazil. The success of the film's violent, yet lyrical, portrait of Brazilian social reality and its personal, almost baroque style made Rocha famous.

DEUX ORPHELINES (LES) see ORPHANS OF THE STORM

DEVDAS
— India 1935. *Dir* Pramathesh Chandra Barua *Scen* Barua based on the novel by Sarat Chandra Chatterjee *Photog* Bimal Roy *Mus* Timir Baran *Cast* Barua (Bengali version); Kundanlal Saigal, Jamuna Devi (Hindi version) *Prod* New Theatres (Calcutta). 12,319 ft.
The life of Devdas, son of a rich man, and his undying love for Parbati.
It appears to have been the greatest success of the New Theatres Ltd. of Calcutta and put Bengali production in the lead in the Indian film industry.

— India 1955. *Dir/Prod* Bimal Roy *Photog* Kamal Bose *Mus* D. S. Burman *Cast* Dilip Kumar, Vyajayanthimala. 95 mins.
Devdas, the hero of the film, is a kind of Hamlet whose resiliency was broken by a deception in his youth. In the very beautiful final sequences, he travels on the trains, hopeless and fatalistic, and dies in a cattle wagon that is carrying him to his true love. There is sometimes the epic feeling of medieval romantic novels in this film, even though its setting is modern.

DEVETI KRUG THE NINTH CIRCLE Yugoslavia 1960. *Dir* France Stiglic *Scen* Zora Dirnbach *Photog* Ivan Marincek *Art Dir* Zeljko Zagota *Ed* Lidija Branis *Cast* Dusica Zegarac, Boris Dvornik *Prod* Jadran Film, Zagreb. 107 mins. (shorter in most foreign release versions).
During the war, a student (Dvornik) loves a young Jewish girl (Zegarac) who is thrown into a concentration camp and then deported.
One of the best works of the young Yugoslav cinema, this film contrasts the lyricism of the young people's love with a powerful portrait of fantastic Nazi atrocities.

DEVIL AND DANIEL WEBSTER (THE) see FAUST

DEVIL AND THE NUN (THE) MATKA JOANNA OL ANIOLOW

DEVIL IN THE FLESH DIABLE AU CORPS (LE)

***DEVIL IS A WOMAN (THE)** USA 1935. *Dir* Josef von Sternberg *Scen* Josef von Sternberg (uncredited), John Dos Passos, S. K. Winston based on *La Femme et le Pantin* by Pierre Louys *Photog* Josef von Sternberg, Lucien Ballard *Art Dir* Josef von Sternberg, Hans Dreier *Mus* Ralph Rainger, Andres Setaro based on Rimski-Korsakov's *Capriccio Espagnol* and Spanish folk songs *Ed* Sam Winston *Cast* Marlene Dietrich, Cesar Romero, Lionel Atwill, Alison Skipworth, Edward Everett Horton *Prod* Paramount. 83 mins.
In Spain at the turn of the century, a beautiful vamp, Concha Perez (Dietrich), captivates an aristocrat, Don Pasqual (Atwill), who protects her but whom she dominates sexually for years. She falls in love with a young man, Antonio

Galvan (Romero), and, after the two men fight a duel, she leaves with him for Paris. But at the border she renounces him and returns to torment Pasqual; both lovers have become her victims.

Sternberg had wanted to call his film "Capriccio Espagnol" but Lubitsch (then head of production at Paramount) rejected both this and the English title of the novel, *The Woman and the Puppet*. Though less indicative of plot, Sternberg's title would have been more fitting: "The integration of the succession of images in the formal sense was extremely accomplished, each sequence having its own rhythmic orientation interrelated with the tempo of the total film. The visual rhythmic qualities were further integrated with the musical score" (Curtis Harrington).

In his autobiography Sternberg wrote: "With the dice loaded so that I could not win, I paid a final tribute to the lady I had seen lean against the wings of a Berlin stage . . . " If *The Devil is a Woman* is a "final tribute" to Dietrich's *femme-fatale* qualities, it is also a successful blending of the decadent romanticism of Pierre Louys's novel and Sternberg's own preoccupations with authoritarianism and personal freedom. Soon after the film's release the Spanish Government objected strongly to certain details, especially those scenes depicting the Guardia Civil. Under threat of a total ban on all Paramount films in Spain, Paramount not only withdrew the film from circulation in Spain, but, in November 1935, pulled the film from general distribution and burned the negative.

The unorthodox qualities of the film infuriated critics and audiences alike in 1935. For many years it had an underground reputation as a "lost" classic. Its recent reappearance in general circulation has only increased its reputation and many now consider it among the most beautiful films ever made.

DEVIL'S ENVOYS (THE) VISITEURS DU SOIR (LES)

DEVIL'S GENERAL (THE) TEUFELS GENERAL (DER)

DEVIL'S WANTON (THE) FÄNGELSE

DEVYAT'DNEY ODNOGO GODA NINE DAYS OF ONE YEAR USSR 1961. *Dir* Mikhail Romm *Scen* Mikhail Romm, Danily Khrabovitsky *Photog* German Lavrov *Art Dir* G. Koltchanov *Ed* D. Tatevsaya *Mus* D. Ter-Tatevosian *Cast* Alexei Batalov, Innokenty Smoktunovsky, T. Lavrova *Prod* Mosfilm. 111 mins.

In an atomic research center a young physicist (Batalov) unquestioningly sacrifices his life and his love (Lavrova) for his research.

Its sincerity and passion, and the freedom with which it discusses major contemporary problems make this Mikhail Romm's best film and one of the best Soviet films of the early Sixties.

Smoktunovsky's slightly cynical speeches are an integral part of his creation of a complex and engaging character.

DHARTI KE LAL CHILDREN OF THE EARTH India 1946. *Dir/Scen* K. A. Abbas *Photog* J. Kapadia *Mus* Ravi Shankar *Cast* nonprofessional actors *Prod* Indian People's Theatre Association.

Tells the story of the terrible Bengal famine of 1943 (in which thousands of people died) which was made worse by greedy landlords who dispossessed peasants unable to pay their debts.

Though often melodramatic, it is memorable for its depiction of the striking contrast between the poverty of the peasants and the luxury in which some Indians continued to live during the famine.

DIABLE AU CORPS (LE) DEVIL IN THE FLESH France 1947. *Dir* Claude Autant-Lara *Scen* Pierre Bost, Jean Aurenche based on the novel by Raymond Radiguet *Photog* Michel Kelber *Art Dir* Max Douy *Mus* René Cloërec *Ed* Madeleine Gug *Cast* Gérard Philipe, Micheline Presle, Jean Debucourt, Denise Grey, Jacques Tati, Richard Francoeur *Prod* Transcontinental-Universal. 110 mins.

During the Armistice celebrations in 1918, François (Philipe), an adolescent, follows Marthe's (Presle) funeral at a distance and recalls (in flashbacks) their tragic love story. He was a college student, she was a young married woman whose husband was away at war. They fell in love, were separated, and she died, alone, giving birth to his child.

Autant-Lara's masterpiece and an important film of the postwar period. Using Radiguet's autobiographical novel set in 1917–18 period, he polemicized against war in general, and expressed many of the sentiments of those who had been adolescents during the Second World War.

It scandalized many who attended the premiere in Bordeaux and the local press wrote: "This production adds the most revolting cynicism to an exaltation of adultery, and ridicules the Family, the Red Cross, as well as the Army. Before this flood of filth gets any further, we demand, in the name of the public, that this ignominious film be removed from the screens." This opinion was shared by the French ambassador to Belgium, who protested and then walked out of the screening when the film was presented at the Brussels Festival. The opposition to it prevented it from winning the Grand Prix, though it did win a well-merited acting award for Gérard Philipe. In Paris many critics agreed in finding the theme "repugnant." Elsewhere, distributors capitalized on the controversy while censors cut or banned it outright.

Famous sequences: the establishment of an ambulance station in a college and the arrival of a group of wounded in April 1917; the meeting between François and Marthe; their first rendezvous on a steamer; a raindrenched François' arrival at Marthe's apartment and their love-making; the lunch in a very elegant restaurant; the armistice celebrations in Harry's Bar, where the pregnant Marthe becomes ill; François' despair in the suburban town as, excluded, he trails behind Marthe's funeral procession while general rejoicing goes on around him.

If the film has a weakness it is perhaps an excessive use of flashbacks and the contrast between the funeral and the armistice celebrations. But its sincerity and compassion are overwhelming. Gérard Philipe justifiably achieved worldwide fame for his performance as François (who was not unlike him) and Micheline Presle confirmed herself as a great actress. Denise Grey and Jean Debucourt are good in cameo roles. Max Douy's sets convey admirably the First World War atmosphere. Michel Kelber's camerawork is excellent and Lebreton's sound track is skillfully constructed, as in the agonized slowing-down of the sound of the church bells to begin each flashback.

DIARY OF A CHAMBERMAID (THE) USA 1945. *Dir* Jean Renoir *Scen* Burgess Meredith based on *Le Journal d'une femme de chambre* by Octave Mirbeau *Photog* Lucien Androit *Art Dir* Eugène Lourié *Mus* Michel Michelet *Ed* James Smith *Cast* Paulette Goddard, Burgess Meredith, Hurd Hatfield *Prod* Burgess Meredith, Benedict Bogeaus for United Artists. 86 mins.

Renoir had dreamed for 10 years of making a film of the Octave Mirbeau novel of the breakdown of French bourgeois society but he shouldn't have made it in Hollywood where he could not re-create the French atmosphere.

See also: *Journal d'une femme de chambre (Le)*

DIARY OF A COUNTRY PRIEST (THE) *Journal d'un curé de campagne (Le)*

DIARY OF A LOST GIRL (THE) TAGEBUCH EINER VERLORENEN

DIES IRAI VREDENS DAG

*DINNER AT EIGHT USA 1933. *Dir* George Cukor *Scen* Frances Marion, Herman J. Mankiewicz based on the play by George S. Kaufman and Edna Ferber *Photog* William Daniels *Ed* Ben Lewis *Art Dir* Frederic Hope, Hobe Edwin *Costumes* Adrian *Cast* Marie Dressler, John Barrymore, Lee Tracy, Wallace Beery, Jean Harlow, Lionel Barrymore, Edmund Lowe, Jean Hersholt, May Robson, Billie Burke, Madge Evans *Prod* MGM. 113 mins.

A social climber, Millicent Jordan (Burke), and her husband (Lionel Barrymore) throw a dinner party. Among the guests are Carlotta Vance (Dressler), a once-famous actress, a self-made industrialist (Beery) and his sluttish wife (Harlow), and a destitute matineé idol, Larry Renault (John Barrymore).

Each of the guests is revealed in a sharp, cynical vignette that exposes the sham and decay of American "high life" during the Depression. The acting, camerawork, and sets are faultless. This is one of Cukor's strongest and most memorable films.

DISGRACE HARAM (EL)

DISTANT JOURNEY DALEKÁ CESTA

DITTE MENNESKEBARN DITTE, CHILD OF MAN Denmark 1946. *Dir* Bjarne Henning-Jensen *Assist Dir* Astrid Henning-

Jensen *Scen* Astrid and Bjarne Henning-Jensen based on the first part of a novel by Martin Andersen Nexö *Photog* Werner Jensen *Art Dir* Kai Rasch *Mus* Herman Koppel *Cast* Tove Maes, Rasmus Ottesen, Karen Poulsen, Karen Lykheus *Prod* Nordisk. 105 mins.

A baby girl is abandoned by an unmarried mother. Later, she becomes a servant and is seduced in her turn by the son of a rich farmer.

Based on a beautiful novel, this film is never melodramatic despite its theme. Apart from Dreyer's *Day of Wrath,* it is the best Danish film of the Forties.

DIVIDE AND CONQUER see WHY WE FIGHT (SERIES)

DIVIDING LINE (THE) LAWLESS (THE)

DIVIDING WALL (THE) Hong Kong 1951. *Dir* Chu Shih-ling *Scen* Win Bay *Cast* Li Chin, Hang Fe, Chang Min. 100 mins. approx.

The arguments and loves of a female schoolteacher (Chang Min), a worker (Hang Fe), and a professor (Li Chin) who share a small room divided into three sections by wooden partitions.

A film of sensitivity, gentleness, and quiet observation (the apple that rolls under the partition, the overloaded bus, the water that fails in the communal toilet). A neorealistic portrait of the housing crisis, superior to de Sica's (then un-made) *Il Tetto.*

DIVORCE, ITALIAN STYLE DIVORZIO ALL'ITALIANA

*****DIVORZIO ALL'ITALIANA** DIVORCE, ITALIAN STYLE Italy 1961. *Dir* Pietro Germi *Scen* Ennio De Concini, Alfredo Giannetti, Pietro Germi *Photog* Leonida Barboni *Mus* Carlo Rustichelli *Art Dir* Carlo Egidi *Ed* Roberto Cinquini *Cast* Marcello Mastroianni, Daniela Rocca, Stefania Sandrelli, Leopoldo Trieste *Prod* Lux/Vides/Galatea. 108 mins.

A Sicilian nobleman, Ferdinando Cefalu (Mastroianni), in love with his cousin Angela (Sandrelli), decides to dispose of his wife Rosalia (Rocca) in a manner appropriate for a society that forbids divorce but is indulgent to crimes of passion. Rosalia's former lover (Trieste) arrives in their home town and Ferdinando pushes them together until finally they run off. Now proved a cuckold in the eyes of the community, he shoots Rosalia, receives only a light sentence as expected, and marries Angela.

Pietro Germi's satire on the Italian divorce laws and aristocracy has a pungency that seems not the less biting in those countries with more enlightened laws. Mastroianni gives one of his best performances in the role of a middle-aged aristocrat so sure of his position and power that he uses other people like pawns in a chess game. The film's deft yet caustic humor is seen best in the scenes where Ferdinando imagines a number of fantastic deaths for his wife, each springing from an ordinary daily situation; in the sequence where Ferdinando, plotting to find a lover for his wife, buys her a new dress and takes her for a walk to see how many stares she still gets from the men; and in the final scene where the aristocrat, having won his young bride, remains so sure of himself that he is unaware she is playing footsie with the boatman. It won an Academy Award for Best Original Screenplay and was voted as one of the Twelve Best Comedy Films of All Time in an international poll of critics in 1967. Its commercial success led to several title imitations.

DIXIEME SYMPHONIE (LA) THE TENTH SYMPHONY France 1918. *Dir/Scen* Abel Gance *Photog* L.-H. Burel *Mus* Michel-Maurice Lévy *Cast* Séverin Mars, Jean Toulout, André Le Faur, Emmy Lynn, Arianne Hugon, Mlle. Nizan *Prod* Le Film d'Art. 4,000 ft.

A composer, Enric Danmor (Mars), who is a widower with a child, Claire (Nizan), marries Eve Dinant (Lynn), who has not told Enric that she had accidentally killed the sister of a former lover, Frederic (Toulout). Frederic blackmails her and courts Claire, while Enric cannot understand Eve's objection to the match and accuses her of being in love with Frederic. He thanks her for the suffering because he says it will be the subject of his next symphony (his 10th). Eventually, Enric discovers the truth and forgives his wife.

"This is a creation. It has character, an idea, an existence. This is a film *by* someone. Everything is in its right place, everything is integrated. The birds, the flowers, the music, the fabrics — what tiny details and what grace. We have the feeling of living intimately with everybody." Delluc, who wrote these words in 1918, avoided, however, referring to the criticism of Gance's misuse of poetic quotations.

Those who have seen the film remember it less for its plot than for its beautiful chiaroscuro photography and its atmosphere. Kevin Brownlow writes: "The visuals are used to create characters, to describe thoughts, to provide metaphors, and not merely to depict incidents."

DO BIGHA ZAMIN TWO ACRES OF LAND India 1953. *Dir* Bimal Roy *Scen* H. Mukherjee based on the story by Salil Chaudhury *Photog* Kamal Bose *Mus* Salil Chaudhury *Ed* H. Mukherjee *Art Dir* Gonesh Basak *Cast* Balraj Sahni, Nirupa Roy *Prod* Bimal Roy Productions. 94 mins. (87 mins. general foreign release).

Ruined by a feudal landowner, an Indian peasant (Balraj Sahni), accompanied by his wife (Nirupa Roy) and their little son, leaves his two acres of land. In Calcutta he finds only slums and poverty and becomes a rickshaw puller, while his son becomes a shoeshine boy and later a thief. The child and his family have various tragic adventures. They return to their village but the landlord has expropriated their land.

One could call this an Indian *Bicycle Thieves* and it is not impossible that neorealism had some influence. However, Bimal Roy was trained in the Thirties by Barau and Debaki Bose of Calcutta, who were themselves interested in portraying social themes. The story is representative of the life of millions of Indians and, though told in a straightforward traditional style, is moving and truthful. One or two romantic episodes are rather pointlessly introduced, as are the numerous songs and dances usual to Indian films. Many of these were deleted from the English release version. The theme music is very beautiful. The film received an award at Cannes in 1954.

DOCKS OF NEW YORK (THE) USA 1928. *Dir* Josef von Sternberg *Scen* Jules Furthman suggested by *The Dock Walloper* by John Monk Saunders *Photog* Harold Rosson *Art Dir* Hans Dreier *Cast* George Bancroft, Betty Compson, Olga Baclanova, Clyde Cook, Gustav von Seyfferitz *Prod* Paramount. 7,200 ft.

A stoker (Bancroft) has one night's leave ashore and rescues a girl (Compson) who has tried to drown herself. They spend the evening together in a dockside bar and, half-drunk, he marries her. Next morning, he starts to return to his ship when the girl is arrested for shooting the third engineer, who had tried to rape her. But the engineer's wife (Baclanova) admits to the crime. The girl tries to persuade her husband to stay but, encouraged by his mate (Cook), he leaves. Back on the ship, he suddenly swims ashore only to find his wife under arrest for possessing stolen clothing. He confesses to the crime, and is sent to jail but he and his wife agree to meet on his release.

Sternberg had clearly been influenced by German *Kammerspiel*. The film's value is mainly in its atmosphere of fog, night, and damp oilskins — a feeling that was to be re-created later in Carné and Prévert's *Quai des brumes* (*q.v.*) and perhaps in some scenes of Pabst's *Dreigroschenoper* (*q.v.*). The photography is superb even if it sometimes seems a little too carefully composed. Betty Compson's face is engaging and Bancroft is robust as the tough stoker.

DR. FAUSTUS see FAUST

DR. JACK USA 1922. *Dir* Fred Newmeyer *Scen* Sam Taylor, Jean Havez *Cast* Harold Lloyd, Mildred Davis, John Prince, Eric Mayne, Normand Hammond *Prod* Rolin for Pathé. 6 reels.

One of Harold Lloyd's first successful features, in which he plays a quack doctor.

DR. MABUSE, THE GAMBLER DOKTOR MABUSE, DER SPIELER

DR. NO see GOLDFINGER

*DR. STRANGELOVE: OR, HOW I LEARNED TO STOP WORRYING AND LOVE THE BOMB Britain 1963. *Dir* Stanley Kubrick *Scen* Stanley Kubrick, Terry Southern, Peter George based on the novel *Red Alert* by Peter George *Photog* Gilbert Taylor *Art Dir* Peter Murton *Special Effects* Wally Veevers *Mus* Laurie Johnson *Ed* Anthony Harvey *Cast* Peter Sellers, George C. Scott, Sterling Hayden, Keenan Wynn, Slim Pickens *Prod* Hawk Films. 94 mins.

Convinced of a Communist plot to demoralize the free world, General Ripper

(Hayden) launches an all-out B-52 attack on the Soviet Union. General Turgidson (Scott) wants to send a second strike but President Muffley (Sellers) offers to help the Russians destroy the planes before the "Doomsday Device" is set off. Meanwhile, land forces attack General Ripper's headquarters and Group Captain Mandrake (Sellers) learns the planes' recall code. All return but one, which, with its radio destroyed, completes its mission. In Washington, the President's adviser, Dr. Strangelove (Sellers), suggests that a few humans might survive in deep shelters. Then the Doomsday weapon is triggered . . .

A bold, sharp, antiwar satire whose humor never gets out of control and collapses into farce, as has happened in so many similar films. The pace of this "nightmare comedy" (Kubrick) is relentless, with superb performances by Peter Sellers (in three roles), Sterling Hayden, and George C. Scott, and brilliant sets by Peter Murton. One of the great films of the Sixties.

DODSKYSSEN THE KISS OF DEATH Sweden 1916. *Dir* Victor Sjöström *Scen* Sam Ask, Victor Sjöström *Photog* Jules Julius (Julius Jaenzon) *Cast* Victor Sjöström, Albin Lavén, Jeny Tschernichin *Prod* Svenska. 1,185 meters.

The engineer, Lebel, is replaced by his double, who tries to steal important plans. A police investigation ends with the discovery of the criminal.

Though not one of Sjöström's great films, it is significant in film history — mainly for a thematic development in which an event is described, through flashbacks, by various witnesses who have different or opposing points of view. Often the characters seem to emerge from darkness while the rear of the sets remain invisible.

DOG'S LIFE (A) USA 1918. *Dir/Scen* Charles Chaplin *Photog* Rollie Totheroh *Cast* Charles Chaplin, Edna Purviance, Chuck Reisner, Henry Bergman, Albert Austin, Tom Wilson, Sidney Chaplin, J. T. Kelly, Billy White *Prod* Chaplin for First National. 2,674 ft.

A tramp (Chaplin) who sleeps in a vacant lot runs afoul of a policeman (Wilson). He tries to get a job but is pushed out of line by the others and arrives at the window only to see it close under his nose. He rescues a little dog, which becomes his faithful friend, and together they steal some sausages from a snackbar owner (Sidney Chaplin). In a cabaret, Charlie meets a pathetic singer (Purviance). Broke, he and the dog return to the vacant lot, where the dog digs up a wallet two crooks had buried (Reisner, Austin). Back in the cabaret, Charlie learns that the girl has been fired and runs into the two crooks, who force him to give up the wallet. By a clever trick he regains the wallet and he and the girl leave the city to live happily with the dog on a little farm.

Louis Delluc described this as "the first complete work of art the cinema has produced."

Famous gags: Charlie, sleeping in the open air in the vacant lot, making a hole in the fence to let in fresh air; Charlie unlacing the boots of the cop who chases him; the line in the employment office where everyone tries to take first place; the dog stealing the sausages while Charlie engages the man's attention; in the cabaret, Charlie trying to hide the dog in his trousers; Charlie putting his hands through the coat of an unconscious man and pretending to make him drink, then stealing the wallet from his accomplice and knocking him out; Charlie planting seeds in a row with his fingers; Charlie and the girl bending over a cradle . . . in which the dog has her puppies.

DOKKOI IKITEIRU AND YET WE LIVE Japan 1951. *Dir* Tadashi Imai *Scen* Kenzo Hirata *Photog* T. Miyajima *Art Dir* Kazuo Kibo *Mus* Masao Oki *Cast* Chojuro Kawaeazaki, Shizue Kawarazaki *Prod* Shinsei. 100 mins. approx.

In postwar Tokyo a day laborer (Chojuro Kawaeazaki) and his wife (Shizue Kawarazaki) and children struggle to reach a living standard above starvation level. They consider collective suicide, but reject it.

Production costs for this independent film were raised by selling shares at leftwing meetings. It is a persuasive and moving portrayal of the life of workers in Japan in the grip of an unemployment crisis and was classed among the Ten Best Films of 1951 by the Japanese critics. However, despite what some critics have written, the film bears little resemblance to *Bicycle Thieves* and Italian neorealism.

DR MABUSE, DER SPIELER DR. MABUSE, THE GAMBLER (Part I: *Der Grosse Spieler;* Part II: *Inferno*) Germany 1922. *Dir* Fritz Lang *Scen* Thea von Harbou, Fritz Lang based on the novel by Norbert Jacques *Photog* Carl Hoffman *Art Dir* Otto Hunte, Stahl-Urach, Erich Kettelhut, Karl Vollbrecht *Cast* Rudolf Klein-Rogge, Alfred Abel, Gertrude Welcker, Lil Dagover, Paul Richter, Bernhard Goetzke, Aud Egede-Nissen *Prod* Ullstein-Uco Films. Part I: 3,496 meters; Part II: 2,560 meters. (Released in the USA and Britain in one part, 9,200 ft.) The evil machinations of the criminal mastermind, Dr. Mabuse (Klein-Rogge), are suspected only by Dr. Wenk (Goetzke), the public prosecutor, assisted by the Countess Told (Welcker), the wife of a millionaire. Mabuse abducts the Countess, systematically ruins her husband (Abel) in gambling, then orders his mistress (Dagover) to seduce him. When she is jailed, he orders her to poison herself. After Mabuse has made two unsuccessful attempts on Wenk's life, he finally hypnotizes him into a suicidal state. But the police intervene in time and, led by Wenk, storm Mabuse's house, free the Countess, and discover Mabuse, a raving maniac, in the cellars.

"The world it pictures has fallen prey to lawlessness and depravity. A nightclub dancer performs in a décor composed of outright sex symbols. Orgies are an institution, homosexuals and prostitute children are everyday characters. The anarchy smoldering in this world manifests itself clearly in the admirably handled episode of the police attack on Mabuse's house — an episode that through its imagery intentionally recalls the tumultuous postwar months with their street fights between Spartacus and Noske troops" (Kracauer). As was not uncommon, the foreign release versions were different from the original. In the Soviet version, which was edited by Eisenstein and Ester Shub, the fighting in the streets was changed into scenes of rebellion.

— Das Testament von Dr. Mabuse/The Last Will of Dr. Mabuse Germany 1933. *Dir* Fritz Lang *Scen* Thea von Harbou, Fritz Lang *Art Dir* Karl Vollbrecht, Emil Hassler *Photog* Fritz Arno Wagner *Cast German version* R. Klein-Rogge, Otto Wernicke, Gustav Diesl, Karl Meixner *French version* R. Klein-Rogge, Jim Gérald, Thomy Bourdelle, Daniel Mendaille, René Ferté, Karl Meixner *Prod* Nero. 122 mins.

Mabuse (Klein-Rogge), an inmate in a lunatic asylum, hypnotizes Baum (Meixner), the head of the asylum, and orders him to carry out his directions. Under Mabuse's guidance, he heads an underworld organization that covers the whole field of crime. When Mabuse dies, Baum believes himself to be a reincarnation of Mabuse. Chief Inspector Lohmann (Wernicke) discovers the plot and tracks him down. Baum flees into Mabuse's former cell where his own madness becomes obvious.

When the film reached New York in 1943, Lang wrote a "Screen Foreword" about his intentions: "This film was made to denounce the terrorist methods of Hitler. Slogans and doctrines of the Third Reich have been put into the mouths of criminals in the film." Mabuse declares in the film: "It is necessary to terrorize people until, losing confidence in the State, they ask us for help. Mankind must be thrown into an abyss of terror." The film was banned by Goebbels, March 24, 1933, and Fritz Lang (whose *Nibelungen* (*q.v.*) Hitler had admired) decided to leave the country after refusing the position of artistic director of UFA. However, his wife and the film's co-scenarist, Thea von Harbou, was already a member of the Nazi party and remained behind. One is perhaps tempted to ask oneself if the political interpretation of a thriller whose theme was much the same as the earlier *Dr. Mabuse* was not invented with the advantage of hindsight. Its style, photography, and sets are remarkable but, even if one admits its anti-Nazi theme, it is inferior to *M*.

— Die 1000 Augen des Dr. Mabuse/The Thousand Eyes of Dr. Mabuse German Federal Republic/Italy/France 1960. *Dir* Fritz Lang *Scen* Fritz Lang, Heinz Otto Wuttig *Photog* Karl Löb *Art Dir* Erich Kettelhut, Johannes Ott *Cast* Gert Fröbe, Dawn Addams, Peter van Eyck, Howard Vernon, Wolfgang Preiss. 103 mins.

A detective (Fröbe) investigates various mysterious crimes in a palace where a millionaire (Van Eyck) has saved an American girl (Addams) from suicide. After an investigation, a car chase, and the discovery of the thousand secret eyes of a television set, Mabuse (Preiss), son of the original mastermind, is unmasked and killed.

It is rather touching that a great director should return 30 years later to his most famous character. The film is pleasing in its simplicity but has none of the rewards of the two earlier films.

— *Die Unsichtbaren Krallen des Dr. Mabuse/The Invisible Dr. Mabuse* German Federal Republic 1961. *Dir* Harald Reinl *Cast* Lex Barker, Karin Dor.

— *Im Stahtnetz des Dr. Mabuse/The Return of Dr. Mabuse* German Federal Republic/Italy/France 1961. *Dir* Harald Reinl *Cast* Gert Fröbe, Wolfgang Preiss. Both the above are distressingly simplistic thrillers using the Mabuse character and are in no way comparable to any of the Lang films.

DOLCE VITA (LA) THE SWEET LIFE Italy/France 1960. *Dir* Federico Fellini *Scen* Federico Fellini, Tullio Pinelli, Ennio Flaiano, Brunello Rondi *Photog* Otello Martelli *Art Dir* Piero Gherardi *Mus* Nino Rota *Ed* Leo Cattozo *Cast* Marcello Mastroianni, Anita Ekberg, Anouk Aímée, Yvonne Furneaux, Alain Cuny, Magali Noël, Nadia Gray *Prod* Riama Film/Pathé Consortium. 173 mins. Totalscope.

The life of a journalist and press agent (Mastroianni) as he mixes with the film world and high life in Rome. Notable sequences: the statue of Christ flown by helicopter over the Eternal City: the arrival of the star (Ekberg), trailed everywhere by photographers, and her visit to Saint Peter's in religious garments; the miracle in a small town and the resultant publicity; the orgy in a nightclub; the abortive suicide of the journalist's girl friend; their scenes together in the apartment; the evening at the home of the philosopher Steiner (Cuny), who fears suicide; the night spent in the palace of a decadent aristocratic family; the orgy in the villa; the journalist finding an enormous dead fish on a beach where he also meets an innocent young girl.

One could criticize this film for its anarchy and grandiloquence but there are many episodes and images that cannot be easily forgotten. Anita Ekberg is all bubbling femininity while Mastroianni conveys the restless bitterness of a man who has "made it" but isn't sure if it's what he wants.

DOLINA MIRU THE VALLEY OF PEACE Yugoslavia 1956. *Dir* France Stiglic *Scen* Ivan Ribic *Photog* Rudi Vavpotic *Art Dir* Ivan Spinic *Cast* John Kitzmuller, Eveline Wohlfeiler, Tugomir Stiglic *Prod* Triglav-Film. 90 mins.

To avoid being deported during the war, two children (Stiglic, Wohlfeiler) escape and meet a black American parachutist (Kitzmuller), who dies to save them. Quietly successful film by an excellent Slovakian director.

DOM NA TRUBNOI THE HOUSE ON TRUBNAYA SQUARE USSR 1928. *Dir* Boris Barnet *Scen* B. Zorich, Anatoli Marienhof, V. Shershenevich, Victor Shklovsky, N. Erdman *Photog* Yevgeni Alexeyev *Art Dir* Sergei Kozlovsky *Cast* Vera Maretskaya, Vladimir Fogel, V. Batalov *Prod* Mezhrabpom-Russ. 1,757 meters.

A peasant girl, Parasha (Maretskaya), becomes a servant in a house on Trubnaya Square in Moscow, the home of a close friend (Batalov). She gets involved in the tangled relations of the occupants, including a hairdresser (Fogel), participates in the municipal election, and forms a trade union.

A comedy of manners and a gentle satire on contemporary everyday life in Moscow at the time of the New Economic Policy. This was Vera Maretskaya's first major role and Vladimir Fogel's (*By the Law, Bed and Sofa*) last: he died less than a year after the film was completed.

DONALD AND PLUTO USA 1936. *Dir/Prod* Walt Disney. 1 reel.

One of the best of the brilliant *Donald Duck* series in which Donald is a plumber. Pluto swallows a magnet during lunch and attracts all kinds of metallic objects. While the overall career of Disney may be open to criticism, one must admire this fountain of perfectly timed gags. Chuck Jones and Tex Avery were probably influenced by this film and some of the earlier ones.

See also *Mickey Mouse* series

DON Q, SON OF ZORRO see MARK OF ZORRO (THE)

DON QUICHOTTE DON QUIXOTE France 1933. *Dir* G. W. Pabst *Scen* Paul Morand, Alexandre Arnoux based on Cervantes' novel. *Photog* Nikolas Farkas, Paul Portier *Art Dir* Andrei Andreiev *Ed* Hans Oser *Mus* Jacques Ibert *Cast* (*French version*): Fédor Chaliapine, Dorville, Mady Berry, Arlette Marchal;

(*British version*): Fédor Chaliapine, George Robey, Sidney Fox. *Prod* Vandor-Nelson-Wester. 82 mins.
Though a highly polished film with beautiful photography (shot in Haute-Provence) and the singer Chaliapine, it lacks warmth. Especially memorable are: the tilting at the windmills, the burning of the books of chivalry, and the rescue of the convicts.
See also *Don Quixote*

DON QUIXOTE USSR 1957. *Dir* Grigori Kozintsev *Scen* E Schwartz based on Cervantes' novel *Photog* Andrei Moskvin, Apollinari Dudko *Art Dir* Yevgeny Yenei *Mus* Kara-Karayev *Ed* E. Manhankov *Cast* Nikolai Cherkassov, Yuri Tolubeyev, T. Agamirova, S. Birman *Prod* Lenfilm. 105 mins. Agfacolor. SovScope.
Undoubtedly the best version of the novel. Kozintsev re-creates in the Crimea a real feeling of the dramatic barrenness of the Spanish plateaus and a sense of the best Velasquez, as in the scene where Sancho is named governor.
OTHER VERSIONS:
— *Don Quichotte* France 1902. *Dir* Ferdinand Zecca (?) 430 meters.
— *Don Quichotte* France 1908. *Dir* Emile Cohl. Animated film.
— **Incident from Don Quixote* France 1908. *Dir* Georges Méliès (?)
— **Don Chisciotte* Italy 1910. *Prod* Cines.
— *Don Quichotte* France 1911. *Dir* Camille de Morlhon. *Cast* C. Garry.
— *Don Quixote* USA 1915. *Dir* Edward Dillon *Cast* DeWolf Hopper, Max Davidson, 5 reels.
— **Don Quixote* Britain 1923. *Dir* Maurice Elvey. *Cast* George Robey, Jerrold Robertshaw.
— *Don Quixote* Denmark 1926. *Dir* Lau Lauritzen *Cast* Carl Schenstrøm, Harald Madsen.
Don Quixote USA 1934. *Dir* Ub Iwerks. 1 reel. color.
— **Don Quijote de la Mancha* Spain 1947. *Dir* Rafael Gil *Cast* Rafael Rivellos, Juan Calvo.
See also *Don Quichotte*.

*DONZOKO THE LOWER DEPTHS Japan 1957. *Dir* Akira Kurosawa *Scen* Hideo Oguni, Shinobu Hashmotu, Akira Kurosawa based on the play by Maxim Gorky *Photog* Ichio Yamasaki *Cast* Toshiro Mifune, Kyoko Kagawa, Isuzu Yamada *Prod* Toho. 125 mins.

An adaptation of Gorky's play in an unusual setting — Edo during the last days of the Tokugawa period. "The cast and crew, with lights, full costume, make-up, and camera positions, rehearsed for forty days before the actual shooting . . . there were no leading characters, the film being entirely a series of vignettes. One of the most important results was an ensemble effect rare on the screen, an acting unit, one part very carefully balanced against the other. Another result was that the film had real style, a consistent set of rules governing characters, camera movements, formal composition and editing" (Donald Richie, Joseph Anderson).
See also *Bas-Fonds (Les)*

DOOMED IKIRU

DOORS OF NIGHT (THE) PORTES DE LA NUIT (LES)

DORGOI TSENOI AT GREAT COST/AT RISK OF LIFE USSR 1957. *Dir* Mark Donskoy *Scen* Irina Donskaya based on works by Kotsubinsky *Photog* N. Topchi *Art Dir* N. Reznik *Mus* Lev Schwartz *Cast* Vera Donskaya, Yuri Dedovich, Olga Petrova *Prod* Dovzhenko Studios, Kiev. 99 mins. Sovcolor.
About 1830, the Ukrainians hold the frontier pass to Bessarabia with the help of some gypsies.
This is considered as Donskoy's masterpiece by those of his admirers who unconditionally follow the *auteur* theory.

*DOUBLE INDEMNITY USA 1944. *Dir* Billy Wilder *Scen* Raymond Chandler, Billy Wilder based on the novel by James M. Cain *Photog* John Seitz *Mus* Miklos Rozsa *Ed* Doane Harrison *Cast* Barbara Stanwyck, Fred MacMurray, Edward G. Robinson, Tom Powers *Prod* Paramount. 106 mins.
An insurance agent, Walter Neff (MacMurray), is seduced by a blonde *femme-fatale*, Phyllis Dietrichson (Stanwyck), in order to gain his help in disposing of her husband (Powers) for the "double indemnity" insurance money. Infatuated, he agrees; they work out a complicated scheme and the husband dies. However, their scheme misfires and an investigator (Robinson) discovers them.
This is perhaps the best example of the Hollywood *film noir* of the Forties — a pitiless study of human greed, sex, and

sadism. Since Raymond Chandler persuaded Wilder that Cain's dialogue needed reworking, the film's ambience, tartness, and cynicism owe more to Chandler and Wilder than to the original novel. The sound track is effectively used, as in the scene where the car stalls after the husband's murder. Superb performances by the three leads, though Stanwyck's blonde seductress now seems a little dated.

DOUCE LOVE STORY France 1943. *Dir* Claude Autant-Lara *Scen* Pierre Bost, Jean Aurenche *Photog* Philippe Agostini *Art Dir* Jacques Kraus *Mus* René Cloërec *Costumes* Claude Autant-Lara *Cast* Odette Joyeux, Madeleine Robinson, Marguerite Moreno, Jean Debucourt, Roger Pigaut *Prod* Société Parisienne de l'Industrie Cinématographique. 106 mins. In 1888, a young woman (Joyeux) from a good family falls in love with a man (Pigaut) who is not of her social position and provokes the opposition of her family (Moreno, Debucourt).
Based on a novel, this is a powerful satire of the French bourgeoisie, despite a happy ending imposed by the producers. It is also Autant-Lara's first important film.

DRACOS (O) Greece 1956. *Dir* Nikos Koundouros *Scen* Iacovos Campanellis *Photog* Costas Théodoridis *Mus* Manos Hadjidakis *Cast* Margarita Papayeorghiou, Dinos Iliopoulos. 90 mins. approx.
A worker (Iliopoulos) runs away because he is the double of a gangster known as the "Beast of Athens." He is mistaken for him in the underworld, arrested, and finally killed in a fight.
"A great film that owes nothing to anybody, full of surprising discoveries, rich and involved, integrating all the details of the action in a breathtaking rhythm. The frenzy of the action is intensified by the forcefulness of the editing" (Gilbert Salachas).

*DRACULA USA 1931. *Dir* Tod Browning *Scen* Garrett Fort based on the novel by Bram Stoker and the play by John Balderston and Hamilton Deane *Photog* Karl Freund *Ed* Milton Carruth *Cast* Bela Lugosi, David Manners, Helen Chandler, Dwight Frye, Edward Van Sloan, Frances Dade *Prod* Universal. 84 mins.
This version of the story of a vampire who moves from his castle in the Carpathian mountains to terrorize the civilized world is one of those rare films that created its own myth and led to the establishment of the screen's perhaps best-known legendary character. Browning based his script on the successful play by Balderston and Deane rather than on the original novel and the film's stage origins are all too obvious when the main plot begins to develop in London. However, Bela Lugosi's embodiment (there is no other word) of the terrible Count Dracula is so complete that the film still retains much of its power. His ominous "I am — Dracula" has become perhaps the most famous phrase in the horror genre. The film was a great commercial success and still ranks as one of Universal's biggest money makers.
OTHER VERSIONS:
— **Dracula/The Horror of Dracula* Britain 1958. *Dir* Terence Fisher *Cast* Peter Cushing, Christopher Lee *Prod* Hammer. 82 mins. Technicolor.
— **Dracula, Prince of Darkness* Britain 1965. *Dir* Terence Fisher *Cast* Christopher Lee, Barbara Shelley, Andrew Keir *Prod* Hammer 90 mins. Technicolor. Techniscope.
— **Dracula Has Risen from the Grave* Britain 1969. *Dir* Freddie Francis *Cast* Christopher Lee, Rupert Davies, Veronica Carlson *Prod* Hammer. 92 mins. Technicolor
— **and many others using the Dracula character, e.g., *Dracula's Daughter* (USA 1936), *Return of the Vampire* (USA 1944), *The House of Dracula* (USA 1946), *The Return of Dracula* (USA 1958), *Billy the Kid Meets Dracula* (USA 1965), *The Fearless Vampire Killers* (USA 1967), etc.
See also *Nosferatu*

DREAM OF A COSSACK KAVALER ZOLOTOI ZVEZDY

DREAMS KVINNODRÖM

DREIGROSCHENOPER (DIE) L'OPÉRA DE QUAT'SOUS/THREE-PENNY OPERA Germany 1931. *Dir* G. W. Pabst *Scen* Belà Balàsz, Ladislao Vajda, Leo Lania based on the play by Bertolt Brecht, freely adapted from *The Beggar's Opera* by John Gay (1728) *Photog* Fritz-Arno Wagner *Art Dir* Andrei Andreiev *Mus* Kurt Weill (arranged Theo Mackeben) *Ed* Hans Oser *Cast German version:* Rudolf Forster, Carola Neher, Valeska Gert, Reinold Schünzel, Fritz Rasp, Lotte Lenja, Herman Thimig, Ernst Busch, Vladimir Sokoloff *French version:* Albert Préjean, Odette Florelle, Gaston Modot, Margo Lion, Jacques Henley, Vladimir Sokoloff *Prod* Warners-First National/Tobis/Nero-Film. 114 mins.

In London at the turn of the century, the best friend of a police chief, the bandit Mack the Knife (Forster/Préjean) marries Polly (Neher/Florelle) without the knowledge of her father, Peachum (Sokoloff), the "king of the beggars." Furious, he provokes a demonstration of beggars against the Queen. Betrayed by Jenny (Lenja/Lion), Mack is arrested. Polly helps him escape after she has established a prosperous bank, in the running of which the three men are reconciled.

The play, freely based on John Gay's *The Beggar's Opera* (1728), was written in Berlin in 1928 and made Bertolt Brecht famous. He disapproved of the film adaptation so strongly that (with Kurt Weill) he sued the producers for altering the content of his work, but lost the case.

Despite Brecht's opposition, Pabst's film is an important work and, though its satire is less astringent than Brecht's, its social polemic equating bandits, police, and bankers remains potent. The Hungarian censor banned the film as "vulgar, ugly, obscene, serving not human culture but revolutions and revolt". In 1940 the German actress who played Polly, Carola Neher, was shot by Hitler. The planned English version was never produced.

Famous sequences: Mack in Jenny's Victorian bordello; the meeting with Flora; the burglary of the shops for the wedding; decorating a dusty hall with elegant furniture; the establishment of the bank; the beggars' demonstration against the Queen, despite the opposition of their "king," Peachum (an extraordinary effect created with a small number of extras).

However, the most memorable aspects of the film are the songs of Kurt Weill and the atmosphere created by the cameraman Fritz-Arno Wagner and the art director Andrei Andreiev. "(They) contrived to clothe everything in chiaroscuro and mist, making the brick walls of the Thames-side docks and Soho slums both real and fantastic at the same time. Swirls of dust and smoke wreath the dwellings of the beggar king and cling to the bare walls . . . and hover in the nuptial shed on the docks, softening the splendor of the tables brimming with fruit and silverware amid the reflections of the gentle candlelight . . . The encounter of the renaissance of Impressionism and the waning of the Expressionism is a happy one . . . It is seen here in the gaudy shots of the brothel, with its Victorian lushness confined in plushness and drapery and its *fin-de-siècle* statue of a negress. In this black and white film, the provocative déshabillés with Edwardian-style corsets, Caligari-ish light-colored gloves with black ribbing and bespatted boots, do even more to heighten the impression of color" (Lotte Eisner).

OTHER VERSIONS:

— German Federal Republic/France 1962. *Dir* Wolfgang Staudte *Cast* Curt Jürgens, Gert Fröbe, Hildegard Knef, Sammy Davis Jnr. 124 mins.

DREI VON DER TANKSTELLE (DIE) THE THREE OF THE FILLING STATION Germany 1930. *Dir* Wilhelm Thiele *Scen* Franz Schulz, Paul Frank *Photog* Franz Planer *Mus* Werner R. Heymann *Cast* Lilian Harvey, Willy Fritsch, Oscar Karlweis, Heinz Rühmann, Olga Tchekhova *Prod* UFA. 80 mins.

Three young penniless men become service station attendants and find happiness and love as they sell gas.

A somewhat ordinary, but lively, operetta with catchy songs that made the sparkling and delicate Lilian Harvey an international star.

REMAKE:

— *Die Drei von der Tankstelle* German Federal Republic 1955. *Dir* Hans Wolff *Supervisor* Willi Forst *Cast* Willy Fritsch, Walter Giller, Hilde Hildebrandt, Wolfgang Neuss, Claude Farell, Rudolf Vogel, Adrian Hoven. 93 mins. Eastman Color.

DREYFUS see AFFAIRE DREYFUS (L')

*DRIFTERS Britain 1929. *Dir/Ed* John Grierson *Photog* Basil Emmott *Prod* New Era for Empire Marketing Board. 3,631 ft.

This story of the North Sea herring fisheries was filmed in the Shetlands, at Lowestoft and Yarmouth, and in the North Sea. It is one of the few films that Grierson personally directed but its influence on the development of the British documentary school of the Thirties was profound. Roger Manvell wrote: "In the opinion of many of those present at the original performance, the excitement it aroused overshadowed the reception of Eisenstein's *Potemkin* . . . *Drifters* arrested the current tendency towards a non-functional artiness in theme or style." Its impact at the time is easy to accept: the British cinema was studio-bound and a film that drew its drama at first hand from real life was revolutionary.

Grierson had studied the work of Russian directors and he applied the principles of dynamic editing and structure to *Drifters*. Writing of the film later, Grierson said: "What seemed possible of development was the integration of imagery with movement . . . In other words, the shots were massed together, not only for description and tempo, but for commentary on it. One felt involved by the tough, continuing, upstanding labour involved, and the feeling shaped the images, determined the background, and supplied the extra details which gave colour to the whole."

DRONES (THE) VITELLONI (I)

DROUGHT VIDAS SECAS

DUBARRY see MADAME DU BARRY

DUBARRY WAS A LADY see MADAME DU BARRY

DUBARRY — WOMAN OF PASSION see MADAME DU BARRY

DUCK SOUP USA 1933. *Dir* Leo McCarey *Scen* Bert Kalmar, Harry Rubin *Additional dialogue* Arthur Sheekman, Nat Perrin *Photog* Henry Sharp *Art Dir* Hans Dreier, Wiard B. Ihnen *Ed* Leroy Stone *Mus* Bert Kalmar, Harry Rubin *Cast* Groucho, Harpo, Chico and Zeppo Marx, Margaret Dumont, Louis Calhern, Raquel Torres *Prod* Paramount. 70 mins.
The Marx Brothers' most striking film is a satire on fascism and war. The director, Leo McCarey, does not seem to have had strong feelings about these so it might be assumed that the Marx Brothers themselves were responsible, with McCarey being only technically the director.
Famous gags: a unanimous Parliament, dancing and singing to opera tunes and blues, including "All God's chillun got guns"; Harpo taking a blow torch from

his pocket or using his scissors to cut cigars, sausages, hair, ties, coat tails, etc; Harpo doing a Paul Revere act and seducing a beautiful woman, after which one sees first, a pair of high-heeled shoes, then Harpo's boots, and, finally, a set of horseshoes; Harpo paddling in a container of lemonade; the shells flying through the window during the battle until Groucho pulls down the blinds; the motorcycle and sidecar that serve as President Groucho's transportation — at one time the motorcycle alone moves, the next only the sidecar; Groucho's call for the world to send help, which brings a runner, swimmers, rowers, elephants, giraffes, gorillas, dolphins, etc; the millionairess (Dumont) constantly baffled by Groucho; the scene before the false mirror in which Groucho finds first one then two reflections of "himself" in white nightgown and nightcap; the entry of the new president heralded by trumpets, girls throwing flowers, guards with raised swords, and Groucho sliding down a fire pole from upstairs and asking, "Who are we waiting for?"
The first part of the film is somewhat weak but the rhythm of the film mounts to a crescendo and the battle in the finale can only be described as inspired.

*DUEL IN THE SUN USA 1946. *Dir* King Vidor *Scen* David O. Selznick, Oliver H. P. Garrett suggested by the novel by Niven Busch *Photog* Lee Garmes, Hal Rosson, Ray Rennahan *Art Dir* James Basevi *Mus* Dimitri Tiomkin *Ed* Hal C. Kern *2nd Unit Dir* B. Reaves Eason, Otto Brower *Cast* Jennifer Jones, Gregory Peck, Joseph Cotten, Lionel Barrymore, Herbert Marshall, Lillian Gish, Walter Huston, Charles Bickford, Tilly Losch *Prod* Selznick. 138 mins. Technicolor.
Lewt (Peck) and Jesse (Cotten) live with their father, Senator McCanles (Barrymore), and his wife Laurabelle (Gish) on the senator's Texas ranch. After a quarrel with her father (Marshall), Pearl Chavez (Jones), a half-breed relative of Laurabelle's, goes to live with them. Lewt seduces Pearl and, to prevent his murderous designs on Jesse, Pearl shoots her lover and kills herself.
A grandiose, passionate, spectacular adaptation of a bestselling novel that David Selznick intended as a tribute to his wife, Jennifer Jones, and which he hoped would become the *Gone With the Wind*

of the Forties. He was eminently successful in all his aims.

Josef von Sternberg and William Dieterle assisted King Vidor in the direction, with Dieterle, in particular, being responsible for the sensual dance scene by Pearl's mother (Tilly Losch). However, Vidor directed most of the film and there is no doubt he found himself again in the splendid plastic style and touches of cruelty. This was his best film for many years.

DUE ORFANELLE (LE) see ORPHANS OF THE STORM

DUE SOLDI DI SPERANZA TWO CENTS WORTH OF HOPE/TWO PENNY WORTH OF HOPE Italy 1952. *Dir* Renato Castellani *Scen* Renato Castellani, Titina de Filippo from a story by Castellani and M. Margadonna *Photog* Arturo Gallea *Mus* Alessandro Cicognini *Ed* Yolanda Benevenuti *Cast* Vincenzo Musolino, Maria Fiore, Filomeno Russo *Prod* Universalcine. 98 mins.

A worker (Musolino) becomes a chauffeur, a lemonade seller, a sexton, a bill poster, and a blood donor, and ends by marrying Carmela (Fiore). Notable sequences: the unemployed waiting in the square; the old country motorbus; the small cinema in Naples and blood sold for a small fee; the accidental fireworks; the boy undressing his fiancée in the square shouting "I only want you naked as your mother made you."

The story was told to the scriptwriters by Vincenzo Musolino. The other actors were all nonprofessionals selected from the people of Bostrecase. Marie-Claire Solleville has described this district: "The houses are hovels, water is scarce, the wells are sour. There isn't a youngster or an old one who does not have bugs and lice in plenty. The women come and plead with us: 'Madam, I have 15 children, give me work' — 'But what of your husband?' — 'He has been unemployed for a long time.' "

On the basis of this tragic poverty, Castellani built a picaresque film, though its picturesque qualities are often somewhat condescending. It is Castellani's best film but its qualities were exaggerated after it received a Grand Prix at Cannes.

DURA LEX PO ZAKONU

DU RIFIFI CHEZ LES HOMMES RIFIFI/RIFIFI SPELLS TROUBLE France 1955. *Dir* Jules Dassin *Scen* René Wheeler, Jules Dassin, Auguste le Breton from a novel by Auguste le Breton *Photog* Philippe Agostini *Art Dir* Auguste Capelier *Mus* Georges Auric *Ed* Roger Dwyre *Cast* Jean Servais, Carl Mohner, Robert Manuel, Marie Sabouret, Janine Darcy, Claude Sylvain, Perlo Vita (Jules Dassin), Robert Hossein *Prod* Indus/Pathé/Prima. 116 mins.

Tony (Servais) leads his confederates, Jo (Mohner), Mario (Manuel), and César (Dassin) in a raid on a jewelry story. The raid su ceeds but a rival gang extracts inf rmation from César, kills Mario an his girl, and kidnaps Jo's small son. Tony liquidates César for squealing, then the rival gang, and, mortally wounded dies after returning the child home.

The se uence that led to the film's merited s ecess was the meticulously detailed, long episode of the obbery during which not a word is spoken. It is a brilliant sequence, as is the performance of Dassin (under the name Perlo Vita) in the role of César.

DU SKAL AERE DIN HUSTRU THOU SHALT HONOR THY WIFE/MASTER OF THE HOUSE Denmark 1925. *Dir* Carl Theodor Dreyer *Scen* Svend Rindom, Carl Dreyer based on the play by Sven Rindom *Tyrannens Feld Photog* George Schnéevoigt *Art Dir* Carl Dreyer *Cast* Johannes Meyer, Mathilde Nielsen, Astrid Holm, Karin Nellemose *Prod* Palladium. 7,000 ft. approx.

An engineer (Meyer) tyrannizes his wife (Holm), son, daughter, (Nellemose), and even the pet canary. The family plots with the old nurse (Nielsen) and brings about the fall of the tyrant.

Dreyer wanted to make his film in only two sets in a middle-class apartment. Because of his reputation he was able to have the apartment constructed in the studio. So realistic was the set that it even included gas, water, and electric installations.

Although a few scenes were shot in the streets of Copenhagen, this domestic drama takes place largely in the obsessive, closed atmosphere of the apartment. The canary in its cage, a clock pendulum swinging, even the corner where the little boy sits, become symbols. It is not difficult to believe that Dreyer, who had just made two films in Berlin, had absorbed something of *Kammerspiel* and incorporated it into his own style. The dialogue plays an important part, as it did later in *Passion de Jeanne d'Arc*, without the titles being wearying. The characters are created with a psychological depth rare in the silent cinema.

The perfect acting is somewhat spoiled by the extravagant make-up that the frequent close-ups emphasize. Dreyer clearly realized his mistake for he later abandoned the use of make-up entirely.

DU SOLLST NICHT EHEBRECHEN see THÉRÈSE RAQUIN

EARRINGS OF MADAME DE (THE) MADAME
DE . . .

EARTH ZEMLYA

EAST OF EDEN USA 1954. *Dir.* Elia Kazan
Scen Paul Osborn based on the novel
by John Steinbeck *Photog* Ted McCord
Art Dir James Basevi, Malcolm Bert
Ed Owen Marks *Mus* Leonard Rosenman *Cast* James Dean, Julie Harris, Jo
Van Fleet, Raymond Massey, Burl Ives,
Richard Davalos *Prod* Warner Bros. 114
mins. WarnerColor. CinemaScope.
In a small town in California before
World War I, Cal (Dean), the young
son of a prosperous and religious farmer,
Adam (Massey), rebels against his environment and searches out his mother,
Kate (Van Fleet), who had left his
father years before. His father thinks
he is a no-good wastrel and clearly
shows he prefers his brother, Aron (Davalos), despite Cal's various attempts to
make his father love him. Cal falls in
love with his brother's fiancée, Abra
(Harris), and, following his father's
birthday party at which his father agai`
has spurned him, reveals that he knows
of his mother's existence.
Some critics (including Roger Vadim) consider this film to be a masterpiece though
it is not Kazan's best film. [The biblical parallels and emotional power of the
original Steinbeck novel now seem less
important than Ted McCord's splendid
use of the CinemaScope camera and
the performances by Raymond Massey and
Jo Van Fleet. This was James Dean's
first major role and both the role and
his performance in it were responsible
for beginning the James Dean myth of
the teenage rebel.]

*EASY RIDER USA 1969. *Dir* Dennis
Hopper *Scen* Dennis Hopper, Peter
Fonda, Terry Southern *Photog* Laszlo
Kovaks *Art Dir* Jerry Kay *Mus* Gerry
Goffin, Carole King, Jaime Robbie Rob-
ertson, Antonia Duren, Elliott Ingber,
Larry Wagner, Jimi Hendrix, Jack Keller,
David Axelrod, Mike Bloomfield, Bob
Dylan, Roger McGuinn performed by
Steppenwolf, The Byrds, The Band, The
Jimi Hendrix Experience, Little Eva,
The Electric Prunes, The Electric Flag,
Roger McGuinn, The Holy Modal Round-
ers, Fraternity of Man *Ed* Donn Cam-
bren *Cast* Peter Fonda, Dennis Hopper,
Jack Nicholson *Prod* Pando Co. in association with Raybert Productions. 95
mins. Technicolor.
Billy (Hopper) and Captain America
(Fonda) sell some cocaine to a pusher
and set off across the States on their
motorcycles towards New Orleans. On
the way they have various encounters:
they are given a meal by a farmer and
his wife; are invited to stay at a New
Mexico "digger" commune where the
people are working the land; are jailed
in a small Texas town and released by
an alcoholic civil rights lawyer (Nicholson), who joins them and is later clubbed
to death by a lynching party antagonized
by the trio's appearance. In New Orleans
they visit the Mardi Gras carnival with
two girls from a brothel and share a
bad LSD trip in a cemetery. The next
day they leave and while riding along a
rural road are shot by two men in a
passing truck.
Peter Fonda described the film as
"cinéma vérité in allegory terms" and
it is, in fact, a 20th-century odyssey
across the States whose pervasive pessimism is focused in the brutal despair of
the ending. Billy's and Captain America's sense of dissatisfaction and quest
for freedom (which they never find) is
contrasted with the violence, bigotry,
and moral bankruptcy they encounter

on their voyage, while the beauty and grandeur of the landscapes they pass through is set against the tawdry vulgarity of the towns. The dialogue was largely improvised; the music track is entirely folk rock. The photography by Laszlo Kovacs (whose name Belmondo took as one of his pseudonyms is *Breathless*) is perhaps his best work to date.

EASY STREET USA 1917. *Dir/Scen* Charles Chaplin *Photog* Rollie Totheroh, William C. Foster *Cast* Chaplin, Edna Purviance, Eric Campbell, Albert Austin, James T. Kelley *Prod* Mutual. 1,680 ft. A derelict, Charlie, wanders into a mission where he is reformed by the minister (Austin) and the beautiful Edna (Purviance). In Easy Street, toughest section of the city, Charlie gets a job as a policeman and overcomes the giant bully (Campbell). With Edna he dispenses charity to the poor. The bully escapes, Charlie overcomes him again, as well as all other opposition, and reforms Easy Street.

One of Chaplin's best shorts and a biting social satire set in slums similar to those Chaplin knew as a child in London. Famous sequences: Charlie's "conversion" in the mission and his return of the collection box he had stolen; his joining the police force; his tossing food at the numerous children in a family as if they were chickens; the bully's arrival in the district and Charlie overcoming him with the gas from a street lamp; Charlie's chase and second fight with the bully during which he drops a stove on him; the reformed crooks of Easy Street walking sedately to the new mission.

*ECLISSE (L') THE ECLIPSE Italy/France 1962. *Dir* Michelangelo Antonioni *Scen* Tonino Guerra, Michelangelo Antonioni, Elio Bartolini, Ottiero Ottieri *Photog* Gianni Di Venanzo *Art Dir* Piero Poletto *Ed* Eraldo da Roma *Mus* Giovanni Fusco *Cast* Monica Vitti, Alain Delon, Lilla Brignone, Francisco R bal *Prod* Interopa Film/Cineriz/Paris Film. 125 mins.

Vittoria (Vitti), a beautiful Roman girl who works as a translator, breaks her affair with Riccardo (Rabal) and shortly afterwards drifts into another affair with her mother's (Brignone) handsome young stockbroker, Piero (Delon).

L'Eclisse can be considered the last part of the trilogy that began with *L'Avventura* (*q.v.*) and *La Notte* (*q.v.*), and again deals with personal relationships in modern society. It is superior to the other two, although less well-received. Notable sequences: the opening scene in which the lovers break off, "having nothing more to say to each other"; the meeting with a neighbor who used to live in Kenya; Vittoria's air trip to Verona; the stock exchange during a market recession; the first meeting of Vittoria and Piero; Piero's car being fished out of an artificial lake with the corpse of the drowned thief inside and Piero worrying only about the car's condition. The end sequence (58 shots, about 7 minutes) is a montage of shots of the area where Piero and Vittoria met, passing from late afternoon to night, but in which neither of the main characters appears. The final group of shots shows only: trees in the wind; the bark of a tree with insects on it; water trickling out of a barrel into a culvert; a building seen almost in silhouette; a huge close-up of a street lamp. This end sequence could suggest that Vittoria and Piero have failed to turn up for their date or could be Antonioni's symbolic generalization on the nature of solitude as man's accustomed state.

ECOLE BUISSONIERE (L') I HAVE A NEW MASTER France 1948. *Dir* Jean-Paul Le Chanois *Scen* Jean-Paul Le Chanois, Elise Freinet *Photog* Marc Fossard, Maurice Pecqueux, André Dumaitre *Ed* Emma Le Chanois *Art Dir* Claude Bouxin *Mus* Joseph Kosma *Cast* Bernard lier, Juliette Faber, Edouard Delmont, Maupi, Pierre Cost etc. *Prod* U.G.C./C.G.C.F. 89 mins.

A teacher (Blier) introduces new teaching methods into a provincial village school, comes into conflict with the parents, but ends by winning his fight. One of the best films of Le Chanois and one of Blier's best performances.

ECSTASY EXTASE

EDGE OF THE CITY A MAN IS TEN FEET TALL USA 1956. *Dir* Martin Ritt *Scen* Robert Alan Aurthur *Photog* Joseph Brun *Art Dir* Richard Sylbert *Mus* Leonard Rosenman *Ed* Sidney Meyers *Cast* John Cassavetes, Sidney Poitier, Jack Warden, Kathleen Maguire, Ruby Dee *Prod* Jonathan for MGM. 84 mins.

A deserter (Cassavetes) becomes a docker with the help of a Negro (Poitier) respected for his intelligence. He fights with an overseer who is a gangster (Warden) and strangles him after his black friend is killed.

This courageous and forceful film was not only anti-*On the Waterfront* (*q.v.*) but was also one of the first Hollywood films to characterize a Negro as a man more sensible and courageous than those around him. Martin Ritt began his career in television and has never directed a film quite as remarkable as this, his first feature. Sidney Meyers, the editor, had been one of the founders of the New York school. In this film he worked with the actor, John Cassavetes, whose later *Shadows* (*q.v.*) echoed something of Meyers' preoccupations and gave a new forcefulness and direction to independent film-making in New York.

EDIPO RE see OEDIPUS REX

8½ (EIGHT AND A HALF) OTTO E MEZZO

1860 MILLE DI GARIBALDI (I)

EISENSTEIN'S MEXICAN FILM: EPISODES FOR STUDY see QUE VIVA MEXICO!

EL THIS STRANGE PASSION/TORMENTS Mexico 1952. *Dir* Luis Buñuel *Scen* Luis Buñuel, Luis Alcoriza based on the novel *Pensamientos* by Mercedes Pinto *Photog* Gabriel Figueroa *Art Dir* Edward Fitzgerald *Ed* Carlos Savage *Mus* Luis Hernández Bretón *Cast* Arturo de Córdova, Delia Garcés, Luis Beristain *Prod* Nacional Film (Oscar Dancigers). 100 mins.

Don Francisco (de Córdova), a wealthy landowner and pillar of the church who is in his early forties, falls in love with a beautiful girl, Gloria (Garcés), whom he sees in church. She is engaged to his friend, Raoul, but breaks off the engagement and marries Francisco. After the marriage, Francisco becomes pathologically jealous, accuses her of infidelity on the slightest provocation, and even threatens to kill her. Gloria finally runs away and Francisco breaks down completely. Years later, Raoul and Gloria, now married and with a small son, visit Francisco in the monastery to which he has retreated. He says he has recovered his serenity, but walks away with the same zig-zag gait that heralded his mental breakdown.

The black humor of the film's official résumé must owe much to Buñuel: "This is the story of a respectable man with a good social position, respected by his friends for his elevated morality, his religious convictions, and his good education, but one who harbors within himself a frightful defect: jealousy. This vice poisons his life and that of his wife until he shuts himself in a monastery to confine his madness."

This is one of the great Buñuel films from his Mexican period. Famous sequences: the feet-washing ceremony in the cathedral on a saint's day; the wedding in Francisco's luxurious and suffocating *fin-de-siècle* villa; the needle in the keyhole to pierce the eye of any potential voyeur; the town seen from a belfry and Francisco's monologue; Francisco's zig-zag walk through the town at night; Francisco preparing the instruments for his erotic vengeance — rope, scissors, needle and thread; Francisco in the convent, his attempt to strangle the priest, and his final zig-zag walk down the garden path.

It is perhaps in this film, in *Los Olvidados* (the most Mexican of Buñuel's films), and in *L'Age d'or* that Buñuel seems closest to de Sade. Francisco seems motivated less by jealousy than by a frenetic, obsessive lust for exclusive possession. *El* was very badly received at the Cannes Film Festival: the jury described it as a bad B-picture and it was booed by 200 war veterans who had gone to the Palais de Festival to applaud *La Vie passionnée de Clemenceau*.

*EL CID USA/Italy 1961. *Dir* Anthony Mann *Scen* Philip Yordan, Frederic M. Frank *Assist Dir* Yakima Canutt, Luciano Sacripanti, etc. *Photog* Robert Krasker *Mus* Miklos Rozsa *Art Dir* Veniero Colasanti, John Moore *Ed* Robert Lawrence *Cast* Charlton Heston, Sophia Loren, Raf Vallone, Andrew Cruickshank, Michael Hordern, Genevieve Page, Herbert Lom, Hurd Hatfield *Prod* Samuel Bronston/Dear Films 184 mins. Technicolor. 70 mm. Super-Technirama. The story of the fight of the Spanish national hero El Cid, Rodrigo Diaz (Heston), against the Moors in Spain and of his love for Chimene (Loren),

Arguably, "one of the most pure and beautiful myths that Hollywood has ever made" (Penelope Gilliatt), *El Cid* was the first spectacular by Anthony Mann, who is better known for his westerns. Perhaps surprisingly, he was not overwhelmed by the film's big budget and created a film whose successful spectacular scenes (such as the siege of Valencia) and beautifully photographed vistas do not crush the character portrayals. Undoubtedly the most memorable shot is the last: El Cid, a corpse on horseback, riding alongside a ridge of surf.

ELDORADO France 1921. *Dir/Scen* Marcel L'Herbier *Photog* Lucas *Art Dir* Le Bertre, Garnier *Mus* Jean-François Gallard *Cast* Eve Francis, J. Catelain, Marcelle Pradot, Philippe Hériat, Paulais, Claire Prelia. 5,000 ft. approx.
In this "melodrama" (described as such by the director), Sibilla (Francis) becomes a dancer in a cabaret in Granada in order to feed her child and meets a Scandinavian painter (Catelain). She is raped by a strange clown (Hériat) and kills herself.
"This is real cinema. I do not believe a better tribute could be offered to a French director. Marcel L'Herbier, in the front rank of the too-small Paris group, has well-proven his artistry and creative independence because he is not surprised by a success that is as enormous as it is just" (Louis Delluc, September 9, 1921).
"L'Herbier knows how to see, and to make us see, all the aspects of nature appropriate to his theme. In order to show that Hedwick is a painter, he shows us the Alhambra, changing as he looks at it; when the habitués of the dance hall are drunk, they appear disfigured; the burning hot countryside seems to dance around Sibilla as she staggers towards her revenge. In all these, the meaning of each image is direct and immediately understandable" (Lionel Landry, *Cinéa*, July 22, 1921).

ELEKTRA ELECTRA Greece 1961. *Dir* Michael Cacoyannis *Scen* Michael Cacoyannis based on the play by Euripides *Photog* Walter Lassally *Ed* L. Antonakis *Mus* Mikis Theodorakis *Art Dir* Spyros Vassiliou *Cast* Irene Papas, Aleka Catselli, Yannis Fertis *Prod* Finos for United Artists. 113 mins.
Though some exaggerated the film's

qualities in describing it as a "masterpiece," this condensed version of the Euripides play performed under the Greek sun, does retain the power of the original. Irene Papas gives a remarkable performance and Walter Lassally's photography is superb.
OTHER VERSION:
— *Elektra/Electra at Epidauros* Greece 1962. *Dir* Ted Zarpas. The play by Sophocles filmed during rehearsals and public performances at Epidauros.

ELMER GANTRY USA 1960. *Dir* Richard Brooks *Scen* Richard Brooks based on the novel by Sinclair Lewis *Photog* John Alton *Art Dir* Ed Carrere *Mus* André Previn *Ed* Marge Fowler *Cast* Burt Lancaster, Jean Simmons, Shirley Jones *Prod* Elmer Gantry Productions for United Artists. 146 mins. Eastman Color.
The story of a hypocritical preacher (Lancaster) in an American revivalist sect.
Richard Brooks had wanted to film Sinclair Lewis's novel for many years and his adaptation admirably conveys the flavor and emotions of the original. His screenplay won an Academy Award.

*ELVIRA MADIGAN Sweden 1967. *Dir/Scen/Ed* Bo Widerberg *Photog* Jörgen Persson *Mus* Mozart's *Piano Concerto No. 21 Cast* Pia Degermark, Thommy Berggren, Lennart Malmer, Nina Widerberg *Prod* Europa Film. 95 mins. Eastman Color.
Based on an actual incident in Sweden in 1889: a young tightrope dancer, Elvira Madigan (Degermark), and Count Sixten Sparre (Berggren) fall madly in love. He deserts the Swedish Army and his wife and children and runs away with her to Denmark. They spend a happy summer together in the countryside until their money runs out. Then, because he cannot look for work, they face starvation. Realizing there is no future for their love, they decide to die together.
"Exquisite" is the word many critics applied to Widerberg's idyllic rendering of a summer passion in which the lovers choose death rather than parting. Certainly, the breathtakingly beautiful color and photography (the images are predominantly golden), the formal loveliness of the Mozart piano concerto, and the graceful performances by the two leads are a total integration of mood and

meaning, of style and content, and give the film a timeless, mythical quality. The most memorable scenes are the lovers' first picnic in the fields and their last breakfast, ending in a frozen shot of Elvira catching a butterfly.

EMIL UND DIE DETEKTIV EMIL AND THE DETECTIVE Germany 1931. *Dir* Gerhard Lamprecht *Scen* Billy Wilder based on the novel by Erich Kästner *Photog* Werner Brandes *Mus* Allan Grey *Cast* Fritz Rasp, Käthe Haack and many children. *Prod* UFA 80 mins.

A group of children discover and chase a crook (Rasp) and succeed in having him arrested. A fresh and charming film that was made in the early days of sound and that has been often imitated.
OTHER VERSIONS:
— *Emil and the Detectives*: Britain 1934. *Dir* Milton Rosmer *Cast* George Hayes, Marion Forster. 70 mins.
— *Emil und die Detektiv* German Federal Republic 1954. *Dir*. R. A. Stemmle *Scen* R. A. Stemmle (from Wilder's original) *Photog* Kurt Schulz *Cast* Kurt Meisel, Peter Finkbeiner, Margaret Haagen. 95 mins. Eastman Color.
A remake that does not match the original.
— *Emil and the Detectives* USA 1964. *Dir* Peter Tewkesbury *Scen* A. J. Caruthers *Cast* Walter Slezak, Heinz Schubert *Prod* Walt Disney. 100 mins. Technicolor.
This latest version is pleasant but without distinction.
See also *Hue and Cry*

EMPEROR'S NIGHTINGALE (THE) CÍSAŘUV SLAVÍK

EMPRESS YANG KWEI-FEI YOKIHI

EN CAS DE MALHEUR LOVE IS MY PROFESSION/IN CASE OF ACCIDENT France/Italy 1958. *Dir* Claude Autant-Lara *Scen* Jean Aurenche, Pierre Bost based on the novel by Georges Simenon *Photog* Jacques Natteau *Art Dir* Max Douy *Ed* Madeleine Gug *Cast* Brigitte Bardot, Jean Gabin, Edwige Feuillère, Franco Interlenghi *Prod* Iéna/U.C.I.L. (Paris)/Incom (Rome). 120 mins. (105 mins., Britain).
A wealthy, middle-aged lawyer (Gabin) who no longer cares for his wife (Feuillère) falls in love and then lives with a young, beautiful client (Bardot) who is

involved in a robbery. She is also loved by a young student (Interlenghi) who stabs her to death out of jealousy.
This was a great box-office success that ran into censorship difficulties in many countries. It lacks, however, the atmosphere and power of the original Simenon novel.

END OF DESIRE UNE VIE

END OF INNOCENCE CASA DEL ANGEL (LA)

END OF ST. PETERSBURG (THE) KONYETS SANKT-PETERBURGA

ENEMIES OF THE PUBLIC PUBLIC ENEMY (THE)

ENFANT DE PARIS (L') France 1913. *Dir* Léonce Perret *Cast* Suzanne Le Bret, Louis Leubas, Maurice Lagrenée *Prod* Gaumont. 3,500 ft. approx.
A serial, but one whose style and technique are remarkable. Perret's imagistic sense was similar to that of D. W. Griffith, though this film was made two years before *The Birth of a Nation* (q.v.).

ENFANTS DU PARADIS (LES) THE CHILDREN OF PARADISE France 1945 (production began 1943). *Dir* Marcel Carné *Scen* Jacques Prévert *Art Dir* Alexandre Trauner, Léon Barsacq, Raymond Gabutti *Photog* Roger Hubert *Mus* Maurice Thiriet, Joseph Kosma *Ed* Henri Rust, Madeleine Bonin *Cast* Arletty, Jean-Louis Barrault, Pierre Brasseur, Maria Casarès, Marcel Herrand, Louis Salou, Pierre Renoir, Gaston Modot, Paul Frankeur, Jane Marken *Prod* Pathé. 195 mins. (Also released in several shorter versions.)
1. "Le Boulevard du crime" In Paris in 1840, Garance (Arletty), the mistress of Lacenaire (Herrand), takes a fancy to the mime, Deburau (Barrault), then leaves him for Frédérick Lemaître (Brasseur).
2. "L'Homme blanc" Seven years later, Deburau has become famous and has married Nathalie (Casarès) whom he doesn't love. Garance is being kept by a rich count (Salou). Frédérick Lemaître, who is also successful as an actor in the role of Othello, is jealous. Lacenaire kills the count. Deburau and Garance meet again and find a brief happiness until Nathalie separates them. Garance leaves and Deburau hopelessly pushes

his way through the carnival crowds searching for her.

Famous sequences: Deburau as a beginner in a side show; his evening at the Rouge Gorge; the pantomime on a tightrope; Lemaître changing *L'Auberge des Adrets* from a melodrama into a farce against the author's wishes; the duel in the inn; Deburau's success in *Chand d'habits;* Garance in the count's mansion; the performance of *Othello* and the actual drama that results; the count's murder in a Turkish bath; Deburau fighting his way through the carnival crowds dressed as Pierrot (a character he created as Chaplin created the "tramp").

The dramatic focal point is the undying love between Garance and Deburau despite the fact that fate (embodied by Lacenaire) always separates them. The misfortunes of their love (which is more enchanting than passionate) are played out against a backdrop of romantic Paris: the Boulevard du Crime, Porte Saint-Martin, mansions, Turkish baths, tightrope walkers, theaters, etc. Prévert seems to have been inspired by Hugo's *Les Misérables,* Eugène Sue's *Les Mystères de Paris* and Balzac's *Splendeur et misère des courtisanes* in developing his major esthetic theme — the relationship between life and theater, real and imaginary characters, tragedy and mime, stage and screen, silence and sound, actors and men; in other words, the relationship between life and art, and art and life.

This is unquestionably both Carné's and Prévert's masterpiece and overflows with art and intelligence. However, it is somewhat cold, even allowing for the fact that Carné and Prévert intended to present a spectacle and that the film's romanticism is breathtaking. Jean-Louis Barrault gives a superb performance and proves himself a mime to equal Deburau. The acting is also notable for Brasseur's truculent Lemaître, Arletty's captivating Garance, and Maria Casarès, spiritual Nathalie, while Marcel Herrand and Louis Salou give well-balanced performances. Jane Marken and Gaston Modot are good in character roles.

Production on the film began in August 1943 but its completion was deliberately delayed until the end of the Occupation. It was an immense international success [even in the shorter versions released outside France. Its recent re-release in the original, complete version has only reinforced critical and public opinion of its qualities.]

*ENJO FLAME OF TORMENT/CONFLAGRATION Japan 1958. *Dr* Kon Ichikawa *Scen* Natto Wada, Keiji Hasebe based on the novel *Kinkaku-ji* by Yukio Mishima *Photog* Kazuo Miyagawa *Mus* Toshio Mayuzumi *Cast* Raizo Ichikawa, Tatsuya Nakadi, Ganjiro Nakamura, Yoko Uraji, Tanie Kitabayshi *Prod* Daiei. 102 mins. Daieiscope.

Based on a true story: a young student-priest (Ichikawa) deliberately burns down his beloved temple to prevent its being polluted by modern commercialism.

Like so many of Ichikawa's films, this is the story of an obsession. Though often cold and replete with overt symbolism, the film's extraordinary, textured visual beauty and formal perfection match that of *Harp of Burma (q.v.).*

EN RADE France 1927. *Dir* Alberto Cavalcanti *Scen* Alberto Cavalcanti, Claude Heymann *Photog* Jimmy Rogers, A. Fairli, P. Enberg *Art Dir* Erik Aaes, A. Cerf, J. Bouissounnouse *Cast* Catherine Hessling, Philippe Hériat, Nathalie Lissenko, Georges Charlia, Thomy Bourdelle *Prod* Néo-Film. 4,540 ft.

A young man (Charlia) dreams of escaping his dreary existence in a large port by eloping with his lover (Hessling), a waitress, but is prevented by his possessive mother and the intervention of a local idiot (Hériat).

Set among the docks and ships of Marseilles, this romantic love story has a delicate sense of environment and atmosphere. It is Cavalcanti's best film, heralded French poetic realism of the Thirties, and is somewhat comparable to Sternberg's *The Docks of New York (q.v.)* made the same year. Catherine Hessling gives one of her best performances.

ENSAYO DE UN CRIMEN THE CRIMINAL LIFE OF ARCHIBALDO DE LA CRUZ Mexico 1955. *Dir* Luis Buñuel *Scen* Eduardo Ugarte, Luis Buñuel based on a story by Rodolfo Usigli *Photog* Agustín Jiménez *Ed* Pablo Gomez *Mus* Jesus Bracho, José Pérez *Cast* Ernesto Alonso, Miroslava Stern, Ariadna Walker, Rita Macedo *Prod* Alianza Cinematografica. 91 mins.

When he was a child, Archibaldo de la Cruz (Alonso) believed he had killed his governess with the magic powers of a music box. Later, when he discovers the music box, the erotic memory of her death leads him to decide to kill all women who cross his path. His plans are continually thwarted when coincidence intervenes: a *cocotte's* protector kills her before Archibaldo can; a model (Stern) escapes and he burns only her wax effigy; the young woman he marries has had an affair with a married man who shoots her as they leave the church; a nun runs away as he tries to kill her and falls down a shaft. The police refuse to believe him, he throws away the music box, and is reunited with the model.

Archibaldo, a self-centered man of property and culture, is clearly related to Francisco in Buñuel's earlier *El* (q.v.), but, as a social portrait, the characterization is not as powerful. Buñuel obviously enjoyed relaxing with the black comedy of this "entertainment." Archibaldo's desire to burn his victims in a furnace is a direct allusion to Nazism. The most famous sequence in the film shows him dragging a wax effigy to the furnace and watching orgasmically as it writhes in the heat.

ENTOTSU NO MIERU BASHO THREE CHIMNEYS/WHERE CHIMNEYS ARE SEEN/CHIMNEY SCENE Japan 1953. *Dir* Heinosuke Gosho *Scen* Hideo Oguni based on the novel by Rinzo Shiina *Photog* Mitsuo Miura *Mus* Yasushi Akutagawa *Cast* Kinuyo Tanaka, Ken Uehara *Prod* Shintoho. 110 mins.

The life of a working family in an industrial district of Tokyo dominated by the obsessive presence of its factory chimneys. A couple without children suddenly become responsible for an abandoned child. At the end "the husband looks once more at the chimneys, so placed that they never appear the same to people in different places, and says: 'Life is whatever you think it is. It can be sweet or it can be bitter—whichever you are . . .' Episodic in structure but with each event relating directly to the central philosophy of the film, it is one of those movies that one cannot adequately summarize. Nothing is irrelevant, every detail adding to the effect of the whole world that is created." (Donald Richie, Joseph L. Anderson). This moving and melancholy social portrait is one of the most important postwar Japanese films.

ENTR'ACTE France 1924. *Dir/Ed* René Clair *Scen/Art Dir* Francis Picabia *Photog* J. Berliet *Mus* Erik Satie *Cast* Jean Borlin, Inge Fries, Francis Picabia, Man Ray, Marcel Duchamp, Erik Satie, Georges Auric, Georges Charensol, Marcel Achard, Pierre Scize, Rolf de Maré, Touchagues, etc. *Prod* Rolf de Maré for Ballets Suédois. 1,398 ft.

René Clair made *Entr'acte* to be shown during the intermission between the two acts of the dadaist ballet *Relâche* (*Performance Suspended*), first performed at the Théâtre des Champs-Elysées on December 4, 1924 by the Ballets Suédois. This company, founded by Rolf de Maré and directed by Jean Borlin, had outraged artistic circles in Paris. Francis Picabia, the author of the ballet and an apostle of dadaism, gave the ballet its ironic title when it was heard that the theater might be closed if the performance were given. Picabia conceived the ballet in typically dadaist terms with an inconsequential succession of rhythms, ideas, shapes, and sounds. The film, however, is entirely Clair's, since, as Picabia wrote, "I gave him a tiny scenario amounting to nothing." Erik Satie, who had also composed the score for the ballet, wrote the music for the film only after its completion and to match the film's own rhythm.

At the time of *Entr'acte*, Clair was associated with the avant-garde and its search for "pure" cinema. He wrote in 1924: "The film is really Picabia's, the man who has done so much to liberate the word and the image. In *Entr'acte*, the image is not required to be 'significant' but has an existence in its own right. These visual babblings seem to me the most correct course for the future of the cinema." Picabia said the film "respects nothing except the right to roar with laughter". These statements, as well as the dadaist background of all those involved, suggest the futility of searching for logical meanings (hidden or not) in the famous sequences and images of the film: a ballet dancer photographed from below; a chess game (between Ray and Duchamp) disturbed by a jet of water; a Tyrolean hunter (Borlin) killed by the author (Picabia); a "legless" man who stands up and runs; the hunter's funeral procession led by a camel, (photographed first in slow motion) and then developing into a crazy chase; the coffin falling open; and the conjuror who makes all the characters disappear before disappearing himself. This delightfully preposterous film is surely the masterpiece of "pure" cinema: "It is still as beautiful as when it first appeared," wrote Alexandre Arnoux twenty years later.

ENTUZIAZM ENTHUSIASM/SYMPHONY OF THE DONBAS USSR 1931. *Dir/Scen* Dziga Vertov *Photog* Zeitlin *Mus* N. Timofeyev *Ed* Svilova *Sound* P. Strom *Prod* Ukrain-film. 96 mins.

A tale of the coal miners of the Don Basin after four years of the first Five Year Plan. "To grasp the feverish reality of life in the Don Basin, to convey as true to life as possible its atmosphere of the clash of hammers, of train whistles, of the songs of workers at rest — this was my aim" (Dziga Vertov). The opening sequence shows the remnants of the past, including churches transformed into clubs, then a procession, a meeting, the mills, factories, and mines. In the finale, a coal train meets a wheat train.

Vertov made a vivid and unusual use of sound that was considerably ahead of its time. Natural sounds (machinery, voices, debates, songs, etc.) recorded in the mines and villages of the Don Basin were edited by Vertov as freely as he cut visuals, creating a kind of *musique concrète*. Chaplin was ecstatic over the film and wrote: "I would never have believed it possible to assemble mechanical noises to create such beauty. One of the most superb symphonies I have known. Dziga Vertov is a musician."

[However, Chaplin's enthusiasm and the enthusiasm of others abroad did not save Vertov from the severe critical attacks on his methods, which had been mounting for some years. He did not make another film for three years.]

ERDGEIST see BÜCHSE DER PANDORA (DIE)

EROICA Poland 1957. *Dir* Andrzej Munk *Scen* Jerzy Stefan Stawinski based on his own novels *Photog* Jerzy Wojcik *Mus* Jan Krenz *Cast* (Part I: *Scherzo alla Pollaca*) Barbara Polemska, L. Niemszyk, Edward Dziewenski; (Part II: *Ostinato lugubre*) K. Rodski, Roman Klosowski, Jozef Kostechi, Josef Nowak, Wojciech Siemion *Prod* Kadr. 83 mins. A two-part film on a war theme. The episodes are distinct but complementary. *Part I:* During the Warsaw uprising of September 1944, a disenchanted volun-

teer (Dziewenski) returns to find his wife (Polemska) entertaining a Hungarian officer (Niemszyk) who offers to help the insurgents. The volunteer crosses the German lines to his superiors but the offer is refused. He finds after all he prefers the Resistance to his wife's company. *Part II:* In a German POW camp for Polish Resistance fighters, two new arrivals (Nowak, Klosowski) find only one man has ever escaped and his escape has supported the prisoners' flagging morale ever since. The escapee, in fact, has been hiding in the roof eluding the Gestapo. One prisoner (Zak) who is especially inspired tries to escape, then dramatically commits suicide. The escapee dies and the Germans and the Poles smuggle his body out, the Germans to save face and the Poles to uphold morale. The title (literally "Heroism") of this biting picture of the Polish cult of heroism, the devotion to lost causes, must have been intended as ironic, since the heroism depicted is the kind associated with pre-1939 Polish officers. This is an excellent film by one of Poland's best directors, who regrettably died in 1961 while still young.

EROTIKON Sweden 1920. *Dir* Mauritz Stiller *Scen* Mauritz Stiller, Gustaf Molander, Arthur Norden based on the play by Franz Herzeg *Photog* Henrik Jaenzon *Art Dir* Axel Esbensen, Mauritz Stiller (?) *Cast* Anders de Wahl, Tora Teje, Karin Molander, Vilhelm Bryde, Lars Hanson, Royal Ballet Company of Stockholm *Prod* Svensk Filmindustri. 5,600 ft.

Professor Charpentier (de Wahl) devotes more time to entomology then to his wife, Irene (Teje), who flirts with Baron Felix (Bryde) but secretly loves Preben (Hanson), a sculptor. Meanwhile, Marthe (Molander), the professor's niece, maneuvers to take over Irene's place. Preben is jealous of the baron and tries to urge the professor into a duel with him. Eventually, Irene divorces the professor to marry Preben while the professor consoles himself with the niece.

"*Erotikon* proves that the Swedes have seen and admired American films," wrote Léon Moussinac, and certainly this film closely resembles Cecil B. De Mille's frivolous comedies, not only because of the amorous intrigues among "sophisticates" but also because it included a "special attraction," the Royal Ballet Company. However, *Erotikon* has the advantage of Stiller's masterly direction. The film's spirited and lively style is also not dissimilar to the sophisticated Hungarian comedies then fashionable in central Europe. Lubitsch seems to have been much influenced by *Erotikon* in his American comedies, themselves often derived from Hungarian musical comedies.

EROTIKON Czechoslovakia 1929. *Dir/Scen* Gustav Machaty *Photog* Vaclav Vich *Cast* Ita Rina, Karel Schleichert, Olaf Fjord, Theo Pistek, Charlotte Suza *Prod* Gem Film, Prague. 7,200 ft. approx.

The pretty daughter (Rina) of a provincial stationmaster (Schleichert) takes a rich lover (Fjord).

Despite its banal story, this Czech film with an international cast conveys marvelously the atmosphere of the little railway station and the contrast between the worlds of the daughter and the lover. These qualities and the film's eroticism (Ita Rina's body was as beautiful as her face) assured the film's international success as they did with Machaty's later *Extase* (*q.v.*).

ESCAPE FROM YESTERDAY BANDERA (LA)

ESPOIR SIERRA DE TERUEL/DAYS OF HOPE/MAN'S HOPE France/Spain 1945 (production began 1938). *Dir* André Malraux *Scen* André Malraux, M. Aub, B. Peskine *Assist* Denis Marion *Photog* Louis Page *Mus* Darius Milhaud *Cast* Mejuto, Nicolas Rodriguez, José Lado and others from Catalana *Prod* Corniglion-Moliniec. 73 mins.

According to Denis Marion (in *Écran français No. 1*), "Production began in June, 1938 in Barcelona in one of the three studios that the city controlled" but in which materials were lacking. "A number of exteriors were shot on airfields between bombardments. For the first time on the screen some scenes were photographed inside a bomber, the descent down the mountain was photographed in the Sierra de Teruel with 2,500 unequipped recruits. The film wasn't completed by January, 1939, when Franco's troops entered Barcelona."

Only one episode was retained from the novel *L'Éspoir:* the raid on the Falangist airfield. However, the main sequence of the film, the descent down the Sierra by a procession carrying dead and wounded pilots, was based on an event in which Malraux had been involved.

There are some remarkable scenes of street fighting, while the scene showing a bomber pilot being guided by peasants unable to recognize familiar country from the air is especially memorable. All the actors in the film were combatants who re-created the events through which they had lived and most of the film conveys an authentic feeling of the anti-Fascist fights during the Civil War. A less effective sequence shows pilots discussing their reasons for fighting.

Although the film was shown to a wide audience, a Swiss critic has written: "The world is beginning to resemble the novels of André Malraux." However, the author wrote no more novels after 1945.

ET DIEU CREA LA FEMME AND GOD CREATED WOMAN/AND WOMAN . . . WAS CREATED France 1956. *Dir* Roger Vadim *Scen* Roger Vadim, Raoul Lévy *Photog* Armand Thirard *Art Dir* Jean André *Ed* Victoria Mercanton *Mus* Paul Misraki *Cast* Brigitte Bardot, Curt Jürgens, Jean-Louis Trintignant, Christian Marquand *Prod* Iéna/U.C.I.L./Cocinor 91 mins. Eastman Color. CinemaScope.

A blond orphan girl (Bardot), indifferent to money and other people's opinions, marries a young man (Trintignant). She is pursued by a rich tycoon (Jürgens) and, out of passion, sleeps with her husband's virile elder brother (Marquand). After a violent altercation, she is won back by her husband.

This was Vadim's first feature and he made a spectacularly successful debut by launching Brigitte Bardot in the USA, where, it is reported, she grossed more dollars in 1957–58 than the sale of Renault cars. "I prefer this of all my films," Vadim has said. "It is the one in which I was free to tell a story that really meant something to me. I attribute its success to Brigitte's personality, initially physical in its appeal, and to her role, which allowed her to show her confidence, dynamism, and totally free sexual behavior. I didn't try to portray a typical 1956 girl but this unique personality who could not have existed at any other time."

The film's daring love scenes helped its success, but it is its portrayal of the

Fifties "amoral" generation that holds the attention. The erotically emancipated female in search of a male passionate yet firm enough to satisfy her was embodied in this film by Bardot. Her character, and that of her husband, contrast sharply with the traditional values of the wealthy tycoon (a role introduced ino the film at the last minute), who still assumes money conquers all, and with the conventional morality of the elder brother, who despises the girl for sleeping with him.

Though Vadim later fell prey to commercializing sexual themes, this first film of his has a special significance. It broke the stranglehold of the established producers in France who, awed by the film's success, allowed the *nouvelle vague* breakthrough.

ETERNEL RETOUR (L') THE ETERNAL RETURN/ LOVE ETERNAL France 1943. *Dir* Jean Delannoy *Scen* Jean Cocteau *Photog* Roger Hubert *Art Dir* Wakhévitch *Mus* Georges Auric *Cast* Jean Marais, Madeleine Sologne, Jean Murat, Yvonne de Bray, Piéral *Prod* André Paulvé. 111 mins.

A modernized version of the legend of Tristan (Marais) and Isolde (Sologne). This was an enormous commercial success during the worst days of the German Occupation of France. [After the war, however, many foreign critics found its Teutonic look disquieting, "The pervading mood of defeatism sublimating itself in death," as Richard Winnington put it.] The photography is often beautiful, and the ending, with a motorboat engine sounding like a heart beat, is effective. But the film's "poetic" style now seems as outmoded as Jean Marais' 1943 sweater and Madeleine Sologne's hair style.

EUROPA 51 THE GREATEST LOVE/EUROPE 51 Italy 1952. *Dir* Roberto Rossellini *Scen* S. de Feo, M. Pannunzio, I. Perilli, D. Fabri, Roberto Rossellini, A. Pietrangeli *Photog* Aldo Tonti *Mus* Renzo Rossellini *Ed* Iolande Benvenuti *Cast* Ingrid Bergman, Alexander Knox, Ettore Giannini, Giulietta Masina *Prod* Ponti/ De Laurentiis. 110 mins.

An American society woman (Bergman) living in Rome after the suicide of her son seeks for some meaning in the chaotic, postwar world. A Communist friend (Giannini) advises her to go to the people; she abandons society and discovers poverty for the first time, but learns that Communist interest is itself often not sincere. She leaves her husband (Knox) and the friend and goes to live with a poor prostitute (Masina). After various attempts by her family and friends to make her see reason, she is committed as insane by her husband and locked up in a clinic.

The opening sequence showing the society lady receiving her guests for a dinner that is suddenly interrupted by her son's suicide, is depicted in a marvelously Stendhalian manner, supple and concise. The overly obvious theme, however, ruins the rest of the film. Nevertheless, it does convey the sense of being the profound and sincere diary of an artist confused by the state of the world around him.

EVANGELIEMANDENS LIV THE LIFE OF THE LAY PREACHER Denmark 1914. *Dir/Scen* Holger-Madsen *Photog* M. Clausen *Cast* V. Psilander, Else Fröhlich, Frederik Jacobsen, August Blad, Rob Schyberg *Prod* Nordisk. 3,600 ft. approx.

Despite a somewhat conventional story line, this is one of the best achievements of the early Danish cinema. It is notable for its attractve photography.

EVIL STREET GERMANIA, ANNO ZERO

EXECUTIONER (THE) VERDUGO (EL)

EXODUS USA 1960. *Dir* Otto Preminger *Scen* Dalton Trumbo based on the novel by Leon Uris *Photog* Sam Leavitt *Art Dir* Richard Day, Bill Hutchinson *Mus* Ernest Gold *Ed* Louis R. Loeffler *Titles* Saul Bass *Cast* Paul Newman, Eva Maria Saint, Ralph Richardson, Sal Mineo *Prod* Carlyle/Alpha for United Artists. 220 mins. Panavision 70. Technicolor.

This film is based on Leon Uris' best-selling novel of the "Exodus" incident and the Israeli fight for independence. The incident is about a group of 400 immigrant Jews and their leader (Newman), who succeed in taking a ship to and landing in Palestine despite the opposition of the British Governor of Cyprus (Richardson).

A large-budget production with good performances and with several good sequences, including one in which a deportee (Mineo) is interrogated. [*Exodus* was the first film that Dalton Trumbo had written under his own name since 1947, when he was blacklisted as a result of his refusal to testify to the House Un-American Activities Committee.] *Exodus* is also the French title of a mediocre (despite an award at Cannes) Italian film by Dullio Coletti: *Il Grido della Terra* (*1949*) based on the events in Palestine and incidentally on the "Exodus" affair.

EXPIATION PO ZAKONU

*EXPLOITS OF ELAINE (THE) (serial) USA 1914. *Dir* Louis Gasnier, George B. Seitz *Scen* Charles W. Goddard, George B. Seitz based on stories by Arthur B. Reeve *Cast* Pearl White, Creighton Hale, Arnold Daly, Sheldon Lewis, Floyd Buckley *Prod* Wharton for Pathé. 14 episodes, each 2 reels.
Chapter titles: 1. The Clutching Hand; 2. The Twilight Sleep; 3. The Vanishing Jewels; 4. The Frozen Safe; 5. The Poisoned Room; 6. The Vampire; 7. The Double Trap; 8. The Hidden Voice; 9. The Death Ray; 10. The Life Current; 11. The Hour of Three; 12. The Blood Crystals; 13. The Devil Worshippers; 14. The Reckoning. (N.B. There is often confusion about these chapter titles since Pathé re-released the serial several times in re-edited versions.)
The heroine, Elaine Dodge (White), assisted by a detective, Craig Kennedy (Daly), goes through various adventures to trap her father's murderer, the archcriminal known as The Clutching Hand (Lewis).
Following the popular success of *The Perils of Pauline* starring Pearl White, Pathé commissioned the Wharton Brothers to produce *The Exploits of Elaine* based on the stories of Arthur B. Reeve about a "scientific" detective, Craig Kennedy. But the serial was to be transformed into a vehicle for the new star, Pearl White.
Unlike *The Perils of Pauline*, in which the chapters were complete in themselves, the chapters in the new serial were "cliffhangers," with Elaine ending each chapter in a difficult situation and Craig Kennedy arriving at the beginning of the next to save her.
The serial was even more successful than *The Perils of Pauline* and netted Pathé over a million dollars. In Europe especially, many eulogies were written about Pearl White's beauty and the extraordinary inventiveness of the films.

— **The New Exploits of Elaine* USA 1915. *Dir* George B. Seitz, Donald MacKenzie, Louis Gasnier, *Scen* George B. Seitz *Cast* Pearl White, Creighton Hale, Arnold Daly, Edwin Arden *Prod* Wharton for Pathé. 10 episodes, each 2 reels. Fans demanded a continuation of the *Elaine* serial; a new villain was introduced — Edwin Arden as Wu Fang.
— **The Romance of Elaine* USA 1915. *Dir* George B. Seitz, Donald MacKenzie, Louis Gasnier *Scen* George B. Seitz *Cast* Pearl White, Creighton Hale, Arnold Daly, Lionel Barrymore *Prod* Wharton for Pathé. 12 episodes, each 2 reels. N.B. In several countries, Pathé combined all three of these serials into one, re-edited version, e.g., in France they were released in one 22-episode serial titled *Les Mystères de New York*.

EXTASE/ECSTASY Czechoslovakia 1932. *Dir* Gustav Machaty *Scen* Gustav Machaty, Frantisek Horky, V. Nezval *Photog* Jan Stallich *Mus* Giuseppe Becce *Cast* Hedy Kieslerova (later Hedy Lamarr) Aribert Mog, Zvonimir Rogoz, Leopold Kramer [German version, 1934 *Dialogue* Robert Horky] *Prod* Universal Elektra Film. 90 mins.
In the countryside, a young woman (Kieslerova) takes a lover (Mog). A theme analagous in its simplicity to Machaty's *Erotikon* (*q.v.*).
Seductive imagery of the summer countryside and animals, Hedy (Kieslerova) Lamarr in the nude, and frank, though often symbolic, depictions of sexual love assured the film's international success. The film's qualities are nevertheless very real — not the least of them being the social criticism, probably the responsibility of the poet, Nezval. Some scenes (such as the work sequence edited in an Eisenstein manner) clearly show the influence of the Soviet cinema.
The film was originally produced under the title *Symphony of Love,* a more meaningful title in view of the film's essentially rhythmic visual style.

EXTERMINATING ANGEL (THE) ANGEL EXTERMINADOR (EL)

EXTRAORDINARY ADVENTURES OF MR. WEST IN THE LAND OF THE BOLSHEVIKS (THE) NEOBYCHAINIYE PRIKLUCHENIYA MISTERA VEST V STRANYE BOLSHEVIKOV

FABULOUS WORLD OF JULES VERNE (THE)
VYNÁLEZ ZKÁZY

FACE IN THE CROWD (A) USA 1957. *Dir* Elia Kazan *Scen* Budd Schulberg from his own short story *Your Arkansas Traveler Photog* Harry Stradling, Gayne Rescher *Mus* Tom Glazer *Cast* Andy Griffith, Lee Remick, Patricia Neal, Walter Matthau, Anthony Franciosa, Rod Brasfield *Prod* Newton Productions for Warner Brothers. 125 mins.

Marcia (Neal), a radio reporter, discovers a drunken down-and-out singer, Lonesome Rhodes (Griffith), in jail. He is given a radio program and becomes very popular. With Marcia and his self-appointed agent, Joe (Franciosa), Rhodes goes to New York where his TV program makes him a national idol. He asks Marcia to marry him but suddenly marries a little majorette (Remick). Marcia and a writer, Mel (Matthau), become more disturbed as Rhodes becomes involved with a group grooming an isolationist senator for the presidency. Appalled by the power he wields and by his megalomania, Marcia smashes him by turning on the sound one night as he is deriding his public after his show has gone off the air.

Some people consider that this film, by the director of *On the Waterfront* (*q.v.*), is an attack on fascism and the personality cult. However, Kazan lays more blame on the "gullible crowd" (who are captivated by Rhodes because they are like him) than on his megalomaniac hero.

This was the film debut of both Lee Remick and Andy Griffith.

FAITHFUL HEART (THE) COEUR FIDÈLE

FAKING WITH SOCIETY CAUGHT IN A CABARET

FALCON TAKES OVER (THE) see FAREWELL, MY LOVELY

FALLEN IDOL (THE) Britain 1948. *Dir* Carol Reed *Scen* Graham Greene based on his own story *The Basement Room Photog* Georges Périnal *Art Dir* Vincent Korda *Mus* William Alwyn *Ed* Oswald Hafenrichter *Cast* Ralph Richardson, Michèle Morgan, Sonia Dresdel, Bobby Henrey *Prod* London Films. 94 mins.

A small boy, Felipe (Henrey), is left in the charge of the butler Baines (Richardson), and his wife (Dresdel) during his parents' absence from the embassy in London where they live. He becomes a bewildered witness to Baines's unhappy love affair with Julie (Morgan) and to Mrs. Baines's accidental death. Because Baines is his hero, and because he thinks Baines actually killed his wife, Felipe lies valiantly to save him but only gets the innocent man more deeply involved. He discovers that Baines himself had been telling many white lies. Eventually the police find a clue that clears the butler.

The subtle creation of atmosphere and the effective, though conventional, characterizations make this Carol Reed's best film.

FALL OF BERLIN (THE) PADENIYE BERLINA

***FALL OF THE HOUSE OF USHER** USA 1928. *Dir* James Sibley Watson *Scen/Art Dir* Melville Webber *Photog* James Sibley Watson *Cast* Melville Webber, Herbert Stem, Hildegarde Watson *Prod* Melville Webber. 1,253 ft.

An experimental fantasy loosely based on the Poe story that creates atmospheric effects by using lights on wall board instead of painted sets, optical distortions through prisms and mirrors, and multiple exposures. An important example of the early American avant-garde though without the strength of the Epstein version.

— *The Fall of the House of Usher* Britain 1949. *Dir/Photog* Ivan Barnett *Cast* Gwendolen Watford, Kay Tendeter, Irving Steen. 70 mins.
An independent production of little merit.

— *The Fall of the House of Usher/The House of Usher* USA 1960. *Dir* Roger Corman *Scen* Richard Matheson based on the Poe story *Photog* Floyd Crosby *Cast* Vincent Price, Myrna Fahey, Mark Domon. 79 mins. Eastman Color. CinemaScope.
This is one of Corman's best early efforts and is replete with an eerie sense of gothic madness that owes much to Floyd Crosby's camerawork.
See also *Chute de la Maison Usher (La)*

FALL OF THE ROMANOV DYNASTY (THE)
PADENIYE DINASTI ROMANOVIKH

FALSTAFF CAMPANADAS A MEDIANOCHE

FANFAN LA TULIPE France 1951. *Dir* Christian-Jaque *Scen* René Wheeler, René Fallet, Henri Jeanson, Christian-Jaque *Photog* Christian Matras *Art Dir* Robert Gys *Mus* Georges Van Parys, Maurice Thiriet *Cast* Gérard Philipe, Gina Lollobrigida, Noël Roquevert, Marcel Herrand. 102 mins.
During the Seven Years War, Fanfan (Philipe) is signed up by a recruiting sergeant (Roquevert) and courts a gypsy (Lollobrigida). He gets into Louis XV's (Herrand) chateau, is condemned to death, and then wins the war all by himself.
Famous sequences: the enlistment by the recruiting sergeant; the bandit attack on a coach; the rooftop battle with the sergeant; the hanging that doesn't succeed; Fanfan's rescue of the gypsy; the chase on horseback.
Christian-Jaque made the film in Provence with great good humor and merriment. Gérard Philipe, cavalier, duellist, and Don Juan, gives a very striking performance that endeared him to millions of admirers, while Gina Lollobrigida's appearance in the film made her an international star. Jeanson's caustic dialogue was prompted by a satire on the "phoney war."
— *Fanfan la tulipe* France 1925. *Dir* René Leprince.

Not an earlier version but a film with the same title.

FANGELSE THE DEVIL'S WANTON/PRISON Sweden 1948. *Dir/Scen* Ingmar Bergman *Photog* Göran Strindberg *Art Dir* P. A. Lundgren *Mus* Erland von Koch *Ed* Lennart Wallén *Cast* Doris Svedlund, Birger Malmsten, Hasse Ekman, Eva Henning, Stig Olin, Irma Christenson *Prod* Terrafilm. 78 mins.
Martin (Ekman), a film director, tells Tomas (Malmsten), a married scriptwriter, of an idea for a film about hell on earth suggested by an old professor. Tomas, who is married to Sofi (Henning), thinks the film might succeed because he has met the ideal heroine, Birgitta-Carolina (Svedlund), a prostitute. She lives with her protector, Peter (Olin), who drowns the child she gives birth to. Exasperated, she runs away with Tomas, who thinks he has murdered his wife, and they live briefly in an attic. But they are forced to part and she commits suicide in a cellar. Tomas returns to Sofi.
The first film that was entirely Bergman's and one of his most personal works. "Life is just a bad curve between birth and death," concludes Tomas who is Bergman's mouthpiece, while in the opening scene the old professor suggests: "Make a film about hell — hell on earth. They would condemn the man who dropped the first atomic bomb equally with the girl who has an abortion. The Devil satisfies the needs of man. As for God, He's dead and life is nothing but a sneering masterpiece."
Memorable sequences in this "meditation on life and death": the satire on studio film production; Tomas and Birgitta-Carolina watching an old slapstick film in the attic; Birgitta-Carolina's oneiric dream in which she sees Peter take from a bath of water a plastic doll that changes in his hands into a fish that he sadistically guts; Birgitta-Carolina's stabbing herself to death in a cellar.
"The borderline is still hazy between the film studio and the real world where other fleeting events are occurring as time flows irrevocably on without even being preserved on celluloid" (Jean Béranger).

FANNY see MARIUS

FANTASIA USA 1940, *Dir* Walt Disney

Story Directors Joe Grant, Dick Huemer, Ford Beebe, etc. *Dir Anim* Kay Nielsen, John Hubley, etc. *Ed* Stephen Csillag *Prod* Walt Disney. 135 mins. Wide screen. Multiplane Technicolor and Fantasound. Shortened in some re-release versions.

Seven animated sequences interpret eight famous musical themes: *Toccata and Fugue in D minor* — J. S. Bach (abstract forms in the manner of Oscar Fischinger); *The Nutcracker Suite* — Tchaikovsky a ballet of flowers, butterflies, etc.); *The Sorcerer's Apprentice* — Dukas (Mickey Mouse); *The Rite of Spring* — Stravinsky (the creation and evolution of the world, "a paleontological cataclysm" according to Stravinsky); *The Pastoral Symphony* — Beethoven (a ballet of fauns, nymphs, centaurs, etc.); *Dance of the Hours* — Ponchielli (a burlesque ballet by elephants and other animals); *Night on Bald Mountain* and *Ave Maria* — Moussorgsky and Schubert (a battle between good and evil, the Devil and God, with good finally triumphant).

The best sequences are those in which Disney was not afraid to burlesque; the worst those in which he tries to be "arty." The traditional and humorous Mickey Mouse sequences in *The Sorcerer's Apprentice* is the most enjoyable. The worst artistic insult is Beethoven's *Pastoral Symphony* used as background for a fairy-like ballet, as unintentionally heavy and elephantine as *The Dance of the Hours* sequence. The Bach sequence is acceptable, although it vulgarizes Fischinger's experiments (he had been hired by Disney for this sequence but was fired before completing it). The ponderous didacticism in the Stravinsky "creation of the world" sequence is matched only by the portentous moralizing in the finale. In this pretentious film, Walt Disney imagined he was Goethe but mainly succeeds in achieving only something at the level of the German turn-of-the-century chromos.

Fantasia is notable in that it was produced with stereophonic sound, a technical innovation in 1940. The musical score was performed by the Philadelphia Symphony Orchestra under the direction of Leopold Stokowski.

FANTOMAS (series) France 1913–14. 5 episodes: 1. *Fantômas* (*Fantomas Under the Shadow of the Guillotine*) in 3 parts; 2. *Juve Contre Fantômas* (*Juve vs. Fantomas*) in 4 parts; 3. *La Mort qui tue* (*The Mysterious Fingerprints*) in 6 parts; 4. *Fantômas contre Fantômas* (*Fantomas, the Crook-Detective*) in 4 parts; 5 *Le Faux Magistrat* (*Fantômas the False Magistrate*) in 1 part. *Dir* Louis Feuillade *Scen* Louis Feuillade based on the serial-novel by Pierre Souvestre, Marcel Allain *Photog/Ed* Guérin *Cast* René Navarre, Bréon, Georges Melchior, Renée Carl, Yvette Andreyor *Prod* Gaumont. 1. 1,146 meters; 2. 1,288 meters; 3. 1,945 meters; 4. 1,274 meters; 5. 1,881 meters.

From October 1911 until early 1914, Editions Fayard published monthly a large volume devoted to the exploits of Fantomas, "the master of terror and torture and the emperor of crime." The characters were Fantomas, the mysterious bandit in a black hood (Navarre), Juve the detective (Bréon), Fandor the journalist (Melchior), his mistress, Lady Beltham (Carl), and her daughter Hélène (Andreyor). Though some episodes and details were omitted, Feuillade's films were a faithful adaptation of the first five volumes (which were not the best). The books were enormously successful and were translated into 40 languages but the outbreak of war brought the series to an end.

Souvestre and Allain wrote their novels (450 pages a month) using Zola's method of setting each volume in a clearly defined social milieu. Feuillade imitated this approach and the sequences in *Fantômas* alternate between the natural landscape of Paris with its suburbs and living rooms full of Dufayel furniture. The films (like the books) have a singular poetic lyricism and sense of fantasy (much admired by Apollinaire and Max Jacob) and are a veritable documentary about life in France on the eve of the First World War. *Fantômas* was an immense worldwide success, especially in Russia, and helped establish the advent of serials in the USA.

OTHER VERSIONS:

— **Fantomas* USA 1920–21. *Dir/Scen* Edward Sedgwick *Prod* Fox. 20 episodes, 2 reels each.

— *Fantômas* France 1931. *Dir* Paul Féjos.

— **Fantômas* France 1936. 8 mm. film made by Alain Resnais.

— *Fantômas* France 1947. *Dir* Jean Sacha *Cast* Marcel Herrand, Simone Signoret. 95 mins.

— *Fantômas contre Fantômas* France 1949. *Dir* Robert Vernay. 95 mins.

— *Fantômas* France/Italy 1964. *Dir* André Hunebelle *Scen* Jean Halain, Pierre Foucaud *Photog* Marcel Grignon *Cast* Jean Marais, Louis de Funès, Mylène Demongeot. 105 mins. Eastman Color. Franscope.

— **Fantômas se déchaîne* (*Fantomas Strikes Back*) France/Italy 1965. *Dir* André Hunebelle *Scen* Jean Halain, Pierre Foucaud *Photog* Raymond Lemoigne *Cast* Jean Marais, Louis de Funès, Mylène Demongeot. 94 mins. Eastman Color. Franscope.

Although "based" on the famous novel, these commercial films by Hunebelle were more of a parody on Arsène Lupin.

See also *Judex; Vampires (Les)*

FAREWELL, MY LOVELY MURDER, MY SWEET USA 1944. *Dir* Edward Dmytryk *Scen* John Paxton based on the novel by Raymond Chandler *Photog* Harry T. Wild *Art Dir* Carroll Clark, Albert S. D'Agostino *Mus* Roy Webb *Cast* Dick Powell, Claire Trevor, Anne Shirley, Otto Kruger *Prod* RKO. 95 mins.

Philip Marlowe (Powell), a private detective, after going through various adventures with the help of a girl (Shirley), unmasks a rich, seductive woman (Trevor) who kills to prevent her past being known. This is a fine example of the American thriller — in its plot, its atmospheric photography and lighting, its brutality (both police and lovers'), and its theatrical touches and twists of plot. It is one of the best films in the genre — and one of Dmytryk's best.

OTHER VERSION:

— **The Falcon Takes Over* USA 1942. *Dir* Irving Reis *Scen* Lynn Root, Frank Fenton based on *Farewell, My Lovely* by Raymond Chandler and the character created by Michael Arlen *Cast* George Sanders, Lynn Bari, James Gleason *Prod* RKO. 63 mins.

One of a long series of films produced at RKO using the character of the Falcon, a sort of Robin Hood of crime. George Sanders appeared in the title role in four of these and Tom Conway in a further nine. Only the "plot" of the original Chandler novel was used in this version, not the characters or atmosphere.

FARREBIQUE: OU LES QUATRE SAISONS THE FOUR SEASONS France 1947. *Dir/Scen* Georges Rouquier *Photog* André A. Dantan, Marcel Fradetal, Daniel Sarrade, Jean-Jacques Rebuffat *Mus* Henri Sauguet *Ed* Madeleine Gug *Cast* Nonprofessionals and the people of Rouerque district of Aveyron *Prod* Films Etienne Lallier/L'Ecran Français. 100 mins.

"A story which unfolds during the four seasons that divide the film and serve as a calendar. A whole family who have known me since my early childhood retraces (with some cheating) its own story in this film. I put myself in the position of a film maker portraying the inhabitants of any country in the world, noting their mores, customs, and religion. I wanted also to capture a sense of nature: insects, plants, the internal life of vegetation, and the intense and external life of nature . . . Involved are the grandfather, who was head of the farm, the quiet grandmother, Roch the elder son, a wily peasant with old-fashioned ideas and the future head of the farm, Bertha his wife, Henri the younger son, more open to modern ideas, and some children" (Georges Rouquier).

At first it is winter, with the family gathered round the hearth and the kerosene lamp discussing of the events of the day and eating homemade bread. Then comes spring, with the awakening of nature and the senses shown lyrically through slow motion, high speed, and microscopic photography. Summer is crops, harvesting, Mass in the village, and the younger son's accident. The film ends in autumn with its new labors; the grandfather dies and the younger son becomes engaged.

Having depicted a family on an isolated farm in this film, Rouquier wanted to make a sequel that showed life on the farm after electrification and that traced the proletarization of a peasant who becomes a worker in the Renault Plant in Paris. But *Farrebique,* though a great artistic success, was a flop at the box office. Because he produced an excellent *cinéma-vérité* film in advance of its time, this disciple of Flaherty had to leave his work unfinished.

FATE OF A MAN SUDBA CHELOVEKA

FAUST: EINE DEUTSCHE VOLKSSAGE Germany 1926. *Dir.* F. W. Murnau *Scen*

Hans Kyser based on Wolfgang von Goethe, Christopher Marlowe, and German folk sagas *Photog* Carl Hoffman *Art Dir* Robert Herlth, Walter Röhrig *Cast* Emil Jannings, Gösta Ekman, Camilla Horn, Yvette Guilbert, Wilhelm Dieterle *Prod* UFA. 7,934 ft.

The story of the man who sells his soul to the Devil. The opening sequence is brilliant: after a discussion between God and the Devil (Jannings), the Devil tempts Faust (Ekman) and, after the pact, places him on his cloak and transfers him across Europe to the home of the Duchess of Parma. Carl Hoffman's camera swirls around above the set in a splendid baroque movement. But the Princess's ball is like a German music hall in the Twenties. More regrettably, the love scenes with Marguerite (Horn) look like 1910 "art" photos while Marguerite herself is insipid and Faust effeminate.

The film regains a sense of style and grandeur in the climax, as Gretchen's face takes on the appearance of a medieval madonna and Faust mounts the stake because he feels responsible for her being condemned.

OTHER VERSIONS:
— *Faust et Marguerite* France 1897. *Dir* Georges Méliès, G. Hatot.
— *Faust* Britain 1897. *Dir* G. A. Smith.
— *Faust aux enfers/La Damnation de Faust* France 1903. *Dir* Georges Méliès.
— *Faust* France 1904. *Dir* Henri Andreani, Georges Fagot.
— **Faust* Italy 1910. *Dir* Enrico Guazzoni.
— *Le Tout-petit Faust* France 1911. *Dir* Emile Cohl. (Animated).
— **Faust* Czechoslovakia 1912. *Dir* Stanislav Hlavsa.
— *Faust* France 1923. *Dir* Georges Bourgeois.
— *Faust and the Devil* Italy 1949. *Dir* Carmine Gallone (Based on Goethe and on Gounod's opera).
— **Faust* Germany 1962. *Dir* Gustaf Gründgens. (Photographed version of the play.)
Plus many modernized versions or films based on the Faust theme, e.g.:
— **All That Money Can Buy/The Devil and Daniel Webster/Daniel and the Devil* USA 1941. *Dir* William Dieterle *Scen* based on *The Devil and Daniel Webster* by Stephen Vincent Benet *Cast* Walter Huston, James Craig, Edward Arnold.

Set in 19th century America; especially notable for Huston's performance as Mr. Scratch.
— **Alias Nick Beal/The Contact Man* USA 1948. *Dir* John Farrow *Scen* Jonathan Latimer *Cast* Ray Milland, Thomas Mitchell.
— **Marguerite de la nuit* France/Italy 1955. *Dir* Claude Autant-Lara *Cast* Michèle Morgan, Yves Montand. 126 mins. Eastman Color.
— **Faust XX* Romania 1966. *Dir* Ion Popesco Gopo.
— **Dr Faustus* Britain/Italy 1967. *Dir* Richard Burton, Neville Coghill *Cast* Richard Burton, Elizabeth Taylor and members of the Oxford University Dramatic Society.
Adaptation of the play by Christopher Marlowe.
— **Bedazzled* Britain 1967. *Dir* Stanley Donen *Cast* Peter Cook, Dudley Moore, Raquel Welch. 103 mins. DeLuxe Color. Panavision.
See also *Beauté du diable (La)*

FELIX THE CAT (cartoon series) USA 1920–28. *Dir/Prod* Pat Sullivan. 1 reel each.
Felix the Cat was the most popular cartoon character of the Twenties, associated forever with the tune "Felix kept on walking, kept on walking still." The series was originated by the Australian, Pat Sullivan, who created the first film around 1914. Felix's popular success started the fashion for caricatured animals who walk on their hind legs and behave like humans. About 90 films in all were released between 1920 and 1928. Included among these was the first cartoon film with sound, released in 1927, a year before Disney's *Steamboat Willie*. Disney's Mortimer (later Mickey) Mouse was at first an obscure rival, but he and other cartoon characters quickly pushed Felix off the screens, though his adventures were continued for some time in a comic strip.
[The *Krazy Kat* series used a similar character with many of the same tricks. transformations, and visual puns and was possibly derivative. The earliest of these seems to have been made in 1916 by Leon Searly, Frank Moser, and Leon Herriman. The *Krazy Kat* series continued through the Thirties under the direction of Charles Mintz at Columbia.]

FEMME DE NULLE PART (LA) THE WOMAN FROM NOWHERE France 1922. *Dir/Scen*

Louis Delluc *Photog* Lucas, Gibory *Art Dir* F. Jourdain *Cast* Eve Francis, Roger Karl, Gine Avril, André Daven, Noémi Suze. 5,000 ft. approx.

A 50-year-old woman (Francis), returning after 30 years to a home that she had left to go off with another man, finds a young woman (Avril) about to leave her husband (Karl) for a younger man (Daven). She convinces Avril that she shouldn't do it and then leaves, alone. "An inspired, unflinching, and complete film. The visual theme develops harmoniously, smoothly, and tenderly. Memories and love and memories of love rather than love of memories. A film of this kind should stir the soul and I know of no film that does it better. The visit to the park where every step brings back another memory, the dizzy climb up the stairs that she had descended in frantic flight thirty years previously in the impulsiveness of passion are the stuff that drama is made of and touch on cinematic genius" (Léon Moussinac, 1922).

Delluc followed the rule of the three unities, experimenting along lines similar to those of German *Kammerspiel*, which was then unkown to him. Some of the most memorable images (e.g. the opening shot of a child's ball rolling towards the viewer) were not included in the script but were improvised during shooting.

FEMME DU BOULANGER (LA) THE BAKER'S WIFE France 1938. *Dir* Marcel Pagnol *Scen* Marcel Pagnol based on part of novel *Jean le Bleu* by Jean Giono *Photog* G. Beniot, R. Lendruz, N. Daries *Mus* Vincent Scotto *Cast* J. Raimu, Ginette Leclerc, Charles Moulin, Charpin, Robert Vattier, Robert Bassac, Maximilienne. 110 mins.

A baker of Provence (Raimu), whose wife (Leclerc) is having an affair with a handsome shepherd (Moulin), refuses to bake any more bread. The despondent villagers seek out the culprit and solve the baker's problem.

One of the most successful in Pagnol's series of films depicting the life and behavior of ordinary people in the south of France. Raimu's performance made him famous and Ginette Leclerc's role was her best. American critics hailed the film as a great work of art.

*FEMME INFIDELE (LA) THE UNFAITHFUL WIFE France/Italy 1968. *Dir/Scen*

Claude Chabrol *Photog* Jean Rabier *Art Dir* Guy Littaye *Mus* Pierre Jansen *Ed* Jacques Gaillard *Cast* Stéphane Audran, Michel Bouquet, Maurice Ronet *Prod* Films la Boétie/Cinegay. 98 mins. Eastman Color.

A prosperous insurance broker (Bouquet) discovers that his wife (Audran) has a lover (Ronet). He tries to be understanding but breaks down and kills him.

One of Chabrol's most accomplished films. His debt to Hitchcock is most evident in the brilliant narrative touches and carefully structured photography, but it is as a study in guilt and of social and sexual mores that the film makes its impact.

*FENG BAO STORM China 1959. *Dir* Chin Shan *Scen* Chin Shan based on his own play *Red Storm Cast* Chin Shan, Li Hsiang, Chang Ping, Tien Hua *Prod* Peking studio. 108 mins. Color.

"The best post-1949 Chinese film I know" (Jay Leyda). The original play and the film are based on the actual events of the Peking-Hankow railway strike of 1922–23 (an important historical event in China's Revolution). The director has incorporated into this realistic story certain elements of Chinese classical theater, giving the whole film an exceptional artistic unity.

FETE ESPAGNOLE (LA) France 1919. *Dir* Germaine Dulac *Scen* Louis Delluc *Photog* P. Parguel *Cast* Eve Francis, Gaston Modot, Jean Toulout *Prod* Nalpas. 6,000 ft. approx.

Two men (Modot, Toulout) vie for the favors of a woman (Francis), who finally chooses a third.

"Nothing has been written in our country that is more cinematic than this tale of blood, voluptuousness, and death. But the director, Germaine Dulac, does not seem to have mastered the art of film impressionism. The execution patently does not match the conception" (Léon Moussinac). The best part of the film is the "Spanish Fiesta" filmed in quasi-documentary style.

— la *Fête espagnole/Spanish Fiesta* France 1961. *Dir* Jean-Jacques Vierne *Cast* Peter Van Eyck, Daliah Lavi. 100 mins.

[Not a remake, but a love story set in the Spanish Civil War and based on the novel by Henri-François Rey.]

FEU FOLLET (LE) THE FIRE WITHIN/WILL O'THE WISP/FOX FIRE/A TIME TO LIVE AND A TIME TO DIE France/Italy 1963. *Dir* Louis Malle *Scen* Louis Malle based on the novel by Pierre Drieu la Rochelle *Photog* Ghislain Cloquet *Art Dir* Bernard Evein *Mus* Erik Satie *Ed* Suzanne Baron *Cast* Maurice Ronet, Herbert Deschamps, Léna Skerla, Bernard Noël, René Dupuy, Jeanne Moreau, Alexandra Stewart *Prod* Nouvelles Editions de Films/Arco. 110 mins.

The last 24 hours in the life of Alain (Ronet), a 30-year-old man, after he leaves the clinic where he had been undergoing a cure for alcoholism. He spends the night with Lydia (Skerla), a friend of his estranged wife. He goes to Paris for the day hoping a revival of the past might give him a reason for living. But his old friends are involved in their own interests and Alain finds their lives a compromise. His disgust starts him drinking. Next morning he cables his wife, packs his belongings, finishes reading a book, then kills himself.

Louis Malle's script transposed the period of the original novel from the late Twenties to 1963. It is one of his finest films, notable for its atmosphere and depiction of social behavior. Maurice Ronet gives a sympathetic and moving portrayal of Alain, a man irrevocably drawn to his death.

FEU MATHIAS PASCAL THE LATE MATTHEW PASCAL France 1925. *Dir* Marcel L'Herbier *Scen* Marcel L'Herbier based on the novel *Il fu Mattia Pascal* by Luigi Pirandello *Photog* Guichard, Letort, Bourgassof, Berliet *Art Dir* Alberto Cavalcanti, Lazare Meerson *Cast* Ivan Mosjoukine, Marcelle Pradot, Lois Moran, Pierre Batcheff, Jean Hervé, Michel Simon, Pauline Carton *Prod* Albatros-Cinegraphic. 11,410 ft.

A young man (Mosjoukine) goes abroad to find consolation from grief. A false report of his own death allows him to enjoy a longed-for freedom but he finds that a lack of identity can create its own problems.

This is Marcel l'Herbier's best film, together with *Eldorado* (*q.v.*). It is notable for Mosjoukine's powerful comic performance and the documentary-like use of exteriors (shot in Italy). The sets by Cavalcanti and Meerson (whose first film this was) are remarkable, not least because they built rooms with ceilings on them. Michel Simon made his screen debut in this film.

— *Il Fu Mattia Pascal/L'Homme de nulle part* Italy/France 1937. *Dir* Pierre Chenal *Scen* Pierre Chenal, Christian Stengel, Armand Salacrou based on the novel by Luigi Pirandello *Photog* André Bac, Joseph-Louis Mundviller *Mus* Jacques Ibert *Cast* Pierre Blanchar, Isa Miranda. 90 mins. approx.

Quite a good version with excellent use of exteriors.

FIEVRE France 1921. *Dir/Scen* Louis Delluc *Photog* A. Gibory, Lucas *Art Dir* Bécan *Cast* Eve Francis, Edmond Van Daële, Elena Sagrary, Gaston Modot, Léon Moussinac, Footitt, Lili Samuel *Prod* Alhambra-Film. 4,000 ft. approx.

Some sailors arrive in a Marseille bar. One of them makes love to the wife (Francis) of the owner (Modot). A brawl develops involving her husband and a regular customer (Footitt) kills the sailor.

"Delluc thinks directly in images. It's about one night in a bar and a port. That's all. From the first and dominant image (the arrival of the sailors) a succession of images emerge that constitute the theme of the film. The story is used only to reinforce the expressive intensity of the tableau. Titles intervene only when absolutely necessary . . . We were enthralled by the acuity of the first part but the film maker has a right to prefer a hasty sketch to a detailed tableau" (Léon Moussinac).

The second part of the film, dominated by the anecdotal story, is the weaker of the two. The first part is an extraordinary, often impressionistic portrait of a bar and its habitués in which Delluc uses the social milieu as background in depicting his characters. The rule of the three unities is followed so closely that the action of the film corresponds with the projection time. Delluc intended to call the film *La Boue* (*Filth*) but the censors not only demanded that this be changed but passed the film only after significant cuts had been made.

FIN DE FIESTA BLOOD FEAST Argentina 1960. *Dir* Leopoldo Torre Nilsson *Scen* Beatriz Guido, Leopoldo Torre Nilsson, Ricardo Luna, based on the novel by Beatriz Guido *Photog* Ricardo Younis

Mus Juan Carlos Paz *Cast* Arturo Garcia Buhr, Lautaro Murua, Graciela Borges, Leonardo Favio *Prod* Angel Productions. 100 mins.

A young man (Buhr) who is in love with his cousin (Borges) gradually realizes that his grandfather (Murua) is a corrupt politician. In the ensuing conflict the politician destroys himself with his own power while the young man emerges more mature.

A portrait of the Argentinian middle class and the political establishment; one of Torre Nilsson's best films.

FINNIS TERRAE France 1929. *Dir/Scen/ Ed* Jean Epstein *Photog* Joseph Barth, Joseph Kottula assisted by Louis Née, Raymond Tulle *Cast* people of the islands of Bannec, Balanec, and d'Ouessant and the crews of the "Pampero" and "Hermine" *Prod* Société Générale des Films. 7,800 ft. approx.

"The film is much more dramatic than poetic. In attempting to dominate the human element Epstein does not entirely master his theme. As a result the film is a flow of esthetic imagery. On the other hand, nonprofessional actors have never been better. One senses that Epstein took great pains to get the actors accustomed to the camera. From this point of view *Finis Terrae* was a complete revelation and a great success" (Henri Langlois).

FIREMAN (THE) USA 1916. *Dir/Scen* Charles Chaplin *Photog* Rollie Totheroh, William C. Foster *Cast* Chaplin, Edna Purviance, Eric Campbell, Lloyd Bacon, Leo White, John Rand, Frank J. Coleman, James T. Kelley. *Prod* Mutual. 1,600 ft.

A great success, with a dazzling display of gags: Charlie extracting coffee and cream from the engine boiler; the excited Frenchman in a top hat (White) who cannot get Charlie and another fireman away from their game of checkers, etc. However, after the film's release, Chaplin received a letter from an admirer which said: "I am very much afraid that you are becoming a slave to your public," and concluded by urging him to "pay no attention to what the public demands," since it only encourages him to become repetitive and stagnated in his art and character. This film marked the end of Chaplin's blithe improvisational films and the beginning of the period in which he exactly refined every gag until it was perfect.

FIRES ON THE PLAIN NOBI

*FIRES WERE STARTED I WAS A FIREMAN Britain 1942 (released 1943). *Dir/Scen* Humphrey Jennings *Photog* Cyril Pennington-Richards *Art Dir* Edward Carrick *Mus* William Alwyn *Ed* Stewart McAllister *Prod* Crown Film Unit. 63 mins.

"A story of one particular unit of the National Fire Service during one particular day and night in the middle of the London Blitz; in the morning the men leave their homes and civil occupations, their taxicabs, newspaper shops, advertising agencies, to start their tour of duty; a new recruit arrives and is shown the ropes; warning comes in that a heavy attack is expected, night falls and the alarms begin to wail; the unit is called out to action at a riverside warehouse, where fire threatens an ammunition ship drawn up at the wharf; the fire is mastered; a man is lost; the ship sails with the morning tide" (Lindsay Anderson).

Although conceived as a documentary, the final form is more dramatic and poetic than pedagogic, an astonishingly intimate portrait of an isolated and besieged Britain. It is perhaps the crowning achievement of the British documentary school — an unforgettable piece of human observation, affectionate, touching, and yet ironic. Although the sequence in which the firemen enter the recreation room to the tune of "One Man Went to Mow" is perhaps the most warmly memorable, it is in the firefighting scenes and their aftermath that Jennings is at his best. Here against a backdrop of extraordinarily photographed and edited visuals, the characters play out Jennings' most profound belief: the willing involvement of the individual in a social act.

FIRE WITHIN (THE) FEU FOLLET (LE)

FIRST YEARS (THE) PIERWSZE LATA

FIVE BOYS FROM BARSKA STREET PIATKA Z ULICY BARSKIEJ

FIVE DAY LOVER AMANT DE CINQ JOURS. (L')

FLAMING YEARS (THE) POVEST' PLAMEN-
NYKH LET

*****FLESH** USA 1968. *Dir/Scen/Photog* Paul
Morrissey *Cast* Joe d'Allesandro, Geraldine Smith, Maurice Bradell, Louis
Waldon, Geri Miller *Prod* Andy Warhol/
Factory Films. 105 mins. (89 mins.
Britain) Eastman Color.
A day in the life of Joe (d'Allesandro),
a hustler in New York's East Village
whose wife (Smith) sends him out to
earn money for a girl friend's abortion.
He earns money from two men, meets
some other hustlers, and calls on a
former girl friend (Miller) who performs fellatio on him and tells him she
once submitted to rape for his sake. He
returns home without sufficient money
only to find his wife's friend does not
need an abortion. He falls asleep and
leaves them to their own devices.
"Flesh was made on about six or seven
weekends, Saturday afternoons . . . while
Andy was in hospital" (Paul Morrissey). It is a documentary-like description of a New York subculture, truthful,
precise, and compassionate. Rejecting
Warhol's passive approach, Morrissey
gives the film a visual structure and overt
meaning, although some of the exterior
shots seem gratuitously designed for effect.

FLESH AND THE DEVIL USA 1927. *Dir*
Clarence Brown *Scen* Benjamin Glazier
based on the novel *The Undying Past*
by Hermann Sudermann *Photog* William Daniels *Ed* Lloyd Nosler *Cast* Greta
Garbo, John Gilbert, Lars Hanson *Prod*
MGM. 8,759 ft.
Leo von Sellenthin (Gilbert) and Ulrich von Kletzingh (Hanson) are friends
with neighboring estates in Austria. Leo's
affair with Felicitas (Garbo) is discovered by her husband; Leo kills
him in a duel and is forced to flee
the country. Ulrich, unaware, of the
affair, marries Felicitas. When Leo returns, Felicitas lures him again into an
affair and then tells Ulrich that Leo
tempted her. In trying to prevent the
ensuing duel, Felicitas falls through the
ice in a river and drowns. Leo wounds
Ulrich but nurses him back to health
and their friendship is renewed.
Based on a typical Sudermann romantic
melodrama, this film is memorable for
its beautifully re-created Austrian atmosphere and for the extraordinary communion service scene in which Garbo
turns the chalice so that her lips will
touch the spot from which her lover
drank.
[This was the first of four films Garbo
made with John Gilbert and the first of
seven in which Clarence Brown directed
Garbo.]

FLESH AND THE WOMAN see GRAND JEU
(LE)

FLIGHT COMMANDER (THE) DAWN PATROL

FLOORWALKER (THE) USA 1916. *Dir/Scen*
Charles Chaplin *Photog* Rollie Totheroh,
William C. Foster *Cast* Chaplin, Edna
Purviance, Eric Campbell, Lloyd Bacon,
Albert Austin, Charlotte Mineau, Leo
White *Prod* Mutual. 1,927 ft.
Chaplin's first film for Mutual in which
the action is built around the escalator
in a department store. [The funniest
scene involves the meeting of the floorwalker (Bacon) and Charlie, with both
thinking they are looking in a mirror.
The final wild chase sequence, including
a chase down the "up" escalator, is inspired slapstick.]

FLORENTINER HUT (DER) see UN CHAPEAU
DE PAILLE D'ITALIE

FOOLISH WIVES USA 1921. *Dir/Scen*
Erich von Stroheim *Assist* Eddy Sowders, Louis Germonprez *Photog* Ben
Reynolds, William Daniels *Art Dir* Erich
von Stroheim, Richard Day *Cast* Erich
von Stroheim, Maud George, Mae Busch,
Cesare Gravina, Malvine Polo, George
Christians, Miss Dupont, Dale Fuller
Prod Universal. Original length 21 reels,
reduced to 14,120 ft. for release; 7,700 ft.
in existing versions.
In Monte Carlo about 1918, "Count"
Wladislas Sergei Karamzin (von Stroheim), his two "cousins" (George, Busch)
and their maid (Fuller), whom the count
has seduced, live on their wits in a luxurious villa. A poor Italian artist (Gravina) gives them counterfeit money in
order to support his beautiful, but idiot,
daughter (Polo) and the count seduces,
then blackmails, rich, foolish wives.
When a wealthy American (Christians)
arrives with his pretty wife (Dupont) he
plans to seduce her, but his attempts
fail and he sends her a note threatening

suicide. She goes to his villa, but the count's maid, jealous because the count's promise to marry her is unfulfilled, sets fire to the house. They are rescued just in time and the American challenges the count. On the night of the duel, the count rapes the counterfeiter's daughter, who has aroused his appetites. The father kills him and throws his body in a sewer and the count's "cousins" are arrested by the police.

The best sequences (of about 20 or 30 memorable ones) are: the count kissing the ugly maid then aristocratically wiping his lips in disgust; the meeting at the villa gates with an armless war veteran; the American wife and the count trapped in a lonely cabin after a storm; the fire started by the jealous maid; the two cousins taking off their wigs; the count's body thrown into the sewer.

Carl Laemmle, head of Universal, gave the film enormous publicity, putting up billboards in the center of large cities announcing, "To date, $423,000 has been spent on von $troheim's *Foolish Wives*" (the S in his name was printed like a $ sign). Each day the figure increased until it exceeded a million. Stroheim himself says the film couldn't have cost more than three or four hundred thousand dollars and that the million dollar figure was a publicist's fiction.

A huge set representing the main square of Monaco complete with casino and hotels was built near Hollywood. Stroheim's penchant for realism was such that he demanded that real bells should be rung in the interiors. This tiny expense was begrudged by the producers more than Stroheim's impressive and minutely correct re-creation of Monte Carlo. Stroheim's obsession with realism pervades this romantic film, which nonetheless offers a true portrait of Europe at the time.

*FOOL THERE WAS (A) USA 1914. *Dir/ Scen* Frank Powell based on Porter Emerson Brown's play, itself based on Rudyard Kipling's poem "The Vampire" *Photog* Roy L. McCardell *Cast* Theda Bara, Edward José, Mabel Frenyear *Prod* Fox. 5,300 ft.

A woman of notorious reputation (Bara), known as the Vampire, seduces a happy family man (José) and drives him to helpless drunkenness. His wife (Frenyear) begs him to return but he falls down dead.

This film precipitated a then unknown Theda Bara into spectacular stardom, introduced the word "vamp" into the language and started a cycle of vamp movies. The famous subtitle, "Kiss me, my fool," affected a generation of movie goers. The film was remade in 1922.

FOOTLIGHTS LUCI DEL VARIETÀ

FORBIDDEN GAMES JEUX INTERDITS

FOREST OF THE HANGED (THE) PADUREA SPINZURATILOR

FOREVER see PETER IBBETSON

FORTY-FIRST (THE) SOROK PERVYI

42ND STREET USA 1933. *Dir* Lloyd Bacon *Scen* Rian James, James Seymour based on the novel by Bradford Ropes *Photog* Sol Polito *Art Dir* Jack Okey *Songs,* Al Dubin, Harry Warren *Choreog* Busby Berkeley *Ed* Thomas Pratt *Cast* Warner Baxter, Bebe Daniels, Gingers Rogers, Dick Powell, George Brent, Ruby Keeler, Una Merkel, Guy Kibbee *Prod* Warner Brothers. 98 mins.

The financial and love mix-ups of a producer (Baxter) trying to mount a musical spectacular.

A banal plot based on the theme of "the show must go on" is the backdrop for the superb dance sequences staged by Busby Berkeley, who is more responsible for the film's success than Lloyd Bacon. This was Ruby Keeler's first major role.

FORTY-SEVEN RONIN (THE) GENROKU CHU-SHINGURA

FOUR FROM THE INFANTRY WESTFRONT 1918

FOUR HORSEMEN OF THE APOCALYPSE (THE) USA 1921. *Dir* Rex Ingram *Scen* June Mathis based on the novel by Vicente Blasco-Ibáñez *Photog* John F. Seitz *Ed* Grant Whytock, June Mathis *Cast* Rudolph Valentino, Alice Terry, Nigel de Brulier, Alan Hale, Jean Hersholt, Pomroy Cannon, Wallace Beery *Prod* Metro. 10,270 ft.

"The unexpected and phenomenal success of *The Four Horsemen* made the reputation of Rex Ingram as a director . . . established Rudolph Valentino, an unknown actor, as a star; and brought recognition and praise to June Mathis, its continuity writer and cutter. The film . . . was a pro-war picture, showing the awakening of an Argentinian (Valentino) to his duty to his father's country, France. Although its story was drawn out, the characters undefined, and the attitude toward war and the Germans was still soured by the bigotry of World War days, it was distinguished by pictorial beauty and many hailed the film as a magnificent work of art. In technique it displayed the influence of Griffith and of the current German importations. Animals and birds were used to point a situation humorously; the symbolic sequences of "The Four Horsemen" (War, Plague, Famine, and Death) galloping through clouds over battle-torn fields were reminiscent of Griffith; the spectacular mass scene suggested the German films. The whole was a blend of exotic settings, striking composition, dramatic lighting, and colorful if sordid atmosphere" (Lewis Jacobs).

The picture grossed $4,500,000 in the United States alone, the record for silent movies (cf. *Ben Hur*, $4,000,000; *The Birth of a Nation*, $3,500,000).

OTHER VERSIONS:

— *The Four Horsemen of the Apocalypse* USA 1961. *Dir* Vincente Minnelli *Scen* Robert Ardrey, John Gay based on the novel *Photog* Milton Krasner *Art Dir* George W. Davis, Urie McCleary, Elliot Scott *Mus* André Previn *Cast* Glenn Ford, Ingrid Thulin, Charles Boyer, Paul Lukas *Prod* Julian Blaustein/MGM. 153 mins. CinemaScope. Metrocolor.

A spectacular (with the plot updated to the Second World War) that cost several million dollars and lost most of them. The opening sequence, in particular, is in very bad taste.

— *Debout les morts* France 1917. *Dir* André Heuze.

This first version of the novel was largely unseen, even at the time.

400 BLOWS (THE) QUATRE CENTS COUPS (LES)

400 MILLION (THE) CHINA'S FOUR HUNDRED MILLION USA 1938–39. *Dir/Scen* Joris Ivens *Commentary* Dudley Nichols *Photog* John Ferno, Robert Capa *Ed* Helen van Dongen *Mus* Hanns Eisler. *Prod* Contemporary Historians. 54 mins. The film's theme is the fight of 400 million Chinese against the Japanese invasion in 1937. It was financed by a company formed by Hemingway, Dudley Nichols, Franchot Tone, Fredric March, Luise Rainer, and several others.

"One of the most striking documents ever produced on any war. The first scenes are unforgettable: the bombing of a large city, streets in flames, women in tears, the corpses of children, old people fleeing, the dead piled up like cattle, and the roar of Japanese aircraft" (Georges Sadoul, 1939). The main section of the film depicts a battle waged against the Japanese in which the Chinese are victorious.

FOUR SEASONS (THE) FARREBIQUE

FOUR STEPS IN THE CLOUDS QUATTRO PASSI FRA LE NUVOLE

FOX FIRE FEU FOLLET (LE)

FRAGMENT OF AN EMPIRE OBLOMOK IMPERII

FRAIL FLOWERS ARE DISAPPEARING (THE) DÉJA S'ENVOLE LA FLEUR MAIGRE

*FRANKENSTEIN USA 1931. *Dir* James Whale *Scen* Garrett Fort, John L. Balderston, Francis Edward Faragoh, Robert Florey (not credited) based on the novel by Mary Shelley and the play by Peggy Webling *Photog* Arthur Edeson *Art Dir* Charles D. Hall *Ed* Clarence Kolster *Make-up* Jack Pierce *Cast* Boris Karloff, Mae Clarke, John Boles, Colin Clive *Prod* Universal. 71 mins.

The famous story of a scientist, Dr. Frankenstein (Clive), who discovers how to create a live man (Karloff).

One of the most famous horror films and one which brought well-deserved fame to Boris Karloff as the monster (a role he was to play three times). "A stark, gloomy film, urelieved by comedy or music . . . the outdoor scenes (are) set in a rocky wasteland under a livid sky . . . Its terror is cold, chilling the marrow but never arousing malaise" (Carlos Clarens). Robert Florey (originally assigned as director) was responsible for the basic change in Mary Shelley's plot, giving the monster the brain of a madman. The film's debt to *The Golem* (*q.v.*) is obvious.

OTHER VERSIONS:

— *Frankenstein USA 1910. *Prod* Edison.

— *Life Without Soul* USA 1915. *Dir* Joseph W. Smiley *Cast* Perry Darrel Standing. 5 reels.

— *The Bride of Frankenstein* USA 1935. *Dir* James Whale *Scen* John L. Balderston, Anthony Veiller *Cast* Boris Karloff, Colin Clive, Elsa Lanchester *Prod* Universal.

Both an elegant gothic horror piece and a delightful parody of them.

— *Son of Frankenstein* USA 1939. *Dir* Rowland V. Lee *Scen* Willis Cooper *Cast* Boris Karloff, Bela Lugosi, Basil Rathbone *Prod* Universal.

— *Frankenstein Meets the Wolf-Man* USA 1943. *Dir* Roy William Neill *Scen* Curt Siodmak *Cast* Lon Chaney, Jr., Bela Lugosi *Prod* Universal.

— *Torticola contre Frankensberg* France 1952. *Dir* Paul Paviot *Cast* Michel Piccoli, Roger Blin.

— *The Curse of Frankenstein* Britain 1956. *Dir* Terence Fisher *Cast* Christopher Lee, Peter Cushing *Prod* Hammer. Color.

— *The Revenge of Frankenstein* Britain 1958. *Dir* Terence Fisher *Cast* Michael Gwynn, Peter Cushing *Prod* Hammer. Color.

— *The Evil of Frankenstein* Britain 1963. *Dir* Freddie Francis *Cast* Kiwi Kingston, Peter Cushing *Prod* Hammer. Color.

— *Frankenstein Created Woman* Britain 1966. *Dir* Terence Fisher *Cast* Peter Cushing *Prod* Hammer. Color.

— *Frankenstein Must Be Destroyed* Britain 1969. *Dir* Terence Fisher *Cast* Peter Cushing, Veronica Carlson *Prod* Hammer. Color.

*And many others using the Frankenstein character, e.g.: *Abbott and Costello Meet Frankenstein; Frankenstein 70; I Was a Teenage Frankenstein; Frankenstein Meets the Space Monster; Jesse James Meets Frankenstein's Daughter.*

FREAKS USA 1932. *Dir* Tod Browning *Scen* Willis Goldbeck, Leon Gordon, Edgar Allan Woolf, Al Boasberg based on *Spurs* by Tod Robbins *Photog* Merritt B. Gerstad *Sound* Gavin Burns *Ed* Basil Wrangell *Cast* Wallace Ford, Leila Hyams, Olga Baclanova, Rosco Ates, Henry Victor, Rose Dione, Harry Earles, Daisy Earles, the Siamese twins Daisy and Violet Hilton, Johnny Eck (boy with half a torso), Angelo (the midget), Randian (Hindu living torso), etc. *Prod* MGM. 64 mins.

"The beautiful trapeze artist Cleopatra (Baclanova) pretends to be in love with a midget (Harry Earles) and marries him in order to steal his inheritance. With the help of her love, Hercules (Victor), she tries to poison him. The film takes place in a Court of Miracles atmosphere involving sword swallowers, fire eaters, bearded ladies, women with prehensile feet, skeleton men, men with bird heads, and living torsos. The bizarre becomes tragically fatal when the freaks discover the plot and wreak a terrible revenge on Cleopatra and Hercules. As the climactic attack develops, close-ups show glimpses of a dwarf playing the ocarina while Johnny Eck, whose torso seems to shoot forth from a chair, nonchalantly caresses his parabellum. The freaks' revenge then takes on the force of old and forgotten rituals. The heights of terror reached in this film have their parallel only in Poe's *Hop Frog*" (Paul Gilson).

[This grisly yet compassionate film ran into trouble on its release: many exhibitors in the USA refused to play it and it was banned in Britain for thirty years.]

FREE TO LIVE HOLIDAY

FRENCH CANCAN France/Italy 1954. *Dir* Jean Renoir *Scen* Jean Renoir based on an idea by André-Paul Antoine *Photog* Michel Kelber *Art Dir* Max Douy *Mus* Georges Van Parys *Costumes* Rosine Delamare *Ed* Boris Lewin *Cast* Jean Gabin, Françoise Arnoul, Maria Félix, J.-R. Caussimon. 105 mins. Technicolor.

Montmartre in the late 1880's: an impoverished middle-aged impresario, Danglard (Gabin), discovers Nini (Arnoul), a laundry girl, and decides she has talent. Baron Walter (Caussimon) agrees to finance a new theater, the Moulin Rouge, in which Nini will star in the Cancan. Danglard's mistress (Félix) is jealous of Nini. When Danglard turns to yet another love on opening night, Nini decides the show must go on and launches the final triumphant dance.

French Cancan was not only Renoir's first film in France for 15 years, but his best film of the Fifties. The film's visual qualities were Renoir's prime concern: "It is rather a piece of tapestry, a composition in colors. The music is not only used as an accompaniment and commentary but rather as counterpoint" (Renoir). The carefully designed street scenes evoke the paintings of the impressionists and the use of color is extraordinarily inventive, but underneath the intense vitality a streak of bitterness is detectable, *French Cancan* is also a social analysis of the conditions that made Montmartre a pleasure spot for wealthy foreign tourists.

Françoise Arnoul gives her best performance and Gabin gives his last great one.

FRENZY HETS

FRERES BOUQUINQUANT (LES) France 1947. *Dir* Louis Daquin *Scen* Louis Daquin, André Cerf based on the novel by Jean Prévost *Photog* Louis Page *Mus* Jean Wiener *Cast* Marcel Préjean, Roger Pigaut, Madeleine Robinson, Jean Vilar, Louis Seigner, Frankeur *Prod* A. Kamenka. 99 mins.

The brothers Bouquinquant (Préjean, Pigaut) are in love with the same woman (Robinson). They fight and one of them is drowned. The woman is arrested and imprisoned, but released when she promises her confessor (Vilar) she will not see the man she loves again. Based on Jean Prévost's popular novel, this is one of Daquin's best films. It is dominated by the personality of Madeleine Robinson, both as a cook in a middle-class home and as a prisoner harassed by her confessor.

FRESHMAN (THE) USA 1925. *Dir* Fred Newmeyer, Sam Taylor *Scen* Sam Taylor, John Grey, Ted Wilde, Tim Wheelan *Photog* Walter Lundin, Henry Kohler *Cast* Harold Lloyd, Jobyna Ralston, Brooks Benedict *Prod* Harold Lloyd Corp. for Pathé. 6,883 ft.

Harold Lloyd, a college student, becomes a football player and through his lucky awkwardness assures his team of victory.

The last reel (the most brilliant) was used later as a preface to Harold Lloyd's last full-length film, *Mad Wednesday* (1946), directed by Preston Sturges. *The Freshman* grossed $2.6 million in the USA compared to $2.5 million for *The Kid, Gold Rush,* and Cecil B. De Mille's *Ten Commandments.*

FREUDLOSE GASSE (DIE) THE JOYLESS STREET Germany 1925. *Dir* G. W. Pabst *Scen* Willy Haas based on the novel by Hugo Bettauer *Photog* Guido Seeber, Curt Oertel, Robert Lach *Art Dir* Hans Sohnle, Otto Erdmann *Cast* Asta Nielsen, Greta Garbo, Werner Krauss, Valeska Gert, Gräfin Agnes Esterhazy, Einar Hanson *Prod* Sofar-Film. 3,734 meters (12,300 ft. approx.).

A study of the inhabitants of one street in inflation-ridden Vienna after the First World War. In order to feed her family, the daughter (Garbo) of an official who has lost his job almost becomes the victim of a procuress (Gert); a kept woman (Nielsen) is almost raped by a butcher (Krauss) but is saved from prostitution by an American (Hanson).

This film brought fame to Pabst during a low period in German cinema. It also made Greta Garbo famous. Though she was then an unknown actress, she was quickly recognized as more the star of the film than the recognized star, Asta Nielsen.

Based on factual accounts and Pabst's own experiences in Vienna, the film astounded audiences everywhere by the accuracy with which it portrayed the economic and moral breakdown, and the poverty and despair of Central Europe after Germany's defeat. Produced entirely in the studio, its sets and lighting show the influence of expressionism. Its success did much to encourage German film makers to use expressionism and *Kammerspiel* as a means of elucidating themes dealing with society and everyday life.

The Joyless Street, however, is not a complete success: the last part is boring and the "happy ending" intolerable.

FROKEN JULIE MISS JULIE Sweden 1951. *Dir* Alf Sjöberg *Scen* Alf Sjöberg based on the play by August Strindberg *Photog* Goran Strindberg *Art Dir* Bibi Lindström *Mus* Dag Wiren *Ed* Lennart Wallen *Cast* Anita Björk, Ulf Palme, Märta Dorff, Anders Henrikson *Prod* Sandrew. 87 mins.

One Midsummer's Eve, Miss Julie (Björk), the daughter of a wealthy count (Henrikson), seduces the count's groom, Jean (Palme). She tells him of her upbringing and they plan to run away. The next morning, Miss Julie realizes she can never regain her former propriety and dignity and cuts her throat.

"The action, which is in two parts, takes place entirely in and around the mansion. There are only three main actors.

While the film is scrupulously faithful to the original text, some of the dialogue is used as voice-over in many short sequences that are set against a variety of backgrounds and that use flashbacks. Sjöberg totally reshapes the story cinematically" (Jean Béranger). The technique of showing these flashbacks is often highly original. Instead of relating them to the present by the usual method of a lap dissolve, Sjöberg superimposes the present over the past with a transition image, so that, for example, Julie the little girl enters the frame behind Julie the young woman.

The film was a great international success, not only because of its atmosphere of passion and its feeling for nature, but also because of Anita Björk's superb portrayal of the capricious, neurotic, tormented Julie and Ulf Palme's restrained performance as the brutally sensual Jean.

OTHER VERSIONS:

— *Fröken Julie* Sweden 1912. *Dir* Anna Hoffman-Uddgren *Cast* August Falk.
— **Plebei/Plebian* Russia 1915. *Dir* Yakov Protazanov.
— *Fräulein Julie* Germany 1921. *Dir* Leopold Jessner *Cast* Asta Nielsen.
— *El Pecado de Julia* Argentina 1947. *Dir* Mario Soffici.

FROM HERE TO ETERNITY USA 1953. *Dir* Fred Zinnemann *Scen* Daniel Taradash from the novel by James Jones *Photog* Burnett Guffey *Art Dir* Cary Odell, *Mus* George Duning *Ed* William Lyon *Cast* Burt Lancaster, Deborah Kerr, Montgomery Clift, Frank Sinatra, Donna Reed, Philip Ober, Ernest Borgnine *Prod* Columbia. 118 mins.

In an army camp at Pearl Harbor in 1941, a soldier, Prewitt (Clift), is victimized by the captain (Ober) because he refuses to box. The captain pays little attention to the camp, which is really run by Sergeant Warden (Lancaster). Warden begins an affair with the captain's wife, Karen (Kerr), and Prewitt falls in love with Lorene (Reed). Prewitt's friend, Angelo Maggio (Sinatra), runs foul of the stockade sergeant, Fatso Judson (Borgnine). Judson beats Maggio to death and is then killed by Prewitt, who runs away to Lorene. When the Japanese attack Pearl Harbor he tries to return to his unit but dies. Karen leaves for the States.

This adaptation of a best-selling novel was an enormous financial success and won eight Oscars and several other awards. Though intended as an attack on the U.S. Army, it is neither powerful nor truly critical. It marks something of a turning point in Zinnemann's career: formerly a fairly good director, from this point on he played the game according to the Hollywood rules.

FROM RUSSIA WITH LOVE see GOLDFINGER

FRONTIER AEROGRAD

FRONTIER MARSHAL see MY DARLING CLEMENTINE

FRONT PAGE (THE) USA 1931. *Dir* Lewis Milestone *Scen* Bartlett Cormack, Charles Lederer based on the play by Ben Hecht, Charles MacArthur *Art Dir* Richard Day *Photog* Glen MacWilliams *Ed* Duncan Mansfield *Cast* Adolphe Menjou, Pat O'Brien, Mary Brian, Edward Everett Horton, George E. Stone, Frank McHugh, Slim Summerville, Mae Clarke *Prod* Howard Hughes for United Artists. 101 mins.

Set in the editorial room of a large newspaper, a comedy involving a cynical editor (Menjou), a fast-talker crime reporter, Hildy Johnson (O'Brien), a whore (Clarke), and an escaped murderer (Stone) whom Johnson hides in a roll-top desk.

["I made them talk even faster in the film than they had in the play . . . We added perhaps just three scenes to the stage piece, going outside for the pranks that Hildy Johnson plays on the editor" (Lewis Milestone).] This robust comedy excelled most other early sound films by its clipped, fast dialogue and movement, its emphasis on cutting, and its use of the moving camera.

See also HIS GIRL FRIDAY.

FU MATTIA PASCAL (IL) see FEU MATHIAS PASCAL

FUNNY FACE USA 1957. *Dir* Stanley Donen *Scen* Leonard Gershe *Photog* Ray June *Art Dir* Hal Pereira, George W. Davis *Ed* Frank Bracht *Mus* arranged by Adolph Deutsch from George and Ira Gershwin, Roger Edens, and Leonard Gershe *Choreog* Fred Astaire, Eugene Loring *Cast* Fred Astaire, Audrey Hepburn, Michel Auclair, Kay Thompson *Prod* Paramount. 103 mins. Technicolor. VistaVision.

A fashion photographer (Astaire) discovers an ideal model (Hepburn) and triumphs over his rival, an existentialist philosopher (Auclair).

One of Stanley Donen's most brilliant musical comedies and almost Fred Astaire's last film (he was 58 when he danced in this film). Donen makes excellent use of natural backgrounds in Paris, Chantilly, and Versailles; the color photography supervised by Richard Avedon (who, as the character portrayed by Fred Astaire, was then working for *Vogue, Harper's Bazaar,* and other fashionable magazines) is delightful. Audrey Hepburn in clothes designed by Givenchy is at her most ravishing and seductive.

FURY USA 1936. *Dir* Fritz Lang *Scen* Bartlett Cormack, Fritz Lang based on a story by Norman Krasna *Photog* Joseph Ruttenberg *Art Dir* Cedric Gibbons, William Horning, E. B. Willis *Mus* Franz Waxman *Ed* Frank Sullivan *Cast* Spencer Tracy, Sylvia Sidney, Walter Abel, Walter Brennan, Bruce Cabot *Prod* Joseph L. Mankiewicz for MGM. 90 mins.

Joe Wilson, a filling station owner (Tracy), driving to meet his fiancée (Sidney), is unjustly accused of kidnapping by the people of a small town who try to lynch him and burn the jail where he is imprisoned. He escapes and, embittered, returns to confront his accusers.

"All converged into a bitter denunciation of mob violence. From the quiet beginning where Joe is picked up on the road, to the scenes of the hysteria of the mob and the burning jail and to the trial of the hypocritical townspeople, Lang's camera piled detail after detail from the point of view of the spectator, the victim, the community, and the law, making them an inspired commentary on bigotry, provincialism, and intolerance. An example of sharp characterization is the scene where Joe is being questioned by the Sheriff . . . Again, during the burning of the jail we see a mother holding her child aloft to get a better view, a moronic adolescent hanging on to a vantage point and crying out gleefully, "I'm Popeye the Sailor Man," and a gaping boy biting into his hot dog as he shifts about for a better look at the conflagration" (Lewis Jacobs). This powerful indictment of mob violence and lynch law was Fritz Lang's first film in America and it matches the best films of his German period. Lang's belief in fate, in man's continual flight from culpability and death is reflected as clearly in *Fury* as it is in his German films.

GAME OF DEATH (A) see MOST DANGEROUS GAME (THE)

GANGA BRUTA Brazil 1933. *Dir/Photog* Humberto Mauro *Scen* Otávio Gabus Mendes *Mus* Radames Gnatalli *Cast* Durval Bellini, Lu Marival, Carls Eugenio, Andrea Duarse, Alfredo Nuñez. 90 mins. approx.

Despite its silly and conventional plot, this is Humberto Mauro's best film and a landmark in the history of Brazilian cinema. The sound is on records and there is only one word of dialogue. The plot is puerile: a villain kills his wife the night they are married, is acquitted, becomes manager of a large factory, courts an innocent young girl, disagrees with an architect and his workers, etc. Excellent sequences: the wedding in a luxurious villa like El's in Buñuel's film; the depiction of a large factory under construction; the love-making in a park; the final battle. The editing is very forceful, using industrial elements as erotic symbols — a penchant that earned Mauro the name of "The Freud of Cascadura" (a suburb of Rio).

GANG WAR ODD MAN OUT

GARDIENS DE PHARE France 1929. *Dir/Ed* Jean Grémillon *Scen* Jacques Feyder based on a Grand-Guignol play *Photog* Georges Périnal *Art Dir* André Barsacq *Cast* Geymond Vital, Fromet, Génica Athanasiou, Gabrielle Fontan *Prod* Société des Films Grand-Guignol. 7,200 ft. approx.

A storm isolates a father (Fromet) and his son in a Breton lighthouse; the son goes mad and the father has to kill him. This semidocumentary masterpiece is just as powerful today, justifying what the young critic Marcel Carné wrote in 1929: "Grémillon really loves the sea. Not content with violent, fast-paced and sustained action, he makes the lighthouse a thing of beauty. He scans it from the most unusual angles and uses light and shadow effectively, ignoring the sea that relentlessly pounds the lighthouse. Enthusiasm like this makes great art. Périnal's photography gives the film atmosphere: grey but not flat, unprecise but not obscure, it adds a great deal to the anguish and oppressiveness of the film. The play on light and shadow has the suavity of a Man Ray image."

GASLIGHT ANGEL STREET Britain 1940. *Dir* Thorold Dickinson *Scen* A. R. Rawlinson, Briget Roland based on the play by Patrick Hamilton *Photog* Bernard Knowles *Art Dir* Duncan Sutherland *Mus* Richard Addinsell *Ed* Sydney Cole *Cast* Anton Walbrook, Diana Wynyard, Frank Pettingell, Robert Newton, Cathleen Cordell *Prod* British National. 89 mins.

In Victorian England a woman is murdered and it is believed that the unknown murdered escaped with the famous Barlow rubies. Fifteen years later, the murdered woman's nephew Paul Mallen (Walbrook) and his gentle wife Bella (Wynyard) move into the house and it becomes apparent that Paul is trying to drive his wife mad while he searches for the missing rubies. A detective, Rough (Pettingell), persuades Bella to let him help her and together they find the rubies and proof that Paul was his aunt's murderer.

One of the finest of all British thrillers, suspenseful, well acted and with a superb re-creation of Victorian England. This is Dickinson's best film, not at all eclipsed by the America remake:

— *Gaslight/Murder in Thornton Square* USA 1944. *Dir* George Cukor *Scen* John Van Druten, Walter Reisch, John

L. Balderston based on the play by Patrick Hamilton *Photog* Joseph Ruttenberg *Art Dir* Cedric Gibbons *Mus* Bronislaus Kaper *Ed* Ralph Winters *Cast* Charles Boyer, Ingrid Bergman, Joseph Cotten, Dame May Whitty, Angela Lansbury *Prod* MGM. 114 mins.

In order to produce this remake, MGM purchased the rights to Dickinson's film and withdrew all copies from distribution, though the story that all copies were destroyed is apocryphal. In this version, Charles Boyer plays the husband, Gregory Anton, and Ingrid Bergman the wife, Paula. Angela Lansbury appears in her first screen role. Despite Bergman's performance (for which she won an Oscar) and excellent sets, Cukor's version doesn't match Dickinson's.

GATE NO. 6 China 1952. *Dir* Liu Pan *Scen* Liu Pan from a play by Wang and Chia *Photog* Tou Yu *Cast* Hsieh Tien. 100 mins. approx.

A powerful, violent, and realistic tableau of the life and exploitation of Chinese dockers during the last years of the Kuomintang, focusing on their strikes and their claims for better conditions. Its forceful realism recalls some of the Soviet films showing life under the Tsars.

GATE OF HELL JIGOKUMON

GATE OF LILACS PORTE DES LILAS

GATES OF NIGHT (THE) PORTES DE LA NUIT (LES)

GATES OF PARIS PORTE DES LILAS

GATTOPARDO (IL) THE LEOPARD Italy/France 1962. *Dir* Luchino Visconti *Scen* Suso Cecchi D'Amico, Pasquale Festa Campanile, Massimo Franciosa, Enrico Medioli, Luchino Visconti based on the novel by Giuseppe Tomasi di Lampedusa *Photog* Giuseppe Rotunno *Art Dir* Mario Garbuglia, Giorgio Pes *Ed* Mario Serandrei *Mus* Nino Rota *Cast* Burt Lancaster, Alain Delon, Claudia Cardinale, Serge Reggiani *Prod* Titanus/SNPC/SGC. 205 mins. (161 mins. Britan, USA, Canada; 185 mins. France.) Technicolor. Technirama. (DeLuxe Color and CinemaScope, Britain, USA, Canada.)

This faithful adaptation of a famous novel is an extraordinary fresco of life in Sicily in the 1860's. Best sequences: the fighting at Palermo; a noble family crossing the ravaged countryside; the final ball — on the screen for almost an hour — during which the prince (forcefully portrayed by Burt Lancaster) realizes that the world he knew has ended and that he is about to die.

GAUCHO WAR GUERRA DES GAUCHOS (LA)

GENBAKU NO KO CHILDREN OF HIROSHIMA/ATOM-BOMBED CHILDREN/CHILDREN OF THE ATOM BOMB Japan 1952. *Dir* Kaneto Shindo *Scen* Kaneto Shindo based on the novel by Arata Osada *Photog* Takeo Itoh *Art Dir* Takashi Marumo *Mus* Akira Ifukube *Ed* Zenju Imaizumi *Cast* Nobuko Otowa, Chikako Hoshawa, Niwa Saito *Prod* Kendai Eiga Kyokai/Gekidan Mingei. 97 mins.

A young teacher (Otowa), returning to Hiroshima seven years after the bomb to visit her parents' grave, meets old friends and pupils. The explosion itself is recalled in several brief but striking flashbacks. This is the first important film directed by Kaneto Shindo, previously well known as a scriptwriter and later famous in the West as director of *The Island*. It was independently produced on a low budget with the backing of the Teachers' Union. [Shindo's version was faithful to the best-selling book but the union was displeased, claiming that he had made the story "into a tear jerker and destroyed its political orientation". They backed another version — Hideo Sekigawa's anti-American polemic, *Hiroshima*.]

Kaneto Shindo's typical understated style is very evident: polemic is avoided and Shindo guides the viewer gently through the horror. For example, the teacher meets a former colleague who seems quite happy. During a friendly conversation, in which the bomb is never mentioned, she learns that radiation has made her friend sterile. At the end, the roar of a plane passing overhead raises the fear of a new Hiroshima.

GENERAL (THE) USA 1926. *Dir* Buster Keaton, Clyde Bruckman *Scen* Al Boasberg, Charles Smith based on a story by Buster Keaton *Photog* J. Devereux Jennings, Bert Haines *Ed* Fred Gabourie, Sherman Kell *Cast* Buster Keaton, Marion Mack, Glen Cavander, Jim Farley *Prod* Buster Keaton Productions for United Artists. 7,127 ft.

During the American Civil War, Buster Keaton tries to enlist in the Confederate Army but, because he drives a train, is not allowed to. His girl friend (Mack) believes him to be a coward. Some Union soldiers steal his train and kidnap the girl, but after several adventures and a hectic chase, Keaton wins both back.

The script was based on an actual event in the Civil War in which a Confederate engine driver, Andrews, had pulled off an analogous exploit.

An old (1860) train had been used previously by Al St. John and by Keaton in *Our Hospitality* (*q.v.*) but in this film it became a character in the drama. Battling the train, rails, bridges, enemy soldiers, and a cannon, "the great stoneface" ridicules machinery and war and a world that seems to find them as inevitable as natural disasters. While Harold Lloyd in a skyscraper or a football game panics over minor incidents and overcomes catastrophes with the obstinacy of a boy-scout, Buster Keaton doesn't even notice the cataclysmic events that threaten him and appears to exorcise them with his impassiveness.

Buñuel's thoughts in 1927 on Keaton's *College* might also refer to *The General*: "Buster's expression is as unassuming as a bottle, although his clear, round pupils reflect his aseptic soul. But Buster's face and a bottle see things from an infinite number of viewpoints that are used in creating the rhythmic and architectonic structure of the film. The editing, the golden key to film-making, is what combines, enhances, and unifies all these points of view. Can greater heights of cinematic virtue be reached? . . . Keaton's comedy derives from a direct harmony with his tools, situations, and other elements. Keaton is full of a humanitarianism that is far beyond the variety that has been on the increase of late."

This is one of Keaton's best films. When it was re-released in 1962 it enjoyed a renewed world-wide success. It was voted one of the "Twelve Best Comedy Films of All Time" in an international poll of critics in 1967.

GENERAL LINE (THE) STAROYE I NOVOYE

GENERATION POKOLENIE

GENROKU CHUSHINGURA THE FORTY-SEVEN

RONIN/THE LOYAL FORTY-SEVEN RONIN OF THE GENROKU ERA

This Kabuki play is very popular in Japan and has been adapted for the screen more often than *The Three Musketeers*. It tells how, during the Genroku Era, 47 Ronin vow vengeance on the man who destroyed their master. To conceal their revenge they spend years pretending to be misfits and debauchers. Finally, they trap their victim, cut off his head, and commit hara-kiri as a final gesture of union with their dead master.

It has been said that there are two times 47 film versions of this story. This is of course exaggerated, but there are at least two or three dozen. The best are those of the father of Japanese film, Makino (1913 and 1927), Kinugasa (1932), notable for its editing, and Mizoguchi (1941/42), whose version was not one of his better films. [A four-hour spectacular color version, directed by Tatsuo Osone in 1957, is one of the most commercially successful films produced in Japan. None of the versions is derived from the formal, traditional style of Kabuki.]

GENTLEMAN'S AGREEMENT USA 1947. *Dir* Elia Kazan *Scen* Moss Hart based on the novel by Laura Z. Hobson *Photog* Arthur Miller *Art Dir* Lyle Wheeler, Mark-Lee Kirk *Mus* Alfred Newman *Ed* Harman Jones *Cast* Gregory Peck, Dorothy McGuire, June Havoc, John Garfield, Celeste Holm, Anne Revere *Prod* 20th Century-Fox. 118 mins.

A magazine writer, Phil Green (Peck), masquerades as a Jew for six months in order to investigate anti-Semitism in the United States. He meets a Jewish serviceman (Garfield) and encounters the "Gentleman's agreement" that excludes Jews from a certain part of society. His impersonation creates difficulties in his private life, with his fiancée (McGuire), his co-worker (Holm), and his mother (Revere).

This is perhaps Elia Kazan's best film, an unsentimental, unbiased approach to its theme. There are several memorable scenes such as that in which the "Jew" is quickly ejected from a "restricted" hotel. The action largely takes place among the upper class and depicts their anti-Semitic behavior. The film won two Oscars for the Best Film and the Best Director.

— *Gentleman's Agreement* Britain 1935. *Dir* George Pearson *Cast* Vivien Leigh. 70 mins.
Romantic comedy about a spendthrift and an unemployed typist.

GENTLEMEN BITTEN ZUR KASSE (DIE) see GREAT TRAIN ROBBERY (THE)

GERMANIA, ANNO ZERO GERMANY, YEAR ZERO/EVIL STREET/ALLEMAGNE, ANNÉE ZÉRO France/Italy 1947. *Dir/Scen* Roberto Rossellini *Assist* Max Colpet *Photog* Robert Juillard *Mus* Renzo Rossellini *Ed* Findeison *Cast* Franz Gruger, Edmund Meschke, Ernst Pittschau, Ingetraude Hinze, Erich Gühne. 78 mins.
In the ruins of Berlin in 1946 a young boy (Gruger), encouraged by his teacher (Gühne), kills his loudmouth father (Pittschau). He is overcome by remorse and commits suicide.
The actors were all nonprofessionals. Made in the neorealist style of films like *Rome, Open City (q.v.)* and *Paisa (q.v.)*, this lyrical view of Germany in the immediate postwar period has some magnificent scenes, even though, as a whole, it does not match the earlier Rossellini films. Among the memorable scenes are the voice of Hitler on a phonograph among the ruins of the Chancellery and the death of the hero in a gutted building, accompanied by the tragic sound of a passing tram. The film was relatively unsuccessful and this prompted Rossellini to move in other directions. ["Although the story of Edmond and his family was invented by me, it is nevertheless the common story of German families. It is a mixture of reality and fiction, treated with the license that is the prerogative of any artist" (Rossellini). The film was made with French financing and the assistance of the East German film company, DEFA.]

GERMANY, YEAR ZERO GERMANIA, ANNO ZERO

GERTRUD GERTRUDE Denmark 1964. *Dir* Carl Theodor Dreyer *Scen* Carl Theodor Dreyer based on the play by Hjalmar Söderberg *Photog* Henning Bendtsen *Art Dir* Kai Rasch *Mus* Jørgen Jersild *Ed* Edith Schlüssel *Cast* Nina Pens Rode, Bendt Rothe, Ebbe Rode, Baard Owe *Prod* Palladium. 116 mins.
Around 1910, a woman (Nina Rode), who is unhappily married to a lawyer meets a famous poet (Ebbe Rode) whom she had loved, has an affair with a young composer (Owe), and decides to live alone in Paris. Dreyer's last film, while not his best, is rigorous, poignant, and profound.

GERVAISE France 1956. *Dir* René Clément *Scen* Jean Aurenche, Pierre Bost based on the novel *L'Assommoir* by Emile Zola *Photog* Robert Juillard *Art Dir* Paul Bertrand *Mus* Georges Auric *Ed* A. Rust *Cast* Maria Schell, François Périer, Suzy Delair, Armand Mestral. 116 mins.
This is a perfect example of a polished and intelligent adaptation and includes an exact reconstruction of 19th century Paris. Good performances by Maria Schell, François Périer, and Armand Mestral. Notable sequences: the fight in the washhouse; the departure of Lantier's young son; Coupeau's alcoholic crisis in the laundry; the ménage à trois in the Goutte d'Or hovel.
OTHER VERSIONS:
— *Les Victimes de l'alcoolisme* France 1902. *Dir* Zecca.
— *L'Assommoir* France 1909. *Dir* Albert Capellani.
— *Les Victimes de l'alcool* France 1911. *Dir* Gérard Bourgeois.
— *L'Assommoir* France 1933. *Dir* Gaston Roudés.

GEZEICHNETEN (DIE) LOVE ONE ANOTHER/THE MARKED ONES Germany 1922. *Dir/Scen* Carl Theodor Dreyer based on the novel by Aage Madelung *Photog* Friedrich Weinmann *Art Dir* Jens G. Lind *Cast (Russian version)* Polina Piekowskaia, Wladimir Gaidarow *(German version)* Richard Boleslawski, Torleiff Reiss, Johannes Meyer *Prod* Prismusfilm. 7 reels.
This little-known film describes the fate of Jews in Russia during the 1905 Revolution. Riccitti Canudo wrote of "polyrhythmic frescoes by a Swedish (sic) film maker. The plastic re-creation of Jewish misfortunes in seething Russia is there, impressive and perfect. The construction of the scenario reminds us of the jammed living conditions, the cupidity, the suffering and anguish, the sorrow to which we forced a great race . . . to become accustomed. The cry of a multitude of souls combines with a thousand often fleeting details and careful photography to create a single and very large vision. Their shapes and

spirits follow us like ghosts" (Article published in *L'Usine aux images,* 1927). This film was made in both Russian and German versions. It was thought to have been lost until a copy was discovered in Gosfilmofond (USSR film archive) in 1961. It is sometimes known, incorrectly, by its Danish title, *Elsker Hverandre.*

GHOST GOES WEST (THE) Britain 1935. *Dir* René Clair *Scen* Robert Sherwood, Geoffrey Kerr based on the story *Sir Tristram Goes West* by Eric Keown *Photog* Harold Rosson *Art Dir* Vincent Korda *Mus* Misha Spoliansky *Ed* William Hornbeck *Cast* Robert Donat, Jean Parker, Eugene Pallette, Elsa Lanchester *Prod* London Films. 91 mins.
An American millionaire (Pallette) is persuaded by his daughter (Parker) to buy a haunted castle from an impoverished Scottish laird (Donat). A ghost (Donat) goes with the castle.
A cleverly fanciful theme (which pokes fun at Americans) and solid, careful direction allowed Clair to avoid becoming a victim of Korda and his (deluxe) sausage machine at London Films. Most memorable are the scenes of the castle being conveyed to Florida and the housewarming with a kilted Negro band playing jazzed-up Scottish tunes. Despite its qualities and its critical and public success, it doesn't match Clair's earlier French films.

GIANT USA 1956. *Dir* George Stevens *Scen* Fred Guiol, Ivan Moffat based on the novel by Edna Ferber *Photog* William C. Mellor *Art Dir* Boris Leven *Mus* Dimitri Tiomkin *Ed* William Hornbeck *Cast* James Dean, Elizabeth Taylor, Rock Hudson Jane Withers, Chill Wills, Mercedes McCambridge, Carroll Baker *Prod* Warner Brothers. 198 mins. WarnerColor.
Based on Edna Ferber's sprawling novel of Texas: a rich landowner (Hudson) marries a beautiful woman (Taylor) who falls in love with an ill-treated adolescent (Dean). He is left some land, discovers oil, and becomes rich.
This film has the failings that similar adaptations of best-sellers usually have, but despite its clichéd story, it paints a colorful and true picture of life in Texas and the United States during the twenty of thirty years between the Old West, with its great herds of cattle, and the advent of industry, oil, and millionaires.

The landscape plays a role in the drama. James Dean died before the film was released; although perfect in the first part of the film as a problem adolescent, he is out of his depth later as an older, successful man who has become a contemptible drunkard.

GILDA USA 1946. *Dir* Charles Vidor *Scen* Marion Parsonnet based on the story by E. A. Ellington *Photog* Rudolph Maté *Art Dir* Stephen Goosson, Van Nest Polglase *Cast* Rita Hayworth, Glenn Ford, George Macready *Prod* Columbia. 109 mins.
Johnny Farrell (Ford) runs a gambling casino in Buenos Aires for Ballin Mundsen (Macready), an overwhelmingly ambitious tycoon. Mundsen's wife, Gilda (Hayworth), used to be Johnny's mistress. Mundsen disappears. Gilda and Johnny quarrel and make love. Mundsen returns but is killed.
Though the plot is weak, *Gilda* is memorable for its erotic strain and Rita Hayworth's ferociously sexual performance. Her barbaric dance in the nightclub, peeling off long black gloves, was every GI's dream.

GION BAYASHI GION FESTIVAL MUSIC Japan 1953. *Dir* Kenji Mizoguchi *Scen* Yoshikata Yoda, Matsutaro Kawaguchi *Photog* Kazuo Miyugawa *Mus* Ichiro Saito *Cast* Michio Kogure, Ayako Wakao, Eitaro Shindo, Haruo Tanaka *Prod* Daiei. 100 mins. approx.
Mizoguchi's remake of his own *Gion no Shimai* (*q.v.*) but set in postwar Japan. It is perhaps even better than the famous 1936 film but doesn't match *Ugetsu Monogatari* (*q.v.*), which Mizoguchi also made in 1953.

GION FESTIVAL MUSIC GION BAYASHI

GION NO SHIMAI THE SISTERS OF GION Japan 1936. *Dir* Kenji Mizoguchi *Scen* Yoshikata Yoda, Kenji Mizoguchi *Photog* Minoru Miki *Cast* Isuzu Yamada, Yoko Umemura, Eitaro Shindo, Benkei Shiganoya *Prod* Daiichi Eigasha. 120 mins. approx.
In Gion, a red-light district of Kyoto, a geisha (Yamada) faithful to the old traditions takes her younger sister (Umemura) as an apprentice. The younger has more modern ideas and the two sisters come into conflict. At the end, the younger is in the hospital, the result of an accident caused by her excesses;

the elder remains too encumbered by tradition to rejoin the man she really loves.

"If Mizoguchi's own sentiments occasionally and by default go to the elder sister, his ending leaves her condemned. The situation is such, however, that the spectator too must make a choice, because, for a Japanese at any rate, the problem suggested by the film is a very vital one and goes beyond the narrow world of the geisha. Aiding this effect of impartiality, which is the effect of realism itself, was Mizoguchi's striving for actuality, and in doing so, successfully evoking the special atmosphere of this single tiny section of Japan . . . To the Japanese this film was more than merely slice-of-life. It went beyond documentation and projected the other-world atmosphere of the Gion itself" (J. L. Anderson and D. Richie).

Although the production company folded after the film, and although badly promoted (the Japanese censors described it as "decadent"), *Sisters of Gion* is considered the best prewar Japanese film and, by many, as Mizoguchi's masterpiece. It is better than his attempt at "new realism" in *Naniwa Elegy* (made the same year) because, as he said, it allowed him "to see human realities more clearly." Its theme was so important to him that he remade it after the war as *Gion Bayashi* (*q.v.*).

GIPSY BLOOD CARMEN

GIRL CAN'T HELP IT (THE) USA 1956. *Dir* Frank Tashlin *Scen* Frank Tashlin, Herbert Baker based on a story by Garson Kanin *Photog* Leon Shamroy *Art Dir* Lyle R. Wheeler, Leland Fuller *Mus* Lionel Newman *Ed* James B. Clark *Cast* Jayne Mansfield, Tom Ewell, Edmond O'Brien, Julie London, Fats Domino, Little Richard *Prod* 20th Century-Fox. 96 mins. Eastman Color. CinemaScope. An alcoholic theatrical agent (Ewell) obsessed with his love for a former girl-friend (London) is ordered by a gang leader (O'Brien) to groom his blonde girl friend (Mansfield) for stardom as a singer. The girl falls in love with the agent and the gangster himself becomes a rock and roll singer.

Jayne Mansfield's caricaturization of Marilyn Monroe in this film made her famous. The script (in which Garson Kanin had a hand) is full of gags, some of which border on vulgarity, but the film is directed with great flair by Frank Tashlin, a former director of cartoons. Tom Ewell, trained at the Actor's Studio, gives a good performance.

GIRL FRIENDS (THE) PODRUGI

GIRL FRIENDS (THE) AMICHE (LE)

GIRL FROM CARTHAGE (THE) AIN EL GHEZAL

GIRL IN BLACK (A) KORITSI ME TA MAVRA (TO)

GIRL IN EVERY PORT (A) USA 1928. *Dir* Howard Hawks *Scen* Seton I. Miller from a story by Hawks *Photog* L. William O'Connell, R. J. Berquist *Ed* Ralph Dixon *Cast* Louise Brooks, Victor McLaglen, Robert Armstrong *Prod* Fox. 5,500 ft. (tinted).

The amorous rivalries of two brawling sailors (McLaglen, Armstrong) who have a girl in every port — one of whom is Louise Brooks, unforgettable for her femininity, lithe body, and fringe of black hair.

The film was discovered by Armand Tallier and made Hawks famous in France before he was really well known in the United States.

— *A Girl in Every Port* USA 1951. *Dir/ Scen* Chester Erskine *Cast* Groucho Marx, William Bendix, Marie Wilson *Prod* RKO. 87 mins.

Not a remake but a slapstick comedy about two sailors who get involved with twin racehorses.

GIRLS IN UNIFORM MÄDCHEN IN UNIFORM

GIRL NO. 217 CHELOVEK NO. 217

*GIULIETTA DEGLI SPIRITI JULIET OF THE SPIRITS Italy/France 1965. *Dir* Federico Fellini *Scen* Federico Fellini, Ennio Flaiano, Tullio Pinelli, Brunello Rondi *Photog* Gianni Di Venanzo *Art Dir* P. Gherardi *Mus* Nino Rota *Ed* Ruggero Mastroianni *Cast* Giulietta Masina, Mario Pisu, Sandro Milo, Sylva Koscina *Prod* Federiz Francoriz. 145 mins. Technicolor.

A woman, Giulietta (Masina), feels her whole world start to crumble when she suspects her husband's (Pisu) infidelity. Her husband is first driven to subterfuge, then a position of guilt. Giulietta seeks out his mistress but finds her own happiness within herself.

Discussing this film, Fellini said "The

majority of people come to marriage completely unprepared because this event has been made into a myth, told in an inexact and treacherous manner . . . I don't believe that marriage is what it is superficially thought to be, and I am certain that it is a matter of far deeper rapport." This theme is explored by Fellini in a film that goes beyond Aristotelian reality in depicting the memories, fears, obsessions, and premonitions that define the mental world of a woman struggling to arrive at a sense of her own identity. It is a fantasy, though not in the usual sense of the word; it is fantasy in that it escapes the limits of what is often dubbed "reality." Though different from his earlier films, it could lay justifiable claim to being his best.

GIVEN WORD PAGADOR DE PROMESSAS (O)

GOHA France/Tunisia 1957. *Dir* Jacques Baratier *Scen* Georges Schehadé based on *Goha le Simple* by A. Adès, A. Josipovici *Photog* Jean Bourgoin *Art Dir* Georges Koskas *Mus* Maurice Ohana *Ed* Léonide Azar *Cast* Omar Cherif (later Sharif), Zina Bouzaïane, Lauro Gazzolo, Daniel Emilfork *Prod* Films Franco-Africains/UGC/Government of Tunisia. 90 mins. Agfacolor.
The story of Goha (Cherif), naive, ignorant, but beloved by all, and his little donkey. In his neighborhood lives a wise man who marries a beautiful young girl, Fulla (Bouzaïane). Fulla and Goha fall in love, Fulla is driven from her husband's house and Goha, cursed by his father and the village, wanders away. The wise man finds him and forgives him. In the face of such charity, Goha clumsily commits suicide.
Baratier's version of this story, famous throughout the Arab world, is charming and poetic. It is the first Tunisian film of international standing, acted by Arab actors in an entirely Tunisian atmosphere, using no sets and with beautiful color photography. Omar Cherif (who later changed his name to Sharif) gives a touching performance as the naive, well-meaning, but foolish Goha.

GOING MY WAY USA 1944. *Dir* Leo McCarey *Scen* Frank Butler, Fran Cavett from a story by Leo McCarey *Art Dir* Hans Dreier, William Flannery *Photog* Lionel Lindon *Mus* Robert Emmett Dolan *Cast* Bing Crosby, Barry Fitzgerald *Prod* Paramount. 130 mins.
An attractive, singing priest (Crosby) in a poor district scandalizes the old parish priest (Fitzgerald) with his modern ideas but wins the kids in the district, the wallets of the rich, and (chastely) the hearts of the girls.
This film was an enormous financial success that won six Oscars but is memorable only for its maudlin sentimentality. [*The Bells of St Mary's,* made the following year (directed by McCarey, with Bing Crosby and Ingrid Bergman), was a successful attempt to repeat the formula. Gene Kelly starred in a TV series, *Going My Way,* in 1963.]

GOLD DIGGERS OF 1933 (THE) USA 1933. *Dir* Mervyn LeRoy *Scen* Avery Hopwood, Ben Markson, David Boehm, Erwin Gelsey, James Seymour based on the play *The Gold Diggers* by Avery Hopwood *Choreog* Busby Berkeley *Photog* Sol Polito *Ed* George Amy *Songs* Al Dubin, Harry Warren *Cast* Warren William, Joan Blondell, Ruby Keeler, Dick Powell, Aline McMahon, Guy Kibbee, Ginger Rogers *Prod* Warner Brothers. 96 mins.
This is the best American musical comedy of the early Thirties. The story of a group of girls in search of millionaire husbands is used only to link up, Ziegfeld-style, a series of stunning ciné-ballets given a new dimension by Berkeley's use of the camera.
One number about the unemployed is particularly memorable, "Remember My Forgotten Man." The film included all the Warner Brothers stars: Dick Powell, Joan Blondell, and the witty Aline McMahon. Ginger Rogers was still a starlet and does not play a feature role. The successful play had previously been produced as a film in 1923 under the title *The Gold Diggers.* It was directed by Harry Beaumont from the Belasco spectacular. Warners also made *Gold Diggers of Broadway* in color in 1929, directed by Roy Del Ruth with songs by Al Dubin and Joe Burke. After the success of the 1933 film, Warner Brothers produced:
— *Gold Diggers of 1935* USA 1935. *Dir* Busby Berkeley.
— *Gold Diggers of 1937* USA 1936. *Dir* Lloyd Bacon.
— *Gold Diggers in Paris* USA 1938. *Dir* Ray Enright.

Busby Berkeley was responsible for choreography on all these films.

Warner Brothers later made another version of *The Gold Diggers:*

— *Painting the Clouds with Sunshine* USA 1951. *Dir* David Butler *Cast* Dennis Morgan, Virginia Mayo, Gene Nelson. 86 mins. Technicolor.

GOLDEN COACH (THE) CARROSSE D'OR (LE)

GOLDEN MARIE CASQUE D'OR

GOLDEN MOUNTAINS ZLATYE GORI

GOLDFINGER Britain 1964. *Dir* Guy Hamilton *Scen* Paul Dehn, Richard Maibaum based on the novel by Ian Fleming. *Photog* Ted Moore *Mus* John Barry *Art Dir* Ken Adam, Peter Murton *Ed* Peter Hunt *Cast* Sean Connery, Gert Fröbe, Honor Blackman, Shirley Eaton *Prod* Harry Saltzman, Albert Broccoli. 109 mins. Technicolor.

The intrepid James Bond (Connery) prevents the evil Goldfinger (Fröbe) from stealing the U.S. gold reserves. Perhaps the best (and certainly the most profitable) of the extraordinary James Bond series, with its weird gadgets, invincible hero, and desperate villains in the *Exploits of Elaine* style. The popularity of the series only began to wane after the shapeless *Casino Royale.*

OTHER JAMES BOND FILMS:

— *Dr. No* Britain 1962. *Dir* Terence Young *Cast* Sean Connery, Ursula Andress. 105 mins. Technicolor.

— *From Russia With Love* Britain 1963. *Dir* Terence Young *Cast* Sean Connery, Daniel Biancha, Lotte Lenya. 116 mins. Technicolor.

— *Thunderball* Britain 1965. *Dir* Terence Young *Cast* Sean Connery, Claudine Auger. 130 mins. Technicolor. Panavision.

— *Casino Royale* Britain 1967. *Dir* John Huston, Ken Hughes, Val Guest, Robert Parrish, Joe McGrath *Cast* Peter Sellers, Ursula Andress, David Niven, Orson Welles, etc. 130 mins. Technicolor. Panavision.

— *You Only Live Twice* Britain 1967. *Dir* Lewis Gilbert *Cast* Sean Connery, Akiko Wakabayshi. 116 mins. Technicolor. Panavision.

— *On Her Majesty's Secret Service* Britain 1969. *Dir* Peter Hunt *Cast* George Lazenby, Diana Rigg. 130 mins. Technicolor. Panavision.

(All except *Casino Royale* were produced by Saltzman and Broccoli).

GOLD FROM THE SEA OR DES MERS (L')

GOLD RUSH (THE) USA 1925. *Dir/Scen* Charles Chaplin *Assist* Charles Reisner, H. d'Abbadie d'Arrast *Photog* Rollie Totheroh, Jack Wilson *Tech Dir* Charles D. Hall *Cast* Charles Chaplin, Mack Swain, Georgia Hale, Tom Murray, Henry Bergman, Betty Morrissey, Malcolm Waite *Prod* Chaplin for United Artists. 8,498 ft. (originally 9,760 ft.) Reissued in a sound version in 1942, 72 mins. (two short scenes were deleted). During the Klondike gold rush of 1898 the Lone Prospector (Chaplin) seeks refuge from a storm in the cabin of a desperado, Black Larsen (Murray), and is joined by Big Jim McKay (Swain). Larsen discovers Big Jim's gold claim and knocks Big Jim out, but dies in an avalanche. Charlie wanders into town where he meets a dance hall girl, Georgia (Hale). Big Jim, his memory gone, retraces his steps with Charlie and, during a storm that blows their cabin half off the cliff, they accidentally rediscover the claim. Later, Charlie as a millionaire meets Georgia again.

Famous sequences: the long line of prospectors trudging up a steep snow-covered hill; the Thanksgiving dinner with Charlie eating the sole of a cooked shoe, enjoying the laces as though they were spaghetti, and sucking the nails as though they were bones; Charlie's first sight of Georgia and his pleasure at her smile until he discovers it is for another man; Charlie's preparations for the New Year's Eve dinner for Georgia and the girls and his dance with two rolls as he imagines they have come; Big Jim, in the delirium of hunger, imagining Charlie as a chicken and chasing him; Charlie sliding about in the teetering cabin during a storm; Charlie, as a millionaire in top hat and fur coat, meeting Georgia on the boat and suddenly becoming awkward and shy again.

Pierre Leprohon has written: "One of Chaplin's most complete works, the one that shows most clearly the tragic greatness of Charlie, but also one of the most difficult and least accessible because of the finesse of its psychology. The characters have richness, scope, and real meaning. *Gold Rush,* glittering with prodigious subtlety, is full of interior nuances. Tragedy is no longer placed beside comedy. It is incorporated into it, it becomes part of it, so that the funniest scenes are also the ones in which there is the most interior tragedy. Hence the impression of greatness with which the film leaves one, comparable to that of a classical tragedy, a fresco that takes place on a higher plane than we are normally able to reach." Chaplin's performance has been characterized by Theodore Huff: "His pantomime is more effective than ever. Turning his back to the camera in the dance hall scene, he says more with his shoulders than many actors do with their eyes and lips. A dreamily raised eyebrow or a movement of his hat produce an astonishing mixture of emotions."

The Gold Rush is perhaps Chaplin's most completely American film, drawing as it does on the traditional theme of men attempting to create civilization out of the wilderness. More than this, it is a parable on his own rapid rise to riches and on the American prosperity that was then at its peak. The universal appeal of its comedy and characters made it a world-wide success.

Chaplin spent much time and money on the production: $650,000 over 14 months of filming, with exteriors shot in the Nevada mountains. It grossed two-and-a-half million dollars in the States and five million in the rest of the world. Chaplin's share of the, for then, enormous profit was two million dollars — the exact amount that Lita Grey asked for in the divorce action she brought soon after.

*GOLEM (DER) THE GOLEM
All these films were based on the legend of the Golem, a popular figure in Jewish tradition, "a body without a soul" created from clay by Rabbi Loew in the 16th century in order to defend the Jews in the Prague ghetto against a pogrom. The character of the Golem bears close relationship to that of the monster in Mary Shelley's *Frankenstein* — both having their origin in the Greek myth of Prometheus. The character of Homunculus in the German film of 1916 was also derived from the Golem.
— *Der Golem/The Monster of Fate* Germany 1914. *Dir* Henrik Galeen, Paul Wegener *Scen* Henrik Galeen *Photog* Guido Seeber *Art Dir* R. A. Dietrich, Rochus Gliese *Cast* Paul Wegener, Henrik Galeen, Lyda Salmonova *Prod* Bioscop. 1,250 meters.

Paul Wegener's first version of the legend mixed contemporary events with the legend: a group of workmen discover the clay figure of the Golem (Wegener); an antiquarian (Galeen) buys it from them and brings it back to life without realizing it should only be revived to fulfill noble tasks. The Golem falls in love with the daughter (Salmonova) but she flees in horror; the Golem goes on a rampage but is finally destroyed when he falls from a tower. "With this film I went further into the domain of pure cinema" (Wegener). Unfortunately, this version (and the following) is lost; all that remains are still photographs suggesting some extraordinary images.
— *Der Golem und die Tänzerin/The Golem and the Dancing Girl* Germany 1917. *Dir/Cast* Paul Wegener *Prod* Bioscop.
— *Der Golem: Wie er in die Welt kam/ The Golem: How He Came into the World* Germany 1920. *Dir* Paul Wegener, Carl Boese *Scen* Paul Wegener, Henrik Galeen *Photog* Karl Freund, Guido Seeber *Art Dir* Hans Poelzig *Costumes* Rochus Gliese *Cast* Paul Wegener, Albert Steinrück, Ernst Deutsch, Lyda Salmonova *Prod* UFA. 5,200 ft.
For this version, Wegener returned to the legend, setting the film in medieval Prague: Rabbi Loew (Steinrück) gives life to the Golem (Wegener) who falls in love with the Rabbi's daughter (Salmonova) and brings fear to the emperor's court. He is destroyed by an innocent child who offers him an apple then removes the Star of David from his chest, sending him crashing to the ground.

Undoubtedly, this is the best version, notable for its extraordinary crowd scenes and the non-expressionistic sets by Hans Poelzig: "Their angular, oblique outlines, their teetering bulk, their hollowed steps, seem the none too unreal ghetto where people actually live . . . (The) alternately terrified and exultant crowd at times recalls the flamboyant outlines and disjointed movement of a painting by El Greco" (Lotte Eisner). Paul Wegener's performance as the inscrutable, enigmatic, hulking claylike figure of the Golem certainly influenced the depiction of the monster in *Frankenstein*.
— *Le Golem/The Legend of Prague* Czechoslovakia 1935. *Dir* Julien Duvivier *Scen* André-Paul Antoine, Julien Duvivier based on the novel by G. Meyrinck

131

(1916) *Photog* Jan Stallich, Vaclav Vich *Art Dir* André Andreyev, S. Kopecky *Mus* Joseph Kumeck *Cast* Harry Baur, Roger Karl, Charles Dorat, Ferdinard Hart, Roger Duchesne, Germaine Aussey, Jany Holt, Marcel Dalio *Prod* A. B. Films, Prague, 83 mins.

Wegener's version emphasized the Golem's revolt against his creator, whereas Duvivier's version, based on Meyrinck's novel, emphasized revolution as the only escape for a slave, the rabbi's young wife discovering the Golem in the emperor's cellar and bringing it to life to save her husband from execution. Duvivier's version is elegant but it doesn't match Wegener's.

In 1951, a two-part comedy in color based on the Golem legend was produced in Czechoslovakia: *Cisaruv pekar* and *Pekaruv cisar* (*The Emperor's Baker* and *The Baker's Emperor*), directed by Martin Fric with Jan Werich in the dual title role.

GOLUBOI EKSPRESS CHINA EXPRESS/BLUE EXPRESS USSR 1929. *Dir* Ilya Trauberg *Scen* L. Ierikhonov, Ilya Trauberg *Photog* B. Khrennikov, Yuri Stilanudis *Art Dir* Boris Dubrovsky-Eshke, Moisei Levin *Mus* Edmund Meisel *Cast* Sun Bo-Yang, Chou Hsi-fan, Chang Kai, Sergei Minin, N. Arbenin *Prod* Sovkino (Leningrad). 1,700 meters.

In the Far East, Chinese workers start a rebellion against colonials, arm themselves, seize a train, and break through the frontier. This is a spirited and convincing film with brilliant montage effects. It was a well-merited success, especially in the sound version, and brought recognition to Leonid Trauberg's younger brother.

GONE WITH THE WIND USA 1939. *Dir.* Victor Fleming *Scen* Sidney Howard based on the novel by Margaret Mitchell *Photog* Ernest Haller, Ray Rennahan *Art Dir* William Cameron Menzies, Lyle Wheeler *Mus* Max Steiner *Ed* Hal C. Kern, James E. Newcom *Cast* Clark Gable, Vivien Leigh, Leslie Howard, Olivia de Havilland, George Reeves *Prod* Selznick International for MGM. 220 mins. Technicolor. Reissued in 1967 in 70 mm Metrocolor.

At Tara in the American South, Scarlett O'Hara (Leigh) imagines herself in love with her cousin, Ashley (Howard), who marries Melanie (de Havilland). When the Civil War begins, Scarlett marries another man who soon dies in battle. In Atlanta, Scarlett is wooed by Rhett Butler (Gable), who saves her during the Battle of Atlanta. When they return to Tara, she marries another man for his money in order to rebuild her property, but he too dies. She finally marries Rhett, mistreats him, and sees her adored daughter die. She realizes her love for Ashley was false when he refuses to marry her after Melanie's death and that it is Rhett she really wants. But he leaves her.

Produced at a cost of four-and-a-half million dollars, this is undoubtedly the world's most commercially successful film. Though its success is to some extent derived from the popular novel on which it was based, its magnificent scenes, its colors, and the vastness of its theme have continued to attract huge crowds all over the world during each of its re-releases over the past 30 years. The best part of this colossal epic is the Battle of Atlanta, depicted in all its horrors.

The film's real director is its producer, David O. Selznick, rather than the unimaginative Victor Fleming, or even George Cukor or Sam Wood, who worked on the film for a while until they were fired. The film was a great triumph for the four lead actors.

GOOD EARTH (THE) USA 1937. *Dir* Sidney Franklin *Scen* Talbot Jennings, Tess Slessinger, Claudine West based on the novel by Pearl S. Buck *Photog* Karl Freund *Art Dir* Cedric Gibbons *Mus* Herbert Stothart *Ed* Basil Wrangell *Montage* Slavko Vorkapich *Cast* Paul Muni, Luise Rainer, Walter Connolly, Tillie Losch *Prod* MGM. 138 mins.

The life of a family in China headed by Wang (Muni) and O-lan (Rainer) and their dependence on the land.

Production of the film took four years; many of the backgrounds were filmed in China and a Chinese landscape was carefully created near Hollywood. The most striking sequence is that depicting the plague of locusts. The Asiatic make-up of the actors is very obvious, but bearable. The film is dedicated to Irving G. Thalberg, its producer, who died during production. Luise Rainer won an Academy Award, as did Karl Freund for the photography.

GORKI TRILOGY See DETSVO GORKOVO

GOSPEL ACCORDING TO ST. MATTHEW (THE) VANGELO SECONDO MATTEO

GOSTA BERLINGS SAGA THE STORY OF GÖSTA BERLING/THE SAGA OF GÖSTA BERLING/THE ATONEMENT OF GÖSTA BERLING Sweden 1924. *Dir* Mauritz Stiller *Scen* Mauritz Stiller, Ragnar Hyltén-Cavallius based on the novel by Selma Lagerlöf *Photog* J. Julius (Julius Jaenzon) *Art Dir* Vilhelm Bryde, Ingrid Günther *Cast* Lars Hanson, Gerda Lundeqvist, Ellen Cederström, Mona Martensson, Otto Elg-Lundberg, Jenny Hasselqvist, Greta Garbo *Prod* Svensk Filmindustri. Originally in two parts, 4,534 meters, approximately 15,000 ft. Extant versions 10,400 ft. (Also reissued in an abbreviated sound version, 93 mins.)

Pastor Gösta Berling (Hanson) is defrocked because of drinking, becomes tutor to Ebba Dohna (Martensson), the granddaughter of Dowager Countess Dohna (Cederström), and develops a friendship with Elisabeth (Garbo), the wife of Count Henry Dohna. He leaves the Dohna family and becomes a pensioner to Margaret (Lundeqvist), wife of Major Samszelius (Elg-Lundberg) at Ekeby Manor, who saves him from suicide. The Major discovers her infidelity, drives her away and turns the manor over to the pensioners. Gösta falls in love with the beautiful Marianne Sinclair (Hasselqvist) and takes her to Ekeby, but her beauty is destroyed by smallpox. Margaret sets fire to Ekeby; Gösta rescues Marianne, who now decides she wants to return home. On his escape Gösta again meets Elisabeth and tries to run away with her, but she urges him to return and rebuild Ekeby. He does so and when it is prosperous offers it to Margaret. Meanwhile, Elisabeth discovers her marriage is not fully legal; she is reunited with Gösta and Margaret gives them the estate.

The original film was in two parts with a running time of over three hours, but Stiller was obliged to make a shorter version to obtain foreign distribution. Existing versions run about two hours, while the later sound version (prepared by Hyltén-Cavallius) runs 93 mins. The continuity of these versions is consequently often obscure and confusing. However, all the scenes at Ekeby have been retained, with their mixture of drama and comedy, theatricality and realism, greediness and passion, set against an almost Shakespearian atmosphere but in exactly realistic backgrounds and exteriors. These scenes force one to agree with Jean Béranger (who had seen the complete film): "Using Selma Lagerlöf's novel, which he had promised to respect, he eliminated accessory scenes, changed the chronology of the narrative and created a gigantic fresco. His film re-created the flamboyant atmosphere of the Wärmlands aristocracy and could well be as great a masterpiece as the novel." Greta Garbo, discovered by Stiller, plays a relatively minor role in the film, but her appearance paved the way to her later stardom.

GOTTERDAMMERUNG CADUTA DEGLI DEI (LA)

GOUPI MAINS ROUGES IT HAPPENED AT THE INN France 1943. *Dir* Jacques Becker *Scen* Pierre Véry, Jacques Becker based on the novel by Pierre Véry *Photog* Pierre Montazel, Jean Bourgoin *Art Dir* Pierre Marquet *Mus* Jean Alfaro *Ed* Marguerite Renoir *Cast* Fernand Ledoux, Georges Rollin, Blanchette Brunoy, Robert Le Vigan, René Génin, Marcel Pérès *Prod* Minerva. 95 mins.

Four generations of Goupis (12 in all), distinguished from one another by their nicknames, live in an isolated hamlet in Charente and resent outside interference. Goupi Tisane is murdered for stealing a hoard of money. Goupi Mains Rouges (Ledoux) discovers that Goupi Tonkin (Le Vigan) was the thief.

The action is centered around an inn run by the Goupis — hence the title *It Happened at the Inn*. Although the mystery plot is somewhat artificial, Becker's portrayal of the peasants and of life in an isolated village is authentic and memorable. The sets and costumes are correct to the last detail, as is the landscape and the bearing and accent of the actors, led by Fernand Ledoux. Becker established himself with this film as a disciple of Renoir, but with a style and personality of his own.

GO WEST USA 1925. *Dir* Buster Keaton *Scen* Raymond Cannon from an idea by Keaton *Photog* E. Lessley, Bert Haines *Cast* Buster Keaton, Howard Truesdall, Kathleen Myers *Prod* Buster Keaton/Metro. 6,256 ft.

Keaton as a cowboy becomes friends with a cow that he takes with him everywhere. Though the film does not have the pace of other Keaton comedies it is full of delightful screwball humor. Best sequences: the herd of cattle in the streets of Los Angeles; the livestock invasion of a large store and a beauty parlor; Keaton and his cow walking across a vast plain.

GO WEST THE MARX BROTHERS GO WEST USA 1940. *Dir* Edward Buzzell *Scen* Irving Brecher *Photog* Leonard Smith *Art Dir* Cedric Gibbons, Stan Rogers *Ed* Blanche Sewell *Cast* Groucho, Chico, Harpo Marx, John Carroll, Diana Lewis, Robert Barratt *Prod* MGM. 81 mins.

A parody on typical westerns, with Groucho wearing a mid-19th century grey top-hat and Harpo a coonskin cap. They have a valuable land deed that brings them into conflict with the town boss (Barratt).

Although the typical, carefully-timed, anarchic humor of the Marx Brothers is marvelous, this film does not measure up to their earlier ones. The best sequences are: the opening scene in a railway station, with Groucho, Chico, and Harpo trying to cheat each other; the climax, with the brothers racing the villains on a train whose carriages they burn for fuel and which jumps the track and pushes a house along in front of it.

*GRADUATE (THE) USA 1967. *Dir* Mike Nichols *Scen* Calder Willingham, Buck Henry based on the novel by Charles Webb *Photog* Robert Surtees *Art Dir* Richard Sylbert *Mus* David Grusin, Paul Simon, songs sung by Simon and Garfunkel *Ed* Sam O'Steen *Cast* Dustin Hoffman, Anne Bancroft, Katherine Ross *Prod* Embassy/Lawrence Turman. 108 mins. Technicolor. Panavision.

Benjamin Braddock (Hoffman), an aimless, recent college graduate is seduced by Mrs. Robinson (Bancroft), the wife of his father's partner, and falls in love with her daughter, Elaine (Ross). Mrs. Robinson tries to separate them by marrying Elaine off to a wealthy student; Ben arrives at the wedding ceremony and runs away with the bride.

Mike Nichols' second feature, set in Los Angeles suburbia, obviously struck a responsive note among audiences. It was an enormous commercial success, not only because of the delightful sexual scenes, but also because of the film's emotional elevation, its central character embodying innocence regained, and its romantic suggestion that true love can still tri-

umph even in the sordid Sixties. Nichols' visual style, clearly derivative of European directors, beautifully conveys the cultural climate of the idealistic, if bumptious hero. Anne Bancroft and Dustin Hoffman give impeccable performances.

GRANDE ILLUSION (LA) France 1937. *Dir* Jean Renoir *Assist* Jacques Becker *Scen* Jean Renoir, Charles Spaak *Photog* Christian Matras, Claude Renoir, Bourgoin, Bourreaud *Art Dir* Eugène Lourié *Mus* Joseph Kosma *Ed* Marguerite Renoir *Cast* Jean Gabin, Pierre Fresnay, Erich von Stroheim, Marcel Dalio, Julien Carette, Gaston Modot, Jean Dasté, Sylvain Itkine, Dita Parlo *Prod* RAC. 117 mins.

Three French prisoners of war are held in German hands during the First World War: an aristocrat, Boieldieu (Fresnay), a mechanic from Paris, Maréchal (Gabin), and a Jewish banker, Rosenthal (Dalio). They are transferred to a prison camp commanded by von Rauffenstein (Stroheim) and unite in escape plans. A friendship develops between von Rauffenstein and Boieldieu, both aristocratic career officers, but von Rauffenstein nonetheless shoots Boieldieu when he helps the other two escape. Maréchal and Rosenthal have a difficult journey across country, are befriended by a German peasant girl (Parlo), and finally cross the border into Switzerland. Famous sequences: downed French pilots welcomed in the mess of their German conquerors; the French prisoners' arrival at the camp; building the escape tunnel under the entrance to the barrack room; the prisoners dressed up as women singing the "Marseillaise" in the theater; the discussions between the stiff-necked Junker camp commandant and Boieldieu about the role of their class after the war; von Rauffenstein shooting down his French friend as he walks along the ramparts playing the flute, and then placing a geranium on his corpse; the violent altercations between Rosenthal and Maréchal as they flee through the snow; Maréchal's love affair with the peasant girl; the final sprint to freedom.

Although it won an award at the Venice Film Festival, the film was banned in Germany and Italy. It was a great success elsewhere, and won an Academy Award. It was voted one of the 12 Best Films of All Time at Brussels in 1957 and enjoyed further success on its re-release.

"The story of *La Grande Illusion* is scrupulously accurate and was told me by several of my wartime friends, particularly Pinsard, whose escapes are the basis of the story. But an escape story, however exciting, isn't enough to make a film. A script must be written and Charles Spaak collaborated with me on this. Our common belief in equality and fraternity was added to the bonds of our friendship" (Renoir, 1958). If Renoir brought his memories as a pilot and prisoner of war to the film, Stroheim considerably enriched the character of von Rauffenstein during production by adding some of his own experience and background.

Introducing his film to the American public in 1938, Renoir wrote: "I hear Hitler yelling on the radio, demanding the partition of Czechoslovakia. We are on the brink of another 'Grand Illusion.' I made this film because I am a pacifist. To me, a true pacifist is a Frenchman, a German, an American. The day will come when men of good faith will find a common meeting ground. Cynics will say that my words at this point in time are naive. But why not?" He added in 1946: "The Frenchmen in this film are good Frenchmen and the Germans good Germans, like those before the 1939 war. I found it impossible to take sides with any of the characters."

GRANDES MANOEUVRES (LES) SUMMER MANEUVERS France/Italy 1955. *Dir* René Clair *Scen* René Clair with Jérome Geronimi, Jean Marsan based on the novel by Courteline *Photog* Robert Lefebvre, Robert Juillard *Art Dir* Léon Barsacq *Costumes* Rosine Delamare *Mus* Georges Van Parys *Ed* Louisette Hautecoeur *Cast* Michèle Morgan, Gérard Philipe, Brigitte Bardot, Yves Robert, Pierre Dux *Prod* Filmsonor/Rizzoli Film. 107 mins. Eastman Color.

In a garrison town before the First World War, Armand (Philipe), a Don Juan Dragoons lieutenant, accepts a bet to seduce the first lady who wins a lottery ticket. Marie-Louise (Morgan), a radiant and sophisticated beauty, wins and Armand sets about his seduction. But he is caught in his own trap and falls in love for the first time. Marie-Louise learns of his other romances, and the bet, and loses faith in him. He goes off to "grandes manoeuvres."

Clair has said that the film could have been called "The Punishment of Don Juan," and, "We didn't choose this era for its picturesque qualities but because affairs of the heart were then of more importance than they are today." He added that its theme of "one shouldn't trifle with love" was also for him "a certain portrait of provincial behavior during the time when the classic image of the seducer was a young cavalry hero". In this case the seducer is caught in his own trap and comedy gradually changes to tragedy. The most typical scenes in the film use the behavior and comments of onlookers as comment on themselves and the conventions of their times.

This is René Clair's only truly romantic film and one that contains more genuine emotion than any of his others. The sets are scrupulously correct and superbly convey the atmosphere and panache of life in a garrison town. Clair's use of color is striking, with compositions most often based on the isolation of one or two vivid hues or the accentuation of two or three shades for their poetic or symbolic values. Michèle Morgan's and Gérard Philipe's performances are among their best.

GRAND JEU (LE) THE GREAT GAME France 1934. *Dir* Jacques Feyder *Assist* Marcel Carné, Henri Chomette *Scen* Charles Spaak, Jacques Feyder *Photog* Harry Stradling, Maurice Forster *Art Dir* Lazare Meerson *Mus* Hanns Eisler *Cast* Marie Bell, Pierre-Richard Wilm, Françoise Rosay, Charles Vanel. 115 mins.

Pierre Martel (Wilm) ruins himself over a blonde demimondaine, Florence (Bell) and joins the Foreign Legion. He meets a prostitute Irma (Bell) who reminds him of Florence, falls in love with her, and gets her a job in a hotel where he is friendly with the manageress, Blanche (Rosay) and her husband, Clement (Vanel). Clement attempts to seduce Irma and Pierre kills him. By chance he meets Florence again but she is contemptuous of him and his love for Irma collapses. Fatalistically he goes to his death.

Feyder's first film in France after his return from the States focuses on the then popular theme of legionnaires and passion in the hot sands of North Africa. It is too melodramatic to be entirely successful and Pierre-Richard Wilm is weak in the lead role. But it does offer an evocative portrait of colonial life. Marie Bell gives a remarkable dual performance as the two women (but with Irma's voice ingeniously dubbed by another actress) and Françoise Rosay and Charles Vanel are excellent as the managers of a large bistro frequented by legionnaires.

— Le Grand Jeu/Flesh and the Woman/ Card of Fate France/Italy 1953. Dir Robert Siodmak Scen Charles Spaak based on the novel Le Grand jeu by Charles Spaak and Jacques Feyder Photog Michel Kelber Art Dir Léon Barsacq Cast Gina Lollobrigida, Jean-Claude Pascal, Arletty. 103 mins. Eastman Color. [This remake loses all the sense of atmosphere of the original, retaining only the novelettish intrigue. Gina Lollobrigida gives a neat double performance as a sparkling sophisticate (with red hair) and a Fille-perdue (with black hair).]

GRAND'RUE CALLE MAYOR

GRAPES OF WRATH (THE) USA 1940. Dir John Ford Scen Nunnally Johnson based on the novel by John Steinbeck Photog Gregg Toland Art Dir Richard Day, Mark-Lee Kirk Mus Alfred Newman Ed Robert Simpson Cast Henry Fonda, Jane Darwell, John Carradine, Doris Bowdon, Russell Simpson, Zeffie Tilbury, Charley Grapewin Prod 20th Century-Fox. 129 mins.

Tom Joad (Fonda), Grandpa (Grapewin), Grandma (Tilbury), Ma (Darwell), Pa (Simpson), sister (Bowdon), Casey (Carradine), a visionary expreacher, and the rest of the family are ruined in the Oklahoma dust bowl and migrate to California to work in the grape harvests. When they arrive, they live for a time in a shanty town and discover terrible labor exploitation. Casey tries to organize a strike but is murdered. In defending him, Tom kills a deputy. They move on and live in a peaceful, well-organized Government camp, but the police are on Tom's trail and they leave again.

Steinbeck's novel was based on his experiences in 1936 as a reporter among the Okies, who were then wandering around the United States, driven from their land by erosion, the Depression, and the usurious methods of bankers. The unity of the film is derived to a great extent from the leitmotiv of the rattling old truck in which the Joad family travels with their clothes, pots and pans, and ramshackle furniture. The stagecoach of Stagecoach is here replaced by the junk pile truck used in the exodus, but it is the same desert that has to be crossed, the trails are just as hazardous and, on top of hunger and lack of work, they are beset by police and roughnecks. Gregg Toland, whose photography in the film is among his best work, described the film this way: "It was the story of unhappy men, men of the soil, suffering men with genuine problems. And it was a difficult film for us. As I recall, we moved the camera only once: a long traveling shot through the streets of Hooverville (the shanty town). This is what the people in the truck saw after the long trip to the promised land of California." This is one of the most important Hollywood films of the Roosevelt era.

GRASS USA 1925. Dir/Scen/Photog Merian C. Cooper, Ernest B. Schoedsack Ed/Titles Terry Ramsaye, Richard P. Carver Prod Famous Players-Lasky. 3,800 ft. approx.

A documentary by Cooper and Schoedsack, who accompanied the nomadic Baktyari tribes of Iran and their herds on their annual migration over mountains and across plains in search of new pasture. It is a fascinating film, showing hundreds of families and thousands of cattle climbing steep snow-covered hills and crossing swift-flowing rivers. The Iranians themselves say the film was largely dramatized, since the tribes agreed to follow an itinerary different from their usual migrations in order to allow the film makers more opportunity for striking photography. This film is nonetheless a beautiful and absorbing piece of work. Schoedsack and Cooper later turned definitely towards the dramatized documentary with Chang (q.v.), and then to the horror film (King Kong (q.v.), etc.).

[The intertitles, written by Terry Ramsaye, are undeniably facetious and diminish the film's qualities, despite his later attempts to justify them by referring to the level of literacy of the average movie audience.]

GREAT ADVENTURE (THE) STORA AVENTYRET (DET)

GREAT CITIZEN (A) VELIKII GRAZHDANIN

GREAT DICTATOR (THE) USA 1940. *Dir/Scen* Charles Chaplin *Photog* Rollie Totheroh, Karl Strüss *Art Dir* J. Russell Spencer *Mus* Charles Chaplin, Meredith Wilson *Ed* Willard Nico *Cast* Charles Chaplin, Paulette Goddard, Jack Oakie, Henry Daniell, Billy Gilbert, Reginald Gardner, Maurice Moscovich (Chester Conklin, Leo White in small roles) *Prod* Chaplin for United Artists. 126 mins.

A Jewish barber (Chaplin), a soldier in the First World War, loses his memory after a plane crash and only regains it after Adenoid Hynkel (Chaplin) has become Dictator of Tomania. He becomes friendly with Hannah (Goddard), a young Jewess and, when Hynkel steps up persecution of the Jews, his barber's shop is burned. He is arrested for hiding an old friend (Gardiner) and sent to a concentration camp; Hannah escapes to Austerlich. Hynkel invites Napaloni (Oakie), the Dictator of Bacteria, to discuss the invasion of Austerlich. The barber escapes, is mistaken for Hynkel, who is duck shooting nearby and who is himself arrested, and is carried in triumph to the grandstand to address the people as conqueror of Austerlich. He delivers a humanistic speech much to the astonishment of his lieutenants Garbitsch (Daniell) and Herring (Gilbert). Famous sequences: the barber trying to escape a shell during the war; the barber flying upside-down in an airplane; Hynkel's speech in guttural German-English double talk and the microphones bending back under his onslaught; the Storm Troopers' attack on the ghetto; the barber leaving the hospital and bickering with the Nazis; Hynkel's ballet with a globe of the world; the barber shaving a man to the tune of a Brahms' "Hungarian Dance"; the barber surrounded by loudspeakers repeating Hynkel's speech; the grotesque meeting between Hynkel and Napaloni that culminates in a cream cake battle; the barber's long (six minutes) speech at the end.

Chaplin originally conceived the story in 1935, revised it in 1938 (under the title *The Dictator*) and began production in 1939 on a third version of the script. Despite the secrecy that surrounded its production, the public was aware of its anti-Fascist theme. The German Ambassador protested, crypto-Nazi organizations in the States sent threatening letters to Chaplin and, after September 1939, the attack was joined by isolationists and the Un-American Activities Committee. The production cost two million dollars, an enormous sum at the time. It was completed just as Nazi troops entered Paris and was one of the few pre-Pearl Harbor American films to attack German fascism. American critical reaction was cool (many felt the final speech was banal and the film's theme was too serious), but the film proved quite popular with the public. Chaplin's final speech is very much an expression of his own sincere feelings. On a dais inscribed with the word "Liberty," he urged the peoples of the world not to despair, not to give in to dictators: "You, the people, have the power to make this life free and beautiful — to make this life a wonderful adventure. Then in the name of democracy — let us use that power, let us unite. Let us fight for a new world — a recent world that will give men a chance to work — that will give youth a future and old age a security."

Paulette Goddard as Hannah, which was the name of Chaplin's mother, gives a graceful and touching portrayal of a member of the persecuted "race." Chaplin's performance in the double role is extraordinary: Hynkel is a "combination of Napoleon and Nijinsky. Playing the dictator and myself, one a tragic figure the other a comic, I can no longer distinguish one from the other" (Chaplin).

GREATEST LOVE (THE) EUROPA 51

GREAT GAME (THE) GRAND JEU (LE)

*GREAT McGINTY (THE) USA 1940. *Dir/Scen* Preston Sturges *Photog* William Mellor *Art Dir* Hans Dreier, Earl Hedrick *Mus* Frederick Hollander *Cast* Brian Donlevy, Muriel Angelus, Akim Tamiroff, William Demarest *Prod* Paramount. 83 mins.

Dan McGinty (Donlevy), a bartender in a banana republic, relates how he came to be elected governor through the intrigues of a corrupt "Boss" (Tamiroff). Beginning as a "voter" for the party machine, he rises to protection collector, then alderman, mayor and finally governor. He rebels against the boss and has to flee with his wife (Angelus).

This gentle, uncynical satire on corrupt political machines was Sturges' first film. Its approach is typical: excellent character dialogue, touches of burlesque, and a superb sense of timing.

GREAT TRAIN ROBBERY (THE) USA 1903. *Dir/Scen* Edwin S. Porter *Cast* Marie Murray, "Bronco Billy" Anderson (Max Aronson), George Barnes, Frank Hanaway *Prod* Edison. 703 ft.

Bandits tie up a telegraph operator and rob a train, celebrate their success, but are arrested by the posse.

Although it was made in a suburb of New York (Patterson, New Jersey), this is the first western. It is also the first important American film. Its script, sophisticated for 1903, was loosely based on a popular play and on true stories and derived to some extent from several successful "chase" films made in Britain. Porter used both studio sets and exteriors, tricks similar to modern process shots, and a pan for dramatic effect (the horses waiting for the bandits). This "feature" film was an enormous success in the Nickelodeons and increased their popularity.

One of the bandits (Barnes) is shown in a close-up at the end, firing at the audience. According to the Edison catalogue, this shot could be shown at the beginning or the end of the film. It is not therefore a sequential element but is similar to the pictures that had been used for some time to open or close a lantern slide show.

— *The Great Train Robbery* USA 1904. *Dir/Prod* Sigmund Lubin.
ter's film.
An attempt by Lubin to cash in on Por-
— *The Great Train Robbery* USA 1941. *Dir* Joseph Kane *Cast* Bob Steele, Claire Carleton. 61 mins.
The sons of a crook fight over a train robbery.
— *Die Gentlemen Bitten zur Kasse / Der Postzug Übersall / The Great Train Robbery* German Federal Republic 1966. *Dir* John Olden, Claus Peter Witt *Cast* Horst Tappert, Hans Cossy, Karl Heinz Hess, Isa Miranda. 104 mins.
Recounts the story of the multimillion dollar train robbery in Britain in 1963.

GREAT TURNING POINT (THE) VELIKI PERE-LOM

GREAT WHITE SILENCE (THE) WITH CAPTAIN SCOTT, R.N., TO THE SOUTH POLE

GREED USA 1924 (production began 1923). *Dir* Erich von Stroheim *Assist* Eddy Sowders, L. Germonprez *Scen* Erich von Stroheim based on *McTeague* by Frank Norris *Photog* Ben Reynolds, William Daniels, Ernest B. Schoedsack *Art Dir* Richard Day, Cedric Gibbons, Erich von Stroheim *Ed* Joe Farnham (first version 42 reels), Erich von Stroheim (second version 24 reels), Rex Ingram (third version, 18 reels), June Mathis (release version, 10 reels) *Cast* Gibson Gowland, ZaSu Pitts, Jean Hersholt, Chester Conklin, Dale Fuller, Sylvia Ashton, Hughie Mack, Cesare Gravina (role removed in editing) *Prod* Goldwyn, then MGM. 10,067 ft. (original commercial release version).

Former miner McTeague (Gowland) sets up as a dentist in San Francisco and marries Trina (Pitts), the daughter of German immigrants (Conklin, Ashton). After winning a lot of money, Trina becomes greedy, and McTeague, having lost his livelihood because of his rival, Marcus (Hersholt), becomes a drunken tramp and ends up killing his wife. He encounters Marcus again in Death Valley and kills him but remains bound to the corpse by handcuffs.

Before making *Greed*, Stroheim wrote: "It is possible to tell a great story in motion pictures in such a way that the spectator . . . will come to believe that what he is looking at is real . . . even as Dickens and De Maupassant and Zola and Frank Norris catch and reflect life in their novels. It is with that idea that I am producing Frank Norris' story *McTeague*." The California writer (1870–1902) had, with Stephen Crane and Theodor Dreiser, established the American naturalistic school; his novel was to some extent derivative of Zola's *L'Assommoir*. Stroheim's original script followed the novel in every detail and he systematically shot scenes in the locations described in it. "Life is not reconstituted, it is captured," said the film maker. "The only truely realistic films are those made at the scene of the action." The final scenes were shot in Deat Valley in the hottest part of the summer in 1923.

Filming took nine months and cost about one-half million dollars. When the shooting was completed in December 1923, Stroheim invited several people to a private screening, including two Frenchmen, Valentin Mandelstam and the journalist, Jean Bertin. Jean Bertin wrote in *Mon Cine* (April 25, 1925): "The film that we saw was no less than 47 reels. I repeat 47 reels. It was long but absorbing. Stroheim 'talked' his film through its screening." The first version Stroheim presented to the Goldwyn Company was 42 reels. He was asked to cut it to a reasonable length and reduced it to 24 reels. Finally, with the help of his friend Rex Ingram, he produced an 18-reel version that he wanted to release in two parts and that he said was the minimum length in which justice to the story could be done. The studio felt otherwise and turned the material over to June Mathis, the story editor at Goldwyn. She trimmed it down to 10 reels and gave it the title *Greed*. It was this version that was inherited by MGM (after the merger) for release. Stroheim argued with Thalberg and Meyer for months about the footage removed by June Mathis, "who had read neither the book nor my script, yet was ordered to cut it" (Stroheim). But to no avail. MGM finally released the Mathis version in December 1924. In 1950, on Henri Langlois's insistence, Stroheim watched the mutilated version. He wept and said afterwards: "This was like an exhumation for me. In a tiny coffin I found a lot of dust, a terrible smell, a little backbone, and shoulder bone." The condensed version is the only one seen by the public, and even in this form (with continuity gaps bridged by long titles) it is a masterpiece, with at least twenty sequences that remain etched in the memories of all cinéphiles. Its theme of the dehumanizing influence of money is projected with an unforgettable realistic power.

Principal sequences: McTeague, fixing the anesthetised Trina's decayed tooth, unable to resist the temptation to kiss her; Marcus giving Trina (then his fiancée) to McTeague in a seaside café; the German-type family on a picnic; the wedding in the apartment while a funeral passes in the street; the drinking bout after the ceremony; Trina on her wedding night able to think of nothing but the $5,000 she has won in a lottery; Marcus' denunciation, which prevents McTeague (without a diploma) from continuing his practice; the penniless McTeague grimacing at the rotten meat served by his wife and then beating her in order to get a few cents for drink; Trina taking the gold coins from her mattress and caressing her naked body with them; McTeague's sordid murder of Trina in the house where she is a scrubwoman; the final confrontation of Marcus and McTeague in Death Valley.

Marcel Defosse (Denis Marion) wrote after *Greed*'s premier in France in 1926: "Everything in the film, people and objects, has been touched by life in a profound and always different way, the alarm clock as well as the pastor, the dentist as well as his canary. The minor characters are equally brought to life often with a small but vivid detail: the servant's disheveled hair, the father-in-law's military mustache, the sister's smile. The principal characters are not merely caricatures or figures of ridicule; their complexities are almost completely portrayed by their appearance, in the way writers like Balzac tried to do. McTeague's crown of curly hair, his wife's great black hat, her habit of placing her finger on her lips, the costumes and Marcus' flashy linen, all these things portray the morals of the characters — complete pigheadedness, implacable greed, false *bonhomie*. Its portrait of the materialistic side of the human soul is the first we have seen, except perhaps in the theater. However, in my opinion the film does it better, more perfectly. And the moral decline of three people, brought on by their lust for gold, is portrayed with a bitterness and cruelty equaled only by the most pessimistic novels of some Russian authors and without their grandiloquence and didactism. The author describes without judging. He gives us a detailed picture of the innermost recesses of this cesspool of hell but it's up to us to decide what he is saying." The acting is powerful, with the sublime ZaSu Pitts and Gibson Gowland giving performances that have rarely been matched in American films. Jean Hersholt, however, overacts a little. None of the three leads were well-known stars at the time.

[Originally, yellow tinting was used throughout for gold, gold teeth, gilt frames and the canary, allowing a persistent visual reiteration of its theme.] (Stroheim's original scenario was published in 1958 by the Cinémathèque Royale de Belgique with the collaboration of Stroheim's widow, Denise Vernac, and later by *L'Avant Scène*. Stroheim's own account of the production is included in Peter Noble's biography, *Hollywood Scapegoat*.)

— *Life's Whirlpool* USA 1915. *Dir* Barry O'Neill *Cast* Fania Marinoff, Holbrook Blinn *Prod* World.

An earlier version of *McTeague,* quite probably seen by Stroheim while he was still a movie extra, but which seems to have disappeared without a trace. Lionel Barrymore made a film with the same title two years later.

GREEN PASTURES USA 1936. *Dir* William Keighley, Marc Connelly *Scen* Marc Connelly, Sheridan Gibney based on the play by Marc Connelly suggested by the story *Ole Man Adam and His Chillun* by Roark Bradford *Photog* Hal Mohr *Art Dir* Allen Saalberg, Stanley Fleischer *Mus* Hall Johnson *Ed* George Amy *Cast* Rex Ingram, Oscar Polk, Eddie Anderson, Frank Wilson, Billy Cumby *Prod* Warner Brothers. 93 mins.

The Bible and Paradise as seen by Blacks, with "De Lawd" (Ingram) smoking a cigar, running heaven from behind a big desk, and discussing affairs on earth with Gabriel (Polk). The film is based on a spectacular that opened on Broadway in 1930 with an all-Negro cast. It was a great success, ran for 557 performances, and enjoyed a triumphant three-year tour. But this show was not by or for Blacks in the South. It was designed to make Broadway laugh at the innocence of Blacks and is as "Negro" as a 1900 imitation commode chair is "Louis XV." It was transferred to film by a tenth-rate director who contented himself with photographing the Broadway production. Marc Connelly is therefore the true auteur of this film, not William Keighley.

The only authentic aspect of the film is its background of beautiful spirituals. These, excellent acting, and the film's exotic stagings, made *Green Pastures* a smash hit in France and elsewhere.

[Although it received a good critical reaction, the film was misunderstood in several countries: it was banned as sacrilegious in Canada and its release was held up for a year in Britain while the censors debated whether to give it a certificate.]

GREY MOTOR CAR (THE) AUTOMÓVIL GRIS

GRIDO (IL) THE CRY Italy/USA 1957. *Dir* Michelangelo Antonioni *Scen* Michelangelo Antonioni, Elio Bartolini, Ennio De Concini *Photog* Gianni Di Venanzo *Art Dir* Franco Fontana *Mus* Giovanni Fusco *Ed* Eraldo Da Roma *Cast* Steve Cochran, Alida Valli, Dorian Gray (dubbed by Monica Vitti), Betsy Blair, Lyn Shaw *Prod* S. P. A. Cinematografica/Robert Alexander Productions. 102 mins.

Because his mistress (Valli) falls in love with another man, Aldo (Cochran) leaves her and travels with his daughter from village to village in the Po Valley. He revisits an old girl friend, Elvira (Blair), takes up for a time with a service station attendant (Gray), then a prostitute (Shaw). Unable to find real love, he returns to Irma for a last look and jumps (or falls) to his death.

This relentless and hopeless voyage across the desolate, bare landscape of the Po Valley in winter culminates in the hero's death while workers are demonstrating against a proposed American air base. Antonioni has described his film: "*Il Grido* has a theme that is very important to me and is the first in which I handled emotional problems in a different way. Previously, my characters were often passive about their emotional crises. In this film we have a man who reacts, who tries to do something about his unhappiness. I treated the character with more compassion. I wanted to use the landscape to express his psychology. It is the landscape I remember from my childhood, but seen through the eyes of a man who returns after an intense cultural and emotional experience."

GRIDO DELLA TERRA (IL) see EXODUS

GRISBI TOUCHEZ PAS AU GRISBI

GUERNICA France 1950. *Dir* Alain Resnais, Robert Hessens *Scen* Robert Hessens *Photog* Henry Ferrand, A. Dumaître *Mus* Guy Bernard *Ed* Alain Resnais *Commentary* Paul Eluard spoken by Maria Casarès, Jacques Pruvost *Prod* Braunberger. 12 mins.

Resnais' first important film is far less of an art film on Picasso than a documentary of the destruction and suffering of war, as expressed through Picasso's enormous fresco, "Guernica," and other paintings, drawings, and sculptures executed by Picasso between 1902 and 1949. Its plastic integration of these (and other elements like newspaper headlines and graffiti) is combined with Paul Eluard's lyrical commentary (a mixture of poetry and prose) and Guy Bernard's evocative score into a stylistic unity suggestive of his later *Hiroshima mon amour* (q.v.).

GUERRA DES GAUCHOS (LA) GAUCHO WAR

Argentina 1942. *Dir* Lucas Demare *Scen* Homero Manzi, Ulyses Petit de Murat based on the poems of Leopoldo Lugones *Photog* Humberto Peruzzi *Cast* Enrique Muiño, Francisco Petrone, Angel Magaña, Sebastian Chiola, Amelia Bence *Prod* Associated Argentine Artists. 90 mins.

The story of the early 19th century guerrilla war fought by the gauchos in the northern mountains against the Spanish Army that tried to crush the newly declared Argentinian independence. It is the best pre-1950 Argentinian film, which, although a bit unpolished, has authentic national character.

[It was the first production of Associated Argentine Artists, a cooperative enterprise founded by Demare, writers, and actors. The company produced several other worthwhile films between 1942 and 1946.]

GUERRE EST FINIE (LA) THE WAR IS OVER France/Sweden 1966. *Dir* Alain Resnais *Scen* Jorge Semprun *Photog* Sacha Vierny *Art Dir* Jacques Saulnier *Mus* Giovanni Fusco *Ed* Eric Pluet *Cast* Yves Montand, Ingrid Thulin, Geneviève Bujold, Dominique Rozan, Françoise Bertin, Michel Piccoli *Prod* Sofracima/Europa Film. 122 mins.

Diego (Montand), a professional revolutionary working to bring revolution to Spain, crosses the Spanish border and travels to Paris. There he meets a young left-wing student, Nadine (Bujold) and makes love to her. He returns to his mistress of nine years, Marianne (Thulin), and reports to his comrades on the situation in Spain, although he is beginning to question the group's effectiveness. Diego is asked to return to Spain. Nadine discovers the police are likely to be waiting for Diego, Marianne flies to Barcelona to warn him, but Diego is already crossing the frontier.

Resnais has defined his theme as "The war in Spain is over but the fight continues." The film is structured not in Resnais' more usual flashbacks but in the "future conditional."

[The film's depiction of a man maintaining faith in his ideals, despite the reality around him, makes this one of Resnais' most satisfying films. Unsentimental about himself, Diego (lucidly characterized by Yves Montand) dissects his own dreams and realities as coldly as he analyzes his involvement with Nadine and Marianne. The ending with Diego's "flash" premonitions merging into actuality suggest Resnais' typical theme that memories and dreams overlap, that time is circular.]

GULLIVER'S TRAVELS (IN LILLIPUT) see NOVYI GULLIVER

GUNNAR HEDES SAGA GUNNAR HEDE'S SAGA/THE JUDGMENT Sweden 1922. *Dir* Mauritz Stiller *Scen* Mauritz Stiller based on the novel *En herrgardssagen* by Selma Lagerlöf *Photog* J. Julius (Julius Jaenzon) *Art Dir* Axel Esbensen *Cast* Einar Hanson, Mary Johnson, Pauline Brunius, Stina Berg, Adolf Olchansky *Prod* Svensk Filmindustri. 2,040 meters.

Nils (Hanson) had been told as a boy how his father Gunnar Hede had made the family fortune by driving a herd of reindeer down from Lapland. He plays the violin and has artistic inclinations. He invites a troupe of strolling players to stay on the estate and falls in love with Ingrid (Johnson), the daughter of one couple (Berg, Olchansky). He joins a group of speculators driving a herd of reindeer south, but while trying to hold the leader of the herd during a blizzard is knocked unconscious and loses his memory. Ingrid nurses him and, by playing her violin, helps him to recover.

Stiller's introduction of reindeers (goats in the novel), after seeing a documentary on reindeers, brought Selma Lagerlöf's wrath down on his head; but in many respects it is his best film, a combination of naturalism, burlesque, and fantasy. The long sequence of Nils' trek south with the reindeer necessitated many documentary-like shots and has a wonderful epic quality. As the herd stampedes, Nils ties the lead reindeer to his belt and is dragged for hundreds of yards over ice and rough forest, Stiller following his flight with a series of dazzling tracking shots. Finally he is knocked unconscious. At the same moment, Ingrid is visited in her dreams by the Lady of Grief, who appears in a sleigh drawn by two black bears and who tells her of the accident and shows her the demented Nils, bound hand and foot. The fantasy sequence matches perfectly the naturalistic sequence: the sleigh enters the bedroom as naturally as the panic-stricken reindeer stampede across the snows.

Mary Johnson gives a touching performance as Ingrid. It is not impossible that the sequence of the arrival of the wandering players in the courtyard of the manor, with the aging tightrope dancer and the pathetic comedy of the clown, influenced Ingmar Bergman when he made *Gycklarnas Afton* (*Naked Night*).

GYCKLARNAS AFTON SAWDUST AND TINSEL/THE NAKED NIGHT/SUNSET OF A CLOWN Sweden 1953. *Dir/Scen* Ingmar Bergman *Photog* Sven Nykvist, Hilding Bladh *Art Dir* Bibi Lindström *Mus* Karl-Birger Blomdahl *Ed* Carl-Olov Skeppstedt *Cast* Harriet Andersson, Ake Grönberg, Hasse Ekman, Annika Tretow, Gudrun Brost, Anders Ek *Prod* Sandrews. 95 mins. (85 mins. USA).

Albert Johansson (Grönberg), the owner of a second-rate traveling circus, leaves his mistress, Anne (Andersson), when the circus arrives in the town where his wife and child live, and pleads with his wife, Agda (Tretow), for a reconciliation. She rejects him. Anne, angered by Albert's visits to his wife, flirts with and is callously seduced by Frans (Ekman), a young actor. Frans taunts Albert about Anne, they fight, and Albert is severely beaten. He tries to commit suicide, then, resigned to his fate, returns to Anne.

Memorable sequences: the flashback of Alma (Brost), wife of the clown, Frost (Ek), bathing naked in front of a group of soldiers, and of Frost, grotesque in his clown's make-up, dragging her clumsily up the beach with incessant drumming on the sound track; the circus column on the road; the bloody fight between Albert and Frans in the circus ring; Alberts inability to shoot himself and his shooting of the bear instead; the final sequence as Albert and Anne trudge along together behind the circus caravan.

"A pessimistic film of life and death that allows only a faint glimmer of hope, though certainly not a Christian one" (Simone Dubreuilh). "Overwhelmed by their terrible destiny, all that the heros can do is to bow their heads and try to carry on, happy to have at least escaped suicide or murder. The film's value lies above all in its pitiless portrayal of the relationships between men and women. The nostalgia of his earlier works gives place here to a total pessimism" (Doniol-Valcroze).

GYPSY BLOOD CARMEN

HADAKA NO SHIMA THE ISLAND Japan 1961. *Dir/Scen* Kaneto Shindo *Photog* Kiyoshi Kuroda *Mus* Hikaru Hayashi *Ed* Toshio Enoki *Cast* Nobuko Otowa, Taiji Tonoyama, Shinji Tanaka, Masanori Horimoto. 92 mins.

The life of a peasant family living on a small waterless island. In the summer, the father (Otowa) and the mother (Tonoyama) look for water on the mainland and water their fields. In the autumn, the family takes a trip to the mainland. The rains bring fresh labors in the winter. In the spring, the elder son catches a large fish whose sale allows them to enjoy themselves in the town. Then the child dies and is buried. The film is largely autobiographical: "I was one of a large family living in the inland sea of western Japan. I saw with my own eyes my parents' hard work, the rice planting in early summer under the harsh sun and the laborious harvesting in autumn. I have an unforgettable memory of my mother carrying two heavy jugs of water on her shoulders. I wanted to express the battle between peasants and the land. Until the day she died, my mother said nothing of her terrible work, her silent battle with nature. This silence was very disturbing and is why I conceived a drama without dialogue. The omission of speech was intended not as a gimmick but to allow the image alone to carry the narrative." This powerful parable, which centers on an overburdened woman's repetitive ascent of a rocky hillside, has great beauty, sensitivity, and humanism, despite its sometimes intrusive music. Though produced on a small budget, it was a great international success.

HAGIVA HILL 24 DOESN'T ANSWER Israel 1955. *Dir* Thorold Dickinson *Scen* Zvi Kolitz, Peter Frye based on a story by Zvi Kolitz *Photog* Gerald Gibbs *Mus* Paul Ben-Haim *Art Dir* Joseph Carl *Ed* Joanna and Thorold Dickinson *Cast* Michael Wager, Edward Mulhare, Haya Hararit, Arie Lavi *Prod* Sik'or Films. 101 mins.

On besieged Hill 24, Israeli soldiers recount their stories: 1. An English police inspector (Mulhare) falls in love with a young resistance worker (Hararit) 2. The Battle of Jerusalem (Wager) 3. The capture of a former Nazi officer (Lavi). With morning, all the soldiers die.

This first success of the young Israeli cinema is superbly directed by Thorold Dickinson. The best episode is that which depicts resistance against the British occupation in Tel Aviv and which incidentally illuminates the beauty of Haya Hararit, who was later a star in *Ben Hur*. The film has dialogue in English.

HAIL THE CONQUERING HERO USA 1944. *Dir/Scen* Preston Sturges *Photog* John Seitz *Art Dir* Hans Dreier, Haldane Douglas *Mus* Sigmund Krumgold *Ed* Stuart Gilmore *Cast* Eddie Bracken, Ella Raines, Bill Edwards, William Demarest, Franklin Pangborn, Jimmy Conlin, Raymond Walburn *Prod* Paramount. 101 mins.

Woodrow Lafayette Pershing Truesmith (Bracken) is discharged from the Marines for chronic hay fever. A bunch of Marine heroes adopt him and foist him off on his home town as a genuine hero. In the ensuing hero-worship, he is elected mayor but allowed to keep his post after admitting his deceit.

A burlesque satire on the manners and mores of small-town America (peopled by typical Sturges character types) and a more acid satire on hero-worship.

HAKUCHI THE IDIOT Japan 1951. *Dir* Akira Kurosawa *Scen* Eijiro Hisaita,

Akira Kurosawa based on Fyodor Dostoyevsky's novel *Photog* Toshio Ubukata *Art Dir* So Matsuyama *Mus* Fumio Hayasaka *Cast* Toshiro Mifune, Masayuki Mori, Setsuko Hara *Prod* Shochiku. 265 mins. (original version); 166 mins. (general release version).

Although Kurosawa transposed the setting to contemporary Japan, this is the best adaptation ever made of this novel and indeed of any of Dostoyevsky's novels. Even without knowing a word of Japanese one sits transfixed during 2½ hours of watching an unsubtitled version. [Kurosawa has said: "I had wanted to make this film since before *Rashomon*. Since I was little I'd read Dostoyevsky . . . he is the one who writes most honestly about human existence . . . He seems terrible subjective, but then you come to the resolution that there is no more objective writing . . . People have said the film is a failure . . . At least as entertainment, I don't think it is a failure. Of all my films, people wrote me most about this one . . . They understood what I was saying." The film was roundly attacked by most Japanese and foreign critics. When the production company asked Kurosawa to cut the film by almost half he made his famous reply: "If you want to cut it, you had better cut it lengthwise."]
See also *Nastasia Filipovna*

HALLELUJAH! USA 1929. *Dir* King Vidor *Scen* Wanda Tuchock, Ransom Rideout, King Vidor *Photog* Gordon Avil *Art Dir* Cedric Gibbons *Mus* Irving Berlin, also Negro spirituals *Ed* Hugh Wynn *Cast* Daniel L. Haynes, Nina Mae McKinney, William Fountaine, Harry Gray, Fannie Belle de Knight, Everett McGarrity, Dixie Jubilee Singers *Prod* MGM. 109 mins. Released in both sound and silent versions.

Zeke (Haynes) falls in love with a semi-prostitute, Chuck (McKinney), the mistress of Hot Shot (Fountaine), and accidentally kills his brother (McGarrity). Forgiven by his father, he becomes a preacher. Chuck is again unfaithful and Zeke kills his rival. He is arrested but then set free.

"For several years I had nurtured a secret hope. I wanted to make a film about Negroes, using only Negroes in the cast . . . I made a list of scenes suitable for an all-Negro sound film — river baptisms, prayer meetings accompanied by spirituals, Negro preaching, banjo playing, dancing the blues . . . We rounded up the cast mostly in the Negro districts of Chicago and New York. Daniel Haynes . . . was understudy for Jules Bledsoe in *Show Boat*. Nina Mae McKinney was third from the right in the chorus of the musical show *Blackbirds* on Broadway . . . In Memphis, Tennessee, which we had chosen for location, we had the technical assistance of a Baptist minister, of Professor and Madame de Knight, and of a Reverend Jackson to help with the baptism scenes . . . The sermons and the baptism were shot without sound and post-synchronized in the studio . . . When *Hallelujah* was finished . . . they opened it in Times Square and Harlem simultaneously and had celebrities and ermine coats in both places, but after that we ran into trouble" (King Vidor). The film was hardly seen outside the large cities and even fared badly in the South. *Hallelujah* was enthusiastically received in Europe and J.-G. Auriol devoted a special issue of *Revue du Cinéma* to it. It is the first sound film with any merit and the first all-Negro film. The virile authority of Daniel Haynes and the rebellious sensuality of Nina McKinney are undeniably admirable as are the beautiful spirituals, scenes like the massed river baptism, the fights, and especially the pursuit in the swamp amid mud, bird screeches, and the panting of the two adversaries. However, the characters of *Hallelujah* are based on the conventional Hollywood view of Negroes as superstitious, mindlessly playful, shiftless, and excessively sentimental. Its portrait of the South, full of chanting and cotton-picking, is as specious as the then common view of a patriarchal society. Nevertheless, the misery of shanty towns and rutted streets is shown in the background and the "black soul" is forcefully expressed in the many scenes that still give the film its strength.

HALLUCINATIONS DU BARON DE MUNCH-HAUSEN (LES) see BARON MÜNCHHAUSEN

HAMLET Britain 1948. *Dir* Laurence Olivier *Text Ed* Alan Dent based on Shakespeare's play *Photog* Desmond Dickinson *Design* Roger Furse *Art Dir* Carmen Dillon *Mus* William Walton *Cast* Laurence Olivier, Jean Simmons, Felix Aylmer, Eileen Herlie, Basil Sydney, Norman Wooland *Prod* Two Cities. 155 mins.

A superb example of filmed theater, using all the resources of the camera to reinforce the text. Olivier's best film. Many critics quarreled with his conception of a Hamlet dominated by an Oedipus complex and with his elimination of the Fortinbras character, but this is not to deny the film's overall qualities.

— *Hamlet* USSR 1964. *Dir* Grigori Kozintsev *Scen* Grigori Kozintsev based on Boris Pasternak's translation of Shakespeare's play *Photog* I. Gritsyus *Art Dir* Y. Enei, G. Kropachev *Mus* Dmitri Shostakovich *Cast* Innokenti Smoktunovsky, Mikhail Nazwanov, Anastasia Vertinskaya *Prod* Lenfilm. 150 mins. Sovscope.

This is perhaps the best film based on Shakespeare. It brings the ancient Kingdom of Denmark face to face with the real world in characterizing Hamlet as sincerely motivated and revolted by injustice, crime, and tyranny. "Into this State, where everyone swims with the stream, there comes a person who is against all of this" (Kozintsev).

This version is very much admired in Britain and North America but is almost unknown in the Latin countries.

OTHER VERSIONS:

— France 1900. *Dir* Clément Maurice *Cast* Sarah Bernhardt (as Hamlet).
— France 1907. *Dir* Georges Méliès.
— *Italy 1908. *Dir* Mario Caserini (?) *Prod* Cines.
— Italy 1910. *Dir* Mario Caserini *Prod* Cines.
— *France 1910. *Dir* Gérard Bourgeois. *Prod* Lux.
— Denmark 1910. *Dir* August Blom *Cast* Alwin Neuss.
— Britain 1913. *Dir* E. Hay Plumb *Cast* Sir Johnston Forbes-Robertson *Prod* Cecil Hepworth. 6 reels.
— Italy 1917. *Dir* Eleuterio Rodolfi *Cast* Ruggero Ruggeri. 3 reels.
— Germany 1920. *Dir* Svend Gade *Cast* Asta Nielsen (as Hamlet). 8 reels.
— *German Federal Republic 1960. *Dir* Franz Peter Wirth *Cast* Maximilian Schell, Hans Caninberg, Wanda Roth. 130 mins.
— *Britain 1969. *Dir* Tony Richardson *Cast* Nicol Williamson, Gordon Jackson, Anthony Hopkins, Judy Parfitt. 119 mins. Technicolor.

HANDFUL OF RICE (A) MAN OCH KVINNA

HANDSOME SERGE BEAU SERGE (LE)

HANDS OVER THE CITY MANI SULLA CITTÀ (LE)

HANGMAN (THE) VERDUGO (EL)

HANIBAL TANAR UR PROFESSOR HANNIBAL Hungary 1956. *Dir* Zoltan Fabri *Scen* Zoltan Fabri, Istvan Gyenes, Peter Szasz based on the novel by Ferenc Moras *Photog* Ferenc Szecsenyi *Mus* Zdenko Tamassy *Art Dir* Ivan Ambrozy *Cast* Ernö Szabo, Zoltan Greguss, Manyi Kiss, Rudolf Somogyvary *Prod* Hunnia Studios. 100 mins.

During the period when the Hungarian dictator Horthy was in power, a professor (Szabo) is persecuted for his researches on the Carthagenian General Hannibal.

This social satire, which is directed as much to the Fifties as to the Twenties, includes an excellent performance by Ernö Szabo.

HAPPINESS BONHEUR (LE)

HAPPY CIRCUS (THE) VESELEY CIRCUS

HAPPY GIPSIES . . . ! SKULPJACI PERJA

HAPPY LOVERS KNAVE OF HEARTS

HARAKIRI SEPPUKU

HARAM (EL) DISGRACE United Arab Republic 1965. *Dir* Henri Baracat *Scen* Saad Eddine Wahba based on the novel by Youssef Idriss *Photog* Diae El Mahdi *Mus* Soliman Gamil *Cast* Faten Hamama, Zaki Rouston, Abdalla Gheith and non-professionals. 105 mins.

An agricultural worker (Hamama) in 1950 kills her illegitimate child, incites the peasants against the seasonal workers, and then brings them together. An unmelodramatic, authentic, and powerful portrait of life in prerevolutionary Egypt.

*HARD DAY'S NIGHT (A) Britain 1964. *Dir* Richard Lester *Scen* Alun Owen *Photog* Gilbert Taylor *Mus* John Lennon, Paul McCartney, George Martin *Ed* John Jympson *Cast* John Lennon, Paul McCartney, George Harrison, Ringo Starr, Wilfred Brambell, Norman Rossington *Prod* Proscenium for United Artists. 84 mins.

The Beatles travel to London for a television show accompanied by their manager (Rossington) and Paul's grandfather (Brambell). They enjoy various escapades but finally complete the show. The exuberant vitality of this episodic film derives less from the Beatles' own admirable charm than from the stylistic effects that Lester contributed. The camera runs, zooms, and swoops, with the fast cuts adding to the sense of hyperactivity. Despite appearances, only a few scenes were improvised; notably among these are sequences at the press conference and on the playing field. Although this is Lester's first important film, his technical training in making TV commercials and the anarchic *The Running, Jumping and Standing Still Film* served him well.

HARP OF BURMA BIRUMA NO TATEGOTO

HARVEST (THE) VOZVRASCHENIE VASILIYA BORTNIKOVA

HAUNTED HOTEL (THE) USA 1907. *Dir* James Stuart Blackton *Prod* Vitagraph. 500 ft.
"A house becomes a monster, a knife cuts slices of sausage and bread by itself, wine, tea and milk upset themselves." (1908 publicity).
This ½-reel film was an enormous international success; 150 copies were sold in Europe alone. It used frame-by-frame photography (one turn, one picture) to animate objects rather than drawings. When such French film makers as Chomon and Emile Cohl saw the film, they called this process *mouvement américain* and it became the basis of the animated cinema. The film even used close-ups, several years before Griffith is credited with their "invention." The name of the cameraman is unknown as perhaps is that of the director; James Stuart Blackton, who founded the prosperous Vitagraph Company, is likely to have been only its artistic producer. [Curiously, despite the film's influence on French film makers, it seems to have been totally ignored by English-language historians. Blackton's technique is now more commonly called "pixilation."]

HAXAN WITCHCRAFT THROUGH THE AGES Sweden 1922. *Dir/Scen* Benjamin Christensen *Photog* Johan Ankarstjerne *Art Dir* Holst-Jørgensen *Sets* Richard Louw *Cast* Oscar Stribolt, Clara Pontoppidan, Karen Winther, Aage Hertel, Tora Teje, Astrid Holm, Emmy Schøenfeld. Elith Pio, Benjamin Christensen *Prod* Svensk Filmindustri. 7,489 ft.
This extraordinary film is in essence a "document" about witchcraft based on the records of numerous trials from the 15th to the 17th centuries. Principal sequences: Satan (Christensen) seducing a witch-wife while her husband sleeps; a poor woman (Schøenfeld) is accused of witchcraft by the neurotic wife (Winther) of a sick man, is tortured by the Inquisition, and forced to admit participating in the Witches' Sabbath. The film concludes with documented scenes of superstition and cases of "possession" in 1920.
Treatment of this theme could have been both ridiculous and pornographic, especially in the explicit depiction of the Witches Sabbath. But Christensen's style is more reminiscent of Bosch, Breughel, Callot, and Goya. In the Inquisition scenes, fantasy gives way to realism and both the costumes and the composition of the images (by Johan Ankarstjerne) make one think of Dreyer's *Passion de Jeanne d'Arc*.
The surrealists were especially enthusiastic about this unique masterpiece. Ado Kyrou described it as: "The most powerful indictment of the criminal Church, its Inquisition and its instruments of torture. This document should be shown in every school in the world."
— **Haxan/La Sorcière/The Sorcerers* Sweden/France 1955. *Dir* André Michel *Cast* Marina Vlady, Maurice Ronet.
A French engineer falls in love with a Swedish half-witch girl who is feared and hated by the inhabitants of the country.

HEARTBEAT ANGÈLE

HEARTS OF THE WORLD USA 1918. *Dir* D. W. Griffith *Scen* Gaston de Tolignac (Griffith) *Photog* G. W. Bitzer *Ed* James Smith, D. W. Griffith *Technical Consult* Erich von Stroheim, Alfred Machin *Cast* Lillian Gish, Dorothy Gish, Robert Harron, Josephine Crowell, Adolphe Lestina, Erich von Stroheim, Noel Coward *Prod* Griffith. 7,100 ft.
In a French village behind the allied lines during the First World War, a young boy (Harron) loves a girl (Lillian Gish), although he is importuned by the Little Disturber (Dorothy Gish), who loves him. When the village is mobilized the boy leaves for the trenches.

The village is bombarded, the girl's grandfather (Lestina) is killed, and the village occupied by Germans. A Prussian officer (Stroheim) tries to ravish the girl but she is saved by the boy and French troops take the village again.

This somewhat sentimental and melodramatic film espousing the virtues of patriotism and democracy was a great commercial success. There are, however, several touching scenes between the lovers and some excellent battle sequences. Noel Coward made his first screen appearance in a small part.

HEAVENLY PLAY (THE) HIMLASPELET

HEIR TO GENGHIS KHAN (THE) POTOMOK CHINGIS-KHAN

HELL ON EARTH NIEMANDSLAND

HELL'S ANGELS USA 1930. *Dir* Howard Hughes. *Scen* Howard Estabrook, Harry Behn based on a story by Marshall Neilan, Joseph Moncure March *Dialogue Dir* James Whale *Art Dir* J. Boone Fleming, Carroll Clarke *Photog* Tony Gaudio, Harry Perry, E. Burton Steene *Ed* Frank Lawrence, Douglas Biggs, Perry Hollingsworth *Cast* Jean Harlow (Greta Nissen in original silent version), Ben Lyon, James Hall, John Darrow, Jane Winton, Lucien Prival *Prod* Caddo for United Artists, 135 mins. Red tints with Technicolor for the ball sequence. Wide screen in two sequences.

In an air squadron in 1917–18, a Don Juan (Lyon) seduces his brother's (Hall) fiancée (Harlow) and is revealed later as a coward. The two brothers are involved in several air fights, are taken prisoner, and the coward dies a hero.

A brilliant aviation film in which the producer-director, millionaire Howard Hughes, introduced platinum blonde Jean Harlow. It was begun in 1927 as a silent film and was later partly reshot as a sound film. Subtitles were used to translate the German dialogue.

HELLZAPOPPIN' USA 1941. *Dir* H. C. Potter *Scen* Nat Perrin, Warren Wilson from a story by Nat Perrin *Photog* Woody Bredell *Ed* Milton Carruth *Cast* Ole Olsen, Chic Johnson, Martha Raye, Mischa Auer, Hugh Herbert *Prod* Universal. 84 mins.

A crazy comedy with a plot impossible to summarize, the action of which partly takes place in a film studio representing hell, where a film is being made in which the Devil (Johnson) meets the Sheriff of Arizona (Olsen). Innumerable crazy scenes develop for no reason other than that they are funny.

This masterpiece of nonsense owes far more to the traditions of American vaudeville and to its scriptwriter, Nat Perrin, who worked with the Marx Brothers and Eddie Cantor, than to its mediocre director.

*HELP! Britain 1965. *Dir* Richard Lester *Scen* Marc Behm, Charles Wood *Photog* David Watkin *Art Dir* Ray Simm *Mus* John Lennon, Paul McCartney, Ken Thorne *Ed* John Victor Smith *Cast* John Lennon, Paul McCartney, George Harrison, Ringo Starr, Leo McKern, Eleanor Bron. Victor Spinetti, Roy Kinnear *Prod* Walter Shenson/Subafilms for United Artists. 92 mins. Eastman Color. The Beatles involved in a plot by villains to take a sacrificial ring from Ringo's finger.

Based on a script that seems to have grown out of the BBC Goon Show via the Marx Brothers and Olsen and Johnson, *Help!* is as visually striking as the earlier film and perhaps even more arresting because of its use of color. The film is full of marvelous gags, of which the most memorable is the "Ode to Joy" whistle taken up by people in a pub, in the street, and finally in a football stadium – a sequence reminiscent of the compilation "rescue" sequence during the battle in *Duck Soup*.

*HENRY V Britain 1944. *Dir* Laurence Olivier *Text Ed* Alan Dent, Laurence Olivier based on the play by Shakespeare *Photog* Robert Krasker *Art Dir* Paul Sheriff *Mus* William Walton *Costumes* Roger Furse *Ed* Reginald Beck *Cast* Laurence Olivier, Robert Newton, Leslie Banks, Renée Asherson, Leo Genn, Felix Aylmer *Prod* Two Cities. 137 mins. Technicolor. Reissued in 1957 in a Superscope version.

The first Shakespearean film to gain not only critical acclaim but a wide measure of public support as well. It was also the first Shakespearean film in color and the first to treat soliloquy as thought, heard on the sound track, but not visibly spoken. For most of the film the viewer is at two removes from reality – in a play at the Globe Theater and then in the world of imagination to which the Chorus is the introduction. This is emphasized by Paul Sheriff's sets, which have the brilliant color, and flat, almost dreamlike quality, of illuminated sets. This is especially evident in the scenes at the French court, where the actors seem to spring to life as though from a medieval paintings. The Battle of Agincourt is a visual high point, which, despite its debt to the battle on the ice in *Alexander Nevsky* (*q.v.*), is immensely exciting and edited with a strong sense of rhythm. The performances are of a very high standard, as in all of Olivier's Shakespeare films. Some critics have felt that the progress from the Globe Theater to the actualities of the French campaign and back again is a confusion of conventions, but the film continues to appeal to audiences.

HERR ARNES PENGAR SIR ARNE'S TREASURE/THE TREASURE OF ARNE Sweden 1919. *Dir* Mauritz Stiller *Scen* Mauritz Stiller, Gustaf Molander based on the novel by Selma Lagerlöf *Photog* J. Julius (Julius Jaenzon), Gustav Boge (exteriors) *Art Dir* Harry Dahlström, Alexander Bakö *Costumes* Axel Esbensen *Cast* Richard Lund, Bror Berger, Erik Stocklassa, Hjalmar Selander, Mary Johnson, Axel Nilsson, Wanda Rothgardt, Stina Berg *Prod* Svenska. 2,219 meters. (7,200 ft. approx.)

In Sweden in the 16th century, Sir Archie (Lund), a Scottish mercenary, escapes from prison with two other mercenaries (Berger, Stocklassa). On their flight to the coast, they come to a rich farm owned by Sir Arne (Selander), steal his treasure, and kill him and his family. While they wait for their ship to free itself from the ice, Arne's daughter Elsalill (Johnson) arrives in the town and, unsuspecting that he is her father's murderer, falls in love with Sir Archie. When she realizes who he is, he tries to escape by using her body as a shield. She is killed and the mercenaries are captured.

This film represents Stiller at the peak of his artistry: perfect sets and costumes, matchless visual beauty in its lyrical use of the countryside and superb acting, especially by the very young Mary Johnson. Stiller also explored new uses of the camera, such as the traveling shot around the prison tower or that following Sir Archie as he crosses the ice smitten with remorse. The film is more powerful after the theft of the treasure and uses snow and the ship

trapped in the ice as leitmotivs. It is as sharp and taut as a sword, but has a delicately inlaid surface that is perhaps too cold in its absolute formal perfection.

The final scene is famous, showing the black-robed women of the village as they follow Elsalill's funeral procession across the snow. Stiller's use of this image must have been derived from avant-garde theater. In its turn its influence can be seen in both the works of Fritz Lang and in the final scene of the first part of Eisenstein's *Ivan the Terrible* (*q.v.*).

HERRIN VON ATLANTIS (DIE) see ATLANTIDE (L')

HERR PUNTILA UND SEIN KNECHT MATTI PUNTILA/MR. PUNTILA AND HIS VALET MATTI Austria 1955. *Dir* Alberto Cavalcanti *Scen* Cavalcanti, Vladimir Pozner, Ruth Wieden based on the play by Bertolt Brecht *Photog* André Bac, Arthur Hämmerer *Art Dir* Erik Aaes, Hans Zehetner, *Mus* Hanns Eisler *Cast* Curt Bois, Heinz Engelmann, Maria Emo, Edith Prager *Prod* Bauer-Film. 95 mins. Agfacolor.

Comedy about the equivocal relationship between master and servant. The rich landowner, Puntila (Bois), is more genial drunk than sober. His patient servant, Matti (Engelmann), is constantly obliged to pacify girls to whom Puntila has proposed.

This is the only adaptation of one of his plays that is said to have satisfied Brecht, who rejected every other film version including *Die Dreigroschenoper*. *Puntila* also makes interesting experimental use of color.

HETS FRENZY/TORMENT Sweden 1944. *Dir* Alf Sjöberg *Scen* Ingmar Bergman *Photog* Martin Bodin *Mus* Hilding Rosenberg *Art Dir* Arne Akermark *Ed* Oscar Rosander *Cast* Stig Järrel, Alf Kjellin, Mai Zetterling, Stig Olin *Prod* Svensk Filmindustri. 101 mins.

A sadistic Latin teacher (Järrel), nicknamed "Caligula," humiliates one of his pupils, Jan-Erik (Kjellin). Jan-Erik meets a girl, Bertha (Zetterling) and falls in love with her. She tells him she fears a sinister man who follows her. One day he finds her dead in her room and, discovers Caligula hiding in a hallway, and accuses him of being responsible for her death. An autopsy gives heart failure as the cause of death. Caligula prevents Jan-Erik from sitting for his matriculation exams and he ends by living alone in Bertha's room.

Stig Järrel as Caligula was made to resemble Himmler, then head of the Gestapo, and was given character details to suggest that he was a Nazi sympathizer: "Many viewers saw Caligula as a symbol of Nazism and applauded his downfall" (Rune Waldekranz). These anti-Fascist allusions were not noticed until the film was screened in France after the war, but the film does not by any means rely on them for its impact. Bergman's vigorous script (his first), Sjöberg's expressive style, and Mai Zetterling's performance (which led to her international career) made the film a world-wide success.

HE WHO MUST DIE CELUI QUI DOIT MOURIR

HIDDEN RIVER RIO ESCONDIDO

HIGH AND DRY MAGGIE (THE)

HIGH NOON USA 1952. *Dir* Fred Zinnemann *Scen* Carl Foreman based on *The Tin Star* by John W. Cunningham *Photog* Floyd Crosby *Mus* Dimitri Tiomkin *Art Dir* Rudolf Sternard *Cast* Gary Cooper, Thomas Mitchell, Grace Kelly, Lon Chaney Jr., Otto Kruger, Lloyd Bridges, Katy Jurado *Prod* Stanley Kramer for United Artists. 85 mins.

Sheriff Kane (Cooper) is deserted by the townspeople (Mitchell, Jurado, Kruger, Morgan, etc.) and even by his own wife (Kelly) and has to stand alone against a bandit and his three accomplices.

"He is alone, this hero: alone against the four bandits who have sworn to kill him but also alone among those he is trying to save. Each of them has reasons: the pure and simple fear of Sam [William, *Ed*] Fuller and the judge, the ambition of Harvey, the religious convictions of his wife and the preacher, the hopeless despair of the old sheriff, the pragmatism of a friend" (Jacques Doniol-Valcroze).

This "intellectual" western, which was unknown in France until André Bazin drew attention to it, has been much overestimated.

Kane's desperate search for support, "a man walking amid treason" (Doniol-Valcroze), the cowardice of the townspeople who let him stand alone, and the theme song by Johnny Mercer and Dimitri Tiomkin, "Do Not Forsake

Me . . . ," are obvious pointers to its allegory of the McCarthy era. The scriptwriter, Carl Foreman, had been cited by the Un-American Activities Committee in 1951 for his alleged Communist associations and had broken his relationship with Stanley Kramer. Much of his own sense of bitterness must have been included in the film.

HIGH SOCIETY see PHILADELPHIA STORY (THE)

HILL OF DEATH KOZARA

HILL 24 DOESN'T ANSWER HAGIVA

HIMLASPELET THE ROAD TO HEAVEN/THE HEAVENLY PLAY Sweden 1942. *Dir* Alf Sjöberg *Scen* Rune Lindström, Alf Sjöberg based on the play by Rune Lindström *Photog* Gösta Roosling *Art Dir* Arne Akermark *Ed* Oscar Rosander *Mus* Lillebror Söderlundh *Cast* Rune Lindström, Eivor Landström, Anders Henrikson, Emil Fjellström, Gudrun Brost *Prod* Wivefilm. 105 mins.

In 18th century Dalecarlia, a girl (Landström) is unjustly accused of witchcraft but dies before she is burnt at the stake. Her fiancé (Lindström) takes the Road to Heaven to demand justice from God (Henrikson). He is helped by four prophets and by Mary and Joseph, is tempted by Satan (Fjellström), and becomes an evil-doer. He dies a rich and lonely man who has lost his soul, but, in death, God restores him to his love. Sjöberg revived the Sjöström tradition of more than twenty years earlier in this blend of fantasy and realism. Sjöberg's style combines Christian mythology, folklore, humor, and imaginativeness without becoming pretentious. The film's qualities owe much to Rune Lindström, who is the principal actor and who, with Sjöberg, wrote the script from his own play.

*HIPPOCAMPE (L') France 1934. *Dir/Scen* Jean Painlevé *Photog* Jean Painlevé, A. Raymond *Mus* Darius Milhaud. 10 mins.

One of the most famous and most beautiful of Painlevé's series of nature films, describing the life cycle and behavior of the sea horse. Its superb photography and wit are typical of Painlevé's work over more than 40 years.

HIROSHIMA MON AMOUR France/Japan 1959. *Dir* Alain Resnais *Scen* Marguerite Duras *Photog* Sacha Vierny, Michio Takahashi *Art Dir* Esaka, Mayo, Petri *Mus* Giovanni Fusco, Georges Delerue *Ed* Henri Colpi, Jasmine Chasney, Anne Sarraute · *Cast* Emmanuèle Riva, Eiji Okada, Stella Dassas, Pierre Barbaud, Bernard Fresson *Prod* Argos-Como-Pathé/Daiei. 90 mins.

A French actress (Riva) working in Hiroshima on an antiwar film meets and falls in love with a Japanese architect (Okada). Their "impossible" love revives her memories of the war and of the German soldier she loved in Nevers who was killed on the day the town was liberated. When the time comes to leave Hiroshima, she tells the architect: "I shall forget you! I have forgotten you!" *Hiroshima mon amour* is not only the most significant film of the French *new wave* but also as cinematically revolutionary as *Citizen Kane*. Its integration of past and present, its images used to counterpoint Marguerite Duras' poetic dialogue, and its original sound track, fusing music and narrative text, broke all previous conventions. The individual drama of the lovers, which awakens the woman's memory of her dead lover, is set against the collective massacre of Hiroshima, provoking the question: "How can humans do that," whether to a single other human being or to millions? The film opens with shots of the naked lovers and then we hear their voices: the woman recounts her experiences over newsreel and documentary shots of the museum, the hospital, and rebuilt Hiroshima while the man insistently rejoins, "No, you have seen nothing in Hiroshima." Next afternoon and evening, the lovers wander through the town and linger in a café and a railway station while the woman relives her memories of Nevers and meditates on forgetfulness and coming to terms with the past.

The acting is remarkable, especially that of Emmanuèle Riva: her characterization bridges the whole range of emotions, from tenderness and passion to despair. *Hiroshima mon amour* was a worldwide success, its complex emotional theme making a powerful impact on all who saw it, even when they didn't understand the full depth of its meaning.

HIS GIRL FRIDAY USA 1940. *Dir* Howard Hawks *Scen* Charles Lederer based on the play *Front Page* by Ben Hecht, Charles MacArthur *Photog* Joseph Walker *Mus* Morris W. Stoloff *Ed* Gene Havlick *Cast* Cary Grant, Rosalind Russell, Ralph Bellamy, Gene Lockhart *Prod* Columbia. 92 mins.

A new version of *Front Page* (*q.v.*) in which Hawks changed the sex of the reporter to a girl (Russell). One of the few remakes as good as the original. Brilliant direction by Hawks and a brilliant performance by Rosalind Russell.

HIS NEW JOB USA 1915. *Dir/Scen* Charles Chaplin *Photog* Rollie Totheroh *Cast* Chaplin, Ben Turpin, Charlotte Mineau, Leo White, Agnes Ayres, Gloria Swanson *Prod* Essanay. 1,098 ft.

Chaplin's first Essanay film, and the only one he made in Essanay's Chicago studios, takes place in a film studio where Charlie gets a job as a carpenter's assistant and causes havoc for the star (Mineau) and the director (White). It is also one of the rare films in which Chaplin uses a moving camera as part of a gag — to reveal him stepping on the leading lady's train.

HISTOIRE D'UNE CHAISE CHAIRY TALE (A)

*HISTOIRE DU SOLDAT INCONNU (L') LE SOLDAT INCONNU Belgium 1932. *Dir/Scen/Ed* Henri Storck. 12 mins. Reissued in sound version, 1959.

A satire on political chicanery and the signing of the Kellogg-Briand Pact (which renounced war as a means of settling international disputes), using only newsreels related to the event. Its ingenious juxtaposition of newsreel images results in a savage attack on armies, religion, and capitalism, and "the silent majority" of the middle classes who give them their power. But, as Marcel Martin put it, it is "more anarchic and surrealistic that Marxist."

*HISTOIRE IMMORTELLE (UNE) IMMORTAL STORY. France 1968. *Dir* Orson Welles *Scen* Orson Welles based on the story by Isak Dinesen (Karen Blixen) *Photog* Willy Kurant *Mus* Erik Satie *Cast* Orson Welles, Jeanne Moreau, Roger Coggio, Norman Ashley *Prod* Albina Films. 58 mins. Eastman Color.

An aging, rich American merchant (Welles) in Macao tells the story of a sailor who was invited to make love to a young woman by her old husband. When the story is disbelieved he decides to make it come true and hires a sailor (Coggio) to go to bed with a woman (Moreau) in his sumptuous home. But things do not go as planned and next morning the merchant is dead in his chair.

Not Welles as his best, but an attractive and romantic film set in muted colors with an impressive performance by Welles himself.

HOLE (THE) TROU (LE) (Becker)

HOLE (THE) ONIBABA (Shindo)

HOLIDAY FREE TO LIVE/UNCONVENTIONAL LINDA USA 1938. *Dir* George Cukor *Scen* Donald Ogden Stewart, Sidney Buchman based on the play by Philip Barry *Photog* Franz Planer *Art Dir* Stephen Goosson, Lionel Banks *Ed* Otto Meyer, Al Clark *Cast* Katherine Hepburn, Cary Grant, Lew Ayres, Henry Kolker, Doris Nolan, Edward Everett Horton *Prod* Columbia. 94 mins.

[Johnny Case (Grant) is engaged to a girl in a rich family but at the last minute rejects his intended for her unconventional sister, Linda (Hepburn). Based on a play by Philip Barry, this comedy of manners, with undertones of satire on the idle rich, is less well known than *The Philadelphia Story* (*q.v.*) (also directed by Cukor from a Philip Barry play), but is at least as graceful and witty with delightful performances by Hepburn and Grant. One of the best scenes shows the father (Kolker) planning the holiday of the future husband and wife.]

— *Holiday* USA 1930. *Dir* Edward H. Griffith *Scen* Horace Jackson based on the play by Philip Barry *Photog* Norbert Brodine *Cast* Ann Harding, Robert Ames, Edward Everett Horton, Mary Astor, William Holden *Prod* RKO-Pathé. 89 mins.

An earlier version of the same play with Ann Harding as Linda, Robert Ames as Johnny Case, and William Holden (not the same Holden as today) as the father.

HOMME DE NULLE PART (L') see FEU MATHIAS PASCAL

HOMME MARCHE DANS LA FOULE (UN) UN HOMME MARCHE DANS LA FOULE

HON DANSADE EN SOMMAR SOMMARDANSEN/ONE SUMMER OF HAPPINESS/SHE ONLY DANCED ONE SUMMER Sweden 1951.

Dir Arne Mattson *Scen* W. Semitjov based on the novel *Sommardansen* by Per Olof Ekström *Photog* Göran Strindberg *Mus* Sven Sköld *Cast* Ulla Jacobsson, Folke Sundqvist, Edwin Adolphson *Prod* Nordisk. 92 mins.

A student (Sundqvist) on holiday falls in love with a young peasant girl (Jacobsson) and causes a scandal among the puritans in the village. Her death in an accident is seen as divine retribution.

The international commercial success of this attack on bigotry stemmed more from the scene (albeit modest and lyrical) in which the naked couple make love in a field than from the theme, acting, or beautifully photographed landscapes. This is, however, one of Mattson's rare good films.

HONEYMOON see WEDDING MARCH (THE)

HONOR AMONG THIEVES TOUCHEZ PAS AU GRISBI

HOPELESS ONES (THE) SZEGENYLEGENYEK

HORROR OF DRACULA (THE) see DRACULA

HORSE FEATHERS USA 1932. *Dir* Norman Z. McLeod *Scen* Bert Kalmar, Harry Ruby, S. J. Perelman, W. B. Johnstone *Photog* Ray June *Mus* Bert Kalmar, Harry Ruby *Cast* Groucho, Chico, Harpo, Zeppo Marx, Thelma Todd, David Landau, James Pierce *Prod* Paramount. 68 mins.

A satire on education, sport, and the Depression, in which Groucho is the new president of a college, Zeppo is his student son and Chico and Harpo are enrolled as students simply to play football for the college. Its absurd, nihilistic script, cascade of gags, (many of them derived from vaudeville), and direct social satire make this one of the Marx Brothers' great films.

HOTEL DES INVALIDES France 1952. *Dir/Scen* Georges Franju *Photog* Marcel Fradetal *Mus* Maurice Jarre *Spoken Commentary* Michel Simon and Museum guides *Prod* Forces et Voix de la France. 23 mins.

The Army intended this film as a prestige documentary but Franju turned it into a sustained attack on war and its effects, juxtaposing banal scenes of a guided tour of the War Museum with shots of the effects of war. "Legend has its heroes, war its victims," says the commentary as the camera moves from a statue of Napoleon to a cripple in a wheelchair.

HOUNDS OF ZAROFF (THE) MOST DANGEROUS GAME (THE)

HOUR OF THE WOLF VARGTIMMEN

HOUSE OF PLEASURE PLAISIR (LE)

HOUSE OF THE ANGEL (THE) CASA DEL ANGEL (LA)

HOUSE ON TRUBNAYA SQUARE (THE) DOM NA TRUBNOI

HOUSE-WARMING (THE) Hong Kong 1954. *Dir* Tsou Se-Ling *Photog* Lo Tchin-chang *Cast* Tsen Tchen-tchouen. 120 mins. approx.
The "proletariazation" of a white-collar worker, the father of a family, and the day-to-day dramas of the housing crisis. There are many truthful touches and excellent character types in this film and some powerfully satiric scenes, such as when the employee loses his job because the real estate company that employs him cannot sell its apartments, even though he himself lives in a hovel so terrible that his children are threatened with sickness and death.

HOW GREEN WAS MY VALLEY USA 1941. *Dir* John Ford *Scen* Philip Dunne based on the novel by Richard Llewellyn *Photog* Arthur Miller *Art Dir* Richard Day, Nathan Juran, Thomas Little *Mus* Alfred Newman *Ed* James B. Clarke *Cast* Walter Pidgeon, Maureen O'Hara, Donald Crisp, Roddy McDowell, Anna Lee, John Loder, Ann Todd, Sara Allgood, Barry Fitzgerald *Prod* Darryl F. Zanuck, 20th Century-Fox. 118 mins.
A man remembers that when he was a small boy in Wales at the turn of the century, Mr. Morgan, his father (Crisp), and his four older brothers worked in the mines. They were happy until labor troubles appeared. A minister (Pidgeon) loved his sister (O'Hara), but she married the mine-owner's son. Mr. Morgan died in a pit explosion.
This adaptation of Richard Llewellyn's best-selling novel about a Welsh mining family is as romantic as Zola's *Germinal* is realistic. Despite its stagey style and somewhat rambling plot, it does contain attacks on bigotry and delivers its

"message" quite forcefully. An elaborate Welsh village set was built in Hollywood for this film, which was a major commercial success and won several Oscars, including Best Picture, Direction, Cinematography, and Art Direction.

HOW THE STEEL WAS TEMPERED KAK ZAKALYALAS STAL

HOW THE WEST WAS WON USA 1962. *Dir* John Ford, Henry Hathaway, George Marshall *Scen* James R. Webb *Photog* William H. Daniels, Milton Krasner, Charles Lang Jr., Joseph LaShelle *Art Dir* George W. Davis, William Ferrari, Addison Hehr *Mus* Alfred Newman *Ed* Harold Kress *Cast* Carroll Baker, Lee J. Cobb, Henry Fonda, Gregory Peck, James Stewart, Richard Widmark, Karl Malden, Carolyn Jones, John Wayne, Agnes Moorehead, etc. *Prod* MGM. 165 mins. Technicolor. Cinerama.
Pioneer days in the West, the gold rush, the Civil War, the building of the railway to the Pacific, and the fight to establish law in the West are depicted in five episodes.
This spectacular western was filmed in three-lens Cinerama (single-lens Cinerama was introduced in 1963) but rarely exploits the possibilities of the giant screen. John Ford directed the Civil War episodes without his usual *élan*.

HUE AND CRY Britain 1947. *Dir* Charles Crichton *Scen* T. E. B. Clarke *Photog* Douglas Slocombe *Art Dir* Norman Arnold *Mus* Georges Auric *Ed* Charles Hasse *Cast* Alistair Sim, Jack Warner, Valerie White, Harry Fowler *Prod* Ealing. 82 mins.
A group of children, an adolescent (Fowler), and a journalist (Sim) track down a crook (Warner). Though its story owes an obvious debt to *Emil und die detektiv* (q.v.), this is a vivid portrayal of life in London in the immediate postwar period and a delightful spoof of authority.

HUMAN CONDITION (THE) NINGEN NO JOKEN

HUMAN DESIRE USA 1954. *Dir* Fritz Lang *Scen* Alfred Hayes based on the novel *La Bête humaine* by Emile Zola *Photog* Burnett Guffey *Art Dir* Robert Peterson *Mus* Daniele Amfitheatrof *Ed* Aaron Stell *Cast* Glenn Ford, Gloria Grahame,

Broderick Crawford, Edgar Buchanan
Prod Columbia. 90 mins.

Alfred Hayes' adaptation of Zola's *La Bête humaine* retained the basic situation but set it in contemporary USA and cleaned up the less wholesome aspects.

Lang screened Renoir's version of *La Bête humaine* (*q.v.*) before shooting to ensure that he took a different approach. Later he said: "Renoir's film is much better. I had a contract, I had to give in to the producer who said 'We don't want sexual perversity but an ordinary American boy.' We also had great difficulty finding a railway company that didn't exclaim 'A murder, on our railway line? Quite out of the question.'" Lang's self-criticism is too severe: there are many excellent exterior sequences and scenes depicting life on the railroad. [Most of the film takes place at night and Lang makes superb use of shadows to create an almost tangible world of fatalistic passion.]

HUMANITY AND PAPER BALLOONS NINJO KAMI-FUSEN

I ACCUSE see AFFAIRE DREYFUS (L')

I ACCUSE J'ACCUSE (Gance)

I AM A FUGITIVE FROM A CHAIN GANG
I AM A FUGITIVE USA 1932. *Dir* Mervyn
LeRoy *Scen* Howard J. Green, Brown
Holmes based on a story by Robert E.
Burns *Photog* Sol Polito *Art Dir* Jack
Okey *Ed* William Homes *Cast* Paul
Muni, Glenda Farrell, Helen Vinson,
Preston Foster, David Landau, Edward
Le Saint *Prod* Warner Brothers. 93 mins.
A jobless veteran (Muni) is framed for
a robbery. He escapes from prison but
is captured and sent to work on a chain
gang. He escapes again but lives his life
a hunted man, despite gaining respectability with a new name and a new life.
This uncompromising indictment of prison brutality was based on a true story
that became a best-seller. Its style is
simple, direct, and forceful, often giving
the feeling of being a documentary. It
is one of the best American films of
social criticism produced in the early
sound era, and has a striking performance by Paul Muni. The most powerful episode depicts conditions in the
prison labor camp — scenes that aroused
public concern and helped bring about
a reformation of the chain-gang system.

I, A NEGRO MOI, UN NOIR

IDIOT (THE) (Japan) HAKUCHI

IDIOT (THE) (USSR) NASTASIA FILIPOVNA

I EVEN MET HAPPY GIPSIES SKULPJACI
PERJA

*IF . . . Britain 1968. *Dir* Lindsay Anderson *Scen* David Sherwin based on
Crusaders by David Sherwin, John How-
lett *Photog* Miroslav Ondricek *Art Dir*
Jocelyn Herbert *Mus* Marc Wilkinson
and the "Sanctus" from *Missa Luba Ed*
David Gladwell *Cast* Malcolm McDowell, David Wood, Richard Warwick,
Robert Swann, Christine Noonan, Peter
Jeffrey, Mona Washbourne *Prod* Memo-
rial Enterprises. 111 mins. Eastman Color.
Mick (McDowell) and some other public
schoolboys (Warwick, Swann, etc.) meet
a girl (Noonan) and rebel against their
school, its headmaster (Jeffrey), and
their environment.
"For me, as I suppose for most of the
public-school educated, the world of
school remains one of extraordinarily
significant vividness; a world of reality
and symbol; of mingled affection and
reserve" (Lindsay Anderson). Though
at first sight a satire on the English public-school system, *If . . .* is more of a
speculation on the nature of individu-
alism and authority. Its anarchic spirit,
style of poetic realism, and refusal to
compromise stem more from the tradition of Jean Vigo than from that of the
British cinema. In fact it can justly be
compared to *Zéro de conduite* (*q.v.*)
— and not to its disfavor.

I HAVE A NEW MASTER ECOLE BUISSIONIÈRE
(L')

IKIMONO NO KIROKU I LIVE IN FEAR/
WHAT THE BIRDS KNEW/RECORD OF A
LIVING BEING Japan 1955. *Dir* Akira
Kurosawa *Scen* Hideo Oguni, Shinobu
Hashimoto, Akira Kurosawa *Photog*
Asakazu Nakai *Art Dir* Yoshiro Muraki
Mus Fumio Hayasaka, Masaru Sato *Cast*
Toshiro Mifune, Eiko Miyoshi *Prod*
Toho. 113 mins. (original length); 104
mins. (foreign release version).
Distressed at the prospect of atomic
war, a rich Japanese (Mifune) dreams of
moving to Brazil and becomes half-mad.
Somewhat slowly paced, but a hauntingly

moving film for those with the patience to allow its feeling to come through.

IKIRU LIVING/TO LIVE/DOOMED Japan 1952. *Dir* Akira Kurosawa *Scen* Hideo Oguni, Shinobu Hashimoto, Akira Kurosawa *Photog* Asakazu Nakai *Art Dir* So Matsuyama *Mus* Fumio Hayasaka *Cast* Takashi Shimura, Nobuo Kaneko, Kyoko Seki, Makoto Koburi, Kumeko Urabe *Prod* Toho. 143 mins.
A mayor's secretary (Shimura) learns he is dying of an incurable cancer and spends the last months of his life creating a children's playground in a poor section of the city.
Kurosawa's most important film and one which was very successful in both Japan and North America. Shimura is perfect in the role of a man of good will who sees behind him a wasted life but surpasses himself before his death. The first part is concerned with his search through the streets and alleys for a meaning to life. The second part shows the funeral vigil, where his colleagues and friends recall his modest and introspective nature and achievements. *Ikiru* also offers a faithful portrait of life in Japan in the early Fifties.

ILA AYN WHITHER? Lebanon 1957. *Dir* George Nasr (Nasser). 90 mins. approx.
The story of a Lebanese peasant who abandons his family to emigrate to the USA, only to return in poverty to his village.
Its sense of atmosphere, conviction, authenticity, and direct style make this the best Lebanese film. Described as an "attempt at Lebanese poetry" and a "living document," it unfortunately had little commercial success in Lebanon.

I LIVE IN FEAR IKIMONO NO KIROKU

ILLICIT INTERLUDE SOMMARLEJ

I MARRIED A WITCH USA 1942. *Dir* René Clair *Scen* Robert Pirosh, Marc Connelly based on the novel *The Passionate Witch* by Thorne Smith, Norman Matson *Photog* Ted Tetzlaff *Art Dir* Hans Dreier, Ernst Fegte *Mus* Roy Webb *Ed* Edna Warren *Cast* Veronica Lake, Fredric March, Susan Hayward, Robert Benchley *Prod* Paramount (United Artists release). 76 mins.
The spirit of a witch is reincarnated in a beautiful blonde (Lake). She falls in love with a politician (March) and marries him after creating havoc.
A very entertaining fantasy-comedy that made the attractive blond "cover girl," Veronica Lake, a star.
[Roger Régent wrote: "All the effects are visual, and the fantasy developed in the images is in the purest René Clair style."
The same story was the basis of the popular TV series *Bewitched*.]

I MET SOME HAPPY GIPSIES SKULPJACI PERJA

IMMIGRANT (THE) USA 1917. *Dir/Scen* Charles Chaplin *Photog* Rollie Totheroh, William C. Foster *Cast* Charles Chaplin, Edna Purviance, Albert Austin, Eric Campbell, Henry Bergman, Stanley Sanford, John Rand *Prod* Mutual. 2,090 ft.
On an immigrants' ship to the USA, Charlie meets a pretty girl (Purviance). Arriving in New York, he fails in his search for work but invites the girl for a meal for which he tries to pay with a counterfeit coin. Finally they were rescued by an artist (Bergman).
Aragon wrote of this film in 1928: "We recall the tragic spectacle of third-class passengers shoved around like cattle, the brutality of the representatives of authority and the filthy hands rubbing the women under the classic gaze of the Statue of Liberty. And then there is this elusive dollar which he is always losing, which in the café keeps falling through a hole in his pants, which is so soft it can be bitten but which, for a moment, allows him to invite a marvelous 'goddess' to his table."
This somewhat autobiographical film, because of its biting social satire, was censored in several later versions. The most commonly deleted scene is that showing the immigrants being herded like cattle as the ship passes the Statue of Liberty.

IMMORTAL STORY HISTOIRE IMMORTELLE (UNE)

IN CASE OF ACCIDENT EN CAS DE MALHEUR

INFIDELITY AMANT DE CINQ JOURS (L')

INFORMER (THE) USA 1935. *Dir* John Ford *Scen* Dudley Nichols based on the novel by Liam O'Flaherty *Photog* Joseph H. August *Art Dir* Van Nest Polglase *Mus* Max Steiner *Ed* George Hively *Cast* Victor McLaglen, Margot

Grahame, Preston Foster *Prod* RKO. 91 mins.

In 1922 during the Irish Rebellion, Gypo (McLaglen) betrays a colleague to the police for money. He spends the money recklessly, which leads to his being accused before a Sinn Fein court of inquiry. He breaks down and hides with his girl friend (Grahame), who unwittingly betrays him. Mortally wounded by the revolutionaries, he drags himself to a church to die.

Although the film had to be more or less sneaked into production through RKO by Ford and Nichols, it was unanimously named Best Film of the Year by the New York film critics, and "proved to be one of the most important contributions to films since sound" (Lewis Jacobs).

The scriptwriter, Dudley Nichols, wrote: "Symbolism is only good when the audience is not aware of it. So when we had to deal with a character like Gypo who is a traitor out of ignorance, out of smallness of mind (but) is overtaken by conscience slowly working up out of his unconscious mind, we gave that a symbol of a blind man. So that when Gypo first gets his money, his 20 pounds . . . as he comes away he sees the blind man, seizes him by the throat and realizes he is blind. It is as if he had seen his own conscience. He passes his hand over his eyes and hurries away and always the tapping of the blind man's stick behind him. I dare say nobody was aware it was a symbol, but it very definitely was."

"A slow, restrained tempo in acting and cutting deepens the sense of tragedy and ominousness; tension and suspense are built on mental rather than physical excitement and action. The heaviness of the slow pace is reinforced by the photography and emphasized by the shadowy, dense Dublin fog and the night that envelopes and pervades the film throughout . . . Inner monologue is cinematically used with effect, less as a stunt than as a necessity" (Lewis Jacobs).

With this film, John Ford returned for the first, but not the last, time to his homeland. Although his (and the cameraman, Joseph August's) previous experience had been in westerns, his style in *The Informer* seems more derivative of expressionism and *Kammerspiel*. Despite Victor McLaglen's weak performance, this is a powerful and intelligent film—though its qualities were somewhat overestimated in the Thirties. Winner of several Academy Awards.

— *The Informer* Britain 1929. *Dir* Arthur Robison *Scen* Benn Levy based on the novel *Photog* T. Sparkuhl, W. Brandes, *Cast* Lya de Putti, Lars Hanson. 82 mins. Later released in a sound version. Jules Dassin's *Uptight* (1968) also uses the same basic plot.

INGEBORG HOLM GIVE US THIS DAY Sweden 1913. *Dir* Victor Sjöström *Scen* Victor Sjöström based on the play by Nils Krook *Photog* Henrik Jaenzon *Cast* Hilda Borgström, Eric Lindholm, William Larsson *Prod* Svenska. 2,006 meters. (6,700 ft. approx.)

An attack on the then Swedish poor-law system in which children of parents in workhouses were auctioned off as forced labor. When the husband of Ingeborg Holm (Borgström) dies, leaving her poverty-stricken, her children are taken from her by the authorities. She learns her daughter is ill and escapes from the police to plead with the authorities. Her daughter dies and she goes mad. Some years later her son returns and brings her back to sanity.

The theme (somewhat similar to Chaplin's *The Kid*) could have been very melodramatic; The story, in fact, is told in episodes, each introduced by a caption and filmed with a fixed camera. But in the scene of Ingeborg's escape, Sjöström takes his camera outside and suddenly the film springs to life. This film is a masterpiece of pre-1914 cinema, perfect in its acting, its classicism, its photography, and in its, albeit primitive, editing.

INHUMAINE (L') France 1923. *Dir* Marcel L'Herbier *Scen* Pierre MacOrlan, Marcel L'Herbier *Photog* George Specht *Art Dir* Fernand Léger, Robert Mallet-Stevens, Claude Autant-Lara, Alberto Cavalcanti *Mus* Darius Milhaud *Cast* Georgette Leblanc, Jacques Catelain, Philippe Hériat *Prod* Cinégraphic. 6,000 ft. approx.

"L'Inhumaine" (Leblanc), a super-vamp, is courted by a retinue of admirers—a Hindu prince (Hériat), a political agitator, and a young industrialist (Catelain)—and has many tragic adventures in an ultramodern mansion.

Its absurd and melodramatic story is reminiscent of 1910 Danish and Italian films but its experimental use of sets, costumes, and photography is interesting. [The film was a total critical and commercial failure and marked the end of the impressionism movement in films.]

IN JENEN TAGEN (literally IN OUR DAYS) German Federal Republic 1947. *Dir* Helmut Käutner *Scen* Ernst Schnabel, Helmut Käutner *Photog* Igor Oberberg *Mus* Bernhardt Eichhorn *Cast* Erich Schellow, Gert Schaefer, Helmut Käutner, Werner Hinz, Winnie Markus, Karl John. 111 mins.

Hitler's rise to power and the fall of the Third Reich told in a series of episodes that center on the adventures of an automobile from 1933 to 1945. This film is very similar to *Paisa* and could have led to the birth of German neorealism.

IN NOME DELLA LEGGE IN THE NAME OF THE LAW/MAFIA Italy 1949. *Dir* Pietro Germi *Scen* Giuseppe Mangione based on the novel *Piccola Pretura* by Giuseppe Guido Loschiavo; in collaboration with Federico Fellini, T. Pinelli, M. Monicelli, Pietro Germi *Photog* Leonida Barboni *Art Dir* Gino Morici *Mus* Carlo Rustichelli *Cast* Charles Vanel, Massimo Girotti, Camillo Mastrocinque *Prod* Lux. 103 mins.

A young magistrate (Girotti) is appointed to a small Sicilian town controlled by the Mafia, who are responsible for a murder. He clashes with a baron (Mastrocinque), whose wife he loves, wins over the townspeople and the head of the Mafia (Vanel), and solves another murder.

Apart from *Divorce, Italian Style* (*q.v.*), this is Germi's best film and a good example of neorealism in the 1948–1952 period.

IN THE NAME OF THE LAW IN NOME DELLA LEGGE

IN THE WOODS RASHOMON

IN THE WORLD see DETSVO GORKOVO

INTIMATE RELATIONS see PARENTS TERRIBLES (LES)

INTOLERANCE USA 1916. *Dir/Scen* D. W. Griffith *Photog* G. W. Bitzer, Karl Brown *Assist Dir* George Siegmann, W. S. Van Dyke, Erich von Stroheim, Edward Dillon, Tod Browning *Mus* Joseph Carl Breil, D. W. Griffith *Ed* James and Rose Smith, D. W. Griffith *Cast* Lillian Gish 1. "The Mother and the Law" Mae Marsh, Robert Harron, Sam de Grasse, Vera Lewis, Ralph Lewis, Miriam Cooper, Lloyd Ingraham, Monte Blue, Edward Dillon, Tod Browning, Walter Long 2. "The Nazarene" Howard Gaye, Lillian Langdon, Gunther von Ritzan, Erich von Stroheim, Olga Grey, Bessie Love 3. "The Medieval Story" Margery Wilson, Eugene Pallette, Spottiswoode Aitken, Frank Bennett, Josephine Crowell, Ruth Handforth 4. "The Fall of Babylon" Constance Talmadge, Elmer Clifton, Alfred Paget, Elmo Lincoln, Seena Owen, Tully Marshall, George Siegmann *Prod* Wark (D. W. Griffith). 13,700 ft. Longest extant version 11,811 ft.

1. "Modern Story (The Mother and the Law)" The struggle between capital and labor in the USA in the early 20th century. After a strike, severely suppressed by a mill magnate (de Grasse), a young man (Harron) goes to live in a town where he marries The Dear One (Marsh) and mixes with crooks (Browning, Dillon). A woman, The Friendless One (Cooper), who kills The Musketeer of the Slums (Long), accuses the young man of the crime and he is convicted. An hour before his hanging, the woman confesses, the governor (Ralph Lewis) reprieves him and he is reunited with his wife, who had striven to save him. 2. "The Judean Story (The Nazarene)" The conflict of Jesus (Gaye) with the Pharisees (Stroheim, von Ritzan) and with Rome. 3. "The Medieval Story" In 1572 a young Huguenot, Brown Eyes (Wilson), her fiancé (Pallette), and parents (Aitken, Handforth) arrive in Paris, where they are killed in the St. Bartholomew's Day Massacre organized by the Catholic Catherine de Medici (Crowell) and Charles IX (Bennett). 4. "The Fall of Babylon" In 539 B.C. the High Priest of Bel (Marshall), helped by the Rhapsode (Clifton), conspires against the tolerant Prince Belshazzar (Paget). During an enormous feast, the troops of Emperor Cyrus of the Persians (Siegmann) invade and conquer Babylon, despite the efforts of Belshazzar's bodyguard (Lincoln) and the Mountain Girl (Talmadge). The "Epilogue" prophesies a future Armageddon followed by the liberation of all men and nations from bondage.

Intolerance is subtitled *Love's Struggle Through the Ages* and the theme is developed by constant cross-cutting between the separate stories (linked by the sym-

157

bolic image of Lillian Gish as The Woman Who Rocks the Cradle until, at the end "they seem to flow together in one common flood of humanity" (original program brochure).

"The Mother and the Law" was conceived and almost entirely produced in 1914, immediately after *The Birth of a Nation* was made. It was originally intended as a separate feature and was later released as such. Griffith based the story on the records of the Stielow murder case and a report of the Federal Industrial Commission that had condemned "the Pinkertons" (the Thugs in the film) — a militant, private army paid by industrialists to break up strikes (and who sometimes even killed the workers). "The Mother and the Law" is a powerful work: its courageous social criticism is directly opposite to the attitudes in *The Birth of a Nation*, even though it was made the same year.

The sequence of Belshazzar's Feast alone cost $650,000 and the sets are the highest, largest and vastest in area ever constructed for a film. Four thousand extras and countless specially trained horses and elephants were used in this sequence. For them, and for the 2,500 extras in "The Medieval Story" and the 3,500 in "The Judean Story," a special railway line was laid to transport food and materials and a camp was constructed to house several thousand people.

Griffith made *Intolerance* without a written scenario or shooting script and shot the film without recourse to a single written note. It took him only two months to edit the film from the 300,000 feet of negative he shot.

The style of *Intolerance* is essentially based on parallel action and cross-cutting, unifying the action taking place in four different times and ten different places. The last section, in which quick cutting is used extensively, is a masterpiece which, nevertheless, must have been difficult for the general public to comprehend.

The four stories are not of equal merit and the spectacular Babylonian sequence is not the most successful. To film the feast of Belshazzar in its entirety, Griffith photographed it from an observation balloon, one of the few uses of the moving camera in a film whose style is almost entirely based on editing.

Its principal failure is Griffith's attempt to use a badly defined theme to unify four stories as different as an American

judicial error in 1914, the fall of Babylon, the St. Bartholomew's Day Massacre, and the story of Christ. In the last analysis, this inspired if uneven film is overburdened by the "massive grandeur" of Belshazzar's feast.

When *Intolerance* was shown in the USSR in 1919 (re-edited and retitled to emphasize the ideological content) it exercised a profound influence on the young Soviet film makers, Eisenstein, Pudovkin, and Kuleshov — not only because of its cinematic techniques but also because of "The Modern Story" depicting a strike and its brutal suppression. *Intolerance* had its premier on September 5, 1916, advertised as *A Sun Play of the Ages*. However, it ran for only 22 weeks in the same theater at which *The Birth of a Nation* had run for 44 weeks. The release pattern was the same elsewhere: box-office records in the opening weeks followed by a rapid dwindling of attendance.

The total cost of production and publicity was two million dollars (MGM rebudgeted the film in 1936 and estimated production cost at ten to twelve million dollars). Because of the film's relative commercial failure and because the entry of the USA into the war in 1917 conflicted with the film's pacifist attitudes, Griffith, who had largely financed the film himself, was financially ruined and was paying debts on the film until his death.

INTRUDER IN THE DUST USA 1949. *Dir* Clarence Brown *Scen* Ben Maddow based on the novel by William Faulkner *Photog* Robert Surtees *Art Dir* Cedric Gibbons, Randell Duell *Mus* Adolph Deutsch *Ed* Robert J. Kren *Cast* David Brian, Juano Hernandez, Claude Jarman Jr., Elizabeth Patterson, Will Geer *Prod* MGM. 89 mins.

In the South, an elderly Negro (Hernandez) is accused of shooting a white man in the back and threatened with lynching. He is proved innocent by a lawyer (Brian), his young nephew (Jarman), (who becomes unwillingly involved), an elderly spinster (Patterson), and the sheriff (Geer).

This harsh, sensitive film, shot almost entirely on location in the author's home town in Mississippi, superbly re-creates the atmosphere and bigotry of small-town life and is one of the best adaptations of a Faulkner novel. Its central Negro character is not a slave or a savage, but a dignified, proud, imposing figure, often scornful of the machinations of the Whites. Remarkable sequences: the headlights of the lynchers' cars terrorizing the black families hiding in their cabins; the midnight exhumation of the murdered man's grave, which is found to be empty; the body emerging from the quicksands where the murderer had thrown it; the preparations for the lynching by the dead man's relatives, who are encouraged by the townspeople as though they were planning a public holiday.

[This is one of Clarence Brown's last and best films, though its qualities are to a considerable extent derived from the script by Ben Maddow (the poet David Wolff), who also wrote Huston's *The Asphalt Jungle* (q.v.).]

*INVASION OF THE BODY SNATCHERS USA 1956. *Dir* Don Siegel *Scen* Daniel Mainwaring based on a story by Jack Finney *Photog* Ellsworth Fredericks *Art Dir* Edward Haworth *Mus* Carmen Dragon *Cast* Kevin McCarthy, Dana Wynter, Carolyn Jones, King Donovan, Ralph Dumke, Larry Gates *Prod* Walter Wanger for Allied Artists. 80 mins.

Dr. Bennell (McCarthy) returns to his home town from a visit to the city and senses that things are not quite right. He meets a woman, Becky (Wynter), and his suspicions are confirmed when they visit his friends (Donovan, Jones) and discover a pseudo human. Next morning he finds huge seed pods that open and release "likenesses" of himself and Becky. Gradually the aliens take over the town. Even the sheriff (Dumke) is supplanted. Dr. Bennell and Becky escape, but at dawn, realizing that Becky, too, has been taken over, the doctor runs hysterically onto the highway, and eventually convinces the authorities of the "invasion."

"This is probably my best film," Siegel has said, "I think that the world is populated by pods and I wanted to show them." Though one of the subtlest films of the genre, containing little graphic horror, it is also one of the most passionate and involving. Its style is typical Siegel: energetic and violent, with clever use of natural locations to create a moody, threatening environment. Its theme is best summed up in the psychiatrist's advice to Bennell to stop fighting the take-over: "There is no need for love or emotion. Love, ambition, desire, faith — without them, life is so simple."

INVENTION FOR (OF) DESTRUCTION (AN) VYNÁLEZ ZKÁZY

INVISIBLE DR. MABUSE (THE) see DR. MABUSE

INVISIBLE MAN (THE) USA 1933. *Dir* James Whale, *Scen* R. C. Sheriff (and Philip Wylie, uncredited) based on the novel by H. G. Wells *Photog* Arthur Edeson *Special Effects* John P. Fulton *Make-up* Jack Pierce *Cast* Claude Rains, Gloria Stuart, Henry Travers, William Harrigan, Dudley Digges, E. E. Clive, Una O'Connor, Holmes Herbert *Prod* Universal. 71 mins.

[Dr. Griffin (Rains) discovers a drug that makes him invisible and leaves the girl he loves (Stuart) and his colleagues (Harrigan, Travers) to seek an antidote. The drug begins to drive him mad and, in the grip of megalomania, he plots world domination through terrorism. The police trap him in a barn. Betrayed by his footprints in the snow, he is shot and regains visibility as he dies.]

"It is a voyage across the impossible, a kind of 'dressed-up mystery play.' Drops of rain outline his silhouette (sic), making him a ghost in the colors of the prism, a phantom trapped by a rainbow. The mist swirls around his outlines and the snow inexplicably carries the mark of his passage. Even objects seem enchanted. One sees a cigarette light itself, a pair of pyjamas slide magically between the bed sheets. When he unties the bandages that serve as a tragic mask, he becomes a talking, headless man. When the Invisible Man is forced out into the snow during the hunt we are in the grip of a fear that doesn't slacken until a policeman shoots at where the heart should be. Finally, the Invisible Man becomes visible and gives us, in his death, the gift of his image at the end of this marvelous film" (Paul Gilson). This Hollywood masterpiece of thrills and special effects is indeed marvelous. Its mood of black comedy and intelligent dialogue completely reflects the original novel. It had a well-merited success throughout the entire world, especially in the USSR. The character of the Invisible Man was used in a TV series in 1958 and in other films, notably:

— *The Invisible Man Returns* USA 1940. *Dir* Joe May *Cast* Cedric Hardwicke, Vincent Price.

— **The Invisible Man's Revenge* USA

159

1944. *Dir* Ford Beebe *Cast* Jon Hall, Leon Errol.

*IN WHICH WE SERVE Britain 1942. *Dir* David Lean, Noel Coward *Scen* Noel Coward *Photog* Ronald Neame *Mus* Noel Coward *Cast* Noel Coward, John Mills, Bernard Miles, Celia Johnson, Michael Wilding, Richard Attenborough *Prod* Two Cities. 114 mins.
The story of a destroyer in the British navy, its captain (Coward), and its officers and sailors. Its quasi-documentary style and effective acting were the basis of its tremendous propaganda impact during the war. It is David Lean's first film as director, though it is very much a Noel Coward film.

IRON CURTAIN (THE) USA 1948. *Dir* William Wellman *Scen* Milton Krims based on the true story of Igor Gouzenko *Photog* Charles G. Clarke *Art Dir* Lyle Wheeler, Mark Lee Kirk *Mus* Alfred Newman (using the works of Soviet composers) *Cast* Dana Andrews, Gene Tierney, June Havoc *Prod* 20th Century-Fox. 87 mins.
Based on the true story of Igor Gouzenko, the Russian cipher clerk who defected to the West in Ottawa. A Soviet diplomat (Andrews) and his wife (Tierney) hold secret documents they want to turn over to the Canadians. They are pursued by Soviet agents but saved by the Canadian mounted police.
This is the first of several "anti-Red" films made in Hollywood in reaction to the investigations of the Un-American Activities Committee. It was largely shot on location to emphasize the "authenticity" of the story.

IRON GATE BAB EL HADID

ISLAND (THE) HADAKA NO SHIMA

ISLAND OF SHAME YOUNG ONE (THE)

ISN'T LIFE A BITCH? CHIENNE (LA)

ITALIAN STRAW HAT (AN) UN CHAPEAU DE PAILLE D'ITALIE

IT ALWAYS RAINS ON SUNDAY Britain 1947. *Dir* Robert Hamer *Scen* Robert Hamer, Angus MacPhail, Henry Cornelius based on the novel by Arthur la Bern *Photog* Douglas Slocombe *Mus* Georges Auric *Art Dir* Duncan Sutherland *Ed* Michael Truman *Cast* Googie

Withers, Jack Warner, Susan Shaw, John McCallum *Prod* Ealing. 92 mins.
In London's Bethnal Green area, an escaped convict (McCallum) seeks refuge with a woman (Withers) who once had loved him, but is finally captured by a policeman (Warner).
Clearly influenced by Marcel Carné, and especially by *Quai des brumes* (q.v.), this tragedy of working-class people takes place one rainy Sunday in London's East End. Its effective low-life atmosphere and portrayal of life in the drab streets, houses, and pubs owes much to the convincing dialogue and to Douglas Slocombe's photography.

IT HAPPENED AT THE INN GOUPI MAINS ROUGES

IT HAPPENED ONE NIGHT USA 1934. *Dir* Frank Capra *Scen* Robert Riskin based on the short story *Night Bus* by Samuel Hopkins Adams *Photog* Joseph Walker *Art Dir* Stephen Goosson *Ed* Gene Havlick *Cast* Claudette Colbert, Clark Gable, Walter Connolly, Roscoe Karns, Alan Hale, Ward Bond, Eddy Chandler *Prod* Columbia. 105 mins.
Ellie Andrews (Colbert), a young heiress running away from her father (Connolly), meets journalist Peter Warne (Gable) on a bus from New York to Miami. They quarrel and have various adventures on their journey, but end by marrying.
This romantic comedy enjoyed an enormous world-wide success and is one of the best-remembered films of the Thirties. Its success disconcerted Hollywood because, according to Lewis Jacobs: "the film had little of the appeals usually regarded as prime necessities for a hit: 'production value', spectacle, gorgeous clothes. It did have other qualities, such as a well-constructed story based on simple human sentiments, fresh locales, witty dialogue, intimacy, informality; and, above all, it was devoid of much of the usual Hollywood affectation."
The film made Clark Gable and Claudette Colbert famous. In 1936, a delegation of manufacturers of underwear made strong protests to the MPPA: because the virile Clark Gable had not worn an undershirt in the film, their sales had slumped by more than half.
It Happened One Night established a new style whose theme became stereotyped in the hundreds of romantic comedies produced in the Thirties. Whether

a millionaire was to marry a girl-reporter or a millionairess a reporter the story was only an excuse for 90 minutes of plot twists, mix-ups, gags, and witty dialogue that flew as fast as a ping-pong ball.

OTHER VERSIONS.

— *Eve Knew Her Apples USA 1945. Dir Will Jason.

— You Can't Run Away From It USA 1956. Dir Dick Powell Cast Jack Lemmon, June Allyson.

Musical version based on a Broadway musical-comedy, itself based on the original film.

IT HAPPENED TOMORROW USA 1943. Dir René Clair Scen Dudley Nichols, René Clair based on stories by Lord Dunsany, Hugh Wedlock, Howard Snyder Photog Archie Stout Tech Dir Eugene Schufftan (Schüfftan) Art Dir Erno Metzner Mus Robert Stoltz Ed Fred Pressburger Cast Dick Powell, Linda Darnell, Jack Oakie, Edgar Kennedy Prod United Artists. 85 mins.

At the turn of the century, a young reporter (Powell) is visited every evening by an obliging ghost who gives him the next day's newspaper. This enables him to make sensational scoops and win at the races. On the third day he learns of his death at the end of the day. He tries to avoid the place where his death was reported but finds himself impelled to the spot, only to learn that press reports can be mistaken.

Clair himself thinks that this is the best of his Hollywood films. It is an entertaining fantasy though the script is overly ingenious. However, Clair's Parisian skills in the end prevail over the Hollywood factory sets, lighting, effects, and acting. The part that depicts the reporter's desperate but unavailing attempts to avoid being at his own death is the best.

IT SHOULD HAPPEN TO YOU USA 1954. Dir George Cukor Scen Garson Kanin Photog Charles Lang Art Dir John Meehan Mus Frederick Hollander Ed Charles Nelson Cast Judy Holliday, Jack Lemmon, Peter Lawford, Constance Bennett Prod Columbia. 85 mins.

A young woman (Holliday), who lives in the same apartment block as a photographer (Lemmon), rents a billboard overlooking a busy section of New York. A publicity agent (Lawford) helps her become a celebrity, but she falls in love with the photographer and eventually rejects fame to marry him.

This Garson Kanin satire on American publicity methods is brilliantly directed by Cukor and contains one of Judy Holliday's best roles.

IT'S IN THE BAG AFFAIRE EST DANS LE SAC (L')

IT'S MY LIFE VIVRE SA VIE

*****IVAN** USSR 1932. Dir/Scen Alexander Dovzhenko Photog Danylo Demutsky, Yuri Yekelchik, Mikhail Glider Art Dir Yuri Khomaza Cast Pyotr Masokha, Stepan Shkurat, Semyon Shagaida Prod Ukrain Film. 103 mins.

"An unheroic hero" (Masokha) and an anarchist "idler" (Shkurat) involved with a hydro project in the Ukraine. "The film is largely unknown because contemporary critics were puzzled and upset by the unorthodox and non-naturalist approach . . . Apart from the obvious appeal of the magnificent poetry of the river and dam sequences, there is the fascination of the elliptical style and sudden shifts of mood in the latter part of the film. The visual beauty of the film even surpasses that of Earth" (Richard Roud).

IVAN GROSNY IVAN THE TERRIBLE Part I: 1944. Part II (The Boyars' Plot): 1946 (released 1958). Dir/Scen/Ed Sergei M. Eisenstein Photog Eduard Tisse (exteriors), Andrei Moskvin (interiors) Art Dir Isaac Shpinel, L. Naumova Mus Sergei Prokofiev Cast Nikolai Cherkassov, Ludmila Tselikovskaya, Serafima Birman, Mikhail Nazvanov, Piotr Kadochnikov, Andrei Abrikosov, Mikhail Zharov, Vslevolod Pudovkin Prod Mosfilm. Part I, 100 mins; Part II, 88 mins. (part in Agfacolor).

Part I: In Moscow in the 16th century, Ivan Alexieff is crowned Tsar Ivan (Cherkassov) and marries Anastasia (Tselikovskaya). He overcomes the Mongols, falls ill, and is threatened by the treachery of the boyars (the Russian feudal nobility), led by his aunt, Euphrosinia (Birman), who poisons Anastasia. Ivan abdicates and retires to Alexandrov to await a new summons to the throne from the people of Moscow. Part II: Ivan is recalled by the people of Moscow. His closest friend, Prince Kurbsky (Nazvanov), deserts to the Poles while his hope for the support of a one-time friend, Philip, Metropolitan of Moscow

(Abrikoːov), is brutally repulsed. With the Oprichniks he sets out to destroy the boyars' power and kills many of them. The boyars plot Ivan's assassination and his replacement by Boyarina Euphrosinia's effeminate son, Vladimir (Kadochnikov). But during a banquet, Ivan becomes suspicious and it is Vladimir who is assassinated, leaving Ivan secure on the throne.

Production began in 1942 in Alma Ata despite terrible difficulties due to the war. Part I was completed in Moscow in 1944 (premiere, December 30, 1944) and Part II (including the long sequence in the Agfacolor process captured from the Germans) in February, 1946. Stalin banned the release of Part II, saying that Eisenstein had misunderstood the "progressive" nature of the "Oprichniks," the secret police guard that protected Ivan. Eisenstein, meanwhile, designed Part III, which was to be in color, but never recovered sufficiently from a heart attack in 1946 to undertake its production. He died in 1948.

The two parts form an inseparable whole. The first part, on its own, seems weaker than *Alexander Nevsky* (*q.v.*) but, seen together with Part II, is unsurpassable. Famous sequences: *Part I:* The coronation of the young Ivan; the peasant insurrection led by a mystic beggar (Pudovkin); the siege of Kazan; Ivan's apparently mortal illness and the boyars' treachery over the succession; the poisoning and funeral of the Tsarina. *Part II:* The procession of people to recall Ivan to the throne; Ivan's conflict with the Metropolitan; the child Ivan's first defiance of the boyars; the murder of the boyars; the allegorical mystery play presented in the cathedral; the assassination plot; the banquet and the extraordinary dance (in color); the entrance of the intoxicated Vladimir into the cathedral, his murder, and the execution of the boyarina. The tragic climax of the complete film, Ivan finally secure on the throne but more lonely than ever, lies in this final scene whose black and white images seem as powerful as the earlier color scenes.

"The grandeur of our theme," wrote Eisenstein, "necessitated a grandiose design. Usually, one tries to show a historical character in a dressing-gown. For *Ivan,* on the other hand, we had to show our characters in a stylized way and make them speak in declamations often with a musical accompaniment." Eisenstein planned his film from a series of sketches without using a shooting script. He forced his actors into the shapes demanded by his visual compositions and designs; everything was sacrificed to the rhythm, design, and emotional structure of the sequences. The unique collaboration of Eisenstein and the composer Prokofiev, which had begun with *Alexander Nevsky,* is here developed to its height, with Prokofiev using a similar contrapuntal technique to mold the score to the images.

Gosfilmofond, the Soviet Film Archives, has two sequences (about 20 minutes long) that were not used in the film. One of these, showing Ivan's childhood, was planned as a prologue to Part I. It isn't clear why it wasn't included in the release version, but a part of it, at least, is used in a flashback in Part II. Perhaps one day it will be possible to see the film complete with its admirable prologue.

OTHER FILMS ON IVAN:

— *Death of Ivan the Terrible* USSR 1909. *Dir/Scen* Vasili Goncharov *Cast* A. Slavin. 1 reel.

— *Krylya kholopa/Wings of a Serf/Ivan the Terrible* USSR 1926. *Dir* Yuri Tarich *Scen* K. Schildkret, V. Shklovsky, Y. Tarich *Photog* Mikhail Vladimirsky, *Art Dir* V. Yegorov *Ed* Esther Shub *Cast* Lo Leonidov, S. Askarova, I. Klyukvin, N. Prozorovsky *Prod* Sovkino. 7 reels.

One of the first Soviet films to be shown in Paris, it depicts the fate of a serf whose invention of a flying machine during the reign of Ivan IV is opposed by the Boyars. A lively film with an excellent portrayal of Ivan by Leonidov.

I WAS A FIREMAN FIRES WERE STARTED

I WAS BORN, BUT . . . UMARETE WA MITA KEREDO

J'ACCUSE I ACCUSE France 1919. *Dir/ Scen/Ed* Abel Gance *Photog* Léonce-Henry Burel, Bujard, Forster *Cast* Séverin-Mars, Romuald Joubé, Marise Dauvray, Maxime Desjardins *Prod* Pathé. 108 mins.

A pacifist poet, Jean Diaz (Joubé), is in love with Edith (Dauvray), who is married to François (Séverin-Mars). Both of the men join the army. Edith is captured and deported by the enemy and, on her return, is pregnant. Both men return to the front, François is killed, while Jean, shell-shocked and unable to face the carnage, is driven insane. Before dying he evokes the ghosts of the war dead.

Abel Gance declared in 1919: "When a soldier wept, accused, or sang, it was only done to continue the tears, the accusation, the laughter of the trenches. *J'Accuse* is a human cry against the bellicose din of armies, an 'objective' cry against the German militarism that destroyed civilized Europe." Originally planned in 1917, when the French privates on the front line mutinied, the first version of the film, Gance's first epic, expressed this rebellious spirit and the confusion of the combatants and was denounced on its release as "antimilitaristic." The allegorical climatic sequence of the Return of the Dead has a unique visual power. Gance revised the plot, titles, and editing in 1922; this version contrasts the Return of the Dead with the Victory Parade of Joffre, Foch, and Clemenceau. The film cost 525,000 Francs (then a considerable sum), earned three and one-half million Francs in France by 1923, and enjoyed considerable success in Britain and North America. A Czechoslovak journalist wrote: "If this film had been shown . . . in every town in the world in 1913, then perhaps there would have been no war."

— France 1937. *Dir* Abel Gance *Scen* Abel Gance, Steve Passeur *Photog* Roger Hubert *Mus* Henri Verdun *Cast* Victor Francen, Jean-Max, Renée Devillers, Line Noro *Prod* Star Films. 116 mins.

A new sound version with which Gance intended to denounce the coming war. It is far from matching the silent version but there are certain epic moments, notably the awakening of the dead sequence.

— France 1956. *Dir* Abel Gance (three-screen version).

Part of the *Magirama (q.v.)* program and based on the 1937 version.

JAGO HUA SAVERA DAY SHALL DAWN Pakistan 1958. *Dir* Aaejay Kardar *Scen* Aaejay Kardar, Faiz Ahmad Faiz *Photog* Walter Lassally, Sadhan Roy *Ed* Bill Bovet *Cast* nonprofessionals from the village of Shaitnol *Prod* Century Films. 91 mins.

Describes the struggle for existence of a group of Bengali fishermen in East Pakistan. It is a film of great beauty and truth, with a similar theme to *La Terra Trema (q.v.)* but stylistically very different, being derived more from the realistic approach developed in the Bengalese cinema since the Thirties.

JAGTE RAHO UNDER COVER OF NIGHT/ KEEP AWAKE India 1956. *Dir* Raj Kapoor *Scen* Shanbhu Mitra, Amit Maitra *Photog* Radhu Karmakar *Mus* Salil Chaudhuri *Ed* Irani *Cast* Raj Kapoor, Nemo, Sumitra Devi, Motilal, Pradap Kumar *Prod* R. K. Films. 115 mins.

The allegorical tale of a poor and simple peasant immersed in the intrigues of modern civilization. A young, unsophisticated man (Kapoor) comes to the city and settles down to sleep in the streets. But, becoming thirsty, he goes into a modern apartment block to look for water and is mistaken for a thief. He is chased, hides in one apartment after another, discovers greed, lechery, and crime, and learns that when "fear and panic shatter the mask of respectability, everybody is revealed in his true colors and hideous appearance" (Raj Kapoor).

This mixture of Chaplinesque comedy and Hollywoodesque pathos, produced and supervised in Bombay by the most famous Indian actor, is not without faults; but it holds one's attention with its sense of life and vitality. It received the First Prize at the Karlovy-Vary Festival in 1957.

JAPANESE TRAGEDY (A) NIHON NO HIGEKI

JAZZ COMEDY VESYOLYE REBYATA

JAZZ SINGER (THE) USA 1927. *Dir* Alan Crosland *Scen* Alfred A. Cohn based on the play by Samson Raphaelson *Photog* Hal Mohr *Mus* Irving Berlin, Gus Kahn, Sam Lewis, Al Jolson and others *Cast* Al Jolson, Warner Oland, Eugenie Besserer, May McAvoy *Prod* Warner Brothers. 88 mins.
Jakie Rabinowitz (Jolson), the son of a Jewish religious cantor (Oland), has a passion for jazz. He leaves his mother (Besserer) to become a blackface singer. The goodhearted son gives up his career for his parents and his religion, but in the end has a triumphant stage career. Although this is a mediocre film, its premier on October 23, 1927, marked the cinema's entrance into a new age and it is usually considered the first sound film.
In 1926, using the Vitaphone system, Warner Brothers had produced *Don Juan*, the first feature length all-synchronized sound film. However this included no dialogue. Its success encouraged Warners to follow up their advantage. They hired Broadway star Al Jolson, who in the film sings seven songs and speaks, ad lib, a few words ("Hello mammy," "You ain't heard nothing yet," etc.). Its success was enormous and Warners quickly produced in 1928 *The Singing Fool* (directed by Lloyd Bacon with Al Jolson), which contained substantial dialogue, and *The Lights of New York* (directed by Bryan Foy with Helene Costello and Cullen Landis), the first all-talking film. These were even more successful and made the fortune of

Warner Brothers, which had previously been fighting for survival.
— *The Jazz Singer* USA 1952. *Dir* Michael Curtiz *Cast* Danny Thomas *Prod* Warner Brothers.
A dull remake that only confirmed the lack of quality in the original. This version doesn't even have the advantage of Jolson's vibrant personality.

JAZZ WAITER (THE) CAUGHT IN A CABARET

JEANNE AU BUCHER see JOAN OF ARC

JEANNE D'ARC see JOAN OF ARC; PASSION OF JEANNE D'ARC (LA) (Dreyer); PROCÈS DE JEANNE D'ARC (Bresson)

JENNY LAMOUR QUAI DES ORFÈVRES

JETEE (LA) THE PIER France 1962 (released 1964). *Dir/Scen* Chris Marker *Photog* Jean Chiabaud *Mus* Trevor Duncan *Ed* Jean Ravel *Cast* Hélène Chatelain, Davos Hanich, Jacques Ledoux *Prod* Argos. 29 mins.
In a ruined France after World War III, a man's vivid experience of a childhood experience enables him to travel backward and forward in time. As a grown man, he meets the girl he had glimpsed as a child on the jetty's end at Orly Airport and falls in love with her. He chooses to remain in the past but is executed by those who hold power in the future.
Undoubtedly Bergsonian in its concern with memory and the philosophy of time, this perfect science-fiction piece uses only still photographs of frozen movement and a detached, literary narration. Only once does an image move: the girl awakening in the early morning after a night of love — a shot with which the screen disarmingly bursts into sensuous life.

JEUX INTERDITS FORBIDDEN GAMES/THE SECRET GAME France 1952. *Dir* René Clément *Scen* Jean Aurenche, Pierre Bost, René Clément, François Boyer *Photog* Robert Juillard *Art Dir* Paul Bertrand *Mus* Narciso Yepes *Ed* Robert Dwyre *Cast* Brigitte Fossey, Georges Poujouly, Lucien Herbert, Suzanne Courtal *Prod* Silver Films. 84 mins.
In June 1940, Paulette (Fossey), a five-year-old girl whose parents are killed in the war, is adopted by peasants and becomes the "lover" of their 11-year-old son, Michel (Poujouly). Influenced by the carnage around them they build

a cemetery for dead animals and devote all their time and care to it. When the "game" is discovered, Paulette is handed over to the Red Cross.

"War was my principal theme in *Jeux interdits*." (René Clément). Produced at the height of the Cold War, it was boycotted by the authorities and excluded from the Cannes Festival but received the major award at the Venice Festival and was a great success from Peking to New York.

Its depiction of life in the French countryside is superficial but its observation of the children's fantasy world and their love is full of gentle poetry. The strikingly edited opening sequence of a column of refugees being machine-gunned is the best, forcefully recalling the brutalities of the Nazi invasion in 1940.

JEW SUSS see JUD SÜSS

JEZEBEL USA 1938. *Dir* William Wyler *Scen* John Huston, Clements Ripley, Abem Finkel based on the play by Owen Davis, Sr. *Photog* Ernest Haller *Mus* Max Steiner *Ed* Warren Low *Cast* Bette Davis, Henry Fonda, George Brent, Donald Crisp, Richard Cromwell *Prod* Warner Brothers. 104 mins.

In New Orleans in the middle of the 19th century, a young woman, Julie Morrison (Davis), creates a scandal at a ball by appearing in a red (rather than a white) ball dress. She loves a dandy, Preston Dillard (Fonda), but he marries another woman while she marries a banker, Buck Cantrell (Brent), who treats her badly and who is killed in a duel. Her true love catches yellow fever and she rushes to nurse him.

This melodramatic story (a sort of *Gone with the Wind* plot) is dominated by Bette Davis as an imperious, arrogant "Siren of the South." Apart from this, there is the well-staged ball sequence and the sequence depicting the yellow-fever epidemic, with its mourners, bodies, smoke, and black signs on the white mansions of the southern aristocrats.

JIGOKUMON GATE OF HELL Japan 1953. *Dir* Teinosuke Kinugasa *Scen* Teinosuke Kinugasa based on a story by Kan Kichuchi *Photog* Kohei Sugiyama *Art Dir* Kisaku Itoh *Mus* Yasushi Aleutagawa *Cast* Kazuo Hasegawa, Machiko Kyo, Isao Yamagata *Prod* Daiei. 89 mins. Eastman Color.

A story of palace intrigue and love during the civil wars in 12th century Japan. A samurai (Hasegawa) falls in love with a woman (Kyo) and tells her that unless she yields he will kill her and her husband (Yamagata). She pretends to agree to kill her husband but takes his place and is herself stabbed to death. The samurai becomes a monk to expiate his crime.

This story, originally based on a true crime in 1159, has inspired many famous stories in Japanese literature; in this case the script was based on a rather poor, but popular novel of the Forties. Kinugasa had been commissioned to make the film and was very surprised that it received the Grand Prix at Cannes in 1954 as well as an Academy Award. He must have been even more surprised when some French critics saw in the film themes similar to those in such great classics as *Phaedra* and *Tristan and Isolde*.

However, the story allowed him to experiment with color and create "the most beautiful color photography ever to grace the screen" (Anderson and Ritchie). Certain colors dominate the screen in specific scenes: red and orange during the palace revolt; blue with touches of purple during a horse race; a warm rose glow breaking through the blackness of night. He would probably have preferred the film's success to have been based on these elements rather than on exotic interpretations. Machiko Kyo's acting is remarkable.

JOAN OF ARC. Films based on the Joan of Arc story:
— *Jeanne d'Arc* France 1900. *Dir* Georges Méliès. 240 meters (800 ft. approx.).
"A magnificent spectacle in 12 scenes. About 500 people are involved in superb costumes" (Méliès).
— *Giovanna d'Arco* Italy 1908. *Dir* Marco Caserini.
— *Jeanne d'Arc* France 1908. *Dir* Albert Capellani.
— *Giovanna d'Arco* Italy 1913. *Dir* Nino Oxilia, U. M. Del Colle.
— *Joan, the Woman* USA 1917. *Dir* Cecil B. DeMille. *Scen* Jeanie Macpherson *Cast* Geraldine Farrar, Wallace Reid, Raymond Hatton, Hobart Bosworth, Theodore Roberts *Prod* Lasky. 6 reels. The story is set in the framework of a prologue and epilogue depicting trench warfare during World War I, with Wallace Reid playing an English soldier in both the modern sequences and the

main story. Released just before the entry of the USA into the war, the film exerted a powerful propaganda effect in favor of France and the Allies. Its considerable success led to DeMille being called by the American press "the Michelangelo of the screen." Although perhaps overpraised at the time, it is nevertheless intelligently and efficiently directed.

— *La Merveilleuse Vie de Jeanne d'Arc/ Saint Joan the Maid* France 1928. *Dir* Marco de Gastyne *Cast* Simone Genevois, Philippe Hériat, Gaston Modot.

— **Das Mädchen Johanna/Joan of Arc* Germany 1935. *Dir* Gustav Ucicky *Cast* Angela Sallocher, Gustaf Gründgens, Heinrich George *Prod* UFA. 87 mins.

An adapted version of the story that presents the feeble Charles VII as "a cool, deliberate sovereign gifted with unusual political insight — a lonely genius" (publicity brochure). Much of the emphasis is switched from Joan to Charles, and his desertion is shown as a farsighted political act. The sets and photography are especially memorable.

— *Joan of Arc* USA 1948. *Dir* Victor Fleming *Scen* Maxwell Anderson, Andrew Solt based on the play *Joan of Lorraine* by Maxwell Anderson *Photog* Joe Valentine *Art Dir* Richard Day *Cast* Ingrid Bergman, Jose Ferrer, Francis L. Sullivan, George Colouris *Prod* RKO. 145 mins. Technicolor.

"I would never have agreed to play the role if I had then seen Dreyer's *La Passion de Jeanne d'Arc*" (*q.v.*) (Ingrid Bergman, 1952).

[This tedious film was an expensive disaster, but Jose Ferrer made an impressive screen debut as the Dauphin.]

— *Destinées/Love, Soldiers, and Women* (Part I: *Jeanne*) France/Italy 1953. *Dir* Jean Delannoy *Cast* Michèle Morgan. Three stories of women and war: the first deals with Joan of Arc (the others are "Elizabeth" and "Lysistrata").

— **Giovanna d'Arco al Rogo/Jeanne au bûcher/Joan at the Stake* Italy/France 1954. *Dir* Roberto Rossellini *Scen* Rossellini based on the oratorio *Jeanne au bûcher* by Paul Claudel *Cast* Ingrid Bergman, Tullio Carminati. Gevacolor.

"It is a strange film; I know they are going to say that my introversion has reached its maximum point, that I have withdrawn from life. This isn't filmed theater at all, it is cinema, and I will even go so far as to say that it is neorealism in the sense that I have always aimed at it" (Rossellini). Ingrid Bergman's second try at the role on the screen was much more successful under Rossellini's direction.

— *Saint Joan* Britain 1957. *Dir* Otto Preminger. *Scen* Graham Greene based on the play by George Bernard Shaw *Photog* Georges Périnal *Art Dir* Roger Furse *Cast* Jean Seberg, Richard Widmark, Richard Todd, Felix Aylmer. 110 mins.

[An ambitious adaptation of Shaw's play, weakened by Graham Greene's rearrangement of the text and Jean Seberg's immaturity as an actress.]

See also *Passion de Jeanne d'Arc* (La); *Procès de Jeanne d'Arc*

JOAN OF THE ANGELS MATKA JOANNA OD ANIOLOW

JOB (THE) POSTO (IL)

JOHNNY GUITAR USA 1954. *Dir* Nicholas Ray *Scen* Philip Yordan based on the novel by Roy Chanslor *Photog* Harry Stradling *Art Dir* James Sullivan *Mus* Victor Young *Ed* Richard Van Enger *Cast* Joan Crawford, Sterling Hayden, Ernest Borgnine, Mercedes McCambridge, Ward Bond, Scott Brady, John Carradine, Ben Cooper *Prod* Republic. 110 mins. Trucolor.

Johnny Guitar (Hayden) a reformed gunfighter, defends Vienna (Crawford), a saloon owner, against the Marshall (Bond), a female banker (McCambridge) who hates her and wants her run out of town, and an attempted lynching.

The film's unexpected success undoubtedly played a part in the development of the "intellectual" western. "This film has a certain depth, a certain point of view. We were using a completely valueless novel. Phil Yordan and I worked like hell on the script to stress the time factor. I would have liked our ideas on the love-hate relationship to have been expressed more clearly" (Nicholas Ray). Ray now thinks of the film as "baroque, very baroque."

JOHNNY IN THE CLOUDS WAY TO THE STARS (THE)

JOLI MAI (LE) France 1962. *Dir* Chris Marker *Scen* Cathérine Varlin *Photog* Pierre Lhomme *Ed* Eva Zora *Mus* Michel Legrand *Commentator* Yves Montand

Prod Sofracima. 180 mins. (under Marker's supervision cut to 123 mins.)

A *cinéma-vérité* study of Paris in May 1962, the month the Algerian War came to an end and France was at peace for the first time since 1939. It is in two parts: "Prayer from the Top of the Eiffel Tower," about personal happiness and ambition; and "The Return of Fantômas," concerned with social and political issues and the relationships of people to each other.

Remarkable sequences: the demonstrations of February (as an introduction); a young couple about to be married; an Algerian workman speaking of his country; a black student from Dahomey; hippies; a slum dweller moving into a new apartment; a group of young right-wing people; three girls from the XVIth District in Paris; a worker-priest turned militant Communist; the Jeanne d'Arc festival celebrated by De Gaulle on May 13 at the Arc de Triomphe. A very moving, personal, and ironic film aided by Pierre Lhomme's superb handling of the "living camera."

JOLLY FELLOWS VESYOLYE REBYATA

JOUR DE FETE THE BIG DAY/THE VILLAGE FAIR France 1948. *Dir* Jacques Tati *Scen* Jacques Tati, Henri Marquet, *Photog* Jacques Mercanton *Art Dir* René Moulaert *Mus* Jean Yatove *Ed* Marcel Moreau *Cast* Jacques Tati, Guy Decomble, Paul Frankeur, Santa Relli *Prod* Francinex. 87 mins.

A traveling fair comes to a small village. The local postman (Tati), characterized by shrunken uniform, ancient bicycle, and oversize shoes, sees a film at the fair about the efficiency of the American postal service and is persuaded to try to imitate their methods. After wild adventures he his converted back to the slow pace of village life.

Tati made a short color film in 1947, *L'Ecole des facteurs,* which is a kind of "rough sketch" for this film even though its jokes are never fully exploited. The adventures of the gangling and bewildered postman on his ancient bicycle take place in a typical French village (Sainte-Sévère-sur-Indre) situated right in the middle of France. *Jour de fête* is, for all intents, silent, the largely unintelligible dialogue being no more important than the film's other sound effects. It is memorable for its fine sense of observation of village life, its jokes

(the wasp, the setting up of the pole, the bicycle running by itself, the military salute, his feverish cycling *à l'américaine,* etc.) but also for its gentle and somewhat melancholy poetry. It also brought to light the best French comedian since Max Linder.

JOURNAL D'UN CURE DE CAMPAGNE (LE) DIARY OF A COUNTRY PRIEST (THE) France 1950. *Dir* Robert Bresson *Scen* Robert Bresson based on the novel by Georges Bernanos *Photog* L.-H. Burel *Mus* Jean-Jacques Grunenwald *Ed* Paulette Robert *Cast* Claude Laydu, Jean Riveyre, Nicole Ladmiral, Balpêtré, Marie-Monique Arkell *Prod* Union Générale Cinématographique. 120 mins.

A young country priest (Laydu) finds his parishioners hostile and indifferent. At the chateau, he earns the enmity of all. The count (Riveyre) is having an affair with his daughter's governess, the daughter is angry, the wife (Arkell) indifferent. The priest discovers he has cancer and goes to die at the home of a defrocked priest living with his mistress.

"Nothing has been lost of the substance of the novel, nothing of the spirit of Bernanos. But everything has been transposed in a vision and esthetic that expresses the real personality of Robert Bresson. Its true merit is in having rejected everything in the novel that could be already thought of as 'cinematic' in the popular sense of the word. Bresson's language is not based on the expressive intensity of each separate element (gestures, facial expressions, isolated scenes, backgrounds) but on their interaction one with another. The words of the characters, or those read from the diary (which gives the events another level of consciousness and memory) are taken directly from the novel" (Albert Beguin). "A work based entirely on interior truth could for the first time be seen on the screen without making any allowances" (Julien Green). "Bresson has reached a rediscovery of the values of the silent film and, for the first time, has succeeded in fusing them with the sound film" (André Bazin).

JOURNAL D'UNE FEMME DE CHAMBRE (LE) THE DIARY OF A CHAMBERMAID France/Italy 1964. *Dir* Luis Buñuel *Scen* Luis Buñuel, Jean-Claude Carrière based on the novel by Octave Mirbeau *Photog* Roger Fellous *Art Dir* Georges Wakhe-

vitch *Ed* Louisette Hautecoeur *Cast* Jeanne Moreau, Michel Piccoli, Georges Géret, Francoise Lugagne, Daniel Ivernel *Prod* Speva/Filmalliance/Filmsonor/ Dear. 98 mins. Franscope.

Buñuel's version of the Mirbeau novel about the decadent French upper classes, while not his best film, has a marvelously eerie atmosphere of incipient evil, and reveals clearly the characters' inhumanities toward themselves and others.

He transposed the setting from the turn of the century to 1928, the time when the French fascist groups were gathering strength for the putsch of February 6, 1934 — the same groups who were responsible for the suppression of *L'Age d'or* (*q.v.*). Excellent performances by Jeanne Moreau as the chambermaid, Célestine, and by Georges Géret as Joseph, her employers' gamekeeper and an extreme right-winger who rapes and murders a young girl.

See also *Diary of a Chambermaid* (*The*)

JOURNEY INTO AUTUMN KVINNODRÖM

JOURNEY TO ITALY VIAGGIO IN ITALIA

JOUR SE LEVE (LE) DAYBREAK France 1939. *Dir* Marcel Carné *Scen* Jacques Viot, Jacques Prévert *Photog* Curt Courant, Philippe Agostini, André Bac *Art Dir* Alexandre Trauner *Mus* Maurice Jaubert *Ed* René Le Henaff *Cast* Jean Gabin, Jules Berry, Arletty, Jacqueline Laurent *Prod* Sigma. 85 mins.

A worker (Gabin) shoots a man (Berry) and locks himself in his attic room. The police lay siege but wait for dawn before making an assault. During this time the worker remembers his meeting with a young girl (Laurent), his affair with another woman (Arletty), the young girl's seduction, and his final quarrel with her seducer, whom he kills. Dawn breaks, and the worker kills himself.

André Bazin has written: "A tragedy of purity and loneliness . . . Carné's realism, while based completely on the versimilitude of its background, is charged poetically, not only by being modified formally and pictorially (as in German expressionism) but in allowing the inherent poetry to free itself and in drawing out the heart of the drama. It is in this sense that one can speak of 'poetic realism.' The perfection of *Jour se Lève* is that its symbolism never outweighs its realism but rather is com-plementary to it . . . Despite its structure and realistic appearance, the film is nothing less than a psychological, or even a social, drama. As with tragedy, the real meaning of its story and its characters is metaphysical. However, this is only precisely valid and convincing in proportion to its realism. And the realism of *Jour se Lève* has the rigor of a poem. Everything is written in verse or at least in a prose invisibly poetic."

Released only a few weeks before the war (June 17, 1939), this film, more than any other by Carné and Prévert, carries a feeling in its opening sequences that its protagonist, "a nice young fellow," is irredeemably trapped by destiny (symbolized by a blind man) and cannot escape his death. Gabin, in one of his best performances, is a hero "from a working-class, suburban Thebes, in which the gods amuse themselves with blind orders, but where everything is also transcended by society" (André Bazin). The influence of German *Kammerspiel* is evident, but the tragedy is presented in quite a different style. The flashbacks (at one time abandoned by the scriptwriters) are subtly used. Every detail of Trauner's sets expresses a state of mind.

Although it was banned as demoralizing by the French military censor in September 1939, during the war it had a wide release abroad and exerted a profound influence in Britain, the USA, Sweden, and other countries.

— *The Long Night* USA 1947. *Dir* Anatole Litvak *Cast* Henry Fonda, Barbara Bel Geddes, Vincent Price. 87 mins.

A very poor remake with a happy ending, the production of which was not worth the suppression, for many years, of all screenings of the original.

— *The Man Upstairs* Britain 1958. *Dir* Don Chaffey *Cast* Richard Attenborough. 88 mins.

Not a remake, but a very similar plot in which a scientist locks himself in an upstairs room because he feels he has killed another man. He is finally persuaded by his fiancée to give himself up to the police.

JOVEN (LA) YOUNG ONE (THE)

JOYLESS STREET (THE) FREUDLOSE GASSE (DIE)

JUDAS WAS A WOMAN BÊTE HUMAINE (LA)

JUDEX (series) France 1916. Prologue and 11 episodes: 1. *L'Ombre mystérieuse* 2. *L'expiation* 3. *La meute fantastique* 4. *Le secret de la tombe* 5. *Le moulin tragique* 6. *Le môme Reglisse* 7. *La femme en noir* 8. *Les souterrains du château rouge* 9. *Lorsque l'enfant parut* 10. *Le coeur de Jacqueline* 11. *L'ondine* 12. *Le pardon d'amour* (English version released in 10 episodes, same total length, but different chapter titles) *Dir* Louis Feuillade *Scen* Arthur Bernède, Louis Feuillade *Photog* Klausse, A. Glattli *Cast* René Cresté, Musidora, Yvette Andreyor, Louis Leubas, Marcel Lévesque, Edouard Mathé *Prod* Gaumont. 1. 1,262 meters; 2. 660 meters; 3. 762 meters; 4. 488 meters; 5. 742 meters; 6. 816 meters; 7. 853 meters; 8. 638 meters; 9. 600 meters; 10. 484 meters; 11. 427 meters; 12. 436 meters. (total 26,000 ft. approx.) A shortened version (2,800 meters) was released in 1923. Judex (Cresté) destroys the evil banker, Favreau (Leubas), falls in love with his daughter (Andreyor), and battles with a crook, Diane Monti (Musidora), and her cohorts.

Feuillade's preceding film series, *Les Vampires,* had been extremely successful, but Minister of the Interior Malvy had complained about the criminal character of the film, which he felt was "demoralizing" while the country was at war. Judex is not a criminal but a kind of Robin Hood character, a righter-of-wrongs. He is played by René Cresté in a black cloak, a wide-brimmed black hat, and a fatalistic air. Though it doesn't match *Les Vampires* (*q.v.*) or *Fantômas* (*q.v.*), this is a remarkable film, especially for its inventiveness, its acting, its sense of landscape and environment, and its blend of fantasy and realism.

— *La Nouvelle mission de Judex* France 1917. 12 episodes. *Dir* Louis Feuillade. Same credits as *Judex.* 27,000 ft. approx.

— *Judex* France 1933. *Dir* Maurice Champreux *Scen* Louis Feuillade, Arthur Bernède *Photog* Georges Raulet *Mus* Francois Gailhard *Cast* René Ferté, René Navarre, N. Constantini, Miahalesco, Blanche Bernis, Louise Lagrange. 6,600 ft. approx.

— *Judex* France/Italy 1963. *Dir* Georges Franju *Scen* Francis Lacassin, Jacques Champreux based on the original scenario by Feuillade and Bernède *Photog* Marcel Fradetal *Mus* Maurice Jarre *Ed* Gilbert Natot *Cast* Channing Pollock, Jacques Jouanneau, Edith Scob, Michel Vitol, Francine Bergé. 100 mins.

An immensely enjoyable film and a brilliant tribute to the silent film serials of Louis Feuillade.

JUDGEMENT (THE) GUNNAR HEDES SAGA

JUD SUSS Germany 1940. *Dir* Veit Harlan *Scen* Ludwig Metzger, Eberhard Wolfgang Möller, Veit Harlan *Photog* Bruno Mondi *Mus* Wolfgang Zeller *Cast* Ferdinand Marian, Werner Krauss, Heinrich George, Kristina Söderbaum (Veit Harlan's wife), Eugene Klöpfer, Hilda von Stoltz, Theodor Loos, Walter Kerner, Erna Morena, Bernhardt Goetzke, Otto Henning, Ursula Deinert *Prod* Terra. 85 mins.

A Jew, Süss Oppenheimer (Marian), ingratiates himself with the Duke of Württemberg (George) and loans him money in return for the tax revenue of the duchy. Against the advice of the old rabbi Loew (Krauss), he increases his power, persecutes the Aryans, puts Jews in powerful positions, and rapes a young girl (Söderbaum). The duchy revolts and Süss is executed.

"Highly recommended for its artistic value and, to serve the politics of the State, recommended for young people" (Goebbels). This is the most notorious film of the Third Reich and one which brought disgrace on almost everyone involved with it. Its production began soon after the "Kristallnacht" at the end of 1938, during which the Nazis swooped down on the Jews, promised them concentration camps, but murdered them instead. It was the epitome of anti-Semitic propaganda in Germany and in the countries they occupied and had a tremendous influence. In some of the occupied countries, partisans attacked theaters in which the film was playing.

Heinrich George died in a Russian concentration camp in 1946; Ferdinand Marian committed suicide in 1950, partly as a result of his guilt over having appeared in the film. Veit Harlan was arrested in 1945 and tried twice for crimes against humanity in 1949–50 but was freed for lack of conclusive proof. The German Federal Republic prosecutor said: "The film, accepted with enthusiasm and executed with undeniable ardor, was an anti-Jewish provocation in the Nazi sense of this expression, a participation in acts which the Nazis described as 'the final solution to the Jewish question.' We are shown a Jew who rapes an Aryan in order to dishonor her, according to Goebbels propaganda." Harlan denied the charges and said he had been forced to make the film. After 1950 he resumed his activities in the German Federal Republic and made nine mediocre films between 1950 and 1958. He died in 1964.

["To an unconcerned viewer today the film may seem more tedious than vicious . . . because of its leaden direction, bombastic acting, and dark-toned photography. Yet the effect of the movie it its own time is undeniable . . . Teenagers who saw the film beat up Jews after seeing it . . . The greatest success of the film was in the Middle East, where Arabic-dubbed prints were still circulating during the 1960's" (David Stewart Hull).]

— *Jew Süss* Britain 1934. *Dir* Lothar Mendes *Scen* based on the novel *Jud Süss* (*Power*) by Lion Feuchtwanger *Cast* Conrad Veidt, Frank Vosper, Cedric Hardwicke. 108 mins.

A faithful adaptation of Feuchtwanger's novel (itself based on the same historical events that inspired Harlan's film), made partly in response to what was then happening in Germany. It is totally opposite in spirit to Harlan's film.

JUJIRO SHADOWS OF THE YOSHIWARA/ CROSSROADS Japan 1928. *Dir/Scen* Teinosuke Kinugasa *Photog* Kohei Sugiyama *Art Dir* Bonji Taira *Cast* J. Bandoha, A. Tschihaya, Yujiko Ogawa, I. Sohma *Prod* Kinugasa Productions/ Shochiku. 5,827 ft.

In 18th-century Japan, a wounded man (Bandoha) who thinks he has killed a rival, takes refuge in his sister's (Tschihaya) house. An official (Sohma) attempts to seduce her and she kills him. The brother sees his sister with the man he thought he had killed and he dies of shock.

This is the only Japanese silent film widely known in the West. Set in the samurai period, it could easily have been a banal melodrama. But Kinugasa turned it into a masterpiece that he himself described as "a film of greys based on the *sumi-e*" (Japanese ink painting). The story is told largely in flashbacks in which past and present,

real and imaginary, are mixed and set against a somber background superbly photographed in a low key by Sugiyama. It is often discussed in relation to the Soviet editing style of "analytical montage," but Kinugasa denies having seen the Soviet films at that time. A German influence is not improbable though the influence is more likely from *Kammerspiel* than from expressionism. *Jujiro,* however, remains profoundly Japanese in spirit and is the equal of any of the best American, French, or German films of the Twenties.

JULES ET JIM France 1961. *Dir* François Truffaut *Scen* François Truffaut, Jean Gruault based on the novel by Henri-Pierre Roché *Photog* Raoul Coutard *Mus* Georges Delerue *Ed* Claudine Bouché *Cast* Jeanne Moreau, Oscar Werner, Henri Serre, Vanna Urbine *Prod* Films du Carosse/SEDIF. 105 mins. Franscope.

Before the First World War, an Austrian, Jules (Werner), and a Frenchman, Jim (Serre), become friends. They meet Catherine (Moreau), who becomes Jule's girl and marries him. When the war comes, the men fight on opposite sides. After the war, Jim visits Jules and Catherine in Germany. Catherine develops a relationship with Jim that Jules encourages. But Jim leaves and returns to Paris. Some years later, Jules and Catherine return to France where they again meet Jim; Catherine drowns herself with Jim.

A sensitive, impassioned, and absorbing work whose poetic re-creation of the period stems from Truffaut's use of natural settings. Remarkable performances by Jeanne Moreau and Oscar Werner. "There are two themes," said Truffaut, "that of the friendship between the two men, which tries to remain alive, and that of the impossibility of living *à trois*. The idea of the film is that the couple is not really satisfactory but there is no alternative."

JULIET OF THE SPIRITS GIULIETTA DEGLI SPIRITI

*JUNGFRUKALLEN THE VIRGIN SPRING Sweden 1960. *Dir* Ingmar Bergman *Scen* Ulla Isaksson based on a 14th century legend *Photog* Sven Nykvist *Art Dir* P. A. Lundgren *Mus* Erik Nordgren *Ed* Oscar Rosander *Cast* Max von Sydow, Birgitta Pettersson, Gunnel Lindblom,

Birgitta Valberg *Prod* Svensk Filmindustri. 87 mins.

Karin (Pettersson), a proud young virgin, is sent by her father, Töre (von Sydow), to ride to church despite her mother's (Valberg) forebodings. She is accompanied by her sister Ingeri (Lindblom), who is jealous of her. In the forest she is raped and murdered by three herdsmen. Later, they ask for shelter at Karin's home and when Töre learns what has happened, he slaughters them. Karin's body is found in a glade and when Töre vows to build a church in her memory, a well springs up.

The script, one of the few Bergman has used that he did not write himself, is based on a 14th century legend whose theme is the abundant grace of God and the miracle of reconciliation. Bergman has observed: "Our whole existence is based on the fact that there are things we may do and others we may not do, and these are the complications that we constantly come into contact with throughout our life." It is this aspect of the story — Ingeri's evil, the father's brutal vengeance, and the miraculous sign of forgiveness — that Bergman concentrates on.

The brutal rape sequence gave the film a certain notoriety at the time but, even in the uncut version, is totally unsalacious.

JUSTICE EST FAITE LET JUSTICE BE DONE France 1950. *Dir* André Cayatte *Scen* Charles Spaak, André Cayatte *Photog* Jean Bourgoin *Art Dir* Jacques Colombier *Mus* Raymond Legrand *Ed* Gaudin *Cast* Valentine Tessier, Claude Nollier, Jacques Castelot, Michel Auclair, Balpêtré *Prod* Silver Films. 105 mins.

Based on a true mercy-killing case, this film is a study of the lives of the jurors and how their own backgrounds and characters inevitably combine to determine the verdict.

"Justice is a difficult thing. Professionals or amateurs serve it as best they are able. This was the theme André Cayatte suggested to me . . . And the film was born with its 83 characters as easily, as mysteriously, as an apple tree grows apples" (Charles Spaak). The film's success was due more to its theme and script than to the direction. This film led André Bazin to speak of "André Cayatte's cybernetics."

KABINETT DES DR. CALIGARI (DAS) CABINET DES DR. CALIGARI (DAS)

KAK ZAKALYALAS STAL HOW THE STEEL WAS TEMPERED USSR 1942. *Dir* Mark Donskoy *Scen* Mark Donskoy based on the autobiographical novel by Nikolai Ostrovsky *Photog* Bentsion Monastirksy *Mus* Lev Schwartz *Art Dir* M. Salokha *Cast* V. Perest-Petrenko, Daniel Sagal, I. Fedotova *Prod* Kiev and Ashkhabad Studios. 92 mins.
A poor adaptation of the original novel about the Civil War. However its production suffered greatly by having to be completed in Central Asia after the Nazi invasion interrupted its production in Kiev. Donskoy's script used only those parts of the novel depicting Ukrainian resistance to the German invaders of 1918 in order to suggest a parallel to the current invasion. The best sequence is the unsuccessful speech of a German officer to the railway workers of an occupied country — coincidentally similar to a scene in Clément's *La Bataille du Rail* (*q.v.*)
— *Pavel Korchagin* USSR 1957. *Dir* A. Alov, Vladimir Naumov *Scen* K. Isayev based on the autobiographical novel by N. Ostrovsky *Photog* I. Minkovetsky, S. Shakhbazian *Cast* V. Lanovoy, E. Lezhdei, T. Stradina *Prod* Kiev. 102 mins. Sovcolor.
A virtuoso version by two young directors that is so different from Donskoy's version that it seems derived from a different source. Unlike Donskoy, they included the whole novel and succeeded in portraying not only the romantic revolutionary feeling but the truth about the difficulties during the terrible Civil War period.

KALPIKI LIRA (I) (literally THE FALSE COIN) Greece 1955. *Dir/Scen* Georges Tzavellas *Photog* Costas Theodoridis *Mus* Manos Hadjidakis *Cast* Vassilis Logothetidis, Ilya Livykov, Orestis Makris, Elli Lambetti, Dimitris Horn, Mamis Fotopoulos, Maria Kalamiotou, Speranza Vrana *Prod* Anzervos. 90 mins. approx.
A comedy film in four sketches involving a counterfeit coin. 1. An engraver spends 100 gold "coins" in making a false one that nobody wants. 2. A beggar (Fotopoulos) pretending to be blind and a prostitute (Vrana) fall in love and quarrel over the coin. 3. A miser (Makris) tries to pass off the false coin in order to help an orphan girl. 4. Found in a Twelfth-Night cake, the coin brings together, then separates, a rich heiress (Lambetti) and a poor painter (Horn).
For the film maker, the meaning of his fable is that falseness is less in the counterfeit coin than in money itself, in the role it plays in society. Produced on a modest budget, it had considerable success in Greece and abroad. It is an imaginative, sensitive, and well-constructed film; a realistic and biting depiction of characters in their social environment and perhaps the best Greek neorealist film.

KAMERADSCHAFT COMRADESHIP Germany 1931. *Dir* G. W. Pabst *Scen* Ladislaus Vajda, Karl Otten, Peter Martin Lempel *Photog* Fritz Arno Wagner, Robert Baberski *Art Dir* Ernö Metzner, Karl Vollbrecht *Ed* Hans (Jean) Oser *Cast* Ernst Busch, Alexander Granach, Fritz Kampers, Gustav Püttjer, Elisabeth Wendt, Daniel Mendaille, Georges Charlin, Pierre Louis, Hélèna Manson *Prod* Nero-Film. 92 mins.
Set in the mines of the Saar shortly after World War I and based on an actual 1906 mine disaster, the film tells

how German miners helped to save their French comrades after a disastrous explosion. After the rescue, the iron barrier between the French and German workings is re-established by the officials. (This last ironic scene has been removed from some versions.) Both French and German are spoken in the film.

Besides emphasizing the solidarity of workers, this left-wing film is a passionate plea for international peace and friendship and, despite some ambiguities, condemns any renewed Franco-German conflict. At the end, as French and German miners pledge unity against war, a Frenchman says. "Why do we not stick together when we need each other? Why not always?" In an earlier sequence, a French miner on the verge of suffocation sees one of the German rescuers approaching him in a gas mask; believing he is back in the war, he attacks his rescuer. This leads to a montage sequence of war horrors.

Pabst's style is sober, restrained and quasi-documentary in approach. There is no musical background, but Pabst's use of natural sounds is very expressive — the rumble of machinery, the sighing and groaning of the mine shaft after the disaster, a popular orchestra, the sound of which is not always synchronized with the image. This is one of Pabst's best films and one of the few films in the West during the Thirties that portrayed truthfully the life of thousands of ordinary workers.

KANAL THEY LOVED LIFE Poland 1956. *Dir* Andrzej Wajda *Scen* J. Stawinski based on his own novel *Photog* Jerzy Lipman *Art Dir* Roman Mann *Cast* Teresa Izewska, Tadeusz Janczar, W. Glinski, Teresa Berezowska *Prod* Kadr. 97 mins.

In September 1944, during the Warsaw Uprising, a group of partisans are ordered to retreat to the center of the city through the sewers ("kanal" in Polish). They become separated. A woman (Berezowska) discovers her lover is already married and kills herself. Two lovers (Izewska, Janczar) reach the Vistula only to find the exit blocked by an iron grill. Another man escapes through a man hole but finds himself in the German barracks. The leader (Glinski) reaches the surface but returns to the sewers to find the others.

A powerful and beautiful work, dominated by a hatred of the horrors of war and its effects. Its epic style carries with it, however, a number of gratuitously "arty" touches: a musician playing amid the ruins; a body floating in the sewers; the too-pretty lighting in the sewers, etc. The film's great success at Cannes made Wajda's name and led to a new critical awareness of the young Polish cinema.

KANI-KOSEN THE CRAB-CANNING SHIP Japan 1953. *Dir* Satoru Yamamura *Scen* S. Yamamura based on the novel by Takiji Kobayashi *Photog* Yoshio Miyajima *Mus* Akira Ifukube *Cast* S. Yamamura, Mori Hidaka, Kono. 103 mins.

During the late Twenties, the captain (Yamamura) of a cannery-factory boat brutally oppresses his workers, who seize control of the ship and make him prisoner. The mutiny is suppressed by a boarding party from a Japanese warship.

The film is based on a popular "proletarian" novel published in 1928, whose author was tortured to death by the Japanese police in 1933. Its action is very violent and Yamamura (whose first film it was) forces the viewer close to the action, the cries, the fights, and the brutality. The story resembles *Potemkin* and Yamamura borrowed many of Eisenstein's techniques. This is an important example of independent, progressive Japanese film-making.

KARIN INGMARSDOTTER KARIN, DAUGHTER OF INGMAR Sweden 1919. *Dir* Victor Sjöström *Scen* Victor Sjöström, Ester Juhlin based on the novel *Jerusalem, Part II*, by Selma Lagerlöf *Photog* Henrik Jaenzon, Gustaf Boge *Art Dir* Axel Esbensen *Costumes* Isak Olson *Cast* Victor Sjöström, Tora Teje, Nils Lundell, Bertil Malmstedt, Tor Weijden *Prod* Svenska. 5,650 ft.

Ingmar (Sjöström) refuses to allow his daughter, Karin (Teje), to marry her true love and forces her to marry a rich man (Lundell). After her father dies, her husband reveals himself as a drunkard and bully. He becomes crippled and eventually drinks himself to death, leaving Karin free to marry her former lover.

"Dressed in ancient folkloric costumes, the characters roam across the landscape and in the rooms of the inn, evoking thoughts of the Flemish school" (Jean Béranger). The most striking scene is when the old man, struck in the side but not believing himself touched, takes his shattered watch from his pocket and then falls down dead. This is a scene that Fellini might have remembered when he made *La Strada* (*q.v.*).

Karin Ingmarsdötter was the sequel to Sjöström's earlier (1918) *Ingmarssönarna* (*The Sons of Ingmar*) filmed in two parts and based on the first part of Selma Lagerlöf's novel *Jerusalem*.

KATKA — BUMAZHNY RANYOT KATKA'S REINETTE APPLES USSR 1926. *Dir* Eduard Johanson, Friedrich Ermler *Scen* M. Borisoglebsky, Boris Leonidov *Photog* Yevgeni Mikhailov, Andrei Moskvin *Art Dir* Yevgeni Enei *Cast* Fyodor Nitkin, Veronica Buzhinskaya, B. Chernova, Valeri Solovtsov *Prod* Sovkino (Leningrad). 5,650 ft.

A young girl, Katka (Buzhinskaya), arrives in Leningrad to look for work in the early days of the New Economic Policy (NEP) and is reduced to selling apples on the street, where she meets various underworld characters. She is seduced and cheated by a wastrel (Solovtsov) before she meets a gentle protector, Fyodor (Nitkin).

This story offers a striking portrait of the Soviet Union during the NEP period, with its profiteers and unemployment, its street vendors, prostitutes, pimps, and whorehouses. Although the phrase was not then invented, this is a "neorealist" film and Ermler's first success. (The co-director, Johanson, has only made mediocre films.) Nitkin, who made several films with Ermler, gives a very good performance. The influence of FEKS (Factory of Eccentric Actors) is evident and perhaps also that of expressionism in some of the sequences and sets.

(Note: a Reinette apple is a variety of apple with very white flesh and a thin skin.)

KAVALER ZOLOTOI ZVEZDY CAVALIER OF THE GOLDEN STAR/DREAM OF A COSSACK USSR 1950. *Dir* Yuri Raizman *Scen* B. Chirksov based on the novel by S. Babayevsky *Photog* S. Urusevsky *Mus* T. Khrennirov *Cast* Sergei Bondarchuk, A. Chemodurov, K. Katayeva. 108 mins.

A Cossack soldier (Bondarchuk) receives the Red Star and returns to his native village. He takes charge of a collective farm, builds a dam, and becomes a deputy.

In the novel on which the film is based, the "cavalier" is a true "Tarzan," concerned only with success. There are still some elements of this (as when the man says condescendingly to his fiancée, "You're catching up on me"), but Raizman's direction makes the characters more human, through the love story and through his feeling for nature. Beautiful photography by Urusevsky, who later photographed *The Cranes Are Flying* (*q.v.*).

KEEP AN EYE ON AMELIA OCCUPE-TOI D'AMÉLIE

KEEP AWAKE JAGTE RAHO

KEEPER OF PROMISES (THE) PAGADOR DE PROMESSAS (O)

KEEPERS (THE) TÊTE CONTRE LES MURS (LA)

KERMESSE HEROIQUE (LA) CARNIVAL IN FLANDERS (German title: DIE KLUGEN FRAVEN) France 1935. *Dir* Jacques Feyder *Assist* Marcel Carné, Charles Barrois *Scen* Charles Spaak, Jacques Feyder based on a novel by Charles Spaak *Dialogue* Bernard Zimmer (French version), A. Rabenalt (German version) *Photog* Harry Stradling *Assist Photog* Louis Page, André Thomas *Art Dir* Lazare Meerson *Assist Art Dir* Alexandre Trauner, Georges Wakhevitch *Costumes* J. K. Benda *Mus* Louis Beydts *Cast French version* Françoise Rosay, Jean Murat, André Alerme, Louis Jouvet, Bernard Lancret, Micheline Cheirel, Alfred Adam *German version* Françoise Rosay, Paul Hartman, Will Dohm, Charlotte Daudert, Albert Lieven, Hans Heninger, Paul Westermaier *Prod* Tobis. 115 mins. (95 mins. in most English versions). Premier, December 1, 1935 in Paris. Banned by Goebbels in September 1939, when war was declared.

In 1616, in the little town of Boom in Spanish-occupied Flanders, the city fathers receive word that a detachment of Spaniards is coming. With past experiences of Spanish brutality in mind, the men hide or leave town. The burgomaster (Alerme/Dohm) pretends to be dead, but the women of the town, led by the burgomaster's wife (Rosay), decide to receive the soldiers warmly and plan a carnival and banquet. The burgomaster's wife is courted by the Duke of Alba (Murat/Hartman), while her daughter (Cheirel/Daudert) becomes engaged to a painter (Lancret). The night is spent in feasting and love-making, the Spaniards' usual harshness disappears, and they reward the women with a year's remission of taxes for the town. Jacques Feyder has said: "After completing *Pension Mimosas* (*q.v.*) I decided to amuse myself with a farce, a safe subject away from reality. With this in mind I returned to a novel that I had asked Charles Spaak to write ten years earlier. The day after the world premier, on the Champs-Elysées, the Parisian press proved cool and very reserved. One minor weekly went out of its way to prove that the film had been inspired by Nazism."

The film was a great world-wide success. But in Belgium, there were hostile, violent demonstrations against the film by the "Rexistes," led by Degrelle, who was a Nazi collaborator in 1940–1945. During this period, Feyder and Françoise Rosay were hunted by the Gestapo and had to leave France, and Goebbels banned the film.

Feyder considers that *"La Kermesse héroïque* remains the most important attempt to popularize and spread the extraordinary art of the great painters of my native country," but that it was not intended "to deride the heroic resistance against invaders for which the Belgians have always been notable" (1944). If Feyder unconsciously sought to bring about a rapport between a country and its occupying forces, it was based on the utopian ideals of the pacifists of the Twenties, who saw non-violence as a means of bringing an end to war.

The magnificent sets by Lazare Meerson, which involved re-creating a little 17th century Belgian town in a Parisian suburb, are based on the paintings of the Dutch masters and convey the feeling that the canvases of Brueghel, Frans Hals, Vermeer are springing into life and movement. The acting is brilliant, with an authoritative Françoise Rosay, a truculent Alerme, a smooth-tongued Alfred Adam, and, as the hypocritical chaplain, a sarcastic Jouvet. However, the Duke of Alba and the Spaniards do not really stand out. This is undoubtedly the best French costume film.

KID (THE) USA 1921. *Dir/Scen* Charles Chaplin *Photog* Rollie Totheroh *Assist Dir* Chuck Reisner *Cast* Charles Chaplin, Jackie Coogan, Edna Purviance, Carl Miller, Tom Wilson, Chuck Reisner, Henry Bergman, Albert Austin, Lita Grey *Prod* Chaplin for First National. 4,600 ft.

Charlie finds the baby of an unmarried mother (Purviance) and decides to bring him up himself. The little boy (Coogan) throws rocks at windows for his adopted father so that Charlie can appear immediately after as an itinerant glazier. Meanwhile, the mother has become a rich opera singer. The authorities attempt to remove the Kid, but Charlie and he run away. A rooming-house owner steals the Kid for the reward. Charlie is awakened from a fantastic dream by a policeman (Wilson), who takes him to the Kid and his mother.

Apart from *Tillie's Punctured Romance* (1914), this was Chaplin's longest film at that time. It is more of a straight drama than a comedy, with a well-constructed plot and realistic characters. Its most striking scene is that in which a group of puritans try to take the Kid away to an orphanage. This episode is autobiographical and the room in which Charlie and the Kid live was based on Chaplin's own childhood memories. One of the best scenes, full of tenderness and humor, is that in which Charlie makes a dressing gown by sticking his head through a ragged blanket, takes a plate of pancakes, and gives the Kid a lesson in good manners. The film even incorporates completely lyrical episodes, as in the final part of Charlie's dream in which the inhabitants of the slum sprout wings like angels and fly about.

Under Chaplin's coaching, the five-year-old Jackie Coogan gives a persuasive, natural, and charming performance as a kind of junior "Tramp." Regrettably, Coogan later became a very mannered child star. Chaplin invested considerable money and time on this feature (a difficult form for a comedian) and, anxious about its success, took it to Europe. It was as great a success there as it was in the States.

KIKU TO ISAMU KIKU AND ISAMU Japan 1959. *Dir* Tadashi Imai *Scen* Yoko Mizuki *Photog* Kiichiro Nakao *Mus* Masao Oki *Cast* Tanie Kitabayashi, Emiko Takahashi, George Okunoyama *Prod* Daito. 117 mins. Tohoscope.

A boy (Okunoyama) and a girl (Takahashi), fathered by Negro American soldiers, live in a village north of Tokyo.

As children of mixed blood they seem to have no place in the world. The boy leaves for the USA while the girl is left alone. A film full of gentle pathos, in which Tanie Kitabayashi, at 40, gives a remarkably sensitive performance as the grandmother.

*KILLERS (THE) USA 1946. *Dir* Robert Siodmak *Scen* Anthony Veiller based on the story by Ernest Hemingway *Photog* Woody Bredell *Art Dir* Jack Otterson, Martin Obzina *Mus* Miklos Rosza *Ed* Arthur Hilton *Cast* Edmond O'Brien, Ava Gardner, Albert Dekker, Sam Levene, Burt Lancaster, Charles McGraw, William Conrad *Prod* Universal. 105 mins.

Two professional killers machine-gun Swede Lunn (Lancaster) to death. James Reardon (O'Brien), an insurance agent, becomes interested and meets Detective Lieutenant Sam Lubinsky (Levene) who tells him that Swede had been seeing Kitty Collins (Gardner), the girl friend of racketeer Jim Colfax (Dekker). Reardon discovers that they had been involved in a holdup and that Swede had learned after the robbery that the others meant to double cross him. Swede is seen by Colfax working at a service station and two days later he is killed. Reardon hunts out Kitty, Colfax, and the rest of the gang.

Only the grim opening sequence was derived from Hemingway's story. However, this taut, intricate, and occasionally brilliant thriller was a notable addition to the genre. It also marked Burt Lancaster's film debut.
— *The Killers USA 1964. *Dir* Don Siegel *Scen* Gene L. Coon based on the story by Ernest Hemingway *Photog* Richard L. Rawling *Art Dir* Frank Arrigo, George Chan *Mus* Johnny Williams *Ed* Richard Belding *Cast* Lee Marvin, Angie Dickinson, John Cassavetes, Ronald Reagan, Clu Gulager *Prod* Universal. 95 mins. Pathécolor.

Siegel's remake was originally intended for television: "I shot it as a feature. I shot it in the style that I feel is my style at its best, very taut and lean, with great economy . . . It was shot at a great pace with no preparation, no color consultant. It just happened" (Don Siegel). The opening sequence of a cold-blooded killing (shot in slow motion) in a home for the blind has a horrific power. The film also has a marginal curiosity value in that Ronald Reagan is shown as a double-crossing mobster just months before he entered politics.

KIMI TO WAKARETE APART FROM YOU Japan 1932. *Dir/Scen* Mikio Naruse *Photog* Suketaro Igai *Cast* Mitsuko Yoshikawa, Akio Isono, Sumiko Mizukubo. 100 mins. approx. Silent film.

In Tokyo, a young geisha (Mizukubo) falls in love with the young son (Isono) of another geisha (Yoshikawa). She is wounded and they separate.

Despite its melodramatic story, this film has gentleness and charm, and a simple, direct, almost "neorealist" style. The best sequence is that in which the young lovers visit the fishing village where the boy was born.

KIND HEARTS AND CORONETS Britain 1949. *Dir* Robert Hamer *Scen* Robert Hamer, John Dighton based on the novel by Roy Horniman *Photog* Douglas Slocombe *Art Dir* Ernest Taylor, Harry Frampton, William Kellner *Ed* Peter Tanner *Cast* Dennis Price, Joan Greenwood, Alec Guinness, Valerie Hobson *Prod* Ealing. 106 mins.

At the turn of the century, a young man (Price) vows vengeance on the d'Ascoyne family, who had spurned his mother when she married a commoner. He murders the eight heirs (all roles played by Guinness) who stand between him and the Dukedom of Chalfont and becomes engaged to the widow (Hobson) of one of his victims. He is accused by his mistress (Greenwood) of a murder he did not commit and is condemned to death. He is reprieved, but when he leaves prison forgets to take his memoirs confessing to the murders he did commit.

Without doubt, this is the best British comedy produced at the Ealing Studios under Michael Balcon. The story is told in a series of flashbacks as the hero writes his memoirs. This satire on the British aristocracy is largely based on "nonsense" humor, but its story evolves with a rigorous logic. Each murder produces its own irresistibly funny gag: the explosion in the laboratory, the priest's poisoned port, the suffragette's balloon shot down by an arrow, the stubborness of the admiral who goes down with his ship, the plastic bomb in a pot of caviar, etc.

Hamer seems to have been influenced by both *La Règle du jeu* (*q.v.*) and

Monsieur Verdoux (*q.v.*), but the humor is also derived from the British satirical tradition of such diverse authors as Swift, Thackeray, and Oscar Wilde. Hamer's own personal style is nevertheless evident in this impertinent film, which proved to be very successful. Alec Guinness' extraordinary performance in eight roles made him world famous.

KING IN NEW YORK (A) Britain 1957. *Dir/Scen/Mus* Charles Chaplin *Photog* Georges Périnal *Art Dir* Allan Harris *Cast* Charles Chaplin, Dawn Addams, Maxine Audley, Oliver Johnston, Jerry Desmonde, Michael Chaplin *Prod* Chaplin. 109 mins.
Fleeing a revolution in his own country, King Shahdov (Chaplin) takes refuge in the USA. He is led by an advertising agent (Addams) into making commercials, is suspected of being a Communist and called before the Un-American Activities Committee, and ends by returning to Europe.
Produced after Chaplin's departure from the USA, this political fable is largely autobiographical.
Famous sequences and gags: the visit to a movie house with its absurd films; a rock-and-roll nightclub; the young journalist breaking into the bathroom; the fashionable party, secretly televised, with commercial interruptions and Hamlet's soliloquy; the king's visit to an ultra-modern school; his commercial for a brand of whiskey; his submission to plastic surgery; his conversation with a young boy (Michael Chaplin), hounded into denouncing his parents before the Un-American Activities Committee.

KING KONG USA 1933. *Dir* Merian C. Cooper, Ernest B. Schoedsack *Scen* James Creelman, Ruth Rose based on a story by Edgar Wallace and Merian C. Cooper *Photog* Edward Linden, Vernon Walker, J. O. Taylor *Special Effects* Willis O'Brien *Art Dir* Carroll Clark, Al Herman *Mus* Max Steiner *Ed* Ted Cheeseman *Cast* Fay Wray, Robert Armstrong, Bruce Cabot *Prod* RKO. 100 mins.
Two explorers (Armstrong, Cabot) find a giant gorilla on a tropical island, capture it with the help of a star (Fay Wray), and exhibit it in New York. The giant ape escapes and seizes the girl but is finally killed.
"Because of the absurdity of the plot (a clumsily contrived script with many inconsistent details), the powerful dream content (frighteningly realistic presentation of a recurrent dream), the unnatural eroticism (the monster's unbounded love for the woman, cannibalism, human sacrifice), the unreality of some of the sets . . . or perhaps because of the combination of these elements, it seems to me that the film is what we would call 'poetic', an adjective we use when we think of cinema as the land of dreams" (Jean Ferry). The monster was based on an idea by Cooper and Schoedsack (not by Edgar Wallace it seems) and brought to life through the designer and the extraordinary trick photography of Willis O'Brien. It is as breathtaking in its first appearance as it is in the climax, when it climbs to the top of a skyscraper carrying the girl in its hand and is attacked by airplanes.
This is one of the first films that used stop-motion trick photography. The same island sets were used in *The Most Dangerous Game* (*q.v.*). King Kong-type monsters have continued to be used both in cartoons and in such films as:
— *Son of Kong* USA 1933. *Dir* Ernest Schoedsack *Scen* Ruth Rose *Photog/Ed* as King Kong *Cast* Robert Armstrong, Helen Mack *Prod* RKO. 70 mins.
A sequel (surprisingly released the same year) to *King Kong* that contains more melodrama and fewer trick effects.
— *Mighty Joe Young* USA 1949. *Dir* Ernest Schoedsack *Scen* Ruth Rose *Cast* Robert Armstrong, Terry Moore, Ben Johnson *Prod* RKO. 93 mins.
[A sort of children's version of *King Kong* with the gorilla being the pet of an orphan girl. Willis O'Brien's special effects, however, won an Academy Award.]
— *King Kong vs. Godzilla* Japan 1963. *Dir* Inoshiro Honda.
— *King Kong no Gyakushu/King Kong Escapes* Japan 1967. *Dir* Inoshiro Honda.

***KINO-GLAZ** KINO-EYE USSR 1924. *Dir/Scen* Dziga Vertov *Photog* Mikhail Kaufman *Ed* Yelizaveta Svilova *Prod* Goskino. 1,627 meters (5,400 ft. approx.)
Dziga Vertov intended this, his first feature-length film, as the first of a series. There was, however, no second film because Vertov decided to apply his approach to single themes. It was also the first opportunity he had to demonstrate his "kino-eye" theory of

capturing life as it is lived and using editing for "the organization of the seen world" (Vertov). Vertov, together with his brother, Mikhail Kaufman, who was his collaborator and cameraman, filmed in every part of Moscow and the vicinity, using every camera device then known, and produced a vision of actuality of epic proportions.

KISS ME DEADLY USA 1955. *Dir* Robert Aldrich *Scen* A. I. Bezzerides based on the novel by Mickey Spillane *Photog* Ernest Laszlo *Art Dir* William Glasgow *Mus* Frank Devol *Cast* Ralph Meeker, Albert Dekker, Paul Stewart *Prod* Parklane for United Artists. 105 mins. (96 mins. Britain).

Mike Hammer (Meeker) hunts down a gang that is trying to smuggle radioactive material to a foreign power. The gang kidnaps his secretary but he tracks them to a beach house and rescues her before the house bursts into flames.

From a mediocre story (Aldrich: "We just took the title and threw the book away.") Aldrich created one of the most extraordinary films of the Fifties. It was shot in only 22 days on a low budget using a relatively unknown cast. In an interview with Truffaut, Aldrich said: "Mike Hammer is an antidemocrat, a fascist. *Truffaut:* You used poetic effects in place of the coarseness of the novel. Should we understand the climax of the film as the end of the world? *Aldrich:* I don't know about that. I made the ending ambiguous to avoid police interference."

[Aldrich said later: "I was very proud of the film. I think it represented a whole breakthrough for me. In terms of style, in terms of the way we tried to make it, it provided a marvelous showcase to display my own ideas of moviemaking . . . It did have a basic significance in *our* political framework that we thought rather important in those McCarthy times: that the ends did not justify the means (but) the French . . . and others read into it all sorts of terribly profound observations."]

KISS OF DEATH (THE) DÖDSKYSSEN

KLEINER MANN, WAS NUN? see LITTLE MAN, WHAT NOW?

KNAVE OF HEARTS MONSIEUR RIPOIS/ LOVERS/HAPPY LOVERS/LOVER BOY Britain 1954. *Dir* René Clément *Scen* Hugh Mills, Raymond Queneau, René Clément based on the novel *Monsieur Ripois et la Némésis* by Louis Hémon *Photog* Oswald Morris *Assist Dir* Claude Clément, Leonard Kiegel, Roger Good, Max Gayton *Art Dir* Ralph Brinton *Mus* Roman Vlad *Ed* Françoise Javet *Cast* Gérard Philipe, Valerie Hobson, Joan Greenwood, Natasha Parry, Germaine Montero *Prod* Transcontinental. 103 mins.

André Ripois (Philipe), the handsome French husband of a wealthy Englishwoman (Hobson), tries to seduce Patricia (Parry), his wife's friend. To seduce her, he tells her of his arrival in London, penniless, his marriage, and three affairs — with his boss's secretary, a sweet young girl (Greenwood), and a motherly prostitute (Montero). Patricia is not persuaded: he threatens to kill himself, then slips and falls. Crippled, he lives in the grip of his wife and Patricia. A sophisticated, witty, and pointed comedy of morals, one of Clément's best films and one of Gérard Philipe's most perfect performances in the role of a libertine, a shabby Don Juan seemingly destined forever to chase, seduce, and abandon women. The best sequence shows Ripois, destitute and unemployed, wandering the streets of London, smashing his last treasure, a transistor radio, sleeping on a bench, and meeting the prostitute who disgusts him but who gives him shelter.

KONGRESS TANZT (DER) CONGRESS DANCES Germany 1931. *Dir* Erik Charell *Scen* Norbert Falk, Robert Liebmann *Photog* Carl Hoffman *Art Dir* Röhrig, Herlith *Mus* Werner R. Heymann *Cast* Lilian Harvey, Willy Fritsch, Conrad Veidt, Lil Dagover, Alfred Abel, Otto Wallburg, Paul Hörbiger *Prod* UFA. 92 mins.

Set during the 1815 Congress of Vienna this quasi-Viennese operetta was designed to evoke "gay Vienna." The songs still retain their charm but the luxuriant UFA decorative style seems too portentous for the material. It was a great commercial success, for which Erich Pommer, the producer, should be given credit rather than Erik Charell. It was banned by the Nazi censors in 1937. [Conrad's Veidt's performance as Metternich is outstanding but Willy Fritsch's heavy romantic approach as Tsar Alexander dates very badly. Lilian Harvey's vivacious performance made her a star.

The film was made in several language versions. In the English and French versions, Henri Garat plays Tsar Alexander.]

KONYETS SANKT-PETERBURGA THE END OF ST. PETERSBURG USSR 1927. *Dir* V. I. Pudovkin *Assist Dir* Mikhail Doller, V. Strauss, A. Ledashev, A. Hendelstein *Scen* Nathan Zarkhi *Photog* Anatoli N. Golovnya, K. Vents *Art Dir* S. Kozlovsky *Cast* Ivan Chuvelev, Vera Baranovskaya, A. P. Chistiakov, Sergei Komorov, V. Obolenski, V. I. Pudovkin *Prod* Mezhrabpom-Russ. 2,500 meters (8,300 ft. approx.).

A peasant (Chuvelev) arrives in St. Petersburg in 1914 to find work and lives with his uncle (Chistiakov) and aunt (Baranovskaya). The workers strike for better conditions but he becomes a blackleg (scab) until his eyes are opened and he understands the reasons. He attacks his employer (Obolenski), is thrown into prison, and is forced to enlist in the army when war is declared. The capitalists become wealthy on war profits. Then the Revolution begins: St. Petersburg becomes Leningrad.

Famous sequences: the monuments of the Tsarist capital overwhelming the young peasant; the declaration of war and the accompanying frenzy; the terrible conditions at the front contrasted with the capitalists' joy in the stock exchange at their increasing profits; the comradeship at the front between Russian and German soldiers; the October Revolution.

As with Eisenstein's *October* (*q.v.*), this film was commissioned to Pudovkin for the 10th Anniversary of the 1917 Revolution.

KORHINTA MERRY-GO-ROUND Hungary 1955. *Dir/Art Dir* Zoltan Fabri *Scen* Laszlo Nadasi, Zoltan Fabri based on a story by Imre Sarkadi *Photog* Barnabas Hegyi *Mus* Gyorgy Ranki *Cast* Bela Barsi, Mari Torocsik, Imre Sos, Adam Szirtes. 90 mins.

A young peasant girl (Torocsik) opposes her landowning father (Barsi) by refusing to marry another landowner (Szirtes). At a country fair she falls in love with a young farmer (Sos) working in a cooperative. Rather than submit to a forced marriage, she runs away; her father reluctantly agrees to let her marry the communist.

A delightful and entertaining film, beautifully photographed. Memorable sequences: the country fair and the Hungarian dance with their exhilarating camerawork; the rebellious young man splashing in the mud.

KORITSI ME TA MAVRA (TO) A GIRL IN BLACK Greece 1955. *Dir/Scen* Michael Cacoyannis *Photog* Walter Lassally *Mus* Argyris Kounadis *Ed* Emile Provelengios *Cast* Elli Lambetti, Georges Foundas, Dimitri Horna *Prod* Hermes. 93 mins.

Pavlo (Horna), an unsuccessful writer, visits the Greek island of Hydra and falls in love with Marina (Lambetti), daughter of his landlady. Marina is persecuted by a fisherman (Foundas) whose passion for her she had rejected and Pavlo becomes involved in the feud. The fisherman stages an accident to provoke Pavlo but his intended joke results in the death of several village children. Marina forces the fisherman to confess his guilt and Pavlo is cleared. Cacoyannis' first successful film, notable for its depiction of the harsh atmosphere of the island, with its little town and broken-down mansion, and for the sensitive portrayal of Marina by the beautiful Elli Lambetti.

KORKARLEN THE PHANTOM CHARIOT/THY SOUL SHALL BEAR WITNESS/THE STROKE OF MIDNIGHT Sweden 1920. *Dir* Victor Sjöström *Scen* Victor Sjöström based on the novel by Selma Lagerlöf *Photog* J. Julius (Julius Jaenzon) *Art Dir* Alexander Bako, Axel Esbensen *Cast* Victor Sjöström, Hilda Borgström, Tore Svennberg, Astrid Holm *Prod* Svensk Filmindustri. 5,600 ft.

On New Year's Eve, while a Salvation Army nurse (Holm) who has sworn to save him is dying, David Holm (Sjöström) is drinking in a graveyard and laughs at the phantom chariot driven by the coachman of Death, who, according to legend, must be replaced that night by the last man to die on December 31. David is hit on the head and knocked senseless at the stroke of twelve and retraces his misspent life: as an honest worker on a picnic with his family; tempted by Georg (Svennberg) he takes to drink, loses his job, and goes to prison; he bullies his wife (Borgström) then, encouraged by the Salvation Army nurse, tries to reform but becomes bitter when his wife leaves him. That New Year's Eve she prepares to kill the children and commit suicide. The Salvation Army nurse dies and saves David, who hurries home to his family.

The most famous, though not the best, Sjöström film despite its moralistic tone and its sermonizing on the evils of alcohol. Its realistic depiction of life in the slums is as brilliant as the fantasy sequences in which the cameraman, Jaenzon, makes superb use of double-exposures. His shots of the phantom chariot driving through the fog and by the sea are the most memorable in the film. These scenes, together with Sjöström's powerful and controlled performance as David Holm, made the film a success at the time and are still impressive.

REMAKES:

— *La Charette fantôme France 1939. Dir/Scen Julien Duvivier Cast Pierre Fresnay, Louis Jouvet, Micheline Francey. 80 mins.
Quite a good version; its depiction of a Salvation Army service is especially notable.

— *Körkarlen Sweden 1958. Dir Arne Mattson Cast George Fant, Ulla Jacobsson, Edvin Adolphson, Anita Björk. 108 mins. Agascope.
Though overly mannered in style, this version has the merit of some excellent photography and fine acting.

KOZARA HILL OF DEATH Yugoslavia 1962. Dir Veljko Bulajic Scen Ratko Djurovic, Steven Bulajic, Veljki Bulajic Photog Aleksander Sekulovic Art Dir Dusko Jericevic Cast Bert Sotlar, Olivera Markovic, Milena Dravic Prod Bosna Film. 130 mins. (96 mins. general foreign release).
In the mountain village of Kozara, partisans fight against German tanks and infantry. Eventually, after bloody fighting, the Germans pull back. One of the best Yugoslav films, notable for its graphic battle scenes.

KRAZY KAT (cartoon series) see FELIX THE CAT (CARTOON SERIES)

KRESTYANIYE PEASANTS USSR 1935. Dir Friedrich Ermler Scen Mikhail Bolshintsov, V. Portnov, Friedrich Ermler Photog Alexander Ginsburg Art Dir Nikolai Suvorov Mus Venedict Pushkov Cast Yelena Yunger, N. Bogolyubov, A. Petrov, Vladimir Gardin, V. Poslavsky Prod Lenfilm. 95 mins.
The struggle for collectivization in the USSR. A man (Petrov) with a profound hatred of collective farms has a wife (Yunger) who is very loyal to the collective. He accidentally kills her after he has tried to sabotage the work of the collective by breaking up its herd of pigs, and then pushes his brother-in-law (Poslavsky) into killing a Party official (Bogolyubov).
Summarized like this, the film might seem very dull. On the contrary, it is a very humanistic film, subtle in portraying the psychology of its characters, and a very true portrait of life in the Soviet countryside and on the collectives during the Thirties.

KRIEMHILDS RACHE NIBELUNGEN (DIE)

KRIEMHILD'S REVENGE NIBELUNGEN (DIE)

KRUZHEVA LACE USSR 1928. Dir Sergei Yutkevich Scen Sergei Yutkevich, Yuri Gromov, Vladimir Legoshin based on a story by M. Kolosov Photog Yevgeni Schneider Art Dir Victor Aden Cast Nina Shaternikova, Boris Poslavsky, K. Gradopolov, Boris Tenin Prod Sovkino. 2,100 meters.
The life of komsomols in a lace factory in which a lazy young man becomes industrious. A fresh and entertaining film and a lively portrait of daily life and the eccentric fashions of the youth of the time. Yutkevich's first film.

KUHLE WAMPE WHITHER GERMANY? Germany 1932. Dir Slatan Dudow Scen Bertolt Brecht, Ernst Ottwald Photog Günther Krampf Art Dir Karl Haaker, Robert Scharffenberg Mus Hanns Eisler, Josef Schmid Cast Herta Theile, Ernst Busch, Martha Wolter, Adolf Fischer, Lili Schönborn Prod Prometheus/Praesens. 73 mins.
The life of some unemployed workers organized into a community near Berlin and the political fights that preceded Hitler's advent to power. The film was banned by the Nazis (March 1933) less than a year after its premier. Ironically, it was also banned by the governments of other countries that were to suffer from Nazism.
Brecht's script incorporated many of his own deepest feelings about life in Germany at the time and Slatan Dudow superbly brings these feelings to life. Those with little knowledge of the history of pre-Hitler Germany might now find some scenes difficult to understand, but the rest is still profoundly moving

in its depiction of working-class life and the hopelessness of the crisis.

["It is certainly true to say that the cinema has never seen a work quite like *Kühle Wampe* in any other country, except for a few socialist experiments in France in the late 1930's . . . Most interesting today are the documentary shots of the Berlin working class on the eve of Hitler, pedaling their bicycles from factory to factory in search of nonexistent work, and the spectacular sports meet and open-air theater which reflected so much the influence of Brecht" (David Stewart Hull).]

KUKSI VALAHOL EUROPABAN

KUMONOSU-JO THE THRONE OF BLOOD/ COBWEB CASTLE/THE CASTLE OF THE SPIDER'S WEB Japan 1957. *Dir* Akira Kurosawa *Scen* Shinobu Hashimoto, Ryuzo Kikushima, Hideo Oguni, Akira Kurosawa adapted from Shakespeare's *Macbeth Photog* Asakazu Nakai *Art Dir* Yoshiro Muraki, Kohei Ezaki *Mus* Masaru Sato *Cast* Toshiro Mifune, Isuzu Yamada *Prod* Toho. 110 mins.

Kurosawa's best period film (jidai-geki), surpassing even *Rashomon* (*q.v.*) and *The Seven Samurai* (*q.v.*). Kurosawa transposed the tragedy of *Macbeth* to medieval Japan and had some of the characters, such as Lady Macbeth (Yamada), play in white masks and with slightly accelerated movements – a direct use of Noh dramatic techniques. Kurosawa's interpretation of Macbeth's character is most evident in the almost operatic finale, when the warriors fire arrow after arrow at him as he flees from them along the ramparts of his castle. ["I decided upon the techniques of the Noh because in Noh style and story are one. I wanted to use the way Noh actors have of walking and the general composition which the Noh stage provides. This is one of the reasons why there are so few close-ups in the picture. I tried to show everything using the full-shot" (Kurosawa).]
See also MACBETH

KURUTTA IPPEIJI A CRAZY PAGE/A PAGE OUT OF ORDER Japan 1926. *Dir/Scen/ Prod* Teinosuke Kinugasa *Cast* Masao Inoue.

According to Donald Richie and Joseph Anderson, this film was "about a sailor, the cause of his wife's insanity, who becomes a servant in the asylum where she is kept. It was shot partly from the point of view of the insane themselves, with impressionistic cutting in the Russian and French avant-garde manner." The film was certainly influenced by European films, especially by *The Cabinet of Dr. Caligari* (*q.v.*), but not, according to the director, by Russian films, which were then unknown in Japan. This experimental film, financed entirely by the director, was a great success and exercised considerable influence on the Japanese cinema.

*KVARTERET KORPEN RAVEN'S END Sweden 1963. *Dir/Scen* Bo Widerberg *Photog* Jan Lindeström *Art Dir* Einar Nettlebladt *Mus* Torelli's *Trumpet Concerto in D Ed* Wic Kjellin *Cast* Thommy Berggren, Keve Hjelm, Ingvar Hirdwall, Emy Storm, Christina Frambäck *Prod* Europa. 100 mins.

In Malmö in 1936, a young factory worker, Anders (Berggren), lives with his alcoholic father (Hjelm) and despondent mother (Storm) and has ambitions to be a novelist. Amid news of the Spanish Civil War and Hitler's rise to power, Anders finishes his novel. He is encouraged by a publisher, but the novel is rejected. He becomes involved with a local girl (Frambäck), whom he makes pregnant, and finally leaves home.

Thematically similar to such films as *Death of a Salesman* (*q.v.*) and *This Sporting Life* (*q.v.*) in its portrait of working-class life, *Raven's End* excels in its re-creation of life in Sweden in the Thirties. The drab atmosphere, the austere tenements, even the amusement designed to break the monotony of daily life, combine to give the film an all-pervasive air of despondency. Keve Hjelm's brilliant performance as the father, a failed underwear salesman, inevitably invites comparison with that of Fredric March in *Death of a Salesman*.

KVINNODROM DREAMS/JOURNEY INTO AUTUMN/WOMEN'S DREAMS Sweden 1955. *Dir/Scen* Ingmar Bergman *Photog* Hilding Bladh *Art Dir* Gittan Gustafsson *Ed* Carl-Olof Skeppstedt *Cast* Eva Dahlbeck, Harriet Andersson, Gunnar Björnstrand, Ulf Palme *Prod* Sandrew. 86 mins.

Susanne (Dahlbeck), the owner of a fashion photography studio, goes to Göteborg, where she telephones her ex-lover, (Palme), who is now married. A model, Doris (Andersson), who has broken with her fiancé goes with her and arouses the infatuation of an elderly consul (Björnstrand), who buys her gifts. Both women learn that the men are egotistic weaklings.

Not Bergman at his best, but a very engaging film in which "the cruelty of shattered hopes is balanced by a sense of serenity, the basis of wisdom" (Jean Béranger).

*LABIRYNT LABYRINTH **Poland 1963. A**
film by Jan Lenica. 15 mins. Color.
Probably one of the most disturbing animated films ever made and certainly
Lenica's richest film. An innocent bowler-
hatted man wanders resignedly through
an eerie city full of monstrous creatures
and places. Flies swarm out of an empty
refrigerator; a butterfly woman kisses
her lover and turns him into a skeleton.
A machine tries to "readjust" the man;
when this fails he is destroyed by hordes
of black vultures. Robert Benayoun says
that Lenica has "an immediately recognizable style rivaling those of Stein-
berg or Miro in its subjective impact."

LACE KRUZHEVA

LADIES OF THE BOIS DE BOULOGNE (THE)
DAMES DU BOIS DE BOULOGNE (LES)

LADRI DI BICICLETTE BICYCLE THIEVES/
BICYCLE THIEF **Italy 1949.** *Dir* Vittorio
de Sica *Scen* Cesare Zavattini based on
a novel by Luigi Bartolini *Photog* Carlo
Montuori *Art Dir* Antonio Traverso *Ed*
Eraldo da Roma *Mus* Alessandro Cigo-
gnini *Cast* Lamberto Maggiorani, Lia-
nella Carnel, Enzo Staiola *Prod* Vittorio
de Sica. 90 mins.
An unemployed man in Rome (Maggiorani) finds a job as a bill poster but
his bicycle is stolen. With his little boy
(Staiola), he searches in vain for the
robber and the bike. In the end he steals
a bike.
The film begins by depicting the family's poor living quarters. Then, the
man learns he needs a bicycle in order
to become a municipal bill poster and
pawns his sheets to buy a bike. He begins work in Rome; while he is sticking
up a sign about the American film
Gilda, a gang steals the bicycle and the
police tell him that they can hardly be
expected to bother about such a small

matter. He goes to a flea market with his
little boy and a friend. He doesn't find
the bike but recognizes the man who
stole it. With the rain pouring down
he chases after a little old man who runs
into a church and then into a Catholic
soup kitchen. He slaps his little boy,
who runs away. He thinks the boy has
drowned in the Tiber. After their reconciliation they go to a black market
restaurant for a meal. He consults a
fortune teller. He finds the thief again,
chases him into a brothel, and then
catches him in the street. He has the
whole district against him when the
police come and take him to see the
thief's mother. When he sees the poverty-stricken circumstances under which
she lives, he drops the charge. Near a
football stadium where a match is just
ending, he steals a bicycle, but is chased
and caught by passers-by and the owner,
who lets him go when he sees his son.
The father cries tears of despair; the
son takes his hand and they are lost in
the crowd.
This is the most important film of the
immediate postwar period; its extension
of the traditional concepts of plot and
dramatic structure exerted considerable
influence on the development of the cinema. Its story of a man searching for
something on which his very life depended was a theme so new that the
film required no artificial drama. Similar
plots were used so often in future years
that the theme lost its freshness.
Zavattini summed up his theme this
way. "What is a bicycle? There are as
many bicycles in Rome as flies. Each day
dozens and dozens of them are stolen
without the newspapers devoting a single word to the fact. But the newspapers might have trouble establishing
the true facts. In Antonio's case they
would have to give the theft of his bike
a banner headline because it was the

instrument that had got him work." An American company proposed that Cary Grant appear in the film but Zavattini and de Sica refused. Lamberto Maggiorani, who was given the lead role, had known unemployment and was working in a large factory in Rome when de Sica found him. De Sica coached him for the role and there were few complaints about his acting. The film's main theme is unemployment in a country where unemployment seemed a chronic disease. Beyond this, however, it is concerned with the loneliness of man in a dehumanized society. When someone remarked to Zavattini that this theme of loneliness was, to some extent, similar to that of Kafka, he replied that the indifference or hostility of others could always be explained. He then added: "My idea is to 'deromanticize' the cinema. I would like to teach men to look at day-to-day life and everyday events with the same passion that they read a book."

LADY FOR A DAY USA 1933. *Dir* Frank Capra *Scen* Robert Riskin based on the story *Madame La Gimpa* by Damon Runyon *Photog* Joseph Walker *Art Dir* Stephen Goosson *Ed* Gene Havlick *Cast* May Robson, Warren William, Guy Kibbee, Glenda Farrell, Ned Sparks, Jean Parker, Walter Connolly, Hobart Bosworth *Prod* Columbia. 95 mins.
Apple Annie (Robson) is transformed into a grand lady "for a day" by a group of crooks (William, etc.) in order to fool her daughter, who thinks she is a rich lady.
Capra and Riskin's first successful comedy, a kind of modern fairy story, very amusing and entertaining.
— *Pocketful of Miracles* USA 1961. *Dir* Frank Capra *Scen* Hal Kanter, Harry Tugend based on the original screenplay *Photog* Robert Bronner *Cast* Glenn Ford, Bette Davis, Hope Lange, Edward Everett Horton, Peter Falk *Prod* Franton for United Artists. 136 mins. Technicolor. Panavision.
An exact remake that lacks the verve and liveliness of the original because Capra had lost his feeling for contemporary America.

LADY FROM SHANGHAI (THE) USA 1947. *Dir* Orson Welles *Scen* Orson Welles based on the novel by Sherwood King *Photog* Charles Lawton Jr. *Mus* Heinz Roemheld *Art Dir* Stephen Goosson, Sturges Carne *Cast* Orson Welles, Rita Hayworth, Everett Sloane, Glenn Anders *Prod* Columbia. 87 mins.
Michael O'Hara (Welles), an Irish adventurer and sailor, is persuaded by Elsa Bannister (Hayworth), the beautiful wife of a crippled lawyer (Sloane), to join the crew of their yacht for a Pacific cruise. The husband's partner (Anders), after persuading O'Hara to pretend to murder him, is killed and O'Hara is tried for the murder. He discovers he was the dupe of all three in their plans to destroy each other. Husband and wife shoot it out in a hall of mirrors and O'Hara leaves Elsa to die.
"I hadn't read the novel when I agreed to write the script and I never understood it" Orson Welles has said. (A statement that others have denied: Sam Spiegel says Welles read the novel before he talked to the producers.) Remarkable sequences: the visit to Acapulco; the chase through a Chinese theater; the love scene and confession in an aquarium; the macabre climax in the Hall of Mirrors; Orson Welles's final soliloquy, "Everybody is somebody's fool sometime . . . Maybe I'll live so long I'll forget her. Maybe I'll die trying."
Production began with typical Hollywood ballyhoo. In front of the press at Columbia Studios, Welles supervised the cutting of the long blond hair of Rita Hayworth, who was then his wife. But the film, strangely accused of obscenity, was a commercial failure (though a critical success) and Welles left Hollywood a little later. He was not forgiven for having made his hero a veteran of the Spanish Civil War, nor for his description of Acapulco: "Oh, there's a fair face to the land, but you can't hide the hunger and guilt," nor for his final bitter and lucid speech. Nor, above all, for having "de-mystified the American woman" for having "denounced her as a monster, a man-eater, a praying mantis who reveals herself through that worst of passions, greed for money." (Maurice Bessy)
["*The Lady From Shanghai* is a morality play without preachment; it can be taken as a bizarre adventure yarn, a bravura thriller, a profound drama of decay, or all three. . . . Behind the magical showmanship, is the voice of a poet decrying the sin and corruption

184

of a confused world" (Peter Bogdanovich).]

LADY IN THE LAKE USA 1946. *Dir* Robert Montgomery *Scen* Steve Fisher based on the novel by Raymond Chandler *Photog* Paul C. Vogel *Cast* Robert Montgomery, Audrey Totter, Lloyd Nolan *Prod* MGM. 103 mins.
A fairly ordinary thriller, notable only for its use of the "subjective" camera in which the camera lens becomes the eyes of both the hero, Marlowe (Montgomery), and the audience. Marlowe is seen only when he is reflected in a mirror. Despite its acrobatic use of this first-person camera technique, the film is mediocre.

LADY OF THE BOULEVARDS see NANA

LADY WITH A (LITTLE) DOG (THE) DAMA S SOBATCHKOI

LAMB (THE) USA 1915. *Dir* Wm. Christy Cabanne *Scen* D. W. Griffith based on the novel *The Man and the Test* by Granville Warwick *Cast* Douglas Fairbanks, Seena Owen (Signe Aven) *Prod* D. W. Griffith for Triangle. 5 reels.
"An effete 'Easterner' (the Lamb) (Fairbanks) becomes mixed up in a Mexican border war and emerges as a two-fisted 'he-man.' This was the screen debut of Douglas Fairbanks . . . Griffith had, in fact, created a new type of hero — the youthful, buoyant, and apparently invincible American 'superman' which then, even as now, became a symbol of wordly optimism and success" (Seymour Stern).

LAMENT OF THE PATH PATHER PANCHALI

*LAND (THE) USA 1942 (production began 1939). *Dir/Scen/Photog* Robert Flaherty *Assist* Irving Lerner, Floyd Crosby, Frances Flaherty *Mus* Richard Arnell *Ed* Helen Van Dongen *Prod* Agricultural Adjustment Agency/U.S. Department of Agriculture. 42 mins.
Flaherty completed this film after the entry of the USA into the war. *"The Land* was Flaherty's unconscious reaction to the war in Europe and all the events which had built up to it" (Arthur Calder-Marshall). The State Department deemed it too depressing for overseas exhibition and the sponsors found it out-of-date. It was given limited non-theatrical circulation in the USA until 1944 and was then withdrawn.
Flaherty had been persuaded to return to the USA by Pare Lorentz (head of the US Film Service) to make a film on a subject that the Roosevelt administration took very seriously: the water and wind erosion that were laying waste once productive areas in the central USA, as well as the problems of overproduction, cash-crop farming, mechanization, and migrant workers. Striking images: the migrant farmers; a scraggy horse in the desert; agricultural machinery blotting out the sun.
Opinions differ markedly about the film; Flaherty himself seems to have been dissatisfied with it. But Basil Wright sees *The Land* as a "watershed in his development as an artist . . . Before *The Land* his conception of *Louisiana Story (q.v.)* could never have existed."

LAND IN A TRANCE TERRA EM TRANSE

LAND WITHOUT BREAD LAS HURDES.

LANK FLOWER HAS ALREADY FLOWN (THE) DÉJÀ S'ENVOLE LA FLEUR MAIGRE

LAS HURDES LAND WITHOUT BREAD/TERRE SANS PAIN Spain 1932. *Dir/Scen/Ed* Luis Buñuel *Assist* Pierre Unik, Sanchez Ventura *Photog* Eli Lotar *Commentary* Pierre Unik *Mus* Brahms *Fourth Symphony Prod* Ramon Acin. 27 mins.
A document of the monstrous conditions of life in the poorest district of northern Spain, "Las Hurdes," not far from the Portuguese border.
Famous sequences: life in the cavelike hovels; the cripples and the 12-fingered monsters; the cretin; the stream used both as a sewer and for drinking water; a goat crashing down from the rocks; bees settling on a dying donkey's eye; a child's coffin carried on the men's shoulders and then set in a brook to drift downstream; the wedding ceremony during which the heads of cocks are pulled off; the contrast between the rich church and the village poverty.
The forcefulness of its images of human degradation is intensified by the apparent matter-of-fact quality of the commentary, written by the poet Pierre Unik as though it were a typical travelogue commentary. *Land Without Bread* reflects the world of Velasquez and Goya: the poor reduced to famine,

obliged to eat unripe cherries (which gave them dysentery), sleeping on heaps of leaves, and forced to beg. Whatever slight relief might exist is shattered by the peasant's own ignorance and superstition.

Buñuel made the film with 20,000 pesetas given to him by a worker friend who had won it in a lottery. It was banned by the Spanish Republican (anti-Franco) Government of 1933–35 as "defamatory." During the Civil War The Popular Front government released this masterpiece of the social documentary, the first to be produced in Western Europe.

It has a special significance in the Buñuel canon, marking a change from the overt surrealism of his two previous films to a direct transcription of reality. Without this concern for reality, the spirit and style of his later work would have been less powerful.

*LASKY JEDNE PLAVOVLASKY THE LOVES OF A BLONDE/A BLONDE IN LOVE Czechoslovakia 1965. *Dir* Milos Forman *Scen* Milos Forman, Jaroslav Papousek, Ivan Passer *Photog* Miroslav Ondricek *Art Dir* Karel Cerny *Mus* Evzen Illin *Ed* Miroslav Hajek *Cast* Hanna Brejchova, Vladimir Pucholt, Vladimir Mensik *Prod* Barrandov Studios. 82 mins.

A young factory girl, Andula (Brejchova), meets a young dance musician, Milda (Pucholt), at a local dance and sleeps with him. But when she later visits him at his home she creates an embarrassing situation.

Antonin Novak has said: "Forman requires no more than an anecdote to depict the social and human universe within its seemingly narrow confines." Though Forman's style is to some extent derived from the *cinéma-vérité* approach, it depends on more than merely a passive recording of behavior for his impact. It depends on an instinctive sense of timing and a consistent vision of life and people. *The Loves of a Blonde*, one of the first films of the Czechoslovak *new wave* to make a impact in the West, is one of the best examples of his gentle style and wry humor. The film has two brilliant sequences: one in a dance hall when three soldiers try to pick up some girls, and the other when Andula arrives unexpectedly at the boy's home with her belongings and stubbornly endures the parents' suspicious reactions.

LAST BRIDGE (THE) LETZTE BRÜCKE (DER)

LAST CHANCE (THE) LETZTE CHANCE (DIE)

LAST LAUGH (THE) LETZTE MANN (DER)

LAST NIGHT (THE) POSLEDNAYA NOCH

LAST STAGE (THE) OSTATNI ETAP

LAST WARNING (THE) USA 1929. *Dir* Paul Leni *Scen* Alfred A. Cohn based on a novel by Thomas Fallon, Wadsworth Camp *Photog* Hal Mohr *Cast* Laura La Plante, Montagu Love, Roy d'Arcy, John Boles, Mack Swain, Margaret Livingston, "Slim" Summerville *Prod* Universal. 7,980 ft. (sound version), 7,920 ft. (silent version).

An excellent comedy-horror film in which Leni made brilliant use of quasi-expressionist sets and the moving camera. Paul Leni died suddenly the same year this and *Puzzles,* his last film, were completed.

— *The Last Warning USA 1938. *Dir* Al Rogell *Scen* Edmund L. Hartmann based on the novel *The Dead Don't Care* by Jonathan Latimer *Cast* Preston Foster, Joyce Compton, Frank Jenks *Prod* Universal. 62 mins.

Not a remake of the Leni film, but a pleasant enough comedy-thriller based on the private-eye character featured in a series of novels by Jonathan Latimer, three of which have been filmed.

LAST WILL OF DR. MABUSE (THE) see DR MABUSE, DER SPIELER

LAST YEAR AT MARIENBAD ANNÉE DERNIÈRE À MARIENBAD (L')

LATE MATTHEW PASCAL (THE) FEU MATHIAS PASCAL

*LAURA USA 1944. *Dir* Otto Preminger *Scen* Jay Dratler, Samuel Hoffenstein, Betty Reinhardt based on the novel by Vera Caspary *Photog* Joseph La Shelle *Art Dir* Lyle Wheeler, Leland Fuller *Cast* Clifton Webb, Gene Tierney, Dana Andrews, Judith Anderson, Vincent Price *Prod* 20th Century-Fox. 88 mins.

A woman's body is found in Laura's (Tierney) apartment and a detective (Andrews) believes Laura has been murdered. Laura reappears and it is discovered that the girl was a friend of one of the suspects (Price). Eventually the detective proves that a cyni-

cal, acid-tongued journalist, Waldo Ly-
decker (Webb), shot the girl by mistake
for Laura.

Rouben Mamoulian claims "I prepared
Laura, cast it, directed some of it, and
Otto Preminger, who was its producer,
decided to take over the shooting . . .
it resulted in my leaving Fox."

The world of Laura is quite different
from that of the conventional American
thriller: it is a world of rich apartments, elegance, sophistication, and taste.
But the script, and Preminger's typically
detached direction, turn the conventions
inside out and present a corrosive portrait of greed and cruelty. In fact, it
seems that Preminger (and perhaps
Mamoulian?) brought to the film the
sense of atmosphere and subtle characterizations typical of central European theater. Clifton Webb, as the cynical columnist turned jealous killer, gives
one of his best performances.

— *Laura USA 1955. Dir John Brahm
Scen Mel Dinelli Photog Lloyd Ahern
Art Dir Lyle Wheeler, Herman Blu-
menthal Cast George Sanders, Dana
Wynter, Robert Stack Prod 20th Cen-
tury-Fox TV Productions. 43 mins.

An abridged remake for television without the atmospheric style of the original
and with the story mostly presented in
a series of dialogue exchanges.

LAVENDER HILL MOB (THE) Britain 1951.
Dir Charles Crichton Scen T. E. B.
Clarke Photog Douglas Slocombe Art
Dir William Kellner Ed Seth Holt Mus
Georges Auric Cast Alec Guinness, Stan-
ley Holloway, Sidney James, Alfie Bass
Prod Ealing. 78 mins.

An apparently meek, respectable, and
honest Bank employee (Guinness) responsible for supervising deliveries of
bullion, organizes a "gang" (Holloway,
James, Bass) to steal the gold, which
they ship out of the country as Eiffel
Tower souvenir paperweights. An innocent schoolgirl buys one and, in their
efforts to trace it, they arouse police
suspicion and are eventually caught.

This lighthearted satire of British middle-class values is one of the best of
the postwar British comedies produced
at Ealing Studios under Michael Balcon. Its pace is continually lively, the
robbery sequence and the final chase incorporate a fine sense of film comedy
timing, and there is an exhilarating
sequence on the Eiffel Tower. Alec
Guinness' brilliant performance in this

and the earlier Kind Hearts and Coronets (q.v.) helped make him famous.

LAWLESS (THE) THE DIVIDING LINE USA
1949. Dir Joseph Losey Scen Geoffrey
Homes Photog Roy Hunt Art Dir L. H.
Creber Mus David Chudnow Ed H.
Smith Cast Macdonald Carey, Gail
Russell, John Sands, Lalo Rios Prod
Pine-Thomas for Paramount. 84 mins.

A young Mexican (Rios) is victimized
by racial prejudice in a small American
town. The owner-editor of the local
newspaper (Carey) and a colleague
(Russell) take up his defense when he
is wrongly accused of raping a girl and
killing a cop. He narrowly escapes lynching and the newspaper's offices are
smashed up by a mob, but he is finally
proved innocent.

Losey's second feature film offers a
jaundiced view of American middle-class
race prejudice in the Fifties. Its style
is typically energetic and forceful and
the music score effectively sustains the
mood. "Notable are Losey's reticences,
his juicy plays with sundry small characters . . . his low-key evocation of a
small Californian town . . . (It) has
a glow reminiscent of the work of
those pioneers of American photography,
Brady and Walker Evans" (Richard
Winnington).

LEAVES FROM SATAN'S BOOK BLADE AF
SATANS BOG

*LEFT HANDED GUN (THE) USA 1958. Dir
Arthur Penn Scen Leslie Stevens based
on a TV play by Gore Vidal Photog
J. Peverell Marley Art Dir Art Loel
Mus Alexander Courage Ed Folmar
Blangsted Cast Paul Newman, John
Dehner, Lita Milan, Hurd Hatfield,
James Congdon, James Best Prod Har-
oll/Warner Brothers. 102 mins. (Also
released in shortened versions.)

William Bonney — Billy the Kid — (Newman) is befriended by a Scottish rancher
and, when he is murdered, Billy sets
out to avenge him. He finds a friend in
Pat Garrett (Dehner) but is then betrayed by him and finally shot.

Arthur Penn's (and Gore Vidal's) Billy
the Kid is a confused adolescent who
only resorts to violence in response to
a world that refuses to live by his rules.
Billy's actions create a legend and he is
destroyed by his inability to live up to
that legend. This violent, expressive film
marked an impressive film debut for

TV and stage director Arthur Penn, even though it is occasionally weighed down by its symbolism. Paul Newman's forceful, Method-oriented portrayal of Billy the Kid is the best of his early performances.

LEGEND OF PRAGUE (THE) GOLEM (DER)

LEGEND OF THE NARAYAMA NARAYAMA BUSHI-KO

LENIN V OKTYABRE and **LENIN V 1918** LENIN IN OCTOBER and LENIN IN 1918 USSR 1937 and 1939. *Dir* Mikhail Romm.
— *Lenin in October: Scen* Alexei Kapler *Photog* Boris Volchok *Art Dir* Boris Dubrovsky-Eshke *Mus* Anatoli Alexandrov *Cast* Boris Shchukin, Nikolai Oklopkov, Vasili Vanin, I. Golshtab *Prod* Mosfilm. 111 mins.
— *Lenin in 1918: Scen* Alexei Kapler, Tatiana Zlatogorova *Photog* Boris Volchok *Art Dir* Boris Dubrovsky-Eshke, V. Ivanov *Mus* Nikolai Kryukov *Cast* Boris Shchukin, Nikolai Cherkassov, Mikhail Gelovani, Nikolai Bogolyubov, Vasili Vanin *Prod* Mosfilm. 132 mins.
The life of Lenin (Shchukin) during the Revolution and the following year in which several historical characters such as Gorky (Cherkassov), Stalin (Golshtab), Voroshilov (Bogolyubov), etc. appear.
[*Lenin in October* was rushed into production in 1937 on Stalin's orders to mark the 20th Anniversary of the Revolution and was completed in three months. Its success prompted the production of *Lenin in 1918*. A good script, excellent direction, and convincing sets outweigh the obvious historical inaccuracies (Lenin discussing Trotsky's "treachery" in 1917!) and prevent these films from being mere propaganda pieces.]
OTHER SOVIET FILMS ON LENIN:
— *Leninskaya Kino-Pravda* 1925. *Dir* Dziga Vertov. 3 reels. (documentary).
— *Three Songs of Lenin* (*q.v.*) 1934. *Dir/Scen* Dziga Vertov. 56 mins. (documentary).
— *The Man With a Gun* 1938. *Dir* Sergei Yutkevich *Cast* M. Strauch (Lenin). 103 mins.
— *The Vyborg Side* (*q.v.*) 1939. *Dir/Scen* Grigori Kozintsev, Leonid Trauberg *Cast* M. Strauch (Lenin). (Part III of the *Maxim* trilogy).

— *Lenin* 1948. *Dir* Mikhail Romm, V. Belyaev. 65 mins. (documentary).
— *Stories About Lenin* 1958. *Dir* Sergei Yutkevich *Cast* M. Strauch (Lenin). 11 reels. Sovcolor.
— *The Last Pages of Lenin* 1963. *Dir* Fedor Tyapkin. (documentary).
— *Lenin in Poland* 1965. *Dir* Sergei Yutkevich *Cast* M. Strauch (Lenin). 97 mins. Sovscope.
— *Three Springs of Lenin* 1964. *Dir* Leonid Kristi. (documentary).
— *Heart of a Mother* 1966. *Dir* Mark Donskoy *Cast* Rodion Nakhapetov. 100 mins. Sovscope.
— *A Mother's Devotion* 1967. *Dir* Mark Donskoy *Cast* Rodion Nakhapetov. Sovscope.
— *Lenin in Switzerland* 1967. *Dir* G. Alexandrov.
— *The Sixth of July* 1967. *Dir* Yuli Karassik *Cast* Yuri Kayurov (Lenin).
— *Lenin in 1903* 1970. *Dir* Yuli Karassik.
— *Red Square* 1970. *Dir* V. Ordinski.
The character of Lenin is also seen briefly in Eisenstein's *October* (*q.v.*), Yutkevich's *Yakov Sverdlov* (1940), and *The Blue Notebook* (1963).

LEON MORIN, PRETRE LÉON MORIN, PRIEST France/Italy 1961. *Dir* Jean-Pierre Melville *Scen* Jean-Pierre Melville based on the novel by Béatrix Beck *Photog* Henri Decaë *Art Dir* Daniel Guéret *Mus* Martial Solal, Albert Raisner *Ed* Monique Bonnot *Cast* Jean-Paul Belmondo, Emmanuèle Riva *Prod* Rome-Paris Films. 117 mins.
During the German Occupation of France a young widow (Riva) who is a Communist and anticlerical meets a young, handsome priest (Belmondo) and a warm relationship develops. She falls in love with him and tries to make him break his vow of celibacy, but he resists and, when the war ends, they part.
This edifying work justifies Pierre Kast's statement in 1953 that "A good film could certainly be made from *Léon Morin, prêtre*." [Melville himself says: "Between you and me there are only two or three ideas that belong to me. It's a film of prudence, smooth and perfect, as comfortable in its moral as in its technique." Riva succeeds admirably in conveying the inner turmoil of the woman, but Belmondo lacks the spiritual authority that his role demands.]

LEOPARD (THE) GATTOPARDO (IL)

LES MISERABLES MISÉRABLES (LES)

LET JUSTICE BE DONE JUSTICE EST FAITE

LETTER TO THREE WIVES (A) USA 1948. *Dir* Joseph L. Mankiewicz *Scen* Vera Caspary, Joseph L. Mankiewicz based on the novel by John Klempner *Photog* Arthur Miller *Art Dir* Lyle Wheeler, J. Russell Spencer *Mus* Alfred Newman *Ed* J. Watson Webb *Cast* Jeanne Crain, Linda Darnell, Ann Sothern, Kirk Douglas *Prod* 20th Century-Fox. 103 mins.

Three wives (Crain, Sothern, Darnell) receive a letter addressed to all of them from a beautiful woman (Celeste Holm speaks the role) telling them that she has run away with one of their husbands. In three flashbacks the relationship of each woman with her husband and the husband's with the woman is shown. Each discovers cause for anxiety but the couples are finally reconciled. A well-made psychological comedy of morals with witty dialogue. One of Mankiewicz's best films.

*LET THERE BE LIGHT USA 1946. *Dir* John Huston *Photog* Stanley Cortez *Prod* Army Pictorial Service. 58 mins.

Together with Huston's *The Battle of San Pietro* this is undoubtedly one of the greatest war documentaries ever made. Banned by the War Department on its completion and never shown publicly, it dealt with the psychiatric treatment of soldiers suffering from the effects of war. As the opening title to the film states "No scenes were staged. The cameras merely recorded what took place in an army hospital." Its deep pacifist implications, its humanitarian attitudes, and its suggestion that war could do such terrible things to people's emotions were clearly too strong for the War Department. Yet for Huston. "It was the most hopeful and optimistic and even joyous thing I had a hand in. I felt as though I were going to church every day out in that hospital." Huston's experiences on this film are clearly evident in *The Red Badge of Courage* (*q.v.*), which itself suffered at the hands of producers.

LETYAT ZHURAVLI THE CRANES ARE FLYING USSR 1957. *Dir* Mikhail Kalatozov *Scen* Victor Rosov from his own play

The Immortal Photog Sergei Urusevski *Art Dir* Y. Svedetelev *Mus* M. Weinberg *Cast* Tatyana Samoilova, Alexei Batalov, Vasili Merkuriev, A. Shvorin *Prod* Mosfilm. 94 mins.

A young Russian girl (Samoilova) whose fiancé (Batalov) is away at the war, marries a man (Shvorin) who has raped her and whom she does not love. Evacuated to Siberia, she has a hard life, becomes a nurse and, after the war, is told of her fiancé's death. She refuses to believe it and waits in vain for his return.

"The script contains none of the conventional propaganda that made us grate our teeth in most films of the Stalin era. The sometimes lighthearted romanticism and lyricism of the images add power to the story. The main 'purple passages': the morning goodbye on the stairway; the departure to the war; the rape during the bombing; finding the demolished house; flight after the speech in the hospital; the final scene on the station platform. There are also a certain number of intimate scenes that are sparklingly natural and vivacious" (J. Doniol-Valcroze). Certain magazine story clichés, such as the rape, are intrusive, but the film, a sort of 1941–1945 *War and Peace* has passion and authenticity. The characters are not cardboard but complex and even the speeches (such as that in the hospital) contain no propaganda.

Along with the virtuoso camerawork by Urusevsky, the film's centerpiece is the performance of Tatyana Samoilova, a touching beauty caught up in all the horrors of war. The film was a great international success and received the Grand Prix at Cannes.

LETZTE BRUCKE (DIE) THE LAST BRIDGE Austria/Yugoslavia 1953. *Dir* Helmut Käutner *Yugoslav Co-Dir* Gustav Gavrin *Scen* Helmut Käutner, Norbert Kunze *Photog* Elio Carniel *Art Dir* Otto Pischinger *Mus* Carl de Groof *Cast* Maria Schell, Bernhard Wicki, Barbara Rütting, Carl Mohner *Prod* Cosmopol, Vienna/UFUS, Belgrade. 95 mins.

A German nurse, Helga (Schell), is taken prisoner by Yugoslav partisans during the war. As time passes, she comes to sympathize with them and their leader (Wicki) and is killed as she tries to bring medical supplies to them across a bridge.

One of the best German films of the

Fifties. Käutner's cool direction (he had to work with a mixed German-Yugoslav unit and cast) is based largely on his use of natural Yugoslav settings, while the theme expresses his hatred for the Hitlerian war. He also makes effective use of the sad smile and bewildered air of Maria Schell, whose performance in this film made her a star.

LETZTE CHANCE (DIE) THE LAST CHANCE Switzerland 1945. *Dir* Leopold Lindtberg *Scen* Richard Schweitzer *Photog* Emil Berna *Mus* Robert Blum *Cast* E. G. Morrison, John Hoy, Ray Reagan, Luisa Rossi, Romano Calo, Giuseppe Galeati, Thérèse Giehse *Prod* Praesens Film. 105 mins.

In northern Italy in September 1943 the SS has installed a Fascist government and is deporting slave-workers and Allied prisoners. Two prisoners, an Englishman and an American, escape from the train during a raid, meet up with a group of civilian refugees of ten nationalities (including several Jews) and, after a terrible journey over the mountains, succeed in crossing into Switzerland.

This semidocumentary film is a sincere and moving attempt to depict the possibilities of all peoples living together in peace, memorable for its striking sense of actuality and for the scenes on the Swiss frontier. It was a tremendous success, though perhaps more because it expressed the feelings of the time than for its style.

LETZTE MANN (DER) THE LAST LAUGH (literally, THE LAST MAN) Germany 1924. *Dir* F. W. Murnau *Scen* Carl Meyer *Photog* Karl Freund *Art Dir* Robert Herlth, Walter Röhrig *Cast* Emil Jannings, Maly Delschaft, Max Hiller, Hans Unterkirchen *Prod* UFA. 6,500 ft.

Because he has become too old, the doorman (Jannings) of a Berlin luxury hotel has his uniform taken away from him and is given the job of looking after the lavatories. Humiliated, he thinks of committing suicide in the cheap tenement where he lives with his daughter (Delschaft) and her fiancé. But (in order to have a happy ending) he inherits a fortune and becomes a client of the hotel.

Carl Mayer's script for this film in the *Kammerspiel* style forms a trilogy with *Scherben* (*q.v.*) and *Sylvester* (*q.v.*) (both directed by Lupu-Pick). Although his original idea undoubtedly came from Gogol's *The Cloak,* his script became a powerful study of the importance Germans attach to uniforms. The final shooting script was developed in collaboration with Jannings, Murnau, and the cameraman, Karl Freund, who later described his own involvement: "He had considered using the moving camera from the start. He asked me if I could film an actress in long shot and then, by traveling forward, show a close up of only her eyes, this being the moment when the doorman's aunt discovers that he has been put in charge of the lavatories. He said he wanted my camera on a dolly at all times." When Mayer saw the possibilities of exploiting this technique he rewrote his script in terms of camera movements.

Mayer, Freund, and Murnau developed effects that were then very new. For example, in the scene in which Jannings, in the depths of despair, gets drunk, he remains still while the camera weaves about. Never have the possibilities of camera movement been so fully exploited. As Marcel Carné, then a young critic, described it in 1929: "The camera on a trolley glides, rises, zooms, or weaves where the story takes it. It is no longer fixed, but takes part in the action and becomes a *character* in the drama. The actors are no longer simply placed before the camera; rather it sneaks up on them when they are least expecting it. This technique in *The Last Laugh* allows us to know the smallest corner of the lugubrious Atlantic Hotel. The camera descends in the elevator, revealing the hall whose vastness is increased by the tracking shot, takes us through the revolving door, and ejects us under Jannings' stately umbrella." This introductory scene described by Carné set the film's tone and style.

Adopting the *Kammerspiel* approach, this tragedy of ordinary people respects the rule of the three dramatic unities — although it uses two locations, the hotel and the doorman's home. It dispenses with titles (though this has recently been questioned) and uses symbolic images such as the revolving door or a wheel of fortune in key scenes. In addition to the moving camera, Murnau uses angle shots to express ideas: high angle shots belittling Jannings in the depths of the lavatory and low angle shots to emphasized his triumph. As the mistreated doorman, Jannings gives a restrained, though occasionally mannered, performance; in the expressionist tradition, he makes much use of his movements and gestures for expressive effect. The film's great success in the USA led Carl Laemmle to object: "Everybody knows that a lavatory attendant makes a lot more money than a doorman."

REMAKE:

— *Der Letzte Mann German Federal Republic 1955. Dir Harald Braun Scen Georg Hurdalek, Herbert Witt based on the original Photog Richard Angst Art Dir Robert Herlth Cast Hans Albers, Romy Schneider, Joachim Fuchsberger, Rudolf Forster. 105 mins. A routine remake in which the doorman becomes head waiter (Albers) at an elegant spa hotel.

LIAISONS AMOUREUSES (LES) MORTE-SAISON DES AMOURS (LA)

LIAISONS DANGEREUSES 1960 (LES) DANGEROUS MEETINGS France 1959. Dir Roger Vadim Scen Roger Vailland, Roger Vadim, Claude Brûlé based on the novel by Choderlos de Laclos Photog Marcel Grignon Art Dir Robert Guisgang Mus Thelonius Monk, Jack Murray, etc. Ed Victoria Mercanton Cast Gérard Philipe, Jeanne Moreau, Annette Vadim, Jean-Louis Trintignant, Jeanne Valéry Prod Films Marceau. 106 mins.

Vadim's version betrayed the splendid novel by de Laclos, not because he updated it to 1960, nor because he made Valmont (Philipe) and Madame de Merteuil (Moreau) husband and wife, but because he vulgarized its passionate free-thinking attitudes and its portrait of a corrupt upper-class society. Gérard Philipe might have made an ideal Valmont and he nevertheless gives a notable performance, as does Jeanne Moreau as Madame de Merteuil.

LIANG SHAN-PO AND CHU YING-TAI THE LOVES OF LIANG SHAN-PO AND CHU YING-TAI/BUTTERFLY LOVERS China 1953. Dir Sang Hu and Huang Sha Scen Hsu Chin based on a Shaohsing opera Photog Huang Shao-fen Mus Liu Ju-tseng Cast Yuan Hsueh-fen, Fan Jui-chuan Prod Shanghai Studio. 76 mins. Agfacolor.

A young woman (Hsueh-fen) disguised as a man falls in love with a student (Jui-chuan). Their parents separate them and she is forced to marry another. On her way to the wedding, the tomb of her lover (who had died of grief) opens and she joins him in death.

A sort of Chinese Romeo and Juliet involving characters from an old Chinese legend that inspired a Shaohsing (a region of Shanghai) opera. This delightful, though occasionally affected, film version is itself virtually an opera in form.

*LIEBE DER JEANNE NEY (DIE) THE LOVE OF JEANNE NEY Germany 1927. Dir G. W. Pabst Scen Ladislaus Vajda based on the novel by Ilya Ehrenburg Photog Fritz Arno Wagner, Walter R. Lach Art Dir Viktor Trivas, Otto Hunte Cast Brigitte Helm, Eugen Jenson, Edith Jehanne, Uno Henning, Fritz Rasp, Vladimir Sokolov Prod UFA. 7,150 ft.

A love story set in Paris and the Crimea during the Civil War, in which the love of a French bourgeois girl (Jehanne) and a young Russian Communist (Henning) is thwarted by an unscrupulous adventurer (Rasp).

Although Ilya Ehrenburg protested to UFA about the adaptation of his novel, Pabst's film is remarkably faithful to its spirit and character. It is, however, Pabst's eloquent style in expressing the psychology of the individuals concerned and his emphasis on realistic detail (albeit studio-made) rather than the melodramatic plot that makes the film memorable. "At Pabst's will, Wagner's camera nosed into the corners and ran with the players . . . Every curve, every angle, every approach of the lens was controlled by the material that it photographed for the expression of mood . . . Mood succeeded mood, each perfect in its tension and understanding" (Paul Rotha).

LIEBELEI Germany 1932. Dir Max Ophüls Scen Hans Wilhelm, Curt Alexander based on the play by Arthur Schnitzler Photog Franz Planer Art Dir G. Pellon Mus Theo Mackeben Ed Friedel Buchott Cast Wolfgang Liebeneiner, Magda Schneider, Luise Ulrich, Gustaf Gründgens, Olga Tschechowa, Willy Eichberger Prod Elite Tonfilm. 88 mins.

In gay Vienna at the turn of the century a young lieutenant (Liebeneiner) falls in love with Christine (Schneider). He is killed in a duel by the baron (Gründgens), whose wife (Tschechowa) had earlier been his mistress, and Christine commits suicide in despair.

"Strong antimilitaristic feelings manifested themselves in Max Ophüls delightful *Liebelei* . . . It contrasts in a very touching way the tenderness of a love story with the severity of the military code of honor" (Siegfried Kracauer). Ophüls style has great charm, especially in his skillful creation of the atmosphere and ostentation of Imperial Vienna. Unforgettable is the sleigh ride through the snowy woods when Fritz and Christine swear eternal love. "*Liebelei* had fascinated me since I first read it," Ophüls has said. "When, after a simple telephone call I found I was to direct, I saw the opportunity of making a picture with young people, unspoiled by stardom. In addition, I had a profound respect for Schnitzler's play. The film was born under a lucky star."

This was Ophüls first major success. He was not able to attend its Berlin premier (March 16, 1933) because, as a Jew, the advent of the Third Reich forced him to leave Germany. It was a great success in many countries but was released in Germany without the name of Ophüls and Schnitzler on the credits. Ironically, it was also banned after the war by an Allied Commission.

While in Paris, Ophüls prepared a French version of *Liebelei,* largely with the original cast:

— *Une histoire d'amour* France 1933. *Dir* Max Ophüls *Dialogue* André Doderet *Photog* Ted Pahle *Cast* Magda Schneider, Wolfgang "Georges" Liebeneiner, Olga Tschechowa, Simone Héliard, Georges Rigaud.

"All we re-did were the close-ups; the rest was the German version dubbed into French. In all, it took about 12 days work" (Max Ophüls).

OTHER VERSIONS:

— *Liebelei* Germany 1927. *Dir* Jacob and Luise Fleck *Scen* Herbert Juttke, George C. Klaren based on Schnitzler's play *Photog* Eduard Hoesch *Cast* Fred Louis Lerch, Henry Stuart, Jaro Fürth, Evelyn Holtz. 7 reels.

— *Christine* France/Italy 1958. *Dir* Pierre Gaspard-Huit *Scen* Pierre Gaspard-Huit, Hans Wilhelm based on Schnitzler's play *Photog* Christian Matras *Mus* Georges Auric *Cast* Romy Schneider, Alain Delon, Micheline Presle, Jean-Claude Brialy. 109 mins. Eastman Color.

A pleasant remake that lacks the beauties of the Ophüls version but that makes excellent use of color and sets in re-creating the atmosphere of Vienna. Romy Schneider plays the role of Christine, which her mother had played in Ophüls' film.

LIEBESKARUSSEL (DAS) see RONDE (LA)

LIED DER STROME (DAS) SONG OF THE RIVERS German Democratic Republic 1954. *Dir* Joris Ivens *Scen* Joris Ivens, Vladimir Pozner *Assist* Joop Huisken, Robert Menegoz *Photog* cameramen in 32 countries *Mus* Dmitri Shostakovich, song written by Bertolt Brecht, sung by Paul Robeson *Prod* DEFA. 102 mins.

A documentary-compilation film about the life of people living near six great rivers — the Mississippi, the Amazon, the Ganges, the Nile, the Yangtse, and the Volga — produced for the Congress (October 11, 1954) of the World Federation of Trade Unions.

"I had always dreamed of making a film showing the workers of the world," Joris Ivens has said, "and the importance of their uniting their power. I wanted to make a fresco, a hymn to the power of man." The composer, Shostakovich, wanted "to develop the essential idea of the film, that all the riches and goodness of life come from the hands of the workers, and only from them." The opening sequence that shows workers denouncing colonialism and their exploitation is the best, while the Volga episode is the weakest. There are some striking editing effects: for example, the sequence that shows the Indians of Brazil lighting their fires as in the Stone Age and then cuts to the explosion of an atomic bomb. Some sequences are reminiscent of *New Earth* (*q.v.*)

The film was released in 18 languages versions and was banned by the censors of several countries.

LIFE (A) UNE VIE

LIFE DANCES ON CARNET DE BAL

LIFE OF A PEKING POLICEMAN (THE) China 1950. *Dir* Shih Hui *Scen* Chang Liu-ching based on a novel by Lao She *Cast* Shi Hui, Wei Ho-ling, Lichi He *Prod* Kun Lun Studio, Shanghai. 100 mins. approx.

A sort of Chinese *Cavalcade* (*q.v.*), full of robust humor. Focusing on the life of one family, it shows the 50 years of Chinese history from the Boxer Rebellion (1900) to the Liberation (1949) and depicts feudalism, the revolutionary movements, the repression of the Kuomintang, and the Japanese occupation.

LIFE OF EMILE ZOLA (THE) USA 1937. *Dir* William Dieterle *Scen* Heinz Herald, Geza Herczeg, Norman Reilly Raine *Photog* Tony Gaudio *Art Dir* Anton Grot *Mus* Max Steiner *Ed* Warren Low *Cast* Paul Muni, Joseph Schildkraut, Donald Crisp, Gale Sondergaard, Vladimir Sokoloff, Henry O'Neill *Prod* Warner Brothers. 116 mins.

A dramatized biography of the writer (Muni) and his friendship with Cézanne (Sokoloff) that concentrates mainly on Zola's involvement with the Dreyfus (Schildkraut) case.

Although Hollywood did a rather poor job of re-creating the French period atmosphere, the film is nevertheless quite well made and often engrossing, with a good, if occasionally overly-mannered performance by Paul Muni. It is the best of Warner Brother's biographical films.

Despite three Academy Awards and a screening at the Venice Festival, the film was banned in France and the Province of Québèc, Canada. It was released in France in 1952 and in Québèc only in 1964.

See also *Affaire Dreyfus* (*L'*)

LIFE OF O'HARU (THE) SAIKAKU ICHIDAI ONNA

LIFE OF THE LAY PREACHER (THE) EVANGELIEMANDENS LIV

LIGHTS OF VARIETY LUCI DEL VARIETÀ

LIGHT WITHIN (THE) MÜDE TOD (DER)

*LILITH USA 1964. *Dir* Robert Rossen *Scen* Robert Rossen based on the novel by J. R. Salamanca *Photog* Eugene Schuftan *Art Dir* Richard Sylbert *Mus* Kenyon Hopkins *Ed* Aram Avakian *Cast* Warren Beatty, Jean Seberg, Peter Fonda, Kim Hunter *Prod* Centaur. 116 mins.

Vincent Bruce (Beatty) is selected by the head therapist, Bea Brice (Hunter), to work as a trainee therapist in an asylum for wealthy schizophrenics. He falls in love with a beautiful patient, Lilith Arthur (Seberg), who gradually draws him into her own private world. Another patient (Fonda) makes a box for Lilith as a sign of his love but, in his jealousy, Vincent returns it to him, saying Lilith had sent it back. The patient commits suicide and Vincent is so shattered he turns to Bea Brice for professional help.

This was Rossen's last film before his death in 1966 and it is undoubtedly his best. Its portrait of the interior world of the mentally disturbed is full of such nuances and subtleties as to make films like Minnelli's *The Cobweb* and *David and Lisa* (*q.v.*), however sincere, seem unreal. Rossen captures beautifully the ambiguity of Lilith and actually makes us experience what madness feels like.

LIMELIGHT USA 1952. *Dir/Scen/Mus* Charles Chaplin *Assist* Robert Aldrich, Jerry Epstein, Wheeler Dryden *Photog* Karl Struss, Rollie Totheroh *Art Dir* Eugène Lourié *Choreog* André Eglevsky, Melissa Hayden, Charles Chaplin *Cast* Charles Chaplin, Claire Bloom, Buster Keaton, Sidney Chaplin, Nigel Bruce, Marjorie Bennett, Snub Pollard *Prod* Celebrated Films for United Artists. 143 mins.

Calvero (Chaplin), once a great comedian, has lost his ability to make people laugh and takes to drink. He prevents a young dancer (Bloom) from committing suicide and gives her confidence in herself. She becomes a star while he leaves to join a group of street musicians. When she finds him he agrees to take part with her in a benefit show. His act is a triumph, but he dies in the wings while the dancer is on stage. This tragedy of Shakespearean grandeur, full of profound wisdom and human warmth, is in part undoubtedly autobiographical. It takes place before 1914 in the London music-hall atmosphere in which Chaplin had been trained as a boy. There is something of his father in the Calvero who asks himself if he isn't successful anymore because he's an alcoholic or if he's alcoholic because he isn't successful anymore. Although old age and the fact that he is forgotten are tearing him apart, he still believes in people and refuses to give in. It is through this "get up and walk" aproach that he cures the young dancer of her paralysis.

Calvero himself has to suffer audiences' whistles and boos, going from bad to worse and ending up begging in pubs as a street singer. When he looks at himself in a mirror, he sees old age and death underneath the make-up. Then taking his handkerchief (like an enormous towel) from his pocket, he creates a veritable "Ecce Homo," abused, scoffed at, beaten, insulted, spat upon, and scourged. His face is spattered with tears, spit, and blood, but he is man triumphing over death and defeat with courage and dignity. "With age comes a keener sense of dignity, which prevents us from ridiculing other men" (Publicity for the film). The climax is a death and rebirth. Man's short span of conscious life is set against infinity and the universe; the man who was once a great comedian hands on the torch to a young dancer. In this way he humbles himself with supreme modesty, presenting himself as a dead leaf to fertilize the earth of the future.

The film's numerous gags and comic routines are never merely diversions but are an integral part of its theme — a theme whose tragic proportions have profound implications for the world in the 20th century. Claire Bloom, then relatively unknown, gives a brilliant performance. Buster Keaton (as Calvero's partner) has little to do but does it delightfully. The film's theme song, "Eternally" is one of the best-remembered songs of the Fifties.

LIMITE Brazil 1930. *Dir/Scen/Ed* Mario Peixoto *Photog* Edgar Brasil *Cast* Iolanda Bernardes, Carmen Santos, Tatiana Rey, Mario Peixoto. 6 reels. Silent.
A unique work by a director who was only 18 years old when he make the film, whose only experience was in film societies, and whose only training was his own love of the cinema. Its theme is man's limitations and it seems to have exercised great influence on the Brazilian cinema through its photography, its editing, its experiments, and its melancholy tone.
N.B. During a visit to Brazil, I was not able to see this "unknown" masterpiece because Peixoto had retired to an almost desert island and was carefully hiding it. (For an analysis of the film see *L'Age du cinéma* no. 6, 1952).

LINE OF DESTINY (THE) REKAVA

*LISTEN TO BRITAIN Britain 1942. *Dir/Scen/Ed* Humphrey Jennings, Stewart McAllister *Prod* Crown Film Unit. 20 mins.
An unforgettable film poem whose subtle rhythms and evocative imagery, freely linked by contrasting and complementary sounds, create an impressionistic portrait of a country at war.

LITTLE CAESAR USA 1930. *Dir* Mervin LeRoy *Scen* Francis Faragoh based on the novel by William R. Burnett *Photog* Tony Gaudio *Cast* Edward G. Robinson, Douglas Fairbanks Jr., Ralph Ince, Glenda Farrell, George Stone, Stanley Fields, William Collier, Jr. *Prod* First National/Warner Brothers. 77 mins.
The story of the rise and fall of a gang leader, Rico (Robinson), and his lieutenant (Fairbanks). After defeating rival gangsters (Ince, Fields), he dominates the town. A woman (Farrell) betrays him and he is killed by the police.
This violent and callous film is, with *Scarface* (*q.v.*), one of the best American gangster films of the Thirties and made Edward G. Robinson's reputation as a "hard-boiled" actor. [His last line ("Mother of God, is this the end of Rico") is famous. "In this gangster film, the audience saw the tough, fighting world where the question of right is thrust aside for the question of might — that world of naked, crude essentials by which they themselves were threatened" (Lewis Jacobs).]

LITTLE FOXES (THE) USA 1941. *Dir* William Wyler *Scen* Lillian Hellman based on her own play *Photog* Gregg Toland *Art Dir* Stephen Goosson *Mus* Meredith Wilson *Ed* Daniel Mandell *Cast* Bette Davis, Herbert Marshall, Teresa Wright, Richard Carlson, Dan Duryea, Carl Benton Reid *Prod* Sam Goldwyn for RKO. 116 mins.
In a small town in the South at the turn of the century the brothers of Regina (Davis), an avaricious woman who is married to a banker (Marshall), need money to finance a cotton mill and Regina agrees to help. One brother, Oscar (Reid), also wants his son (Duryea) to marry Regina's daughter (Wright). Oscar's son steals some bonds from Regina's husband who discovers the loss. He threatens to disinherit Regina but dies of a heart attack. Regina promises to keep silent in return for

a large interest in the mill. Her daughter stalks out of the house in disgust.

Together with *Dead End* (*q.v.*), which Lillian Hellman also wrote, this is Wyler's best film and includes an extraordinary performance by Bette Davis as an avaricious but still beautiful woman.

The best known sequence is that in which her sick husband, having discovered her greed and trickery, refuses to give her money. She tells him that she has always hated him. He has a heart attack and she coldly watches him die.

For André Bazin, in this death scene: "The maximum cinematic coefficient coincides paradoxically with the minimum possible *mise en scène*. Nothing could better increase the dramatic power of this scene than the absolute immobility of the camera. The camera does not behave like an itinerant viewer. Rather, because of the frame of the screen and the ideal coordinates of dramatic geometry the camera arranges the action." This was a key work for André Bazin, whose famous analysis of the film is in Part I of his *Qu'est-ce que le cinéma?*

LITTLE FUGITIVE (THE) USA 1953. *Dir/Scen* Morris Engel, Ray Ashley, Ruth Orkin *Photog* Morris Engel *Ed* Ruth Orkin, Lester Troos *Mus* Eddy Manson *Cast* Rickie Andrusco, Ricky Brewster, Winifred Cushing, Jay Williams. 73 mins.

Lenny (Brewster) and Joey (Andrusco), two young boys, are left alone when their widowed mother (Cushing) has to leave town. Lenny tricks Joey into thinking he has killed a friend and Joey runs away. He goes to Coney Island, where he forgets his troubles among the side shows and merry-go-rounds and spends the night on the beach. A pony-ride attendant (Williams) gets in touch with Lenny, who takes Joey home before their mother returns.

This low-budget film by a group of semiprofessionals is one of the best films of the New York school and an authentic observation of American life.

LITTLE MAN, WHAT NOW? USA 1934. *Dir* Frank Borzage *Scen* William Anthony McGuire based on the novel *Kleiner Mann, was nun?* by Hans Fallada *Photog* Norbert Brodine *Ed* Milton Carruth *Cast* Margaret Sullavan, Douglas Montgomery, Alan Hale, Muriel Kirkland, Alan Mowbray, Mae Marsh *Prod* Universal. 90 mins.

Based on an excellent novel by Fallada, this is one of Borzage's best films. It is a touching and authentic portrait of Germany in the grip of unemployment, with remarkable performances by Margaret Sullavan and Alan Hale.
— *Kleiner Mann, was nun?* Germany 1933. *Dir* Fritz Wendhausen *Scen* based on the novel by Hans Fallada *Cast* Herta Thiele, Viktor de Kowa, Hermann Thimig.

An excellent version of the novel and according to many contemporary critics, the best German film of 1933.

LITTLE MATCH GIRL (THE) PETITE MARCHANDE D'ALLUMETTES (LA)

LIVING IKIRU

LIVING DESERT (THE) USA 1953. *Dir* James Algar *Scen* James Algar, Winston Hibler, Ted Sears *Photog* N. Paul Kenworthy, Jr., Robert H. Crandall *Special Processes* Ub Iwerks *Anim Effects* Josh Meador, John Hench, Art Riley *Mus* Paul Smith *Ed* Norman Palmer *Prod* Walt Disney. 72 mins. Technicolor.

The first of the *True Life Adventure* series. It is a compilation of footage (some shot by nauralists) showing the habits of various animals and insects that inhabit the desert areas of the USA. Trick editing and special animation process work was used to manipulate many of the scenes in order to "humanize" the animals, as, for example, when scorpions are made to "dance" the bolero in time with the music. [The film has the same cosy anthropomorphism as a Disney cartoon and its facetious commentary and vulgar musical score are typical of many other films in this series.]

LOLA France/Italy 1960. *Dir/Scen* Jacques Demy *Photog* Raoul Coutard *Art Dir* Bernard Evein *Mus* Michel Legrand *Ed* Anne-Marie Cotret *Cast* Anouk Aimée, Jacques Harden, Marc Michel, Elina Labourdette, Margo Lion *Prod* Rome-Paris Films/Euro-International. 91 mins. Franscope.

In Nantes, a cabaret dancer, Lola (Aimée), is courted by a childhood friend (Michel). However, she is still in love with Michel (Harden), who had left her with their child when he went off to seek his fortune. Lola spends the night with another man, then Michel reappears, rich, and takes Lola away.

A lighthearted, precisely constructed film about love, with an almost balletic sense of rhythm set against the urban background of Nantes. It belongs very much to a kind of "poetic neorealism" of the Sixties and owes much to Raoul Coutard's evocative camerawork. A subtle relationship is developed between Anouk Aimée and Elina Labourdette, who is a Lola-grown-old, but who also suggests Bresson's *La Dame du bois de Boulogne*.

[Demy dedicated the film to Ophüls and, in fact, the style is not dissimilar to *La Ronde* (*q.v.*).]

LOLA MONTES France/Germany 1955. *Dir* Max Ophüls *Scen* Max Ophüls, Annette Wademant, Franz Geiger based on the novel *La Vie Extraordinaire de Lola Montès* by Cecil Saint-Laurent *Photog* Christian Matras *Art Dir* Jean d'Eaubonne, Willy Schatz *Mus* Georges Auric *Ed* Madeleine Gug *Cast* Martine Carol, Anton Walbrook, Peter Ustinov, Ivan Desny, Will Quadflieg, Oscar Werner, Henri Guisol, Lise Delamare, Hélèna Manson *Prod* Gamma Films-Florida/Oska Films. 140 mins. Eastman Color. CinemaScope. (Cuts reduced the original length to 110 mins. and the re-edited general release version was 90 mins.)

A ringmaster (Ustinov) introduces Lola Montès (Carol), who recalls her unhappy marriage in Scotland, her romances with Liszt (Quadflieg), and a shy student (Werner), her boisterous affair with the King of Bavaria (Walbrook), and the 1848 Revolution that cost him his throne.

Lola Montès, based on Saint-Laurent's popular (but historically inaccurate) novel, was planned as a super production with an international cast. It was made in French, English, and German versions and cost 650 million francs. But what might have been only a spectacular about the scandalous life of Lola Montès was transformed by Ophüls into what many consider his masterpiece. Though there are weak sequences (the romance with Liszt is tasteless and too long) Ophüls's unorthodox narrative technique works brilliantly. The circus scenes are visually stunning and the flashbacks exuberantly baroque, while Ophüls' ingenious "poly-visual" fragmentation of the CinemaScope image and use of non-naturalistic color and sound aroused the admiration of many critics.

[Ophüls said that he "was struck by a series of news items which, directly or indirectly, took me back to Lola: Judy Garland's nervous breakdown, the sentimental adventures of Zsa Zsa Gabor . . . The questions asked by the audience in *Lola* were inspired by certain radio programs."

Despite its qualities, *Lola Montès* was one of the biggest commercial flops of all time and led to the bankruptcy of the powerful Gamma Company. Audiences found the unusual narrative technique difficult to follow and the first reaction of the producers was to cut the film by 30 minutes. When this didn't help, they re-edited the film behind Ophüls' back, put the story in chronological order, and reduced it to 90 minutes. This too fared badly commercially. Ophüls died a few weeks after the re-edited French version was shown in Paris. In 1969, the original version was reconstituted and re-released and received enthusiastic critical response.]

OTHER VERSIONS:

— *Lola Montez* Germany 1919. *Dir* Rudolf Walther-Fein *Scen* Robert Heymann *Cast* Marija Leiko, Hans Albers. 5 reels.

— *Lola Montez, die Tänzerin des Königs* Germany 1922. *Dir* Willi Wolff *Scen* Paul Merzbach, Willi Wolff *Cast* Ellen Richter, Arnold Korff, Georg Alexander. 6 reels.

*LONELY BOY Canada 1962. *Dir* Wolf Koenig, Roman Kroiter *Photog* Wolf Koenig *Ed* John Spotton, Guy Coté *Prod* National Film Board of Canada. 26 mins.

A *cinéma-vérité* study of pop singer Paul Anka and the adolescent hysteria he generated. It is a powerful social document, whose impact is heightened by brilliant sound and picture editing. It was one of the first films to prove the merits of the portable camera-sound systems in probing character and social phenomena.

LONELY WOMAN (THE) VIAGGIO IN ITALIA

LONESOME USA 1928. *Dir* Paul Fejos *Scen* Edmund T. Lowe based on a story by Mann Page *Photog* Gilbert Warrenton *Ed* Frank Atkinson *Cast* Glenn Tryon, Barbara Kent *Prod* Universal. 6,193 ft. Released in part-dialogue and silent versions.

A young worker (Tryon) and a telephonist (Kent) meet by chance, go to Luna Park, and are separated again by the crowds. Both are miserable at having lost their first love until they discover they are neighbors.

Lonesome was Hungarian Paul Fejos' second film and one of the rare Hollywood films of the Twenties that showed the world of ordinary people and life in a big city with its crowds and amusement areas. The film is full of poetic charm and is often humorous, but its gentle sentiment never falls into sentimentality. It does not contain the inherent bitterness of Vidor's *The Crowd* (*q.v.*), but the justice of its observation, its deep gentleness, its feeling for gesture and expression raise it above the level of just another entertainment film.

[Fejos made extensive use of a hand-held camera to follow the couple through the crowds.]

— **The Affair of Susan* USA 1935. *Dir* Kurt Neumann *Cast* Zasu Pitts, Hugh O'Connell *Prod* Universal. 61 mins. A remake of no distinction.

*LONESOME COWBOYS USA 1968. *Dir/ Scen* Andy Warhol *Cast* Viva, Taylor Mead, Tom Hompertz, Louis Waldon, Joe d'Allesandro, Francis Francine *Prod* Factory Films. 110 mins. Eastman Color.

In a ghost town in the West, Romona (Viva) and her male nurse (Mead) are both desperate for male companionship. Romona remarks about the homosexuality of a gang of "brothers" who ride into town, and the gang, unrestrained by the Sheriff (Francine), rapes Romona. The nurse strikes up a friendship with Little Joe (d'Allesandro), the Sheriff is revealed as a transvestite, and Romona finally seduces the lethargic Julian (Hompertz).

The first Andy Warhol film to enjoy a relatively wide commercial release in the USA (though *Chelsea Girls* made a lot of money). It is a hilariously funny mockery of the conventional Hollywood western and a sort of *Romeo and Juliet* in reverse — with superstar Viva playing Romeo.

LONE WHITE SAIL (THE) BYELEYET PARUS ODINOKY

LONGEST DAY (THE) USA 1962. *Dir* Darryl Zanuck (American interiors), Andrew Marton (American exteriors), Ken Annakin (British scenes), Bernhard Wicki (German scenes) *Scen* Cornelius Ryan based on his own book *Photog* Jean Bourgoin, Henri Persin, Walter Wottitz, Guy Tabary *Mus* Maurice Jarre (title song by Paul Anka) *Art Dir* Léon Barsacq, Vincent Korda, Ted Aworth *Cast* Richard Burton, Jean-Louis Barrault, Richard Todd, Kenneth More, Henry Fonda, Mel Ferrer, Arletty, etc. *Prod* 20th Century-Fox. 180 mins. CinemaScope.

Four directors, fifty stars, 20,000 extras and many millions of dollars were used to produce this gigantic "actuality" reconstruction of the Allied landing in Normandy on June 6, 1944. Jean Grémillon's modest *Le 6 juin à l'aube* (*q.v.*) is far superior to this super spectacle, which was an enormous commercial success.

LONG NIGHT (THE) see JOUR SE LÈVE (LE)

LONG PANTS USA 1927. *Dir* Frank Capra *Scen* Arthur Ripley *Photog* Elgin Lessley, Glen Kershner *Cast* Harry Langdon, Gladys Brockwell, Alan Roscoe, Alma Bennett, Betty Francisco *Prod* Harry Langdon Corp. for First National. 5,250 ft.

When Harry (Langdon), a country adolescent, gets his first pair of long pants he falls in love with a city vamp. Deserting his girl friend, he absconds to the city and gets mixed up with a policeman, a crocodile, several shootings, and sundry other adventures.

A typical Langdon scene is that in which he rides his bicycle foolishly round and round the car where the vamp is sitting.

LOST CHILD (THE) MUNNA

LOST CONTINENT (THE) CONTINENTE PERDUTO (IL)

LOST IN THE DARK SPERDUTI NEL BUIO

LOST PATROL (THE) USA 1934. *Dir* John Ford *Scen* Dudley Nichols, Garrett Fort based on the story *Patrol* by Philip MacDonald *Photog* Harold Wenstrom *Mus* Max Steiner *Ed* Paul Weatherwax *Cast* Victor McLaglen, Boris Karloff, Wallace Ford, Reginald Denny, J. M. Kerrigan, Alan Hale, Brandon Hurst, Billy Bevan *Prod* RKO. 74 mins.

About 1917, in the Middle East, a dozen British soldiers are lost among the dunes of the North Arabian desert and are picked off one by one by unseen Arabs. One (Karloff) who becomes mad is killed by a friend (Ford) as he tries to run away. Only the sergeant (McLaglen) survives and destroys the Arabs as they attack.

Although the story is a typical colonial adventure, Dudley Nichols stressed the characterizations and the drama of a group of men trapped by destiny and sent one by one to their deaths at the hands of an enemy they can never see. According to Jean Mitry, the film was made in a desert near Hollywood, with its only sets a mosque and several artificial palm trees. However, it gave the impression of having been produced in the studio, largely because of its emphasis on dialogue and its deliberately impersonal style. As Jean Mitry has said: "The theatricalization of reality here became pictorial." It had a warm critical reception at the time, but has aged badly.

— *The Lost Patrol* Britain 1929. *Dir* Walter Summers *Scen* based on Philip MacDonald's story *Cast* Cyril McLaglen, Sam Wilkinson, Terence Collier, Hamilton Keene. 80 mins.
An earlier version produced by Fox in Britain under the "quota" rule, and well thought of by British critics at the time. [The same story was used as a basis for *Badlands* USA 1939, *Sahara* USA 1943 and *The Sabre and the Arrow* USA 1952.]

LOST WEEK-END (THE) USA 1945. *Dir* Billy Wilder *Scen* Charles Brackett, Billy Wilder based on the novel by Charles R. Jackson *Photog* John F. Seitz *Art Dir* Hans Dreier, Earl Hedrick, Bertram Granger *Mus* Miklos Rozsa *Ed* Doane Harrison *Cast* Ray Milland, Jane Wyman, Phillip Terry, Howard Da Silva *Prod* Paramount. 101 mins.
Three days in the life of a dipsomaniac (Milland) who is deserted by his brother (Terry) and his girl friend (Wyman). In a rather unlikely happy ending, he renounces his vice.
A good film by Wilder, especially notable for its New York atmosphere, Ray Milland's admirable performance, the sympathetic psychology, and Wilder's quasi-expressionistic camera style.

LOUISIANA STORY USA 1948. *Dir* Robert J. Flaherty *Scen* Robert and Frances Flaherty *Photog* Richard Leacock *Ed* Helen Van Dongen *Mus* Virgil Thompson *Cast* Joseph Boudreaux, Lionel LeBlanc, Frank Hardy (all nonprofessionals) *Prod* Robert Flaherty for the Standard Oil Company. 77 mins.
In the Louisiana bayous, where a young boy (Boudreaux) lives close to nature, an oil crew arrives, erects a derrick to search for oil, and makes a strike.
Robert Flaherty has explained how he conceived the film, which was his last masterpiece: "It was a story built around a derrick which moved so silently, so majestically in the wilderness; probed for oil beneath the watery ooze and then moved on again, leaving the land as untouched as before it came . . . For our hero, we dreamed up a half-wild Cajun boy of the woods and bayous (and) we developed the character of an oil driller who would become a friend of the boy, eventually overcoming his shyness and reticence. Then came the difficult business of casting. I spend perhaps more time on this aspect of picture-making than any other, for I believe the secret of success lies in finding the right people." The right boy was difficult to find but was eventually located by Richard Leacock and Frances Flaherty. Flaherty continues. "We worked day after day, shooting reams of stuff. But somehow we never could seem to make that pesky derrick come alive . . . Then we hit on it. At night. That's when it was alive! At night, with the derrick lights dancing and flickering on the dark surface of the water, the excitement that is the very essence of drilling for oil became visual."
More than three months was spent just on the scenes of the boy with the animals. Then, since the film had been shot silent, came the recording of the noises of the machines ("There are seven separate sound tracks running through the drilling scenes" — R. F.), of animals, of nature, and of silence ("because one cannot leave a sound track blank and it was finally at four in the morning in a cemetery that we found the perfect silence" — R. F.) Eight months were spent in editing, reducing the 300,000 feet of film shot to 7,000.
The film cost $280,000. Famous sequences: the lyrical opening; the derrick

in action (superbly edited by Helen van Dongen); the boy's walk through the bayous and his fight with a crocodile. This last sequence took Flaherty many weeks of work because he wanted it to be dramatic. It is obvious in this film as in his others that the great director believed in a "constructed" actuality, an "acting out" of a real life situation.

In 1964, Frances Flaherty assembled *The Louisiana Story Study Film* from scenes shot by her husband but not used in the film. This assemblage is more than 15 hours long but enables one to see this great film maker's creative spirit in action.

LOVE ETERNAL ETERNEL RETOUR (L')

LOVE IN THE CITY AMORE IN CITTÀ

LOVE IS MY PROFESSION EN CAS DE MALHEUR

LOVEMAKER (THE) CALLE MAYOR

LOVE OF JEANNE NEY (THE) LIEBE DER JEANNE NEY (DIE)

LOVE ONE ANOTHER GEZEICHNETEN (DIE)

*LOVE PARADE (THE) USA 1929. *Dir* Ernst Lubitsch *Scen* Ernest Vajda, Guy Bolton based on the play *The Prince Consort* by Leon Xanrof, Jules Chancel *Photog* Victor Milner *Art Dir* Hans Dreier *Mus* Victor Schertzinger *Ed* Merrill White *Cast* Maurice Chevalier, Jeannette MacDonald, Lupino Lane, Lillian Roth, Edgar Norton, Eugene Pallette *Prod* Paramount. 110 mins.

The bored prince consort (Chevalier) of the imperious Queen of Sylvania (MacDonald) revolts against his position and finally manages to tame his bride. Their peccadillos are observed by their valet (Lane) and maid (Roth). Lubitsch's first sound film has been justifiably identified as "the first truly cinematic screen musical in America" by Theodore Huff. It was a great critical and commercial success. In fact, its witty dialogue, delightfully staged songs, and visual fluidity make it one of the most memorable musicals of all. This was Jeanette MacDonald's film debut.

LOVER BOY KNAVE OF HEARTS

LOVERS KNAVE OF HEARTS

LOVERS (THE) AMANTS (LES)

LOVES OF A BLONDE (THE) LASKY JEDNE PLAVOVLASKY

LOVES OF CARMEN (THE) see CARMEN

LOVES OF LIANG SHAN-PO AND CHU YING-TAI (THE) LIANG SHAN-PO AND CHU YING-TAI

LOVES OF MADAME DE (THE) MADAME DE . . .

LOVE STORY DOUCE

LOWER DEPTHS (THE) (Renoir) BAS-FONDS (LES)

LOWER DEPTHS (THE) (Kurosawa) DONZOKO

LOYAL FORTY-SEVEN RONIN (THE) GENROKU CHUSHINGURA

LUCI DEL VARIETA FOOTLIGHTS/LIGHTS OF THE MUSIC HALL/LIGHTS OF VARIETY Italy 1950. *Dir* Alberto Lattuada, Federico Fellini *Scen* Federico Fellini, Alberto Lattuada, Tullio Pinelli *Photog* Otello Martelli *Art Dir* Aldo Buzzi *Mus* Felice Lattuada *Cast* Peppino De Filippo, Carla Del Poggio, Giulietta Masina, John Kitzmiller. 94 mins.

Liliana (Del Poggio) becomes a success with a second-rate touring stage company, whose aging manager (De Filippo) falls in love with her, to the chagrin of his faithful mistress (Masina). Eventually, Liliana uses her influence with a businessman to get a break in a bigger show and leaves the company. This is Fellini's film rather than Lattuada's. Already present is his special "universe": his sense of irony, his baroque qualities, his sympathy for and delight in downtrodden eccentrics, and his portraits of "bidones" striving comically to find themselves.

LULU BÜCHSE DER PANDORA (DIE)

LUMIERE D'ETE France 1943. *Dir* Jean Grémillon *Scen* Jacques Prévert, Pierre Laroche *Photog* Louis Page *Art Dir* Max Douy, Léon Barsacq *Cast* Paul Bernard, Pierre Brasseur, Madeleine Renaud, Madeleine Robinson, Georges Marchal, Aimos, Blavette, Marcel Levesque *Prod* Discina. 112 mins.

Michèle (Robinson) arrives at a small inn in Provence to meet her fiancé, Roland (Brasseur), a second-rate, alcoholic artist. The inn is run by an ex-dancer, Cri-Cri (Renaud), on behalf of Patrice le Verdier (Bernard), an aging playboy, whose mistress she is. Patrice falls passionately in love with Michèle who, deserted by Roland, seems easy prey. However, she falls in love with Julien (Marchal), a young engineer working on a dam nearby. After a fancy dress ball, the drunken Roland is killed in a car crash and Patrice attempts to kill Julien. He is prevented by some workers from the dam and Michèle and Julien leave together.

Produced during the German occupation of France, this uneven, but lyrical and courageous, film was banned by the Vichy censors for its polemic (albeit allusive) against the ruling classes. Grémillon allegorically set evil against good. If the latter (represented by the workmen from the valley) is rather briefly sketched, its portrayal of a corrupt, wealthy playboy (who almost seems taken from de Sade) is as potent and true as that of his aging mistress and the debauched painter who, dressed as Hamlet during the ball says, "There is something rotten in that state of Denmark." Its mordant humor recalls *La Règle du jeu* (*q.v.*), although Grémillon's own forceful personality had not been influenced by Renoir.

LUMIÈRE FILMS France 1895. *Dir* Louis Lumière. First program: 1. *La Sortie des Usines Lumière;* 2. *La Voltige;* 3. *La Pêche aux poissons rouges;* 4. *Le Débarquement du Congrès de photographie à Lyon* (*Arrivée des congressistes à Neuville-sur-Saône*); 5. *Les Forgerons;* 6. *Le Jardinier* (*L'Arroseur arrosé*); 7. *Le Repas de bébé* (*Le Déjeuner de bébé*); 8. *Le Saut à la couverture;* 9. *La Place des Cordeliers à Lyon;* 10. *La Mer.*

Together with these ten films (screened December 23, 1895, in the Salon Indien of the Grand Café, 14 Boulevard des Capucines, Paris), one should include the following films, which made the new camera a world-wide success: 11. *Partie d'écarté;* 12. *La Sortie du port;* 13. *Démolition d'un mur;* 14, 15, 16, and 17. *Pompiers.*

Almost all of these films had been made by Louis Lumière in 1895, either in Paris or in La Ciotat near Marseilles, by using the "Cinématographe" that he had patented February 18, 1895. At the time there was only one camera (made by the mechanic Moisson) in existence. It was a square box that weighed around five kilos and would operate anywhere. Louis Lumière, who was 31 at the time, used his camera in much the same way as an amateur photographer does today. He took pictures of relatives, friends, babies, streets, landscapes, the sea, and family excursions as the fancy struck him. At the end of his long life he said that his ambition had been to reproduce life. "Nature in the raw" and "life as it happens" were the expressions used most often by journalists and film viewers of 1896–97.

After 1920, Louis Lumière said that he had made his first film (*La Sortie des usines/Workers Leaving the Lumière Factory*) in August, 1894. There were at least two versions of it and it was shown in Paris for the first time on March 22, 1895. There is no question about this date, but it is almost certain that this film could not have been made during the summer of 1894, when Louis Lumière had just become interested in moving pictures. He didn't finish designing his camera until the end of 1894. The well-known version of *La Sortie des usines* was filmed on a very hot day and may have been made in the summer of 1895. There is another version that ends with the owners leaving the factory in horse-drawn carriages. This may be the one that was shown March 22, 1895 in Paris; there could have been a third, of poor photographic quality, that might have been lost.

This film, which was an advertisement for the largest camera factory in Europe at that time, showed everyday life (like *Les Forgerons*). In *Séance de voltige* and *La Saut à la couverture* Louis Lumière also showed barracks and the army. But he was largely inspired by life in his own family of prosperous industrialists and gentlemen, proud of their success at the end of the last century. In *Le Repas du bébé/Baby at the Breakfast Table*, his brother, Auguste, puts porridge in the mouth of his little daughter under the tender eyes of her mother. It was widely noted that the leaves of the trees in the background of this film moved. *La Sortie du port/*

A Boat Leaving Harbor, with its remarkably composed frame, shows waves, as does La Mer/The Sea, which made a deep impression on spectators at the Grand Café. The little girl in Le Repas du bébé appears in La Pêche aux poissons rouges/Fishing for Goldfish trying to catch the fish in a jar, and her father, Auguste, is present at Démolition d'un mur/Demolition of a Wall, which collapses in a cloud of dust. This film was run in reverse at the Grand Café and thus became the first film trick shot — a scene in which the wall seemed to rise from the rubble. La Partie d'écarté/A Game of Cards is played by Louis's father, Auguste, Winkler the brewer, his father-in-law, and the magician Trewey, who later took the Cinématographe to London. Also in the film is the Lumières' butler, who tries to be funny; but he is less effective than Winkler blowing the froth from the actors' glasses.

Louis Lumière made a "documentary" with the four films called Les Pompiers/ The Firemen, which showed a fire, then firemen going through the streets, bringing the fire under control, and making a rescue. These four films were the beginning of editing and pioneered "the last-minute rescue." As for the "documentary," a simple street scene in La Place des Cordeliers was deeply moving. But it wasn't as effective as L'Arrivée d'un train/Train Entering a Station where Louis Lumière used background

perspective so dramatically that the viewers in the Grand Café slid down in their seats, thinking that they were about to be run over by the La Ciotat locomotive. As for Le Débarquement du Congrès de Photographie à Lyon it may have been filmed (according to a review of the time) by Auguste Lumière, although he never contested his brother Louis's claim that he directed it.

LURDZHA MAGDANY MAGDANA'S DONKEY USSR 1955. Dir T. Abuladze, Revaz Chkeidze Photog L. Sukhov, Alexander Digmelov Art Dir I. Sumbatishvili Mus A. Keresilidze Cast T. Tserodze, Akaki Vasadze Prod Georgia Films. 67 mins. The story takes place in 1896 in a Georgian village where a poor widow Magdana (Tserodze) ekes out a living selling sour milk. A donkey is abandoned near her home and she and her children nurse it back to health until the real owner recognizes it and takes it back. This was the first film by these two young film makers who had only just finished their training at the All-Union State Institute of Cinematography (VGIK) in Moscow. It is a simple film but full of compassionate insight. It marked the beginning of a "new wave" in Soviet films and a revival of Georgian cinema, which, however, was not influenced by Italian neorealism but instead returned to the style of the Thirties.

M Germany 1931. *Dir* Fritz Lang *Scen* Thea von Harbou, Paul Falkenberg, Adolf Jansen, Karl Vash *Photog* Fritz Arno Wagner *Art Dir* Karl Vollbrecht, Emil Hasler *Ed* Paul Falkenberg *Cast* Peter Lorre, Otto Wernicke, Gustaf Gründgens *Prod* Nero-Film. 118 mins. (original length); most current versions 99 mins.

In a large town a sadistic murderer (Lorre) kills little girls. The police (Wernicke) try in vain to catch him, but in the end he is trapped by the denizens of the underworld and condemned to death by their leader (Gründgens). The police arrive in time to prevent his execution.

The story was based on a news story about a real murderer in Dusseldorf. It was to have been called *Mörder unter uns* (*Murderer Among Us*) but this title was abandoned when a Nazi thought it might dishonor Germany. The film, produced almost entirely in a studio, has no music but a very expressive sound track. Peter Lorre (who was a stage actor trained by Bertolt Brecht) became world famous for his portrayal of the murderer, an outwardly gentle man who is trapped by his mental sickness and afraid to discover himself. He is characterized best by his whistling of the theme from Grieg's *Peer Gynt* whenever his desires overwhelm him, but otherwise he hardly says a word until his final despairing cry of protest at the end, "I can't help it."

The stylized realism of the sets, the sense of destiny overshadowing the characters, the use of symbols (a balloon offered to one of the victims, the glinting blade of a pocket knife, the sexuality of some of the ads) owe more to *Kammerspiel* than to expressionism.

"A Town Hunts a Murderer" was one provisional title for the film, an appropriate title since the town is one of the main characters in the drama. *M* is a film in which buildings play a major role, especially in the best sequence, where the thief drives the murderer into a deserted building, and traps him as though he were locked in a vault. The climax, where the thief "squeals" to the police, seems to have been influenced by Brecht and *Threepenny Opera* (*q.v.*). The band of beggars and thieves in the film included some real criminals. *M* also offers a portrait of the profound troubles that gripped Germany in the years immediately before Hitler came to power.

— *M* USA 1951. *Dir* Joseph Losey *Assist Dir* Robert Aldrich *Scen* Norman Reilly Raine, Leo Katcher, Don Weiss based on Lang's film *Photog* Ernest Laszlo *Art Dir* Martin Obzina *Mus* Michel Michelet *Ed* Edward Mann *Cast* David Wayne, Howard Da Silva, Martin Gabel, Steve Brodie *Prod* Columbia. 82 mins.

An almost exact remake of the original version but since it is set in Los Angeles it has an American rather than German atmosphere. Losey's version is not simply a hack copy but an original and sometimes powerful work in its own right, and is especially notable for the way Losey used the streets of Los Angeles.

MABUSE DR. MABUSE, DER SPIELER

MACBETH USA 1948. *Dir/Scen* Orson Welles *Photog* John L. Russell *Art Dir* Fred Ritter, John McCarthy, James Redd *Mus* Jacques Ibert *Cast* Orson Welles, Jeanette Nolan, Dan O'Herlihy, Roddy McDowell *Prod* Mercury. 86 mins.

Shot in 23 days in Hollywood on an extremely low budget. Most critics disliked its use of extravagant costumes, its cardboard sets, and its exaggerated theatrical style. Orson Welles' *Othello* (*q.v.*) is far better [This version is more Welles than Shakespeare, with Welles using the play as a basis for his own Macbeth. It is most memorable for its rhythm, its murky atmosphere of evil, and Welles's imaginative visualizations. Most of the acting is uniformly bad.]

OTHER VERSIONS:
— USA 1908. *Dir* James Stuart Blackton. 1 reel.
— Italy 1909. *Dir* Mario Caserini.
— France 1909. *Dir* Calmettes.
— France 1910. *Dir* Andreani (?).
— Britain 1911. *Dir* F. R. Benson.
— *Germany 1913. *Cast* Arthur Bouchier, Violet Vanbrugh. 5 reels.
— *France 1916. *Cast* Georgette Leblanc-Maeterlinck.
— USA 1916. *Dir* John Emerson *Cast* Herbert Beerbohm Tree.
— Germany 1922. *Dir* Heinz Schall. 3 reels.
— *USA 1951. *Dir* Katherine Stenholm. 78 mins. Color.
— *Britain 1960. *Dir* George Schaefer *Cast* Maurice Evans, Judith Anderson. 108 mins. Technicolor.
See also KUMONOSU-JO.

*MADAME DE . . . THE LOVES OF MADAME DE/THE EARRINGS OF MADAME DE France/ Italy 1953. *Dir* Max Ophüls *Scen* Max Ophüls, Marcel Achard, Annette Wademant based on the novel by Louise de Vilmorin *Photog* Christian Matras *Art Dir* Jean d'Eaubonne *Mus* Oscar Strauss, Georges van Parys *Ed* Borys Lewin *Cast* Danielle Darrieux, Charles Boyer, Vittorio de Sica, Jean Debucourt, Lia de Léa. 192 mins.

Madame De (Darrieux) is given a pair of earrings by her husband (Boyer) and sells them to pay off her debts. Monsieur De buys them back and gives them to his mistress (De Léa), who also sells them when she returns to South America. They are bought by a diplomat (de Sica) who goes to Paris, falls in love with Madame De, and gives her the earrings. Monsieur De thus discovers her infidelity and tells the whole story to her lover, who throws her over. Having lost her one true love, Madame De dies of a broken heart.

Ophüls changed the chaste prose of the original short novel into a dazzling visual symphony and a remarkable por-trait of the vanity and frivolity of the lives of the main characters. The extraordinary coordination of Ophüls' design is perhaps best seen in the series of dance scenes between Madame De and her lover. Claude Beylie contends the film has little to do with Louise de Vilmorin and much more to do with La Fayette and the Tolstoy of *Anna Karenina. Madame De . . .* "is Ophüls' swan song, his requiem. It remained for him to sign his testament, a glowing testament, which will be the high point of the fresco, the allegro furioso of the symphony, his *Zauberflöte: Lola Mon-tès*."

MADAME DUBARRY (also DU BARRY) PAS-SION Germany 1919. *Dir* Ernst Lubitsch *Scen* Fred Orbing, Hanns Kräly *Photog* Theodor Sparkuhl *Art Dir* Karl Machus, Kurt Richter *Costumes* Ali Hubert *Cast* Pola Negri, Emil Jannings, Harry Liedtke, Eduard von Winterstein *Prod* Union-UFA. 7,600 ft. approx.

The romanticized "private life" of the mistress (Negri) of Louis XV (Jannings), her affair with a courtier (Liedtke), and the passion that led to the French Revolution and her death on the guillotine in 1793.

This is the most famous of Lubitsch's historical spectaculars whose great success in the USA and the rest of the world did much to encourage the further production of costume dramas in the luxurious UFA style. It also established Pola Negri's international reputation.

Lubitsch's skillful style was largely inspired by the stage designs of Max Reinhardt, whose pupil Lubitsch had been and from whom he also took many of his actors. The film's brilliant sets are matched by the handling of crowd scenes, notably in the guillotine scene with the raised fists of the mob demanding the death of the King's favorite. However, the rebels are caricatured; this undoubtedly contributed to the film's success when it was premiered at the UFA Palast am Zoo (then the largest theater in the world) in September 1919 — a period when Berlin was recovering from the Spartacist revolutionary riots of 1918–19.

[The American version of the film ended with a long-shot of Dubarry on the guillotine. The original detailed ending was apparently removed by First National to avoid offending the sensibilities of American audiences.]

— *Dubarry* France 1913. *Prod* Eclectic-Pathé.

— *La Dubarry* Italy 1914. *Dir* Edoardo Bencivenga *Scen* based on the play by David Belasco *Cast* Leslie Carter, Hamilton Revelle *Prod* Ambrosio. 6 reels.
Leslie Carter went to Italy to re-create the role that she had made famous in David Belasco's Broadway success.

— *Du Barry/Madame Dubarry* USA 1917. *Dir* J. Gordon Edwards *Scen* Adrian Johnson *Cast* Theda Bara, Charles Clary, Fred Church *Prod* Fox. 7 reels.

— *Madame Dubarry* USA 1928. *Dir* R. William Neil *Prod* MGM. 2 reels.

— *Dubarry — Woman of Passion* USA 1930. *Dir* Sam Taylor *Scen* based on the David Belasco play *Cast* Norma Talmadge, Conrad Nagel.
A contemporary critic remarked: Norma Talmadge "speaks the Belascoan rodomontades with a Vitagraph accent."

— *Madame Du Barry* USA 1934. *Dir* William Dieterle *Scen* Edward Chodorov *Cast* Dolores Del Rio, Reginald Owen.

— *I Give My Heart/Du Barry* Britain 1935. *Dir* Marcel Varnel *Scen* Frank Launder, Roger Burford, Kurt Siodmak *Cast* Gitta Alpar, Patrick Waddington *Prod* B.I.P. 90 mins.
A version derived from a then popular operetta by Paul Knepler and J. M. Welleminsky.

— *Dubarry Was a Lady* USA 1943. *Dir* Roy del Ruth *Cast* Red Skelton, Lucille Ball, Gene Kelly. 101 mins. Technicolor.
A burlesque version of the story.

— *Madame Du Barry/Mistress Du Barry* France/Italy 1954. *Dir* Christian-Jaque *Cast* Martine Carol, André Luguet. 96 mins. Eastman Color.

MADCHEN IN UNIFORM GIRLS IN UNIFORM Germany 1931. *Dir* Leontine Sagan *Scen* F. O. Andam, Christa Winsloe based on the play *Gestern und Heute* by Christa Winsloe *Photog* Reimar Kuntze, Fritz Weihmayr *Art Dir* F. Maurischat, F. Winkler-Tannenberg *Mus* Hanson Milde-Meissner *Supervised* Carl Froelich *Cast* Dorothea Wieck, Ellen Schwannecke, Emilie Lunda, Herta Thiele. 90 mins.
A young girl (Thiele) arrives at an aristocratic boarding school for girls, heavy with the traditions of Prussian authoritarianism. She is obstinate, is almost crushed by the regulations, goes wild with love for one of the teachers (Wieck), and is driven to suicide.
Christa Winsloe's occasionally mawkish play had been also directed on the stage by Leontine Sagan. It is a sensitive and restrained attack on German militarism and its simple yet forceful portrayal of the authoritarian milieu still seems effective. Leontine Sagan and the principal actors had to leave Germany when Hitler came to power.

— *Mädchen in Uniform* German Federal Republic 1958. *Dir* Geza Radvanyi *Scen* Franz Hollering based on the play *Photog* Werner Krien *Cast* Romy Schneider, Lilli Palmer. 94 mins. Color.
A disappointing remake whose color merely glamorizes the boarding-school background. However, Lilli Palmer is commendable as the teacher.

MAFIA IN NOME DELLA LEGGE

MAGDANA'S DONKEY LURDZHA MAGDANA

MAGGIE (THE) HIGH AND DRY Britain 1953. *Dir* Alexander Mackendrick *Scen* William Rose *Photog* Gordon Dines *Art Dir* Jim Morahan *Mus* John Addison *Ed* Peter Tanner *Cast* Paul Douglas, Alex Mackenzie, Hubert Gregg, James Copeland *Prod* Ealing Studios. 90 mins.
The adventures of the "Maggie," one of the few remaining small ships that sail among the islands of western Scotland. A rich American (Douglas) is tricked by the "Maggie's" skipper (Mackenzie) into letting the ship carry his cargo. He tries to remove it but eventually falls under the ship's charm and agrees to jettison the cargo so the little ship can be saved.
Very good satirical comedy in which the canny Scottish sailors "put one over" on an overbearing, quick-tempered American.

*MAGIC FOUNTAIN PEN (THE) USA 1909. *Dir/Anim* James Stuart Blackton *Prod* Vitagraph. 335 ft.
One of the earliest examples of animation (it was released the same year as *Gertie the Dinosaur*) and one which combines drawings and live action. Stuart Blackton sits at a desk and with a fountain pen draws quick sketches, each of which is transformed into something else — for example, Napoleon becomes Kaiser Wilhelm and then Washington;

a man and a woman becomes two birds. The same idea was to be used later by Fleischer in the *Out of the Inkwell* series (*q.v.*).

MAGIRAMA France 1956. *Dir* Abel Gance, Nelly Kaplan.

A spectacular that uses several screens, lasts about two hours, and is made up of three short color films: *Fête foraine* (*Dir* Abel Gance *Scen* Abel Gance, Nelly Kaplan, Steve Passeur *Photog* Pierre Petit, J. Lemare *Mus* H. Verdun, Magne) *Auprès de ma blonde* (*Art Dir* Henry Mahé *Cast* Maurice Baquet, other credits as for *Fête foraine*); *Châteaux de nuages* (*Dir* Nelly Kaplan *Mus* Debussy, other credits as for *Fête foraine*) It also included a three-screen version of *Begone Dull Care* (*Anim* Norman McLaren) and Abel Gance's 1937 version of *J'accuse* (*q.v.*).

This extraordinary spectacle was premiered in December 1956 at Studio 28 in Paris, but unfortunately did not have the success merited by its exciting exploration of the possibilities of three screens. *Magirama's* experiments in multiscreen were preceded by those of *Quatorze Juillet* in 1953, a 13-minute color film shown at the Gaumont-Palace in Paris and by Gance's own short films *Marines* and *Cristaux* in 1928.

MAGNIFICENT AMBERSONS (THE) USA 1942. *Dir* Orson Welles *Scen* Orson Welles based on the novel by Booth Tarkington *Photog* Stanley Cortez *Art Dir* Mark-Lee Kirk *Ed* Robert Wise *Mus* Bernard Herrmann *Costumes* Edward Stevenson *Cast* Joseph Cotten, Dolores Costello, Anne Baxter, Tim Holt, Agnes Moorehead *Prod* Mercury for RKO. 88 mins.

Isabel Amberson (Costello), a member of an important family whose husband has died, falls in love with Eugene Morgan (Cotten), whom she had earlier loved but who is despised by her family because he designs automobiles. Her son, George (Holt), intervenes to prevent their marriage. Isabel leaves on a long voyage and George is too proud to marry Lucy (Baxter), Morgan's daughter, even though he loves her. Eventually Isabel dies unhappily and George is left ruined and alone except for his aunt Fanny (Moorehead). He is involved in an automobile accident and, in hospital, asks Morgan for forgiveness. This somewhat Balzacian story, which

contrasts the decadence of the landed gentry and founders of an American town with the rise of the new industrialists, is dominated by the egocentric, spoilt George Minafer Amberson. The 19th-century Amberson mansion, magnificent at first, crumbling at the end, and Stanley Cortez' high-contrast lighting are equally expressive of the personality of the Ambersons.

Famous sequences: the childhood of the spoiled son, George; George's carriage ride down a town street (specially built for this single scene); the last ball in the Amberson mansion; George and Lucy's ride through the snow and the beginning of their love; the death of Isabel; Aunt Fanny's anguish at the breakup of the old family home.

There has been much discussion of the 167-second sequence involving Aunt Fanny and George; André Bazin's analysis is famous: "The camera obstinately refuses to guide us through the labyrinth of an action we sense is becoming more tense — who knows if it is not at the precise moment we are looking at George that Fanny has a revealing facial gesture? And, throughout the scene, objects totally foreign to the action (cakes, food, kitchen utensils, coffee pot, etc.) solicit our attention though no movement of the camera recognizes their presence." *Magnificent Ambersons* might have been a complete masterpiece if the newly appointed directors of RKO had not taken advantage of Welles' absence in South America to re-edit the last three reels and add a final scene. However, its qualities could not be totally destroyed and it remains one of his most beautiful films.

— *Pampered Youth USA 1925. *Dir* David Smith *Scen* based on the novel *The Magnificent Ambersons* by Booth Tarkington *Cast* Alice Calhoun, Cullen Landis, Allan Forest, Wallace MacDonald *Prod* Vitagraph. 6,640 ft.

This earlier version of the novel had Cullen Landis playing the boorish young Amberson.

MAGNIFICENT SEVEN (THE) see SHICHI NIN NO SAMURAI

MAHIRU NO ANKOKU DARKNESS AT NOON/ A MIDDAY DARKNESS Japan 1956. *Dir* Tadashi Imai *Scen* Shinobu Hashimoto based on the book *The Judge* by Hiroshi Masaki *Photog* Shun Ichiro Nakao *Mus*

Akira Ifukube *Cast* Kojiro Kusanagi, Teruo Matsuyama, Masatsugu Makita *Prod* Gendai. 107 mins.

This vigorously realistic film was based on a judicial *cause célèbre* that caused a sensation in Japan and that had not reached final judgement when the film was released. It involves a young man (Kusanagi) who is unjustly accused of murder and condemned to death. The police investigation with its brutalities serves as background for a series of flashbacks that explain the judicial error and also offer a very pertinent social portrait of contemporary Japan.

MALDONE France 1927. *Dir* Jean Grémillon *Scen* Alexandre Arnoux *Photog* Georges Périnal, Christian Matras *Art Dir* André Barsacq *Mus* Jacques Brillouin, Marcel Delannoy (with Maurice Jaubert) *Cast* Charles Dullin, André Bacque, Roger Karl, Génica Athansaiou, Marcelle Charles Dullin, Annabella *Prod* Films Charles Dullin. 3,800 meters (original length) reduced to 2,800 meters for release.

Oliver Maldone (Dullin), who has wandered for 20 years as a vagabond and sailor, returns home to the family chateau after the death of his brother. He marries a young girl (Annabella), then takes to the road again with a bohemian (Athansaiou).

This excellent film was a commercial failure because it was mutilated by the distributor and rendered incoherent. Its marvelous use of landscapes and an excellent sequence of a country dance is a direct antecedent of the "poetic realism" of the Thirties. Charles Dullin, seemingly ill-served by his appearance, is weak in the lead role but nevertheless convincing in the sequence where he returns to his habits as a vagabond.

MALTESE FALCON (THE) USA 1941. *Dir* John Huston *Scen* John Huston based on the novel by Dashiell Hammett *Photog* Arthur Edeson *Art Dir* Robert Haas *Mus* Adolph Deutsch *Ed* Thomas Richards *Cast* Humphrey Bogart, Peter Lorre, Mary Astor, Sidney Greenstreet *Prod* Warner Brothers. 100 mins.

A private eye, Sam Spade (Bogart), to help a pretty client, (Astor), gets involved in a fight with a gang (Greenstreet, Lorre) for possession of a jeweled statuette known as "the Maltese Falcon." He discovers his client is one of the crooks and that the statuette is a fake.

John Huston already had an established reputation as a scriptwriter when he directed this, his first film. It is a faithful adaptation of the original novel with a style that reflects the essence of Hammett. In fact, its style and pace still make it one of Huston's most memorable films. Although the two earlier versions passed almost unnoticed, they are part of the development of the American *film noir* in the literary tradition of Hammett and James Cain. Humphrey Bogart was well known as an actor at the time, but this film was really the first to introduce the famous "Bogie" characteristics that made him a star. Sidney Greenstreet gives one of his most unforgettable performances as Kasper Gutman.

— *The Maltese Falcon/Dangerous Female* USA 1931. *Dir* Roy Del Ruth *Scen* Brown Holmes, Maude Fulton, Lucien Hubbard based on the Hammett novel *Photog* William Rees *Cast* Ricardo Cortez, Bebe Daniels, J. Farrell MacDonald, Otto Matieson *Prod* Warner Brothers. 75 mins.

[The plot and behavior of the heroine (Daniels) seems to have puzzled audiences at the time; Ricardo Cortez makes a good try at the role of Sam Spade but his pose of careless ease is not quite in character.]

— **Satan Met a Lady* USA 1936. *Dir* William Dieterle *Scen* Brown Holmes based on the Hammett novel *Photog* Arthur Edeson *Cast* Warren Williams, Bette Davis *Prod* Warner Brothers. 75 mins.

A delightfully amusing version, with Bette Davis giving a memorable performance as a wide-eyed innocent.

MAN-ABOUT-TOWN SILENCE EST D'OR (LE)

*MAN DIE ZIJN HAAR KORT LIET KNIPPEN (DE) THE MAN WHO HAD HIS HAIR CUT SHORT Belgium 1966. *Dir* André Delvaux *Scen* André Delvaux, Anna de Pagter based on the novel by Johanne Daisne *Photog* Ghislain Cloquet *Art Dir* Jean-Claude Maes *Mus* Freddy Devreese *Ed* Suzanne Baron *Cast* Senne Rouffaer, Beata Tyszkiewicz, Hector Camerlynck. 94 mins.

When he was a teacher, Govert (Rouffaer) developed an obsession for a beautiful pupil, Fran (Tyszkiewicz). Some years later he sees her again when she has become a famous actress. He dreams he reveals his love to her, that she at first responds then shatters his illusions about her, and he shoots her. Waking, he is taken to an asylum and finally understands that the murder was only in his mind.

This film, depicting, like *Le Feu follet* (*q.v.*), the complex path from idealism to despair and insanity, marked one of the most impressive directorial debuts of the Sixties. The brilliant depiction of Govert's sense of isolation in the first half, the subtle psychology in the second, and its Bosch-like alliance of horror and beauty have rarely been matched.

MAN ESCAPED (A) UN CONDAMNÉ À MORT S'EST ÉCHAPPÉ

MANHATTAN MADNESS USA 1916. *Dir* Alan Dwan *Scen* E. V. Durling *Cast* Douglas Fairbanks, Jewel Carmen, George A. Beranger, Warner P. Richmond *Prod* D. W. Griffith for Triangle. 4 reels.

A man (Fairbanks) returns from the West and, to amuse him, some friends stage some mysteries in an old mansion and a love affair with a young girl (Carmen) develops.

Louis Delluc hailed this film as "one of the first films that indicated both the serenity and recklessness of a splendid art. A great actor has appeared . . . impeccable and crazy, scattering his precious youth. He is simplicity itself, naturalness, life . . . In the mad evening of mystery, love, and hate in which he is involved, observation, violence, sentimentality, and slapstick are mixed as in life itself. It is the new force of modern poetry, which you can note for yourself in the streets, and which a film maker isolates. The landscape, dogs, horses, furniture, a lamp, a hand, all take on a fantastic character" (1928).

This superb film (and many of Fairbanks' other pre-1920 films when he was still the all-American boy) is a predecessor of the American screwball comedy of the Thirties.

— *Manhattan Madness* USA 1925. *Dir* John McDermott *Scen* E. V. Durling *Cast* Jack Dempsey, Estelle Taylor. 5,600 ft.

A remake with, curiously, the former boxer Jack Dempsey appearing in Fairbanks' role.

MAN IN THE WHITE SUIT (THE) Britain 1951. *Dir* Alexander Mackendrick *Scen* Roger Macdougall, John Dighton, Alexander Mackendrick *Photog* Douglas Slocombe *Art Dir* Jim Morahan *Mus* Benjamin Frankel *Ed* Benjamin Gribble *Cast* Alec Guinness, Joan Greenwood, Cecil Parker *Prod* Ealing Studios. 85 mins.

An inventor (Guinness) who works as a laboratory assistant at a textile mill invents a fabric that will never wear out and never get dirty. After initial opposition, he is supported by a mill owner (Parker) and his daughter (Greenwood). But the trade unions and the mill owners form an alliance to keep the fabric off the market. In the end, the fabric falls to pieces as they chase the "man in the white suit."

This entertaining satirical fable pokes derisive fun at convention and the establishment and makes clever use of picture and sound editing. Together with *Kind Hearts and Coronets* (*q.v.*), this is one of the best films of the postwar British comedy school, which unhappily soon went into decline.

MAN IS TEN FEET TALL (A) EDGE OF THE CITY

MANI SULLA CITTA (LE) HANDS OVER THE CITY Italy 1963. *Dir* Francesco Rosi *Scen* Enzo Provenzale, Enzo Forcella, Raffaele La Capria, Francesco Rosi *Photog* Gianni Di Venanzo *Mus* Piero Piccioni *Art Dir* Massimo Rosi *Cast* Rod Steiger, Salvo Randone, and nonprofessionals *Prod* Galatea. 105 mins.

Set in Naples, and based on fact (though the story is fictitious), this film depicts how a property developer (Steiger) schemes to modify a city planning scheme and direct expansion northwards into property he owns. An old building in the poor district collapses because of his building activities on the next site, but his maneuvrings with the leaders of the Left, Center, and Rightist parties in the election get him what he wants.

This is mainly a political film whose essence is in the debates and in the bargainings for power between the political parties. Using entirely natural sets, it is a powerful and courageous work. Rosi used nonprofessional actors except for the remarkable Rod Steiger and Salvo Randone.

MAN OCH KVINNA EN HANDFULL RIS/A HANDFUL OF RICE Sweden/Thailand 1939. *Dir* Gunnar Skoglund, Paul Fejos *Photog* Gustav Boge *Mus* J. Sylvain, G. Johansson *Cast* Po'Chai, Me'Ying, Thailand peasants.

One year in the life of a young Siamese peasant couple: their marriage, the clearing of the jungle, the capture of a tiger, the loss of their harvest, and the purchase of a buffalo after the man goes to work in a timber concession.

A sort of romanticized documentary that remains generally unconvincing despite its sedate style.

MAN OF ARAN Britain 1934. *Dir/ Scen/ Photog* Robert Flaherty in association with Frances Flaherty *Assist* David Flaherty *Mus* John Greenwood *Ed* John Goldman *Cast* (nonprofessionals) Tiger King, Maggie Dirrance, Mikeleen Dillane *Prod* Gainsborough (Gaumont-British). 76 mins.

The daily life of the inhabitants of an isolated island, 30 miles off the west coast of Ireland: fishing in the tiny curraghs, a storm, the difficulties of existence, the hunting of a basking-shark. After *Moana* (*q.v.*) and his break with Hollywood, Flaherty went to England at John Grierson's request. He had long wanted to make a film about a "man of the sea" and, after he saw the Aran Islands, he discussed the idea with John Grierson while making *Industrial Britain*. Grierson persuaded Michael Balcon (production chief) and Angus McPhail (head of the story department) of Gaumont-British to let Flaherty make the film. He spent almost two years making the film at Kilmurvey on the island of Inishmore, studying the customs of the people and then selecting his "actors" and re-creating with them their daily life. Flaherty installed a small processing laboratory on the island so that he could screen the rushes as soon as possible, which probably explains why the photographic quality of *Man of Aran* is superior to his other films. Some episodes were artificially reconstructed; for example, Flaherty included a sequence depicting the hunting of the basking-shark although the islanders had not hunted it for almost a century. For the sequence, perhaps the most dramatic in the film, Flaherty had the islanders retrained in harpooning, using an 1840 harpoon gun, and photographed the

hunt from a small motorboat, mainly with a telephoto lens. But the best sequence is perhaps also the simplest: the boy fishing on top of an enormous cliff. It might be possible to criticize Flaherty for choosing a woman to play the wife who was a bit too beautiful and for misusing some beautiful photography. However, in *Man of Aran*, as in *Nanook* (*q.v.*) and *Louisiana Story* (*q.v.*), his passionate devotion to the portrayal of human gesture and of a man's fight for his family makes the film an incomparable account of human dignity. Better than anyone, he knew how to show the true face of Man.

MAN OF THE WEST USA 1958. *Dir* Anthony Mann *Scen* Reginald Rose from the novel *The Border Jumpers* by Will C. Brown *Photog* Ernest Haller *Mus* Leigh Harline *Ed* Richard Heermance *Cast* Gary Cooper, Julie London, Lee J. Cobb, Arthur O'Connell *Prod* Mirisch for United Artists. 100 mins. DeLuxe Color. CinemaScope.

A reformed gunman (Cooper) is entrusted with the savings of his community and is on his way to hire a schoolteacher for the town when he is robbed by members of his old gang led by Tobin (Cobb). He takes refuge with another man (O'Connell) and a singer (London) in his old hideout, which is also the bandits' hideout. Eventually he recovers the money, destroys the bandits, and the singer becomes the schoolteacher.

"But a step forward in which direction? Towards a style of the western that will recall Conrad, certainly, and Simenon also, and which, for me, will be derived from nothing else, because I have seen nothing quite as new since, why not, Griffith. Just as the director of *Birth of a Nation* gave us the impression in each shot that he was inventing the cinema, each shot of *Man of the West* gives the impression that Anthony Mann is reinventing the western just as, let us say, the pencil of Matisse reworked Piero Della Francesca . . . The amorphous face of Gary Cooper is like stone in *Man of the West*. It is the proof that Anthony Mann has returned to the primary verities" (Jean-Luc Godard).

MAN ON THE TRACKS CZLOWIEK NA TORZE

MAN'S CASTLE (A) USA 1933. *Dir* Frank Borzage *Scen* Jo Swerling based on the play by Lawrence Hazard *Photog* Joseph August *Ed* Viola Lawrence *Cast* Spencer Tracy, Loretta Young, Glenda Farrell, Walter Connolly *Prod* Columbia. 75 mins.

During the worst days of the Depression, an unemployed American, Bill (Tracy), meets Trina (Young), gives her the protection of a roof in Shanty Town, and they fall in love. She meets an assortment of broken humanity and Bill is involved in a robbery. Eventually they flee from the town to begin a new life. One of Borzage's best romantic films but also one of the few films that show directly how millions of unemployed Americans lived in the Thirties. In the opening of the film, Bill is shown all dressed up and wearing a top hat as though he were rich; but on his chest is a publicity sign – he is a sandwich-board man. This is Loretta Young's best film; she is especially touching in the scene where she makes a dignified entrance into their poor shack. Joseph August's photography is unaffected and beautiful.

MAN'S DESTINY (A) SUDBA CHELOVEKA

MAN'S HOPE ESPOIR

*MA NUIT CHEZ MAUD MY NIGHT AT MAUD'S France 1969. *Dir/Scen* Eric Rohmer *Photog* Nestor Almendros *Art Dir* Nicole Rachline *Ed* Cecile Decugis *Cast* Jean-Louis Trintignant, Françoise Fabian, Marie-Christine Barrault, Antoine Vitez *Prod* Films du Losange. 110 mins.

Jean-Louis (Trintignant), a quiet, devout Catholic, moves to a new job in a dull provincial town. He develops an ambivalent relationship with Maud (Fabian), an elegant divorcee, but sets out to marry a young Catholic girl (Barrault) he meets at Church. Years later, Maud and Jean-Louis meet briefly on a beach.

This intensely literate and cinematic film is the third of Eric Rohmer's *contes moraux*. Its story of apparently banal lives has tremendous power and is, ultimately, an intelligent and moving examination of morality, solitude, and human relationships. The focal point of the film is the dialogue between Maud and Jean-Louis in which "each talks with an affected charm born of some private knowledge that the others lacks"

(Peter Cowie). The final encounter on the beach, in which hardly a word is spoken, has the kind of discreet brilliance in its use of the camera that one finds elsewhere in the film.

MAN WHO HAD HIS HAIR CUT SHORT (THE)
MAN DIE ZIJN HAAR KORT LIET KNIPPEN (DE)

MAN WHO KNEW TOO MUCH (THE) Britain 1934. *Dir* Alfred Hitchcock *Scen* A. R. Rawlinson, Edwin Greenwood from the original story by Charles Bennett, D. B. Wyndham-Lewis *Photog* Kurt Courant *Art Dir* Alfred Junge *Mus* Arthur Benjamin, Louis Levy *Ed* H. St. C. Stewart *Cast* Leslie Banks, Peter Lorre, Edna Best, Nova Pilbeam, Pierre Fresnay, Frank Vosper *Prod* Gaumont-British. 84 mins.

Before he is shot, a spy (Fresnay) passes on a message for the authorities to the Lawrences (Banks, Best), on holiday in St. Moritz. Their daughter (Pilbeam) is kidnapped by a rival spy group led by a mysterious European (Lorre). Lawrence refuses to give the message to the police because he knows his daughter will be killed. Eventually, after an assassination attempt is foiled, Mrs. Lawrence saves her daughter on the roof of the gang's hideout and the gang are rounded up or killed by the police.

"Because of its frank refusal to indulge in subtleties, (it is) the most promising work that Hitchcock has produced since *Blackmail*" (C. A. Lejeune, *The Observer*, December 8, 1934). A marvelous suspense film whose story, while not always easy to follow, is always engrossing.

– *The Man Who Knew Too Much* USA 1955. *Dir* Alfred Hitchcock *Scen* John Michael Hayes, Angus McPhail from the story by Charles Bennett, D. B. Wyndham-Lewis *Photog* Robert Burks *Art Dir* Sam Comer, Hal Pereira, Henry Bumstead, Arthur Krams *Mus* Bernard Herrmann *Ed* George Tomasini *Cast* James Stewart, Doris Day, Daniel Gélin, Brenda de Banzie, Bernard Miles *Prod* Filwite for Paramount. 119 mins. Technicolor. VistaVision.

An exact remake of the earlier film but reworked and enlarged to transpose the action from Switzerland to Morocco The dramatic high point remains the concert scene in the Albert Hall where a cymbal crash coincides with the murder. Not as good as the original.

MAN WITH A MOVIE CAMERA (THE) CHE-LOVEK S KINOAPPARATOM

MAN WITH THE GOLDEN ARM (THE) USA 1955. *Dir* Otto Preminger *Scen* Walter Newman, Lewis Meltzer based on the novel by Nelson Algren *Photog* Sam Leavitt *Art Dir* Joe Wright *Mus* Elmer Bernstein *Ed* Louis R. Loeffler *Cast* Frank Sinatra, Eleanor Parker, Kim Novak, Arnold Stang *Prod* Otto Preminger for United Artists. 119 mins.
Frankie (Sinatra), a drug addict cured of his addiction in jail, tries to become a jazz drummer. Pressure from his wife (Parker), who is a neurotic cripple, and a dope peddler drives him back to his former occupation as a poker dealer and eventually to drugs. Encouraged by a faithful girl friend (Novak), he tries to break free but comes under suspicion when the dope peddler is found dead. In fact his wife had killed him because he had discovered her paralysis was a pretense to keep Frankie. His wife kills herself, Frankie undergoes a violent cure in his girlfriend's apartment, and they start a new life.
This is Preminger's best film and Frank Sinatra's best role as a troubled, disgraced man, trapped in a vicious circle of drugs, guilt, and an apparently impossible love. The somewhat melodramatic plot is less important than the film's sense of atmosphere, its description of American "flesh-pots," its characters, and the rapport between the players. Kim Novak's blond sensuality in this film made her famous, though her apparent personality is mainly due to strong direction.

MARAT/SADE PERSECUTION AND ASSASSINATION OF JEAN-PAUL MARAT AS PERFORMED BY THE INMATES OF THE ASYLUM OF CHARENTON UNDER THE DIRECTION OF THE MARQUIS DE SADE

MARGUERITE DE LA NUIT see FAUST

MARIA CANDELARIA PORTRAIT OF MARIA/XOCHIMILCO Mexico 1945. *Dir* Emilio Fernandez *Scen* Maurico Magdalena, Emilio Fernandez *Photog* Gabriel Figueroa *Mus* Francisco Dominguez *Cast* Dolores Del Rio, Pedro Armendariz, Manuel Indan *Prod* Films Mundiales.

102 mins. (Dubbed English version 77 mins.)
A painter, in a flashback, recalls how he came to paint a portrait of a beautiful girl. In Xochimilco, near Mexico City, a young girl, Maria (Del Rio) is persecuted by the other people for her mother's misconduct and finds difficulties in selling the flowers from her plot of ground. She is engaged to Lorenzo (Armendariz). A rich merchant (Indan) who lusts after her, takes revenge by refusing her quinine when she is ill. Lorenzo steals the quinine and is arrested. A painter asks to paint her portrait and she agrees. Then some natives see the nude portrait and not knowing she posed only for the head, stone her to death as they had her mother.
This poignant film was the first Mexican film to make an impact in Europe. Its success enabled Dolores Del Rio to begin a new career. Figueroa's typical camera style is first identifiable in this film, while Pedro Armendariz created the moustached Mexican peon type he was to make famous. The film is, however, not exempt from conventional folkloric elements and the image of the "happy natives" that typify some of Fernandez' work.

MARIE — A HUNGARIAN LEGEND TAVASZI ZAPOR

MARIUS, FANNY, CESAR (trilogy) France 1931–36.
— *Marius* France 1931. *Dir* Alexander Korda *Scen* Marcel Pagnol based on his own play *Photog* Ted Pahle *Mus* Francis Grammon *Cast* Raimu, Pierre Fresnay, Charpin, Orane Demazis, Robert Vattier, Alida Rouffe, E. Delmont, Milly Mathis, Paul Dullac, Mihalesco *Prod* Marcel Pagnol for Paramount. 125 mins.
— *Fanny* France 1932. *Dir* Marc Allégret *Scen* Marcel Pagnol based on his own play *Assist Dir* Pierre Prévert, Yves Allégret *Photog* Nicholas Torporkoff *Art Dir* Scognamillo *Mus* Vincent Scotto *Cast* as for *Marius Prod* Marcel Pagnol for Paramount. 128 mins.
— *César* France 1936. *Dir/Scen* Marcel Pagnol based on his own play *Photog* Willer *Mus* Vincent Scotto *Cast* as for *Marius Prod* Marcel Pagnol for Paramount. 117 mins.
Although *Marius* was directed by Alexander Korda and *Fanny* by Marc Al-

légret, Marcel Pagnol himself is the true *auteur* of all three films. The story is about Marius (Fresnay), whose father, César (Raimu), runs a Marseilles waterfront bar. Marius abandons his fiancée, Fanny (Demazis), because of his love of the sea. She marries the wealthy widower Panisse (Charpin) and provides him with an heir who is really Marius' son. Twenty years later, Panisse is dead and the son succeeds in reuniting his mother and Marius.

Despite its peripatetic plot, this trilogy is far from being a simple melodrama. Its robust observation of the behavior of the ordinary people of Marseilles, unrivaled performances by actors trained by Pagnol, and brilliant use of the natural settings of Marseilles made it a world-wide success.

OTHER VERSIONS:

— *Der Schwarze Walfish / The Black Whale* Germany 1934. *Dir* Fritz Wendhausen *Cast* Emil Jannings, Max Gülstorff, Angela Salloker.

A stylized version of Pagnol's *Fanny*, with some material from *Marius*.

— *Port of Seven Seas* USA 1938. *Dir* James Whale *Scen* Preston Sturges based on the Marcel Pagnol trilogy *Photog* Karl Freund *Cast* Wallace Beery, Frank Morgan, John Beal, Maureen O'Sullivan *Prod* MGM.

Despite the talent involved, this version is only a crude reflection of the original, with an incredibly hammy performance by Wallace Beery as César. Curiously, the name Fanny was changed to Madelon (O'Sullivan) presumably because of Code objections to the possible vulgar implications of the original name.

— *Fanny* USA 1960. *Dir* Joshua Logan *Cast* Leslie Caron, Maurice Chevalier, Charles Boyer. 133 mins. Technicolor. Joshua Logan's unmemorable version is based on a musical version of the original play, but without the songs.

MARKED ONES (THE) GEZEICHNETEN (DIE)

MARK OF ZORRO (THE) USA 1920. *Dir* Fred Niblo (and Ted Reed for the action scenes) *Scen* based on the story *The Curse of Capistrano* by Johnston McCulley *Photog* William McGann, Harry Thorpe *Art Dir* Edward Langley *Cast* Douglas Fairbanks, Marguerite de la Motte, Claire McDowell, Noah Beery, Robert McKim, Walt Whitman *Prod* United Artists. 8 reels.

In Spanish-controlled California, Zorro (Fairbanks) combats the evil Sergeant Pedro (Beery) and Captain Ranson (McKim), courts a beautiful woman (de la Motte), and wins in the end, after we have learned that the mysterious masked avenger, Zorro, is also a mannered and effeminate aristocrat.

This delightful tongue-in-cheek spoof marked a major change in the Fairbanks character from the all-American boy to action-costume roles. "Douglas' vigorous healthiness" (Moussinac) is perhaps best seen in this work. Fred Niblo, a mediocre craftsman, is credited as director but Fairbanks is largely responsible for all his films.

— *Don Q, Son of Zorro* USA 1925. *Dir* Donald Crisp *Scen* based on a story by K. and H. Pritchard *Cast* Douglas Fairbanks, Mary Astor, Donald Crisp, Jack McDonald, Jean Hersholt *Prod* United Artists. 10,264 ft.

Produced to capitalize on the success of *Mark of Zorro* but far from being as good. However this did not prevent the multiplication of a surfeit of "Zorros" (Spanish for fox) in films, serials, cartoons, etc.

— *The Mark of Zorro* USA 1940. *Dir* Rouben Mamoulian *Scen* Bess Meredith, Garret Ford based on the story by Johnston McCulley *Photog* Arthur Miller *Cast* Tyrone Power, Linda Darnell, Basil Rathbone *Prod* 20th Century-Fox. 93 mins.

A pictorially elegant remake by Mamoulian, though with less action and comedy than the original.

MARRIED WOMAN (A) UNE FEMME MARIÉE

MARSEILLAISE (LA) France 1937. *Dir* Jean Renoir *Assist Dir* Jacques Becker, J.-P. Dreyfus, Claude Renoir, Demazure, Marc Maurette, Corteggiani *Scen* Jean Renoir, Carl Koch, N. Martel, J.-P. Dreyfus *Photog* Jean Bourgoin, Jean Douarinou, Maillols *Art Dir* Léon Barsacq, Georges Wakhévitch, Jean Perrier *Shadow theatre* Lotte Reiniger *Mus* Joseph Kosma, Sauveplane and various 18th century composers *Ed* Marguerite Renoir *Cast* Pierre Renoir Lise Delamare, Louis Jouvet, Maurice Escande, Aimé Clariond, Jaque Catelain, Jean-Louis Allibert, Gaston Modot, Ardisson and others *Prod* Syndicats CGT and general subscription. Original length 145 mins; released in several shorted versions ranging from 80 to

104 mins.; 1967 re-release version is 130 mins.
The story of 150 revolutionary volunteers from Marseilles at the time they assembled and adopted a new marching song and marched to Paris. It describes the events of August 10, 1789, and the capture of the king, and ends on the eve of the Battle of Valmy. Produced during the days of the Popular Front and financed by the trade unions, this important film encountered more political attacks than artistic ones. Although its plot is a little uneven, it contains some extremely beautiful sequences: Louis XVI (Renoir) in Versailles on the morning of July 15, 1789, being told of the storming of the Bastille; the three revolutionaries in the mountains of Provence; the meeting in the Club des Jacobins in Marseilles; the march of the Marseilles volunteers to Paris; the exiled aristocracy in Coblenz plotting their return; the storming of the Tuileries and the flight of the royal family; the Marseillais and the federate army on the road to Valmy. Louis XVI, as conceived by Jean Renoir and portrayed by Pierre Renoir, is not the conventional feeble-minded idiot, but an intelligent and sensible man who tries to conserve his rights as an absolute monarch but is overwhelmed by the march of history. The Marseillais (actors from the south of France, trained by Pagnol and in *caf'conc'*) form a very true collective portrait.
[Renoir's aim in *la Marseillaise* was to create a kind of "documentary" film of the people who took part in the Revolution. There is no idealization in the film and no dramatization; its impact lies in its naturalness, its attempt to portray human details against a background of history.]

MARTY USA 1955. *Dir* Delbert Mann *Scen* Paddy Chayevsky based on his own TV play *Photog* Joseph La Shelle *Mus* Roy Webb *Cast* Ernest Borgnine, Betsy Blair *Prod* Hecht-Lancaster-Steven for United Artists. 99 mins.
The love story of a warmhearted, shy butcher (Borgnine) and a plain, wistful schoolteacher (Blair) in the Bronx.
This film, which was acclaimed a little too highly after it received the Palme d'or at Cannes, has qualities that derive less from Delbert Mann's direction than from Paddy Chayevsky's "neorealist" script. Chayevsky, who had experience as a writer for radio, reveals here his marvelous sense of observation and of naturalistic dialogue. His heros come, not from Hollywood, but from American daily life. The commercial success of this low-budget film encouraged the development of independent production in the USA as well as a search for new themes.

MARX BROTHERS GO WEST (THE) GO WEST

*****MASCULIN-FEMININ** MASCULINE-FEMININE France 1966. *Dir* Jean-Luc Godard *Scen* Jean-Luc Godard freely based on *La Femme de Paul* and *Le Signe* by Guy de Maupassant *Photog* Willy Kurant *Mus* Francis Lai *Ed* Agnès Guillemot *Cast* Jean-Pierre Léaud, Chantal Goya, Marlène Jobert, Michel Debord, Catherine-Isabelle Duport. 103 mins.
Paul (Léaud) comes home from his military service to Paris in December 1965, when presidential elections are being held. He loves Madeleine (Goya), who finds him a job with a popular show. She is a singer and makes her first record. Paul seeks warmth and tenderness but finds only despair.
According to Scott Burton: "In *Masculin-Féminin,* Godard compiles a natural history of this period (adolescence). His film is also a version of *Kulturroman,* very much about a particular society at a particular time and place, and about how its issues and obsessions touch its young — now intimately, now peripherally . . . Godard's movie is full of dualities, of ambivalence and opposition. But the terms of its antitheses are as shifting as the loyalties of its characters, who are themselves described as the product of an extraordinary dialectic: they are 'the children of Marx and Coca-Cola' . . . The form of the film shifts back and forth between inclusive, open improvisation and considered articulated design."

MAT MOTHER USSR 1926. *Dir* V. I. Pudovkin *Scen* N. Zarkhi, V. I. Pudovkin based on the novel by Maxim Gorky *Photog* A. Golovnia *Art Dir* Sergei Kozlovsky *Cast* Vera Baranovskaya, Nikolai Batalov, A. Chistyakov, Ivan Koval-Samborsky *Prod* Mezhrabpom-Russ. 6,325 ft.
A free adaptation of the novel. The mother (Baranovskaya) is married to a worker (Chistyakov) who is a strike

breaker and a drunkard. After his death she reveals to the police where her son (Batalov) has hidden the arms his comrades have entrusted to him. She realizes her error when he is condemned to prison by the authorities. He escapes and meets her again in a demonstration in which they are killed.

Famous sequences: the death of the father (a character not in the original novel); the arrival of the police, their search, and the mother's pleading with them; the trial; the prison revolt; the son's escape over the ice that is breaking up on a river; the clash with the police; the mother raising the fallen Red flag; the final sequence suggesting the Revolution with the Soviet flag flying over the Kremlin.

It was largely in relation to *Mother* that Léon Moussinac wrote: "Pudovkin's 'types' are pure and complete because they represent not a 'bit' of humanity but that which is eternal and inevitable in human nature itself. These 'types' are also unforgettable because they are intimately and powerfully related to an overall theme of significant social acts in which, whether they like it or not, men endlessly participate."

The sequence on the ice was not taken from the novel but from Griffith's *Way Down East* (q.v.). In the film's climax, which includes this sequence, the arrival of spring at the prison as the escape begins presages the theme of the breakup of the ice; the movement of the river matches that of the marching crowds in the May Day demonstration, while the smashing of the ice against the metallic bridge matches the clash with the police. The lyricism of the climax is in this way derived from a metaphor taken directly from the action. It is a classic example of the art of editing in silent film.

At Brussels in 1958, *Mother* was voted as one of the 12 Best Films of All Time. Since its release it has had a profound influence everywhere, almost equaling that of *Potemkin*.

OTHER VERSIONS:

— *Mat/Mother* USSR 1920. *Dir* Alexander Razumni *Scen* M. Stupina from Gorky's novel *Cast* Vladimir Karin, L. Sychova. 3,700 ft. approx.

— *Mat/Mother/1905* USSR 1955. *Dir* Mark Donskoy *Scen* Mark Donskoy, N. Kovarsky based on Gorky's novel *Photog* A. Mishurin *Art Dir* V. Agranov *Mus* Lev Schwartz *Cast* Vera Maret-

skaya, Alexei Batalov *Prod* Kiev Studio. 105 mins. Sovcolor.

Donskoy's version is a very faithful adaptation of the novel. The first part, showing the factory under the Tsar is very beautiful, but after the demonstration and a flight of doves, the style becomes weak and the story begins to meander. It regains its forcefulness in the finale, in which the mother is arrested in a station and addresses the crowd. Vera Maretskaya gives a very moving performance. Although this version doesn't match Pudovkin's, it is important to see it in the complete version and not in the various re-edited and cut versions shown outside the USSR.

MATER DOLOROSA France 1917. *Dir/Scen* Abel Gance *Photog* L.-Henri Burel *Cast* Emmy Lynn, Armand Tallier, Firmin Gémier, Gaston Modot *Prod* Films de France. 4,290 ft.

Dr. Berliac (Gémier) neglects his wife (Lynn), who falls in love with the doctor's brother (Tallier) and has a child by him. The affairs ends with her attempted suicide. In trying to stop her, the lover accidentally kills himself, but before dying he makes her swear she will never reveal their affair and writes a suicide note. The doctor is suspicious, and takes the child away from her. She becomes frantic when the child falls ill and eventually tells the doctor the whole story. He is so moved by her despair that he reunites her with the child.

Abel Gance's first major commercial success, not only in France but also especially in the USA. It is notable not for its plot but for its authoritative direction and its striking "chiaroscuro photography stressing facial expressions" (Delluc).

— *Mater Dolorosa* France 1932. *Dir/Scen* Abel Gance *Photog* Roger Hubert *Cast* Line Noro, Gaby Triquet, Samson Fainsilber, Jean Galland, Antonin Artaud.

Gance's attempt to re-create his earlier film was not a success.

The following have the same title as Gance's films:

— **Mater Dolorosa* France 1909. *Dir* Louis Feuillade *Prod* Pathé.

The story of a mother who sacrifices her farm and her life to satisfy her son's love for the village coquette.

— **Mater Dolorosa/Die Schmerzensreiche Mutter* Germany 1924. *Dir* Joseph Delmont. *Scen* B. E. Lüthge. 6 reels.

MATKA JOANNA OD ANIOLOW MOTHER JOAN OF THE ANGELS/THE DEVIL AND THE NUN/JOAN OF THE ANGELS Poland 1960. *Dir* Jerzy Kawalerowicz *Scen* Tadeusz Konwicki, Jerzy Kawalerowicz based on the novel by Jaroslav Iwaszkiewicz *Photog* Jerzy Wojcik *Art Dir* Roman Mann, Tadeusz Borowczyk *Mus* Adam Walacinski *Cast* Lucyna Winnicka, Mieczyslaw Voit, Anna Ciepielewska *Prod* Kadr. 108 mins.

In a 17th century Polish convent, Mother Joan (Winnicka) and the nuns are "possessed" by devils. The local parish priest, who has been burned at the stake, and several other priests have tried in vain to exorcise the spirits. A new priest, Suryn (Voit), arrives but finally he, too, becomes possessed and ends by killing two innocent people.

Based on the famous French case of Devils of Loudon and Urban Grandier, this passionate, visually stylized, almost mannered film accurately depicts hysterical possession in the time of Callot and La Tour.

MAUDITE SOIT LA GUERRE LE MOULIN MAUDIT Belgium 1913. *Dir/Scen* Alfred Machin *Assist* André Jacquemin *Photog* Jacques Bizeuil, Paul Flon *Cast* Baert, La Berni, Albert Hendricks, Fernand Crommelynck, Nadia d'Anjély, Goidsen *Prod* Belge-Cinéma Film. 1,050 meters. Pathécolor.

Produced on the brink of World War I and set against a background of war between two imaginary nations, the film tells of the rivalry between two pilots and shows their fights, the burning of a mill, aerial battles, etc. While not matching the promise of its title (literally "War be damned") this is an interesting and spectacular film directed by a French film maker who almost alone before 1914 used the cinema as a weapon in the fight for progress.

MAUDITS (LES) THE DAMNED France 1947. *Dir* René Clément *Scen* Jacques Rémy, René Clément, Henri Jeanson based on a story by Jacques Companeez, Victor Alexandrov *Photog* Henri Alekan *Art Dir* Paul Bertrand *Mus* Yves Baudrier *Ed* Roger Dwyre *Cast* Paul Bernard, Henri Vidal, Dalio, Michel Auclair, Fosco Giachetti, Florence Marly, Jean Didier, Jo Dest *Prod* Spéva-Film. 105 mins.

In 1945, while Germany is collapsing, a group of influential Nazis kidnap a French doctor (Vidal) and flee in a submarine to South America. Only a few of them believe they have a mission and when the submarine has to refuel from a freighter many escape. A fanatical Nazi (Didier) orders the sinking of the freighter and a fight ensues in which the remnants of the party escape or are killed.

One of René Clément's best films, in which he conveys brilliantly the claustrophobic feeling of a submerged submarine where the rivalries and quarrels are made more explosive by the oppressive atmosphere.

MAUVAISES RENCONTRES (LES) France 1955. *Dir* Alexandre Astruc *Scen* Alexandre Astruc, Roland Laudenbach based on the novel *Une sacrée salade* by Cécil Saint-Laurent *Photog* Robert Lefebvre *Art Dir* Max Douy *Ed* Maurice Serain *Mus* Maurice Leroux *Cast* Anouk Aimée, Jean-Claude Pascal, Philippe Lemaire, Gianni Esposito, Claude Dauphin *Prod* Films Marceau. 102 mins.

As she is interrogated by the police on a charge of procuring an abortion a young journalist, Catherine (Aimée), relives her past relationships with various men: an editor (Pascal), a photographer (Lemaire), a man from the provinces trying to establish himself (Esposito), and a somewhat unscrupulous doctor (Dauphin).

Astruc's first feature is stylistically expressive and full of interesting visual effects, but the untalented Laudenbach's adaptation of Saint-Laurent's conventional crime melodrama made it difficult for Astruc to develop the "Education sentimentale" theme — though he made a film of Flaubert's novel six years later. Nevertheless, its stylistic qualities exercised great influence on some members of the future *nouvelle vague*.

MAX (series) France 1907–1916.

Before he left for the USA in 1917, Max Linder made between 100 and 200 short comedies in France featuring the dapper comic, Max. Chaplin was a great admirer of his work. Among the best of his early films are:

— *Max et le quinquina/Max victime du quinquina* France 1911. *Dir* Max Linder *Assist* René Leprince *Scen* Maurice Delamare, Max Linder *Cast* Max Linder, Vandenne, Gabrielle Lange, Paulette

Lorsy, Maurice Delamare *Prod* Pathé. 1 reel.

Having drunk too much quinquina (an aperitif wine), Max receives three challenges to duels; the drunken man visits the homes of his adversaries and provokes various mix-ups. The film contains only 27 shots. Famous gag: Max collapses in the street; faced with a policeman, he seizes his sword and transforms himself into a bullfighter fighting this "cow."

— *Max, professeur de tango/Max, Tango Teacher/Too Much Mustard* France 1912. *Dir* Max Linder *Assist* René Leprince *Scen* Max Linder *Cast* Max Linder, Leonora *Prod* Pathé. 1 reel.

The exterior scenes of this film were improvised in Berlin during one of Linder's stage tours. Max courts a pretty girl (Leonora) and tries to teach her the tango after getting tight in a nightclub. Since the dance was new and few knew how to do it, the family imitates Max's drunken blunderings believing that they are the tango steps. When Max crosses the Unter den Linden gathering up fresh snow and using it as confetti, he reveals a deep understanding of mime and the comic use of objects from which Chaplin was later to profit.

— *Max toréador* France 1912. *Dir* Max Linder *Assist* René Leprince *Scen* Armand Massard *Cast* Max Linder, Stacia Napierkowska *Prod* Pathé. 1 reel.

Dreaming of becoming a bull fighter, Max practices on a cow in his Parisian apartment, then goes into a Spanish arena to fight a real bull. The first part, with the gentleman installing a cow in his bedroom, is marvelous, but the second part, filmed in the arena of Barcelona, is not as good.

See also: *Seven Year's Bad Luck; The Three Must-Get-Theres*

MAXIM TRILOGY see YUNOST MAKSIMA

*****MEET ME IN ST. LOUIS** USA 1944. *Dir* Vincente Minnelli *Scen* Irving Brecher, Fred F. Fomklehoffe based on the stories by Sally Benson *Photog* George Folsey *Art Dir* Cedric Gibbons *Ed* Albert Akst *Songs* Hugh Martin, Ralph Blane *Cast* Judy Garland, Margaret O'Brien, Mary Astor, Lucille Bremer, Leon Ames, Tom Drake, Marjorie Main, Hank Daniels *Prod* MGM. 113 mins. Technicolor.

The story of the Smith family of St. Louis during one summer, autumn, and winter at the turn of the century. Esther (Garland) takes a fancy to the boy next door; Rose (Bremer) is awaiting a proposal from her beau; Tootie (O'Brien) is up to mischief. The father (Ames) says they have to move to New York but, after a minor family tragedy, everything ends up happily.

Minnelli's first major film is a delightful integration of songs and dances with the nostalgic, gently comic stories of childhood by Sally Benson. The dialogue of these stories was retained almost intact in the film. Judy Garland is at the peak of her talents in the memorable songs. This film's blend of story and songs in the style of *The Love Parade* (*q.v.*) was to become almost a trademark of the postwar MGM musicals.

MELODIE DER WELT (DIE) MELODY OF THE WORLD/WORLD MELODY Germany 1929. *Dir/Scen/Ed* Walther Ruttmann *Photog* Reimar Kuntze, Wilhelm Lehne, Rudolph Rathmann, Paul Holzki *Mus* Wolfgang Zeller *Prod* Tonbild Syndikat. 1,115 meters (3,600 ft. approx.)

A compilation film whose basic idea (every man, woman and child goes through the same daily routine whatever the color of their skin) is very good. Using material from the UFA newsreel archives, Ruttmann's editing gives some of the sequences (the swimming and diving for example) an astonishing visual impact. *Melodie der Welt* created immense excitement in the early days of sound and still remains interesting, despite the pedantry of a script that catalogues some activities in ponderous detail (getting up, the morning wash, breakfast, daily exercises, etc.). In order to put a sound track over silent footage, (involving a change from 16 to 24 frames per second) the film had to be "stretched" by printing one extra frame every three. The result is a sometimes hilarious distortion of movement.

MEN (THE) BATTLE STRIPE USA 1950. *Dir* Fred Zinnemann *Scen* Carl Foreman *Photog* Robert De Grasse *Art Dir* Edward G. Boyle *Mus* Dimitri Tiomkin *Ed* Harry Gerstad *Cast* Marlon Brando, Teresa Wright, Everett Sloane *Prod* Stanley Kramer for United Artists. 86 mins.

Ken (Brando) is paralyzed from the waist down as a result of a war wound. In the hospital he feels himself incurable and is very bitter and resentful. He hesitates to marry his fiancée (Wright) but a doctor (Sloane) helps them and they marry. Their first night is a disaster when the girl betrays her uncertainty and Ken reverts to self-pity and leaves. In the hospital, his companions refuse to sympathize with him and he returns to his wife.

"The most admirable thing about this film is the relentless honesty that prevents it from becoming melodramatic" (Jean Queval). Zinnemann's sparse style, the discrete presentation of the couple's sexual problems, and the moving collective portrait of the young paraplegics (most of whom were real) add much to the success of this early Stanley Kramer production. Tiomkin's music is effective and unobtrusive. This was Marlon Brando's film debut.

MENILMONTANT France 1926. *Dir/Prod/ Scen* Dimitri Kirsanoff (Kirsanov) *Photog* Léone Crovan, Dimitri Kirsanoff *Cast* Nadia Sibirskaia, Yolande Beaulieu, Guy Belmont, Jean Pasquier, Maurice Ronsard. 2,850 ft.

A young girl (Sibirskaia), the rival of her sister (Beaulieu), is seduced by a fickle youth (Belmont) who deserts her when she is pregnant. She contemplates suicide, meets her sister, who has since become a prostitute, is reconciled with her, and regains her own enjoyment of life.

This film without titles is not a melodrama but an antecedent to neorealism, portraying life itself with a sensitive use of natural sets and a feeling for poetry and truth. Nadia Sibirskaia is as simple and moving as the work of her husband, a Russian who emigrated to France.

MENSCHEN AM SONNTAG PEOPLE ON SUN-DAY Germany 1929. *Dir* Robert Siodmak, *Assist* Fred Zinnemann, Edgar Ulmer *Scen* Billy Wilder based on an idea by Kurt Siodmak *Photog* Eugen Schüfftan *Cast* Brigitte Borchert, Christl Ehlers, Annie Schreyer, Wolfgang von Walterschausen, Erwin Splettstösser *Prod* Filmstudio 1929. 2,014 meters (6,600 ft. approx.).

Two couples spend a holiday in the countryside around Berlin. This low-budget semidocumentary uses nonprofessional actors in natural sets and is the last notable German silent film. Though Bela Balasz criticized its "fanaticism of facts," *People on Sunday* is derived from

the work of Flaherty and Vertov and is a contemporary social document. The authors went on to very diverse careers in the cinema.

MEPRIS (LE) CONTEMPT France/Italy 1963. *Dir* Jean-Luc Godard *Scen* Jean-Luc Godard based on the novel *Il Disprezzo* (*A Ghost at Noon*) by Alberto Moravia *Photog* Raoul Coutard *Mus* Georges Delerue *Ed* Agnès Guillemot, Lila Lakshmanan *Cast* Brigitte Bardot, Jack Palance, Michel Piccoli, Georgia Moll, Fritz Lang, Jean-Luc Godard *Prod* Rome-Paris Film/Films Concordia/Cinematografia Champion. 103 mins. Technicolor. Franscope.

Paul Javal (Piccoli), a scriptwriter in Rome, is working on a rewrite of an adaptation of *The Odyssey* that is being produced by Jeremy Prokosch (Palance) and directed by Fritz Lang. Though once deeply in love, Paul and his wife Camille (Bardot) are drifting apart in mistrust. Camille's developing contempt for Paul is increased after an incident with the producer who invites them to his villa in Capri. Paul refuses to work on the script, hoping to regain his wife's respect, but she leaves with Prokosch and they are both killed in an automobile accident. Fritz Lang continues to shoot the film.

["*Le Mépris* is the story of men cut off from themselves, from the world, from reality. They awkwardly seek their way back to the light, but they are enclosed in a dark room . . . Paul Javal is the first of my characters to be realistic, whose psychology is justifiable . . . Bardot not at all" (Godard).] This is one of Godard's finest films: taut, vibrant, and sensitive, whose tragedy unfolds relentlessly, reaching its climax in the strangely transfigured landscapes of Capri. Fritz Lang made his acting debut in this film as the director of *The Odyssey* — a witness to the vengeance of the gods.

MERRY-GO-ROUND KORHINTA

***MERRY WIDOW (THE)**
— USA 1925. *Dir* Erich von Stroheim *Scen* Erich von Stroheim, Benjamin Glazier based on the operetta *Photog* William Daniels, Oliver T. Marsh, Ben Reynolds *Art Dir* Cedric Gibbons, Richard Day *Ed* Frank Hull *Mus* David Mendoza, William Awt based on the music of Franz Lehàr *Cast* John Gil-

bert, Mae Murray, Roy D'Arcy, Tully Marshall *Prod* MGM. 10,027 ft. (reduced from 14 reels by MGM).

Stroheim's satire on the Viennese aristocracy has lost none of its bite and visual elegance with the years. Stroheim took the operetta's central theme — a Prince (Gilbert) who falls in love with an American actress (Murray) — and used it to portray a decadent aristocracy and court intrigue. Some of his more sardonic scenes were apparently removed in the producer's release version but this did not prevent it from becoming an enormous popular success. The difference between the Stroheim and Lubitsch versions is perhaps best described in Stroheim's own words: "Lubitsch shows you first the king on the throne, then as he is in the bedroom. I show you the king in the bedroom so you'll know just what he is when you see him on his throne."

— *USA 1934. *Dir* Ernst Lubitsch *Scen* Ernest Vajda, Samson Raphaelson based on the operetta *Photog* Oliver Marsh *Art Dir* Cedric Gibbons, Gabriel Scognamillo, Fredric Hope, Edwin B. Willis *Mus* Franz Lehàr, adapted and arranged by Herbert Stothart *Cast* Maurice Chevalier, Jeanette MacDonald, Edward Everett Horton, Una Merkel *Prod* MGM. 110 mins.

Undoubtedly this charming, tongue-in-cheek version by Lubitsch comes closest to the composer's and librettists' intentions, even though only half the score is sung and that almost entirely by Jeanette MacDonald. Although the silent version had made a fortune for MGM, the public did not respond to this film at all. It was the fourth and last appearance together of Maurice Chevalier and Jeanette MacDonald.

— *USA 1952. *Dir* Curtis Bernhardt *Scen* Sonya Levien, William Ludwig based on the operetta *Photog* Robert Surtees *Art Dir* Cedric Gibbons, Paul Groesse *Cast* Lana Turner, Fernando Lamas, Una Merkel, Richard Haydn *Prod* MGM. 104 mins. Technicolor.

A top-heavy version, with colossal sets, elaborately staged numbers, and dreadful reorchestrations, it totally lacks the deft spirit of the original

*MESHES OF THE AFTERNOON USA 1943. *Dir/Photog/Ed/Cast* Maya Deren in collaboration with Alexander Hammid (Hackenschmied). 13 mins. Silent.

Together with *At Land* (*q.v.*) this is one of the seminal films of the American experimental cinema. It is Maya Deren's first film and was made in collaboration with her husband, the film maker Alexander Hammid. A girl (Deren) comes home one afternoon, falls asleep, and sees herself in a dream returning home, tortured by loneliness and frustrations, and eventually committing suicide.

Maya Deren wrote: "This first film is concerned with the relationship between the imaginative and objective reality. The film begins in actuality and, eventually, ends there. But in the meantime the imagination, here given as a dream, intervenes. It seizes upon a casual incident and, elaborating it into critical proportions, thrusts back into reality the product of its convolutions. The protagonist does not suffer some subjective delusion of which the world outside remains independent, if not obvious; on the contrary, she is, in actuality, destroyed by an imaginative action."

METROPOLIS — DAS SCHICKSAL EINER MENSCHHEIT IM JAHRE 2000 Germany 1926. *Dir* Fritz Lang *Scen* Thea von Harbou *Photog* Karl Freund, Günther Rittau (special effects Eugen Schüfftan) *Art Dir* Otto Hunte, Erich Kettelhut, Karl Vollbrecht *Mus* Gottfried Huppertz *Cast* Brigitte Helm, Alfred Abel, Gustav Fröhlich, Rudolf Klein-Rogge, Fritz Rasp, Heinrich George *Prod* UFA. 4,189 meters (13,700 ft. approx.) Existing English versions range from 8,400 to 9,300 ft.

In the 21st century a gigantic metropolis is controlled by an authoritarian industrialist (Abel) who lives with his son, Freder (Fröhlich), and his collaborators in a paradise-like garden. The workers live in a subterranean portion of the city. Maria (Helm), a saintly agitator, exhorts the workers to be patient; soon the Mediator will come. Freder becomes a devotee of Maria. The industrialist hears Maria and entrusts a mad inventor with the job of creating a robot that looks exactly like her and that will incite the workers to revolt. The inventor is successful and the workers destroy the machines, releasing flood waters that threaten to drown their own children. Freder and Maria save the doomed city and, in the finale, a foreman (George) shakes hands with the industrialist and Maria and Freder are married: labor and capital are united. "The path to human dignity and happiness lies through the master of us all, the great Mediator, Love," says the industrialist at the end of Thea von Harbou's scenario.

The film cost 7 million Marks. Its production lasted from May 22, 1925 to October 30, 1926. Almost 2 million feet of negative were shot and (according to the publicity) the following were used: 8 stars, 25,000 men, 11,000 women, 1,100 bald people, 250 children, 25 negros, 3,500 pairs of special shoes, 50 cars.

Famous sequences: the luxurious quarters of the ruling class with the statues, swimming pools, hanging gardens, and places of pleasure; the underground city where the workers have to live and work like robots; the electric Moloch machine controlling everything; the suggestion of slaves building the pyramids; the old house of the mad inventor where he gives life to the artificial woman; the destruction of the Moloch machine; the children drowning in the underground city and the robot-woman burned as a witch. Fritz Lang said in 1959, "I don't like *Metropolis*. The ending is false. I didn't like it even when I made the film." Fritz Lang also recalled in an interview in 1941 that, immediately after Hitler's rise to power, Goebbels had sent for him " . . . he told me that, many years before, he and the Führer had seen *Metropolis* in a small town, and Hitler had said at that time that he wanted me to make Nazi pictures." Later, deportees in the death camp at Mauthausen, constructing a gigantic stairway in 1943, said, "It's like *Metropolis*."

In 1926, however nationalism, in full retreat, appeared liquidated and Thea von Harbou's propaganda fable supported the aims of the coalition (Social Democrats and Christian party) government then in power. This was not only because of its "Christian" and reformist reconciliation between capital and labor but because it "revealed" that the first victims of a revolution fomented by irresponsible intellectuals were the children of the workers.

This science-fiction drama was derived both from the traditions of expressionism and medieval myths. *The Golem* (*q.v.*) and *Homunculus,* as well as *Caligari* (*q.v.*) and *Nosferatu* (*q.v.*) were ancestors of the film's evil female robot.

METROPOLITAN SYMPHONY TOKAI KOKYO-GAKU

MEXICAN BUS RIDE SUBIDA AL CIELO

MICHURIN USSR 1947 (revised for 1948 release). *Dir/Scen* Alexander Dovzhenko *Co-Dir* Yulia Solntseva *Photog* Leonid Kosmatov, Yuli Kun *Art Dir* M. Bogdanov, G. Myasnikov *Mus* Dmitri Shostakovich *Cast* G. Belov, A. Vasilieva, F. Grigoriev *Prod* Mosfilm. 103 mins. Sovcolor.

The life of the famous naturalist, Michurin (1855–1936), (Belov), who was a simple gardener in Kozlov in the Ukraine at the turn of the century but after the Russian Revolution became world famous for developing 350 new fruit species.

[Dovzhenko had long wanted to make this film (which he originally conceived as a play) but its production coincided with the international controversy about the theories of Michurin's most famous follower, Lysenko.] The Stalin regime ordered Dovzhenko to revise the film and these revisions so irritated him that a considerable part of the final version was made without him. However, it does include some beautiful sequences that only Dovzhenko could have created: Michurin's early failures and difficulties; the scene following his wife's death; and especially the lyrical sequence in an autumn landscape, where the aging Michurin reminisces with his wife about their happy youth. This is immediately followed by the October Revolution and the raising of the Red flag. The lyricism of this piece of cinema, whose color harmonies are incomparable with any previous film, is heightened by Shostakovich's very beautiful score. This was Dovzhenko's last film; he died in 1956 before completing his long-planned *Poem of the Sea* (*q.v.*), which was completed by his widow, Yulia Solntseva.

MICKEY MOUSE (cartoon series) USA 1928–1960 (?). *Dir* Ub Iwerks, Walt Disney, and various others.

This anthropomorphic mouse, wearing big shoes and short trousers with his long tail hanging out, began his career as "Mortimer Mouse" (in two films only, *Plane Crazy* 1927 and *Galloping Gaucho* 1928) and adopted his new name after appearing in the first animated film with synchronized sound, *Steamboat Willie,* 1928. Later, dialogue was added and, when a three-color process became practicable, Mickey Mouse cartoons were among the first to use it. Disney himself provided Mickey's voice in the early days.

In the "Film Daily Year Book" for 1929, the following advertisement appears: "Mickey Mouse Sound Cartoons. Produced by Walt Disney. Drawn by Ub Iwerks." This announcement of his birth (which was repeated in 1930 in the same terms) suggests that the original creator of Mickey was in fact Ub Iwerks who later became head of the production service at Walt Disney Productions, Inc. [Mickey's character, however, must owe much to Walt Disney's conception: Mickey is a quiet, kindhearted, "ordinary guy," an innocent who nevertheless manages always to defeat his more spectacular opponents. It is on this characteristic, apart from the series' technical expertise and gags, that Mickey's world-wide popularity was based.]

Ub Iwerks also created Mickey's wife, Minnie, alongside her stubborn husband a very retiring character – lucky, incurably optimistic, and incredibly naive. Later in the Thirties other anthropomorphic animals were introduced: Donald Duck dressed in sailor's clothes, angry, nasal, and always tilting at windmills; Pluto the idiotic dog, toadying, blundering, and faithful; Goofy, timid and bewildered; and an entire menagerie of other animals.

Mickey's worldwide popularity was enormous and since 1935, he has actually been included with a thousand other divinities in the pantheon of a Hindu Temple. The date of his death is not exactly known. However, it appears that Mickey Mouse was withdrawn from production in about 1955, the Disney factory thereafter restricting itself to revising and re-releasing earlier productions. A complete filmography of the 100 or so Mickey Mouse cartoons has never been established; at least a dozen, such as *Clock Cleaners* and *The Band Concert,* are true masterpieces whose influence is still evident in many American and European animated films.

See also: *Silly Symphonies* (cartoon series)

MIDDAY DARKNESS (A) MAHIRU NO ANKOKU

MIDSUMMER NIGHT'S DREAM (A) USA 1935. *Dir* Max Reinhardt, William Dieterle *Scen* Charles Kenyon, Mary McCall based on the Shakespeare play *Photog* Hal Mohr, Byron Haskin and others *Mus* Erich Korngold arranging Mendelssohn's

A Midsummer Night's Dream Choreog Bronislawa Nijinska *Cast* James Cagney, Joe E. Brown, Mickey Rooney, Hugh Herbert, Olivia de Havilland, Frank McHugh, Dick Powell, Anita Louis *Prod* Warner Brothers. 132 mins.

The only sound film by the genius of the German theater, Max Reinhardt, made in collaboration with his disciple William Dieterle, a former actor. Though it captures much of the spirit of the play, the text is heavily edited to allow full rein to Reinhardt's penchant for production effects. The Warner Studios expended great effort on the million dollar spectacular. It is full of major stars (in somewhat unorthodox roles), sumptuous sets, and soft photography and lighting designed to produce a romantic, magical quality, but it was a total commercial failure.

OTHER VERSIONS:

– *France 1909. *Cast* Footitt, Stacia Napierkowska.

– *USA 1909. *Dir* Charles Kent (?) *Cast* Maurice Costello, Billy Ranous, Julia Swayne *Prod* Vitagraph.

– *Germany 1913. *Dir* Stellan Rye *Scen* Hanns Heinz Ewers *Prod* Deutsche Bioscop.

– *Italy 1913 (?) *Cast* Socrate Tommasi, Maria Hübner.

– *Germany 1925. *Dir* Hans Neumann *Photog* Reimar Kuntze, Guido Seeber *Art Dir* Ernö Metzner *Cast* Werner Krauss, Hans Albers, Valeska Gert, Fritz Rasp.

– *USA 1968. *Dir* Peter Hall *Cast* Diana Rigg, Judy Dench, David Warner, Ian Richardson, and members of the Royal Shakespeare Company. 124 mins. Eastman Color.

See also: *Sen Noci Svatojanske*

MIGHTY JOE YOUNG see KING KONG

MIKRES APHRODITES YOUNG APHRODITES Greece 1962. *Dir* Nikos Koundouros *Scen* Costas Spikas, Vassilis Vassilikos based on *Daphnis* by Longus and the poems of Theocritus *Photog* Giovanni Variano *Mus* Yiannis Markopoulos *Ed* George Tsaoulis *Cast* Cleopatra Rota, Eleni Prokopiou, Takis Emmanouel, Vangelis Joannides *Prod* Minos Films/ Anzervos Studios. 98 mins. (88 mins. North America/Britain).

This pastoral romance in which the senses and sensuality of two adolescents (Rota, Joannides) are awakened is very freely based on the pastoral poems of Theocritus and the Greek myth of Daphnis and Chloe.

A pagan hymn to the sensuality and dignity of ancient Greece set against a stark landscape. "Love, in the modern sense of the word, existed in ancient societies only for the ruling classes. The shepherds, about whose joys and miseries of love Theocritus sings, were only slaves" (Frederic Engels).

MILLE DI GARIBALDI (I) *1860* Italy 1933. *Dir* Alessandro Blasetti *Scen* Alessandro Blasetti, Gino Mazzuchi based on a story by Gino Mazzuchi *Photog* A. Brizzi *Art Dir* Cafiero, Carnevari *Cast* Aita Bellia, Antonio Gulino, Mario Ferrari, Maria Denis, Gianfranco Giachetti *Prod* Cinès. 90 mins. approx.

The adventures of a Sicilian mountaineer who, after the liberation of Sicily, leaves his new wife to join Garibaldi's Red Shirts at Genoa and stays to fight with Garibaldi until the defeat of the Bourbon troops.

This excellent film, produced largely in natural sets and using many nonprofessional actors, admirably re-creates the Garibaldi period and was clearly influenced by the Soviet cinema. The film originally ended with a sequence glorifying the Black Shirts, but this was deleted after 1945.

MILLION (LE) France 1931. *Dir* René Clair *Scen* René Clair based on the musical comedy by Georges Berr and Guillemaud *Photog* Georges Périnal *Art Dir* Lazare Meerson *Mus* Georges Van Parys, Armand Bernard, Philippe Parès *Cast* René Lefèvre, Annabella, Louis Allibert, Wanda Gréville, Paul Olivier, Odette Talazac, Raymond Cordy *Prod* Tobis. 8,029 ft. 89 mins.

A painter (Lefèvre), hounded by his creditors, wins a million on a lottery ticket. But the ticket is left in the pocket of a coat sold to a secondhand shop dealer (Olivier). The hero, in his pursuit of the fortune, is closely followed by his creditors, a false friend (Allibert), their girl friends (Annabella, Gréville), crooks, and the police. All ends happily.

The original musical comedy appealed to Clair because it centered around a chase similar to that in *An Italian Straw Hat* (*q.v.*). But he confided to Charensol as he began the film: "It is obvious the flow (of the play) is based on words.

I want to change this. I am hoping, however, to preserve the irreality of vaudeville by replacing dialogue with music and songs. I am pleased to have discovered this operatic formula in which everybody sings except the main character and I have developed musical elements directly based on the action."

Famous sequences: the chorus of creditors, "the butcher, the baker, the milkman," types similar to those in Commedia dell'Arte; the chase in the opera house; the stout tenor and the even more enormous primadonna singing the sentimental duet, "Nous sommes seuls dans la fôret"; the fight over the coat in the form of a football match, with whistles and the thud of a ball on the sound track; the poetic bric-a-brac in the secondhand shop, "where wax policemen wear fencing masks, where shadows among the collections of top hats and dinosaur skeletons are all alone on the walls, and the feet of hanging models falls naturally from the ceiling" (Paul Gilson).

This film is the best European musical comedy of the early sound period. Several dance sequences are incorporated into the action, though the film is not a ballet — except perhaps in its precise construction and movement arranged symmetrically around the main theme. Meerson's sets, sometimes unreal and dreamlike, sometimes realistic, are perhaps his masterpiece and influenced the future course of art direction in film. This is the young René Lefèvre's best role.

MILLION DOLLAR LEGS USA 1932. *Dir* Edward Cline *Scen* Henry Myers, Nick Barrows based on an original story by Joseph L. Mankiewicz *Photog* Arthur Todd *Cast* W. C. Fields, Jack Oakie, Andy Clyde, Lyda Roberti, Ben Turpin, Susan Fleming, Hugh Herbert, Vernon Dent, Dickie Moore *Prod* Paramount. 65 mins.

A brash American brush salesman (Oakie) arrives in Klopstockia, a country on the brink of economic ruin. He meets the president (Fields), falls in love with his daughter (Fleming), and promotes various schemes to stave off bankruptcy. Because of the athletic prowess of the inhabitants, he advises them to participate in the Olympic Games: the major-domo (Clyde) is the fastest runner on earth. The president wins out in the end, despite the machinations of the secretary of the treasury (Herbert), a mystery man (Turpin), and a vamp, Mata Machree (Roberti).

This nonsense comedy masterpiece features the enormous, insolent W. C. Fields in his first starring role in the talkies. He more than proved himself a match for the Marx Brothers on their own ground, while the lunatic inventiveness of the plot surpasses that of *Hellzapoppin* (*q.v.*). One brief dialogue exchange is characteristic of the film: "Why are all the women called Angela and the men George?" "Why not?"

MIRACLE IN MILAN MIRACOLO A MILANO

MIRACLE WOMAN (THE) USA 1931. *Dir* Frank Capra *Scen* Jo Swerling, Dorothy Howell based on the play *Bless You, Sister* by John Meehan, Robert Riskin *Photog* Joseph Walker *Ed* Maurice Wright *Cast* Barbara Stanwyck, David Manners, Sam Hardy *Prod* Columbia. 90 mins.

A thinly veiled recapitulation of the career and methods of the notorious woman evangelist Aimee Semple Macpherson — Florence Fallon (Stanwyck) in the film — who preached "miracles" in a commercial circus-like atmosphere.

This potent, accurate satire on American evangelism is Capra's first notable sound film and includes a brilliant performance by Barbara Stanwyck.

MIRACOLO A MILANO MIRACLE IN MILAN Italy 1950. *Dir* Vittorio de Sica *Scen* Cesare Zavattini, Vittorio de Sica based on Zavattini's novel *Toto il Buono Photog* Aldo Graziati *Art Dir* Guido Fiorini *Mus* Alessandro Cicognini *Ed* Eraldo Da Roma *Cast* Francesco Golisano, Brunella Bovo, Emma Gramatica, Paolo Stoppa, G. Barnabo *Prod* Productions de Sica/ E.N.I.C. 101 mins.

Toto (Golisano), an abandoned foundling, is raised by a kindly old lady, Lolotta (Gramatica). When she dies he joins a group of poor people and beggars living in a shanty town in the outskirts of Milan and becomes involved in their fight against a rich man (Barnabo) who wants to take away their land because oil has been found on it. Lolotta sends Toto a magic dove to grant the poor people's wishes but pursuing angels remove it and the people are evicted. Lolotta returns the dove to Toto in time

for him, his girl friend (Bovo), and the people to fly away to a better land.

Zavattini's script was based on a novel he had written in 1940. In it, he turns from the precepts of neorealism to an allegorical fantasy that makes a powerful social protest about postwar Italian life.

Notable sequences: Lolotta's unattended funeral; Toto creating a river of milk; the people naively paying admission to a charlatan (Stoppa) for a view of the sunset; the erection of the barricades and the battle with the police; the contrast between the shacks and the luxury trains that pass close by; the police chief singing opera as he orders the assault; the final flight on broomsticks high over Milan.

MISERABLES (LES)

Few novels, except perhaps *The Three Musketeers,* have been so often adapted into films as this novel by Victor Hugo.

— *Les Misérables* France 1911. *Dir* Albert Capellani *Cast* Henry Krauss, Marie Ventura, J. P. Etiévant, Mistinguette, Gabriele de Gravone *Prod* Pathé. 3,450 meters. Released in 4 parts, each 3 reels. Pathécolor.

Capellani's visualization was largely derived from the illustrations (approved by Hugo) in the popular French edition of the novel. The barricades episode is not included in this adaptation.

— *Les Misérables* France 1925. *Dir/Scen* Henri Fescourt *Photog* Merobian, Laffont, Donnot, Abourdier *Cast* Gabriel Gabrio, Sandra Milovanoff, Andrée Rolane, Renée Carl, Jean Toulout, Jeanne-Marie Laurent, Paul Jorge, Georges Saillard, Paul Guidé, Rozet, Charles Bandole *Prod* Ciné-Romans Nalpas. Released in France in 4 parts; in the English version in 2 parts, 32 reels. 1. *Les Misérables;* 2. *The Barricades.* Released in the USA in 1927 in 1 part, 11,500 ft.

Henri Fescourt described this novel by "a great imagist with words": "Great ideas, great emotions, and great action in the old style but mixed with the romantic spirit. In settings depicted by a master's hand the characters are portrayed so strongly that they seem drawn from living reality." Henri Fescourt's film fulfills perfectly his own description of the novel and is the best adaptation of the novel ever made.

— *Les Misérables* France 1934. *Dir* Raymond Bernard *Scen* André Lang, Raymond Bernard *Photog* Jules Kruger *Art Dir* Louis Carré *Mus* Arthur Honegger *Cast* Harry Baur, Charles Vanel, Henry Krauss, Florelle, Josseline Gael, Max Dearly, Jean Servais, Yvette Guilbert *Prod* Pathé-Natan. Released in 2 parts: 1. *Jean Valjean* 109 mins; 2. *Cosette* 100 mins. Released in the USA in 1 part, 165 mins.

The premier of this film was held on February 3, 1934, only a few days before the bloody riots in Paris. This creditable adaptation conveys the spirit of the novel and includes a powerful (sometimes too powerful) performance by Harry Baur. The sets are excellent but the photography somewhat affected.

— *El Bouassa* Egypt 1944. *Dir* Kamal Selim *Cast* Abbas Farès, Amina Rizk, Serag Mounir, Fakher Kakher *Prod* Nil Film. 120 mins. approx.

The characters in this adaptation are 20th century Egyptians in national costumes: Jean Valjean is changed to El Charkawi then Sherif Pasha (M. Madeleine) while Mgr. Myriel becomes El Shiekh Abdallan, and Javert becomes Colonel Fahune, etc.

"The social injustice suffered by Jean Valjean is identical with that born by millions of Egyptians who also suffer from poverty, ignorance, and sickness. In order to satisfy popular taste, Kamal Selim put in the film a song and a dance scene for the marriage between Marius (Fathy) and Cosette (Soad)" (Galal El-Charkawi *History of the Cinema in Egypt*). Despite its commercial ending, this version is one of the best.

— *Les Misérables* France/Italy 1957. *Dir* Jean-Paul Le Chanois *Scen* René Barjavel, Michel Audiard, Jean-Paul Le Chanois *Photog* Jacques Natteau *Mus* Georges Van Parys *Art Dir* Serge Pimenoff *Cast* Jean Gabin, Bernard Blier, Bourvil, Gianni Esposito, Serge Reggiani, Fernand Ledoux, Danièle Delorme, Sylvia Montfort, Jimmy Urbain, etc. *Prod* Pathé/Serena with cooperation of DEFA. Released in 2 parts: 1. 97 mins., 2. 120 mins. Technicolor. Technirama. "The difficulty is to adapt without betraying, to follow faithfully the texture and bring out the spirit of a work that remains young and alive" (J.-P. Le Chanois). Jean Gabin gives one of his last good performances and totally overshadows Bernard Blier's camped-up version of Javert.

OTHER VERSIONS:

— *Le Chemineau* France 1907. *Prod* Pathé.

— *Les Miserables* USA 1909. *Prod* Vitagraph. In 4 parts, each 1 reel.

— *Les Miserables* USA 1918. *Dir* Frank Lloyd *Cast* William Farnum, George Moss, Jewel Carmen *Prod* Fox. 10 reels.

— *Les Misérables* Britain 1922. *Dir* Edward J. Collins *Cast* Lyn Harding. 1 reel.

— *Les Miserables* USA 1935. *Dir* Richard Boleslawski *Photog* Gregg Toland *Art Dir* Richard Day *Cast* Fredric March, Charles Laughton, Rochelle Hudson, John Beal *Prod* 20th Century. 108 mins.

— *Gavroche* USSR 1937. *Dir* T. Lukatchevich.

— *Los Miserables* Mexico 1944. *Dir* Fernando Rivero *Cast* Domingo Soler, Manolita Saval. 103 mins.

— *I Miserabli* Italy 1946. *Dir* Riccardo Freda *Photog* Rodolfo Lombardi *Cast* Valentina Cortesa, Gino Cervi, Giovanni Hinrich. 140 mins.

— *Ezai Padam Padu* India 1950. *Dir* K. Ramnoth (Tamil version.).

— *Re Mizeraburu* Japan 1950. In 2 parts: 1. *Dir* Daisuke Ito 2. *Dir* Masahiro Makino *Cast* Sessue Hayakawa.

The novel was transposed to Meiji-period Japan.

— *Les Miserables* USA 1952. *Dir* Lewis Milestone *Photog* Joseph LaShelle *Art Dir* Lyle Wheeler, J. Russell Spencer *Cast* Michael Rennie, Robert Newton, Debra Paget *Prod* 20th Century-Fox. 104 mins.

MISERE AU BORINAGE BORINAGE

MISFITS (THE) USA 1960. *Dir* John Huston *Scen* Arthur Miller *Photog* Russell Metty *Art Dir* Stephen Grimes, William Newberry *Mus* Alex North *Ed* George Tomasini *Cast* Marilyn Monroe, Clark Gable, Montgomery Clift, Eli Wallach *Prod* Seven Arts for United Artists. 124 mins.

A beautiful, lonely stranger, Roslyn (Monroe), waiting for her divorce in Reno, meets a part-time cowboy (Gable), a widowed motor mechanic (Wallach), and later a rodeo rider (Clift). She lives with the cowboy, Gay. All the men confide in her because they sense her "gift for life," but they are all misfits, callous and indifferent to cruelty while pretending to live a "free" life.

The Misfits is essentially a life portrait of Marilyn Monroe (the script was written by Miller for his ex-wife) but its theme is also a demystification of the great American dreams of success and the West. Its sense of bitterness took on a special irony with the death of Clark Gable almost immediately after the film was finished and the later suicide of Marilyn Monroe. For both, this was their last screen appearance. This is Huston's best film since *The African Queen* (*q.v.*) in 1951.

MISS JULIE FRÖKEN JULIE

MR. ARKADIN CONFIDENTIAL REPORT

MR. DEEDS GOES TO TOWN USA 1936. *Dir* Frank Capra *Scen* Robert Riskin based on *Opera Hat* by Clarence Buddington Kelland *Photog* Joseph Walker *Art Dir* Stephen Goosson *Ed* Gene Havlick *Cast* Gary Cooper, Jean Arthur, Raymond Walburn, H. B. Warner, George Bancroft, Lionel Stander *Prod* Columbia. 115 mins.

A backwoods poet (Cooper) inherits a fortune and goes to New York, where he immediately becomes famous. A young woman reporter (Arthur) gains his confidence and fills the newspaper with stories about him. Disillusioned, he gives away his money to alleviate poverty. Scheming relatives try to have him committed for insanity but he puts up such a spirited defense that the judge (Warner) releases him. He is reconciled with the reporter and marries her.

Graham Greene wrote of this film: "Capra's (happy ending) is natural and unforced. He *believes* in the possibility of human happiness; he *believes,* in spite of the controlling racketeers, in human nature. Goodness, simplicity, disinterestedness: these in his hands become fighting qualities. Deeds sees through opera directors, fashionable intellectuals, solicitors, and psychologists who prove that he is insane merely because he likes playing the tuba and isn't greedy for money . . . he is never a helpless victim . . . he comes back into the ring with folk humor and folk shrewdness to rout his enemies for the sake of the men they have ruined."

Capra, like his hero, with whom he might be identified, is naive, committed, and artful. Mr. Deeds himself can be seen as a kind of Roosevelt accused by his opponents of instituting the New Deal and "wasting millions" in helping the poor and unemployed. Riskin's script

is excellent: never mawkish and never merely sermonizing. And Gary Cooper, a gawky rube, fitted his role perfectly.
Memorable sequences: Mr. Deed's meeting an unemployed man who wants to kill him; his "eccentric" way of playing the tuba so he can think better; his artfulness in demolishing witnesses, psychiatrists, and lawyers during the trial.

MR. HULOT'S HOLIDAY VACANCES DE M. HULOT (LES)

MR. MAGOO (cartoon series) USA 1949. *Dir* John Hubley, Pete Burness, Robert Cannon and, later, others *Prod* UPA. 1 reel each.

This nearsighted, short-tempered, and terrifyingly energetic character unwittingly involves himself in catastrophes from which he always emerges unscathed. His characteristics seem to have sprung from Donald Duck and Buster Keaton. The series degenerated in the late Fifties when they were turned out on an assembly line by the producer, Stephen Bosustow.
[John Hubley, with Robert Cannon, created the original Mr. Magoo character in *Mr. Magoo* (1949). When the series began, it brought a freshness of style, colour, and comic invention to the animated film. Among others, Hubley directed *Ragtime Bear* (1949) and *Fuddy Duddy Buddy* (1949). Burness was responsible for, among others, *Bungled Bungalow* (1950), *Trouble Indemnity* (1950), *Magoo Goes West* (1953), *Destination Magoo* (1954), and *Stagedoor Magoo* (1955).]

MR. PUNTILA AND HIS VALET MATTI HERR PUNTILA UND SEIN KNECHT MATTI

MR. SMITH GOES TO WASHINGTON USA 1939. *Dir* Frank Capra *Scen* Sidney Buchman based on a story by Lewis R. Foster *Photog* Joseph Walker *Art Dir* Lionel Banks *Mus* Dimitri Tiomkin *Ed* Gene Havlick *Montage Effects* Slavko Vorkapich *Cast* James Stewart, Claude Rains, Edward Arnold, Guy Kibbee, Eugene Pallette, Jean Arthur *Prod* Columbia. 129 mins.

Jefferson Smith (Stewart), an idealistic young Boy Scout leader, is elected to succeed a US Senator who has died because the crooked politicians think he is too naïve to discover their misdeeds. After he arrives, his secretary (Arthur)

tells him why he was elected. He battles the party machine and a corrupt senator (Rains), fights for lost causes, makes a 23½-hour speech to the Senate, and triumphs in the end.

"Naive, simplistic, and boyish as it might be, the film possesses a sincere honesty that is more important than its humor, its perfect acting, and the punctilious exactitude of the action and the settings" (Lewis Jacobs). In this, Capra's most Rooseveltian film and perhaps his best, the Rangers and their mimeographed newspaper ensure Mr. Smith's victory over the press and the big party machine. Much of the action takes place in the US Senate Chambers, an exact copy of which was built in the studio.

MR. WONDERBIRD BERGÈRE ET LE RAMONEUR (LA)

MISTRESS DU BARRY see MADAME DUBARRY

MOANA — A ROMANCE OF THE GOLDEN AGE MOANA OF THE SOUTH SEAS USA 1925. *Dir* Robert Flaherty *Scen* Robert Flaherty, Frances Flaherty *Photog* Robert Flaherty, Bob Roberts *Assist* David Flaherty *Ed/Titles* Robert Flaherty, Julian Johnson *Prod* Famous Players-Lasky (Paramount). 6,055 ft.

The world-wide success of *Nanook* (*q.v.*) led Paramount to hire Flaherty to direct a documentary about life in the South Seas. Flaherty, with his wife and brother, spent two years (1923–24) on Savai'i one of the Samoan islands. They lived with the native population, gradually evolving the story out of their lives and choosing the principal characters. Famous sequences: the tattooing of Moana, part of his initiation into manhood; dancing the Siva before a village virgin; the preparations for a feast; the hunt for a robber crab.

Flaherty has said: "I like at all times to entrust the roles in my films to 'natives.' They are excellent actors, quite simply because they don't act and it is the natural things done unconsciously that count the most on the screen. This is why the greatest actors appear never to act. But few of them can be as unaware of external things as a child or an animal. However, a South Seas islander is as little affected by the camera as a baby or a kitten."

While not the equal of *Nanook*, this "in-tensely lyrical poem on the theme of the last paradise" (Herman Weinberg) was warmly greeted by the critics. It was a commercial failure in America, Britain, and Germany, but it ran for years in Paris and Stockholm. It seems audiences were disappointed at the lack of tropical sex appeal, Hawaiian guitars, and Tahitian dances.

MODERN TIMES USA 1936. *Dir/Scen/Mus/Ed* Charles Chaplin *Photog* Rollie Totheroh, Ira Morgan *Art Dir* Charles D. Hall *Cast* Charles Chaplin, Paulette Goddard, Chester Conklin, Stanley Sandford, Allan Garcia, Hank Mann, Lloyd Ingraham, Henry Bergman, Wilfred Lucas, Louis Natheax *Prod* Chaplin for United Artists. 85 mins.

Charlie is a worker in a big factory, goes to jail, has various other jobs, and becomes unemployed; but he refuses to be defeated.

Main sequences: Charlie mechanically tightening bolts on an endless conveyor belt and the chaos that results when he is distracted for a moment; the boss (Garcia) in his office overseeing the whole factory by television; Charlie's unhappy involvement in the trials of a new mechanical feeder; Charlie going berserk from the regimentation of his job and dancing like a faun; the parade of the workers in which Charlie, after picking up a red danger flag from a truck, is arrested as an agitator; the visit of a patronizing lady in jail; Charlie inadvertently preventing a jailbreak; working in a shipyard where he is fired again for accidentally launching an unfinished ship that sinks; getting arrested and meeting the Gamin (Goddard), who has stolen some food; his meal in a restaurant that he cannot pay for; Charlie and the Gamin living in a little shack on the waterfront; working as a night watchman in a department store, his getting mixed up with a mechanic (Conklin) and an enormous machine; skating in the department store; going to jail again after getting involved with burglars (Mann, Sanford, Natheax). After his release he sings a double-talk song to the tune of "Titiana"; the final scene as Charlie and the Gamin walk jauntily down the road towards the sunrise.

The film has a sound track but no dialogue, apart from a few words heard over radio or television.

The theme is automation, the assembly

line, unemployment and the world crisis — in brief "modern times" in the early Thirties. The most outstanding scene is that involving the feeding machine for which Charlie is both guinea pig and victim. An inventor persuades the boss he can make more money and gain time by installing a machine so the workers don't have to take a lunch hour. Charlie is told to try one and is strapped down while the machine feeds him automatically, wipes his mouth, etc. But something goes wrong — he is fed steel nuts, soup is spilled down his shirt, corn is pushed up his nose and he is pelted with food. And the little man howls with pain and terror. Such was the world of the early Thirties, where an abundance of food and machinery existed alongside starvation and unemployment.

The film cost one and a half million dollars and lost a half million dollars in the USA, where it was coldly received and even accused of "Red propaganda" by some. It was banned in Germany and Italy but was very successful in Britain, France, USSR, and other countries.

Based directly as it was on the world situation in the early Thirties, one might assume that it would later lose some of its forcefulness and sense of actuality. However, when it was re-released in the Fifties, a period of full employment and automation, it had lost none of its freshness. The passing years have only increased its power and affirmed its brilliant structure.

MOI, UN NOIR TREICHVILLE/I, A NEGRO France 1957. *Dir/Photog* Jean Rouch *Mus* directed by Japi Joseph Degre *Ed* Marie-Joseph Yoyotte, Catherine Dourgnon *Cast* (nonprofessionals) Oumarou Ganda, Petit Touré, Alassane Maigu, Amadou Demba, Seydou Guedé. 70 mins. Agfacolor. (Produced in 16mm and originally titled *Treichville;* released commercially in 1959 with the title *Moi, un noir.*)

The lives, dreams and ambitions of dockers and others in a shanty town in Abidjan, capital of the Ivory Coast (then a French colony). The dockers are nicknamed Lemmy Caution and Edward G. Robinson; a taxi driver, Tarzan; and a prostitute, Dorothy Lamour.

The most remarkable sequence: on the edge of a lagoon where water skiers skim about, Oumaru Ganda describes how he went to war in Indochina, had to kill Vietnamese, and when he returned was condemned by his father for having "lost the war."

The film was made in 16mm without a sound track. Later, Rouch invited the film's principal character, Oumarou Ganda (Edward G. Robinson) to record a commentary (in French) on the events he had filmed. The spontaneity and sense of authenticity that this produced encouraged ethnographer-film maker Rouch to develop his ideas on *cinéma-vérité.*

This is one of the first films in which African Blacks were able to speak their minds freely and describe their poverty, unhappiness, hopes and loves, and their wages since arriving in the big city as peasants. With this film Rouch abandoned traditional ethnography in favor of social argument and made one of the most important French films of the Fifties.

MOLODAYA GVARDIYA YOUNG GUARD (THE) USSR 1947 (revised and released in 1948). *Dir* Sergei Gerasimov *Scen* Sergei Gerasimov based on the novel by Alexander Fadeyer *Photog* Wulf Rapoport *Art Dir* I. Stepanov *Mus* Dmitri Shostakovich *Cast* Tamara Makarova, V. Ivanov, Sergei Bondarchuk *Prod* Soyuzdetfilm. In 2 parts: 1. 101 mins., 2. 84 mins.

Based on a popular postwar novel, this is the story of a group of young people who voluntarily form "the Young Guard" to sabotage the Nazis occupying their village. They are denounced and shot.

This is one of the best Soviet films from the 1947–52 period, containing many sequences that have a robust humor. The cast was selected largely from recent graduates of the State Institute of Cinematography, among whom was Sergei Bondarchuk.

MONDE DU SILENCE (LE) THE SILENT WORLD France 1955. *Dir* Jacques-Yves Cousteau, Louis Malle *Photog* Edmond Séchan, Louis Malle, Jacques-Yves Cousteau, Frédéric Dumas, Albert Falco *Ed* Georges Alépée *Mus* Yves Baudrier *Prod* Filmad/F.S.J.Y.C. 82 mins. Technicolor. This film and *Le Monde sans soleil* (1964) are the best of Cousteau's underwater work. It is, in essence, the discovery of an unknown universe and includes some brilliantly staged sequences, such as the ballet of swimmers with their torches. The editing and music are remarkable.

MONKEY BUSINESS USA 1931. *Dir* Norman Z. McLeod *Scen* S. J. Perelman, W. B. Johnstone, Arthur Sheekman *Photog* Arthur L. Todd *Cast* Groucho, Chico, Harpo, Zeppo Marx, Thelma Todd, Ruth Hall, Harry Woods, Tom Kennedy, Rockcliffe Fellows, *Prod* Paramount. 77 mins.

The Marx Brothers are stowaways on an ocean liner where Groucho and Zeppo on the one hand and Chico and Harpo on the other get mixed up with rival gangs and are involved in a kidnapping. Remarkable sequences: the Marx Brothers in their hiding place in kippered herring barrels carrying on with their day-to-day activities; the hairdressing salon where Chico and Harpo work; Groucho as a seductive ship's officer; Harpo hiding in a Punch and Judy show; Groucho's parody of an interview with a star; the burlesque scenes at the Customs.

This is one of the fastest and most malicious of the Marx Brothers films and brought to the screen some of their best vaudeville gags.

*MONKEY BUSINESS USA 1952. *Dir* Howard Hawks *Scen* Ben Hecht, I. A. L. Diamond, Charles Lederer based on a story by Harry Segall *Photog* Milton Krasner *Art Dir* Lyle Wheeler, George Patrick *Mus* Leigh Harline *Cast* Cary Grant, Ginger Rogers, Charles Coburn, Marilyn Monroe *Prod* 20th Century-Fox. 97 mins.

A research chemist (Grant) experimenting to find a formula to restore youthful vigor, drinks by mistake a mixture that a monkey has concocted. He behaves like a young boy and takes a secretary (Monroe) for a day out. Later, his wife (Rogers) drinks some and reverts to adolescence, as do his boss (Coburn) and the board of directors.

Though not one of Hawks' best films, this is a curious return to the "screwball" comedies of the Thirties with an interesting comic performance by Marilyn Monroe, who was not then a star. Hawks himself doesn't believe that "the premise of *Monkey Business* was entirely believable and for that reason the film was not as funny as it should have been."

MON ONCLE France/Italy 1958. *Dir/Scen* Jacques Tati *Photog* Jean Bourgoin *Art Dir* Henri Schmitt *Mus* Alain Romans, F. Barcellini *Ed* Suzanne Baron *Cast* Jacques Tati, Jean-Pierre Zola, Alain Bécourt, Adrienne Servantie *Prod* Specta-Films/Gray-Film/Alter-Film/Film del centauro. 120 mins. Eastman Color.

Mr. Hulot (Tati) lives in an old house; his nephew (Bécourt) and his parents, Mr. and Mrs. Arpel (Zola, Servantie) in an ultramodern "functional" house. The film contrasts the life style of the gentle Hulot with the regimentation and soullessness of the Arpels' life.

Remarkable sequences: the opening and closing shots of a group of stray dogs that run across the strip of wasteland between the old and new districts; Mr. Arpel's departure to the factory in his car; Hulot passing through a rambling maze of passages and stairways to reach his attic room; the Arpel's plagued by their own gadgets; Hulot's misadventures in Arpel's factory; the bizarre garden party in the Arpels' geometrical, ornamental garden; the arrival of an upper-class neighbor.

This is a satire not on modernism but on the middle class who think they are being modern. "What upsets me," Tati has said, "is not that we build new buildings but that they become barracks. I don't like to be always rushing about, I don't like mechanization. I have defended the back streets, the tranquil corners against freeways, airports, businesses, forms of modern life, because I don't believe geometric lines create likeable people . . . I meant to suggest a return to gentleness through a defense of individuality in the film's ultimately optimistic point of view."

MONSIEUR VERDOUX USA 1947. *Dir/Mus* Charles Chaplin *Scen* Charles Chaplin based on an idea by Orson Welles *Associate Dir* Robert Florey, Wheeler Dryden *Photog* Curt Courant, Rollie Totheroh, Wallace Chewing *Art Dir* John Beckman *Ed* Willard Nico *Cast* Charles Chaplin, Mady Correll, Allison Roddan, Martha Raye, Margaret Hoffman, Almira Sessions, Audrey Betz, Isobel Elsom, Marilyn Nash *Prod* Chaplin for United Artists. 122 mins.

"A comedy for murders," suggested by the crimes of Landru. Monsieur Verdoux (Chaplin) had been a bank clerk for thirty years but is dismissed during the Depression. Unable to find honest work he turns to marrying, bigamously, rich women in various parts of France, securing their property, murdering them, and then returning to his unsuspecting and crippled wife. When this wife and his son die, Verdoux is caught and submits bravely to the death sentence.

Famous sequences: Verdoux fastidiously cutting roses in a garden while in the background an incinerator smokes with his latest victim; counting his money very fast; his courting of the snobbish Marie Grosnay (Elsom); after a murder he sets two places for breakfast then stops to remove one; the obstreperous Annabella (Raye) avoiding the poison then later saving him from the water after he tries to drown her; the abandoned marriage; his arrest, trial, and execution.

It is only by chance that the film is set in France, since its heroines are basically American in character. Chaplin has explained his theme: "Von Clausewitz said that war is a logical extension of diplomacy. Verdoux feels that murder is a logical extension of business. He should express the feeling of the times we live in — out of catastrophe come people like him. He typifies the psychological disease of depression. He is frustrated, bitter and, at the end, pessimistic. But he is never morbid."

In prison, Verdoux becomes philosophical, argues against the atomic bomb and adds, "Wars, conflict, it's all business. One murder makes a villain; millions a hero. Numbers sanctify." Offered rum before he leaves for the guillotine, Verdoux at first refuses and then, "Just a minute. I've never tasted rum." For a moment on his way to the execution, Charlie's famous walk returns, though in this film Chaplin had completely abandoned his tramp in favor of an elegant, elderly man, fashionably attired and sporting a little French mustache; a cynical and intelligent character.

The film's release in the USA coincided with the start of the witch hunts and it was a total disaster. Chaplin withdrew it from distribution after a disappointing two years and only 2,075 play dates (an average B picture will get about 12,000 dates). In Europe it was a great success, especially in Paris, where 500,000 people saw the film.

MONSTER (THE) WAHSH (EL)

MONSTER OF FATE (THE) see GOLEM (DER)

MOONBIRD USA 1959. *Dir* John Hubley *Anim* Robert Cannon, Edward Smith *Prod* Storyboard Inc. 10 mins. Color.

Two small children sneak out at night in search of the "moon bird." Its remarkably free and inventive design, and its flat, pure colors reminiscent of the paintings of Pierre Bonnard and the Nabis group, is combined with dialogue improvised by the Hubley children.

MOONTRAP (THE) POUR LA SUITE DU MONDE

MORANBONG: CHRONIQUE COREENE France/Democratic Republic of Korea 1959 (released 1964). *Dir* Jean-Claude Bonnardot *Scen* Armand Gatti, Jean-Claude Bonnardot *Photog* Pak Gwieeng-Ovan *Mus* Djoevng Nam-lu *Cast* Oeu Do Soun, Ovan Djoeng Hi, Sin Hou Soeun *Prod* Films d'Aujourd'hui/Ombre et Lumière. 95 mins. Dyaliscope.

In Korea in 1950, two young lovers are separated by the hostilities. The man (Oeu Do Soun) leaves South Korea, joins the communist forces, and is captured by the South Koreans. The girl (Ovan Djoeng Hi) takes refuge in North Korea and joins a theater group. After the armistice in 1953, they find each other again.

The French Minister of Information banned this film in 1959 for interfering in "the foreign policies of France." This "profoundly pacifist film" (Pierre Kast) was finally authorized for release in 1964. Michèle Manceaux considers it, "Perhaps the *Paisa* of Korea." Best sequences: the hero crossing the barbed-wire frontier; the performance in the underground opera in Pyong-Yang during a bombing raid; the arrival of war in a still peaceful town.

MORDER SIND UNTER UNS MURDERERS ARE AMONG US German Democratic Republic 1946. *Dir/Scen* Wolfgang Staudte *Photog* Friedl Behn-Grund, Eugen Klagemann *Art Dir* Otto Hunte, Bruno Monden *Mus* Ernst Roters *Cast* Hildegarde Knef (Neff), Ernst Wilhelm Borchert, Arno Paulsen *Prod* DEFA. 86 mins.

In the ruins of Berlin a man (Borchert) discovers a Nazi criminal (Paulsen), wants to execute him, but is prevented by his landlady (Knef). This first postwar German film revealed the talents of Staudte and the actress Hildegarde Knef (who later changed her name to Neff).

MORT DU DUC DE GUISE (LA) ASSASSINAT DU DUC DE GUISE (L')

MORTE-SAISON DES AMOURS (LA) THE SEASON FOR LOVE France 1960. *Dir* Pierre

Kast *Scen* Pierre Kast, Alain Aptekman *Photog* Sacha Vierny *Art Dir* Jacques Saulnier *Mus* Georges Delerue *Cast* Daniel Gélin, Françoise Arnoul, Françoise Prèvost, Pierre Vaneck. 100 mins.

A jaded young writer, Sylvain (Vaneck), and his wife, Geneviève (Arnoul), settle in the village of La Saline des Chaux and become involved with a decadent politician, Jacques (Gélin), and his wife (Prévost), who live on a large estate. Jacques falls in love with Geneviève while Sylvain, his creativity dried up, has an affair with Jacques's wife. Eventually, Geneviève tries to leave Sylvain for Jacques but finds she still loves him and they decide to live in a *ménage à trois*.

This is Pierre Kast's best film and superficially is a conventional sophisticated "French" film about sex and love. However, it is more of a tragedy than a comedy. The setting (an "ideal" town built but never finished by the 18th century architect, Claude-Nicholas Ledoux) is very expressive both of the characters' lives and of time being suspended.

MOSCOW LAUGHS VESYOLYE REBYATA

MOST DANGEROUS GAME (THE) THE HOUNDS OF ZAROFF USA 1932. *Dir* Ernest B. Schoedsack, Irving Pichel *Scen* James Ashmore Creelman based on the short story by Richard Connell *Photog* Henry Gerrard *Mus* Max Steiner *Art Dir* Carroll Clark *Cast* Leslie Banks, Fay Wray, Joel McCrea *Prod* RKO Radio. 63 mins.

A once-famous explorer, Count Zaroff (Banks), lives on a tropical island and finds he cannot recapture the thrill of hunting unless he hunts human beings instead of animals. He causes shipwrecks to provide himself with victims. Among these are another explorer (McCrea) and a girl (Wray) who finally kill him.

This is one of the most taut American horror films of the Thirties [with unusually restrained performances in the leading roles. It was produced while Schoedsack and Cooper were working on *King Kong* (*q.v.*) and benefited from using many of the same technicians and sets.]
— *A Game of Death* USA 1945. *Dir* Robert Wise *Scen* Norman Houston based on Richard Connell's story *Photog* J. Roy Hunt *Cast* John Loder, Audrey Long, Edgar Barrier, Russell Wade, Jason Robards *Prod* RKO Radio. 72 mins.
An almost exact copy that even includes some of the original scenes. Count Zaroff

becomes a Nazi but still hunts for pleasure.
— *Run for the Sun* USA 1956. *Dir* Roy Boulting *Scen* Dudley Nichols, Roy Boulting based on Richard Connell's story *Photog* Joseph LaShelle *Cast* Richard Widmark, Trevor Howard, Jane Greer, Peter Van Eyck. 99 mins. Technicolor. Superscope.
Yet a further variation on the original: Count Zaroff becomes a Nazi but is concerned only with self-preservation and no longer hunts for pleasure.
Johnny Allegro/*Hounded* (1949), *Kill or Be Killed* (1950), *The Naked Prey* (1966), and *Blood Feast* (1966) all use the same basic plot.

MOTHER (USSR) MAT

MOTHER (JAPAN) OKAASAN

MOTHER JOAN OF THE ANGELS MATKA JOANNA OD ANIOLOW

MOUCHETTE France 1966. *Dir* Robert Bresson *Scen* Robert Bresson based on *La Nouvelle Histoire de Mouchette* by Georges Bernanos *Photog* Ghislain Cloquet *Art Dir* Pierre Guffroy *Mus* Monteverdi's *Magnificat Ed* Raymond Lamy *Cast* Nadine Nortier, Marie Cardinal, Paul Hébert, Jeanne Vimenet, J.-C. Guilbert *Prod* Parc Films/Argos. 90 mins.
A 14-year-old friendless schoolgirl, Mouchette (Nortier), lives with her alcoholic bootlegger father (Hébert) and bedridden dying mother (Cardinal). One day she witnesses a fight between Arsène (Guilbert) and Mathieu. Later, Arsène takes her back to his cabin, but when she tries to console him after he accuses himself of killing Mathieu, he misinterprets her actions and rapes her. The death of her mother and other encounters only increase her hostility and isolation from the world around her. She kills herself.
"If I chose *La Nouvelle Histoire de Mouchette,* it is because I found neither psychology nor analysis in it. The substance of the book seemed usable. It could be sieved. Mouchette offers evidence of misery and cruelty. She is found everywhere: wars, concentration camps, tortures, assassinations" (Robert Bresson). [This faultless film is a fusion of realism and allegorical fable in which Mouchette's suicide becomes an inexorable yet longed-for destiny. Her isolation and the

intensity of her suffering is conveyed not only in the images but through Bresson's brilliantly orchestrated sound track.]

MOULIN MAUDIT (LE) MAUDITE SOIT LA GUERRE

MOULIN ROUGE Britain 1952. *Dir* John Huston *Scen* Anthony Veiller, John Huston based on the book by Pierre La Mure *Photog* Oswald Morris *Art Dir* Paul Sheriff *Mus* Georges Auric *Cast* Jose Ferrer, Colette Marchand, Suzanne Flon, Zsa Zsa Gabor *Prod* Romulus. 120 mins. Technicolor.

A romanticized impression of the life of Toulouse-Lautrec (Ferrer) and his awareness of his infirmity. Most of the story focuses on the Moulin Rouge, and Lautrec's relationships with its habitués: Marie (Marchand), a debauched street girl, Jane Avril (Gabor), and Myriam (Flon), a lonely, cultured model who finally rejects him. Lautrec drinks more and more, becomes increasingly bitter, and is finally taken home to die in the family chateau.

This was a great commercial success despite its slick story that occasionally lapses into bad taste; Auric's theme music became one of the most popular tunes of the Fifties. However, its superb photography often brings to life some of Toulouse-Lautrec's most famous scenes. A little known detail is that the famous news photographer, Robert Capa, was the film's still photographer.

Not surprisingly, perhaps, several other films have used the same title:
— *Moulin Rouge* Britain 1928. *Dir/Scen* E. A. Dupont *Photog* Walter Brandos *Cast* Olga Tschechowa, Eva Gray, Jean Bratin, Forrester Harvey *Prod* British International Pictures. 100 mins. Re-released with sound track in 1929. 89 mins.

This story of a dancer's sacrifice for her daughter's happiness set amid Parisian night life was the first British "super production." It is sumptuously mounted and pictorially elegant but ultimately unsatisfying.
— *Moulin Rouge* USA 1933. *Dir* Sidney Lanfield *Scen* Nunnally Johnson, Henry Lehrman *Photog* Charles Rosher *Cast* Constance Bennett, Franchot Tone, Russ Columbo. 72 mins.

A comedy-drama with musical interludes about infidelity in the theater. Constance Bennett plays a dual role.
— *Moulin-rouge* France 1939. *Dir* Yves

Mirande *Cast* Lucien Barroux, René Dary. 65 mins.
A musical comedy of little merit.

MUDDY WATERS RUN DOWN AGUAS BAJAN TURBIAS

MUDE TOD (DER)—Ein Deutsches Volkslied in 6 Versen *Destiny/The Weary Death/ Between Worlds/The Three Lights/The Light Within* Germany 1921. *Dir* Fritz Lang *Scen* Thea von Harbou, Fritz Lang *Photog* Fritz Arno Wagner, Erich Nitzschmann, Hermann Saalfrank *Art Dir* Robert Herlth, Walter Röhrig, Hermann Warm *Cast* Lil Dagover, Rudolf Klein-Rogge, Bernhard Götzke, Walter Janssen *Prod* Decla-Bioscop. 2,311 meters. (7,500 ft. approx.).

In the early 19th century a young woman (Dagover) tries to save her lover (Janssen) from Death (Götzke). Death evokes three tragic destinies (Baghdad in the 9th century, Renaissance Venice, and a legendary China) all of which lead to the same conclusion: the girl's efforts to save her lover only cause his destruction. Eventually, after failing to find someone to die in her lover's place, she joins him in death.

The three "destinies" are the least successful parts of the film, since their mannered theatrical style seems closer to Lubitsch's than to Fritz Lang's own style. The carnival in Venice is mainly of decorative interest but the ending of the "Arabian Nights" sequence in Baghdad, as Francis Courtade noted, is striking: "In the garden where the infidel whom she loves is buried, Zobeide, daughter of the Caliph, embraces the head of the man," and, in the Chinese sequence, he noted "the transformation of the magician into a cactus and the army of midgets passing between the gigantic feet."

However, it is the continuing dialogue between the young woman and Death that is of principal interest and that made the film successful. In a flashback it is shown that Death had long ago bought land near the little German town and had surrounded his house with walls so tall that one could not see where they ended. Inside, "Lang soon realized what the judicious handling of light could bring to an atmosphere. He opens up a wall and erects a steep staircase whose steps compose a ladder of light in an arch; a bamboo thicket with its smooth shafts bathed in a swirl of phosphorescent light . . . Extraordinary oddness of appearance is found in the laboratory of the little apothecary. A real alchemist's laboratory this, with bottles and innumerable utensils glimmering mysteriously; skeletons and stuffed animals jut out from the darkness like phosphorescent phantoms" (Lotte Eisner). Sets such as these certainly came from the expressionistic influence of the art directors (the same as for *Caligari*) but also owe much to Fritz Lang's own architectural genius.

In the crypt of a thousand candles, "the Weary Death (der Müde Tod), tired of killing, agrees to return her lover's life if she can bring him another life in exchange. This leads to the highly ambiguous and melodramatic finale in which Lang reveals his talents as a master scenarist: the young woman asks a beggar and several old sick women to give up their lives to save her lover's. All refuse vigorously. Then she saves a baby from a fire, although allowing it to die would have saved her lover" (Luc Moullet).

Although initially not well received by public or critics in Germany, the film's success elsewhere rivaled that of *The Cabinet of Dr. Caligari* (*q.v.*) [and established Lang's reputation. According to one story, Alfred Hitchcock was so impressed by *Destiny* that he decided to become a film maker himself. Douglas Fairbanks adopted many of the film's special effects for his oriental fantasy, *The Thief of Bagdad* in 1924.]

MUERTE DE UN CICLISTA DEATH OF A CYCLIST/AGE OF INFIDELITY Spain/Italy 1955. *Dir* Juan-Antonio Bardem *Scen* Juan-A. Bardem based on a story by Luis F. de Igoa *Photog* Alfredo Fraile *Art Dir* Enrique Alarcon *Mus* Isidro B. Maztegui *Ed* Margarita Ochoa *Cast* Lucia Bosè, Alberto Closas, Carlos Casaravilla. 100 mins. (85 mins. North America, Britain).

The wife (Bosè) of a rich industrialist is the mistress of a young university professor (Closas). They accidentally kill a worker who is bicycling along the road and abandon him. After several crises between the lovers, the professor says they must tell the police. The woman kills him and later, swerving to avoid a cyclist, accidentally kills herself. This story might have been used to produce a conventional melodrama or a thriller, but Bardem used it to probe beneath the glossy surface of Madrid society and of those who became rich as supporters of the Franco regime. The professor goes through a crisis of conscience and discovers the workers' poverty, the students' rebellion, and the corruption of his environment. Abrupt crosscutting emphasizes the social contrasts. This and *Calle Mayor* (*q.v.*) are Bardem's best films.

Some critics have noted an Antonioni influence in this film, especially Antonioni's *Cronaca di un amore* (*q.v.*), but this resemblance probably owes more to Lucia Bosè appearing in both films. Other influences apart, *Death of a Cyclist* is directly descended from those Spanish novels of social criticism published between 1880 and 1930.

MUJER DEL PUERTO (LA) (literally: HARBOR WOMAN) Mexico 1933. *Dir* Arcady Boytler *Scen* Guzman Aguila based on a story by Guy de Maupassant adapted by Raphael J. Sevilla *Photog* Alex Phillips *Mus* Max Urban *Cast* Andrea Palmas, Elisa Altamira, Lina Boytler, Domingo Soler, Joaquin Busquets, Consuelo Segarra. 76 mins.

This powerfully atmospheric and sensitive film is not dissimilar to some examples of French poetic realism and marked the start of a renaissance of the Mexican cinema.

MUNCHHAUSENS ABENTEUER see BARON MÜNCHHAUSEN

MUNEQUITAS PORTENAS Argentina 1931. *Dir* José A. Ferreyra *Photog* Gunner Barriero, T. Lempard *Mus* Hans Brend *Cast* Maria Turgenova, Floren Deblene, Mario Soffici, A. Berciano. 73 mins. (sound on discs).

One of the first Argentinian sound films. The story takes place in the poor district of Buenos Aires and the few sequences that have been conserved have great charm. Its director, José Ferrayra, had a reputation as an "anarchical artist" who refused to see films and worked without scripts.

*MUNNA THE LOST CHILD India 1954. *Dir/Ed* K. A. Abbas *Scen* K. A. Abbas, Mahendra Nath based on a story by Mohan Bali *Photog* Ramchandra *Art Dir* Kanwal Nayyar *Mus* Anil Biswas *Cast* Romi Kapoor, Sulochana Chatterjee,

Shammi, Jai Raj, Om Prakash, Tripti Mitra *Prod* Nayar Sansar. 85 mins.

A seven-year-old boy, Munna (Kapoor), escapes from the orphanage where he had been left by his widowed mother during a famine and sets out to seek his identity. He is caught up in the ruthless underworld of Bombay and is involved with a gang of homeless children who are exploited as child thieves. He is rescued by a poor clerk but wrongfully accused of theft and turned out. He is adopted by the childless wife of a rich industrialist but, when he has to choose between comfort with his foster parents and poverty with his mother, he chooses his mother.

This is one of the first Indian realist films to achieve international recognition and is marked by its simplicity, warmheartedness, appealing characters, and nicely judged balance of comedy and pathos. The episode about Munna's exploitation as a child thief as well as other sequences, give the film a Dickensian flavor. It was well received in India despite its being the first Indian film without songs.

MURDERERS ARE AMONG US MÖRDER SIND UNTER UNS (DIE)

MURDER IN THORNTON SQUARE GASLIGHT (USA)

MURDER, MY SWEET FAREWELL MY LOVELY

MURIEL OU LE TEMPS D'UN RETOUR France/ Italy 1963. *Dir* Alain Resnais *Scen* Jean Cayrol *Photog* Sacha Vierny *Art Dir* Jacques Saulnier *Mus* Hans Werner Henze *Ed* Kenout Peltier, Eric Pluet *Cast* Delphine Seyrig, Jean-Pierre Kérien, Nita Klein, Jean-Baptiste Thierée *Prod* Argos/Alpha/Eclair/Films de la Pléiade /Dear Films. 116 mins. Eastman Color.

Hélène (Seyrig), a widow of about forty, lives in Boulogne-sur-met with her stepson, Bernard (Thierée), who is haunted by the memory of Muriel, a girl tortured to death in Algeria. Hélène meets her lover (Kérien) of 22 years earlier, who arrives with his mistress (Klein), but neither she nor Bernard can exorcise the ghosts of the past.

Jean Cayrol has written: "It is a tentative attempt to recapture the world around us, the actuality, the politics, the social life, the regrets. It is an essay on man's rehabilitation in the midst of his trials. It is a testament to 'things could always be worse.' The real story could begin when the film ends."

In *Muriel,* fantasy is born out of daily life, beauty from the apparently commonplace, drama out of everyday language. Though this difficult film puzzled some, it must be included among the best French films of the early Sixties.

*MUSIC BOX (THE) USA 1932. *Dir* James Parrott *Cast* Stan Laurel, Oliver Hardy, Billy Gilbert, Charley Hall *Prod* Hal Roach Studios. 25 mins.

As delivery agents, Laurel and Hardy have to deliver an electric piano to a house at the top of a long flight of stairs. After many labors they finally succeed but the owner (Gilbert) returns and destroys the piano.

This is the only Laurel and Hardy film to win an Academy Award and has always been their most famous. Stan Laurel himself considers it their best film. Certainly, its brilliant sense of timing and carefully modulated destructiveness make it the quintessence of Laurel and Hardy. Much of the film's continuing strength and appeal is generated by the central symbol of the stairs, which Raymond Durgnat sees as "the myth of Sisyphus in comic terms." Like most of their shorts it was shot in a few days and in sequence.

MY DARLING CLEMENTINE USA 1946. *Dir* John Ford *Scen* Samuel G. Engel, Winston Miller based on the novel *Wyatt Earp, Frontier Marshal* by Stuart N. Lake *Photog* Joe MacDonald *Art Dir* Lyle Wheeler, James Basevi *Mus* Alfred Newman *Ed* Dorothy Spencer *Cast* Henry Fonda, Linda Darnell, Victor Mature, Grant Withers, John Ireland, Walter Brennan, Tim Holt, Ward Bond, Alan Mowbray, Cathy Downs *Prod* 20th Century-Fox. 97 mins.

Wyatt Earp (Fonda) becomes Marshal of Tombstone in order to avenge the murder of his youngest brother. He is helped by Clementine (Downs), "Doc" Holliday (Mature), and Chihuahua (Darnell) and finally kills Old Man Clanton (Brennan) and his sons (Ireland, Withers) in the famous gunfight at the O.K. Corral.

"John Ford conveys to us the true face of everything about which the West sang, loyalty and courage, in reaching for the summit of gallantry" (J.-L. Rieupeyrout). Much of *My Darling Clementine* was based directly on true stories of the American West, especially that of the famous gunfight between Wyatt Earp and his brothers and the Clanton gang, which took place in 1880 near the Arizona mining town of Tombstone. However, historical incidents were used freely — "Doc" Holliday was not involved in Tombstone nor was there a Clementine Carter.

The film's settings and atmosphere are comparable to those of *Stagecoach* (q.v.), In fact, many consider this film the purest, most classically beautiful western of the Forties, as *Stagecoach* was for the Thirties. Its depiction of life in a western town, the arrival of the traveling theater group, and the final gunfight are brilliant, and the lyrical, open-air sequence of the dedication of the Tombstone Church is among the greatest Ford has created. Fonda, in one of his greatest roles, dominates the acting.

OTHER VERSIONS:

— *Frontier Marshal* USA 1934. *Dir* Lew Seiler *Scen* Stuart Anthony, William Conselman based on Stuart Lake's novel *Photog* Robert Planck *Cast* George O'Brien, Irene Bentley, George E. Stone *Prod* 20th Century-Fox. 66 mins.

— *Frontier Marshal* USA 1939. *Dir* Allan Dwan *Scen* Sam Hellman based on Stuart Lake's novel *Photog* Charles Clarke *Cast* Randolph Scott, Nancy Kelly, Cesare Romero, Binnie Barnes *Prod* 20th Century-Fox. 71 mins.

A routine western with an effective period atmosphere. Randolph Scott plays Earp with Romero as Holliday.

— *Gunfight at the O.K. Corral* USA 1957. *Dir* John Sturges *Scen* Leon Uris *Photog* Charles B. Lang *Mus* Dimitri Tiomkin *Cast* Burt Lancaster, Kirk Douglas, Rhonda Fleming, Jo Van Fleet, John Ireland *Prod* Wallis-Hazen for Paramount. 122 mins. Technicolor. Vista-Vision.

Only the climax of this lavishly mounted but dull western is similar to the climax of Lake's novel. Burt Lancaster plays Earp with Kirk Douglas as Holliday.

MY FAIR LADY USA 1964. *Dir* George Cukor *Scen* Alan Jay Lerner from his own musical play based on George Bernard Shaw's *Pygmalion Photog* Harry Stradling *Prod Design/Costumes* Cecil Beaton *Art Dir* Gene Allen *Mus* Frederick Loewe *Ed* William Ziegler *Cast* Audrey Hepburn, Rex Harrison, Stanley Holloway, Wilfred Hyde-White, Gladys Cooper *Prod* Warner Brothers. 175 mins. Technicolor. Super Panavision 70.

Although this is an overly sumptuous production by Jack L. Warner of the Broadway hit (originally called *Lady Liza*) George Cukor's typical style and approach often come through. Cecil Beaton's costumes are delightful and the music entertaining. Dainty Audrey Hepburn (whose songs were sung by Marni Nixon) cannot match Wendy Hiller in the 1938 *Pygmalion* (q.v.) and Rex Harrison is heavy handed as Professor Henry Higgins.

MY IZ KRONSTADT WE FROM KRONSTADT/ WE ARE FROM KRONSTADT USSR 1936. *Dir* Yefim Dzigan *Co-Dir* G. Berezko *Scen* Vsevolod Vishnevsky *Photog* N. Naumov-Strazh *Art Dir* Vladimir Yegorov *Cast* Vasili Zaichikov, Oleg Zhakov *Prod* Mosfilm. 97 mins.

The story of the defense of Petrograd against the Whites by sailors from Kronstadt during the Civil War in 1919. One of the best Soviet films of the Thirties. Especially memorable are the night scene with the sailors sleeping on the stairs of a large house, and the scene of the sailors' execution in which they are thrown into the Baltic from a high cliff. The direction is excellent but the true *auteur* of the film seems to have been the playwright, Vishnevsky. He refused to allow a film adaptation of his poetic play about a Bolshevik defeat, "An Optimistic Tragedy," but agreed to write a scenario with a similar theme. He discussed his approach in a series of letters to Dzigan in which he revealed his search for a strong, new treatment for hackneyed themes.

MY LIFE TO LIVE VIVRE SA VIE

MY NIGHT AT MAUD'S MA NUIT CHEZ MAUD

MYSTERE PICASSO (LE) THE PICASSO MYSTERY France 1956. *Dir/Scen* Henri-Georges Clouzot *Photog* Claude Renoir *Mus* Georges Auric *Ed* Henri Colpi *Prod* Filmsonor. 75 mins. Eastman Color. Final two reels in CinemaScope.

A documentary that shows Picasso at work, creating his drawings and sketches under the eyes of the spectator, revealing the inevitable failures and changes that go into his work before he is satisfield with the result.

Some sequences, as edited by Henri Colpi, have tremendous dramatic intensity especially the CinemaScope finale. André Bazin found this "Bergsonian film" of "incomparable importance" and added, "Some time would be necessary to discover and examine the body of criticism that has erupted from it like a volcano and that penetrates deep into the heart of the mass of cinema and painting."

MY UNCLE MON ONCLE

MY UNIVERSITIES See DETSVO GORKOVO

NAKED CITY (THE) USA 1948. *Dir* Jules Dassin *Scen* Malvin Wald, Albert Maltz based on a story by Malvin Wald *Photog* William Daniels *Art Dir* John F. DeCuir *Mus* Miklos Rozsa, Frank Skinner *Ed* Paul Weatherwax *Cast* Howard Duff, Barry Fitzgerald, Dorothy Hart, Don Taylor *Prod* Universal. 96 mins.

Lieutenant Dan Muldoon (Fitzgerald) and his aide (Taylor) investigate a murder in New York City.

The banal plot of this crime thriller is merely an excuse for a semidocumentary portrait of the life of ordinary people in a major city. It continued the approach of such films as *Brute Force* (*q.v.*), was shot largely on location in New York, and used a hidden camera in many sequences to capture a candid, real, and unadorned view of the bared face of a city.

Although Universal re-edited the film without his consent, this is one of Dassin's best films. William Daniel's photography (which won an Oscar) is superb; Barry Fitzgerald's acting is somewhat forced. The film ends with "There are eight million stories in the naked city: this has been one of them." — a tag made famous by the TV series of the same name produced twelve years later.

NAKED NIGHT (THE) GYCKLARNAS AFTON

NANA France 1926. *Dir* Jean Renoir *Scen* Pierre Lestringuez based on the novel by Emile Zola *Photog* Jean Bachelet, Carl Edwin Corwin, M. Asselin and others *Art Dir* Claude Autant-Lara *Cast* Catherine Hessling, Werner Krauss, Jean Angelo, Raymond Guérin, Valeska Gert, Pierre Champagne *Prod* Films-Renoir. 8,500 ft. approx.

A slum girl becomes a demimondaine and sets out to humiliate the class responsible for her former misery.

Jean Renoir: "I reduced *Nana* to three main characters: Nana (Hessling), Muffat (Krauss), and Vandoeuvres (Angelo), who themselves personify everything I had to delete. The ambience is only in the background. The three characters hold all the attention. Also, I tried to give my protagonists a range of feelings. But I did try my best to recreate the period at the end of the Second Empire and I must be forgiven a small intentional historical error: I dressed my actors in the very curious 1871 fashions."

Best sequences: the Grand Prix races; Nana dancing the cancan in the Bal Mabille; the civil servant, Muffat, sleeping at Nana's feet like a dog; an exhibition of "Blonde Venus."

Lucien Wahl could thus draw attention to the influence of Auguste Renoir and of Manet. *Nana* cost Renoir the then considerable sum of a million francs; although it was a public and critical success in France and abroad, Renoir lost most of the money he had put into it through the fault of the distributors. Of his silent films Renoir has said, "I made only one film worth talking about: *Nana*. The rest were harmless, cut-to-pattern films, made for fun or for 'commercial' reasons."

OTHER VERSIONS:

— **Nana/Storstadens Hyaene* Denmark 1912. *Scen* Knud Lumbye *Photog* M. A. Madsen *Cast* Holger Reenberg, Ellen Lumbye, Jon Iverson.

— *Nana/Lady of the Boulevards* USA 1934. *Dir* Dorothy Arzner *Scen* Willard Mack, Harry Wagstaff Gribble *Photog* Gregg Toland *Cast* Anna Sten, Lionel Atwill *Prod* Goldwyn 89 mins.

— *Nana* Mexico 1943. *Dir* Celestino Cerostiza *Photog* Alex Phillips, M. A.

Ferriz, C. de Castro *Cast* Lupe Velez. 107 mins.

— *Nana* France/Italy 1955. *Dir* Christian-Jaque *Scen* Jean Ferry, Albert Valentin, Henri Jeanson, Christian-Jaque *Photog* Christian Matras *Mus* Georges Van Parys *Cast* Martine Carol, L. Boni, D. Doll. 120 mins. Eastman Color.

A typically glossy Christian-Jaque effort, sumptuously mounted but totally inadequate to the material.

— **Nana/Take Me, Love Me* Sweden/France 1970. *Dir* Mac Ahlberg. Modernized, and abysmally bad, version.

NANIWA HIKA or NANIWA EREJI NANIWA ELEGY/OSAKA ELEGY Japan 1936. *Dir* Kenji Mizoguchi *Scen* Yoshikata Yoda, Kenji Mizoguchi *Photog* Miki Minoru *Cast* Isuzu Yamada, Benkei Shigaroya, Eitaro Shindo, Kensaku Hara *Prod* Daiichi. 90 mins. approx.

To help her family, a young telephone operator (Yamada) allows herself to be seduced by her boss (Shindo) and her boss's wife takes it out on the girl's family. She is abandoned by her fiancé (Hara), a typically unambitious white-collar worker, and returns to her family. She cannot live there and finds herself alone. (Naniwa is the old name for Osaka.)

The main thread of Mizoguchi's work begins to appear with this film: the depiction of society and the condition of women within that society. It marks also his search for a "new realism," a difficult task under a militaristic government concerned only with "ideological" films. In fact, it was banned by the government censors in 1940 for its "decadent tendencies."

When Mizoguchi said late in his life, "I only found my true voice after I was 40," he was undoubtedly thinking of this film, a simple, story simply directed. It is the first film on which he worked with Yoshikata Yudo, whose sympathies were close to his own and whose collaboration he valued highly. He also recalled later the "passion and devotion to her work" of the actress Isuzu Yamada, whose role was written for her and who gives an extraordinary performance as a modern woman struggling against commercialization.

The film is an incomparable artistic achievement, matching the best work of Jean Renoir at this time and, like Renoir's films, has a profound sense of social realities.

NANOOK OF THE NORTH USA 1920–21 (released 1922). *Dir/Scen/Photog/Ed* Robert Flaherty *Sponsored by* Revillon Frères. 5,400 ft. Reissued in a sound version in 1947, 50 mins.

The life of an Eskimo, Nanook, his wife Nyla, and their children. Famous sequences: the family emerging from the kayak; Nanook at the trading post and his excitement over a phonograph; the seal hunt; the feast of raw meat; the preparation of the seal skin; Nanook with the dog team; the building of the igloo; life inside it; the snow storm and the dogs in the snow.

When he was exploring the Arctic, Robert Flaherty had made a film about Eskimos in 1916 in the Baffin Bay area. The negative of this film burned in a fire in Toronto, leaving only one print from which Flaherty was able to make a duplicate. Several screenings of this film confirmed his dissatisfaction with his approach and he decided to go back to make a film of Eskimos "as they really are, not as civilized people see them." The French fur company, Revillon Frères, provided him with the backing. *Nanook* is a film whose heroes are Eskimos, a people with whom Flaherty became very friendly and with whom he lived for 15 months during 1920–21 in Hopewell Sound, Northern Ungava. They "acted out" for him their daily life and behavior, with which he had made himself completely familiar.

Flaherty defined his approach after making this film: "I think it is essential to work with unfamiliar material among peoples whose way of life is completely different from ours. If the theme is a new one, the camera can be used to record the most simple effects — and these are often the best. That is why I have taken an ethnological approach. I am convinced it is possible to discover a grace, a dignity, a culture, a refinement among peoples who have been placed by circumstances outside the mainstream. It is true that there are races in Labrador, Mexico, South America, and Asia who have been badly affected by their contacts with the White race, ridiculed for their 'colonial' costumes and often ruined by alcohol. However, one must believe strongly that these people cut off from the rest of the world have a way of life very different from our own. Each time I produce a film in a little known country I shall have for the people the same sympathy, the same desire to present an exact and favourable portrait. The camera is a super-eye which captures every nuance of feeling and movement; thanks to this, the rhythm is truly magical."

Of the scenes in the igloo, Flaherty said: "The average Eskimo igloo, about 12 feet in diameter, was much too small. On the dimensions I laid out for him, a diameter of 25 feet, Nanook and his companions started in to build the biggest igloo of their lives." They worked for days to build it and then, when they discovered that the light from the windows proved inadequate, "the dome's half just over the camera had to be cut away, so Nanook and his family went to sleep and awakened with all the cold of out-of-doors pouring in." Because he used a constructed "set" and because in many sequences Nanook and his family were "directed" as though they were non-professional actors, Flaherty aroused resentment among some for his misuse of "facts." The episode where Nanook listens to the phonograph "for the first time," for example, gives the impression not of having been taken from life but of being based on a prearranged idea. However, even if one could criticized this, one cannot condemn the method. As Flaherty himself said: "One often has to distort a thing to catch its true spirit." And there are many moments (Nanook absorbed in the hunt, Nyla feeding and washing the baby) where the characters are oblivious to the presence of the camera and which reveal Flaherty's genius for waiting patiently for exactly the right moment to capture a significant gesture or event.

When Flaherty had finished the film he had great difficulty selling it to a distributor. Even when Pathé (US) bought it, there were difficulties deciding how to exploit it. Eventually it was such a great public success around the world that some ice creams were dubbed "Nanooks" in Germany, USSR, Czechoslovakia, etc., "Esquimaux" in France, and "Eskimo pie" in Britain and North America. Nanook himself knew nothing of his fame; he died of hunger on the ice shortly after the film was released.

If this unknown Eskimo achieved the fame usually accorded to a film star it is because, without romanticizing, Flaherty shows the Eskimos as human beings with their own particular way of life but with the same aspirations and emotions as men everywhere. Flaherty's ability not only to capture real life on film but also to use characters in what Paul Rotha called a "slight narrative" is seen best in *Nanook*. And, apart from this, he made the public at large aware of these people, their culture and dignity. Even such objects as igloos, kayaks, and anoraks (until this film known only to ethnographers) were adopted elsewhere because of the "cultural exchange" between the far North and the rest of the world.

The world-wide success of *Nanook* encouraged the development of the documentary, while its approach exerted considerable influence in every country, even in the USSR, where Vertov was searching for a different approach.

*NAPOLEON VU PAR ABEL GANCE: PREMIÈRE ÉPOQUE: BONAPARTE France 1927 (production began January 1925). *Dir/Scen/ Ed* Abel Gance *Assist* Alexandre Volkoff, V. Tourjansky, Louis Osmont, André Andréani, Henry Krauss, Lemaire (explosions) *Photog* Jules Kruger, L.-H. Burel (Color only), Jean-Paul Mundviller, Roger Hubert, Emile Pierre, Lucas, Briquet *Art Dir* Schildknecht, Alexandre Benois, Jacouty, Meinhardt, Eugène Lourié, Schnitt *Mus* Arthur Honegger *Cast* Albert Dieudonné, Antonin Artaud, Pierre Batcheff, Armand Bernard, Harry Krimer, Albert Bras, Georges Cahuzac, Van Daele, Chakotouny, Koubitzky, Boris Fastovitch, Favière, Abel Gance, Philippe Hériat, Jean d'Yd, Gina Manès, Annabella, Marguerite Gance, Eugénie Buffet, Suzy Vernon *Prod* WESTI/Société Générale de Films. 17 reels. Parts in Polyvision. (About 28 reels screened at the premier.) Released by MGM generally in an 8 reel version without the Polyvision. Gance originally intended to depict Bonaparte's life in six separate films. The first film, "Bonaparte," was to be split into three parts: the youth of Bonaparte, Bonaparte and the French Revolution, and the Italian Campaign. The second film was to be "From Arcole to Marengo"; the third, "From 18th Brumaire to Austerlitz"; the fourth, "From Austerlitz to the Hundred Days"; the fifth "Waterloo"; and the sixth "Saint Helena." Financial difficulties prevented his producing any but the first film, *Bonaparte*.

Léon Moussinac summarized the film immediately after its premier on April 7, 1927 at the Opéra in Paris: "After a prologue showing Napoléon as a boy in the military academy of Brienne, the film shows the first singing of the "Marseillaise" in the club des Cordeliers with Danton (Koubitzky) and Rouget de Lisle (Krimer). Then we see Napoléon (Dieudonné) in Corsica, condemned to death by his compatriots and chased across the countryside in the style of American westerns. Scenes of Napoléon fighting a storm at sea in an open boat with the French flag as sail are intercut with scenes of the Convention with its gathering 'storm' (literary symbolism) of struggle between Girondish and Jacobin. The Terror. Popular dictators are transformed into purveyors of the guillotine with emphasis on Robespierre's (Van Daele) idiosyncrasies, the hemoptysis of Marat (Artaud), and Saint-Just (Gance) smelling a rose each time the blade falls. Thermidor (July–August in the French Republican calendar). The confusions of and attacks on the Revolution intercut with Bonaparte's love. Barras suggests Bonaparte as leader to suppress the Royalist insurrection and Josephine (Manès) looks for a male." He takes command of the army and crosses the Italian Frontier.

Moussinac didn't like the script at all, going so far as to call it "a Bonaparte for apprentice fascists" (the fascists were very active in France at that time). But he added that the film's originality was heightened by its visual richness and marked "an undeniable progress, an important date in the history of the evolution of cinematic techniques." He stressed the importance of the triple screen: "There were four Polyvision sections: the storm in the convention and the storm at sea, which I called Les Deux Tempêtes, the Return to Corsica, Le Bal des Victimes, and the Entry into Italy" (Gance), intended the Polyvision process to be used only for the last two reels — the Entry into Italy. But when he was cutting and saw the exciting material for the *double tempête* of the Convention, he decided to convert that to triptych — three shots side by side . . . But only at the end of the film did the panoramic Cinerama effect appear" (Kevin Brownlow).

There is no doubt that Gance's triple screen, especially when he combined it with stereophonic sound in 1934, suggested the development of Cinerama. Henri Chrétien, inventor of the Cinema-Scope lens, wrote to Gance that "it was your film *Napoléon* which gave me the idea of applying this panoramic technique." As Léon Moussinac wrote, "There isn't a single passage in the film without original technique." Apart from the triple screen, Gance's experiments in the use of the camera and movement were especially original and powerful. In the Corsican episode, the camera is strapped to a galloping horse during the chase; during the Marseillaise sequence, Gance strapped a camera to the chest of Alexandre Koubitzky to capture the rhythm of the song; and he mounted the camera on a huge pendulum to achieve the vertigo-inducing storm in the convention, which he intercut with the pitch of Napoléon's boat.

Similar original techniques were used for the Bal des Victimes (where the camera "dances" with the participants) and the Battle of Toulon. However, exciting as is the famous snowball fight at Napoléon's military academy, the story of Gance throwing the camera about like a snowball is apocryphal. As Kevin Brownlow describes this scene: "The camera is completely subjective, and becomes one of the struggling mass. Snowballs are thrown at you, little boys appear to punch you on the nose, and as the rolling, swirling mass loses control, the boyish face of Napoleon breaks into a smile of victory. The cutting reaches a frenetic climax in which the face appears for one frame every four."

One might apply to the director himself the phrase that Napoléon uses in the script: "I have pushed back the frontiers of glory. That's quite something." Gance pushed back the frontiers of the cinema. According to Kevin Brownlow, the complete version of the film was shown in eight European cities only. MGM bought it for $450,000 and then showed it complete only in London. "They never released the full version in America, being unwilling to risk a Polyvision revolution on top of the talkie upheaval."

In 1934, Gance prepared a stereophonic sound version from the original, adding some dialogue scenes and a 12-minute prologue that is set in 1815 and that introduces the film itself in a flashback.

Additional *Cast* Marcel Delaître, Armand Laville, Jane Marken and the voices of Fainsilber and Sokoloff *Mus* Henri Verdun. 130 mins. approx.

In 1955, Gance prepared a new version of the 1934 sound film under the title *Napoléon-Bonaparte*. It runs for 135 minutes and includes the three-screen scenes. Both sound versions suffer from a speeding-up of the original scenes that had been photographed at 16-20 frames-per-second. In 1971, Gance prepared a revised sound version, incorporating the three-screen scenes and with an introductory color sequence: *Bonaparte et la Revolution*. Additional *Ed* Max Sindlinger. 275 mins. Financing came largely from Claude Lelouch.

[NOTE: As Kevin Brownlow (*The Parade's Gone By*) points out: "The definitive version of *Napoléon* is as extinct as the original, ten-hour *Greed*. Many different copies have been pieced together, some of them such travesties that the picture's reputation has suffered." The version at the Cinémathèque Française is 17 reels in length but confusingly mounted with repetitive shots of the same scene. From the best material available from several film archives, Brownlow himself has compiled a version for the National Film Archive in London. This is 19,600 ft. in length, runs 4 hours 10 mins., and includes the Polyvision sequences on one strip of film. I am indebted to Kevin Brownlow for checking this entry against his own researches and for supplying additional information. *Ed*.]

NARAYAMA BUSHI-KO LEGEND OF THE NARAYAMA/BALLAD OF THE NARAYAMA/ SONG OF THE NARAYAMA Japan 1958. *Dir* Keisuke Kinoshita *Scen* Keisuke Kinoshita based on the story by Shichiro Fukazawa *Photog* Hiroyuki Kusuda *Art Dir* Kisuka Ito *Mus* R. Kineya, M. Nozawa *Ed* Yoshi Sugihara *Cast* Kinuyo Tanaka, Teiji Takahashi, Yuko Machizuki *Prod* Shochiku. 103 mins. Fujicolor. Grandscope.

[Based on folk legend and a prize-winning short story about the people in a remote part of Japan who traditionally abandon their aged on the top of a high mountain to maintain the economic status quo.] When Orin (Tanaka), a hale and hearty 69-year-old woman, turns 70, she forces her reluctant and loving son to carry her to the top of the mountain,

there to die of starvation and exposure. "I wanted to try something difficult with this film," Kinoshita said, "to create a work that would be very personal and would also develop a truly folkloric tradition for the Japanese cinema." This is a singular, virtuoso work, notable both for its kabuki-like, though untheatrical, style and for its moving allegory. ["The moving camera was used to superlative effect, both color and wide-screen were employed in the most imaginative fashion, and the pacing and general tempo of the film was cinema at its most creative" (J. L. Anderson and Donald Richie).]

NASTASIA FILIPOVNA THE IDIOT, PART ONE USSR 1958. *Dir/Scen* Ivan Pyriev based on Fëdor Dostoevski's novel *Photog* Valentin Pavlov *Art Dir* S. Volkov *Mus* N. Kryukov *Cast* Yuri Yakovliev, Yulia Borisova, Leonid Parkomenko, Nikita Podgorny, Nikolai Pazhitnov *Prod* Mosfilm. 124 mins. Sovcolor.

An adaptation of the first part of the novel for which Pyriev creates a kind of filmed theater, dividing the action into a series of "acts" which take place in single sets. This is an interesting and often powerful film with a well directed, uniformly excellent cast. The second part of the film seems to have been either abandoned or never begun.

OTHER VERSIONS:

— *Idiot* USSR 1910. *Dir* Pyotr Chardynin.

— *Dummkopf* Germany 1921. *Dir* Lupu Pick.

— *l'Idiot* France 1946. *Dir* Georges Lampin *Scen* Charles Spaak *Photog* Christian Matras *Cast* Gérard Philipe, Edwige Feuillère. 98 mins.

This somewhat underestimated version has a moving performance by Gérard Philipe.

— *Hakuchi* (*q.v.*) Japan 1951.

NATIVE LAND USA 1942. *Dir/Scen* Paul Strand, Leo Hurwitz *Commentary* David Wolff (Ben Maddow) *Photog* Paul Strand *Ed* Leo Hurwitz *Mus* Marc Blitzstein *Narrator* Paul Robeson *Cast* Fred Johnson, Mary George, Howard Da Silva, Housely Stevens, Louis Grant, Tom Connors *Prod* Frontier Films. 80 mins.

This is not, strictly speaking, a documentary, but, like Jean Renoir's *La Vie est à nous* (*q.v.*), a series of social studies photographed in natural sets largely with professional actors and a script. Production began in 1939 with a script based on the report of the Senate Civil Liberties Committee, which had been investigating violations of constitutional liberties. Lewis Jacobs described it at that time as a "feature-length picture dramatizing America's heritage of freedom, the Bill of Rights, in terms of modern America."

Frontier Films had been founded as a "cooperative" in 1936 by Paul Strand, Leo Hurwitz, the poet David Wolff (Ben Maddow), Irving Lerner, Sidney Meyers (Robert Stebbins), John Howard Lawson, and others. The film was financed by small contributions from thousands of people, but it was not until a grant was received from the Roosevelt administration in 1940 that it could be completed.

Native Land is a perfect example of the first New York school. Though it is mainly a powerful plea for unionism and rights of workers, it is as subtle as *Citizen Kane* even though its style is quite different. From this great film one especially recalls the sequence about union gangsters and another about racism, in which the Ku Klux Klan and a lynch party pursue a Negro across the fields.

*NATTVARDSGASTERNA WINTER LIGHT Sweden 1962. *Dir/Scen* Ingmar Bergman *Photog* Sven Nykvist *Art Dir* P. A. Lundgren *Ed* Ulla Ryghe *Mus* none *Cast* Ingrid Thulin, Gunnar Björnstrand, Max von Sydow, Gunnel Lindblom *Prod* Svensk Filmindustri. 80 mins.

Tomas Ericsson (Björnstrand), a village pastor who feels that since the death of his wife he has been deserted by God, celebrates Holy Communion with a handful of parishioners, including Märta (Thulin), his mistress, and Jonas (von Sydow) and Karis (Lindblom) Persson. After the service, Karin begs him to help her husband, who has an obsessive dread of the Chinese using nuclear weapons, but he is unable to comfort him. In a letter Märta begs him to marry her but he cannot respond to her love. Jonas commits suicide and, after breaking the news to Karin and a climactic row with Märta in the schoolroom, Tomas goes to another church in his parish to celebrate evensong, though the church is empty except for Märta.

"The theme of these three films is a 're-duction,' in the metaphysical sense of that word. *Through a Glass Darkly* (*q.v.*), certainty achieved. *Winter Light* certainty unmasked. *The Silence* (*q.v.*) — God's silence — the negative impression" (Ingmar Bergman). Less satisfying, perhaps, than the other two films in the trilogy, *Winter Light* is a moving evocation of the agonies of doubt and the search for self-awareness. As Raymond Lefèvre puts it, Tomas 'plays out his role like an artist who can no longer believe in his art; like a lover caressing the woman whom he no longer loves." Though the starkness of the church and the bleakness of the snowy landscape outside reflect a mood, it is the dialogue that is of paramount importance in revealing the characters' inability to respond to each other's needs.

NAVIGATOR (THE) USA 1924. *Dir* Buster Keaton, Donald Crisp *Scen* Jean Havez J. A. Mitchell, Clyde Bruckman *Photog* Elgin Lessley, Byron Houck *Art Dir* F. Gabourie *Cast* Buster Keaton, Kathryn McGuire *Prod* Metro-Goldwyn. 5,600 ft. Keaton has recalled that their first idea had simply been to have a boy and a girl marooned on a dead ship in the middle of the Atlantic. But it was no use their being poor — how could they be on a transatlantic liner in the first place? Then scriptwriter Jean Havez suggested "I want a rich boy and a rich girl who never had to lift a finger . . . I put these two beautiful spoiled brats — the two most helpless people in the world — adrift on a ship, all alone. A dead ship. No lights, no steam." Keaton: "So we worked it out. I'm Rollo Treadway, a really useless millionaire who can't even shave himself. I've proposed to this girl. She wants no part of me, my money or my position . . . And there we are, neither one knowing the other is on the ship, drifting off to nowhere in the dark." As this suggests, Keaton's comic style is often based directly on social observation. *The Navigator* is full of wonderful gags, especially those involving the sleeping and cooking problems, but its theme stems from Keaton, a little man at the mercy of The Machine.

NAZARIN Mexico 1958. *Dir* Luis Buñuel *Scen* Luis Buñuel, Julio Alejandro based on the novel by Benito Pérez Galdós *Photog* Gabriel Figueroa *Art Dir* Edward Fitzgerald *Ed* Carlos Savage *Cast* Francisco Rabal, Marga Lopez, Rita Macedo, Jesus Fernandez *Prod* Manuel Barbachano Ponce. 94 mins.

In the Mexico of 1900, during the era of the dictator Porfirio Diaz, Father Nazarin (Rabal) lives in a slum house. Defrocked for protecting a whore, Andara (Macedo), who has killed a woman, he decides to follow precisely the teachings of Christ and leaves to wander around Mexico. He is followed by Andara, another woman, Beatriz (Lopez), and Ujo, the dwarf (Fernandez). After many wanderings and attempts to practice a pure Christianity, which the world resists, he is jailed and mocked. His humiliations cause him to weaken. In the end he accepts a gift of charity and continues on his way, now aware of his existence as a man as well as a priest.

There is a great deal of Don Quixote in Nazarin: just as Don Quixote believed in an imaginary chivalry, Nazarin believes in a form of Christianity that can never be more than illusory. His wanderings are also described in a synopsis of the film (somewhat condensed): "Nazarin sparks off a worker's rebellion and shooting when he tries to work in a factory for little pay. In a plague-stricken village, a dying girl refuses divine consolation in favor of the passionate embrace of her lover. An unjust society remains unmoved by the example of pure Christianity. In prison he is mocked and beaten by a murderer and befriended by a sacrilegious thief who asks him 'What good is your life? You're on the right side. I'm on the wrong side — we're both equally useless.' Nazarin is led out in chains, exhausted. His doubts increase. And because he doubts, he accepts his fate and his failure as reaffirmation of his moral conviction to rebel and not submit. Now the road of a good man, a moral hero, opens before him, the road which leads to the death established by society for perpetual rebels." However, this film relates less to the Mexico of 1900 than to the Spain of 1958 under another dictator and seen through the eyes of memory as a new *Las Hurdes* (*q.v.*).

Octavio Paz has written: "In *Nazarin*, whose style avoids condescension and any suspect 'lyricism,' Buñuel tells a story of a quixotic priest, whose conception of Christianity prompts him to oppose the church, society, and the police. Nazarin follows in the great tradition of mad Spaniards, originated by Cervantes. His madness consists in taking seriously great ideas and big words, and trying to live accordingly. . . . Don Quixote saw Dulcinea in a farmer's daughter; Nazarin sees a helpless image of "the fallen people" behind the monstrous features of Andara and Ujo; and behind the erotic frenzy of Beatriz — the echo of divine love."

Some critics felt that, with *Nazarin*, Buñuel had returned to his origins. But he responded to this by making *Viridiana* (*q.v.*).

NAZIS STRIKE (THE) see WHY WE FIGHT (SERIES)

*NEIGHBORS Canada 1952. *Dir* Norman McLaren *Photog* Wolf Koenig *Cast* Jean-Paul Ladouceur, Grant Munro *Prod* National Film Board of Canada. 8 mins. Kodachrome.

A parable about two men who live tolerantly as neighbors until one day a flower emerges on the borderline between their properties. At first they share its beauty but, as each becomes more possessive, a violent struggle begins.

This famous, award-winning parable on the futility of violence for settling disputes is a pixilation (animation of actors and objects) film without dialogue or narration but accompanied by synthetic music and effects. McLaren's control over this blend of realism and stylization is perfect.

NEOBYCHAINIYE PRIKLUCHENIYA MISTERA VESTA V STRANYE BOLSHEVIKOV THE EXTRAORDINARY ADVENTURES OF MR. WEST IN THE LAND OF THE BOLSHEVIKS USSR 1924. *Dir* Lev Kuleshov *Assist* V. Pudovkin, Sergei Komarov, P. Podobed and others *Scen* V. Pudovkin, Nikolai Aseyev *Art Dir* V. Pudovkin *Photog* Alexander Levitsky *Cast* Porfiri Podobed, Boris Barnet, Valya Lopatina, V. Pudovkin, Alexandra Khokhlova, Komarov, Vladimir Fogel, Leonid Oblensky *Prod* Goskino. 2,680 meters.

An American, Mr. West (Podobed), arrives in Moscow believing it to be populated with savages and bandits. A gang "plays up" to him and shows him everything he expects to see. Just as he is about to pay an enormous ransom he is rescued and shown the real Moscow. An intelligent, funny, absorbing, and stylistic film whose exaggerated plot is derived from American serials, and contains a number of inside jokes. [It was the first effort by the Kuleshov "workshop" group and was a great success in the USSR, though not released abroad. In recent years it has been seen outside the Soviet Union and still seems as fresh in its humor and characterization as it must have in 1924.]

NEOKONCHENNAYA POVEST UNFINISHED STORY (AN) USSR 1955. *Dir* Friedrich Ermler *Scen* K. Isayev *Photog* Anatoli Nazarov *Art Dir* I. Kaplan *Mus* G. Popov *Cast* Sergei Bondarchuk, Yelina Bystritskaya, Yevgeni Samoilov, Sophia Giatsintova *Prod* Lenfilm. 92 mins.

The story of an attractive woman doctor (Bystritskaya), her self-centered suitor, and a paralyzed patient (Bondarchuk) whom she really loves. Because he is paralyzed he refuses to encourage her love, but all ends happily when he learns to walk.

The talents of the two main actors, the lyricism of the urban scenes, and the film's psychological nuances make it a success. It is not, however, one of Ermler's best films.

*NEVER GIVE A SUCKER AN EVEN BREAK WHAT A MAN! USA 1946. *Dir* Edward Cline *Scen* Otis Criblecobis (W. C. Fields) *Photog* Jerome Ash *Art Dir* Jack Otterson, Richard H. Riedel *Mus* Frank Skinner *Cast* W. C. Fields, Gloria Jean, Franklin Pangborn, Leon Errol, Margaret Dumont *Prod* Universal. 63 mins.

Field's last personal film has a plot that almost makes *Hellzapoppin* (*q.v.*) look sane. Fields (as himself) tries to persuade a producer (Pangborn) to buy a script in which Fields has various adventures with his niece (Jean), lands in a mountain sanctuary owned by Mrs. Hemoglobin (Dumont), and sets out to sell wooden nutmegs to the Russian colony in Mexico City. Fields originally scribbled this plot on the back of a grocery bill and sold it to Universal for $25,000.

Full of inspired inanities, this is Fields at his best: "Whether he is offering a cure for insomnia ('Get plenty of sleep'), refusing a bromo ('Couldn't stand the noise'), nasally vocalizing ('Chickens have pretty legs in Kansas'), meticulously blowing the head off an ice cream soda, Fields is a beautifully timed exhibit of

mock pomposity, puzzled ineffectualness, subtle understatement and true-blue nonchalance" (James Agee). The final chase is a masterpiece of its kind that recalls the best of silent slapstick. Unfortunately, Gloria Jean sings.

NEVER ON SUNDAY POTE TIN KYRIAKI

NEW BABYLON (THE) NOVYI VAVILON

NEW EARTH (THE) NIEUWE GRONDEN

NEW EXPLOITS OF ELAINE (THE) see EXPLOITS OF ELAINE (THE)

NEW GULLIVER (A) NOVYI GULLIVER

*NEW YEAR SACRIFICE China 1956. *Dir* Sang Hu *Scen* Hsia Yen based on a story by Lu Hsun *Photog* Chien Chiang *Art Dir* Chih Ning *Mus* Liu Ju-tseng *Cast* Pai Yang, Wei Hao-ling, Li Chingpo, Shih Lin *Prod* Peking Studio. 94 mins. Agfacolor.

Based on a 1924 novel set in the time of the 1911 revolution, the film tells of a woman (Pai Yang) sold into marriage, the death of her husband and son, and her rejection by society.

This is a gentle film, quietly acted and slowly paced, made by the director of *Liang Shan-po and Chu Ying-tai* (*q.v.*). Pai Yang gives a beautiful performance and the final sequences as she wanders in the snow are extremely moving. The director's sympathetic portrayal of his characters far outweighs the somewhat unsophisticated melodramatic coincidences upon which the plot hangs.

NEW YEAR'S EVE SYLVESTER

NEW YORK HAT (THE) USA 1912. *Dir* D. W. Griffith *Scen* Anita Loos *Photog* Billy Bitzer *Cast* Mary Pickford, Lionel Barrymore, Lillian Gish, Dorothy Gish, Jack Pickford, Mack Sennett, Robert Harron, Mae Marsh *Prod* Biograph. 719 ft.

In a small town, a minister (Barrymore) gets into trouble when he buys a hat for a young girl (Pickford) for whom he is holding money in trust. She is attacked by bigots and the town gossips but the truth finally puts them to shame.

The accuracy and humor in its depiction of puritanical and hypocritical small-town America make this a masterpiece of the early American cinema. Its theme is not dissimilar to that of Chaplin's *Sunnyside* (*q.v.*), though it is considerably less astringent. The original story was the first submitted to Griffith by the then eleven-year-old Anita Loos.

NIBELUNGEN — EIN DEUTSCHES HELDENLIED (DIE) 1 Teil: SIEGFRIED 2 Teil: KRIEMHILDS RACHE Part I: SIEGFRIED Part II: KRIEMHILD'S REVENGE/THE VENGEANCE OF KRIEMHILD Germany 1924 (production began 1922). *Dir* Fritz Lang *Scen* Thea von Harbou *Photog* Carl Hoffman, Günther Rittau *Art Dir* Otto Hunte, Karl Vollbrecht, Erich Kettelhut *Costumes* Paul Gerd Gudesian, Anne Willkomm *Make-up* Otto Genath *Mus* Gottfried Huppertz *Anim* (dream of the hawks sequence) Walther Ruttman *Cast* Paul Richter, Margarete Schön, Theodor Loos, Hanna Ralph, Rudolf Klein-Rogge, Hans Adalbert Schlettow, Georg John, Bernhard Goetzke, Gertrud Arnold, Erwin Biswanger, Frida Richter, Rudolf Rittner, Iris Roberto *Prod* Decla-Bioscop. Part I: 3,216 meters (10,500 ft. approx.). Part II. 3,576 meters (11,800 ft. approx.). English language release version was 9,000 ft. for both parts; extant versions are shorter.

The scenario is based less on Wagner's opera than on original sources of the Nibelungen legend.

Siegfried: Siegfried (Richter) destroys a dragon and becomes invulnerable by bathing in the dragon's blood. He visits the court of Burgundy to propose to Kriemhild (Schön), sister of King Gunther (Loos). Hagen (Schlettow), the king's adviser, demands that before the marriage Siegfried help conquer the fierce queen Brunhild (Ralph). By means of his magic hood, Siegfried cheats Brunhild into becoming Gunther's wife. When she learns of this, Brunhild demands Siegfried's death and Hagen contrives to kill him. At the bier of her husband, Kriemhild swears revenge.

Kriemhilds Rache: Kriemhild (Schön) marries Attila (Kleine-Rogge), king of the barbaric Huns, and persuades him to invite Gunther and Hagen to visit them. At a banquet, she incites the Huns to attack the guests. A terrible massacre follows, with the Burgundians trapped in a hall that Attila orders set on fire. Kriemhild kills Gunther and Hagen and is herself killed. Attila, her corpse in his arms, buries himself in the blazing hall. Preparation for the film took two years

and the shooting seven months. Its production was very costly, although it is impossible to estimate the amount because of the gigantic inflation in Germany at that time.

The two parts are in quite different styles. *Siegfried* is dominated by architectural structures that often reduce the characters to decorative elements against landscapes or vast buildings. *Kriemhild's Revenge,* on the other hand, is dominated by the fire, the massacre, the chaos, and the awe-inspiring "Twilight of the Gods."

In the opening scenes of *Siegfried,* which introduce the characters of the tragedy and reveal warriors frozen into living pillars, Lang introduces a living architecture. His decorative compositions seem often like frozen bits of life, as if any movement would disturb the geometry. In the constructional austerity of his geometrical universe, any irregular plant life would seem out of place. Produced entirely in the studio, its most typical shot is the image of Siegfried riding through a mystical Germanic forest whose trees are silhouetted against the artificial light. Too much has been made of the so-called expressionism of this film's monumental images. They are much more derivative of the style of Germanic painting influenced by Arnold Böcklin and of the Munich style of architecture that characterized the last period of the Second Reich and to which the expressionists were intensely opposed. Famous sequences of *Siegfried:* Alberic's treasure cavern where Siegfried finds his sword; the conquest of the dragon; the scenes on the great stairway of the cathedral; Brunhild's castle and the fight; the death of Siegfried in a flower meadow; Kriemhild swearing revenge.

Where *Siegfried* is architectural, *Kriemhild's Revenge* is dynamic. As Francis Courtade wrote: "The static harmonies of the first part are followed by the entrancing and dynamic sequences of the second." Luc Moullet notes that "The climax is a long battle lasting three-quarters of hour with encirclements and identical attacks, defenses against the encirclements, and renewed attacks; the movements of the assailants are similar, but Lang creates shots with different details and builds a rhythm of variations. It is at the same time vehement, dynamic, and the opposite."

The two-part film was conceived as a

monumental tribute to the German nation. UFA, which controlled Decla-Bioscop, was in turn controlled by heavy industry, especially by Krupp and Farben who were subsidizing national movements. Hitler admired *Nibelungen* very much and it has often been noted that the gigantic mosaic designs of *Triumph of the Will* (*q.v.*) resemble many passages in *Nibelungen*. However, Hitler was only a discredited agitator in 1924 and it was Minister Streseman who released it "to create a feeling of unity among the people." And yet, according to *Mon Ciné* (October 8, 1924), militant German nationalists were highly indignant about the film because it showed their "ancestors as bandits." Under the Nazis, the sound version of *Siegfried* continued to be shown but not *Kriemhild's Revenge*.
— *Siegfrieds Tod/The Death of Siegfried* Germany 1933. A sound version of *Siegfried,* narrated by Theodor Loos with music by Gottfried Huppertz and based on Wagner and classical themes. 7,590 ft. Premiered May 29, 1933 — after Fritz Lang's departure from Germany.
— **Die Nibelungen/Whom the Gods Wish to Destroy* Part I: *Siegfried von Xanten* Part II: *Kriemhilds Rache* German Federal Republic/Yugoslavia 1966. *Dir* Harald Reinl *Cast* Uwe Beyer, Maria Marlow, Karin Dor, Siegfried Wischnewski, Rolf Henniger. Part I, 91 mins. Part II, 104 mins. Eastman Color. Ultrascope. English version released in 1 part, 153 mins.
Yet another Harald Reinl pastiche of a Fritz Lang classic.
Two Italian films, *Invisible Sword,* 1962, and *Dragon's Blood,* 1963, were based on the Siegfried legend.

NIEMANDSLAND HELL ON EARTH/NO MAN'S LAND Germany 1931. *Dir* Viktor Trivas *Scen* Viktor Trivas based on an idea by Leonhard Frank *Photog* Alexander Lagorio, Georg Stilianudis *Art Dir* Arthur Schwartz *Mus* Hanns Eisler, Kurt Schröder *Cast* Ernst Busch, Georges Péclet, Douglas Hughes, Renée Stobrawa, Louis Douglas, Vladimir Sokoloff, Elisabeth Lennartz *Prod* Resco-Filmproduktion. 93 mins.
A prologue shows scenes of Germany, France, and England as war breaks out in 1914. Then in 1918, five soldiers of different nations get lost in the front lines and seek shelter in an abandoned trench in no-man's land. They are a Frenchman (Péclet), an American Negro singer

(Douglas), a German (Busch), a British officer (Hughes), and a Jewish tailor (Sokoloff). While the war rages around them they change from "enemies" into friends and learn to understand and respect each other.
This intensely pacifist film was made with the collaboration of people like Ernst Busch and Hanns Eisler, both of whom had worked with Brecht. It is one of the most progressive films of pre-Hitler Germany, powerful, true and original, and one which never merely sermonizes.

NIEUWE GRONDEN THE NEW EARTH/ZUIDERZEE Netherlands 1934. *Dir/Scen* Joris Ivens *Photog* Joris Ivens, John Fernhout (Ferno), Joop Huisken, Helen van Dongen *Ed* Helen van Dongen *Mus* Hanns Eisler, words for the song by Bertolt Brecht *Prod* CAPI. 28 mins.
A documentary on the reclamation of the Zuiderzee in the late Twenties and early Thirties.
In 1929 the Nederlands Bouwakarbeidersbond (Netherlands building workers union) commissioned Joris Ivens to make a documentary. The 7-reel silent film that he made *Wij Bouwen* (*We Are Building*) was premiered "at the end of 1929" (Ivens) to celebrate the union's 25th anniversary. From the footage he had been unable to use he made four other documentaries: *Nieuwe Architectuur* (*New Architecture*), 1 reel; *Zuid-Limbourg* (*South Limbourg*), dealing with the construction of a railway line, 3 reels; *Heien* (*Pile-Driving*), and impressionistic film on the use of wooden piles as foundations, 1 reel; and *Caisson-bouw* (*Caisson Building*), 1 reel. He also compiled a technical film of 9 or 10 reels called *Zuiderzeewerken.* In 1933, he took material from *Wij Bouwen* and some new material and with Helen van Dongen edited the 3-reel silent film, *Zuiderzee,* dealing with the land reclamation project. In 1933–34, with the financial assistance of the government, he returned to the Zuiderzee project with a team of collaborators and completed *Nieuwe Gronden.*
According to A. Saltzman, "The photography was handled separately by three teams: the first was 'the camera of the land' and covered the fight against the sea; the second, 'the camera of the sea,' covered the fight against the invasion of the land; and the third covered men and their machines. This production approach

provided three dramatic themes and the conflict and antagonism was emphasized by Hanns Eisler's music. Everything led up to the dramatic finale with the closing of the dike."

This magnificent sequence is the conclusion of the first two reels of *New Earth*. The third reel contrasts this magnificent technical endeavor with a world in the grip of economic depression, a world in which grain is poured back into the sea to support wheat prices despite the millions of unemployed on the bread lines. For this sequence Bertolt Brecht wrote the "Ballad of people who throw away sacks." The explicit social criticism of the sequence led to its being banned in several countries and the French censor's comments are probably typical: "Such a sequence cannot be shown to the public: it describes reality too bluntly." Though *New Earth* loses its main import when deprived of its exemplary last reel, the lyrical, epic, yet realistic style of the first two reels still makes the film a masterpiece.

In 1941, the Dutch Government-in-exile released *New Earth* without the third reel but with a brief introductory sequence of the Dutch resistance to aggression. 22 minutes.

NIGHT (THE) NOTTE (LA)

NIGHT AND FOG NUIT ET BROUILLARD

NIGHT AND THE CITY Britain 1950. *Dir* Jules Dassin *Scen* Jo Eisinger based on the novel by Gerald Kersh *Photog* Max Greene *Art Dir* C. P. Norman *Mus* Benjamin Frankel *Ed* Sidney Stone *Cast* Richard Widmark, Gene Tierney, Googie Withers, Hugh Marlowe, Francis L. Sullivan *Prod* 20th Century-Fox. 101 mins. A small-time crook (Widmark) with the help of his aging father, a former wrestling champion, sets out to develop a racket around wrestling in opposition to a Greek (Sullivan) who controls all London wrestling. His father is killed and the crook is hunted across London by the rival gang and murdered.

Set in London's Soho district and clearly a follow-up to his earlier *Naked City* (*q.v.*), *Night and the City* is a sharp, violent, and explosive film whose most famous sequence is that in which a fat, aging wrestler dies. Widmark has a great sense of presence but his performance is at times a little too hysterical. This

was Dassin's first European film after falling victim to the witch hunts in Hollywood.

NIGHT AT THE OPERA (A) USA 1935. *Dir* Sam Wood *Scen* George S. Kaufman, Morrie Ryskind *Photog* Merritt B. Gerstad *Art Dir* Cedric Gibbons, Ben Carré, Edwin B. Willis *Mus* Herbert Stothart *Ed* William Levanway *Cast* Groucho, Chico, and Harpo Marx, Margaret Dumont, Kitty Carlisle, Allan Jones, Siegfried Rumann *Prod* MGM. 96 mins. After various comic adventures on a transatlantic liner, the Marx brothers cause havoc in the opera house in their attempts to promote the career of a young singer (Jones).

After the high point of *Duck Soup* (*q.v.*), this film began the slide down hill that became more marked in their later films. There are however, many superb gags: the tiny cabin with thirty people crammed into it; the three Italian pilots with long beards; Harpo silently slitting the evening coat of the maestro; the chase in the opera house with a melée of costumes and changing backdrops as the singers try to perform. This was the Marx Brothers' first film for MGM and their first without Zeppo.

NIGHT BEAUTIES BELLES DE NUIT (LES)

NIGHT MAIL Britain 1936. *Dir/Scen* Basil Wright, Harry Watt *Photog* J. Jones, H. E. (Chick) Fowle *Mus* Benjamin Britten *Dir Sound* Alberto Cavalcanti *Poem* W. H. Auden *Ed* R. Q. McNaughton *Prod* John Grierson for G.P.O. Film unit. 24 mins. This documentary about the nightly journey of the Postal Special from London to Glasgow is, in essence, a "film-poem" in which the images, natural sounds, Britten's music, and Auden's verse are edited together to create a rhythmic unity. One of the best films of the British documentary school. It marked a real advance in the approach and technique of the documentary and is a tribute to Cavalcanti's experiments in the use of sound.

NIGHT OF REMEMBRANCE (A) CELULOZA

*NIGHT OF THE DEMON CURSE OF THE DEMON Britain 1958. *Dir* Jacques Tourneur *Scen* Charles Bennett, Hal E. Chester based on the story *Casting the Runes* by Montagu R. James *Photog* Ted Scaife *Art Dir* Ken Adam *Mus* Clifton Parker *Ed* Michael Gordon *Cast* Dana Andrews, Peggy Cummins, Niall MacGinnis, Maurice Denham, Reginal Beckworth, Athene Seyler *Prod* Sabre. 82 mins.

Professor Harrington (Denham) dies suddenly after threatening to expose Dr. Karswell (MacGinnis), known as a specialist in the occult. Harrington's niece, Joanna (Cummins), explains this to John Holden (Andrews), an American psychologist. After Karswell predicts Holden's death within four days, Holden receives a piece of parchment similar to one Harrington received. Joanna and Holden unite against Karswell, who dies a horrible death after they return the parchment to him.

Jacques Tourneur's first venture into the horror genre since his collaboration with Val Lewton on such films as the thematically similar *Cat People* (*q.v.*) and *I Walked with a Zombie* in the early Forties. Based on the classic short story by M. R. James, it "abounds in prosaic situations turning implacably into nightmares" (Carlos Clarens). Its understated, elliptical style and brilliant final sequence make this one of the great films of the supernatural.

NIGHT ON BALD (BARE) MOUNTAIN (A) UNE NUIT SUR LE MONT CHAUVE

NIGHTS OF CABIRIA (THE) NOTTI DI CABIRIA (LE)

NIGHT TRAIN POCIAG

NIGHT WATCH TROU (LE)

NIHON NO HIGEKI A JAPANESE TRAGEDY Japan 1953. *Dir/Scen* Keisuke Kinoshita *Photo* Hiroyuki (Hiroshi) Kusuda *Mus* Chuji Kinoshita *Cast* Yoko Mochizuki, Yoko Katsuragi, Masami Taura *Prod* Shochiku. 100 mins. approx.

The life of a Japanese family in the immediate postwar years centering on the life of a war widow (Mochizuki) who has fallen into prostitution. An authoritatively directed work, this is one of Kinoshita's best films and is justfiably admired in Japan.

— *Nihon no Higeki/A Japanese Tragedy* Japan 1945. *Dir* Fumio Kamei.

A documentary banned by the American Occupation authorities because of its communist theme.

NIJUSHI NO HITOMI TWENTY-FOUR EYES Japan 1954. *Dir* Keisuke Kinoshita *Scen* Keisuke Kinoshita based on the novel by Sakae Tsuboi *Photog* Hiroyuki (Hiroshi) Kusada *Mus* Chuji Kinoshita *Cast* Hideko Takamine, Takahiro Tamura, Yumeji Tsukioka *Prod* Shochiku. 110 mins.

The story of Japan from 1927–1946 as seen through the eyes of a teacher (Takamine) educating children on a small Japanese island.

Based on a very popular Japanese novel and similar to Donskoy's *A Village Schoolteacher* (*q.v.*), this sensitive film avoids stylization in favor of a more direct realism and includes an excellent performance by Hideko Takamine.

NINE DAYS OF ONE YEAR DEVYAT' DENEY ODNOGO GODA

1905 see MAT

NINETY DEGREES SOUTH WITH CAPTAIN SCOTT, R. N., TO THE SOUTH POLE

NINGEN NO JOKEN THE HUMAN CONDITION Japan 1958–61. Part I: *No Greater Love* Japan 1958–59. Part II: *Road to Eternity* Japan 1959. Part III: *A Soldier's Prayer* Japan 1961. *Dir* Masaki Kobayashi *Scen* Masaki Kobayashi, Zenzo Matsuyama based on the 6-volume novel by Jumpei Gomikawa *Photog* Yoshio Miyajima *Mus* Chuji Kinoshita *Ed* Keiichi Uraoka *Cast* Tatsuya Nakadi, Michiyo Aratama, Shinji Nambara, Ineke Arima *Prod* Shochiku. Part I, 211 mins. (138 mins. USA); Part II, 181 mins. Part III, 190 mins. Grandscope.

The action of the trilogy takes place in Japanese-occupied Manchuria between 1943 and 1945. *Part I:* Kaji (Nakadi), a young pacifist, takes a job as a labor supervisor in a remote mine. He and his wife (Aratama) try to better the lot of the Chinese laborers. He is accused of conspiracy, tortured, then forced into military service. Part II: Kaji is appalled at the inhuman treatment of army recruits. He is promoted and tries to introduce less harsh measures but he earns the hatred of other officers. At the head of a detachment during combat he is one of three survivors. Part III: The Japanese collapse. Kaji starts the journey home to his wife. He is imprisoned by the Russians, escapes, but dies in the snow before reaching his wife.

245

This nine and one-half hour long humanistic, antiwar fresco is magnificent, including many forceful scenes that depict the horrors and cruelties of war. Its director, Kobayashi, said: "I had some of the same experiences during the war as Kaji. I wanted to bring to life the tragedy of men who are forced into war against their will. Kaji is both the oppressor and the oppressed and he learns that he can never stop being an oppressor while he himself is oppressed. Of course I wanted to denounce the crimes of war but I also wanted to show how human society can become inhumane."

NINJO KAMI-FUSEN HUMANITY AND PAPER BALLOONS/THE PAPER BALLOONS Japan 1937. *Dir* Sadao Yamanaka *Scen* Shintaro Mimura *Photog* Akira Mimura *Art Dir* Sentaro Iwata *Cast* K. Nakamura, Ch. Kawarazaki, S. Suketakaya *Prod* Toho/P.C.L. Studio. 90 mins. approx.
The lives of the people who live in an alley in Edo (Tokyo) at the end of the 18th century: the goldfish seller, the blind masseur, the noodle seller, the street gambler and a samurai and his wife. The time is known as the most artistically vital period in Japanese history, but these poor people play no part in it.
Yamanaka, who greatly admired René Clair, reveals in this film an admirable ability to capture the nuances of gesture and behavior. Soon after its release, he was drafted into the army and died in northern China in 1938 when he was only 31. The actors were all members of the Zenshinza (Progress) Group, who then represented the progressive trends in Kabuki drama.

NINOTCHKA USA 1939. *Dir* Ernst Lubitsch *Scen* Charles Brackett, Billy Wilder, Walter Reisch from an original story by Melchior Lengyel *Photog* William Daniels *Art Dir* Cedric Gibbons *Mus* Werner R. Heymann *Ed* Gene Ruggiero *Cast* Greta Garbo, Melvyn Douglas, Ina Claire, Bela Lugosi, Sig Rumann, Felix Bressart, Alexander Granach *Prod* MGM. 111 mins.
A dedicated (but attractive) Soviet commissar (Garbo), sent to Paris to check up on three incompetent emissaries (Rumann, Bressart, Granach) who are supposed to be selling jewels to buy machinery, is deflected from her pur-

pose) by romance with an aristocrat (Douglas). She buys a hat, loses the jewels, and then loses her lover through the jealousy of a duchess (Claire). Ninotchka's honor and career are saved and in the end she meets her lover again in Istanbul.
A sophisticated, spirited comedy but one which was also used as political propaganda in 1939-41 (before the Americans entered the war) and later in Europe in 1948-52 during the "hottest" period of the cold war.
Even without Garbo, this would be one of Lubitsch's best films. The script still sparkles and is still irresistibly funny; Lubitsch's sense of timing is as fine as ever.
— *Silk Stockings* USA 1957. *Dir* Rouben Mamoulian *Scen* Leonard Gershe, Leonard Spigelgass based on the musical play suggested by *Ninotchka Photog* Robert Bronner *Mus* Cole Porter *Cast* Fred Astaire, Cyd Charisse *Prod* MGM. 117 mins. Metrocolor. CinemaScope.
[A remake based on the musical play but without the flair, wit, and grace of the Lubitsch version. Cole Porter's score and Fred Asttaire's dancing are the main redeeming features.]

NINTH CIRCLE (THE) DEVETI KRUG

NOBI FIRES ON THE PLAIN Japan 1959. *Dir/Ed* Kon Ichikawa *Scen* Natto Wada based on the novel by Shohei O-oka *Photog* Setsuo Kobayashi *Art Dir* Tokuji Shibata *Mus* Yasushi Akutagawa *Cast* Eiji Funakoshi, Osamu Takizawa, Micky Curtis *Prod* Daiei. 108 mins. Daieiscope.
During the collapse of the Japanese army in the Philippines, Tamura (Funakoshi) is sent to a hospital, which turns him away. He is forced to wander in the hills without food, harassed by American tanks and terrified by the "fires on the plain" that are set by Filipinos bent on revenge against the Japanese. He meets several soldiers who have turned cannibal and joins two of them (Takizawa, Curtis), unsuspectingly sharing human flesh ("monkey meat") with them. After the two fight and kill each other, Tamura tries to surrender to the Americans but is shot.
Though not equaling *Ningen no Joken* (*q.v.*), this is one of the most powerful Japanese antiwar films and includes several explicit scenes of the horrors and

cruelties to which men are reduced by war.

NOCES DE SABLE (LES) DESERT WEDDING/ DAUGHTER OF THE SANDS France/Morocco 1948. *Dir* André Zwobada *Scen* André Zwobada, Jean Besancenot based on a Moroccan legend; commentary written and spoken by Jean Cocteau *Photog* André Bac *Mus* Georges Auric *Cast* Denise Cardi, Itto Bent Lahsen, Larbi Tounsi *Prod* Studio Maghreb. 90 mins. (75 mins., North America; 50 mins., Britain.)

[Abandoned by her father and raised by a woman, "The Mad One" (Lahsen), a young girl (Cardi) falls in love with the son of a sheik (Tounsi). The sheik dies and his son, the prince, is not allowed to see the girl, who is imprisoned and tortured by the court jester. She escapes and, believing the prince responsible, kills herself. "The Mad One" kills the prince to reunite them in death. From their graves, a spring appears to irrigate the land.]

This Arabian *Tristan and Isolde* is the best preindependence Moroccan film but it didn't have the success in the Arab countries its quality and authenticity deserved.

NO GREATER GLORY USA 1934. *Dir* Frank Borzage *Scen* Jo Swerling based on the novel *The Paul Street Boys* by Ferenc Molnar *Photog* Joseph August *Ed* Viola Lawrence *Cast* George Breakston, Jimmy Butler, Jackie Searl, Frankie Darro, Donald Haines, Julius Molnar *Prod* Columbia. 117 mins.

An adaptation of Molnar's antimilitaristic novel, which depicts the war games of a group of Hungarian children in 1914. Marcel Lapierre summarized the film: "Rival gangs of boys carry out organized war over the possession of a playground with all of the protocol of their elders: honor of the flag, respect of rank, punishment books . . . The only boy of Paul Street who is not an officer strives for distinction in order to merit the peaked cap he has coveted since he joined. Because of his initiative he is laid up with a bad cold and has to stay in bed . . . On the day of the "war" he escapes to rejoin his comrades, but his display of loyalty and fortitude on the battlefield aggravates his illness and he dies. The 'soldiers' of the two armies weep as they follow the mother carrying the little

corpse." This is probably one of Borzage's best films and one of the best American films of the early Thirties.

— *A Pal utcai fiuk/The Boys of Paul Street* Hungary 1968. *Dir* Zoltan Fabri *Scen* Fabri, Endre Bohem based on the novel *Photog* G. Illes *Mus* Emil Petrovics *Cast* Anthony Kemp, William Burleigh, John Moulder-Brown. 105 mins. Eastman Color. Produced simultaneously in English and Hungarian language versions.

NO GREATER LOVE (Japan) NINGEN NO JOKEN (*Part I*)

NO GREATER LOVE (USSR) ONA ZASCHISHCHAYET RODINU

NO MAN'S LAND NIEMANDSLAND

NON C'E PACE FRA GLI ULIVI NO PEACE AMONG THE OLIVES Italy 1950. *Dir* Giuseppe De Santis *Scen* Giuseppe De Santis, Libero De Libero, Carlo Lizzani, Gianni Puccini *Photog* Pietro Portalupi *Mus* Goffredo Petrassi *Cast* Raf Vallone, Lucia Bosè, Folco Lulli *Prod* Lux. 99 mins.

Francesco (Vallone), returning to his village after the war, finds his flock of sheep have been stolen by a local racketeer (Lulli). He attempts to steal back his sheep helped by Laura (Bosè), a girl forced to become engaged to the racketeer. He is imprisoned and no one will testify on his behalf. Francesco escapes from prison and takes his revenge. Produced in the Fondi region where the director was born, this is a sincere and vigorous social drama, even though the photography is often pretentious with characters carefully composed against expressive and baroque landscapes.

NON UCCIDERE TU NE TUERAS POINT/ THOU SHALT NOT KILL Italy/Yugoslavia/ Leichtenstein 1961. *Dir* Claude Autant-Lara *Scen* Jean Aurenche *Photog* Jacques Natteau *Art Dir* Max Douy *Ed* Madeleine Gug *Cast* Laurent Terzieff, Suzanne Flon, Horst Frank. 129 mins. Dyaliscope.

In France in 1949 an army tribunal is about to try two men: a German priest (Frank) who was forced to kill a French resistance fighter and a conscientious objector (Terzieff). The priest is acquitted while the conscientious objector is sentenced to a one year prison term, which, according to French law, can be repeated indefinitely if the objector does not retract.

The script (originally titled *L'Objecteur*) was written in 1950 and was based on a true story. It was to have been made in France with Gérard Philipe as the objector but financial backing quickly evaporated when the army made its disapproval known. It was finally made in Yugoslavia with Italian backing. When it was shown at the 1961 Venice Festival (before the end of the Algerian War) it created a profound impression, attested to by the prize for acting awarded to Suzanne Flon, who plays the objector's mother. The problem of whether a soldier ought to obey orders under any circumstances, including shooting hostages, had a special significance in France at the time and led to its being banned there as in Italy.

[Despite the power of its arguments, the film lacks emotion and any real sense of characterization and remains largely polemic.]

NO ORCHIDS FOR LULU see BÜCHSE DER PANDORA (DIE)

NO PEACE AMONG THE OLIVES NON C'È PACE FRA GLI ULIVI

NORA-INU STRAY DOG Japan 1949. *Dir* Akira Kurosawa *Scen* Ryuzo Kikushima, Akira Kurosawa *Photog* Asakazu Nakai *Art Dir* So Matsuyama *Mus* Fumio Hayasaka *Cast* Toshiro Mifune, Takashi Shimura, Keiko Awaji, Ko Kimura *Prod* Shintoho. 122 mins.

A young detective (Mifune) has his pistol stolen from him on a crowded bus. Several murders are committed with his gun before he eventually captures the criminal (Kimura).

Though it has some of the feeling of a Hollywood *film noir,* this is not a thriller as much as it is a portrait of postwar Tokyo, where the detective's search brings him into contact with the unemployed, the defeated, the carpetbaggers, crooks, and prostitutes. One long sequence, entirely without dialogue, depicts his search among the homeless. The final sequence is very beautiful: after a fight in which both detective and murderer are covered in mud, they lie undistinguishable from each other in a field of flowers.

The hero, played by Kurosawa's favorite actor, is a restless and complex character

and in some respects is pursuing his own reflection. This is an even more important film than *Rashomon* (*q.v.*) but regrettably is still relatively unknown.

NORTH BY NORTHWEST USA 1959 *Dir* Alfred Hitchcock *Scen* Ernest Lehman *Photog* Robert Burks *Art Dir* Robert Boyle, William A. Horning, Merrill Pyle, Henry Grace, Frank McKelvey *Mus* Bernard Herrmann *Ed* George Tomasini *Cast* Cary Grant, Eva Marie Saint, James Mason, Leo G. Carroll *Prod* MGM. 136 mins. Technicolor. VistaVision.

The professor (Carroll), a CIA agent, invents a mythical spy to force the hand of a foreign spy (Mason). An advertising executive, Thornhill (Grant), mistaken for the professor, is hunted across the USA and gets involved with a girl (Saint) before the final showdown.

North by Northwest is not dissimilar in its shape to *The 39 Steps* (*q.v.*) and *Saboteur.* Its fantastic chase across America, its deft wit, and its spirited style make this one of Hitchcock's best Hollywood films. Best known sequences: the hero lured to a remote Indiana prairie and attacked by a biplane "crop-dusting where there ain't no crops"; the climax on Mount Rushmore with the chase and fight on the gigantic sculptured faces of American presidents.

NOSFERATU — EINE SYMPHONIE DES GRAUENS NOSFERATU, THE VAMPIRE/ NOSFERATU, A SYMPHONY OF HORROR Germany 1921 (released 1922). *Dir* F. W. Murnau *Scen* Henrik Galeen based on the novel *Dracula* by Bram Stoker *Art Dir* Albin Grau *Photog* Fritz Arno Wagner *Cast* Max Schreck, Gustav von Wangenheim, Greta Schröder, Alexander Granach, Max Nemetz *Prod* Prana. 1,967 meters. (6,500 ft. approx.). Re-released in 1930 in a sound version with the title *Die Zwölfte Stunde: Eine Nacht des Grauens.*

In the 1830's, Hutter (von Wangenheim), the clerk of a real estate agent (Granach), leaves his young wife Nina (Schröder) to arrange the sale of a property with the mysterious Count Orlock (Nosferatu, the Vampire) (Schreck) in the Carpathians. He falls into the clutches of the count but escapes. The count leaves his castle in a coffin full of earth taking several other coffins with him. He travels to Bremen on a ship whose crew dies and from which, when he arrives, a swarm of plague rats emerge to scourge the town. Hutter returns to Nina and explains. She resolves to destroy the count by keeping him at her bedside until sunrise, when the count's body dissolves in the sun's rays and the wife dies.

The film only really begins when the clerk enters the region of the castle. "And when he crossed the bridge, the phantoms came to meet him." A mysterious black draped coach appears and hurtles him along the roads to Count Orlock's castle.

Famous sequences: Nosferatu carrying a coffin on his shoulders through the streets; the coffins full of earth and rats; the plague killing the ship's crew; the dead ship entering Bremen harbor; the madman eating flies; Nosferatu vanishing when the cock crows.

For Siegfried Kracauer, "Nosferatu is a 'Scourge of God' and, only as such, identifiable with the pestilence. He is a bloodthirsty, bloodsucking tyrant figure looming in those regions where myths and fairy tales meet. It is highly significant that during this period German imagination, regardless of its starting point, always gravitated towards such figures — as if under the compulsion of hate-love. The conception that great love might force tyranny into retreat (was) symbolized by Nina's triumph over Nosferatu." This interpretation is based more on theory than facts. Can one really accept that Murnau, even unconsciously, was devising propaganda for the eventual Nazi triumph? Ado Kyrou felt on the contrary that "Across the bridge of Nosferatu we reach the perfect expression of love and revolution." In any case, this fascinating film is superior to Bram Stoker's Victorian novel and to the many other film versions.

Only in its theme can Nosferatu be called expressionistic. It was produced mainly in exteriors. Albin Grau's sets, such as the Carpathian castle or the three empty houses sold to Nosferatu, are more realistic than deformed, and in any case are less fantastic than many natural sets. The romantic couple are stiff and awkward. But Max Schreck, with his exaggerated makeup, bald head, long pointed ears, talons, jerky walk, and gangly black silhouette, creates a Nosferatu who is a convincing "symphony of horror."

The film was a great success in Germany and France, where the surrealists were especially enthusiastic. However, it was ridiculed by many in Britain and the USA, where later it led to a series of Dracula (q.v.) films.

A version of the film was released in North America in 1929 based on a scenario by Conrad West with editing by Symon Gould and titles by Ben de Casseres. Its length was 6,942 ft. and it included many additional sequences.

NOT AGAINST THE FLESH VAMPYR

NOT ON YOUR LIFE VERDUGO (EL)

NOTORIOUS USA 1946. *Dir* Alfred Hitchcock *Scen* Ben Hecht *Photog* Ted Tetzlaff *Art Dir* Darrell Silvera, Carroll Clark, Albert S. D'Agostino *Mus* Roy Webb *Ed* Theron Warth *Cast* Cary Grant, Ingrid Bergman, Claude Rains, Louis Calhern *Prod* RKO. 102 mins.

A beautiful American agent (Bergman) in South America marries the head of a group of German spies (Rains) in order to watch him, although she loves another American agent (Grant). The Americans get the secrets but the wife nearly dies from slow poisoning.

This spy thriller includes some brilliant stylistic exercises: a traveling shot beginning in a ballroom and ending in close-up on a key held in a hand; an enormous close-up of a poisoned cup of coffee; close-up of dancers' faces, etc.

NOTTE (LA) THE NIGHT Italy/France 1960. *Dir* Michelangelo Antonioni *Scen* Michelangelo Antonioni, Ennio Flaiano, Antonio Guerra *Photog* Gianni Di Venanzo *Art Dir* Piero Zuffi *Mus* Giorgio Gaslini *Ed* Eraldo Da Roma *Cast* Jeanne Moreau, Monica Vitti, Marcello Mastroianni, Bernhard Wicki *Prod* Nepi-Film/Sofitedip/Silver Film. 121 mins.

Giovanni (Mastroianni), a novelist who feels himself written out, and his wife, Lidia (Moreau), begin to question their marriage after visiting a dying friend (Wicki). A visit to an all-night party increases their confusion. Giovanni is attracted to another woman (Vitti) and Lidia is pursued by another man. At dawn, their self-awareness has increased but not their hope.

Part of Antonioni's "trilogy" with *L'Avventura* (q.v.) and *L'Eclisse* (q.v.). Famous sequences: the visit to the dying man; Lidia's wanderings through Milan and its outskirts; the jaded atmosphere in the nightclub; the guests at the party jumping into the swimming pool; the last sequence on the golf course at dawn.

Antonioni describes Lidia and Giovanni as, "A couple in which the woman is more lucid than the man because the female sensibility is a much more precise filter than anyone else's and because the man, in the area of feelings, is almost always incapable of understanding reality, since he tries to dominate. Male egoism assumes out of self-interest a total abstraction of the woman's personality."

*NOTTI BIANCHE (LE) THE WHITE NIGHTS Italy/France 1957. *Dir* Luchino Visconti, Suso Cecchi D'Amico based on the story by Dostoevski *Photog* Giuseppe Rotunno *Art Dir* Mario Chiori, Mario Garbuglia *Mus* Nino Rota *Ed* Mario Serandrei *Cast* Maria Schell, Marcello Mastroianni, Jean Marais *Prod* CIAS/Vides/Intermondia. 107 mins.

Mario (Mastroianni), a shy young man, meets a mysterious young girl, Natalia (Schell), sobbing on a canal bridge. She tells him she is in love with a sailor (Marais) who left on a long journey and promised to return in one year. The year is up and he hasn't arrived, but she is convinced he will. Mario falls in love with her and has just persuaded her that the sailor will not return and she can be happy with him when the sailor appears and Natalia leaves with him.

The White Nights disappointed many critics at the time of its release. Its "neo-romanticism" seemed gross and its sets glaringly artificial in comparison with Visconti's earlier *Senso* (*q.v.*). However, though a minor Visconti, its baroque style now seems a direct step towards the development of *Rocco and His Brothers* (*q.v.*) and, curiously, more Stendhalian than Dosoevskian in its attempt to capture the "emotional crystallization of experience."

OTHER VERSIONS:

— **Belye nochi/White Nights* USSR 1959. *Dir* Ivan Pyriev *Scen* Pyriev based on the Dostoyevsky story *Photog* Valentin Pavlov *Cast* Ludmilla Marchenko, Oleg Strijanov, M. Peklhoban. 95 mins. Sovcolor.

— **Quatre nuits d'un rêveur* France/Italy 1970. *Dir* Robert Bresson *Scen* Bresson based on the story *Photog* Pierre Lhomme *Cast* nonprofessionals. 90 mins. Color.

NOTTI DI CABIRIA (LE) THE NIGHTS OF CABIRIA Italy/France 1956. *Dir* Federico Fellini, *Scen* Federico Fellini, Ennio Flaiano, Tullio Pinelli, Pier Paolo Pasolini *Photog* Otello Martelli, Aldo Tonti *Art Dir* P. Gherardi *Mus* Nino Rota *Ed* Leo Cattozza *Cast* Giulietta Masina, François Périer, Amedeo Nazzari, Franca Marzi, Dorian Gray *Prod* de Laurentiis/Films Marceau. 110 mins.

Cabiria (Masina), a streetwalker in Rome, dreams of success and happiness. Thinking she has found love with a young man (Périer) whom she has met in a theater, she sells her house and withdraws her savings in order to marry him. But he betrays and robs her and she returns to the streets.

Famous sequences: the tarts, including an enormous fat one, in the streets; Cabiria's adventures when she is picked up by a famous film star (Nazzari) and taken to his luxurious villa; the little house she has built in the suburbs; the pilgrimage: her attempt at suicide; her exaggerated makeup; the picnic by the lake where she becomes aware of having been cheated; the ending as she is surrounded by a group of young people singing, dancing, and playing.

Giulietta Masina, the passive Gelsomina of *La Strada* (*q.v.*), is here an indomitable fighter, a kind of Don Quixote, always ready to tilt at windmills and possessing, in spite of all her troubles, an unconquerable belief in life and happiness.

— **Sweet Charity* USA 1968. *Dir* Bob Fosse *Scen* Peter Stone based on the musical play by Neil Simon (book), Cy Coleman (music), Dorothy Fields (lyrics) derived from Fellini's film *Photog* Robert Surtees *Art Dir* George C. Webb, Alexander Golitzen *Cast* Shirley MacLaine, Sammy Davis Jr., Ricardo Montalban, John McMartin, Chita Rivera, Paula Kelly, Stubby Kaye *Prod* Universal. 149 mins. Technicolor. Panavision 70.

This is choreographer Bob Fosse's first film as director. It is memorable not only for its use of New York locations but for some brilliantly choreographed numbers such as "Hey Big Spender."

NOUS LES GOSSES US KIDS France 1941. *Dir* Louis Daquin *Scen* Maurice Hilero, Marcel Aymé, Gaston Modot *Photog* Jean Bachelet *Art Dir* Lucien Aguettand *Mus* M. F. Gaillard *Cast* Louise Carletti, Gilbert Gil, Larquey, Raymond Bussières, André Brunot, Louis Seigner, Marcel Pérès. 90 mins.

The children of a suburban school break a huge window and spend their Easter holidays acquiring money to pay for it. Released during the somber winter of the second year of the Nazi Occupation, this unpretentious, lively, and entertaining film brought with it a breath of fresh air and hope.

The script was written before the war by militants of the Ciné-Liberté Group (part of the *Front Populaire*); its production showed that films of poetic realism could still be made in France despite the Nazi and Vichy censors.

NOUS SOMMES TOUS DES ASSASSINS WE ARE ALL MURDERERS/ARE WE ALL MURDERERS? France 1952. *Dir* André Cayatte *Scen* Charles Spaak, André Cayatte *Photog* Jean Bourgoin *Art Dir* Jacques Colombier *Ed* Paul Cayatte *Cast* Marcel Mouloudji, Raymond Pellegrin, Claude Laydu, Louis Seigner, Antoine Balpêtre *Prod* UGC. 115 mins.

A very persuasive dramatized sermon against capital punishment. The best sequence shows life in the condemned cell. Curiously, the British release title turned Cayatte's statement into a question.

NOUVEAUX MESSIEURS (LES) France 1928. *Dir* Jacques Feyder *Assist* Marcel Carné *Scen* Charles Spaak, Jacques Feyder based on the play by Robert de Flers and Francis de Croisset *Photog* Georges Périnal, Maurice Desfassiaux *Art Dir* Lazare Meerson *Cast* Albert Préjean, Gaby Morlay, Henri Roussel *Prod* Albatros-Sequance. 3,700 meters (12,000 ft. approx.). 135 mins.

Suzanne (Morlay), a dancer without much talent, is the mistress of the Comte de Montoire (Roussel). Jacques (Préjean), a handsome trade union leader, falls in love with her. When Jacques becomes a minister he takes Suzanne under his protection. A change of government gives the count a cabinet post, Jacques is sent abroad as a diplomat and Suzanne returns to the count. "Its key sequences: the dance class at the Opéra, the meeting at Saint-Denis, the discussion in the Chamber of Deputies and the opening of the block of tenement housing exhibited a stunning sense of rhythm and timing" (Marcel Carné).

This film was banned by the authorities in 1928 for attacking "the dignity of Parliament and its ministers." It was based, however, on "a boulevard drama that was not in the least polemical. But when its gentle ironies were recorded by the camera they played the role of incendiary bombs, sarcasm and insults to parliamentary institutions." The Left, with Léon Moussinac, sprang to the defense of this political satire.

The satire of the Opéra predates that by Clair in *Le Million* (*q.v.*) while the accelerated speech sequence of the opening of the tenement housing is delightfully ironic. The film was finally released in 1929 after a year of arguments. But the discouraged Feyder had already left for Hollywood.

NOUVELLE MISSION DE JUDEX (LA) see JUDEX

NOVYI GULLIVER A NEW GULLIVER USSR 1935. *Dir* Alexander Ptushko *Scen* Grigori Roshal, Alexander Ptushko derived from Swift's story *Photog* N. Renkov *Art Dir* Sara Mokil, Y. Schwetz *Mus* Lev Schwartz *Cast* V. Konstantinovich *Prod* Mosfilm. 80 mins.

This is certainly the best Soviet animated film, the result of three years of work with caricatured puppet's. [Swift's satire is framed by a reading in a camp of Young Pioneers: in a boy's dream, Gulliver (Konstantinovich) arrives in an updated Lilliput controlled by an effete, mad King, his court, and the secret police. In a workers' revolt Gulliver comes to the aid of the oppressed.]

OTHER GULLIVER FILMS:
— *Les Voyages de Gulliver* France 1902. *Dir* Georges Méliès. 80 meters.
— *Gulliver's Travels* USA 1903. *Dir/Prod* Sigmund Lubin.

Probably an attempt by Lubin to cash in on Méliès' version.

— *Gulliver's Travels/Gulliver's Travels in Lilliput* USA 1939. *Dir* Dave Fleischer *Scen* Dan Gordon, Cal Howard, Ted Pierce, I. Sparber, E. Seward based on the story by Swift *Anim* Graham Place, Arnold Gillespie, and others *Photog* Charles Schettler *Prod* Max Fleischer. 77 mins. Technicolor.

Apparently spurred by the success of Disney's cartoon features, Fleischer produced this somewhat simplified version of the first part of Swift's book. Although pleasant and amusing it was not a great success.

— *Garibah no Uchu Ryoko/Gulliver's Travels Beyond the Moon* Japan 1966. *Dir* Yoshio Kuroda. 85 mins. Eastman Color.

Animated fantasy of a boy who travels on Dr. Gulliver's time machine.

— *Pripad pro zacinajiciho kata/A Case for the New Hangman* Czechoslovakia 1969. *Dir/Scen* Pavel Juracek *Photog* Jan Kalis *Art Dir* Milan Nejedly *Mus* Zdenek Liska *Cast* Lubomir Kostelka, Klara Jernekova, Milena Zahrynowska. 100 mins.

A free, modernized adaptation of the third part of the novel recounting Gulliver's adventures in Balnibarbi and Laputa. Originally produced under the title *Krajina vlidnych bludicek/A Country of Affable Spirits*.

NOVYI VAVILON THE NEW BABYLON USSR 1929. *Dir/Scen* Leonid Trauberg, Grigori Kozintsev *Photog* Andrei Moskvin, Yevgeni Mikhailov *Art Dir* Yevgeni Enei *Mus* Dmitri Shostakovich *Cast* Yelena Kuzmina, Pyotr Sobolevsky, D. Gutman, Sophie Magarill, Sergei Gerasimov, Andrei Kostrichkin, V. Pudovkin *Prod* Sovkino (Leningrad), 2,200 meters (7,300 ft. approx.).

The rise and fall of the French Commune in 1871, focusing on the life and death of a girl, Louise (Kuzmina), employed in a Parisian store, The New Babylon. The film is in eight parts: 1. The War of 1870. In the big department store, The New Babylon, a frenzied sale is in progress. 2. In a café are an over-gallant shop assistant (Pudovkin), a journalist (Gerasimov), and a Nana-like singer (Magarill), who hear the news of the defeat of the French Army. 3. The Prussians march through the snow towards Paris. The common people take up arms and fraternize with the soldiers while the government surrenders. 4. The women take the cannons, rise against the government, and march on Versailles. 5. Paris sets up its own government — the Commune. The cannons at Versailles are aimed on Paris. 6. Barricades are established in the streets. The Communards fight heroically for 49 days. 7. The Communards are arrested and insulted by the prosperous merchants. 8. After a mockery of a trial the Communards are ordered to dig their own graves and are then shot.

The actress Kuzmina wrote of her role: "Louise is not to be found in the literature of the time. We sought her in the whole epoch. This was the synthetic image of a communist girl at the time of the Paris Commune. . . . While working on *The New Babylon* it was Zola who gave us the most. All of us read all his works."

Best sequences: the evening in the café; the Germans marching on Paris; the Montmartre Commune facing the cannons at Versailles; the mourning over the first Communard mortalities; the savage executions during the "Week of Blood."

This magnificent film by Kozintsev and Trauberg (their last silent one) is not as well known as it deserves to be. Enei's sets, especially those for the luxurious Parisian department store, are excellent. The direction, despite some occasional historical errors, carries one forcefully from the sardonic opening scenes to the moving climax as the heroic tragedy of the Paris Commune gradually unfolds. The music was Shostakovich's first film score.

NUIT ET BROUILLARD NIGHT AND FOG France 1956. *Dir/Ed* Alain Resnais *Commentary* Jean Cayrol *Photog* Sacha Vierny, Ghislain Cloquet *Assist Dir* Chris Marker, André Heinrich, Jean-Charles Lauthe *Sound Assist* Henri Colpi, Jasmine Chasney *Prod* Como-Films/ Argos-Films/Cocinor. 30 mins. Eastman Color in parts.

One of the key films of its author, conceived as a "warning siren" against the Nazi extermination camps and against war. It is a moving compilation of black and white archival footage of the camps and color shots of the camps as they are today. [Resnais' subtle counterpoint of present and past, color and stark black and white, is heightened by the lyrical narrative of Cayrol, who himself said, "Not only is it a film of memory, it is also a film of great uneasiness."]

NUIT SUR LE MONT CHAUVE (UNE) UNE NUIT SUR LE MONT CHAUVE

NUTTY PROFESSOR (THE) USA 1963. *Dir* Jerry Lewis *Scen* Jerry Lewis, Bill Richmond *Photog* Wallace Kelley *Art Dir* Hal Pereira, Walter Tyler *Cast* Jerry

Lewis, Stella Stevens, Del Moore *Prod* Jerry Lewis Enterprises. 107 mins. Technicolor.

Broadly based on a Dr. Jekyll and Mr. Hyde theme, this a farce about a myopic, mild chemistry professor (Lewis) who concocts an elixir that turns him at will into a swaggering, virile lover. Jerry Lewis is in every sense the complete *auteur* of this wild, burlesque, though occasionally creaking, comedy, which is also his best.

*OBCHOD NA KORZE THE SHOP ON MAIN STREET/THE SHOP ON THE HIGH STREET Czechoslovakia 1965. *Dir* Jan Kadar, Elmar Klos *Scen* Jan Kadar, Elmar Klos, Ladislav Grosman based on a story by Ladislav Grosman *Photog* Vladimir Novotny *Art Dir* Karel Skvor *Mus* Zdenek Liska *Cast* Josef Kroner, Hana Slivkova, Ida Kaminska, Frantisek Svarik. 128 mins.

In a small provincial town in German-occupied Slovakia in 1942, Tono (Kroner) and his wife (Slivkova) have difficulty making a living because he does not sympathize with the regime. His brother-in-law makes him "Aryan controller" of a button shop owned by an old Jewish lady (Kaminska) who is nearly deaf. Tono finds he cannot explain his position to the woman and gradually accepts her belief that he is her "assistant." In return, the local Jews pay him a handsome salary. When the Jews are ordered deported the woman's name is mistakenly omitted from the list. Tono is afraid he will be arrested for shielding her from the Hlinka Guards and tries to push her into the street. Finally he locks her in a cupboard until the deportation is over but his rough treatment kills her and he hangs himself.

The first Czechoslovakian feature to win an Academy Award, this film is not only an engrossing study in guilt and the failure of a generation to fight anti-Semitism, but also an affectionate and often lyrical portrait of life in a small provincial town. However, the film is not entirely successful. The first half, detailing Tono's domestic life, meanders and the film in general often falls into sentimental whimsy when the irony of, for example, Munk's *Eroica* (*q.v.*) would be more appropriate.

OBLOMOK IMPERII FRAGMENT OF AN EMPIRE USSR 1929. *Dir* Friedrich Ermler *Scen* Friedrich Ermler, Katerina Vinogradskaya *Photog* Yevgeni Schneider, G. Bushtuyev *Mus* V. Desheyov *Art Dir* Yevgeni Enei *Cast* Fyodor Nikitin, Yakov Gudkin, Ludmila Semyonova, Valeri Solovtsov, Vyacheslav Viskovsky, Sergei Gerasimov *Prod* Sovkino (Leningrad). 7,900 ft.

A young man (Nikitin) who lost his memory in World War I regains it in 1928, unaware of the social changes that had occurred in the previous decade. Memories of his wife (Semyonova), the Civil War, his being wounded by a White (Gerasimov), and his former employer (Viskovsky) return and he rushes back to the city he knew as St. Petersburg but which is now Leningrad.

The complex psychological characterization of the hero as he regains his memory through a series of visual associations is the principal quality of this exceptional film. Superb photography of contemporary Leningrad and the Soviet Union blend with a kaleidoscopic cluster of images from the hero's memories to create a gradually recognizable pattern of present and past. Although the last few sequences are weak, on the whole this is an excellent satiric portrait of life in the USSR at the beginning of the first Five Year Plan.

OCCUPE-TOI D'AMELIE OH, AMELIA!/KEEP AN EYE ON AMELIA France 1949. *Dir.* Claude Autant-Lara *Scen* Pierre Bost, Jean Aurenche based on the play by Georges Feydeau *Photog* André Bac *Art Dir* Max Douy *Mus* René Cloërec *Ed* Madeleine Gug *Cast* Danielle Darrieux, Bervil, Carette, Jean Desailly, Coco Aslan *Prod* Lux. 98 mins.

At the turn of the century, a Parisian coquette, Amélie (Darrieux), agrees to go through a mock marriage with a young man (Desailly) who can only inherit his fortune when he marries. Amélie's protector discovers the trick and arranges for a real marriage. After several comic mix-ups Amélie and the young man decide they really love each other and elope.

Feydeau's typical boulevard farce is handled by Autant-Lara in a conventional theatrical style, but it is a style that allows him to satirize the hypocrisy and pettiness of the Parisian bourgeois while including all the usual intrigues and comic set pieces.

OCTOBER OKTYABR'

ODD MAN OUT GANG WAR Britain 1947. *Dir* Carol Reed *Scen* R. C. Sherrif, F. L. Green based on the novel by F. L. Green *Photog* Robert Krasker *Art Dir* Roger Furse, Ralph Brinton *Mus* William Alwyn *Cast* James Mason, Robert Newton, Kathleen Ryan, F. J. McCormick, Denis O'Dea, Fay Compton *Prod* Two Cities. 115 mins.

Johnny MacQueen (Mason), leader of an illegal political organization in Northern Ireland, is wounded during a raid on a bank to raise funds for the organization. The police hunt him through the city while his fiancée (Ryan) tries to help him. People he comes into contact with try to help in various ways but don't want to become involved. His fiancée tries to get him to the local priest but he is betrayed and, at dawn, he and his fiancée are shot by the police.

This brilliant film established Carol Reed as a major director. Its theme is not dissimilar to *Quai des brumes* (*q.v.*) while its use of a chase through city streets is derivative of *M* (*q.v.*) and *The Informer* (*q.v.*). James Mason, in a role with little dialogue, gives a brilliant performance and the supporting characters, largely actors from the Abbey Theatre, are sharply drawn.

— *The Lost Man* USA 1969. *Dir* Robert Alan Aurthur *Scen* Robert Alan Aurthur based on the novel by F. L. Green *Photog* Jerry Finnerman *Cast* Sidney Poitier, Joanna Shimkus, Al Freeman, Jr. *Prod* Universal. 122 mins. Technicolor. Panavision.

A stylistically fashionable but pedestrian version in which the IRA leader becomes a Negro (Poitier) who robs a factory in Philadelphia to acquire funds for an underground Civil Rights organization.

ODNA ALONE USSR 1941. *Dir/Scen* Grigori Kozintsev, Leonid Trauberg *Photog* Andrei Moskvin *Art Dir* Yevgeni Enei *Mus* Dmitri Shostakovich *Cast* Yelena Kuzmina, Pyotr Sobolevsky, Sergei Gerasimov, Bal Liou-Sian *Prod* Soyuzkino. 80 mins.

A young girl (Kuzmina) engaged to a student (Sobolevsky) is assigned as a teacher to the almost medieval wilds of the Altai. She comes into conflict with a kulak (Liou-Sian) and a Soviet civil servant (Gerasimov) with almost fatal results.

Main sequences: the carefree life in Leningrad; the marriage preparations; the girl's arrival on a high plateau and her first sight of the tents, strange costumes, and idols; the civil servant, who is bourgeois at heart, treating his wife like a dog; the order to destroy the sheep; the protest meeting; the search for the teacher in bitterly cold weather.

Alone was planned and photographed as a silent film; a sound track was added only after its completion in 1930. This track includes a few words of dialogue but depends largely on Shostakovich's exemplary music score. This is the best film score he ever wrote and incorporates not only certain musical themes used for dramatic effect but also natural sounds as a typewriter, telegraph, and a radio.

Since it had little dialogue, this film had only a limited release outside the USSR. It is nonetheless a work of great significance and beauty, equaling *Road to Life* (*q.v.*). These two films, in fact, were the most important Soviet sound films until *Chapaev* (*q.v.*)

*OEDIPUS REX

— *Edipo Re/Oedipus Rex* Italy 1967. *Dir* Pier Paolo Pasolini *Scen* Pier Paolo Pasolini based on the play by Sophocles *Photog* Giuseppe Ruzzolini *Art Dir* Andrea Fantacci, Luigi Scaccianoce *Ed* Nino Baragli *Mus* mainly Romanian and Japanese *Cast* Franco Citti, Silvana Mangano, Carmelo Bene *Prod* Arco Film. 110 mins. Technicolor.

Pasolini's own translation of the original Sophocles play set within a modern prologue and epilogue. Pasolini said: "I wanted to make the film freely. When I made it I had two objectives: first, to make a 'kind of completely metaphoric — and therefore mythicized — autobiography; and second to confront both the problem of psychoanalysis and the problem of the myth. But instead of projecting the myth on to psychoanalysis, I have reprojected psychoanalysis on to the myth. This was the fundamental operation in *Oedipus*. But I kept very free, I followed up all my aspirations and impulses. I didn't deny myself a single one. Now, the father's resentment towards his son is something I felt more distinctly than the relationship between the son and the mother, because the relationship between a son and his mother is not a historical relationship, it is a purely interior, private relationship, which is outside history, indeed is meta-historical, and therefore ideologically unproductive, whereas what produces history is the relationship of hatred and love between father and son, so naturally this interested me more than the one between son and mother. I have felt my love for my mother very, very deeply, and all my work is influenced by this, but it is an influence whose origin is deep down inside me and, as I said, rather outside history. While everything ideological, voluntary, active, and practical in my actions as a writer depends on my struggle with my father. That's why I put in things that weren't in Sophocles, but which I don't think are outside psychoanalysis, because psychoanalysis talks about the superego represented by the father repressing the child; so in a way I just applied psychoanalysis notions in the way I felt."

—*Oedipus Rex* Canada 1956. *Dir* Tyrone Guthrie *Cast* Douglas Campbell, Eleanor Stuart, Douglas Rain. 75 mins. Eastman Color.

Tyrone Guthrie's film of his own stage production in 1955 at Stratford, Ontario. Notable for its costumes, masks, and music score. Although filmed on a single set, Guthrie makes good use of a mobile camera and forceful editing.

—*Oedipus the King* Britain 1967. *Dir* Philip Saville *Photog* Walter Lassally *Cast* Christopher Plummer, Lilli Palmer, Richard Johnson. 97 mins. Technicolor. An elaborate production, overly acaddemic and without much force or cinematic merit. It was staged in a ruined Greek theater at Dodoni in Greece.

OF A THOUSAND DELIGHTS VAGHE STELLE DELL'ORSA

OH, AMELIA! OCCUPE-TOI D'AMÉLIE

O'HARU SAIKAKU ICHIDAI ONNA

OH! FOR A MAN! WILL SUCCESS SPOIL ROCK HUNTER?

*OH, MR. PORTER! Britain 1937. *Dir* Marcel Varnel *Scen* Val Guest, J. O. C. Orton, Marriott Edgar based on a story by Frank Launder *Photog* Arthur Crabtree *Art Dir* Vetchinsky *Mus* Louis Levy *Cast* Will Hay, Graham Moffatt, Moore Marriott, Dennis Wyndham. *Prod* Gainsborough. 85 mins.

William Porter (Hay), an incompetent railway worker, wants to become a stationmaster. Through influence, he is sent to the derelict station of Buggleskelly in Ireland where his other staff are Albert (Moffatt) and Jeremiah Harbottle (Marriott). In trying to organize a day excursion he gets mixed up with gun runners but captures the gang after a hectic journey on the train.

Oh, Mr. Porter! is the best of the series of comedies made by music hall comedian Will Hay between 1934 and 1943, and one of the best comedies of the Thirties, though this and his other films such as *Ask a Policeman, The Goose Steps Out* and *My Learned Friend*, remain relatively unknown outside Britain. His characteristic air of decrepit gentility, of being both a victim of events and their unwitting cause, is seen at its best in this film. As always, innocence prevails and Hay displays that peculiarly British virtue of "muddling through." The film has vigor, double-talk routines, and well-timed gags, climaxing in the famous windmill sequence and a long locomotive chase.

Oh, Mr. Porter! and many of Hay's other films include considerable implicit social satire, mocking a number of British sacred cows from the police to imperialism. The postwar Ealing comedies owe much to Hay's films.

OKAASAN MOTHER Japan 1952. *Dir* Mikio Naruse *Scen* Yoko Mizuki *Photog* Hiroshi Sezuki *Art Dir* M. Kato *Mus* Ichiro Saito *Cast* Kinuyo Tanaka, Kyoko Kagawa, Masao Mishima, Daisuke Kato *Prod* Shin-Toho. 95 mins.

A widow (Tanaka) faces life with three children and, with the eldest daughter (Kagawa), runs a dyeing and cleaning business. Her story is told through the eyes of the eldest daughter.

This modest story is set in the poor section of postwar Tokyo, but the film does not stress the poverty nor is it excessively sentimental. Its style seems similar to that of Italian neorealism but in fact is derived from the Japanese "new realism" of the mid-Thirties. Kinuyo Tanaka, who later was Mizoguchi's *O'Haru* (*q.v.*), gives a beautiful performance.

OKRAINA OUTSKIRTS/PATRIOTS **USSR** 1933. *Dir* Boris Barnet *Scen* Boris Barnet, Konstantin Finn based on his own story *Photog* M. Kirillov, M. Spiridonov *Art Dir* Sergei Kozlovsky *Mus* Sergei Vasilenko *Cast* Yelena Kuzmina, Nikolai Bogolyubov, Mikhail Zharov, Sergei Komarov, A. Chistyakov, Hans Klering *Prod* Mezhrabpomfilm. 97 mins.

The life of a young girl (Kuzmina), the daughter of a cobbler (Komarov) in a small provincial town in Russia during World War I, and her love affairs with a student and a German prisoner.

One of the best films made anywhere in the Thirties — droll, pathetic, powerful, charming, and atmospheric. "In the pictorial structure of *Okraina* there is something of Chekhov's plays, with an action of interior development as well as an outer action. In it an important role is played by everything that goes on *beneath* the words — the concealed and repressed emotions of the characters, the pauses and hints, the circumstances and atmosphere of the events, the combination of comic and dramatic elements, all building a profound inner rhythm" (Nikolai Lebedev, quoted by Jay Leyda). Only the justly famous *Gorki* (*q.v.*) trilogy has evoked the ambience of Tsarist Russia as sensitively as *Okraina*.

OKTYABR' OCTOBER/TEN DAYS THAT SHOOK THE WORLD USSR 1927 (released 1928). *Dir/Scen* Sergei M. Eisenstein, G. Alexandrov *Assist* Maxim Strauch, Mikhail Gomarov, Ilya Trauberg *Photog* Eduard Tisse *Assist Photog* Vladimir Nilsen, Vladimir Popov *Art Dir* Vasili Kovrigin *Cast* nonprofessionals, including Nikandrov (Lenin), N. Popov (Kerensky) Boris Livanov, Eduard Tisse *Prod* Sovkino. 9,500 ft. (U.S.-Britain commercial release version, 1928, 8,600 ft.).

October was commissioned to Eisenstein to commemorate the tenth anniversary of the 1917 Revolution and was screened on November 7, 1927 as part of these celebrations. It was released to the public, somewhat revised, on March 14, 1928.

Almost unlimited resources were placed at Eisenstein's disposal for his production of *October* and he was even put in control of the Winter Palace in Leningrad for several months. As usual, he used no professional actors, relying entirely on "types," — found by his assistant, Strauch, in the streets, factories, and offices — to play the aristocrats, workers, soldiers, Mensheviks, etc. in the film. Many of these had themselves been involved in the October Revolution. Eisenstein also drew much from the "mass pantomime" of the attack on the Winter Palace that the people of Leningrad had staged each year since 1920.

October is the film in which Eisenstein most rigorously followed his own theories of "intellectual montage." The most famous sequences (such as the "bridge raising" or the depiction of Kerensky's lust for power) not only incorporate images of objects as metaphorical elements but also integrate the titles into a total dynamic and plastic unity. These sequences seem to have baffled the general public at the time.

[*October* was not well received in the Soviet Union. Not only did its montage sequences lead to the first attacks on Eisenstein for his "formalism," but its production coincided with the power struggle in the Soviet Union in which Stalin consolidated his position and Trotsky was ousted. Eisenstein had made no distinction between the roles played by members of the then present government and those of the present opposition. Trotsky's anti-Stalin campaign came into the open during the jubilee celebrations. After a few showings during the jubilee, Eisenstein was obliged to re-edit *October* to eliminate opposition figures. Trotsky can still be seen, however, in two sequences but is not identified by name. Eisenstein also write in late 1927 of a two-part film, *Before October* and *October,* which was to be 13,000 ft. The fact that the release version is a little over 9,000 ft. indicates how much material for *October* has never been seen. In 1967, for the Fiftieth Anniversary celebrations, Alexandrov reconstituted the "original" version of *October* based on Eisenstein's notes, with original music by Shostakovich.]

The version released in Britain and North America in 1928 titled *Ten Days*

That Shook the World is considerably shorter than the Soviet version, many of the montage sequences having been deleted from it.

OLD AND THE NEW (THE) STAROYE I NOVOYE

OLD CZECH LEGENDS STARÉ POVĚSTI ČESKÉ

OLVIDADOS (LOS) THE YOUNG AND THE DAMNED Mexico 1950 *Dir* Luis Buñuel *Scen* Luis Buñuel, Luis Alcoriza *Photog* Gabriel Figueroa *Mus* Rodolfo Halffter *Art Dir* Edward Fitzgerald *Cast* Alfonso Mejia, Robert Cobo, Estela Inda, Miguel Inclan *Prod* Ultramar Films (Oscar Dancigers). 88 mins.
A tale of "loving and loveless children, of adolescent destroyers and the destroyed" (Jacques Prévert), set in the outskirts of Mexico City. Famous sequences: a gang of young boys led by Jaibo (Cobo) tip a legless beggar out of his cart and torment a blind man (Inclan); Jaibo killing a friend; Pedro's (Mejia) dream, his witnessing a crime, his work with a cutler, his meeting with a pederast, his arrest on a false accusation by Jaibo; Pedro, in the reformatory, given 50 pesetas by the liberal-minded humane director and sent into the city; his being ambushed by Jaibo, who steals the money; life in the shanty town; the blind man caressing a young girl; Jaibo killing Pedro then being hunted and killed by the police; Pedro's body thrown onto a garbage dump.
Octavio Paz wrote in 1951: "Buñuel has constructed a film as precise as clockwork, as hallucinating as a dream, as implacable as the silent march of lava, whose social theme is juvenile delinquency. Its basic plot was taken from police records. Its characters are our contemporaries. They are the age of our own sons. But it is more than a realistic film. Dream, design, chance, and the dark side of life are here given their due. Reality is impossible to endure. That is why men kill and die, love and create. Refusing to be tempted by the beauty of the Mexican countryside, Buñuel sticks close to the often forgotten sordid desolation of the urban landscape. *Los Olvidados* (the forgotten ones) live in those slums and shanty towns that modern cities spawn, a world of its own from which there is no escape except death. It is in other worlds where chance opens doors. Here they are shut tight. Pedro struggles against chance, the bad luck that Jaibo embodies. When he faces them, chance becomes destiny: the collision between human conscience and the exterior fatalism becomes tragedy. This is not a documentary film. Even less is it a thesis, a piece of propaganda, or a morality fable. But while it doesn't preach — despite its admirable objectivity — neither is it correct to describe it as a film where purely superficial artistic values are paramount. The relentless passion with which Buñuel treats the theme recalls the great art of Spain. The blind beggar we have met before in 'Lazarillo de Tormès.' The women, the drunkards, the killers, the simpletons, the innocents appear in the works of Quevedo, Pérez Galdós, and Cervantes; Velasquez, Murillo, and Goya have painted their portraits. And Figueroa, the cameraman, has created a style so completely functional that it almost seems to disappear. This is a profitable loss: what the images may have lost in static beauty they have gained in dramatic effectiveness."

OLYMPISCHE SPIELE 1936 THE OLYMPIAD/ OLYMPIA Part I: *Fest der Völker/Festival of the Nations;* Part II: *Fest der Schönheit/Festival of Beauty* Germany 1938 (production began 1936). *Dir/Ed* Leni Riefenstahl *Assist* Walther Ruttman *Photog* Hans Ertl, Walter Frantz, Guzzi Lantschner, Kurt Neubert, Willy Zielke, Hans Schneib, Wilfried Basse and 38 others *Mus* Herbert Windt *Prod* Leni Riefenstahl. Part I, 118 mins. Part II, 107 mins. Lengths vary slightly according to the various versions.
Leni Riefenstahl was given full artistic freedom and almost unlimited facilities to produce this film of the 1936 Olympic Games in Berlin. One and a half million feet of film were shot and the editing by Riefenstahl, assisted by Ruttman, took 18 months. It was released in Germany in two parts in 1938 and released abroad in at least four language versions and several differently edited versions.
Some sequences, such as the marathon, the men's diving, Jesse Owen's sprint races, are beautiful not only because of their content but also because of Riefenstahl's use of slow motion and telephoto lenses. However, others are ridiculous, such as the sequence in which Riefenstahl compares the naked bodies of ath-

letes to Greek statues. One of the most extraordinary pieces of bravura is the sequence that shows the carrying of the Olympic torch from Olympia in Greece to Berlin. Five years later the SS retraced this journey, planted the Swastika, and drowned Greece in blood and fire.
[Although the film is still engrossingly beautiful, it provides strange glimpses of the Nazi mystique and about its idealization of the young male body whose implications may seem disturbing today. Many sequences suggest a deeply suspicious attitude on Riefenstahl's part toward physical reality. Its numerous shots of figures silhouetted against the sun or searchlights illustrates this visual obscurantism. More than a hymn to the glory of athletics, its compelling beauty remains only a monument to the Nazi ideal of *Kraft durch Freude*.]

ONA ZASCHISHCHAYET RODINU SHE DE-FENDS HER COUNTRY/NO GREATER LOVE USSR 1943. *Dir* Friedrich Ermler *Co-Dir* K. Gakkel *Scen* Mikhail Bleiman, I. Blondin *Photog* Wulf Rapoport *Mus* Gavril Popov *Art Dir* Nikolai Suvorov *Cast* Vera Maretskaya, L. Smirnova, Nikolai Bogolyubov *Prod* Central Studios. 80 mins. English version, 68 mins.
A peasant woman (Maretskaya) whose husband and baby have been killed by the Nazis, wanders half-mad through the countryside, but later becomes Comrade P, the heroic leader of a group of partisans.
This was one of the few Soviet films to be dubbed into English for foreign release. The dubbing makes it difficult to judge the quality of the film, but it does not appear to be one of Ermler's more important works. The film was written for Vera Maretskaya and she gives a superb performance as the peasant woman.

ONE A.M. USA 1916. *Dir/Scen* Charles Chaplin *Photog* Rollie Totheroh, William C. Foster *Cast* Charles Chaplin *Prod* Mutual. 2 reels.
A tour de force in which Chaplin alone holds the screen with pantomime for about 30 minutes, with only a brief appearance at the beginning by Albert Austin. Charlie, in evening dress and top hat, comes home drunk to a house full of nightmarish objects that seem to attack him but in the face of which he never loses his dignity. His performance is straight out of the music hall.

ONE LIFE UNE VIE

ONESIME (series) France 1910–14. *Dir/Scen* Jean Durand *Photog* Paul Castanet *Cast* Ernest Bourbon and the Pouitte troupe, Gaston Modot, Aimos, Paulos, Max Bonnet, Sarah Duhamel *Prod* Gaumont. ½–1 reel each.
The complete series of these films featuring "Onésime" (a sort of Simple Simon character) probably involved over a hundred films. Some examples of the stories:
— *Onésime coeur de tzigane*. At Saintes-Maries-de-la-Mer, a gypsy plays such an entrancing waltz that Onésime and a girl whirl over the beach, over the roof of a church, etc.
— *Onésime horloger*. Hopelessly in love, Onésime speeds up the Observatory clock and time accelerates with it. Crowds rush through the streets. A couple gets married and has a child who grows up, quickly outstripping his father, etc.
— *Le Noël d'Onésime*. An angel warns Onésime that he is being deceived by his wife who is at the Gaumont Palace. He takes a cab in which many accidents occur. He is refused admittance and, chased by a Negro hunter and the Pouitte troupe dressed as cops, he climbs the roof and opens a trapdoor. Then the spectators at the Gaumont see him descending in flesh and blood onto the stage.
This series was very influential on Mack Sennett and, later, René Clair. [*Onésime horloger* (1910), particularly, is a minor masterpiece; Clair's *Paris qui dort* (*q.v.*) is its most direct descendant.] The rigorous "Cartesianism of the absurd" of this series, improvised by acrobats and caricaturists, represents the summit of crazy comedy.

ONE SUMMER OF HAPPINESS HON DANSADE EN SOMMAR

ONE WEEK USA 1920. *Dir/Scen* Buster Keaton, Eddie Cline *Cast* Buster Keaton, Sybil Seely *Prod* Metro. 2 reels.
This minor comic masterpiece is Keaton's first venture as his own scriptwriter and director. The "great stone face" is no longer merely Fatty Arbuckle's sidekick but has a character and style of his own that almost invariably involves a con-

flict with objects. In *One Week,* he is at odds with a model house that he never properly completes and that finally collapses in a shambles.

ON HER MAJESTY'S SECRET SERVICE see GOLDFINGER.

*ONIBABA THE HOLE Japan 1964. *Dir/ Scen/Art Dir* Kaneto Shindo *Photog* Kiyomi Kuroda *Mus* Hikaru Hayashi *Ed* Toshio Enoki *Cast* Nobuko Otowa, Jitsuko Yoshimura, Kei Sato, Jukichi Uno. 105 mins. Tohoscope.
A mother (Otowa) and her daughter-in-law (Yoshimura) live in a hut by a river in war-ravaged 16th-century Japan. They earn money by selling armor from dead soldiers. A neighbor (Sato) deserts the army and he and the daughter have a violent love affair. In order to frighten the lovers, the jealous mother wears a devil mask from a general (Uno) she has killed. But she discovers the mask is infected and her face decomposes.
A film whose blend of murder, nudity, sex, violence, and superstition made it a great success on the art-house circuit in North America. Totally unlike Shindo's stark *The Island (q.v.),* made with the same group as this film, it made a vivid, sometimes sickening, impression on most viewers. Its sensuous photography, fine acting, and forceful rhythm are compensations for its simplistic, melodramatic theme and Shindo's failure to achieve the mythical quality he was apparently aiming at.

ONLY ANGELS HAVE WINGS USA 1939. *Dir* Howard Hawks *Scen* Jules Furthman based on a story by Hawks *Photog* Joseph Walker, Elmer Dyer *Art Dir* Lionel Banks *Mus* Dimitri Tiomkin, Morris W. Stoloff *Cast* Cary Grant, Jean Arthur, Richard Barthelmess, Rita Hayworth *Prod* Columbia. 121 mins.
The lives and loves of the pilots of a small commercial airline in Latin America.
"Every character was taken from life. Barthelmess was a man I saw jump from an airplane leaving another behind. The character of Jean Arthur and her relationship with that of Cary Grant is a true story based on facts, though the linking of the various incidents was fictional. The bird coming through the windscreen was true and the place was

real – a small Grace Line port in South America" (Howard Hawks).
One could describe this as the most beautiful of Hawks's aviation films and the one in which the sense of peril is most evident. In agreeing with this, Jean Douchet adds, "Once again the real peril is neither the Andes nor the miserable planes of the broken-down airline but the Woman. Together with nature (the bird breaking the windshield), she is the root of every disaster. On the other hand, man is unaware of himself and only finds himself in and through his profession . . . In this extraordinary adventure film, which includes shots of the plane on the mountain tops, . . . the confrontation of man, his labors, and his grandeur with the world – a confrontation that he both desires and rejects – has a truly breathtaking beauty."

ONNA HITORI DAICHI O IKU A WOMAN WALKS THE EARTH ALONE Japan 1953. *Dir* Fumio Kamei *Scen* Kaneto Shindo *Photog* H. Nakazawa *Cast* Isuzu Yamada *Prod* Kinuta. 120 mins. approx.
Centering on the life of a woman (Yamada) who works in a large mine, this film is a portrayal of Japan before, during, and after World War II. It is a remarkable independent production, an exposure of the terrible working conditions in Japanese mines, in which the main role is played by Mizoguchi's favorite actress, Isuzu Yamada. It was largely shot in the Hokkaido mines with the support of the local unions, some members of which appear in the film.

ON THE BEACH USA 1959. *Dir* Stanley Kramer *Scen* John Paxton, James Lee Barrett based on the novel by Nevil Shute *Photog* Giuseppe Rotunno *Art Dir* Fernando Carrere *Mus* Ernest Gold *Ed* Frederick Knudtson *Cast* Gregory Peck, Ava Gardner, Fred Astaire, Anthony Perkins, Donna Anderson *Prod* Stanley Kramer for United Artists. 133 mins.
The survivors of an atomic war, fatally affected by fallout, live out their last days in Australia.
Though one can sympathize with its aims, this is not always a successful film. Best sequences: the car race in which the drivers commit suicide; the husband (Perkins) giving his wife (Anderson) some pills before he leaves so she can kill herself and the children at the first

sign of radiation sickness; a survivor (Peck) landing in a dead and deserted San Francisco.

ON THE LOOKOUT FOR TRAINS OSTRE SLEDOVANÉ VLAKY

*ON THE TOWN USA 1949. *Dir* Gene Kelly, Stanley Donen *Scen* Adolph Green, Betty Comden based on their own musical play *Photog* Harold Rosson *Art Dir* Cedric Gibbons, Jack Martin Smith *Mus* Leonard Bernstein *Ed* Ralph Winters *Cast* Gene Kelly, Frank Sinatra, Ann Miller, Vera-Ellen, Jules Munshin, Betty Garrett *Prod* MGM. 98 mins. Technicolor.

Three sailors (Kelly, Sinatra, Munshin) spend a day's shore leave in New York City and meet three girls (Miller, Vera-Ellen, Garrett).

Undoubtedly the first masterpiece of the postwar musical and a film whose style established a convention for the many similar films that MGM produced in the Fifties. Shot largely on location in New York City and very freely adapted from the 1944 stage musical, its songs and dances (designed by Kelly) flow naturally out of the story without the usual "cues." Its exuberance, inventiveness, choreographic style, and use of urban settings were to become a trademark of later Kelly-Donen musicals such as *Singin' in the Rain* (*q.v.*) and *It's Always Fair Weather*, and Minnelli's *An American in Paris* (*q.v.*). But the vitality of the number on top of the Empire State Building has rarely been matched.

ON THE WATERFRONT USA 1954. *Dir* Elia Kazan *Scen* Budd Schulberg based on articles by Malcolm Johnson *Photog* Boris Kaufman *Art Dir* Richard Day *Mus* Leonard Bernstein *Ed* Gene Milford *Cast* Marlon Brando, Karl Malden, Eva Marie Saint, Lee J. Cobb, Rod Steiger *Prod* Horizon for Columbia. 108 mins. Terry Malloy (Brando) is the strongarm boy for a group of gangsters led by Johnny Friendly (Cobb) who control the dockers' union. He is involved in the murder of a rebellious docker but his allegiance begins to waver when he meets Edie (Saint), the dead man's sister. Terry's brother (Steiger) is ordered to secure Terry's loyalty but fails and is brutally murdered. Encouraged by a dockland priest (Malden), Terry agrees to testify to the Crime Commis-

sion and, although he is beaten up, the police finally break the gang's power. Some American unions had been in the hands of gangsters but in 1954 this was not true of the dockers' union, which was then being hounded by McCarthyism and whose leader's Kazan describes in this film as gangsters. His position provoked a response from some American intellectuals. Arthur Miller's *A View From the Bridge* was, for example, an anti-*On the Waterfront*. Miller replied in the affirmative to this question by Doniol-Valcroze: "Doesn't it (*On the Waterfront*) take an antiunion position and doesn't it tarnish its own purity by suggesting that a denunciation to the police is the correct attitude?"

Chardère felt that, "This defense of informing by two well-known informers for the Un-American Activities Committee is very unappetizing." André Bazin however wrote, "It's true that what I know of Kazan makes me feel antipathetic to the theme. However, there is Brando's extraordinary performance and two unforgettable love scenes — the first in the church the other as he forces in the door to meet his girl."

This is Brando's best role and the film owes much to his performance as it does to the photography by Boris Kaufman, Dziga's Vertov's brother and Vigo's cameraman. However, the film's use of natural locations does not outweigh the pretentiousness and unnecessary effects of many scenes nor the very theatrical performances of Karl Malden and Eva Marie Saint. It won several Academy Awards including that for Best Picture.

OPEN CITY ROMA, CITTÀ APERTA

OPERA DE QUAT'SOUS (L') DREIGROSCHENOPER (DIE)

OR DES MERS (L') GOLD FROM THE SEA France 1932. *Dir/Scen/Ed* Jean Epstein *Photog* Christian Matras *Mus* Devaux, Kross-Hertman *Cast* the inhabitants and fisherman of the islands of Houat and Hoedick (Britanny) *Prod* Synchro-Ciné. 73 mins.

"A magical work steeped in a feeling for Britanny whose enchantment is derived only from a distillation of the most simple realities. This is not a drama, it is a Murnau tragedy. Unfortunately, this film, which was made silent, has been buried under its music, a Wagerian commentary that totally disfigures it" (Henri Langlois).

ORDET THE WORD
— Sweden 1943. *Dir* Gustaf Molander *Scen* Rune Lindström, Björn Berglund based on the play by Kaj Munk *Photog* Aka Dahlquist *Art Dir* Arne Akermark *Mus* Sven Sköld *Ed* Oscar Rosander *Cast* Victor Sjöström, Wanda Rothgardt, Stig Olin, Holger Löwenadler, Ludde Gentzel, Gunn Wallgren, Rune Lindström, Inga Landgré *Prod* Svensk Filmindustri. 108 mins.

A tyrannical old widower (Sjöström) has three sons. Inger (Rothgardt) the wife of the eldest son (Löwenadler), who is often rebellious, acts as mistress of the farm. Johannes (Lindström), the middle son, has studied for the church, but when his fiancée (Wallgren) dies he turns half-mad and broods. The youngest son (Olin) falls in love with Ester (Landgré), the daughter of his father's mortal enemy, a preacher (Gentzel). Inger dies in childbirth. On the day of the funeral, Johannes orders Inger to wake up and, as she is restored to life, Johannes regains his own mental stability.

This first film version of Kaj Munk's play was produced only a year before he was assassinated by the Nazis. It is an excellent film, with splendid performances by Sjöström as an authoritarian old farmer and by Lindström as a mystical fanatic, and with a sensitive portrayal of landscape, nature, and country life by veteran director Molander.

— Denmark 1955. *Dir* Carl Theodor Dreyer *Scen* Dreyer based on the play by Kaj Munk *Photog* Henning Bendtsen *Art Dir* Erik Aaes *Mus* Poul Schierbeck *Cast* Henrik Malberg, Emil Hass Christensen, Preben Lerdorff Rye, Cay Kristiansen, Birgitte Federspiel *Prod* Palladium. 125 mins.

Dreyer wanted to film Munk's play ever since its premier in 1932, after which he had said "Kaj Munk's courage in setting in counterpart sometimes paradoxical problems is astonishing." His adaptation is more faithful to the original than is Molander's and he filmed part of it in the village (Verdersø in Jutland) where Munk had been vicar. However, most of the action takes place on the farm soon after the death of the wife (Federspiel) and, apart from the prologue, scenes in the countryside are very rare.

Dreyer mainly stresses the conflict between accepted religion and the sect to which the fanatic belongs. In spite of the film's length and even if one cannot accept the notion that faith in the Word can raise the dead, *Ordet's* hypnotic rhythm and the geometric world of the farm designed by Erik Aaes are spellbinding.

ORFEU NEGRO BLACK ORPHEUS France/Italy/Brazil 1958.
Dir Marcel Camus *Scen* Jacques Viot, Marcel Camus based on the play *Orfeu da Conceicao* by Vinicius de Moraes *Photog* Jean Bourgoin *Mus* Luis Bonfa, Antonio Carlos Jobim *Ed* Andrée Feix. *Cast* Breno Mello, Marpessa Dawn, Adhemar Da Silva, Lourdes De Oliveira *Prod* Dispatfilm/Gemma Cinematografica/Tupan Filmes. 105 mins. Eastman Color. CinemaScope.

The myth of Orpheus (Mello) and Eurydice (Dawn) pursued by Death (Da Silva) through the slums and carnival of Rio de Janeiro. All the roles are played by Blacks.

Notable sequences: the sunrise; wandering among the old records; the encounter with Death in a power plant; the carnival and the final chase. The film's brilliant, apparently spontaneous, performances by black actors (many of them nonprofessionals), its entertaining Latin-American music, its beautiful color photography by Bourgoin, and its use of Rio's exotic character and carnival led to a well-merited Palme d'or at Cannes and world-wide commercial success.

ORPHANS OF THE STORM USA 1921.
Dir D. W. Griffith *Scen* D. W. Griffith based on the Palmer-Jackson version of the play *The Two Orphans* by Adolphe Philippe D'Ennery and Eugène Cormon *Photog* Hendrick Sartov, Paul Allen *Art Dir* Charles M. Kirk *Mus* Louis F. Gottshalk, William F. Peters *Ed* James and Rose Smith *Cast* Lillian Gish, Dorothy Gish, Creighton Hale, Joseph Schildkraut, Lucille LaVerne, Monte Blue, Frank Losee *Prod* Griffith for United Artists. 11,340 ft.

Two innocent orphans, Henriette (Lillian Gish) and the blind Louise (Dorothy Gish), arrive in Paris just prior to the French Revolution. They are exploited by Mother Frochard (LaVerne) and delivered to the debauched Chevalier de Vaudry (Schildkraut). They are separated and nearly find each other several times but each time are parted again. In the second half of the film they become involved with the French Revolution. In the climax, Henriette is about to be guillotined when Danton (Blue) races to her rescue with a pardon. All ends well with Louise regaining her sight.

This large-budget historical spectacle, based on a popular melodrama, took six months to produce and one set alone cost $60,000. Griffith was clearly influenced by Lubitsch's *Madame Dubarry* (*q.v.*) and its style is smothered by the luxurious, and luxuriant, costumes. The film was cut and re-edited in France because it didn't condemn the monarchist movements but its climax still remained quite improbable.

[Although the reviews were favorable it was not a commercial success. This was not only because the public was turning to more sophisticated themes and away from Griffith's "old values and virtues" but also because First National took advantage of the usual huge Griffith publicity to launch a German film on the French Revolution — *Danton/All For a Woman* with Emil Jannings — in advance of Griffith's. Griffith eventually bought this to keep it off the market and changed the title of his film from the original *The Two Orphans* to avoid confusion with an earlier film he discovered after the initial publicity had been released.]

OTHER VERSIONS:

— *Les Deux orphelines* France 1910. *Dir* Albert Capellani.

— *The Two Orphans* USA 1911. *Cast* Kathlyn Williams, Winifred Greenwood *Prod* Selig.

— *The Two Orphans* USA 1915. *Dir* Herbert Brenon *Cast* Theda Bara *Prod* Fox. 7 reels.

— *The Two Orphans* USA 1916. *Dir* Otis Turner *Scen* Kate Claxton *Prod* Selig. 3 reels.

— *Les Deux orphelines* France 1933. *Dir* Maurice Tourneur *Cast* Yves Guilbert, René Saint-Cyr, Rosine Dorean *Prod* Pathé-Natan.

— *Le Due orfanelle/The Two Orphans/ The Two Sisters* Italy 1942. *Dir* Carmine Gallone *Cast* Alida Valli, Maria Denis, Gilda Marchio 92 mins.

— *Le Due orfanelle/The Two Orphans* Italy 1954. *Dir* Giacomo Gentilomo *Cast* Myriam Bru, Milly Vitale, Franco Interlenghi.

— *les Deux orphelines* France/Italy 1965. *Dir* Riccardo Freda *Cast* Sophia Darès, Valeria Ciangottini, Mike Marshall. 95 mins. Eastman Color.

ORPHÉE ORPHEUS France 1949. *Dir/Scen* Jean Cocteau *Photog* Nicolas Hayer *Art Dir* Jean d'Eaubonne *Mus* Georges Auric *Ed* Jacqueline Sadoul *Cast* Jean Marais, Maria Casarès, François Périer, Juliette Greco, Maria Déa, Édouard Dermithe *Prod* André Paulvé/Films du Palais Royal. 112 mins. (95 mins. English version).

Broadly derived from Cocteau's first play (1926), this is a modern version of the legend of Orpheus (Marais) and Eurydice (Déa), their involvement with Death (Casarès), the "angel" Heurtebise (Périer), Cégeste (Dermithe), and the bacchantes (Greco and others).

Cocteau has said: *"Orphée* is a film that could exist only on the screen. I tried to use the camera not like a pen but like ink. I interwove many myths. It is a drama of the visible and the invisible. In *Orphée,* Death is a spy who falls in love with the man on whom she is spying. She condemns herself in order to help the man she is duty bound to destroy. The man is saved but Death dies; it is the myth of immortality."

The film is replete with poetic tricks — the mirrors, the messengers of Death dressed in black leather and riding motorcycles, and especially the creation of an imaginary town out of Paris locations. When Orpheus pursues Death through the streets, the action seems continuous and in one locale but was actually composed of a series of shots photographed miles apart.

— *Le Testament d'Orphée* France 1959. *Dir/Scen* Jean Cocteau *Photog* Roland Pontoiseau *Art Dir* Pierre Guffroy *Mus* Georges Auric, Martial Solal, Glück, Richard Wagner, Johann-Sebastian Bach arranged by Jacques Metehan *Ed* Marie-Josèphe Yoyotte *Cast* Jean Cocteau, Édouard Dermithe, Maria Casarès, Jean Marais, François Périer, Charles Aznavour, Yul Brynner, Jean-Pierre Léaud, Pablo Picasso, Daniel Gélin, etc. 83 mins.

[*Le Testament d'Orphée* is subtitled "And Don't Ask Me Why" and is introduced by Cocteau announcing "I shall present a striptease in which I shed my body to expose my soul."]

Unfortunately this film mixing life and death, present and future, nightmare and dream was Cocteau's last film. Many of his friends were involved in its production. It forms the third part, with *le*

Sang d'un Poète (q.v.) and Orphée, of a private diary whose allegory and metaphorical obsessions are confessions and whose esotericism is an expression of his sincerity. The film is a series of poetic gags that cannot be adequately summarized but that illustrate Cocteau's theme: "My great desire is to live a reality which is truly mine and which is beyond time. Having discovered that this state was my privilege, I improved myself and plunged in deeper."

OSAKA ELEGY NANIWA HIKA

OSSESSIONE Italy 1942. *Dir* Luchino Visconte *Scen* Antonio Pietrangeli, Giuseppe de Santis, Gianni Puccini, Mario Alicata, Luchino Visconti based on the novel *The Postman Always Rings Twice* by James Cain *Photog* Aldo Tonti, Domenico Scala *Ed* Mario Serandrei *Mus* Giuseppe Rosati *Cast* Massimo Girotti, Clara Calamai, Juan de Landa, Elio Marcuzzo *Prod* ICI. 135 mins. Never released commercially in North America or Britain for copyright reasons.

A wanderer, Gino (Girotti), arrives at a country inn and falls in love with Giovanna (Calamai), the wife of the innkeeper (Marcuzzo). They decide to leave together but she turns back. Some weeks later Gino meets the couple again and the husband insists he return with them. On the journey Gino and Giovanna murder the husband in a faked accident and get away with it. After a while, Gino begins to mistrust Giovanna and believes she only killed her husband for the insurance money. They are reconciled but, as they leave in the car to escape impending arrest, it skids off the road.

Though unknown for many years (copyright on the James Cain novel prevented public release outside Italy), this is the first great Italian neorealist film. Visconti, who had been an assistant to Jean Renoir before the war, had hoped to make his directorial debut with an adaptation of a novel by Giovanni Verga but the Fascist censors obliged him to fall back on an American thriller, which he adapted very freely. The film still created difficulties, however, since it showed both adultery and poverty — subjects "banned" in Fascist Italy.

In an article in 1948, co-scenarist Angelo Pietrangeli describes this film, which was to change the face of the Italian cinema

and establish its world-wide influence. "A long traveling shot *à la* Renoir ends in front of a service station erected along the road like a frontier post. Suddenly, in a lyrical break so abrupt that it takes one's breath away, a camera flight introduces us royally to a character, a character still without a face, his vest unbuttoned over his sunburned skin, exhausted and hesitant, as a man would be who is stretching his legs after a long sleep in a truck. Are we the Gino of *Ossessione?* Let us call it simply Italian neorealism.

"Ferrara, its squares, its grey and deserted streets; Ancona and its San Ciriaco Fair; the Po and its sandy banks; a landscape streaked with a rubble of cars and men along the network of highways. Against this backdrop are silhouetted the wandering merchants, mechanics, prostitutes and inn boys who have all the typical innocent exuberances, beset by violent proletarian love affairs, primitive anger, and the sins that flesh is heir to." One can recognize the dominant influence on Visconti of Renoir and Marcel Carné and also that of the naturalist writer, Giovanni Verga. Even in this, his first film, "Visconti transformed everything he touched — actors, houses, objects, light, dust — into symbolic elements of his personal lyricism" (J.-G. Auriol).

— *Le Dernier tournant* France 1939. *Dir* Pierre Chenal *Scen* based on the novel by James Cain *Cast* Fernand Gravet, Corinne Luchaire, Michel Simon. 93 mins.

[A fine psychological thriller with a brilliant performance by Michel Simon as the husband. Inexplicably it was banned by the Hays Office in the USA]

— *The Postman Always Rings Twice* USA 1946. *Dir* Tay Garnett *Scen* Harry Ruskin, Niven Busch based on the novel by James Cain *Photog* Sidney Wagner *Art Dir* Cedric Gibbons, Randall Duell *Cast* Lana Turner, John Garfield, Cecil Kellaway, Hume Cronyn *Prod* MGM. 113 mins.

[This harshly lit, tense version is one of the best of the Hollywood *film noir* of the Forties, perfectly bringing to life the atmosphere of the novel and its suggestion of soulless American ambition in the character of the wife.]

OSTATNI ETAP THE LAST STAGE Poland 1948. *Dir* Wanda Jakubowska *Assist Dir*

J. Kawalerowicz *Scen* Wanda Jakubow-
ska, Gerda Schneider *Photog* Boris
Monastyrski *Art Dir* Roman Mann,
C. Piaskowski *Mus* Roman Palester *Cast*
Wanda Bartowna, Huguette Faget, Bar-
bara Drapinska, Antonina Gorecka *Prod*
Film Polski. 110 mins.

The horrors and heroism of the inhabitants of the Auschwitz death camp. The
two women who wrote it and several of
the actresses had themselves been prisoners in Auschwitz and the film is in some
respects an actuality reconstruction. Its
various episodes — the arrival of the
train, the forced labor, the promiscuity
in the barracks, the orchestra playing
during roll call, the trucks taking the
victims to the crematoria, the columns
of exhausted prisoners, the announcement of Allied victory — comprise a
unity whose moral power is overwhelming.

*OSTRE SLEDOVANE VLAKY CLOSELY
WATCHED TRAINS/CLOSELY OBSERVED
TRAINS/ON THE LOOKOUT FOR TRAINS/
SPECIAL PRIORITY TRAINS Czechoslovakia
1966. *Dir* Jiri Menzel *Scen* Jiri Menzel,
Bohumil Hrabal based on the novel by
Bohumil Hrabal *Photog* Jaromir Sofr
Art Dir Oldrich Bosak *Mus* Jiri Pavlik
Ed Jirina Lukesova *Cast* Vaclav Neckar,
Jitka Bendova, Vladimir Valenta, Josef
Somr, Libuse Havelkova, Jitka Zeleno-
horska, Jiri Menzel *Prod* Barrandov Stu-
dio. 92 mins.

In Czechoslovakia during World War II,
a diffident youth (Neckar) starts his
first job at a village railway station run
by a stationmaster (Valenta) who tends
geese and pigeons. He enviously observes
the amorous exploits of the regular
guard (Somr) and tries to develop a
romance with a pretty conductress (Bendova) but fails miserably in bed with
her and tries to commit suicide. A doctor (Menzel) advises him to try an
older woman and he finally succeeds with
an obliging and beautiful partisan. His
confidence renewed he makes a date
with the conductress and goes off to
sabotage a German ammunition train.
He succeeds but is killed.

Jiri Menzel's first feature recalls the work
of Forman in its elliptically funny, but
tender observation of the quirks of
humanity. Its funniest scenes are up-
roarious: the regular guard tearing up the
stationmaster's couch in a moment of
passionate abandon; the same guard

rubber-stamping the backside of a peasant girl; the visits of a Nazi controller.
But it is also marvelously perceptive
both in its observation of everyday behavior and in the way it reveals the
boy's maturation; the scene of the boy
losing his virginity to the partisan girl
has an especial charm. *Closely Watched
Trains* was the second Czechoslovak film
in three years to win an Academy Award.

OTHELLO
— Morocco 1951. *Dir* Orson Welles *Scen*
Orson Welles based on Shakespeare's
play *Photog* Anchise Brizzi, G. R. Aldo,
George Fanto, Robert Fusi, Obadan
Troiani *Art Dir* Alexandre Trauner *Mus*
Francesco Lavagnino, Alberto Barberis
Cast Orson Welles (Othello), Suzanne
Cloutier (Desdemona), Michéal MacLi-
ammoir (Iago), Robert Coote, Fay
Compton *Prod* Films Marceau. 91 mins.

According to Maurice Bessy, "(Welles)
made it without a production company,
without money in his pocket, working as
an actor to raise additional funds. It
was produced, with good luck, in Morocco. He set the assault on Cassio in a
Turkish bath because he didn't think he
could find tailors there capable of cutting
Renaissance doublets. This filmic adventure forced him to move his crew and
cast around from Morocco to Venice,
Rome, Paris, and London, stopping
shooting for several months as funds
ran out, starting and stopping again, re-
starting some scenes after a gap of two
years. On one occasion he even shot
some scenes himself when he had no
money to pay the cameraman. Even the
seashore, the citadel, birds, waves, and
ramparts joined in this private exuberance."

Othello is far better than Welles' earlier
Macbeth (*q.v.*), with the influence of
Lang and Eisenstein evident in some of
the scenes. It was filmed in the old
citadel at Mogador, whose battlements,
overlooking the sea, are the setting for
Othello's and Iago's walk together, a
scene dominated by the shrill cries of
gulls.

Welles said of the Shakespearean tradition: "The great actor, like an ancient
god, must kill his father. And when the
wheel returns to its starting point, he
too perishes under the assault of a new
savior. . . . That is the true, the only
tradition."

— USSR 1955. *Dir* Sergei Yutkevich

Scen Sergei Yutkevich based on Boris Pasternak's translation of Shakespeare's play *Photog* Yevgeni Andrikanis *Art Dir* A. Weisfeld, V. Dorrer, M. Karykin *Mus* Aram Khachaturian *Cast* Sergei Bondarchuk (Othello), Irina Skobtseva (Desdemona), Andrei Popov (Iago), Vladimir Soshalsky *Prod* Mosfilm. 108 mins. Sovcolor.

Yutkevich cherished for 20 years his ideas for a film adaptation of *Othello*. As early as 1938 he described his conception of the play: "The essence of the tragedy is the pathetic struggle for truth. . . . It is chaos that terrifies Othello. Shakespeare shows us the rise of an honest and impassioned man, a man searching for the highest spiritual refinement. . . . Desdemona's betrayal is a total downfall for Othello, the loss of his faith in man's noble destiny. Its hero's tragedy is in loss of faith, in trust betrayed." Conceived in this way, Othello (powerfully portrayed by Sergei Bondarchuk) "is not, as Pushkin thought, jealous but trustful. He is good and generous and it is a false story that drives him to commit the crime."

Many of the scenes were shot on location in the Crimea, in the Genoese fortress at Soudak, and in Bielgorod. Cocteau later said to Yutkevich, "You expended the inheritance of Eisenstein, who bequeathed to you the secrets of a somewhat primitive savagery, and of a classical romanticism in the Pushkin manner."

OTHER VERSIONS:

— Italy 1907. *Dir* Mario Caserini *Prod* Cines.

— *Austria 1908. *Prod* Pathé. With sound.

— *USA 1908. *Dir* William V. Ranous *Cast* William V. Ranous, Hector Dion, Paul Panzer, Julia Swayne Gordon *Prod* Vitagraph.

— *Italy 1909. *Dir* Gerolama Lo Savio *Cast* Ferrucio Garavaglia, Vittoria Lepanto, Cesare Dondini *Prod* Film d'Arte Italiana. 1,105 ft.

— *Italy 1914. *Prod* Ambrosio. 4,215 ft.

— Germany 1922. *Dir* Dimitri Buchowtzki *Scen* Buchowetzki, Carl Hagen based both on Shakespeare's play and Cinthio's original narrative *Photog* Karl Hasselman, Friedrich Paulmann *Cast* Emil Jannings. Ica von Lenkeffy, Werner Krauss. 2,662 meters.

— *Britain 1965. *Dir* Stuart Burge *Cast* Laurence Olivier, Frank Finlay, Maggie Smith. 166 mins. Technicolor. Panavision. A filmed version of the British National Theater production.

8½ (OTTO E MEZZO) EIGHT AND A HALF Italy 1963. *Dir* Federico Fellini *Scen* Tullio Pinelli, Ennio Flaiano, Brunello Rondi, Federico Fellini *Photog* Gianni Di Venanzo *Art Dir* Piero Gherardi *Mus* Nino Rota *Ed* Leo Catozzo *Cast* Marcello Mastroianni, Anouk Aimée, Claudia Cardinale, Sandra Milo, Jean Rougeul, Barbara Steele, Guido Alberti *Prod* Cineriz. Original length, 188 mins. reduced to 162 mins. Foreign release length, 138 mins.

A successful film maker (Mastroianni) is committed to an ambitious new production but is bankrupt of ideas. Exhausted and hounded by his wife (Aimée) and mistress (Milo), but stimulated by a famous actress (Cardinale), he escapes into childhood memories and sexual fantasies. He finally realizes his own artistic future lies within his own experiences of life.

Famous sequences: the people at the spa; the evocation of life in a religious college; the hero's dream of a harem in which his wives serve his every wish; the fat prostitute dancing on the beach for some young boys; the fantastic ballet in the finale around a gigantic "spaceship ramp that is intended in his film to take the survivors of an atomic war to another planet" (Fellini).

This unique work, which received the first prize at the 1963 Moscow Festival, focuses on a "film maker who is trying to pull together the pieces of his life till now and make sense of them" (Fellini). However, Fellini ends by "portraying the many facets of a man's character at the age of 45" and creating in some ways a 20th-century version of *The Inferno*. Its theme does not relate only to the world of the cinema, and its extremely elaborate story and style cannot be considered "jumbled" as some critics have claimed.

Fellini himself considers that his film "can be described as something between a muddled visit to a psychiatrist and an examination of a disordered conscience with Limbo as the setting. It is a melancholy film, almost funereal, but emphatically comic. . . . Most people have written that *8½* is autobiographical. In a certain sense I am always autobiographical even if I am recounting the life history of a sole. And yet I swear that this is a work of fantasy and that, of all my films, this has the least reference to little personal facts. . . . I would like to think that people will go to see the film with a completely open mind, recognizing that I have just been telling a fable and that there's nothing in it beyond what can be seen. . . . Perhaps underneath it's the story of a film I didn't make."

OUR DAILY BREAD USA 1934. *Dir* King Vidor *Scen* Elizabeth Hill based on a story by King Vidor *Photog* Robert Planck *Mus* Alfred Newman *Ed* Lloyd Nossler *Cast* Karen Morley, Tom Keenes, John T. Qualen, Barbara Pepper, Addison Richards, Harry Holman *Prod* King Vidor for United Artists. 80 mins.

King Vidor (in his autobiography *A Tree is a Tree*) has described how this very personal film came into being:

"It is difficult for many young people to realize that the early 1930's were a period of real crisis for the United States, with widespread unemployment and depression. Hunger marchers and "Hooverville" stories took up a lot of space in our press, while farmers and their neighbors blocked the selling of foreclosed lands for nonpayment of taxes. I wondered how I could corral this nationwide unrest and tragedy into a film. I wanted to take my two protagonists out of *The Crowd* and follow them through the struggles of a typical young American couple in this most difficult period. . . .

"Here was the nucleus of my story. John (Keenes) and Mary (Morley), as I had called them in *The Crowd,* unemployed and in desperate straits in the city, would inherit a broken-down bankrupt farm. . . . Then John, realizing his ignorance and incompetence as an agriculturist, would at this moment of frustration meet an unemployed farmer. In their ensuing conversation, the idea of turning the farm into a "co-op" would be born in John's mind. The idea would be expanded until the two originators would take in a carpenter, a plumber, a machinist, a stonemason, a bookkeeper, and so on, until one hundred out-of-work souls were managing to work out a subsistence livelihood from the unused land. . . .

"Having exhausted the supply of big companies, I was left with one alternative: to raise the money and make the picture myself. . . . I appealed to my friend, Charles Chaplin, who was one of the owners of United Artists, to assist in getting the releasing contract. I knew Charlie would not be one to shy away from a picture in which the principal character was somewhat, shall we say, impoverished. Charlie became an immediate ally and was most voluble in his praise of the subject.

"With a releasing arrangement in my pocket, I approached the banks. When a banker reads a script in which a bank forces a sheriff to make a foreclosure sale that a disreputable-looking group of neighbors won't permit, he doesn't feel kindly toward your venture. Nor, as I learned at firsthand, does he mince words in refusing to lend you the money to make the film.

"Well, I didn't want to eliminate that scene. It was true to the period; such scenes were occurring all over the country. I decided I would have to borrow the money by going into hock for everything I had accumulated to date. This included my home, my automobile, and everything that looked valuable in my safe-deposit box. We would have to pull some miracles of production to get by with what I could scrape together on my own. . . . At this time the ever-mounting production costs of Hollywood had reached an average budget of three hundred thousand to five hundred thousand dollars per film. I convinced myself that I would have to be content with a budget of half this amount."

Famous sequence: the arrival of water to irrigate the land after long and arduous work. Although somewhat utopian in its solution it has great sincerity and it is not impossible that it influenced Renoir and Prévert in *Le Crime de Monsieur Lange* (*q.v.*) and Duvivier and Spaak in *La Belle équipe* (*q.v.*).

— ***Our Daily Bread/City Girl** USA 1928. *Dir.* F. W. Murnau *Scen* based on *The Mud Turtle* by Elliott Lester *Photog* Ernest Palmer *Cast* Charles Farrell, Mary Duncan *Prod* Fox. 8,217 ft.

A film on the life of wheat farmers. Originally made as a silent film by Murnau under the title *Our Daily Bread,* it was shortened by Fox, the producers, a sound track was added, and it was released in 1930 under the title *City Girl,* with a running time of 67 minutes. Those who have seen the film compare it favorably to *Sunrise* (*q.v.*).

— *Unser täglich Brot/Our Daily Bread* German Democratic Republic 1949. *Dir* Slatan Dudow *Scen* Slatan Dudow, Hans Joachim Beyer, Ludwig Turek *Photog* Robert Baberske *Mus* Hanns Eisler *Cast* Paul Bildt, Viktoria von Ballasko, Inge Landgut, Harry Hindemith, Alfred Balthoff, Paul Edwin Roth, Irene Korb *Prod* DEFA. 103 mins.

The daily life of a Berlin family between 1945 and 1948. One of the best postwar German films, though quite dissimilar to Vidor's film except in title. [It is also the title of a 1929 German fictionalized documentary (*Dir/Photog* Phil Jutzi) about the Waldenburg coal mines.]

OUR HOSPITALITY USA 1923. *Dir* Buster Keaton, Jack Blystone *Scen* Jean Havez, Joseph Mitchell, Clyde Bruckman *Photog* Elgin Lessley, Gordon Jennings *Cast* Buster Keaton, Natalie Talmadge, Joe Keaton, Buster Keaton, Jr., Kitty Bradbury, Joe Roberts *Prod* Buster Keaton Prod. for Metro. 6,300 ft. approx.

A situation comedy about a blood feud in the American South. A prologue establishes the baby, William McKay (Keaton, Jr.), as the last of his line, which has been decimated by the Canfields. Twenty-one years later in the middle of the 19th century, William (Keaton) returns to the South from New York to claim his family estate and falls in love with Virginia Canfield (Talmadge). The Canfields must kill him because of the blood feud but, because of their code of chivalry, he is safe while he is a guest in their home. After a breathless chase, the lovers are married and the feud ended.

Many of the gags stem from Keaton's attempts to remain in the Canfield house. He makes excellent use of an antediluvian locomotive as later he was to do in *The General* (*q.v.*). Both *The General* and *Our Hospitality* are among Keaton's best films.

OUTCRY SOLE SORGE ANCORA (IL)

OUT IN THE WORLD see DETSVO GORKOVO

OUTLAW AND HIS WIFE (THE) BERG-EJVIND OCH HANS HUSTRU

OUT OF THE INKWELL (cartoon series) USA 1921–29. *Dir* Dave Fleischer *Anim*

Max Fleischer *Prod* Max Fleischer Studio. 1 reel each.

The Fleischer brothers made many dozens of cartoons in this series, all of which have the same basic plot: Max Fleischer, sitting in his office, draws Koko the Clown, who then begins to move freely on his own and performs many tricks until his creator returns him to the inkwell from which he came. These cartoons, produced by a careful, craftsman-like blend of drawings and live photography, have an originality, verve, and individuality that were lacking in the Disney and Fleischer factory cartoons after 1935.

Fleischer wrote: "I like to give the impression that everything is effortless but it isn't as easy as one might believe. I devote an average of four weeks to the production of one *Inkwell Comedy*. Six artists collaborating with me makes seven consistently hard-working people."

OUTRAGE (THE) see RASHOMON

OUTSIDERS (THE) BANDE À PART

OUTSKIRTS OKRAINA

OVERCOAT (THE) SHINEL

OVERLANDERS (THE) Britain 1946. *Dir/Scen* Harry Watt *Photog* Osmond Borrodaile *Mus* John Ireland *Cast* Chips Rafferty, John Nugent Howard, Daphne Campbell, Jean Blue *Prod* Ealing. 91 mins.

In Australia in 1942, when a Japanese invasion threatened the country, two cattlemen (Rafferty, Howard) save 1,000 head of cattle by taking them 2,000 miles overland across near desert country.

The simple yet dramatic theme of this film in the tradition of the British documentary is sparked by the endless landscapes and the movement of the immense herd of cattle.

OX-BOW INCIDENT (THE) STRANGE INCIDENT USA 1943. *Dir* William A. Wellman *Scen* Lamar Trotti based on the novel by Walter Van Tilburg Clark *Photog* Arthur Miller *Art Dir* Richard Day, James Basevi *Mus* Cyril J. Mockridge *Ed* Allen McNeil *Cast* Henry Fonda, Dana Andrews, Anthony Quinn, Henry Morgan, Jane Darwell, Francis

Ford, Frank Conroy *Prod* 20th Century-Fox. 75 mins.

In 1885 in Nevada, the inhabitants (Darwell, Conroy, Fonda, etc.) of a small town lynch three suspected criminals (Quinn, Ford, Andrews), only to discover after the hanging that they were innocent.

This courageous polemic against lynch law made a great impression in the USA during the war. However, its direction is pedestrian, its sets patently artificial, and it has none of the power of Lang's *Fury* (*q.v.*). Its success at the time was probably due to an intelligent script and dialogue by one of Dudley Nichols' collaborators. The same story has appeared at least twice as a play on American TV.

OYSTER PRINCESS (THE) AUSTERPRINZESSIN (DIE)

PACIFIC EXPRESS UNION PACIFIC

*PACIFIC 231 France 1949. *Dir/Scen/Ed*
Jean Mitry *Photog* André Tadie, André
Périer, Jean Jarret *Mus* Arthur Honegger. 11 mins.
Honegger's music for this favorite of
film societies and classes in editing was
originally written in the late Twenties
to accompany a silent film that was never
made. Jean Mitry became interested in
it and produced this brilliantly edited
visual interpretation of a fast run on a
Pacific 231 engine of the French rail-
ways.

PADENIYE BERLINA THE FALL OF BERLIN
(Parts I and II) USSR 1949. *Dir* Mikhail Chiaureli *Scen* Pyotr Pavlenko,
Mikhail Chiaureli *Photog* Leonid Kosmatov *Art Dir* Vladimir Kaplunovsky,
A. Parkhomenko *Mus* Dmitri Shostakovich *Cast* Mikhail Gelovani, Boris Andreyev, Oleg Froelich, V. Savelyov, V.
Stanitsin, M. Kobaleva *Prod* Mosfilm.
165 mins. Sovcolor.
Part I: Alexis Ivanov (Andreyev), a soldier engaged to a schoolteacher (Kobaleva), is decorated by Stalin (Gelovani)
and participates in the Battle of Stalingrad after the Nazi invasion. *Part II:*
As the Soviet troops cross Germany
he once again finds his fiancée, who had
been deported. He participates in the
taking of Berlin, Hitler (Savelyov) kills
himself, and the fall of Nazism is celebrated by the liberated people.
Remarkable sequences: Nazi bombs ex-
ploding in a poppy field; the liberation
of the deportees; the suicides of Eva
Braun and Hitler in the Chancellery
bunker.
The dramatic events of the 1941–45 period are shown through the eyes of a
"typical" Russian family in the manner

of *Cavalcade* (*q.v.*). However, Alexis
Ivanov is nothing less than a brave, dis-
ciplined, and taciturn giant of a man.
The violent battle scenes and caricatures
of Hitler and Churchill (Stanitsin) are
contrasted with the Olympian calm of
Stalin in his majestic Kremlin office, winning the war by gently indicating to his
marshals key strategy on a map.
This film was the high point of the personality cult. [Kruschev refers to it in
his condemnation of Stalin in the famous
1956 Party Congress: "Let us recall the
film *Fall of Berlin*. In it only Stalin acts,
issuing orders from a hall in which there
are many empty chairs . . . Stalin acts
for everybody."]
Enormous funds, on a scale comparable
to a De Mille epic, were poured into this
"monumental" film. However, it is not
entirely without merit. Visually it is full
of plastic beauty and sometimes seems
like a massive fresco that reflects the
truth of its time, as in the final apo-
theosis when the people dance in the
ruins of the Reichstag.

PADENIYE DINASTI ROMANOVIKH THE
FALL OF THE ROMANOV DYNASTY USSR
1927. *Dir/Scen/Ed* Esther Shub *Prod*
Sovkino. 1,700 meters (5,600 ft. ap-
prox.).
This remarkable feature-length compi-
lation film was produced for the 10th
anniversary celebrations of the Soviet
Revolution. It shows Tsarist Russia,
World War I, and the events of Feb-
ruary and October, 1917.
— *The Fall of the Romanoffs* USA
1917. *Dir* Herbert Brenon *Cast* Nance
O'Neil, Edward Connelly, Conway
Tearle, Iliodor *Prod* Iliodor Pictures.
A dramatization of the immediate pre-
Revolutionary period with "the role of
the monk Iliodor played by Iliodor him-
self."

PADUREA SPINZURATILOR THE FOREST OF THE HANGED Romania 1965. *Dir* Liviu Ciulei *Scen* Titus Popovici based on the novel by Liviu Rebreanu *Photog* Ovidiu Gologan *Mus* Theodor Grigoriu *Cast* Victor Rebengiuc, Liviu Ciulei, Ana Szeles *Prod* Bucarest Studios. 157 mins. CinemaScope.

Set in Transylvania during World War I, the film opens with the hanging of a Czechoslovakian lieutenant (Rebengiuc) for desertion from the Austro-Hungarian army. The film explores the differing reactions of the main characters, particularly that of a Romanian officer who was a member of the court martial.

Although the best postwar Romanian film, it has too many wordy exchanges and drags a little after a very taut first half. There are some poignant scenes, such as that in which a young peasant girl (Szeles) prepares the last meal for the condemned man.

*PAGADOR DE PROMESSAS (O) THE GIVEN WORD/THE KEEPER OF PROMISES Brazil 1961. *Dir* Anselmo Duarte *Scen* Anselmo Duarte based on the play by Dias Gomes *Photog* Chick Fowle *Mus* Gabriel Migliori *Ed* Carlos Coimbra *Cast* Leonardo Vilar, Gloria Menezes, Dionizio Azevedo, Geraldo del Rey. 97 mins.

Ze (Vilar), a Brazilian peasant, vows to carry a heavy cross thirty miles to the altar of a Church if his donkey doesn't die. When it recovers, he fulfills his promise. But the priest (Azevedo) refuses to allow him and his wife, Rosa (Menezes), to enter the church because the vow was made at a Macumba (voodoo) ceremony. Ze refuses to budge and the townspeople take sides. A local pimp (del Rey) seduces Rosa but when she repulses him he denounces Ze to the police as a Communist agitator. When the police arrive to arrest him, Ze goes berserk and a riot breaks out during which Ze is killed. The townspeople carry Ze's body to the altar.

Together with *Barravento* (*q.v.*), this is one of the best of the early Brazilian *cinema novo*. Its theme of simple people fighting blind authority is a crucial one for these Brazilian film makers who are noted for their social conscience. Chick Fowle's photography graphically portrays the film's completely natural settings and the participation of the local population. As a minor masterpiece of the Brazilian cinema, the film fully deserved the Palm d'or at Cannes.

PAINTING THE CLOUDS WITH SUNSHINE see GOLD DIGGERS OF 1933.

PAISA PAISAN 1946. *Dir* Roberto Rossellini *Scen* Roberto Rossellini, Federico Fellini from ideas by Sergio Amidei, Klauss Mann, Federico Fellini, Marcello Pagliero, Alfred Haynes, Roberto Rossellini *Photog* Otello Martelli *Ed* Eraldo Da Roma *Mus* Renzo Rossellini *Assist Dir* Federico Fellini, E. Handimar, I. Limentarus *Cast* Nonprofessionals plus Maria Michi, Gar Moore, Dale Edmonds, Dots Johnson, Harriet White, Bill Tubbs *Prod* Foreign Films Productions/OFI. 115 mins.

A journal in six episodes of the Battle of Italy from 1943 to 1945: 1. Sicily: the American landing; a GI meets a young Sicilian girl and both are shot. 2. Naples: a drunken American Negro soldier (Johnson) is tormented by some children and has his boots stolen by a shoeshine boy. When he sees the miserable conditions in which the boy lives he leaves the boots. 3. Rome: an American soldier (Moore) meets a prostitute (Michi) whom he does not recognize as the innocent young girl he had met earlier when Rome was liberated. 4. Florence: an American nurse (White) searches for her lover, a leader of the partisans, during the battle of Florence. 5. Three American chaplains are welcomed by the monks of a monastery. When they discover only one is a Catholic priest (Tubbs) and the others are a Protestant and a Jew, they do penance for the two souls who have strayed from truth. 6. The Po valley: partisans fight alongside soldiers of the OSS led by Dale (Edmonds) but are massacred after a hopeless fight.

When *Paisà* was first shown in Paris, Paul Eluard described it as, "A film in which we are impassioned rubber-neckers and greedy voyeurs but one in which, like all good rubber-neckers, we are both actors and spectators. We see and we are seen, and this upsets us. Life surrounds us, involves us, overwhelms us. For this is continuously the story of the first coming, taken in the streets with men, women, children, civilians, and soldiers revealing their typical behavior. It is a people fighting, as others have done so often, against tyranny and their own weakness, against injustice and poverty; a film in which people bare not only their feelings but also their innocence, merits and goodness; not only their miseries but also their joys and hopes for love and truth — a truth in turns miserable and glorious. Not wishing to show the people of his country better than they are, the auteur of this film, with a calm audacity, compensates and redresses his victims' past with his heros' hopes."

Having discovered, almost by chance, this film with my friend Paul Eluard, I wrote: "A revelation such as I have rarely seen since I was first excited by my first viewings of *Caligari* (*q.v.*), *Potemkin* (*q.v.*), or *Peter Ibbetson* (*q.v.*). I have no doubt that, if it fulfills the promise of this film, the postwar Italian cinema will match the importance of those of Sweden and Germany during the Twenties." (*Ecran Francais*, November 12, 1946). Rossellini had earlier told me: "In order to choose my actors for *Paisà*, I began by establishing myself with my cameraman in the middle of the district where such-and-such an episode of my film was to be shot. The rubber-neckers than gathered around us and I chose my actors from among the crowd . . . Amidei and I never finished our script before we arrived on location. We adapted ourselves to the existing circumstances and to the actors we selected. The dialogue and intonation were determined by our nonprofessional actors . . . *Paisà* is a film without actors in the accepted sense of the term."

The best episodes are those in the Po Valley and Florence; the portrayal of the massacre of the partisans and Allied parachutists having become a classic in iself. The episode in Florence [This episode aroused a storm of protest in Britain. *Ed.*] is extraordinary but has been misunderstood by those who have forgotten that the town became a battlefield because the British refused to cross the Arno for three months and left the partisans alone to fight the Germans. In these episodes, as in the others, Rossellini damned the horrors that war had brought to his country and his heart cry was emotionally and enthusiastically understood around the entire world.

Paisà was not a low-budget film despite what is often claimed. Rossellini's technique of improvisation was expensive and the film was in fact the most costly Italian film in 1946. The cameraman, Otello Martelli, was then the most famous in Italy.

[Most of the ideas seem to have stemmed from Amidei though Fellini, then a journalist, assisted in both script and direction; and certainly worked on research and liaison with the local population.

Rossellini received backing for the production from Rod Geiger, an American GI who had taken *Rome, Open City* (*q.v.*) to the States in 1945 and formed a company (Foreign Films Productions) to release it. In 1946, Geiger returned to Italy with film stock and a few unknown actors and actresses and successfully persuaded Rossellini to make a successor to *Open City*. As with the earlier film, *Paisà* received critical adulation in the USA and Britain.]

PANDORA'S BOX BÜCHSE DER PANDORA (DIE)

PAPERHANGER (THE) WORK

PARAPLUIES DE CHERBOURG (LES) THE UMBRELLAS OF CHERBOURG France/German Federal Republic 1964. *Dir/Scen* Jacques Demy *Photog* Jean Rabier *Mus* Michel Legrand *Art Dir* Bernard Evein *Ed* Anne-Marie Cotret *Cast* Catherine Deneuve, Anne Vernon, Nino Castelnuovo, Marc Michel, Ellen Farner *Prod* Parc Film/Madeleine Films/Beta Film. 92 mins. Eastman Color.

Geneviève (Deneuve), who works in an umbrella shop, is in love with Guy (Castelnuovo) a service station attendant, but he has to leave for military service. He does not write to Geneviève because he is wounded. She discovers she is pregnant and marries Roland (Michel) for security. When Guy returns he marries Madeleine (Farner). Several years later, Guy and Geneviève meet briefly.

This charming musical comedy in which all the dialogue is sung, as in an operetta, could be described as "poetic neorealism." It has exemplary sets by Bernard Evein.

PAREH, HET LIED VAN DE RIJST PAREH, SONG OF THE RICE Netherlands East Indies 1935. *Dir/Scen* Manus Franken *Cast* R. Mochtar, Tassim Effendi, Soekarish. 90 mins. approx.

Directed by Iven's co-director on *Rain* (*q.v.*), this was the first Indonesian film of merit, possessing a semidocumentary style that contributed greatly to its quality. Franken used nonprofessional actors and the film's success made them local "stars."

[C. Boost wrote: "With the limited means at his disposal, he gave us a glimpse of his feelings in *Pareh, Het Lied van de Rijst,* feelings which were later on to cause him to return again and again to the East. He gave us an absorbing picture of the grandeur of the natural scene and of the customs and superstitions of the inhabitants of an exotic world."]

PARENTS TERRIBLES (LES) THE STORM WITHIN France 1948. *Dir/Scen* Jean Cocteau based on his own play *Photog* Michel Kelber *Art Dir* Christian Bérard, Guy de Gastyne *Mus* Georges Auric *Ed* Jacqueline Sadoul *Cast* Jean Marais, Yvonne de Bray, Gabrielle Dorziat, Marcel André, Josette Day *Prod* Sirius. 98 mins. (86 mins. USA.)

A study of a neurotic middle-class family. Sophie (de Bray), a hysterical, possessive mother, and Georges (André), her weak, philandering husband, oppose the marriage of their adolescent son, Michel (Marais), to Madeleine (Day). An aunt, Léonie (Dorziat) is secretly in love with Georges. When it is revealed that Georges, under an assumed name, has been Madeleine's "protector," the terrible parents and the aunt plot to disrupt the affair between Michel and Madeleine. The situation is resolved by Léonie's change of heart and the mother's suicide.

This is perhaps Cocteau's best film. His adaptation of his own play (with the original cast) is set only in the family's oppressively untidy apartment cluttered with knick-knacks and in Madeleine's neat and airy apartment. In the hands of Christian Bérard, however, these two apartments are not merely sets but are characters in the drama. The brilliant acting is dominated by the two eldest actresses: Gabrielle Dorziat as the spinsterish, spiritual Léonie, and Yvonne de Bray as the neurotic mother with an incestuous suicidal infatuation for her son. Michel Kelber's close-ups are very expressive. At the end of this "vaudeville tragedy" the sound of a fire truck's siren emphasizes the silent, inbred world of the apartment as the camera slowly tracks away.

— *Intimate Relations* Britain 1953. *Dir* Charles Frank *Scen* Charles Frank based on Cocteau's play *Photog* Wilkie Cooper *Art Dir* Duncan Sutherland *Mus* René Cloërec *Cast* Marian Spencer, Harold Warrender, Ruth Dunning, Russell Enoch, Elsy Albiin *Prod* Adelphi. 86 mins.

Although based closely on the original play and modeled on Cocteau's film, this version totally fails to convey any of the mood or feeling of the original. The photography and acting are equally dull.

PARIS BELONGS TO US PARIS NOUS APPARTIENT

PARIS 1900 France 1947. *Dir/Scen* Nicole Vedrès *Mus* Guy Bernard *Ed* Myriam *Prod* Pierre Braunberger. 81 mins.

This compilation film, a re-creation of Paris from the turn of the century to 1914, shows that this form is capable of being used for personal artistic expression. Sometimes satirical, sometimes picturesque, but always thought-provoking, it is an assemblage of old newsreels, early fiction films, theater programs and Méliès' trick films. Great artists and beauties, politicians, ordinary people in the streets, and official state visits are all included. The second, more serious, half portrays the increasing crisis after 1910: the strikes, demonstrations, maneuvers on both sides of the Rhine, the Balkan wars, and finally the crowds at the Gar de l'Est waving farewell to the mobilized troops.

Paris 1900 clearly owes much to the many anonymous film researchers, as it does to Guy Bernard's expressive music and Myriam's brilliant editing.

*PARIS NOUS APPARTIENT PARIS BELONGS TO US France 1960 (production began 1958). *Dir* Jacques Rivette *Scen* Jean Gruault, Jacques Rivette *Photog* Charles Bitsch *Mus* Philippe Arthuys *Ed* Denise de Casabianca *Cast* Betty Schneider, Françoise Prévost, Jean-Claude Brialy, Gianni Esposito, Daniel Croheim, Jean-Marie Robain and Jean-Luc Godard, Claude Chabrol and Jacques Demy in bit parts *Prod* AYJM/Films de Carosse. 140 mins. (128 mins. Britain; 124 mins. USA; 135 mins. Canada).

Anne (Schneider), a student in Paris, meets Gérard (Esposito), his mistress Terry (Prévost), and a group of young actors staging Shakespeare's *Pericles.* A Spaniard dies in curious circumstances and an American political refugee, Philip (Croheim), is alleged to possess a terrible secret concerning the clandestine acts of an all-powerful fascist society. De Georges, a sinister character, who at the same time is a gang boss, mystic, and financier, seems to control Philip, Anne's brother, and the actors. All seem to be his victims, all seem to be futilely struggling to resist his subversive ends. But are the plots real? Or are the characters only undergoing the consequences of their own and Philip's imaginings?

Jacques Rivette was a critic for *Cahiers du cinéma* when he began production on this, his first feature, in July 1958, at the age of 30. The film stock was purchased from day to day with help from Françoise Truffaut, *Cahiers du cinéma*, and Rivette's family. The camera was borrowed from Claude Chabrol. No one in the film received any payment until after the film was released.

Rivette described his film as being "in the spirit of 16 mm production. I know that it will please only one person in ten . . . The characters are all tragic puppets, taking themselves too seriously, living in a sort of dream world and sickened by the real world, which they cannot reform."

A group of *Cahiers du cinéma* critics (Resnais, Chabrol, Godard, Demy, Varda, Melville, Kast) issued a joint statement about the film, calling it, "primarily the fruit of an astonishing persistence over several years to bring to the screen a personal vision of the world as rich and diverse as if expressed by any other means. But the universe that Rivette shows us — one of anguished confusion and conspiracy — is not merely a reflection of sensibility and interrogation. One would have to be totally shortsighted to miss seeing in it a vision of the modern world. Perhaps it is this fusion of a poetic vision and an expression of reality that makes *Paris nous appartient* of such foremost importance to us."

When the film was premiered in Paris in June 1960, OAS terrorism was at its height, making the film's comments on contemporary personal and political confusions that much more pertinent.

PARIS QUI DORT LE RAYON INVISIBLE/THE CRAZY RAY/AT 3:25 France 1923 (released 1924). *Dir/Scen/Ed* René Clair *Assist* Claude Autant-Lara, Georges La-

combe *Photog* Maurice Desfassiaux, Paul Guichard *Art Dir* André Foy *Cast* Henri Rollan, Albert Préjean, Marcel Vallée, Madeleine Rodrigue, Pré fils Martinelli, Stacquet *Prod* Films Diamant. 3,660 ft. Short version released in the USA under the title *At 3:25*, 1,750 ft.

A mad scientist (Martinelli) invents an invisible ray that brings all of Paris to a halt except for six people beyond its range: the guard at the Eiffel Tower (Rollan), the pilot (Préjean) of a plane and his four passengers, a thief (Vallée), a detective (Pré fils) guarding him, a woman (Rodrigue), and an industrialist (Stacquet). Eventually movement is restored and the people of Paris carry on, unaware of the break that has occurred.

This lyrical vision of Paris, with its theme contrasting immobility and motion, was made by 25-year-old René Clair in three weeks between July and September 1923. [As a film critic he was an ardent advocate of a revival of the intrinsic possibilities of the film medium, which he felt were "the external movement of objects (and) the internal movement of the action."] In his manifesto he wrote, "The main task of each new generation should be to guide the cinema back to its origins, to remove all the false art that strangles it. It seems possible to me to make films as they were made when the cinema began, using scripts written directly for the screen and some of the unique resources of the film camera." Clair's friend, Georges Charensol, later wrote, "He had been weaned on (Alfred) Jarry and Apollinaire and one can also see in *Paris qui dort* touches of Mack Sennet and dada. It is, however, this film that revealed his own nature." Dadaism and the prewar avant garde are both keys to this extraordinary first film.

PARIS UNDERGROUND TOUCHEZ PAS AU GRISBI

PARTIE DE CAMPAGNE (UNE) UNE PARTIE DE CAMPAGNE

PASAZERKA PASSENGER Poland 1963 (production began 1961). *Dir* Andrzej Munk (completed by Witold Lesiewicz) *Scen* Andrzej Munk, Zofia Posmysz-Piasecka based on the novel by Zofia Posmysz-Piasecka *Photog* Krzysztof Winiewicz

Art Dir Tadeusz Wybolt *Ed* Zofia Dwornik *Cast* Aleksandra Slaska, Anna Ciepielewska *Prod* Kadr. 62 mins. Dyaliscope.

On board a liner, a German woman, Liza (Slaska), sees a woman on the gang plank she thinks she recognizes. She admits to her husband that she had once been an SS guard in Auschwitz and that the woman, Marta (Ciepielewska), was someone she had tried to help by bringing her and her lover together for what happiness they could get. But Marta's haunting face stirs Liza's conscience and she relives and questions the incidents in the camp.

This unfinished masterpiece (but still a masterpiece) by Andrzej Munk, who died in a car crash in 1961 while still shooting the film, was completed by Witold Lesiewicz. Because shooting of the liner scenes was interrupted when Munk died, Lesiewicz sensitively and simply uses still photographs to fill in the gaps. [Jean-Luc Godard once said that, "The only true film to make about the concentration camps . . . would be a picture of the camp from the point of view of the executioners. The executioners with their daily problems — how to burn a hundred women with only enough gasoline for ten? It would also be necessary to show the typists doing inventories. It would not be the horror of such scenes that would be insupportable, but their normality and human appearance." Munk's impassioned film, a humanistic portrayal of guilt and anguish, largely follows this thesis.]

PASSENGER PASAZERKA

PASSION MADAME DUBARRY

PASSION DE JEANNE D'ARC (LA) THE PASSION OF JOAN OF ARC France 1928. *Dir* Carl Theodor Dreyer *Scen* Carl Theodor Dreyer, Joseph Delteil *Photog* Rudolf Maté, Kotula *Art Dir* Hermann Warm, Jean Victor-Hugo, Valentine Hugo *Mus* Leo Pufet, Victor Allix *Cast* Marie Falconetti, Eugène Sylvain, André Berley, Antonin Artaud, Michel Simon, Maurice Schutz, Louis Ravet, Jean d'Yd *Prod* Société Genérale des Films. 6,720 ft.

The trial of Joan of Arc (Falconetti) and her death at the stake. The script was derived from Joseph Delteil's novel about Joan of Arc but Dreyer used little material from the actual story and Delteil was only credited as co-scenarist for publicity reasons. In fact the largest part of the screenplay was taken from the authentic records of the trial. Actual shooting lasted from May to October 1927 and chronologically followed the sequence of the trial, the death sentence, and Joan's execution. The trial and execution are concentrated into one day from the eighteen months actually involved. Dreyer's approach in this respect is similar to the methods of *Kammerspiel* by which he had been earlier influenced on *Thou Shalt Honor Thy Wife* (*q.v.*).

When Dreyer arrived in Paris he announced that Jeanne d'Arc was to be a sound film. Lack of equipment forced him to abandon this but he nevertheless had his actors speak their lines. While shooting was still in progress he said: "It is necessary to give the public the true impression of watching life through a keyhole in the screen . . . I am searching for nothing but life. Only when the film is finished does one know if one has found it. The director is nothing, life is everything and is the real director. It is the objective drama of the spirit that is important, not the objective drama of the images" (September 9, 1927 *Cinémagazine*). The enormous sets, designed by Hermann Warm, were built on a piece of land between Montrouge and Petit-Clamart in Paris. The stark "white" walls were tinted pink to make them more photogenic. Dreyer chose Marie Falconetti for the title role though nothing in her career seemed to indicate she could handle it. She had never appeared in films (and never did again) and was most well known for her performance in *Miche* with André Brûlé at the Théâtre de la Madeleine.

Valentine Hugo has described Dreyer's methods on the set: "At all times we suffered the enveloping sense of horror, of an iniquitous trial, of an eternal judicial error . . . I saw the most mistrustful actors, carried away by the will and faith of the director, unconsciously continuing to play their roles after the cameras had stopped. A judge, after a scene in which he appeared moved by Joan's suffering, mumbling, 'At heart she's a witch!' he was living the drama as though it were real. Another, boiling with rage, hurls a string of invective at the accused and finally interjects this apostrophe: 'You are a disgrace to the

275

Army!' . . . (It was) particularly moving the day when Falconetti's hair was cropped close to her skull in the wan light of the execution morning and in the total silence on the set. We were as touched as if the mark of infamy were truly being applied and we were in the grip of ancient prejudices. The electricians, the mechanics held their breaths and their eyes were full of tears." Falconetti herself cried. "Then the director slowly walked towards the heroine, caught some of her tears on his finger and touched them to his lips" (*Ciné-Miroir,* November 11, 1927).

The film is in three parts: the first uses the moving camera to a large extent to introduce the judges and describe the tribunal hall and the setting up of the tribunal. The second part, which depicts, the trial itself, the death sentence, and the preparation of the torture, is handled almost entirely in close-ups or extreme close-ups. Objects take on more significance than the white walls of the set and the cutting and intertitles render the rare camera movements almost invisible. The third part, Joan's exit from prison and march through the crowds in the market place to the stake, is full of many audacious camera movements.

Moussinac has noted that "Dreyer made maximum use of close-ups and all the expressive possibilities of camera angles. His refusal to use make-up gives the faces a strange and terrible force, allowing them to express internal feelings and thoughts with a singular power. All the fingerprint techniques in the world identify less from the outside than such a facial detail reveals from the interior only by means of a close-up of a mouth, and eye, or a wrinkle."

Since 1928, *Jeanne d'Arc* has been hailed as a masterpiece and in 1958 was voted among the Twelve Best Films of All Time. Jean Cocteau wrote that, "*Potemkin* imitated a documentary and threw us into confusion. *Jeanne d'Arc* seems like an historical document from an era in which the cinema didn't exist." The reference to Eisenstein is pertinent, since Dreyer has often said he was influenced by him.

Moussinac pinpointed the film's significance. "Dreyer wanted to convey only the profound *human* meaning of the trial and death of the Maid. The pervasive sense of realism and the sharp power of the images emphasize this, though it is also to be found in the implacable unfolding of the story and in the poor, noble, and inspired girl in the all-powerful grip of the judges. The tribunal has a symbolic significance . . . Its hypocrisy and contemptible actions are its own accusers, even if one has the impression not of taking part in a trial carefully set in its own time but, beyond a conventional era, in a drama the likes of which might be found in many more obscure examples in the history of class warfare."

Jeanne d'Arc was originally released in France in a version censored by the Catholic Church. It was also banned in all the Nazi-occupied countries between 1940–44.

See also *Procès de Jeanne d'Arc; Joan of Arc*

PASSPORT TO FAME WHOLE TOWN'S TALKING (THE)

PASSPORT TO PIMLICO Britain 1948. *Dir* Henry Cornelius *Scen* T. E. B. Clarke *Photog* Lionel Banes *Art Dir* Roy Oxley *Mus* Georges Auric *Ed* Michael Truman *Cast* Stanley Holloway, Hermione Baddeley, Margaret Rutherford, Basil Radford, John Slater, Jane Hylton, Betty Warren, Naunton Wayne *Prod* Ealing. 84 mins.

The accidental explosion of a long-buried bomb in Pimlico brings to light a 15th-century Royal Charter, which decrees that the estate shall be forever recognized as Burgundian territory. The inhabitants, led by Arthur Pemberton (Holloway), are delighted with finding themselves exempt from the restrictions imposed on postwar Britain and make many attempts to "go French." However, their independence creates its own difficulties until a solution is found.

The film's theme, based on the division of Berlin into two zones, provides some hilarious comedy and delightful examples of character acting. Most of the best gags are derived from actuality and from the lives of ordinary people or are brilliant bits of crazy comedy. [This is the first of the famous Ealing comedies produced under Sir Michael Balcon's supervision. Unfortunately, though still appealing, it has dated badly since many of its funniest scenes are too closely linked with the contemporaneous situation in Britain.]

PATHER PANCHALI (trilogy)

— *Pather Panchali/The Song of the Road/The Saga of the Road/The Lament of the Path* India 1955. *Dir* Satyajit Ray *Scen* Satyajit Ray based on the novel by Bibhutti-bhusan Bandapaddhay *Photog* Subrata Mitra *Art Dir* B. Chandragupta *Mus* Ravi Shankar *Ed* Dulat Dutta *Cast* Kanu Bannerjee, Karuna Bannerjee, Uma Das Gupta, Subir Bannerjee, Runki Bannerjee, Chunibala Devi *Prod* Ray in cooperation with the government of West Bengal. 115 mins.

A would-be writer (Kanu Bannerjee) and his wife (Karuna Bannerjee) live poorly in a Bengal village and try to raise their children, Apu (Subir Bannerjee) and his sister Durga (Runki Bannerjee, then Das Gupta), and support an aged relative (Chunibala Devi). The father leaves for the city and the mother is left to raise the children on her own. She becomes shrewish and eventually drives out the old relative into the countryside where she dies. Durga also dies before the father returns. The family pack their belongings and sadly leave for Benares.

Famous sequences: the young child in tropical nature; the daily life of the family in their poor house; Apu's first sight of a train; "Auntie's" death in the forest; Durga's fever and death; Apu destroying the evidence of a small, forgotten crime of his dead sister as the family leave for Benares.

— *Aparajito/The Unvanquished* India 1956. *Dir/Scen* Satyajit Ray. Other credits as above except for *Cast* Pinaki Sen Gupta, Kanu Bannerjee, Karuna Bannerjee, Smaran Ghosal, Subodh Ganguly, Ramani Sen Gupta *Prod* Epic. 113 mins.

The ten-year-old Apu (Pinaki Sen Gupta) goes to live in Benares with his mother (Karuna Bannerjee) and his father (Kanu Bannerjee), who earns a living by reading scriptures on the banks of the Ganges. The father dies. The mother first works for a rich landlord then goes to a village to keep house for an old uncle (Ramani Sen Gupta) who is a priest and begins to train Apu for the priesthood. But Apu persuades his mother to send him to school. As an adolescent (Ghosal), Apu goes to university in Calcutta where he works to support himself. Life in the city draws him farther away from his mother and village life. While he is studying, his mother falls ill, dying before he can reach home. He returns to Calcutta.

Famous sequences: life in the religious city of Benares; Apu's arrival in Calcutta; his mother's death.

— *Apur Sansar/The World of Apu* India 1958. *Dir/Scen* Satyajit Ray. Other credits as above except for *Cast* Soumitra Chatterjee, Sharmila Tagore, Shapan Mukerjee *Prod* Satyajit Ray Productions. 106 mins.

Apu (Chatterjee) leaves the university and, in poverty, tries to earn a living as a writer. An old friend of his, Pulu (Mukerjee), invites him to the country wedding of his cousin Aparna (Tagore). But the bridegroom is mad and Apu is persuaded by Pulu to accept tradition and marry Aparna himself. They return to Calcutta where the marriage is idyllically happy. Aparna dies in childbirth and Apu is shattered. He refuses to see his son, Kajole, and wanders alone through the country. Five years later Pulu seeks him out and persuades him to return to his son. When Apu sees Kajole his feelings of bitterness become love and, after much difficulty, he persuades Kajole to leave with him.

Famous sequences: Apu looking for work; the arrival in the village for the wedding; the marriage; Aparna's first sight of Apu's miserable room in Calcutta; their married life; Apu's half-mad wanderings after her death; his meeting with his son.

[Satyajit Ray spent three years studying painting and had long been seriously interested in films. In 1947 he founded the Calcutta Film Society, where he saw the work of Flaherty and films like *Bicycle Thieves* (*q.v.*). In 1950–51 he worked as an assistant on Jean Renoir's *The River* (*q.v.*). He was very much taken with the filmic possibilities of the popular Bengali novel *Pather Panchali* and its characterizations. When he couldn't get financial backing for his script he set out to make it himself at nights and on weekends while continuing his work as a commercial artist. His crew with one exception was equally inexperienced. The cameraman, Subrata Mitra, was a young musician who had done some still photography. Filming began in 1952 but lack of funds forced him to stop work on it several times. When it seemed the film would never be finished, the West Bengal government supplied the funds to complete it.]

Ray said he chose the novel "for those qualities that make it great: its humanity, its lyricism, its sense of truth. I knew it would be wrong to force its story into a rigid mold. I wanted to retain the somewhat rambling qualities of the novel because it is this very sense that gives it its feeling of authenticity."

When *Pather Panchali* was screened at the Cannes Festival it bored the audiences and most critics. But the enthusiasm of a few critics, including André Bazin, led to its winning the "Prix du document humain" and to the subsequent adulation of Ray. Later the film won many other awards and *Aparajito* received the Golden Lion at the Venice Film Festival.

Ray incorporates various leitmotivs into the films, the most notable of which is his use of trains to punctuate stages in Apu's destiny.

The pervasive warmth, simplicity, and artistry of this trilogy place it among the world's best films of the Fifties and it was hailed as such in the USA, Britain, and many other countries. All three parts owe much to Subatra Mitra's lyrical photography and to Ravi Shankar's memorable music.

PATHETIC FALLACY (THE) AJAANTRIK

PATHS OF GLORY USA 1957. *Dir* Stanley Kubrick *Scen* Stanley Kubrick, Calder Willingham, Jim Thompson based on the novel by Humphrey Cobb *Photog* George Krause *Art Dir* Ludwig Reiber *Mus* Gerald Fried *Ed* Eva Kroll *Cast* Kirk Douglas, Ralph Meeker, Adolphe Menjou, George Macready, Wayne Morris *Prod* Bryna for United Artists. 86 mins.

During the First World War on the French front, General Mireau (Macready) orders Colonel Dax (Douglas) to lead an attack on an almost impregnable German strong point. When the exhausted men advance only a few yards, Mireau orders his own artillery to fire on them and becomes hysterical when the officer refuses. Mireau persuades General Broulard (Menjou) that an example should be made to re-establish discipline and three men, including Corporal Paris (Meeker) are arbitrarily chosen from Dax's regiment to be court-martialed for cowardice. Although Dax defends his men, they are sentenced to death. Dax reports to Broulard that Mireau had been prepared to fire on his own troops but Broulard takes no action and the three soldiers are executed.

Best sequences: the night reconnaissance; the confused attack; the war council in the baroque room of a chateau; the court martial; Dax's confrontation of Broulard and the final showdown; the execution by firing squad, with a dying man carried out on a litter in order to be shot.

This independent production by Kubrick is one of the best American films of the Fifties. It is based on a novel that is itself derived from an actual incident in World War I. Kubrick has said he read the novel when he was 15 and it branded itself on his memory, "not because of its literary qualities but because of its disturbing and tragic theme of three characters, three guiltless soldiers who are accused of cowardice and mutiny and shot 'as an example.' This *historical* situation could have happened in any other army in the world. I considered setting it in an imaginary army. I would have preferred that the soldiers were American but nothing comparable to the mutinies of 1917 took place in our army. My aim was to make an antiwar film." *Paths of Glory* was banned in France.

PATH TO HOPE (THE) CAMMINO DELLA SPERANZA (IL)

PATRIOTS OKRAINA

PAUVRE PIERROT France 1891. *Dir/Prod* Émile Reynaud.

Based on the classic story of the rivalry of Harlequin and Pierrot for the hand of Colombine, Émile Reynaud's first "pantomime lumineuse" is also the first masterpiece of the animated cartoon. Reynaud presented it many times a day to crowds at the Musée Grévin, the show of about ten minutes in length delighting the spectators with its rhythm, colors, backgrounds, and sound effects.

The strip of drawings is conserved by the Musée des Arts et Métiers in Paris and some years ago Grimoin-Sanson photographed its images, but did so rather poorly. One hopes that some day a modern animator, using new technical resources and Gaston Paulin's score, will bring back to life this forgotten masterpiece.

PAVEL KORCHAGIN see KAK ZAKALYALAS STAL

*PAWNBROKER (THE) USA 1964. *Dir* Sidney Lumet *Scen* David Friedkin, Morton Fine based on the novel by Edward Lewis Wallant *Photog* Boris Kaufman *Art Dir* Richard Sylbert *Mus* Quincy Jones *Ed* Ralph Rosenblum *Cast* Rod Steiger, Geraldine Fitzgerald, Jamie Sanchez, Thelma Oliver *Prod* Ely Landau. 115 mins.

Sol Nazerman (Steiger), a Jewish pawnbroker in New York, is haunted by his experiences in a Nazi concentration camp where his wife and children were exterminated. He tries to exist without interest in or involvement with anyone else but his world begins to crumble and he is forced to face the reality of the present.

Lumet's "big" theme — the problem of human responsibility — emerges from this relentlessly dramatic film only as an intellectual one. Its contrived style (the almost subliminal flashbacks) and dramatic tricks never truly reveal Nazerman's character and he remains a dehumanized symbol, despite Rod Steiger's technically faultless performance. Its pretentious parable and arty style made it a considerable success as a "provocative" film on the art-house circuit in North America.

PAWNSHOP (THE) USA 1916. *Dir/Scen* Charles Chaplin *Photog* Rollie Totheroh, William C. Foster *Cast* Charles Chaplin, Albert Austin, Edna Purviance, Henry Bergman, John Rand, Eric Campbell *Prod* Mutual. 1,844 ft.

Charlie is employed by a pawnbroker (Bergman), courts his daughter (Purviance), fights with another clerk (Rand), and foils a thief (Campbell).

Chaplin's first masterpiece and one of the most famous of his Mutual comedies. Famous gags: Charlie drying dishes and his hands by putting them through a wringer in the kitchen; courting the daughter by putting a necklace of dough round his neck and strumming a ladle as if it were a guitar. The most famous scene is that in which Charlie, having been tricked by a crook, is offered a clock as security by a customer (Austin) and examines it with a stethoscope as though he were a doctor; then he opens it with a can opener, extracts the insides like teeth, squirts oil on the wriggling springs, hands back the whole mess to the customer and refuses the loan. When the customer protests Charlie brains him and the customer revenges himself on an innocent passer-by.

PAY DAY USA 1922. *Dir/Scen* Charles Chaplin *Photog* Rollie Totheroh *Cast* Charles Chaplin, Phyllis Allen, Mack Swain, Edna Purviance, Syd Chaplin, Allen Garcia *Prod* Chaplin for First National. 1,810 ft.

Charlie is a laborer on a building site. He arrives late for work, admires the pretty daughter (Purviance) of the foreman (Swain), and tries to hide his pay from his enormous shrewish wife (Allen). He takes the money from her bag, has a night out with the boys, and, returning home just as the alarm clock rings, pretends he is getting up. His wife drives him off with a rolling pin.

This last but one Chaplin short is one of his best. Gags: Charlie offering a lily to the foreman to pacify him; juggling bricks on a high scaffold; Charlie collecting his lunch from several sources as the elevator moves up and down; Charlie and his friends singing in the street, and, when a woman douses them with water, Charlie raising his umbrella; the trolley car that is so full that when Charlie dives in he is shoved out the other end; Charlie oiling his squeaky shoes; Charlie trying to sleep in a bathtub full of dirty laundry.

PAYING THE PENALTY UNDERWORLD

PEASANTS KRESTYANIYE

PEDAGOGICAL POEM (A) see PUTYOVKA V ZHIZN

PENSION MIMOSAS France 1934 (released 1935). *Dir* Jacques Feyder *Assist* Marcel Carné *Scen* Charles Spaak, Jacques Feyder *Photog* Roger Hubert *Art Dir* Lazare Meerson *Mus* Armand Bernard *Cast* Françoise Rosay, Paul Bernard, Alerme, Lise Delamare, Arletty, Paul Azaïs *Prod* Tobis. 110 mins.

A man (Bernard) who was adopted as a child by a woman (Rosay) and her croupier husband (Alerme), managers of the Pension Mimosas, becomes a crook and is forced to hide out with his adopted mother. To save him from the consequences of his actions she wins a large sum of money gambling at the casino, but he has already killed himself. Best sequences: the croupier teaching new recruits how to run a gaming table; gambling in Paris society; the secret gambling den in the suburbs; daily life in the shabby boarding house and the behavior of the guests, especially the gamblers; the "son" surprised by his "mother" as he forces open a desk; the bank notes falling on the body.

This and *La Kermesse héroïque* (*q.v.*) are Feyder's best sound films. It is a direct descendant of French naturalist novels. The mother is a modern Phaedra who is in love with her adopted son, but the basic theme is gambling: upper class gambling in Paris and Monte Carlo, gambling among the crooks and gangsters. Lazare Meerson's precisely realistic sets and a careful choice of exteriors have an immense importance, and the shabby Pension Mimosas becomes a major protagonist in the film. Léon Moussinac considered the film "highly representative of an artist's sensitivity and an idealism."

Pension Mimosas was the root from which grew the French poetic realism of the Thirties as it was to be developed by Marcel Carné.

PEOPLE ON SUNDAY MENSCHEN AM SONNTAG

PEPE LE MOKO France 1936 (released 1937). *Dir* Julien Duvivier *Scen* Ashelbé, Henri Jeanson based on the novel by Ashelbé (Henri La Barthe) *Photog* Jules Kruger *Art Dir* Jacques Krauss *Mus* Vincent Scotto, Mohamed Yguerbuchen *Cast* Jean Gabin, Mireille Balin, Gabriel Gabrio, Lucas Gridoux, Line Noro, Fréhel, Marcel Dalio, Saturnin Fabre, Fernand Charpin, Gaston Modot, Roger Legris *Prod* Paris-Film. 90 mins.

Pépé Le Moko (Gabin), a Parisian gangster, defies the police by hiding with his gang in the Casbah while a cunning Algerian police inspector (Gridoux) awaits the inevitable false step that will draw him from his security. Pépé falls in love with the mistress (Balin) of a fat tourist. He tries to leave with her on a boat but is killed.

The inspiration for *Pépé le Moko* was a mediocre story by Ashelbé, an ex-commissioner of the Paris police. Duvivier, hoping to make a typical American gangster film, drew his characterizations of the gang members directly from Howard Hawks' *Scarface* (*q.v.*) and gave them such identifiable mannerisms as continually tossing a coin or playing with a flick knife. Some typical gangster scenes are well handled, such as that in which the insidious stool-pigeon, Regis (Charpin), is unmasked and shot and collapses screaming on a mechanical piano as the piano plays a tune. Jeanson's superb adaptation contains many thematic elements, such as Pépé's nostalgia for the refinements of Paris, as in the scene where he looks at a Métro ticket and recites the names of the stations like a litany.

Though it has all the entertainment value of a gangster film it is in the context of films like *Quai des brumes* (*q.v.*) and *Le Jour se lève* (*q.v.*) that *Pépé le Moko* can be best appreciated. As with these other films it has a fatalistic despondency, a background of poverty and violence, a revelation of character through milieu, and a central character who is destroyed by a woman. Pépé the gangster is neither explicitly nor implicitly condemned. He is trapped in urban squalor, finds love, and tries to break away with his ideal woman on a beautiful ship. He runs towards the sea through a cobweb of tenement-lined alleys (a dramatically charged scene) but finds his way to love and freedom barred by destiny in the shape of an iron gate and a police ambush. He dies as the boat's siren announces its departure. Thus a new myth, a form of "modern tragedy," was born — to be used over and over again in the ensuing years. The film's considerable international success is attested to by the two Hollywood remakes.

— *Algiers* USA 1938. *Dir* John Cromwell *Scen* John Howard Lawson, James M. Cain based on the novel by Ashelbé *Photog* James Wong Howe *Mus* Vincent Scotto, Mohamed Yguerbuchen *Cast* Charles Boyer, Hedy Lamarr, Sigrid Gurie *Prod* Walter Wanger. 97 mins.

A shadow of the original despite its commercial success and the appearance of some famous names among the credits.

— *Casbah* USA 1948. *Dir* John Berry *Cast* Tony Martin, Peter Lorre, Yvonne De Carlo *Prod* Universal. 94 mins.

A mediocre, semimusical remake.

— *Toto Le Moko* Italy 1949. *Dir* D. Baraglia *Cast* Toto. A parody with the Italian comedian, Toto.

PERFECT LADY (THE) WOMAN (A)

*PERSECUTION AND ASSASSINATION OF JEAN-PAUL MARAT AS PERFORMED BY THE INMATES OF THE ASYLUM OF CHARENTON UNDER THE DIRECTION OF THE MARQUIS DE SADE (THE) Britain 1966. *Dir* Peter Brook *Scen* Adrian Mitchell based on the English translation of the play by Peter Weiss *Photog* David Watkin *Art Dir* Ted Marshall, Sally Jacobs *Mus* Richard Peaslee *Ed* Tom Priestley *Cast* Ian Richardson, Patrick Magee, Glenda Jackson, Michael Williams, Robert Lloyd, Clifford Rose, John Steiner *Prod* Marat-Sade Productions for United Artists. 116 mins. DeLuxe Color.

Peter Brook's film version of the brilliant play about revolution and society by Peter Weiss is in some ways merely a cinematic record of the stage production. The forty-one members of the original British cast were retained, including the superb performances by Ian Richardson as Marat and Patrick Magee as de Sade. But it succeeds brilliantly as cinema, not only because the original play itself seems nearer to cinema than conventional theater, but also because Brook uses his cameras imaginatively to concentrate attention on details or to emphasize emotional mood in a way a stage production could never achieve.

PETER IBBETSON USA 1935. *Dir* Henry Hathaway *Scen* Vincent Lawrence, Waldemar Young, Constance Collier, John Meehan, Edwin Justus Mayer based on the play by John Nathan Raphael adapted from the novel by George Du Maurier *Photog* Charles Lang, Gordon Jennings *Mus* Ernst Toch *Ed* Stuart Heisler *Cast* Gary Cooper, Ann Harding, John Halliday, Ida Lupino *Prod* Paramount. 88 mins.

In the mid-19th century, a small boy and girl are devoted to each other. The boy's mother dies, he is taken to England and becomes Peter Ibbetson (Cooper). Years later, as a promising architect, he is sent to design new stables for the Duke of Towers and meets his childhood friend Mary (Harding), who had married the duke. They are irresistibly drawn to each other, but the duke's jealousy leads to a quarrel in which Peter accidentally kills the duke. He is imprisoned for life, treated brutally by the warders, and is on the point of death when Mary appears to him and begs him

not to die so they might continue to meet in his dreams. This they do for many years until a final vision after Mary's death leads to Peter's death so that he can join her.

André Breton described this as "a stupendous film, a triumph of surrealist thought" in his analysis of the connexion between dream and reality in *L'Amour fou* and one can only echo his enthusiasm, which was not restricted to his surrealist friends. It is one of the most beautiful films about love ever made, a lyrical "hymn to *l'amour fou.*" Its brilliance is even more remarkable since the George Du Maurier novel does not match the film and since Henry Hathaway is not a director of consequence. But perhaps he had known that rare thing, true love.

It is difficult to discuss this film without tending to invent certain details more than 25 years after being burnt by its flame, its profound understanding of love and death. But Ado Kyrou is not wrong in writing that "The dream attains its true grandeur; as it materializes it unites the two bodies. Human constraints, even death itself, are as nothing to a love more powerful than all the notions of overt life."

OTHER VERSIONS:
— **Forever* USA 1921. *Dir* George Fitzmaurice *Cast* Elsie Ferguson, Wallace Reid *Prod* Paramount.

PETITE MARCHANDE D'ALLUMETTES (LA) THE LITTLE MATCH GIRL France 1928. *Dir* Jean Renoir, Jean Tedesco *Assist* Claude Heymann, Simone Hamiguet *Scen* Jean Renoir based on the story by Hans Christian Andersen *Photog* Jean Bachelet *Art Dir* Erik Aaes (Aèss) *Mus* Manuel Rosenthal *Cast* Catherine Hessling, Jean Stor, Amy Wells, Manuel Raaby, 3,600 ft. Released in a sound version in 1929, 887 meters.

A version of the Andersen fairy tale in modern dress.

"I made *La Petite marchande d'allumettes* in collaboration with Jean Tedesco [director of Le Vieux-Colombier, a major avant-garde film theater in Paris. *Ed*] in a tiny studio carved out of the attic of the Vieux-Colombier. The reason behind its production rested on our belief in the importance of using panchromatic stock in place of orthochromatic from then on. We constructed a plant that is the basis of every studio and we also made our own sets, make-up, costumes, and so on. We did the developing and printing. The end result was a film, in the fantasy sequences, not worse than any other. Unfortunately a somewhat stupid trial made our artisans' company a failure" (Jean Renoir, 1938).

The fantasy sequences are in fact the best. Catherine Hessling, sometimes known as the French Mae Murray, gives a somewhat simpering performance.

*PETULIA Britain 1968. *Dir* Richard Lester *Scen* Lawrence B. Marcus based on the novel *Me and the Arch Kook Petulia* by John Haase *Photog* Nicolas Roeg *Art Dir* Tony Walton *Mus* John Barry *Ed* Tony Gibbs *Cast* Julie Christie, George C. Scott, Richard Chamberlain, Shirley Knight, Joseph Cotten *Prod* Petersham Films. 105 mins. Technicolor.

Petulia (Christie) is married to David (Chamberlain), an immature playboy still dominated by his wealthy father (Cotten). She first attempts to seduce a doctor, Archie (Scott), then leaves him. When she finally sleeps with Archie she is beaten up by David. David's father bullies the hospital into releasing Petulia. Archie is powerless to break the family's hold over her and she tries to come to terms with her situation. A year later, Archie sees Petulia in the hospital's maternity wing. She agrees to leave David but Archie cannot bring himself to make the necessary arrangements and he kisses her goodbye.

Richard Lester's first attempt at a psychological drama, an attempt to portray the impossibility of romantic love in a rapacious society, struck a responsive chord among audiences as had *The Graduate* (*q.v.*) earlier. The fragmentary narrative technique — flashbacks, jump cuts, flash images — brilliantly reflects the swinging world and its disjointed relationships. Julie Christie, as the kooky but intangibly sad heroine, gives one of her best performances.

PHANTOM CHARIOT (THE) KÖRKARLEN

*PHILADELPHIA STORY (THE) USA 1940. *Dir* George Cukor *Scen* Donald Ogden Stewart based on the play by Philip Barry *Photog* Joseph Ruttenberg *Art Dir* Cedric Gibbons *Mus* Franz Waxman *Ed* Frank Sullivan *Cast* James Stewart, Katherine Hepburn, Cary Grant, Ruth Hussey, John Howard, Roland Young,

John Halliday *Prod* MGM. 112 mins.
Tracy Lord (Hepburn), a brittle heiress, is divorced from her husband, C. K. Dexter Haven (Grant), who still pursues her, and is courted by a gossip columnist, Mike Connor (Stewart).

George Cukor's version of Philip Barry's glossy comedy about manners and morals of the upper class is deft and engaging. Often hailed as one of the most successful films of its type, it is especially memorable for the brilliant performances by Katharine Hepburn and Cary Grant. Cukor's sense of timing, pacing, and use of dialogue has rarely been more evident.

— **High Society* USA 1956. *Dir* Charles Walters *Scen* John Patrick based on the play *The Philadelphia Story* by Philip Barry *Photog* Paul Vogel *Art Dir* Cedric Gibbons, Hans Peters *Mus* Cole Porter *Cast* Grace Kelly, Bing Crosby, Frank Sinatra, Celeste Holm, John Lund, Louis Calhern, Louis Armstrong *Prod* MGM. 107 mins. Technicolor. VistaVision.

This version, with music and lyrics by Cole Porter, has a somewhat shortened plot and many defects that only emphasize Cukor's command of his material in the 1940 version. None of the three leads are a match for the originals.

PIATKA Z ULICY BARSKIEJ FIVE BOYS FROM BARSKA STREET Poland 1953. *Dir* Aleksander Ford *Scen* Aleksander Ford, Kazimierz Kozniewski based on the latter's novel *Photog* Jaroslav Tujar, Karol Chodura *Mus* K. Serocki *Art Dir* Anatol Radzinowicz *Ed* W. Otocka, H. Kubik *Cast* Aleksandra Slaska, T. Janczar, T. Lomnicki, A. Kozak, W. Skoczylas, W. Rulka, M. Stoor *Prod* Film Polski. 115 mins. Afgacolor.

Five boys, demoralized by the war, are placed on probation for robbery with violence. Their guardian, a bricklayer on the new East-West Highway, finds them jobs. One of them Kazek (Janczar) falls in love with Hanka (Slaska). After a savage fight with their old leader, who wants them to destroy the highway, the boys set out to rebuild their futures.

This is one of the first postwar films about juvenile delinquency and has many good sequences. Ford received the director's award at the 1954 Cannes Festival.

PICASSO MYSTERY (THE) MYSTÈRE PICASSO (LE)

PICKPOCKET France 1959. *Dir/Scen* Robert Bresson *Photog* Léonce-Henry Burel *Art Dir* Pierre Charbonnier *Mus* Jean-Baptiste Lulli *Ed* Raymond Lamy *Cast* Martin Lasalle, Pierre Leymarie, Jean Pelegri, Marika Green, Dolly Scal, Pierre Etaix *Prod* Agnès Delahaie. 75 mins.

Michel (Lasalle) is a petty thief who, after an unsuccessful theft, tries to justify his sense of exhilaration to a police inspector (Pelegri). The death of his mother (Scal) and the reactions of his friends, Jacques (Leymarie) and Jeanne (Green), stir his conscience, but when he meets a master pickpocket who trains him he reverts to crime. The inspector continues to observe him. When Michel learns of Jeanne's attachment to him, he leaves for London and spends all his spoils on women and gambling. Some years later he finds Jeanne alone and abandoned and, having been arrested, realizes his love for her.

Famous sequences: the races at Longchamp as an introduction and conclusion; his timid beginnings in the Métro; the thefts among the crowds in a railway station; Michel's discussion with the friendly police inspector in a café in the Latin Quarter; the cell-like apartment resounding with all the noises of the city; Michel's flight before his arrest; his final meeting with Jeanne in prison when he accepts his love for her.

Though this is the first time Bresson composed an entirely original script, its theme is to some extent inspired by Dostoevski's *Crime and Punishment*. This was initially quite unconscious on Bresson's part, but when he became aware of it he accentuated this aspect in his script. Bresson offers none of the conventional reasons for Michel's life of crime. He doesn't steal for money and always wears the same poor clothes. Nor is it a taste for the *acte gratuit* or a desire to live dangerously. Rather he is urged towards his "vocation" as though it were a vice, a temptation, a sin. One wonders if Bresson felt that Michel's ultimate redemption also seizes him "like a thief."

This is very much a film of objects; it is also a film of noises, carefully recorded and orchestrated. Jean Pelegri, one of Bresson's nonprofessional actors, offers this portrait of the director at work. "He knows what he wants but he doesn't know why. Nobody could be less dogmatic or more obstinate than he. He relies entirely on his instinct."

PICKUP ON SOUTH STREET USA 1953. *Dir* Samuel Fuller *Scen* Samuel Fuller based on a story by Dwight Taylor *Photog* Joe MacDonald *Art Dir* Lyle Wheeler, George Patrick *Mus* Leigh Harline *Ed* Nick De Maggio *Cast* Richard Widmark, Jean Peters, Thelma Ritter *Prod* 20th Century-Fox. 80 mins.

Skip McCoy (Widmark), a pickpocket, steals a wallet from a girl, Candy (Peters), who is unknowingly carrying an ultrasecret microfilm from one communist agent to another. Skip denies all knowledge of the film to the FBI. Candy is ordered to recover the film. Skip discovers a conscience after Moe (Ritter) is murdered, falls in love with Candy, and together they round up the spy ring.

This lurid piece of anti-Red propaganda in which the hero "seduces the (Red's) courier and obtains as reward for his patriotic act the obliteration of all criminal charges against him" (P.G., *Index de la Cinemato*, 1962), is treated in the typical Hollywood thriller style of the Forties. It was designed by the MPPA during the McCarthy era to represent the USA at the Venice Festival. The French offices of Fox refused to release the film and it was shown only eight years later in a version whose dubbed French dialogue changed the political propaganda into a story about the drug traffic.

PICNIC USA 1955. *Dir* Joshua Logan *Scen* Daniel Taradash based on the play by William Inge *Photog* James Wong Howe *Art Dir* Jo Mielziner, William Flannery *Mus* George Duning *Ed* Charles Nelson, William Lyon *Cast* William Holden, Susan Strasberg, Kim Novak, Rosalind Russell, Betty Field, Cliff Robertson, Arthur O'Connell *Prod* Columbia. 113 mins. Technicolor. CinemaScope.

Hal Carter (Holden) arrives in a small Kansas town to visit his friend Alan (Robertson). He is taken to the town picnic along with Alan's girl, Madge (Novak), her young sister (Strasberg), his mother (Field), and Rosemary (Russell), a frustrated schoolmistress. Madge is elected local beauty queen. A slightly drunk Rosemary makes advances to Hal and then creates an ugly scene. Hal leaves the picnic followed by Madge and they discover an instinctive affinity. A jealous Alan informs the police that Hal has stolen his car but Hal eludes arrest and persuades Madge to marry him before he leaps on a passing train. This entertaining film, offering a rare portrait of small-town American life, appeals mainly through its excellent cast: William Holden as the brawny hero, Kim Novak as the local blond beauty, and a delightful burlesque performance by Rosalind Russell.

PIER (THE) JETÉE (LA)

*PIERROT LE FOU France/Italy 1965. *Dir* Jean-Luc Godard *Scen* Jean-Luc Godard based on the novel *Obsession* by Lionel White *Photog* Raoul Coutard *Art Dir* Pierre Guffroy *Mus* Antoine Duhamel *Ed* Françoise Collin *Cast* Jean-Paul Belmondo, Anna Karina, Dirk Sanders, Raymond Devos, Graziella Galvani *Prod* Rome-Paris Films/Dino de Laurentis. 110 mins. Eastman Color. Techniscope. One evening, Ferdinand (Belmondo) leaves his wife (Galvani) in the middle of a boring party. He meets Marianne (Karina), a girl with whom he was in love five years earlier and who is involved with a gang of criminals. After Ferdinand finds a dead man in her room they leave Paris, travel across France, and go to live on a deserted island. She leaves him. He chases her and kills her and then commits suicide with dynamite. One of Godard's most poetic films, full of the anguish of love, aptly summarized in his own words over the first images of the film: "At the age of fifty, Velasquez no longer painted precise objects; he painted what lay between precise objects." Godard's style attempts to evoke this absence of precision in the struggles of love and life. The final sequence on the island ("A Season in Hell"), where Marianne and her "brother" are shot by Pierrot-Ferdinand, who then kills himself, is one of the most brilliant Godard has ever created.

PIERWSZE LATA THE FIRST YEARS Czechoslovakia/Poland/Bulgaria 1949 (production began 1947). *Dir/Ed* Joris Ivens *Assist Dir/Scen* Marion Michelle *Commentary* Catherine Duncan (spoken by Stanley Harrison and Anne Shortreed in the English version) *Photog* Ivan Fric (Czechoslovakia), Zachari Shandoff (Bul-

garia), Wladislaw Forbert (Poland) *Mus* Jan Kapr *Prod* Statni Film, Prague/Wytornia Filmow Dokumentalnych, Warsaw/Bulgarischer Staatsfilm, Sofia. 110 mins. 95 mins. in English version.
[In June 1947, Joris Ivens began work on a combined production by the nationalized film industries of Bulgaria, Czechoslovakia, Poland, and Yugoslavia designed to show life in these four new socialist countries. Czechoslovakia was selected as the administrative and technical production center. The Bulgarian, Yugoslav, and Polish episodes had been filmed by May 1948 when Yugoslavia's break from the Soviet bloc made it necessary to drop this episode. Then a new administration in the Czechoslovakian film industry, uninterested in the film, delayed production on its episode so that it was not completed until 1949. Finally, while editing and recording was in progress, the Bulgarian authorities decided its episode could not be included. So the film that was intended to show four People's Democracies was screened at its premier in December 1949 in a version that included only the Polish and Czechoslovakian episodes. The Bulgarian authorities eventually allowed its episode to be included.]
Bulgaria: life in a village of tobacco farmers, the farming, the children, a peasants dance, and the development of irrigation for the fields. *Czechoslovakia:* a reconstruction of the struggle of the national hero, Jan Hus, against the Roman Catholic church; the exploitation by the capitalists in the Bata factories; the liberation of the country by the Soviet armies; new industrial developments. *Poland:* the story of a woman widowed in the bombardment of Warsaw; the horrors of the Nazi Occupation; after the war she finds work in the laboratory of a steel foundry and discovers a new purpose in life. *Yugoslavia* (never released): the construction of a railroad by young people.
The Czechoslovakian episode is the least satisfactory; the dramatized Polish episode touching. The Bulgarian episode is the best, perhaps because of its pastoral mood. This film has, over the years, developed a special historical, social, and political importance and one hopes that one day it can be seen in an integral version.

PILGRIM (THE) USA 1923. *Dir/Scen* Charles Chaplin *Associate Dir* Chuck

Reisner *Photog* Rollie Totheroh *Cast* Charles Chaplin, Edna Purviance, Kitty Bradbury, Mack Swain, Tom Murray, Sydney Chaplin, Chuck Reisner, Loyal Underwood, Dinky Dean, Mai Wells *Prod* Chaplin for First National. 4,300 ft. "The Pilgrim" (Chaplin), an escaped convict, steals a minister's clothes and is mistaken for the new minister by the deacon (Swain) of a small Texas town. He lives at the home of a girl (Purviance) and her mother (Bradbury). A former cellmate (Reisner) arrives and steals the mother's mortgage money. The Pilgrim's true identity is revealed when he tries to recover the money. The sheriff (Murray) arrests him but turns him loose at the Mexican border.

Outstanding sequences: Charlie's train trip sitting near the sheriff; his welcome by the deacon and congregation; the deacon's hidden bottle of "hooch"; the church collection with Charlie testing the coins to see if they are counterfeit; his impromptu pantomimed sermon on David and Goliath; his welcome into the home where he will live and the family photo album; the visit of the mother (Wells) and starchy father (Sydney Chaplin) of an abominable child (Dean); the child's putting a derby hat over a plum pudding that Charlie covers with sauce and serves. The ending is especially famous: Charlie is freed by the sheriff at the Mexican border which he doesn't want to cross because of gun battles by bandits on the other side. He uses various excuses to come back including offering the sheriff some flowers. The final image shows him running down the border-line with one foot in each country, the sheriff on one side and lawlessness on the other.

This is Chaplin's last short film and one of his most perfect; for this Molière of the cinema it is in some respects his *Tartuffe*. It is a powerful satire on hypocrisy, bigotry, and puritanical narrow-mindedness. The Pennsylvania censors banned it because "it made the Ministry look ridiculous." It is not impossible that the various attacks on Chaplin by religious and quasi-religious groups a few years later were a direct response to his aggressive social criticism in *The Pilgrim*.

PILGRIMAGE TO THE VIRGIN MARY PROCESÍ
K PANENCE

PLACE IN THE SUN (A) USA 1951. *Dir* George Stevens *Scen* Michael Wilson, Harry Brown based on *An American Tragedy* by Theodore Dreiser and the Patrick Kearney play adapted from the novel *Photog* William C. Mellor *Art Dir* Hans Dreier, Walter Tyler *Mus* Franz Waxman *Ed* William Hornbeck *Cast* Montgomery Clift, Elizabeth Taylor, Shelley Winters, Ann Revere, Raymond Burr, Keefe Braselle *Prod* Paramount. 122 mins.

George Eastman (Clift) escapes from a life of poverty and fierce puritanism with his mother and is offered a job in a mill by his rich uncle. He falls in love with Alice Tripp (Winters), who works in the mill. He is taken up again by his rich relatives and meets an attractive and wealthy girl, Angela Vickers (Taylor). Alice discovers she is pregnant and tries to persuade George to marry her. Georges sees her as the only obstacle to a successful business future and a life with Angela and contemplates murder. He plans to drown her but discovers he cannot go through with it. The boat overturns in an accident and Alice is drowned. George is arrested and sentenced to death.

This is George Stevens best film. It owes much to a concise and forceful script and to the dazzling femininity of Elizabeth Taylor, then at the height of her talent and appeal. Montgomery Clift's performance admirably conveys the restlessness of his character.

[As with Sternberg's earlier *An American Tragedy* (*q.v.*) George Stevens concentrates on the love story and plays down Dreiser's social criticism. Sternberg's version succeeds as an effective romantic melodrama; Stevens doesn't seem sure what his theme is. Though hailed by many at the time of its release as one of the best American films, it now seems overblown and pretentious and curious in its romanticized portrait of Angela and her circle.]

PLAISIR (LE) HOUSE OF PLEASURE France 1951. *Dir* Max Ophüls *Scen* Jacques Natanson, Max Ophüls based on the stories *Le Masque*, *La Maison Tellier*, and *Le Modèle* by Guy de Maupassant *Photog* Christian Matras (episodes 1 and 2), Agostini (episode 3) *Art Dir* Jean d'Eaubonne *Mus* Maurice Yvain, Joë Hajos *Ed* Léonide Azar *Cast Le Masque:* Claude Dauphin, Gaby Morlay,

Balpêtré, Jean Mayer; *Le Modèle:* Daniel Gabin, Pierre Brasseur, Pauline Dubost. Jean Galland; *La Maison Tellier:* Madeleine Renaud, Danielle Darrieux, Jean Gélin, Jean Servais, Simone Simon *Prod* C.C.F.C./Stera Films. 95 mins.

Derived from three short stories by Guy de Maupassant: *Le Masque:* a wife (Morlay) describes to a doctor (Dauphin) how her husband, despite his age, visits a dance hall wearing a mask to hide his wrinkles. *La Maison Tellier:* Madame Tellier (Renaud) closes her brothel so she and her girls can attend her niece's first communion. One of them, Rosa (Darrieux), has a brief love affair with a farmer (Gabin) before they all return to work. *Le Modèle:* a young painter (Gélin) has an affair with a model (Simon). She throws herself from a window because of her love for him and breaks her legs. The artist marries her and devotes his life to caring for his crippled wife. The stories are linked by a narrator — Jean Servais in the original, Peter Ustinov in the English version.

This brilliant film is Ophüls second after his return from the States and marks the beginning of his greatest period. [Its unifying theme is, as Claude Beylie put it, that "if pleasure is an easy thing, happiness is not." The first story contrasts pleasure and old age, the second pleasure and purity, and the third pleasure and marriage. Ophüls had originally hoped to film *La Femme de Paul* for the third episode to contrast pleasure and death but this was abandoned at the producer's insistence.]

The best episode is the humorous *La Maison Tellier,* which opens with the camera circling the exterior of the brothel and peering voyeuristically through the windows at the 1880 furnishings and the activity within. Later, Ophüls takes his camera to the Normandy plains for some beautiful, idyllic country scenes which, under the hot July sun, seem directly inspired by the impressionists.

POCIAG NIGHT TRAIN Poland 1959. *Dir* Jerzy Kawalerowicz *Scen* Jerzy Lutowski, Jerzy Kawalerowicz *Photog* Jan Laskowski *Art Dir* Ryszard Potocki *Mus* Andrzej Trzaskowski based on "Moon Rays" by Artie Shaw *Cast* Lucyna Winnicka, Leon Niemczyk, Teresa Szmigie-

lowna, Zbigniew Cybulski *Prod* Kadr. 100 mins.

Marthe (Winnicka) buys a sleeping car ticket and finds herself sharing a compartment with a doctor (Niemczyk) who wanted it to himself. Gradually they are drawn together despite sporadic appearances by Marthe's ex-lover (Cybulski).

A flirtatious blonde (Szmigielowna) tries to seduce the doctor. The police come aboard the train looking for a murderer and the doctor is arrested since the suspect was supposed to be in that compartment. But Marthe recognizes a man hiding behind his overcoat as the one who sold her the ticket and informs the police. The man escapes but is caught by the police. When the train arrives the doctor's wife is waiting for him and Marthe is left alone.

Though this is a typical thriller with touches of comedy it is also a psychological study of carefully characterized people and their ultimate separateness.

POCKETFUL OF MIRACLES see LADY FOR A DAY

POD GWIAZDA FRYGISKA CELULOZA

PODRUGI THE GIRL FRIENDS/THE SONG OF POTEMKIN USSR 1936. *Dir/Scen* Lev Arnstam *Co-Dir/Art Dir* Moisei Levin *Photog* Wulf Rappaport, A. Shafran *Mus* Dmitri Shostakovich *Cast* Boris Babochkin, I. Zarubina, Yanina Zheimo, Zoya Fyodorova, B. Blinov *Prod* Lenfilm. 90 mins.

During the First World War and the Civil War, the story of the youthful friendships of three young nurses and their first romances.

The first part of the film, showing in a somewhat "neorealist" manner the life of the young people, is remarkably expressive and perceptive. Especially memorable is the scene in which a group of trapped workers get drunk and break out into a revolutionary song.

POEMA O MORE POEM OF THE SEA USSR 1958 (production began 1955). *Dir* Alexander Dovzhenko, Yulia Solntseva *Scen* Alexander Dovzhenko *Photog* Georgy Yegiazarov *Art Dir* A. Borissov, V. Plastinkin *Mus* G. Popov *Cast* Boris Livanov, Boris Andreyev, Mikhail Tsaryov, Zinaida Kiriyenko *Prod* Mosfilm. 112 mins. Sovcolor. Sovscope.

A hydroelectric station is under construction on the Dnieper River near the small Ukrainian town of Kakhovka. A huge dam will cause the river to flood an extensive area, putting one of the villages under water. The collective farm chairman Zarudny (Andreyev) invites many of the natives to return to see it for the last time. Some of these have achieved success and fame, such as General Fedorchenko (Livanov), the son of an old man who refuses to leave his home. The action takes place in the present, in the past, through the reminiscences of the characters, and occasionally in the future. For example, the general recalls the battles he fought against the Nazis on the Ukrainian plains. In the present is a story of the seduction of the chairman's daughter Katerina (Kiriyenko) by the chief of the construction job (Tsaryov). At one point the chairman imagines that the technician has abandoned his daughter, that she commits suicide, and that he delivers a speech over her grave.

Fereydoun Hoveyda said that this is "truly the first posthumous film in the history of the cinema." [Dovzhenko had planned this film with great care. He lived among the builders of the hydroelectric station and spent two years writing his script and taking documentary shots during different stages of the construction. He made numerous drawings to indicate the style of the film. On the night before shooting began Dovzhenko died of a heart attack and the film was completed by Dovzhenko's wife and colleague, Yulia Solntseva.]

This paean to the Soviet Union and socialism is not always entirely positive. For example, the general has a frightful little monster of a son who wants to become an attorney in order to prosecute people. A self-centered female minister has become so myopic that she no longer recognizes her childhood friends. The construction chief, an ambitious cynic but a good worker, says (in substance) to the girl he has seduced, made pregnant, and abandoned, "Don't use cheap psychology; what's the use of that when we are building a glorious future." Later, he says of himself, "I may be a bastard but I am a builder of communism and that is more important." Dovzhenko offers a sympathetic portrait of the Ukrainian peasants still tied to their land, as in the case of Grandfather Maxim, who is reluctant to leave the house in which he was born and in which he has lived all his life. Unfortunately, Solntseva's direction does not always match Dovzhenko's conception, although many sequences have Dovzhenko's typical epic breadth and lyricism.

POINT DU JOUR (LE) France 1948. (released 1949). *Dir* Louis Daquin *Scen* Vladimir Pozner *Photog* André Bac *Art Dir* Paul Bertrand *Mus* Jean Wiener *Ed* Claude Nicole *Cast* Jean Desailly, René Lefèvre, Catherine Monot, Loleh Bellon, Michel Piccoli, Marie-Hélène Dasté, Jean-Pierre Grenier *Prod* Ciné-France. 101 mins.

Louis Daquin said, "our script was written on location and the natural settings were often selected before the scenes that were to be shot in them had been conceived in their final form." The film's theme is the daily life of people from various walks of life who work among the coal fields of northern France. The three principal characters have been described by Claude Roy: "The engineer (Desailly) is a very gentle and kindhearted man from the upper-class districts who feels his way with caution. The miner (Grenier) is the image of one of those new men who are the heroes of our times, as clumsy as innocence, as shabby as work, as gentle as goodness, as beautiful as purity. Loleh Bellon is simply the image of gracefulness to whom grace is refused."

Memorable sequences: dawn in the mining village; the room where the miners change their clothes; the descent into the mine; the love making between a young girl and a miner; the conflict between the young engineer and an older one (Lefèvre); the evocation of old strikes.

This excellent film was poorly distributed and failed to reach a large public, although it might have been the *point du jour* (dawn) of a French neorealist movement.

POINTE-COURTE (LA) France 1955. *Dir/Scen* Agnès Varda *Photog* Louis Stein *Mus* Pierre Barbaud *Ed* Alain Resnais *Cast* Sylvia Montfort, Philippe Noiret, and the inhabitants of La Pointe-Courte *Prod* Films Tamaris. 80 mins.

A man (Noiret) and a woman (Montfort) who have grown apart during four years of marriage visit a little fishing village called La Pointe-Courte, where the husband was born. Around them the simple pattern of work, play, marriage, birth, and death continues in the village. This gradually changes their perspective and they are drawn together again.

This is certainly the first film of the French *nouvelle vague*. [The production company was a cooperative formed by the crew and actors; the film was shot in the summer of 1954. Its interplay between conscience, emotions, and the real world make a direct antecedent of *Hiroshima, mon amour* (*q.v.*). Agnès Varda said that she, "tried to establish a system of correspondences between human beings and objects. The hero is constantly associated with wood . . . the heroine is constantly associated with steel . . . For the couple, objects are filled with psychological significance. At the beginning of the film when the two are farthest from each other, objects have the most important role. In moments of crisis their objects have an aggressive impact. But as the film progresses this world is transformed and human beings regain ascendancy over objects." In its concern for the ambiguous relationship between the apparent world of things and the interior world of feelings and thoughts *La Pointe Courte* reflected a theme that was to occupy many of the new French film makers of the Sixties.]

POKHOZDENIYA OKTYABRINI THE ADVENTURES OF OKTYABRINA USSR 1924. *Dir/Scen* Grigori Kozintsev, Leonid Trauberg *Photog* F. Verigo-Darovsky, Ivan Frolov *Art Dir* Vladimir Yegorov *Cast* Z. Tarkhovskaya, Sergei Martinson *Prod* Sevzapkino/FEKS. 970 meters.

This burlesque comedy by the youthful FEKS (Factory of the Eccentric Actor) group involves a fantastic attempt by Curzon, Poincaré, and Coolidge (clowns symbolizing the capitalists) to rob the State Bank, but they are foiled by a Young Pioneer. [Yuri Tinyonov wrote in 1929: "*The Adventures* made liberal use of all the tricks the FEX people had been panting to utilize once they had entered that paradise – the cinema. The least pretentious episode I remember from it is a crowd bicycling across roofs!"]

POKOLENIE A GENERATION Poland 1954. *Dir* Andrzej Wajda (supervision Alek-

sander Ford) *Scen* Bodhan Czeszko *Photog* Jerzy Lipmann *Art Dir* Roman Mann *Mus* A. Markowski *Cast* Tadeusz Lomnicki, Urszula Modrzynska, T. Janczar, Roman Polanski, Zbigniew Cybulski *Prod* Film Polski. 90 mins.

In Nazi-occupied Warsaw, a youth (Lomnicki) finds a job and through his new friends joins a resistance group headed by a girl, Dorota (Modrzynska). On the day of the Ghetto uprising the group helps some of the fighters escape through the sewers. Soon after the youth and Dorota realize they are in love, Dorota is arrested by the Gestapo and he takes over as leader of a new Youth Fighters group.

This is Wajda's first feature and forms a kind of trilogy with the later *Kanal* (*q.v.*) and *Popiol i Diamant* (*q.v.*). Its theme – the inconsistencies of the Polish Resistance – is not new, but Wajda's romantic style and pictorial talent give it a freshness and absorbing quality.

POLIKUSHKA USSR 1919 (released 1922). *Dir* Alexander Sanin *Assist* Fyodor Otsep (Ozep) *Scen* Valentin Turkin, Fyodor Otsep, Nikolai Efros based on the story by Leo Tolstoy *Photog* Yuri Zheliabuzhsky *Art Dir* Sergei Kozlovsky S. Petrov *Cast* Ivan Moskvin, V. Pashennaya, Y. Rayevskaya, V. Bulgakov *Prod* Russ. 4,514 ft.

Based on the story by Leo Tolstoy about a serf, Polikushka (Moskvin), who is a notorious drunkard, liar, and thief. His mistress is determined to make him reform but he loses a sum of money entrusted to him and hangs himself in despair.

This is the first successful film of the post-Revolution Soviet cinema. [It was produced under conditions of extreme difficulty in an unheated film studio during a severe winter and with a shortage of both food and raw film stock. The production company, Russ, was a collective composed of many (including the director) who had worked in the Moscow Art Theater.] Though its style is primitive and gives no hint of the later Soviet style, Moskvin's impressive and moving performance and the evocation of the Russian landscape gives the film a singular quality.

POPIOL I DIAMANT ASHES AND DIAMONDS Poland 1958. *Dir* Andrzej Wajda *Scen* Andrzej Wajda, Jerzy Andrzejewski based on the latter's novel *Photog* Jerzy Wojcik *Art Dir* Roman Mann *Ed* Halina Nawrocka *Cast* Zbigniew Cybulski, Ewa Krzyzanowska, B. Kobiela, Adam Pawlikowski *Prod* Kadr. 104 mins.

On the first day of peace in a small Polish town, Maciek (Cybulski) is ordered by a nationalist underground unit to assassinate the newly arrived Communist District Secretary. Maciek moves into a room at the hotel next door to his quarry and falls in love with the hotel barmaid, Christina (Krzyzanowska). The mayor attends a victory banquet downstairs at which his drunken secretary (Kobiela) disgraces himself. Maciek's love affair makes him question whether he believes in a cause that sets Pole killing Pole, but his superior Andrzej (Pawlikowski) forces him to continue and he shoots his quarry in the early hours of the morning. Maciek flees, runs into a military patrol, and is shot trying to escape.

Wajda felt that it would be a marvelous theme to show, during the first night of peace, "the fate of a young man weary of heroism and having had a taste of a better life. Past and future sit at the same table to the sound of tangos and fox trots. The hero has to resolve the soldier's eternal dilemma: to obey orders or think for himself. However, he kills rather than give up his arms, typical of a generation that relies only on itself and on the concealed revolver. I wanted to show the complex and difficult world of the generation of which I was part."

[In *Ashes and Diamonds,* the third part of an unplanned trilogy with *Pokolenie* (*q.v.*) and *Kanal* (*q.v.*), a pattern of gradual disillusionment reveals itself. Its hard-hitting bitterness and the restlessness of its central characters, a young man searching for a way out of his confusion, seems as much a reflection of the youth of Poland in the Fifties as of postwar youth. This parallel is reinforced by Cybulski's anachronistic dark glasses.]

Wajda's re-creation of a small war-torn town celebrating the end of peace gives the film much of its depth. The film opens with a violent massacre. The bodies from the opening sequence are later seen again in the film's most famous sequences: the love scene in a bombed church under a baroque Christ hanging upside down. It ends with Maciek's death on a garbage dump — surely one of the most powerful scenes Wajda has created.

None of the characters is merely a black and white symbol. Cybulski is a complete incarnation of the complex, disoriented Maciek, and Kobiela is excellent as the drunken secretary. Regrettably, there are several touches that suggest an unnecessary striving after effect: the drinks being slid along the bar in the manner of an American western and then set alight as though to suggest the flame on the Tomb of the Unknown Soldier.

PORTE DES LILAS GATES OF PARIS/ GATE OF LILACS France/Italy 1957. *Dir* René Clair *Scen* René Clair, Jean Aurel based on the novel *La Grande Ceinture* by René Fallet *Photog* Robert Lefebvre *Art Dir* Léon Barsacq *Mus* Georges Brassens *Ed* Louisette Hautecoeur *Cast* Pierre Brasseur, Georges Brassens, Henri Vidal, Dany Carrel, Raymond Bussières, Annette Poivre *Prod* Filmsonor/Rizzoli. 95 mins.

Juju (Brasseur), an aging idler and drunkard in Paris, has a friendship with a mendicant guitarist, the artist (Brassens). A gangster (Vidal) on the run after a holdup takes refuge in the artist's house and Juju devotes himself to caring for him. The gangster beguiles the girl (Carrel) for whom Juju has a sentimental affection and tricks her into providing money for his escape. In trying to prevent this, Juju accidentally shoots the gangster.

"The aim of *Porte des Lilas*", said René Clair, "is to blend the themes of friendship and love with that of altruism and to show the way a simple man is brought to think of others. Our main task has been to suggest without adopting words that wouldn't fit with the characters' roles." All the characters speak in popular French, though not in slang, because "one can't achieve realism merely by reproducing what is real. For a dog, a photograph of his master is not a reproduction of reality, it is only a piece of cardboard. What is true for images is also true for words and sounds" (René Clair).

PORTES DE LA NUIT (LES) THE GATES OF THE NIGHT/THE DOORS OF NIGHT France 1946. *Dir* Marcel Carné *Scen* Jacques Prévert based on his ballet *Le Rendez-Vous Photog* Philippe Agostini *Art Dir* Alexandre Trauner *Mus* Joseph Kosma *Ed* Jean Feyte *Cast* Pierre Brasseur, Serge Reggiani, Yves Montand, Nathalie Nattier, Saturnin Fabre, Raymond Bussières, Carette, Mady Berry, Jean Vilar, Dany Robin, Syvia Bataille *Prod* Pathé. 106 mins.

In Paris after the liberation, Diego (Montand) is introduced to "the most beautiful woman in the world" (Nattier) by a vagrant musician who calls himself Destiny (Vilar) and makes some disturbing prophecies. Between night and dawn the drama of their relationship with the woman's husband (Brasseur) and brother, a Fascist collaborator (Reggiani), is played out. The brother commits suicide and the woman dies as dawn breaks. The film opens with a voice announcing "Paris during the difficult winter that followed the liberation." It is excellent when it offers a realistic description of the immediate postwar problems of France: the black market, the return of war profiteers from London, the collaborator who dreads punishment, and his father (Fabre) who had grown rich building Nazi fortifications. But the melodramatic theme with its characters drawn into a pattern woven by "destiny" is unconvincing and its gloomy atmosphere seems prewar in style.

Carné was given a large budget for this production. It was a resounding commercial failure, though this was due less to its weaknesses than to its good qualities. [It was based on a ballet that Prévert had written in 1945. This was the last film in the long collaboration between Carné and Prévert, except for the uncompleted *La Fleur de l'age* a year later. The part of the woman had been originally written for Marlene Dietrich.]

PORT OF SEVEN SEAS see MARIUS (trilogy)

PORT OF SHADOWS QUAI DES BRUMES

PORTRAIT OF MARIA MARIA CANDELARIA

POSLEDNAYA NOCH THE LAST NIGHT USSR 1937. *Dir* Yuli Raizman *Co-Dir* Dmitri Vasiliev *Scen* Yuli Raizman, Yevgeni Gabrilovich *Photog* Dmitri Feldman *Art Dir* Alexander Utkin *Mus* A. Veprik *Cast* A. Konsovsky, I. Peltser, M. Yarotskaya, Nikolai Dorokhin *Prod* Mosfilm. 100 mins.

In Briansk in October 1917, the son of a poor worker falls in love with the daughter of a rich industrialist.

The events of the Revolution are reflected in this very touching love story based on a kind of *Romeo and Juliet* theme. Final sequence: the wait in the station for a train that is supposed to be carrying Whites but is instead occupied by Bolshevik soldiers.

POSTMAN ALWAYS RINGS TWICE (THE) see OSSESSIONE

POSTO (IL) THE JOB Italy 1961. *Dir/Scen* Ermanno Olmi *Photog* Lamberto Caimi *Art Dir* Ettore Lomardi *Ed* Carla Colombo *Cast* Sandro Panzeri, Loredana Detto *Prod* The Twenty Four Horses. 90 mins.

An adolescent (Panzeri) looks for a job and is offered one as messenger boy in a big Milan industrial concern until a position as clerk is available. At the interview he meets a girl (Detto) who gets a job as a typist. He goes to the office dance to meet her again but she doesn't turn up. One of the clerks dies and he takes his place at his desk in the back of the room, his job secure at last. Olmi's first feature has almost no story but is endowed with quiet, truthful humor and concentrated observation of everyday happenings. Though its style seems simple, it has a precise sense of timing and reveals Olmi's brilliant talent for capturing the comic, pompous, and sometimes sad way people behave. The cast is entirely nonprofessional.

POTEMKIN BRONENOSETS POTYOMKIN

POTE TIN KYRIAKI NEVER ON SUNDAY Greece 1959. *Dir/Scen* Jules Dassin *Photog* Jacques Natteau *Art Dir* A. Zonis *Mus* Manos Hadjidakis *Ed* Roger Dwyre *Cast* Melina Mercouri, Jules Dassin, Georges Foundas, Tito Vandis *Prod* Lopert Pictures/Melinafilm. 97 mins.

An American pedant, Homer (Dassin), meets Ilya (Mercouri), the most cheerful and popular prostitute in the Port of Piraeus. He becomes infatuated with her and tries to reform and educate her. She undertakes a course in self-improvement but revolts and organizes a prostitutes' strike against the rents charged by their landlord. Homer, recognizing defeat sails away.

The theme song of this entertaining comic fairy tale became enormously popular. Under the romantic fable is a somewhat acrid theme that suggests, in the way "civilized values" are defeated by older instincts, that an intellectual is wrong in wanting to reform the world.

POTOMOK CHINGIS-KHAN STORM OVER ASIA/THE HEIR TO GHENGHIS KHAN/THE DESCENDENT OF GHENGHIS KHAN USSR 1928. *Dir* V. I. Pudovkin *Assist Dir* A. Ledashev, L. Bronstein *Scen* Osip Brik *Photog* A. N. Golovnya *Art Dir* Sergei Kozlovsky, M. Aaronson *Cast* I. Inkizhinov, Valeri Inkizhinov, A. Chistiakov, L. Dedintstev, L. Biliniskaya, Anna Sudakevich, V. Tsoppi, Boris Barnet, P. Ivanov *Prod* Mezhrabpomfilm. 8,430 ft. Re-released in 1950 with music and dialogue prepared under Pudovkin's supervision.

In Soviet Central Asia in 1920, a young Mongolian trapper, Amogolan (V. Inkizhinov), flees to the north and joins Soviet partisans after an argument with an American fur trader (Tsoppi) who has cheated him. He is captured by interventionist forces and is shot, but a general (Dedintstev) finds an amulet among his belongings that identifies him as a descendent of Ghenghis Khan. He is nursed back to health and made puppet ruler over Buryat Mongolia, but eventually turns against his oppressors and starts a "storm over Asia."

Main sequences: the life of the nomadic Mongols; the argument with the fur trader in the market; the fighting against interventionist troops and the Whites (many of these scenes were cut by censors in Western countries when the film was first released); the Mongol led out to be shot by an English soldier; the visit of the general and the masculine-looking female officer (Biliniskaya) to the Dalai Lama (Ivanov), with the parallel scenes of preparations for the ceremony in the temple and in the soldiers' quarters; the puppet ruler covered with bandages, as silent as an idol; his sudden rebellion and the final victory ride across the open plains.

Since Osip Brik's scenario was a three or four page synopsis, the film only began to take shape after Pudovkin and his crew arrived in Soviet Central Asia. The location photography often gives the film the feel of a documentary. Perhaps the most typical Pudovkin sequence is that of the Mongol's execution. The soldier ordered to shoot him marches him through muddy streets taking care to keep his own boots clean, but after he has sadly and reluctantly shot him, he drags his feet back through the same streets, seemingly unaware of the mud. Pudovkin's film seemed almost prophetic of the Japanese control over a puppet emperor they placed on the throne of Manchuria in 1932 and of the numerous storms of liberation that crossed Asia after the Second World War. One of the most curious stories in connection with the film is that French distributors were allowed to show the film in Hanoi and Saigon while the Indochina War was at its height.

— *Tempête sur l'Asie/Storm over Asia* France 1937. *Dir* Richard Oswald *Cast* Conrad Veidt, Sessue Hayakawa, Madeleine Robinson, Roger Duchesne *Prod* Rio.

An "epic" about how a Mongolian with a handful of followers takes over his country. It has no relationship to Pudovkin's film.

POUR LA SUITE DU MONDE THE MOONTRAP/SO THAT THE WORLD GOES ON Canada 1963. *Dir/Scen* Michel Brault, Pierre Perrault *Photog* Michel Brault, Bernard Gosselin *Sound* Marcel Carrière *Ed* Werner Nold *Prod* National Film Board of Canada. 105 mins. English version, 84 mins.

A *cinéma-vérité* study of how the people of the Ile-aux-Coudres in the St. Lawrence river set about trapping the white beluga whale, a practice they had abandoned in 1920. Because of the archaic French spoken by the inhabitants of the island subtitles were necessary when the film was screened in Paris.

This brilliant and poetic ethnographic film in the tradition of Flaherty, Rossellini, and Rouquier marked the birth of a new French-Canadian cinema.

POVEST' PLAMENNYKH LET THE FLAMING YEARS/STORY OF THE TURBULENT YEARS USSR 1961. *Dir* Yulia Solntseva *Scen* Alexander Dovzhenko *Photog* Fyodor Provorov, Alexei Temerin *Art Dir* Alexander Borisov *Mus* Gavriel Popov *Ed* K. Moskvina *Cast* Boris Andreyev, Nikolai Vingranovsky, Zinaidi Kirienko, Sergei Loukianov, Vassili Merkouriev, Zvetlana Zhgun *Prod* Mosfilm. 105 mins. Sovcolor. 70 mm Cinerama.

A story of the Ukraine during the Second World War focusing on a heroic soldier (Vingranovsky) who fights many courageous battles, is wounded, but is finally reunited with his sweetheart (Zhgun) and married by the general (Andreyev).

Solntseva's version of a script written in 1945 by her late husband, Dovzhenko, is full of sweeping battle scenes and lyrical moments but seems much more dated than the splendid *Poem of the Sea* (*q.v.*).

PO ZAKONU DURA LEX/BY THE LAW/THE UNEXPECTED/EXPIATION USSR 1926. *Dir* Lev Kuleshov *Scen* Victor Shklovsky based on the story *The Unexpected* by Jack London *Photog* K. Kuznetsov *Art Dir* Isaac Makhlis *Cast* Sergei Komarov, Alexandra Khokhlova, Vladimir Fogel, Pyotr Galadzhev, Porfiri Podobed *Prod* Goskino. 1,673 meters.

Two men are murdered in Alaska and the three people involved — Edith (Khokhlova), Nelson, her husband (Komarov), and Jack, their servant (Fogel) — are isolated in their cabin by winter storms. Eventually, the guilty one is condemned by the other two and hung "By the Law."

Shklovsky's excellent script was based on a Jack London story (though with some added episodes) and Kuleshov's recreation of the Alaskan atmosphere is brilliant. Though made with a restricted budget and as an experiment, it is Kuleshov's best film. Its study of three characters in conflict is intensified by Kuleshov's isolation and accumulation of significant gestures and details. The two men give restrained performances but Khokhlova's is often unnecessarily exaggerated.

PRELUDE TO WAR see WHY WE FIGHT (SERIES)

PREY FOR THE SHADOWS PROIE POUR L'OMBRE (LA)

PRIMARY USA 1960. A film by Richard Leacock, Robert Drew, Don Pennebaker, Al Maysles *Prod* Time-Life Inc. 27 mins.

A record, originally made for television, of one of John F. Kennedy's 1960 primary campaigns against Hubert Humphrey. It was made entirely with the "living camera," silent running, light, and flexible equipment able to record both image and synchronous sound and run by a single operator who could move about while filming. It is more than a mere physical record however, for it succeeds in capturing the emotional tensions and crises, the moments of relaxation, and the overwhelming sense of pleasure and relief in the Kennedy camp as the votes are finally counted. The film makers' depended for their effect on not interfering with any scene, on making their filming as unintrusive as possible, and on being able to persuade Kennedy, Humphrey, and others involved to accept the camera's participation in the action as though it were just another item of furniture.

["In *Primary*, Ricky Leacock, Robert Drew, Don Pennebaker, and Al Maysles have caught the scenes of real life with unprecedented authenticity, immediacy, and truth. They have done so by daringly and spontaneously renouncing old controlled techniques; by letting themselves be guided by the happening scene itself . . . We see *Primary* as a revolutionary step and a breaking point in the recording of reality in cinema." — Independent Film Award Citation (1961) to *Primary*.]

The most famous sequence is that in which the camera shows Kennedy in his car, then follows him into a meeting hall as he shakes hands with large numbers of his followers, and finally follows him up a small stairway and shows him on the stage receiving the applause of the crowd. This sequence photographed by Al Maysles is in one single take. In a later scene, Jacqueline Kennedy addresses the crowd and the camera revealingly shows her nervously twisting her hands behind her back.

Despite its new techniques and the use of highly sensitive 16mm film to avoid the use of special lighting, the "living camera" method is not cheap. This TV film cost more than $200,000 and the shooting ratio was between ten and twenty to one.

PRINCE BAYAYA BAJAJA

PRINCESS YANG (THE) YOKIHI

PRISIONEROS DE LA TIERRA PRISONERS OF THE EARTH Argentina 1939. *Dir* Mario Soffici *Scen* U. Petit de Murat, Dario Quiroga based on three stories by Quiroga *Photog* Pablo Tabernero *Art Dir* Ralph Pappier *Mus* Lucio Demare *Cast*

Francisco Petrone, Angel Magnana, Raoul de Lange, Elisa Calva *Prod* Pampa Film. 85 mins.

There is a certain imbalance between the film's two themes: the revolt of "yerba maté" collectors against their cruel treatment, and the story of an old alcoholic doctor who kills his daughter. The first theme, which probably inspired Hugo del Carril when he made *Aguas Bajan Turbias* (*q.v.*), is the better of the two and produces the film's best sequences: the hiring of the maté collectors in a saloon; their long trip up river; their cruel exploitation; the revolt; the "slave trader" beaten with a cudgel and put on a raft that is swept away by the river; the leader of the revolt hiding in the ruins of a mission. This is Soffici's best film and started the social folkloric trend in Argentina cinema.

Jorge Luis Borges wrote in 1939, "Superior to those that have been recently sent to us from California or Paris. Its vigorous script has been contaminated neither by North American prudishness (the protagonist comes from a brothel) nor by the neoprudishness of French films. A memorable moment is when the woman flees at night in the mountains. The photography is admirable."

PRISON FÄNGELSE

PRISONERS OF THE EARTH PRISIONEROS DE LA TIERRA

PRIVATE LIFE OF HENRY VIII (THE) Britain 1933. *Dir* Alexander Korda *Scen* Lajos Biro, Arthur Wimperis *Costumes* John Armstrong *Photog* Georges Périnal *Mus* Kurt Schroeder *Art Dir* Vincent Korda *Ed* Harold Young, Stephen Harrison *Cast* Charles Laughton, Merle Oberon, Elsa Lanchester, Robert Donat, Binnie Barnes, Wendy Barrie *Prod* London Films. 93 mins.

King Henry (Laughton) has Anne Boleyn (Oberon) executed and then marries Jane Seymour (Barrie), who gives him a longed-for male heir but who dies in bed while giving birth. His marriage with Anne of Cleves (Lanchester) is a fiasco and is annulled. Next is the flirtatious Katherine Howard (Barnes), who is executed for adultery, and finally, Katherine Parr, who "nurses" the no longer lustful king.

[This highly irreverent and witty portrait of a British monarch was Korda's first successful British production and the first British film to make a significant mark on the American market — even though (or perhaps because) it was condemned by the U.S. Legion of Decency. Though often described as a "spectacular" it was in fact made on the relatively low budget of £53,000 but with a rare technical polish.] Périnal's photography and Vincent Korda's luxurious sets are superb. Laughton's virtuoso performance as the roistering, gluttonous, lascivious Henry established his international reputation. According to Richard Griffith (1949), the film's success was based on its "story of a man who had six wives" and he pointed out that it had been "generally overlooked that this, the most famous and successful of British films overseas, had little that was British about it except its subject, its stars, and the fact that it was made near London. Its story, direction, photography, settings, and music were all by continentals. In an interview with Stephen Watts at the time, Korda said: 'An outsider often makes the best job of a national film. He is not cumbered with excessively detailed knowledge and associations . . . I know there are people who think it odd that a Hungarian from Hollywood should direct an English historical film but I can't see their argument' . . . The basic formula of the Private Life idea was probably derived from the Lubitsch films of the early twenties."

PROCES (LE) THE TRIAL France/Italy/German Federal Republic 1962. *Dir* Orson Welles *Scen* Orson Welles based on the novel by Franz Kafka *Photog* Edmond Richard *Art Dir* Jean Mandaroux *Mus* Jean Ledrut *Pin screen prologue* A. Alexeieff *Cast* Orson Welles, Jeanne Moreau, Anthony Perkins, Madeleine Robinson, Elsa Martinelli, Suzanne Flon, Akim Tamiroff, Romy Schneider, Arnoldo Foa, Maurice Teynac *Prod* Paris Europa/FI-C-IT/Hisa Films. 120 mins.

Welles's version of Kafka's novel (which he says in the prologue "has the logic of a dream, of a nightmare") is the only one of his films apart from *Citizen Kane* (*q.v.*) over which he has exercised complete control, including control of the editing. Even though it contains necessary transpositions and adaptations to update the action, it is entirely faithful to the novel; beyond this, it is Welles's reflections on himself and on the modern world.

Much of the action was filmed in the vast, fantastic setting of the disused Gare d'Orsay, which Welles turns into a kind of antechamber of hell. Though one could fault Tony Perkins' uncertain and often ambiguous performance as Joseph K, the film is replete with traditional Wellesian baroque images: the enormous office echoing with the sound of typewriters; K and Leni (Schneider) making love amid a sea of files and papers; Hastler's (Welles) office full of rococo furniture, files, and candles; a pseudo Gothic cathedral at night in central Europe (part of the film was shot in Zagreb); the endless corridor; the disturbed women — Hilda (Martinelli), Leni, and Miss Burstner (Moreau) — with whom K has amorous interludes; the servility of the Jew, Block (Tamiroff), toward Hastler; the dominating, ubiquitous, grotesque presence of the cruelly indifferent Hastler; K's death accompanied by an atomic explosion.

Most of the acting is unexceptionable, but in this extraordinary film the atmosphere and sets should perhaps be more important than the characters. This voyage through a 20th century hell often seems directly descended from the Méliès of *Voyage dans la lune* (*q.v.*).
— *Der Prozess/The Trial* Austria 1947. *Dir* G. W. Pabst *Scen* Rudolf Brunngraber, Kurt Heuser, Emeric Roboz based on the novel by Rudolf Brunngraber *Photog* Oskar Schnirch, Helmut Fischer-Ashley *Cast* Ewald Balser, Marianne Schönauer, Ernst Deutsch, Gustav Diessl *Prod* Hübler-Kahla for Star-Film. Pabst's first postwar film is a study of the roots of anti-Semitism based on the notorious "ritual murder" trial in Tisza-Eszlar, Hungary, in 1882. It received awards for best direction and best acting at the 1948 Venice Biennale.

PROCES DE JEANNE D'ARC THE TRIAL OF JOAN OF ARC France 1962. *Dir/Scen* Robert Bresson *Photog* L.-H. Burel *Art Dir* Pierre Charbonnier *Mus* Francis Seyrig *Ed* Germaine Artus *Cast* Florence Carrez, Jean-Claude Fourneau, and non-professionals *Prod* Agnès Delahaie. 65 mins.

Bresson's film, like Dreyer's *La Passion de Jeanne d'Arc* (*q.v.*), was based on the actual transcript of the trial and follows Joan's prolonged interrogation, her refusal to submit, and the inevitable burning at the stake. In various interviews Bresson has discussed his film: "I wanted to make a film that would re-create the visual and aural integrity of the 'trial and death of Joan of Arc' . . . The problem was that of a film entirely in questions and answers. But I was content to use the monotony like a unified background against which the nuances would be more clearly seen . . . Joan's replies to the questions put to her serve not so much to give information about present or past events as to provoke significant reactions on Joan's face, the movements of her soul . . . I see her with the eyes of a believer. I believe in the marvelous world whose doors she opens and closes . . . One might say she was a more perfect being than we are, more sensitive. She combines her five senses in a new way. She sees her voices. She convinces us of a world at the farthest reach of our faculties. She enters this supernatural world but closes the door behind her."

Though Bresson makes considerable use of close-ups of hands, feet, or objects, the film is mainly in medium close-ups of Joan and her judges with their dialogue emphasized by the cross-cutting. Much of the force of this austere film derives from the fugitive facial expressions that this approach reveals, and from the perfect tempo and sound track. See also *Passion de Jeanne d'Arc; Joan of Arc.*

PROCESI K PANENCE PILGRIMAGE TO THE VIRGIN MARY Czechoslovakia 1960. *Dir* Vojtech Jasny *Scen* Miloslav Stehlik *Photog* Jaroslav Kucera *Mus* Milos Vacek *Cast* Vaclav Lohnisky, Pavlina Filipovska, Josef Kemr, Martin Tapak *Prod* Barrandov Studios. 81 mins.

A satirical comedy showing how a group of villagers joins the traditional village procession to the local shrine in order to avoid political involvement and the various problems that are settled on the way.

The gentle satire and lyrical sense of fantasy make Jasny's film one of the best early examples of the new Czechoslovak cinema of the Sixties.

PROFESSOR HANNIBAL HANIBÁL TANÁR ÚR

PROFESSOR MAMLOCK USSR 1938 *Dir* Adolf Minkin, Herbert Rappoport *Scen*

Adolf Minkin, Friedrich Wolf, Herbert Rappoport based on the play by Friedrich Wolf *Photog* G. Filatov *Art Dir* P. Betaki *Mus* Y. Kochurov, N. Timofeyev *Cast* Sergei Mezhinsky, Olev Zhakov, E. Zharov, Nina Shaternikova, Vasili Merkuriev *Prod* Lenfilm. 105 mins. In Germany in the early Thirties, a Jewish surgeon, Professor Mamlock (Mezhinsky), believes himself immune from the Nazis because of his position and distinguished war record. He reproves his son (Zharov) for becoming a communist but is vilely persecuted because of his Jewish blood.

Though this film was directed by Rappoport, a recent German emigré who had been Pabst's assistant, it owes much more to Friedrich Wolf, who adapted the script from his own play. Wolf, a friend of Brecht, had himself suffered from Nazi persecution and his script brilliantly brings to life the bitter atmosphere of the early days of Nazi terrorism. The most famous sequence shows Mamlock, his white overall inscribed with the yellow star and the word "Jude," marching with great dignity through a crowd of Brown Shirts.

— *Professor Mamlock* German Democratic Republic 1961. *Dir* Konrad Wolf *Scen* Konrad Wolf, Karl-Georg Egel based on the play by Friedrich Wolf. 100 mins.

This remake by the son of Friedrich Wolf (who had died in 1953) is far from matching the original.

PROIE POUR L'OMBRE (LA) SHADOW OF ADULTERY/PREY FOR THE SHADOWS France 1960. *Dir/Scen* Alexandre Astruc *Photog* Marcel Grignon *Art Dir* Jacques Saulnier *Mus* Richard Cornu and J.-S. Bach's Cantata 51 *Ed* Denise Casabianca *Cast* Annie Girardot, Daniel Gélin, Christian Marquand *Prod* Marceau Cocinor. 99 mins.

For Anna (Girardot), independence is all-important. Contented in her work running an art gallery she lives in a friendly fashion with her husband (Gélin), whom she doesn't love. She meets a man (Marquand) she feels she can love and leaves her husband. But the man also seems to fail her in a small crisis and she leaves him lest she become dependent on him. She wins independence but is left alone.

Derived from an original scenario, *La Plaie et le Couteau,* written with Fran-çoise Sagan, *Shadow of Adultery* is one of Astruc's most personal films and the only one over which he has had sole control. It was shot on a relatively low budget and is far less visually elaborate than his earlier study of marriage, *Une Vie (q.v.).* Astruc has described his heroine as "a woman who feels in herself a very real need for freedom that is as much moral as social so that she sets about matching a man's work; but at the same time, because she is a woman, she feels the need to be passive, dominated, submissive." As with so many of Astruc's films, this was not as well received as it deserved.

*PSYCHO USA 1960. *Dir* Alfred Hitchcock *Scen* Joseph Stefano based on the novel by Robert Bloch *Photog* John L. Russell *Art Dir* Joseph Hurley, Robert Clatworthy *Mus* Bernard Herrmann *Ed* George Tomasini *Cast* Anthony Perkins, Vera Miles, Janet Leigh, John Gavin, Martin Balsam *Prod* Alfred Hitchcock for Paramount. 109 mins.

Marion Crane (Leigh), in love with Sam Loomis (Gavin), robs her employer in the hope that this will enable them to marry. She drives to meet Sam but, exhausted, stops at the Bates Motel just outside the town where Sam lives. Norman Bates (Perkins), the proprietor, talks to her and gives her supper. Later that night she is stabbed in the shower apparently by Norman's maniacally possessive mother. Marion's sister, Lila (Miles), and an insurance investigator, Arbogast (Balsam), arrive to investigate Marion's disappearance. Arbogast talks to Norman but is himself stabbed to death. Lila and Sam visit the motel and survive an encounter with the killer, who is revealed as Norman dressed as his mother, whom he had killed years before. *Psycho* was a relatively low-budget film, produced in black and white with the methods used for shooting television serials. However, the famous 45 second Marion Crane murder sequence alone took seven days to create. Hitchcock says that it was "made with a great sense of amusement on my part. To me it's a *fun* picture. The processes through which we take the audience, you see, it's rather like taking them through the haunted house at the fairground." Certainly *Psycho* is Hitchcock's most visually involving film and his most successful in terms of audience participation.

Even those critics unable to find profound poetry in Hitchcock's films accept this. For Robin Wood, "No film conveys — to those not afraid to expose themselves fully to it — a greater sense of desolation, yet it does so from an exceptionally mature and secure emotional viewpoint. And an essential part of this viewpoint is the detached sardonic humor. It enables the film to contemplate the ultimate horrors without hysteria."

*PUBLIC ENEMY (THE) ENEMIES OF THE PUBLIC USA 1931. *Dir* William Wellman *Scen* Harvey Thew from a story by Kubec Glasmon, John Bright *Photog* Dev Jennings *Ed* Ed McCormick *Cast* James Cagney, Jean Harlow, Edward Woods, Joan Blondell, Beryl Mercer, Donald Cook, Mae Clarke *Prod* Warner Brothers. 83 mins.

Tom Powers, a boy from a middle-class family, is excited by the lures of saloons and pool rooms and becomes a petty crook as an adolescent (Cagney). Under the guidance of a local gangster, he eventually graduates into organized robbery and the liquor racket. His progress is watched with dismay by his mother (Mercer). He becomes very successful, lives a high life with his women (Harlow, Blondell) in luxurious apartments, but in the end is killed by rival gangsters and his corpse is delivered to his mother's doorstep.

One of the most successful of the early gangster films, which, depite its overall dated air, still retains some powerful sequences: the opening pan establishing the boy's environment; the piano player "hero" teaching the boys dirty songs; the final gun battle; the corpse falling in through the opened doorway, not to mention the famous scene where Cagney pushes a grapefruit into the face of the mistress (Harlow) who is boring him. As Richard Griffith points out, "The gangster cycle, growing more harrowing with each picture, was box-office throughout the early years of the talkies . . . The Daughters of the American Revolution, the American Legion, and that greater league of women's clubs and business men's clubs . . . disliked this focusing upon 'America's shame!' They pointed out, truly enough, that audiences sentimentalized the gangster and envied his life of unrestrained violence and excitement . . . By the end of 1931 the gangster film had vanished from the screen." Cagney, who made his name with this film, revealed his earlier experience as a dancer in his superb sense of movement and gesture.

PUNTILA HERR PUNTILA UND SEIN KNECHT MATTI

PUTYOVKA V ZHIZN THE ROAD TO LIFE/ A PASS TO LIFE USSR 1931. *Dir* Nikolai Ekk *Scen* Nikolai Ekk, Alexander Stolper, R. Yanushkevich *Photog* Vasili Pronin *Art Dir* I. Stepanov, A. Yevmenenko *Mus* Y. Stolyar *Cast* Nikolai Batalov, Mikhail Zharov, I. Kyrla *Prod* Mezhrabpomfilm. 121 mins. English version 100 mins. Re-released in 1957, re-edited by Ekk with a new sound track, 98 mins.

In 1923, the Children's Commission VGIK rounds up a group of *bezprizorni* (homeless children abandoned or orphaned during the Revolution and Civil War). One gang is led by Mustafa (I. Kyrla), a Mongolian. A commission inspector, Sergeyev (Batalov), proposes to the gang that they establish their own commune. Eventually they learn trades and Sergeyev suggests they build a railroad. When it is completed, Mustafa is killed by Zhigan (Zharov), their former leader who has tried to regain Mustafa's confidence.

The film is directly based on the methods used by Makarenko, the author of *A Pedagogical Poem* (1935). In an introduction V. J. Katchalov (Professor John Dewey in the American version) describes the social reasons for the homelessness of thousands of children and the methods used to rehabilitate these victims of war, famine, and revolution. In 1931 the problem had still not been entirely eradicated and the opening sequence showing the band of children in the streets of Moscow is quasi-documentary.

Famous sequences: the teacher setting out alone with the wild boys without any guards; his techniques for developing confidence and encouraging them to work; Zhigan trying to regain his influence by forming his own gang; Mustafa's death; his body being carried back to the camp on the front of the locomotive.

This effective exposition of social case work was the first success of the Soviet sound cinema. However the dialogue plays little part in a film whose style is derived from the montage approaches of Eisenstein and Pudovkin. Ivan Kyrla gives a remarkable performance as the Mongolian leader, and himself seems to have been an abandoned child. Nikolai Ekk, whose background was partially in the theater, never again directed a film to match this.

— *Pedagogicheskaya Poema/A Pedagogical Poem/Road to Life USSR 1955. Dir I. Manevich, M. Mayevskaya Scen I. Manevich, A. Maslyukov based on the book by Anton Makarenko Photog I. Shecker Art Dir M. Lipkin Cast V. Yomelyanov, M. Prokotilo, Y. Litskanovich, N. Krashkovskaya Prod Kiev. 108 mins. Sovcolor.
A new version based directly on the book about his experiences that Makarenko wrote in 1935. It is one of the dullest Soviet films of the Fifties, stuffed full of speeches and sermonizing.

— *Wild Boys of the Road/Dangerous Days USA 1933. Dir William Wellman Scen Daniel Ahearn, Earl Baldwin Cast Frankie Darro, Dorothy Coonan, Edwin Phillips, Rochelle Hudson. 77 mins. With much the same theme as the Russian film, this Wellman version is perhaps the most hard-hitting of his "social" films of the early Thirties and is unjustly neglected.

PYGMALION Britain 1938. Dir Anthony Asquith, Leslie Howard Scen Cecil Lewis, W. P. Lipscomb, Anthony Asquith, Ian Dalrymple based on the play by George Bernard Shaw Photog Harry Stradling Art Dir Laurence Irving Mus Arthur Honegger Ed David Lean Cast Wendy Hiller, Leslie Howard, Wilfrid Lawson, Scott Sunderland, Marie Lohr, Jean Cadell, Esme Percy Prod Gabriel Pascal. 96 mins.
Based on Shaw's famous play about a professor (Howard) who teaches a Cockney flower seller (Hiller) to speak educated English and become a lady and who ends up falling in love with his own creation.
An intelligent, satisfying, and tasteful adaptation with an excellent cast. Leslie Howard's skillful performance as Professor Higgins is surpassed only by Wendy Hiller's superb creation of Eliza Doolittle. Wilfrid Lawson is delightful in the comic role of Eliza's father. The play was later adapted as a Broadway musical and, when filmed in 1964 as My Fair Lady (q.v.), all copies of this film

were withdrawn from distribution. However, contrary to rumor, these and the negative were not destroyed by Warner Brothers.

— Pygmalion Germany 1935. Dir Erich Engel Scen Heinrich Orberländer, Walter Wassermann based on Shaw's play Photog Bruno Mondi Cast Jenny Jugo, Gustaf Gründgens, Anton Edthofer, Eugen Klöpfer. 2,561 meters.
[This first version upset Shaw and he wrote that the producers "had spent huge sums in altering it out of all recognition. They spoiled every effect, falsified all the characters." Copyright problems prevent public screenings of this version but those who have seen it have praised the acting, sets, and costumes.]

— Pygmalion Netherlands 1937. Dir Ludwig Berger Scen Ludwig Berger based on Shaw's play Cast Lily Bouwmeester, Johann de Meester, Mattieu van Eijsden.
[This version by a German and Hollywood director also departed from the original dialogue and staging and also infuriated Shaw. But it was commercially successful and for a time encouraged Dutch hopes for a flourishing feature film industry.]

— *Pygmalion USSR 1958. Dir S. Alexeyev Cast M. Tsarev, K. Royek.

PYSHKA BOULE DE SUIF USSR 1934. Dir Mikhail Romm Scen Mikhail Romm based on the Maupassant story Photog Boris Volchok Art Dir Isaac Shpinel, P. Beitner Mus Chulaky Cast Galina Sergeyeva, Anatoli Goryunov, Andrei Fait, Faina Ranevskaya Prod Mosfilm. 1,893 meters. (6,300 ft. approx.) Re-released in a sound version in 1958, 65 mins.
Mikhail Romm's silent version of the first Maupassant story to appear in print is also his first feature and the best adaptation from Maupassant ever made. Romm added a love story between a servant and a Prussian soldier to the main theme, but the whole reveals a brilliant feeling for characterization, for the French ambience, and for human relationships. The film is almost entirely in close-ups and the editing is excellent but the numerous scenes in the coach have too much of a studio feel about them.

— Boule de suif/Angel and Sinner France 1945. Dir Christian-Jaque Scen Henri Jeanson, Louis d'Hélo based on Boule de suif and Mam'zelle Fifi by Maupassant *Photog* Christian Matras *Art Dir* Léon Barsacq, Clavel *Cast* Micheline Presle, Louis Salou, Alfred Adam, Berthe Bovy, Suzet Maïs, Roger Carel *Prod* Artis. 105 mins. (84 mins. North America).

The script is an adaptation of both *Boule de suif* and *Mam'zelle Fifi* and cleverly suggests a World War II parallel in the setting of the Franco-Prussian War of 1870. It is a well-made film with some superb landscape photography by Matras. Jeanson's dialogue, however, is too glossy. Micheline Presle and Louis Salou give good performances.

— *Mademoiselle Fifi* USA 1944. *Dir* Robert Wise *Scen* Josef Mischel, Peter Ruric based on Maupassant's *Boule de suif* and *Mam'zelle Fifi Photog* Harry Wild *Art Dir* Albert D'Agostini, Walter E. Keller *Cast* Simone Simon, John Emery, Kurt Kreuger, Alan Napier, Helen Freeman, Jason Robards *Prod* RKO. 69 mins.

Robert Wise's second feature (nestling curiously between *The Curse of the Cat People* (*q.v.*) and *The Body Snatchers* is also an amalgamation of *Boule de suif* and *Mam'zelle Fifi*. Less well known than it deserves, it, too, offers a parallel with World War II that is in many ways more biting than Christian-Jaque's glossy version. It has a very satisfying performance by Simone Simon.

QUAI DES BRUMES PORT OF SHADOWS
France 1938. *Dir* Marcel Carné *Scen*
Jacques Prévert based on the novel by
Pierre Mac Orlan *Photog* Eugène Schüf-
tan (Schüfftan) assisted by Louis Page,
Marc Fossard, Henri Alekan, Philippe
Agostini *Art Dir* Alexandre Trauner
Mus Maurice Jaubert *Ed* René Le He-
naff *Cast* Jean Gabin, Michèle Morgan,
Michel Simon, Pierre Brasseur, Robert
Le Vigan, Aimos, Delmont *Prod* Rabin-
ovitch. 89 mins.

In a busy port, a deserter from the Colonial Army, Jean (Gabin), meets a
young orphan girl, Nelly (Morgan), and
her villainous guardian, Zabel (Simon).
The girl and the soldier fall in love. The
soldier mixes with the underworld and
Lucien (Brasseur), the leader of a local
band of crooks tries to force his attentions on Nelly. Jean kills Zabel when
he attacks Nelly and tries to escape by
ship, but Lucien kills him and the ship
leaves the harbor.

The original novel is used very freely
as a basis for Prévert's script and is set
in Le Havre in 1938 rather than Montmartre in 1912. As in *Pépé le Moko*
(*q.v.*), a man is trapped in a town where
he meets his true love but is killed before
he can escape on a boat with her. Unity
of space, time, and action give the film
a classical finish and suggest the influence of *Kammerspiel*. Fate, of course,
is present – in the shape of the painter
(Le Vigan) and the tramp (Aimos) –
and this and the evil of the other characters prevent the lovers from reaching
the ship, the symbol of an unknown and
impossible "elsewhere."

The center of the action, an underworld
bistro, suggests less Les Lapin Agile of
1912 than Les Deux Magots and other
Parisian cafés frequented by artists in
the mid-Thirties. Roger Leenhardt wrote
in 1936: "The Prévertian spirit can be
best defined by Les Deux Magots, the
headquarters of heretical communists,
film makers who refuse to yield to commercial pressures, and dissident surrealists. This charming café is one of the
places where the mind is set free."
Carné's direction is masterful, not only
in his handling of the actors, but in the
visual suggestiveness he obtains from
Schuftan's images and from Trauner's
perfect settings. Jean Gabin and Michèle
Morgan (working together for the first
time) convey a real warmth of love that
is rare in Carné's work.

The film expresses so clearly (though
unconsciously) the pessimistic mood of
France before the 1940 debacle that
Vichy spokesmen claimed, "If we have
lost the war it is because of *Quai des
brumes.*" Carné replied that one can't
blame a storm on the barometer and
that one of the aims of a film maker
should be to be the barometer of his
times. It was because this film was a
"sign of the times" that it was admired
around the world. Its theme has been
so often imitated that it has become
trite.

QUAI DES ORFEVRES JENNY LAMOUR
France 1947. *Dir* H.-G. Clouzot *Scen*
H.-G. Clouzot, Jean Ferry based on the
novel *Légitime Défense* by Stanislas-An-
dré Steeman *Photog* Armand Thirard
Art Dir Max Douy *Mus* Francis Lopez
Cast Bernard Blier, Louis Jouvet, Suzy
Delair, Perre Larquey, Charles Dullin,
Simone Rennant *Prod* Majestic. 105
mins.

Maurice (Blier) and Jenny (Delair) are
married music hall artists, but Maurice is jealous and Jenny ambitious.
When Jenny goes to the house of the
lecherous head of a film company (Dullin) who has offered her a job, Maurice
rushes off to kill him but finds him al-

ready dead. Dora (Rennant), a friend of Jenny's, persuades Maurice that Jenny was responsible but the murder is eventually solved by Chief Inspector Antoine (Jouvet).

This thriller is saved from banality by a clever sense of character and suspense that is often worthy of Hitchcock.

QUATRE CENTS COUPS (LES) THE FOUR HUNDRED BLOWS France 1959. *Dir* François Truffaut *Scen* François Truffaut, Marcel Moussy *Photog* Henri Decaë *Art Dir* Bernard Evein *Mus* Jean Constantin *Ed* Marie-Josèphe Yoyotte *Cast* Jean-Pierre Léaud, Claire Maurier, Albert Rémy, Guy Decomble, Patrick Auffay *Prod* Films du Carosse/SEDIF. 94 mins. Dyaliscope.

Antoine Doinel (Léaud), a twelve-year-old schoolboy, lives at home in an atmosphere of indifference, falsehood, and quarrels between his father (Rémy) and mother (Maurier) and suffers ignorance and punishment from his teacher (Decomble) at school. He and his friend René (Auffay) play truant and later Antoine hides out at René's home. They steal a typewriter but can't sell it and Antoine is caught trying to return it. He is sent to an observation camp for juvenile delinquents but escapes and reaches the sea.

This story of young adolescence is largely autobiographical, being based on Truffaut's own childhood and experiences in a reform school. Notable sequences: the opening, credit title sequence exploring the Eiffel Tower neighborhood, the family's life in their apartment in a poor quarter of Paris; the truant wandering through the streets; the amusement park; the theft of a typewriter; Antoine's conversations with his teacher; his trip in the Black Maria to the police station; his interview with a psychologist in the observation camp; his escape across country to the sea; the final frozen close-up of Antoine's face.

This warm and personal film, made with limited finances, is the then 27-year-old Truffaut's first feature. It was shot entirely in locations and superbly captures the moods of the city that surround the boy. Its lyrically realistic and totally unsentimental portrait of adolescence has never been matched in the cinema. *Les Quatre Cents Coups* was a world-wide success, encouraging other producers to support young inexperienced directors and helping to establish the French *new wave*.

QUATRE NUITS D'UN REVEUR see NOTTI BIANCHE (LE)

QUATTRO PASSI FRA LE NUVOLE FOUR STEPS IN THE CLOUDS Italy 1942. *Dir* Alessandro Blasetti *Scen* Cesare Zavattini, Giuseppe Amato, Piero Tellini, Aldo de Benedetti *Photog* Vaclav Vich *Art Dir* Virgilio Marchi *Mus* Alessandro Cicognini *Cast* Gino Cervi, Adriana Benetti, Giuditta Rissone, U. Sacripante *Prod* Cines Amato. 90 mins.

A young married salesman, Paolo (Cervi), meets a young and pretty girl, Maria (Benetti), on a bus. She is pregnant but had been deserted by the man she loved. She persuades Paolo to go with her to her parent's farm and pretend to her father (Sacripante) that he is her husband. He does so, hoping to leave in a few hours. But he becomes so lost in his surroundings that he spends the night. Maria's parents discover the truth, but under Paolo's eloquent pleading, forgive her and Paolo returns to his wife and children.

Largely due to Zavattini, this film and the far better *Ossessione* (*q.v.*) laid the foundations of Italian neorealism. Its theme was derived from Hollywood comedies of the Thirties and the idea of the meeting on a bus probably came from *It Happened One Night* (*q.v.*). Its fresh humor, realistic characters, and unsentimental sentiment were like nothing seen before and its portrait of everyday Italian life was extraordinary under a regime concerned only with making "the trains run on time." However, the sequences on the farm are not up to the rest of the film.

Carlo Lizzani described it as "a return to the real world and to everyday life. The man in the street, for too long obliged to dress himself for parades, could find himself again in the commercial traveler and in the modest streets and suburbs where the action took place. Its absorbing story of daily life offered a welcome contrast to the official face of the war."

— *Sous le ciel de Provence/The Virtuous Bigamist/Era di Venerdi 17* Italy/France 1957. *Dir* Mario Soldati *Scen* as original version *Photog* Nicolas Hayer *Cast* Fernandel, Alberto Sordi, Giulia Rubini. 90 mins. Eastman Color.

A routine Fernandel comedy that is totally unlike the original, despite making use of the original script.

QUEEN BESS, HER LOVE STORY AMOURS DE LA REINE ELISABETH (LES)

QUEEN ELIZABETH AMOURS DE LA REINE ELISABETH (LES)

QUEEN KELLY USA 1928. *Dir/Scen* Erich von Stroheim *Assist* Eddy Sowders, Louis Germonprez *Photog* Gordon Pollock, Paul Ivano, Ben Reynolds *Art Dir* Harry Miles *Mus* Adolf Tandler *Cast* Gloria Swanson, Walter Byron, Seena Owen, Sidney Bracey, William von Brincken *Prod* Joseph Kennedy for United Artists. Release version, 10 reels. [The release version (see below) of *Queen Kelly* is only the prologue to a story intended to be largely set in Africa. The following is Stroheim's own synopsis of the plot: "The life history of a young girl, Kitty Kelly (Swanson), brought up in a convent school in one of the Duodec States of Imperial Germany . . . The cousin (Byron) of the Queen (Owen), the beloved enfant terrible, "Wild Wolfram" — and the Queen's fiancée — is punished by her for one of his escapades with some extra duty with his escadron of cuirassiers outside of the little capital where he encounters the convent girls herded by their nuns. As the girls curtsey before the Prince one girl's panties fall to the ground. They are Kitty Kelly's. He laughs, to the dismay of the girl, who, in her anger, throws her pants into the Prince's face. He keeps them as a souvenir. He falls madly in love with her. He kidnaps her from the convent and brings her to his apartment in the palace, where he is surprised by his cousin, the queen. She puts him under arrest and whips the girl out of the palace. After an unsuccessful attempt at suicide, Kitty is brought back to the convent where a cable awaits her. It is from her aunt in Dar-es-Salam in German East Africa, who has paid for her niece's education and who suffered a stroke. Kitty is shipped to Africa. On her arrival she finds that her aunt is the proprietor of a saloon-bawdy house. At the death bed of her aunt, she is married to an old but very rich degenerate and inherits the establishment. After the death of her aunt she declines to live with her husband but takes charge of the house. On account of her regal ways and carriage everybody nicknames her 'Queen Kelly.' The Prince had been sentenced to Custodia Honesta and on his return from the fortress finds out the whereabouts of Kitty. He has himself transferred into the Imperial German Schutztruppe in Africa. He meets Kelly in her saloon but finds that she is married. After harrowing experiences during which the husband dies, he marries Kitty. The Queen, meanwhile, has been assassinated and he is recalled to ascend the throne. He refuses to come unless his wife, a commoner, would be accepted as Queen. She is accepted and Kitty now really becomes 'Queen Kelly,' residing in the palace from which she had been forcibly ejected."

In the late Twenties Gloria Swanson decided to produce her own films; her financial backer was Joseph Kennedy, later American Ambassador to London, whose son was to become President of the USA. Stroheim was commissioned to write and direct *Queen Kelly* and the script was passed by the Hays Office. According to Gloria Swanson, "(Stroheim) agreed to stick to this, which he did for a while. But then we got to the scene in the brothel — well, in the script it was dance hall, but Stroheim had other ideas, and proceeded to spend a fortune — of my money — shooting stuff he knew perfectly well would never get into the finished picture . . . this was sheer waste and enraged me, so we halted the picture to see what could be done. By that time sound was coming in, and we had shot only the first third of the film, so while we were considering what to do I made very quickly with the English director Edmund Goulding a talkie, *The Trespasser*, and then somehow *Queen Kelly* just stayed on the shelf. Finally I myself directed a sort of patched-up last scene (the Prince discovers Kelly's drowned corpse and kills himself) to tie up the story and it was shown a little in Europe and South America, in places where they didn't yet have talking apparatus and that was that. A year or two before his death Stroheim and I talked about it and wondered if we couldn't do something with it, but neither of us had time." Stroheim disowned Swanson's release version but said, "Any stories of friction between myself and Gloria Swanson were entirely fictitious." However, he justifiably complained that the editing

301

was atrocious: scenes he had intended to run three feet ran twenty feet in the release version in order to pad out the film.

In 1964 an additional twenty minute fragment came to light. This shows Kelly and the rich aunt in the brothel in Africa with a bespectacled Negro priest giving the last sacrament as whores snigger; and also Kelly's marriage, with a mosquito net for a veil, to the old degenerate.]

Despite its mutilation *Queen Kelly* is perhaps Stroheim's most perfect work if not his richest. Striking sequences: the Queen's champagne bath in a fantastic bath tub; the convent girls; the Prince's arrival; Kelly's panties falling around her feet; the jealous Queen in fur-trimmed, black velvet negligee whipping Kelly out of the palace.

QUE VIVA MEXICO! Mexico 1931–32. *Dir/ Scen* Sergei M. Eisenstein in collaboration with Grigori Alexandrov *Photog* Eduard Tisse *Cast* nonprofessionals from various parts of Mexico *Prod* Upton Sinclair. Unfinished film for which some 285,000 ft. (about 50 hours) of negative were shot.

[As envisaged by Eisenstein, the film was to be "four novels framed by prologue and epilogue, unified in conception and spirit, creating its entity." The six sections were to have been: "Prologue," set in Yucatan, is designed to establish the link between past and present. "Fiesta," set in pre-1910 Mexico under the dictatorship of Diaz, depicts a romance of Spanish-influenced colonial life. "Sandunga," set in Tehuantepec, is a story of the Mexican Indian uncontaminated by alien cultures. "Maguey," also set in pre-1910 Mexico, is a story of the Mexican inheritance of the colonial peonage. "La Soldadera," set in the Mexican Revolution of 1910–16, is a story of those who made the Revolution. "Epilogue," set in modern Mexico, shows the carnival pageant of Death Day. Each of the four central stories concerns the love of a man and a woman.]

In October 1930, Paramount rejected Eisenstein's various proposals for film projects. On November 24, 1930, he signed a contract with the novelist Upton Sinclair and various other investors (including the Gillette razor company) under the name, "The Mexican Picture Trust," to shoot a film in Mexico. None

of the three Russians was to receive a salary for his work. By the end of 1931, they had shot some 285,000 feet of film, including the "Prologue," "Fiesta," "Maguey," "Sandunga" and the "Epilogue." Sinclair, meanwhile, became restive at the apparently unending flow of film, and a series of misunderstandings developed between him and Eisenstein (an account of this is given in Marie Seton's biography of Eisenstein). On January 15, 1932, as Eisenstein was preparing to film "La Soldadera" with government help and a large crowd of extras, Sinclair ordered Eisenstein to stop shooting. All the footage had been sent to Hollywood for processing because of lack of laboratories in Mexico. Eisenstein was refused a USA visa to edit his film in Hollywood and since his contract with Sinclair did no give him control over the editing, the footage was legally as well as physically in Sinclair's hands. In March, 1932, the three Russians were given a visa to cross the United States and, in New York, before he left for the USSR, Eisenstein saw the rushes of his film for the first time. After protracted negotiations, Sinclair finally agreed to send the negative to Moscow for Eisenstein to edit. Alexandrov remained in New York until June to ensure the material was shipped, but after Alexandrov left Sinclair cabled for it to be returned from Hamburg to the United States. He then made an agreement with Sol Lesser to produce a film from the rushes. Eisenstein was not involved in the editing of any of the following films, all of which use material from his unfinished masterpiece.

— *Thunder over Mexico* USA 1933. *Ed* Harry Chandlee *Mus* Hugo Riesenfeld *Prod* Sol Lesser. 69 mins.

Sol Lesser drew his material largely from what Eisenstein had shot for the "Maguey" episode and loosely based his film on Eisenstein's scenario. In a feudal hacienda about 1900, Sebastian, a young peon who is betrothed to Maria, sees her raped by a drunken guest. Unable to get justice, he plans revenge and becomes a rebel. With three friends he tries to rescue Maria, but all three are captured, buried in the ground up to their necks, and trampled to death by horses. Despite its terrible music, and editing that is clearly not Eisenstein's, there are many memorable sequences: the peons waiting in the courtyard of the hacienda; the love scene in the field of cacti (Maguey); the party in the hacienda and the rape; Sebastian's flight and the final "crucifixion" of the three naked Christ-like figures.

— *Death Day* USA 1933. *Prod* Sol Lesser. 2 reels.

Derived from fragments Eisenstein had intended for the Epilogue in which abysmal music and commentary are set against some extraordinary images.

— **Eisenstein in Mexico* USA 1933. *Prod* Sol Lesser. 2 reels.

Bits from the footage, together with stills and some film of Eisenstein at work.

— **Time in the Sun* USA 1930. *Ed* Marie Seton with Paul Burnford *Prod* Marie Seton. 56 mins.

After corresponding with Eisenstein, Seton was given access to all the footage not previously used. From this she tried to reconstruct Eisenstein's conception, whose connecting theme, in her words, "was that of the eternal circle — the idea of the passing of one life and the birth of the next . . . I took the memory of what he had told me and attempted to reconstruct his dream in order that it might not be entirely lost." The film certainly had a wide critical success. The photography is impressive — especially in the final sequences showing the Indians attitude to death — but the construction is uneven and episodic and is surely only a pale shadow of what might have been.

Marie Seton attempted to purchase the rest of the footage from Sinclair, but lacked funds. In 1941, Upton Sinclair made arrangements with Bell and Howell of Chicago to prepare (*Ed* William F. Kruse) six educational films about Mexico: *Mexico Marches; Conquering Cross; Idol of Hope; Land and Freedom; Spaniard and Indian; Zapotec Village*. The first five of these were sometimes shown together as a feature under the title *Mexico Symphony*. In the mid-Fifties, Sinclair donated all the remaining nitrate negative to the Museum of Modern Art Department of Film.

— *Eisenstein's Mexican Film: Episodes for Study* USA 1958. Compiled and annotated by Jay Leyda. 255 mins.

Jay Leyda, a former student of Eisenstein, reconstituted the original rushes as they came from the camera without trying to convey the final form they might have taken. Each take appears in its original, unedited sequence. It includes material from the "Prologue,"

"Sandunga," "Fiesta," and "Maguey." The result gives an astonishing insight into the mind of a great artist.

QUIET MAN (THE) USA 1952. *Dir* John Ford *Scen* Frank S. Nugent based on a story by Maurice Walsh *Photog* Winton C. Hoch, Archie Stout *Art Dir* Frank Hotaling *Mus* Victor Young *Cast* John Wayne, Maureen O'Hara, Barry Fitzgerald, Victor McLaglen, Francis Ford, Ward Bond *Prod* Argosy for Republic. 129 mins. Technicolor.

Sean Thornton (Wayne), an American boxer, returns to his native Ireland to forget a fight in which he killed an opponent. He incurs the wrath of the neighboring squire, Red Will Danaher (McLaglen), and falls in love with Danaher's sister, Mary Kate (O'Hara). After the intervention of the local priest (Fitzgerald), Danaher consents to the marriage but refuses to part with his sister's dowry. Sean refuses to fight Danaher for the dowry until he learns his wife and the village are beginning to despise him as a coward. The fight, a marathon affair with everyone involved, ends in the pub with Sean victorious.

John Ford's first return to Ireland since *The Informer* (*q.v.*) was one of his most commercially successful postwar films, though not his best. It is too full of gay 'blarney' and picturesque characters — among whom is Barry Fitzgerald's stage Irish priest. [There are however some beautifully observed scenes, notably the delightful formal courtship and the village steeplechase. Ford's vision of a fairy-tale Ireland may not be realistic but it is as affectionate as his vision of the West.]

QUIET ONE (THE) USA 1948. *Dir* Sidney Meyers *Scen/Ed* Sidney Meyers, Helen Levitt, Janice Loeb *Photog* Richard Bagley *Commentary* James Agee *Mus* Ulysses Kay *Cast* Donald Thompson, Sadie Stockton, Clarence Cooper, Estelle Evans *Prod* Film Documents. 67 mins. Produced in 16 mm.

The story is presented in the form of a case history of a Negro boy, Donald Peters (Thompson), who lives in Harlem with his grandmother. Rejected by his mother and stepfather, he becomes lonely and miserable, and commits acts of delinquency that lead to his detention at the Wiltwyck School. There, with psychiatric help he takes the first steps back from the emotional solitude to which his family's instability has condemned him.

This is the first feature from the New York school, made by Sidney Meyers on 16 mm for $20,000. It received theatrical release and earned more than its investment. It reveals a powerful and sensitive vision of the cluttered streets and poor apartments of Harlem and its theme is disturbingly relevant. Donald Thompson is engaging as the boy, though the most significant moments of his "performance" owe more to Meyers' editing.

QUO VADIS? The only famous novel (1896) by the Nobel Prize-winning Polish author, Henryk Sienkiewicz, has been filmed three times.

— Italy 1912. *Dir* Enrico Guazzoni *Scen* Enrico Guazzoni based on the novel by Henryk Sienkiewicz *Cast* Amleto Novelli, Gustavo Serena, Lea Gunghi, Amelia Cattaneo, Bruto Castellani, Giovanni Gizzi, Leo Orlandini *Mus* (USA) Frank Byng *Prod* Cinès. 7,800 ft.

This first Italian spectacular was an enormous world-wide success and earned its producers ten to twenty times their investment of the then considerable half a million liras. The sculptor, Rodin, hailed it as "a masterpiece." The acting was especially praised, particularly Gustavo Serena as the wily Petronius and Bruto Castellani as the athletic Ursus. Castellani was even congratulated on his exploits by King George V of England. A chariot race, a fire, gladiators in the circus, and Christians thrown to the lions, were star attractions. This *Quo Vadis?* was successfully re-released many times (the latest in the the USA in 1919–20), encouraged the production of "feature length" films, and in the ensuing years was often imitated.

— Italy/Germany 1924. *Dir* Georg Jacoby, Gabriellino d'Annunzio *Photog* Kurt Courant, Giovanni Vitrotti, Alfredo Donelli *Cast* Emil Jannings, Elena Sangro, Andrea Habay, Bruto Castellani, Lilian Hall-Davis, Gino Viotti *Prod* U.C.I. 7,500 ft.

This Italian-German coproduction (shot in Rome) was an almost total commercial failure.

— USA 1951. *Dir* Mervyn LeRoy *Scen* John Lee Mahin, S. N. Behrman, Sonya Levien based on the novel by Henryk Sienkiewicz *Photog* Robert Surtees, William V. Skall *Art Dir* William A. Horning, Cedric Gibbons, Edward Carfagno *Mus* Miklos Rosza *Ed* Ralph Winters *Cast* Robert Taylor, Deborah Kerr, Leo Genn, Peter Ustinov, Felix Aylmer, Finlay Currie *Prod* MGM. 171 mins. Technicolor.

This spectacular cost $8.5 million and was two years in production at the Cinecittà Studios in Rome. Its enormous sets, chariot races, spectacular fire, and a sea of extras are more forgettable than Peter Ustinov's brilliant performance as an effeminate Nero.

RADUGA THE RAINBOW USSR 1944. *Dir* Mark Donskoy *Scen* Wanda Wasilewska based on her own novel *Photog* Bentsion Monastirsky *Art Dir* V. Khmelyova *Mus* Lev Schwartz *Ed* Gorbenko *Cast* Natalia Uzhvi, Nina Alisova, Yelena Tyapkina, Hans Klering *Prod* Kiev/Ashkhabad Studios. 95 mins.

The story of a Ukrainian village occupied by the Nazis; neither savage brutalities nor promises of better treatment pacify the villagers or subdue their hatred for their conquerors.

This faithful adaptation of a novel that won the Stalin Prize does not hide cowardice and in fact shows one of the village women (Alisova) prostituting herself to the German Commandant (Klering). The central character is a partisan girl (Uzhvi) who leaves the woods to have her baby in the village, is captured, tortured, and finally forced to walk barefoot in the snow to her death. Another harrowing scene shows children trampling on their father's secret grave in order to fool the Nazis. Donskoy said that it was "as an artist in soldier's uniform that I made my films on the strength, beauty, and intelligence of Soviet men and women fighting Nazism." *The Rainbow* is one of his best films: more perfect, though perhaps less rich, than his *Gorki* trilogy (*q.v.*).

RAICES ROOTS Mexico 1954. *Dir* Benito Alazraki *Scen* Carlos Velo, Manuel Barbachano Ponce, J. M. Garcia Ascott, F. Espeyo based on four short novels by Francisco Rojas *Photog* Hans Beimler, Walter Reuter *Art Dir* Fernando Gamboa *Mus* Silvestro Revueltas, Rodolfo Halfter, and others *Ed* Luis Sobreyra, Miguel Campos *Cast* Olimpia Alazraki, Doctor Gonzalez, Juan Hernandez, Miguel Negron, Antonia Hernandez, Alicia Del Lago, Carlos Robles Gil, Teodulo Gonzalez *Prod* Manuel Barbachano Ponce. 105 mins. approx. Released in the English version with only three episodes ("The Beast" deleted), 78 mins.

Four episodes: 1. "Our Lady" — A woman anthropologist (Alazraki) goes to a remote village to observe the "natives" and concludes they are savages when they seemingly fail to respond to reproductions of great paintings. When she returns, the village is hostile: they believe she has come to take back her reproduction of the Mona Lisa which they have hung over the altar in the church. 2. "The One-Eyed Boy" — A small boy (Negron), blind in one eye, is taken by his mother (A. Hernandez) on a pilgrimage to a religious shrine where he is injured and loses the sight of his remaining eye. His mother finds comfort in this "miracle" because he will now encounter pity instead of cruelty. 3. "The Filly" — An archeologist (Gil) becomes obsessed with a village girl (Del Lago) but is rejected. He tries to buy her from her father (T. Gonzalez), who agrees if the archeologist will sell him his own wife. 4. "The Beast" — An Indian sells his wife as a wet nurse. This episode film offers a striking portrait of contemporary Mexican Indian life and avoids the extravagant pictorial style of many previous Mexican films. "The One-Eyed Boy," with its combination of cruelty and sentiment is a perfect filmic short story. In "The Filly," the panting archeologist's pursuit of the Indian girl is naively overdone, but "The Beast" has a memorable and pointed sequence in which a luxurious car, its radio blaring, drives past a crowd of Indians with bare feet. "Our Lady" is less successful but has an amusing moment when the Indians, having taken the Mona Lisa as an icon, baptize their child Velo because of a bicycle. From this it might seem that the Spanish film maker Carlos Velo and the producer Barbachano Ponce who co-authored the script are mainly responsible for the film's success.

RAIL (THE) SCHERBEN

RAIN REGEN

RAINBOW (THE) RADUGA

RAINBOW DANCE Britain 1936. *Dir/Ed* Len Lye *Sound* Jack Elliott *Mus* Ricco's Orchestra *Prod* GPO Film Unit. 4 mins. Gasparcolor.
This abstract film (like Lye's *Color Box,* 1935), in which all the colors of the rainbow "dance" to jazz music, is not derived from the earlier German abstract musical films but was made from drawing and painting that Lye did directly on the film. Norman McLaren took up and developed this new technique in such films as *Love on the Wing,* 1937 and *Dollar Dance,* 1943.

RASHOMON IN THE WOODS Japan 1950. *Dir/Ed* Akira Kurosawa *Scen* Shinobu Hashimono based on a story by Ryonosuke Akutagawa *Photog* Kazuo Matsuyama *Mus* Takashi Matsuyama *Cast* Toshiro Mifune, Machiko Kyo, Masayuki Mori, Takashi Shimura, Minoru Chiaki, Kichijiro Ueda *Prod* Daiei. 88 mins.
In a period of civil war and famine in medieval Japan, a woodcutter (Shimura), a priest (Chiaki), and a servant (Ueda) take shelter from the rain under the ruined Rasho gateway to the city of Kyoto and the woodcutter describes a recent event that disturbs him. A bandit (Mifune) was captured and confessed to the murder of a nobleman (Mori) and the rape of his wife. He admits that he lured the nobleman away, tied him up, and then attacked the wife, who succumbed to his attentions. Later he killed the nobleman in a duel fought at the wife's request. The wife's story is that the bandit tied up her husband, raped her, and left. She released her husband, then fainted, and when she recovered the dagger was in his breast. The dead nobleman, through a medium, said that, after the attack, the wife begged the bandit to kill her husband, but he refused. The wife had run away and the nobleman killed himself. Finally the woodcutter admits having seen the attack. According to him, the husband refused to risk his life for a worthless woman and had to be goaded into a duel in which he was killed. And the woodcutter stole the dagger. At the end, the three men discover an abandoned baby under the gate and the woodcutter agrees to take it.
This powerful drama was the first Japanese film to have a wide impact in the West. It was selected as the Japanese entry for the Venice Festival (by the then head of Unitalia Film) and received the Golden Lion. Kurosawa was astonished and said he would have preferred the award to have gone to "a film reflecting contemporary Japanese life." Though its appeal in the West rested largely on its fascinating exoticism, it is not without contemporary allusions. Its four contradictory stories helped end the "samurai" stereotype: the bandit, the nobleman, and his wife are revealed as cowardly, untruthful and vicious in the final story of the woodcutter. In the epilogue, the action of the woodcutter, an ordinary man terrified of the three in the wood, restores a faith in humanity.
Each of the episodes has its own particular style but at the same time is dominated by the conflicts in the forest. The somewhat westernized music is based on Ravel's *Bolero.* The acting, particularly that of Machiko Kyo and Toshiro Mifune, is excellent.
— *The Outrage* USA 1964. *Dir* Martin Ritt *Scen* Michael Kanin based on the play by Michael and Fay Kanin based on Kurosawa's film *Photog* James Wong Howe *Mus* Alex North *Cast* Paul Newman, Claire Bloom, Laurence Harvey, Edward G. Robinson, Howard Da Silva, William Shatner. 96 mins. Panavision.
This remake is absolutely faithful to the original plot line except that it is set in the American West at the end of the nineteenth century. It is also a complete disaster, unconvincing and melodramatic.

RAVEN (THE) CORBEAU (LE)

RAVEN'S END KVARTERET KORPEN

RAYON INVISIBLE (LE) PARIS QUI DORT

REBEL WITHOUT A CAUSE USA 1955. *Dir* Nicholas Ray *Scen* Stewart Stern, Irving Shulman based on a story by Nicholas Ray *Photog* Ernest Haller *Art Dir* Malcolm Bert *Mus* Leonard Rosenman *Ed*

William Ziegler *Cast* James Dean, Jim Backus, Natalie Wood, Ann Doran, Rochelle Hudson, William Hopper, Dennis Hopper, Corey Allen *Prod* Warner Brothers. 111 mins. Warnercolor. CinemaScope.

Jim (Dean), the adolescent son of a weak father (Backus) and domineering mother (Doran), is involved in acts of violence and gets in trouble with the police. At school he is attracted to Judy (Wood), a girl unbalanced by her father's (William Hopper) sudden withdrawal of affection, while Plato (Mineo), the son of divorced parents, is drawn to him. Jim quarrels with Judy's boyfriend, Buzz (Allen), and, after an inconclusive knife fight, they meet in an "endurance test" in which Buzz accidentally dies. Jim's parents object to his going to the police and Buzz's gang threaten to beat him up. Jim and Judy flee to a deserted house in the hills and are joined by Plato. When Buzz's gang arrives Plato shoots one of them and is himself shot as the police arrive. As a result the parents of Jim and Judy reach a new understanding of their problems. Notable sequences: Jim's aproned father dominated by his wife; the "chicken run" involving driving a car as near as possible to the edge of a cliff before jumping out; Jim's parents' reaction after the accident; the three adolescents exploring the deserted house; the dénouement. *Rebel Without a Cause* is dominated by its character study of Jim. The late James Dean's moving portrayal of a tormented adolescent was a reflection of his own character and his blue jeans and T-shirt became the standard dress of other "rebels without a cause" during the late Fifties. This remarkable study of disturbed youth, ironic, tender, and understanding, is certainly one of Nicholas Ray's most personal films.

RECORD OF A LIVING BEING IKIMONO NO KIROKU

RED BADGE OF COURAGE (THE) USA 1951. *Dir* John Huston *Scen* John Huston, Albert Band based on the novel by Stephen Crane *Photog* Harold Rosson *Art Dir* Cedric Gibbons, Hans Peters *Mus* Bronislau Kaper *Ed* Ben Lewis *Cast* Audie Murphy, Bill Mauldin, Royal Dano, Andy Devine, John Dierkes, Douglas Dick *Prod* MGM. 69 mins.

During the last days of the American Civil War, a young northern recruit's (Murphy) second experience of battle confirms his own fears of cowardice and he runs away. Behind the lines he joins a line of retreating soldiers and strikes up a friendship with the Tattered Soldier (Dano). Together they helplessly watch the agonizing death of the Tall Soldier (Dierkes), who had been the recruit's confidant. On his way to his unit, the recruit is hit by a soldier hurrying from the front. This wound, his "red badge of courage," resolves his personal doubts. Having come to terms with death he leads his unit in a heroic and victorious charge.

The theme of Stephen Crane's novel is fear, or perhaps better, the fear of fear. [Huston considered it his dream project and put all his energies into it. But from the beginning Huston and his sympathetic producer Gottfried Reinhardt had to face one obstacle after another erected by the MGM "front office." (These events are wryly chronicled by Lillian Ross in *Picture*.) A million dollars were cut from the budget just as shooting began and, to save money, the battle scenes were filmed in the San Fernando Valley on Huston's own ranch. The entire production was completed in only 47 days. Even after shooting was completed, MGM intervened: important scenes were omitted, others transposed, and action sequences extended.]

Despite this, *The Red Badge of Courage* remains one of Huston's best films. André Bazin wrote, "This is not a lyrically pessimistic film; its conclusion is rather a positive stoicism, an active scepticism that is not devoid of humor. Its emphasis is on interior development. This is not psychological but *romanesque:* not a spectacle but a narrative wedded to a critical intelligence."

RED BALLOON (THE) BALLON ROUGE (LE)

RED BEARD AKA HIGE

RED DESERT (THE) DESERTO ROSSO (IL)

RED INN (THE) AUBERGE ROUGE (L')

REDES (LOS) THE WAVE Mexico 1935. *Dir* Fred Zinnemann, Emilio Gomez Muriel *Scen* Paul Strand, Velasquez Chavez, Henwar Rodakiewicz *Photog* Paul Strand *Mus* Silvestre Revueltas based on Mexican folk themes *Ed* Gunther von Fritsch

Cast (all nonprofessionals) Silvio Hernandez, Miguel Figueroa, Antonio Lara, David Valles Gonzales, and the fishermen of Alvarado *Prod* Paul Strand, Carlos Chavez for the Secretariat of Education of the Mexican Government. 63 mins.

A semidocumentary set in the village of Alvarado on the Gulf of Vera Cruz that depicts a fisherman's strike against exploiters who paid them seven cents an hour during the depression years.

In 1933, the New York photographer, Paul Strand, was invited by Velasquez Chavez, the Secretary of Culture in the then left-wing Mexican government, to submit a proposal for the development of the Mexican sound cinema. Paul Strand wrote: "We assume that these films are being made for the great majority of rather simple people to whom elementary facts should be presented in a direct and unequivocal way, a way that might be boring to more complicated sensibilities — though we believe otherwise." This, the first of an uncompleted series of films on Mexican life, was based on a draft script, *Pescados,* by Velasquez Chavez himself. It was adapted by Paul Strand who drew much from the stories of the people of Alvarado and who took a series of photographs in order that he might reflect accurately the way of life and the fishing techniques of the people. It was shot silent and was later synchronized in Mexico City. The actors, all nonprofessionals, were directed according to methods that were later those of Italian neorealism. Production took ten months.

Paul Strand photographed the film himself and, as producer, supervised the editing. Fred Zinnemann, then a young film maker who had left Germany to escape fascism, was responsible for the direction of the actors. His experience on *Menschen am Sonntag* (*q.v.*) probably stood him in good stead. The Mexican, Emilio Gomez Muriel, credited as co-director, was in fact the first assistant director.

The film's simple and moving story has a visual dynamism that makes it one of the most esthetically satisfying Mexican films of its period. It is also one of the first successes of the New York school of the Thirties, which was strongly influenced by Paul Strand. The social content and visual style of *The Wave* had considerable influence on the Mexican

cinema over the ensuing decade, much more so than Eisenstein's unfinished *Que Viva Mexico!* (*q.v.*). In many ways it is similar to *La Terra Trema* (*q.v.*) even though it is impossible to claim that it influenced Visconti.

RED SHOES (THE) Britain 1948. *Dir* Michael Powell, Emeric Pressburger *Scen* Emeric Pressburger, Michael Powell, Keith Winter based on the story by Hans Christian Andersen *Photog* Jack Cardiff *Art Dir* Hein Heckroth *Mus* Brian Easdale *Choreog* Robert Helpmann *Cast* Moira Shearer, Anton Walbrook, Marius Goring, Leonide Massine, Robert Helpmann, Ludmilla Tcherina *Prod* Archers. 136 mins. Technicolor.

A young dancer, Vicky Page (Shearer), joins the famous Lermontov Company, whose director (Walbrook) demands complete dedication. She reaches fame in the "Red Shoes" ballet, dancing to music by Julian Craster (Goring). She is torn between her love for Julian and devotion to the ballet and its jealous master. Their three lives are shaken by a torment that is echoed in the story of their new ballet. As does the character in the fairy story, Vicky dances herself to death.

The backstage story of the world of ballet is basically used to introduce a series of dance numbers in which Massine and Helpmann are superb and Shearer appealing. This is one of the first successful attempts at a difficult genre. [Apart from the dancing, Jack Cardiff's brilliantly evocative color photography is the most memorable aspect of the film; the story now seems even more ponderous than it did on its release and Anton Walbrook's mannered performance as the impresario is extremely dated.]

REGEN RAIN Netherlands 1929. *Dir/Scen* Joris Ivens, Mannus Franken *Photog/ Ed* Joris Ivens *Assist Photog* Chang Fai *Prod* CAPI. 1 reel. (*Mus,* for 1932 sound version, Lou Lichtveld).

A film poem depicting the moods and visual patterns produced by a rain shower in Amsterdam. It was made in four months with limited resources by two young founders of an Amsterdam film society, Filmliga, and was photographed entirely with a hand-held camera. It is one of the last great silent films and uses no titles. According to Ivens, the main job of his assistant, a young Chinese sailor, "was to hold an umbrella over my camera." Salzman wrote, "Each drop of rain revealed a smile. They had unconsciously filmed in moments when everything that moved in the town was smiling, not brightly but tenderly."

REGLE DU JEU (LA) THE RULES OF THE GAME France 1939. *Dir* Jean Renoir *Scen* Jean Renoir, Carl Koch *Assist Dir* Carl Koch, André Zwoboda, Henri Cartier-Bresson *Photog* Jean Bachelet, Alain Renoir, Alphen *Art Dir* Eugène Lourié, Max Douy *Mus* Joseph Kosma, Roger Désormières based on Mozart, Monsigny, Saint-Saëns *Ed* Marguerite Renoir *Cast* Marcel Dalio, Nora Grégor, Jean Renoir, Roland Toutain, Mila Parély, Julien Carette, Gaston Modot, Paulette Dubost, Pierre Magnier, Eddy Debray, Pierre Nay, Lise Elina, André Zwoboda *Prod* La Nouvelle Edition Francaise. 113 mins. Released generally in 80, 85, and 90 mins. versions.

The rich Marquis Robert de la Cheyniest (Dalio) organizes a weekend house party at his country chateau that is attended by his mistress, Geneviève (Parély), Octave (Renoir), and André Jurieux (Toutain), a pilot and the lover of the Marquis' wife, Christine (Grégor). After a hunt, the complicated love intrigues among the high society guests are mirrored by parallel activities among the servants. The gamekeeper, Schumacher (Modot), is jealous of his wife, Lisette (Dubost), and, after a comic chase sequence during a fancy dress ball, sets out to hunt his wife's lover with a gun but ends up shooting the pilot.

Famous sequences: the employment of a poacher, Marceau (Carette), as a domestic; the arrival of the guests at the chateau; the hunted animals being forced out into the open by the beaters and shot by the waiting hunters; the fancy-dress ball like a *danse macabre;* Schumacher hunting his wife's lover.

Jean Renoir has said that the germinal idea of *La Règle du jeu* — that honest sincerity is rare and catastrophic in a world where everyone "has his reasons" — occurred to him during the filming of *La Grande Illusion* (*q.v.*). After completing *La Bete humaine* (*q.v.*), Renoir and a group of his friends decided to form their own production company (La Nouvelle Edition Francaise). Re-

noir's declared ambition for the company's first film, *La Règle de jeu,* was "to make a *drame gai."* The first draft of the script was several pages long and was vaguely inspired by Musset's *Les Caprices de Marianne.* By 1939 many recognized that Europe was approaching disaster and Renoir has said that he hoped his film would do for France at that time what Beaumarchais's *The Marriage of Figaro* had done for France on the eve of the Revolution: "I knew the evils that were gnawing at my contemporaries . . . The very knowledge that the danger existed gave me my basic situations and my comrades seemed to react to it in the same way I did."

[Shooting began in the Sologne on February 15, 1939; interiors were shot later in the Joinville studios in Paris. Renoir developed a schematic scenario much of which was reworked during shooting as the actors improvised certain scenes. By the time the film was completed in July 1939, bad weather and casting problems had increased its costs to five million francs, double its original budget, and had necessitated a loan from Gaumont. At the first screening for members of the N.E.F. it ran for 113 minutes. Gaumont insisted it was too long and, after protesting, Renoir finally agreed to cut 13 minutes. It was premiered on July 7, 1939, at the Colisée and Aubert-Palace Cinemas in this 100 minute version. The audience didn't appreciate what Renoir called "an exact depiction of the bourgeois of our time" and the premiere was an unmitigated disaster. The appearance of a Jew (Dalio) and an Austrian (Grégor) in the cast allowed French anti-Semites and ultra-nationalists to condemn the film as evidence of the corruption of France. Others felt that French society was being dragged through the mud; others that it was morally decadent or incomprehensible. The first showing provoked a riot and successive showings brought hisses and boos. Five days after the premiere, the film was cut again, bringing its running time to about 85 minutes. These cuts gave a different meaning to the end of the film. The film ran only three weeks and was then withdrawn. In October, 1939, it was banned by the military censors as "demoralizing." Later the ban was lifted, but with the Nazi occupation the ban was reimposed for the duration of the war. In 1942, Allied bombs destroyed the negative of the complete version of the film. In 1956, two film enthusiasts Jean Gaborit and Jacques Maréchal established a distribution company and acquired the rights to *La Règle du jeu*. They discovered that there were in existence some 200 cans of film, soundtrack, positive and negative, all relating to *La Règle du jeu*. After months of painstaking effort they were finally able to re-create the complete, integral version of the film. Only one short scene (about a minute) is missing — a conversation between Octave and Jurieux before the hunt. Since its re-release many critics have concluded that this satirical anatomy of polite society, with its mixture of farce and bitterness, is Renoir's masterpiece. In 1962 and 1972, it was classed among the Ten Greatest Films of All Time in an international poll of film critics.]

REIMEI IZEN BEFORE DAWN Japan 1931. *Dir* Teinosuke Kinugasa *Prod* Shochiku Kinema.
According to Anderson and Richie, this film "was a period drama about women sold into prostitution, their misery and, eventually, their revolt. " If it is true that parts of this film are included in the fragments preserved by the Cinémathèque Française under the title *Nippon* then its photography is beautiful (such as the close-up of a sword in movement) and its editing original. It also contains a lively polemic against samurais and priests.

REISE NACH TILSIT (DIE) see SUNRISE

REKAVA THE LINE OF DESTINY Ceylon 1957. *Dir/Scen* J. Lester Peries *Photog* William Blake *Mus* Sunil Santha Dayaratne *Ed* Titus de Silva *Cast* (nonprofessionals) Dharma Pryia, Myrthle Pernando. 97 mins.
In a small village in Ceylon, a young boy is told by a minstrel he will be a great healer. On his first try, his playmate recovers his sight, but his next patient dies. The village blames him for the current drought and for all the misfortunes of the village until the rains finally bring peace.
This first film by Lester Peries is an affectionate and sympathetic chronicle of Sinhalese life and customs and an attack on the evils of superstition. It is the best film ever made in Ceylon. Un-

fortunately, when it was shown at the Cannes Festival it did not win a prize. However this may be because it was screened on Friday the 13th during a lunar eclipse!

REMORQUES STORMY WATERS France 1941 (production began 1939). *Dir* Jean Grémillon *Scen* Jacques Prévert, André Cayatte based on the novel by Roger Vercel *Assist* Louis Daquin *Photog* Armand Thirard, Louis Née *Art Dir* Alexandre Trauner *Mus* Roland-Manuel *Ed* Louisette Hautecoeur *Cast* Jean Gabin, Michèle Morgan, Madeleine Renaud, F. Ledoux, R. Blavette *Prod* M.A.I.C. 80 mins.
Captain Laurent (Gabin), master of a tugboat, is married to an invalid wife (Renaud) whom he sees at rare intervals. His real love is the sea, until he rescues a woman (Morgan) during a storm and falls in love with her. The wife falls seriously ill and Captain Laurent goes to her bedside. She dies contented he has always loved her.
Grémillon had intended to include what he felt was an essential documentary sequence of a storm. The shooting of this was scheduled for the end of September 1939, but the outbreak of war prevented it. Early in 1940 a few substitute scenes were shot in order to complete the film. Nevertheless, it remains a remarkable, beautifully photographed film. Memorable sequences: a walk along a deserted beach; the little tugboat battling the waves; the wedding celebration interrupted by an S.O.S.

RENDEZ-VOUS DE JUILLET France 1949. *Dir* Jacques Becker *Scen* Jacques Becker, Maurice Griffe *Photog* Claude Renoir *Art Dir* Robert-Jules Garnier *Mus* Jean Wiener, Mezz Mezzrow *Ed* Marguerite Renoir *Cast* Daniel Gélin, Maurice Ronet, Pierre Trabaud, Bernard Lajarrige, Nicole Courcel, Brigitte Auber, Louis Seigner, Claude Luter orchestra *Prod* U.G.C./S.N.E.G. 112 mins. English version (Britain), 68 mins.
A study of a group of young people in postwar Paris, their love affairs, ambitions, and family conflicts, Lucien (Gélin) wants to make a film in the Congo and, at the end, leaves Paris and his girl friend (Courcel), an aspiring actress. Though not comparable to the later *Casque d'or* (q.v.), this is a sympathetic and stylistic portrait of the in-

habitants of St.-Germain-des-Prés and the Latin Quarter, perfectly set within its period.

*REPULSION Britain 1965. *Dir* Roman Polanski *Scen* Roman Polanski, Gerard Brach *Photog* Gilbert Taylor *Art Dir* Seamus Flannery *Mus* Chico Hamilton *Ed* Alistair McIntyre *Cast* Catherine Deneuve, Yvonne Furneaux, John Fraser, Ian Hendry, Patrick Wymark *Prod* Compton/Tekli. 104 mins.

Carol (Deneuve) shares an apartment with her sister, Helen (Furneaux), but seems obsessed by the frequent presence of Helen's lover, Michael (Hendry), and is cold and indifferent to her own boyfriend, Colin (Fraser). When Helen and Michael go on holiday, Carol suffers from hallucinations, is fired from her job as a manicurist, and locks herself up in the apartment. When the landlord (Wymark) calls for the rent, he makes advances to her and she kills him with Michael's razor. When Helen and Michael return they find her lying inert on the floor.

Polanski's first English language feature is a *grand guignol* study of madness in a girl repelled by sex. Though the dialogue is stilted, Polanski's creation of atmosphere, hallucination, and Carol's increasing sense of isolation is superb. Memorable sequences: the opening close-up of an eyeball; the women in the beauty parlor gossiping about men; Carol overhearing the excited moans of her sister making love; Carol walking, unseeing, past a road accident; Carol's delusions of rape as she imagines solid plaster turning into a clawing hand and the walls cracking apart; the final scene as Michael carries Carol down to the waiting ambulance. Catherine Deneuve is perfect as the jealously sadistic schizophrenic.

*RESCUED BY ROVER Britain 1905. *Dir* Cecil M. Hepworth (?), Lewin Fitzhamon *Scen* Mrs. C. M. Hepworth *Cast* Cecil M. Hepworth, Mrs. C. M. Hepworth, Barbara Hepworth, Mabel Clarke, Sebastian Smith, Mrs. Sebastian Smith *Prod* Hepworth, 416 ft.

A child (Barbara Hepworth) is stolen from her carriage in the park by a beggar woman (Mrs. Smith). Rover, the dog, discovers where the child is hidden, fetches the father (Hepworth), and the child is returned to her mother (Mrs. Hepworth).

Cecil Hepworth was one of the pioneers of the British cinema and this is perhaps his most famous film. It was shot in the lanes and streets around the Hepworth home in Walton-on-Thames, had a script by Hepworth's wife, and involved the whole Hepworth family (including the eight-month-old daughter and the pet dog) in the cast, as well as two professional actors, Mr. and Mrs. Sebastian Smith. The total cost was under £8 ($25) and the film was so popular it had to be remade twice because the negatives wore out.

RETURN OF MAXIM (THE) see YUNOST MAKSIMA

RETURN OF VASILI BORTNIKOV (THE) VOZ-VRASHCHENIE VASILIYA BORTNIKOVA

RIDEAU CRAMOISI (LE) THE CRIMSON CURTAIN France 1952. *Dir* Alexandre Astruc *Scen* Alexandre Astruc based on the short novel by Barbey d'Aurevilly *Photog* Eugène Schuftan (Schüfftan) *Art Dir* Mayo *Mus* Jean-Jacques Grunenwald *Ed* Jean Mitry *Cast* Jean-Claude Pascal, Anouk Aimée, Jim Gérald, Marguerite Garcia, narration by Yves Furet *Prod* Argos Films/Como Films. 44 mins.

In the early 19th century, a young neophyte officer (Pascal) is billeted at the home of a dull, bourgeois couple (Gérald, Garcia) whose daughter, Albertine (Aimée), returns home after completing convent school. She makes bold advances to him, then bewilders him by ignoring him. When he is desperate with longing, she comes to his bedroom. One night she dies in his arms and the soldier leaves the house.

[This is the first film by the then 28-year-old Alexandre Astruc, apart from two 16 mm shorts. It is based on a Romantic *nouvelle* by Barbey d'Aurevilly which is presented in the form of a long conversation between the story teller and a hoary old officer who recalls his extraordinary adventure as a young man.] Astruc has said: "I made my film as a visual illustration of a literary text whose intrinsic style I tried to retain. The visual and the verbal develop in complement, without one duplicating the other, in an attempt to re-create the atmosphere and retain the flow of this Barbey tale whose inexorable development towards death makes it more than a strange love story, almost a tragedy. I tried to retain its 'indirect' style, half-way between memory and dream, confession and story." In order to create the sound track "we found it necessary to entirely rewrite the film, to develop a second *mise en scène* in which the narration, natural sounds, and music played as great a role as the lighting or the acting."

Le Rideau cramoisi is striking and stylish; in it, Astruc makes more use of the dramatic setting of the interior of the house (the ornate dining room, the complex iron stairways, the mirrors) than of the actors. Anouk Aimée as the silent Albertine is moving and more convincing than Jean-Claude Pascal as the overly handsome cavalry officer. It enjoyed considerable success, won several prizes and helped pave the way for the future *nouvelle vague*.

*RIDE THE HIGH COUNTRY GUNS IN THE AFTERNOON USA 1961. *Dir* Sam Peckinpah *Scen* N. B. Stone, Jr. *Photog* Lucien Ballard *Art Dir* George W. Davis, Leroy Coleman *Mus* George Bassman *Ed* Frank Santillo *Cast* Randolph Scott, Joe McCrea, Ronald Starr, Mariette Hartley, James Drury *Prod* MGM. 94 mins. Metrocolor. CinemaScope.

A once-respected lawman, Steve Judd (McCrea), accepts the job of transporting gold from a remote mining camp. Assisting him are Gil Westrum (Scott), another forgotten lawman turned carnival sharpshooter, and his young assistant, Heck (Starr), who secretly plan to hijack the gold. En route, they are joined by Elsa (Hartley), the daughter of a religious zealot running away to the mining camp to join her boyfriend, Billy (Drury). When they arrive, Elsa marries Billy but, after a riotous brawl, she refuses to stay with him and leaves with Steve, Gil, and Heck, who have collected Billy and his brothers, Gil and Heck (who loves Elsa) attempt to steal the gold. But in a gunfight with the pursuing Billy and his brothers, Gil and Heck prove their worth. Steve is also mortally wounded, but before he dies Gil promises him that he will deliver the gold.

This first feature by a former director of TV westerns (*The Westerner*), Sam Peckinpah, is unpretentious, intelligent, droll, and full of quiet charm. Its theme — the waning of the old West — and its heroes — tough but aging vestiges of the old days — are ones Peckinpah was to

make his own and that appear in their most complete form in his masterpiece, *The Wild Bunch* (*q.v.*). Peckinpah lovingly reflects the beauty of the landscapes, obtains performances from Scott and McCrea that are among their best, and creates some of his most memorable scenes: the saloon wedding (beautifully tinted); the race between a horse and a camel; the reminiscent dialogue between Scott and McCrea; a moronic gunman firing in wild fury at a flock of chickens; McCrea's death.

RIFIFI DU RIFIFI CHEZ LES HOMMES

RIFIFI SPELLS TROUBLE DU RIFIFI CHEZ LES HOMMES

RIFLEMEN (THE) CARABINIERS (LES)

RINK (THE) USA 1916. *Dir/Scen* Charles Chaplin *Photog* Rollie Totheroh, William C. Foster *Cast* Chaplin, Edna Purviance, Eric Campbell, James T. Kelley, Albert Austin, Henry Bergman, John Rand, Charlotte Mineau, Lloyd Bacon *Prod* Mutual. 1,830 ft.

Charlie, a waiter, spends his lunch hour in a roller-skating rink, where he saves a girl (Purviance) from the flirtatious Mr. Stout (Campbell), knocking the big man and others off their feet. Later, at a skating party, he creates havoc but escapes by hooking his cane to an automobile. It is a film full of agile and graceful movements and precise editing, which Delluc described as "a ballet."

RIO BRAVO USA 1959. *Dir* Howard Hawks *Scen* Jules Furthman, Leigh Brackett based on a short story by B. H. McCampbell *Photog* Russell Harlan *Art Dir* Leo K. Kuter *Mus* Dimitri Tiomkin *Ed* Folmer Blangsted *Cast* John Wayne, Dean Martin, Ricky Nelson, Walter Brennan, Ward Bond, Angie Dickinson, Claude Akins, John Russell *Prod* Armada for Warner Bros. 141 mins. Technicolor.

Sheriff John Chance (Wayne) arrests Joe Burdette (Akins), a murderer, but the town is blockaded by Joe's brother, Nathan (Russell), who wants to rescue him before the arrival of the state marshal. The Sheriff's only supporters are an old cripple, Stumpy (Brennan), a self-pitying drunk, Dude (Martin), and a wagonmaster (Bond), who is murdered by one of the gang. Dude tracks down the killer but is captured by the gang. To save him, the sheriff agrees to hand over Joe but during the exchange, a gunfight breaks out, started by the Sheriff's love (Dickinson), and the gang is finally forced to surrender.

Francis Lacassin describes this as "a classically refined Western." For Luc Moullet, "Hawks, who not so long ago gave little evidence of support for the fallen individual and rarely suggested that redemption was possible, is now particularly concerned with this rebirth of man, the best theme of *Rio Bravo*."

RIO ESCONDIDO HIDDEN RIVER Mexico 1948. *Dir* Emilio Fernandez *Scen* Emilio Fernandez, M. Magdaleno *Photog* Gabriel Figueroa *Art Dir* M. Parra *Mus* Francisco Dominguez *Cast* Maria Felix, Carlos Lopez-Moctezuma, Fernando Fernandez *Prod* Raoul de Anda. 90 mins.
A young girl (Felix) goes as a teacher to a small, isolated village dominated by a cruel tyrant (Lopez-Moctezuma). She contends with him and an epidemic while educating the Indian peasants and ends by killing him. After being thanked by the president she herself dies of a heart attack.
Though the reference to a president (who was in fact corrupt) is propaganda, this film has considerable charm and beauty and shows, without pretentious "folklore," the poverty of the Mexican countryside.

RIO, QUARENTA GRAUS (40°) RIO, FORTY DEGREES (40°) Brazil 1955. *Dir* Nelson Pereira dos Santos *Scen* Arnaldo de Farias *Photog* Helio Silva *Art Dir* J. Romito, A. Samailoff *Mus* Radamès Gnatalli *Cast* José Valadào, G. Rocha, Modesto de Souza. 90 mins. approx.
One Sunday in the life of the Brazilian metropolis, involving various stories and characters, and showing a football match, samba schools, and the shabby slums of the "favelas."
An extremely interesting film, full of the sense of real life, by a young Brazilian director. His later *Rio, Zona Norte* (1957) is not as good (though its theme is similar) but includes a fine performance by an excellent black actor, Grande Otello.

RIPTIDE UNE SI JOLIE PETITE PLAGE

RISO AMARO BITTER RICE Italy 1949. *Dir* Giuseppe De Santis *Scen* Carlo Lizzani,

Carlo Musso, Gianni Puccini, Corrado Alvaro, Ivo Perelli, Giuseppe De Santis *Photog* Otello Martelli *Mus* Goffredo Petrassi *Ed* Gabriele Barriale *Cast* Raf Vallone, Silvana Mangano, Vittorio Gassman, Doris Dowling *Prod* Lux. 108 mins.
Walter (Gassman), a thief, and his girl (Dowling) are obliged to hide in the rice fields of the northern Po Valley. There he meets Silvana (Mangano), a rice girl addicted to cheap luxury and strong men, who tries to steal his loot. Walter tries to flood the rice fields and, after a violent gun battle in an abattoir with Mario (Vallone), Silvana leaps to her suicide.
Using a deliberately melodramatic and lurid plot, the young director, De Santis, set out to reveal life in the rice fields, in which Italian girls worked every year under appalling conditions. He developed two effective characters in major roles: Mario, a recently demobilized sergeant, generous, chivalrous and full of hate for war and the police; and Silvana, a passionate rice worker who adores "fumetti" (strip cartoons) and Hollywood films and who works in the mud up to her knees while her head is lost in dreams. She was for De Santis "typical of unaware youth, incapable of understanding their condition or changing it because they are diverted towards a synthetic life that condemns them to self-destruction." However, this attack on the "americanization of culture" is too often overstressed.
Bitter Rice was a great commercial success (exceeding even that of *Paisa* and *Sciuscia* in the USA) and made Silvana Mangano and Raf Vallone famous.

RIVER (THE) USA 1929. *Dir* Frank Borzage *Scen* Philip Klein, Dwight Cummings based on a story by Tristram Tupper *Photog* Ernest Palmer *Ed* Barney Wolf *Cast* Charles Farrell, Mary Duncan, Ivan Lenow, Margaret Mann, Alfred Sabato *Prod* Fox. 7,814 ft. Released in silent and sound versions.
In a forest beside a river, a forester (Farrell) meets a woman (Duncan) and falls in love with her.
Famous sequences: the man ferociously felling trees in frustrated passion; the woman warming her naked and chilled body.
The version of this film released in France (almost certainly re-edited as was usual) was extremely successful and

made Borzage's name as a romantic director.

*RIVER (THE) USA 1937. *Dir/Scen/Ed* Pare Lorentz *Photog* Willard van Dyke, Stacey Woodward, Floyd Crosby *Mus* Virgil Thomson *Commentary* Thomas Chalmers *Prod* Farm Security Administration, U.S. Government. 30 mins.

This famous documentary by Pare Lorentz, "a tragedy of land twice impoverished," depicted the Mississippi flood problem and the work of rehabilitating the land and lives of the people in the Mississippi basin. It focused on the development of the TVA. Superbly photographed, with memorable music and a free-verse commentary, it is undoubtedly a masterpiece of the American documentary and has had considerable influence on many subsequent films.

RIVER (THE) India 1951. *Dir* Jean Renoir *Scen* Rumer Godden, Jean Renoir based on the novel by Rumer Godden *Assist* Satyajit Ray *Photog* Claude Renoir *Art Dir* Eugène Lourié *Mus* M. A. Partha Sarathy *Ed* George Gale *Cast* Nora Swinburne, Esmond Knight, Arthur Shields, Thomas E. Breen, Patricia Walters, Adrienne Corri, Suprova Mukerjee, Radha *Prod* Oriental-International for United Artists. 97 mins. Technicolor.

Harriet (Walters), the daughter of an English couple (Knight, Swinburne) living in Bengal, falls romantically in love with Captain John (Breen), an American ex-soldier. Her two best friends — Valerie (Corri) and Melanie (Radha), an Anglo-Indian — are her rivals. Harriet's brother is killed by a snake and she discovers Valerie in Captain John's arms. She tries to commit suicide but is rescued and consoled. Captain John leaves.

This is not a film about India but an episode in the life of a small English community living on the banks of the Ganges as seen through the eyes of an awkward, fourteen-year-old girl. But Renoir does convey a constant sense of the Indian scene with the river flowing eternally on in the background. The acting is largely undistinguished but Radha dances enchantingly and Claude Renoir's color camerawork (including a superb camera movement around a gigantic tree) is striking.

RIVER FLOWS EAST IN THE SPRING (THE) China 1948. *Dir* Tsai Tsou-sen, Chen Chun-ly *Cast* Tao Ching, Pai Yang, Sou Shou Won, Wou Ying, Chan Wan-Yuen-tsou, Yen Koun Sang. 2 parts. 3–4 hours approx.

In Shanghai in 1934, a teacher (Tao Ching) marries a working girl (Pai Yang). When the Japanese invade in 1937, he joins the army, is taken prisoner, escapes, and joins Choung-King. While his wife and son suffer the hardships of occupation in Shanghai, he allows himself to be corrupted by his mistress (Sou Shou Won) and the black market in the provisional capital. When he returns to liberated Shanghai his behavior disgusts both his son, who had become a newspaper boy, and his wife, who finally kills herself.

This important work, with its peripatetic plot (somewhat similar to *Les Misérables*) contrasts the life of the people with that of the corrupt Kuomintang officials during the war and includes many moving sequences on the hardships of the occupation, with its deportation camps, hangings, and escapes through flooded rice fields. Curiously enough, it was produced while the Kuomintang regime was still in power; censorship was severe but officials could easily be bribed. It was a tremendous success throughout China and Southeast Asia because it depicted the sufferings endured by many millions of men, women, and children. In Shanghai the public lined up from midnight for the 2 P.M. performance and sometimes were so impatient that they broke down the doors.

ROAD (THE) STRADA (LA)

ROAD A YEAR LONG (THE) CESTA DUGA GODINU DANA

ROAD TO ETERNITY NINGEN NO JOKEN (PART II)

ROAD TO GLORY (THE) see CROIX DE BOIS

ROAD TO HEAVEN (THE) HIMLASPELET

ROAD TO HOPE (THE) CAMMINO DELLA SPERANZA (IL)

ROAD TO LIFE PUTYOVKA V ZHIZN

ROARING TIMBER COME AND GET IT

*ROBBER SYMPHONY (THE) Britain 1936. *Dir* Friedrich Feher *Scen* Friedrich Feher, Anton Kuh, Jack Trendall *Photog* Eugen Schüfftan *Art Dir* Ernö Metzner *Mus* Friedrich Feher *Cast* Vinette (Françoise Rosay in French version), Hans Feher, Magda Sonja, George Graves, Jim Gérald, Tela Tchai, Webster Booth, Alexandre Rigneault *Prod* Concordia. 136 mins. (Original length); existing versions 104 mins. Produced in English and French versions (*La Symphonie des Brigands*).

A stolen sum of money is hidden in a small boy's (Hans Feher) piano organ by a gang of robbers led by their chief (Rigneault). The boy's mother (Sonja) is arrested in error as one of the gang. To recover the gold, the gang pursues the boy, his piano organ, and donkey through the countryside of fields and snowy mountains, but in the end they are discovered and arrested.

Produced in England by an international group of artists and technicians, this musical burlesque fantasy is one of the most eccentric films in cinema history. It opens with an overture played by an orchestra wearing false moustaches and bowler hats and develops a series of exhilarating comic scenes combined by the pervasive presence of a series of musical motifs and by a deliberately rhythmic cutting tempo. Speech is reduced to a minimum; even the donkey has a syncopated bray and the dog's bark is in rhythm. Its extraordinary sense of anarchy comedy and satire recall the Marx Brothers while its dark undercurrents are reminiscent of the German films of the Twenties.

Friedrich Feher played Francis in *The Cabinet of Dr. Caligari* (*q.v.*) and later directed *Mary Stuart* and *Le Loup Garou* in Germany. After completing *The Robber Symphony* he left for the United States where he apparently disappeared from public view. *The Robber Symphony* is much admired in Europe but is almost totally unknown in Britain and North America.

ROBE (THE) USA 1953. *Dir* Henry Koster *Scen* Philip Dunne, Gina Kaus based on the novel by Lloyd C. Douglas *Photog* Leon Shamroy *Art Dir* Lyle Wheeler, George W. Davis, *Mus* Alfred Newman *Ed* Barbara McLean *Cast* Richard Burton, Jean Simmons, Victor Mature, Michael Rennie, Jay Robinson, Dean Jagger, Richard Boone, Dawn Addams *Prod* 20th Century-Fox. 134 mins. Technicolor. CinemaScope.

Marcellus (Burton), a Roman officer, is ordered to Jerusalem as a punishment for differing with Caligula (Robinson), commands the execution party at Christ's crucifixion, and gives Christ's robe to his slave, Demetrius (Mature). Diana (Simmons), who loves Marcellus, intercedes for him and he is ordered home. But he is in a state of melancholy and believes the robe has bewitched him. Sent back to Palestine, he meets Demetrius and Peter and is converted to Christianity. When Demetrius is captured and tortured in Rome, Marcellus leads a rescue but is himself captured. When he refuses to recant his faith, he and Diana face martyrdom.

This mediocre Biblical spectacular merits attention only as the first feature made in CinemaScope and stereophonic sound. In the USA alone it earned more than 19 million dollars.

ROBIN HOOD USA 1922. *Dir* Allan Dwan *Scen* Elton Thomas (Douglas Fairbanks) *Photog* Arthur Edeson *Art Dir* Wilfred Buckland, Irvin J. Martin *Cast* Douglas Fairbanks, Wallace Beery, Alan Hale, Enid Bennett, Sam De Grass, Paul Dickey, Willard Louis *Prod* Fairbanks for United Artists, 11,250 ft.

Fairbanks' version of the legend of Sherwood Forest is his best spectacular. It has an elaborate plot, colossal sets (in shots from the top of the castle the extras seem like ants) and, especially in the second half, is full of some of Fairbanks' most exciting athletic feats.

[Robin Hood is one of the screen's favorite characters and had appeared in five films before Fairbanks' version. By far the most exhilarating of the Robin Hood films that followed this version is the 1938 production.]

— **The Adventures of Robin Hood* USA 1938. *Dir* Michael Curtiz, William Keighley *Scen* Norman Reilly Raine, Seton Miller *Photog* Sol Polito, Tony Gaudio, W. Howard Green *Art Dir* Carl Jules Weyl *Cast* Errol Flynn, Olivia De Havilland, Claude Rains, Basil Rathbone, Alan Hale, Eugene Pallette *Prod* Warner Brothers. 105 mins. Technicolor.

Splendid color, sets, and action whose appeal has not diminished with time.

Alan Hale plays Little John as he did in Fairbanks' film.

Other versions include: *Bandit of Sherwood Forest*, USA 1946; *Prince of Thieves*, USA 1948; *Tales of Robin Hood*, USA 1952; *The Story of Robin Hood and His Merrie Men*, Britain 1952; *Sword of Sherwood Forest*, Britain 1961 (with Richard Greene, who had also appeared in the 165 episodes of the Robin Hood TV series); *A Challenge for Robin Hood*, USA 1967.

ROCCO E I SUOI FRATELLI ROCCO AND HIS BROTHERS Italy/France 1960. *Dir* Luchino Visconti *Scen* Luchino Visconti, Vasco Pratolini, Suso Cecchi D'Amico, Pasquale Festa Campanile, Massimo Franciosa, Enrico Medioli inspired by the novel *Il Ponte della Ghisolfa* by Giovanni Testori *Photog* Giuseppe Rotunno *Art Dir* Mario Garbuglia *Mus* Nino Rota *Ed* Mario Serandrei *Cast* Alain Delon, Annie Girardot, Renato Salvatori, Katina Paxinou, Roger Hanin, Spiros Focas, Suzy Delair, Claudia Cardinale, Paola Stoppa, Max Cartier *Prod* Titanus/Films Marceau. 180 mins.

The film is made up of five episodes and is spread over half-a-dozen years. Each episode concentrates on one of five peasant brothers who, with their widowed mother, Rosaria (Paxinou), migrate to industrial Milan from poverty-stricken Southern Italy.

Vincenzo (Focas) is already living in Milan and is engaged to Ginetta (Cardinale) when his mother and four brothers arrive. They move into the dark basement of a lower-class apartment block in the suburbs of the city. A snowfall allows them to earn a little money shoveling it away. Rocco (Delon) and Simone (Salvatori) meet Nadia (Girardot), an attractive prostitute.

Simone is ambitious, trains as a professional boxer, and wins his first fight set up by Morini (Hanin), a homosexual impresario. He sleeps with Nadia but later becomes jealous when he learns her interest in him is not serious. Rocco gets a job in a dry-cleaner's, the manageress (Delair) of which Simone seduces while stealing a brooch to give to Nadia. The discovery of the theft leads Nadia to meeting Rocco again and she falls in love with him.

Rocco does his military service and meets Nadia again as she is leaving prison. They return to Milan where Ciro (Cartier) has a job at an automobile factory and Nadia decides to change her way of life. Simone drifts in petty crime and learns that Rocco and Nadia are lovers. He surprises them during a walk and rapes Nadia in front of a helpless Rocco. The two brothers fight savagely but Rocco senses the depths of Simone's despair. On the terrace of Milan cathedral Rocco tells Nadia they must separate because his brother needs him. Nadia goes back to Simone.

Ciro becomes his mother's hope for support as Rocco moves in with Vincenzo. Nadia, obsessed with revenging herself on Simone, is thrown out of her apartment. Simone gives himself to Morini then robs him after a brawl. To save him, Rocco signs a ten-year contract as a professional boxer. Rocco wins his first big fight. These scenes are intercut with Simone's brutal murder of Nadia.

Luca is still a child and uncorrupted by the city. The family celebration of Rocco's victory is interrupted by Simone, who confesses to Nadia's murder then throws himself onto the bed in an outburst of despair and grief that is matched by Rocco and his mother. Ciro rushes out for the police and Simone is arrested. Rosaria's last hope is Luca.

This epic saga has been said to be a continuation of the story of the Valastros in *La Terra Trema* (*q.v.*). Visconti has said he was most influenced by literary works: the inevitable Giovanni Verga (for his psychological study of the individual in relation to society), Dostoevski (the "goodness" of Rocco is similar to that of *The Idiot*) and the biblical story of Joseph and his brethren. Though Visconti's aim is naturalistic in its indictment of contemporary society, his style is one in which the acting and photography are deliberately stylized and intensified in the manner he returned to in *The Damned* (*q.v.*). His control of his actors, especially Annie Girardot, Renato Salvatori, and Alain Delon, is superb and amply justifies his own statement: "Experience has taught me that an expression of the burden of being human is the only thing that really counts on the screen."

ROMA, CITTA APERTA ROME, OPEN CITY/OPEN CITY Italy 1945. *Dir* Roberto Rossellini *Scen* Sergio Amidei, Federico Fellini, Roberto Rossellini *Photog* Ubaldo Arata *Mus* Renzo Rossellini *Cast* Aldo Fabrizi, Anna Magnani, Marcello Pagliero, Maria Michi, Francesco Grandjacquet *Prod* Excelsa Film (Rossellini). 101 mins.

The story of a group of workers and a local priest in the Rome of 1943–44, declared an "open city" by the Nazis, who were ruling it with ruthless tyranny. Underground leader, Manfredi (Pagliero), seeks refuge from the Gestapo in the home of Francesco (Grandjacquet) and is received by Pina (Magnani), Francesco's pregnant girl friend whom he is planning to marry. Because Manfredi is wanted by the Gestapo, he gets Father Don Pietro (Fabrizi) to deliver some money to the underground. The Gestapo raid the apartment block, Francesco is arrested and, as Pina rushes after him, she is shot. Francesco escapes and rejoins Manfredi, who is hiding in the apartment of his mistress, Marina (Michi), an actress who has turned to prostitution and who has become a drug addict. Unknown to Manfredi, her supplier is a Gestapo woman agent. She betrays Manfredi, who is arrested with Don Pietro. Manfredi dies under torture, refusing to betray the resistance movement, and Don Pietro is shot.

Open City was planned in secret by Rossellini and his colleagues while the Nazis still occupied Rome. In order to avoid conscription by the Fascist government, Rossellini hid in a worker's apartment with Sergio Amidei and a communist leader of the resistance. In this way they were kept up to date with the activities and tragedies of the underground, many of which they incorporated into their script. The priest, Don Pietro, was modeled on Father Don Morosini who was executed by the Nazis in 1944.

Rossellini said in 1956: "We began our film only two months after the liberation of Rome, despite the shortage of film stock. We shot it in the same settings in which the events we re-created had taken place. In order to pay for my film I sold my bed, then a chest of drawers and a mirrored wardrobe . . . *Rome, Open City* was shot silent, not by choice but by necessity. Film stock cost 60 liras a meter on the black market and it would have involved us in additional expense if we had recorded the sound. Also the Allied authorities had only given us a permit to produce a docu-mentary film. After the film was edited, the actors dubbed their own voices."

It was to some extent the warm performance by Anna Magnani as the ungainly, gesticulating, but proud and dignified Pina that made the film's international popularity. Audiences everywhere were astonished to see ordinary people in an Italian film instead of the endless parades of Black Shirts, or romantic, frilly actors.

The latter half of the film is weaker but it regains its power in the finale: the small black-frocked figure of the priest tied to a chair, waiting for death as the local children whistle a resistance song to comfort him.

Its realistic treatment of everyday Italian life heralded the postwar renaissance of the Italian cinema and the development of neorealism. In addition, as Rossellini jokingly said, "*Rome, Open City* was worth more than the persuasion of our Ministry of Foreign Affairs in helping Italy regain its place in the concert of nations." As his country's spokesman, in this film, Rosellini showed that Italians had fought as hard as anyone against fascism and for freedom.

ROMANCE IN A MINOR KEY ROMANZE IN MOLL

ROMANCE OF ELAINE (THE) see EXPLOITS OF ELAINE (THE)

ROMAN D'UN TRICHEUR (LE) STORY OF A CHEAT/THE CHEAT France 1936. *Dir/ Scen* Sacha Guitry *Photog* Marcel Lucien *Cast* Sacha Guitry, Serge Grave, Marguerite Moreno, Pauline Carton, Jacqueline Delubac *Prod* Cinéas. 83 mins.

An elderly card sharp and adventurer writes his memoirs in a Paris bistro. From his boyhood on, he had felt that cheating pays. After a long life in Monte Carlo, meetings with adventuresses, and successes and failures, he reforms and becomes a poor man.

This film is told entirely from the point of the leading character, Sacha Guitry, who describes the action in a running commentary while the characters act in pantomime. It is not the first attempt at this technique but the first and only truly cinematic success by Guitry, the author of innumerable farces and lightweight comedies designed to display his verbal virtuosity and talents as a comedian. Guitry not only wrote and directed *Story of a Cheat* but also played seven or eight character roles.

ROMAN HOLIDAY USA 1953. *Dir* William Wyler *Scen* Ian McLellan Hunter, John Dighton based on a story by Ian McLellan Hunter *Photog* Franz Planer, Henri Alekan *Art Dir* Hal Pereira, Walter Tyler *Mus* Georges Auric *Ed* Robert Swink *Cast* Gregory Peck, Audrey Hepburn, Eddie Albert, Harcourt Williams, Margaret Rawlings *Prod* Paramount. 118 mins.

In Rome on a goodwill tour, Princess Ann (Hepburn) runs away and meets an American newspaperman, Joe Bradley (Peck). When Joe discovers who she is he decides to exploit her for a scoop, with his cameraman (Albert) taking photographs. In the process, he falls in love with her. After various adventures, the princess decides to return to her duties and, at a press conference, Joe gives her the photographs.

This entertaining romantic comedy has some beautiful location photography, won an Oscar for and made famous the relatively unknown Audrey Hepburn, and was nominated for several other Oscars (but only won those for Best Costume and Best Story).

ROMANZE IN MOLL ROMANCE IN A MINOR KEY Germany 1943. *Dir* Helmut Käutner *Scen* Willy Clever, Helmut Käutner *Photog* Georg Bruckbauer *Mus* Lothar Brühe, Werner Eisbrenner *Cast* Marianne Hoppe, Paul Dahlke, Ferdinand Marian *Prod* Tobis. 99 mins.

Loosely based on *Les Bijoux* by Maupassant (an author on the Nazi blacklist), a story about a woman (Hoppe), married to an elderly civil servant (Dahlke), who falls in love with a famous composer-conductor (Marian). He buys her a strand of pearls because she inspired him to compose his greatest work, the "romance" of the title. Later he acquires a new mistress. His former mistress begs him to put the main theme of his new work in a minor key, but at the first performance, she leaves before hearing the aria in a minor key and kills herself in her anguish.

This is the only film of real quality, and certainly the most elegant, produced in Germany during the war. The fact that it is set in late nineteenth-century Paris and almost entirely in interiors suggests a kind of veiled rebellion against the Nazi regime and certainly its romantic story about infidelity infuriated Goebbels. It was a great commercial success.

Louis Marcorelles wrote: "Marianne Hoppe displays a sensitivity and emotion that comes from the interior. When, during the concert, we see tears flowing down her glassy face we know she is living her character in a physical sense."

ROMA, ORE 11 ROME, ELEVEN O'CLOCK Italy/France 1951. *Dir* Giuseppe De Santis *Scen* Cesare Zavattini, Giuseppe De Santis, B. Franchini, Elio Petri, R. Sonego, G. Puccini *Photog* Otello Martelli *Art Dir* Léon Barsacq *Mus* Mario Nascimbene *Cast* Lucia Bosè, Carla del Poggio, Massimo Girotti, Raf Vallone, Paola Stoppa, Elena Varzi, Lea Padovani, Delia Scala *Prod* Paul Graetz/ Transcontinental Films. 102 mins.

In Rome in 1950, over 200 young girls wait on an office staircase to apply for a typist's job. Luciana (del Poggio), the wife of an unemployed workman, Mando (Girotti), pushes ahead of the others, a squabble develops, and the staircase collapses. Luciana runs away panic-stricken and many casualties are taken to hospital. The story describes the lives of a number of the injured girls: Simona (Bosè) whose marriage to a penniless artist (Vallone) brought her the disapproval of her upper-class relatives; Adriana (Varzi) who decides to live on her own when she becomes pregnant; a prostitute, Caterina (Padovani), trying to start a new life; Angelina (Scala) trying to break away from her life as a domestic servant. Luciana, tortured by her conscience, contemplates suicide, but is deterred by Mando.

This is a key example of the last period of Italian neorealism. Zavattini's script was based on the Rome staircase tragedy in 1950 (earlier included in Genina's *Tre Storie Proibite*) and on the detailed study on women's unemployment that stemmed from it. From this study, written by the young journalist, Elio Petri, the scriptwriters created a persuasive and well-balanced story in which women from many backgrounds converge inexorably on the central tragedy.

Rome, Eleven O'Clock is more than merely a series of sketches performed by well-known Italian actors. It is a deeply motivated protest against unemployment and social conditions in Italy and is perhaps De Santis' best film. However, his orthodox background in neorealism did not prevent him from using a number of excellent professional actors and studio sets. It enjoyed considerable success in Rome, New York, and Moscow, but not in Paris.

ROME, ELEVEN O'CLOCK ROMA, ORE 11

ROME, OPEN CITY ROMA, CITTÀ APERTA

RONDE (LA) France 1950. *Dir* Max Ophüls *Scen* Jacques Natanson, Max Ophüls based on the play *Reigen* by Arthur Schnitzler *Photog* Christian Matras *Art Dir* Jean d'Eaubonne, Marpaux, M. Frederik *Costumes* Georges Annenkov *Mus* Oscar Strauss, Joë Hajos *Ed* Léonide Azar, S. Rondeau *Cast* Anton Walbrook, Simone Signoret, Serge Reggiani, Daniel Gélin, Simone Simon, Danielle Darrieux, Jean-Louis Barrault, F. Gravey, Gérard Philipe, Isa Miranda, Odette Joyeux *Prod* Sacha Gordine. 97 mins.
Based on Schnitzler's play, which shows love as a bitterly comic merry-go-round. A young whore (Signoret) meets a young soldier (Reggiani), who leaves her for a chambermaid (Simon), who later educates a young man (Gélin) into the ways of love-making. He seduces a married lady (Darrieux), whose husband (Gravey) is keeping a *grisette* (Joyeux), who adores a poet (Barrault), who prefers an actress (Miranda), who is attracted to a Lieutenant (Philipe), who visits the whore (Signoret) from the beginning. Thus love's roundabout turns full circle as explained by the narrator and master of ceremonies (Walbrook).
Delightfully witty and enjoyable, although not all the episodes work equally well, especially in the last half of the film. It is noticeably less successful than *Le Plaisir* (*q.v.*) though it does form something of a transition to *Lola Montès* (*q.v.*). [It was a great box-office success in France, Britain and North America despite (or perhaps because of) censorship problems. With it, Ophüls gathered around him the collaborators who remained with him until he died.]
— *La Ronde/Circle of Love* France 1964. *Dir* Roger Vadim *Scen* Jean Anouilh based on the play by Arthur Schnitzler *Photog* Henri Decaë *Art Dir* François de Lamothe *Mus* Michel Magne *Ed* Victoria Mercanton *Cast* Anna Karina, Claude Girard, Jean-Claude Brialy, Jane Fonda, Maurice Ronet, Marie Dubois, Catherine Spaak *Prod* Hakim. 110 mins. Eastman Color.
This tediously luxurious remake by Vadim has none of the graceful subtleties of the Ophüls' version and relies on a romanticized sexuality for effect.
Two Austrian films *Das Grosse Liebesspiel/And So To Bed* (1963) and *Das Liebeskarussel/Who Wants to Sleep?* (1965) are based on the *Reigen* formula but totally lack charm and wit.

*ROOM AT THE TOP Britain 1958. *Dir* Jack Clayton *Scen* Neil Paterson based on the novel by John Braine *Photog* Freddie Francis *Art Dir* Ralph Brinton *Mus* Mario Nascimbene *Ed* Ralph Kemplen *Cast* Laurence Harvey, Simone Signoret, Heather Sears, Donald Wolfit, Donald Houston, Raymond Huntley *Prod* Remus. 117 mins.
Joe Lampton (Harvey) arrives in an English industrial town for a job in the Borough Treasurer's office, where he makes friends with Soames (Houston). He is ambitious and begins to court Susan Brown (Sears), the daughter of a local industrial magnate (Wolfit) who discourages the courtship by sending Susan abroad. Joe seeks comfort with an older, married woman, Alice (Signoret), who falls in love with him. Susan returns, Joe seduces her, then returns to Alice. Susan becomes pregnant and Mr. Brown first tries to buy Joe off then forces him to give up Alice and marry Susan. Alice goes on a drinking bout that ends in her death in a car accident. Joe disappears and, after being beaten unconscious by a gang of toughs, is found by Soames in time for the wedding.
Undoubtedly the most significant British feature of the Fifties, not merely because it was the first to reflect life in an industrial town nor because of its sexual frankness but because of its brilliant delineation of character and environment. Its theme is not dissimilar to those of Dreiser's *An American Tragedy* or Stendhal's *The Red and the Black* in that its slum-bred hero tries to break into the establishment and gain power but is trapped by sex and destroys his only true love. Clayton (who had pre-

viously directed only the sensitive *The Bespoke Overcoat*) creates a vivid sense of the environment and of the system that creates Joe Lamptons. He draws from Simone Signoret one of her most outstanding performances (for which she won an Oscar). Even Laurence Harvey's apparently ambiguous performance is exactly right. *Room at the Top* was an international box-office success (the first British film to manage this for many years) and ushered in the era of British "kitchen sink" films of which, in retrospect, only *This Sporting Life* (*q.v.*) matches this film's depth and intensity.

An uninteresting sequel, *Life at the Top*, was produced in 1965 (*Dir* William T. Kotcheff *Cast* Laurence Harvey, Jean Simmons, Honor Blackman) in which Harvey's performance only confirms Clayton's skill in the original. A British TV series, *Man at the Top*, 1970–71, continued, *à la* Peyton Place, Joe's steamy adventures.

ROOTS RAICES

ROPE USA 1948. *Dir* Alfred Hitchcock *Scen* Arthur Laurents based on the play by Patrick Hamilton *Photog* Joseph Valentine, William V. Skall *Art Dir* E. Kuri *Mus* Leo F. Forbstein based on Poulenc *Ed* William Ziegler *Cast* James Stewart, John Dall, Farley Granger, Joan Chandler, Sir Cedric Hardwicke, Constance Collier, Edith Evanson *Prod* Transatlantic (Hitchcock/Sidney Bernstein). 81 mins.

Two young intellectuals (Dall, Granger) strangle their friend in order to prove the right of the "superior being" to place himself above conventional morality. They arrange a party consisting of the murdered man's relatives and fiancée and their ex-teacher (Stewart) and serve food from the unlocked chest in which they have hidden the body. The teacher becomes suspicious, discovers the body, and, despite their argument that it was he who first expounded the idea of "superiority," he calls the police.

A piece of technical virtuosity in which the story, apart from the first shot, takes place within a single apartment without time lapses. It is filmed entirely in ten-minute takes, without cuts, in which the camera moves continuously through each complete scene. Days of rehearsal allowed Hitchcock to develop complicated tracking shots and extraordinarily complex actions that involve several actors moving in and out of close-up.

ROSSIYA NIKOLAYA II I LEV TOLSTOY THE RUSSIA OF NICHOLAS II AND LEV TOLSTOY USSR 1928. *Dir/Scen/Ed* Esther Shub *Prod* Sovkino. 1,700 meters.

The last film in Shub's trilogy on Russian history covering the pre-1912 period; she had covered the 1912–1917 period in *The Fall of the Romanov Dynasty* (*q.v.*) and the first post-Revolutionary decade in *The Great Road*. She had originally intended to compile a film on Tolstoy to commemorate the centenary of his birth. Tolstoy adored the cinema and had produced between 1906 and 1910 several important film documents on his life in Yasnaya Polyana in collaboration with several photographers, chiefly Alexander Drankov. After his death in 1910, some of this had been used in a successful film, *The Life of Count Tolstoy*. Not much of this footage had survived, however, and Shub decided to cover the period using Tolstoy as a linking figure and drawing on additional archive footage. Some of this was footage shot by cameramen officially attached to the court of Tsar Nicholas who filmed the tsar in every conceivable situation, even when he went swimming in the nude with his family.

Shub also included material from a film purportedly "written and directed personally by Tolstoy." It was titled *A Peasant Wedding*, and was released by Alexander Drankov, with the approval of Tolstoy's daughter, soon after Tolstoy's death. And she certainly followed Tolstoy's advice that "Russian life must be shown as it is by the cinema; instead of continuing to chase after fabricated subjects."

ROUE (LA) France 1922 (production began 1919). *Dir/Scen/Ed* Abel Gance *Assist* Blaise Cendrars *Photog* L.-H. Burel, Bujard, Duverger, Brun *Mus* Arthur Honegger *Cast* Séverin-Mars, Ivy Close, Gabriel de Gravone, Gil Clary, Pierre Magnier, Georges Terof, Maxudian *Prod* Gance for Pathé. First version (1922), 32 reels, 10,500 meters in 3 parts; general release (and existing) version (1924), 4,200 meters.

An old railway mechanic, Sisif (Séverin-Mars), and his son, Elie (de Gravone), are both in love with Norma

(Close), Sisif's adopted daughter whom he had rescued from a crash as a baby. Elie is uaware that Norma is not his sister. Norma marries an engineer, de Hersan (Magnier), but it is a failure. Sisif becomes partially blind, is discharged, and goes to drive a funicular railway in the Alps accompanied by Elie. Elie meets Norma and de Hersan and, after a fight, Elie falls over a cliff. Sisif becomes blind and Norma moves into his chalet to look after him till he dies.

Main sequences: the crash in which Sisif rescues and adopts Norma; the canteen fight between a railwayman (Terof) and Sisif, who has been informed the man had attacked Norma; life in the Sisif household (which was erected amidst the railway lines); Sisif's attempt to wreck the train taking Norma to her marriage (rapid cutting of pistons, rails, smoke etc.); Sisif's passion for his locomotive, Norma-Compound, "transferring his love to his long-time mate with the smoky hair" (Gance); the steam-valve accident that partially blinds Sisif; Sisif's attempt to destroy his locomotive; Sisif driving a funicular railway in the Alps; life in the snowy landscape after the grime and soot of the railway yards; Elie's gift to Norma, a violin that conceals a love-letter; de Hersan's discovery of the letter and his fight with Elie on the mountainside; Norma's discovery of Elie suspended over an abyss and his recollection of his past life with Norma (rapid cutting) before he falls to his death; Sisif's blindness and his life in the squalid mountain chalet; Norma's return, an Antigone leading a blind Oedipus; Sisif's death, while, in the snow, Norma joins with the local people in a rondel dance for the Festival of Saint-Jean.

La Roue was originally called La Roue du rail. Gance shot the film in 16 months between 1919 and 1921, first in the railway yards at Nice and then in the Alps at St. Gervais.

Léon Moussinac wrote of this "tragedy of modern times" that its "melodramatic pattern with, at the same time, a universal theme, used a world made for the cinema." The mechanic, Sisif, is a combination of Sisyphus, Prometheus, Oedipus, and Christ. His son, searching for the secret of the violin makers of Cremona, is suddenly transformed into a troubador and his adopted sister into a princess.

Léon Moussinac wrote in 1924: "This film is a combination of forces. In it, the purity of the water matters less than the power of its gushing forth. We should have the courage to forget that which is unbearable and even odious: the exaggerated effects, the visual excesses, literature that only appears in these bits of visuals, and the extreme bad taste, because it is the price we have to pay for the dazzling glimpses of something to admire. It matters little whether we are mistaken. It is sufficient that it is ventured. Gance is the first to have captured, and, albeit confusedly, he *has* captured, exuberance, movement, depth — in a word, original beauty."

La Roue had an enormous impact and has long been considered revolutionary. Fernand Léger said that, "With La Roue, Abel Gance has elevated cinematographic art to the level of the plastic arts," while Jean Cocteau said, "There is the cinema before and after La Roue as there is painting before and after Picasso".

La Roue had considerable influence, especially on the developing French avant-garde. However it is unlikely that Eisenstein was influenced by the plastic symphonies of the film: Dziga Vertov was also, independently, exploring the patterns of cutting at this same time in the USSR.

— *La Roue/Wheels of Fate France 1956. Dir Andre Hagnet Cast Jean Servais, Catherine Anouilh. 100 mins.

ROUNDUP (THE) SZEGENYLEGENYEK

RULES OF THE GAME (THE) RÈGLE DU JEU (THE)

RUN FOR THE SUN see MOST DANGEROUS GAME (THE)

RUSSIA OF NICHOLAS II AND LEV TOLSTOY ROSSIYA NIKOLAYA II I LEV TOLSTOY

SAD SACK (THE) SEE TIRE AU FLANC

SAFETY LAST USA 1923. *Dir* Sam Taylor, Fred Newmeyer *Scen* Harold Lloyd, Hal Roach, Sam Taylor, Tim Whelan *Photog* Walter Lundin *Ed* Fred Guiol *Cast* Harold Lloyd, Mildred Davis, Noah Young, Bill Strother, Anna Townsend, Mickey Daniels *Prod* Hal Roach. 6,300 ft.

Harold (Lloyd) travels to the big city from a small town and becomes an assistant in a department store. In order to impress his fiancée (Davis) he poses as the general manager and gets involved in climbing a skyscraper as a publicity stunt for the store.

Harold's Lloyd's first complete masterpiece and one that made him world-famous as the timid "ordinary guy" in spectacles who is always inadvertently getting involved in dangerous stunts.

Harold Lloyd (who controls the rights to his features) re-released an abridged version of the film in his *Harold Lloyd's World of Comedy* in 1961.

SAGA OF GOSTA BERLING (THE) GÖSTA BERLINGS SAGA

SAGA OF THE ROAD (THE) PATHER PANCHALI

SAIKAKU ICHIDAI ONNA O'HARU/THE LIFE OF O'HARU/THE LIFE OF A WOMAN BY SAIKAKU Japan 1952. *Dir* Kenji Mizoguchi *Scen* Yoshikata Yoda, Kenji Mizoguchi based on the novel *Koshuku Ichidai Onna* by Ibara Saikaku *Photog* Yoshimo Kono *Art Dir* Hiroshi Mizutani *Mus* Ichiro Saito *Ed* Toshio Goto *Cast* Kinuyo Tanaka, Ichiro Sugai, Tsuki Matsura, Toshiro Mifune, Masao Shinizu, Tashiaki Konoe, Eitaro Shindo *Prod* Shintoho. 147 mins. (original version); 118 mins. (foreign release versions).

In 17th century Japan, a prostitute, O'Haru (Tanaka), recalls her unfortunate life. As the young and beautiful daughter of a samurai she serves in the imperial palace in Kyoto, where she is seduced by a serving man (Mifune). She is caught, her lover executed, and she and her parents driven out of the capital according to the severe moral code of the Genroku era. She is sold as a concubine to a prince, who drives her out after she bears him a son. Her father (Sugai) sells her to a brothel. She is married to a merchant, but when he dies she is forced down the path of degradation. As an old prostitute she catches a glimpse of her son, now a prince, and finally turns to religion to find peace at last.

"This film was very close to me ever since I went to Kyoto," Mizoguchi has said. "It is a true maxim that 'If you want something badly enough, you will get it.' It is essential that one should reflect for five or six years before beginning to film. Films produced quickly are never very good. Among the books of Saikaku are many others I would like to film because it would allow me to depict men and women as part of the social system of the time."

In the eyes of some critics this is Mizoguchi's masterpiece. It is a criticism of feudal Japan (with modern overtones) as seen through the eyes of a woman and depicts the problems of social predestination and destiny in a way that recalls Maupassant's *Une Vie*. In its cast of characters and its depiction of low-life adventures and the social system, the original novel would also seem to be similar to Spanish picaresque novels of the 17th century.

O'Haru is not merely an exotic period

piece. The gradual degradation of the central character never becomes melodramatic nor is it shown simply to exploit degradation for its own sake. The film's slow, simple style, its perfectly constructed and controlled images, and its striking use of the moving camera are characteristic of Mizoguchi's work in the Fifties. Kinuyo Tanaka gives a sensitive performance as O'Haru. Toshiro Mifune appears in a cameo role. *O'Haru* received the Silver Lion Award at the Venice Festival.

SAINT JOAN see JOAN OF ARC

SALAIRE DE LA PEUR (LE) THE WAGES OF FEAR France/Italy 1953. *Dir* Henri-Georges Clouzot *Scen* H.-G. Clouzot, Jérôme Géronimi based on the novel by Georges Arnaud *Photog* Armand Thirard *Art Dir* René Renoux *Mus* Georges Auric *Ed* Madeleine Gug, Henri Rust *Cast* Yves Montand, Charles Vanel, Véra Clouzot, Peter van Eyck, Folco Lulli. 156 mins. English versions, 140 mins. and 128 mins.

In a squalid little South American town virtually owned by an American oil company, four down-and-outs take on the job of driving two trucks of nitroglycerine 300 miles to a burning oil well. The high reward of two thousand dollars apiece tempts them as a means of escape from the town, though their chances of success are slim. The first truck is driven by Luigi (Lulli), a cheerful Italian bricklayer and Bimba (van Eyck), a narcissistic and fearless German. The second consists of Jo (Vanel), a middle-aged gangster who has killed to get the job, and Mario (Montand), a young Corsican. Jo loses his nerve at the first dangerous encounter and Mario comes to despise him as his illusions of his toughness are shattered. The first truck is blown up, Jo is fatally injured, and Mario alone reaches the oil well. Returning with an empty truck, Mario, ironically, crashes on the mountainside.

"I avoided exotism," Clouzot has said, "though it might have masked the absence of a solid construction. A significant setting, complex human material and the gripping accessory of a truck loaded with nitroglycerin allowed me to develop not the picaresque story but the epic qualities; yes, this is an epic whose main theme is courage. And the opposite."

Though based on the unrelenting tension of its construction, *Wages of Fear* also offers a comment on the exploitation of South America by United States oil companies. Pierre Kast found it "A drama of failure, a tragedy about the absurdity of blind industry. Its mesmeric development towards the conclusion is perhaps what most moves us on first seeing it. The double twist at the end surprises us as unnecessary but this ending is inseparable from the total design."

It was an outstanding international success and, unlike most foreign films, had a full-circuit release in Britain and North America in both subtitled and dubbed versions.

SALERNO BEACHHEAD WALK IN THE SUN (A)

SALT FOR SVANETIA SOL SVANETII

SALT OF THE EARTH USA 1954. *Dir* Herbert J. Biberman *Scen* Michael Wilson *Mus* Sol Kaplan *Cast* Rosaura Revueltas, Juan Chacon, Will Geer, David Wolfe, and members of Local 890 of the International Union of Mine, Mill, and Smelter Workers *Prod* Paul Jarrico. 94 mins.

[This social drama depicts the struggle for equality of Mexican-American zinc miners and their wives — the men for equality of working and living conditions with white "Anglo" miners, and the women for equality with men. It is broadly based on the 1951–52 strike of the Mexican-American zinc miners against Empire Zinc, Silver City, New Mexico. It was made as a cooperative endeavor during the height of the McCarthy era by Herbert J. Biberman, Michael Wilson, Sol Kaplan, and the producer Paul Jarrico, in close collaboration with Local 890 of the Union. Juan Chacon, the union president in real life and in the film, wrote that a production committee had "the responsibility of seeing that our picture ran true to life from start to finish. *Salt of the Earth* was not intended as a documentary record of that particular strike but . . . it is a true account of our people's lives and struggles." Biberman, Wilson, and Kaplan were all black-listed after investigations by the House Un-American Activities Committee and Biberman had served a jail sentence for "contempt of Congress". Michael Wilson had won an

Oscar in 1952 for his script for *A Place in the Sun* (*q.v.*) and later broke through the black-list by collaborating on the scripts for *Friendly Persuasion* and *Bridge on the River Kwai* (*q.v.*).]

Main sequences: the wives of the miners establishing a Ladies Auxiliary Strike Committee that adds its demands to those of the miners; the women, led by Esperanza (Revueltas), take over the picket line despite violence and tear gas; the arrest of the wives, their demonstration in jail, and their consequent release; Esperanza's quarrel with her husband, Ramon, the union president (Chacon); Ramon being beaten up; the arrival of deputies of the Sheriff (Geer) with an eviction order and their flight before the crowd's anger.

Apart from the miners' struggle for economic equality, the film's dramatic core is the struggle by the women for equality with their men, who consider them capable only of looking after the home and the children. The attitude of the men is not dissimilar to that of Zampano in *La Strada* (*q.v.*). In fact, it is the struggle for "women's liberation" that gives the film much of its power. The central character is portrayed with sincerity and conviction by the Mexican professional actress, Rosaura Revueltas. [Not surprisingly for the period, charges of "communist propaganda" were leveled at the film on its release and it received only limited exhibition in North America until a belated general release in 1965. Even *Sight and Sound* called it "extremely shrewd propaganda for the business of the USSR . . . (whose) situation is grotesquely far from typical." It was a great success, in France, however, where it was described as a "human document" and received an award as the Best Film Exhibited in France in 1955.]

SALVATION HUNTERS (THE) USA 1925. *Dir/Scen* Josef von Sternberg *Photog* Edward Gheller, Josef von Sternberg *Cast* George K. Arthur, Georgia Hale, Bruce Guerin, Otto Matiesen, Stuart Holmes, Nellie Bly Baker, Olaf Hytten *Prod* Sternberg, George K. Arthur (Academy Photoplays) for United Artists. 5,930 ft.

In San Pedro, just south of Los Angeles, a Boy (Arthur) fights successfully for a Girl (Hale) against a Brute (Hytten). [Josef von Sternberg's first film was made independently in Hollywood for the amazingly small cost of $4,800 provided by a British actor, George K. Arthur, who was trying to break into films. Sternberg used largely obscure actors and a maximum of natural settings in and around the mud flats of San Pedro] Chaplin said "The unreality of its characters might be criticized but it is this which gives the work its grandeur. They were not intended to be real and must be considered as symbols." This symbolism is reinforced by the grandiloquent titles comparing the trio of derelicts with children of the sun.

The film reveals the influence of German *Kammerspiel* not only in its dramatic structure and visual style, but in its use of symbolic objects: the dredge scooping up mud, the manikin symbolizing sensuality, the coat rack characterizing the Brute as "a demon," the way the Brute scratches his thigh when he is aroused, etc.

The symbolism has dated badly, but the film's sense of realism, engrossing story, attractive characters from American daily life, and portrait of the sordid side of America made it a success at the time and still retain their power. *Salvation Hunters* is a key film for an understanding of the general development of Sternberg's work.

SALVATORE GIULIANO Italy 1961. *Dir* Francesco Rosi *Scen* Francesco Rosi, Susi Cecchi d'Amico, Enzo Provenzale, Franco Solinas *Photog* Gianni Di Venanzo *Art Dir* Sergio Canevari *Mus* Piero Piccioni *Ed* Mario Sarandrei *Cast* Frank Wolff, Salvo Randone, Pietro Cammarata, and other nonprofessionals *Prod* Lux/Vides/Galatea. 125 mins.

The story of a Mafia leader, Salvatore Giuliano, in postwar Sicily: his guerrilla activities aimed at Sicily's independence, his banditry and war against the police, his betrayal by his right-hand man, and his assassination. Interwoven with this story are details of Giuliano's laying-out and burial and the trial of his associates.

Famous episodes: the police occupying Giuliano's village; the women whose husbands have been arrested attacking the long rows of Carabinieri; the bloody massacre by Giuliano's followers of peasants attending a Communist rally; the bandit's death; the trial; the continuation of the vendetta as another Mafia follower is liquidated.

Rosi himself calls this "an exposition on the corpse of Julius Caesar" and its portrait of the character of Giuliano in fact offers a complex social reportage on postwar Sicily. The cast is almost entirely nonprofessional and the film was shot entirely on location in Sicily, Rosi's birth place. The narrative structure, elliptical and chronologically diffuse, is extremely complex, depending largely on an interwoven structure of flashbacks. This extension of the neorealist heritage is the most important Italian film of the early Sixties.

*SAMMA NO AJI AN AUTUMN AFTERNOON/ THE TASTE OF MACKEREL (literally, A TASTE OF THE FISH CALLED SAMMA) Japan 1962. *Dir* Yasujiro Ozu *Scen* Yasujiro Ozu, Kogo Noda *Photog* Yushun Atsuta *Art Dir* Tatsuo Hamada *Mus* Takanobu Saito *Ed* Yoshiyasu Hamamura *Cast* Chishu Ryu, Shima Iwashita, Shinichiro Mikami, Keiji Sada, Mariko Okada *Prod* Shochiku. 113 mins. Agfacolor.

Shuhei Hirayama (Ryu) is a contented widower with a married son, Koichi (Sada), a son at College, Kazuo (Mikami), and an unmarried daughter, Michiko (Iwashita). During one of his regular sake sessions with friends he learns that his daughter is interested in marriage, though she denies it. The man she wants has recently become engaged to another girl and she finally marries a man chosen by the wife of her father's old friend. After the wedding, Shuhei returns to his house, now empty except for Kazuo, and contemplates his coming loneliness.

Ozu's last completed film before his death in 1963 is like a final summation of all the familiar themes of his work: the older and younger generations of a traditional Japanese family, serenity, contemplation, and the traditional ways of life (though here Ozu integrates certain aspects of modern Japan such as the neon-lit little bars). His style, as always, is simple yet rigorous — the reposeful, non-moving shot just above floor level that he uses to such consummate effect. However, he has rarely matched the emotional intensity of the scenes depicting Shuhei after the wedding of his daughter, his visit to a little bar, and his return to the empty home. The delicate use of color gives the film something of the spirit of traditional Japanese art.

SAMSON Poland 1961. *Dir* Andrzej Wajda *Scen* Andrzej Wajda, Kazimierz Brandys based on the novel by K. Brandys *Photog* Jerzy Wojcik *Art Dir* Leszek Wajda *Mus* Tadeusz Baird *Cast* Serge Merlin, Alina Janowska, Elzbieta Kepinska *Prod* Kadr/Droga. 105 mins. The life and death of a young Jew (Merlin) in Warsaw during the German occupation, a story that echoes the biblical legend of Samson.

Best sequences: a fight over anti-Semitism in the university; life in prison; the flight through a Jewish cemetery; the Jew hiding in a black marketeer's peculiar apartment.

This is one of Wajda's best films, a blend of sober quasi-documentary sequences and extravagantly "baroque" episodes.

SANDRA VAGHE STELLE DELL'ORSA

SANG DES BETES (LE) THE BLOOD OF BEASTS France 1949. *Dir/Scen* Georges Franju *Photog* Marcel Fradetal *Mus* Joseph Kosma *Ed* André Joseph *Narration* Jean Painlevé spoken by Nicole Ladmiral, Georges Hubert *Prod* Forces et Voix de France. 22 mins.

Georges Franju's first professional short film established his international reputation. [Franju records his subject, the everyday work of the abattoir of La Vilette in Paris, with dreadful directness. However, he does not condemn the sickening brutality involved; as he himself termed it, butchering is "hard work that men must do so that others may eat," and the abattoir sequences are set within carefully composed atmospheric shots of Parisian suburbs. Jean Cocteau said it "proved that the cinema is the vehicle for realism and lyricism." *Le Sang des bêtes* is one of the most poetic postwar documentaries, full of strangely surrealistic touches.]

Franju said he was attempting (and he succeeded) "to restore to documentary reality its appearance of artifice and to natural sets their real attribute of seeming constructed. In order to reveal the almost ritual nature of the slaughtering process, we placed strange mutterings over an ensemble in which gleams diffused by the steam from the blood seemed to officiate under a conical beam light."

SANG D'UN POETE (LE) BLOOD OF A POET France 1930. *Dir/Scen* Jean Cocteau

Photog Georges Périnal *Art Dir* Jean Gabriel d'Eaubonne *Mus* Georges Auric *Ed* Jean Wiedmer *Commentary* Jean Cocteau *Cast* Lee Miller, Pauline Carton, Odette Talazac, Jean Desbordes, Enrique Rivero, Fernand Duchamps, Barbette *Prod* Vicomte de Noailles. 58 mins.

[The film is in four episodes ("The Wounded Hand" or "The Poet's Scars"; "Do Walls Have Ears?"; "The Battle of the Snowballs"; "The Profanation of the Host") linked by a commentary, all of which supposedly occurs in the fraction of second that elapses before a falling chimney, shown in the film's opening sequence, hits the ground, shown in the film's last sequence.]

Privately commissioned by the Vicomte de Noailles — who also commissioned *L'Age d'or* (*q.v.*) — it was Cocteau's first venture into the cinema and the only film on which he claims to have been completely free. As Cocteau himself has said many times, it is not a surrealist film but was made as an "answer" to the surrealists. He himself described it as a poem on celluloid and said, "I am trying to picture the poet's inner self." Despite its stylistic artificiality and visual fireworks, it is a sincere and personal film, replete with his personal iconography and the themes, obsessions, and dream associations he had already used in his poems, novels, drawings, and plays. Examples of these in the film include: the poet with a star on his left shoulder; the mouth in a drawing that comes alive; the mirror that leads to another world; the poet moving down the corridor, apparently against a strong wind; the elderly governess in buttoned boots and the mutinous child; the opium addict, the hermaphrodite with the "Danger de Mort" sign in its crotch; the childrens' snowball fight in which one is killed; the game of cards; the triumphant petrification of Death when she wins the game; the horns of a bull forming a lyre while Cocteau's voice proclaims "L'Ennui mortel de l'immortalité."

SANSHO DAYU SANSHO, THE BAILIFF Japan 1954. *Dir* Kenji Mizoguchi *Scen* Fuji Yahiro, Yoshikata Yoda based on the novel by Ogai Mori *Photog* Kazuo Miyagawa *Art Dir* Fumio Itoh *Mus* Fumio Hayasaka *Cast* Kinuyo Tanaka, Yoshiaki Hanayagi, Masao Shimizu, Eitaro Shin-do, Kyoko Kagawa, Kikue Mori *Prod* Daiei. 120 mins.

In Heian era (11th century) Japan, a mother (Tanaka) sets off with her two children to find her husband, a former deputy governor who has been in exile for some years. They suffer hardships and the family is broken up by a priestess who sells all three to kidnappers. The mother is taken to Sado Island to become a courtesan, while the brother and sister are sold as slaves to Sansho (Shindo), a rich and cruel bailiff in control of a distant region. Ten years later the brother (Hanayagi) has become brutalized despite his gentle sister's (Kagawa) remonstrances. After they escape, she commits suicide because she feels she is a burden to him. The brother comes under the influence of a Buddhist monk, the eldest son of Sansho, and decides to devote his life to helping humanity. After some adventures, he learns that his father has died and that he has been made governor of a province once under Sansho's brutal rule. He frees the slaves and sets out to Sado Island for a reunion with his mother, now old and blind.

From a rather melodramatic novel, Mizoguchi created a powerful work with strong humanistic overtones. Focusing on the influence the two women in the story have on the hero, the film alternates the idyllic atmsophere of some scenes with the violent cruelty of others.

SANS LAISSER D'ADRESSE France 1950. *Dir* Jean-Paul Le Chanois *Scen* J.-P. Le Chanois, Alex Joffé *Photog* Marc Fossard *Art Dir* Max Douy, Pimenoff *Mus* Joseph Kosma *Cast* Danièle Delorme, Bernard Blier, Julien Carette, Gérard Oury *Prod* Corena. 90 mins.

A young girl (Delorme) from the provinces wanders around Paris looking unsuccessfully for the father of her child and is saved from hopelessness by an ebullient taxi driver (Blier).

This is Le Chanois' best film. It had considerable commercial success and was remade in Hollywood as:

— *Taxi USA 1953. *Dir* Gregory Ratoff *Scen* Daniel Fuchs, D. M. Marshman based on the Le Chanois film *Photog* Milton Krasner *Cast* Dan Dailey, Constance Smith *Prod* 20th Century-Fox. 77 mins.

An uninteresting, but mildly amusing, sentimental remake.

*SASOM I EN SPEGEL THROUGH A GLASS DARKLY Sweden 1961. *Dir/Scen* Ingmar Bergman *Photog* Sven Nykvist *Art Dir* P. A. Lundgren *Mus* J. S. Bach, *Suite No. 2 in D Minor for Violincello Ed* Ulla Ryghe *Cast* Harriet Andersson, Gunnar Björnstrand, Max von Sydow, Lars Passgard *Prod* Svensk Filmindustri. 91 mins.

On a remote Baltic island, Karin (Andersson), a schizophrenic, lives with her doctor husband, Martin (von Sydow), her father, David (Björnstrand), a famous novelist, and her teen-age brother, Minus (Passgard). All feel an inability to express feelings for each other. Minus is worried about sexual problems and his father's departure on a lecture tour. Karin's mental illness is intensified when she learns that her father is almost clinically observing her deterioration and she rejects reality for the world where her mysterious voices announce the coming of God. In this state, she seduces Minus then asks to be sent back to the hospital with Martin. David and his son are left alone and David tries to explain his new understanding of what love and God mean.

Through a Glass Darkly forms the first part of a kind of trilogy with *Winter Light* (q.v.) and *The Silence* (q.v.). In it Bergman seems to search for a new interpretation of "God" other than the conventional one with which he was raised. Though the ending of the film is unconvincingly rhetorical (Minus declaring joyfully "My father spoke to me," and David orating on the nature of God) its theme is lucidly developed and it is full of some of Bergman's most unforgettable sequences — Karin lost in her own world, the seduction of Minus, and the slow descent of the helicopter as Karin screams "God is a spider!"

SATAN MET A LADY see MALTESE FALCON (THE)

SATURDAY NIGHT AND SUNDAY MORNING Britain 1960. *Dir* Karel Reisz *Scen* Alan Sillitoe based on his own novel *Photog* Freddie Francis *Art Dir* Ted Marshall *Mus* Johnny Dankworth *Ed* Seth Holt *Cast* Albert Finney, Shirley Anne Field, Rachel Roberts, Hylda Baker, Norman Rossington *Prod* Woodfall. 89 mins.

Arthur (Finney) is a factory worker in Nottingham who spends his Saturday nights with Brenda (Roberts), the wife of another factory worker. Brenda becomes pregnant and he takes her to his Aunt Ada (Baker), hoping for advice on abortion but without result. He is also taking out Doreen (Field), a young girl set on marriage. Brenda's husband learns of the affair and his brother and a friend waylay Arthur after an evening at a fair and beat him up. Arthur feels he deserved it; responsibility is catching up with him and it seems he will marry Doreen and settle down in a new housing estate.

This raw, low-life drama followed such films as *Room at the Top* (q.v.) and Richardson's *Look Back in Anger*. Like them it was concerned with the provincial, industrial milieu and reflected the new provincial English literature of the Fifties, the "angry young men" (led by John Osborne), and the *free cinema* movement in which both Karel Reisz and Tony Richardson (who produced this film) were involved. It is of especial interest because it broke with the rigidly conformist style represented in the British cinema by "J. Arthur Rank presents. . . ." As A. S. Lebarthe wrote, "The English cinema is totally paralyzed. We should remember that Karel Reisz has taken the first steps forward." According to Louis Marcorelles, "it demystified the capitalist order and is above all one of those rare films made west of the Elba whose hero is an authentic worker." It also made Albert Finney internationally famous.

SAVAGE PRINCESS AAN

SAWDUST AND TINSEL GYCKLARNAS AFTON

SCARFACE — Shame of a Nation USA 1932. *Dir* Howard Hawks *Scen* Ben Hecht, Seton I. Miller, W. R. Burnett, John Lee Mahin, Fred Pasley based on the novel by Armitage Trail *Photog* Lee Garmes, L. W. O'Connell *Art Dir* Harry Olivier *Ed* Edward Curtiss *Cast* Paul Muni, Ann Dvorak, George Raft, Osgood Perkins, Karen Morley, Boris Karloff, Tully Marshall *Prod* Howard Hughes for United Artists. 99 mins.

Tony Camonte, "Scarface" (Muni), destroys rival gangs, defeats his own leader (Perkins), becomes all-powerful, and controls bootlegging and politics alike. Though he has a mistress, Poppy (Morley), he seems to have an incestuous love for his sister (Dvorak). She falls for Scarface's lieutenant, coin-flipping "Little Boy" (Raft), and Scarface murders him. Later, when he is trapped by the police, his sister returns to help him and is killed in the gun battle. Finally, shaking like a coward, Scarface is shot down by the police.

Loosely based on the career of Al Capone, *Scarface* was released as "the gangster film to end all gangster films," but in fact triggered off a whole series of imitations. It is Hawks's best prewar film, despite the fact that some of the acting (such as that of Paul Muni) and the costumes have dated badly. Its violent visual style, its cutting, and its cynicism and sense of character are as arresting today as they were then. The opening sequence, in which the guest of honor is cold-bloodedly shot down after a mob party, is perhaps the best of the film's numerous memorable sequences.

Hecht and Hawks create a world for Scarface and his mob that is not unlike the court of the Borgias in Renaissance Italy with similar intrigues, double crosses, and gratuitous murders. Scarface himself is more arrogant and stupid than his counterpart in *Underworld* (*q.v.*) and gets to the top only through ambition and the fact that he has what was then a new absolute weapon, the machine-gun. His lieutenant, Little Boy, is characterized by his habit of perpetually flipping a coin and other mobsters are identified by their own special peculiarities of behavior — a device often imitated in gangster films. Though it has often been copied, *Scarface* still remains one of the best of its genre.

SCARLET LETTER (THE) USA 1926. *Dir* Victor Seastrom (Sjöström) *Scen* Frances Marion based on the novel by Nathaniel Hawthorne *Photog* Hendrik Sartov *Art Dir* Cedric Gibbons *Cast* Lillian Gish, Lars Hanson, Karl Dane, Henry B. Walthall, William H. Tooker, Marcello Corday, Fred Herzog, Jules Cowles *Prod* Jury-Metro-Goldwyn. 8,200 ft.

In 17th century New England, an adulteress, Hester Prynne (Gish), rather than endanger the reputation of her lover, suffers punishment and humiliation for years by being forced to wear a scarlet "A" on her breast. She devotes herself to raising her child. Her lover, the Reverend Dimmesdale (Hanson),

makes atonement by public confession, revealing the scarlet letter he has himself burnt into his flesh, and then dies in Hester's arms.

Léon Moussinac described this as "a film that stigmatizes the vicious, odious puritanism rampant in New England and that still exists in small communities in America and elsewhere." The passions and suffering of the couple and their terrible persecution as depicted in Hawthorne's beautiful novel (he himself was born in Salem in 1804) is superbly caught in Sjöström's direction and in the remarkable performances of Lillian Gish and the Swedish Lars Hanson. The sets and costumes (almost certainly by Cedric Gibbons, who joined MGM in 1924) are historically accurate but unimaginative. However, Hendrik Sartov's sensitive photography makes the most of them.

OTHER VERSIONS:

— *USA 1908. *Prod* Kalem.

— *USA 1911. *Cast* Lucille Young, King Baggot *Prod* Imp.

— *USA 1913. *Dir* David Miles *Cast* Linda Arvidson, Charles Perley *Prod* Kinemacolor.

— USA 1917. *Dir/Scen* Carl Harbaugh *Cast* Vivian Martin, Stuart Holmes *Prod* Fox. 5 reels.

— *USA 1920. *Dir* Herbert Kaufman *Prod* Selznick. 1 reel.

— *Britain 1922. *Cast* Sybil Thorndike, Tom Fraser. 1 reel (Only includes highlights of the story).

— USA 1934. *Dir* Robert Vignola *Scen* Leonard Fields, David Silverstein *Cast* Cora Sue Collins, Hardie Albright *Prod* Majestic. 8 reels.

An independent production that didn't achieve a major release.

SCARLET STREET USA 1945. *Dir* Fritz Lang *Scen* Dudley Nichols based on *La Chienne* by Georges de la Fouchardière *Photog* Milton Krasner *Art Dir* Alexander Golitzen, John B. Goodman *Mus* Hans J. Salter *Ed* Arthur Hilton *Special Effects* John P. Fulton *Cast* Edward G. Robinson, Joan Bennett, Dan Duryea, Margaret Lindsay, Vladimir Sokoloff *Prod* Diana Productions for Universal. 103 mins.

Lang's version of the story of an ordinary, middle-aged man, Chris Cross (Robinson), who gets involved with a *femme fatale* (Bennett), her boyfriend (Duryea), and murder. It was made independently for Diana Productions, a new company formed by Lang, Walter Wanger, and Joan Bennett. Despite Lang's reputation, it is not equal to Renoir's version in 1931, *La Chienne* (*q.v.*). [Its structure is predictably melodramatic and its sordidness and ceaseless degradation are not substitutes for the naturalism the story required. Edward G. Robinson is no match for Michel Simon in Renoir's version.]

SCEICCO BIANCO (LO) THE WHITE SHEIK Italy 1952. *Dir/Art Dir* Federico Fellini *Scen* Federico Fellini, Tullio Pinelli, Ennio Flaiano, Michelangelo Antonioni *Photog* Arturo Gallea *Mus* Nino Rota *Ed* Rolando Benedetti *Cast* Alberto Sordi, Leopoldo Trieste, Brunella Bovo, Giulietta Masina. 86 mins.

A young provincial woman (Bovo) and her husband (Trieste) arrive in Rome for their honeymoon. While her husband busies himself with arrangements to meet relatives and be presented to the Pope, she sets out to meet her idol — the White Sheik (Sordi), hero of a photographed magazine strip (the popular *fumetti*). She discovers her idol has feet of clay in an encounter with him on a boat that is interrupted by the arrival of his domineering wife. She throws herself into the Tiber only to discover it is but a few inches deep. Her husband finds her in the hospital and together they set out to meet his relatives.

The first film Fellini directed alone, this is a delightful, shrewd and sardonic satire on popular "heart-throb" heros. Though it is firmly rooted in orthodox neorealism, many of Fellini's characteristic motifs and subtle tones are present, event though in embryonic form. Alberto Sordi's performance as the romantic hero who turns out to have earthy tastes made him famous. Giulietta Masina appears in a supporting role as the prostitute, Cabiria.

SCHATTEN — EINE NACHTLICHE HALLUZINA-TION WARNING SHADOWS Germany 1922. *Dir/Ed* Arthur Robison *Scen* Rudolf Schneider, Arthur Robison based on an idea by Albin Grau *Photog* Fritz Arno Wagner *Art Dir* Albin Grau *Cast* Fritz Körtner, Ruth Weyher, Fritz Rasp, Gustav von Wangenheim, Alexander Granach, Max Gülstorff, Ferdinand von Alten *Prod* Deutsches Film Union. 5,650 ft.

A count (Körtner) is bitterly jealous of the favors his wife (Weyher) bestows on "the Lover" (von Wangenheim) and other cavaliers (von Alten, Gülstorff). An itinerant showman (Granach) presents a shadow play that parallels their lives and in which they act out their passions. In the play, the count, in mad jealousy, forces the cavaliers to stab his wife, then is overcome by remorse and is thrown out of the window by the furious cavaliers. After the shadow play, the count and his wife see the errors of their ways and are reconciled.

Warning Shadows is a product of expressionism in its use of light and shadow and of *Kammerspiel* in its unity of time, place, and theme and its almost titleless narrative. Paul Rotha described it as "a remarkable achievement. Its purely psychological direction, its definite completeness of time and action, its intimate ensemble were new attributes of the cinema. It was a rare instance of complete filmic unity, with the possible exception of the unnecessary roof-garden scene. The continuity of theme, the smooth development from one sequence into another, the gradual realization of the thoughts of the characters, were flawlessly presented. It carried an air of romance, of fantasy, of tragedy."

SCHERBEN — EIN DEUTSCHES FILMKAMMER-SPIEL THE RAIL/SHATTERED Germany 1921. *Dir* Lupu Pick *Scen* Carl Mayer, Lupu Pick *Photog* Friedrich Weinmann *Cast* Edith Posca, Werner Krauss, Paul Otto *Prod* Rex Film. 1,356 meters. (4,400 ft. approx.).

A railroad trackwalker (Krauss) lives with his wife, and daughter (Posca) in their small house. A railway inspector (Otto) arrives and seduces the girl. When the mother discovers it she wanders into the snow to pray and dies. When the inspector refuses to take the girl with him, she informs her father of the seduction and he strangles the inspector. The daughter goes mad and her father gives himself up to the engine driver of an express train.

The action takes place in 24 hours as is indicated by an alarm clock and a calendar. "The theme is simple, the characters equally so," wrote Lionel Landry in 1922. Unity of place is the trackwalker's small house, the snow-covered landscape, and the railroad track. Red tinting is used for the trackwalker's lantern as he signals to stop the express. Only one title appears: the trackwalker announcing to the engine driver, "I am a murderer."

Carl Mayer was the most significant influence behind *Kammerspiel* and *Shattered* is part of a series with *Backstairs*, 1921, *Sylvester* (*q.v.*), and *Der Letzte Mann* (*q.v.*). All four are "modern tragedies" about the lower middle-class world whose heros are trapped by the workings of fate.

As with other *Kammerspiel* films, objects are used symbolically as part of the dramatic action. Siegfried Kracauer describes how the alarm clock of *Backstairs* "reappears in *Shattered* along with such significant objects as the miserable scarecrow trembling in the wind before the trackwalker's house, and the shining boots of the inspector . . . In addition, *Shattered* offers details of locomotives, wheels, telegraph wires, signal bells, and other pertinent items . . . The repeated close-ups of broken glass . . . have no purpose other than to denote the fragility of human design in the face of fate . . . In *Shattered,* so-called pan shots . . . deliberately advance the narrative. For instance, the camera pans from the trembling scarecrow to a corner window, with the silhouette of the inspector and the daughter behind it, in a slow and steady movement designed not only to divulge the starting love affair, but also to relate its meaning to that of the desolate effigy in the wind." Another example — which was also used by Carné in *Le Jour se lève* (*q.v.*) — is the alarm clock that begins to ring beside the empty bed of the dead mother. [As with *Backstairs* and *Sylvester*, *Shattered* received considerable critical acclaim but limited commercial success. The public responded only to *The Last Laugh,* the last of Mayer's four "screen poems."]

SCIUSCIA SHOESHINE Italy 1946. *Dir* Vittorio de Sica *Scen* Cesare Zavattini, Sergio Amidei, Adolfe Franci, C. G. Viola *Photog* Archise Brizzi, Elio Paccara *Art Dir* Ivo Battelli, G. Lombardozzi *Mus* Alessandro Cicognini *Cast* Rinaldo Smordini, Franco Interlenghi, Angelo D'-Amico, Aniello Mele, Bruno Ortensi. 90 mins.

In Nazi-occupied Rome, two young shoeshine boys, Giuseppe (Interlenghi) and Pasquale (Smordini) want to buy a horse. They become involved in a black-market deal for the needed money and buy the horse. But they are caught and sent to prison. Pasquale is tricked into informing and Giuseppe encouraged to betray his friend in revenge. Giuseppe escapes but Pasquale leads the police to his hiding place and it is Pasquale who finally kills his friend. (The title of the film is the Italian word derived from the English "shoeshine." Phonetically it is pronounced "shoo-shai" and is what young boys used to shout at passing Americans to persuade them to have their shoes cleaned.)

Famous sequences: the life of the "sciuscia" in the streets of Rome; the two boys riding their horse proudly down the street; the stolen goods taken to a clairvoyant's and the arrival of the gangsters; the arrest of the two boys; their interrogation and the apalling conditions in the prison; the two locked in separate cells; the fire; Giuseppe's escape. The finale, in studio sets is weak, but the prison scenes, shot in an actual prison, are unforgettable. *Shoeshine* is far from an equal to *Rome, Open City* (*q.v.*) or *Paisà* (*q.v.*), but it was a great popular success, which allowed De Sica and Zavattini to continue creating their portraits of life in postwar Italy — *Bicycle Thieves* (*q.v.*), *Miracle in Milan* (*q.v.*), and *Umberto D* (*q.v.*)

*SCORPIO RISING USA 1963. *Dir/Scen/ Photog/Ed* Kenneth Anger *Songs* sung by Elvis Presley, Bobby Vinton, Ray Charles and others *Cast* Bruce Byron, Johnny Sapienza, Frank Carifi *Prod* Puck. 31 mins. 16 mm. Ektachrome.

Anger's stunning evocation of contemporary American myth and mysticism as symbolized in the tribal motorcycle cult is one of the most powerful films to come from the American underground. Its drag party, initiation ceremonies, and fascist religious overtones quickly found a Hollywood home in such films as *Wild Angels* (*Dir* Corman, 1966). One of its most telling sequences intercuts scenes of Mickey Rooney as Puck from *A Midsummer's Night Dream* (*q.v.*). Anger says that "What *Scorpio* represents is me cluing in to popular American culture after having been away for eight years . . . every single song that I used in *Scorpio* came out at the time that I made the film . . . I see the bike boys as the last romantics of this particular culture. They're the last equivalents of the riders of the range, the cowboys . . . The (astrological) sign of Scorpio, which is death and resurrection, is like the poisonous bite that makes the fever that makes you well."

SCOTT OF THE ANTARCTIC/SCOTT'S LAST JOURNEY see WITH CAPTAIN SCOTT, R.N., TO THE SOUTH POLE

SEARCH (THE) Switzerland/USA 1947. *Dir* Fred Zinnemann *Scen* Richard Schweizer, David Wechsler, Paul Jarrico *Photog* Emil Berna *Mus* Robert Blum *Ed* Hermann Haller *Cast* Montgomery Clift, Aline MacMahon, Wendell Corey, Ivan Jandl, Jarmila Novotna *Prod* Praesens-Film, Zurich for MGM. 105 mins.

A group of refugee children are on their way to an UNRRA home when they become panic-stricken that the ambulance is a gas chamber and break out. One of the boys (Jandl), is found by an American soldier in the US Zone of Germany, looked after by him and a nurse (MacMahon), and taught to speak. Eventually he is found by his Czech mother (Novotna), who has been searching through Germany for him.

This excellent film using many nonprofessional actors is largely in the semi-documentary style of the New York school. It was produced in Switzerland and in the shattered United States-Occupied Zone of Germany by the same producers as *The Last Chance (q.v.)*. It enjoyed considerable success in the USA and won an Oscar for Best Story as well as a special award for Ivan Jandl.

SEASHELL AND THE CLERGYMAN (THE) CO-QUILLE ET LE CLERGYMAN (LA)

SEASON FOR LOVE (THE) MORTE-SAISON DES AMOURS (LA)

SECRET GAME (THE) JEUX INTERDITS

SECRET LIFE OF WALTER MITTY (THE) USA 1947. *Dir* Norman Z. McLeod *Scen* Ken England, Everett Freeman based on a story by James Thurber *Photog* Lee Garmes *Art Dir* George Jenkins, Perry Ferguson *Mus* David Raksin *Ed* Monica Collingwood *Cast* Danny Kaye, Virginia

Mayo, Boris Karloff, Fay Bainter *Prod* Goldwyn for RKO. 105 mins. Technicolor.

Walter Mitty (Kaye), a typical American dominated by his mother (Bainter), imagines himself as various heroic figures — a famous surgeon, a daring pilot, a brave captain, a cowboy, etc.

The quality of its script and its gags make this Danny Kaye's best film.

SEINE A RENCONTRE PARIS (LA) THE SEINE MEETS PARIS France 1957. *Dir* Joris Ivens *Scen* Georges Sadoul *Poem* Jacques Prévert, spoken by Serge Reggiani *Photog* André Dumaître, Philippe Brun *Mus* Philippe Gérard *Ed* Gisèle Chézeau *Prod* Garance Films. 40 mins.

This poetic documentary about Paris was shot from barges on the River Seine using the methods of the "camera-eye." Its only commentary is the poem by Prévert. It received a Palme d'or at Cannes.

SELSKAYA UCHITELNITSA A VILLAGE SCHOOLTEACHER USSR 1947. *Dir* Mark Donsky *Scen* Maria Smirnova *Photog* Sergei Urusevsky *Art Dir* D. Vinitsky, P. Pashkevich *Mus* Lev Schwartz *Cast* Vera Maretskaya, Daniel Sagal, P. Olenev, M. Maritka *Prod* Soyuzdet film. 105 mins.

In Tsarist Russia, Varvara (Maretskaya) sees her fiancé arrested by the police and travels to Siberia as a teacher in order to marry him. He is killed in 1914. After the Revolution, she dedicates herself to teaching and, in 1941, sees the children she had taught leave for a new war.

One of Donskoy's best films with memorable scenes evoking Tsarist Russia and the romanticism of the revolutionaries. Vera Maretskaya gives a brilliant performance, first as a gay, young girl in the opening episodes and finally as an old teacher at the end of the film.

SEN NOCI SVATOJANSKE A MIDSUMMER NIGHT'S DREAM Czechoslovakia 1959. *Dir* Trnka *Scen* Jiri Brdecka, Jiri Trnka based on the Shakespeare play *Anim* B. Pojar, Jan Adam, V. Juradova, Jan Karpas, S. Latal, B. Sramek *Photog* Jiri Vojta *Mus* Vaclav Trojan. 74 mins. Eastman Color. CinemaScope.

Trnka's story is very freely based on the Shakespeare play: for example, Bottom becomes a Czech peasant not unlike the "Good Soldier Schweik." It is not a puppet film but uses animated sculptures in sets directly derived from the Czech baroque era and is Trnka's most determined effort to create a new form of plastic cinema. It was three years in production. Though it does not always entirely achieve its aims, the bold approach of this experiment deserved more success than it received.

SENSO THE WANTON COUNTESS/SENTIMENT Italy 1953. *Dir* Luchino Visconti *Scen* Luchino Visconti, Suso Cecchi D'Amico, G. Prosperi, C. Alianello, G. Bassani based on the short story by Camillo Boito *Photog* G. R. Aldo, Robert Krasker *Art Dir* Ottavio Scotti *Costumes* Marcel Escoffier, Piero Tosi *Mus* Anton Bruckner's *Seventh Symphony Ed* Mario Serandrei *Cast* Alida Valli, Farley Granger, Massimo Girotti, Heinz Moog, Christian Marquand *Prod* Lux. 115 mins. Technicolor. (Abridged English version, 100 mins., released under title *The Wanton Countess* with dialogue by Tennessee Williams and Paul Bowles.) In 1866 in Venice, where patriots are conspiring against the occupying Austrians, Countess Livia Serpieri (Valli) meets a young Austrian officer, Franz Mahler (Granger), and finds herself so desperately in love that she forgets family and patriotic obligations. She tries to break with him when liberation forces approach Venice but is unable to resist his persistence. She gives him money intended for the partisans so that he can buy his way out of the army. He leaves for Verona, and when she joins him, she finds him wrecked by drink and aware of his cowardice. When she discovers he had loved her for her wealth and had betrayed her cousin (Girotti), she goes to the Austrians to denounce him and he is shot.

This large-budget spectacular is one of the most beautiful Italian films ever made and one whose expressive colors and luxurious period setting are never used merely as a decorative backdrop. Its style seems almost operatic and, in fact, the film opens with a tribute to Giuseppe Verdi, whose opera gives rise to an Italian demonstration in the theater. Visconti makes brilliant use of the Italian landscape and existing settings: the old streets of Venice through which the countess goes to meet her lover; the splendid country house at Aldano,

which shelters their love; and the stone ramparts of Verona before which Franz is led to be shot. Each and every word and phrase of the dialogue is used to develop the drama and the psychology of the characters.

Visconti (aristocrat by birth, Marxist by conviction) offers in *Senso* an extraordinary portrait of a decadent and corrupt aristocracy in which Livia's seduction and treachery and Franz's cowardice and deceit are an inevitable result of their environment.

Senso also depicts the Risorgimento of the Italian people as they fight for the freedom and unification of their country. A high point of the film is the battle during which a young marquis (Girotti) vainly pleads with his superiors for the use of the ordinary Italian people in the fighting. This sequence was cut by the Italian censors and, without it, the tragic destiny of the two lovers no longer seems so closely tied to the destiny of a nation.

Alida Valli gives a superb interpretation of the countess ravaged by age, passion, and misery, and Farley Granger is convincing as the wretched Franz.

Senso was a critical failure and had only a limited commercial success. [Many critics bewailed Visconti's betrayal of neorealim in favor of "neoromanticism." But, in retrospect, Visconti's baroque qualities are evident even in *La Terra Trema* (*q.v.*) and *Ossessione* (*q.v.*) and reached their height in *The Leopard* (*q.v.*) and *The Damned* (*q.v.*) *Senso's* reputation has only increased over the years and it is now recognized as a great classic.]

SENTIMENT SENSO

SENZA PIETA WITHOUT PITY Italy 1948. *Dir* Alberto Lattuada *Scen* Federico Fellini, Tullio Pinelli based on an idea by E. M. Margadonna *Photog* Aldo Tonti *Mus* Felice Lattuada *Cast* Carla del Poggio, John Kitzmiller, Giulietta Masina, Pierre Claude, Lando Muzio *Prod* Lux Films. 94 mins.

An Italian girl, Angela (del Poggio), befriends a Negro soldier, Jerry (Kitzmiller), who is attempting to desert. Later, he finds her again in the port of Leghorn, where she has become a prostitute working for a group of black marketeers. They plan to steal a large sum of money but Angela is killed in the attempt. Jerry drives himself and her body over a cliff.

This portrait of the aftermath of war is also antiracist. Its style is mainly influenced by French poetic realism, especially by the films of Marcel Carné.

SEPPUKU HARAKIRI Japan 1962. *Dir* Masaki Kobayashi *Scen* Shinobu Hashimoto based on a novel by Yasuhiko Takiguchi *Photog* Yoshio Miyajima *Art Dir* Junichi Ozumi, Shigemasa Toda *Mus* Toru Takemitsu *Ed* Hisashi Sagara *Cast* Tatsuya Nakadai, Shimai Iwashita, Akira Ishihama, Rentaro Mikuni, Yoshio Inaba *Prod* Shochiku. 135 mins. Grandscope.

In Japan in the early 17th century many samurai have no means of existence and resort to pretending to commit harakiri in the hope that a clan will enroll them as retainers. A samurai, Tsugumo (Nakadai) arrives at a clan seeking permission to commit harakari and the leading retainer, Saito (Mikuni) tells him of another samurai, Motome Chijiwa (Ishihama), who had arrived on the same quest but with an imitation sword of bamboo. The clan force him to go through with the ritual. Tsugumo then reveals that Motome had been entrusted to his care and had married his daughter (Iwashita). Driven to desperation by the times, he had first sold his sword and then feigned a desire to commit harakiri. Tsugumo also reveals that he has waylaid the three men mainly responsible for forcing the boy to go through with his harakiri and dishonored them by cutting off their topknots. Saito orders his men to kill Tsugumo but he defeats them and Saito orders that the events shall remain a strict secret.

Though a "gendai-geki" (period film), *Harakiri* has serious contemporary overtones in its depiction of the meaninglessness of harakiri and honor. Its style is almost ritualized in its precise visual structure, careful camera movements, and intricate flashbacks — all dominated by the recurring image of Tsugumo sitting calmly in the center of a white harakiri mat. In Motome's harakiri scene and Tsugumo's final fight against Saito's men, it is also graphically brutal.

SERGEANT YORK USA 1941. *Dir* Howard Hawks *Scen* Aben Finkel, Harry Chandlee, Howard Koch, John Huston based on three books by Sam K. Cowan and Tom Skeyhill *Photog* Sol Polito *Mus*

Max Steiner *Cast* Gary Cooper, Joan Leslie, Walter Brennan, George Tobias, David Bruce, Margaret Wycherley, Ward Bond, Noah Beery, Jr., Howard Da Silva *Prod* Warner Brothers. 134 mins.

The story is based on the diary of an actual Alvin C. York (Cooper), who farms in the mountains of Tennessee to support his mother (Wycherley), brother, and sister, and dreams of owning fertile land in the lowlands so he can marry Gracie Williams (Leslie). When the USA enters the war in 1917, Alvin claims exemption as a conscientious objector, since he thinks war is wrong, but his claim is denied. He makes a model soldier, rethinks his attitudes, and becomes a corporal. In the battle of the Argonne, after his sergeant is killed, Alvin, as a sniper, single-handedly kills 20 Germans and captures 132 prisoners. He is hailed as a war hero and returns to Tennessee to find he has been given a fine house and fertile land so he can marry Gracie.

A film notable for its carefully composed atmosphere and sense of the Tennessee landscape, its slow rhythm, and its quiet humor. Gary Cooper is a complete incarnation of Alvin C. York, a religious, meditative farmer, scratching a living from the soil. One of the most striking of these early sequences shows him winning two shooting contests in order to gain money to buy his land, only to find it sold under his nose; angry, he drinks heavily and strides into the rain with death in his heart, but his gun is struck by lightning and he walks into a church service and becomes converted.

SERA'A FIL WADI THE BLAZING SUN/STRUGGLE IN THE VALLEY Egypt 1953. *Dir* Youssef Shahin *Scen* Ali El Zorkani *Cast* Omar El-Sherif (Omar Sharif), Faten Hamama, Zaki Rostom. 95 mins.

A young engineer (El-Sherif), the son of a fellah, struggles against exploitation and the princes and defeats one of them, as well as the bandits in his pay.

An excellent Egyptian film made in the year following the Revolution, with interesting portraits of the life of the fellahs and the luxurious palace life of the feudal prince. The climax, a chase and fight to the death in the ruins of Karnak, is a little too "Hitchcockian."

*SERVANT (THE) Britain 1963. *Dir* Joseph Losey *Scen* Harold Pinter based on the novel by Robin Maugham *Photog* Douglas Slocombe *Prod Design* Richard MacDonald *Art Dir* Ted Clements *Mus* Johnny Dankworth *Ed* Reginald Mills *Cast* Dirk Bogarde, Sarah Miles, James Fox, Wendy Craig, Catherine Lacey, Richard Vernon, Patrick Magee, Alun Owen *Prod* Springbok-Elstree. 115 mins.

A servant, Hugo Barrett (Bogarde), is hired by an upper-class indolent young man, Tony (Fox), who has moved into a new house in Chelsea where he plans to live with his fiancée (Craig) after their marriage. Gradually the relationship of servant and master changes as Tony falls under Barrett's control. Vera (Miles), Barrett's girl friend, seduces Tony and later leaves the house. In a final "orgy" sequence, Barrett's control over Tony, in an almost homosexual relationship, is made absolute.

Losey's brilliant socio-psychological drama is both a study in the ultimate sterility of an outdated class warfare (Tony's self-centeredness and arrogance being as self-destructive as Barrett's aggressive hostility) and an exploration of fear and guilt in human relationships. The servility-domination theme of Barrett and Tony is echoed in other relationships throughout the film and is most clearly seen in the brilliant restaurant scene in which three couples are revealed in relationships lacking real contact. Losey himself sees "the last third of *The Servant* (as) a resolution (however negative) of the consequences of living by false values — turning the relationship upside down to expose the falsity of values on both sides." *The Servant* is one of Losey's most assured films, a total integration of acting, fluid camerawork, and design.

SETUP (THE) USA 1949. *Dir* Robert Wise *Scen* Art Cohn based on the narrative poem by Joseph Moncure March *Photog* Milton Krasner *Art Dir* Albert D'Agostino, Jack Okey *Mus* C. Bakaleinikoff *Ed* Roland Gross *Cast* Robert Ryan, Audrey Totter, George Tobias, Alan Baxter, Wallace Ford *Prod* RKO. 72 mins.

Stoker Thompson (Ryan), an aging boxer, refuses to retire despite the pleadings of his wife, Julie (Totter). He agrees to fight a much younger man, unaware that his manager (Tobias) has accepted a bribe from Little Boy (Baxter) for Stoker to "lie down." In spite of terrible punishment, Stoker persists and wins in the last round. On the way home he is set upon by Little Boy and his gang and his right hand is injured so that he cannot fight again.

Set entirely at night in a seedy provincial town, this harsh portrait of the boxing world, with its petty crooks and its sadistic, hysterical crowds, has rarely been matched. Robert Ryan gives a good characterization of the battered, but indefatigable, boxer.

— **The Setup* Britain 1962. *Dir* Gerard Glaister *Cast* Maurice Denham, John Carson, Maria Corvin. 58 mins.

Not about the boxing world, but one of the seemingly endless British series of B-pictures based on Edgar Wallace stories.

SEVEN MEN FROM NOW USA 1956. *Dir* Budd Boetticher *Scen* Burt Kennedy *Photog* William H. Clothier *Art Dir* Leslie Thomas *Mus* Henry Vars *Ed* Everett Sutherland *Cast* Randolph Scott, Gail Russell, Lee Marvin, Walter Reed, John Larch *Prod* Batjac for Warner Brothers. 77 mins. WarnerColor.

After seven bandits raid a Wells Fargo office, and in the process kill his wife, Ben Stride (Scott), the former sheriff, seeks revenge. On his journey he meets John Greer (Reed) and his wife, Anne (Russell), and two outlaws, one of whom, Masters (Marvin), covets both Anne and the stolen gold. After Ben has killed several of Pat Bodeen's (Larch) men he discovers that Greer had been an unwilling accomplice of the bandits. Greer is then killed by Bodeen. The remaining bandits ride to where Ben is hiding the gold but are shot down by Masters, who is himself killed in a final gun duel with Ben.

André Bazin's brilliant analysis of this film was the first time serious critical attention had been paid to Boetticher. "Possibly the best western I have seen since the war . . . One complicating factor is that it is difficult to discern how much of this exceptional film's quality derives directly from the director's style, from the scenario, and from the brilliant dialogue, not to mention the anonymous virtues of the western tradition . . . It is indeed one of the most intelligent westerns I know but at the same time the least intellectual, the subtlest and the least esthetic, the simplest and the most beautiful . . . Budd

Boetticher and his scriptwriter did not set out to "dominate" their theme by being patronizing, nor to "enrich" it by psychological asides, but simply to force it to its logical extremes . . . [The film's power lies in its use of abstraction in the characters' relationships set against the very concrete beauty of the landscape . . . The style is a combination of extreme realism and extreme conventionality . . . A color process is used . . . that gives *Seven Men From Now* the tone and feeling of transparency that old book engravings have; it is as though conventions of color were being used to emphasize conventions of action."]

SEVEN SAMURAI (THE) SHICHI-NIN NO SAMURAI

SEVENTH HEAVEN USA 1927. *Dir* Frank Borzage *Scen* Benjamin Glazer based on the play by Austin Strong *Photog* Ernest Palmer, J. A. Valentine *Cast* Janet Gaynor, Charles Farrell, Gladys Brockwell, Albert Gran, David Butler *Prod* Fox. 8,500 ft.
In 1914, Chico (Farrell), a young man working in the sewers of Paris, reaches Diane (Gaynor), a young girl, from the clutches of her older sister (Brockwell). He gives the girl shelter in his garrett, tells the police she is his wife, and they fall deeply in love. Just as they are about to be married he is drafted and sent to the war. She works in a munitions factory until the end of the war, when he is reported killed. But he returns, blind, and they are reunited.
This Borzage romance was a great success in the United States and made the "ideal couple," Janet Gaynor and Charles Farrell, famous. In France, this beautiful love story fared badly but was recognized by the surrealists after André Breton discovered it in a small theater. Ado Kyrou wrote: "The two lovers, separated by life, are joined together by a force that one can only call 'Love,' which tells each of the least movement or thought of the other and guides their steps through a universe in which we believe ourselves to be blind."
— **Seventh Heaven* USA 1937. *Dir* Henry King *Scen* Melville Baker based on the play *Photog* Merritt Gerstad *Mus* Louis Silvers *Cast* Simone Simon, James Stewart, Jean Hersholt, Gale Sondergaard *Prod* 20th Century-Fox. 102 mins.

Henry King's remake has a charming romantic atmosphere and pleasant performances but is often heavy-handed, especially in the final scenes.

SEVENTH SEAL (THE) SJUNDE INSEGLET (DET)

SEVEN YEAR ITCH (THE) USA 1955. *Dir* Billy Wilder *Scen* Billy Wilder, George Axelrod based on the play by George Axelrod *Photog* Milton Krasner *Art Dir* Lyle Wheeler, George W. Davis *Mus* Alfred Newman *Ed* Hugh Fowler *Cast* Marilyn Monroe, Tom Ewell, Evelyn Keyes, Sonny Tufts, Oscar Homolka *Prod* 20th Century-Fox. 105 mins. De-Luxe Color. CinemaScope.
A faithful husband (Ewell) is left alone when his wife (Keyes) leaves for a holiday to escape the New York summer heat. He is tempted by a pretty neighbor (Monroe), invites her into his apartment, but, in the end, remains faithful to his wife.
This skillful, but essentially vulgar farce, was a great commercial success, although it is not at all like Wilder's other films on sexual mores. Tom Ewell indulges himself with histrionics but Marilyn Monroe appears in one of her most seductive and appealing roles.

SEVEN YEARS' BAD LUCK USA 1921. *Dir/ Scen* Max Linder *Assist* Paul Ivano *Photog* Charles Van Enger *Cast* Max Linder, Alta Allen, Thelma Percy, Harry Mann, Lola Gonzales *Prod* Linder for United Artists. 4,000 ft.
Having celebrated too freely, Max breaks a mirror. His fiancée breaks with him and he leaves on a long trip. When he returns he meets his former fiancée about to marry his best friend, but all ends happily.
Max Linder's first film in Hollywood, where he lived a life of rich ease in a luxurious house with many servants. The most famous comic sequence shows Max's valet breaking a mirror and then persuading the cook to dress up like Max who, thinking he sees himself reflected in what is actually an empty frame, tries to shave. This gag was already a vaudeville classic in 1921 and has since been used in several later films (e.g. *Duck Soup*) but here it has an almost balletic gracefulness. Later, Max has his ticket and luggage stolen and finds himself in an extremely diffi-

cult situation. Disguised as a Negro, he terrifies a woman traveler, then finds himself in a cage of lions, is arrested by a monkey dressed as a policeman, and battles with a fly-paper.

Sequences such as these are somewhat Keatonesque; certainly Linder's comic style must have had some influence on Keaton.

Seven Years' Bad Luck is included in the recent compilation *En compagnie de Max Linder*.

SHADOW OF A DOUBT USA 1943. *Dir* Alfred Hitchcock *Scen* Thornton Wilder, Alma Reville, Sally Benson *Photog* Joseph Valentine *Mus* Dimitri Tiomkin *Ed* W. Carruth *Cast* Joseph Cotten, Teresa Wright, Macdonald Carey, Henry Travers, Hume Cronyn *Prod* Universal. 108 mins.

A widow-murderer, Charley (Cotten) dodges the police and joins his relatives in a small California town. There, his niece, Charley (Wright) takes Uncle Charley to her heart but eventually recognizes him as the murderer. Though someone else is accused, Uncle Charley commits suicide.

Hitchcock has said many times in interviews that he considers *Shadow of a Doubt* his best American film. One can easily agree with him even though this film is often less admired than his other films, which usually sacrifice more to technical effects and black comedy. Its classically effective style is used not only to develop the suspense but also to characterize the world of Charley's small-town relatives and to disclose the psychotic tension under Charley's gentle exterior. Joseph Cotten's silences count more than his dialogue in his very effective performance as Charley. The various subtle camera movements seem that much more perfect because they are never used gratuitously.

— *Step Down to Terror/The Silent Stranger* USA 1958. *Dir* Harry Keller *Photog* Russell Metty *Cast* Charles Drake, Rod Taylor, Colleen Miller *Prod* Universal. 75 mins.

This is virtually a remake (except that it is a son returning to his mother after six years who is the psycopathic killer), but its script sags and it totally lacks subtlety, atmosphere, and reasonable acting.

SHADOW OF ADULTERY PROIE POUR L'OM-BRE (LA)

SHADOW OF THE THIN MAN see THIN MAN (THE)

*SHADOWS USA 1959. *Dir* John Cassavetes *Photog* Erich Kollmar *Mus* Charlie Mingus *Ed* Len Appelson, Maurice McEndree *Cast* Lelia Goldoni, Ben Carruthers, Hugh Hurd, Anthony Ray *Prod* Cassavetes/McEndree/Cassel. 81 mins.

Two Negro brothers and a sister, Hugh (Hurd), Ben (Carruthers), and Lelia (Goldoni), share an apartment in New York. Ben is light skinned and roams the streets with two friends searching for his identity. Lelia is seduced by Tony (Ray), who leaves her when he learns she is a mulatto. Later she goes with an attractive Negro to a dance. Ben and his friends are beaten up by a rival group. Hugh accepts a third-rate engagement in a nightclub.

This episodic film was shot without a script for about $15,000 in 16 mm and then enlarged to 35 mm for release. It is primarily a series of improvisations that gradually reveal the mood of the city and the life and relationships of the three characters. Its sense of spontaneity is comparable to that achieved by Rouch in *Moi, un noir* (*q.v.*) and its approach had considerable impact on the developing "new American cinema." Two versions of *Shadows* were made. The first has much less of a formal construction than the second for which Cassavetes reshot certain scenes. He also completely re-edited the second version at the request of distributors, who wanted it more "commercial."

SHADOWS OF THE YOSHIWARA JUJIRO

SHAGAI, SOVIET STRIDE, SOVIET! USSR 1926. *Dir/Scen/Ed* Dziga Vertov *Assist* Y. Svilova *Photog* I. Belyakov *Ciné-explorer* Ilya Kopalin *Prod* Goskino. 1,650 meters.

This "symphony of creative work" was commissioned by the Moscow Soviet. Although largely concerned with life in Moscow, it is ultimately a tableau of life in the USSR during the reconstruction period. Vertov makes constant use of contrasting opposites: life then and now; life here and in other countries. The opening sequence has a discourse on the destruction caused by the Civil War and what had been done to repair the damage. The titles are never merely explicative but are an indispensable part of the visual sequence. Like illustrated alphabets and spelling books, or like words in a futurist collage, even the typography is an essential visual element. Each object or subject thus becomes a kind of ideogram or hieroglyph with as precise a significance as a drawing in a dictionary this illustrates the meaning of a word. The whole film is constructed and has a rhythm like a poem by Mayakovsky.

One of the most striking sequences in this "two thousand meters of the Bolshevik country" (another title for the film) is the meeting in front of the Mos-Soviet. Here, Vertov's use of elements like the loudspeakers and the taxis becomes a kind of lyrical, Futurist exaltation of the machine.

SHAME OF A NATION WESTFRONT 1918

SHANE USA 1953. *Dir* George Stevens *Scen* A. B. Guthrie, Jr. based on the novel by Jack Schaefer *Photog* Loyal Griggs *Art Dir* Hal Pereira, Walter Tyler *Mus* Victor Young *Ed* William Hornbeck, Tom McAdoo *Cast* Alan Ladd, Jean Arthur, Van Heflin, Brandon De Wilde, Jack Palance *Prod* Paramount. 118 mins. Technicolor.

At the turn of the century, Joe Starrett (Heflin), his wife, Marion (Arthur), and son Joey (De Wilde) are trying to homestead with their neighbors in Wyoming despite Ryker, who wants to keep the land free for open-range farming. Shane (Ladd), a mysterious stranger with a gunfighting past, arrives in the district, is befriended by the Starretts and idolized by Joey. Ryker hires a professional gunfighter, Wilson (Palance), to drive away the homesteaders and he kills one of them. Starrett wants to fight him, but Shane, knowing of Wilson's prowess, prevents him, goes to the fight himself, and kills both Wilson and Ryker. Then he rides off as mysteriously as he arrived.

This psychological western was produced by Paramount to celebrate the 80th birthday of its founder, Zukor. Richly atmospheric, with a persuasive evocation of the period, it is structured like a modern tragedy — the symbolic hero figure only prepared to apply his powers in a righteous cause and refusing to take advantage of the unspoken love between himself and the wife of his host. Though

not revolutionary, it is a superior western [that enjoyed an enormous commercial success and whose appeal seems not to have lessened with the years. In retrospect, Shane seems also like an embryonic Peckinpah hero whose services are needed one more time before the settlers finally establish their civilization and take over the "open range" of the West. The "settled West" is beautifully caught by Stevens in the Starrett family scenes and in the party and burial sequences — places where Shane does not, and cannot, belong.]

SHANGHAI DOCUMENT (A) SHANGHAISKY DOKUMENT

SHANGHAIED USA 1915. *Dir/Scen* Charles Chaplin *Photog* Rollie Totheroh *Cast* Charles Chaplin, Edna Purviance, Wesley Ruggles, John Rand, Leo White, Billy Armstrong, Paddy McGuire, Fred Goodwins. *Prod* Essanay. 1,670 ft.

One of Chaplin's best Essanay films, in which Charlie is shanghaied on to a ship as the cook's assistant and has great difficulty serving food when the sea gets rough. Later, after he has discovered the shipowner's (Ruggles) daughter (Purviance) is a stowaway, he foils a plot to destroy the boat for the insurance. As in *The Bank* (*q.v.*) made just prior to this film, Chaplin's elemental Keystone style evolves here towards social satire.

SHANGHAI EXPRESS USA 1932. *Dir* Josef von Sternberg *Scen* Jules Furthman, Josef von Sternberg based on a story idea by Harry Hervey *Photog* Lee Garmes *Art Dir* Hans Dreier *Costumes* Travis Banton *Cast* Marlene Dietrich, Clive Brook, Anna May Wong, Warner Oland, Louise Closser Hale, Eugene Pallette, Lawrence Grant, Emile Chautard *Prod* Paramount. 84 mins.

On the express train from Peking to Shanghai are Captain Harvey (Brook), Shanghai Lily (Dietrich) with whom Harvey had had an affair five years before, a Chinese girl, Huie Fei (Wong), on her way to be married, and several other passengers (Grant, Pallette, Chautard, Hale, etc.). On the way, the train is stopped by a rebellious Chinese war lord, Henry Chang (Oland). In order to save Huie Fei and the Captain, Lily offers herself to Chang, who dupes her but is killed by Huie Fei. Finally, the train arrives in Shanghai with the Captain realizing he still loves Lily.

[Sternberg has said that he "took great pleasure in recreating China in Hollywood according to my imagination. Later on (1934) I went there. I took the Shanghai Express and it was quite different. That is why I'm glad I made this film before, following my fancy. I'm sort of a poet." Certainly, his portrait of China, despite its visual evocativeness, is a conventional one.]

The best episode in the film is the opening in Peking station with the bustle of the crowds and the various passengers preparing for their departure. When the train finally departs, it puffs it way slowly down a street teeming with coolies, shopkeepers, hucksters, and women shoppers and is held up by a cow in the middle of the track. After this the plot becomes melodramatic. Marlene Dietrich's extraordinary clothes were designed by Travis Banton as they had been for *Morocco* and *The Scarlet Empress.*

— *Peking Express* USA 1951. *Dir* William Dieterle *Scen* John Meredyth Lucas based on the story of *Shanghai Express Photog* Charles Lang, Jr. *Art Dir* Hal Pereira, Franz Bachelin *Mus* Dimitri Tiomkin *Cast* Joseph Cotten, Corinne Calvert, Edmund Gwenn, Marvin Miller *Prod* Paramount. 85 mins.

This remake was produced at the height of the McCarthy era: Warner Oland's role becomes that of a Communist "gangster" and the whole film is used as an excuse for anti-Red propaganda, with Edmund Gwenn (in an added priest role) delivering little homilies about peace, love, and man's inhumanity to man.

SHANGHAISKY DOKUMENT A CHINESE DOCUMENT USSR 1928. *Dir* Yakov Blyokh *Photog* V. Stepanov *Prod* Soyuzkino. 1,700 meters.

An unforgettable documentary on life in the Chinese metropolis, with its skyscrapers, coolies, theaters, international companies, and children working at looms specially built for ten-year-olds.

SHATTERED SCHERBEN

SHCHORS USSR 1939 (production began 1936). *Dir/Scen* Alexander Dovzhenko *Co-Dir* Yulia Solntseva *Assist* Lazar Bodik *Photog* Yuri Yekelchik *Art Dir* Maurice Umansky *Mus* Dmitri Kabalevsky *Cast* Yevgeni Samoilov, Ivan Skuratov,

Hans Klering, P. Krassilich *Prod* Kiev. 142 mins.

A biographical portrait of the Ukranian partisan leader, Nikolai Shchors (Samoilov) during the latter period of the First World War and the Civil War.

Best sequences: the meeting with the Germans after the Kaiser's abdication; the wedding procession during a Civil War bombardment; the political meeting in a theater with an old peasant Bozhenko (Skuratov); the Red cavalry entering a palace with its elaborate staircases and luxurious rooms; the discussion between Shchors and Bozhenko; the dirgelike ending; the burial of Bozhenko, carried by eight soldiers with heads bowed in grief.

[In 1935, Stalin had suggested to Dovzhenko that he "give us a Ukrainian *Chapayev (q.v.)*" but when Dovzhenko accepted the proposal he found himself in the middle of a production hampered by political and bureaucratic interference. Preparation of the script took 11 months and the shooting twenty because of endless discussions about each character and episode.] In the end, Shchors becomes an authoritarian, godlike figure whose decisions have an unbreakable, moral force (designed to reflect the leader, Stalin) both in the script and in the performance by Samoilov (father of Tatyana Samoilova of *The Cranes are Flying* fame). Dovzhenko himself "felt more at ease with the old peasant" and this historical invention, an emotional, undisciplined, earthy old man, is far more the hero of the film than the unrealistic partisan leader whose men adore him unquestioningly.

Despite its rhetoric and somewhat rambling dramatic structure, *Shchors* has many epic sequences and unforgettable images "of death and passionate life" (Jay Leyda) and has long been accepted as a classic in North America and Britain.

SHE DEFENDS HER COUNTRY ONA ZASHCHISHCHAYET RODINU

SHE DONE HIM WRONG USA 1933. *Dir* Lowell Sherman *Scen* Harvey Thew, John Bright based on the play *Diamond Lil* by Mae West *Photog* Charles Lang *Art Dir* Bob Usher *Mus* Ralph Rainger *Ed* Alexander Hall *Cast* Mae West, Cary Grant, Gilbert Roland, Noah Beery, Rafaela Ottiano, David Landau, Rochelle Hudson *Prod* Paramount. 66 mins.

Diamond Lil (Mae West) a chanteuse in the Bowery during the Gay Nineties, plays Gus (Beery) off against Serge (Roland) and eventually settles for Captain Cummings (Grant). This is the first starring vehicle by the splendidly fleshy, vulgar, yet self-mocking Mae West, who is much more the *auteur* of this film than the obscure Lowell Sherman. [It was Mae West's repertoire of one-liners ("Is that a gun in your pocket or are you just glad to see me?") and songs like "Where Has My Easy Rider Gone?" in this and in *I'm No Angel* that led to the imposition of the Hollywood Production Code.]

SHEIK (THE) see SON OF THE SHEIK (THE)

SHE ONLY DANCED ONE SUMMER HON DANSADE EN SOMMAR

SHEPHERDESS AND THE CHIMNEY SWEEP (THE) BERGÈRE ET LE RAMONEUR (LA)

SHERLOCK, JR. USA 1924. *Dir/Ed* Buster Keaton *Scen* Clyde Bruckman, Jean Havez, Joseph Mitchell *Photog* Elgin Lessley, Byron Houck *Art Dir* Fred Gabourie *Cast* Buster Keaton, Kathryn McGuire, Ward Crane, Joseph Keaton, Horace Morgan, Jane Connelly, Ford West *Prod* Metro. 4,065 ft.
Buster, a film projectionist, is falsely accused by his girl friend's (McGuire) father of stealing a watch. At work, he falls asleep and dreams he is a famous film detective on a similar case. When he wakes he solves his real life difficulties and wins back his girl friend.
Although perhaps not Keaton's most well known film, this is one of his perfectly realized pieces of imperturbable frenzy. René Clair, in 1925, drew attention to the surrealistic aspects and added. "The remarkable *Sherlock, Jr.* was a kind of dramatic critique comparable to *Six Characters in Search of an Author*, which Pirandello wrote for the theater." In 1947, Clair wrote: "Keaton, in the role of a film projectionist, fell asleep, slid down the beam of light from his machine, entered the screen, and took part with the characters in the drama being played out there. Subsequently, the unfortunate dreamer got lost in the middle of a world whose face changes in an unforeseen manner around him. Diving off a high rock to save a blond heroine struggling in the waves, he landed on desert sand under the astonished gaze of a lion."
J. A. Fieschi finds "the dream embracing, and finally taking the place of, reality, with the synthesis resolved in the world of the screen, a world at once acted in and observed by Keaton and true to his actual situation. At the same time he offers one of the most perfect definitions of our art."

SHESTAYA CHAST MIRA A SIXTH OF THE WORLD USSR 1926. *Dir/Scen/Ed* Dziga Vertov *Assist* Mikhail Kaufman, Yelizaveta Svilova, Ilya Kopalin *Photog* Mikhail Kaufman, Ivan Belyakov, Samuel Bendersky, P. Zotov, A. Lemberg, N. Konstantinov, N. Strukov, Yakov Tolchan *Prod* Goskino. 1,767 meters.
This lyrical film-poem was commissioned by the Soviet government's trade agency and made the same year as *Stride, Soviet! (q.v.)*. It is an exotically beautiful, animistic documentary that brings together in a "universal song" the various European and Asiatic regions of the Soviet Union. It had considerable influence on the development of the documentary in many countries. In particular, Walther Ruttman took the idea for his *Melodie der Welt (q.v.)* from this key film by Vertov.

SHICHI-NIN NO SAMURAI THE SEVEN SAMURAI/THE MAGNIFICENT SEVEN Japan 1954. *Dir/Ed* Akira Kurosawa *Scen* Akira Kurosawa, Hideo Oguni, Shinobu Hashimoto *Photog* Asaichi Nakai *Art Dir* Takashi Matsuyama *Mus* Fumio Hayasaka *Cast* Takashi Shimurai, Toshiro Mifune, Kuninori Kodo, Yoshio Inaba, Seiji Miyaguchi, Minoru Chiaki, Daisuke Kato, Ko Kimura, Keiko Tshushima *Prod* Toho. 200 mins. (original version); various English versions 161 mins., 155 mins., 148 mins.
In 16th century Japan, the inhabitants of a small village decide to hire samurai to defend themselves against the annual raid by bandits but they can only afford those that are poor and hungry. A deputation led by the village elder (Kodo) wins over a veteran, Kambei (Shimurai), and with his help six others are recruited, including Shichiroji (Kato), the young Katsushiro (Kimura), Kyuzo (Miyaguchi), and Kikuchiyo (Mifune), a crazy braggart posing as a samurai. The seven samurai help organize the villagers' defenses while convincing them of their

good intentions. Katsushiro falls in love with Shino (Tshushima), a young peasant girl. After a series of violent battles, victory is won for the villagers, but only three (Kambei, Shichiroji, and Katsushiro) of the original seven sumurai survive.

This expensive spectacular was more than a year in production. Like *Rashomon* (*q.v.*) it is a period film with a humanistic theme: seven mercenaries who sacrifice themselves to ensure peace for the ordinary people. As Kambei says at the end: "It is not we who have won. It is the peasants — they have their earth, but we have nowhere." *Seven Samurai* was a great success in the West: its narrative power, rich imagery, virtuoso battle scenes, and sharply etched and well-acted characters have often been noted.

[The original version (which Kurosawa himself felt was "too long") was shown only in major cities in Japan; shortened versions were prepared for general release and export. The original version is apparently no longer extant. *Seven Samurai* was awarded the Silver Lion at the Venice Festival and an Academy Award as Best Foreign Film.]

— *The Magnificent Seven* USA 1960. *Dir* John Sturges *Scen* William Roberts based on Kurosawa's film *Photog* Charles Lang, Jr. *Art Dir* Edward Fitzgerald *Mus* Elmer Bernstein *Ed* Ferris Webster, *Cast* Yul Brynner, Steve McQueen, Horst Buchholz, James Coburn, Eli Wallach, Charles Bronson, Robert Vaughan, Brad Dexter, Rosenda Monteros *Prod* Mirisch-Alpha for United Artists. 128 mins. Eastman Color. Panavision.

[This lively, pictorially impressive western transposes the action to a Mexican village that seven American gunmen (Brynner, McQueen, Buchholz, Coburn, Vaughan, Bronson, Dexter) defend against the plunderings of bandits led by Calvera (Wallach). It includes several well-characterized roles, notably Steve McQueen as the relaxed Vin and James Coburn as the knife expert. The most memorable sequence is that in which Chris (Brynner) and Vin meet while driving a hearse to Boot Hill. A remarkably dull sequel was produced in 1966, *The Return of the Seven,* directed by Burt Kennedy in Technicolor and Panavision and an even duller follow-up in 1968, *The Guns of the Magnificent Seven,* directed by Paul Wendkos in De-Luxe Color and Panavision. The former still retained Yul Brynner from the original cast but the latter, which had no actors from the original, starred George Kennedy and James Whitmore.]

SHINEL' THE CLOAK/THE OVERCOAT USSR 1926. *Dir* Grigori Kozintsev, Leonid Trauberg *Scen* Yuri Tinyanov based on short stories, *The Cloak* and *Nevsky Prospect* by Gogol *Photog* Andrei Moskvin, Yevgeni Mikhailov *Art Dir* Yevgeni Enei *Cast* Andrei Kostrichkin, Anna Zheimo, Sergei Gerasimov, A. Kapler *Prod* Leningradkino. 1,921 meters.

This "comedy in the Gogol manner" (the subtitle of *The Cloak*) by the founders of the FEKS group used not only Gogol's most famous story, but another, *The Nevsky Prospect,* in a prologue showing a youthful adventure of the clerk, Bashmachkin (Kostrichkin). *The Cloak* is more expressionistic than merely "eccentric." Moskvin's black and white images (of the robbery in the snow, for example) create a fatalistic world of elongated shadows while Enei's expressive interior sets blend superbly with the many scenes shot on the streets of St. Petersburg. The cloak (both the old and the new one) itself becomes a character in the drama. Kozintsev and Trauberg also convey a precise atmosphere of the epoch with the pervasive presence of authoritarian, military officialdom. The tailor (Gerasimov) and his wife (Zheimo) give typical, acrobatic, FEKS performances.

The various battered 16 mm copies of this film circulating in the West make it impossible to fully appreciate its visual experiments and original style.

— *Le Manteau* France/German Democratic Republic 1951. *Co-Dir/Cast* Marcel Marceau. 50 mins. approx.

This pantomime by Marcel Marceau may have been influenced by the Soviet film, particularly in the tailor's scenes.

— *Il Cappotto/The Overcoat* Italy 1952. *Dir* Alberto Lattuada *Scen* Cesare Zavattini, Alberto Lattuada, Enzo Currel, Giorgio Prospero, and others based on Gogol's story *Photog* Mario Montuori *Art Dir* Gianni Polidori, Baldachini *Mus* Felice Lattuada *Cast* Renato Rascel, Yvonne Sanson, Giulio Stival, Antonella Lualdi *Prod* Enzo Currel/Faro Films. 95 mins.

A modernized version set in a village in northern Italy in winter. This "neorealist fantasy" is perhaps Lattuada's best film, lyrical and persuasively realistic and with an excellent performance by ex-cabaret artist Renato Rascel as the little clerk, Carmine de Carmine.

— *The Bespoke Overcoat* Britain 1955. *Dir* Jack Clayton *Scen* Wolf Manko-witz *Photog* Wolfgang Suschitzky *Art Dir* Anthony Masters *Ed* Stanley Hawkes *Cast* Alfie Bass, David Kossof, Alan Tilvern *Prod* Remus. 33 mins.

This short feature derived from the Gogol story is Jack Clayton's first film and is a minor gem in the skillful crea-tion of mood and atmosphere through its acting and (extremely modest) staging. It won several awards, including an Oscar and a Venice Festival award.

— *Shinel/The Overcoat* USSR 1959. *Dir* Alexei Batalov *Scen* Li Soloviev based on Gogol's story *Photog* G. Marangian *Cast* R. Rykov, I. Tolubiev, A. Ezkina *Prod* Lenfilm. 93 mins.

This latest version not only returns to Gogol's original setting and period, but also, in some ways, to the style of the 1926 Soviet Film

SHOESHINE SCIUSCIA

SHOOT THE PIANO PLAYER TIREZ SUR LE PIANISTE

SHOP ON MAIN (THE HIGH) STREET (THE) OBCHOD NA KORZE

SHOULDER ARMS USA 1918. *Dir/Scen* Charles Chaplin *Photog* Rollie Totheroh *Cast* Charles Chaplin, Edna Purviance, Sydney Chaplin, Jack Wilson, Henry Bergman, Albert Austin *Prod* Chaplin for First National. 2,100 ft.

This biting satire on war and the army is a perfect blend of realistic description (muddy trenches, water-filled dugout) and free lyricism as Charlie, camouflaged as a tree, moves into the realm of dreams, rescues a beautiful French girl (Pur-viance), captures the Kaiser (Syd Chap-lin), the Crown Prince (Wilson), and a German general (Bergman) and winds up the war singlehandedly. After a work of this stature Elie Faure could justifi-ably compare Chaplin to Shakespeare. Although Louis Delluc found it "a film that, dreadfully, bays at the moon," he also felt it "justifies everything one could hope for in the cinema."

Chaplin had originally intended to pro-duce a five-reel film but First National objected to some of the more polemical scenes. Among these was the film's original ending in which Charlie, after his victory, is feted by Poincaré, King George V, and Wilson, steals their but-tons as souvenirs, and forces them to flee clutching their trousers. Even with the deletions, First National was wary of its "bad taste" and finally released it with some trepidation shortly before the Armistice. It was a great popular success and, for some, still remains Chaplin's masterpiece.

SIEGFRIED NIBELUNGEN (DIE)

SIERRA DE TERUEL ESPOIR

SI JOLIE PETITE PLAGE (UNE) UNE SI JOLIE PETITE PLAGE

SILENCE (THE) TYSTNADEN

SILENCE DE LA MER (LE) France 1947 (re-leased 1949). *Dir* Jean-Pierre Melville *Scen* Jean-Pierre Melville based on the short story by Vercors *Photog* Henri Decaë *Mus* Edgar Bischoff *Ed* Jean-Pierre Melville, Henri Decaë *Cast* Howard Vernon, Nicole Stéphane, Jean-Marie Robain, Denis Sadier *Prod* Mel-ville Productions. 86 mins.

During the Nazi occupation of France, an aristocratic German officer (Vernon) is stationed in the provinces with an old man (Robain) and his niece (Stéphane) who are bitterly hostile and silent in his presence. Just as he overcomes their enmity and at the same time discovers the realities of Nazism in France, he is ordered to the eastern front.

The short story by Vercors had been written during the German occupation and published clandestinely. Melville shot this, his first feature, in the house Vercors had used for the setting of the story. "The use of a commentary over the images seemed to me to be open to criticism . . . then, a true miracle hap-pes: the repetitions, the occasionally maladroit use of trifles, the buried im-agery, and especially the insistent fidelity to the original give birth finally to that unremitting, forceful tension so admir-able in the famous book . . . It goes right to the heart because its director's heart was in it. *Le Silence de la mer* must be seen and applauded" (G.S. *Les Lettres françaises,* May 5, 1949).

SILENCE EST D'OR (LE) MAN-ABOUT-TOWN
France 1947. *Dir/Scen* René Clair
Photog Armand Thirard *Art Dir* Léon
Barsacq, de Gastyne *Mus* Georges Van
Parys *Ed* Louisette Hautecoeur, Taverna
Cast Maurice Chevalier, François Périer,
Dany Robin, Marcelle Derrien, Robert
Pizani, Raymond Cordy *Prod* Pathé-
RKO. 99 mins.

René Clair wrote that it was "without
doubt youthful memories that gave birth
to this comedy. The action is set in the
pioneer era of the French cinema. These
souvenirs of artisans who, between 1900
and 1910, gave birth to the first film industry in France, is a tribute to their
memory by their pupil . . . The plot
is not a new one. It is about a middle-
aged flirt, a theme used very often in
the theater and never better than by the
author of *L' Ecole des Femmes* . . . *Le
Silence est d'or*, nevertheless, is not completely a reflection of Molière. Arnolphe-
Emile (Chevalier), a seducer on the re-
bound, has an almost paternal friendship for Horace-Jacques (Périer) . . .
He teaches him tricks of seduction and
ends up the victim of his own lessons."
Emile falls in love with a young girl
(Derrien) only to discover that she has
already fallen in love with Jacques, his
assistant.

Memorable sequences: an evening in a
caf'conc'; the production of an "oriental"
film in a glass-lined studio; the visit of a
sultan to the film factory; the conclusion in a traveling cinema — "You like it
when all ends happily and, Mademoiselle,
so do I."

Clair's director-hero seems less like
Méliès than Feuillade, whose style greatly
influenced Clair. Its historical re-creation
of the silent film era is much more than
"a backdrop," which is the way Clair has
described it. Its witty and accurate portrait of the people and the period is the
heart of the film and gives it much of its
appealing warmth.

SILENT STRANGERS (THE) see SHADOW OF A
DOUBT

SILENT WORLD (THE) MONDE DU SILENCE
(LE)

SILK STOCKINGS see NINOTCHKA

*SILLY SYMPHONIES (cartoon series) USA
1929–39. *Dir* Walt Disney, Ub Iwerks,
and various *Prod* Walt Disney. 1 reel
each.

This inventive series began in 1929 with
Skeleton Dance, an all-sound cartoon
with images brilliantly synchronized to
the music of Saint-Saëns' *Dance Macabre.* It is in this series that Disney encouraged his animators to express their
and his imaginations more freely. In
Flowers and Trees (1932), the first film
in full Technicolor, the color is used
kinetically for mood and comedy, while
others like *Music Land* (1935), *Wynken,
Blynken, and Nod* (1938), *The Farm-
yard Symphony* (*The Battle Between
Classic and Jazz*) (1938), and *Who
Killed Cock Robin?* (1935) have an extraordinary range of graphic design and
an imaginative use of sound. Perhaps the
most famous film in the series is *The
Three Little Pigs* (1933), whose theme
song "Who's Afraid of the Big Bad
Wolf?" achieved national popularity almost overnight. The *Silly Symphonies*
were, however, generally far less lucra-
tive than Disney's *Mickey Mouse series*
(*q.v.*) and were phased out of production in 1939.

SINGIN' IN THE RAIN USA 1952. *Dir*
Gene Kelly, Stanley Donen *Scen* Adolph
Green, Betty Comden *Photog* Harold
Rosson *Art Dir* Cedric Gibbons, Randall
Duell *Mus* Nacio Herb Brown, Lyrics by
Arthur Freed *Ed* Adrienne Fazan *Cast*
Gene Kelly, Jean Hagen, Donald O'Con-
nor, Debbie Reynolds, Millard Mitchell,
Cyd Charisse *Prod* MGM. 102 mins.
Technicolor.

Don Lockwood (Kelly), an immensely
popular film star of the Twenties teamed
with the equally famous Lina Lamont
(Hagen), meets and falls in love with
Kathy Selden (Reynolds), a young actress. Don and Lina's next film together
is a talkie and is a fiasco because of
Lina's voice. Don and his partner, Cosmo
(O'Connor), turn it into a musical using
Kathy to dub Lina's voice. Lina threatens
to sue the studio if the public learns the
truth and, after the film is a success at
the premier, announces she plans to
continue making musicals using Kathy's
voice. She makes a speech to the audience
then sings with Kathy stationed behind
the curtains but Don and Cosmo raise
the curtain revealing Kathy as the film's
real star.

This is undoubtedly one of the best
musicals of the Fifties, matching *An*

342

American in Paris (q.v.) in its pace, rhythmic structure, and memorable songs, and On the Town (q.v.) in its smoothly constructed and witty script by Adolph Green and Betty Comden (who also wrote On the Town). Its background of the Roaring Twenties and its satire on Hollywood during the introduction of sound add much to the film's appeal, as do the numerous excellent visual and sound gags — such as that revealing Kathy's dubbing of Lina. The imaginative choreography includes several (ironic) tributes to Busby Berkeley (such as "All I Do is Dream of You" and "Beautiful Girl") and a striking semiabstract ballet by Kelly and Cyd Charisse in "Broadway Rhythm." In supporting roles, Jean Hagen is memorable as the dumb star and Donald O'Connor brings a touch of American vaudeville, especially in his number "Make 'Em Laugh" (originally used in The Pirate). Gene Kelly is the true creative genius behind this film, which many consider his masterpiece.

SI PITJANG (literally, The Cripple) Indonesia 1952. Dir/Scen Kotot Sukardi Photog R. H. Jusuf Ganda Art Dir H. B. Angin Ed B. Supardi Cast nonprofessionals Prod Perusahaan Film Negara (Government Film Unit). 110 mins.
A small boy, crippled from birth, loses all his family during the war and is reduced to begging and vagabondage in the streets of Djakarta. He joins forces with other lost children and together they form a small community. Eventually a local army officer helps start a school for the children and the cripple decides to stay in order to be trained as a useful member of society.
Si Pitjang is not unlike Road to Life (q.v.) and is mainly of interest for its somewhat neorealist style and as the first important work to come from the young Indonesian cinema soon after Indonesia's independence. The children were all from a juvenile rehabilitation center. The last part of the film showing the public-spirited efforts to train the children in the rehabilitation school, is less convincing.

SIR ARNE'S TREASURE HERR ARNES PENGAR

SIREN OF ATLANTIS (THE) see ATLANDTIDE (L')

SISTERS OF GION (THE) GION NO SHIMAI

SIX ET DEMI-ONZE (UN KODAK) SIX AND A HALF BY ELEVEN (A KODAK) France 1927. Dir Jean Epstein Scen Marie Epstein Photog Georges Périnal Art Dir Pierre Kefer Cast Edmond Van Daele, Suzy Pierson, Nino Constanini, René Ferté, Jeanne Hebling Prod Jean Epstein Films. 2,000 meters approx. (6,540 ft. approx.).
Marie (Pierson), a young woman raised by Harry Gold (Ferté), an impresario, marries Jerome de Ners (Van Daele), a famous doctor. When he develops an old roll of Kodak film, he discovers that his wife is loved desperately by his young brother, Jean (Constanini), who is believed dead. She contemplates suicide.
The film was originally to have been called Un Kodak but the company objected to this. Epstein described it as "a visualization of movement, of appearances, and of tentative experiments less of spatial movements than of movements in time," based on a theme "still very Pierre Frondaie."

SIX JUIN A L'AUBE (LE) — Notes Cinématographiques sur le Débarquement Anglo-Americain France 1945. Dir/Scen/Mus/Commentary Jean Grémillon Photog Louis Page, André Bac, Alain Douarinou, Maurice Pecqueux, Henri Ferrand Ed Louisette Hautecoeur Prod Coopérative du cinéma francais. 56 mins.
Despite its subtitle, Grémillon deals only briefly with the actual landings. The main part of the film is an elegy, a requiem with Goya-like images, on war's tragic aftereffects. Grémillon described it as "an extremely exact report on conditions in Normandy after the battles in the summer of 1944. The cinema can and must accept the obligation of 'rendering account' without in any way having to give up its purity and its intrinsic nature. It is, and will be, an essential historical document of our times."

SIXTH OF A WORLD (A) SHESTAYA CHAST MIRA

SJUNDE INSEGLET (DET) THE SEVENTH SEAL Sweden 1956. Dir/Scen Ingmar Bergman Photog Gunnar Fischer Art Dir P. A. Lungren Mus Erik Nordgren Ed Lennart Wallen Cast Max von Sydow, Gunnar Björnstrand, Nils Poppe, Bibi Andersson, Bengt Ekerot Prod Svensk Filmindustri. 95 mins.
A knight, Antonius Blok (von Sydow), and his squire, Jöns (Björnstrand) re-

turn from the Crusades to a Sweden stricked by the plague. As they travel toward his castle, the knight plays a game of chess with Death (Ekerot). He meets Jof (Poppe), a wandering player, his wife, Mia (Andersson), and their small son and takes them with him. Later, he diverts Death's attention while Jof and Mia escape. He and his company are trapped in the castle and find themselves led away in the Dance of Death.

Bergman has recalled how, as a child, he used to accompany his father to small rural churches around Stockholm. "While the assembly of the faithful prayed, I directed my attention . . . to the medieval paintings. My intention has been to portray in the manner of these frescoes. My characters laugh, weep, mourn, are afraid, speak, reply, question — always question. They dread the Plague and the Last Judgement. Our anguish is of a different kind but the words remain the same." In this way, Bergman relates the Apocalypse to the modern fear of a nuclear catastrophe.

The Seventh Seal is Bergman's most ambitious film and is somewhat his "Faust" (and even his "Second Faust") in its allegory of the knight vainly grappling with Death. Despite its simplistic philosophy it has an engaging lyricism and a power of imagery perhaps unequaled in the Swedish cinema. Preferable to the final Dance of Death or the chess game on the seashore are the scenes of medieval Sweden, the band of flagellants, the life of the three wandering players, and the young girl condemned as a witch.

*SKULPJACI PERJA I EVEN MET HAPPY GYPSIES/I MET SOME HAPPY GYPSIES/HAPPY GYPSIES . . . ! (Alternative Yugoslav title: *Steo Sam Cak I Srecne Cigane*) Yugoslavia 1967. *Dir/Scen* Aleksander Petrovic *Photog* Tomislav Pinter *Art Dir* Veljko Despotovic *Mus* gipsy melodies arranged by Aleksander Petrovic *Cast* Bekim Fehmiu, Olivera Vuco, Bata Zivojinovic, Gordana Jovanovic *Prod* Avala. 90 mins. Eastman Color.

Bora (Fehmiu), a gypsy who trades goose feathers, is attracted to Tisa (Jovanovic), the stepdaughter of a fellow dealer, Mirta (Zivojinovic). She is married off to a young boy who, when he is unable to consummate the marriage, is thrown out by Tisa. Bora tries to buy Tisa from Mirta, who refuses the offer and tries to rape Tisa, who runs away.

Bora finds her, marries her, and takes her home to live with his two children and commonlaw wife. Tisa soon becomes bored and leaves for Belgrade. On the way back in a truck, she makes love to one of the drivers but not to the other, who throws her out at her village. She is taken back to her stepfather. Enraged, Bora fights and kills Mirta then disappears.

This, the first film in the gypsy language, is one of the most engaging and visually impressive films from Yugoslavia in the Sixties. It is Petrovic's fourth film and its unromantic portrait of the cruel yet beautiful life of the gypsies is well served by the muted color photography of the gay cottages and the flat, gray landscape and by Fehmiu's exhilarating, Belmondo-like performance as the hero.

SMILES OF A SUMMER NIGHT SOMMARNATTENS LEENDE

SMILING MADAME BEUDET (THE) SOURIANTE MADAME BEUDET (LA)

SMULTRONSTALLET WILD STRAWBERRIES Sweden 1957. *Dir/Scen* Ingmar Bergman *Photog* Gunnar Fischer *Art Dir* Gittan Gustafsson *Mus* Erik Nordgren *Ed* Oscar Rosander *Cast* Victor Sjöström, Ingrid Thulin, Bibi Andersson, Gunnar Björnstrand, Folke Sundquist, Björn Bjelvenstam, Gunnar Sjöberg, Gunnal Broström, Naima Wifstrand, Max von Sydow. *Prod* Svensk Filmindustri. 95 mins.

Old Professor Isak Borg (Sjöström) drives to Lund to receive an honorary doctorate accompanied by his daughter-in-law, Marianne (Thulin), who resents him because his son (Björstrand) reflects too many of his own egotistical traits. On the way they pick up a quarreling couple, Alman (Sjöberg) and his wife (Broström), and later three young hikers, Sara (Andersson), Anders (Sundquist), and Evald (Bjelvenstam). The professor also stops to visit his aged mother (Wifstrand). On the journey, Borg has been haunted by nightmares and memories of his past failings. Sara awakens memories of his childhood and his love for another Sara (Andersson). After the ceremony in Lund, it seems Sara and her friends truly like Borg and he goes to sleep with his conscience at peace.

Wild Strawberries is constructed around dream sequences (notably the nightmare at the beginning) and flashbacks and is, in addition to a voyage through modern Sweden, a voyage through time, the past, and the unconscious. An old man approaching death (this was the last role of the great Victor Sjöström) takes stock of his life and its failings and is confronted by those who loved him, admired him for his contributions to science, and those who detested him as an inhuman, self-centered idiot. Sara, in the present, brings him back to the human simplicity of his youth and the time of "wild strawberries" and gives him a new sense of serenity.

This is the best Bergman film of the Fifties, much closer to a true philosophical tragedy than his more ambitious *The Seventh Seal* (*q.v.*).

SNOW WHITE AND THE SEVEN DWARFS USA 1937. *Supervising Dir* David Hand *Scen* Ted Sears, Richard Creedon, Earl Hurd, Otto Englander, Dick Richard, Dorothy Ann Blank, Merrill de Maris, Webb Smith based on the fairy tale by the Grimm brothers *Sequence Dir* Larry Morey, Perce Pearce, William Cottrell, Wilfred Jackson, Ben Sharpsteen *Anim Dir* Hamilton Luske, Vladimir Tytla, Fred Moore, Herman Ferguson *Anim* Frank Thomas, Les Clark, Dick Lundy, Robert Stokes, James Algar, Ward Kimball, Eric Larson and others *Art Dir* Charles Philippi, Hugh Hennesy, Terrell Stapp, McLaren Stewart, Harold Miles, Tom Codrick, Kenneth Anderson, Hazel Sewell, Gustaf Tenngren, Kendall O'Connor *Mus* Frank Churchill, Leigh Harline, Paul Smith *Songs* Larry Morey, Frank Churchill *Character Design* Joe Grant, Albert Hunter *Prod* Walt Disney. 82 mins. Technicolor. Re-released 1962.

The familiar story of how the Wicked Queen attempts to destroy Snow White because she is jealous of her beauty. Snow White escapes with the help of the queen's huntsman and takes refuge with the Seven Dwarfs (Happy, Grumpy, Sneezy, Doc, Bashful, Sleepy, and Dopey) in the forest. The queen disguises herself as an old woman and gives Snow White a poisoned apple. She dies but is later revived by the kiss of Prince Charming. [Walt Disney's first feature-length cartoon was made at the height of his talents and was three years in production. His colleagues tried to dissuade him from the venture on the grounds that it only accentuated the problems of *The Silly Symphonies* (*q.v.*) in relation to the popular and financially successful *Mickey Mouse* (*q.v.*) series. But it was a great critical and commercial success and grossed as much as most popular dramatic features. Its more horrific scenes (Snow White's flight through the forest; the witch's brew; the Wicked Queen as a kindly old lady) terrified young children and many who saw the film as children still remember these scenes vividly.]

The film's international success derived mainly from the delightful caricatures of the Seven Dwarfs with their comedy and their memorable songs, and from the episodes with animals in such sequences as the housecleaning and the music hour, with penguins acting as organ pipes. The "poetic" and sentimental sequences, however, are marred by extreme bad taste and by a "cute" style that is a mixture of Christmas Card designs and German Kitsch. The Prince and Snow White are supposed to be realistic and were modeled on two unknown actors (Marge Champion for Snow White) but are tasteless, insipid, and unconvincing.

The film's financial success was increased by the sale of reproductions of the characters. Each time their likeness appeared "on toilet soap, a handkerchief, a wardrobe or an effigy, Disney received extremely important payments for author's rights," Maurice Bessy noted in 1938, after visiting the Disney factories where at the time 735 somewhat poorly paid craftsmen ($30–40 per week for a colorer) worked on an assembly line. As a creator, this "smiling Führer," as Bessy characterized him, "makes no contribution or almost none," but "mainly supervises the administration of his company and, even more actively, the assignment of rights. Some films are made without his knowing the details." After the success of *Snow White and the Seven Dwarfs*, Disney became even more of an executive producer wielding enormous power and influence. The film was re-released in 1962 in a version whose backgrounds and music were rejuvenated.

SOLDAT INCONNU (LE) HISTOIRE DU SOLDAT INCONNU

SOLDIERS (THE) CARABINIERS (LES)

SOLDIER'S PRAYER (A) NINGEN NO JOKEN (PART III)

SOLE SORGE ANCORA (IL) OUTCRY/THE SUN ALWAYS RISES/THE SUN RISES AGAIN Italy

345

1946. *Dir* Aldo Vergano *Scen* Giuseppe De Santis, G. Gorgerino, Carlo Lizzani, Guido Aristarco *Photog* Aldo Tonti *Art Dir* Fausto Galli *Mus* Giuseppe Rosati *Cast* Elli Parvo, Lea Padovani, V. Duse, M. Serrato, Carlo Lizzani, M. Levi, G. Pontecorvo *Prod* E.N.I.C. 95 mins.

A film about life on a large agricultural estate on the Lombardy plains and about the exploitation of peasants at the end of the Second World War. A deserter (Duse) hides on the estate and becomes intimate, first with the daughter (Padovani) of a worker-partisan, then with a tenant's wife (Parvo). He rejoins the resistance movement. A priest (Lizzani) and a Communist are shot together and the rebellious workers hunt down the tenants.

With the passing years this excellent film has also become a document of historical interest on the Italian resistance movement. Carlo Lizzani, who co-authored the script, also appears as the priest in the film's best sequence, which depicts the shooting of the hostages with the crowd chanting "Ora pro nobis." He has described this film: "The point of view chosen by the director and his collaborators allowed the observation of the social structure of occupied Italy. Around the large agricultural industry gather the peasants, workers, the priest of the mansion's chapel, and the tenants, who prefer the peace of the countryside to a famine-stricken and bombed Milan. In this milieu the miseries of war and the occupation were enlarged and the seeds of the resistance took root. The reactions of the various social groups formed the focal point of the story."

SOL SVANETII SALT FOR SVANETIA USSR 1930. *Dir* Mikhail Kalatozov *Scen* Mikhail Kalatozov based on an idea by Sergei Tretyakov *Photog* Mikhail Kalatozov, M. Gegelashvili *Prod* Goskinprom (Georgia). 1,500 meters. (4,900 ft. approx.)

This documentary, originally based on Tretyakov's prewritten script about Svanetia, is as memorable as Buñuel's *Land Without Bread* (*q.v.*). The people of Svanetia, an isolated valley, 6,000 feet up in the Caucasus, were then as backward as the people of Las Hurdes in Buñuel's film. They were totally cut off from the outside world except for a single mountain pass that was open only during the brief snowless period. [The official cata-

logue description characterizes life there as "patriachal, primitive; the struggle for existence among the snow-capped mountains entails such constant want and hunger, and particularly, the tormenting hunger for salt, that each new birth is regarded as a terrible curse, while death becomes a solemn feast."] The hopeless life of the inhabitants is dominated by their need for salt, which they must carry on their backs across the mountains where, even in the middle of summer, snow still falls. Many of the images are Buñuelian; a woman, close to childbirth, driven from her house; a horse galloping until its heart bursts; the pagan offering of a slaughtered horse; a cow thirstily drinking human urine for its salt; a new-born torn apart by a dog; a widow dripping her milk into the grave; money counted on a crucifix. The last part, urging the construction of a road to bring salt and civilization to Svanetia is un-unnecessary; as Harry Alan Potamkin put it "the entire film cries that convincingly enough".

Mikhail Kalatozov had been trained as a cameraman and this was his second film as director. Its bold and striking images certainly reflect his background, but its editing is influenced by Eisenstein and its lyricism is reminiscent of Dovzenko. In some scenes one can detect the future director of *The Cranes Are Flying* (*q.v.*) [*Salt for Svanetia* is almost unknown outside the Soviet Union and has received only limited screenings. The original negative was destroyed during the German invasion but copies still exist in the USSR.]

SOME CAME RUNNING USA 1959. *Dir* Vincente Minnelli *Scen* John Patrick, Arthur Sheekman based on the novel by James Jones *Photog* William H. Daniels *Art Dir* William A. Horning, Urie McCleary *Mus* Elmer Bernstein *Ed* Adrienne Fazan *Cast* Frank Sinatra, Dean Martin, Shirley MacLaine, Martha Hyer, Arthur Kennedy *Prod* Sol Siegel Productions for MGM. 136 mins. Metrocolor. CinemaScope.

Dave Hirsch (Sinatra), a disillusioned writer, returns to his small home town where, despising his hypocritical brother (Kennedy), he takes up with a gambler, Bama (Martin), and a pixy-like waif, Ginny (MacLaine), who is fleeing from a rejected lover in Chicago. Dave's brother is discovered to be having an affair with his secretary, while Dave himself falls in love with Gwen (Hyer), a local college teacher. Gwen finally rejects him and Dave decides to marry Ginny. After the wedding, Ginny's ex-lover takes a shot at Dave but Ginny stops the bullet and is killed.

This intelligent and sensitive adaptation of a best-selling novel is, apart from his musical comedies, Minnelli's best romantic film.

*SOME LIKE IT HOT USA 1959. *Dir* Billy Wilder *Scen* Billy Wilder, I. A. L. Diamond based on an unpublished story by R. Thoeren, M. Logan *Photog* Charles Lang, Jr. *Art Dir* Ted Hawarth *Mus* Adolph Deutsch *Ed* Arthur Schmidt *Cast* Marilyn Monroe, Jack Lemmon, Tony Curtis, George Raft, Pat O'Brien, Joe E. Brown, Nehemiah Persoff *Prod* Ashton for Mirisch. 121 mins.

Two unemployed muscians, Joe (Curtis) and Jerry (Lemmon), involuntarily witness the St. Valentine's Day Massacre in Chicago and are forced to escape the gang boss, Spats Colombo (Raft). Disguised as women, they join the all-girl jazz band en route to Florida and become friendly with Sugar Kane (Monroe), the singer. In Florida, Jerry is courted by a millionaire, Osgood (Brown), while Joe, in love with Sugar, pretends to be a millionaire (male). Spats Colombo and his men arrive in the hotel for a gangsters convention, spot Joe and Jerry, and pursue them. Spats is killed by a more powerful gang boss, Bonaparte (Persoff), and his men chase Joe and Jerry who, with Sugar, escape to sea on Osgood's boat.

Perhaps Wilder's most successful and popular comedy, fast, racy and zany, though less astringent than many of his satires. Famous sequences: the opening evocation of speak-easy Chicago; the St. Valentine's Day massacre; Jerry, Sugar Kane, and the other girls in a party on the upper berth of a train; Osgood's meeting with Jerry-as-a-girl; their romantic evening together; Joe disguised as a millionaire with a Cary Grant voice; Joe's evening with Sugar on board the yacht; the assassination of Spats with the killers emerging from a big birthday cake; the slapstick chase through the hotel; the final scene on Osgood's boat as Jerry reveals he is a man. *Some Like It Hot* grossed over 14 million dollars, of which

three million went to Monroe as a partner in the production company.]

SOMEWHERE IN EUROPE VALAHOL EUROPÁBÁN

SOMMARDANSEN HON DANSADE EN SOMMAR

SOMMAREN MED MONIKA SUMMER WITH MONIKA/MONIKA Sweden 1952. *Dir* Ingmar Bergman *Scen* Ingmar Bergman, P. A. Fcgelström *Photog* Gunnar Fischer *Art Dir* P. A. Lundgren, Nils Svenwall *Mus* Erik Nordgren *Ed* Tage Holmberg, Gösta Lewin *Cast* Harriet Andersson, Lars Ekborg, Ake Fridell, John Harryson *Prod* Svensk Filmindustri. 97 mins.

Harry (Ekborg) a young errand boy, falls in love with Monika (Andersson), a wild, seductive shop girl. Monika quarrels with her father (Fridell) and she and Harry take a boat for an idyllic holiday on a remote island in the archipelago outside Stockholm. At the end of the holiday, Monika is pregnant and Harry agrees to marry her. Monika soon becomes bored with the routine of motherhood and housekeeping and takes a lover. Harry discovers this, Monika walks out, and Harry is left to look after the baby.

This is one of the first of Bergman's films to achieve a wide release through art houses outside Sweden partially because of its sensuality. The best part is that portraying the young couple on the remote island. Harriet Andersson gives a memorably moving performance as a self-centered, self-willed, but erotic adolescent. In North America, an atrociously dubbed version with new music by Les Brown even played the drive-in circuits.

SOMMARLEK SUMMER INTERLUDE/ILLICIT INTERLUDE Sweden 1951. *Dir* Ingmar Bergman *Scen* Ingmar Bergman, Herbert Grevenius *Photog* Gunnar Fischer *Art Dir* Nils Svenwall *Mus* Erik Nordgren *Ed* Oscar Rosander *Cast* Maj-Britt Nilsson, Alf Kjellin, Birger Malmsten, Georg Funkquist *Prod* Svensk Filmindustri. 96 mins.

Marie (Nilsson), a ballerina in Stockholm, falls in love with Henrik (Malmsten) one summer in the archipelago, despite the bitter jealousy of her uncle (Funkquist), who was once in love with Marie's mother. As the summer ends and they return to Stockholm, Henrik is accidentally killed. Marie is grief-stricken, though her faithful friend, David (Kjellin), tries to comfort her. Finally, she forces herself to visit the island again, purge herself of her memories, and look forward to a new future with David.

This evocation of past happiness is one of Bergman's most moving films. The flashbacks to Marie's affair with Henrik during an idyllic summer on an island, with its wild strawberries and trees in blossom, is set against the melancholy of the present and Marie's attempt to break away from the sterility that has stifled her since Henrik's death.

SOMMARNATTENS LEENDE SMILES OF A SUMMER NIGHT Sweden 1955. *Dir/Scen* Ingmar Bergman *Photog* Gunnar Fischer *Art Dir* P. A. Lundgren *Mus* Erik Nordgren *Ed* Oscar Rosander *Cast* Ulla Jacobsson, Gunnar Björnstrand, Eva Dahlbeck, Margit Carlquist, Harriet Andersson, Jarl Kulle, Ake Fridell, Björn Bjelvenstam *Prod* Svensk Filmindustri. 104 mins.

A group of men and women spend a weekend party at a country mansion at the turn of the century: Fredrik Egerman (Björnstrand), a prosperous lawyer; Anne (Jacobsson), his young, virgin wife; Desirée (Dahlbeck), an actress and Egerman's former mistress; Count Malcolm (Kulle), Desirée's current lover; Charlotte (Carlquist), the count's wife; Henrik (Bjelvenstam), Egerman's son by a former marriage, who is constantly being ogled by Petra (Andersson), the maid. During a single midsummer's night, their relationships change and interchange. Egerman is seduced by Charlotte; Henrik finds himself attracted to Anne and they run off together. Petra rolls in the hay with Frid (Fridell), the groom. As a result of his escapade with Charlotte, Egerman has to fight a duel by Russian roulette — but the gun has a blank cartridge filled with soot and Egerman is merely humiliated.

This witty, sophisticated comedy is one of series of Bergman films about women and their relationships. Though superficially a frothy farce in the Feydeau (or even Flers and Cavaillet) manner, it is in fact a profound satire of mores and social conventions comparable to *La Règle du jeu* (*q.v.*). But where Renoir's film is realistic, Bergman's is more philosophical, at times, even metaphysical — and

one can find in it traces of Beaumarchais, Marivaux, Musset, Shakespeare, Laclos, Pirandello, and Kafka.

Some of the characters, such as Egerman, are caricatures. But the blond, earthy, and erotic Petra, played by Harriet Andersson in the manner of her *Monika* (*q.v.*) role, and Charlotte, the man-hating feline seducer of Egerman are especially memorable. Nor should one forget Bergman's use of mechanical objects, clocks, mechanical beds, etc., which add their own humor to his lusty, tragi-comedy.

Smiles of a Summer Night was a great international success and led to a (belated) general critical recognition of Ingmar Bergman.

*SONG OF CEYLON (THE) Britain 1934. *Dir/Scen/Photog* Basil Wright *Mus* Walter Leigh *Sound* Alberto Cavalcanti *Commentary* Lionel Wendt's adaptation of Robert Knox's account of Ceylon in 1680 *Prod* John Grierson for the Ceylon Tea Propaganda Board. 40 mins.

A documentary about Ceylon in four sections: "The Buddha" deals with the coming of the Buddha to liberate the people from their devil-worship; "The Virgin Island" depicts the native Ceylonese culture and economy; "The Voices of Commerce" contrasts traditional methods with new technology introduced from Europe; "The Apparel of a God" reflects the continuity of life and tradition.

This lyrical impression of Ceylon and its people is justifiably considered one of the masterpieces of the British documentary movement. Its evocative sensual imagery, its construction, and its skillful, often contrapuntal, use of natural sound still have a powerful impact. Most memorable is "The Voices of Commerce" section in which the images show the natives working in the fields while contrasting sound effects on the sound track depict how the British exploited this labor.

SONG OF POTEMKIN (THE) PODRUGI

SONG OF THE NARAYAMA NARAYAMA BUSHI-KO

SONG OF THE RIVERS LIED DER STRÖME (DAS)

SONG OF THE ROAD (THE) PATHER PANCHALI

SONG OF THE SEA CANTO DO MAR (O)

SONG OF THE THIN MAN see THIN MAN (THE)

SON OF MONGOLIA SYN MONGOLII

SON OF THE SHEIK (THE) USA 1926. *Dir* George Fitzmaurice *Scen* Frances Marion, Fred de Gresac derived from the novel by E. M. Hull *Photog* George Barnes *Art Dir* William Cameron Menzies *Mus* James C. Bradford, Arthur Gutman *Cast* Rudolph Valentino, Vilma Banky, George Fawcett, Montague Love, Karl Dane, Bull Montana, Agnes Ayres *Prod* Feature. 6,685 ft. Re-issued in 1938 in a sound version with music and effects.

Ahmed (Valentino) falls in love with Yasmin (Banky) but believes she has betrayed him to his enemies. Eventually it is proved she is faithful and he vanquishes his enemies and rides off with Yasmin.

This romantic melodrama full of rescues, fights, and stunts, was the sequel to Valentine's earlier romantic success *The Sheik* (see below). However, unlike most sequels, this one enjoyed a popular success ten times as great as the original. This is perhaps because it was heartthrob Valentino's last film before his premature death. He plays a dual role, that of father and son, while Agnes Ayres (who was the English heiress in the original) appears briefly as the mature mother of the young Sheik.

This often re-released film is a social document on taste and mores — but of Hollywood during the Golden Twenties, not of the Arabs

— *Sheik (The)* USA 1921. *Dir* George Melford *Scen* Monte M. Katterjohn based on the novel by E. M. Hull *Photog* William Marshall *Cast* Rudolph Valentino, Agnes Ayres, Adolphe Menjou, Walter Long, Lucien Littlefield *Prod* George Melford for Famous Players-Lasky. 6,580 ft.

Sheik Ahmed (Valentino) captures Diane Mayo (Ayres) a proud English girl disguised as a slave. She refuses to submit to him, is captured by enemy bandits, rescued, and all ends happily.

Although he had already appeared in *The Four Horsemen of the Apocalypse* (*q.v.*) it was his role in this film that made Valentino the idol of millions of women.

SORCERERS (THE) see HÄXAN

SORCIERE (LA) see HÄXAN

SOROK PERVYI THE FORTY-FIRST

— USSR 1927. *Dir* Yakov Protazanov *Scen* Boris Lavrenyov, Boris Leonidov based on the novel by Boris Lavrenyov *Photog* Pyotr Yermolov *Art Dir* Sergei Kozlovsky *Cast* Ada Voitsik, Ivan Koval-Samborsky, I. Strauch *Prod* Mezhrabpom-Russ. 1,885 meters.

During the Civil War in Turkestan, a detachment of Red soldiers encounters a detachment of the White Guard led by a lieutenant (Koval-Samborsky). The best sharpshooter of the Reds, a girl (Voitsik), fires at her "forty-first" victim, but misses. The Whites are captured and eventually the girl and the lieutenant become separated from the rest on an island. There they fall in love but when an enemy ship approaches to rescue them, the girl carries out her orders and shoots her "forty-first."

Lavrenyov's excellent novel (which he also adapted for the screen) gave Protozanov the opportunity of directing what is undoubtedly his best film A newly graduated actress, Ada Voitsik, was chosen for the demanding role of Maryutka after Vera Maretskaya fell ill; she gives an extraordinary performance.

— USSR 1956. *Dir* Grigori Chukrai *Scen* G. Koltunov based on the novel by Boris Lavrenyov *Photog* Sergei Urusevsky *Art Dir* V. Kamsky, K. Stepanov *Mus* Nikolai Kryukov *Cast* Isolda Izvitskaya, Oleg Strizhenov, Nikolai Kryuchkov *Prod* Mosfilm. 90 mins. Sovcolor.

Chukrai's remake of the classic story of the moving, tragic, and ill-fated love between two believable characters came at the end of an era in the Soviet Union when it had been heresy to show a Red in love with a White or to show the White as anything but a fiend. Chukrai found that the story (which also portrays sexual love, another taboo subject at the time) allowed him to return to the source of the best Soviet cinema. Avoiding the stereotyped characters that marred the postwar Soviet cinema, Chukrai used the romantic story to portray the hopelessness and misery that war inevitably brings. Its sincerity and superb photography and the subtle character portrayal of the two protagonists brought this version a success that marked a turning point in Soviet cinema.

349

SO THAT THE WORLD GOES ON POUR LA SUITE DU MONDE

SOUPIRANT (LE) THE SUITOR France 1962. *Dir* Pierre Etaix *Scen* Pierre Etaix, J.-C. Carrière *Photog* Pierre Levant *Mus* Jean Paillaud *Ed* Pierre Gillette *Cast* Pierre Etaix, Laurence Lignères, France Arnell, Karin Vesely *Prod* C.A.P.A.C. 85 mins.

The misadventures of a studious young man (Etaix) attempting to get married: first to a predatory brunette (Lignères), then to a famous pop singer (Arnell), and finally to a Swedish *au pair* girl (Vesely).

Pierre Etaix's first feature revealed a new, original, and fertile comic imagination, not without its origins in Max Linder's style, despite a physical resemblance (the dead-pan gaze) to Buster Keaton.

SOURIANTE MADAME BEUDET (LA) THE SMILING MADAME BEUDET France 1922. *Dir* Germaine Dulac *Scen* André Obey based on the play by Denys Amiel, André Obey *Photog* Amédée Morrin *Cast* Germaine Dermoz, Alexandre Arquillière, Jean d'Yd, Madeleine Guitty *Prod* Vandal/Dulac/Aubert. 3,200 ft. approx.

The romantic, "smiling" Madame Beudet (Dermoz) is married to a dull and insensitive tradesman (Arquillière) who irritates her so much that she dreams of other lovers and of killing him.

Germaine Dulac's best film is derived from a play by André Obey and Denys Amiel, the exponents of the "theater of silence" involving formalized, mimetic staging. Its theme is clearly theatrical but it is also very cinematic. The action, set in a dreary, provincial town, takes place in the back-shop living quarters of the couple. The style is set by Dulac's impressionistic camera and by metaphors established through editing devices — the angry Monsieur Beudet becoming an ogre or Madame Beudet's romantic daydreams of streams and ponds as she plays Debussy on the piano. Slow-motion photography shows handsome young men stepping into her arms out of the pages of a magazine. Objects, too, (the vase that the wife, then the husband, keep moving about) are used to express the domestic conflict but are not "symbols." Germaine Dermoz as the wife gives a sensitive performance, unforgettable in the shot in which her ravaged face is reflected by three mirrors.

The theme and approach are not dissimilar to *Sylvester* (*q.v.*) or *Scherben* (*q.v.*) but it is unlikely that Germaine Dulac, always a convinced "impressionist," was then aware of German *Kammerspiel*.

SOUS LE CIEL DE PROVENCE see QUATTRO PASSI FRA LE NUVOLE

SOUS LES TOITS DE PARIS UNDER THE ROOFS OF PARIS France 1930. *Dir/Scen* René Clair *Assist Dir* Marcel Carné, Georges Lacombe, Houssin, de Schaak *Photog* Georges Périnal, Georges Raulet *Art Dir* Lazare Meerson *Mus* Raoul Moretti, R. Nazelles, Armand Bernard *Cast* Albert Préjean, Pola Illery, Gaston Modot, Edmond Gréville, Paul Olivier, Jane Pierson, Aimos, Bill Blockett *Prod* Tobis. 92 mins.

A street singer, Albert (Préjean), has a mistress, Pola (Illery), a pretty Romanian girl who also flirts with his best friend, Louis (Gréville). While Albert is in jail for a theft he is innocent of, Louis and Pola become lovers. When he is released Albert and Louis quarrel but when Albert sees that Pola really loves Louis he abandons his claim and the three remain friends.

Famous sequences: the opening with the camera gliding over Meerson's memorable sets of Paris accompanied by a similar "gliding movement" on the sound-track; the lovers' quarrel in the dark; the fight near a railway momentarily hidden first by the steam of a passing train then by its roar; the argument behind a glass door preventing the words from being heard; the ending with a reverse camera movement to that of the opening.

Initially, René Clair was passionately opposed to the introduction of dialogue in films and in 1927 had described the talking cinema as "a redoubtable monster, an unnatural creation, thanks to which the screen will become poor theater." This film "must be considered," as Georges Charensol put it, "as a manifesto of those who oppose the supremacy that dramatic authors from now on intend to give to words over images." René Clair himself says he used a bare minimum of dialogue, "because I thought it needed from the first to be amalgamated with the achievements of the silent cinema, that is to say, expressed essentially in images with words used only when helpful and to avoid lengthy visual explanations."

Its release in May 1930 at the Moulin-Rouge as a "100% French-talking and singing film" was not an immediate success. Only after a spectacular opening in Berlin in August 1930 under the slogan "The most beautiful film in the world," did it receive full recognition. Its successful run of many months in Berlin was echoed in New York (December, 1930), London (December, 1930), Tokyo, Shanghai, Moscow, Buenos Aires, etc. Its success was certainly in part due to its merits as a musical comedy whose songs and mime expressed much without recourse to dialogue. But, more than this, it derived from its portrayal of the lives of ordinary people at a time when most internationally successful films dealt with life among the upper classes. Its portrait of ordinary Parisians, the midinettes and the street singers in cloth caps, and Meerson's unusually realistic sets had an impact around the world, similar to that which Ince's first westerns had in France.

SOUTHERNER (THE) USA 1945. *Dir* Jean Renoir *Assist Dir* Robert Aldrich *Scen* Jean Renoir based on the novel *Hold Autumn in Your Hand* by George Sessions Perry *Photog* Lucien Andriot *Art Dir* Eugène Lourié *Mus* Werner Janssen *Ed* Gregg Tallas *Cast* Zachary Scott, Betty Field, Beulah Bondi, J. Carroll Naish *Prod* Producing Artists for United Artists. 91 mins.

In the American South, Sam Tucker (Scott) tries to set up his own cotton farm with his wife (Field), Granny (Bondi), and the children. During one year, everything goes wrong: the crops are ruined by a storm, a malicious neighbor (Naish) ruins their vegetable patch, one of the children falls sick from malnutrition, and nobody will help.

This poetic, simple, and realistic chronicle of a man's attempt to establish himself is Renoir's best American film. He sensitively captures the pressures and anxieties, and the pride and the hopes of the "poor Whites" as they try to wrest their existence from the poor southern soil. Its realistic style is similar to that of *Toni* (*q.v.*), though it is not as good as that earlier film, and its theme seems to have its origin in *Le Crime de M. Lange* (*q.v.*). But here, a farm laborer who wants to become his own

master is even farther from achieving his ambition.

SPALICEK THE CZECH YEAR Czechoslovakia 1947. *Dir/Scen/Art Dir* Jiri Trnka *Mus* Vaclav Trojan *Anim* Bretislav Pojar, B, Sramek, Z. Hrabe, S. Karpas, S. Latal, A. Tovarev. 74 mins. Agfacolor. A compilation of seven short puppet films: *Carnival; Spring; The Legend of Saint Procopius; Pilgrimage; Harvest Festival; Village Feast; Bethlehem,* all of which had been released separately.

Trnka's first puppet films were an absolute revelation when they were first shown at Venice and turned upside down the long accepted Disney animation techniques. Trnka says he turned from cartoons to puppet films because "marionettes have more *presence*" and one can see what he meant in the three-dimensional qualities of this film whose carved, wooden dolls with impassive faces are made expressive by the lighting, sets, songs and music based on Bohemian folklore themes. Trnka's revolutionary approach revealed new perspectives for animation and recalled techniques long forgotten during the Disney years.

As J.-P. Coursodon noted, this feature "juxtaposes realism and the simplicity of everyday life with the popular taste (which is also that of Trnka) for legend, marvels, and phantasmagoria. The horned devil who temps Saint Procopius, the monsters and masks that terrify the peasants in *The Village Feast* are used as dazzling baroque exercises that make *The Czech Year* a deeply magical film fantasy . . . The three-dimensional sets and the pure and simple designs are very subtly blended. The tortuous pines in the forest of *Procopius* and the mellow colors of the hazy sky of *Bethlehem* are both equally essential elements in the film's style and atmosphere."

SPANISH EARTH (THE) USA 1937. *Dir/Scen* Joris Ivens *Photog* Joris Ivens, John Ferno (Fernhout) *Mus* Marc Blitzstein, Virgil Thomson based on Spanish folk music *Ed* Helen van Dongen *Sound Ed* Irving Reis *Commentary* Ernest Hemingway, who also speaks it *Prod* Contemporary Historians Inc. 54 min.

In the small Spanish village of Fuenteduena near Madrid and on the road between Madrid and Valencia, the villagers develop plans for the irrigation of land recently confiscated from the feudal landowners while military forces take part in the defense of Madrid.

The beautiful commentary for this extraordinarily moving document on the Spanish Civil War and the attendant land reform was written by Ernest Hemingway. [An example of the style is in the sequence of the bombed village where Hemingway says: "Before, death came when you were old or sick. But now it comes to all this village. High in the sky and shining silver it comes to all who have no place to run. No place to hide."] Orson Welles, then a young actor, was hired to read the commentary (this reading was used in the White House screening described below) but his voice was found too declamatory for Hemingway's stark style and Hemingway himself recorded it "like that of a sensitive reporter who has been on the spot" (Ivens). The film was previewed at the White House in a special screening for President F. D. Roosevelt, Mrs. Roosevelt, and others. The president apparently liked it very much and Mrs. Roosevelt wrote a warm review of it in her column the following day. [However, when generally released, critics in the USA attacked its lack of "objectivity" and in Britain it was banned by the censor until all references to Italian and German intervention in Spain were deleted from the commentary.]

SPANISH FIESTA see FÊTE ESPAGNOLE (LA)

SPECIAL PRIORITY TRAINS OSTRE SLEDOVANE VLAKY

SPELLBOUND USA 1945. *Dir* Alfred Hitchcock *Scen* Ben Hecht, Angus McPhail based on the novel *The House of Dr. Edwardes* by Francis Beeding *Photog* George Barnes *Art Dir* James Basevi, John Ewing *Mus* Miklos Rozsa *Ed* William Ziegler *Dream Sequence* Salvador Dali *Cast* Gregory Peck, Ingrid Bergman, Jean Acker, Donald Curtis, Rhonda Fleming, John Emery, Leo G. Carroll *Prod* Selznick International/Vanguard for United Artists. 111 mins.

J. B. (Peck), head psychiatrist in a sanatorium, believes himself a murderous amnesiac who killed the previous director, but the developing love and mutual trust between himself and Dr. Constance Peterson (Bergman), a staff psychiatrist, returns him to sanity and they finally uncover the real murderer.

This psychological thriller in the typical somber Hollywood thriller style of the Forties is persuasively directed by Hitchcock, who nevertheless amused himself with some bits of gratutious technical virtuosity — the rather mediocre Salvador Dali dream sequence and the audience identification in the "first-person" suicide of the murderer at the end.

— *Spellbound/Passing Clouds* Britain 1940. *Dir* John Harlow *Cast* Derek Farr, Vera Lindsay, Hay Petrie, Felix Aylmer. 82 mins.

Not an earlier version of the novel but the story of a man whose girl friend dies and who seeks solace in spiritualism.

SPERDUTI NEL BUIO LOST IN THE DARK Italy 1914. *Dir* Nino Martoglio *Scen* Nino Martoglio, A. Moretti based on the play by Romano Bracco *Photog* L. Romagnoli *Cast* Giovanni Grasso, Virginia Balistrieri, Maria Carmi, Dillo Lombardi *Prod* Morgana Film. 2,000 meters approx.

In Naples, the mistress (Carmi) of a duke (Lombardi) is abandoned by him after giving birth to his child and becomes a famous star. The child is given into the care of a blind man (Grasso) and when she becomes a young woman (Balistrieri) learns the secret of her birth. The duke, persecuted by his former mistress, dies of a heart attack.

This somewhat melodramatic story was based on a "naturalistic" dialect play by Romano Bracco. But Umberto Barbaro's developing theory of "neorealism" (baptized thus by him in 1942) is reflected in his analysis of this film written in 1938: "The presentation of two contrasting environments, one ostentatious, the other poor, led the director to use, from the prologue on, parallel editing in the Griffith manner. The camera angles and composition are often astoundingly adroit and very beautiful.

"There is considerable feeling of visual depth and the compositions emphasize the most significant details. The relentless sun of Naples illuminates both the frock coat of Dillo Lombardi and the rags of the striking Virginia Balistrieri. The enormous and profound human warmth of the director is manifest even in the cotton check robes, striped trousers, and battered hats of Giovanni Grasso and in Maria Carmi's earrings and long, flowing hair. It touches also the worn steps leading to the blind man's room and the horribly cracked walls of the streets of ill-fame. With perfect stylistic coherence, the realism becomes more marked during the story until it goes beyond this to become metaphor and signification; it is a way of looking at the world which, through its expression, becomes art."

Umberto Barbaro was a professor at the Centro Sperimentale in Rome, whose archive, the Cineteca Nazionale, had a copy of this film until 1944 when the Germans took it. It now seems to be lost forever, but this unknown masterpiece played a decisive role in the gestation of neorealism.

— *Sperduti nel buio* Italy 1947. *Dir* Camillo Mastrocineque *Scen* based on the play by Romano Bracco *Photog* Renato Del Frate *Art Dir* Virgilio Marchi *Cast* Vittorio de Sica, Jacqueline Plessis, Enrico Glori, Florella Betti.

This new version of the play was made during the heyday of neorealism, with De Sica playing the blind man and Betti the girl he rescues.

SPIVS (THE) VITELLONI (I)

SPRING VESNOY

SPRING SHOWER TAVASZI ZAPOR

STACHKA STRIKE USSR 1924 (released 1925). *Dir/Ed* Sergei M. Eisenstein *Assist* Grigori Alexandrov, I. Kravchunovsky, A. Levshin *Scen* Proletkult Collective (Valeri Pletnyov, Eisenstein, Alexandrov, Kravchunovsky *Photog* Eduard Tisse, Vassili Khvatov, V. Popov (?) *Art Dir* Vasili Rakhals *English titles* Ivor Montagu *Cast* Grigori Alexandrov, Maxim Strauch, Mikhail Gomarov, Alexander Antonov, Judith Glizer, Boris Yurtsev, I. Ivanov *Prod* Goskino/Proletkult. 6,250 ft.

The story of a strike by factory workers in Tsarist Russia about 1912 and its brutal suppression by the authorities.

This is the first film by 26-year-old Sergei Eisenstein. A 1925 press release described it in these terms: "A masterpiece and a brilliant achievement of the Soviet cinema. *Strike,* a filmic drama in six acts is one of a series of films on the development of the workers' struggle. This is the only one of the projected seven films to be made. Directed by S. M. Eisenstein with artists from the Proletkult workers theater: 1, . . . ; 2. The reasons for the strike; 3. The factory brought to a halt; 4. The strike gathers momentum; 5. The provocators set about their work; 6. The repression. The savage aggression of the local police. The Tsarist secret police disguised as vagabonds. The workers procession broken up by water from fire hoses. *Strike* has the solution to the age-old problem of dramatic creation because its hero and principal character is the *mass."*

Strike was shot entirely in the real sets and backgrounds like a reconstruction of actuality. Famous sequences: the worker's meeting in the factory; the clandestine meeting among scrap iron; the first appearance of the police agents and their fantastic disguises; the factory owners' evening of luxury when they turn down the workers' demands; the workers happily enjoying their unaccustomed leisure; the crooks hiding in barrels in a piece of waste ground; the peaceful procession, the provocation, and the firemen turning their hoses on the workers; the mounted police attacking and killing the workers and their children in the apartment block; the final massacre intercut with shots of the slaughter of cattle in an abattoir.

Though not always successful in its inventiveness and stylistic devices, *Strike* is in some ways a rough sketch for *Battleship Potemkin* (*q.v.*).

STAGECOACH USA 1939. *Dir* John Ford *Scen* Dudley Nichols based on the short story *Stage to Lordsburg* by Ernest Haycox *Photog* Bert Glennon, Ray Binger *2nd Unit* Yakima Canutt, Jack Mohr, John Eckert *Mus* Richard Hageman, Frank Harling, Louis Gruenberg *Ed* Dorothy Spencer, Walter Reynolds *Cast* John Wayne, Claire Trevor, Thomas Mitchell, George Bancroft, Andy Devine, John Carradine, Louise Platt, Donald Meek, Berton Churchill, Tim Holt *Prod* Walter Wanger for United Artists. 96 mins.

Aboard a stagecoach bound for Cheyenne driven by Buck (Devine) are: Dallas (Trevor), a saloon-girl being hounded from town; Dr. Boone (Mitchell), an alcoholic doctor; Mrs. Mallory (Platt), the pregnant wife of a cavalry officer trying to join her husband; Hatfield (Carradine), a gambler; Mr. Peacock (Meek), a timid liquor salesman; Mr. Gatewood (Churchill), who is absconding with his bank's funds. Sheriff Wilcox (Bancroft) rides shotgun in order to recapture the Ringo Kid (Wayne), who is probably on his way to Cheyenne to settle an old score with Luke Plummer. On the way the Ringo Kid joins the coach after losing his horse. There are rumors that Indians are on the warpath and the coach is at first given a cavalry escort. When it has to leave them, the passengers vote to continue. During an enforced stop Mrs. Mallory's baby is born, then the Indians attack, but after a desperate fight the stagecoach is saved by the cavalry. In Cheyenne, the Ringo Kid kills the Plumers and leaves with Dallas with the Sheriff's connivance.

This classic western by a pioneer director of westerns has a favorite John Ford theme: the behavior of and revelation of character in a group of people under stress. Though the plot is from an American short story, Dudley Nichols' script has many of its roots in Maupassant and especially in *Boule de suif,* not only in its heroine, Dallas, but also in its depiction of the changing relationships in a group of characters during a voyage in a country at war. The most famous sequence is the Indian attack with a swift pan revealing the Indians on the skyline, but this superbly mounted and edited sequence is perhaps of lesser value than the film's memorable portraits of typical American pioneers.

— *Stagecoach* USA 1966. *Dir* Gordon Douglas *Scen* Joseph Landon based on the original by Dudley Nichols *Photog* William H. Clothier *Mus* Jerry Goldsmith *2nd Unit* Ray Kellogg *Cast* Alex Cord, Van Heflin, Bing Crosby, Red Buttons, Ann-Margret, Michael Connors, Robert Cummings, Stefanie Powers, Slim Pickens *Prod* Martin Rackin/20th Century-Fox. 114 mins. Deluxe Color. CinemaScope.

A lush but pallid remake with some added scenes at the beginning. The Indian attack is well staged, despite the absence of the marvelous cavalry rescue in the original.

Alex Cord is no match for John Wayne in that most famous of his early roles and the rest of the cast are but pale shadows of the original characters.

STARE POVESTI CESKE OLD CZECH LEGENDS Czechoslovakia 1953. *Dir/Art Dir* Jiri Trnka *Scen* M. Kratochvil, J. Brdcka based on the collection of legends by Alois Jirasek *Photog* L. Hajek, E. Franck *Mus* Vaclav Trojan. 83 mins.

Seven legends portraying the history of Czechoslovakia: *The Legend of Forefather Czech* depicts how slaves led by Czech settled in a new country; *The Legend of Bivoj* depicts the hero's defeat of the wild boar; *The Legend of Premysl the Ploughman* depicts how a poor ploughman married a princess and founded the dynasty of the Premyslids; *The Legend of the Women's War,* the rebellion of women against male tyranny ending in reconciliation; *The Legend of Kresomysl and Horymir,* the evil influence of gold; *The War Against the Lukanians,* the invasion of Czech lands, the cowardice of the leaders, and the people's resistance. (Some of these episodes were released separately as short films.)

Old Czech Legends was for Trnka what *The Nibelungen* (*q.v.*) was for Fritz Lang: an epic full of noble deeds. It uses animated figures rather than marionettes and many scenes have large numbers of "extras." The most impressive sequence is in the last legend: the attack of the wolves and birds of prey, a metaphor of the Nazi aggression in Europe.

STARKER ALS DIE NACHT STRONGER THAN THE NIGHT German Democratic Republic 1954. *Dir* Slatan Dudow *Scen* Kurt Stern, Jeanne Stern *Photog* Karl Plintzner, Horst Brandt *Mus* Ernst Roters *Cast* Helga Göring, Kurt Oligmüller, Rita Gödikmeier, Harald Halgardt *Prod* DEFA. 106 mins.

The clandestine resistance of an anti-Fascist (Göring) against the Nazis soon after Hitler's rise to power. It ends with his arrest and execution.

This is one of the best East German films — beautiful, quietly moving, and totally ungratuitous in its effects.

STARS STERNE

STAROYE I NOVOYE OLD AND NEW/THE GENERAL LINE USSR 1929 (production began 1926). *Dir/Scen* Sergei M. Eisenstein *Co-Dir/Co-Scen* Grigori Alexandrov *Assist* Maxim Strauch, Mikhail Gomorov, A. Antonov, A. Gonkarov *Photog* Eduard Tisse *Assist Photog* V. Popov, V. Nilsen *Art Dir* Vasili Kovrigin, Vasili Rakhals *Models* A. K. Burov *Cast* Marfa Lapkina, Vasya Buzenkov, Kostya

354

Vasiliev, M. Ivanin, I. Yudin, M. Gomorov (mainly nonprofessionals) *Prod* Sovkino. 8,050 ft.

Martha (Lapkina) lives in a typical village in the USSR where farming conditions are poor and the rich kulaks of the village will not help. When a commissar is sent to organize a village cooperative, Martha becomes its most devoted supporter, despite the superstition and suspicions of the villagers. She procures for the village a cream separator, a bull, and, despite bureaucratic resistance, a tractor. The cooperative is triumphant.

Famous sequences: the Izba sawn in half as a partition between the heirs; the prayer for rain; the government commissar urging the establishment of a cooperative; the kulaks, fat in their prosperity, spurning Martha; the cream separator demonstration; the arrival and mating of the bull; the satire on bureaucrats who, under enormous portraits of Lenin, refuse to listen to Martha; the arrival of the tractor and the "knowledgeable" tractor-driver (Vasiliev), who is soon humiliated in a comic breakdown; the old fences between plots of land broken down by the tractor; the final "dance" of the tractors.

[Eisenstein began production on this film under the title *General Line* in 1926 immediately after completing *Battleship Potemkin* (*q.v.*) but dropped it for a time to make *October* (*q.v.*). He returned to it in the spring of 1928, though there is dispute as to whether he adopted a new approach to the theme or merely completed his original intentions. The final cut was finished in the spring of 1929 when, at the personal request of Stalin, the film makers had to spend an additional two months shooting a new ending. Even with this, the authorities were cool and, to avoid identification with "the general line" of Party policy changed its release (November, 1929) title to *Old and New*. Outside the Soviet Union, however, it is still known mainly by its original title.]

In 1929, *The General Line* did not represent actuality. The kolkhozes did not become common until after 1930 and the shots of model farms were, in fact, merely models inserted by trick photography.

Though it seems to take place in a single place, it was shot by Tisse and his assistants in regions of Moscow, Leningrad, Baku, Ryazan, Rostov, Penza, and even Soviet Central Asia. The central character of the peasant women is essential and carefully portrayed. Eisenstein did not want to use a professional actress and finally, after a long search, an illiterate peasant with a remarkable face, Marfa Lapkina, was discovered on a state farm. Other actors and actresses were found in other parts of the USSR. During the cutting of *The General Line,* Eisenstein developed a new approach to editing that he later called "polyphonic montage" and that used "thematic minors" and "thematic majors" with "emotive structures applied to nonemotional material." He used blacks, whites, and grays like the sounds and tones of a symphony orchestra: ["The whole intricate, rhythmic and *sensual* nuance scheme of the combined pieces (of certain sequences) is conducted almost exclusively according to a line of work on the 'psychophysiological' vibrations of each piece." (*Film Form*). Though the montage of the cream separator sequences is famous, Eisenstein's cutting throughout the film is highly complex and at least as subtle and powerful as anything he achieved before or since.] *The General Line,* more successful than *October* but far from achieving the critical and public acclaim of *Battleship Potemkin,* was later used as evidence in many of the Soviet attacks on Eisenstein's "formalism." Many of the versions released outside the USSR were re-edited in a manner that destroyed the film's cohesive structure.

*STARS LOOK DOWN (THE) Britain 1939. *Dir* Carol Reed *Scen* J. B. Williams based on the novel by A. J. Cronin *Photog* Mutz Greenbaum *Art Dir* James Carter *Ed* Reginald Beck *Cast* Michael Redgrave, Margaret Lockwood, Emlyn Williams, Edward Rigby, Nancy Price, Cecil Parker *Prod* Grafton. 96 mins.

In northeast England, David Fenwick (Redgrave) is the son of a miner who leads a strike against the working of an unsafe mine. He is doing well at university and meets Joe Gowlan (Williams), an ambitious young man from his home village. David falls in love with Joe's former girl friend, Jenny (Lockwood), and they marry. To support her, David becomes a teacher in his home village of Sleesdale, but Jenny becomes bored and discontented, especially after Joe returns to Sleesdale with a contract that will involve the miners agreeing to re-open the unsafe mine. David opposes this as his father had, but Joe persuades the union it is due to personal antagonism. Soon after work begins, the mine is flooded and a terrible disaster follows, with David's father and brother among the dead.

Carol Reed's first successful feature, based on A. J. Cronin's novel about the life of miners, is not only one of the best British films of the Thirties but also bears more than favorable comparison with John Ford's later *How Green Was My Valley* (*q.v.*). Its delineation of life in a mining village, its sensitive creation of atmosphere, and such scenes as the lock-out, the pillaging of a local shop, and the disaster have a persuasive air of realism and deeply-felt sincerity. At the time, Graham Greene, commenting on the inevitable comparison with Pabst's *Kameradschaft* (*q.v.*), felt it "can bear the comparison," while Richard Griffith felt "it was, rather, less symbolic and more deeply rooted in human living than any film dealing with the working class that I can recall." Michael Redgrave gives one of his most persuasive performances.

STEAMBOAT BILL, JR. USA 1928. *Dir* Charles F. Reisner *Scen* Carl Harbaugh, Buster Keaton *Photog* J. Devereux Jennings, Bert Haines *Ed* Sherman Kell, Buster Keaton *Cast* Buster Keaton, Ernest Torrence, Marion Byron, Tom Lewis, Tom McGuire *Prod* Joseph Schenk/Buster Keaton Productions for United Artists. 6,400 ft.

A foppish student (Keaton) returns to his father's (Torrence) old Mississippi river boat and after many misadventures ends up marrying the daughter (Byron) of his father's rival, the owner of a new boat.

This is one of the best Keatons, almost as good as *The General* (*q.v.*). The student arrives fashionably dressed with a mustache and "Oxford bags." He tries on a number of hats and rejects in horror the typical Keaton flat hat. The dramatic and comic high point of the film is the sequence of the cyclone that blows everything in front of it: houses fly away and a house front collapses on Keaton who is not at all astonished that he is saved by a window opening in the

facade. Toward the end, he flies away on a tree. Only the old boat resists the storm. All the forces of nature attack Keaton, who makes no attempt to control them and doesn't even seem to resent them, but uses them instead to perform a kind of free ballet.

*STELLA DALLAS — USA 1925. *Dir* Henry King *Scen* Frances Marion based on the novel by Olive Higgins Prouty *Photog* Arthur Edeson *Cast* Lois Moran, Belle Bennett, Jean Hersholt, Douglas Fairbanks, Jr., Ronald Colman, Alice Joyce *Prod* Goldwyn for United Artists, 10,000 ft.

Stella (Bennett), an uneducated lower-class girl, marries Stephen Dallas (Colman) after he breaks off his engagement to Helen Morrison (Joyce) following his father's financial ruin and suicide. The marriage is not a success and after their daughter, Laurel (Moran), is born, Stephen leaves for New York. Stella adores her daughter and, to improve her social chances, takes her to a smart holiday resort. There Laurel falls in love with Richard Grosvenor (Fairbanks, Jr.) but is shamed by her mother's uncouth behavior. Stephen meanwhile renews his liaison with Helen, and Stella, hoping that Helen can give Laurel a social advantage, agrees to a divorce. But Laurel refuses to desert her mother who, to force the issue, goes off with Ed Munn (Hersholt), a coarse riding master she had earlier been involved with. On the eve of Laurel's marriage to Richard, Stella stands outside in the rain, alone.

This melodramatic story, a kind of *East Lynne*, becomes, in the hands of the director of *Tol'able David* (*q.v.*) a delicate, deeply emotional, and subtle character study that reveals a masterly handling of the actors. Lois Moran and Jean Hersholt are memorable, but Belle Bennett's performance, ranging from buxom youth to blowsy middle-age, is one of the great performances of the Twenties. King's evocation of the social background — Stella's subtly vulgar home contrasting with the well-bred refinement of Helen's — is outstanding.

— USA 1937. *Dir* King Vidor *Scen* Harry Gribble, Victor Heerman, Sara Mason based on the novel *Photog* Rudolph Maté *Art Dir* Richard Day *Mus* Alfred Newman *Ed* Sherman Todd *Cast* Barbara Stanwyck, Anne Shirley, John Boles, Alan Hale, Tim Holt, Barbara

O'Neil *Prod* Goldwyn for United Artists. 105 mins.

Vidor's remake twelve years later (made during his most undistinguished period) reveals the plot as an outdated tear-jerker despite polished photography from Rudolph Maté and a touching performance by Stanwyck as Stella Dallas. Anne Shirley plays the daughter, Tim Holt her boyfriend and John Boles the father.

STEP DOWN TO TERROR see SHADOW OF A DOUBT

STERNE STARS Bulgaria/German Democratic Republic 1959. *Dir* Konrad Wolf *Scen* Angel Wagenstein *Photog* Werner Bergmann *Mus* Simeon Pironkov *Cast* Sascha Kruscharska, Jürgen Frohriep, Erik S. Klein. 95 mins.

In 1943, a German soldier (Frohriep) falls in love with a Jewish girl (Kruscharska) in a convoy of Greek deportees as it passes through a small Bulgarian town on its way to a concentration camp, but he is unable to save her.

A modestly conceived and sensitive film with a convincing creation of atmosphere.

STORA AVENTYRET (DET) THE GREAT ADVENTURE Sweden 1953. *Dir/Scen/Photog /Ed* Arne Sucksdorff *Mus* Lars-Erik Larsson *Commentator* Gunnar Sjöberg *Cast* Anders Nohrborg, Kjell Sucksdorff *Prod* Sucksdorff/Sandrews. 73 mins.

One winter, on a farm in central Sweden, two young brothers (Nohrborg Sucksdorff) rescue and tame an otter, hiding it from their parents. At the same time, the life of the animals in a neighboring forest is shown. When spring comes, "Otty" escapes.

The script, editing, and photography of this fictionalized documentary may at times be sentimental but Sucksdorff's ability to capture the rhythms of nature and the images of "a divided world" gives the film a moving sense of beauty — as in the delicate opening sequence as the forest wakes to a bright new dawn.

STORM FENG BAO

STORM OVER ASIA POTOMOK CHINGIS-KHAN

STORM WITHIN PARENTS TERRIBLES (LES)

STORMY WATERS REMORQUES

STORY FROM CHIKAMATSU (A) CHIKAMATSU MONOGATARI

STORY OF A CHEAT ROMAN D'UN TRICHEUR (LE)

STORY OF GOSTA BERLING (THE) GÖSTA BERLINGS SAGA

STORY OF THE TURBULENT YEARS POVEST' PLAMENNYKH LET

STRADA (LA) THE ROAD Italy 1954. *Dir* Federico Fellini *Scen* Federico Fellini, Ennio Flaiano, Tullio Pinelli *Photog* Otello Martelli *Art Dir* Mario Ravasco *Mus* Nino Rota *Ed* Leo Cattozo *Cast* Giulietta Masina, Anthony Quinn, Richard Basehart, Aldo Silvani, Marcella Rovena *Prod* Ponti/De Laurentiis. 94 mins.

Gelsomina (Masina), a half-witted peasant girl, is sold to Zampanò (Quinn) an itinerant strong-man, to replace her sister Rosa. She travels around the country with him, gradually becoming more expansive in human society and in relationship to Zampanò, an unfeeling brute who picks up other women in her presence. She refuses to steal for him and he strikes her. Becoming jealous she leaves him. But she returns and they join a circus, where Zampanò is arrested for attacking Il Matto (Basehart), a tightrope walker. When Zampanò is released from prison he gets involved in another fight with Il Matto and kills him. Gelsomina loses her grip on sanity and, after a time, Zampanò abandons her. Years later he hears of her death.

Famous sequences: Gelsomina sold by her mother to Zampanò for a plate of pasta; the wanderings along the roads in a battered old truck; the country wedding party and Gelsomina's encounter with a sick child; Gelsomina's first meeting with Il Matto as he plays a tune she had sung earlier; Gelsomina's conversation with a nun in a convent; Zampanò's fight with Il Matto, who looks at his shattered watch before falling down dead; Gelsomina's illness followed by Zampanò's abandonment of her; the final scene as Zampanò wanders alone by the seashore with Gelsomina's tune playing on the sound track.

La Strada was bitterly attacked by left-wing critics in Italy as a perversion and betrayal of neorealism. There is no doubt that Il Matto (The Fool), a kind of archangel soaring on his tightrope, suggests a Christian parable when he tells Gelsomina: "If I knew what this pebble is for I would be God who knows everything. When you are born. And when you die also. This pebble certainly has a purpose. If it is useless, everything is useless, even the stars. And you also, with your artichoke head, you have a purpose."

But this theme is far from being the main one of this complex film. Fellini seems most concerned with an analysis of the feminine condition represented by the "woman-as-object," as passive as a pebble, created for no other purpose than to make love and food. Gelsomina's search for her own sense of identity is central to the film. Fellini told me he knew he had achieved his aim when he received a letter from a woman who said, in substance: "My husband treats me like a Gelsomina. We went together to see *La Strada* and he cried and asked my forgiveness." Fellini's ending has been discussed at length but this letter would seem to prove that the important aspect of it is Zampanò's tears. Zampanò is a symbol of all men for whom women are predestined household drudges, the counterpart in the home of the exploited workers.

It is this theme that lies at the heart of *La Strada*'s success with the public, for it profoundly moved the majority of women and exasperated many men. Far from betraying neorealism, Fellini enriched it by guiding it along a new path.

STRANGE ADVENTURE OF DAVID GREY (THE) VAMPYR

STRANGE INCIDENT OX-BOW INCIDENT (THE)

STRANGERS VIAGGIO IN ITALIA

STRANGERS ON A TRAIN USA 1951. *Dir* Alfred Hitchock *Scen* Raymond Chandler, Czenzi Ormonde based on the novel by Patricia Highsmith *Photog* Robert Burks *Art Dir* Ted Haworth *Mus* Dimitri Tiomkin, Ray Heindorf *Ed* William Ziegler *Cast* Farley Granger, Robert Walker, Ruth Roman, Leo. G. Carroll, Patricia Hitchcock, Laura Elliott *Prod* Warner Brothers. 101 mins.

A stranger, Bruno (Walker), meets Guy (Granger) on a train and suggests that he will kill Bruno's wife (Elliott) if Guy will kill his father in exchange. Since they are strangers to each other both will have perfect alibis. Guy refuses but seems to agree in theory since he wants to marry Ann (Roman), whose father, Senator Morton (Carroll), can assist his political career. Bruno goes ahead with the plan, picks up Miriam in a fairground, and strangles her. Guy becomes enmeshed in guilt and Bruno's pressure on him to murder his father. When he still refuses, Bruno tries to use a cigarette lighter to implicate him in his wife's murder but is eventually killed after a fight on a merry-go-round.

This otherwise conventional thriller contains many typical Hitchcock themes and his typical development of suspense. Some of its editing effects (the cross-cutting between the tennis match and Bruno with the lighter) and photographic images (the murder of Miriam reflected in a pair of glasses with one lens shattered) are famous and the dramatic final chase and climax are among Hitchcock's most unforgettable sequences. Robert Walker gives a memorably disturbing performance as the unbalanced killer, especially in the scene at the Mortons' party where he discusses murder and demonstrates silent strangling techniques.

STRASSE (DIE) THE STREET Germany 1923. *Dir* Karl Grune *Scen* Karl Grune, Julius Urgiss based on an outline by Carl Mayer *Photog* Karl Hasselmann *Art Dir* Karl Görge, Ludwig Meidner *Cast* Eugen Klöpfer, Aud Egede-Nissen, Lucie Höflich, Leonhard Haskel *Prod* Stern-Film. 2,057 meters. (6,700 ft. approx.)

A middle-aged, middle-class man (Klöpfer), dissatisfied with his wife and the monotony of everyday existence, one night rebels. He meets a prostitute (Egede-Nissen) who lures him into a nightclub. There, he meets a man from the provinces. Two friends of the prostitute kill the provincial for his money and contrive to make the bourgeois appear the murderer. In the police station he tries to hang himself but the real murderer confesses. Released, he staggers home to submit to domestic routine.

The story of *The Street* takes place entirely in one night and is told without titles. Almost totally shot in studio sets, its style suggests the influence of Carl Mayer and *Kammerspiel* more than that of expressionism. Karl Grune was a former pupil of Max Reinhardt and his characters are typified by gestures, dress, and symbols. *The Street* is undoubtedly a source of *La Chienne* (*q.v.*), which Renoir made eight years later with a comparable theme but in a quite different style.

STRAY DOG NORA-INU

STRAY LAMB (THE) China 1936. *Dir* Tsai Tsou-sen. 90 mins. approx.
A small boy arrives in Shanghai from the country and soon joins a band of children who have been abandoned like him. A rich man wants to adopt him but he runs away and joins a community set up by a poor man.
This excellent film is comparable to *Road to Life* (*q.v.*) and *Munna* (*q.v.*) but has many comic sequences and sequences critical of life in China under the Chiang Kai-shek regime. It is the best film by the best Chinese director of the Thirties and Forties.

STREET (THE) STRASSE (DIE)

STREETCAR NAMED DESIRE (A) USA 1951. *Dir* Elia Kazan *Scen* Tennessee Williams, Oscar Saul based on the play by Tennessee Williams *Photog* Harry Stradling *Art Dir* Richard Day *Mus* Alex North *Ed* David Weisbart *Cast* Vivien Leigh, Marlon Brando, Kim Hunter, Karl Malden, Rudy Bond, Nick Dennis *Prod* Elia Kazan/Warner Brothers. 125 mins.
Blanche (Leigh), the daughter of a once wealthy southern family, goes to live with her sister, Stella (Hunter), and her husband, Stanley (Brando). Her refined nature is disgusted at their squalid apartment and animal-like vulgarity. She is courted by Mitch (Malden), a shy, middle-aged man, but he leaves after Stanley recounts her past history and how she had to leave the town where she was a schoolteacher because of her numerous men. While Stella is having a baby in the hospital, Blanche is raped by Stanley and goes mad.
Elia Kazan had originally directed the play on the stage with Brando and Hunter in the same roles. This skillful screen adaptation is much aided by the sets and low-key lighting, which convey an atmosphere of tawdry squalor. Kazan himself describes it as "a beautiful play that I shot without softening or deepening it, filming it as it was because there was nothing to change." The performances of Vivien Leigh and Marlon Brando (convincingly vigorous and primitive as a Polish immigrant) won them a number of awards.

STRIDE, SOVIET! SHAGAI, SOVIET

STRIKE STACHKA

STROKE OF MIDNIGHT (THE) KÖRKARLEN

STRONGER THAN THE NIGHT STÄRKER ALS DIE NACHT

STRONG MAN (THE) USA 1926. *Dir* Frank Capra *Scen* Frank Capra, Arthur Ripley, Hal Conklin, Robert Eddy *Photog* Elgin Lessley, Glenn Kershner *Cast* Harry Langdon, Gertrude Astor, Tay Garnett, Priscilla Bonner, Robert McKim *Prod* Harry Langdon Corp. 6,840 ft. Dream sequence in color.
A young man (Langdon) returns from the war and searches in a big city for a girl he knows only through correspondence. He finally discovers her in a small town and also saves the town from corrupt crooks. In between he is used as a front by a group of gangsters and joins a "strong man."
Langdon's second feature is one of his most endearing and has many outstanding comic sequences and a typical thrilling climax in the Lloyd and Keaton manner. It is difficult to say whether its success owes more to Langdon or to Frank Capra. [This is Capra's first feature as director though he was also a scriptwriter on *Tramp, Tramp, Tramp* (*q.v.*). He later directed *Long Pants* (*q.v.*) for Langdon, whose career soon fell into decline when they parted after this film.]

STRUGGLE IN THE VALLEY SERA'A FIL WADI

SUBIDA AL CIELO ASCENT TO HEAVEN/ MEXICAN BUS RIDE Mexico 1951. *Dir* Luis Buñuel *Scen* Manuel Altolaguirre *Photog* Alex Phillips *Art Dir* Edward Fitzgerald, José Rodriguez Granada *Mus* Gustavo Pittaluga *Cast* Lilia Prado, Carmelita Gonzales, Esteban Marquez, Manuel Donde, Roberto Cobo *Prod* Islas. 85 mins.
Oliviero (Marquez), a young peasant, is forced to leave his bride (Gonzalez) on their wedding night in order to get

his dying mother to regularize her will. On the bus journey he meets a diverse group of passengers and has various adventures. The bus driver insists on diverting the bus to attend his mother's birthday party; the bus gets stuck in a flooded river; Oliviero meets Raquel (Prado), a beautiful girl who seduces him. Because of the delays on the journey, Oliviero's mother dies alone but by a clever trick Oliviero saves her legacy.

"I liked making this," Buñuel has said, "very simple, very static . . . nothing happens in it, nothing at all; no progression, but a nice film." It is this amiable assertion of the moment when "nothing happens" that pervades this picaresque portrait of Mexican country life. Its story is a happy one; Buñuel is in a relaxed mood and he enjoys himself and amuses us. But, as Freddy Buache points out, "this popular farce should not be confused with mere vaudeville entertainment. It has a kind of second depth. Its unusual characteristics are to be found in its mockery, as, for example, in the scene where the bus is so bogged down that a tractor cannot move it. Two oxen are then harnessed to the bus and suddenly it moves, the oxen following a little girl who is leading them by a piece of string. The passengers take their seats again then suddenly notice the man who has got his wooden leg stuck in the mud. The droll caricatures have anarchic undertones that owe much to surrealism." This surrealism is most evident in the dream sequence in which the earthy Raquel appears in his bride's wedding gown and in which unending rolls of apple peel appear like an umbilical cord.

SUCH A PRETTY LITTLE BEACH UNE SI JOLIE PETITE PLAGE

SUCH IS LIFE TAKOVÝ JE ŽIVOT

SUDBA CHELOVEKA DESTINY OF A MAN/ FATE OF A MAN/A MAN'S DESTINY USSR 1959. *Dir* Sergei Bondarchuk *Scen* Y. Lukin, F. Shakhmagonov based on the novel by Mikhail Sholokov *Photog* Vladimir Monakhov *Art Dir* A. Golovanov, I. Novodereshkin, S. Voronkov *Mus* V. Basner *Ed* V. Leonov *Cast* Sergei Bondarchuk, Zinaida Kirienko, Pavlik Boriskin, P. Volkov *Prod* Mosfilm. 98 mins. English version 77 mins.

Andrei Sokolov (Bondarchuk) is a prosperous married man with a wife (Kirienko) and family when war breaks out. He joins the army and is captured by the Nazis, who treat him brutally. He escapes but is recaptured and sent deeper into Germany to slavery and humiliation. He escapes again and rejoins the Soviet army and is told of his son's death as a hero. Returning to his home, he learns his wife has been killed and his house destroyed by a bomb. He finds a homeless orphan and decides to pose as the boy's father and start a new life.

Notable sequences: the arrival at the camp; the escape; his return to the Ukraine, undefeated by all the animadversions of fate.

Making a prisoner of war the hero of this film was considered bold at the time, since this theme was suspect under Stalin. This unsentimental, humanistic tragedy is the first film directed by the famous actor, Bondarchuk.

SUITOR (THE) SOUPIRANT (LE)

SULLIVAN'S TRAVELS USA 1941. *Dir/Scen* Preston Sturges *Photog* John Seitz *Art Dir* Hans Dreier *Ed* Stuart Gilmore *Cast* Joel McCrea, Veronica Lake, William Demarest, Robert Warwick, Franklin Pangborn, Porter Hall *Prod* Paramount. 91 mins.

John L. Sullivan (McCrea), a famous Hollywood director, disguises himself as a vagabond and sets off to search for the meaning of poverty. He meets a young blonde (Lake), is accused of his own murder, and is sentenced to a chain gang before he proves his identity. He returns to Hollywood and marries the blond, having determined that the public really want comedies.

Best sequences: the rich Sullivan, disguised as a poor vagabond, in the luxurious rooms of his beautiful Hollywood mansion; his departure on foot down the road — followed by numerous cars, a secretary, and radio reporters; the fight with a bum in a railway marshaling yard, in which the bum knocks him out but is then crushed by a locomotive; Sullivan's life in a chain gang like that in *I Am a Fugitive From a Chain Gang* (q.v.).

This eccentric satire of a protean director of musical comedies who wants to make social treatises (with titles like *Brother, Where Art Thou?*) is Preston Sturges's best film. It is also something of a self-justification: after watching the prisoners laugh at a *Mickey Mouse* cartoon, the director decides he can better achieve his social aims through comedy than through "pretentious" social dramas.

SUMMER INTERLUDE SOMMARLEK

SUMMER MANEUVERS GRANDES MANOEUVRES (LES)

SUMMER WITH MONIKA SOMMAREN MED MONIKA

SUN ALWAYS RISES (THE) SOLE SORGE ANCORA (IL)

SUNA NO ONNA THE WOMAN OF THE DUNES Japan 1964. *Dir* Hiroshi Teshigahara *Scen* Kobo Abe *Photog* Hiroshi Segawa *Mus* Toru Takemitsu *Ed* F. Susui *Cast* Eiji Okada, Kyoko Kishida *Prod* Teshigahara. 127 mins.
A young entomologist (Okada) is persuaded by villagers to spend the night in a shack in a sand pit with a widow (Kishida) whose task is endlessly to shovel away sand, which is hauled up on ropes. Next day he finds he cannot leave, but his initial hostility gives way to sexual attraction and he becomes the woman's lover as well as her helper. When he has a chance to escape he does not take it.
This bizarre allegory on modern life has a complex visual poetry and texture and sensitive performance. It is an impressive and powerful example of the Japanese *new wave*.

SUNLESS STREET (THE) TAIYO NO NAI MACHI

SUNNYSIDE USA 1919. *Dir/Scen* Charles Chaplin *Photog* Rollie Totheroh *Cast* Charles Chaplin, Edna Purviance, Tom Wilson, Albert Austin, Henry Bergman *Prod* Chaplin for First National. 2,900 ft.
Charlie is the hired help at a country hotel owned by a puritanical slave driver (Wilson). Working from dawn to midnight, his only solace is his love for the Village Belle (Purviance). A City Slicker (Austin) arrives and steals the heart of his sweetheart but Charlie eventually triumphs.
Famous sequences: at dawn, Charlie making a pretense of getting up; Charlie losing and attempting to recapture the cows on the way to pasture; his dream in which he burlesques Pan and dances with a bevy of wood nymphs; his visit to his sweetheart at her family's home; the arrival of the elegant City Slicker at the hotel; Charlie's attempts to compete with him in dress and mannerisms.
This satire on rural life is one of the best of Chaplin's shorts, as perfect an alliance of lyrical fantasy and realistic social criticism as *Shoulder Arms* (*q.v.*). It was a great success in France, where it was hailed as the masterpiece it is. But in the United States it received only a lukewarm response from the public: Theodore Huff describes it as "a gentle pastle pastoral idyll . . . many sat through it wondering when a laugh was in order."

SUNRISE USA 1927. *Dir* F. W. Murnau *Scen* Carl Mayer based on *A Trip to Tilsit* by Hermann Sudermann *Photog* Karl Strüss, Charles Rosher *Art Dir* Rochus Gliese *Mus* Hugo Riesenfeld *Assist Art Dir* Edgar Ulmer, Alfred Metscher *Titles* Katherine Hilliker, H. H. Caldwell *Cast* George O'Brien, Janet Gaynor, Margaret Livingston *Prod* Fox. 8,730 ft. Sound version with synchronized music, 97 mins.
A man (O'Brien) lives happily with his wife (Gaynor) and their child in a small village until he is seduced by a woman from the city (Livingston). She persuades him to drown his wife and leave with her for the city. He takes his wife across the lake but cannot drown her. She runs away, he follows her; they are reconciled, re-discover their love, and have a happy day in the city. On the way home, a storm capsizes the boat and the wife is lost. The city woman assumes her plan has succeeded but the man, insane with grief and anger, tries to strangle her. Suddenly, news comes that the wife is safe; the city woman leaves.
Sunrise opens with a title that describes it as "the song of two humans. This story of a Man and his Wife is of nowhere and everywhere, you might hear it anywhere and at any time. For everywhere, the sun rises and sets — in the city's turmoil or under the open sky on the farm, life is much the same, sometimes bitter, sometimes sweet, tears and laughter, sin and forgiveness."
[Murnau was invited to Hollywood by William Fox after the success of *The Last Laugh* (*q.v.*). Murnau signed a contract on the understanding that his first film would be *Sunrise* and that it would

be made without studio interference. According to Charles Rosher, the cameraman, the script was written by Mayer in Berlin, where Murnau completely planned the film before he left for Hollywood. William Fox kept to his agreement; no one at the studio except Murnau, Rosher, Strüss, and the editor, saw any part of the film until it was finished. Murnau spent huge sums of money on the sets: the vast sets for the city and the trolley-ride sequence; mechanized rain and dust storms; even the interiors were built with slanted walls and ceiling to create a "psychological" perspective rather than a realistic one. Mayer's script, perhaps his most perfect, was derived from a typical Sudermann story but underwent several basic changes. Sudermann's peasant is boorish and unpleasant and, in the end, accidentally drowns; the city woman is a servant in their house. In the film the peasant is portrayed as an essentially simple man who truly loves his wife but is seduced against his better nature. These changes are basic to the film's essentially fable-like structure.]

Murnau's most perfect film, though made in Hollywood, is entirely Germanic in style. Its style is dominated by fluid camera movements that are so masterfully handled that they also seem invisible. This is best seen in the sequence in which Murnau defines the man's relationship to the city woman — the seduction scene. The camera slowly follows the man as he moves through the misty meadows, creating, as Lewis Jacobs describes it, a mood of "quiet sensuality (in which) the overhanging mists, the dew, the full moon, the sinuous and constant movement of the camera — all combined to create a dark, somnolent mood."

The lyrical, unreal mood of the first half gives way to a more realistic one after the drowning attempt on the lake. When the boat reaches the shore, the terrified wife runs away and boards a trolley. He follows her, and, both numb and miserable, they travel into the city. Behind them the landscape flows past the window, first the lake and the woods, then the outskirts, and finally the city itself. Throughout, they are oblivious to the increasing activity around them. The sets throughout are brilliant and contribute effectively to the theme.

Both Janet Gaynor and George O'Brien

(then a famous "ideal couple") are well directed: Janet Gaynor as the wife is an image of pure goodness (as the city woman is one of evil).

Sunrise was a financial flop from which Murnau never recovered; his remaining two films for Fox were entirely controlled by the studio. His independently made *Tabu* (q.v.) was his last film before his death.

— die Reise nach Tiltsit (Germany 1939. *Dir* Veit Harlan *Scen* Veit Harlan based on Sudermann's novelette *Photog* Bruno Mondi *Mus* Hans Otto Bergmann *Cast* Fritz van Dongen (Philip Dorn), Kristina Söderbaum, Anna Damman, Albert Florath *Prod* Tobis. 92 mins.

[Made by the director of *Jud Süss* (q.v.), this is reportedly a beautifully photographed work with performances by Fritz van Dongen and Kristina Söderbaum that a least equal those of O'Brien and Gaynor in the Murnau version. Veit Harlan has said: "I did my version in Memel, where the story takes place. Murnau's *Sunrise* was a poem, but, if you'll excuse me, mine was a real film."]

SUN RISES AGAIN (THE) SOLE SORGE ANCORA (IL)

SUNSET BOULEVARD USA 1950. *Dir* Billy Wilder *Scen* Charles Brackett, Billy Wilder, D. M. Marshman, Jr. based on the story *A Can of Beans* by Charles Brackett and Billy Wilder *Photog* John F. Seitz *Art Dir* Hans Dreier, John Meehan *Mus* Franz Waxman *Ed* Doane Harrison, Arthur Schmidt *Cast* Gloria Swanson, William Holden, Erich von Stroheim, Nancy Olson, Jack Webb, Fred Clark, Buster Keaton, Cecil B. De Mille, Hedda Hopper, Anna Q. Nilsson, H. B. Warner *Prod* Paramount. 111 mins.

Norma Desmond (Swanson), at one time a famous star of silent films, lives in a luxurious Hollywood mansion on Sunset Boulevard attended only by Max von Mayerling (Stroheim), once her director now her servant. She employs Joe Gillis (Holden), a disillusioned young writer, to work on the script with which she hopes to make a comeback, even though Cecil B. De Mille has turned it down. Joe finds himself in servitude and a love affair, enmeshed in her fantasies of coming glory. He tries to escape but she attempts suicide and he returns. He sneaks out at night to write his own scripts with a girl he is in love with

(Olson). When he eventually tells her the truth about her own fantasies, she shoots him. The shock tips the balance in her mind and she walks downstairs to be arrested, believing the cameras and crowds are to welcome her return to the screen. The story is told by the writer whose body floating in the swimming pool is seen at the beginning of the film.

This film was hailed on its release as a ruthless portrait of Hollywood but it remains essentially superficial. Wilder's creation of atmosphere is fascinating but is compounded by clever devices and exaggerated characterizations that remain unconvincing or even cheap — as in the ceremonial bridge party for (real) forgotten ex-stars. However, Gloria Swanson's magnetic performance is unforgettable as is that of the servile Stroheim trying to sustain the star's belief in herself. [Cecil B. De Mille is shown on the set of *Samson and Delilah* and an extract from *Queen Kelly* (*q.v.*) is included.]

SUNSET OF A CLOWN GYCKLARNAS AFTON

S.V.D. THE CLUB OF THE BIG DEED USSR 1927. *Dir* Grigori Kozintsev, Leonid Trauberg *Scen* Yuri Tinyanov, Yuri Oxman *Photog* Andrei Moskvin *Art Dir* Yevgeni Enei *Cast* Pyotr Sobolevsky, Sergei Gerasimov, Sophie Magarill, Andrei Kostrichkin *Prod* Sovkino (Leningrad). 2,100 meters.

In a St. Petersburg Garrison in 1825, a "Decembrist" officer (Sobolevsky) in love with a countess (Magarill), involves his comrades in a revolt against Tsarist tyranny, but because of a traitor (Gerasimov) the insurrection fails.

This romantic story by the FEKS (Factory of Eccentric Actors) group has striking sets and Moskvin's always memorable photography. In style it is somewhat reminiscent of *Fantômas* (*q.v.*) and westerns: pistols are fired by people hiding in barrels, an underground escape ends up at the altar of a church, a single weapon holds back a crowd until it shatters a chandelier, a circus is interrupted by the arrival of the police, etc.

SWEET LIFE (THE) DOLCE VITA (LA)

SWEET SMELL OF SUCCESS USA 1957. *Dir* Alexander Mackendrick *Scen* Clifford Odets, Ernest Lehman based on the novelette by Ernest Lehman *Photog* James Wong Howe *Art Dir* Edward Carrere *Mus* Elmer Bernstein *Ed* Alan Crosland, Jr. *Cast* Burt Lancaster, Tony Curtis, Susan Harrison, Marty Milner *Prod* Hecht, Hill, and Lancaster for United Artists. 96 mins.

J. J. Hunsecker (Lancaster), an influential New York columnist, tries to break up his sister Susan's (Harrison) romance with Steve Dallas (Milner), a musician. He gains the help of Sidney Falco (Curtis), a press agent who needs access to Hunsecker's column. Falco bribes another columnist to smear Dallas as a dope addict and communist. Later, Hunsecker instructs Falco to plant marijuana on Dallas and have him picked up by the police. Susan is saved from suicide by Falco but Hunsecker misinterprets the situation and beats him up. Falco tells Susan of her brother's role in the plot and Hunsecker informs the police of Falco's planting the dope.

A tough and bitter portrait of New York journalism and power corruption whose sinister, decadent atmosphere owes much to James Wong Howe's photography. [This was Alexander Mackendrick's first film in the USA, a total contrast to his work at Ealing on such films as *The Maggie* (*q.v.*) and *The Ladykillers*. It includes a remarkably persuasive performance by Tony Curtis but the film was not a commercial success.]

SWINDLERS (THE) BIDONE (IL)

SYLVESTER — TRAGODIE EINER NACHT NEW YEAR'S EVE Germany 1923. *Dir* Lupu Pick *Scen* Carl Mayer *Photog* Karl Hasselmann (interiors), Guido Seeber (exteriors) *Art Dir* Robert A. Dietrich *Cast* Eugen Klöpfer, Edith Posca, Frieda Richard *Prod* Rex-Film. 1,529 meters (5,000 ft. approx.).

The owner (Klöpfer) of a cheap café is torn by the discord between his wife (Posca) and his mother (Richard), who lives with them. As merry crowds outside celebrate New Year's Eve, the conflict reaches its climax in a scene of bitter jealousy. Torn between them, overcome with self-pity and besotted with punch, the man is pushed to suicide.

This is the masterpiece of *Kammerspiel* and part of Carl Mayer's trilogy with *Scherben* (*q.v.*) and *Der Letze Mann* (*q.v.*). As with the other two, a heavy sense of fatalism dominates the action: once the nature of the three characters has been established, the ultimate tragedy is inevitable and the man kills himself just as the new year begins. Mayer's scenario follows the law of the Three Unities: the action takes place in a single set (the dining room behind the café) and the time of the action is the time of the projection. The camera (like a Greek chorus) only leaves this closed world to reveal crowds celebrating in the streets, in an elegant restaurant and in a tavern, or to picture the sea, a cemetery, or a heath in the manner of a lietmotiv. The linear simplicity of the story makes the use of titles unnecessary. Everything is expressed through the gestures and behavior of the three characters, the use of visual metaphors, and camera movements. The sets are highly simplified but are realistic and not expressionistic. The acting is stylized using expressive gestures that are almost pantomimic.

The best examples of Mayer's use of objects as symbols come as the tragedy reaches its climax: the mother clinging to the stove when the man seems prepared to send her away; her poking about with the child's pram; the two family portraits (son and mother, husband and wife) that spark a jealous scene between the two women; the wife setting two places at the table then unwillingly adding a third on the part of the table without a cloth.

SYMPHONY OF THE DONBAS ENTUZIAZM

SYMPHONY OF THE METROPOLIS TOKAI KOKYOGAKU

SYN MONGOLII SON OF MONGOLIA USSR 1936. *Dir* Ilya Trauberg *Scen* B. Lapin, Lev Slavin, Z. Khatzrevin, *Co-Dir* R. Suslovich *Photog* M. Kaplan, V. Levitin, E. Shtirtskober *Art Dir* I. Vuskovich *Mus* Isaac Rabinovich, E. Grikurov *Cast* Tse-Ven, Sosor-Barma, Gam-bo, Bato-Ochir *Prod* Lenfilm. 90 mins.

A Mongolian shepherd (Tse-Ven) loses his way in a storm and finds himself in Japanese-controlled Manchuria. After many adventures he destroys evil and finds love.

A beautiful achievement in the form of a ballad sung and acted by the hero. A reflection of Mongolian folkloric themes entirely performed by Mongols, though

it isn't clear if they were nonprofessionals.

*SZEGENYLEGENYEK THE ROUND-UP/THE HOPELESS ONES/THE POOR OUTLAWS Hungary 1966. *Dir* Miklos Jancso *Scen* Gyula Hernadi *Photog* Tamas Somlo *Art Dir* Tamas Banovich *Ed* Zoltan Farkas *Cast* Janos Gorbe, Tibor Molnar, Andras Kozak, Gabor Agardy, Zoltan Latinovits *Prod* Studio IV, Mafilm. 94 mins. Agascope. Shorter in foreign releases.

Twenty years after the abortive Hungarian revolt against Austrian rule in the mid-19th century, several hundred outlaws, peasants, and herdsmen are rounded up and incarcerated in a prison stockade in Hungary in the hopes of identifying active Hungarian rebels. Janos Gajdor (Gorbe) is identified as a killer and is told if he can find a man who has killed more than he has he will go free. The first man he betrays tries to escape and is hanged. He then identifies Veszelka (Latinovits), who, when he sees his woman tortured in front of him, leaps to his death. The other inmates kill Janos for his treachery but Kabai (Molnar) and his son unwittingly betray the murderer, Torma (Agardy). Kabai and Torma are forced to compete in a horsemanship match. When Torma wins he is asked to pick a cavalry squadron from the prisoners who have now been conscripted into the army. His group consists of active rebels and when this is known they are led away for punishment.

Jancso's savage and often ironic epic about the effects of imprisonment, fear, and torture in a police state was one of the first films to reveal a new trend in the Hungarian cinema. *The Round Up* is austere, detached, almost Bressonian in visual style, but entirely without introspective character development. Its emotional eloquence comes entirely from a series of often ruthlessly cruel incidents depicted against a stark vast plain, spotless white buildings, and featureless grey sky. Individual nobility has no place in Jancso's film, as he portrays the prisoners' resolution inevitably crumbling beneath psychological weapons that play on their own fears and weaknesses. Jancso himself says the film was made as "an appeal to face our illusions, which go back over a thousand years."

TABU USA 1931 (production began 1929). *Dir* F. W. Murnau, Robert Flaherty *Assist* David Flaherty *Scen* F. W. Murnau, Robert Flaherty based on an original story by Flaherty *Photog* Floyd Crosby, Robert Flaherty *Mus* Hugo Riesenfeld *Ed* F. W. Murnau *Cast* Reri (Anna Chevalier), Matahi, Hitu, and other nonprofessionals from Bora-Bora in Tahiti *Prod* Colorart Synchrotone (Murnau) for Paramount. 80 mins. (synchronized music version).

In Tahiti, a young pearl fisherman (Matahi) loves a maiden (Reri) who is consecrated to the gods and is thus taboo to all men. Their love leads them to break the code and tragedy results.

Main sequences: the idyllic love scene between the young couple; Reri being declared taboo by Hitu, priest and chief of the tribe, and taken to another island; Matahi carrying her off; their life together on an unpopulated island where he gathers pearls that he goes to sell in Tahiti; Hitu finding Reri and telling her he will fetch her in three days; Matahi trying to get Reri a passage on a boat but losing his money; Hitu taking Reri away in his boat pursued by the swimming Matahi, who drowns when the rope from Hitu's boat that he had grabbed is cut by the priest.

[In 1928, Murnau broke with the Fox Studios following a disagreement over his production of *Our Daily Bread* (*q.v.*). He proposed a collaborative production to Robert Flaherty. They bought a yacht, the "Moana," and set sail around the world intending to film as they went. In Tahiti in July 1929, they began production of a film based on a theme proposed by Flaherty: the impact of civilization on a primitive society. But as the production developed, problems arose. Murnau wanted more "plot," which he felt lay in the Polynesian taboo custom; Flaherty felt Murnau's story was "imposed" on the people. Both were sincere in their approach and they agreed to differ. Flaherty sold his interests in the film to Murnau and relinquished control over its content. He continued to work on the film and supervised the photography but left Tahiti before the film was completed. Murnau finished it and supervised the editing. As Richard Griffith points out, although Flaherty's "name looms large in the screen credits . . . it is a Murnau treasure, not a Flaherty one."]

"When our yacht arrived in the harbor at Bora-Bora," Murnau said, "the natives had never seen even a kodak snapshot camera. I had the idea that the taboos of these islands could form the theme of my story. Around this idea, Flaherty and I wove a romantic plot that was as simple as possible. It would be possible to make a striking film if we could find actors capable of living this plot. Where to find them? Among the natives, not from among Hollywood actors. Ever since I arrived in Bora-Bora, I felt it was *my* island, a precious stone in the middle of an immense sea. Its natives knew almost nothing of the outside world and lived in perpetual play without false modesty." The evocation of an "enchanted isle" is found especially in the idyllic bathing scene, somewhat obviously staged, but glowing with seductive imagery.

Murnau returned to the States to edit the film and died in an automobile accident one week before the first public showing in March 1931. It was released by Paramount (with a banal musical score by Hugo Riesenfeld) and was a world-wide success, returning profits of over $150,00 to the Murnau estate.

TAGEBUCH EINER VERLORENEN THE DIARY OF A LOST GIRL/THE DIARY OF A

LOST ONE Germany 1929. *Dir* G. W. Pabst *Scen* Rudolf Leonhardt based on the novel by Margarete Böhme *Photog* Sepp Allgeier *Art Dir* Ernö Metzner, Emil Hasler *Cast* Louise Brooks, Fritz Rasp, Josef Rovensky, Sybille Schmitz, Valeska Gert, André Roanne, Andrews Engelmann, Franziska Kinz *Prod* G. W. Pabst Film. 2,863 meters (9,400 ft. approx.).

Thymian (Brooks), the daughter of a wealthy pharmacist, is seduced by her father's assistant (Rasp) and has an illegitimate child. She is placed in a house of correction run by a sadistic governess (Gert) and finds herself in a brothel. She inherits some money when her father dies but gives it to her stepmother, since her child had since died. A degenerate nobleman marries her, then commits suicide. Finally her uncle takes her into his house.

Based on Margarete Böhme's popular novel, this is a graphically frank account of the sordid downfall of a middle-class girl reflected in the marvelous face of Louise Brooks. [The film was badly mutilated by censors everywhere, including Germany. According to Rudolf Leonhardt, "entire filmed sequences were cut without mercy . . . The film comes to an end shortly after the middle of our script, inconclusively and incomprehensibly."] Especially memorable for its rhythmic cutting is the scene in the brothel/reformatory with the sadistic governess beating with a cane the rhythm with which the girls must eat each spoonful of soup.

Louise Chavance, later scriptwriter on *Le Corbeau* (*q.v.*), wrote: "The meaningless actions of the puppets are treated with a passive psychology. A vulgar realism is stuck onto sordid details of existence." But the film nevertheless remains "naturalistic" in the polished perfection of its script, exposing the social structures and conditions that lead to wasted lives and youth.

— *Das Tagebuch einer Verlorenen* Germany 1918. *Dir* Richard Oswald *Scen* Richard Oswald based on the Böhme novel *Photog* Max Fassbender *Art Dir* August Rinaldi *Cast* Reinhold Schünzel, Erna Morena, Conrad Veidt, Werner Krauss. In two parts: 1,934 meters and 1,890 meters. First part known as *das Tagebuch einer Toten.*

TAIYO NO NAI MACHI THE SUNLESS STREET Japan 1953. *Dir* Satsuo Yama-

moto *Scen* T. Saburo based on the novel by Sunao Tokunaga *Mus* N. Yda *Cast* H. Sumiko, M. Katisura, S. Susukida, Y. Nagata *Prod* Shinsei Eiga. 142 mins.

This adaptation of a 1929 "proletarian" novel about a prolonged strike at a large Tokyo printing plant is one of the best independently produced Japanese films. Its forceful cutting (often using very brief flashbacks) effectively contrasts dramatically intense scenes of the capitalist adversaries, such as the torture of a militant striker by the police, with lyrical outdoor scenes of the strikers, such as that of the festival.

TAKOVY JE ZIVOT SUCH IS LIFE Czechoslovakia 1929. *Dir/Scen* Karl Junghans *Photog* Laszlo Schäffer *Art Dir* Ernst Meiwers, A. Kavalirka *Cast* Vera Baranovskaya, Theodor Pistek, Wolfgang Zilzer, J. Plachta, Mana Zeniskova, Manja Kellerova, Valeska Gert *Prod* Bukac/Pistek. 6,050 ft. Re-released with synchronized music in 1959, 67 mins.

Set in Prague, this is the story of an old washerwoman (Baranovskaya), her drunken philandering husband (Pistek), his girl friend (Gert), and their daughter (Zeniskova), a manicurist. The daughter becomes pregnant, the mother scalds herself, dies, and is buried.

Though the script is not excellent and sometimes verges on melodrama, this realistic portrait of the life of ordinary people in Prague is one of the best Czechoslovak films of the Twenties, authentically true to life. Life in the working-class districts is often calamitous, dirty, and hopeless, but Junghans does not merely report and often reveals his own sense of indignation at these conditions. The sets and photography are remarkable but are not influenced by expressionism nor even by Pabst. In fact, the style often seems closer to neorealism.

The best sequence is that of the Sunday country outing during which the washing is done in the Moldava. Also especially memorable are the final sequences: the mother's death, her funeral with family and friends in unaccustomed black clothes, and the funeral repast, which ends up in a wine shop.

TALES OF THE PALE AND SILVERY MOON AFTER THE RAIN UGETSU MONOGATARI

TARAS SHEVCHENKO USSR 1951. *Dir/Scen* Igor Savchenko *Assist* A. Alov, Vladimir

Naumov *Photog* Abram Kaltsati, Danylo Demutsky *Art Dir* L. Shengelaya, B. Nemechek, M. Solokha *Mus* Boris Lyatoshinsky *Cast* Sergei Bondarchuk, Natalia Uzhvi, Yevgeni Samoilov, Alexei Konsovsky, I. Timofiev *Prod* Kiev. 118 mins. Agfacolor.

The life of Taras Shevchenko (Bondarchuk), poet and Ukrainian hero (1814–1861), who fought for Slav democratic union and was sentenced by Tsar Nicholas to penal army service in Central Asia and forbidden to write.

The sequences in the penal camp and the persuasive performance by Bondarchuk are far more memorable than several somewhat pompous episodes; such as that in which Shevchenko meets several famous Russian writers. Savchenko died defore the film was finished and it was completed by his young assistants, Alov and Naumov.

TASTE OF HONEY (A) Britain 1961. *Dir* Tony Richardson *Scen* Shelagh Delaney, Tony Richardson based on the play by Shelagh Delaney *Photog* Walter Lassally *Art Dir* Ralph Brinton *Mus* John Addison *Ed* Tony Gibbs *Cast* Rita Tushingham, Dora Bryan, Murray Melvin, Robert Stephens, Paul Danquah *Prod* Woodfall. 100 mins.

In an industrial city in Lancashire, Jo (Tushingham), a gawky adolescent, lives with Helen (Bryan), her restless, effusive mother until Helen decides to marry Peter (Stephens). Jo meets a Black sailor, Jimmy (Danquah), and sleeps with him. She takes a job in a shoe store, and lives alone in a big, bare room until she meets Geoffrey (Melvin), a homeless homosexual who moves in with her and looks after the house. Jo discovers she is going to have Jimmy's baby and, although Geoffrey offers marriage, appears not to want the child. Geoffrey tells Helen of Jo's pregnancy and, having been deserted by Peter, Helen moves in with Jo and drives Geoffrey out.

One of several significant British films that grew out of the *free cinema* movement and the developments in British drama in the Fifties, this appealing and compassionate portrait of life in a large industrial town in Lancashire is never gratuitously squalid. The story focuses on an independently minded and spirited, but gawky, adolescent girl (lovingly portrayed by Rita Tushingham) who tries to seize any tiny moment of happiness from the hopelessness of her surroundings.

Walter Lassally's photography of the non-studio urban background is among his best work.

TASTE OF MACKEREL (A) SAMMA NO AJI

TAUSEND AUGEN DER DR. MABUSE (DIE) see DR. MABUSE, DER SPIELER

TAVASZI ZAPOR MARIE/SPRING SHOWER Hungary/France 1932. *Dir* Paul Fejös *Scen* Ilona Fülor *Photog* Istvan Eiben, Pawerell, Marleyi *Mus* Vincent Scotto, Laszlo Angyal *Cast* Annabella, Istvan Gyergyai, Ilona Dajbukat, Erzsi Barsony, Margit Ladomerszky *Prod* Osso. 66 mins. Sound, but without dialogue.

Marie (Annabella), a Hungarian peasant, is seduced by the local farm bailiff, becomes pregnant, and is driven by her shame from the village into the town. There, she becomes a servant in a disreputable café and brothel. The authorities try to remove her child to an orphanage. She resists but dies, goes to heaven, and returns in triumph to her natal village.

Good sequences: the preparations for a fête on the prosperous farm where Marie is a servant; her seduction under an apple tree in blossom; her distress when she cannot find work in Budapest; her welcome into the brothel and the kindnesses shown to her by the prostitutes and the madame; her child taken away by the police; Marie driven from a church by bigots. The finale, in which Marie is seen in a heavenly kitchen with gold utensils, is open to criticism but less so than her triumphant return to her village in gaudy, spurious folk costume.

At the invitation of the Paris producers, Osso, Paul Fejös returned to his native Hungary to direct two films, of which this is the first. It is undoubtedly the best Hungarian film of the Thirties, though it was more admired abroad than in Hungary. Its script, based on a popular Hungarian legend, is never melodramatic and seems to have been influenced by Chaplin's *The Kid* (*q.v.*). With clever stylization and symbolism, an extensive use of sound effects (which now, however, seem dated), and the omission of audible dialogue, Fejös paints a social portrait of the poverty and distress of most of his countrymen. Unhappily, the ending, in contrast to the delicate style and sense of tragic reality of earlier scenes, is entirely artificial and more typical of the postcard style of contemporaneous Hungarian films.

TAXI see SANS LAISSER D'ADRESSE

TEMPEST BARRAVENTO

TEN COMMANDMENTS (THE) USA 1923. *Dir* Cecil B. De Mille *Scen* Jeanie Macpherson *Tech Dir* Roy Pomeroy *Photog* Bert Glennon and others *Art Dir* Paul Iribe *Cast* (Biblical story) Theodore Roberts, Estelle Taylor, Charles de Roche, James Neill; (Modern story) Rod La Rocque, Edythe Chapman, Richard Dix, Leatrice Joy, Nita Naldi *Prod* Famous Players-Lasky, 12,397 ft. Biblical sequences in two-color Technicolor.

The biblical story of Moses (Roberts), the flight from Egypt under Ramses (De Roche) and the giving of the Ten Commandments is followed by a modern story about two brothers, one (La Rocque) of whom breaks all the commandments while the other (Dix) observes them.

Costing $1.5 million, this is the first of the De Mille spectaculars. The modern story is melodramatic and dull. The biblical prologue is staged with thousands of extras and enormous sets. The trick photography (in color) of the parting of the Red Sea and the drowning of the pursuing Egyptians, Moses receiving the Ten Commandments from the blazing heavens, and the orgies of the Golden Calf were considered amazing spectacles.
– USA 1956. *Dir* Cecil B. De Mille *Scen* A. MacKenzie, Jesse Lasky, Jr., Jack Gariss, Frederick M. Frank *Photog* Loyal Griggs *Art Dir* Hal Pereira, Walter Tyler, Albert Nozaki *Mus* Elmer Bernstein *Ed* Anne Bauchens *Special Effects* John P. Fulton *Cast* Charlton Heston, Anne Baxter, Yvonne De Carlo, Yul Brynner, Judith Anderson, John Derek, Edward G. Robinson, Debra Paget, H. B. Warner, Sir Cedric Hardwicke, Vincent Price *Prod* Paramount. 219 mins. Technicolor. VistaVision.

Not a remake of the 1923 film but a biblical charade about Moses (Heston) and the Exodus. De Mille spared nothing: the spectacular parting of the Red Sea; a protracted orgy of the Golden Calf; the Burning Bush; the giving of the Ten Commandments; a bald Yul Brynner (as Rameses) and Charlton Heston in a false beard. This is the last film De Mille

personally directed and it was an enormous success.

TEN DAYS THAT SHOOK THE WORLD OKTYABR'

TENDRE ENNEMIE (LA) France 1936. *Dir* Max Ophüls *Scen* Max Ophüls, Curt Alexander, André-Paul Antoine based on the play *L'Ennemie* by André-Paul Antoine *Photog* Eugène Schuftan (Schüfftan), Lucien Colas *Art Dir* Jacques Gotko *Mus* Albert Wolff *Ed* Pierre de Hérain *Cast* Simone Berriau, Georges Vitray, Catherine Fonteney, Roger Legris, Jacqueline Daix, Marc Valbel, Maurice Devienne *Prod* Eden Productions. 69 mins.

During a party celebrating her daughter's (Daix) engagement to a man (Devienne) she does not love, Annette (Berriau) is taken through her past life: how her mother (Fonteney) would not let her marry the man she loved and how she made the lives of her husband (Vitray) and lover (Valbel) miserable in retaliation and eventually killed them. The ghosts of her husband and lover help Annette's daughter escape to true love.
"A sense of pessimism and an icy humor pervade this carefully mounted and excessively experimental film. In it can be found the lastest influences of expressionism: its fractionizing of people and things, its taste for caricatured characters and for the past, its flirtation with the hereafter . . ." (G. S. *Regards,* November 5, 1936).

TERESA USA 1951. *Dir* Fred Zinnemann *Scen* Stewart Stern, Alfred Hayes *Photog* William J. Miller *Art Dir* Leo Kerz *Mus* Louis Applebaum *Ed* Frank Sullivan *Cast* Pier Angeli, John Ericson, Patricia Collinge, Richard Bishop, Peggy Ann Garner, Ralph Meeker *Prod* Fred Zinnemann for MGM. 101 mins.

Philip (Ericson), in an interview with a psychiatrist, recalls how when he joined the army during World War II he was freed from the stifling presence of his domineering mother (Collinge). In Italy, he meets Sergeant Dobbs (Meeker), who befriends him, and falls in love with Teresa (Angeli). He is wounded and then marries Teresa but has to return home leaving Teresa to follow alone. At home he is again dominated by his mother and makes little effort to get a job. When Teresa arrives they have to live with his family in an East Side tenement apartment. She recognizes his weakness but cannot persuade him to break away from his mother and leaves him when she is pregnant. After the interview with the psychiatrist, Philip leaves home, gets work, and is reunited with Teresa in the hospital after she has her baby.

Despite some melodramatic plot conventions (notably in depicting Philip's change), this is one of Zinnemann's best films and a good example of the ephemeral "American neorealism" of the postwar years. Especially memorable is the scene in which the young Italian girl arrives in New York and discovers it is not at all a "paradise." Pier Angeli gives a sensitive performance and her exceptional beauty dominates the film.

*TERRA EM TRANSE LAND IN A TRANCE Brazil 1966. *Dir/Scen* Glauber Rocha *Photog* Luis Carlos Barreto *Mus* Sergio Ricardo and the music of Verdi, Carlos Gomes, Villa Lobos *Ed* Eduardo Escorel *Cast* Jardel Filho, Glauce Rocha, Paulo Autran, José Lewgoy, Paulo Gracindo, Danunza Leao *Prod* Mapa/Difilm. 112 mins.

A young poet and journalist is persuaded by his lover to become involved in the politics of his country.

Terra em transe is perhaps Rocha's most personal film and the most politically committed and polemical film of the Brazilian *cinema novo*. In Brazil it was attacked as fascist by the academic left and hailed by the extreme left as a revolutionary film, but, according to Glauber Rocha, it was not understood in the provinces and this led to his making the more conventional *Antonio das Mortes*. *Terra em transe* is full of extremely moving and provocative images – including footage from a Rocha documentary, *Maranhao*, about the elections in that province. Rocha has said, "it is for me my most important film . . . (and) represents a more profound expression of my life, a more intellectual work . . . Although the style is irregular, you will see, if you study the technique, that the camera is always positioned as in a documentary . . . There is no surrealism, it is not Buñuelian. I filmed newspapers and television, yet even in Brazil people said it was made up . . . Because I chose an asymmetrical presentation this was confused with staging and the film was con-

sidered baroque. The editing is straightforward and is more similar to a Mondrian painting than a baroque sculpture." *Terra em transe* won both the Luis Buñuel Award and the International Film Critic's Award at Cannes.

TERRA TREMA (LA): EPISODIO DEL MARE Italy 1948. *Dir/Scen* Luchino Visconti *Assist* Francesco Rosi, Franco Zeffirelli *Photog* G. R. Aldo *Mus* Luchino Visconti, Willy Ferrero *Ed* Mario Serandrei *Sound* Vittorio Trentino *Cast* inhabitants of Aci Trezza, Sicily *Prod* Universalia. 160 mins.

Derived from a novel by Verga, *I Malavoglia*, set in Sicily and intended as the first part of a trilogy (the sea; the sulphur mines; the countryside). Only this first part was completed. It is the story of the Valastros, a fisherman's family, poverty-stricken and exploited by canotieri (the men of the fish market). The grandfather falls ill and is taken to a home; the eldest son battles to maintain their precarious existence; the younger son runs away and works for a suspicious stranger; they mortgage their house to bolster their finances but, despite a good fishing trip, find themselves ruined; they have to leave their home and the family is unemployed; the eldest son sets out to work for others.

Visconti wrote, "In *La Terra trema* I was trying to express the whole dramatic theme as a direct outcome of an economic conflict." After several years in the theater, Visconti returned to the cinema with this film, shot under difficult conditions in carefully selected locations in Sicily and with an entirely nonprofessional cast recruited on the spot. The *canotiero* was in fact a mercenary fish merchant. Maria, the daughter, a servant at the inn, had a face which, as Visconti said, "took on a Leonardoesque beauty as soon as I put a black veil over her hair." The characters all speak Sicilian and use everyday words. But Visconti directed them as rigorously as if they were true actors.

Though *La Terra trema* follows the neorealist approach, its style is quite different from *Paisà* (*q.v.*) and *Bicycle Thieves* (*q.v.*). Visconti planned many of his shots very carefully in advance and draws from G. R. Aldo's photography an almost classical visual quality. André Bazin drew attention to the operatic nature of the characters. Antonioni, contrasting it to Olivier's *Hamlet* (*q.v.*), whose "technique was an end in itself," found "Visconti's technique always used poetically . . . every shot expresses something, even a simple spiritual state, and the photography always powerfully creates the atmosphere." He also noted "in the angry voices, the twilight murmurs as the fishermen leave, the masons' songs, the livid light of the storm, the inflections of N'Toni, and the resignation of his mother, is found not only the inevitable social polemic but also the most sincere tone of Visconti's poetic voice." Although somewhat too elaborate in its style, the original, complete version of *La Terra trema* has a powerful realism and sense of lyrical grandeur, almost a kind of operatic *cinéma vérité*.

La Terra trema was hailed as a revelation by critics at the Venice Festival but it appeared very low down in the list of awards and was a commercial disaster. The Sicilian dialect baffled even Italian audiences. After the production company, Universalia, went bankrupt (because of its spectaculars not on accout of this modestly budgeted film), it was cut severely and dubbed into Italian. In France, it was ruined by an overlaid commentary that reversed its meaning. It was not released commercially in Britain or North America and screenings have been restricted to film societies and specialized film theaters. After this film, Visconti again return to the theater for several years.

TERRE (LA) France 1921. *Dir* André Antoine *Scen* André Antoine based on *Earth* by Zola *Co-Dir* Georges Denola *Cast* Jean Hervé, Alex Ravet, Hieronymus, Armand Bour, Monnier, Berthe Bovy *Prod* Pathé. 6 reels.

This adaptation of Zola's epic novel of peasant life was shot largely in natural settings in the Beauce, the region where Zola had set his story. It is a film of great force and beauty as far as I can recall after seeing it once in 1922. Especially memorable is the image of père Fouan wandering across the vast expanses of a ploughed field.

TERRE SANS PAIN LAS HURDES

TESTAMENT D'ORPHEE (LE) see ORPHÉE

TESTAMENT VON DR. MABUSE (DAS) see DR. MABUSE, DER SPIELER

TETE CONTRE LES MURS (LA) THE KEEPERS France 1958. *Dir* Georges Franju *Scen* Jean-Pierre Mocky, Jean-Charles Pichon based on the novel by Hervé Bazin *Photog* Eugène Schuftan (Schüfftan) *Art Dir* Louis Le Barbenchon *Mus* Maurice Jarre *Ed* Suzanne Sandberg *Cast* Jean-Pierre Mocky, Pierre Brasseur, Paul Meurisse, Charles Aznavour, Anouk Aimée, Jean Galland, Thomy Bourdelle, Roger Legris *Prod* Sirius/Atica/Elpénor. 98 mins.

François (Mocky), a wild, amoral young man, is in love with Stéphanie (Aimée) and steals from his father (Galland), who discovers the theft and has him committed to a lunatic asylum. There he is declared insane by the reactionary psychiatrist, Dr. Varmont (Brasseur), unsuccessfully attempts to escape, and tries to be transferred to the care of the more progressive Dr. Emery (Meurisse). He becomes friendly with an epileptic (Aznavour), who kills himself. He escapes to Stéphanie, finds a job, and hides in her apartment. But, refusing to let her become involved, he leaves and is recaptured.

This free adaptation of a well-known novel is Franju's first feature, a work of undeniable power that is often strangely beautiful. His visualization of the asylum world, the use of natural sounds, and Maurice Jarre's score combine to create a sense of oppressive encirclement. The photography by veteran cameraman Schuftan is outstanding. It was enthusiastically hailed by Jean-Luc Godard as "a crazy film on madmen, thus a film of crazy beauty." In this film, Franju discovered a great actor — Charles Aznavour, until then known only as a singer. *La Tête contre les murs* had neither the critical nor the commercial success it deserved. It is, however, an important example of the early *nouvelle vague*.

TEUFELS GENERAL (DES) THE DEVIL'S GENERAL German Federal Republic 1955. *Dir* Helmut Käutner *Scen* Georg Hurdalek, Helmut Käutner based on the play by Carl Zuckmayer *Photog* Albert Benitz *Art Dir* Herbert Kirchoff, Albrecht Becker, Friedrich-Dieter Bartels *Ed* Klaus Dudenhofer *Cast* Curt Jurgens, Victor de Kowa, Karl John, Eva-Ingeborg Scholz, Marianne Koch *Prod* Real. 121 mins.

In Germany in 1941, General Harras (Jurgens), one of the Luftwaffe's air aces, is contemptuous of the Nazis and is arrested by the S.S. After 10 days of pressure he is released, falls in love with a young actress (Koch), and helps save from deportation a Jewish couple, who later commit suicide. He discovers his closest friend (John) also hates the regime and has been responsible for a number of test-flight crashes. Realizing there is no escape from the S.S., he deliberately crashes his plane.

This is Curt Jurgens' best performance and made his name international. Käutner contributes a striking re-creation of the atmosphere of Berlin during the war, ranging from nightclubs frequented by the Nazis and the Wehrmacht to the suicide of a despairing Jewish couple in a park.

THAT CAT AZ PRIJDE KOCOUR

THAT OTHERS MAY LIVE ULICA GRANICZNA

THEIR FIRST TRIP TO TOKYO TOKYO MONO-GATARI

THERESE RAQUIN. Adaptations of Zola's novel (1867) about Thérèse, who falls passionately in love with Laurent. Together they drown Thérèse's shopkeeper husband but fall prey to bitter remorse.
— *Teresa Raquin* Italy 1915. *Dir* Nino Martoglio *Scen* Nino Martoglio based on the Zola novel *Photog* L. Romagnoli *Cast* Maria Carmi, Dillo Lombardi, Giacinta Pezzana *Prod* Morgana.

This first adaptation is the only one to have been set during the Second Empire in France and seems to have exercised an influence on the development of neorealism. Antonio Chiaccone wrote: "It is largely set, like the novel, in interiors: the Raquin household, the dining room, the hallway leading to the shop, the married couple's bedroom. The only exterior is the river where the crime is committed. Here, with the Tiber used instead of the Seine, the director created some admirable images, using aquatic elements — barges, pilots, the bridge — in his shots. In this, his work predated a famous sequence in Murnau's *Sunrise* (*q.v.*)."

As with Martoglio's *Sperduti nel buio* (*q.v.*), this film was removed from the archives in Rome by the Nazis and seems to have disappeared.
— *Du Sollst Nicht Ehebrechen/Thérèse Raquin/Thou Shalt Not* Germany/

France 1928. *Dir* Jacques Feyder *Assist* Charles Barrois *Scen* Fanny Carlsen, Willy Haas based on the Zola novel *Photog* Hans Scheib, Frédéric Fuglsand *Art Dir* Andrei Andreiev, Erik Zander *Mus* Pasquale Perris *Cast* Gina Manès, Wolfgang Zilzer, Jeanne-Marie Laurent, Hans-Adalbert von Schlettow *Prod* Zelznick, Defu (Berlin). 7,828 ft.

All copies of this version have apparently disappeared. As far as one can tell from recollections of seeing it at the time of its release and from contemporary reviews, it seems to have been one of the best films at the end of the silent period. Léon Moussinac wrote: "Feyder has selected a style of adaptation that allowed him, in the first part, to create the atmosphere, to develop and *stress* the milieu in which the heroine was shaped, to evoke the daily life against whose *petit bourgeois* spirit Thérèse (Manès) continually rebels. The mediocrity, the despicable background, is made evident in details of the staging, which alternately involve the accessories, the sets, the actors (except for von Schlettow, who plays Laurent without force or conviction) and especially the extremely creative lighting. In the second part, Feyder came to the melodramatic action without trying to fake, and develops in detail the odius and cruel psychology of his characters. Over everything is an oppressive atmosphere in which there are no concessions to public taste except in the final shots." After the murder on the river the lovers become terrified under the perpetual stare of the now mute and paralyzed mother Raquin — sequences which give Jeanne-Marie Laurent the opportunity for a striking performance. The action throughout is dominated by the sensual and frustrated personality of Thérèse, as played by Gina Manès, and by the haunting presence of Andreiev's sets — a dirty window dominating a hallway, a kind of bell-jar under-which the bourgeois trio stagnate and decompose.
— *Thérèse Raquin/The Adulterers* France 1953. *Dir* Marcel Carné *Scen* Charles Spaak, Marcel Carné based on Zola's novel *Photog* Roger Hubert *Art Dir* Paul Bertrand *Costumes* Mayo *Mus* Maurice Thiriet *Ed* H. Rust *Cast* Simone Signoret, Raf Vallone, Roland Lesaffre, Sylvie, Jacques Duby, Anna-Maria Casilio *Prod* Paris Film/Lux. 108 mins.

A free adaptation of the novel brought

up to date and set in Lyons in 1950. Laurent (Vallone) becomes an Italian truck driver who falls in love with Thérèse (Signoret). The husband, Camille (Duby), is not drowned in the river but is pushed from a moving train during an argument. The mother (Sylvie) becomes paralyzed and the couple decide to part, but a sailor (Lesaffre) who had seen the argument tries to blackmail Thérèse. They decide to pay him but he is run down accidentally by a truck and the letter he had left at his hotel as a safeguard is sent to the police.

This is Carné's best postwar film, with the studio-built exteriors creating an oppressive and drab background. The acting is of a high standard, especially that of Simone Signoret and Jacques Duby.

THESE ARE THE DAMNED DAMNED (THE)

THEY LOVED LIFE KANAL

THEY WERE FIVE BELLE ÉQUIPE (LA)

THIEVES' HIGHWAY USA 1949. *Dir* Jules Dassin *Scen* Albert Isaac Bezzerides based on his novel *Thieves' Market Photog* Norbert Brodine *Art Dir* Lyle Wheeler, Chester Gore *Mus* Alfred Newman *Ed* Nick De Maggio *Cast* Richard Conte, Lee J. Cobb, Valentina Cortese, Barbara Lawrence, Jack Oakie *Prod* 20th Century-Fox. 94 mins.

A truck driver (Conte) sets out to avenge his father, who lost his legs through the actions of a crooked fruit dealer (Cobb), who controls the San Francisco market. The gangster lures him to a hotel room through a girl (Cortese) but the truck driver defeats the gangster and he and the girl fall in love. Dassin's last film in Hollywood has a carefully developed story line, well-composed photography, and an effective construction.

*THIN MAN (THE) USA 1934. *Dir* W. S. Van Dyke *Scen* Albert Hackett, Frances Goodrich based on the novel by Dashiell Hammett *Photog* James Wong Howe *Art Dir* Cedric Gibbons *Mus* William Axt *Ed* Robert J. Kern *Cast* William Powell, Myrna Loy, Maureen O'Sullivan, Nat Pendleton, Edward Ellis, Minna Gombell, Porter Hall *Prod* MGM. 93 mins.

An eccentric inventor (Ellis) disappears and shortly afterwards two people are murdered. He is suspected but his daughter (O'Sullivan) has faith in his innocence. She asks Nick (Powell), an urbane, alcoholic ex-detective now living on his wife's (Loy) income, to investigate. With his unorthodox methods, Nick discovers the inventor's dead body. He gives a party for all the suspects and reconstructs the crime so convincingly that the real murderer, the dead man's lawyer (Hall), falls into the trap and reveals himself.

This comedy-thriller is a classic of its kind and established a new trend of urbane, witty, detectives. Though its style seems effortless it is highly skillful, with a marvelous sense of informality and naturalism, crisp dialogue, and taut action. William Powell and Myrna Loy give subtly amusing performances as the husband and wife team and their domestic scenes are a delight — one of the first times an affectionate marriage had been honestly portrayed in the cinema.

Although the *Thin Man* is not, of course, the name of the detective, the tag stuck and was used in five sequels produced by MGM and, later, in a TV series based on the Hammett characters.

— **After the Thin Man* USA 1936. *Dir* W. S. Van Dyke *Scen* Frances Goodrich, Albert Hackett *Photog* Oliver T. Marsh *Cast* William Powell, Myrna Loy, James Stewart, Elissa Landis. 110 mins.

— **Another Thin Man* USA 1939. *Dir* W. S. Van Dyke *Scen* Frances Goodrich, Albert Hackett *Photog* Oliver T. Marsh, William Daniels *Cast* William Powell, Myrna Loy, Virginia Grey, Otto Kruger, C. Aubrey Smith. 105 mins.

— **Shadow of the Thin Man* USA 1941. *Dir* W. S. Van Dyke *Scen* Irving Brecher, Harry Kurnitz *Photog* William Daniels *Cast* William Powell, Myrna Loy, Barry Nelson, Donna Reed. 97 mins.

— **The Thin Man Goes Home* USA 1944. *Dir* Richard Thorpe *Scen* Robert Riskin, Dwight Taylor *Photog* Karl Freund *Cast* William Powell, Myrna Loy, Gloria De-Haven, Lucille Watson, Donald Meek. 100 mins.

— **Song of the Thin Man* USA 1947. *Dir* Edward Buzzell *Scen* Nat Perrin, Steve Fisher *Photog* Charles Rosher *Cast* William Powell, Myrna Loy, Keenan Wynn, Dean Stockwell. 86 mins.

THIRD MAN (THE) Britain 1949. *Dir* Carol Reed *Scen* Graham Greene based on his own then unpublished story *Photog*

Robert Krasker *Art Dir* Vincent Korda, John Hawkesworth, Joseph Bato *Mus* Anton Karas *Ed* Oswald Hafenrichter *Cast* Joseph Cotten, Orson Welles, Alida Valli, Trevor Howard, Bernard Lee, Ernst Deutsch, Erich Ponto, Wilfrid Hyde-White *Prod* London Films. 93 mins.

Martins (Cotten), a writer of westerns, arrives in Vienna to work for his friend, Harry Lime (Welles), but is told by Calloway (Howard), a British police officer, that Lime died in an accident. Martins does not accept this and begins to track down those who knew him, including Anna (Valli), an actress who was his lover, and the effete Kurtz (Deutsch). He learns that Lime, who turns out to have been the "third man" who witnessed the accident-murder, is a notorious racketeer who traffics in penicillin. Martins struggles with his conscience and eventually is involved in the pursuit of Lime through the sewers, where he kills him.

This thriller is set in postwar Vienna and is in some ways a portrait of the "cold war," then in its early stages. Carol Reed's perfectly controlled technique, somewhat reminiscent of Lang and Hitchcock, creates an overwhelming melancholy atmosphere that is heightened by the haunting, relentless zither music and the sharply drawn and well-acted characters. Most notable of these, and an important element in the film's international success, is Orson Welles as Harry Lime. According to Carol Reed (quoted by Peter Noble), Welles nearly refused the role, which he thought too small: "Orson suddenly turned up one morning, just as we had set up our cameras in the famous sewers. He told me that he felt very ill, had just got over a bout of influenza, and could not possibly play the role . . . I entreated him, in any case, just to stay and play the scene we had prepared, where he is chased along the sewers . . . Reluctantly he agreed. 'Those sewers will give me pneumonia!' he grumbled, as he descended the iron steps. We shot the scene. Then Orson asked us to shoot it again, although I was satisfied with the first 'take.' He talked with the cameraman, made some suggestions, and did the chase again. Then again. The upshot was that Orson did that scene ten times, became enthusiastic about the story — and stayed in Vienna to finish the picture." However, as much as Welles

dominates the film, one should not assume that Graham Green's dialogue reflects his own attitudes.

THIRST TÖRST

13TH LETTER (THE) see CORBEAU (LE)

39 STEPS (THE) Britain 1935. *Dir* Alfred Hitchcock *Scen* Charles Bennett, Alma Reville, Ian Hay based on the novel by John Buchan *Photog* Bernard Knowles *Art Dir* Otto Werndorff *Mus* Louis Levy, *Ed* Derek Twist *Cast* Robert Donat, Madeleine Carroll, Godfrey Tearle, John Laurie, Lucie Mannheim, Wylie Watson, Peggy Ashcroft *Prod* Gaumont-British. 87 mins.

A secret service agent (Mannheim) is assassinated in the London apartment of Richard Hannay (Donat), but Hannay escapes both the police and the assassins in order to find the members of the spy ring called "The 39 Steps" in Scotland and thus clear his name. Evading his pursuers on the train north he arrives at a rich house to seek the advice of the professor (Tearle) but is again driven off by the police. In a girl's school he seeks the help of a teacher (Carroll), but she betrays him to the police. He escapes again and gets involved in a political meeting, is arrested by the gang, posing as detectives, and manacled to the teacher. They escape and he drags her across Scotland seeking a solution. Eventually she believes his story and they set out to London together and unmask the gang in a London music hall.

Freely adapted from Buchan's novel, this is Hitchcock's most virtuoso and most famous work during his English period. Its chase is handled with great technical finesse and with marvelous touches of macabre humor and banter, moving the hero from a train to a leap from a bridge, across the nicely observed Scottish landscape to a party in a large house (whose owner turns out to be the chief of the spy ring), to a political meeting, to a Salvation Army rally, through yet another flight across the landscape handcuffed to a girl, and finally to a musical hall in London. Though its plot is unbelievable, Hitchcock's continual mastery of suspense keeps it alive. He was to return many times in later films to similar situations, but he never truly matched the finesse of this one.

— *Britain 1959. *Dir* Ralph Thomas *Scen*

373

Frank Harvey based on the Buchan novel *Photog* Ernest Steward *Cast* Kenneth More, Taina Elg, Barry Jones, James Hayter *Prod* Betty Box/Ralph Thomas. 93 mins. Eastman Color.

A plagiaristic remake heavily dependent on vintage Hitchcock that can't make up its mind whether it is playing "tongue-in-cheek" or not with the melodrama.

*THIS SPORTING LIFE Britain 1963. *Dir* Lindsay Anderson *Scen* David Storey based on his own novel *Photog* Denys Coops *Art Dir* Alan Withy *Mus* Roberto Gerhard *Ed* Peter Taylor *Cast* Richard Harris, Rachel Roberts, Alan Badel, William Hartnell, Colin Blakely, Vanda Godsell *Prod* Independent Artists. 134 mins.

Frank Machin (Harris), a miner, lives with Mrs. Hammond (Roberts), a widow with two children. Aggressive and ambitious, Frank seeks a trial with the city rugby team and is taken on by Weaver (Badel), a local industrialist who runs the team as a hobby. Mrs. Hammond becomes his lover but with emotional reservations and Frank is obsessed with his need to force an emotional admission from her. She resents his physical dominance and forces him away in anger. He returns one day to find she has been taken to hospital with a brain hemorrhage and finally he is able to speak to her with tenderness. But she dies, and Frank, with a sense of futility and loss, returns to the physical violence of the rugby field.

This Sporting Life (Anderson's first feature) represented a significant breakthrough in the British cinema from the rhetoric and "objective" social analysis of such films as *Saturday Night and Sunday Morning* (*q.v.*). Though set against an industrial background, its theme (Frank's inability to reconcile his need to be loved with his essentially violent, physical temperament) and its portrayal of inner tension and personal conflict is the film's main focus and is brilliantly conveyed by Anderson's complex visual style — the shock cuts set against flexible and often hypnotically intriguing stagings. Though Anderson was a graduate of *free cinema*, this film owes more to French poetic realism and to the style of Central European directors like Wajda.

THIS STRANGE PASSION EL

THISTLES OF THE BARAGON (THE) CIULINI BARAGANULUI

THOUSAND EYES OF DR. MABUSE (THE) see DR. MABUSE, DER SPIELER

THOU SHALT HONOR THY WIFE DU SKAL AERE DIN HUSTRU

THOU SHALT NOT see THÉRÈSE RAQUIN

THOU SHALT NOT KILL NON UCCIDERE

THREE AGES USA 1923. *Dir* Buster Keaton, Eddie Cline *Scen* Clyde Bruckman, Joseph Mitchell, Jean Havez *Photog* Elgin Lessley, William McGann *Art Dir* Fred Gabourie *Cast* Buster Keaton, Margaret Leahy, Wallace Beery, Joe Roberts, Horace Morgan *Prod* Buster Keaton Productions for Metro. 5,251 ft.

The hero (Keaton) copes with a lover's problems in three periods. In the Stone Age he and the villain (Beery) fight with pebbles and he captures the girl (Leahy) by dragging her off by the hair. In the Roman period he is involved in a chariot race. In a modern period (1920) he has to combat a wealthy suitor.

The action in these three ages is intercut and the film is something of a parody on *Intolerance* (*q.v.*). This is Keaton's second feature and, although it has many good gags, it does not match either *Our Hospitality* (*q.v.*) made the same year or most of his later films.

THREE CHIMNEYS ENTOTSU NO MIERU BASHO

THREE LIGHTS MÜDE TOD (DER)

THREE MUST-GET-THERES (THE) USA 1922. *Dir/Scen* Max Linder *Photog* Max Dupont *Cast* Max Linder, A. J. Cooke, Clarence Wertz, Charles Metzetti, Jack Richardson, Harry Mann, Sam de Grasse, Bull Montana, Jean de Limur, Jobyna Ralston, Caroline Rankin *Prod* Max Linder Inc. for United Artists. 5 reels.

This delightful parody of *The Three Musketeers* (especially the Fairbanks' film version) has Lind'Dart-in-Again (Linder) in period costume meeting his cohorts (Wertz, Metzetti), falling in love with Constance (Ralston), and fighting against the cardinal (Montana). The film is full of marvelous anachronisms: Max Linder in Louis XIII costume but wearing a straw hat; motorcycles mixed-up with horses; telephones with sword fights.

Very French in comic style (although made in Hollywood), it has a great sense of comic pace and is always entertaining. It was not, however, a commercial success in North America or Britain. Sequences from it are included in the compilation *En Compagnie de Max Linder/Laugh with Max Linder,* 1963.

THREE OF THE FILLING STATION (THE) DRIE VON DER TANKSTELLE (DIE)

THREEPENNY OPERA DREIGROSCHENOPER (DIE)

THREE SONGS OF LENIN TRI PESNI O LENINYE

THREE STRANGE LOVES TÖRST

3:10 TO YUMA USA 1957. *Dir* Delmer Daves *Scen* Halsted Welles based on a story by Elmore Leonard *Photog* Charles Lawton, Jr. *Art Dir* Frank Hotaling *Mus* George Duning *Ed* Al Clark *Cast* Glenn Ford, Van Heflin, Felicia Farr, Leora Dana, Richard Jaeckel, Robert Emhardt, Henry Jones *Prod* Columbia. 92 mins.

A notorious bandit, Ben Wade (Ford), is captured in a small town. Fearing reprisals from his gang, Dan Evans (Heflin) and Alex Potter (Jones) agree to deliver Wade to the train bound for Yuma while other townspeople try to divert the gang elsewhere. They take him to a small hotel and hold him prisoner, though he is confident he will be rescued. The gang discover his whereabouts and murder Alex. Dan manages to get Wade to the station and aboard the train through a barrage of gunfire.

A western whose theme rests on mounting tension and careful characterization of the two main protagonists. Delmer Daves saw in it "the possibilities of a documentary approach drawing on the prints of (Matthew) Brady."

THREE WAX MEN WACHSFIGURENKABINETT

THROUGH A GLASS DARKLY SÅSOM I EN SPEGEL

THUNDERBALL see GOLDFINGER

THUNDER OVER MEXICO see QUE VIVA MEXICO!

THY SOUL SHALL BEAR WITNESS KÖRKARLEN

TIGHT LITTLE ISLAND WHISKY GALORE

TIME IN THE SUN see QUE VIVA MEXICO!

TIME TO LIVE AND A TIME TO DIE (A) FEU FOLLET (LE)

TIME WITHOUT PITY Britain 1956. *Dir* Joseph Losey *Scen* Ben Barzman based on the play *Someone Waiting* by Emlyn Williams *Photog* Freddie Francis *Prod Layout* Richard MacDonald *Art Dir* Bernard Sarron *Mus* Tristram Cary *Ed* Alan Osbiston *Cast* Michael Redgrave, Ann Todd, Leo McKern, Peter Cushing, Alec McCowen, Renee Huston, Lois Maxwell *Prod* Harlequin. 88 mins.

Alec Graham (McCowen) is condemned to death for a murder he did not commit. His father, David Graham (Redgrave), a chronic alcoholic, returns to London 24 hours before the execution to seek new evidence that might permit a stay of execution. He visits Mrs. Harker (Huston) and her daughter (Maxwell), who have been bought off. He visits Robert Stanford (McKern), a wealthy industrialist in whose apartment the murder took place, and his suspicions are aroused. A stay of execution is refused and David gets drunk. In this state he discovers that Stanford is really the murderer and forces Stanford to shoot him, thus incriminating the real murderer and saving Alec.

[Based on an Emlyn Williams play attacking the evils of capital punishment in which the action takes place after the execution of the innocent young man, this is the first feature Losey made in Britain under his own name.] Although Philip Oakes wrote in the London *Evening Standard,* "As a social document, it runs out of ink. But as a thriller it is first-rate," the traditional suspense qualities of *Time Without Pity* are of less interest than its depiction of people coping with the pressures of society. The film focuses on the father himself, an alcoholic writer who shirks his responsibilities to society, and on the people with whom he comes into contact: his son, lied to, neglected by his father and swept away by events he does not properly understand; the eccentric Mrs. Harker, who lives surrounded by clocks; and the guilty Stanford, a rich, powerful, self-made automobile mechanic. More than just a protest film about capital punishment, this fevered film is a protest about

375

the malaises of contemporary society and owes as much to its writer, Ben Barzman as it does to Losey.

*TIRE-AU-FLANC

— *Tire-au-flanc* France 1928. *Dir* Jean Renoir *Scen* Jean Renoir, Claude Heymann based on the play by André Mouézy-Eon and Sylvane *Photog* Jean Bachelet *Art Dir* Erik Aaes (Aèss) *Cast* Georges Pomiès, Michel Simon, Fridette Faton, Félix Oudart, Jeanne Helbling *Prod* Néo-Films/Braunberger. 2,200 meters.

Jean Dubois d'Ombelles (Pomiès), a member of the fading aristocracy, is drafted into service with the French army at the same time as his valet, Joseph (Simon). Though both wear the same uniforms, Jean attempts to continue their civilian status but Joseph has other ideas. He declares his independence and slips off without leave to a romantic rendezvous. Jean, at a loss in the classless situation, becomes the company scapegoat and even ends up in prison. His fiancée, Solange, is much taken by the martial presence of a lieutenant and becomes engaged to him. But Jean becomes engaged to her cousin, Lily, while Joseph marries the chambermaid, Georgette.

This satirical comedy is based on a 1904 vaudeville farce that has become a classic, constantly performed by amateur groups and frequently revived on the Paris stage. One of the most unjustly neglected of Renoir's films, it is in some ways comparable to *Un chapeau de paille d'Italie* (q.v.) with roots in the improvised slapstick of Sennett and links to the poetic caricatures of Vigo's *Zéro de conduite* (q.v.) and Renoir's own *Boudu sauvé des eaux* (q.v.). A sense of poetic fantasy and an almost balletic rhythm unites the marvelous gags, the satire on barracks life, and the derisive portrait of the upper classes as seen through the eyes of Joseph. Its depiction of the parallel love affairs of master and servant, though in the original play, is a typical part of the Renoir world and appears again in later films, most notably *La Règle du jeu* (q.v.). Michel Simon gives a memorable comic parody of Chaplin.

Tire-au-flanc France 1949. *Dir/Scen* Fernand Rivers based on the play by Mouézy-Eon and Sylvane *Photog* Jean Bachelet *Cast* M. Baquet, F. Blanche, V Donde. 87 mins.

— *Tire au flanc 62/The Sad Sack/The Army Game* France 1961. *Dir* Claude de Givray *Co-Dir* François Truffaut *Scen* Claude de Givray, François Truffaut, André Mouézy-Eon based on the play *Photog* Raoul Coutard *Mus* Ricet-Barrier, J. M. Defaye *Ed* Claudine Bouche *Cast* Ricet-Barrier, Christian De Tilière, Jacques Balutin, Serge Davri, Annie Lefebvre, Germaine Risse, Odile Geoffrey, Annette Augay, Bernadette Lafont *Prod* Les Films du Carrosse/SEDIF. 87 mins. Franscope.

This first feature by de Givray (though he had assisted on Chabrol's *Le Beau Serge* (q.v.) and Truffaut's *Les Mistons*) was made following his own military service. Truffaut agreed to produce the film and lend his name to the credit, though he also apparently helped with the shooting, for some scenes have a characteristic Truffaut touch, recalling especially, *Tirez sur le pianiste* (q.v.). Full of fast scene changes, abrupt changes of pace, cinematic puns, music hall jokes, and many improvised scenes, this version is often genuinely funny. Best sequences: cleaning the barracks to a Schubert march; burlesque of army training methods; Joseph (Ricet-Barrier) getting a date with a girl he meets in the street; the three soldiers going to leave on a scooter; the hair-cutting. Mouézy-Eon himself (at 85) appears briefly, near the end of the film, watching the performance of his original play.

*TIREZ SUR LE PIANISTE SHOOT THE PIANO PLAYER France 1960. *Dir* François Truffaut *Scen* Marcel Moussy, François Truffaut based on the novel *Down There* by David Goodis *Photog* Raoul Coutard *Art Dir* Jacques Mély *Mus* Jean Constantin *Ed* Cécile Decugis *Cast* Charles Aznavour, Maria Dubois, Nicole Berger, Michèle Mercier, Albert Rémy, Jacques Aslanian, Daniel Boulanger, Claude Mansard *Prod* Films de la Pléiade. 80 mins.

Charlie (Aznavour), a timid piano player in a small Parisian bar, is forced to hide his brothers (Rémy, Aslanian) from two gangsters (Boulanger, Mansard) they have double crossed. Lena (Dubois), a waitress in the bar, becomes Charlie's lover and discovers that he is actually the concert pianist, Edouard Saroyan, whose wife, Theresa (Berger), had killed herself. Later, Charlie fights with the bar owner and kills him in self-defense. While he and Lena are involved in this fracas, Charlie's youngest brother is kidnapped by the two gangsters. At a farm in the mountains where his brothers are hiding, Lena is killed during a gunfight and Charlie is again left alone.

Truffaut's second feature, a complete contrast to the style and social theme of *Les 400 coups* (*q.v.*), was an almost total critical failure, attacked for what was called its perplexing shifts of mood from farce to near-tragedy. Truffaut himself says that "my only rule in making *Shoot the Piano Player* was my own pleasure . . . I would call the film a respectful pastiche of the Hollywood B-film." However, Truffaut's ironic style conceals a kind of existentialist tragicomedy about a timid man who is driven from society by malignancy but who also mistrusts himself and because of this mistrust breed "accidents" around him. As Pierre Kast wrote: "The externally imposed framework of a thriller allows the individuality of the characters to be rendered more sensitively . . . The plastic beauty of the ending in the snow and the emotion brought about by the death of the heroine are not diminished but magnified by the grotesque counterpoint of the gangsters." Charlie (marvelously played by Aznavour) is a typical 20th century hero — destroying when he tries to be kind, killing the two women he loves most, despite his good intentions. Even on a superficial level, the film has a marvelous sense of bizarre comedy, delightful songs, and is pictorially magnificent.

TO BE OR NOT TO BE USA 1942. *Dir* Ernst Lubitsch *Scen* Edwin Justus Mayer from a story by Lubitsch, Melchior Lengyel *Photog* Rudolph Maté *Art Dir* Vincent Korda, Julia Heron *Mus* Werner Heymann *Cast* Jack Benny, Carole Lombard, Robert Stack, Felix Bressart, Sig Rumann, Stanley Ridges, Lionel Atwill *Prod* Korda for United Artists. 99 mins.

In Nazi-occupied Warsaw a troupe of actors headed by Josef Tura (Benny) and his wife Maria (Lombard) become involved with an Allied agent (Stack) and a Polish traitor (Ridges) selling information on the Polish underground to the Gestapo. Josef disguises himself first as the Polish traitor then as a Gestapo officer (Rumann), hoodwinks the enemy, and escapes with the whole troupe to England.

This witty, satirical comedy (almost a black comedy) was attacked at the time of its release for its "callous, tasteless effort to find fun in the bombing of Warsaw." It remains, however, immensely entertaining with a steadily rising crescendo of comedy toward the climax. It even ends on one of the film's running gags. This was the last appearance of Carole Lombard who died in a airplane accident before the film's premiere.

TO CATCH A THIEF USA 1955. *Dir* Alfred Hitchcock *Scen* John Michael Hayes based on the novel by David Dodge *Photog* Robert Burks *Art Dir* Hal Pereira, Joseph MacMillan Johnson *Mus* Lyn Murray *Ed* George Tomasini *Cast* Cary Grant, Grace Kelly, Jesse Royce Landis, Charles Vanel, John Williams, Brigitte Auber, Jean Martinelli, Roland Lesaffre *Prod* Paramount. 107 mins. Technicolor. VistaVision.

On the Riviera, a once celebrated jewel thief, John Robie (Grant) is suspected of a series of burglaries and decides to track down the real thief. He becomes friendly with the rich Mrs. Stevens (Landis) and her daughter, Frances (Kelly), who is attracted to him until her mother's jewels are stolen. Robie again escapes and the police announce the thief is Foussard (Martinelli). Robie, however, sets a trap and reveals the thief is a girl (Auber). This comedy thriller, not one of Hitchcock's best, gave Grace Kelly the opportunity to become Princess of Monaco.

TOKAI KOKYOGAKU METROPOLITAN SYMPHONY/SYMPHONY OF THE METROPOLIS/CITY SYMPHONY Japan 1929. *Dir* Kenji Mizoguchi *Scen* Hamamoto Akiichi, Tadashi Kobayashi based on the works of Teppei Kataoka, Fusao Hayschi, Rokuro Asahara, Saburo Okada *Photog* Tatsuyuki Yokota *Cast* Shizue Natsukawa, Takako Irie, Isamu Kosugi, Eiji Takagi, Reiji Ichiki *Prod* Nikkatsu. 7 reels.

A working girl (Natsukawa) is seduced by a rich man and, with the help of a young man inspired by ideals of social justice, revenges herself.

This "social tendency" film contrasts the proletarian and bourgeois worlds as seen by a working girl and her upper-class counterpart (Irie). Mizoguchi said in 1954: "The producers did not know that the script was based on works of extreme left-wing writers. If they had, they would never have approved the project. We had great difficulties with the police when the film was finished. We shot it in a very lawless section of the city and were obliged to disguise ourselves as workers and hide the equipment."

It would seem that this film (which disappeared years ago and was never shown outside Asia) was of major importance, anticipating not only French poetic realism and Italian neorealism but also the works of postwar independent Japanese film makers.

TOKYO CHORUS TOKYO NO GASSHO

*TOKYO MONOGATARI TOKYO STORY/THEIR FIRST TRIP TO TOKYO Japan 1953. *Dir* Yasujiro Ozu *Scen* Kogo Noda, Yasujiro Ozu *Photog* Yushun Atsuta *Art Dir* Tatsuo Hamada *Mus* Takanori Saito *Ed* Yoshiyasu Hamamura *Cast* Chishu Ryu, Chiyeko Higashiyama, So Yamamura, Haruka Sugimura, Setsuko Hara, Kyoko Kagawa, Shiro Osaka *Prod* Shochiku. 135 mins.

An elderly man (Ryu) and his wife (Higashiyama) decide to visit their two married children in Tokyo. But the son (Yamamura) and daughter (Sugimura) are busy with their own lives and send them off to a resort. Only the widow (Hara) of a son killed in the war is kind to them. When they return, the mother falls sick and the children are sent for. But she can no longer recognize them and, after the funeral, they rush away again. Only the daughter-in-law stays on until the father advises her to get married again. Then he is left alone in an empty house.

This moving account of the sad but necessary differences between generations is one of the few Ozu films to have been shown abroad and the one on which, for most occidentals, his critical reputation rests. It is also one of Ozu's own favorites. Donald Richie's description of Ozu's films applies well to this: "You have seen the goodness and beauty of everyday things and everyday people; you have had experiences indescribable because of cinema and no words can describe them; you have seen a few small, memorable, unforgettable actions, beautiful because sincere." Although superficially slow, *Tokyo Story* has an inner strength and drive that draws one inexorably into the

Japanese world and its universal human problems.

TOKYO NO GASSHO CHORUS OF TOKYO/ TOKYO CHORUS Japan 1931. *Dir* Yasujiro Ozu *Scen* Kogo Noda based on the novel by Komatsa Kitamura *Photog* Hideo Mobara *Cast* Tokihiko Okada, Rieko Yaguma, Hideo Suguwara, Mitsuko Ichimura, Takeshida Sakamoto *Prod* Shochiku. 9 reels. Silent.

An awkward, timid man (Okada) loses his job after taking the side of an older colleague when he is dismissed. He faces bleak poverty, becomes a sandwich-man but all ends happily.

This social comedy about the life of a middle-class man is one of the first to reveal the talents of Ozu. Best sequences: the argument (in slow motion) with the employer; the wage packets examined in the toilet; the behavior of an insufferable small boy (Suguwara) because his unemployed father has only brought him a scooter; the meal in the vegetarian restaurant, Calories, run by an old professor.

TOKYO STORY TOKYO MONOGATARI

TOL'ABLE DAVID USA 1921. *Dir* Henry King *Scen* Edmund Goulding, Henry King based on the novel by Joseph Hergesheimer *Photog* Henry Cronjager *Ed* Duncan Mansfield *Cast* Richard Barthelmess, Gladys Hulette, Ernest Torrence, Warner Richmond, Walter P. Lewis, Edmund Gurney, Marion Abbott, Forrest Robinson, Lassie the dog *Prod* Inspiration for First National. 7,200 ft.

A quiet farming community is disrupted by the three villainous Hatburn brothers led by Luke Hatburn (Torrence), an escaped convict. David Kinemon (Barthelmess), a farmer's son, sees his father killed and his brother crippled. Torn between fear and duty, David finally battles Luke and defeats him.

This modern version of David and Goliath was a tremendous popular and critical success in North America and Britain; in the USSR it exercised considerable influence on the developing Soviet cinema. Pudovkin, especially, was impressed by the film and cited it repeatedly for its cinematic construction and use of plastic material. It was never released in France.

Lewis Jacobs wrote: "Its subject matter — the tale of a poor mountain boy — was fresh and unstereotyped; its setting was real; its characterizations were honest and rounded; the narrative was simple and unmelodramatic; the whole picture was frank and pungent rather than sentimental . . . King's technique throughout stemmed from Griffith. Whether or not King was conscious of this influence is hard to say." Paul Rotha wrote that, "King learnt from Griffith all that was good, combining the spoil with his own filmic knowledge."

Though one cannot compare the film, as Rotha does, to *La Passion de Jeanne d'Arc* (*q.v.*), *The Last Laugh* (*q.v.*), or *Turksib* (*q.v.*), its atmosphere of rural America is solidly believable and its characterizations effective despite the occasional "Mary Pickfordisms." In some ways, *Tol'able David* is comparable to Sjöström's *The Wind* (*q.v.*) or Renoir's *The Southerner* (*q.v.*), while its poetic sense of landscape may have influenced John Ford.

— *Tol'able David* USA 1930. *Dir* J. George Blystone *Scen* Benjamin Glazer based on the novel *Photog* T. Tetzlaff *Cast* Richard Cromwell, Noah Beery, Joan Peers, Henry B. Walthall *Prod* Columbia. 81 mins.

A rather unenterprising, melodramatic remake.

TO LIVE IKIRU

TOM JONES Britain 1963. *Dir* Tony Richardson *Scen* John Osborne based on the novel by Henry Fielding *Photog* Walter Lassally *Prod Design* Ralph Brinton *Art Dir* Ted Marshall *Mus* John Addison *Ed* Tony Gibbs *Cast* Albert Finney, Susannah York, Hugh Griffith, Joan Greenwood, Edith Evans, Diane Cilento, George Devine, Rosalind Knight, David Tomlinson, Joyce Redman, David Warner *Prod* Woodfall. 128 mins. Eastman Color.

In 18th century Somerset, England, a Tom Jones (Finney), supposedly the illegitimate son of a servant, Jenny Jones (Redman), is raised by Squire Allworthy (Devine) along with his own son Blifil (Warner). He is in love with Sophie Western (York), the daughter of Squire Western (Griffith), but her aunt (Evans) wants Sophie to marry Blifil. Tom has an adventure with Molly (Cilento), a local trollop, and, after his name is blackened by Blifil and his tutors, is banished by Squire Allworthy and sets off to London.

He has a series of amorous adventures with Mrs. Waters (formerly Jenny Jones) and Lady Bellaston (Greenwood) and is followed to London by Sophie in the company of Mrs. Fitzpatrick (Knight), who is fleeing her husband. Sophie is courted by Lord Fellamar (Tomlinson) while Tom is involved in a fight with Mr. Fitzpatrick, who is wounded. Blifil bribes two rogues to swear that Tom was committing robbery and Tom is sentenced to death. He is saved by the revelation of Blifil's treachery while a further discovery shows that Tom is the illegitimate son not of Jenny Jones but of the Squire's deceased sister.

This full-blooded, joyful, adaptation of Fielding's famous novel is full of fashionable cinematic tricks but its bawdy good humor brought it a justifiable commercial success. Albert Finney makes a perfect Tom Jones and Walter Lassally's images in muted colors are excellent.

TONI France 1934. *Dir* Jean Renoir *Scen* Carl Einstein, Jean Renoir from an idea by J. Levert *Photog* Claude Renoir *Art Dir* Bourelly *Mus* Eugène Bozzi *Ed* Marguerite Renoir, Suzanne de Troeye *Cast* Charles Blavette, Edouard Delmont, Max Dalban, Jenny Hélia, Andrex, Célia Montalvan, Kovachevitch, Bozzi *Prod* Films d'Aujourd'hui (Marcel Pagnol). 90 mins.

A group of Italian immigrants arrive to work in a quarry. Toni (Blavette) lives with Maria (Montalvan), who loves him, but he falls in love with Josépha (Hélia). Their foreman, Albert (Dalban), a brutish man, marries Josépha and beats her. She and Toni try to run away but Albert catches them. Albert is killed and Toni is accused of the murder. He is found guilty and executed, then Marie reveals she was the murderess.

It is essential to quote from Renoir's introduction to a 1956 revival of his film: "The cinema is based above everything on photography and the art of photography is the least subjective of all the arts. Good photography (as with Cartier-Bresson), sees the world as it is, selects it, determines what merits being seen and seizes it as if by surprise, without change . . . At the time of *Toni*, I was opposed to make-up. My ambition was to integrate the non-natural elements of my film, the elements not dependent on chance encounter, into a style as close as possible to everyday life. The same thing for the sets. There is no studio used in *Toni*. The landscapes, the houses are those we found. The human beings, whether interpreted by professional actors or the inhabitants of Martigues, tried to resemble people in the street. Moreover, the professional actors themselves, with some exceptions, were of the same social classes, nations, and races as their roles. The script was from a true story told by Jacques Mortier, the Martigues police commissioner. No stone was left unturned to make our work as close as possible to a documentary. Our ambition was that the public would be able to imagine that an invisible camera had filmed the phases of a conflict without the characters unconsciously swept along by it being aware of its presence."

Toni anticipated the methods of Italian neorealism though the Italian film makers (except for Visconti) were completely unaware of the film until 1950. But they could understand its lessons through *La Grande Illusion* (*q.v.*). The actors were largely from Marseilles *caf'conc'* and the film was produced with backing from Marcel Pagnol, the influence of whose own style on Jean Renoir is discernible. Léon Moussinac wrote at the time of *Toni*'s release: "Who could fail to be affected by the direct, simple, spare, and so touching expression of the realistic psychology of these men and women, the primitive brutality of some, the dignity of many, the violence of those on whom 'the town' (another word for the bourgeois social structure) has unleashed cynicism, the assertion of social violence? Who could avoid the feeling of naturalness that the film maker has created with such ability, tenderness, and technical understanding? Jean Renoir's images overflow with that feeling of reality that the screen demands. In *Toni* are sound foundations on which it is possible to build the necessary experiences of the sound cinema. Doubtless the true story will not be the only starting point for such development but the realism that this makes necessary will in fact be one of the surest."

— *Toni* Britain 1928. *Dir* Arthur Maude *Cast* Jack Buchanan, Dorothy Boyd, Henry Vibart, Moore Marriott. 6 reels.
A British comedy-thriller about a young idler (Buchanan) who changes places with a famous detective, solves a crime and wins a princess.

*TOP HAT USA 1935. *Dir* Mark Sandrich *Scen* Dwight Taylor, Allan Scott derived from the musical *The Gay Divorcee* by Dwight Taylor and a play by Alexander Farago, Aladar Laszlo *Photog* David Abel, Vernon Walker *Art Dir* Van Nest Polglase, Carroll Clark *Mus* Irving Berlin *Ed* William Hamilton *Choreog* Fred Astaire, directed by Hermes Pan *Cast* Fred Astaire, Ginger Rogers, Edward Everett Horton, Helen Broderick *Prod* RKO Radio. 101 mins.
Jerry Travers (Astaire) falls in love with Dale Tremont (Rogers) after he meets her while tap dancing in his friend's (Horton) hotel room. Later, in Venice, she thinks he is his married friend until all is straightened out.
This scintillating, zestful, and professional musical is one of the classics of the Thirties and the best of the famous series that Astaire and Rogers made together. It includes many of Irving Berlin's most memorable numbers (including "Cheek to Cheek," "Isn't it a Lovely Day?") and Mark Sandrich's direction is fluently deft, especially in the "Piccolino" number.

TORERO! Mexico 1955. *Dir* Carlos Velo *Scen* Hugo Mozo, Carlos Velo *Photog* Ramon Muñoz *Mus* Rodolfo Affter *Cast* Luis Procuña, Manuel Rodriguez (Manolete), Carlos Arruza *Prod* Manuel Barbachano Ponce. 80 mins.
The re-created true story of Luis Procuña, a matador of humble origins who becomes rich and famous. After the tragic death of Manolete he becomes afraid and is seriously wounded in the ring. He rebuilds his career but in the ring is jeered by the crowd. Nevertheless, he goes on to defeat a bull and regains praise and glory.
This fictionalized documentary uses both newsreels (including those of Procuña regaining his fame in the last sequence) and re-created sequences in which Procuña acts out his own role. Totally unsentimental in approach, *Torero!* is a brilliant achievement that owes much to the talents of the Spanish film maker Carlos Velo and to its powerful script, which conveys universal truths that go beyond the world of bull-fighting. Everyone, at least once in his career, faces an *hora de verdad* in which those who had once praised him demand his death. This is true for all great artists and perhaps

more so in the cinema than in the other arts. Certainly, critical attacks on a great film maker do not immediately deprive him of his physical life but they can take away from him his means of creation and even his livelihood if he is not able, as Procuña does in *Torero!*, to face the taunts and go on to greater achievements.

TORMENT HETS

TORMENTS EL

TÖRST THIRST/THREE STRANGE LOVES Sweden 1949. *Dir* Ingmar Bergman *Scen* Herbert Grevenius based on four short stories by Birgit Tengroth *Photog* Gunnar Fischer *Art Dir* Nils Svenwall *Mus* Erik Nordgren *Ed* Oscar Rosander *Cast* Eva Henning, Birgit Tengroth, Birger Malmsten, Hasse Ekman, Mimi Nelson, Bengt Eklund *Prod* Svensk Filmindustri. 88 mins.
Bertil (Malmsten) and his wife, Rut (Henning), return in a train from Basle across a shattered Germany and contemplate their marriage, which has become a vindictive relationship. Rut had had an affair with a ship's captain (Eklund). In a parallel story, Viola (Tengroth), Bertil's former wife, tries to overcome loneliness, visits a psychiatrist (Ekman) who tries to seduce her, meets a Lesbian (Nelson) who wants to exploit her, and commits suicide. As the train nears Stockholm, Bertil dreams he has murdered his wife but both realize they cannot live in loneliness and decide that, "Hell together is better than hell alone." Described by Jean Béranger as "a kind of *Viaggio in Italia* (*q.v.*) revised by Sartre," this somber film is one of the more notable of Bergman's early films with typical Bergman themes of loneliness, personal strife, and "the difficulty of being." The main story, largely set in a compartment of the train, is intercut with flashbacks to show Rut's affair and Bertil's brief marriage to Viola and to show Viola's current life in parallel action.

TOUCHEZ PAS AU GRISBI HONOUR AMONG THIEVES/ GRISBI/ PARIS UNDERGROUND France/Italy 1953. *Dir* Jacques Backer *Scen* Maurice Griffe, Jacques Becker, Albert Simonin based on the novel by Albert Simonin *Photog* Pierre Montazel *Art Dir* Jean d'Eaubonne *Mus* Jean Wiener *Ed* Marguerite Renoir *Cast* Jean Gabin, René Dary, Jeanne Moreau, Gaby Basset, Paul Frankeur, Lino Ventura, Daniel Cauchy, Dora Doll *Prod* Del Duca/Silver/Anteres. 94 mins.
Two Montmartre gangsters, Max le Menteur (Gabin) and Riton (Dary) have successfully stolen a *grisbi* (treasure) of 50 million francs worth of gold bars but Riton reveals this to his mistress (Moreau), who tells Angelo (Frankeur), a rival gangster with whom she is in love. Angelo attempts to kidnap Max and Riton, but he fails and they move into hiding. Riton, however, leaves to revenge himself on his mistress and is captured by Angelo's gang. Max agrees to exchange the gold for Riton. The exchange takes place but Angelo still tries to kill them and in the ensuing gun battle Angelo and his gang are killed and Riton fatally wounded. Max is left alone.
This film is based, as was Dassin's *Du rififi chez les hommes* (*q.v.*), on a conventional Simonin *série noire* novel whose chief merit was its characters' argot. But Becker uses his technical mastery to weave the strands of the action into a study of loyalty and friendship and a sympathetic portrait of a man of action becoming too old for his way of life. Jean Wiener contributes an excellent, haunting theme tune that was very popular in France.

TOUCH OF EVIL USA 1957. *Dir* Orson Welles *Scen* Orson Welles based on the novel *Badge of Evil* by Whit Masterson *Photog* Russell Metty *Art Dir* Alexander Golitzen, Robert Clatworthy *Mus* Henry Mancini *Ed* Virgil Vogel, Aaron Stell *Cast* Orson Welles, Charlton Heston, Janet Leigh, Akim Tamiroff, Joseph Calleia, brief appearances by Marlene Dietrich, Joseph Cotten, Zsa Zsa Gabor *Prod* Universal. 95 mins.
In a seedy Mexican-American border town, the town boss is killed by a bomb. Mike Vargas (Heston), special narcotics investigator for the Mexican government, investigates with the reluctant cooperation of Captain Hank Quinlan (Welles), the American detective in charge of the case. Vargas and his wife, Susan (Leigh), stay at a motel owned by a gangster, Grandi (Tamiroff), who is looking for ways to blacken the reputation of Vargas. Quinlan, who allies him-

self with Grandi, is discovered by Vargas planting two sticks of dynamite on the dead man's son-in-law, Sanchez. Vargas also discovers that Quinlan's remarkable record of captured criminals has been achieved by fake proofs. Susan is kidnapped from the motel and left in a room with evidence of narcotics. Quinlan then strangles Grandi and leaves him in the same room. Susan is arrested on a murder charge. Vargas persuades Quinlan's assistant (Calleia) that his boss is corrupt and he persuades Quinlan, while drunk, to confess everything. Quinlan discovers this and shoots the detective who himself shoots Quinlan before he dies. Meanwhile news come through that Sanchez has confessed to the murder, justifying Quinlan's hunch.

This "Goya-like vision of an infected universe" (Peter Bogdanovich) is based on a banal thriller whose plot appealed to Charlton Heston. Despite the producer's interference (67 pages of the script were cut), Welles turned it into his most technically impressive film. The pervasive atmosphere of the Mexican town with its slums and dives and the singularly believable characters (including the cameo roles such as the very brief appearance by Marlene Dietrich) create their own world, while Welles's lens twists visible space into a strange and baroque universe. Welles himself, as the ugly, fleshy, satanic Quinlan, gives one of his most memorable performances.

Maurice Bessy wrote: "Welles confirms that what is personal in the film is his hatred for police abuse of their authority. He could not have dealt with this problem if Quinlan had been only an ordinary cop." Welles affirmed, "I firmly believe that in the modern world we have to choose between the morality of the law and the morality of basic justice. That is to say, between lynching someone and letting him go free. I prefer to let a murderer go free than to let the police arrest him by mistake."

TRAGIC HUNT CACCIA TRAGICA

TRAMP (THE) USA 1915. *Dir/Scen* Charles Chaplin *Photog* Rollie Totheroh *Cast* Charles Chaplin, Edna Purviance, Leo White, Bud Jamison, Lloyd Bacon, Paddy McGuire, Billy Armstrong *Prod* Essanay. 1,643 ft.

A tramp (Chaplin) rescues a farmer's daughter (Purviance) from robbers and is given a job on her father's farm. He falls in love with the daughter, who nurses him after he is shot while chasing the robbers away again. But when her handsome boyfriend (Bacon) arrives he sadly leaves the farm alone.

One of the first Chaplin's to include straight dramatic scenes among the gags. The ending, with Charlie, back to the camera, walking sadly away down the road, is famous.

TRAMP, TRAMP, TRAMP USA 1926. *Dir* Harry Edwards *Scen* Frank Capra, Tim Whelan, Hal Conklin, Gerald Duffy, Murray Roth, J. Frank Holliday *Cast* Harry Langdon, Joan Crawford, Alec B. Francis *Prod* Harry Langdon. 5,830 ft.

Harry attempts to win a cross-country marathon walking contest in order to win a $25,000 prize and a girl (Crawford). He succeeds in spite of everything, including imprisonment in a chain gang and a cyclone.

This was doleful comedian Harry Langdon's first feature. It was written by a battery of gag writers led by Frank Capra, who was later to direct Langdon in *The Strong Man* (*q.v.*) and *Long Pants* (*q.v.*).

TREASURE OF ARNE (THE) HERR ARNES PENGAR

TREASURE OF THE SIERRA MADRE (THE) USA 1947. *Dir* John Huston *Scen* John Huston based on the novel by B. Traven *Photog* Ted McCord *Art Dir* John Hughes *Mus* Max Steiner *Ed* Owen Marks *Cast* Humphrey Bogart, Tim Holt, Walter Huston, Bruce Bennett, Barton MacLane, Alfonso Bedaya *Prod* Warner Brothers. 126 mins. 98 mins in some re-release versions.

In Mexico in 1920, Dobbs (Bogart) and Curtin (Holt), two down-and-out hoboes, meet an old-timer, Howard (Walter Huston), who tells them he knows where gold is to be found if they can raise the money for equipment. They set off for the bandit-ridden Sierra Madre and strike it rich. But they are haunted by suspicions of each other and are raided by bandits led by the evil Gold Hat (Bedaya). They try to make it back but in an ironic twist of fate the wind blows the gold dust away to mingle with the sand from which it came.

A morality fable on greed and human nature in a typical adventure setting. Huston sets the harsh realities of Mexico against two North Americans whose main desire is for wealth and for the luxury, comfort, and women it will buy. In contrast is the philosophic old-timer (played by John Huston's father) who learns true wisdom from the peaceful life of the Indians and who laughs ironically as the gold dust blows away among the cactus in the final shot. The fable is not at all schematic and is brought brilliantly to life by the powerful characterizations of the men continually at each other's throats and by the harsh re-creation of a hostile nature and a primitive urban environment. To reduce it to a "tragedy on greed and the poetry of failure" is to simplify it, since its apparent simplicity covers many levels of meaning. This is Bogart's most famous role, but Walter Huston, though less impressive, is a match for him all the same and [won an Oscar for his performance. John Huston won Oscars for direction and scriptwriting and himself appears in a bit part as the man in the white suit.]

TREICHVILLE MOI, UN NOIR

TRIAL (THE) PROCÈS (LE)

TRIAL OF JOAN OF ARC (THE) PROCÈS DE JEANNE D'ARC

TRI PESNI O LENINYE THREE SONGS OF LENIN USSR 1934 (production began 1931). *Dir/Scen/Ed* Dziga Vertov *Photog* Bentsion Monastirsky, Surensky, M. Magidson *Mus* Yuri Shaporin *Prod* Mezhrabpomfilm. 68 mins.
Structured around three Uzbekistan "folk songs" about Lenin, an evocation of the effect of Lenin's life and teaching, especially on the women of Central Asia. The first song recounts the lifting of oppression, the second, Lenin's death, the third the future life built on Lenin's teachings.
Three Songs of Lenin is unquestionably Vertov's most perfect film and his last important one. Rigorously based on his theories about picture and sound editing, it is a skillful blend of archive films and recordings of Lenin with specially photographed film to create a unity of extraordinary emotional impact.

TRIP TO THE MOON VOYAGE DANS LA LUNE (LE)

TRIUMPH DES WILLENS TRIUMPH OF THE WILL Germany 1936 (production began 1934). *Dir/Ed* Leni Riefenstahl *Photog* Sepp Allgeier and 36 assistants *Mus* Herbert Windt *Architecture* Albert Speer *Prod* NSDAP (Nazi party). 120 mins.
The official film record of the sixth Nazi Party Congress held at Nuremberg, Germany, September 4–10, 1934. It was commissioned to Leni Riefenstahl (who also made short films about the 1933 and 1935 congresses) by Adolf Hitler personally. The 1934 Congress came soon after President Hindenburg's death in August and Hitler's rise to ultimate power as Chancellor and Führer. Riefenstahl was granted almost unlimited funds and given every cooperation by the leaders of the Party, who worked closely with her in planning the details of the 1934 congress to facilitate making the film. Thirty cameras, a crew of 120, and the most advanced photographic devices were put at her disposal. The editing took 18 months. In her book about the film, Leni Riefenstahl noted, "The preparations for the Party congress were made in concert with the preparations for the camerawork." [This comment on the willingness of the Party to fit their plans in with hers has often been taken to mean that the congress was actually staged for the purpose of making the film. There is no factual basis for this supposition, which is a little like suggesting that moon shots are staged only for television. Certainly Albert Speer designed some monumental constructions for the congress but similar edifices were built elsewhere in Germany and are typical of Nazi architecture. The mass adulation, torchlight processions, and marching were evident in other congresses.]
In a prologue, the Führer descends from the clouds like a Messiah arriving for the second coming. From the clouds he makes his way through streets amid scenes of quasi-religious adoration. This is followed by processions, by day and by torchlight, men staged against the architecture like statues, and endless speeches by the Führer. Some of the most revealing sequences of the film are those behind the scenes: the SS and Hitler Youth with their naked chests, their apparent gaiety only thinly covering their animal ferocity.
This powerful piece of propaganda by the officially appointed "Film Expert of the National Socialist Party," was banned in

Britain, the USA, and Canada. It furnished much footage during the war for American propaganda against the Nazis, most notably for the *Why We Fight* (*q.v.*) series.

TROU (LE) THE HOLE/NIGHT WATCH France/Italy 1959. *Dir* Jacques Becker *Scen* Jean Aurel, José Giovanni, Jacques Becker based on the novel by José Giovanni *Photog* Ghislain Cloquet *Art Dir* René Mondellini *Mus* non *Ed* Marguerite Renoir *Cast* Michel Constanin, Jean Keraudy, Phillippe Leroy, Marc Michel, Raymond Meunier (nonprofessionals), Catherine Spaak *Prod* Play Art/Filmsonor/Titanus. 123 mins.

In a prison cell, four men planning an escape are joined by a fifth, a car salesman accused of the murder of his wife. After some misgivings the four decide to include the fifth in their plan and begin digging an escape tunnel. But at the last minute they are betrayed.

Jacques Becker's last film (he died in February 1960 after completing the sound editing) is a study in idealism, loyalty, and betrayal based on a true story written by one of the participants in the attempted escape. Almost documentary-like in its details of the escape preparations and completely assured in its style, it is also Becker's most deeply felt film. Five men in a common desire for freedom struggle against the inhuman prison life and every obstacle put in their path, but in the end they cannot escape any more than a man can escape his own death. No music is used, only brilliantly orchestrated natural sounds. This superb portrait of man's persistence and courage, entirely unromanticized, did not have the commercial success it deserved.

TROUBLE IN PARADISE USA 1932. *Dir* Ernst Lubitsch *Scen* Samson Raphaelson, Grover Jones based on the play *The Honest Finder* by Laszlo Aladar *Photog* Victor Milner *Art Dir* Hans Dreier *Mus* W. Franke Harling *Cast* Miriam Hopkins, Kay Francis, Herbert Marshall, Charlie Ruggles, Edward Everett Horton, C. Aubrey Smith, Robert Greig *Prod* Paramount. 83 mins.

In Venice in the early Thirties, two jewel thieves, Gaston (Marshall) and Lily (Hopkins), meet and fall in love. They join the household staff of a rich widow, Marianne (Francis), in order to rob her. Lily, jealous of Gaston's infatuation for Marianne, decides to rob her alone and leave him. But Gaston, realizing he really loves Lily, goes with her and they pool their separate spoils.

Broadly based on a Hungarian farce, this is the masterpiece of Lubitsch's sophisticated comedies. Its witty badinage and excellent character performances give it the exhilaration of a championship tennis match. It has never been bettered in its genre. [Jean Mitry finds it "employing an often cruel sarcasm aimed at moral institutions and principles . . . With it he became the most mordant, most subtle ironist of the cinema." Grover Jennings is credited as "adapter" but contributed nothing to the final screenplay. This film was Lubitsch's own favorite.]

TROUBLE WITH HARRY (THE) USA 1955. *Dir* Alfred Hitchcock *Scen* John Michael Hayes based on a novel by Jack Trevor Story *Photog* Robert Burks *Art Dir* Hal Pereira, John Goodman *Mus* Bernard Herrmann *Ed* Alma Macrorie *Cast* Edmund Gwenn, Shirely MacLaine, John Forsythe, Mildred Dunnock, Mildred Natwick *Prod* Alfred Hitchcock Productions for Paramount. 99 mins. Technicolor. VistaVision.

One autumn morning in a Vermont wood, Captain Wiles (Gwenn) stumbles across the body of a man wearing bright red socks and, assuming he must have accidentally shot him, decides to bury him. He is interrupted successively by Miss Gravely (Natwick), a middle-aged spinster who had hit the dead Harry when he tried to assault her; Jennifer Rogers (MacLaine), Harry's estranged wife who had hit him with a milk bottle when he arrived at her house; and Sam Marlow (Forsythe), an artist. Harry is buried, exhumed, and buried again until Jennifer and Sam (who have meanwhile fallen in love) realize they want proof of his death in order to marry. The body is disinterred again, a doctor certifies that he died of natural causes, and Harry is returned to the place where he was first found.

This irreverent, sardonic, black comedy, largely set amid the rich fall colors of Vermont, is perhaps Hitchcock's best postwar film.

TRUE HEART SUSIE USA 1919 *Dir* D. W. Griffith *Scen* D. W. Griffith based on a story by Marian Fremont *Photog* G. W. Bitzer *Cast* Lillian Gish, Robert Harron,

Clarine Seymour, George Fawcett, Kate Bruce, Wilbur Higby, Loyola O'Connor, Carol Dempster *Prod* Artcraft. 5,580 ft. In a small village, Susie (Gish), a country girl, secretly sells her own cow in order to send her sweetheart, William (Harron), to college. But when he returns to the village as a minister he is trapped into marriage by a worthless city girl (Seymour), who ruins him by her unfaithfulness. Only after his wife dies through catching cold by going to a party does William learn how much he owes Susie. This sentimental rural melodrama (thematically close to many of Mary Pickford's films) about a country girl's loyalty and devotion bears no comparison with *Broken Blossoms* (*q.v.*), made the same year. However, the writing has a sympathetic sureness of touch, Griffith's style has a perfect natural simplicity, unobtrusively skillful and technically uncomplicated, and the whole film is illuminated by the fragile grace, gentle humor, and appealing timidity of Lillian Gish.

TRUTH (THE) VÉRITÉ (LA)

*TUMBLEWEEDS USA 1925. *Dir* King Baggot *Scen* C. Gardner Sullivan based on a story by Hal G. Evarts *Photog* Joseph August *Cast* William S. Hart, Barbara Bedford, Lucien Littlefield, J. Gordon Russell, Monte Collins *Prod* William S. Hart for United Artists. 7,250 ft. Re-released in 1939 with music and sound effects and an eight-minute introduction by William S. Hart, 88 mins.
In the area of the Cherokee Strip in 1889, an itinerant cowboy, Don Carver (Hart), meets a family of settlers and falls in love with the daughter (Bedford). The strip is being opened to settlers and "sooners" are trying to take choice land by "jumping the gun" before the fixed time. Carver tries to prevent this but is himself arrested as a "sooner" for crossing the line. Imprisoned when the strip is opened, he escapes, captures the villains, finds the girl's family the land they want and reveals the girl's half-brother as a scoundrel.
William S. Hart's last film (at the age of 55) is not only his own masterpiece and a summation of everything he felt about the West but also one of the greatest silent westerns. The opening sequence in which Hart laments the passing of the wilderness is one of the silent western's most lyrical sequences. The evocation of

the actualities of the Old West and of the frontier code is clearly by a man who understood and felt deeply about them and not by the hack director, King Baggot, assigned by the producers. The climactic land rush is one of the cinema's most bravura action sequences, impeccably constructed and edited and with some virtuoso trick riding by Hart. The pure morality of Hart's character may seem naive, but the authentic flavor of a "wild, lost America" and the evocation of the pioneering spirit gives *Tumbleweeds* a sense of poignant poetry. The re-release version has an introduction by Hart himself, extremely moving in its revelation of Hart's personal feelings for the West.

TU NE TUERAS POINT NON UCCIDERE

TUNTEMATON SOTILAS THE UNKNOWN SOLDIER Finland 1955. *Dir* Edvin Laine *Scen* Juha Nevalainen based on the novel by Vaino Linna *Photog* Pentti Unho, Osmo Harkimo, Olavi Tuomi, Antero Ruuhonen *Art Dir* Aarre Koivisto *Mus* Sibelius, Ahti Sonninen *Ed* Armas Vallasvuo *Cast* Kosti Klemela, Jussi Jurkka, Matti Ranin. 132 mins.
An episodic account of the Russo-Finnish War from 1941 to 1944 as seen from the point of view of the ordinary soldiers and with a powerful sense of the terrible conditions of the fighting.

TURKSIB USSR 1929. *Dir* Victor Turin *Scen* Victor Turin, Victor Shklovsky, Alexander Macheret, Y. Aron *Photog* Yevgeni Slavinsky, Boris Frantzisson *Prod* Vostok-kino. 1,666 meters. (5,400 ft. approx.) English version, *Titles* John Grierson, 5,300 ft.
A documentary describing the building of the Turkistan-Siberian Railway.
Nikolai Lebedev wrote: "Certain scenes are unforgettable: the camel indifferently gazing at the railway line appearing for the first time in the desert; the Kazak horsemen and camel drivers trying at full gallop to race the first train; the enthusiasm of the workers as they finish laying the last rails at fantastic speed." *Turksib* was a great success, not only in the USSR but also abroad, and was influential on the British documentary school. However, it doesn't seem that this Ukrainian director's other films are of comparable importance.

TURNING WIND (THE) BARRAVENTO

385

12 ANGRY MEN USA 1957. *Dir* Sidney Lumet *Scen* Reginald Rose based on his own TV play *Photog* Boris Kaufman *Art Dir* Robert Markell *Mus* Kenyon Hopkins *Ed* Carl Lerner *Cast* Henry Fonda, Martin Balsam, Lee J. Cobb, Ed Begley, E. G. Marshall, Jack Warden, John Fielder, Jack Klugman *Prod* Orion-Nova (Fonda, Reginald Rose). 95 mins.

A jury in a murder case retires to consider its verdict about which there seems little doubt. But when a vote is taken, Juror No. 8 (Fonda) votes not guilty. The others are reluctant to re-examine the issues but his persistence gradually reveals questions that throw doubt on the prisoner's guilt and one by one the others also admit to doubts. Among the last to change are a man with racial prejudice (Begley) and a sadist (Cobb). Finally the accused is acquitted.

This compelling drama of the interplay of personalities is based on a television play and retains the original's unity of place, time, and theme. Its success, however, is due more to the scriptwriter, Reginald Rose, and to the leading actor, Henry Fonda, than to its director, Sidney Lumet, whose first film this was.

TWENTIETH CENTURY USA 1934. *Dir* Howard Hawks, *Scen* Ben Hecht, Charles MacArthur based on their own play adapted from the play *Napoleon of Broadway* by Charles Bruce Milholland *Photog* Joseph August *Ed* Gene Havlick *Cast* John Barrymore, Carole Lombard, Roscoe Karns, Walter Connolly, Ralph Forbes, Dale Fuller, Etienne Girardot *Prod* Columbia. 91 mins.

A famous Broadway producer, Oscar Jaffe (Barrymore), having discovered and married an unknown actress, Lilly Garland (Lombard), who had left him to go to Hollywood, finds her again on the Twentieth Century Limited train en route to New York. He spends the whole trip trying to cajole her into appearing in his next show and finally gets her to sign a contract after feigning a fatal illness. Back on Broadway he is as tyrannical as ever.

One of the earliest of the "screwball" comedies but with dramatic, and even tragic, overtones, this film has tremendous pace and vitality deriving not only from the rapid-fire dialogue but also from the continual sense of motion of the train. John Barrymore's performance as the producer reflects something of his own image as does that of Carole Lombard, who was then a rising star and whom this film made famous.

— **Streamline Express* USA 1935. *Dir* Leonard Fields *Scen* Leonard Fields, David Silverstein based on an original story by Wellyn Totman *Photog* Ernest Miller *Cast* Victor Jory, Evelyn Venables, Esther Ralston *Prod* Mascot. 72 mins.

Not exactly a remake but a curiously similar copy of the plot and comic approach, with a playwright manager (Jory) pursuing an erring actress (Venables) on the express from New York to Los Angeles.

TWENTY-FOUR EYES NIJUSKI NO HITOMI

TWO ACRES OF LAND DO BIGHA ZAMIN

TWO CENTS WORTH OF HOPE DUE SOLDI DI SPERANZA

TWO ORPHANS (THE) see ORPHANS OF THE STORM

TWOPENNY WORTH OF HOPE DUE SOLDI DI SPERANZI

*2001: A SPACE ODYSSEY Britain 1968 (production began 1965). *Dir* Stanley Kubrick *Scen* Stanley Kubrick, Arthur C. Clarke based on the short story *The Sentinel* by Arthur C. Clarke *Photog* Geoffrey Unsworth *Special Effects Design and Dir* Stanley Kubrick *Special Effects* Wally Veevers, Douglas Trumbull, Con Pederson, Tom Howard *Prod Design* Tony Masters, Harry Lange, Ernie Archer *Art Dir* John Hoesli *Mus* Richard Strauss (*Thus Spake Zarathustra*), Johann Strauss ("The Blue Danube"), Aram Khachaturian (*Gayne Ballet Suite*), György Ligeti ("Atmospheres," "Lux Aeterna," "Requiem") *Ed* Ray Lovejoy *Costumes* Hardy Amies *Cast* Keir Dullea, Gary Lockwood, William Sylvester, Daniel Richter, Douglas Rain (voice only) *Prod* MGM. 141 mins. (Reduced by Kubrick from 160 mins. after New York premiere. Metrocolor. Super Panavision presented in Cinerama.

1. A group of apemen learn how to use tools after finding a monolithic slab. 2. Several million years later, Dr. Heywood Floyd (Sylvester) arrives on the moon to investigate a similar slab that has been found buried deep below the surface. 3. Eighteen months later, a giant spaceship is en route to Jupiter manned

by astronauts Bowman (Dullea) and Poole (Lockwood) with three colleagues kept in a state of hibernation and a new computer, HAL 9000 (voice by Rain), in overall control. HAL deliberately causes a failure and when Poole goes outside the ship to repair it maroons him in space. Bowman attempts a rescue but HAL terminates the life functions of the hibernating crewman and refuses to let Bowman back. Bowman forces his way in and, disconnecting HAL's memory banks, reduces him to impotence. Arriving at Jupiter he is sucked into a new dimension, encounters the monolith again and is reborn as a new kind of Man.

Almost 2½ years (December 29, 1965 to April 1968) in production at a cost of over $10 million (twice the original budget), *2001: A Space Odyssey* is an epic (in the true sense), breathtakingly sensuous and an extraordinary visual experience. Arthur C. Clarke (the title of whose most famous novel *Childhood's End* might be an appropriate title for the film) said: "It's about concern with man's hierarchy in the universe which is probably pretty low . . . We set out with the deliberate intention of creating a myth. The Odyssean parallel was in our minds from the beginning, long before the film's title was chosen." Stanley Kubrick pointed out that it is "essentially a non-verbal experience. Less than half the film has dialogue. (There are no spoken words in the film's first 30 minutes. *Ed*) It attempts to communicate more to the subconscious and to the feelings than it does to the intellect." This science-fiction spectacular is also as personal and original a metaphysical vision of humanity as the cinema has produced.

The film received an extremely mixed critical reception. This ranged from the National Catholic Office for Motion Pictures award citation ("the scope of its imaginative vision of man . . . immerses the eye, the ear, and the intuitive responses of the viewer in a uniquely stimulating human experience") and the *Saturday Review* description of it as "an extraordinary masterpiece . . . a major challenge to some of the assumptions that dominated serious writing for at least a hundred years" to Renata Adlers' "like three hours of Tolkien without the ring," Andrew Sarris's "merely a pretext for a pictorial spread in *Life* magazine" and John Simon's dubbing it "a shaggy God story."

More than any previous science-fiction film, it gripped public imagination and was a world-wide commercial success.

TYSTNADEN THE SILENCE Sweden 1963. *Dir/Scen* Ingmar Bergman *Photog* Sven Nykvist *Art Dir* P. A. Lundgren *Mus* J. S. Bach's *Goldberg Variations* (25th Movement) *Ed* Ulla Ryghe *Cast* Ingrid Thulin, Gunnel Lindblom, Jörgen Lindström, Hakan Jahnberg, Birger Malmsten *Prod* Svensk Filmindustri. 96 mins.

Two women, Ester (Thulin), who is seriously ill, and Anna (Lindblom), who is perhaps her sister, sensual and indolent, arrive by train in a foreign city with Anna's son, Johann (Lindström), and stay in a large hotel. The language around them is totally incomprehensible. The two have a Lesbian relationship but are at odds with each other. Ester seeks relief in chain-smoking, alcohol, and masturbation, while Anna, after seeing a couple copulate in a cabaret, sleeps with a barman (Malmsten). Later, after a quarrel, Ester is forced to watch a repetition. She trys to talk to the old waiter in the hotel (Jahnberg) and to communicate with Johann but is left in a fatal coma as Anna and Johann leave the city.

[The last part of the trilogy with *Through a Glass Darkly* (*q.v.*) and *Winter Light* (*q.v.*) and one of Bergman's most perfectly realized films, oppressive in its atmosphere and disquieting in its human implications.] The best scenes show the small boy wandering around the strange world in which he finds himself, a world that amuses and excites him more than it disturbs him. Anna is entirely carnal and libidinous but the scenes of intercourse are not at all erotically stimulating (though parts of them were censored outside Sweden and Germany), being presented objectively and dispassionately. *The Silence* has little dialogue, and conflict between the two women being presented almost entirely in visual terms and through a sound track made up of incomprehensible words and sound effects such as tanks rumbling past the hotel. The Bach music is heard only via the radio that Ester switches on to soothe herself.

UGETSU MONOGATARI TALES OF THE PALE AND SILVERY MOON AFTER THE RAIN Japan 1953. *Dir/Ed* Kenji Mizoguchi *Scen* Yoshikata Yoda, Matsutaro Kawaguchi, Kenji Mizoguchi based on two stories *Asaji Ga Yade* and *Jasei No In* from the classic collection of stories by Akinari Ueda *Photog* Kazuo Miyagawa *Art Dir* Kisaku Ito *Mus* Fumio Hayasaka *Cast* Machiko Kyo, Masayuki Mori, Sakae Ozawa, Kinuyo Tanaka, Mitsuko Mito *Prod* Daiei. 96 mins.

In 16th century Japan, Genjuro (Mori), a village potter and his farmer brother-in-law, Tobei (Ozawa), are both ambitious: Genjuro longs for wealth, Tobei craves military glory. With their wives they set out across the lake for the nearest city to sell Genjuro's pots. But on the way they are frightened by tales of pirates; Genjuro puts his wife, Miyagi (Tanaka), ashore while Tobei's wife, Ohama (Mito), insists on staying. In the city, Genjuro is seduced by a sensuous phantom, Lady Wakasa (Kyo), and, forgetting his wife and child, goes to live with her in her mansion. Tobei acquires samurai armor and, by claiming another's conquest as his own, is given a military command. The neglected Ohama is raped by a gang of soldiers and in despair becomes a prostitute. Miyagi is killed by two starving soldiers. Genjuro is warned by a priest that he is living with ghosts and, protected by cabalistic signs, breaks the spell. He returns disconsolately home and is greeted by Miyagi only to discover next morning that she, too, is an apparition. Tobei meets his wife by chance in a geisha house and their bitter reunion smashes his ambitions; they return together to the village. Genjuro continues his work protected by the ghostly presence of his wife.

[These two parallel tales about ambition are based on two 16th century classic stories, one derived from an ancient Chinese legend often called "the lewdness of the female viper" (filmed at least twenty times in China and Japan) and the other a longer story *The House in the Broken Reeds*. Mizoguchi has said: "I had wanted to make this film also for a long time but I am not happy with the result. I think the original *Ugetsu* has a more lasting quality. For example, the man played by Ozawa should not change his mind at the end but should continue regardless with his ambitious social climb. But Daiei didn't want the ending and forced me to change it."

Ugetsu Monogatari, like so many of Mizoguchi's films, is a study in feminine psychology, social mores, and the intense correlation between women and love. The phantom princess and the wife are similar in their love for the potter, who destroys both of them because he doesn't give them the love they need. The wife of the ambitious farmer is degraded because he, too, fails her. Its parallel stories with a unifying moral theme give it something of the force of a classical tragedy.

Mizoguchi's depiction of his characters' 16th century world has an almost palpable air of realism, with impeccable period reconstructions and an all-pervasive sense of continuous war that permeates the film. Though Mizoguchi saw in it a parallel to postwar Japan and its problems, its success clearly lies beyond its own time. Both allegorical and realistic, it is an intensely moving film experience. Stylistically it is one of Mizoguchi's most accomplished films, full of beautiful images that have the mystical beauty of classical Japanese paintings and are even occasionally reminiscent of the paintings of the 16th-century Flemish artist, Breughel. The scene on the lake, the potter and the phantom princess breakfasting on the lawn, and the final shot as the camera slowly rises to take in the whole village have a poetic simplicity. Throughout, fantasy is given the force of reality and the power of tragedy. Its stylistic perfection and the rich overtones of its theme make *Ugetsu Monogatari* one of the most beautiful films of all time.]

ULICA GRANICZNA BORDER STREET/THAT OTHERS MAY LIVE Poland 1948. *Dir* Aleksander Ford *Scen* Jean Force, Ludwig Stolarski *Photog* Jaroslav Tuzar *Art Dir* A. Radzinowicz, A. Sachicki *Cast* J. Leszczynski, Maria Broniewska, Jurek Zlotnicki, W. Godik, W. Walter *Prod* Film Polski. 116 mins.

A tragedy about the Warsaw Ghetto during the Nazi occupation involving an old tailor (Godik), a doctor (Leszczynski) who tries to save his daughter (Broniewska), and others. Under pressure of German persecution the Jews seize arms, but the Nazis murder the population and level the entire district.

A humanistic film even though Ford's belief in his theme leads him into an affected style. This and *The Last Stage* (*q.v.*) are the best Polish films of the postwar period.

UMARETE WA MITA KEREDO I WAS BORN, BUT . . . Japan 1932. *Dir* Yasujiro Ozu *Scen* Akira Fushimi, James Maki *Photog* Hideo Mobara *Cast* Tatsuo Saito, Hideo Sugawara, Tokkan Kozo, Mitsuko Yoshikawa *Prod* Shochiku. 8,020 ft. Silent, shot at 20 f.p.s.

A young boy (Sugawara) and his younger brother (Kozo) live with their father (Saito) and mother (Yoshikawa) in the suburbs; during a brief period they are shown discovering adult society and its attendant problems. They love their father and cannot understand why he should have to bow obsequiously to his employer and suffer various humiliations when they themselves can rule the employer's son.

This sympathetic and acutely perceptive observation of the changing relations between members of a family captures the foibles of adults and middle-class behavior with a delightful sense of humor. Though rigidly formal in style, it has a lightness of touch and a sense of the unconscious comedy of everyday life. Especially perfect are: the introductory sequence with the father and his two sons moving into the suburbs; the scene in which the two brothers watch home movies in which the father acts the fool for his employer's camera and later run home in shame.

This portrait of the life of a white-collar worker has its roots in the Japanese social "tendency films" and has undertones of social analysis and criticism. In some ways, it is possible to speak of Ozu's "poetic realism" during this period as it is of René Clair's at the same time.

UMBERTO D Italy 1952. *Dir* Vittorio De Sica *Scen* Cesare Zavattini, Vittorio De Sica *Photog* G. R. Aldo *Art Dir* Virgilio Marchi *Mus* Alessandro Cicognini *Ed* Eraldo Da Roma *Cast* Carlo Battisti, Maria Pia Casilio, Lina Gennari. 89 mins.

Umberto (Battisti), a retired civil servant whose only real friend is his dog, has to survive on a very meager pension, living in a furnished room and eating cheaply. He sacrifices part of his pension for his dog, cannot pay his rent, is turned out by his landlady (Gennari), and contemplates suicide.

Memorable sequences: the demonstration by pensioners; Umberto's solitary life in his shabby room; his attempts at begging stopped by his own pride; his discussions with the melancholy maid (Casilio) who becomes pregnant and who occasionally helps him in his squabbles with the landlady; his stay in the hospital; the loss of his dog; his decision to kill himself; his efforts to put his dog in boarding kennels, and his change of heart; his attempt to throw himself with his dog under a train and the dog's wriggling away making him change his mind.

Vittorio De Sica has described his "favorite film" as: "the tragedy of those people who find themselves cut off from a world that they nevertheless helped to build, a tragedy hidden by resignation and silence but one that occasionally explodes in loud demonstrations or that is pushed into appalling suicides. A young man's decision to kill himself is taken seriously but what does one say of the suicide of an old man already close to death? It's terrible. A society that allows such things is a lost society." Zavattini saw it as a continuation of the three earlier films he had made with De Sica, which he defined as an appeal to public solidarity. Is it possible to describe *Umberto D* as "pessimistic" because the demonstration takes place at the beginning and the attempted suicide at the end? The public would surely be more likely to be aroused by this portrait of a man in the depths of distress than by suggesting the demonstration was immediately effective. The film's uncompromising approach to its theme made it only a limited commercial success. Nevertheless, this and *Bicycle Thieves* (*q.v.*) are the best of the five films from *Sciuscia* to *Il Tetto* in which De Sica and Zavattina depicted life in postwar Italy.

UMBRELLAS OF CHERBOURG (THE) PARA-PLUIES DE CHERBOURG (LES)

UN CHAPEAU DE PAILLE D'ITALIE AN ITALIAN STRAW HAT France 1927. *Dir* René Clair *Scen* René Clair based on the play by Eugène Labiche, Marc Michel *Photog* Maurice Desfassiaux, Nicolas Roudakoff *Art Dir* Lazare Meerson *Costumes* Souplet *Ed* Henri Dobb *Artistic Dir* Alexandre Kamenka, Georges Lacombe, Lily Jumel *Cast* Albert Préjean, Olga Tschekowa (Tchekova), Marise Maia, Alice Tissot, Yvonneck, Alex Bondi, Paul Olivier, Jim Gérald, Pré fils *Prod* Albatross (Kamenka). 6,623 ft.

Fadinard (Préjean) is on his way to be married when his horse casually chews a lady's (Tschekowa) straw hat. The lady is married and on a clandestine excursion with her lover. They insist Fadinard find an identical hat in order to keep the lady's husband from becoming suspicious. Fadinard is forced to postpone his marriage and neglect his bride (Maia) while he searches the town for an identical hat. Each of the guests at the wedding has his own personal worry at any loss of his "respectability."

Best sequences: the troop of lancers; the horse eating the hat; the wedding ceremony officiated by the mayor; the mix-ups with the cravat, boots, and footbath, etc.

Clair had been attracted by the Labiche and Michel farce for some time, but declared: "I wanted to retain the spirit of the work (which is alone important) and not its form, which was designed for the stage. I have written the script as it seems to me Labiche and Michel would have written it if they had known the cinema." But, he also said, "I have filmed the intermission," changing the original vaudeville farce into a comic chase in the Mack Sennett and Jean Durand manner and replacing Labiche's verbal jokes with visual gags. The period was changed from 1851 to 1895. The characters are presented rather like turn-of-the-century puppets, identified by conventions of costumes and accessories, and the period sets and ornamental furnishings are minutely accurate. Clair relied much on "indirect comedy" and "deliberately literary devices" (Léon Moussinac) to bring out the satirical allusions.

Léon Moussinac wrote: "He has accentuated the outdated, ridiculous touches of the comedy, notably through the 1895 sets and costumes, and the obsolete behavior of the characters, which sometimes evokes that of prewar films. By caricaturing the era and its spirit in this filmic parody of a work that had a special success during a mediocre period, René Clair brought to the screen all the idiosyncrasies, failings, and excesses of the *fin de siecle* bourgeoisie."

An Italian Straw Hat was Clair's first major success (though a critical rather than a commercial one). At the age of 30, through his encounter with Labiche, he reached in this film a maturity of style and a theme that was to typify his work in the future.

— *der Florentiner Hut* Germany 1939. *Dir* Wolfgang Leibeneiner *Scen* B. Hofmann, H. Budjuhn based on the play *Photog* Carl Hoffman, Karl Löb *Cast* Heinz Rühmann, Herti Kirchner, Christl Mardayn. 90 mins.

Apparently a pleasing version with amusing performances.

UN CHIEN ANDALOU France 1928 *Dir/Ed* Luis Buñuel *Scen* Luis Buñuel, Salvador Dali *Photog* Albert Dubergen (Duverger) *Art Dir* Schilzneck *Cast* Pierre Batcheff, Simone Mareuil, Jaime Miravilles, Luis Buñuel, Salvador Dali *Prod* Buñuel. 430 meters. Version with music track prepared under Buñuel's supervision in 1960, 17 mins.

Any synopsis of this film would necessarily be meaningless since the power of the film depends on its succession of surrealistic images. However the main sequences of the film are as follows: "Once Upon A Time" — close-ups of a man (Buñuel) smoking a cigarette and sharpening a razor; the eye of a young woman (Mareuil) being slit with a razor as a cloud passes across the moon. "Eight years later" — a young cyclist (Batcheff) rides down a street dressed in a winged cap, stiff collar, and a frilly skirt over his suit and with a striped box hanging round his neck; a young woman (Mareuil) sees him from her window and rushes out when he falls off his bicycle; in the room the cyclist's hand crawling with live ants; a masculine-looking young woman, dressed like a man and with a man's hair cut, is seen in the street poking at a severed hand with a stick and watched by a crowd of curious onlookers; a policeman picks up the hand and puts in the striped box; the androgyne is beset by passing cars and then run over by one; the cyclist grabs the young woman and paws her breasts, seen clothed and then naked, with the shot dissolving to a pair of naked buttocks; the woman runs away; in following her the cyclist begins to drag on ropes an enormous cargo; two grand pianos on which are two dead and decaying donkeys, cork mats, two priests; as the woman escapes, the cyclist's hand is trapped in the door and is again seen covered with live ants. "Towards Three in the Morning" — a stranger arrives, tears off the cyclist's frills and throws them out of the window and makes him stand against the wall. "Sixteen Years Before" — in the same room, the stranger gives the man some books; in his hands they become revolvers and he shoots the stranger who, as he falls, ends up in a meadow; as he dies he is carried away by two men; back in the room, the cyclist's mouth becomes covered with hair as the woman discovers her armpit is hairless; the woman leaves, arrives on a pebbly beach and embraces a man in striped jersey and knickerbockers; among the pebbles are the frills and striped box of the cyclist; they walk away along the beach. "In the Spring" — the man and the woman are buried up to their necks in sand.

It would be absurd to try to explain logically all the symbols and metaphors in this film, derived as they were from a phrase of Lautréamont's, "Beautiful as the chance meeting of an umbrella and a sewing-machine on a dissection table." Indeed a phrase from "La Révolution surréaliste" (though Buñuel and Dali had not then joined the group) could have served as a guide in their conception: "The cinema is the bringing into play of chance." This is not to say that the film is without meaning. It is the expression of a generation's passionate revolt, its theme (as Dali described it in 1928) is "the pure and correct line of 'conduct' of a human who pursues love through

wretched humanitarian, patriotic ideals and the other miserable workings of reality."

Jean Vigo in *Vers un cinéma social* in 1930 wrote: *"Un chien Andalou,* though primarily a subjective drama developed like a poem, is nonetheless for me a film with a social theme . . . M. Buñuel is a fine marksman who disdains the stab in the back. A kick in the pants to macabre ceremonies . . . A kick in the pants to those who have sullied love in rape. A kick in the pants to sadism, of which clowning is its most disguised form . . . Shame on those who kill in youth that which they themselves could have become, who seek in the forests and along the beaches, where the sea casts up our memories and regrets, the shriveled projection of their first blooming. *Cave canem.* Beware of the dog. It bites."

UN CONDAMNE A MORT S'EST ECHAPPE or LE VENT SOUFFLE OÙ IL VEUT/A MAN ESCAPED France 1956. *Dir* Robert Bresson *Scen* Robert Bresson based on a true story by André Devigny *Photog* Léonce-Henry Burel *Art Dir* Pierre Charbonnier *Mus* Mozart (*C Minor Mass*) *Ed* Raymond Lamy *Cast* (nonprofessionals) François Leterrier, Roland Monod, Charles Le Clainche, Maurice Beerblock, Jacques Ertaud *Prod* SNE Gaumont/ NEF. 102 mins.

In France in 1943, Lt. Fontaine (Leterrier) is captured by the Gestapo and imprisoned in Fort Montluc. He carefully plans his escape but procrastinates until he is sentenced to death. Jost (Le Clainche), a young boy known to have worked with the Germans is placed in his cell. Fontaine is faced with having to kill him or trust him. Finally they escape together.

Famous sequences: the first, unsuccessful, attempt to escape from a moving car in Lyons; his bloody beating at the hands of the Gestapo; his contacts with other prisoners through windows, tapping on walls, etc; the preparations for the escape with a sharpened iron spoon and ropes made out of bed springs, blankets and clothing; the sudden arrival of the new prisoner; the escape over the roofs of the prison.

Based on a true account of a wartime escape, this film was described by Simone Dubreuilh as "the advent of unsordid realism," by François Truffaut as "the most crucial French film of the past ten years," and by André Bazin as "an

unusual film that resembles no other."
In what was his first film since *Journal
d'une curé de campagne* (*q.v.*) Bresson
creates what Eric Rohmer called "a
miracle of objects" in this story of a man
almost entirely alone in his blank-walled
cell. A pin is used to undo handcuffs, a
spoon is used to dismantle the cell
door, bed springs and blankets become a
rope to escape with, a door-handle
stresses the theme. The numerous close-
ups of Fontaine's face and his hands at
work take on an added significance in relation to Bresson's rich and complex
use of sound. The sound track contains
not only a kind of "musique concrète"
of noises that convey a sense of being
in a prison (footsteps, keys jangling,
locks being opened or shut, a train passing outside) but also the "Kyrie" from
Mozart's *Mass in C Minor* and the voice
of the hero, linking the action and revealing his own thoughts.
All the actors were nonprofessionals
(though Leterrier later became a director) but were directed with as much
discipline as if they were professionals,
often made to repeat an action a hundred
times in order to catch just the right
expression. The characters themselves
are stylized rather than naturalistic:
despite his long weeks of incarceration,
the hero's facial stubbles remains the
same length and he is still wearing the
same bloody shirt at the end of the film
as he wore at the beginning. "I avoided
all deliberate dramatic effects," said
Bresson, "in searching for the utmost
simplicity so that the emotion would
arise from the general development of
the action rather than from details."
Bresson's original title for the film, *Le
Vent souffle où il vent* ("The Spirit
breathes where it will", from St. John's
Gospel) was retained as a subtitle in the
release version and suggests a clear link
with his previous film, *Diary of a Country Priest* (*q.v.*). Though it uses the minimum of conventional filmic devices and
says little in order to express more, this
film truthfully transmits the atmosphere
of occupied France and the spirit of the
French Resistance.

UNCONVENTIONAL LINDA HOLIDAY

UNDER COVER OF NIGHT JAGTE RAHO

UNDER THE PHRYGIAN STAR CELULOZA

UNDER THE ROOFS OF PARIS SOUS LES
TOITS DE PARIS

UNDERWORLD (THE) BAS-FONDS (LES)

UNDERWORLD PAYING THE PENALTY USA
1927. *Dir/Ed* Josef von Sternberg *Scen*
Ben Hecht, Robert N. Lee, Josef von
Sternberg, Jules Furthman *Photog* Bert
Glennon *Art Dir* Hans Dreier *Cast*
George Bancroft, Evelyn Brent, Clive
Brook, Larry Semon, Fred Kohler, Helen
Lynch *Prod* Paramount. 7,453 ft.
Bull Weed (Bancroft), a Chicago gang-
ster, kills a rival (Kohler) and is sent
to prison. His moll, Feathers McCoy
(Brent), and his lieutenant, Rolls Royce
(Brook) organize a successful escape.
Later he thinks they have betrayed him
and leaves but they find him when he is
trapped by the police. Realizing that
Feathers and Rolls Royce are in love
he forces them to leave and remains
alone to fight the police.
Based on an 18-page film treatment that
Ben Hecht says he wrote with Harold
Rosson, this low-budget film was an
enormous international box-office success
and made Sternberg, Hecht (who won
an Oscar), Bancroft, and Brent famous.
It was the first film to use gangsters as
heroes and established the gangster film
vogue that lasted through the Thirties.
George Bancroft's Bull Weed is sympathetic and humane, even sentimental, a
man rebelling as much against society as
were the anarchists. Clive Brook's character is a kind of failed intellectual, alcoholic, cautious and melancholy, while
Evelyn Brent plays the kind of sensuous
role that Sternberg was later to make his
trademark with Marlene Dietrich. When
she leaves the besieged apartment several
feathers float behind her, symbolizing
not only her characteristic costume but
her personality and strange charm. All
that remains is for the gangster to die.
Lewis Jacobs wrote: "Von Sternberg
brought to it a realistic atmosphere,
striking lighting effects and compositions,
characterization expressed through close-
ups shot from carefully chosen angles
and through a selection of types, a sense
of timing, and an economy of means (the
jewelry store holdup was shocking in its
impressionistic effect . . .), and above
all a freshness and discipline that made
the melodrama outstanding. Unquestionably a new director had 'arrived' in this
picture."

Underworld was of considerable influence on European directors, notably on Jacques Prévert and Marcel Carné.

UNDYING STORY OF CAPTAIN SCOTT AND ANIMAL LIFE IN THE ANTARCTIC (THE) WITH CAPTAIN SCOTT, R.N., TO THE SOUTH POLE.

UNE FEMME MARIEE (originally LA FEMME MARIÉE) A MARRIED WOMAN France 1964. *Dir/Scen* Jean-Luc Godard *Photog* Raoul Coutard *Art Dir* Henri Nogaret *Mus* Beethoven, Claude Nougaro *Ed* Agnès Guillemot, Françoise Collin *Cast* Macha Méril, Bernard Noël, Philippe Leroy, Roger Leenhardt *Prod* Anouchka/Orsay. 94 mins.

Charlotte (Méril) visits her lover, Robert (Noël), an actor, and promises to make up her mind about leaving her husband, Pierre (Leroy), a pilot. She spends that evening with Pierre and their son. Next day her doctor confirms that she is pregnant and she admits she doesn't know who the father is. She does research for a magazine article on love, sex, and modern youth. She meets Robert at Orly Airport, since he is about to go to Marseilles to play Racine's *Bérénice*. They make love in a hotel and Charlotte explains why she cannot reach a decision about leaving Pierre. Robert tells her that the affair must therefore end and Charlotte seems to agree.

Godard described this as "a film in which individuals are considered as things, in which chases in a taxi alternate with ethnological interviews, in which the spectacle of life is intermingled with its analysis, in brief a film in which the cinema horses around and is happy to be only what it is." This sociological study of the alienation of the modern woman is expressed largely through a graphic pop art style rather than through dramatic exposition. [The French censors insisted on a change in the title from *La Femme Mariée* on the grounds that this might cast a slur on French womanhood in general, although a change from the generic to the particular contradicted Godard's sociological approach.]

UNE NUIT SUR LE MONT CHAUVE A NIGHT ON BALD MOUNTAIN/A NIGHT ON BARE MOUNTAIN France 1933. *Dir/Prod* Alexandre Alexeieff *Co-Dir* Claire Parker *Mus* Moussorgsky's tone poem *Night on Bald Mountain,* arranged by Rimski-Korsakov. 8 mins.

This experimental phantasmagoria by Alexeieff and his wife (their first) uses the pinboard technique to give an impression of animated engravings. It contains so many explorations of the possibility of creating mood through a plastic flow of images that it must be considered one of the germinal works of the animated cinema.

UNE PARTIE DE CAMPAGNE A DAY IN THE COUNTRY France 1936 (released 1946). *Dir* Jean Renoir *Scen* Jean Renoir based on the story by Guy de Maupassant *Assist* Luchino Visconti, Jacques Becker, Henri Cartier-Bresson *Photog* Claude Renoir, Jean (Yves) Bourgoin *Mus* Joseph Kosma *Ed* Marguerite Renoir *Cast* Sylvia Bataille, Georges Darnoux, Jane Marken, Gabriello, Paul Temps, Jacques Brunius, Jean Renoir, Marguerite Renoir, Pierre Lestringuez *Prod* Pierre Braunberger. 40 mins.

In the mid-19th century, Monsieur Dufour (Gabriello), a Parisian ironmonger, takes his wife (Marken), his daughter, Henriette (Bataille), and her fiancé (Temps) for a Sunday excursion into the country. In a restaurant by the river, they meet two men who take the mother and Henriette in a boat up the river. Henri (Darnoux) falls in love with Henriette and they kiss. But their love has no future.

This unfinished masterpiece, with all the revelation and freshness of touch of a sketch by a great painter, was shot in 1936 but never completed. It was eventually edited and released as a short feature in 1946. The atmosphere and fashions are those of 1880, the period when the banks of the Seine were frequented by impressionist painters and naturalist authors, both of whom were capturing aspects of contemporary life. Pictorially, it reveals Renoir's relationship not only to his father, Auguste Renoir, but also to Manet, Monet, Degas, and other impressionists. Its theme derives as much from Zola as from Maupassant. This endearing, romantic film has nonetheless a heart of sadness in its meditation on solitude and the difficulties of human relationships.

The young critic, Alexandre Astruc, wrote in 1946: "The royal tradition of this family of artists (the Renoirs) runs through this film like sap through the trees, traces exactly the winding, swollen Marne until it becomes a bubbling sheet in which everything is drowned, mixed, intermingled, in which is found the exquisite lace-trimmed face of Sylvia Bataille like a crumpled flower, seizes an eyeblink and becomes tangled up in the frothy linens. Who is prisoner in time and space, prisoner of the thousand invisible touches of impressionism?"

UNE SI JOLIE PETITE PLAGE RIPTIDE/SUCH A PRETTY LITTLE BEACH France 1948. *Dir* Yves Allégret *Scen* Jacques Sigurd *Photog* Henri Alekan *Art Dir* M. Colasson *Mus* Maurice Thiriet *Ed* Léonide Azar *Cast* Gérard Philipe, Madeleine Robinson, Jean Servais, Jane Marken, Mona Dol. 91 mins.

An orphan (Philipe) returns to the inn where he had been mistreated by the owner (Marken) when he had worked there as a child. He is befriended by a servant (Robinson) but she cannot prevent his suicide, which is provoked by a composer (Servais) who knows he has committed murder.

Yves Allégret's best *film noir* with an excellent script that not only allows one to understand, without monologues, flashbacks or asides, that the former ward of Public Assistance had killed his lover, an aging, famous actress, but also captures the fatalistic melancholy that drives the hero back to seek his childhood on a "pretty little beach" out of season, bare and blurred by rain and mist. Gérard Philipe was attracted to the role written by his friend Jacques Sigurd and made it one of his best.

UNE VIE A LIFE/ONE LIFE/END OF DESIRE France/Italy 1958. *Dir* Alexandre Astruc *Scen* Roland Laudenbach, Alexandre Astruc based on the novel by Guy de Maupassant *Assist Dir* Claude Clément, Paul Saban *Photog* Claude Renoir *Art Dir* Paul Bertrand *Mus* Roman Vlad *Ed* Claudine Boucher *Cast* Maria Schell, Christian Marquand, Ivan Desny, Antonella Lualdi, Pascale Petit *Prod* Agnès Delahie/Nepi Film. 88 mins. Eastman Color.

Jeanne (Schell), the daughter of an aristocratic country family, marries Julien (Marquand), a cynical philanderer. She learns that a baby that Rosalie (Petit), a servant girl, has had is her husband's but tries to revive his love. She herself has a child and finds a new meaning in life. Julien carries on as before and has an affair with Gilberte (Lualdi) the wife

of a friend of his who discovers the affair and kills both of them. Jeanne is left alone without purpose in life.

Alexandre Astruc said: "I didn't choose the subject. The film was offered to me on the condition that Maria Schell was the lead. I re-read the novel and felt I could do it. For Maupassant, *Une Vie* was the story of an unhappily married woman who couldn't obtain a divorce because divorce then was impossible. I insisted on what was still relevant in it: the difficulty of two people living together. The drama is the impossibility of married life, for Maria Schell and Marquand have completely different conceptions of marriage. For her, despite her dread, marriage is the beginning of life. She wants to build and possess. For him on the other hand, marriage is an end and he suffers under his marriage and its chains."

Astruc's second feature, three years after *Les Mauvaises rencontres* (*q.v.*), was an expensive coproduction, shot in color in period settings, with Maria Schell at the height of her international fame playing the lead role, but it achieved only a limited success. It is, nevertheless, one of Astruc's best films with a dramatic and symbolic use of color and some excellent atmospheric photography of the Normandy farm setting by Claude Renoir.

UNEXPECTED (THE) PO ZAKONU

UNFAITHFUL WIFE (THE) FEMME INFIDÈLE (LA)

UNFINISHED STORY NEOKONCHENNAYA POVEST

UNHOLY THREE (THE) USA 1925. *Dir* Tod Browning *Scen* Waldemar Young based on a story by Clarence Aaron Robbins *Photog* David Kesson *Ed* Danny Gray *Cast* Lon Chaney, Harry Earles, Victor McLaglen, Mae Busch, Matt Moore, Matthew Betz, Edward Connelly, Walter Perry, John Merkyl, Percy Williams *Prod* Metro-Goldwyn. 6,948 ft. Tinted.

A ventriloquist, Echo (Chaney), runs a pet shop disguised as an old woman. With his assistant, a dwarf (Earles) disguised as a child, a girl, Rosie (Busch), and a strong man (McLaglen) disguised as an honest citizen, he carries out a series of crimes that end in a murder. Suspicion falls on Hector

(Moore), an innocent assistant in the shop whom Rosie loves. She agrees to marry Echo, if he saves Hector. In the courtroom, Echo tells the true story by throwing his voice into Hector's. The strong man is killed by a gorilla from the pet shop and Hector is freed.

A marvelous piece of fantasy and one of the most bizarre films in the history of the cinema, tinged with moments of black humor. [This is the first of eight silent films Tod Browning, the master of horrific beauty, made with Lon Chaney and (with the possible exception of *London After Midnight* in 1927) by far the best. Its macabre vision of evil has been matched only in *Freaks* (*q.v.*)]

— *The Unholy Three* USA 1930. *Dir* Jack Conway *Scen* Elliott Nugent, J. C. Nugent based on the story by Robbins *Photog* Percy Hillburn *Ed* Frank Sullivan *Cast* Lon Chaney, Lila Lee, Elliott Nugent, Harry Earles, John Miljan, Ivan Linow *Prod* MGM. 70 mins.

[This remake is Lon Chaney's first and only sound film (he died soon after production was completed) in which he uses four different voices (his own, an old woman, a parrot, and a baby) as Echo the ventriloquist. Harry Earles also repeats his original role. The ending, however, is changed to a melodramatic climax in a courtroom with justice meted out by a prosecuting attorney who strips the woman's wig off Echo to reveal the criminal.]

UN HOMME MARCHE DANS LA VILLE France 1949 (released 1950). *Dir* Marcel (Marcello) Pagliero *Scen* Marcel Pagliero based on the novel by Jausion *Photog* Nicolas Hayer *Art Dir* Maurice Colasson *Ed* Pierre Cholot *Cast* Jean-Pierre Kérien, Robert Dalban, Ginette Leclerc, Yves Diniaud, Coco Aslan *Prod* Sacha Gordine. 95 mins.

André (Dalban), a docker, is jealous of his wife, Madeleine (Leclerc), whom he suspects is the mistress of his foreman, Jean (Kérien). The two men quarrel and, when André's body is discovered, Jean is arrested. Madeleine, thinking him guilty, kills herself. Jean, though proved innocent, is too late to save Madeleine and is left alone in the hostile city.

This film was produced with the support of the docker's union but ran into severe critical attacks on its release. It remained without a distributor for some time,
then, in the middle of a long docker's strike, it was suddenly shown at two of the largest theaters in Paris in May 1950. This led to attacks on Pagliero (whose first French film this is) for "demoralizing the working class."

My own views were expressed in *Les Lettres francaises,* March 1950. After pointing out that P. Lafargue had no basis for criticizing Zola for having shown drunken workers in *L'Assommoir* soon after the Commune (he described it as "a novel warmly welcomed by reactionaries"), I added: "Zola proved that he considered people as something other than material for a naturalistic study. Marcel Pagliero will show by what follows whether *Un homme marche dans la ville* was an error or a premeditated insult."

UNION PACIFIC PACIFIC EXPRESS USA 1939. *Dir* Cecil B. De Mille *Scen* C. Gardner Sullivan, Walter DeLeon, Jesse Lasky, Jack Cunningham based on a story by Ernest Haycox *Photog* Victor Milner, Dewey Wrigley *Art Dir* Hans Dreier, Roland Anderson *Mus* George Antheil *Ed* Ann Bauchens *Cast* Barbara Stanwyck, Joel McCrea, Akim Tamiroff, Brian Donlevy, Robert Preston, Lynn Overman, Anthony Quinn, Henry Kolker, Evelyn Keyes, Julia Faye *Prod* Paramount. 133 mins.

The story of the building of the trans-American railroad about 1870 when the two rival companies, stimulated by government subsidies, fought to finish first, took enormous risks, and allowed nothing to stand in their way, not the lives of their workers, nor the Indians, nor the buffalo.

This is one of the best westerns ever made. Hollywood pioneer, Cecil B. De Mille, identified strongly with the railroad pioneers he depicts and brings history strikingly to life in this film's many spectacular scenes, full of savage power.

UNKNOWN SOLDIER (THE) TUNTEMATON SOTILAS

UNSICHTBAREN KRALLEN DES DR. MABUSE (DIE) see DR. MABUSE

UNVANQUISHED (THE) see PATHER PANCHALI

US KIDS NOUS LES GOSSES

VACANCES DE M. HULOT (LES) MR. HULOT'S
HOLIDAY France 1953. *Dir* Jacques Tati
Co-Dir Bernard Maurice, Pierre Aubert
Scen Jacques Tati, Henri Marquet *Photog*
Jacques Mercanton, Jean Mousselle *Art
Dir* Henri Schmitt, Roger Briaucourt
Mus Alain Romans *Ed* Suzanne Baron,
Charles Bratoneiche, Grassi *Cast* Jacques
Tati, Nathalie Pascaud, Louis Perrault,
Michèlle Rolla, Suzy Willy, André
Dubois *Prod* Cady Films/Discina/Eclair
Journal. 96 mins. Re-released in 1961
with a new sound track.
Pipe-smoking, middle-class Mr. Hulot
(Tati) arrives in his battered old car
(Hamikar, 1924 model) to spend his
holiday in a family hotel at a seaside
resort in Britanny. He is attracted to a
pretty girl, Martine (Pascaud), but makes
only a few tentative advances and nothing comes of it.
Main gags and sequences: the railway
station with its loudspeakers calling out
gibberish; Hulot's arrival at the hotel;
his room at the top of the building;
Hulot painting a boat at the water's edge
with the paint pot always floating within
reach; his encounter with a collapsible
dinghy that folds up beneath him; the
long trail of wet footprints he leaves behind him as he enters the hotel; the
breakdown of his car in a cemetery
where his leaf-covered spare tire is mistaken for a wreath and he gets involved
in a funeral; the game of tennis; the
masked ball where Hulot in disguise
makes timid advances to Martine; the
picnic during which the car runs away;
Hulot, chased by dogs, hiding in a hut
and setting off a "display" of fireworks;
the nostalgic ending as the guests depart
for home.
The humor is largely visual. Words are
used only as noises and rarely have direct meaning in themselves. The hero
himself uses only one word — "Hulot."

The carefully composed sound track is
even better in the new 1961 version.
Tati said: "The images are put at the
disposal of the viewer, who must tell
his own story as if he had his hands on
the camera. He chooses from among the
various elements (gags, impressions of
the beach) I have included the details
that recall to him his own impressions of
holidays. Instead of treating him like a
passive being who submits to a well-
greased, rapid exposition of a story, I
offer him a world that everyone knows
and I believe he will find pleasure in
recognizing people and situations he
knows."

VAGABOND (THE) AWARA

VAGHE STELLE DELL'ORSA SANDRA/OF A
THOUSAND DELIGHTS Italy 1965. *Dir*
Luchino Visconti *Scen* Luchino Visconti,
Suso Cecchi d'Amico, Enrico Medioli
Photog Armando Nannuzzi *Art Dir*
Mario Garbuglia *Mus* César Franck *Ed*
Mario Serandrei *Cast* Claudia Cardinale,
Jean Sorel, Michael Craig, Renzo Ricci,
Marie Bell, Fred Williams *Prod* Vides.
100 mins.
[Sandra (Cardinale) returns with her
American husband, Andrew (Craig), to
her native Volterra to attend a ceremony
in memory of her Jewish father, who
died in a concentration camp. She meets
again her brother, Gianni (Sorel), with
whom she had been deeply involved in
their adolescence. For her it is a memory
of which she is ashamed but for him it is
still alive and he is engaged in an autobiographical novel about it. Both think
that their mother (Bell), now mentally
unbalanced, denounced their father in
order to marry her lover (Ricci). Andrew
naively tries to bring about a reconciliation but this only results in disaster.
Andrew leaves for America and Gianni

destroys his novel and kills himself. Sandra decides to forget the past and join her husband.

This rococo vision of corruption and despair is not among Visconti's better films, despite some memorable images and a brilliant creation of the claustrophobic atmosphere of the house. It is comparable to the later film, *The Damned* (*q.v.*), in that both are "symbolic" social dramas, almost Greek tragedies in a quasi-operatic style. But this film falls uneasily at times into lurid melodrama that makes one more aware of the inadequacies of the acting.]

VALAHOL EUROPABAN SOMEWHERE IN EUROPE/KUKSI Hungary 1947. *Dir* Geza Radvanyi *Assist Dir* Felix Mariassy *Scen* Bela Balasz, Felix and Judith Mariassy, Geza Radvanyi *Photog* Barnabas Hegyi *Art Dir* Joseph Pan, B. Mikoz *Mus* Denas Buday *Ed* Geza Radvanyi, Felix Mariassy *Cast* Miklos Gabor, Arthur Sonlay, Ladislas Horvath, Z. Banky *Prod* Mafirt/Radvanyi. 104 mins. English version, 80 mins.

A band of wild, lawless children, made homeless in the aftermath of war, wander with their leader (Gabor) into a crumbling castle owned by a famous musician (Somlay). He gives them a more positive attitude towards society. The local villagers, encouraged by a fascist, attack the castle and one of the children, Kuksi (Horvath), is killed in a fight with the police. But the children are taken back into society.

The first part of the film — the wild life of the children on the roads of a country devastated by war — is particularly effective and striking and suggests (as does the revelry scene in the castle) the influence of the German silent cinema. The later sequences depicting the children's re-education are less convincing. *Somewhere in Europe* owes more to its scriptwriters and cameraman than to its director, whose only memorable film this is. It is one of the best films of the immediate postwar period and obtained a well-merited international success.

VALKOINEN PEURA THE WHITE REINDEER Finland 1952. *Dir/Photog* Erik Blomberg *Scen* Erik Blomberg, M. Kuosmanen *Art Dir* Osmo Osva *Mus* Einar Englund *Cast* Mirjami Kuosmanen, Kalervo Nissila, Arvo Lehesmaa, Ake Lindman, J. Tapiola. 65 mins.

In Lapland, a young woman with magical powers, Pirita (Kuosmanen) marries a hunter (Nissila) and after consulting a wizard (Lehesmaa) is transformed into a vampiric white reindeer that is hunted by the villagers and finally killed by the husband.

Based on a Nordic legend, this fantasy film has some delicately expressive photography but is largely unknown even to enthusiasts of the genre.

VALLEY OF PEACE DOLINA MIRU

VAMPIRES (LES) (series) France 1915–1916. [Ten episodes: 1, 2 (released together). *La Tête coupée, La Bague qui tue;* 3. *Le Cryptogramme rouge;* 4. *Le Spectre;* 5. *L'Évasion du mort;* 6. *Les Yeux qui fascinent;* 7. *Satanas;* 8. *Le Maître de la foudre;* 9. *L'Homme des poisons;* 10. *Les Noces sanglantes*] *Dir/Scen* Louis Feuillade *Photog/Ed* Guérin (?) *Art Dir* Garnier *Cast* Edouard Mathé, Jean Aymé, Musidora, Stacia Napierkowska, Marcel Levesque, Louis Leubas, Fernand Hermann, Delphine Renot *Prod* Gaumont. 1, 2. 1,500 meters approx; 3. 1,016 meters; 4. 815 meters; 5. 1,000 meters; 6. 1,300 meters; 7. 1,300 meters; 8. 1,300 meters; 9. 1,252 meters; 10. 1,410 meters. Total approx. 37,000 ft.

A band of criminals led by the Grand-Vampire (Aymé) and Irma Vep (Musidora) commit a series of brilliant crimes. They are tracked down by a journalist (Mathé). After many adventures, the Vampires are discovered in their hideout during an orgy and killed by the police, the journalist, and his assistant (Levesque).

The plot of this "series-film" (whose true heroine is Musidora in molded black-silk tights) was improvised by Feuillade during production. Unlike the usual serial films (such as the contemporary *Exploits of Elaine*) the episodes did not appear weekly but at intervals of two to five weeks. The first and second parts were released on November 13, 1915 and the last on June 30, 1916. After their initial screenings, they were presented elsewhere in weekly episodes. Stylistically, *Les Vampires* is a blend of realism, fantasy, and comedy. It also reveals a singular poetry in the use of landscapes. Though largely ignored by intellectuals, *Les Vampires* was much admired by such people as Aragon, Breton, and Eluard, the future founders of surrealism.

Aragon wrote in 1918: "I could defend these thrillers as being as significant of our era as the novels of chivalry, the precious novels, or the free-thinking novels. I could talk of the exaltation we are going to find, youthful and free of literary prejudices, when the Tenth Muse, Musidora, plays across the screen the weekly epic of *Vampires*." Aragon and Breton wrote in 1928: "One day it will be understood, that there was nothing more realistic or poetic than the serial film that was formerly the joy of strong spirits. It is in *The Exploits of Elaine (q.v.)* and *Les Vampires* that the grand reality of our century will be found. They are beyond fashion, beyond taste." The episode (*L'Évasion du mort*) in which the guests at a ball are sealed in a room and gassed could have inspired Buñuel when he made *The Exterminating Angel (q.v.)*. Since he began, Buñuel has proclaimed himself a disciple not of Feuillade (whose name he didn't know) but of his films, which he greatly admired.

VAMPYR THE STRANGE ADVENTURE OF DAVID GRAY/NOT AGAINST THE FLESH/ CASTLE OF DOOM Germany/France 1931 (released 1932). *Dir/Ed* Carl Theodor Dreyer *Scen* Christen Jul, Carl Theodor Dreyer based on the story *Carmilla* from *In a Glass Darkly* by Sheridan Le Fanu *Photog* Rudolf Maté, Louis Née *Art Dir* Hermann Warm, Cesare Silvani *Mus* Wolfgang Zeller *Cast* Julian West (Baron Nicolas de Gunzburg), Sybille Schmitz, Maurice Schutz, Rena Mandel, Jan Hieronimko Henriette Gérard, Albert Bras, N. Babanini *Prod* Dreyer-Filmproduktion for Tobis Klangfilm. 83 mins. Produced in French, German and English language versions. Existing English versions, 73 mins.

David Gray (West) arrives at an inn in the village of Courtempierre. That night an old man (Schutz) gives him a package to be opened in the event of his death. David leaves the inn and sees a one-legged gamekeeper keep a rendezvous with the village doctor (Hieronimko) and an old woman (Gérard). He follows him further to a nearby chateau whose owner is revealed as the old man David has seen earlier. The old man is shot and dies in the arms of his younger daughter, Gisèle (Mandel), while the older daughter, Leone (Schmitz), lies ill with a strange sickness. David opens the package and discovers it is a book on vampires. Later that night, Leone is found prostrate in the castle grounds, the old woman seen briefly by her side. The doctor asks David for blood for a transfusion. He agrees and weak from blood, has a vision of his own death and burial. He awakens in the cemetery and drives an iron stake through the heart of the old woman in her grave. The body crumbles to dust and Leone is freed from her curse. The gamekeeper is hurled down a flight of stairs and killed and the doctor is buried in the flour in the mill.

Produced independently by Dreyer's own company with the financial assistance of a film enthusiast, Baron Nicolas de Gunzburg, *Vampyr* was shot outside the studios in real settings in France (an inn, a chateau, an unused factory) and with only two professional actors, Maurice Schutz and Sybille Schmitz (a young disciple of Max Reinhardt). The rest of the cast was drawn from friends and acquaintances selected for their resemblance to the characters. Dreyer described his film during its production to Ebe Neergard: "Imagine that we are sitting in a very ordinary room. Suddenly we are told that there is a corpse behind the door. Instantly, the room we are sitting in is completely altered. Everything in it has taken on another look. The light, the atmosphere have changed, though they are physically the same. This is because *we* have changed and the objects *are* as we conceive them. This is the effect I wanted to produce in *Vampyr*."

Elliptical in style, hauntingly sinister in atmosphere, and with a spare use of dialogue, *Vampyr* is, as Lotte Eisner wrote, "a worthy successor to Murnau's *Nosferatu (q.v.)*. It is bathed in an atmosphere whose magic only the cinema could express; it would be impossible for the theater to give shapes the characteristic fuzziness of the world of nightmares." The most famous sequence shows a burial as seen through the eyes of a corpse, David Gray, with the camera taking David's place in the coffin, watching the old woman peer through the glass, then glimpsing treetops, the sky, and corners of buildings as the coffin is carried to the cemetery.

*VANGELO SECONDO MATTEO (IL) THE GOSPEL ACCORDING TO ST. MATTHEW Italy/

France 1964. *Dir* Pier Paolo Pasolini *Scen* Pier Paolo Pasolini based on the Gospel according to St. Matthew *Photog* Tonino Delli Colli *Art Dir* Luigi Scaccianoce *Mus* Bach, Mozart, Prokofiev, Webern, and the *Misa Luba Ed* Nino Baragli *Cast* (nonprofessionals) Enrique Irazoqui, Margherita Caruso, Susanna Pasolini, Marcelle Morante, Mario Socrate, Settimio Di Porto *Prod* Arco/Lux. 142 mins. English version, 135 mins.

Made by an avowed Marxist, this version of the life of Christ (Irazoqui) from the Annunciation to the Resurrection sticks strictly to the spirit of the Gospel and avoids the usual Hollywood sentimentalities. Its sense of dynamic immediacy (largely obtained through the use of hand-held cameras in the *cinéma-vérité* manner to get in into the center of the action), its use of visual devices and music overlaying an apparently stark and simple style, and its forceful performances create a dramatic account of a man spiritually determined to fulfill his destiny and a persuasive revelation of why that man dominated the history of the world for two thousand years.

*VARGTIMMEN HOUR OF THE WOLF Sweden 1968. *Dir/Scen* Ingmar Bergman *Photog* Sven Nykvist *Art Dir* Marik Vos-Lundh *Mus* Lars Johan Werle, extracts from Mozart's *Der Zauberflöte* and J. S. Bach's *Experiment Ed* Ulla Ryghe *Cast* Max von Sydow, Liv Ullman, Erland Josephson, Ingrid Thulin, Gertrud Fridh, Bertil Anderberg *Prod* Svensk Filmindustri. 89 mins.

An artist Johan Borg (von Sydow), and his wife, Alma (Ullmann), who live in an island cottage, are invited to dinner at the castle of the island's owner, Baron von Merkens (Josephson). Johan is mocked and intimidated by his hosts. Alma discovers Johan's diary in which he recalls incidents on a beach with his former mistress, Veronica Vogler (Thulin), and the death of a boy. Johan becomes insane and tries to shoot Alma and then goes up to the castle again where in a vault he sees Veronica lying like a corpse on a bier. She awakes and embraces him to the amusement of guests in the castle. Johan later wanders into a swamp while Alma is herself on the verge of a breakdown.

Bergman has described his theme: "According to the ancient Romans, the Hour of the Wolf means the time between night and dawn, just before the light comes, and people believed it to be the time when demons had a heightened power and vitality, the hour when most people died and most children were born and when nightmares came to one." Undoubtedly the most visually impressive and engaging of Bergman's recent films, almost hallucinatory and Bosch-like in its impact. Typically isolating his characters in a remote environment, Bergman here explores the nature of artistic creation and the relationship of the artist to society, finding his spiritual inspiration in *The Magic Flute*.

VARIETE VARIETY/VAUDEVILLE Germany 1925. *Dir* Ewald André Dupont *Scen* E. A. Dupont, Leo Birinsky based on the novel *Der Eid des Stephan Huller* by Friedrich Hollaender *Photog* Karl Freund *Art Dir* Oscar F. Werndorff *Mus* Ernö Rappée *Cast* Emil Jannings, Maly Delschaft, Lya de Putti, Warwick Ward, Georg John, Alice Hechy, Kurt Gerron *Prod* UFA. 2,844 meters. (9,300 ft. approx.) American version, 7,800 ft. British version 8,400 ft.

A formerly talented acrobat (Jannings), leaves his wife (Delschaft) and child to elope with a young foreign girl. They form a trapeze act with a young acrobat (Ward), who quickly seduces the girl. The man discovers this and kills his rival in a fight, leaves the girl, and surrenders to the police. The story is framed by scenes of the acrobat in prison telling his story in "flashback."

Léon Moussinac wrote: "One is aware of the coarse thread of melodrama that is saved from vulgarity only by the clearly defined personality of the characters and by the rich and easily exploitable photogenic background. The protagonists are well-defined 'types' rather than personalities. The intelligent machinery of the technical direction, including the editing, takes the place of genius."

The editing is especially remarkable, since the change from one shot to another is often used to suggest shifts of viewpoint on the part of the characters. "Not a scene was staged," wrote Moussinac, "except in relationship to the camera. A continually roving lens seizes the best angle for every detail, expression, and scene." However, one might question whether the incessant camera movements and unusual angles are due to Dupont or to his cameraman, Karl Freund, who also shot *The Last Laugh* (*q.v.*). The use of the subjective camera is derivative of this earlier film. Dupont is more likely responsible for the sense of environment and detail in a manner that anticipated Pabst's "new objectivity." Jannings gives what is certainly his best performance and for once plays with remarkable restraint. Lya de Putti radiates a convincing sense of voluptuous eroticism. *Variety* was an enormous public success, especially in the USA, and exerted considerable effect on Hollywood technique.

— **Varieté* Germany/France 1935. *Dir* Nicolaus Farkas *Scen* Nicolaus Farkas, Rolf Vanloo based on the novel *Photog* Viktor Arménise *Cast* Hans Albers, Annabella, Attila Hörbiger, Karl Etlinger *Prod* Bavaria Film/Vandor Films. 95 mins.

VASILI BORTNIKOV'S RETURN VOZVRASH-CHENIE VASILIYA BORTNIKOVA

VAUDEVILLE VARIETÉ

VELIKII GRAZHDANIN A GREAT CITIZEN
— *Part I* USSR 1938. *Dir* Friedrich Ermler *Scen* Mikhail Bleiman, Mikhail Bolshintsov, Friedrich Ermler *Photog* Arkadi Kaltsati *Art Dir* Nikolai Suvorov, A. Wechsler, Semyon Menken *Mus* Dmitri Shostakovich *Cast* Nikolai Bogolyubov, Ivan Bersenev, Oleg Zhakov, Alexander Zrazhevsky *Prod* Lenfilm. 118 mins.
— *Part II* USSR 1939. *Dir/Scen/Photog/Mus* as above *Art Dir* Semyon Menken *Cast* Nikolai Bogolyubov, Oleg Zhakov, Ivan Bersenev, Boris Poslavsky, Yuri Tolubeyev *Prod* Lenfilm. 134 mins.
Inspired by the assassination of Serge Kirov in 1934, this film presents an account of the life and death of Shakhov (Bogolyubov) from the official party viewpoint. There was then by no means unanimous agreement with the official version of the assassin's motives and this version has since been contested. However, the events themselves mark a dramatic turning point in the history of the USSR. *Part I* deals largely with the events of 1925, the preparations for the Fourteenth Party Congress and the exposure of those who opposed the plans for industrialization. *Part II* is concerned with the events of 1934, the Seventeenth Party Congress and leads up to Shakhov's assassination.

Apart from its historical interest as the "film to explain the Moscow trials," it has carefully drawn characters in the hero and his opponents, all of whom are set against the social background. Though both parts together run over four hours, it never fails to hold one's attention by the fidelity of its characterizations and the forcefulness of its dialogue. Most of the film is carried by the dialogue, usually discussions or arguments involving two, three, or four characters in an office or apartment. This technique takes the spectator through the thinking processes of the protagonists without ever becoming like a play or novel. Occasional excursions to exteriors, especially in mass scenes like the factory meeting, relate the characters (positive and negative) to the social life of the country. Without question, this is Ermler's masterpiece, better than *Veliki Perelom* (*q.v.*), which uses a similar approach to its material.

VELIKI PERELOM THE GREAT TURNING-POINT USSR 1945. *Dir* Friedrich Ermler *Scen* Boris Chirskov *Photog* A. Kaltsati *Art Dir* Nikolai Suvorov *Mus* Gavril Popov *Cast* P. Andriyevsky, Mikhail Derzhavin, Andrei Abrikosov, Alexander Zrazhevsky, Mark Bernes, Soviet army soldiers in the region of Leningrad *Prod* Lenfilm. 108 mins.
An account of the Battle of Stalingrad seen from the point of view of the generals who have to make decisions involving thousands of lives. It focuses on General Muravyov (Derzhavin), a composite of several actual generals, as he discusses with his colleagues the various problems of military strategy. The film ends with the surrender of the German general.
Ermler called this not "a battle film but a psychological film," and in fact it reveals to the viewer the psychological strain on generals, their debates, and arguments. It takes place largely in closed sets and by means of dialogue but it never seems theatrical. Views of the battle are infrequent, though one memorable sequence shows a soldier rejoining a cut telephone wire with his teeth. The German opponent is neither caricatured nor underestimated, especially when one compares the role with similar figures in contemporary Soviet and Hollywood films.
Neither Stalingrad nor the name of

Stalin himself are mentioned. This was not at the request of the Supreme Commander but at the request of those generals who had been involved in the actual battle.

This is one of Ermler's best films, but after its release in 1946 he became inactive for ten years, his various projects being neglected by the Minister of the Cinema. His first film after the minister left the scene in 1955 was *The Unfinished Story*.

VENT SOUFFLE OU IL VEUT (LE) UN CONDAMNÉ A MORT S'EST ÉCHAPPÉ

VERDUGO (EL) THE EXECUTIONER/THE HANGMAN/NOT ON YOUR LIFE Spain/Italy 1963. *Dir* Luis Garcia Berlanga *Scen* Luis Garcia Berlanga, Rafael Azcona, Ennio Flaiano *Photog* Tonino Delli Colli *Art Dir* José Antonio de la Guerra *Mus* Miguel A. Arbo *Ed* Alfonso Santacana *Cast* Nino Manfredi, José Isbert, Emma Penella *Prod* Naga/Zebra. 110 mins. English version, 91 mins.

José Luis (Manfredi), an undertaker's assistant is attracted to Carmen (Penella), the daughter of Amedeo (Isbert), the executioner. They decide to marry when Amedeo is allocated a new apartment, but later discover that they are only entitled to the apartment until Amedeo retires. When he does, José Luis is persuaded to become his successor. He is reluctant and plans to resign before his first job. He is called to an execution in Palma de Mallorca and, so they can have a holiday, Amedeo and Carmen convince José Luis to remain because they are sure the man will be reprieved. He is not and, half-fainting with terror, José Luis has to officiate.

This black comedy whose dominant symbol is the sight and sound of the executioner's garrotting equipment is also a tableau of life in modern Spain. It is full of that sharp and malicious humor that has made Berlanga one of the best Spanish directors.

VERITE (LA) THE TRUTH France 1960. *Dir* Henri-Georges Clouzot *Scen* H.-G. Clouzot, Jérôme Géronimi, Simone Drieu, Michèle Perrein, Vera Clouzot *Photog* Armand Thirard *Art Dir* Jean André *Mus* Beethoven, Stravinsky excerpts *Ed* Albert Jurgenson *Cast* Brigitte Bardot, Sami Frey, Marie-José Nat, Charles Vanel, Paul Meurisse *Prod* Iéna/CEIAP. 130 mins.

In a French criminal court during the trial of Dominique (Bardot) for the murder of her lover (Frey), the prosecutor (Meurisse) and defense advocate (Vanel) present different versions of the events. In flashbacks, Dominique's life story is shown from her arrival in Paris with her sister (Nat), her meeting her sister's boyfriend (Frey), and their stormy love affair. When he leaves her to return to the sister, she shoots him. In the court, the judges seem not to believe her version of the story and she commits suicide in her cell before the verdict is known.

A professionally made but glib film with a good dramatic performance by Brigitte Bardot.

*VERTIGO USA 1958. *Dir* Alfred Hitchcock *Scen* Alec Coppel, Samuel Taylor based on the novel *D'entre les morts* by Pierre Boileau, Thomas Narcejac *Photog* Robert Burks *Art Dir* Hal Pereira, Henry Bumstead *Mus* Bernard Herrmann *Ed* George Tomasini *Special Effects* John P. Fulton *Titles* Saul Bass *Cast* Kim Novak, James Stewart, Barbara Bel Geddes, Tom Helmore *Prod* Hitchcock Productions for Paramount. 128 mins. Technicolor. VistaVision.

Scottie Ferguson (Stewart) resigns from the police force when he discovers he suffers from vertigo. He is asked by an old college friend, Gavin (Helmore) to follow his wife, Madeleine (Novak). He does so and falls in love with her. The night they confess their love, Madeleine seems to throw herself to her death. Scottie has a nervous breakdown and months later meets a girl, Judy (Novak), who resembles Madeleine so much that he begins to fall in love with her. Meanwhile, it is shown in a flashback that Judy had posed as Madeleine as part of a plot to kill another woman. Scottie persuades Judy to dress in Madeleine's clothes and dye her black hair blond, but when she puts on a necklace Madeleine used to wear, Scottie begins to guess the truth. He confronts her in the tower from which "Madeleine" jumped and after a violent altercation, Judy accidentally falls to her death.

Based on a novel by Boileau and Narcejac (who also wrote the novel that became Clouzot's *Les Diaboliques*), this is certainly one of Hitchcock's most poetic films, a meditation on the destructive power of romantic illusion. The nightmarishly effective opening (with its simultaneous tracking in and zooming out) leads inevitably through the obsessional quality of Scottie's involvement with Madeleine/Judy to the emotional shocks of the ending. Some find the plot construction contains basic flaws, but whether they are rationalized or not in terms of the "thematic structure," they matter little in relation to Hitchcock's total control over spectator identification and involvement.

VESELY CIRKUS THE HAPPY CIRCUS Czechoslovakia 1951 *Dir/Scen* Jiri Trnka *Art Dir* Frantisek Tichy, Kamil Lhotak, Zdenek Seydl, Jiri Trnka *Mus* Vaclav Trojan, Jan Rychlik *Prod* Kratky Film. 12 mins. Agfacolor.
This gayly colored animated film uses paper cutouts, a forgotten technique that Trnka revived.

VESNOY SPRING/SPRINGTIME USSR 1929. *Dir/Scen/Photog/Ed* Mikhail Kaufman *Prod* VUFKU. 5,000 ft. approx.
Less of a traditional documentary than a "film poem," which, as Paul Rotha described it, "attempted to show the gradual transition from the Russian winter to the first signs of Spring: the awakening of new life. It was admirably photographed and well composed into a beautiful pattern of shots." This deeply moving film by the brother of Dziga Vertov is one of the masterpieces of the *kino-eye* group and exercised a strong influence on the British documentary movement.
— *Vesna/Spring* USSR 1947. *Dir* Grigori Alexandrov *Scen* Alexandrov, A. Raskin, M. Slobodskoy *Photog* Y. Yekelchik *Mus* Isaac Dunayevsky *Cast* L. Orlova, Nikolai Cherkassov, N. Konovalov. 90 mins.
One of several misguided attempts by Alexandrov to recapture his musical comedy successes of the Thirties, *Circus* (*q.v.*) and *Vesyolye Rebyata/Jazz Comedy* (*q.v.*). This one, a comedy with music and ballet, deals with the efforts of a Russian film director (Cherkassov) to make a biographical film about a famous scientist (Orlova) who hates films. It won an award at the Venice Festival.

VESYOLYE REBYATA JAZZ COMEDY/JOLLY FELLOWS/MOSCOW LAUGHS USSR 1934. *Dir* Grigori Alexandrov *Scen* Alexan-

drov, Nikolai Erdman, V. Mass *Photog* Vladimir Nilsen *Art Dir* Alexander Utkin *Mus* Isaac Dunayevsky *Cast* Lubov Orlova, Leonid Utyosov, Maria Strelkova, Yelena Tyapkina *Prod* Mosfilm. 93 mins.
A shepherd (Utyosov) from the Crimea is mistaken by an ambitious female opera singer (Orlova) for a famous conductor and is entertained at her home. He brings his flocks with him and the sheep, pigs, and goats turn the house upside down. In Moscow, he is again mistaken for the conductor and has to conduct for him in his place. He eventually reaches fame as the leader of a jazz band.
Famous sequences: the orchestra rehearsing behind a hearse; the ridiculous sunbathers on a beach; the animals carried away by the jazz music and "dancing" like people.
A musical comedy, gay and lively, with many gags inspired by cartoons and American slapstick and with appealing music by Dunayevsky (though its best tune is a Mexican song intended for use in *Que Viva Mexico!*). It was a considerable international success.

VIAGGIO IN ITALIA THE LONELY WOMAN/ JOURNEY TO ITALY/VOYAGE TO ITALY/ STRANGERS Italy/France 1953. *Dir* Roberto Rossellini *Scen* Roberto Rossellini, Vitaliano Brancati *Photog* Enzo Serafin *Art Dir* Piero Filippone *Mus* Renzo Rossellini *Ed* Jolanda Benvenuti *Cast* Ingrid Bergman, George Sanders, Paul Muller, Maria Mauban, Anna Proclemer. 105 mins. General foreign release, 70 mins.
Alex (Sanders), a rich English businessman, and his wife, Isabelle (Bergman), take their first trip together since their honeymoon when they travel to Italy to sell a piece of property. They have grown bored with each other. Though Isabelle finds Naples and its people exciting, Alex feels alienated from his strange environment and goes to Capri. When he returns, they go together to Pompeii and reach a point at which they agree on a divorce. But next day, caught up in a religious festival and a warm, noisy crowd, they realize the emptiness of the life ahead of them if they separate.
Rossellini says this "is a film that I like very much. It was very important for me to show Italy, Naples, that strange atmosphere in which is found a very real, very immediate, very profound feeling: the feeling of eternal life, something that has

entirely disappeared from the world."
Viaggio in Italia is something of a private
diary, a meditation on the problem of
lack of communication in a couple who
know each other too well, comparable
in theme to Bergman's *Törst* (*q.v.*).
Rossellini's style is built on an accumulation of small details without any apparent
relationship, a use of landscape in which
well known touristic vistas suddenly become entirely strange. Though some prefer *Europe 51* (*q.v.*) to this film in
Rossellini's "Bergman period," it was profoundly admired by the young critics of
Cahiers du Cinéma and influenced many
new wave directors.

VIDAS SECAS DROUGHT/BARREN LIVES Brazil 1963. *Dir* Nelson Pereira dos Santos
Scen Nelson Pereira dos Santos based on
the novel by Graciliano Ramos *Photog*
Luis Carlos Barreto, José Roza *Ed* Rafael
Justo *Cast* Atila Iorio, Maria Ribeiro,
Orlando Macedo, Jofre Soares. 105 mins.
In barren Northeast Brazil, the story of
the life and struggles of a peasant family.
This dramatization of the realities of Brazil, direct in style and restrained in its
portrayal of violence, is one of the best
films from the *cinema novo* group of
which Pereira dos Santos is in some ways
the founder.

VIE (UNE) UNE VIE

VIE EST A NOUS (LA) France 1936. *Dir/
Scen* Jean Renoir assisted by Jacques
Becker, Jean-Paul Le Chanois, Jacques
Brunius, Henri Cartier-Bresson, Maurice
Lime, Pierre Unik, A. Zwoboda *Photog*
Jean Bourgoin, Claude Renoir, Alain
Douarinou, Jean Isnard *Mus* songs of the
Front Populaire *Ed* Marguerite Renoir
Cast Julian Bertheau, Madeleine Sologne,
Jean Dasté, Marcel Duhamel, Gaston
Modot, Charles Blavette, Sylvain Itkine,
Nadia Sibirskaia, Roger Blin, Max Dal-
ban, Jacques Becker, Fabien Lorris, J.-P.
Le Chanois, J.-B. Brunius, Emile Drain,
O'Brady, Jean Renoir, Yolande Oliveiro
Prod French Communist Party. 66 min.
Re-released 1969.
This is a cooperative production made in
early 1936 as part of the electoral propa-
ganda of the French Communist Party. A
blend of newsreels and staged scenes, it is
the first militant left-wing film made in
France and was thought to have been lost
until a copy was discovered in 1969. It
is unarguably a brilliant work of art,

stylistically characteristic of Renoir during his best period.
Main sequences: the beauty and richness
of France; a teacher (Dasté) telling his
pupils about unemployment; the portraits
of the 200 patrician families said to rule
France; the chairman (Brunius) of a
board of directors discussing excess production and the reduction of staff; a
demonstration by Croix de Feu (French
fascists) on the 6, 9, and 12 of February
1934 (newsreels); a newspaper vendor
selling *L'Humanité* beaten up by fascists;
in the newspaper's office Marcel Cachin
reads three letters: 1 — in a factory, a
worker (Sologne) is at odds with the
foreman who opposes a victorious strike;
2 — in a village, a bailiff (Drain) tries to
seize the furniture and livestock of a
farm but, led by a communist (Modot),
is driven off by the peasants; 3 — an intellectual, unemployed man (Bertheau)
leaves his girl friend (Sibirskaia), almost
joins the Croix de Feu, and is welcomed
by the Young Communists. The film ends
with several speeches by communist leaders (Thorez, Duclos etc.) that lead into
a lyrical poem to the unity of the people
as the "Internationale" is heard on the
sound track.
In order to satirize Colonel de la Rocque,
Renoir devised trick photography of
newsreels that makes the fascist leader
appear to be dancing. More than in his
earlier films, Renoir employs deep-focus
photography for dramatic purposes, using
it with particular success in the episode
about the unemployed man (written by
Pierre Unik) and in that of the peasant.
[Ivor Montagu's ironical film for the British Communist Party (*Peace and Plenty*
Britain 1939, 18 mins.) seems to have
derived much inspiration in its approach
from Renoir's film.]

VILLA! see VIVA VILLA!

VILLAGE FAIR (THE) JOUR DE FÊTE

VILLAGE SCHOOLTEACHER (A) SELSKAYA
UCHITELNITSA

VIRGEN DE LA CARIDAD (LA) VIRGIN OF
CHARITY Cuba 1930. *Dir* Ramón Peón
Scen Ernesto Caparrós *Photog* Ricardo
Delgado *Cast* Diana V. Marde, Miguel de
Santos *Prod* B.P.P. Pictures. Silent.
Despite a melodramatic plot, this film's
use of natural sets and its portrait of
social types make it one of the first films

of quality from the rather unenterprising Cuban film industry of the time.

VIRGIN OF CHARITY VIRGEN DE LA CARIDAD

VIRGIN SPRING (THE) JUNGFRUKÄLLEN

VIRIDIANA Spain/Mexico 1961. *Dir* Luis Buñuel, *Scen* Luis Buñuel, Julio Alejandro *Photog* José Aguayo *Air Dir* Francisco Canet *Mus* Handel *Ed* Pedro del Rey *Cast* Silvia Pinal, Francisco Rabal, Fernando Rey, Margarita Lozano, Teresa Rabal, Victoria Zinny *Prod* Gustavo Alatriste/Uninci Films 59. 90 mins.

Viridiana (Pinal), about to take religious vows, returns to visit her uncle, Don Jaime (Rey), who is struck by her resemblance to his wife, who died on their wedding night. He persuades Romano (Lozano), the servant, to drug her, intending to seduce her. However, he is inhibited and cannot do it. But the next morning, in an effort to get her to stay with him, he tells her he did seduce her and then hangs himself. Viridiana now seems bound to the estate, which she shares with Don Jaime's illegitimate son, Jorge (Rabal). Viridiana invites a band of beggars to live in the estate's abandoned workers' houses, hoping to reclaim them through prayer. One day when Jorge and Viridiana are away, the beggars take over the house and have an orgy. When they return, one of the beggars rapes Viridiana. Disillusioned, Viridiana later joins Jorge and his new mistress, Ramona, in a game of cards.

Famous sequences: Don Jaime meeting his niece in religious garb in the convent; the arrival at the estate with its enormous villa, antiquated furnishings, and almost deserted fields; Viridiana, who peels apples with a crucifix-knife and carries religious appurtenances in a suitcase, agreeing to wear the wedding dress of her dead aunt; the drugged Viridiana laid out on the bed by her uncle who begins to undress her, then stops; next morning, after he lies to her, Viridiana leaves, but is stopped at the bus by the news that her uncle has hanged himself with a jump rope; Viridiana collecting the outcasts of the world, an ugly leper, a blind beggar, a dwarf woman, etc.; the cousin buying a dog made to trot along under a cart, then seeing another dog tied up in the same way a few seconds later; the orgy in the villa, the table covered with food and drink, the slaughtered sheep, the leper dressed as a bride, the beggars suddenly frozen in a reproduction of Leonardo da Vinci's "Last Supper" before a beggar woman, who raises her skirt to "photograph" them; the return of Viridiana and her cousin, who is knocked out while she is tied up and eventually forced by the leper to "acquiesce" in the rape (these scenes are set to Handel's "Hallelujah Chorus," which is blaring from a phonograph); the final scene, which suggests that Viridiana has acquired a new awareness of herself and is settling for a ménage-à-trois with her cousin and the servant.

[*Viridiana* was shot in Spain from a script approved by the Spanish authorities. After production was completed, the authorities became aware of its "subversive" implications and attempted to seize all copies. But a few had already left for France and, despite strenuous protests by the Spanish government, it was the official Spanish entry at the Cannes Festival in 1961 where it won the Palme d'or. The film was immediately denounced by *l'Osservatore Romano,* the official Vatican organ, and by Catholic organizations as an insult to Christianity. In Spain, the head of the state film organization was dismissed, the film was banned, and the press was not even allowed to report that Buñuel's film had received an award. It was distributed internationally by the Mexican co-producer.]

Viridiana, like the priest in *Nazarin* (*q.v.*), is a "saint" whose virtues lead to terrible misfortunes, not only for her but for others. *Viridiana,* the only fiction film Buñuel has made in his natal Spain, is profoundly Spanish in feeling. Though it certainly includes pictorial influences, especially that of Goya, it is even more derived from novelists like Benito Perez Galdos and Ramon del Valle-Inclan, who at the turn of the century wrote social portraits of the decadence, bigotry, and spitefulness of provincial Spanish "high society." That society has not changed since its privileges were confirmed by Franco.

VIRTUOUS BIGAMIST (THE) see QUATTRO PASSI FRA LE NUVOLE

VISITEURS DU SOIR (LES) THE DEVIL'S ENVOYS France 1942. *Dir* Marcel Carné *Scen* Jacques Prévert, Pierre Laroche *Photog* Roger Hubert *Art Dir* Alexandre Trauner, Georges Wakhevitch *Mus* Joseph Kosma, Maurice Thiriet *Ed* Henri Rust *Cast* Arletty, Jules Berry, Marie Déa, Fernand Ledoux, Alain Cuny, Marcel Herrand, Gabriel Gabrio *Prod* André Paulvé. 110 mins.

In the Middle Ages, the Devil (Berry) sends two envoys, Gilles (Cuny) and Dominique (Arletty), who were selfish lovers on earth, to a chateau to intervene in the betrothal between the count (Ledoux) and Lady Anne (Déa). Disguised as minstrels, the two cast a spell and use their charms to seduce the couple. Since Anne and the count were not truly in love, their betrothal is destroyed, but Gilles finds true love in his seduction of Anne. The Devil himself arrives and sets everyone at odds while Dominique engages the attention of Anne's pious father, who finally relinquishes everything and follows her to his doom. The Devil cannot destroy the true love of Gilles and Anne. In the end he turns them into stone, though he cannot stop their hearts from beating.

In this adaptation of a 15th century legend, Jacques Prévert intended the Devil (earthily played by Jules Berry) to represent Hitler and hoped to present the story as a fantasy in modern dress. However, the existence of the Nazi censors necessitated setting the story in the past and the rather buried allusions to modern times were lost on even the most aware spectators.

Though neither the theme nor the actors are convincing and the sense of fantasy is rather forced, it has some exquisite compositions and portraits of a medieval court. Especially notable are the ride through the stony landscape, the arrival at the white chateau, the buffoons and jesters performing during a banquet, and the dancers suddenly frozen in mid-step during a ball. The images and sets often have the charm of medieval miniatures. *Les Visiteurs du soir* was a considerable success in France and after 1945 was also successful abroad, helping to pave the way for the success of such other period films as *L'Eternel retour* (*q.v.*) and *Les Enfants du paradis* (*q.v.*)

VITELLONI (I) THE DRONES/THE SPIVS/THE YOUNG AND THE PASSIONATE Italy/France 1953. *Dir* Federico Fellini *Scen* Federico Fellini, Ennio Flaiano, Tullio Pinelli *Photog* Otello Martelli, Luciano Trasatti, Carlo Carlini *Art Dir* Mario Chiari *Mus* Nino Rota *Ed* Rolando Benedetti *Cast* Franco Interlenghi, Alberto Sordi, Franco Fabrizi, Eleonora Ruffo, Leopoldo Trieste, Riccardo Fellini, Lida Baarowa, Arlette Sauvage, Jean Brochard. 109 mins.

This is the story of the "vitelloni," five well-fed but rootless and directionless not-so-young men, the sons of middle-class families in a town on the Adriatic. Fausto (Fabrizi), the leader of the group, forced by his father (Brochard) to marry Sandra (Ruffo), who is pregnant, takes a job in an antique shop but continues to seek romantic conquests and is left by his wife. Alberto (Sordi) is a sentimental baby trapped in his childhood, who dresses up as a woman during the fête. Leopoldo (Trieste) is an intellectual writer who seeks fame and finds consolation in an affair with a chambermaid. Moraldo (Interlenghi), the youngest, and some would say the sanest, of the group, rebels against his family and the stagnant culture of the town and leaves. It has been suggested he leaves for Rome and becomes the journalist in *La Dolce Vita* (*q.v.*)

Fellini has described his characters: "They shine during the holiday season and waiting for this takes up the rest of the year. They are the unemployed of the middle-class, mothers' pets. But they are also friends to whom I wish well. Flaiano, Pinelli, and I started to talk and, having all been ex-vitelloni, found we had a host of stories to tell. After all the funny stories, we finally became greatly depressed and we made a film." Fellini drew on his own memories of life in Rimini. However, the plot of *I Vitelloni* is far less important than its characters, the sense of environment, and the various episodes in their lives: the boredom in the small town, the chit-chat, the familiar jokes, the sordid romantic adventures, the long arguments at night in the deserted streets, the depressing absurdities of the feast days and the nostalgic walks along the empty beach in winter. *I Vitelloni*, one of Fellini's best films, is still neorealist in approach. It was a considerable critical and commercial success and established Fellini's international reputation.

VIVA VILLA! USA 1934. *Dir* Jack Conway (and Howard Hawks, uncredited) *Scen* Ben Hecht (and Howard Hawks, uncredited) based on the book by Edgcumb Pinchon, O. B. Stade *Photog* James Wong Howe, Charles Clarke *Art Dir* Edwin B.

Willis *Mus* Juan Aguilar *Ed* Robert J. Kern *Montage Effects* Slavko Vorkapich *Cast* Wallace Beery, Fay Wray, Leo Carrillo, Donald Cook, Stuart Erwin, George E. Stone, Joseph Schildkraut, Henry B. Walthall, Katherine De Mille, *Prod* MGM. 115 mins.

At the time of the 1890 Diaz decree expropriating communal village lands, Francisco (Pancho) Villa avenges the murder of his father and takes to the hills. In 1910, Villa (Beery) has married Rosita (DeMille) and become leader of one of the peasant armies supporting Madero (Walthall). In a fight he revenges himself on a treacherous general (Schildkraut), refuses the presidency, retires to his hacienda, and is assassinated by an old friend (Cook).

[*Viva Villa!* was begun on location in Mexico with Howard Hawks as director and co-scriptwriter with Ben Hecht. However, Louis B. Mayer interfered with the production and Hawks was replaced by Jack Conway, who completed the film. It is generally agreed that Hawks directed about half the finished film, mainly the exteriors, with Conway handling the interiors. It is impossible, however, to separate Hawks's footage from Conway's and ultimate credit for the film must rest with Conway.]

In its many epic scenes, *Viva Villa!* conveys the violent spirit of the Mexican Revolution, which was then quite recent. In any case, it is far superior to *Viva Zapata!* (*q.v.*). However Beery's crude and sometimes hysterical performance as Villa characterizes him as a simpleminded glutton. The American journalist (Erwin) who follows Villa around like a diarist could have been (historically) the famous John Reed, who was a witness of the Mexican Revolution. Contrary to rumor, no shots from Eisenstein's *Que Viva Mexico!* (*q.v.*) are included in the film, though parts of it were shot at the hacienda Eisenstein had used for the "Maguey" episode in that film.

— **Villa!* USA 1958. *Dir* James B. Clarke *Scen* Louis Vittes *Photog* Alex Phillips *Cast* Brian Keith, Cesare Romero, Margia Dean *Prod* 20th Century-Fox. 72 mins. Eastman Color. CinemaScope.

Another far less interesting version of the same story, with Cesare Romero as Villa and Brian Keith as the American journalist.

VIVA ZAPATA! USA 1952. *Dir* Elia Kazan *Scen* John Steinbeck *Photog* Joe Mac-Donald *Art Dir* Lyle Wheeler, Leland Fuller *Mus* Alex North *Ed* Barbara McLean *Cast* Marlon Brando, Anthony Quinn, Jean Peters, Joseph Wiseman, Frank Silvera, Alan Reed, Harold Gordon *Prod* 20th Century-Fox. 113 mins.

In 1909, the Mexican Revolutionary leader, Emilio Zapata (Brando), joins in the overthrow of the dictator, Porfirio Diaz, marries the daughter (Peters) of a rich landowner, supports President Madero (Gordon), accepts his order to disarm the peasants, and, with Pancho Villa (Reed), revenges himself on Madero's assassin by putting into flight the ambitious General Huerta (Silvera). He is appointed to the presidency. "Some peasants come to complain to him about taxes imposed by his brother (Quinn). He marks them down as dangerous elements. He then recognizes that he is going to commit the same injustices as his predecessor, Porfirio Diaz. He resigns and is killed in an ambush he had foreseen" (C. B., *Index de la Cinémato,* 1953).

Kazan's style, though calculated, cold, and a little declamatory, is often very effective, reminiscent especially of Eisenstein. But, as René Guyonnet pointed out, "*Viva Zapata!* attempts to show that all revolutions are destined to fail, that power inevitably corrupts the leaders, that a Zapata is inescapably driven to speak to the humble like a Porfirio Diaz, in brief, that there is no other end for the good (Madero) and the pure (Zapata) but martyrdom. Coming from men like Steinbeck and Kazan, such a film becomes a saddening attempt at self-justification."

VIVRE SA VIE IT'S MY LIFE/MY LIFE TO LIVE France 1962. *Dir/Scen* Jean-Luc Godard *Photog* Raoul Coutard *Mus* Michel Legrand *Ed* Agnès Guillemot, Lila Lakshmanan *Cast* Anna Karina, Sady Rebbot, Brice Parain, André-S. Labarthe, Guylaine Schlumberger, Gérard Hoffmann, Paul Pavel, Eric Schlumberger *Prod* Films de la Pléiade. 85 mins.

[A film in 12 episodes: Nana (Karina), a salesgirl in a record shop, can't pay her rent and is evicted by her landlady. She becomes a prostitute and meets a pimp (Rebbot) who takes her under his protection. She meets a philosopher (Parain) and a man (Eric Schlumberger) who apparently loves her. Her pimp tries to sell her to another pimp (Hoffmann) and she is shot down in the street.

Jean-Luc Godard described his heroine in his script: "The few episodes in her life that I am going to film are very likely of little interest to others but most important to Nana S. Indeed Nana, like the song in Max Ophüls' *Lola Montès* (*q.v.*), is gracious . . . and will be able to safeguard her soul while selling her body. In other words (it) will prove Montaigne's saying that you have to give yourself to others and not only to yourself." And, later, in an interview, he characterized the film as "really a collection of shots placed side by side, each of which should be self-sufficient . . . *Vivre sa vie* is a very realistic film and at the same time unrealistic. It is very schematic: a few bold lines, a few fundamental principles. I was thinking, in a way, as a painter, of confronting my characters head on as in the paintings of Matisse or Braque, so the camera is always upright."

Vivre sa vie is one of the most beautiful, touching, and original films by Godard, an extremely complex blend of social document, theatricality, and interior drama in the Bresson manner. As Susan Sontag wrote: "It triumphs because it is intelligent, discreet, delicate to the touch. It builds edifies and gives pleasure because it is about what is most important . . . the nature of our humanity."]

VOINA I MIR WAR AND PEACE USSR 1967 (production began 1963). *Dir* Sergei Bondarchuk *Scen* Sergei Bondarchuk, Vasili Solovyov based on the novel by Leo Tolstoy *Photog* Anatoli Petrinsky *Art Dir* Mikhail Bogdanov, Gennady Myasnikov *Mus* Vyacheslav Ovchinnikov *Ed* Tatiana Likhacheva *Special Effects* Alexander Shelenkov, Chen Yu-Lan *Cast* Lyudmila Savelyeva, (Natasha) Sergei Bondarchuk (Bezukov) Vyacheslav Tikhonov (Prince Andrei) Anastasia Vertinskaya, Vasili Lanovoi, Viktor Stanitsin, Oleg Tabakov *Prod* Mosfilm. In four parts, 507 mins. 70 mm. Sovcolor. English language version (*Adaptation* Lee Kressel *Ed* Sidney Katz *Commentary* Andrew Witwer spoken by Norman Rose), in two parts, 357 mins.

Sergei Bondarchuk said, "We wanted to neither invent nor add anything. Tolstoy is the author of the film." And indeed his film is more faithful to the novel than Vidor's *War and Peace* (*q.v.*). Almost five years in production at a cost of forty million dollars, it was originally released in four parts running eight and a half hours. The dubbed version in two parts runs approximately six hours. More than in the sheer scale of its battle scenes, its merit lies in its sense of the Russian landscape — its plains, rivers, and forests. [Though perhaps an impressive example of film-making on a large scale, Bondarchuk's film is ponderous by any standards, a tediously faithful rendition of the book, with none of Tolstoy's narrative flair or spirit of the novel. The occasional bravura or touching episodes are not adequate compensations for the dogged pedantry of the whole — in neither the original nor the English versions].

OTHER RUSSIAN VERSIONS:

— *Voina i mir* USSR 1915. *Dir/Scen* Vladimir Gardin, Yakov Protazanov *Photog* Alexander Levitsky *Cast* Olga Preobrazhenskaya (Natasha), N. Nikolsky, V. Vasiliev, V. Gardin (Napoleon). 10 reels in two series.

— *Natasha Rostova* USSR 1915. *Dir* Pyotr Chardynin *Cast* Vera Coralli, Vitold Polonsky, Ivan Mozhukhin (Mosjoukine). 1,600 meters.

— *Voina i Mir* USSR 1915. *Dir* Anatoli Kamensky. 1,200 meters.

For other versions, see *War and Peace*

VOYAGE A TRAVERS L'IMPOSSIBLE (LE) AN IMPOSSIBLE VOYAGE/VOYAGE ACROSS THE IMPOSSIBLE France 1904. *Dir/Scen* Georges Méliès *Prod* Star Film. 380 meters. (1,233 ft.) Also released with a variant in the ending. 1,414 ft. Color.

A group of scientists from the *Institut de géographie incohérente* invent an "automaboulof" (a kind of high speed train) that takes off from the summit of a Swiss mountain and travels through space. They reach the sun, float back to earth, fall into the ocean, and arrive back safely on dry land.

In some ways this is a new version of *Voyage dans la lune* (*q.v.*), but more comical and more developed in its tricks. It should be noted that the editing is not in sequence. When the "automaboulof" hits the inn at Righi, the wall is shown being hit, then the diners in the inn are shown still undisturbed, followed by the surprise entry of the vehicle.

VOYAGE DANS LA LUNE (LE) A TRIP TO THE MOON France 1902. *Dir/Scen* Georges Méliès *Photog* Michaut *Art Dir* Claudel, Georges Méliès *Costumes* Mme. Georges Méliès *Cast* Georges Méliès, Victor André, Depierre, Farjaux, Kelm, Brunet,

Bleuette Bernon, dancers and acrobats from the Folies-Bergère *Prod* Star Film. 280 meters. (845 ft.)

Produced in May 1902; placed on sale in August, 1902. Production cost 10,000 gold francs.

Summary of the 30 tableaux: 1. Congress of the astronomy club. 2. The plans for the trip explained. 3. The enormous factory; construction of the projectile. 4. Casting of the cannon. 5. The scientists embark. 6. Loading the cannon. 7. The cannon fires. 8. The moon gets nearer. 9. The rocket falls into the moon's eye. 10. The rocket on the moon; earth light. 11. The plain covered with craters. 12. The dream of "stars." 13. The snowstorm; first sight of the Selenites (acrobats from the Folies-Bergère). 14. Descent into a crater. 15. The grotto with giant mushrooms. 16. The fight with the Selenites. 17. Taken prisoner. 18. The king of the moon. 19. The escape. 20. The pursuit. 21. The departure in the rocket. 22. The rocket falling vertically. 23. The rocket falls into the ocean. 24. Submerged. 25. The return to land. 26. Celebrations. 27. Decoration of the heroes. 28. March past. 29. The erection of a commemorative statue. 30. The exhibition of the Selenite.

Famous sequences: the firing of the projectile after a display by a chorus of pretty girls; approaching the moon's face and the rocket hitting the moon squarely in the eye; the explorers escaping from the Selenites followed by the rocket falling off the edge of the moon. This was not Méliès' first "long" (1 reel) film, but it was the film that brought him universal fame. Méliès has described how itinerant showmen, his main outlet in France, said the film was too long and therefore too expensive. He agreed to loan it for nothing and it was shown at a fair: more probably in the Invalides than in the Place du Trône. At first the public hesitated at the door of the booth, muttering that it must be a trick since no one had ever been to the moon and therefore it couldn't have been filmed. But the first spectators were so amused that word of mouth quickly attracted large crowds and the news of its success led to the sale of dozens of copies among other showmen. Printing material for the film was sent to the USA and Méliès later established a branch office of his "Star Films" there.

A Trip to the Moon is of considerable significance in the history of the cinema. Its success laid the foundations for the international preeminence of French films until the First World War. More than this, it established the appeal of films with "staged" scenes over the everyday incidents, rudimentary documentaries, and outdoor scenes that had dominated film production since the days of Louis Lumière.

VOYAGE SURPRISE France 1946. (released 1947). *Dir* Pierre Prévert, assisted by Lou Bonin *Scen* Pierre Prévert, Jacques Prévert, Claude Accursi based on *Paris, Paris,* an operetta by Diamant-Berger, Jean Nohain, Mireille *Photog* Jean Bourgoin *Art Dir* Alexandre Trauner, assisted by Auguste Capelier *Mus* Joseph Kosma *Ed* Jacques Desagneaux *Cast* Martine Carole, Sinoël, Maurice Baquet, Jacques-Henri Duval, Annette Poivre, Thérèse Dorny *Prod* Pathé. 108 mins. (85 mins. original release) Re-released 1968.

In order to win customers from his more up-to-date rival, Grandpa (Sinoël) organizes a "mystery tour" for his coach and sells all his furniture to finance the scheme. He is joined by two revolutionaries from "Stromboli" (Baquet, Duval) who have hidden the crown jewels in the coach toolbox. Grandpa's daughter, Isabelle (Carole), joins the tour, which is pursued by two detectives who are convinced the coach is carrying a gang of terrorists. After many misadventures, the coach returns and Grandpa is appointed head of the Strombolian tourist service. René Clair had originally hoped to film the original operetta before the war. In Prévert's version the original plot is barely followed. This nonsense comedy about a slapstick chase across the beautiful landscape of Haute-Provence has numerous, typically Prévertian, poetic gags, often eccentric and sometimes tinged with sadness. It was a commercial failure, unfortunately, especially since the Prévert brothers could have possibly regenerated French comedy after the war.

VOYAGE TO ITALY VIAGGIO IN ITALIA

VOZVRASHCHENIE VASILIYA BORTNIKOVA THE RETURN OF VASILI BORTNIKOV/VASILI BORTNIKOV'S RETURN/THE HARVEST USSR 1953. *Dir* V. I. Pudovkin *Scen* Galina

Nikolayeva, Yevgeni Gabrilovich based on the novel *Harvest* by Galina Nikolayeva *Photog* Sergei Urusevsky *Art Dir* A. Freidin, B. Chebotaryov *Mus* K. Molchanov *Cast* S. Lukyanov, N. Medvedeva, N. Timofeyev, I. Makarova, K. Luchko *Prod* Mosfilm. 110 mins. Agfacolor.

Vasili (Lukyanov), who was believed to have died during the war, returns five years later to discover his wife (Medvedeva), has married another man (Timofeyev). He joins their communal life, but his authoritarian attitude, both at home and in the collective farm, leads to a quarrel and separation. However, Vasili is eventually reconciled.

Remarkable sequences: the return of the husband; the changing life during the four seasons; the storm during the harvest.

Pudovkin's best sound film (and his last film before his death in 1953), while not matching his silent masterpieces, has something of their lyrical beauty, character portrayal, and social attitude. Since this film was made during the most difficult period of the Stalinist cinema, Pudovkin showed considerable daring in the way he handled its theme, ending the film, for example, not with collectivization but on a note of love.

VREDENS DAG DAY OF WRATH/DIES IRAE Denmark 1943. *Dir* Carl Theodor Dreyer *Scen* Carl Theodor Dreyer, Poul Knudsen, Mogens Skot-Hansen based on the play *Anne Pedersdotter* by Wiers Jensen *Photog* Carl Andersson *Art Dir* Erik Aaes, Lis Fribert *Mus* Poul Schierbeck *Cast* Thorkild Roose, Lisbeth Movin, Sigrid Neiiendam, Preben Lerdoff, Anna Svierkier *Prod* Palladium. 105 mins.

In a Danish village in 1623, an old peasant woman, Marthe (Svierkier). is accused of witchcraft and the elderly Pastor Absolon (Roose) — who had earlier spared the mother of his young wife, Anne (Movin), when she was accused — sits in judgment. She is tortured and finally burned at the stake as she hurls a curse at the pastor. Meanwhile, Martin (Lerdoff), the pastor's son by a former marriage, has returned from the seas; he and Anne are attracted to each other and fall in love. Anne begins to defy her mother-in-law (Neiiendam), who hates her, while the pastor is haunted by the memory of what he had done to the old woman. He tells Anne he wronged her by marrying her and she

tells him of her love for Martin and that she wishes him dead. He suffers a stroke and dies. At the funeral, the mother-in-law accuses Anne of witchcraft and, deserted by Martin, she finds she cannot take the oath and swear she did not kill her husband through witchcraft.

Dreyer began production of this film in 1942 and it was premiered on November 13, 1943 during the blackest period of the Nazi occupation in Denmark. The sequence near the beginning, showing Marthe's arrest in the pastor's house, the preparations for the execution, and the burning itself as the choir sings "Herlof's Marthe was safely burnt to the Glory of God," is especially striking. The ending, however, with Anne seemingly convinced of her own evil, is ambiguous. As André Bazin put it: "The despair at the end could as well indicate confession as a lie." However, it seems that Dreyer *believed* in witchcraft as he did in vampires in *Vampyr* (*q.v.*) and in the resurrection of the dead in *Ordet* (*q.v.*).

Day of Wrath has great atmospheric intensity, visual beauty, and, in some scenes, a sense of nature. And not least, it has a sense of anguish, brilliantly mirrored in Lisbeth Movin's tormented face.

VSTRECHNYI COUNTERPLAN USSR 1932. *Dir* Friedrich Ermler, Sergei Yutkevich *Scen* Leo Arnstam, D. Dell (Leonid Lyubashevsky), Ermler, Yutkevich *Co-Dir* Leo Arnstam *Assist* Boris Poslavsky, G. Kazansky, Victor Eisimont *Photog* Wulf Rappaport, I. Martov, Alexander Ginsburg *Art Dir* Boris Dubrovsky-Eshke, N. Pavlov, A. Ushin, *Mus* Dmitri Shostakovich *Cast* Vladimir Gardin, Boris Poslavsky, Maria Blumenthal-Tamarina, T. Guretskaya, Andrei Abrikosov, Boris Tenin *Prod* Rosfilm (Leningrad). 116 mins.

A story of the rivalries in a Leningrad factory where a turbine is being built: Babchenko (Gardin), an old foreman, and his friends in the machine shop are opposed by an engineer (Poslavsky) who wants to wreck the production plans. The combined forces of the workers defeat the engineer.

One of the best of the early Soviet sound films about the problems of modern life and the Five Year Plan, with a brilliant performance by the experienced stage actor, Vladimir Gardin. Both Ermler and Yutkevich were at this time part of the "Leningrad school," which was more interested in social psychology than in "heroic" themes. The theme song by Shostakovich was adopted as the United Nations hymn in 1945.

VYBORG SIDE (THE) see YUNOST MAKSIMA

VYNALEZ ZKAZY AN INVENTION FOR (OF) DESTRUCTION/THE FABULOUS WORLD OF JULES VERNE Czechoslovakia 1957. *Dir/Art Dir* Karel Zeman *Scen* Frantisek Hrubin, Karel Zeman based on *Face au drapeau* by Jules Verne *Photog* Jiri Tarantik *Mus* Zdenek Liska *Models* Zdenek Rozkopal *Cast* Arnest Navratil, Lubor Tokas, Jana Zaklouvova, 83 mins. (US version *Mus* Sidney Fox, 95 mins.). A scientist, Professor Roch (Navratil), is seized by adventurers who intend to dominate the world with his invention of a terrible explosive. An engineer (Tokas) rescues him and the scientist destroys his invention.

"I used ideas from different novels by Jules Verne," Karel Zeman said. "My film reaches the imagination through the engravings of Benett and Riou who illustrated the novels during his lifetime. In some scenes cartoons and puppets are used alongside live actors. I have stylized even the smallest details." Zeman's trick photography, which brings to life 19th century wood engravings and has the actors playing their roles among typical Jules Verne inventions — strange flying machines and Victorian-looking submarines — also gives the modern cinema a touch of the ingenuous Méliès tradition.

WACHSFIGURENKABINETT (DAS) WAXWORKS/
THREE WAX MEN Germany 1924. *Dir*
Paul Leni *Scen* Henrik Galeen *Photog*
Helmar Lerski *Art Dir* Paul Leni, Ernst
Stern, Alfred Jünge *Cast* William Dieterle, Emil Jannings, Conrad Veidt,
Werner Krauss, Olga Belajeff, John
Gottowt, Georg John *Prod* Neptun-Film.
5,600 ft.
A young poet (Dieterle) visits a waxworks booth in a fair and concocts
stories about three of the figures: Haroun
al Raschid (Jannings) and his tyrannical
rule; Ivan the Terrible (Veidt) and his
insatiable lusts and terrible cruelties,
especially when he makes a bride his
mistress for a night. He is finally driven
mad by a vengeful conspirator. The final
episode is in the form of a dream inter-
linking the poet, the daughter (Belajeff)
of the fairground showman, and Jack the
Ripper (Krauss), who pursues them relentlessly through the fairground.
Directed and designed by Paul Leni,
Waxworks is something of the swan
song of expressionism in its attempt to
create a fantastic atmosphere through
curiously deformed sets and ingenious
lighting effects. The best episode is the
short sequence of Jack the Ripper, nightmarishly effective in its construction and
visual effects. The gay burlesque of the
Arabian nights episode sits uncomfort-
ably next to these horrors. William
Dieterle, who plays the poet, later became a director himself.

WAGES OF FEAR (THE) SALAIRE DE LA PEUR
(LE)

WAHSH (EL) THE MONSTER Egypt 1954.
Dir Salah Abu Saif *Scen* Naguib Mah-
fouz, Salah Abu Saif, El Said Bedair
Cast Anwar Wagdi, Samia Gamal,
Mahmud el Moligui. 90 mins. approx.
A social thriller based on an authentic

police case about police pursuit of a
drug-addicted gangster (Wagdi). It is
filmed in a quasi-documentary style and
portrays, in the background, life in the
Egyptian countryside.

WAITER (THE) CAUGHT IN A CABARET

WALK IN THE SUN (A) SALERNO BEACHHEAD
USA 1945. *Dir* Lewis Milestone *Scen*
Robert Rossen based on the novel by
Harry Brown *Photog* Russell Harlan *Art
Dir* Max Bertisch *Mus* Fredric Efrem
Rich *Ed* Duncan Mansfield *Cast* Dana
Andrews, Richard Conte, John Ireland,
George Tyne, Herbert Rudley, Lloyd
Bridges, Sterling Holloway, Huntz Hall
Prod Lewis Milestone Productions. 116
mins.
A platoon of American soldiers lands
with other American forces at Salerno in
1943 and is ordered to capture a farmhouse six miles from the beach. The
platoon's lieutenant is killed during the
landing, a sergeant (Bridges) going for
further orders is also killed, and a second
sergeant (Rudley) collapses into hysteria.
Sergeant Tyne (Andrews) takes over and
finally takes the farmhouse after heavy
losses.
This remarkable film (originally made
for 20th Century-Fox but subsequently
repudiated by them) is a portrait of war
as it is seen by those fighting it; as one of
the film's ballads puts it, it is the story
of some men who "came across the sea
to sunny Italy, and took a little walk in
the sun." Because of its semidocumentary
style, even the well-known actors cease to
be "stars" and become individuals. Undoubtedly the best American film on the
last war, directed by the same man who
made *All Quiet On the Western Front*
(*q.v.*).

WANTON COUNTESS (THE) SENSO

WAR AND PEACE Italy/USA 1955. *Dir* King Vidor *Co-Dir* Mario Soldati *Scen* Bridget Boland, Robert Westerby, King Vidor, Mario Camerini, Ennio De Concini, Ivo Perelli based on the novel by Leo Tolstoy *Photog* Jack Cardiff, Aldo Tonti *Art Dir* Mario Chiari *Mus* Nino Rota *Ed* Stuart Gilmore, Leo Catozzo *Cast* Audrey Hepburn, Henry Fonda, Mel Ferrer, Vittorio Gassman, Anita Ekberg, Oscar Homolka, Herbert Lom, John Mills, Helmut Dantine *Prod* Ponti/De Laurentiis. 208 mins. Technicolor. Vista-Vision.

This large-budget spectacular version — though not as expensive as the Russian version *Voina i mir* (*q.v.*) — was filmed in Italy and Yugoslavia, resulting in "Russian" landscapes that look strangely Mediterranean. The studio scenes are turgid and lifeless and the sets rather shabbily designed. But the film comes to life in the spectacle scenes, with a number of impressively staged battles (largely directed by Mario Soldati) and a sense of visual power in the retreat from Moscow. Audrey Hepburn is an appealing Natasha who seems to have stepped out of the pages of the novel and Henry Fonda is an excellent Bezukhov.

[The British Broadcasting Corporation is producing (1971) a 20-episode TV adaptation of the novel that will run for a total of 15 hours. The Japanese *War and Peace* (1947), directed by F. Kamei and S. Yamamoto, is not an adaptation of the novel but the story of two soldiers returning from the last war to their families.]

WAR COMES TO AMERICA see WHY WE FIGHT (series)

*WAR GAME (THE) Britain 1965. *Dir/Scen* Peter Watkins *Photog* Peter Bartlett *Art Dir* Tony Cornell, Anne Davey *Ed* Michael Bradsell *Narrators* Michael Aspel, Dick Graham *Prod* BBC Television. 50 mins.

This "staged" documentary on the subject of nuclear warfare was produced by the BBC but refused a television screening as being unsuitable for home viewing. It aroused considerable controversy at the time and was eventually released by the BBC for theatrical and non-theatrical exhibition. A blend of simulated newsreels and street interviews with a neutral commentary, it details the escalation of war, a missile attack, its physical effects, and the eventual breakdown of public morale and the social structure. Though intermittently brilliant and full of powerful shock effects, *The War Game* is too often patently manipulative in its technical effects and heavy-handed in its propaganda.

WAR IS OVER (THE) GUERRE EST FINIE (LA)

WARNING SHADOWS SCHATTEN — EINE NÄCHTLICHE HALLUZINATION

WAVE (THE) REDES

WAXWORKS WACHSFIGURENKABINETT (DAS)

WAY DOWN EAST USA 1920. *Dir* D. W. Griffith *Scen* Anthony Paul Kelly, Joseph R. Grismer, D. W. Griffith based on the play (1898) by Lottie Blair Parker *Photog* G. W. Bitzer, Hendrik Sartov *Ed* James E. Smith *Cast* Lillian Gish, Richard Barthelmess, Lowell Sherman, Burr McIntosh, Kate Bruce, Creighton Hale, Porter Strong, Mary Hay, Mrs. Morgan Belmont *Prod* Griffith Prod. 10,500 ft. Part color. Re-released with music track in 1931, 110 mins.

A poor orphan girl (Gish) is seduced and gives birth to a baby that dies. She becomes a servant on a farm with some kindly people and the son (Barthelmess) is attracted to her. Her seducer arrives and reveals her "shame" to the farmer, who throws her out into the snow. But the son rescues her from drowning and marries her.

Based on an old stage melodrama, the rights to which cost Griffith $175,000, and filmed in Griffith's Marmaroneck studios on Long Island, *Way Down East* is the best of Griffith's later films, despite its Victorian sentimentality, morality, and heroics. In total contrast to *Broken Blossoms* (*q.v.*), Griffith shot about thirty times as much footage as he eventually used in the film. At the time of its production, he declared: "We live in a time when *ideas* have supplanted technical form in the cinema. The idea, the theme, the subject, the basic thought is the only element to consider in the choice of a film story, and it must be able to be expressed briefly, in 300 words, as is that of *Way Down East*." Louis Delluc wrote, "Griffith describes in his black and white style the story of an unmarried mother, a dead child, and a brave hero. The key scene of the break-up of the ice on the river, questionable in intention, is unquestionable in effect, because of the marvelous talent of Lillian Gish, the vigorous healthiness of Barthelmess, and the beneficial grandeur of the snowy landscape, which the producers have interferred with only when it was necessary." This famous sequence, which influenced Pudovkin when he made *Mother* (*q.v.*), shows the young girl being rescued from river ice that is breaking up and carrying her towards a waterfall. Griffith made this sequence out of an unusual collection of material that included not only specially filmed exteriors on the frozen Connecticut River and studio shots, but also shots taken out of various documentaries (including one on Niagara Falls), which were then convincingly intercut. Some of the sequences (such as the dress parade) were filmed in color.

Way Down East was the most popular Griffith film after *Birth of a Nation* (*q.v.*), and, according to the publicity, grossed over $4.5 million.

*Way Down East USA 1935. *Dir* Henry King *Scen* Howard Estabrook, William Hurlbutt based on the play *Photog* Ernest Palmer *Cast* Rochelle Hudson, Henry Fonda, Slim Summerville *Prod* 20th Century-Fox. 85 mins.

Considering that the plot, by 1935 standards, was almost totally ludicrous, Henry King manages to convey a sense of character and environment and obtains a sympathetic performance from Henry Fonda as the hero. There are a number of comic scenes and even a kind of documentary at the beginning on American farm life at the time.

WAY TO THE STARS (THE) JOHNNY IN THE CLOUDS Britain 1945. *Dir* Anthony Asquith *Scen* Terence Rattigan, R. Sherman, Anatole de Grunwald *Photog* Derek Williams *Art Dir* Paul Sheriff, Carmen Dillon *Mus* Nicholas Brodsky *Ed* Fergus McDonell *2nd Unit Photog* Jack Hildyard, Guy Green *Cast* Michael Redgrave, John Mills, Rosamund John, Renée Asherson, Douglas Montgomery, Bonar Colleano, Stanley Holloway, Basil Redford, Joyce Carey *Prod* Two Cities. 109 mins.

In 1940, Peter (Mills), a young pilot, arrives at an RAF bomber station where he shares a room with David (Redgrave). David marries Toddy (John),

the manageress of a local hotel, and Peter falls in love with Iris (Asherson), a guest at the hotel. Soon after David and Toddy's son is born, David is killed on a bombing mission and Peter concludes it would be wrong to marry Iris because of the chance of his death. Later, men from the US Army Air Force arrived and Toddy becomes friendly with Johnny (Montgomery), a married American pilot, whose friend Joe (Colleano) courts Iris. Johnny is also killed making a crash landing on the airfield. Peter is persuaded by Toddy that he ought to marry Iris and he proposes to her.

This convincing portrait of the life of pilots at war, continuing their private lives while courting death on bombing missions, is undoubtedly Asquith's best film. Successful sequences: a long traveling shot across the deserted camp; the lovers' meeting in a room looking out on a schoolyard full of children.

WE ARE ALL MURDERERS NOUS SOMMES TOUS DES ASSASSINS

WE ARE FROM KRONSTADT MY IZ KRONSTADT

WEARY DEATH (THE) MÜDE TOD (DER)

WEDDING MARCH (THE) (sequel, THE HONEYMOON) USA 1928 (production began 1926). *Dir* Erich von Stroheim *Scen* Harry Carr, Erich von Stroheim *Assist* Eddy Sowders, Louis Germonprez *Photog* Hal Mohr, Ben Reynolds *Mus* G. S. Zamecnik, Luis de Francesco *Art Dir* Erich von Stroheim, Richard Day *Ed* P. A. Powers, Stroheim, Josef von Sternberg *Cast* Fay Wray, Erich von Stroheim, ZaSu Pitts, Maude George, Matthew Betz, George Fawcett, Cesare Gravina, George Nichols *Prod* Celebrity Pictures/Paramount. 10,852 ft. (*The Wedding March*); 10,789 ft. and 7,000 ft. (*The Honeymoon*). *The Honeymoon* released in France in 1929, 3,000 meters. Part color.

In Vienna during the last years of the Hapsburg dynasty, Prince Nicki (Stroheim) sees a poor but beautiful girl, Mitzi (Wray), while he is on parade and falls in love with her. But his father, the archduke (Fawcett), and mother (George) are determined he should marry to gain a dowry and force him to marry the lame daughter (Pitts) of Vienna's cornplaster king (Nichols). Part I ends with impending marriage of the prince to the cripple and the tragic grief of Mitzi. Part II depicts the wedding and honeymoon trip to the mountains, the death of the crippled princess, and the death of the prince at the hands of the butcher (Betz), Mitzi's former sweetheart bent on her revenge.

[Following the worldwide success of *The Merry Widow* (*q.v.*), Pat Powers of Celebrity Pictures gave Stroheim carte blanche to make a film of his own choosing. Production began in June 1926 and Stroheim had shot 200,000 ft. by the time the alarmed producers called a halt in the spring of 1927 when Stroheim hadn't quite completed the second part. In the meantime Powers had appealed to Paramount for additional funds after the original budget of $750,000 had been exceeded and Paramount had consequently acquired a controlling interest in the film.

Stroheim's first cut of *The Wedding March* was 25,795 ft. Subsequent versions (cut by Sternberg at Paramount's request but with Stroheim's agreement) ran 17,993 ft., 11,147 ft., 11,062 ft., and finally the released length of 10,852 ft. Stroheim's original cut of *The Honeymoon* ran 22,484 ft., reduced by Sternberg to 10,789 ft. This latter version was further reduced by Paramount to 7,000 ft., without Stroheim's agreement. Moreover, this second part of what Stroheim had conceived of as a unity was separated from the first. *The Wedding March* was premiered on October 6, 1928. The second part was never released in the USA but was given a limited release in Europe in 1929. Stroheim disowned this version of Part II.

According to Sternberg, "I showed him the shortened version and he thanked me. Had he objected to anything, I would not only have restored the film to its original length but would have refused to have anything more to do with it. I am explicit about this . . . I know nothing about the division of the film into two parts."]

The film has such a pitilessly authentic portrait of decadent Imperial Austria that one is almost inclined to believe Stroheim's claim to have been an Imperial Army officer instead of his actual background as a member of Mitzi's class. The two parts of this film form an inseparable whole. The first part, seen alone, seems confusing in theme, with a number of apparently pointless digressions. But in the second part, more stylistically aggressive and powerful, all the various threads of the tragedy and the behavior of the characters are brought together. The symbol of the flowering apple tree whose blossoms fall on Mitzi and the prince making love in an abandoned coach, recurs again, preceded by shots such as a sow suckling its young. Stroheim's style is not so much in his editing but in the stagings and creation of atmosphere through an accumulation of details. It is of interest to read Freddy Buache's summary of the bordello sequence, which is intercut with the prince and Mitzi's lovemaking: "Black servants with chastity belts, heart-shaped clasps, chains, open bottles of champagne. Orgy. Orchestra. The prince's father crawls across the floor through groups of drunken men and undressed women. The cornplaster king puts a plaster on the corn that is giving him pain, then, totally drunk, they haggle over the amount of the daughter's dowry: '500,000 crowns,' 'No, a million,' 'Done, we're agreed.' Around them the orgy takes on demoniacal dimensions – a number of the more daring scenes were censored."

[Shortly before his death in 1957, Stroheim recut both parts to approximate more closely to his original conception and the original music score was transferred from discs onto the film. However, *the Honeymoon* was apparently lost in a fire at the Cinémathèque française and no other copy has been located. Part I is still extant.]

WE FROM KRONSTADT MY IZ KRONSTADT

WELCOME MR. MARSHALL BIENVENIDO MR. MARSHALL

WESTFRONT 1918 SHAME OF A NATION/ FOUR FROM THE INFANTRY/COMRADES OF 1918 Germany 1930. *Dir* G. W. Pabst *Scen* Ladislaus Vajda, Peter Martin Lampel based on the novel *Vier von der Infanterie* by Ernst Johannsen *Photog* Fritz Arno Wagner, Charles Métain *Art Dir* Ernö Metzner *Cast* Fritz Kampers, Gustav Diessl, Claus Clausen, Hans Joachim Moebis, Gustav Püttjer, Jackie Monnier, Hanna Hoessrich *Prod* Nero-Film, 98 mins. 85 mins. in existing English versions (apparently the result of censorship deletions of the more "gruesome" scenes).

The life and death of four average

soldiers attached to the same company on the French front during the last months of World War I. Karl (Diessl), from Berlin, goes home on leave and finds his wife (Hoessrich) in bed with another man. A Bavarian (Kampers) takes life as it comes, while the lieutenant (Clausen) sticks to his duty. An ex-student (Moebis) falls in love with a French girl (Monnier) but loses her when the company moves on. All of them, sooner or later, meet a terrible end. Best sequences: the men buried alive during a bombardment; the first romantic meeting between the young student and Yvette; Berlin in the midst of food rationing with queues at all the shops; the death of the student at the hands of a wounded soldier in no-man's-land; the tank attack; the lieutenant going mad; the wounded and the dying in the ruined church converted into a field hospital.

Far better than the contemporary *All Quiet on the Western Front* (*q.v.*), *Westfront 1918* has little dialogue but gives tremendous dramatic force to natural sounds (Pabst refused to use music). As John C. Moore describes the final sequences: "Pabst makes one last desperate effort to convey to us not only the horror of war but its futility and its gross stupidity as well." Released to tremendous international acclaim, it still must be included among the finest war films ever made.

WEST SIDE STORY USA 1961. *Dir* Robert Wise, Jerome Robbins *Scen* Ernest Lehman based on the musical, book by Arthur Laurents, lyrics by Stephen Sondheim *Photog* Daniel L. Fapp *Art Dir* Boris Leven *Mus* Leonard Bernstein *Ed* Thomas Stanford, Marshall M. Borden *Choreog* Jerome Robbins *Special Effects* Linwood Dunn *Titles* Saul Bass *Cast* Natalie Wood, Richard Beymer, George Chakiris, Russ Tamblyn, Rita Moreno, Simon Oakland, William Bramley *Prod* Mirisch/Seven Arts for United Artists. 155 mins. Technicolor. Panavision 70.

On New York City's West Side, the Jets, led by Riff (Tamblyn), are rivals of the Puerto Rican Sharks, led by Bernardo (Chakiris). At a dance in a gym, Riff challenges Bernardo to a fight. Bernardo's sister, Maria (Wood), who is in love with Tony (Beymer), ex-member of the Jets, begs Tony to stop the fight but his efforts misfire. Bernardo calls

Tony a coward, Riff rushes to his defense, Bernardo kills Riff and Tony instinctively stabs Bernardo. Maria wants to hate him for killing her brother but agrees to run away with him. Tony goes into hiding. Maria is detained by the police and she sends Anita (Moreno), Bernardo's girl friend, to take a message to Tony. On the way she is mauled by the Jets and is so enraged that she tells him that Maria is dead. The grief-stricken Tony is killed in revenge by a member of the Sharks.

This *Romeo and Juliet* musical is based on a successful stage musical that ran for three years on Broadway. The book and lyrics were retained but the dances were almost entirely restaged, being shot in five weeks largely on location in West Side areas scheduled for demolition. Production was completed over six months in reconstructed sets representing the urban background.

Its choreographic style is in distinct contrast to the early Busby Berkeley or Ziegfield style of musical and even to the later developments of Minnelli, Gene Kelly, and Stanley Donen. Based on interracial tensions its story is dramatic and almost all the dance sequences, designed and directed by Jerome Robbins, are excellent. Especially memorable sequences: the opening "Jet Song" danced in the streets; the sequence in the gymnasium where "Romeo" meets "Juliet" followed by the "In America" number; the satirical "Gee, Officer Krupke"; the bloody fight between the two gangs in a garage; the final sequence of Tony's dead body being borne away.

The sentimental love songs, shot largely in close-ups that give the faces the gargantuan dimensions of the wide screen, are slick and unappealing. Natalie Wood's voice was dubbed by Marni Nixon and that of Richard Beymer by Jimmy Bryant.

One of the most successful aspects of the film is Saul Bass's credit titles, which start with abstract lines and end up coinciding with an aerial view of New York as the overture develops into excellent stereophonic sound effects.

West Side Story cost six million dollars and was an enormous international success.

WHAT A MAN! NEVER GIVE A SUCKER AN EVEN BREAK

WHAT THE BIRDS KNEW IKIMONO NO KIROKU

WHEELCHAIR (THE) COCHECITO (EL)

WHEN THE CAT COMES AZ PRIJDE KOCOUR

WHERE CHIMNEYS ARE SEEN ENTOTSU NO MIERU BASHO

WHISKY GALORE TIGHT LITTLE ISLAND Britain 1948. *Dir* Alexander Mackendrick *Scen* Compton Mackenzie, Angus Macphail based on the novel by Campton Mackenzie *Photog* Gerald Gibbs *Art Dir* Jim Morahan *Mus* Ernest Irving *Cast* Basil Radford, Joan Greenwood, James Robertson Justice, Gordon Jackson, Jean Cadell, Duncan Macrae, Wylie Watson *Prod* Ealing. 82 mins.
In 1943, the inhabitants of an island in the Outer Hebrides off the west coast of Scotland are without whisky because of the war. The local Home Guard, commanded by an Englishman, Captain Waggett (Radford), are totally demoralized. Then a ship carrying thousands of cases of whisky is wrecked off the island. Since it is Sunday, the islanders have to wait to salvage it and in this time Captain Waggett and Sergeant Odd prepare plans to prevent looting. But the islanders, led by George Campbell (Jackson), salvage it and hide it in a cave and George uses it to celebrate his betrothal to Catriona (Greenwood). Captain Waggett discovers the whisky and reports it to the excise officer but when the excise men appear, the whisky has again vanished.
One of the best of the Ealing comedies, full of disrespectful allusions to the army, bureaucracy, puritanism, the Americans, and, last but not least of course, the English.

WHITE-HAIRED GIRL (THE) China 1950. *Dir* Wang Pin, Chouei Houa *Scen* Ho Tsing-Tche, Ting Yi, Yang Jouen-Chen, Wang Pin, Chouei Houa *Photog* Wou Yu-Yun *Mus* Tchou Wei, Tchang Lou, Ma Ko *Ed* Wang Lien *Cast* Tien Houa, Hou Peng, Tchen Tsiang, Li Po-Wan, Tchao Lou *Prod* North-East Studios. 120 mins.
Hsi Erh (Tien Houa), the daughter of an exploited peasant family, is engaged to Ta Tchouen (Li Po-Wan), but the son (Tchen Tsiang) of a rich landowner forces her to become his servant and then rapes her. When she is preg-nant he sells her to a slave trader. She escapes, hides in the mountains, and her child is born dead. Because her hair has turned prematurely white through her sufferings she is thought by the peasants to be a white-haired goddess. Meanwhile, Ta Tchouen, having joined the People's Army, returns as an officer to his village, finds his sweetheart again, and punishes the evil landlord.
This film is a talented and convincing adaptation of an opera that was based on a legend that grew up around 1935 in the People's Army and in the areas that had been liberated. It has a moving performance by the young Tien Houa. The songs that are sung throughout are not incongruous in relation to the somewhat neorealist style of the drama.

WHITE MANE CRIN BLANC

WHITE NIGHTS NOTTI BIANCHE (LE)

WHITE REINDEER (THE) VALKOINEN PEURA

WHITE SHADOWS IN THE SOUTH SEAS USA 1928. *Dir* W. S. Van Dyke (and Robert Flaherty, uncredited) *Scen* Ray Doyle, Jack Cunningham based on the book by Frederick J. O'Brien *Photog* Clyde de Vinna, George Nogle, Bob Roberts, (Robert Flaherty, uncredited) *Titles* John Colton *Cast* Monte Blue, Raquel Torres, and Tahitian nonprofessionals *Prod* MGM. 7,968 ft. Released in sound and silent versions.
A doctor (Blue) who is rescued from a ship settles down in Tahiti, loses hope, and becomes alcoholic. He falls in love with a native girl (Torres) and finds happiness until he is killed by a group of white colonials.
[Robert Flaherty was hired by MGM to film the book by Frederick J. O'Brien whose advice had first sent Flaherty to Samoa to make *Moana* (*q.v.*). However, MGM wanted a "story" and appointed a co-director, W. S. Van Dyke, who was a specialist in "action" films. Soon after production began, Flaherty found himself at odds with Van Dyke's approach and Thalberg's insistence on using two "stars." He resigned and left Van Dyke to complete the film alone. There is considerable disagreement as to how much of the final film is Flaherty's but certainly some of the sequences seem to have his touch.]
The plot, though it dealt with the cor-

rupting influence of Western civilization, was considered puerile in North America and Britain. But its touching love story and the theme song were much admired by the French surrealists. Ado Kyrou echoed their feelings when he wrote of it as "one of the most beautiful poems about love we have been given to see," and of "the magnetic beauty of this flood of love" and of "this miracle that plunges us into total wonder."

WHITE SHEIK (THE) SCEICCO BIANCO (LO)

WHITE STALLION CRIN BLANC

WHITHER? ILYA AYN

WHITHER GERMANY? KÜHLE WAMPE

WHOLE TOWN'S TALKING (THE) PASSPORT TO FAME USA 1935. *Dir* John Ford *Scen* Robert Riskin, Jo Swerling based on the novel *Jail Break* by William Riley Burnett *Photog* Joseph August *Art Dir* Lionel Banks *Ed* Viola Lawrence *Cast* Edward G. Robinson, Jean Arthur, Wallace Ford, Arthur Byron, Arthur Hohl, Donald Meek *Prod* Columbia. 95 mins.
Jones (Robinson), a timid clerk shyly in love with a girl (Arthur), resembles Killer Manion (Robinson), a desperate gangster. Jones is arrested by mistake and when released is given a passport by the police to protect him from arrest. The gangster tries to kill him in order to take his place but fails.
An appealing comedy-thriller, "the height of unaffectedness at heart the same as artifice" (Alexandre Arnoux), but one which seems less typical of John Ford than of another Columbia director of the time, Frank Capra. However, this may be due to the fact that it was co-written by Robert Riskin, Capra's scenarist.

*WHO'S AFRAID OF VIRGINIA WOOLF? USA 1966. *Dir* Mike Nichols *Scen* Ernest Lehman based on the play by Edward Albee *Photog* Haskell Wexler *Art Dir* Richard Sylbert *Mus* Alex North *Ed* Sam O'Steen *Cast* Richard Burton, Elizabeth Taylor, Sandy Dennis, George Segal *Prod* Warner Brothers. 132 mins.
George (Burton), a professor in a small college, and his wife, Martha (Taylor), verbally tear each other to pieces during an evening and a night spent with a

younger couple, Nick (Segal) and Honey (Dennis).
This obsessional portrait of emotional cannibalism in marriage is Mike Nichols' first feature. It is less memorable for his occasionally irritating stylistic tricks than for the verbal force retained from the original play, brilliantly transmitted by Burton and Taylor.

*WHY WE FIGHT (series)
— *Prelude to War* USA 1942. *Dir* Frank Capra *Scen* Eric Knight, Anthony Veiller *Mus* Dimitri Tiomkin *Ed* William Hornbeck *Commentary* Walter Huston *Prod* Orientation Branch, US War Department. 53 mins.
Deals with the rise of fascism up to 1938.
— *The Nazis Strike* USA 1942. *Dir* Frank Capra, Anatole Litvak *Scen* Eric Knight, Anthony Veiller *Mus* Dimitri Tiomkin *Ed* William Hornbeck *Commentary* Walter Huston, Anthony Veiller *Prod* as above 42 mins.
The fall of Austria and Czechoslovakia and the attack on Poland.
— *Divide and Conquer* USA 1943. *Dir* Frank Capra, Anatole Litvak *Scen* Anthony Veiller, Robert Heller *Mus* Dimitri Tiomkin *Ed* William Hornbeck *Commentary* Walter Huston, Anthony Veiller *Prod* as above. 58 mins.
The attacks on Western Europe.
— *The Battle of Britain* USA 1943. *Dir/Scen* Anthony Veiller *Mus* Dimitri Tiomkin *Ed* William Hornbeck *Commentary* Walter Huston *Prod* as above. 54 mins.
— *The Battle of Russia* USA 1944. *Dir* Anatole Litvak *Scen* Robert Heller, Anatole Litvak *Mus* Dimitri Tiomkin *Ed* William Hornbeck *Commentary* Walter Huston, Anthony Veiller *Prod* as above. 80 mins.
— *The Battle of China* USA 1944. *Dir* Frank Capra, Anatole Litvak *Scen* Eric Knight, Anthony Veiller *Mus* Dimitri Tiomkin *Ed* William Hornbeck *Commentary* Walter Huston *Prod* as above. 60 mins. (Not given public release.)
— *War Comes to America* USA 1945. *Dir* Anatole Litvak *Scen* Anthony Veiller *Mus* Dimitri Tiomkin *Ed* William Hornbeck *Commentary* Walter Huston *Prod* as above. 70 mins.
The impact on American public opinion of the events depicted in the early films and the nation's entry into the war.
These seven feature-length compilation films were all produced under the supervision of Major (later Colonel) Frank

Capra in Hollywood. Richard Griffith (who handled film research for the series) points out: "Every member of the armed forces was required to see these before going overseas. Some of them were shown to civilian audiences in the USA and abroad . . . The whole series was compiled entirely from existing documentary and newsreel film (and even fictional films from Hollywood and elsewhere *Ed*), drawn from every conceivable source, including the enemy." All of the films are still in general circulation with two exceptions: *The Battle of China*, which was not given a public release because of its unbalanced assessment of the politics (the Communist armies are not mentioned and Chiang Kai-Shek only barely); *The Battle of Russia* was withdrawn during the McCarthy era and public showings forbidden because its warm portrayal of the USSR did not accord with US policy during the cold war.

The films in this series, following methods developed in the *March of Time* series, are highly original and often brilliant examples of the compilation film technique and could be profitably studied by all film makers. The first three films are the most remarkable, with their brilliant amalgamation of Tiomkin's rhythmic music, Huston's strident commentary, and William Hornbeck's frenetic editing. *Prelude to War*, in particular, is a model of the genre.

[To the *Why We Fight* series should be added the following films, all produced by Frank Capra's US War Department Documentary Film Unit:
— *Tunisian Victory* Britain/USA 1943. *Dir* Roy Boulting, Frank Capra. 79 mins.
— *Know Your Ally: Britain* USA 1944. *Dir* Anthony Veiller. 42 mins.]
— *Know Your Enemy: Japan* USA 1945. *Dir* Joris Ivens. Not completed for release.
— *Two Down, One to Go* USA 1945. *Dir* Frank Capra. 9 mins.

WHY WORRY? USA 1923. *Dir* Sam Taylor, Fred Newmeyer *Cast* Harold Lloyd, Jobyna Ralston, Leo White, John Aasen, Wallace Howe, *Prod* Roach for Pathé. 5,500 ft.
A wealthy young hypochondriac (Lloyd), in South America to recover his health and forget his illnesses, gets mixed up in a revolution and rescues his nurse (Ralston) with the aid of a giant (Aasen).

One of all-American Harold Lloyd's rare excursions outside the USA in which he behaves like a superman in an underdeveloped country with much of the vigor (though not the manner) of Douglas Fairbanks.

WILD BOYS OF THE ROAD see PUTYOVKA V ZHIZN

*WILD BUNCH (THE) USA 1969. *Dir* Sam Peckinpah *Scen* Walon Green, Sam Peckinpah *2nd Unit Dir* Buzz Henry *Photog* Lucien Ballard *Art Dir* Edward Carrere *Mus* Jerry Fielding *Ed* Louis Lombardo *Cast* William Holden, Robert Ryan, Ernest Borgnine, Edmond O'Brien, Warren Oates, Jaime Sanchez, Ben Johnson, Emilio Fernandez, Albert Dekker *Prod* Warner Brothers/Seven Arts. 145 mins. Technicolor. Panavision 70.
In Texas in 1914, Pike Bishop (Holden) and his gang rob a railroad office unaware that Deke Thornton (Ryan), Bishop's ex-partner now in the pay of the railroad, has set an ambush for them. They shoot their way out through a hail of indiscriminate killings only to discover that they have stolen bags of steel washers. The gang moves to Mexico, where they meet Mapache (Fernandez), a bandit general, who promises them ten thousand dollars if they will rob an ammunitions train for him. Though pursued by Thornton and a group of bounty hunters, they pull off the robbery only to have Mapache try to steal the arms from them by force. They outwit him and he has to pay the gang one by one. When it is the turn of a Mexican, Angel (Sanchez), Mapache captures him and allows his men to torture him. The gang demand his return, Mapache cuts Angel's throat in front of them and a bloody battle breaks out in which Bishop and his men are killed along with Mapache's. Later Thornton arrives. His bounty hunters steal from the corpses but are killed by Angel's revolutionary peasant comrades. Thornton rides away.
Peckinpah's first credited feature since his troubles with the producers over *Major Dundee* in 1965 is at once a lament for the Old West and its "real" men and a lugubrious prophecy of the bloody world the numerous children seen in the film were heir to. Its blend of nostalgia for the American Dream with a sense of hopeless despair is found also in the contemporary *Easy Rider* (*q.v.*). Perhaps

one of the most telling sequences of the film is when Sykes (O'Brien), an aging member of the gang, is abandoned to Thornton. The set-pieces are justifiably famous: the opening ambush, the blowing-up of the bridge, the bloody massacre at the end. But *The Wild Bunch* is better characterized by the brutal lyricism of the closing sequences as the bounty hunters compete with the vultures for pickings from the corpses.

WILD ONE (THE) USA 1954. *Dir* Laslo Benedek *Scen* John Paxton based on the story *The Cyclists' Raid* by Frank Rooney *Photog* Hal Mohr *Art Dir* Walter Holscher *Mus* Leith Stevens *Ed* Al Clark *Cast* Marlon Brando, Mary Murphy, Robert Keith, Lee Marvin, Jay C. Flippen, Peggy Maley, Ray Teal *Prod* Stanley Kramer for Columbia. 79 mins.

A gang of motorcyclists, clad in black leather and led by Johnny (Brando), terrorize a small town. Johnny falls for Kathie (Murphy), the sheriff's (Flippen) daughter. The population eventually rebel against the behavior of the gang and attempt to mete out rough justice to Johnny, who is saved by the sheriff.

Pierre Kast, in an article titled "The Martians Have Landed," described this as "a film without explanations, judgements or justifications. An absurd, brutal, awkward film; an abstruse, fascinating, animalistic Marlon Brando, who searches out and provokes distress, disquiet, and discomfort because, I imagine, Benedek and the authors find the world disquieting and uncomfortable." Though Stanley Kramer had a hand in this success, the contribution of Laslo Benedek should not be ignored. Though perhaps most famous as the first film to typify and characterize the attitudes of a certain kind of delinquent, it also contains a muted antifascist polemic. *The Wild One* was banned at the time by the British censors and was only recently released for public exhibition.

WILD STRAWBERRIES SMULTRONSTALLET

WILL (THE) AZIMA (EL)

WILL O' THE WISP FEU FOLLET (LE)

WILL SUCCESS SPOIL ROCK HUNTER? OH! FOR A MAN! USA 1957. *Dir* Frank Tashlin *Scen* Frank Tashlin based on the play by George Axelrod *Photog* Joe Mac-Donald *Art Dir* Lyle Wheeler, Leland Fuller *Mus* Cyril J. Mockridge *Ed* Hugh S. Fowler *Cast* Tony Randall, Jayne Mansfield, Betsy Drake, Henry Jones, Joan Blondell, Lili Gentle, Mickey Hargitay *Prod* 20th Century-Fox. 95 mins. Eastman Color. CinemaScope.

A New York advertising agent, Rockwell Hunter (Randall), is led to develop an idea for a lipstick advertisement featuring Hollywood actress, Rita Marlow (Mansfield), who accepts on condition that Rockwell poses as the world's greatest lover in order to make her boyfriend (Hargitay) jealous. The stunt grows out of proportion and Rockwell's fiancée, Jenny (Drake), grows jealous. Meanwhile, Rita's companion, Violet (Blondell), finds romance with Rufus (Jones), Rockwell's colleague. Eventually, Rockwell learns that success isn't everything and returns to chicken-farming with Jenny.

Something of a continuation of Tashlin's earlier *The Girl Can't Help It* (*q.v.*) but more satirical, especially in the amusing parody of TV commercials in the opening sequence.

WIND (THE) USA 1927. *Dir* Victor Sjöström (Seastrom) *Scen* Frances Marion based on the novel by Dorothy Scarborough *Photog* John Arnold *Art Dir* Cedric Gibbons, Edward Withers *Ed* Conrad A. Nervig *Titles* John Colton *Cast* Lillian Gish, Lars Hanson, Montagu Love, Dorothy Cummings, William Orlamond, Edward Earle, Carmencita Johnson, Leon Ramon, Billy Kent Schaeffer *Prod* MGM. 6,400 ft. (silent version released in Europe in 1927); 6,721 ft. (sound version released in the USA in 1928).

A sensitive young girl (Gish) from Virginia goes to live with her cousin (Orlamond) and his coarse and insensitive wife (Cummings) on the lonely and windy Texas prairie. The wife resents the additional burden of keeping the girl and, to escape, she agrees to marry a rough cowboy (Hanson). She does not love him but at least he can support her. Revolted by the coarseness of her husband, she is further depressed by the endless wind and dust. One night, she is attacked by a former acquaintance (Love) who tries to rape her. Maddened by terror, she kills him. Later the husband returns and helps his wife bury the body. She adjusts to her surroundings and finds contentment with her husband.

The Wind is one of the masterpieces of the silent cinema and Sjöström's best American film, matching his Swedish achievements. Throughout the film, Sjöström emphasizes the impact of the elements, especially the wind, on his characters. Exteriors were shot in the blistering hot Mojave Desert in Southern California, and so penetrating is the atmosphere that one can almost *feel* the wind oneself and taste the endless dust. In the opening sequence, the girl arrives by train from Virginia, a land where the grass is always green, and is suddenly hit by a windstorm. Here and elsewhere, Sjöström's realistic portrayal of landscape, psychology, and the elements is similar to the style of his Swedish films though, as Lewis Jacobs points out, it has something in common with Stroheim: "Seastrom achieved effects with a technique similar to that of *Greed* (*q.v.*); the use of details within the scene itself rather than the building of the scene with an assemblage of detail shots. In one scene, for example, the woman (Cummings), cuts a carcass for food and is covered with blood. The girl (Gish), who is going for an iron to press her clothes (here is an ironic contrast between purposes), sees the blood and draws away in revulsion. This incident was depicted in the whole scene with a minimum of cutting."

Though Lillian Gish is as perfect here as she was under Griffith's direction in *Broken Blossoms* (*q.v.*), Lars Hanson is her equal. Seen first as a brutal, coarse, idiotic cowboy to whom the wife quite naturally refuses to give herself after their marriage, he later becomes a man whose love gives him stature and dignity. The ending is courageous, especially in a Hollywood film: the husband returns home, sees the body, is pleased with his wife for killing the attacker and never dreams of telling the sheriff. Together they bury the body in the sand and become truly bound as husband and wife in their common knowledge.

[After Sjöström had supervised the first cut, MGM recut it and added synchronized sound-effects on discs for its 1928 release in the USA. It was released silent outside the USA and was more admired by critics in Europe, especially in France, than it was in the USA. The original story did not have a happy ending.]

WINTER LIGHT NATTVARDSGÄSTERNA

WITCHCRAFT THROUGH THE AGES HÄXAN

WITH CAPTAIN SCOTT, R.N., TO THE SOUTH POLE THE GREAT WHITE SILENCE/NINETY DEGREES SOUTH/THE UNDYING STORY OF CAPTAIN SCOTT AND ANIMAL LIFE IN THE ANTARCTIC Britain 1912 (production began (1910). *Dir/Scen/Photog/Prod* Herbert George Ponting. 7 reels. Re-released in 1924 as *The Great White Silence*, 7,021 ft. Re-released in 1933 with sound track *Commentary* Commander F. A. Worsley, narrated by Herbert G. Ponting *Mus* Sir Walford Davies, 73 mins.

A film record of the final expedition of Captain Robert Scott to the Antarctic and his attempt to reach the South Pole ahead of Amundsen. It begins with the departure of the scientists and explorers in 1910 on the "Terra Nova," depicts their grim struggle against the ice and cold, and ends with the last ill-fated dash for the Pole and Scott's death in March 1912. This latter episode is depicted through still photographs with the aid of Scott's diary.

Herbert Ponting, an experienced photographer, turns what might have been merely an actuality record into a striking and often highly dramatic film. During more than a year spent in the polar wastes, Ponting photographed a true diary of the expedition that allows the viewer to identify with the explorers during their privations on the great ice fields, and with their discovery of the unearthly and terrible beauty of Antarctica and its native fauna. Even today, the splendor of Ponting's photography is striking.

Ponting filmed, developed, and printed his original footage under impossibly bleak conditions. His camera occasionally froze solid and Ponting himself not only suffered from the cold but was even attacked by the animals he was trying to film. However, some of the footage he shot was discovered about 1950 still in perfect condition, having been preserved by the intense cold.

Ponting's film is very much an ancestor of the documentary film as we know it today. It was a considerable world-wide success and was reissued twice. King George V ordered that it be shown to every boy in the British Empire as an example of supreme courage and self-sacrifice.

— *Scott's Last Journey* Britain 1962. *Dir* John Read *Prod* BBC TV. 58 mins.

A prize-winning documentary that drew much from Ponting's original footage.

— *Scott of the Antarctic* Britain 1948.

Dir Charles Frend *Mus* Vaughan Williams *Cast* John Mills, Derek Bond, Harold Warrender, James Robertson Justice, Regnald Beckwith, Diana Churchill, Kenneth More *Prod* Ealing. 111 mins. Technicolor.

A rather "stiff-upper-lip" fictionalized version of the Scott saga shot on location in Norway and Switzerland. Memorable for Vaughan Williams' evocative symphonic score.

WITHOUT PITY SENZA PIETÀ

WOMAN (A) CHARLIE, THE PERFECT LADY/ THE PERFECT LADY USA 1915. *Dir/Scen* Charles Chaplin *Photog* Rollie Totheroh *Cast* Charles Chaplin, Edna Purviance, Charles Insley, Marta Golden, Billy Armstrong, Leo White, Margie Reiger *Prod* Essanay. 1,800 ft.

Charlie is thrown out of his girl's (Purviance) home by her father (Insley) whom he had previously pushed into a lake. Finding himself in Edna's dressing room he dresses himself in women's clothes and coyly foments a rivalry between the father and the suitor (Armstrong) until he is discovered and kicked out again.

Chaplin's pantomime in "drag" is extraordinary, but the rest of the film is quite mediocre.

WOMAN FROM NOWHERE (THE) FEMME DE NULLE PART (LA)

WOMAN IN THE WINDOW (THE) USA 1944. *Dir* Fritz Lang *Scen* Nunnally Johnson based on the novel *Once Off Guard* by J. H. Wallis *Photog* Milton Krasner *Art Dir* Duncan Cramer *Mus* Arthur Lang *Ed* Gene Fowler, Marjorie Johnson *Cast* Edward G. Robinson, Joan Bennett, Raymond Massey, Dan Duryea, Edmund Breon *Prod* International Productions/ Christie Corporation for RKO. 99 mins.

A psychology professor, Wanley (Robinson), visits the apartment of Alice Reed (Bennett), a woman he has just met and whose portrait he had admired. Suddenly a man enters and jealously attacks Wanley, who stabs him with a pair of scissors Alice hands him. The situation becomes increasingly complex as the police attempt to locate the killer. Wanley happens to be friendly with the District Attorney (Massey) and this gives him access to knowledge of his own mistakes in hiding the crime. The dead man's bodyguard, Heidt (Duryea), knows the truth and blackmails Wanley and Alice but, later is shot by the police who have deduced he is the murderer. Wanley, however, has already taken poison – but wakes in his club to discover it has all been a nightmare.

One of Fritz Lang's better American films, with a fine performance by Edward G. Robinson, *à la* Emil Jannings, as a middle-aged philanderer trapped by his own emotional weakness.

WOMAN OF PARIS (A) USA 1923. *Dir/ Scen* Charles Chaplin *Assist* H. d'Abbadie d'Arrast, Eddie Sutherland, Jean de Limur *Photog* Rollie Totheroh, Jack Wilson *Art Dir* Arthur Stibolt *Ed* Monta Bell *Cast* Edna Purviance, Adolphe Menjou, Carl Miller, Lydia Knott, Charles French, Betty Morrissey, Malvina Polo *Prod* Chaplin for United Artists. 7,700 ft.

In a small French village, Marie (Purviance) plans to elope with her sweetheart, Jean (Miller). While she waits at the station, Jean's father (French) dies and, misunderstanding the delay, Marie leaves for Paris alone. Later, in Paris, she is elaborately gowned as the mistress of Pierre (Menjou), a wealthy gentleman who plans to marry her. In Montmartre, Marie accidentally meets Jean again, now an artist, but when his mother (Knott) objects to a renewal of their relationship, Marie returns to Pierre. At a party, Jean fights with Pierre and shoots himself. The mother is about to shoot Marie until she finds her weeping by Jean's body. The two women return to the country.

Famous sequences: the reflections from the windows of an unseen train passing over Marie's face as she leaves the station; the contrast between the bustle in the kitchens and the rich diners; Jean's discovery that Marie is a kept woman through finding a collar in her bureau; Marie tossing her diamond necklace out the window then changing her mind and rushing after it as Pierre plays his saxophone; Marie gossiping with two excited girls as she is massaged by a stone-faced masseuse with a disinterested air; Jean's grotesque and tragic suicide amid the splendors of a ballroom; the final, unrecognized, meeting between Marie and Pierre in the country. Chaplin himself appears, unbilled, only in the bit part of a porter at the station.

Subtitled "a drama of fate," *A Woman of Paris* was originally to have been called *Destiny* and later became *Public Opinion*. It opens with this preface: "Humanity is not made up of heroes and traitors but

421

simply of men and women. And passions stir them, good and bad. Nature has given these to them. They wander in blindness. The ignorant condemn their mistakes, the wise man has pity on them."

"I treated the subject," Chaplin said, "in the simplest possible manner, avoiding emphasizing or underlining in a conscious attempt to show as much as possible through suggestion. Without exception, people questioned here remarked on two things: at the begining, the arrival and departure of the train without showing it; later, the gap of a year in the life of the woman." Later he said, "My film did not have all the hoped for success because its ending leaves one without hope."

"*A Woman of Paris* did not have a success comparable to that of his other films," René Clair noted, then added: "The silent American cinema was renewed through this failure. He proved with this film that above everything he was an artist. It isn't important that other actors lend him his mask. He is everywhere, he creates each character. Can I have seen its scenes ten or twelve times? Each time, I admire their precise rhythm, their enchantment, their ease . . . Each detail of these well-known scenes can be anticipated, but their human value never becomes exhausted."

Stylistically it is extremely simple, with a classical concision and a lack of effects. Above all, it is notable for its introduction of character psychology insight into the dramatic film, developed mainly through the use of a third-person narrative and the use of suggestive details, accessories, and metaphorical allusions. In order to obtain a natural quality from his actors, Chaplin handled them in the studio as if it were real life.

The film's underlying theme is what would be called, thirty years later, "lack of communication." A critic in 1923 in *Cinémagazine* shuddered "in the face of a nothingness greater than death, that of the mutual lack of understanding between two human beings, all human beings, the profound Chaplin, following Maupassant, seems to imply. Is not a human being always alone, alone, alone . . . ?"

WOMAN OF THE DUNES (THE) SUNA NO ONNA

WOMAN WALKS THE EARTH ALONE (A) ONNA HITORI DAICHI O IKU

WOMEN OF RYAZAN BABI RYAZANSKYE

WOMEN'S DREAMS KVINNODRÖM

WORD (THE) ORDET

WORK THE DECORATOR/THE PAPERHANGER USA 1915. *Dir/Scen* Charles Chaplin *Photog* Rollie Totheroh *Cast* Charles Chaplin, Edna Purviance, Charles Insley, Billy Armstrong, Marta Golden, Leo White, Paddy McGuire *Prod* Essanay. 1,700 ft.

Charlie, an assistant to a paperhanger (Insley), creates havoc in a middle-class household, courts the maid (Purviance), and gets mixed up in a mad chase with the husband (Armstrong) and the secret lover (White) of the wife (Golden).

A largely slapstick film without much characterization. Famous gags: Charlie seals his pockets with safety pins after the wife locks up her valuables; Charlie pantomiming the sad story of his life; Charlie, playing around with a naked statuette, puts a lamp shade on it and makes it "dance."

WORLD MELODY MELODIE DER WELT (DIE)

WORLD OF APU (THE) see PATHER PANCHALI

WUTHERING HEIGHTS. Emily Brontë's romantic novel of the eternal love between Cathy and Heathcliff on the Yorkshire moors has been filmed several times, notably by Buñuel in *Cumbres Borrascosas* (*q.v.*)

— *Wuthering Heights* USA 1939. *Dir* William Wyler *Scen* Ben Hecht, Charles MacArthur based on the novel *Photog* Gregg Toland *Art Dir* James Basevi *Mus* Alfred Newman *Ed* Daniel Mandell *Cast* Laurence Olivier (Heathcliffe), Merle Oberson (Cathy), David Niven (Edgar), Geraldine Fitzgerald (Isabella), Flora Robson, Donald Crisp, Leo G. Carroll *Prod* Samuel Goldwyn Productions for United Artists. 104 mins.

A careful, workmanlike, academic version that simplifies much of the action, changes the period, and ends before the novel does. It was shot in California in synthetic "Yorkshire moors." Laurence Olivier gives one of his most outstanding performances as Heathcliffe but Merle Oberon is an uninspiring Cathy.

OTHER VERSIONS:

— *Wuthering Heights* Britain 1920. *Dir* A. V. Bramble *Scen* Eliot Stannard based on the novel *Cast* Warwick Ward, Milton Rosmer, Annie Trevor (Cathy).

A critically well-received and commercially popular version, with high praise for Milton Rosmer's performance as Heathcliffe.

— *El Gharib/The Stranger* Egypt 1955. *Dir* Kamal el Sheikh, Fatine Abdel Wahab *Cast* Yahia Shahin, Magda, Kameil El Chennaoui.

— *Cumbres Borrascosas (q.v.)*

— **Wuthering Heights* Britain 1970. *Dir* Robert Fuest *Scen* Patrick Tilley based on the novel *Photog* John Coquillon *Mus* Michel Legrand *Cast* Anna Calder-Marshall, Timothy Dalton, Harry Andrews, Pamela Brown, Judy Cornwell *Prod* American International. 104 mins. Color. Unimaginative and stagnant adaptation directed like a routine TV soap opera.

XOCHOMILCO MARIA CANDELARIA

*

YANG KWEI FEI YOKIHI

YANKI NO! USA 1960. *Dir* Richard Leacock *Scen* Robert Drew *Photog* Richard Leacock, Albert Maysles *Prod* Drew Associates for Time-Life Inc. 58 mins.

This television documentary on life in Latin America was photographed in Venezuela by Richard Leacock and in Cuba and San José by Albert Maysles. It was produced by Drew Associates for Time-Life Inc. at a time when the USA had not yet broken off diplomatic relations with Cuba. It was withdrawn from circulation in 1961.

A series of excellent sequences pose a number of essential Latin American problems: at the San José conference, the Venezuelan Minister of Foreign Affairs supports Cuba, only to be dismissed by Betancourt when he returns home; not far from the air-conditioned skyscrapers of Caracas, an unemployed man living in a slum cries out his bitterness at his position, that of millions of Latin Americans; in Cuba, a family leaves a slum to move into a home with every comfort and marvels at its running water and electricity. The film ends with the image of a Soviet cargo boat in Havana and a note of warning to the people of the United States.

*YELLOW SUBMARINE Britain 1968. *Dir* George Dunning *Scen* Lee Minoff, Al Brodax, Jack Mendelsohn, Erich Segal *Design* Heinz Edelman, John Cramer, Gordon Harrison *Anim Dir* Jack Stokes, Bob Balser *Mus* John Lennon, Paul McCartney *Ed* Brian Bishop *Voices* John Clive, Geoffrey Hughes, Paul Angelus, Dick Emery, Lance Percival *Prod* King Features/Subafilms, presented by Apple Films. 87 mins. DeLuxe Color.

Pepperland is invaded by the Blue Meanies as Old Fred, conductor of Sergeant Pepper's Lonely Hearts Club Band, escapes in his yellow submarine to get help. He surfaces in Liverpool and encounters Ringo, John, Paul, and George. Together they travel back to Pepperland in the submarine through may strange worlds and on the way meet a superintellectal, the Boob. In Pepperland, they disguise themselves as an Apple Bonker and, after a battle, drive out the Blue Meanies and restore life and color to the people.

This pop art cartoon with brilliant, vibrant, almost incandescent colors is an extraordinary amalgam of nearly every 20th century graphic design style. Especially memorable sequences in this weird fantasy are: "Eleanor Rigby" in a Borowczyk-like Liverpool; the magical underwater mystery tour where the Beatles encounter several lunatic, surrealist monsters; "The Nowhere Man"; and, throughout, the John Lennon brand of whimsical, nonsense humor. This is the first British feature-length cartoon since *Animal Farm* (*q.v.*) and, in itself, is an anthology of the changes animation has gone through since then.

YOKIHI THE EMPRESS YANG KWEÏ-FEÏ/THE PRINCESS YANG/YANG KWAÏ-FEÏ Japan/ Hong Kong 1955. *Dir* Kenji Mizoguchi

424

Scen Yoshikata Yoda, Matsutaro Kawaguchi, Tou Shing, Masashiga Narosawa *Photog* Kohei Sugiyama *Art Dir* Hiroshi Mizatani *Mus* Fumio Hayasaka *Cast* Machiko Kyo, Masayuki Mori, Yamamura So, Sakae Ozawa, Eitaro Shindo, Isao Yamamoto *Prod* Daiei/Shaw Brothers. 100 mins. Eastman Color.

In 18th century China, the daughter of a cook, Yang Kwei-Fei (Kyo), becomes the favorite of the Emperor Tang (Mori). They fall deeply in love and decide to marry. But the new empress is surrounded by jealous relatives who foment a palace rebellion. The rebels demand that the emperor sacrifice Yang Kwei-Fei but he refuses to do so. Nevertheless, she insists on going to her death in the hope of saving him.

This was Mizoguchi's first color film, a coproduction between Daiei and Shaw Brothers of Hong Kong. It was filmed on location in Hong Kong. Despite the difficulties of a large-budget coproduction (which necessitated including sequences like the empress's bath), Mizoguchi succeeded in creating a film with a marvelous integration of color with the tragedy. Though it does not equal *Ugetsu Monogatari* (*q.v.*) or *O'Haru* (*q.v.*), it has some memorably beautiful sequences: the confinement in the imperial palace; the sovereigns wandering through the town on a feast day; a procession of the court through an orchard in blossom; the tumult of the rebellion and the fighting; Yang Kwei-Fei being draped in a purple cap and covered with jewels before being hung from a dead tree.

YOLANDA AND THE THIEF USA 1945. *Dir* Vincente Minnelli *Scen* Irving Brecher from a story by Ludwig Bemelmans, Jacques Thery *Photog* Charles Rosher *Art Dir* Cedric Gibbons, Jack Martin Smith *Songs* Arthur Freed, Harry Warren *Dances* Eugene Loring *Special Effects* Arnold Gillespie, Warren Newcombe *Ed* George White *Cast* Fred Astaire, Lucille Bremer, Frank Morgan, Mildred Natwick, Leon Ames, Mary Nash *Prod* MGM. 107 mins. Technicolor.

Yolanda (Bremer), an orphaned heiress from the American South who was raised in a convent, meets two unscrupulous adventurers, Johnny (Astaire) and Victor (Morgan). Johnny discovers she believes in a "guardian angel" and persuades the girl to accept the notion that he is the angel's earthly embodiment. When he tries to escape with shares he has swindled out of her, the bag of shares is neatly purloined by a strange character who seems to be actually the "guardian angel." This character also prevents Johnny from escaping and brings him back to marry Yolanda.

[An extravaganza with ornate sets and costumes in which much of the story is danced. It was a commercial failure on its release but its visual grace now seems no less appealing than the nostalgic glow of Minnelli's earlier *Meet Me in St. Louis* (*q.v.*).] A. Johnson describes it as "the first film of the decade to reintroduce modern ballet into musical comedy. The colors seem to have come out of a child's paint box, and Minnelli defines the film as a kind of 'Southern American baroque.' The most appealing sequences are the dazzling 'Coffee Time' and the dream ballet whose first images are not fanciful until Fred Astaire asks for a light from a man who has a disturbing number of arms."

YOU CAN'T TAKE IT WITH YOU USA 1938. *Dir* Frank Capra *Scen* Robert Riskin based on the play by George S. Kaufman, Moss Hart *Photog* Joseph Walker *Art Dir* Stephen Goosson *Mus* Dimitri Tiomkin *Ed* Gene Havlick *Cast* Jean Arthur, Lionel Barrymore, James Stewart, Edward Arnold, Mischa Auer, Ann Miller, H. B. Warner, Spring Byington, Mary Forbes *Prod* Columbia. 127 mins.

Tony (Stewart), the son of a millionaire, Anthony P. Kirby (Arnold), falls in love with a poor girl, Alice (Arthur), who lives with her eccentric family in a ramshackle old house. Kirby wants to buy the house in order to build a huge office building but Alice's grandpa (Barrymore) refuses to sell. Alice refuses to marry Tony without his father's consent. Mr. and Mrs. Kirby (Forbes) pay an official visit to her family, get caught up in all its eccentricities, and finally become involved with the police. Alice flees into hiding, Grandpa decides to sell the house, and Tony leaves his father's business. At this, plus some wise words from Grandpa, Kirby relents, the house is restored, and Tony marries Alice.

This adaptation of a Broadway success won Oscars for Best Picture and Direction. It owes much of its appeal to "crazy things such as the Big Apple impromptu with the children in the street, the fireworks episode, the harmonica playing, the gadgets and inventions, the dancing and the writing — all expressive of the self-indulgent eccentricities of the Vanderhof household" (Lewis Jacobs). It contrasts a rich man and a poor but "free" Grandpa who makes impassioned speeches against money, "progress," various "isms," and the income tax. Around him, his family and the other inhabitants of the house go their own merry ways with pet interests that give rise to many gags. The rich man rediscovers the joys of playing the harmonica and consequently the secret of happiness and thereafter dedicates himself to bringing happiness to all around him.

YOUNG AND THE DAMNED (THE) OLVIDADOS (LOS)

YOUNG AND THE PASSIONATE (THE) VITELLONI (I)

YOUNG APHRODITES MIKRES APHRODITES

YOUNG GUARD MOLODAYA GVARDIYA

YOUNG ONE (THE) ISLAND OF SHAME/LA JOVEN Mexico 1960. *Dir* Luis Buñuel *Scen* Luis Buñuel, H. B. Addis (Hugo Butler) based on the novel *Travellin' Man* by Peter Matthiesen *Photog* Gabriel Figueroa *Art Dir* Jesus Bracho *Mus* Jesus Zarzosa, song "Sinner Man" sung by Leon Bibb *Ed* Carlos Savage *Cast* Zachary Scott, Kay Meersman, Bernie Hamilton, Graham Denton, Claudio Brook *Prod* Producciones Olmeca. 96 mins. (Produced in English, not Spanish.)
Travers (Hamilton), a Negro pursued by a lynch mob, lands on an offshore island inhabited only by Miller (Scott), the game warden, and Ewie (Meersman), the inocent 14-year-old daughter of Miller's recently dead handyman. He first sees Ewie and, when Miller returns, is attacked by him until Ewie convinces Miller that Travers did not molest her. Miller forces Travers to become his handyman and later himself assaults Ewie. Next day a minister (Brook) arrives with Jackson (Denton), the boatman, to take Ewie to a children's home. When Miller learns that Travers is wanted for rape, he and Jackson want to lynch him, but the minister says he believes Travers is innocent and should merely be tied up to prevent his escaping.

That night he learns of Ewie's lost innocence but promises not to report Miller if he can take both Travers and Ewie to the mainland. Ewie cuts Travers' bonds and Jackson hunts him down but is overpowered by Travers. The minister leaves with Ewie; Miller, stricken by conscience, assists Travers in his flight to freedom. Buñuel's only English dialogue film, set in the American South, is an attack on racism, hypocrisy and religion, perfectly controlled in its style. Peaceful though violent, relaxed though extremely tense, complex though apparently simple, it is a blend of De Sade with Rousseau and Robinson Crusoe. Though the minister, as Freddy Buache points out, "makes order and moral truth triumph" it is "through moral blackmail which, even though he is a protestant, has something very Catholic about it . . . the only use of physical and natural elements ridiculing the artificial morality of the clergy."

YOU ONLY LIVE ONCE USA 1937. *Dir* Fritz Lang *Scen* Graham Baker based on a story by Gene Towne *Photog* Leon Shamroy *Art Dir* Alexander Toluboff *Mus* Alfred Newman *Ed* Daniel Mandell *Cast* Henry Fonda, Sylvia Sidney, Barton MacLane, Jean Dixon, William Gargan, Jerome Cowan, "Chic" Sale, Margaret Hamilton, Ward Bond, Jean Stoddard *Prod* Walter Wanger Productions for United Artists. 86 mins.
Eddie Taylor (Fonda), a petty criminal leaves prison after his third sentence, marries Joan (Sidney) who has waited for him, and settles down to a normal life. But because of circumstantial evidence and his past record he is convicted and condemned to death for the murder of six men during a bank raid. With his wife's help he escapes from prison a few hours before his execution but shoots a priest (Gargan) who has brought him news of his pardon. He is joined by his wife, who has a child in a wayside hut that they are eventually forced to abandon. They are hunted across America and mortally wounded at a roadblock as they cross the border into Canada.
This and *Fury* (*q.v.*) are Fritz Lang's best Hollywood films, an exposition of Lang's favorite theme of guilt. As in *Fury,* it is society not destiny that is responsible, but whereas in *Fury* Lang focused blame on the mob, here society's guilt is more diffuse. Visually striking,

the composition and lighting, in their brooding, atmospheric effects, sometimes recall those of expressionism. Though its plot is largely melodramatic, the total effect of the film (much helped by the touching warmth of Sylvia Sidney and Fonda) is very powerful.

The first part, with its indictment of unemployment, injustice, prejudice, prison conditions and police brutality, offers a portrait of the USA in the Thirties. The last half, the couple's flight through nocturnal, oppressive landscapes, the rain, the forests and marshes, leads inevitably to the conclusion — their death in each other's arms as the disembodied voice of the dead priest announces "Eddie, you are free."

YOU ONLY LIVE TWICE see GOLDFINGER

YOUTH OF MAXIM (THE) YUNOST MAKSIMA

YUNOST MAKSIMA THE YOUTH OF MAXIM USSR 1935. *Dir/Scen* Grigori Kozintsev, Leonid Trauberg *Photog* Andrei Moskvin *Art Dir* Yevgeny Enei *Mus* Dmitri Shostakovich *Cast* Boris Chirkov, Stepan Kayukov, Valentina Kibardina, Mikhail Tarkhonov *Prod* Lenfilm. 97 mins.

In Russia in 1910, after a prologue showing the underground revolutionary movement under the Tsars, a young worker, Maxim (Chirkov), falls in love with Natasha (Kibardina) and through a militant Bolshevik (Kayukov) himself becomes a revolutionary. He is drawn into the struggle against repression and is arrested.

— *Vozvrashcheniye Maksima/The Return of Maxim* USSR 1937. *Dir* Grigori Kozintsev, Leonid Trauberg *Scen* Kozintsev, Trauberg, Lev Slavin *Photog/Art Dir/Mus* as above *Cast* Boris Chirkov, Valentina Kibardina, A. Kuznetsov, Alexander Zrazhevsky, Mikhail Zharov *Prod* Lenfilm. 114 mins.

In 1914, Maxim, Natasha, and their comrades take part in the worker's demonstrations against the war. They are joined by a clerk (Zharov).

— *Vyborgskaya storona/The Vyborg Side* USSR 1939. *Dir/Scen* Grigori Kozintsev, Leonid Trauberg *Photog* Andrei Moskvin, G. Filatov *Art Dir* V. Vlasov *Mus* Dmitri Shostakovich *Cast* Boris Chirkov, Valentina Kibardina, Mikhail Zharov, Natalia Uzhvi, Maxim Strauch, Mikhail Gelovani *Prod* Lenfilm. 120 mins.

After the Revolution in 1917, Maxim is put in charge of the State Bank as political commissar and has meetings with Lenin (Strauch) and Stalin (Gelovani). Natasha becomes a judge and the clerk an anarchist "activist."

Remarkable sequences in the trilogy: two lengthy meetings of the Constituent Assembly, one in 1914, the other in 1917; a meeting with the clerk, St. Petersburg's billiard king; Maxim, hunted by the police, encroaches on a picnic party; the demonstrations in the streets of St. Petersburg just prior to the outbreak of war; Maxim's departure for the war front; his embarrassment when he is put in charge of the State Bank.

The *Maxim* trilogy was conceived as a unit, Kozintsev's and Trauberg's plan to make three films about a synthetic party worker evolving from their dissatisfaction with *Alone* (*q.v.*). Kozintsev wrote: "We began by carefully reading memoirs by old Bolsheviks . . . We quickly realized that all previous experience in the so-called 'revolutionary adventure' film — such as *Red Imps, Traitor, Gay Canary*, and the like — was no help to us, neither in dramaturgy, nor in direction, nor in acting. All those enigmatic provocateurs, those effective escapes from prison, underground secrets, and the rest of the romantic paraphernalia, not only did not come from the documents of revolutionary activity, but were actually distortions of that material, transforming the Bolsheviks into heroes of adventure fiction." Jay Leyda points out that, "Out of their search for a more truthful dramatic representation of revolutionary and underground activity came, also, a fresh dramatic form. Their 'story' is a freeflowing series of episodes that often seem accidentally or arbitrarily chosen. (The film) is built on artistic selection — of words, gestures, faces, moments."

Even after the script had been written, many months were spent in preparations and rehearsals. In order to make his Maxim character more true to life, Boris Chirkov spent considerable time with revolutionaries who had lived through the 1910–18 period and worked for two or three months in a Leningrad factory to get the feel of being a worker.

This dramatic epic is not lacking in humor, nor in gaiety, nor in almost vaudeville-like episodes in the eccentric tradition of FEKS. The photography,

427

somewhat expressionistic in the first part, becomes more simple and direct in the last two parts. Some themes, sketched briefly in early sequences, are later returned to and developed. As a unity, the *Maxim* trilogy is one of the most important films produced in the USSR (and the world) during the Thirties.

✱

ZAZIE DANS LE METRO ZAZIE France 1960. *Dir* Louis Malle *Scen* Louis Malle, Jean-Paul Rappeneau based on the novel (1959) by Raymond Queneau *Photog* Henri Raichi *Art Dir* Bernard Evein *Mus* Fiorenzo Carpi *Ed* Kenout Peltier *Cast* Catherine Demongeot, Philippe Noiret, Vittorio Caprioli, Hubert Deschamps, Antoine Roblot, Annie Fratellini, Carla Marlier *Prod* N.E.F. 88 mins. Eastman Color.

Ten-year-old Zazie (Demongeot) arrives in Paris to stay with her uncle Gabriel (Noiret). Zazie's one desire is to ride on the Métro, which is closed by a strike. She meets Gabriel's wife (Marlier), a café owner (Deschamps), and other characters, is taken to see the sights of Paris and spreads havoc wherever she goes. At the end they all meet in a nightclub, where a terrible battle develops between diners and waiters.

Raymond Queneau's novel, with its emphasis on puns and word plays, offered a real challenge in adaptation. Malle and his co-scriptwriter, Rappeneau, looked for visual equivalents while remaining faithful to the novel's anarchic logic and series of incidents. Malle said: "I hope that this film, described as a comedy, will convey the difficulty of being a man in a 20th century Western city. Queneau destroys the foundations through his style. We have tried to find equivalents in cinematic writing that would enable us to bring out the same basic points."

Full of parodic allusions to literature and to other films, from *Hiroshima mon amour* (*q.v.*) to Malle's own *Les Amants* (*q.v.*), and containing many "private jokes," *Zazie* is Malle's best film. Among its inventive sequences, welter of techniques, and deliberate sense of anarchy, Malle's indictment, not only of the insane life of Paris but also of war and fascism remains in the memory.

ZEMLYA EARTH/SOIL USSR 1930. *Dir/Scen/Ed* Alexander Dovzhenko *Assist* Yulia Solntseva, Lazar Bodik *Photog* Danylo Demutsky *Art Dir* Vasili Kri-chevsky *Mus* (not on film) L. Revutsky *Cast* Semyon Svashenko Stepan Shkurat, Mikola Nademsky, Yelena Maximova, V. Mikhailov, Pyotr Masokha, Yulia Solntseva *Prod* VUFKU (Kiev). 5,670 ft. Shorter (approx. 5,200 ft) in original foreign release version.

In a Ukrainian village, a rich kulak refuses to divide his land up for a collective farm. Vasili (Svashenko), the young village chairman who is betrothed to a village girl (Maximova), buys a tractor, takes the land by force and makes the collective a success. One day, Vasili is killed. The Kulak's son (Masokha) is accused but denies the charge. Vasili's father (Shkurat) asks that his son have a "modern" burial by the young people, not the priest, and that they sing songs of the new life. As a comrade preaches peace, rain begins to fall on the new crops.

Main sequences: the prologue, with the old man biting joyfully into an apple and dying in peace; a family looking depressed that in fact turns out to be kulaks upset because a meeting is taking place to found the collective; the arrival of the tractor whose radiator boils over but when filled with urine starts again; the harvesting and the beautiful harvesters; the love scene between Vasili and the village girl; he leaves and dances out of sheer joy and suddenly falls, killed by the kulak's son; the family, mourning Vasili, drive away the priest (Mikhailov); the funeral with the young singing with joy as the branches of fruit trees brush the face of the dead Vasili, the priest praying alone in his church, the fiancée's naked agony, a woman so moved by sorrow as the coffin passes that she goes into labor (these four scenes are intercut); the speech over the grave; the kulak's son's mad dance and confession among the graves; the rain falls on the crops, then the clouds pass and there is sunshine and peace again.

Dovzhenko wrote in 1930 of his aims and methods: "I wanted to show the state of a Ukrainian village in 1929, that is to say, at the time it was going through an economic transformation and a mental change in the masses. My principles are: 1. Stories in themselves do not interest me; I choose them in order to get the greatest expression of essential social forms. 2. I work with typical material and apply synthetic methods; my heroes and their behavior are representative of their classes. 3. The material of my films is extremely concentrated temporally and, at the same time, I make it pass through the prism of the emotions, which gives it life and eloquence. I never remain indifferent in the face of this material. It is necessary to both love and hate deeply and in great measure if one's art is not to be dogmatic and dry. I work with actors, but above all with people taken from the crowd. My material demands it. One should not be afraid of using nonprofessional actors because one should remember that everyone at least once can act out his own role on the screen." Dovzhenko also said: "I decided from the beginning to use no effects, no tricks, no acrobatic techniques, but only simple methods. I took as a theme the earth. On this earth, an isba; in this isba, men, simple people; events in themselves commonplace. My film was screened 32 times for various organizations before being released to the public."

The central sequence is dominated by what Dovzhenko called a "biological, pantheistic conception." Under the moonlight of a warm, peaceful summer's night, groups of loving couples lie in ecstasy, the hands of the boys in the bodices of the girls. Among them are Vasili and his betrothed. They leave. Alone on a dusty road, he begins to dance, to express all his joy, all his spiritual and physical happiness. He falls. Horses start up from their grazing. He hasn't merely stumbled; he is dead, shot by the murderer hiding in the hedge.

[Three sequences at least were cut by Soviet censors before release abroad: the replenishment of the tractor's radiator with urine; the fiancée tearing off her clothes in grief; the woman in labor during the funeral.]

Though its basic story (collectivization in the Ukraine and kulak defiance) is very much set in its own time, Earth has universal themes that transcend this: the fruitfulness of the earth, its annual rebirth, life, love, and death. It is Dovzhen-

ko's portrayal of these themes that gives Earth its moving lyrical power and that has twice justifiably led to its inclusion by a panel of critics as one of the Twelve Best Films of All Time. The deceptively simple photography, reducing every element to its essential meaning, has incredible beauty and brilliantly captures the sense of vast plains, fruit trees, and enormous sunflowers under an overpowering sky. And over everything lies Dovzhenko's love for his native Ukraine.

ZERO DE CONDUITE France 1933. *Dir/Scen/Ed* Jean Vigo *Assist* Albert Rièra, Henri Storck, Pierre Merle *Photog* Boris Kaufman *Art Dir* Henri Storck, Jean Vigo *Mus* Maurice Jaubert *Cast* Jean Dasté, Louis Lefebvre, Gilbert Pruchon, Coco Goldstein, Gérard de Bedarieux, Robert Le Flon, le nain Delphin, Louis de Gonzague-Frick, Larive, Raya Diligent, Henri Storck *Prod* Gaumont/Franco Film/Aubert (J. L. Nounez). 47 mins. Existing versions 43–45 mins.

Three young boys, Caussat (Lefebvre), Colin (Pruchon), and Druel (Goldstein), return from the holidays to a sordid little French boarding school. In their rebellion against the petty, dictatorial regime of the school, they are joined by Tabart (De Bedarieux), whose mother dresses him like a girl. A new teacher, Huguet (Dasté), who behaves like Charlie Chaplin, gets their sympathy, but their hatred is directed against the principal (Delphin) and "Sourpuss" (Le Flon). They develop a conspiracy that starts with hidden marbles, develops into a dormitory revolt, and ends with full-scale rebellion as the group throw rubbish into the schoolyard full of assembled dignitaries, including the prefect (de Gonzague-Frick) and a bishop (Storck).

Main sequences: the opening, without dialogue, in which two boys in a railway compartment play with toys and tricks; the first night in the dormitory with the sleepwalker; playtime in the schoolyard with Huguet imitating Chaplin; the slow passing of time on Sunday; the headmaster's study; the Sunday walk; the refectory; the science lesson with the skeleton and the libidinous teacher's behavior, which leads to the revolt; the dormitory pillow fight that develops into an ecstatic "religious" procession (shot in slow motion); the teacher tied to his bed and propped up as though "crucified"; Tabart raising the skull-and-crossbones flag on the roof; the bombardment of the dignitaries, who are forced to flee; Huguet waving from the yard and the final shot of the four conspirators on the roof.

Zéro de conduite is, to some extent, an autobiographical work. "Certainly I return again," Vigo said, "in the compartment in which the two boys on their return leave behind their holidays. Certainly my memories are reflected in those thirty identical beds, the dormitory of my boarding school years. I see also Huguet, whom we all loved, and his colleague Sourpuss and that silent supervisor with the crepe soles of a phantom. In the dimmed-down gaslight, will the little sleepwalker still haunt my dreams tonight?"

"There are two worlds in *Zéro de conduite*," according to Salès Gomes, "on the one hand that of the children and the people, on the other that of the adults, the bourgeois. Vigo bases the children in reality, but with the grown-ups he has not hesitated to accentuate their traits, almost to the limits of caricature . . . This division into two worlds and the film's conclusion gives us all the elements of Vigo's ideology and the social intentions of *Zéro de conduite*."

Maurice Jaubert, who wrote the music, has also described one of his "secrets": "The composer had to accompany a procession of rebellious children (quite ghostly in fact and shot in slow motion). Once the necessary music was obtained and wanting to use an unreal sonorousness, he transcribed it backwards, the last bar before the first and within each bar, the last note before the first. The bit of music in this form was then recorded and recalled little of the original music. The music thus obtained was then used with the film and one found again the shape of the basic melody but the 'transmission' was entirely reversed and derived all its mystery from this simple mechanical operation."

The dormitory revolt is especially brilliant, not only for its music but also for its visual symphony of the boy's white nightgowns and the slow-motion storm of pillow feathers.

[When the film was shown to the press in Paris, Cavalcanti recalls that "the bourgeois sentiments of the audience were deeply shocked by the behavior of the children as shown by Vigo. During the projection the house lights had to be switched on several times, and the show almost ended in a free fight." It was banned by the French censors until 1946 on the grounds of its malicious attack on the French educational system. Certainly it is one of the masterpieces of the French cinema. Its blend of poetry and realism, its psychological depth, and its profound sense of anarchy exerted considerable influence on many directors. Truffaut pays overt homage to it in *Les Quatre cents coups* (*q.v.*), and Lindsay Anderson's *If . . .* (*q.v.*) owes its anarchic approach to it, not least in the similar endings.]

ZLATYE GORI GOLDEN MOUNTAINS USSR 1931. *Dir* Sergei Yutkevich *Scen* A. Mikhailovsky, V. Nedrobrovo, Leo Arnstam, Sergei Yutkevich *Photog* I. Martov, Wulf Rappoport, A. Vol *Art Dir* Nikolai Suvorov *Mus* Dmitri Shostakovich *Cast* Boris Poslavsky, I. Strauch, B. Fedosyev, Boris Tenin, N. Michurin *Prod* Soyuzkino (Leningrad). 95 mins.

In 1914, a peasant (Poslavsky) arrives in St. Petersburg expecting to find the streets paved with gold (the "golden mountains" of the title) and is transformed from subservience into solidarity with his worker-comrades.

Yutkevich's first sound film is also one of his best, a conscious attempt, according to Yutkevich, to "base the action, not on editing, but on the movement of the actor." Its sense of popular life is perfectly matched by Shostakovich's beautiful score. Especially memorable is the turn-of-the-century song played on the accordion by Boris Tenin. Jay Leyda notes, "Its interesting idea (transformation of a peasant's attitude on being exposed to city and revolution between 1912 and 1917) was sometimes obscured by the more immediately interesting execution of each scene, cleverly staged with a touch of stylization (it is one of the few films influenced by Dovzhenko), and photographed by a group of young cameramen whom Yutkevich encouraged to do their best. The sound track . . . was also 'advanced,' with a serious attempt at the audio-visual counterpoint proposed by the Eisenstein-Pudovkin-Alexandrov 'Statement.' The film was cast with customary sensitivity of Yutkevich."

ZONE (LA) France 1928. *Dir* Georges

Lacombe *Photog* Georges Périnal. 2,000 ft. approx.

A documentary about the terrible shanty towns – the "Zone" – which then encircled Paris, and the life of some of its inhabitants, the rag-men. Through the influence of this important film, the French avant-garde began to evolve toward poetic documentaries and the portrayal of social themes.

*ZORBA THE GREEK Greece/USA 1964. *Dir/Ed* Michael Cacoyannis *Scen* Michael Cacoyannis based on the novel by Nikos Kazantzakis *Photog* Walter Lassally *Art Dir* Vassilis Photopoulos *Mus* Mikis Theodorakis *Ed* Roger Dwyre *Cast* Anthony Quinn, Alan Bates, Irene Papas, Lila Kedrova, George Foundas *Prod* Cacoyannis/Rochley. 141 mins.

Basil (Bates), a young English writer on his way to Crete, meets Zorba (Quinn), a lusty Greek peasant who offers to act as his cook, miner, and guide. In a Cretan village they stay at the hotel of Hortense (Kedrova) whom Zorba gallantly courts. Basil also meets a beautiful young widow (Papas) who lives in seclusion, and Mavrandoni (Foundas), a village idiot who is devoted to her and who has been looking after the land Basil has inherited. While Zorba is away buying equipment, Basil visits the widow but is seen. Mavrandoni's son, himself in love with the widow, drowns himself. Soon after Zorba's return the villagers stone the widow to death. Hortense dies and the villagers pillage the hotel. Zorba's plan for developing the mine fails completely but he sees this and everything as a great joke.

Though not at all a good adaptation of the novel, with a theatrical and often confusing script, *Zorba the Greek* succeeds through sheer verve, Lassally's splendidly stark images of the island, and the colorful portrait of Zorba by Anthony Quinn. Though not perhaps matching his Zampanò in *La Strada* (*q.v.*), it is an unforgettable performance, lusty and primitive. The film was a considerable commercial success and was nominated for several Oscars while its theme music also became very popular.

ZUIDERZEE NIEUWE GRONDEN

ZVENIGORA USSR 1928. *Dir* Alexander Dovzhenko *Scen* Yuri Yurtik, Mikhail Johansen *Photog* Boris Zavelyov *Art Dir* Vasili Krichevsky *Cast* Mikola Nademsky, Semyon Svashenko, Alexander Podorozhny, V. Uralsky *Prod* VUFKU (Odessa). 1,799 meters. (6,000 ft. approx.)

During the Civil War in the Ukraine, Grandpa (Nademsky) tells stories of a legendary Scythian treasure buried in the place called Zvenigora. These stories range from the Viking invasion through more modern wars and Grandpa is always the hero. One of his grandsons, Pavlo, is so filled with the stories that he turns his back on the revolution and leaves for foreign parts, dreaming of sudden wealth. Meanwhile, the other grandson stays with the revolution to fight. Pavlo becomes an adventurer and steals the box-office receipts from a Paris theater filled with people expecting to see his public suicide. He returns to the Ukraine to become a counter-revolutionary. When Grandpa fails to derail a train, Pavlo kills himself and Grandpa joins forces with his good grandson.

Zvenigora was much criticized by critics at the time for its confusing and complicated story but this was largely due to the versions re-edited for foreign release. The original film is very clear, with flashbacks used in the manner of a film poem.

Dovzhenko was still an unknown director when, in 1928, the VUFKU representative in Moscow invited Eisenstein and Pudovkin to see *Zvenigora* because, "We can't make head nor tail of it." In 1940, Eisenstein described this screening: "Goodness gracious, what a sight! We saw sharp-keeled boats sailing out of double exposures. The rump of a black stallion being painted white. A horrible monk with a lantern being either disinterred or buried – I am not sure which . . . We saw 'grandpa' – symbolizing the old – instigated by his villainous son, putting dynamite on the rails over which a train – the symbol of progress – was to pass. Traveling in the train was 'grandpa's' other son, one of us, a good Soviet citizen. He sat drinking tea. But no catastrophe occurred. And all of a sudden, 'grandpa' . . . was shown in a 3rd class compartment . . . drinking tea with his son from an ordinary teapot . . . We felt we were succumbing to the irresistible charm of the picture. To the charm that lay in its original ideas, in the wonderful feeling of what was real and what was a profoundly national poetic invention, of contemporaneity and legend, of the humorous and the pathetic. In some way, reminiscent of Gogol . . . The show was over . . . But the atmosphere was tense with a feeling that a new talent had appeared in film art. A talent with an original personality. A talent in his own *genre*. A talent with his own ego . . . (Pudovkin and I) had to say (to the audience) that we had just seen a remarkable film and met an even more remarkable man; and be the first to congratulate him . . . That is how Dovzhenko was 'ordained' a director" (From *Notes of a Film Director*). Somewhat later, after the premiere of *Arsenal* (*q.v.*), Pudovkin, Eisenstein, and Dovzhenko celebrated their meeting with an impromptu party. They drew lots for the characters of three artists of the past. "I was to impersonate Leonardo da Vinci, Dovzhenko, Michelangelo, and Pudovkin, gesticulating wildly, proclaimed he wanted to be Raphael." With *Zvenigora* a new artist of the cinema was born and was recognized as such by his peers.